Gillette®

LEAGUE
Publications Ltd

RUGBY LEAGUE 2007-08
Onwards and upwards

League Publications Ltd

First published in Great Britain in 2007 by
League Publications Ltd
Wellington House
Briggate
Brighouse
West Yorkshire HD6 1DN

Copyright © League Publications Ltd

A CIP catalogue record for this book is available from the British Library
ISBN 978-1-901347-18-0

Designed and Typeset by League Publications Limited
Printed by TJ International, Padstow, Cornwall

Contributing Editor	Tim Butcher
Statistics, production and design	Daniel Spencer
Contributors	Gareth Walker
	Malcolm Andrews
	Mike Latham
	Tony Hannan
	Raymond Fletcher
	Mike Sterriker
	Martyn Sadler
	Andrew Foster
	Phil Caplan
	Ian Bridge
	Neil Barraclough
	Martyn Sadler
	James Gosling
	Steve Mascord
	Dave Lawrenson
	Mike Rylance
	Richard de la Riviere
Pictures	Rugby League Photos
	Varley Picture Agency
	Peter Morley
	Action Photographics, Australia
	Max Flego
	Gordon Clayton
	Ian Lovell
	Mike McKenzie

CONTENTS

ACKNOWLEDGEMENTS

Gillette Rugby League 2007/2008 is the 12th in League Publications Ltd's annual series of Rugby League Yearbooks, the fourth year of its production with the backing of world-leading brand Gillette.

Once again we have to recognise the hard work and dedication of all the contributors to Rugby Leaguer & Rugby League Express and Rugby League World magazine, who provide such a tremendous service to the game of Rugby League. Without their efforts this yearbook would not be possible.

As always we are lucky to be able to include some wonderful action photography provided by, in particular Varley Picture Agency, Dave Williams of RLphotos.com, Col Whelan of Action Photographics in Sydney and Peter Morley.

Thanks are due to the Rugby Football League for their help during the year, and in particular Alice Scott for her assistance in tracking down the dates of birth of players.

The magnificent statistical review was put together meticulously, as always, by Daniel Spencer, who also designed the majority of the book again. Thanks also to Tony Hannan for his help with the colour sections.

Special mentions for Gareth Walker, Malcolm Andrews, Raymond Fletcher and Mike Latham, who have contributed so much again in the writing of this book.

Thanks also to Opta Index, who compiled the Opta Index Analysis in our jam-packed statistical section; and to Mike Latham, who proofed many pages.

TIM BUTCHER
Contributing Editor
Rugby League 2007-2008

INTRODUCTION

The aftermath of the 2007 Rugby League season was highly unusual.

With the pattern of internationals following the domestic season on both sides of the world by now firmly established, British fans had become used to brushing off another defeat for Great Britain and looking ahead to the season to come.

2007 was different. Great Britain had won a series, and in some style. The annual round of navel-gazing that had afflicted the British game for the past decade never happened. 2008 was a World Cup year, and although an eight-year wait between drinks was longer than it should have been, here was a big event for us all to look forward to. Great Britain has been dropped in favour of England, but the 3-0 series win over New Zealand raised hopes that we can actually win it.

The Gillette Fusion Series was a great way to finish the year, and rumblings about the new Great Britain coach Tony Smith being a 'bloody Aussie' faded away as Great Britain turned on the style.

It wasn't a bad domestic year either

Twelve years on from the revolution heralded by Super League and the change of the game's season, the landscape of British Rugby League was changing.

The game now had a genuine European angle with the establishment of Catalans Dragons in Super League and their march into a historic Challenge Cup final, as the showpiece returned the re-built Wembley Stadium after seven years sojourn. The Dragons' return to the re-furbished Stade Gilbert Brutus also paid dividends with average crowds of over 8,000, almost 25 per cent up on the year before.

In fact, ten clubs out of 12 registered increased attendances in 2007, with promoted club Hull Kingston Rovers more than doubling their average crowd, while Huddersfield Giants, Hull FC and Wakefield Trinity Wildcats, as well as the Catalans, all experienced grown in excess of 20 per cent.

If Rugby League's progress shuffled forward after over a decade of development, 2009 will represent a seismic shift. The Rugby Football League announced this year that 18 clubs - among them Celtic Crusaders, promoted to National League One - were expected to apply for Super League licences, with a decision to be announced in July 2008 on which clubs will be competing.

It will mark the game's abandonment of promotion and relegation based purely on on-field results - although automatic promotion had not been in place for several years, with Hunslet (1999) and Dewsbury (2000) both being denied promotion after NL grand final victories.

Many supporters of lower leagues have cried foul, but a mechanism for promotion will still exist for those clubs with ambition and the right infrastructure in place. A three-year cycle will be put in place.

The new system should ensure clubs don't implode by failing to achieve standards, although in 2007 Hull Kingston Rovers certainly blew away the theory that promoted National League clubs could never survive in Super League. They were hot favourites for the drop but made the bookies, and most pundits, look daft by winning ten games, beating eventual champions Leeds early in the season, as well as pulling off an away double at Wigan, and thrashing Hull FC on their own patch.

Their coach Justin Morgan must have been a hot contender for the Coach of the Year award, which on the Tuesday before the Grand Final, was handed to St Helens Daniel Anderson, a sure-fire way of making sure Saints lost at Old Trafford.

Hull KR must surely be one of the clubs to be granted a Super League licence in 2008. The return of the Hull derby - and we had four of them for good measure, including one in Cardiff - was the biggest success of SLXII. And Paul Cooke's 'defection' from west to east in April added spice to a rivalry that will endure forever. The Robins' opening-round win over Wakefield at Craven Park was a brilliant night as well, with Ben Cockayne's last-minute winner the stuff of legend.

St Helens were proven to be fallible on Grand Final night in October, as Leeds Rhinos proved themselves the true Champions - despite finishing second in the table - in spectacular fashion. Scott Donald's second-half try was the best seen in the ten years of the finale, as Tony Smith booked his place in the Headingley history books with his second Championship in four years. New Rhinos coach Brian McClennan has got a mighty hard act to follow.

Saints were beatable, but not very easily, as Brisbane Broncos found out at the Reebok Stadium in February, when Paul Sculthorpe made the first several comebacks from injury to win the man of the match award in Saints' 18-14 World Club Challenge win. The Catalans came to the same conclusion at Wembley when a typical St Helens performance - fired by the 33rd minute try from eventual Man of Steel James Roby - beat them 30-8.

Karl Harrison was the only coaching casualty of SLXII, a 66-6 hammering in Perpignan being the final straw. A change of coach mid-season, with Shaun McCrae taking up the mantle, didn't make any difference as the City Reds were relegated, although if work does start on a new stadium in the new year as planned, they must be strong candidates for Super League in 2009.

Wakefield Trinity Wildcats enjoyed a wonder start to the year when they reached the top of the table in the early rounds, despite looking like relegation fodder when they lost at Hull KR. But they got themselves clear of that perennial battle with several rounds to spare and the end-of-season run-in must have seemed unexciting for the Wakefield support. They too had a new council-backed stadium in the pipeline.

Improving stadia was one of the themes of Rugby League by the end of the year. As well as Wakefield and Salford, St Helens' long-held dream of a stadium fit for a top club looked like happening. And promoted Castleford Tigers' new ground was also expected to be given the green light.

The Tigers bounced straight back into Super League with a track record of bringing colour and spectacle to the competition, and they will be welcomed back by everybody. Their only serious challengers in NL1, Widnes, after a financial crisis, are thankfully showing signs that they can regroup in time for 2009.

Bradford Bulls were predicted to drop off this year, but they didn't and must still be having collective nightmares about the Elimination play-off at Odsal which they controlled almost totally for first minute to 55th when they led 30-6. Cue Trent Barrett starting to weave some magic and the Bulls were eliminated, Pat Richards, who did a sterling job for Wigan with the boot all season, kicking his first ever field goal to seal a 31-30 win.

Hull FC started like a slug and finished like a train but even they couldn't stop Wigan's momentum the week after they'd knocked Huddersfield Giants out. The Giants themselves started even slower, losing their first seven games before clicking into gear with a 50-point thrashing of then table-toppers Wakefield, then going on to make the play-offs for the first time. And they beat their long-time nemesis Bradford, twice.

Leeds Rhinos and St Helens take to the field at Old Trafford for the Super League Grand Final

Harlequins coach Brian McDermott assembled a side that didn't look to have any strength in depth and proceeded to beat champions St Helens on their own patch in round one, and contend for the play-offs.

Warrington coach Paul Cullen was under pressure with some mini-slumps along the way, the victim of a horror injury list. Adrian Morley fractured his cheekbone twice and ended the season in the stands after a one-match ban for a high tackle on St Helens teenage forward Paul Clough in round 26.

And the year ended with great sadness with the news that former Great Britain captain Mike Gregory had finally succumbed to the degenerative illness that had struck him down when he was coaching with great success at Wigan in 2004. Rugby League had lost one of its finest sons.

In this year's Gillette Yearbook you will find the story of the domestic year, full details of the international season and the Australian NRL season, and match facts for every Super League and Challenge Cup games involving professional teams, as well as National League One and Two and Northern Rail Cup games. We have also selected five individuals who we judge to have made the biggest impact on Rugby League in 2007.

League Publications produces the weekly newspaper Rugby Leaguer & Rugby League Express, as well as the monthly glossy magazine Rugby League World and the website 'totalrugbyleague.com'.

We hope you enjoy looking back over the year with us.

Lastly, heartfelt thanks once again to Gillette for their support for both this yearbook, and for the sport of Rugby League.

TIM BUTCHER
Contributing Editor
Rugby League 2007-2008

1
THE 2007 SEASON

DECEMBER 2006
All Saints Day

The final month of 2006 created a great stir in the game and beyond. It all began when St Helens made the shortlist of three teams for 'Team of the Year' at the BBC Sports Personality of the Year Awards following their historic treble of Super League, Challenge Cup and League Leaders' Shield.

They faced seemingly unbeatable competition from Europe's victorious Ryder Cup golf team, who had enjoyed saturation media coverage that summer, and cricket's county champions Sussex for an award that was, for the first time, to be decided by a public vote.

St Helens not only won the popular vote, they were selected by a landslide. A total of 15,848 votes were cast by text message, with Saints gaining 10,720 votes, at 67.64 per cent, just over two-thirds of the total.

Sussex came second, with 2,716 votes, 17.14 percent of the total, while the Ryder Cup team came third, with 2,412 votes, 15.22 per cent of the votes.

The reaction in the national press in the days following was almost hysterical, with denouncements of the result and suggestions of 'sinister voting patterns in the north of England'. The golfers should have won it they opined, failing to notice they had come third in the poll.

The man who organised the vote flatly rejected suggestions there was anything untoward. 'I can assure you that we felt Saints were absolutely worthy winners after an amazing year,' BBC Sports Personality editor Carl Doran told *Rugby Leaguer & League Express*. Saints coach Daniel Anderson added to the jubilation at Knowsley Road by being voted the BBC's Coach of the Year.

There were other good news stories doing the rounds. Aussie winger Matt King of the Melbourne Storm, a member of the Australian squad that won the 2006 Gillette Tri-Nations tournament, donated his winner's medal to a young disabled English supporter. King met 17-year-old Scott Walker, who suffers from cerebral palsy, in the Australian dressing-room after the final.

But there was also bad news from down under when it was revealed that the great Wally Lewis had been battling epilepsy - a condition that forced him to freeze mid-sentence while reading a sports bulletin on television - since his playing days with the Brisbane Broncos in the late 1980s.

The New Zealand RL confirmed there would be no mid-season Test between Great Britain and the Kiwis in 2007 - with a tour at the end of the year that always looked unlikely. It left the Rugby Football League with a free weekend for international football in 2007 and no obvious opposition for Great Britain.

The pressure was also growing for a change of coach for the international side, incumbent Brian Noble's contract set to come up for renewal. Leading the criticism was Great Britain legend Garry Schofield who called for the resignation of Noble in his column December's issue of *Rugby League World*: He pressed for former GB prop Karl Harrison, who had worked wonders with his club Salford City Reds in 2006, to be given the job.

Current Great Britain captain Jamie Peacock was the only British player named in the 2006 World XIII in *Rugby League World*, after he was voted the best forward in the game at the Rugby League International Federation awards night in Sydney.

The RFL had some pressing problems. Firstly they were still struggling to find new sponsors for the Challenge Cup and National Leagues for the forthcoming season. And they also had the task of selling the 'Millennium Magic' weekend, which would involve staging a complete round of Super League matches at the Millennium Stadium on the first weekend of May. Promoted Hull Kingston Rovers were less than enthusiastic about the RFL's decision to stage re-runs of derby matches in Cardiff. It meant the two Hull-based sides were drawn together four times during the season, with two of the games at Hull's Kingston Communications Stadium and only one at Craven Park. Having to play SLXI's runners up four times was forecast to be a huge disadvantage. Wigan assistant coach Phil Veivers also criticised the 2007 Super League fixture list for giving Wigan four matches against their derby rivals, champions St Helens.

The timing of the Carnegie World Club Challenge game was also posing the RFL problems. The game between St Helens and NRL champions Brisbane Broncos was scheduled to be played at Bolton's Reebok Stadium on 23rd February - on the weekend of SLXII round three. It meant that St Helens' round three tie at Huddersfield would kick-off the new season, the week before round one. When the fixtures were announced, Friday 2nd February was the date published, but this was almost immediately rescheduled for Sunday night 4th February at the request of Sky TV.

Super League clubs were gearing up for SLXII, with promoted Hull KR the busiest as they tried to build a side able to compete and survive. After spending six seasons at Hull FC, Chris Chester crossed to the east side after agreeing a switch to Rovers. Chester followed the signings of former international front-rowers Danny Ward and Michael Vella, Huddersfield's experienced Jim Gannon, plus NRL Premiership winning prop Mark O'Neill, released by Leeds, and the returning fans favourite Stanley Gene. They also signed little known New Zealander Andreas Bauer from Mount Albert Lions, as well as retaining most of the backline that had won them promotion from NL1.

Michael Platt officially became a Bradford Bulls player, with the Bulls paying Castleford a transfer fee, an RFL Tribunal ruling that the fullback was still registered to the Tigers, despite their relegation from Super League. The Tigers, aiming to bounce straight back into Super League after their dramatic relegation, were handed a Christmas present with the news that an outline planning application for a new stadium at Glasshoughton had been submitted.

Bradford also signed David Solomona, who was threatening to sue his former club Wakefield - who were also boosted by the news the Wakefield MDC had plans for a new stadium close to the city centre - for unpaid wages. The Bulls were cleared of making an illegal approach for the New Zealand international when he was under contract to the Wildcats towards the end of the 2006 season during the club's fight against relegation from Super League. Glenn Morrison arrived at Odsal as well in this month.

Wigan announced the close-season signings of Thomas Leuluai, Michael Withers and Shane Millard, dispelling rumours they were unable to fit the three players into their 2007 salary cap. Star signing Trent Barrett landed with the big job of solving Wigan's problem number-six shirt.

The man aiming to replace the departed Jamie Lyon, Newcastle Knight Matthew Gidley, arrived in St Helens on the eve of the new year, as the club, along with plenty of others, announced record season ticket sales.

Salford City Reds denied they had received any enquiries for Andy Coley. Coley, who was promoted from the stand-by list to the full Great Britain squad for the Tri-Nations, had been linked with moves to Leeds and Wigan.

Warrington Wolves coach Paul Cullen refused to comment on reports that Andrew Johns could be ready to tear up the last year of his contract with Newcastle Knights and head to the Halliwell Jones Stadium in 2008.

The exit door at Harlequins was in use. New signing Sione Faumuina quit the club, citing family reasons for an unscheduled return to Auckland. On the same day Tongan captain Solomon Haumono announced his retirement from Rugby League in order to resume his career as a heavyweight boxer. Faumuina was unveiled as a North Queensland Cowboys player.

The 'Rumble by the Humber' - a charity boxing match between Hull FC's Lee Radford and Wigan's Stuart Fielden to raise money for stricken former Hull star Steve Prescott - scheduled for February 2nd - was switched from the KC Stadium to the Hull Arena to accommodate the demand for tickets.

The highlight of the Festive Friendlies played over the Christmas period was in Doncaster, where the Lakers had first use of the new Keepmoat Stadium for a friendly against South Yorkshire rivals Sheffield Eagles on the Wednesday after Christmas. After the game the club promised to revise their matchday procedures after many of the 5,264 spectators who turned out had to wait at least 30 minutes for admission to the ground. Sheffield won the game 16-10.

In other games, Warrington's Lee Briers masterminded a 62-6 win at neighbours Widnes; Leeds Rhinos edged a feisty game with Wakefield 22-14 and Whitehaven won the inaugural Ike Southward Trophy by beating Workington 18-6.

None of those games made any difference to the bookies' assessment of how SLXII would go, with St Helens 11/8 to retain their title and Hull KR favourites for relegation.

The Australian Combined High Schools won the two-match Test series against the England Academy side 2-nil following up a 36-22 win at Odsal's Grattan Stadium with a 32-20 success at Widnes.

After being behind 16-8 at half-time in the first Test the Aussies blitzed their opponents with five tries in a 12-minute spell at the start of the second half. England scored tries through the St Helens pair of Paul Clough (2) and Kyle Eastmond, while Hull's Craig Hall also touched down and landed three goals.

Israel Folau, who went on to storm the NRL with Melbourne, scored two tries in the second game as the Australians, led by Mitchell Pearce, son of former great Wayne Pearce, edged an exciting tussle, with Warrington trio Ben Harrison, Kevin Penny and Chris Riley, and St Helens' Scott Moore, getting the English tries.

The Australians wrapped up their tour in France with two wins against the French Cadets.

COMBINED AUSTRALIAN HIGH SCHOOLS TOUR 2006

FIRST TEST

Saturday 9th December 2006

ENGLAND UNDER 18S ACADEMY 22
AUSTRALIAN COMBINED HIGH SCHOOLS 36

ENGLAND: 1 Chris Riley (Warrington Wolves); 2 Sean Gleeson (Wigan Warriors); 3 Darrell Goulding (Wigan Warriors); 4 Craig Hall (Hull FC); 5 Dean McGilvray (St Helens); 6 Kyle Eastmond (St Helens); 7 Tommy Lee (Hull FC); 8 Joe Walsh (Bradford Bulls); 9 Scott Moore (St Helens); 10 Steve Bannister (St Helens); 11 Ben Harrison (Warrington Wolves); 12 Luke Adamson (Salford City Reds); 13 Paul Clough (St Helens). Subs (all used): 14 Ben Kavanagh (Wigan Warriors); 15 Brett Robinson (Wigan Warriors); 16 Rob Draper (Widnes Vikings); 17 Chris Hill (Leigh Centurions).
Tries: Hall (9), Clough (25, 67), Eastmond (32); **Goals:** Hall 3/4.
AUSTRALIA: 1 Chris Lawrence; 2 Shannon Walker; 3 Joel Thompson; 4 Israel Folau; 5 Obadiah Geia; 6 Chris Sandow; 7 Mitchell Pearce; 8 Aiden Tolman; 9 Nathan Strudwick; 10 Tim Mannah; 11 Joseph Paulo; 12 Kevin Proctor; 13 Jay Aston. Subs (all used): 14 Luke Capewell; 15 Will Matthews; 16 Tim Robinson; 17 Luke Muttdon.
Tries: Thompson (16), Walker (28, 52), Lawrence (43), Geia (48, 50), Strudwick (55); **Goals:** Sandow 4/7.
Sin bin: Paulo (32) - dissent.
Half-time: 16-8; **Referee:** Ben Thaler (England).
(At Grattan Stadium, Odsal).

SECOND TEST

Friday 15th December 2006

ENGLAND UNDER 18S ACADEMY 20
AUSTRALIAN COMBINED HIGH SCHOOLS 32

ENGLAND: 1 Chris Riley (Warrington Wolves); 2 Sean Gleeson (Wigan Warriors); 3 Darrell Goulding (Wigan Warriors); 4 Craig Hall (Hull FC); 5 Kevin Penny (Warrington Wolves); 6 Tommy Lee (Hull FC); 7 Thomas Coyle (Wigan Warriors); 8 Joe Walsh (Bradford Bulls); 9 Scott Moore (St Helens); 10 Ben Harrison (Warrington Wolves); 18 Steve Bannister (St Helens); 12 Luke Adamson (Salford City Reds); 13 Paul Clough (St Helens). Subs (all used): 14 Ben Kavanagh (Wigan Warriors); 15 Brett Robinson (Wigan Warriors); 16 Anthony Rourke (Warrington Wolves); 17 Danny Colquitt (Warrington Wolves).
Tries: Harrison (13), Penny (22), Riley (35), Moore (53); **Goals:** Hall 2/4.
AUSTRALIA: 1 Chris Lawrence; 2 Shannon Walker; 3 Joel Thompson; 4 Israel Folau; 5 Obadiah Geia; 6 Mitchell Pearce; 7 Chris Sandow; 8 Aiden Tolman; 9 Nathan Strudwick; 10 Tim Mannah; 11 Tim Robinson; 12 Kevin Proctor; 13 Joseph Paulo. Subs (all used): 14 Joel Brown; 15 Will Matthews; 16 David Hala; 17 Luke Muttdon.
Tries: Geia (1), Folau (26, 55), Pearce (47), Muttdon (78);
Goals: Sandow 6/6.
Half-time: 14-14; **Referee:** Peter Taberner (England)
(At Halton Stadium, Widnes).

AUSTRALIAN ACADEMY OF SPORT TOUR 2006

Great Britain U18 Community Lions 14 Australian Institute of Sport 18
(at Rochdale Mayfield)
England Academy U17s 22 Australian Institute of Sport 32
(at South Leeds Stadium)

OTHER RESULTS

Wales U19s 14 Australian Combined High Schools 68
(at Blackwood RFC)
Great Britain U18 Community Lions 8
Australian Combined High Schools 38 *(at Doncaster RUFC)*
BARLA Under 18s 12 Australian Combined High Schools 58
(at Copeland Stadium)
France Juniors 18 Australian Combined High Schools 32
(at Carcassonne)
France Juniors 18 Australian Combined High Schools 58 *(at Toulouse)*

JANUARY
Going home

It was an optimistic start to 2007, with strong rumours that the RFL were on the verge of a broadcast deal for the National Leagues with the Eurosport satellite channel. Negotiations did take place but after they broke down, BSkyB stepped in to agree to televise live NL games on Thursday evenings.

2007 was also the year that the Rugby League Challenge Cup Final was set to return to Wembley, albeit a year late, and the RFL was to announce its plans for 2009, when its strategy for the franchising of Super League was due to come into place.

The RFL made two significant moves which were to alter the domestic game in 2007 - they changed the points structure in the three divisions below Super League, and they appointed six referees to full-time positions.

The decision to introduce the 'bonus point' for Northern Rail Cup and National League games met with a mixed reaction. Under the new rules a team was to be awarded three points for a victory, two points for a drawn game and one point for a loss by 12 points or fewer. 'We believe this is a progressive move and will generate increased levels of competition and interest in the National Leagues and Northern Rail Cup,' said Nigel Wood, the RFL's Chief Operating Officer. 'The RFL believes it will encourage an exciting, attacking brand of Rugby League for spectators to enjoy throughout the forthcoming season. The points system creates additional possible outcomes to games.'

Full-time referees were hailed as 'a vital development' by one of the men appointed, Steve Ganson. 'Crucially, being professional allows us the time, which we never had before, to improve our game in every element,' he said. 'There are only positive things to come out of that, and it will be of great benefit to Rugby League.' Richard Silverwood, Ben Thaler, Ashley Klein, Ian Smith and Phil Bentham were the other full-timers.

League Express also revealed that the RFL was to appoint a new member to its board of directors, following the retirement of Yorkshire businessman Tony Gartland - 63 year old Bob Stott, until last year the chief executive of the Bradford-based William Morrison Supermarkets PLC.

The RFL also employed a new marketing executive at its Red Hall headquarters in Rhodri Jones, former marketing and media manager with Bradford Bulls and Hull FC.

The Challenge Cup had a new sponsor in Leeds Metropolitan University, only weeks before the start of the competition. The RFL announced that the University, using its 'Carnegie' identity, would sponsor the Cup for six years for a 'seven-figure sum', refusing to give any more financial detail about the agreement. Northern Rail, the sponsors of the National League Cup, extended their sponsorship of the competition for another three years.

Man of Steel Paul Wellens crowned an imperious year for him and his club St Helens when he was unveiled as Fans' Player of the Year by *Rugby Leaguer & League Express* in the first issue of the New Year. Royal Navy Rugby League coach, Warrant Officer PTI Wayne Okell was awarded the MBE in the Queen's New Year's Honours List for services to Rugby League.

Huddersfield Giants, searching for their first ever place in the Super League play-offs, welcomed their new signings from Wests Tigers, Shane Elford and Jamahl Lolesi, to the Galpharm Stadium. The two joined former Wests Tigers teammate John Skandalis, who had arrived before Christmas.

And later in the month, Giants coach Jon Sharp said he was impressed by Ryan Hudson's contribution, as Hudson made a return to professional Rugby League after a two-year drugs ban, in a friendly with Wigan, which Huddersfield edged 24-22.

His two-year ban had ended at midnight on the Saturday night before the game. There was no comment about Hudson's reported arrest a week earlier in Portugal following a night's celebration with his new teammates at the pre-season training camp.

Hudson was not supposed to be training with the Giants until the end of his ban, but a Portuguese newspaper reported that he had caused damage to a car wing mirror and had been involved in pushing a policeman. The story was front-page news back in Huddersfield and Hudson issued an apology through his lawyer.

The Giants and Hudson were found to have no case to answer after a RFL inquiry, but their preparations for Super League XII took a blow when they were beaten 50-0 in their final pre-season friendly by Leeds Rhinos at Headingley in a joint testimonial match for the Rhinos' Keith Senior and Huddersfield's Paul Reilly. Winger Martin Aspinwall was ruled out for the start of the season after a groin operation.

Hull Kingston Rovers were preparing to make their Super League debut and installed a temporary stand at the 'away' end at Craven Park. The stand had come from the 16th green at the Wentworth golf course. They kicked off their pre-season with a 16-8 home victory against Bradford Bulls. But their close-season signing from the Bulls, Stanley Gene was out for up to eight weeks after he underwent an operation to clean out a knee.

The Robins said goodbye to one of their favourite sons as around two thousand mourners attended a snowy Craven Park for the funeral of Peter 'Flash' Flanagan, who died at the age of 65. As the coffin was carried out of the tunnel, the Rovers anthem of 'Red, Red Robin' rang out in his memory amid a spontaneous standing ovation.

Lee Radford was appointed captain of Hull FC, replacing hooker Richard Swain, who stepped down from the role after the previous season's Super League Grand Final. Former Hull FC coach Shaun McRae said he was ready to listen to any offers, either for a coaching role or for a job in the media, following his resignation as South Sydney Director of Football. He was immediately linked to the Great Britain coaching job.

Wakefield Trinity Wildcats were the only Super League club that hadn't recruited any players from the NRL for the 2007 season. But one of their overseas players returned to Belle Vue. Semi Tadulala came back from his loan spell at rugby union club Gloucester. His career in the 15-man game never got underway, due to his failure to obtain a work permit. One of Wakefield's Brit recruits, Danny Sculthorpe, turned his ankle during the club's pre-season training camp at Torremolinos, damaging ligaments and ruling himself out of the opening rounds of the campaign.

Stacey Jones was set to miss Catalans Dragons' first game of the season after knee surgery. The Dragons beat a French Presidents XIII, a team comprised of players from the French Elite competition, 38-22 in St Estève.

Bradford Bulls' scrum-half Paul Deacon was appointed captain for the 2007 season, replacing 2006 skipper Iestyn Harris. St Helens coach Daniel Anderson signed an extension to his contract to keep him at Knowsley Road until the end of the 2008 season.

Warrington Wolves were planning ahead and announced they had already signed New Zealand Warriors star Louis Anderson, the younger brother of the Wolves' 2007 recruit Vinnie Anderson, for the 2008 season.

Widnes Vikings owner Stephen Vaughan reassured Widnes fans that he was 'going nowhere', after rumours circulated the town that a Widnes-led consortium was about to take over the club.

Tommy Martyn put his Challenge Cup winners medal from 1996 on ebay to raise money for his former teammate Steve Prescott, battling a rare form of stomach cancer. The charity XIII Heroes bought the medal for £2,605. Another former St Helens clubmate, Chris Smith, auctioned his Grand Final winner's ring from 2000 for over £1000 for the same cause.

Workington Town's hopes of a new stadium moved a step closer to reality, with Allerdale Council publishing planning documents proposing the redevelopment of Derwent Park to house Town, Workington Reds soccer team and possibly speedway.

Dean Bell ended a 25-year association with British Rugby League, after arriving in England in 1982 to play for Carlisle, by leaving the role of Rugby Executive at Wigan. Meanwhile Warriors coach Brian Noble said he would hand the goal-kicking duties in 2007 to winger Pat Richards.

Wigan chairman Maurice Lindsay published a proposal to reduce the regular Super League season from 27 to 22 fixtures ahead of the meeting of Super League clubs. Lindsay was convinced that Test stars suffered burnout, while young players were over-exposed to intense Super League matches too quickly in their careers.

It was opposed by St Helens chairman Eamonn McManus, who pointed to the damaging lack of revenue that clubs would suffer if the proposal were implemented. 'In an ideal world I have a high degree of sympathy with Maurice's suggestion,' McManus told *Rugby Leaguer & League Express*.

John Wilkinson OBE, the longest serving chairman in British Rugby League, celebrated 25 years as the helm of Salford Reds on 3rd January. But the Reds' hopes of silverware in 2007 were damaged with the news that fullback Karl Fitzpatrick was to be sidelined for at least three months after he tore an Achilles tendon. He underwent surgery to repair the serious damage as the rest of the Salford squad flew out to Florida for their pre-season training camp.

Meanwhile Reds coach Karl Harrison poured cold water on stories linking him with the newly vacant, and now full-time Great Britain coaching job.

RFL Executive Chairman Richard Lewis admitted that the decision not to re-appoint Brian Noble to the post was a hard one. 'It was a very difficult decision, because I have a lot of respect for Brian Noble, and for the way he did the job,' said Lewis. 'But on balance I believe the international game has moved forward significantly since the Tri-Nations started. Its profile and its importance have grown, we have a World Cup next year, and a Tri-Nations or Four-Nations in 2009, and it's important we do everything we can to be successful in those tournaments.'

Harrison was many people's favourite for the role but he ruled himself out. 'I've just signed a new contract and am really happy here. We are building for the future,' said Harrison. 'I've not applied for the Great Britain job, and not spoken to anybody regarding the Great Britain job, so as far as I'm concerned that's that.'

FEBRUARY
Sshh...it's Super League

Super League XII crept into life on a bitterly cold and dry Sunday evening at the Galpharm Stadium in a slightly surreal fashion. Champions St Helens began the defence of their Super League title by earning a hard-fought 18-10 victory over the Giants - in a Round 3 encounter brought forward to accommodate their forthcoming World Club Challenge with Brisbane Broncos at the Reebok Stadium later that month. The build-up was low key and the kick-off, advertised widely as 7.05pm, was delayed until 7.15pm - decided in midweek but given no publicity. It was an inconvenient kick-off time, but a large travelling support from St Helens lifted the occasion.

Saints fielded 13 of their Grand Final-winning team, with Paul Wellens injured, Willie Talau suspended after being sent off for punching in a pre-season game with Leigh, Jamie Lyon departed, and Paul Anderson retired and now assistant coach at Huddersfield, all missing. Matt Gidley, stepping into Lyon's shoes, made his Saints bow after 11 seasons in the NRL with Newcastle Knights. Nick Fozzard, left out of the Grand Final-winning side, got a chance to stake his claim for a starting spot, while Bryn Hargreaves, signed from Wigan, was on the bench alongside teenager Scott Moore. James Roby demonstrated his versatility by filling in for Wellens at fullback. The Giants, missing the injured Martin Aspinwall, handed debuts to five players - the Wests Tigers trio of Jamahl Lolesi, Shane Elford and John Skandalis alongside Darrell Griffin and Ryan Hudson.

Despite scoring four tries to one, Saints struggled to put daylight between themselves and the Giants, Sean Long successful with only one kick at goal. Lee Gilmour, with a broken nose, led the way with two slickly-finished tries, while Leon Pryce was behind Saints' best attacking moves.

But this opening game of the season was dominated by the whistle of referee Ashley Klein - one of the six full-time referees - who dished out 27 penalties, many in a clamp down on a new interpretation on obstruction and dummy and decoy runners.

There was other controversy as Giants coach Jon Sharp suggested that Jon Wilkin should have been sent off and not yellow-carded for a late challenge that saw captain Chris Thorman miss the last 23 minutes with a head injury. Wilkin was referred to the RFL Disciplinary the following Tuesday and received a two-match ban. In the week leading up to the game the Giants had complained about the appointment of video referee Steve Ganson, another full-timer, who lived in St Helens. Ganson disallowed a 'try' by Giants star Eorl Crabtree in the second half, refusing to give him the 'benefit of the doubt'.

The RFL also investigated a complaint by Huddersfield that St Helens failed to name an 18-man squad for the match in accordance with Super League regulations.

Round One was scheduled for the following weekend and the other ten clubs made their final preparations. There was an early blow for SLXI runners-up Hull FC when Paul Cooke looked set to miss the first half of the season after he hobbled off in the 63rd minute of his side's friendly 30-24 victory over Castleford at the Jungle

Bradford Bulls signed their former threequarter Nathan McAvoy. McAvoy, 30, who played 17 games for Wigan in SLXI after moving from Leeds Rhinos, for whom he played one Challenge Cup tie, was a replacement for winger Marcus Bai who had surprisingly retired in the off-season. McAvoy promised to repay the faith of coach Steve McNamara. Wakefield Trinity Wildcats prop forwards Ricky Bibey and Richard Moore, signed from Leigh, made the same commitment to their coach John Kear.

Wigan's decision to send a second-string side to face Whitehaven in their last friendly upset the Cumbrian club, who claimed it cost them at least £20,000. They claimed Wigan reneged on a promise to send a first-team squad as part of the transfer deal that saw Oliver Wilkes join the Super League club in 2006. After a near full-strength Warriors side beat Salford at the Willows the previous Wednesday, coach Brian Noble announced he would be sending a squad of fringe and Academy players.

In the first round of the Challenge Cup, Carnegie's sponsorship received a boost when Leeds Metropolitan University team blasted NCL Premier Division side Wigan St Patricks out of the competition. Inspired by hat-trick hero Rob Worrincy – the ex London Broncos and Sheffield Eagles winger - the students progressed with 38-24 away victory.

Off the field, Hull captain Lee Radford fought his former Bradford teammate Stuart Fielden at Hull Arena on the night of Friday 1st and raised £60,000 for Steve Prescott. The referee stepped in to stop the fight soon after the start of the second round after Radford caught Fielden with a flurry of punches.

The RFL and Sky Sports reached an agreement for the broadcaster to show 25 National League games a year for the next two seasons, including the play-offs and the Grand Finals.

Round 1

Hull Kingston Rovers remained hot favourites for relegation despite their opening-day 14-9 win against Wakefield Trinity Wildcats at a delirious Craven Park in the Saturday TV game. But they eased from 4/6 to 5/6 to finish bottom of the league, with the bookmakers not impressed by the Wildcats. Rovers' coach Justin Morgan, the youngest head coach in Super League at the age of 31, was delighted with the club's first ever Super League victory, after a sensational win that was secured by a last-minute try from fullback Ben Cockayne.

It was a huge night in east Hull that looked like ending in disappointment for the passionate Robins support. When Jamie Rooney potted a 35-metre field goal on 72 minutes to give the Wildcats a 9-8 lead, an heroic show from Super League's new boys looked in vain. When Gareth Morton was bundled into the corner flag by Ryan Atkins and Semi Tadulala with only three minutes left, there was no hope.

But red and white prayers for a Wakefield mistake were answered when the hitherto faultless Sam Obst lost the ball almost straight after the 20-metre restart. There was only time for one last attack and a clever ploy from captain James Webster - dummying the field goal and then shifting the ball left - and a slick inside ball from Chris Chester sent Cockayne in by the posts.

Wakefield's discipline let them down - they lost Tevita Latu, who revealed his surname was really Leo-Latu, and Richard Moore for ten minutes each to the sin bin, both of them for fighting - and were on the wrong end of a 14-11 penalty count, though John Kear had no complaints about referee Ashley Klein. At 15/8, the bookies saw them as Hull KR's only serious rivals to be relegated.

The Robins attracted a crowd of 7,154 to their opening fixture, and were banking on a large following to the Galpharm in round two, with sponsor Lloyds TSB bank putting on ten free 48-seater coaches to Huddersfield for season-ticket holders.

Warrington Wolves' opening-night bone-jarring 16-10 win at Wigan came at a cost, with Adrian Morley and Chris Bridge facing lengthy lay-offs. Bridge limped off early in the game, with a suspected torn hamstring, whilst Morley accidentally clashed heads with Wigan substitute Eamon O'Carroll while attempting a king-hit and suffered a fractured cheekbone.

February

Bradford Bulls' 18-year-old prop forward Sam Burgess was knocked out in a tackle at Odsal as the Bulls defeated Huddersfield Giants 18-14 at the Grattan Stadium. Burgess was injured in the first minute of the second half, when he went crashing to the floor after making a tackle. The clock was stopped as he lay motionless for several minutes before being stretchered off.

The Bulls needed an early-morning pitch inspection for the game to go ahead, following a week's wintry weather, while their stand-off Iestyn Harris missed the clash when he went down with a flu bug. A 71st minute try from Glenn Morrison won the game for the Bulls.

Leeds Rhinos coach Tony Smith paid tribute to his team's clinical finishing as they racked up 22 points in the first half on the way to a 30-26 win at Salford City Reds, despite being on the wrong end of the possession and territory statistics. A total of 13 first-half penalties threatened to ruin the spectacle, with Leeds conceding nine successive penalties at one stage.

Brent Webb made a two-try debut, and the other new signing Kylie Leuluai impressed up front. Winger Ashley Gibson was helped from the field with a knee injury in the 19th minute.

Hull FC and Catalans kicked-off the season without their main halfback playmakers - Paul Cooke, whose knee injury wasn't as bad as first predicted, and Dragons' Stacey Jones sidelined following a knee operation - and emerged from the opening round at KC Stadium with a point each after a 10-10 draw. Three Danny Tickle goals were crucial as the Dragons scored two tries to one in an impressive performance, with new signings Aaron Gorrell, Casey McGuire, Jason Croker and Adam Mogg standouts, along with French debutants Vincent Duport, Sebastian Raguin and David Ferriol. Tickle could have pinched the win, but his late penalty kick sailed wide of the posts.

St Helens were still favourites to finish at the top of the table, but they eased from 5/6 before the start of the season to 11/8 after a shock Friday-night 14-6 defeat to Harlequins, in freezing conditions and steady snowfall. It took two pitch inspections to get the go ahead to play.

Ian Hardman played at fullback for Saints in the absence of Paul Wellens (ankle), with James Roby moving to loose forward in place of Jon Wilkin (suspended) and Willie Talau back at centre in place of Lee Gilmour (broken nose).

For the Quins the debutant halfback pairing of Scott Hill and Danny Orr was impressive. Orr was outstanding in scoring one and creating another try, whilst former Kangaroo Hill grew increasingly influential. Another new boy, Chris Melling, signed from Wigan, replaced the injured Mark McLinden (back injury) at fullback and played with assurance, making the key break to create Quins' second try by Lee Hopkins.

Meanwhile, former Great Britain coach Phil Larder warned against the RFL looking for a full-time coach to take on the Great Britain job for the New Zealand Test series in the autumn and the World Cup in 2008. Larder advised the RFL not to combine too many roles in one job.

Round 2

After two rounds of competition, Bradford Bulls sat at the top of the table, with four points from their two matches, ahead of Leeds Rhinos and Hull Kingston Rovers on points difference, while champions St Helens languished in seventh place with just two points from their three games.

The Rhinos, after their impressive 18-4 win against Hull FC on the Friday night, took over as favourites to finish the regular season at the top of the table.

St Helens suffered a shock 29-22 defeat at Wakefield, after a 23-point second-half Wildcats blitz, hardly the preparation Saints would have wanted for their Carnegie World Club Challenge against the Brisbane Broncos the following Friday. St Helens coach Daniel

Anderson criticised the fixture schedule that had his side backing up so soon after a Super League game: 'Sunday to Friday is a tough back-up, whatever the competition, whether it's between Super League rounds or ahead of a World Club Challenge. It certainly doesn't enhance your preparation for a game that is supposed to be seen as the game of the year.'

Wakefield welcomed back Australian packman Duncan MacGillivray, who missed the previous week's trip to Craven Park, while winter acquisition from York Matt Blaymire came in at fullback. Paul Wellens returned for his first competitive match since suffering a leg injury in Sean Long's pre-season testimonial and Lee Gilmour was also back after missing the previous weekend's 14-6 home defeat to Harlequins with a broken nose. But Jason Hooper missed out with a shoulder injury, while Jon Wilkin was serving the last of his two-game suspension. Jamie Rooney claimed a try and four conversions, plus a field goal, as well as having a crucial hand in a Ned Catic touchdown, which began to turn the tide.

Leeds' 18-4 home win over Hull FC evoked memories of the 'watersplash' cup final of 1968. Kevin Sinfield's try at the start of the second half pushed Leeds two scores ahead and left Hull, still missing Paul Cooke and flu victim Lee Radford, almost literally, swimming against the tide.

The Bulls recovered from 14-6 down to post an ultimately convincing 36-20 victory over the Wolves at the Halliwell Jones, with Glenn Morrison's awesome work-rate in attack and defence and Michael Platt's predatory hat-trick the key. Morrison had been the match-winner on debut against the Giants and looked set to be one of the outstanding players of Super League XII. 'No-one's getting carried away, we are only two games into the season but it was a great result for us,' said Bulls coach Steve McNamara.

Warrington were missing Vinnie Anderson with a groin strain and flu victim Martin Gleeson, as well as Adrian Morley and Chris Bridge. In New Zealand, former Wolves back-rower Logan Swann, in an article in the New Zealand Herald, slammed what he claimed was an unprofessional culture at the club. 'I didn't learn a lot at Warrington,' said Swann. 'It was a bit tough with some of the senior players in that team running amok.' Swann subsequently claimed he was misquoted.

Hull Kingston Rovers were clear and deserved 17-10 winners at Huddersfield to maintain their 100 per cent start. The Robins established a commanding 16-4 lead at the break and James Webster's late field goal wrapped up the two points.

Coach Justin Morgan praised Michael Smith, after the 30-year-old made his first senior appearance of the season from the bench. Smith had been told at the start of the year to prove his fitness and was left in England when his teammates jetted out to Spain for warm weather training.

A freak deluge, the very first rain of the winter, spoilt Catalan Dragons' opening parade, when they returned to their spiritual home at the Gilbert Brutus Stadium. But worse was to come. They had led all night and were heading for the reprise of last season's first-day victory over Wigan, until along came Sean O'Loughlin to pinch the game.

After Gareth Hock had been sin-binned for dissent and Catalan hooker Aaron Gorrell had kicked a penalty to open up a 16-12 lead, Wigan showed some of the class which had only been glimpsed in the preceding 70-odd minutes. As the Dragons gave away successive penalties, captain O'Loughlin took full advantage of Adam Mogg's attempt to knock down Trent Barrett's pass, and strode over the line for a try which, converted by Pat Richards from a simple position, gave Wigan more than they deserved.

Wigan chairman Maurice Lindsay made a plea to the RFL to choose any club other than Wigan to send to Perpignan for the Dragons' first home game of the season next year. Around 2,000 Wigan fans made the trip to the south of France, and were drenched by some of the heaviest rainfall seen in the region for many years. Lindsay insisted the fans deserved a warm-weather trip.

Harlequins - who had signed former Kangaroo tourist Richard Villasanti that week -

and Salford shared the points at the Stoop in an 18-all draw. Paul Sykes for Harlequins and David Hodgson for Salford converted only one out of four attempts at goal as Quins looked to be coasting to a second successive win at 14-0 up after 25 minutes. But a John Wilshere try on the half hour turned the tide. Michael Korkidas's try with two minutes left could have pinched it for the Reds but Hodgson - who had a fine game otherwise - missed the conversion.

Sheffield Eagles made history when they were awarded the first ever bonus point in British Rugby League, when they lost 20-18 to Doncaster Lakers in a second round Northern Rail Cup game at the Don Valley Stadium on the Friday night.

World Club Challenge

Paul Sculthorpe came off the bench and produced a man of the match performance in a thrilling 18-14 win over Brisbane Broncos at Bolton's Reebok Stadium. Sculthorpe, whose last game had been against Wakefield Trinity Wildcats on 1st September 2006, was a surprise selection, not originally having been named in the St Helens 18-man squad just 24 hours before the game.

He had undergone surgery to try to cure a chronic knee problem that had plagued him over the last two years - the latest in a series of operations that had not provided a complete cure, and had only begun running on the knee two weeks before the World Club Challenge. He admitted that being the man of the match was the last thing on his mind as he warmed up on the side of the field before entering the pitch after 20 minutes. 'Just to play the game and come through it well, that was my main aim,' Sculthorpe told *Rugby Leaguer & League Express*.

Saints captain Sean Long, an inspirational leader, and two-try Ade Gardner, whose second touchdown gave his side the lead for the first time with ten minutes left, were other top Saints performers, with Jon Wilkin, Mike Bennett and James Roby heroes in the pack. Daniel Anderson's side, who were under the cosh for much of the opening stages and fell 0-8 behind, capped a triumphant hat-trick, adding the World Club Challenge to the Challenge Cup and Grand Final successes in the space of seven memorable months.

Saints had four survivors from their 20-18 victory over the Broncos at the Reebok six years before - Paul Wellens, Long, Keiron Cunningham and Sculthorpe. The Broncos had captain Darren Lockyer, Shaun Berrigan, Petero Civoniceva and Dane Carlaw from their 2001 line-up.

The attendance of 23,207 was also impressively higher than the 16,200 gate in 2001. The Broncos, who had prepared with an extended stay in this country that included a warm-up game in Bridgend, had 14 of their 2006 grand final winning team, while Saints had 13 of theirs.

CARNEGIE WORLD CLUB CHALLENGE

Friday 23rd February 2007

ST HELENS 18 BRISBANE BRONCOS 14

SAINTS: 1 Paul Wellens; 2 Ade Gardner; 3 Matt Gidley; 4 Willie Talau; 5 Francis Meli; 6 Leon Pryce; 7 Sean Long (C); 8 Nick Fozzard; 14 James Roby; 10 Jason Cayless; 11 Lee Gilmour; 15 Mike Bennett; 12 Jon Wilkin. Subs (all used): 13 Paul Sculthorpe; 17 James Graham; 18 Bryn Hargreaves; 9 Keiron Cunningham.
Tries: Gardner (40, 70), Sculthorpe (57);
Goals: Sculthorpe 3/3.
BRONCOS: 1 Karmichael Hunt; 5 Steve Michaels; 4 Justin Hodges; 3 Brent Tate; 2 Darius Boyd; 6 Darren Lockyer (C); 7 Shane Perry; 8 Dane Carlaw; 9 Shaun Berrigan; 10 Petero Civoniceva; 11 Corey Parker; 12 Brad Thorn; 13 Tonie Carroll. Subs (all used): 14 Sam Thaiday; 15 Greg Eastwood; 16 Ben Hannant; 17 Michael Ennis.
Tries: Parker (6), Boyd (43); **Goals:** Parker 3/4.
Rugby Leaguer & League Express Men of the Match:
Saints: Sean Long; *Broncos:* Darren Lockyer.
Penalty count: 6-5; **Half-time:** 6-8;
Referee: Steve Clark (Australia);
Attendance: 23,207 *(at Reebok Stadium, Bolton).*

Round 3

Leeds Rhinos suffered two injury blows in their shock 30-22 defeat against the Catalans Dragons in Perpignan on the Saturday night, with stand-off Danny McGuire breaking a knuckle, while prop forward Ryan Bailey suffered a sternum injury.

A second-half 18-point blitz from the Catalans, with hooker Aaron Gorrell providing key passes for two of their tries and his penalty seven minutes from time capping a superb fightback. Two minutes later he was being stretchered from the field with a season-ending knee injury.

Bulls halfback and captain Paul Deacon scored his 2000th point for the club in the Saturday-night home 32-28 win over Wigan. The victory took Bradford to the head of Super League with the only 100 per cent success record from three matches; as Lesley Vainikolo hit top form with three tries. Coach Steve McNamara's main concern was that after coming back from 10-0 down inside 13 minutes to lead 30-10, the Bulls almost lost it in the last quarter, with Wigan down to 12 men - Chris Ashton in the sin bin - when they got to within two points three minutes from time.

Jamie Rooney grabbed a personal haul of 20 points to propel relegation-fancied Wakefield into Super League's top three after a 36-24 win over Salford at Belle Vue. Rooney kicked eight goals from eight attempts and added a try late on that killed off an unlikely Salford comeback. 'Some of the players need to look at themselves and come to work on Monday ready to buckle down,' was Reds coach Karl Harrison's reaction.

The Wolves held on for a thrilling 25-24 victory against Hull FC at the Halliwell Jones Stadium. They overcame a 12-0 first-quarter deficit, fighting back to claim two precious points as Lee Briers 77th-minute field goal finally ended Hull's determined but shaky challenge. The returned Martin Gleeson's surge down the right centre channel and pin-point inside pass that sent Jon Clarke in for the opening try of the second half was the crucial score.

Hull had skipper Lee Radford and creative mainspring Paul Cooke returning, whilst Peter Sharp opted to include Motu Tony at fullback in preference to Shaun Briscoe. Willie Manu made his club debut off the bench.

Hull KR's bubble looked to have burst after a 26-10 home defeat by unbeaten Harlequins at Craven Park. As early as the first minute when debutant Mark O'Neill spilled possession on his own 20-metre line, it wasn't going to be Rovers' day. From the resulting scrum Scott Hill sent Chris Melling racing through a huge gap on Rovers' right flank for the Quins opening try - and Paul Sykes added the first of his three conversions. Quins were 18-0 up after Louie McCarthy-Scarsbrook's try on 18 minutes as Danny Orr continued his rich vein of form with another stand-out display.

Meanwhile the Wolves were fined £500 by the RFL for assistant coach Gary Chambers encroaching onto the field of play when the Wolves played Wigan at the JJB Stadium in round one. Chambers was alleged to have transgressed when the Wolves were bringing Chris Bridge off the field, while trying to get substitute Michael Sullivan onto the pitch early in the game. Warrington coach Paul Cullen believed his side has been harshly treated by the RFL.

SUPER LEAGUE TABLE - *Sunday 25th February*

	P	W	D	L	F	A	D	PTS
Bradford Bulls	3	3	0	0	86	62	24	6
Harlequins	3	2	1	0	58	34	24	5
Wakefield T Wildcats	3	2	0	1	74	60	14	4
Leeds Rhinos	3	2	0	1	70	60	10	4
Hull Kingston Rovers	3	2	0	1	41	45	-4	4
Warrington Wolves	3	2	0	1	61	70	-9	4
Catalans Dragons	3	1	1	1	56	50	6	3
St Helens	3	1	0	2	46	53	-7	2
Wigan Warriors	3	1	0	2	56	64	-8	2
Hull FC	3	0	1	2	38	53	-15	1
Salford City Reds	3	0	1	2	68	84	-16	1
Huddersfield Giants	3	0	0	3	34	53	-19	0

CARNEGIE CHALLENGE CUP - ROUND 1

Saturday 3rd February 2007

Army 20 Leigh Miners Rangers 28; Bradford-Dudley Hill 42 Brighouse 4; Crosfields 6 West Bowling 34; Dewsbury Celtic 36 Ovenden 20; Drighlington 44 Askam 0; East Leeds 56 Warrington Wizards 0; Eastmoor 28 Shaw Cross 6; Eccles & Salford Juniors 20 Blackbrook 2; Egremont 34 Oldham St Annes 18; Heworth 10 Hull Isberg 36; Hull Dockers 52 Thatto Heath 8; Hull Victoria 14 Castleford Lock Lane 44; Ince Rose Bridge 12 Widnes St Maries 35; RAF 0 East Hull 42; Rochdale Mayfield 50 Millom 16; Royal Navy 30 Waterhead 28; Saddleworth 34 Halton Simms Cross 20; Seaton 50 Queens 10; Siddal 18 York Acorn 14; Skirlaugh 74 Milford 0; Stanningley 20 Leigh East 26; Thornhill 58 South London 18; Wath Brow 22 Oulton 26; West Hull 38 Castleford Panthers 12; Wigan St Patricks 24 Leeds Metropolitan University 38

Sunday 4th February 2007

Bramley Buffaloes 12 Wigan St Judes 18; Normanton Knights 46 Fife Lions 8

CARNEGIE CHALLENGE CUP - ROUND 2

Saturday 24th February 2007

Bradford-Dudley Hill 26 Castleford Lock Lane 28 (aet); East Hull 50 Dewsbury Celtic 4; Eccles & Salford Juniors 40 Egremont 28; Leigh East 10 Oulton Raiders 25; Leigh Miners Rangers 34 Leeds Metropolitan University 18; Rochdale Mayfield 50 East Leeds 0; Royal Navy 26 Normanton 28; Saddleworth 21 Siddal 14; Thornhill 38 Strela Kazan 20; West Hull 23 Skirlaugh 16; Widnes St Maries 22 Hull Isberg 6; Wigan St Judes 22 Drighlington 30

Saturday 1st March 2007

Hull Dockers 8 Eastmoor 28; Seaton 4 West Bowling 22

MARCH
Cats go wild

Round 4

Wakefield reached the Super League summit for the first time in their history, following a 19-6 triumph at Hull FC in torrential rain and wind. After their opening-round defeat at relegation-fancied Hull KR, the Wildcats had six points from their four matches, ahead of Bradford, Leeds Rhinos, Hull Kingston Rovers and Warrington on points difference.

'It's only round four,' said their coach John Kear. 'We're a seventh of the way through the season. It's a Grand National, not a sprint.' It was the first time Wakefield had won three successive games since 2005. Halfbacks Ben Jeffries and man of the match Jamie Rooney ran the show. Wakefield sealed their win ten minutes from time when Jeffries' sublime pass sent Rooney away again down the centre and Brett Ferres was perfectly placed to complete the 50-metre move. Kear, sacked by Hull in 2006, found it impossible to hide his delight at his side's performance on his first return to former employers. Hull started without playmaker Paul Cooke, sidelined for up to five weeks with a torn hamstring suffered in training, whilst for the Wildcats Danny Sculthorpe and Waine Pryce both made their debuts from the bench.

Trinity's elevation to the top of Super League came at an opportune time, with club officials due to meet the leaders of the local council that week to discuss plans for their new stadium.

Despite being among the frontrunners, bookmakers still had Hull KR favourites to finish at the bottom of the table at the end of the regular season of 27 rounds - even after they defeated Wigan 26-16 at the JJB Stadium, which gave them six points in the Super League table.

It was a Friday night to remember for Rovers and their fans, their first win on Wigan soil since 1984, and a day to forget for the Warriors, missing star turn Trent Barrett through a calf injury and trailing by 26-0 at the interval. 'The first half was embarrassing,' coach Brian Noble admitted. 'I'm reasonably excited,' counterpart Justin Morgan said.

Rovers' game plan was deceptively simple but devastatingly effective, driving the ball forward, with Michael Vella setting the lead, kicking astutely and then mounting an efficient kick chase. They set the tone with a second-minute try, forcing the position when Chris Ashton, who endured a nightmare first half, put a foot in touch attempting to gather James Webster's raking kick. Chris Chester, revelling on his return to the JJB, capitalised with a slick pass and Byron Ford squeezed in at the corner.

St Helens, after their World Club Challenge win and a stunning performance against Bradford Bulls on the Friday night, were re-installed as favourites to finish at the top of Super League. The home win ended 34-22, but Bradford had been blown away in a blistering start that saw them 28-0 adrift after just 21 minutes.

Eighth-placed Saints entered the clash against the undefeated table-topping Bulls with just one win from their opening three league games. To compound the pressure they were deprived of the services of Jason Hooper (shoulder), Maurie Fa'asavalu (ankle), Paul Sculthorpe (knee) and Mike Bennett (face), with coach Daniel Anderson giving a debut bench spot to youngster Steve Bannister, and a start to Steve Tyrer, two weeks before his 18th birthday. Tyrer (whose only previous appearance was as a substitute against Catalans in July 2006) scored a crucial second-half try and five conversions for a 14-point haul. But the show was stolen by James Roby with an electrifying creative display from dummy-half, and some solid defence.

Anderson was unhappy with knocks to the head suffered by Lee Gilmour and Jon Wilkin, with Bulls hooker Terry Newton going on report for the incident involving Wilkin, for which he received a two-match ban. Saints' injury woes meant that they finished the game with eleven men.

Anderson was concerned too that the RFL's new policy on restricting trainers' access to the playing field would impact on player health. 'Anyone who watches it can see it has flaws in it ... it's just not working. I'm not a lone voice in this,' said the Saints coach. 'We played a World Club Challenge last week under last year's rules, with no issues whatsoever, but for some reason we've got to do something different in Super League.'

Salford City Reds, according to the Sydney media, on the weekend they registered their first win of the season, had made a massive offer to Bulldogs goal-kicking machine Hazem El Masri. They beat Catalan Dragons 10-nil in a dour televised Saturday game. A poor spectacle was worsened by the Salford club's decision to hand out free horns to children who created an ear-splitting noise all game. Malcolm Alker's try nine minutes from time sealed it.

Leeds Rhinos beat win-less Huddersfield Giants in the Headingley mud. The Giants pulled back to 16-12 with barely a minute left, and – with a man to the good after the sin-binning of Brent Webb for dissent – launched a final assault; Keith Mason, Brad Drew and Ryan Hudson sending Stephen Wild clear, only for Lee Smith to crucially bat down what would have been a scoring pass for Jamahl Lolesi.

Paul Cullen was delighted to report no additional injury concerns following the Wolves' 19-12 victory, after trailing 12-0, against Harlequins in London on the Saturday, with Chris Bridge making his return.

After four rounds the Challenge Cup finalists Huddersfield and Grand Final runners-up Hull – two of the movers and shakers of Super League XI – were propping the table.

Meanwhile the RFL announced that the Wolves would play host to Andrew Johns once again when the Halliwell Jones Stadium staged the Gillette Fusion Centenary International between sides representing the RFL and the New Zealand Rugby League, with Johns joining the Kiwis as a guest player for a one-off match.

Round 5

At last Hull KR were no longer the favourites to finish at the bottom of Super League. The Robins stayed at the top of the table after a 22-20 win over Leeds Rhinos at Craven Park, with 11 of the squad having taken them to the National One title the previous season.

James Webster scored a brilliant solo try, and debutant Andreas Bauer's 56th minute try followed by Gareth Morton's angled goal made it 22-10 and proved to be just a wide enough margin. There were rumblings among the Headingley faithful about coach Tony Smith.

The new favourites for relegation were Huddersfield Giants, after suffering their fifth successive defeat of the season at home, to Hull FC - their first win of the season – by 16-12. Shaun Briscoe was man of the match after his re-inclusion at fullback.

Bradford Bulls chairman Peter Hood denied rumours that Gloucester rugby union club had made a bid for winger Lesley Vainikolo. But *Rugby Leaguer & League Express* confirmed that Wigan fullback Chris Ashton had signed a contract with the Northampton rugby union club.

The Volcano failed to score in the 56-18 victory against Salford City Reds at Odsal. Bulls coach Steve McNamara highlighted Michael Platt and David Solomona, two of his new recruits, after they produced five-star performances in the demolition. Platt, grabbed a hat-trick of tries, while Solomona, the Bulls' major off-season capture, produced his best performance in a Bradford shirt.

Iestyn Harris and Shontayne Hape were also in top form. Hape grabbed two tries – an effort equalled by Chris McKenna – while Harris's excellent distribution led directly to five of Bradford's ten scores.

Salford City Reds football manager Steve Simms dismissed reports linking the Reds with a bid for Hazem el Masri.

Trent Barrett returned to the Wigan line-up after a calf tear ruled him out of the home defeat to Hull KR, and the Warriors edged Harlequins 16-12 in a Friday night game at the JJB Stadium.

David Vaealiki's 65th-minute try, the only score of the second half, decided the contest. Vaealiki, loitering with intent on the wing, fell over the line to score in the left corner after Thomas Leuluai, a Quins old boy, produced a long cut-out pass.

Lee Briers' eight points before leaving the field with a hamstring injury in the Wolves' 48-12 home hammering by St Helens took him past a career total of 2,000 in front a capacity crowd.

Saints rode their luck in a controversial first half - with Martin Gleeson denied a try by the video referee - to accumulate a 16-0 lead, weathering a brief 12-point Wolves rally in the dying moments of the half before securing victory in style with 32-unanswered second-half points, Matt Gidley ending with a hat-trick.

As well as Briers' injury, Paul Wood (shoulder) and Chris Bridge (groin) didn't finish the game.

Catalans Dragons signed Newcastle Knights hooker Luke Quigley for the rest of the season to plug the gap created by the loss of Aaron Gorrell. Another top performance from Wakefield stand-off Jamie Rooney helped Wakefield Trinity to a 40-20 home win over the French - their fourth win in a row - and maintained their position in the leading pack.

And as the Irish satellite TV channel Setanta's coverage of Australian NRL matches began, its Head of Programmes Jim McMunn admitted he was looking further down the track at a possible Super League deal, with BSkyB's current contract set to run out at the end of 2008.

Round 6

Warrington went into the home game with Hull KR without captain Lee Briers and Chris Bridge, with Paul Cullen shuffling his troops to create a makeshift halfback partnership of back-rower Vinnie Anderson and hooker Jon Clarke. The changes worked, however, with the Wolves registering a 30-12 victory, and Clarke scoring two tries.

Paul Johnson also scored two tries and showed no ill-effects from a head-clash with teammate Adrian Morley, who, after only 16 minutes of the game, fractured the same cheekbone he injured on his debut for Warrington in the first game of the season against Wigan at the JJB Stadium.

Warrington ran in six tries in all to strike a psychological blow before the teams met again in a fourth-round Carnegie Challenge Cup-tie a fortnight later.

The defeat was a double-blow for Rovers, with inspirational captain and halfback James Webster sustaining ankle ligament damage in the 39th minute. In the week the Robins agreed to release their New Zealand forward Michael Smith from his contract 'for personal reasons' after three games off the bench.

Harlequins got themselves 12-4 in front of the Bulls at half-time of their clash at the Stoop, but Bradford came through to win 36-22. The turning point was Lesley Vainikolo's interception try from a pass that was intended for an unmarked Matt Gafa. Instead of restoring their lead, Quins found themselves more than a score down with just over ten minutes left to play.

Bulls coach Steve McNamara hailed Joe Vagana as one of Super League's best ever overseas players after his 200th game for the Bradford club.

Quins chairman Ian Lenagan claimed his club came close to persuading former Wigan and Great Britain star Brian Carney, who had left Gold Coast at the start of the season, to sign for his club, before he opted to sign for Irish rugby union province Munster.

Hull's Kiwi hooker Richard Swain suffered concussion in their 24-12 win over St Helens at the KC Stadium. Hull's two tries in two minutes mid-way through the second half from top performer Shaun Briscoe, and Kirk Yeaman put them 22-6 ahead and proved too much, even for the high-scoring Saints to claw back. Samoan prop Hutch Maiava had his best game in the black and white shirt, but Sid Domic was found guilty of a reckless high tackle on Lee Gilmour and suspended for two matches.

Paul Sculthorpe confirmed that his knee came through the game unscathed after he came off the bench.

Salford went down 25-6 to Wigan at the Willows in a low-quality clash, with captain Malcolm Alker suffering medial ligament damage on the half hour. Second-rower Mark Edmondson also left the field with a dislocated shoulder. Wigan skipper Sean O'Loughlin again led from the front and capped his inspirational display with a fine try.

Wakefield Trinity Wildcats looked dead and buried when Leeds Rhinos led 24-0 at Belle Vue with only a few first-half seconds remaining. But within 14 minutes the Wildcats had clawed their way back to be only four points behind.

In the end it was three penalty goals that proved the difference. After matching Leeds' five tries, Wakefield deserved at least a point. Unfortunately, the penalty count (26 in all) once again caused as much discussion as the spectacular play. At one first-half stage it was 11-2 to Leeds and on the back of that they swept in for four unanswered tries.

Referee Ashley Klein also sent three Wakefield players to the sin bin, plus one from Leeds, to put Wildcats coach John Kear in an accusing mood at the post-match press conference. 'We will analyse our own performance, but I hope the man in the middle's performance is analysed as well,' he said. Fijian winger Semi Tadulala broke his forearm.

Catalans Dragons produced a 23-22 win over Huddersfield in Perpignan on the Saturday night, to leave the Giants still without a win. Stacey Jones' field goal with the last kick of the first half proved the difference as the Giants came back from 23-12.

Round 7

Catalans Dragons pulled Bradford Bulls back to the chasing pack with their first away win of the season - the most significant display in their short history - a 29-22 success at Odsal.

More bad news for the Bulls was that Shontayne Hape picked up cruciate ligament damage, thought likely to rule him out for the rest of the season - the third time that the New Zealand international had suffered the injury, undergoing surgery on his other knee in 2003 and 2005.

The Dragons led 10-0 midway through the first half - despite a 7-1 first-half penalty count in Bradford's favour - and then 23-10 with only 15 minutes remaining, but had to withstand two attempted Bradford comebacks. Their winger Thomas Bosc collected 16 points in total, with ten of those ensuring the Dragons made a perfect start.

Stacey Jones was magnificent for Catalans, but Casey McGuire pipped his halfback partner for gamestar honours. But the Dragons' injury list lengthened when Sébastien Raguin suffered a broken arm and Gregory Mounis a broken thumb.

Pre-season relegation fancies Wakefield recorded their fifth win to stay joint top - a 30-24 televised Sunday evening home win over Warrington Wolves. Warrington fought back from an early 10-0 deficit to lead 24-16, before tries by Waine Pryce, Ben Jeffries and Tevita Leo-Latu in the space of eight minutes took the Wildcats home. Pryce had a clinching try contentiously ruled out before the Wolves went desperately close to a leveller in a tense finish. Already without the injured Adrian Morley and Lee Briers, they lost Paul Johnson to a broken finger.

Rugby Leaguer & League Express reported that Rhinos coach Tony Smith was in pole position to be offered the Great Britain coaching job following the RFL's decision to reject the application of former St Helens, Gateshead and Hull coach Shaun McRae. Smith - whose contract with the Rhinos expired at the end of the 2007 season - was duly unveiled that week, and would take up the job full-time at the end of Leeds' season.

The Rhinos ended the weekend joint top on ten points after Danny McGuire and Brent Webb scored two tries apiece in Leeds' 28-16 win over Harlequins at Headingley, with Rob Burrow outstanding.

Harlequins coach Brian McDermott insisted there was no need to panic after watching his side - missing Scott Hill - slip to a fourth consecutive defeat

Paul Sculthorpe made his second Super League appearance as a substitute following his long-standing knee troubles in an ultimately comprehensive eight-try 42-14 victory over Hull KR at Knowsley Road.

After falling behind to an early Jon Steel try, the Saints responded with their other bench players - James Graham, James Roby and Maurie Fa'asavalu - all impressing.

Hull KR captain James Webster was missing after suffering ankle ligament damage in the previous weekend's defeat at Warrington. But there was no fracture and the Aussie talisman was expected to be out for only four to six weeks.

Chris Ashton received high praise from Wigan Warriors coach Brian Noble after Wigan's 30-20 win at Hull FC. The 19-year-old fullback had that week announced his move to Northampton RU at the end of the season, and was booed every time he had the ball. And after the game it was revealed he had been injured in a car crash the night before.

Trent Barrett had his best game for Wigan. The former Australia Test stand-off scored his first Super League try after 31 minutes, followed with another in the second half, and also created one for Pat Richards.

'I'm very disappointed, a pile of rubbish to tell you the truth,' Hull coach Peter Sharp said.

Huddersfield were left five points adrift after an 18-16 defeat by Salford City Reds at the Galpharm Stadium - their seventh straight defeat - all by eight points or less. Chris Thorman had a late chance to level things, with a penalty for obstruction, but his kick drifted narrowly wide

Calls were made for the removal of coach Jon Sharp. A much more comfortable looking Reds boss Karl Harrison was in no doubt how important a first away win of the season was to a Salford side still striving to rediscover the form that took them to the play-offs in 2006.

With captain Malcolm Alker set to be sidelined for between four to six weeks after picking up medial knee ligament damage in the 25-6 defeat to Wigan the previous weekend, David Berthezene was signed on a month's loan from Catalans Dragons. He had arrived on the Wednesday and made an impressive debut. Huddersfield winger Martin Aspinwall made his seasonal debut for the Giants and told *Rugby Leaguer & League Express* that one win would kick start the Giants' season.

SUPER LEAGUE TABLE - *Sunday 25th March*

	P	W	D	L	F	A	D	PTS
Bradford Bulls	7	5	0	2	222	165	57	10
Wakefield T Wildcats	7	5	0	2	189	142	47	10
Leeds Rhinos	7	5	0	2	166	136	30	10
St Helens	7	4	0	3	182	125	57	8
Wigan Warriors	7	4	0	3	143	128	15	8
Warrington Wolves	7	4	0	3	146	172	-26	8
Hull Kingston Rovers	7	4	0	3	115	153	-38	8
Catalans Dragons	7	3	1	3	128	144	-16	7
Harlequins	7	2	1	4	120	133	-13	5
Hull FC	7	2	1	4	104	126	-22	5
Salford City Reds	7	2	1	4	120	181	-61	5
Huddersfield Giants	7	0	0	7	96	126	-30	0

APRIL
Cooke-ing up a storm

April opened with the fourth round of the Carnegie Challenge Cup and the gap between Super League and the National Leagues was illustrated again, with some one-sided scorelines. The two exceptions were at Odsal and the Halton Stadium.

NL1 Castleford went down at Bradford by only 24-16 on the Friday night. At 18-16 with less than 20 minutes left, the Tigers - with scrum-half Danny Brough in top form - were in with a real shout until David Solomona's converted try took the Bulls into the fifth round. In the Sunday TV game Wigan came away from Widnes with a 34-24 win thanks to a four-try seven-minute period just after the hour mark, with Gareth Hock having a hand in all four scores.

Leeds winger Scott Donald scored four tries in the first 22 minutes as the Rhinos demolished Workington Town 72-10 at Headingley on the Friday night. And in France, Featherstone coach David Hobbs received a rare first-half red card from referee Phil Bentham for protesting against a Catalans challenge in their 70-12 defeat.

Paul King was missing in Hull FC's 78-0 win over Hunslet Hawks after being disciplined for a breach of Hull's disciplinary code, although the club refused to elaborate on King's offence.

Hull Kingston Rovers were the only Super League club knocked out of the Cup, following their 38-10 defeat on the Saturday at Warrington - who that week had been linked with Huddersfield's giant forward Eorl Crabtree. Ben Westwood was placed on report for alleged use of the elbow while carrying the ball on Robins loose forward Tommy Gallagher. Westwood received a two-match suspension.

Round 8

It finally all came good for Huddersfield on Good Friday night as they hammered table-topping Wakefield 56-12 at the Galpharm Stadium. Right from the kick-off the fired-up Giants - led by Brad Drew - tore ruthlessly into their neighbours, and were on the scoreboard when Stephen Wild powered over in the corner after only three minutes. Twenty-five minutes later it was 28-0.

Leeds Rhinos were left clear at the top after their 18-14 win over the Bulls at Odsal on the Thursday night. Bradford's tremendous defence seemed to have earned them victory with only three minutes left, but a sensational late Scott Donald try won the game.

Champions St Helens moved smoothly into second place with an accomplished 32-14 six-try demolition of derby rivals Wigan at a sold-out JJB Stadium. Saints overcame an early Pat Richards try to compile a tidy 16-8 half-time lead through tries by Francis Meli, Willie Talau and James Roby before going on to dominate the second half with further tries from Maurie Fa'asavalu, Matt Gidley and Mike Bennett. A Thomas Leuluai strike was the Warriors' only reply. Roby was at the heart of Saints' attacking efforts, grabbing his first try of the season.

Paul Rauhihi scored two tries to sink the struggling City Reds in a thrilling 34-32 Warrington win at the Willows. Salford, second bottom in the table, now three points above the Giants, had beaten Warrington in all three of their Super League meetings in 2006.

Four tries in 18 minutes at the beginning of the second half took Catalans Dragons into the top six for the first time in their history - and condemned Hull KR to their fourth league defeat of the season - by 34-20 at Craven Park. Although Rovers had clawed their way back into the match with two tries in five minutes just before the break to turn around all square at 10-points each, a superb third quarter from the French ended their hopes of completing an unlikely comeback.

With the Hull derby looming on Easter Monday, Hull FC also sunk to defeat - by 30-28 at Harlequins - leaving last season's grand finalists third from bottom.

The coaches of both Hull clubs voiced their concerns about the two-games-in-four days fixture schedule and St Helens coach Daniel Anderson said he was expecting a lull. 'Last year I reckon we were playing at about 60 per cent of our capacity after Easter,' he said. 'I think the whole competition goes backwards for a couple of weeks in terms of intensity after Easter.'

Round 9

A capacity 23,002 Easter Monday crowd was kept in a state of hysteria throughout the first Hull derby since 1997, as Rovers pushed Hull FC right to the last few seconds before conceding the try that finally finished them off.

But for that try by Sid Domic, Rovers could have claimed equal bragging rights in the city after matching Hull's three tries at that late stage. They had battled back from being 12-0 down inside 18 minutes to make it a tension-packed derby right to the end.

Hull welcomed back Paul Cooke after a six-match injury absence and he proved to be the main difference between the teams. Cooke missed the opening two rounds of Super League with a knee injury, and, after playing just one game against Warrington, tore a hamstring in training and had not played since. His brilliant distribution set up Hull's first three tries. The 20-metre pass that sent in Matt Sing for Hull's third try was exceptional. A similar one opened the way for Gareth Raynor to put in Danny Tickle for the first and Cooke produced a shorter one that Shaun Briscoe shot onto to score. Cooke also added three goals, including a great touchline effort.

Rovers also took a risk in bringing back their key man, James Webster, after injury, and he seemed to be struggling despite putting in Luke Dyer for Rovers' first try. He also linked with Scott Murrell to get Andreas Bauer over to make it 16-14 after David Tangata-Toa had charged over off Ben Fisher's pass a few minutes earlier to set the stage for a nerve-wracking last 20 minutes. There was a huge sigh of relief from Hull players and fans when Domic dashed in for the match-clinching try seconds from the end.

St Helens hit top spot with a 48-4 home demolition of the struggling Salford City Reds - who confirmed they were looking to sign New Zealand Test centre Paul Whatuira from Wests Tigers. Saints never missed a beat from their Good Friday victory over Wigan, despite drafting-in youngsters Paul Clough and Scott Moore to replace Paul Sculthorpe and Jon Wilkin (broken hand), with James Roby starting at loose forward.

Harlequins completed a perfect Easter with a resounding 38-16 win over the Dragons in front of over 9,000 fans in Perpignan. The game ended on a controversial note as Alex Chan appeared to use his forearm on Henry Paul. Chan was placed on report as Paul was carried from the field, although he was found to have no case to answer.

Four second-half Wakefield tries at Belle Vue were not enough to stop high-flying Bradford getting back to winning ways by 36-24 after successive defeats against Catalans and Leeds.

Trinity were always playing catch-up after falling 12-0 behind to scores from Lesley Vainikolo and former Belle Vue hero David Solomona, who was booed every time he was involved the game. A soul-destroying 80-metre interception try from Vainikolo just before the break, sent the visitors in 24-6 ahead at half-time. Paul Deacon defied a blustery wind to only miss one in seven attempts on goal, ensuring it would remain a pointless Easter for the Wildcats.

Chris Thorman booted seven goals from seven attempts to grab Huddersfield's second win of the weekend - a 26-18 success at Warrington. On the downside Shane Elford needed surgery to repair a shoulder he damaged in the win. Warrington – and Henry Fa'afili in particular – threw everything at the visitors in a frantic second half, but a couple of Thorman goals kept the Wolves at bay.

On Easter Tuesday night Leeds' two-point lead at the top was wiped out as Wigan beat them 20-18 at Headingley. Phil Bailey's breathtaking last-gasp try in the corner gave the Warriors the win. After the majestic Trent Barrett had conjured a ripping 40/20 with 100 seconds left, Keith Senior went for a miracle play 20 metres from his own line, succeeding only in putting the ball into touch - Bailey securing the points from the resulting scrum.

Wigan lost Michael Withers with a knee injury. It proved to be the Aussie's last game in Super League since arriving at Bradford for the 1999 season.

Meanwhile in one of the more left-field stories of the year, RFL Executive Chairman Richard Lewis downplayed reports in New Zealand that suggested a New Zealand team based in the capital city of Wellington could join the Super League in 2009.

Round 10

Huddersfield's 41-16 home win over Wigan saw them move off the bottom of the table for the first time in SLXII, and equalled the club record of three consecutive Super League victories.

Wigan started well enough and led 10-8 after 30 minutes. Then Huddersfield stepped up the pace and at one stage in the second half ran them ragged. Former Wigan player Kevin Brown was switched from centre to stand-off to face Trent Barrett, with match honours going to the young Englishman. Barrett looked rattled, giving away a penalty when the pair had a minor confrontation late on. Chris Thorman made two tries with kicks and also converted nine goals including a field goal. A year before, Brian Noble had ended a Wigan slump with a 46-14 victory at Huddersfield in his first match in charge, but this year the Warriors were well beaten.

The Giants' win put Salford on the bottom of the table after a 35-18 defeat to Hull FC at the Willows. The City Reds led 12-0 after only 12 minutes. But the Airlie Birds scored 22-unanswered points before half-time, as they extended their winning run against Salford to 14 games. There was more woe for the Reds as captain Malcolm Alker's comeback game lasted only 12 minutes, as he suffered another knee injury.

Hull had picked up four points out of four since Paul Cooke had returned to action, and he slotted over five goals, scored a game-turning try on 16 minutes, and set up two other touchdowns with pinpoint kicks. Gareth Raynor also performed heroics, scoring two tries.

Hull Kingston Rovers meanwhile slumped to a 52-22 defeat at Bradford. The Bulls ran in nine tries – including four in a devastating six-minute spell midway through the second half – to inflict Hull KR's sixth successive defeat. And Rovers' miserable afternoon was completed by news that winger Jon Steel had suffered a broken leg during a collision with Lesley Vainikolo. Hull KR coach Justin Morgan gave debuts to St Helens winger Ian Hardman and Wigan's Danny Hill, who both joined the club on a month's loan.

Wakefield and Harlequins ended the weekend fourth and fifth in the table after fighting out an 18-all draw at a sun-lit Stoop. Wakefield led 10-0 early on but Quins fought back to lead 22-16 before Matt Blaymire's try, converted by Jamie Rooney, 64 minutes in levelled the scores. A late flurry of field-goal efforts from Rooney, Orr and Tyrone Smith added to the drama.

April

The Rhinos eventually cut loose to post a convincing nine-try 52-10 victory over an injury-depleted Wolves side at a sun-baked Halliwell Jones Stadium. Warrington competed spiritedly for most of the first half, deservedly holding a 6-0 lead until Gareth Ellis's try opened the floodgates. Keith Senior's 200th career try set up the Rhinos for a dominant second-half display.

A four-try performance from Man of Steel fullback Paul Wellens helped Saints to a 53-10 victory over Catalan Dragons at Knowsley Road, to keep the champions top of the table on points difference.

Round 11

The weekend of round 11 was dominated by the news that Paul Cooke was poised to sign for Kingston Rovers, with the Robins adamant they would not have to pay a transfer fee, because Cooke himself was sure he did not have a valid signed contract with Hull FC. Cooke, 26, was reported to have signed a three-year extension to his contract with Hull in June 2005, but no one from the club was able to confirm that the contract was actually signed.

Hull FC chairman Kath Hetherington was insistent he would be playing for the black and whites when they visited Wakefield Trinity Wildcats on the following Saturday evening. Hetherington also dismissed reports from Australia that Hull were lining up Canterbury Bulldogs halfback Brent Sherwin as a replacement for Cooke.

On the field, David Hodgson's late try pulled Salford to within a point of Hull KR at the foot of the table after a thrilling clash at Craven Park. Salford had led 16-0 inside the first eight minutes but, helped by 13 consecutive penalties from rookie referee Gareth Hewer, Rovers managed to claw their way back into the tie to set up a frantic finish. Salford scrum-half Luke Robinson scored one try, created two others and was the difference between the sides.

Rovers coach Justin Morgan had that week put pen to paper on a new contract keeping him at the club until the end of 2010, despite being linked with the Leeds Rhinos job, which became vacant at the end of the current campaign. New signing Mark Lennon made his debut.

Hull also lost out at home - in a 32-22 defeat to Bradford Bulls, Andy Lynch crashing over in the 78th minute to seal a thrilling win. Cooke kicked three goals as David Solomona starred for the Bulls, reported to be close to signing Melbourne Storm and Australian Test winger Matt King. Current Bulls winger Lesley Vainikolo was thought likely to follow former Bulls star Karl Pryce to Gloucester rugby union club at the end of the season.

Bradford went back to the top of the table on points difference after Leeds' Saturday night victory over St Helens at a jam-packed Headingley. Lee Smith starred in the 38-19 win, making breaks for the last two Leeds tries by Brent Webb and Rob Burrow. Clinton Toopi's try a minute into the second half set his side up for a near faultless 40-minute barrage that rocked the champions.

Saints coach Daniel Anderson had given his squad some time off in the week after the heavy Easter programme, and was without Matt Gidley, taken ill on the team bus, and Ade Gardner, who sustained an eye injury after being attacked on a night out in Barrow.

Catalans Dragons parted company with their chief executive Nicolas Rayer, but it didn't affect them, as they beat Warrington 27-16 at Gilbert Brutus. Winger Thomas Bosc made an excellent transition to stand-off, kicked five goals from five and scored the clinching try two minutes from time.

Huddersfield Giants created a club record when their 46-16 home victory over Harlequins became their fourth successive league victory, the most ever registered by the Giants since they first joined Super League in 1998. And there was a personal record for skipper Chris Thorman, whose try and seven goals took his career tally to more than

1,000 points.

Wigan moved into the top four with a Friday night 44-10 victory over Wakefield Trinity Wildcats at the JJB, with fullback Chris Ashton scoring two tries, and Pat Richards netting 20 points with a try and eight goals.

On the Sunday of that weekend, over 5,700 people turned up at Knowsley Road to see St Helens Legends beat a Rugby League Legends side 46-28, raising in the region of £60,000 for former Saints fullback Steve Prescott.

Round 12

Paul Cooke made his Hull KR debut in their 28-16 home defeat to Huddersfield Giants on the Friday night of round 12, after the RFL accepted his registration less than an hour before the 5.00pm deadline. The RFL did so after fresh evidence was brought to light by Cooke's legal team, confirming that Hull FC had accepted his resignation. Hull FC immediately issued a statement saying that their acceptance of Cooke's resignation had been taken 'out of context'. Cooke's second game would be against his former club in the second game of the Millennium Magic weekend the following Saturday.

The Giants moved up to eighth after their fifth straight win. With the score 16-18 and only ten minutes remaining, the sin-binning of Mark O'Neill ended the Robins' chances, as Brad Drew once again stood out.

Adrian Morley played 67 minutes of the Wolves' 36-24 defeat at Bradford - his second comeback of the year, after twice fracturing his cheekbone, in the opening game against Wigan and again, five matches later, against Hull KR. Morley, who helped Bradford to Grand Final success in 2005, quickly incurred the home fans' wrath, and had already been warned twice for illegal challenges by referee Ashley Klein when he was put on report for a late tackle on Iestyn Harris. A 17-7 penalty count in their favour helped the Bulls shake off the Wolves. Morley was found to have no case to answer.

New Zealand Test winger Tame Tupou, released by the Brisbane Broncos, was being reported down under as having joined the Bulls with immediate effect.

Leeds climbed back on top on points difference after a 54-8 home win over Catalans Dragons. Rhinos skipper Kevin Sinfield scored 26 points, with Brent Webb recording a hat-trick. But young utility threequarter Ashley Gibson was ruled out for the remainder of the season after rupturing an anterior cruciate ligament.

Hull FC were stepping up the search for potential new halfback, with the club flooded with offers from agents based in Australia. Manly halfback Michael Monaghan was linked with the club, although debutant Anthony Thackeray made a sparkling Super League debut while helping his team to a 20-18 win at Wakefield on the Saturday.

Wildcats coach John Kear signed a two-year extension to his contract, to keep him at Belle Vue until the end of the 2009 season. The news was revealed to a crowd of over 7,000 prior to Trinity's defeat in front of the TV cameras. The Wildcats also extended the contracts of front-row duo Richard Moore and Tevita Leo-Latu. Ryan Atkins' try three minutes from time gave Wakefield the chance of a draw but Jamie Rooney's kick was astray.

St Helens trounced Harlequins at the Stoop 44-6, And Wigan produced a nine-try 50-24 barrage at the Willows to keep Salford bottom, with Trent Barrett scoring his first Super League hat-trick.

SUPER LEAGUE TABLE - *Sunday 29th April*

	P	W	D	L	F	A	D	PTS
Leeds Rhinos	12	9	0	3	346	207	139	18
Bradford Bulls	12	9	0	3	392	275	117	18
St Helens	12	8	0	4	378	197	181	16
Wigan Warriors	12	7	0	5	287	253	34	14
Hull FC	12	5	1	6	231	238	-7	11
Wakefield T Wildcats	12	5	1	6	275	320	-45	11
Catalans Dragons	12	5	1	6	223	325	-102	11
Huddersfield Giants	12	5	0	7	293	204	89	10
Harlequins	12	4	2	6	232	289	-57	10
Warrington Wolves	12	5	0	7	248	345	-97	10
Hull Kingston Rovers	12	4	0	8	211	317	-106	8
Salford City Reds	12	3	1	8	226	372	-146	7

MAY
Chaos in Wales

Round 13

The return in 2007 to the Challenge Cup's traditional home of Wembley Stadium led to the creation of Rugby League's latest innovation on the Mayday Bank Holiday weekend - 'Millennium Magic'.

The venture had received plenty of criticism in the months before the weekend, not least because the RFL had created an extra derby fixture for all the clubs, meaning that Super League XII involved at least four derbies for some clubs Many of the clubs themselves were worried that the weekend - despite a huge cash injection from the Welsh Tourist Board over three years - would be a financial disaster.

A reported total of 58,831 spectators came through the gates of Cardiff's Millennium Stadium on the first Saturday and Sunday of May, leading RFL Executive Chairman Richard Lewis to express confidence that the weekend would be repeated the next year.

From the opening game between Harlequins and the Catalans, won 32-28 by the Quins, to the final game between Bradford Bulls and Leeds Rhinos on the Sunday night, the entertainment was excellent, with two games each day being televised live.

But there was plenty of controversy, right up to the last minute, with Steve Ganson awarding a matchwinning try to Leeds when the scorer Jordan Tansey touched down Kevin Sinfield's last-second penalty miss from an offside position.

The penalty, which bounced back from the crossbar, should never have been awarded in the first place. Bradford second-rower Matt Cook had been penalised for picking the ball up in an offside position, but replays revealed the ball had actually come off a Rhinos boot. That week, refs boss Stuart Cummings was forced to admit that video referee Ashley Klein had wrongly advised Ganson on the penalty award - overstepping his brief. But there was still puzzlement over why Ganson decided not to go to the video referee for the ninth time and immediately awarded the try.

It ended 42-38, harsh on a Bulls side that led for virtually the entire match. Bulls coach Steve McNamara - who had just been named as Tony Smith's assistant in the new Great Britain coaching set-up - wasn't impressed. 'The referee decided the game,' he said. 'It was ludicrous, ridiculous and I'm sick to the teeth.'

In the following week, the Bulls threatened to pursue the two lost league points with a legal challenge. McNamara met with Stuart Cummings and Ganson and Klein, and confirmed afterwards that he had settled his differences with the officials.

That week the Bulls failed to overturn a three-match suspension imposed on hooker Terry Newton - a top performer in Cardiff - for a foul committed on the Rhinos' Jamie

Thackray. The 200th Hull-Rovers derby ended in a 14-10 triumph for the Robins. There were a few jeers early on, but Paul Cooke soon silenced them as his kick through brought a try for Makali Aizue after only four minutes. Cooke popped over the goal, added a 20th minute penalty goal, and Rovers never looked back, as they dug in to end a run of eight successive cup and league defeats.

After the game, Cooke described the last two weeks as 'murder. I can't even go down the street without getting abuse. But I'm broad shouldered and I'm better than that. I love playing football, and now I play for Hull Kingston Rovers.'

Paul Wellens scored four tries as St Helens cruised to a 34-18 victory over Wigan to round off day one. Saints coach Daniel Anderson had some harsh words for the performance of the officials, saying, 'The win was very satisfying. I was filthy at the end of the game. I thought the officiating was inconsistent. Sometimes you get good calls, but tonight I thought we got every dumb call possible.'

Warrington eased the pressure on coach Paul Cullen with their first win in five matches since their Good Friday success at the Willows - hammering Salford 50-18 and leaving the Reds three points adrift at the foot of the table.

'Nobody likes being bottom of the table, but somebody has to be, and at the moment it's our turn,' said Reds coach Karl Harrison. 'But I'm sure that we won't be there at the end of the season. People have to remain confident in what we're trying to build here.'

A ten-try effort from the Wolves lifted the gloom that had been gathering at the Halliwell Jones Stadium, and club stalwart Cullen's spirits were raised by the best Wolves performance since the opening night win at Wigan. 'Our intention is very clear,' he said. 'We intend to make the second half of the season ours.'

The opening game of the weekend between Catalans and Quins was the most entertaining clash of the first day. Harlequins edged a topsy-turvy match 32-28, ending a superb Catalans comeback with a controversial winning try. With Stacey Jones pulling the strings at scrum-half, the French had recovered from an early 0-12 deficit to lead 28-18 going into the final 15 minutes. But then, after Paul Sykes' score had hauled Quins back into the contest, Chad Randall snatched it, despite there being the hint of a knock-on in the build-up to his 74th minute try.

The Sunday clash between Huddersfield and Wakefield failed to rise to the occasion, the Giants winning 36-12 - a seventh consecutive victory against their West Yorkshire rivals, and their sixth Super League win on the bounce, after losing their first seven. Brad Drew was once again the thorn in the Wildcats side.

Coaches Brian McDermott, Jon Sharp, John Kear, Paul Cullen and Brian Noble were among those to give firm backing to the event after their respective games. 'I'm proud to be involved in Rugby League,' Harlequins boss McDermott said. 'We're always coming up with innovative ideas like this and the Grand Final at Old Trafford.

Challenge Cup Round 5

Catalans Dragons were joint 25/1 outsiders - with Harlequins, who beat Oldham at Sedgley Park 66-6 - following an unconvincing fifth round 24-14 victory at Whitehaven. The Catalans were in talks to play their quarter-final match in Barcelona, if they received home advantage in the draw, made bizarrely on the fringe BBC News24 TV channel the following Tuesday afternoon. BBC sources had confirmed that a Catalans home game in the sixth round, whether or not held in Barcelona, would almost certainly be one of the two matches to be broadcast on the weekend of 9th/10th June. The Catalans drew Hull FC away.

Meanwhile Dragons coach Mick Potter dismissed rumours circulating in the Australian media that centre Adam Mogg was about to return home to Canberra Raiders. And he appeared confident that halfback Stacey Jones would remain at the club beyond his current contract, which expired at the end of this season.

May

St Helens were hot evens favourites to retain the Challenge Cup, and eased through the fifth round with a 70-10 home win over Rochdale Hornets. Calf-injury victim Sean Long was replaced by youngster Matty Smith - his first outing of the season - and he caught the eye with a busy display, particularly with his shrewd kicking game. The star of the show was second-rower Paul Sculthorpe, who played the full 80 minutes and finished with a 26-point haul.

According to Australian media reports, Wayne Bennett was set to take over as St Helens coach in 2008, with incumbent Daniel Anderson returning to Sydney to pick up the reins at Sydney Roosters from former Australian Test mentor Chris Anderson.

Saints loose forward Jason Hooper announced his retirement from Rugby League after succumbing to shoulder problems, which had dogged him for nearly two years. His last appearance was the first game of SLXII, when the injury forced him from the field in the home defeat to Harlequins.

In a compelling Saturday TV game, Wigan - aiming to be the first club to win at the new Wembley, as they had at the old stadium in 1929 - edged Leeds Rhinos 22-18 in a superb match at Headingley. Trent Barrett produced another virtuoso attacking performance.

Again according to the Sydney press, Wigan were emerging as the hot favourites to sign St George Illawarra prop forward Jason Ryles.

Giants coach Jon Sharp talked up a number of his in-form stars for Great Britain's June Test against France, in particular loose forward Stephen Wild, after his side's convincing 36-10 Challenge Cup win over Salford on the Friday night.

Bradford coach Steve McNamara admitted it was not pretty, but he was happy with the way his team ground out a hard-fought 14-4 victory at Wakefield in wet conditions in the Sunday TV game. Bradford's victory was marred by an injury to Chris Feather, who was taken off on a stretcher in the 41st minute after sustaining a dislocated and fractured ankle, which sidelined him until August.

Hull FC battled their way into the last eight with a comfortable, if at times unconvincing 44-6 victory over Sheffield Eagles in torrential rain. Willie Manu's tremendous second-half display was the main highlight.

And Warrington made it an all-Super League last-eight with a 48-16 home win over NL2 Barrow Raiders, thanks to a hat-trick of tries from stand-off Vinnie Anderson.

Round 14

Salford City Reds director Dave Tarry dismissed speculation that the job of coach Karl Harrison was under threat after the Reds lost 66-6 to Catalans Dragons in Perpignan on the Saturday evening of round 14. The result left the club four points adrift at the bottom of Super League, just over half way through the season, and to deepen the gloom, captain and hooker Malcolm Alker broke his hand early in the game. It was the Dragons' Super League record win as they posted 12 tries, Adam Mogg setting Justin Murphy free for a walk-in in the seventh minute, and by the half hour, it was 36-0. Mogg scored two tries and had a hand in several others, and David Ferriol's crunch tackle on Michael Korkidas will long be remembered, although it was the Frenchman who left the field on the stretcher.

At the other end of the table, St Helens went top on points difference after their 34-14 victory over Wakefield Trinity Wildcats, and Leeds' subsequent 16-12 defeat at Hull FC.

At Knowsley Road on the Friday night, trailing by eight points at half-time, Wakefield needed to score first in the second half but didn't, with Matt Gidley's second try putting the game out of the Trinity's reach. The loss left the Wildcats in a deep slump, and without a Super League win since March 25th (30-24 at home to Warrington) and now in 11th spot, only four points ahead of Salford. Meanwhile Saints reported they were unlikely to suffer any serious financial consequences, after their sponsor, Earth Money, went into administration.

Leeds were rumoured to be trying to tempt Brian Noble to Headingley to take over the reins at the Rhinos at the end of the season from his Great Britain successor Tony Smith. And on the Sunday the Rhinos were edged 16-12 by Hull, who were in tenth place before kick-off. Richard Swain led his side impeccably throughout a thrilling match that could have gone either way. Ali Lauitiiti missed the game after having surgery on a knee injury.

Huddersfield moved up into fourth spot - ending a 35-year wait for a league victory over Bradford on the Friday night at the Galpharm - winning 36-12 after leading 24-0 at the break. It came after 27 successive defeats, with Huddersfield's only other victory against Bradford in the period being a Yorkshire Cup-tie in 1980. Chris Thorman netted a 20-point haul from two tries and six goals.

Harlequins, shorn of several leading players, virtually shut out Warrington and moved above them into sixth in the table. The 17-4 win at the Halliwell Jones was built on a rock-solid team performance. Halfbacks Mark McLinden and Danny Orr outplayed their opposite numbers, while Wigan cast-off Chris Melling enhanced his growing reputation at fullback. The Leeds loan duo of Luke Burgess and Joe Walsh both earned praise from their coach Brian McDermott after the game.

Hull Kingston Rovers' early-season win at Wigan in Round 4 could have been attributed to a newly-promoted team still playing on adrenaline. But Rovers did it again in round 14 and emerged deserved 12-10 victors at the JJB Stadium. Two first-half tries, with Luke Dyer involved in both, enabled Rovers to gain the initiative. Paul Cooke's 54th-minute penalty, awarded for a high Gareth Hock tackle on Michael Vella, ultimately proved decisive.

Round 15

The Tuesday after Salford's 66-6 defeat to Catalans Dragons, Salford coach Karl Harrison parted company with the Reds after five years at the helm. Harrison's assistant, Jimmy Lowes, applied for the head-coach vacancy even though he wasn't given the chance to prove himself in a caretaker capacity, football manager Steve Simms taking charge.

However, the Reds produced their best display of the season on the Friday night of round 15 as they stunned Huddersfield Giants with a 14-12 win at the Willows. The Reds' thrilling win - their first in five games that completed a seasonal double over the Giants - breathed new fire into their hopes of avoiding relegation. It was the Giants' first defeat since they lost to Salford at the Galpharm Stadium two months before, ending a nine-match winning sequence, and was their sixth defeat of the season by a margin of four points or less. Their biggest of eight defeats had been by eight points.

Salford showed tenacious defence and opportunism in attack, with David Hodgson and Gray Viane scoring excellent second-half tries. Hodgson streaked 70 metres away from the trailing cover after John Wilshere's great kick-return from a Brad Drew chip. Viane then eclipsed that, finishing off a length-of-the-field move sparked by Stuart Littler's clever offload to Luke Robinson close to his own line. Kevin McGuinness, linking well with Luke Dorn, then supplied the assist for Viane to finish triumphantly in the corner.

Sitting in the crowd, and heavily linked with the job at the Willows was former St Helens, Gateshead and Hull coach Shaun McRae, who arrived in the UK the day before in order to work with Sky Sports.

That week Huddersfield announced the immediate signing of Rod Jensen from North Queensland Cowboys and tied up forward Eorl Crabtree on a new three-year contract.

Salford's win on the Friday put pressure on Wakefield, only two points off the bottom going into their Sunday game with the Catalans, and on a run of seven games without a win. The return from injury of Adam Watene and Tevita Leo-Latu helped the Wildcats to an 18-12 victory in the rain which took them up to ninth place in the table. Having not won a league match since the 30-24 success against Warrington back in March, Wildcats' boss John Kear admitted: 'We could have played like a bunch of dogs today, as long as we won.' It wasn't until Jamie Rooney's last-gasp penalty that Wakefield were finally able to breathe easily.

The Dragons suffered another injury blow as Jamel Fakir was stretchered off midway through the second half in his second game back after returning from a knee injury. It was the end of his season.

The top four had a familiar look by the end of May, with Wigan moving up to fourth after an astounding 47-16 win over Hull at the JJB Stadium. Astounding because Willie Manu's third try for Hull put the Warriors 16-2 behind after 30 minutes.

It took an inspired spell by powerhouse Iafeta Palea'aesina, either side of the break, coupled with a stunning brace of tries on the stroke of half-time from Trent Barrett, to set the scene for a remarkable and unlikely revival. There was also a 30-point haul from hat-trick hero Pat Richards. The game's turning point came when Hutch Maiava gave away what looked like an innocuous penalty for a flop. Forty-five-unanswered points silenced the jeers from their fans that had greeted the Warriors' error-strewn first half hour. Warriors scrum-half Thomas Leuluai was found not guilty of attempting a 'slide tackle' on Hull FC captain Lee Radford.

Hull KR sank to 11th spot in the table when they couldn't manage a second home success of the season over Leeds, the Rhinos emerging from a wet and windy Craven Park with an 18-10 win. Jordan Tansey's converted try 14 minutes from time put the Rhinos 14 points ahead and left Rovers with too much to make up, as prop Ryan Tandy made his debut for the Robins following his signing from financially-strapped Doncaster Lakers.

Bradford remained in third spot after a 44-18 home win over Harlequins, who were rocked by another injury - this time to prop forward Daniel Heckenberg, who popped a shoulder in the opening stages and was ruled out for the rest of the season. Bulls captain Paul Deacon celebrated his 300th career appearance with a 16-point haul and Lesley Vainikolo maintained his promise to hold nothing back since deciding to switch to rugby union as he powered in for a hat-trick of tries. There was relief for Bulls star Chris McKenna who had been in court charged with affray after an incident outside a Leeds nightclub in 2006. A jury at Leeds Crown Court took just 15 minutes to find the Australian not guilty.

On the Spring Bank Holiday Monday, Saints, eventually, cruised back to the top of the table with a 40-12 win at the Halliwell Jones Stadium. Warrington looked good in the early stages, Adrian Morley in particular producing some trademark big hits, and deserved their 12-6 lead at the half-time break. But the stuttering Wolves - who had been booed from the field nine days previously after their home defeat by Harlequins - had no answer to the champions' 34-point blitz in the second half. Leon Pryce scored a hat-trick.

Saints had been busy that month securing players. Jason Cayless agreed a contract extension to the end of 2009, Sean Long and Keiron Cunningham signed two and one-year contracts respectively. The club also extended the contracts of Maurie Fa'asavalu and Scott Moore – each to the end of the 2010 season. The Wolves confirmed the signing of Michael Monaghan from the Manly Sea Eagles for 2008 on a four-year deal.

SUPER LEAGUE TABLE - *Monday 28th May*

	P	W	D	L	F	A	D	PTS
St Helens	15	11	0	4	486	241	245	22
Leeds Rhinos	15	11	0	4	418	271	147	22
Bradford Bulls	15	10	0	5	486	371	115	20
Wigan Warriors	15	8	0	7	362	315	47	16
Huddersfield Giants	15	7	0	8	377	242	135	14
Harlequins	15	6	2	7	299	365	-66	14
Hull FC	15	6	1	8	273	311	-38	13
Catalans Dragons	15	6	1	8	329	381	-52	13
Wakefield T Wildcats	15	6	1	8	319	402	-83	13
Warrington Wolves	15	6	0	9	314	420	-106	12
Hull Kingston Rovers	15	6	0	9	247	355	-108	12
Salford City Reds	15	4	1	10	264	500	-236	9

JUNE
Reds revival

Round 16

Harlequins moved up into fifth after a Saturday afternoon 18-8 home win over Wigan which put them level on points with the Warriors. Bathed in glorious sunshine, a boisterous crowd - Quins' biggest of the season at only 5,657 - saw only four tries, shared two apiece. The kicking of Paul Sykes proved to be the difference, his five from five contrasting with Pat Richards' failure to convert any of his three attempts. Danny Orr gave a battling performance against his old side, and came up with the assist for the try which put Quins more than a score in front. Another former Wigan player, Chris Melling, celebrated the signing of a new two-year contract by putting in a fine performance.

Hull Kingston Rovers' Papuan prop Makali Aizue became the first player in Super League XII to be dismissed from the field. Aizue was sent off in the Robins' televised defeat at Wakefield for a high, dangerous tackle on Wakefield winger Paul White in the 34th minute. Rovers were ahead 8-2 at the time, and they went in at the break seemingly in control with a 9-2 lead after Paul Cooke dropped a goal. But in the second half they struggled to hold the Wildcats, who surged to a 30-15 victory. Aizue was banned for three games.

Wakefield's second straight win had them sitting just outside the play-off places, behind Huddersfield on points difference. The home side's storming start to the second half saw them score 16 points in 11 minutes to turn the game on its head.

New Zealand national coach Brian McClennan refused to discuss whether he was a candidate for the Leeds Rhinos job that was to become vacant at the end of the season, although he hinted he was ready for a Super League or NRL post. The Rhinos stayed level top with a 42-26 win over Warrington at Headingley in what *Rugby Leaguer & League Express* reporter Phil Caplan described as 'bubblegum rugby', neither side showing a ruthless streak.

England Academy winger Kevin Penny scored two notable tries and Mike Sullivan came off the bench after an eight-week absence. But Danny McGuire was the evening's standout, with a hand in every Leeds touchdown and his try in the closing stages of the first half to make it 24-8 established a lead that was seldom really threatened.

Wolves star Adrian Morley told his club's supporters to stop criticising coach Paul Cullen, following the Wolves' recent string of bad results that saw them sink to tenth place in the Super League table.

St Helens denied revived Salford a first win at Knowsley Road for 27 years in a dramatic ending, securing two points with a 27-26 win. Having recovered from 14-26 down midway through the second half to tie the scores, Daniel Anderson's side earned the spoils through Matty Smith's field goal - with just one minute of normal time remaining.

Smith, who had put an earlier attempt well wide, kept his cool to pot the ball through the uprights after Lee Gilmour's run set up the position. The Reds had just failed with two similar attempts, David Hodgson's audacious attempt from halfway being charged down by James Graham and Luke Robinson's rushed effort anticipated by Moore, who charged that effort down. Robinson had one last effort to earn Salford what would have been a deserved share of the spoils, only to see his field-goal attempt deep into injury time rebound off a post.

Daniel Anderson defended his decision to rest a number of key players, with Paul Wellens, Matt Gidley, James Roby, Jon Wilkin and Maurie Fa'asavalu all missing.

In a very windy Perpignan, the Bulls had to come from behind to prevent the Dragons from claiming a double over them, winning 28-20. The result was only confirmed in the final minute when James Evans, playing on the wing rather than his usual position of centre, crossed unmarked in the corner following a half-break from Chris McKenna, who had shaken off an earlier wrist injury.

But things could have worked out very differently had Casey McGuire had his second try of the evening allowed by the video referee. The stand-off appeared to have grounded the ball in the 77th minute, but the fourth official confirmed the touch judge's call that winger Justin Murphy had a foot in touch as he passed to his teammate and the score was chalked off.

Huddersfield coach Jon Sharp slammed referee Ian Smith, following the Giants' 9-9 draw with Hull at the KC Stadium on the Sunday.

The game ended controversially when Hull's Sid Domic was apparently in an offside position when he collected a ball from Motu Tony's knock-on from a kick in the last minute. The final hooter sounded as Domic kicked the ball into touch. Smith was then surrounded by angry Huddersfield players pointing out that Domic had been offside, and insisting that they should be awarded a penalty straight in front of the posts.

'I do know now how (Bradford coach) Steve Mac feels after Cardiff,' said Sharp. 'I haven't had a chance to speak to the referee, I think it's better for me not to, and to give myself about three years to calm down.' In the week, referees controller Stuart Cummings confirmed that Ian Smith's decision had been correct.

Challenge Cup Quarter Finals

St Helens were odds-on favourites to win the Challenge Cup, at 8/13 following their 25-14 Challenge Cup quarter-final victory over Warrington Wolves at Knowsley Road in the Saturday TV game.

Captain Paul Sculthorpe was absent after having been carried from the training field on Friday afternoon with an Achilles injury that ended his campaign. But Saints came from behind against the Wolves for the second time in a fortnight. On Bank Holiday Monday they came from a 12-6 half-time deficit with 34-unanswered points to win 40-12. In this game they were behind 4-12 at the interval, and they again come through in the second half, once more preventing the Wolves from scoring a try in the final 40 minutes.

The Wolves lost Adrian Morley in the first minute of the game, following a head clash with Nick Fozzard. The departure of Morley, who returned for the last 20 minutes, was closely followed by a Saints try for Lee Gilmour. But an avalanche of points never came. Kevin Penny broke brilliantly down the left touchline from a pass by Paul Johnson, and beat Ade Gardner, Matt Gidley and Paul Wellens on a dash down the wing. Lee Briers' touchline conversion gave the Wolves a 6-4 advantage. Then Brent Grose's long pass created an opening for Henry Fa'afili to crash through Willie Talau's tackle for a try at the right corner. Briers' conversion opened the 12-4 advantage at the break.

The first ten minutes of the second half were crucial as Saints pulled back two tries through Talau and Gardner. Briers' goal put the Wolves back in front, but Gilmour's superb second try emphasised Saints' ability to raise their game when needed. Sean Long had a relatively quiet game, but his field goal from the half-way line put a seven-point gap between the teams. James Roby sealed the win on 75 minutes, spinning out of a tired Mark Gleeson tackle 20 metres out to sprint clear.

Catalans Dragons were rank outsiders at 16/1, despite their sensational and thoroughly deserved win over Hull FC at the KC Stadium. Fullback Clint Greenshields led the way with a terrific display, whilst centre Adam Mogg, with two tries, and the evergreen Stacey Jones and stand-off Thomas Bosc were also key contributors.

The home fans made their feelings known, sending their men to the dressing rooms at both half and full time with boos ringing in their ears. Hull could have stolen victory too, after coming from 16-12 down to lead 17-16 with Richard Horne's field goal, only to see Wayne Godwin sin-binned with ten minutes remaining, allowing Catalans to press on. Jerome Guisset replied with a one-pointer before Greenshields cruised through a gap to post a deserved try, before Bosc, fresh from converting, added a further field goal. Gareth Raynor scored a late consolation.

Stacey Jones gave the club a boost by committing himself to the Catalans for a further season after signing a one-year extension to his contract, and the Dragons also confirmed that they would have a senior Academy side by 2009.

Wigan were still on course for a Wembley return after a 25-6 Friday night win over Harlequins at the JJB. Jon Wells became the second Super League player to be red carded for a 53rd minute elbow on Darrell Goulding (sending off sufficient) and with him went Quins' chances.

Steve Bannister, who made a big impact on his first appearance after signing from St Helens, scored after fine approach play by Mark McLinden. But Trent Barrett, who by his own high standards had a quiet evening, confirmed Wigan's entry into the last four with a coolly struck field goal, and when Sean O'Loughlin sliced through a rare gap in the close-range Quins cover, Wigan were home and dry. Mike McIlorum, Wigan's Academy hooker, made his first-team debut.

Bradford Bulls fans welcomed giant new winger Tame Tupou with ecstatic applause when he entered the Odsal field in the 51st minute, with the Bulls already 34-4 up against Huddersfield. Tupou scored two tries, overshadowing Lesley Vainikolo, who was making his 150th appearance for the Bulls. Iestyn Harris injured a hamstring in the Bulls' eventual 52-20 thrashing of the Giants. The Giants gave Rod Jensen his debut days after his arrival in the UK.

Round 17

Shaun McRae signed a four-and-a-half year deal to coach Salford, despite their precarious position at the foot of the Super League ladder, and made a winning start the following Friday night to move the City Reds within one point of 11th-placed Hull KR.

The Reds won a 5-2 home victory over Harlequins in the first try-less game of the summer era. As a result of incessant rain, flowing rugby was kept to a minimum, but it was a compelling battle that pitted the likes of Michael Korkidas, Andy Coley and Lee Jewitt against Karl Temata, David Mills and Jon Grayshon. Mark Edmondson, Malcolm Alker and Aaron Moule all made returns from injury as Salford looked like they could have turned the corner.

Harlequins that week released former Kangaroo prop forward Richard Villasanti, with him not having played a game for the London club. Villasanti, 26, had failed to recover from a knee injury he suffered playing with NRL club Cronulla Sharks the previous year.

Hull KR needed to produce a win at home to St Helens on the Sunday to stay three points clear of Salford, but they crashed 40-0 against the champions. Paul Wellens was at his faultless best and chipped in with a typical support player's try. To add to Rovers' problems, they also lost Stanley Gene and Ben Fisher with early injuries that disrupted their chances.

St Helens signed Sydney Roosters back row forward Chris Flannery on a three-year deal, and he was expected to arrive in July, although he had been registered too late to play in the Challenge Cup campaign.

Leeds kept level with St Helens at the top after a 25-12 win at Huddersfield. It was 12-12 with only five minutes left. Then Kevin Sinfield edged Leeds Rhinos ahead with a low-flying field goal from 40 metres and converted two quick tries. Both the tries came from well-placed kicks. First Danny McGuire put in a short stab that Jordan Tansey touched down. And that was followed by a booming effort by Sinfield from behind a scrum in his own quarter, with Scott Donald easily winning the chase to pick up and score. Gamestar McGuire also snapped up two quick early tries.

The draw for the semi-finals of the Carnegie Challenge Cup had paired Wigan and Catalans and on the Friday they met in a league encounter at the JJB Stadium.

The Warriors blew the French side away on a dull, chilly evening by 30-0. Stuart Fielden led from the front as Trent Barrett's glorious individual try on 26 minutes saw Wigan take full advantage of Adam Mogg's costly first-half sin-binning for holding down.

The game will best be remembered for an horrific incident when Catalans Dragons winger Justin Murphy fell at speed over the advertising hoardings and the fence surrounding the pitch to crash heavily on the floor of the stand. The 29-year-old landed on his neck and back on a concrete step. He appeared to have a very fortunate escape and most observers were amazed that Murphy was alive, let alone able to resume his place on the field. The RFL said they might investigate the incident, emphasising that the JJB Stadium had passed all its safety tests.

Lesley Vainikolo made an emotional farewell to the Bradford supporters in the televised Sunday 34-8 victory over Hull FC at Odsal.

'We started Lesley's party 80 minutes too early and had to address that at half-time,' was Bulls coach Steve McNamara's assessment, after watching his side overturn an 8-6 first-half deficit in a manner that did little justice to Hull's contribution to an enjoyable match.

Terry Newton ended up scoring four tries, with Vainikolo not crossing the whitewash at all, although his last-minute conversion to Paul Deacon's try will go down in Bradford legend. Another player in his last season at Odsal was Ian Henderson, set to move back to the NRL at the end of the season to take up a two-year deal at New Zealand Warriors.

Meanwhile Hull confirmed that they had signed 30-year-old Cronulla Sharks stand-off Adam Dykes on a two-year contract from 2008, and Brisbane's State of Origin rep Shaun Berrigan on a four-year deal. Their fullback Shaun Briscoe suffered a broken jaw in the Odsal defeat that kept him out of action until round 23.

Warrington eased their relegation fears with a more convincing than expected 31-12 home win over Wakefield, who fell away in the second half. The Wildcats were hampered by the absence of Jamie Rooney - who had undergone keyhole surgery to repair a torn cartilage, ruling him out of the end-of-month Test against France - and they suffered further problems after just three minutes when Paul March limped from the field with an ankle injury. Young winger Chris Riley's 43rd minute try set the tone for a one-sided second half as Ben Westwood had a great game against his old club.

Off the field, Wigan and Great Britain fullback Kris Radlinski was awarded the MBE in the Queen's birthday honours.

And St Helens hooker Keiron Cunningham topped *Rugby League World* magazine's list of the 100 best Super League players of all time. The summer era had seen St Helens and Bradford Bulls share most of the trophies, and the two clubs were represented by nine of the top ten players, with Cunningham beating departing Bulls winger Lesley Vainikolo into second place, with Paul Sculthorpe third.

The 12 Super League clubs met over two days in Perpignan in June and agreed several changes at the behest of the Rugby Football League.

From 2008 clubs would no longer only be able to spend a maximum of 50 per cent of their total income on players' salaries. In a move designed to equalise the competition, all the clubs would be able to spend the maximum figure of £1.65 million, regardless of their income.

The salary cap system would also be tightened. The RFL would from 2008 calculate a club's salary cap position at the start of and throughout the season. If a club wished to sign a new player, the impact of that new salary would be assessed before the player was allowed to register. Clubs would have to justify the signing at the time they made it, rather than retrospectively at the end of the season. The new regulations were meant to eliminate the danger of clubs gaining advantage one season by exceeding the salary cap, and having points deducted and paying a fine the following season.

RFL Operations Director Nigel Wood introduced a new 'home grown player' rule designed to reduce the competition's reliance on overseas players, although, the clubs also agreed to raise the overseas quota from its current limit of three players to five from 2008.

Under the new rules, in 2008 at least five members of a club's first team squad of 25 players must be players who had graduated from a club's Academy system, or were aged under 21 years. The number was to increase by one player each year, so that by 2011 a squad must have eight 'home-grown' players.

During the same period the number of 'overseas trained' players attached to any club must drop from 40 per cent (10 players) to 20 per cent (5 players), with the remaining players in a 25-man squad to be made up of players who have been trained by other clubs in the same Federation (the RFL and the French Rugby League were to be counted as two distinct federations, so that that British players recruited by the Catalans, or French players recruited by English Super League clubs, would count in either case as overseas trained players).

It was also announced that the Millennium Magic weekend would go ahead in Cardiff on the May Bank holiday weekend in 2008, with an almost identical set of derby fixtures to those that were played at the Millennium Stadium in 2007.

SUPER LEAGUE TABLE - *Sunday 17th June*

	P	W	D	L	F	A	D	PTS
St Helens	17	13	0	4	553	267	286	26
Leeds Rhinos	17	13	0	4	485	309	176	26
Bradford Bulls	17	12	0	5	548	399	149	24
Wigan Warriors	17	9	0	8	400	333	67	18
Harlequins	17	7	2	8	319	378	-59	16
Huddersfield Giants	17	7	1	9	398	276	122	15
Wakefield T Wildcats	17	7	1	9	361	448	-87	15
Hull FC	17	6	2	9	290	354	-64	14
Warrington Wolves	17	7	0	10	371	474	-103	14
Catalans Dragons	17	6	1	10	349	439	-90	13
Hull Kingston Rovers	17	6	0	11	262	425	-163	12
Salford City Reds	17	5	1	11	295	529	-234	11

JULY
French revolution

Round 18

On the first Monday of July, *Rugby Leaguer & League Express* revealed that three clubs were suspected of having infringed the salary cap rules in 2006, with Wigan, Bradford Bulls and St Helens in the frame. The three clubs were to be given a right to make a presentation to an independent panel as to why they shouldn't be punished, either with a fine or a points deduction, or both. Clubs had agreed the previous year to double the possible points deductions, so it was thought that up to 12 points could be docked from a team's record if their transgression was large enough.

The same weekend, Wigan coach Brian Noble slammed the attitude of some of his players after a 32-6 defeat at Wakefield, who moved back up into the play-off spots. Trent Barrett had a difficult afternoon, after scoring an early try and then being sin-binned in the second half for a high tackle on Wakefield prop Adam Watene.

Ben Jeffries was in superb form for the Wildcats, who introduced another halfback signing to the crowd at Belle Vue in Maxime Grésèque, who had a brief spell at Wakefield at the end of the previous season without playing. He had been in outstanding form for his country against Great Britain the previous weekend, and signed until the end of the season after Salford had also shown interest.

New Hull FC halfback Mathew Head arrived in England claiming to be fully fit after knee and shoulder injuries dogged his promising career with St George Illawarra Dragons. The 25-year-old signed initially until the end of the season, with the possibility of staying longer if the move was successful.

Head should have made his Hull debut against Salford in round 18, but had to kick his heels when the game was postponed in anticipation of more bad weather in flood-hit Hull. The game was re-arranged for Sunday 29th July, the weekend of the Challenge Cup semi-finals.

At the end of a week that saw the departure of prime minister Tony Blair from Downing Street after ten years, Lesley Vainikolo played his last game for Bradford in a superlative 38-14 win at Headingley.

His opening try for the Bulls saw him take a superb round-the-corner pass from Terry Newton, before he batted Leeds fullback Brent Webb out of the way, ran backwards for a few yards, shrugged off Jamie Peacock and charged down the wing to score a trademark try.

The turning point of the game came just before the 60-minute mark, with the score at 14-20 after Webb's superb try. At that point Ryan Bailey and Kevin Sinfield got into a muddle and seemed to knock the ball on between them. The Bulls then won a penalty and Andy Lynch beat three defenders to touch down for a try that was given by the video referee, Richard Silverwood.

In another event related to the changes in Westminster, Gerry Sutcliffe, the MP for Bradford South, was appointed as the government's Sports Minister under new Prime Minister Gordon Brown. Almost a third of the new Cabinet represented constituencies in the Rugby League heartland

That week the Bulls pulled out of the chase for Melbourne's Australian Test star Matt King, with Wigan now thought favourites to land the Test centre.

The result at Headingley meant St Helens went two points clear at the top after their 54-4 hammering of Huddersfield. Teenage winger Steve Tyrer ended the game with 22 points from two tries and seven goals. Saints had announced that the club hoped to be playing in a new stadium by the 2010 season, after revealing they had submitted a planning application for a new facility to replace their ageing Knowsley Road home.

Harlequins coach Brian McDermott described the 32-18 home win over Hull KR as 'beautiful'. A patched-up Harlequins outfit produced a gritty defensive display in the rain. Guided in attack by the brains and boots of Henry Paul and Mark McLinden, they were deserved winners. McDermott praised Rikki Sheriffe, who made his second debut after short stints at Halifax and Doncaster. Quins were now fifth, while the Robins were still just one point ahead of bottom-placed Salford.

Catalans recorded their second home win over Warrington, themselves only three points off the bottom, but this time only by a whisker - 22-20. The on-song Lee Briers seemed to have stolen the game for Warrington after his second try had brought them back to within two points 12 minutes from the end. A precise chip in his own half was regathered and he broke away. He kicked again for Chris Riley to chase and the winger beat the covering Thomas Bosc to the ball. But just when the winger was crossing the line Bosc got enough contact to make Riley fumble as he tried to touch down.

It was revealed that the Dragons could be facing competition for the best French players in the near future. Toulouse Olympique's bid for a place in Super League from 2009 was be taken a step further when the French club received a visit from top RFL officials in early August.

Round 19

There was talk of St Helens going through the rest of the season undefeated, but Leeds exploded the theory on the Friday night of round 19 at Knowsley Road, beating them 22-10. Saints' search for a tenth successive win faltered as the Rhinos muscled-up in defence to inflict their second victory of the season over the champions, after their 38-19 victory at Headingley in April - the last time St Helens had lost. After their home defeat against the Bulls the previous week, the Rhinos were now back level with St Helens at the top of the ladder.

Leeds had recalled Ali Lauitiiti - back from a knee injury for the first time since May - and young winger Ryan Hall, and he scored his first try for the club, with Saints fielding an unchanged 17 for the third game in a row. Matty Smith, continuing his impressive run at halfback, was lining up against Rob Burrow, who was playing in his 200th game for Leeds - at the age of 24 - and took the gamestar award. Jordan Tansey's sharp interception of Nick Fozzard's desperate offload on 78 minutes sealed the win, with the substitute streaking the 50 metres to touch down to the left of the posts.

Bradford missed their chance to go level top, losing 25-18 on the same night at Wigan. The Warriors' performance eased some of the worries over a potential points deductions for salary cap misdemeanours. Their forwards, with Bryan Fletcher outstanding, refused to be intimidated by the Bulls' mighty pack and eventually wrested control of a physical and fast-moving game.

Stuart Fielden, Gareth Hock, Iafeta Palea'aesina and skipper Sean O'Loughlin were other stand-outs, with Trent Barrett and two-try centre Phil Bailey providing the cutting edge. Barrett's late field goal gave Wigan breathing space at last in a breathless and tense encounter.

Five people were arrested and Hull FC captain Lee Radford was spat on and threatened, after spectators invaded the pitch after the Sunday derby clash between Hull

July

Kingston Rovers and Hull FC at Craven Park

Reports suggested that the invasion was begun by Hull supporters rushing onto the field to congratulate their team after Hull's 30-20 victory, and a section of Hull KR fans responding, coming onto the pitch and, in some cases, confronting their rivals. The whole incident was witnessed by RFL Executive Chairman Richard Lewis, himself a spectator at the match, and the RFL was awaiting a report from both clubs before deciding whether to take further action.

In a game of thrills and spills before a ground-record capacity crowd of 9,035, Hull just about deserved their win after holding back Rovers' all-out bid to grab a late victory.

Both teams gave debuts to a former St George-Illawarra player. Mathew Head gave indications of his distributive and kicking skills for Hull before retiring injured at half-time, while Rhys Lovegrove produced a strong display in the centre for Rovers, highlighted by a try. Hull KR back-rower Chris Chester suffered a broken hand early in the game.

Fortunately for Hull KR they stayed a point above Salford after the Reds lost at home to Wakefield 35-18. Reds prop Lee Jewitt was out for the rest of the season after breaking his leg. Shaun McRae had also lost assistant coach James Lowes, who moved to become Paul Cullen's assistant at Warrington Wolves. Ben Jeffries - amid top displays from many, including Jason Demetriou and the back from-injury Jamie Rooney - was again the major architect of the Wildcats' win that had them three points clear in sixth.

Wolves coach Paul Cullen refused to be drawn on report that Australian Test centre Matt King had agreed a four-year contract with the club. On the Sunday the Wolves blew away the challenge of Huddersfield in an impressive 47-28 win at the Galpharm Stadium. Lee Briers' masterful display saw stand-off Chris Bridge finish with a hat-trick of tries. Kevin Penny continued his remarkable start to life in the professional game with two well-taken tries.

In a further blow for the Giants, winger Martin Aspinwall suffered a knee injury which needed a major reconstruction, threatening to sideline him for up to a year.

Harlequins winger Rikki Sheriffe capped a fine display with two tries – including the final four-pointer - that sealed an absorbing and highly entertaining 30-22 win over the Catalans at the Stoop.

Meanwhile, as well as Wigan, St Helens and Bradford were charged with breaching the salary cap during the 2006 season. Wigan made a presentation at a preliminary tribunal to determine what scale of deductions would apply to any breaches. It was unclear whether the new doubled scale of penalties applied to breaches in 2006, or whether it applied only to 2007 onwards.

Round 20

On the Thursday night before round 20, Bradford found themselves four points adrift of Leeds and St Helens after having two points deducted for a salary cap infringement in 2006. St Helens were fined £22,000 for a smaller infringement.

Wigan's tribunal was put back to 25th July, but the maximum points deduction, which would be applied to an overspend of 10 per cent or more, would now be six points, rather than twelve as thought, after a 'preliminary hearing' in which Wigan and St Helens both pursued a claim that 2006 breaches should be calculated under the old rules.

Bradford pegged back two points on Saints as they beat them 10-4 on the Friday night at a rainy Odsal. It was a double blow for St Helens, with the dismissal of Jon Wilkin and a second successive Super League defeat. Wilkin was sent off by referee Phil Bentham after 59 minutes after a high tackle on Matt James. Wilkin copped a one-match ban, meaning he would be back for the Challenge Cup semi-final against the Bulls. Jamie Langley left the field during the first-half with an injury to the AC joint in his shoulder. It was the end of his season.

Leeds missed their chance to go clear at the top as they lost 18-2 at Wigan. Bryan Fletcher was again outstanding in a Wigan pack that laid the foundation for an ultimately convincing display over a Rhinos side coming off a huge win at St Helens.

Leeds' only points were from a Kevin Sinfield penalty goal. But for that the Warriors would have 'nilled' their visitors on their way to a third victory of the season over the Rhinos. It was the first time since May 2000, when Leeds lost 2-44 at home to Bradford, they had failed to score a try in a game.

The Rhinos announced that New Zealand Test coach Brian McClennan would take over the reins at Headingley after the departure of Tony Smith at the end of the season to become the full-time coach of Great Britain. McClennan had wanted to retain his Kiwi coaching position until after next year's World Cup in Australia. But the NZRL refused to employ a national coach not resident in New Zealand.

Wakefield Trinity Wildcats skipper Jason Demetriou signed a one-year contract extension to keep him at Belle Vue until the end of 2008 and limped off with a deadleg in the 24-23 home defeat to Huddersfield Giants, while Wildcats prop Danny Sculthorpe was put on report late in the game, and tore a hamstring. Huddersfield staged an astonishing second-half comeback to snatch their first win in six matches. The buoyant Wildcats, on a run of four wins in their previous five matches, had led 13-0 at the break, having tailored their game to the dreadful muddy conditions. In the week, Giants GB international Steve Wild had turned down a move to St Helens in order to remain at the Giants, signing a new three-year contract to run until the end of 2010.

Warrington Wolves halfback Michael Sullivan suffered a season-ending broken arm after 23 minutes in the 42-6 home win over Salford City Reds. It proved to be Sullivan's last game in a Wolves shirt, as he signed for Canterbury Bulldogs. Kevin Penny grabbed a quick-fire second-half hat-trick for his ninth try in six starts – and the Wolves were never in danger.

Hull KR spoiled the Catalans' Bastille Day celebrations to win a crucial two points in a 22-20 win at the Stade Gilbert Brutus that took them three points clear of Salford. Mark Lennon's touchline conversion after Ian Hardman's try on 24 minutes was the eventual winner.

Harlequins were only two points behind fourth-placed Wigan, and could move above them if Wigan were docked points at their rearranged RFL tribunal hearing, despite a 20-8 defeat against Hull on the Friday night at the KC Stadium. Led superbly by Paul King, Hull finally came up with the type of performance that suggested they were play-off material, despite Richard Swain having announced his shock retirement due to a back injury.

That weekend Barrie McDermott's Ambassadors won the Fairfax Cup at the York International Nines Festival, defeating Dewsbury Rams 20-8 in the final, and donated the full £2,000 prize money to the Brennan Rooney Appeal, set up to provide support for Wakefield star Jamie Rooney's cerebral palsy suffering son, Brennan.

Round 21

Salford grabbed a lifeline in their battle against relegation with a stunning 14-10 win over third-placed Bradford Bulls in the Saturday TV game at the Willows. The basement-dwelling City Reds faced a tough run-in, with Hull away, Leeds away, and St Helens and Wigan at home, so this was a vital success, that moved them to within one-point of pre-season relegation favourites Hull KR.

The Reds were bolstered by three new signings - Richie Barnett and Mike Wainwright from Warrington, and Tom Saxton from Castleford Tigers - as Bradford's indiscipline led to Salford imposing their authority on the first half. Despite being temporarily overhauled before the hour by two Tame Tupou tries, the Reds rallied to regain the lead and finish the stronger, Luke Robinson's 66th minute try converted by John Wilshere sealing the win and the two precious points.

Hull KR fans had reasons for becoming slightly nervous - Salford still had the postponed away game at Hull in hand - after seeing their side, with Paul Cooke surprisingly left out, suffer an 11-try 60-20 home demolition at the hands of Warrington. Skipper Lee Briers scored 28 points - from three tries and eight goals - as the Wolves romped into the top-six. Kevin Penny surprisingly didn't score after signing an enhanced four-year deal to remain at the Halliwell Jones Stadium until November 2011.

Wigan - due to face an RFL tribunal the following Wednesday to face salary cap charges - were heartened by a Friday night 19-12 defeat at St Helens. It was Saints' eighth win in a row against the Warriors. Sean Long, returning after a calf injury, was playing just his second game in the last ten matches. And only when he succeeded at the third attempt in potting a field goal could Saints coach Daniel Anderson be sure of continuing a remarkable unbeaten record against Wigan.

Wigan lost fullback Pat Richards, victim of an alleged swinging arm from Keiron Cunningham in a three-man tackle midway through the second half. But the in-form Australian happily returned to the fray eight minutes later. Cunningham was placed on report for the incident but escaped with just a fine from the RFL Disciplinary Committee.

Chris Flannery made his St Helens debut, playing his first game since breaking his leg playing for the Sydney Roosters earlier in the year, after joining on a three-and-a-half year deal.

That weekend Wigan rejected suggestions they were about to swoop for Warrington Wolves star Martin Gleeson and for former Leeds Rhino Chev Walker, who joined Bath rugby union club at the end of the previous season.

On the Saturday night, Hull - without scrum-half Mathew Head - got the better of Catalans at the third attempt with a 34-18 win in Perpignan. Matt Sing's try just after the hour made the game safe, as Danny Tickle stood out with two tries and five goals. Dragons form centre Adam Mogg scored the first try of the game after putting an end to rumours that he was looking to return to Canberra by confirming he would see out the final year of his contract with the Catalans in 2008. Thomas Bosc broke an arm in the game.

On the same day, Harlequins dropped from fifth to eighth place in the table, after a 22-10 defeat by Huddersfield Giants at the Stoop, though their coach Brian McDermott remained confident his side would reach the play-offs. The Giants looked the more likely top-six candidates after their horrendous start to 2007 - a seven-match win-less run. Huddersfield's forwards dominated their inexperienced rivals and on the back of that playmakers Ryan Hudson, Brad Drew and Robbie Paul pinned Quins in their own half for long periods. Paul in particular was an increasingly influential figure as the game wore on, rolling back the years as he created one try for Steve Snitch and provided a constant menace in midfield.

Two points separated the clubs from fourth to ninth positions in the table after round 21, and one of them, Wakefield, moved into fifth after one of the biggest upsets of the season, a 23-16 Friday night win over Leeds at Headingley.

Scott Donald's 66th minute try looked to have seen off the Wildcats as the Rhinos led 16-10. But a Ryan Atkins try four minutes later, converted by Jamie Rooney levelled and Rooney's field goal edged the Wildcats in front. Luke George's converted try two minutes from time settled it. Ben Jeffries was a standout for Wakefield, who that week had announced they had agreed to release him from his contract a year early, with Castleford Tigers star Danny Brough rumoured to be on his way back to Belle Vue in 2008.

Challenge Cup Semi-finals

The Dragons blazed to a rousing, historic 37-24 victory over the Wigan Warriors at Halliwell Jones Stadium on the last Sunday in July to seal a first ever Wembley appearance and deny Wigan a record-breaking 29th Challenge Cup final appearance.

Wigan fans were stunned as the Dragons stormed into an early 22-0 lead. The prompting of halfbacks Stacey Jones and Casey McGuire, coupled with the strong running of Alex Chan and centre Adam Mogg, repeatedly caused the Warriors problems in a blistering opening quarter. McGuire, John Wilson, Mogg and Vincent Duport all crossed for tries before the Warriors had entered the Dragons' '20'. Thomas Leuluai crossed from a quick play-the-ball, and Pat Richards' conversion closed the gap to 22-6 by half-time.

But the Dragons struck first in the second half. Darrell Goulding looked to have defused the threat when he leapt to take Jones' chip to the left corner. But Jones was quickly in on the tackle, and the ball spilled out to Duport, who scooped it up to touch down for his second try. Jones again landed a superb touchline conversion to make it 30-6. And Jones tagged on a field goal moments later to open a 25-point gap.

The 62nd minute sin-binning of Jones for interfering with a 20-metre restart then presented Wigan with one final golden opportunity for a do-or-die push. While Jones was off the field, tries from threequarters Goulding and then Mark Calderwood, who went 90 metres to touch down, cut the deficit to just seven points by the time Jones came back onto the field.

But with his first touch of the ball on his return Jones delivered a pin-point kick to Wigan's line that was intended to force a goal-line drop-out. Veteran second-rower Jason Croker pounced on it for the match-clinching try.

The Cup exit completed a bad week for Wigan. The previous Wednesday an independent RFL tribunal found the club guilty of infringing the salary cap in 2006 and deducted them four league points, sending them from fourth to ninth spot in the ladder. The Warriors were found to have spent £222,314 (6.3 per cent) over the salary cap in 2006.

To compound their misery, the Warriors faithful saw arch-rivals St Helens march through to their second consecutive Challenge Cup final on the Saturday lunchtime, with a 35-14 victory against Bradford Bulls at the Galpharm Stadium.

Keiron Cunningham stole most of the headlines in the sunshine by picking up the man of the match award in his 400th game for the club. Cunningham was the only current St Helens player who played in both their Wembley triumphs against the Bulls in 1996 and 1997.

Another big plus for St Helens was the return to commanding form of Sean Long after injury. Starting only his second game in 11 matches, the Saints scrum-half ruled the midfield, produced two try-making passes, and landed a great 48-metre field goal. He also resumed his goal kicking duties to score four out of five. Leon Pryce's 69th minute try, when he intercepted Iestyn Harris's kick and raced 80 metres, knocked the stuffing out of Bradford just as they were threatening a late victory bid. The Bulls had decided not to recall Lesley Vainikolo for the game.

In the round 18 catch-up game postponed because of the terrible flooding in the city, Hull FC moved into fourth after a 48-26 win over Salford after going 26-0 up after half an hour, in Reds coach Shaun McRae's first return to the KC Stadium. Mathew Head made his home debut for the black and whites.

SUPER LEAGUE TABLE - *Sunday 29th July*

	P	W	D	L	F	A	D	PTS
St Helens	21	15	0	6	640	315	325	30
Leeds Rhinos	21	14	0	7	539	398	141	28
Bradford Bulls *	21	14	0	7	624	456	168	26
Hull FC	21	10	2	9	422	426	-4	22
Wakefield T Wildcats	21	10	1	10	474	512	-38	21
Warrington Wolves	21	10	0	11	542	552	-10	20
Harlequins	21	9	2	10	399	460	-61	20
Huddersfield Giants	21	9	1	11	476	410	66	19
Wigan Warriors **	21	11	0	10	461	404	57	18
Catalans Dragons	21	7	1	13	433	547	-114	15
Hull Kingston Rovers	21	7	0	14	342	567	-225	14
Salford City Reds	21	6	1	14	359	664	-305	13

* *2 points deducted for 2006 salary cap breach*
** *4 points deducted for 2006 salary cap breach*

AUGUST
Uncatchable Saints?

Round 22

In the wake of Wigan's Challenge Cup exit and the four-point fine for the club's second salary cap transgression in two years, club chairman Maurice Lindsay announced he would step down at the end of the season. Wigan owner Dave Whelan announced his intention to sell the Warriors, with Whelan claiming that the RFL was engaged in a witch-hunt against his club.

On the first Sunday afternoon of August, the Warriors' chances of making the play-offs receded at the Halliwell Jones Stadium after a 43-24 defeat to the Wolves. Warrington moved up to fourth as coach Paul Cullen celebrated a two-year extension to his contract.

For the second week in a row the Warriors were punished for a slow start, falling to a 25-6 half-time deficit. Lee Briers was allowed to dominate the game as he compiled a 19-point haul, while Kevin Penny's ninth-minute scorcher underlined his outstanding potential as a match-winning winger.

In one of the most significant results of the season, Hull KR beat Salford 30-24 at the Willows on the Friday night to move three points ahead of the Reds, with a superior points difference, with just five games to go.

The returning from injury duo of Mick Vella and Chris Chester were standouts and Paul Cooke and James Webster combined brilliantly at halfback. The recalled Cooke scored a solo try, and caused Salford no end of problems with his kicking and distribution. Webster used his pace and trickery to make several clean breaks and set up two of Rovers' five tries.

Kiwi prop Phil Leuluai - signed on a two-and-a half-year contract - ran the ball in hard and defended extremely well on his Salford debut, while David Hodgson made an impressive return from injury, scoring a try and looking dangerous every time he had the ball. Mark O'Neill's second try of the game at the start of the second half turned the tide in Hull KR's favour.

Salford coach Shaun McRae still believed that his side could gain the necessary wins in the last five rounds and avoid relegation. 'There's still ten points to play for over five games,' said McRae. 'My attitude doesn't change at all, even after tonight.' McRae had lost ever-present loose forward Simon Finnigan for the remainder of the season with a sternum injury.

St Helens stayed two points clear of Leeds at the top of the table after a 31-20 home win over Hull FC. A second-half hat-trick from Francis Meli, and another powerful display from the in-form Nick Fozzard were the highlights. Sean Long nipped over for a trademark first-half try, only his second of an injury-ravaged season, before clinching the points with a late field goal.

Saints were without Leon Pryce who was suspended for three matches by the RFL disciplinary committee for grabbing Bradford Bulls' Sam Burgess by the testicles in the Challenge Cup semi-final. Pryce claimed that there was an absence of malice in the illegal action, but the committee rejected the defence.

Catalans Dragons stand-off Casey McGuire was thought likely to miss the Challenge Cup Final after suffering a pectoral injury in the Dragons' 42-22 loss at Huddersfield Giants. McGuire missed the rest of the season. The Catalans had now lost four successive Super

League matches. Huddersfield's star was Rod 'Rocket' Jensen, who lived up to his nickname when launching himself on an 80-metre sprint for the first try after collecting a high kick inside four minutes. It was his first try for the club in his seventh match. He also blasted through in the 20th minute to send Shane Elford in for the first of his two tries.

The Giants were now sixth after both Wakefield and Harlequins lost. The Wildcats went down 38-24 at Odsal, despite the dismissal by Steve Ganson of Joe Vagana just before half-time, for running into Wakefield defender Luke George with a raised elbow. With the Bulls leading only 16-10 at the time, their supporters were stunned by the decision. It was Ganson's first return to Odsal since the Bulls' controversial last-minute defeat by Leeds Rhinos at the Millennium Stadium in May. He had taken to the field to a chorus of boos from the Odsal faithful. Vagana got two matches.

Bradford were missing Michael Platt, banned for two matches, reduced to one on appeal, for punching Maurie Fa'asavalu in the Challenge Cup semi-final, and the injured Iestyn Harris. Paul Deacon had withdrawn from the game with an injury picked up while warming up, and 18-year-old Sam Burgess took over Deacon's goalkicking responsibilities, ending up the gamestar. Kevin Henderson's 62nd minute try brought the scores to 26-24 but James Evans and Burgess scored tries to keep the game in Bradford's pocket. Former London Broncos goal-kicker Tony Martin, now at NZ Warriors, was signed by the Wildcats on a two-year deal from the 2008 season.

Leeds coach Tony Smith singled out Kiwi Brent Webb for praise after the 54-20 win at Harlequins. The fullback suffered a mixed afternoon, committing three high tackles early in the first half – one of which landed him in the sin bin, and two of which were put on report – but he scored two second-half tries and created another for Jamie Peacock. The following Tuesday Webb was banned for four matches, reduced to three on appeal.

The Rhinos, who had previously suffered consecutive losses against Wigan and Wakefield, were losing 16-6 at half-time, only to post 48 second-half points to keep the pressure on leaders St Helens. The defeat was the Londoners' third on the bounce.

Round 23

Two weeks before they were due to meet in the first Challenge Cup final to be played at the re-built Wembley Stadium, Catalans and St Helens played out a dress rehearsal at the Stade Gilbert Brutus, with a stunning outcome, as the French side won 21-0.

Unlike in 2006, when St Helens were defeated in France, there was no question of an under-strength line-up. With the exception of the highly-rated youngster Kyle Eastmond, the rest of the Saints players were front-line squad members. In fact the home side were missing more first choices. Adam Mogg moved from centre to stand-off to cover the loss of Casey McGuire, with Sebastien Raguin taking his place as a makeshift centre.

Clint Greenshields was a handful for the Saints defence throughout, scoring the final Dragons try nine minutes from time. Saints had chances, but determined defence kept them out.

To compound a miserable weekend, St Helens' management and several players were left high and dry in Perpignan after a strike by local firemen prevented flights from leaving the local airport.

Saints' shock defeat allowed Leeds to move level at the top, as they had beaten Salford 52-14 at Headingley the night before. The Reds had never beaten the Rhinos in the Super League era, and that record never looked like being threatened. For their part, Leeds shrugged off the loss of their two most potent strike players this season – Brent Webb to suspension and Rob Burrow to injury – to post nine tries, some of them spectacular. Jamie Thackray crowned another rip-roaring display with two unstoppable surges for tries. But prop Nick Scruton was ruled out for the rest of the season after breaking his right hand.

Bradford stayed two points behind the leaders with a 28-10 win at Hull KR. Rovers suffered from the loss of Ben Cockayne and Ian Hardman in the opening ten minutes. Makali Aizue was already missing, suspended for one match for a careless high tackle in the win against Salford. And then a disastrous first half, where a clinical Bulls attack ran in five tries in the opening 33 minutes, put the visitors 28-0 ahead and ended the game as a contest. The Robins had only two home wins to boast - the worst record in Super League.

Meanwhile the Robins allowed threequarters Byron Ford and Gareth Morton to go on loan to Oldham until the end of the season. The Bulls were reported to have completed the signing of Wakefield halfback Ben Jeffries for the 2008 season, with Wildcats chief executive Steve Ferres admitting his club was very interested in signing Huddersfield Giants' Brad Drew. The Bulls were also thought to be in line to sign Giants centre or back-rower Chris Nero. Wests Tigers centre Paul Whatuira was to join Huddersfield for 2008, on a three-year deal.

Hull coach Peter Sharp paid tribute to Motu Tony after the Kiwi Test star's two-try performance in the 46-14 victory over Warrington Wolves at the KC Stadium. The outcome was in doubt throughout the first half, before Gareth Raynor's 42nd minute score saw Hull take the game by the scruff of the neck. Paul Wood's dismissal just after the hour for a high shot on Scott Wheeldon did little to help Warrington's cause. Wood was fined but not suspended for a 'careless tackle'.

After a tumultuous three weeks which had seen the club docked four league points and lose three games, Wigan kept their play-off chances alive with a 20-12 home win over Huddersfield. The Giants were missing Brad Drew after the club gave him permission to travel to Australia because of a serious family illness. The Giants would have gone into the weekend sitting proudly in fourth position had they extended their winning run to four games. But Pat Richards' faultless kicking - he kicked six from six, including four penalties to pass 100 goals for the season - and Trent Barrett's ability to create Wigan's two tries with kicks proved decisive. Later that week refs boss Stuart Cummings confirmed that the 37th minute try scored by Mick Higham was wrongly awarded by video referee Ian Smith, as Higham had been offside.

There was an unusual incident when referee Steve Ganson took action late in the match after a complaint from Huddersfield centre Jamahl Lolesi over remarks he alleged had been made to him by Fielden. Subsequently, however, Lolesi withdrew his complaint, and when the RFL investigation took place Fielden was cleared of any wrongdoing.

But that wasn't the case with Wakefield hooker Tevita Leo-Latu, who was suspended for six matches for racially abusing Warrington Wolves winger Kevin Penny in the match between the two clubs on 17th June at the Halliwell Jones Stadium. During the game the Warrington winger reported the incident to a touch judge, and the RFL Compliance Unit subsequently investigated it.

On the field Wakefield bounced back to winning ways and forced their re-entry into the top six with a five-try-to-two 28-14 home victory over Harlequins, with prop Richard Moore the gamestar.

It was a busy time for the RFL, who that week announced it had charged both Hull KR and Hull FC with misconduct following incidents at the end of their Super League clash at Craven Park on 8th July. Both clubs would face an independent hearing later in the year.

Round 24

Huddersfield coach Jon Sharp labelled the 26-22 victory over Bradford Bulls that moved the Giants into the top six as the best in his four years in charge at the club. The Giants lost Shane Elford early on through a hamstring injury, and then had Keith Mason sent off just after the hour mark for butting David Solomona in a fiery encounter that also saw Bradford's Tame Tupou dismissed two minutes earlier for releasing a flurry of punches on Stuart Jones.

The Giants were without captain Chris Thorman, who failed to recover after suffering a blow to the kidneys at Wigan the previous week, but with Robbie Paul reverting to fullback they welcomed back Brad Drew from compassionate leave. Bradford's hopes of Paul Deacon returning from a nagging hamstring injury proved premature as he limped out of training on the Saturday.

Jamahl Lolesi scored a well taken hat-trick, which could easily have been four, as Bradford were left four points adrift in third behind St Helens and Leeds, who both recorded victories.

St Helens won 32-20 against Salford at the Willows on the Friday night. The Reds had mighty Saints on the ropes for much of the game. But they bombed too many chances and Saints inevitably made them pay - scoring 20 points in the final 17 minutes. The points were in the balance until two-try Saints winger Ade Gardner caught Salford in the 76th minute, breaking clear and showing his searing pace out wide to score his second try. John Wilshere was in inspired form at halfback, for the second time this season scoring two tries against Saints and ending up on the losing side.

The defeat left the Reds' Super League status hanging by a thread, with relegation rivals Hull KR three points ahead and just three games left to go.

Leeds beat Hull KR at Headingley Carnegie on the same night. A superb long-range try on 55 minutes halted a terrific Rovers comeback after they had trailed 16-0 at the break. Danny McGuire started it with an offload on the left. Keith Senior fed Matt Diskin, Kevin Sinfield's precise pass unleashed Carl Ablett and he trampled through the cover out wide on the South Stand side, making 50 metres before turning the scoring pass inside to the trailing Clinton Toopi.

Wolves coach Paul Cullen heaped praise on his injury-hit squad side following their 22-18 home win over Wembley-bound Catalans Dragons. They were inspired by the distribution and work-rate of hooker Mark Gleeson and the clinical finishing of fullback Brent Grose. Grose struck for two crucial tries to turn the game the way of the Wolves, his second score breaking a 12-12 deadlock to edge them into the lead for good. Lee Mitchell made a debut appearance off the bench.

Dragons coach Mick Potter hit-out at the RFL and Sky TV for rearranging the fixture to Sunday evening. That left his side facing a Monday morning trip back to Perpignan and a short three-day turnaround in France before a trip back to London for that Cup-final clash against St Helens.

It was a bruising encounter, with three sin-binnings (Lee Briers, Clint Greenshields and John Wilson) and one on-report incident involving David Ferriol, although he was found not guilty of leading with a forearm on Mark Gleeson.

Wigan, who had decided not to appeal against their deduction of four points for breaking the 2006 salary cap, remained eighth after a 16-all draw at Harlequins.

It was a strange situation for Harlequins owner Ian Lenagan, strongly tipped to be in takeover talks for the Warriors, and both clubs, now two points adrift of the play-offs, viewed the game as a point lost. Once again Trent Barrett dug his side out of a hole with two tries. Mark McLinden had the opportunity to win the game with the last kick of the game, but his field-goal attempt sailed wide.

There was massive controversy over the refereeing in the TV game between Wakefield and Hull FC on the Friday. Three late Hull tries when Wakefield were down to 11 players gave Hull a flattering 42-24 victory margin and left the Wildcats coach John Kear fuming.

Hull were leading a terrific contest 26-24 when referee Phil Bentham sent two Trinity players - Olivier Elima for a tackle on Gareth Raynor after he had defused a bomb, and Adam Watene for a high tackle - to the sin bin within 60 seconds. Both were contentious decisions and before they returned Hull had taken full advantage to clinch victory with three tries in six minutes.

SUPER LEAGUE TABLE - *Sunday 19th August*

	P	W	D	L	F	A	D	PTS
St Helens	24	17	0	7	703	376	327	34
Leeds Rhinos	24	17	0	7	679	450	229	34
Bradford Bulls *	24	16	0	8	712	516	196	30
Hull FC	24	12	2	10	530	495	35	26
Warrington Wolves	24	12	0	12	621	640	-19	24
Huddersfield Giants	24	11	1	12	556	474	82	23
Wakefield T Wildcats	24	11	1	12	550	606	-56	23
Wigan Warriors **	24	12	1	11	521	475	46	21
Harlequins	24	9	3	12	449	558	-109	21
Catalans Dragons	24	8	1	15	494	611	-117	17
Hull Kingston Rovers	24	8	0	16	400	653	-253	16
Salford City Reds	24	6	1	17	417	778	-361	13

* 2 points deducted for 2006 salary cap breach
** 4 points deducted for 2006 salary cap breach

CHALLENGE CUP FINAL
Capital return

St Helens, surviving temperatures reminiscent of their 1976 Challenge Cup Final victory over Widnes, won their sixth Challenge Cup in the 12 years of Super League, and their eleventh overall, as they deservedly made history in the first final to be played at the redeveloped national stadium.

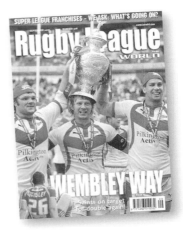

The 30-8 scoreline was harsh on the Dragons, carving out their own niche in history as the first French club to reach the Cup final, but no-one could deny Saints' superiority as they won the great trophy for a second year in row. In the absence of Paul Sculthorpe, Keiron Cunningham - the only survivor from Saints' Cup-winning teams in 1996 and 1997 - lifted the Cup in front of 84,241 fans, a larger crowd than expected. With 17,000 'Club Wembley' members expected not to take up their seats. RFL officials were celebrating the fact that over 11,000 of them were filled.

It was a superb all-round performance by St Helens - presented with their Cup Final jerseys by Mal Meninga, one of their old heroes from the 1980s. The result of there being no obvious contender for man of the match was that the vote for the Lance Todd Trophy was split between Paul Wellens and Leon Pryce. It was only the second time there had not been an outright winner, and once again a fullback and a stand-off shared the honour. But in 1965 they were in opposition; Wigan fullback Ray Ashby added the trophy to his winners' medal, while it was some consolation for Hunslet's Brian Gabbitas. Both were at Wembley again to join the pre-match parade of past Lance Todd Trophy winners.

It was Pryce's first game after a three-match ban for squeezing Sam Burgess's testicles in the semi-final. 'I was a bit surprised to win it,' said Pryce. 'I don't think anybody stood out. The first 20 minutes was like a game of chess. In the next ten minutes I thought James Roby made a massive difference, and also James Graham.' Roby and Graham had played in the 1997 Wembley curtain-raiser as 11-year-olds.

Substitute Roby scored a brilliant individual try to break a deadlock after 33 minutes, the first by a professional at the new Wembley, although the first try was scored by Castleford High School pupil Luke Metcalfe in the Year 7 Champion Schools Final that preceded the Cup Final.

Saints could have been behind 6-0 at that stage. After 24 minutes of nip and tuck, Jason Croker, the oldest player in SLXII, collected a Stacey Jones chip-kick behind the posts in spectacular fashion and touched down. After a lengthy video review that made it obvious that it was impossible to come down firmly one way or the other, video referee Phil Bentham ignored the 'benefit of the doubt' rule, and decided against a try.

The wait for the decision took about four minutes, allowing Saints to re-gather their breath and composure. Almost immediately Mike Bennett broke to within five metres of the Dragons' line and Ade Gardner dropped the ball going over trying to collect a Gidley pass.

There was more sustained Saints pressure, as Croker knocked on inside his own 30-metre line, and the Catalans held up Pryce on the line twice within three minutes, with Greg Mounis showing remarkable strength to turn Pryce over.

Ultimately the pressure would tell, as the brilliant Roby went on an individual run from acting halfback from 25 metres out, beating attempted tackles by Mounis, Rémi Casty, Greenshields, Croker and Cyril Gossard to touch down. Long's goal gave Saints a 6-0 lead after 33 minutes.

The Catalans were in no mood to give in, however, and when Saints fumbled the rebound from a Long kick they put on a superb move for Younes Khattabi to go in at the left corner after receiving a great ball by Adam Mogg. The 23-year old, who just eighteen months before was playing for the defunct Marseille club, became the first Frenchman and the first player of Moroccan origin to score in a Challenge Cup final, and probably the first Muslim of any nationality to touch down at Wembley. Jones couldn't convert, and a two-point margin at the interval would have been a fair reflection of the game.

But Saints received another penalty for a high tackle, and they took advantage for Gidley to put Gardner in at the corner, after running through an off-colour Clint Greenshields. Long added the goal for a 12-4 interval score.

After six minutes of the second half, the game swung further St Helens' way when Greenshields failed to drop on a low grubber from Long, and Wellens pounced on the ball for a try that was awarded by the video referee, with Long's goal giving Saints a 14-point lead.

Saints cranked up the pressure, with Long's next kick winning a goal-line drop-out, and, although Greenshields made a superb tackle from behind on Long, Saints spread the ball through Cunningham and Pryce to Paul Clough, the youngest player

CARNEGIE CHALLENGE CUP FINAL

Saturday 25th August 2007

CATALANS DRAGONS 8 ST HELENS 30

DRAGONS: 1 Clint Greenshields; 2 Justin Murphy; 11 Sebastien Raguin; 3 John Wilson; 25 Younes Khattabi; 4 Adam Mogg; 7 Stacey Jones (C); 10 Jerome Guisset; 26 Luke Quigley; 19 Alex Chan; 12 Jason Croker; 17 Cyril Gossard; 13 Gregory Mounis. Subs (all used): 8 David Ferriol; 18 Vincent Duport; 24 Remi Casty; 27 Kane Bentley.
Tries: Khattabi (37), Murphy (58); **Goals:** Jones 0/2.
SAINTS: 1 Paul Wellens; 2 Ade Gardner; 3 Matt Gidley; 4 Willie Talau; 5 Francis Meli; 6 Leon Pryce; 7 Sean Long; 8 Nick Fozzard; 9 Keiron Cunningham (C); 10 Jason Cayless; 11 Lee Gilmour; 15 Mike Bennett; 12 Jon Wilkin. Subs (all used): 14 James Roby; 17 James Graham; 22 Paul Clough; 23 Maurie Fa'asavalu.
Tries: Roby (33), Gardner (40, 78), Wellens (46), Clough (51); **Goals:** Long 5/6.
Rugby Leaguer & League Express Men of the Match:
Dragons: Jason Croker; *Saints:* Paul Wellens.
Penalty count: 9-12; **Half-time:** 4-12; **Referee:** Ashley Klein; **Attendance:** 84,241 *(at Wembley Stadium).*

on the field at the age of 19, who touched down. Long missed the conversion.

The Dragons didn't collapse despite the game being clearly beyond them. Justin Murphy pounced on a spilled ball that Jon Wilkin tried to pass to Lee Gilmour, instead hitting him in the back, and giving the Catalans winger a straight run into the right corner. After Long put a ball out on the full, from his own 40-metre line, the Dragons lost their chance when Alex Chan dropped a crucial pass from Jones with the line in sight.

Gardner broke downfield as the Dragons fumbled again, but was tackled from behind by Khattabi, but then, after a high tackle by Luke Quigley on Nick Fozzard, Long's goal extended the lead to 16 points.

The last ten minutes saw the match winding down, with Saints winning three more penalties, and showing some fine work, with Roby prominent, and with a penalty for a dangerous tackle on Gilmour by Croker and Vincent Duport, before they scored their final try by Gardner in the 78th minute from a pass by the excellent Wellens.

Long's final conversion sealed the success, and the Saints fans celebrations began. The Challenge Cup final had returned to the venue, that since 1929, had been its spiritual home.

SEPTEMBER
Robins fairytale

Round 25

Justin Morgan had said before the Cup Final that beating Hull FC to maintain Hull KR's Super League status would be a fairytale. And on the first Sunday of September Rovers celebrated their survival after a stunning 42-6 win at KC Stadium. Eight tries-to-one emphasised Rovers' superiority, which gave them their second victory of the season over last year's Grand Finalists and condemned Salford to National League One.

With their future secured, Rovers were set to announce the signings of a number of new players, one of them Hull's due-to-be released Shaun Briscoe. Wests Tigers pair Ben Galea and Daniel Fitzhenry, Wakefield's Peter Fox, Melbourne Storm's highly-rated second-rower Clint Newton were all expected to sign. Rovers had already announced the capture of Jake Webster, 23, the New Zealand international centre or winger from Gold Coast Titans.

Salford went down fighting at Wigan on the Friday night, leading 10-6 at half-time, but Trent Barrett put on another vintage master-class to rescue the Warriors from a dire first-half showing. Wigan's 40-16 victory condemned the Reds to relegation for the second time in five years. Iafeta Palea'aesina's try midway through the second half killed off Salford's hopes of Super League survival, though Palea'aesina and Harrison Hansen both received one-match bans for their parts in a fight.

City Reds chairman John Wilkinson celebrated 25 years at the helm earlier in the year and relegation was a highly disappointing outcome after being a play-off club in 2006.

With two Super League rounds remaining, St Helens and Leeds Rhinos were still battling for the League Leaders' Shield, after the Rhinos scrapped for a 16-16 draw against Bradford Bulls at Odsal on the Sunday night. The game celebrated the 100-year history of the club in its previous guise of Bradford Northern and, since 1995, the Bulls.

James Evans' 78th-minute try rescued a share of the spoils for Bradford, but their top-two hopes all but faded after Paul Deacon's missed conversion cost them the chance to claim both points.

The draw meant St Helens now led the table by one point from the Rhinos after a 32-10 home win over dogged but ultimately out-gunned Harlequins. The loss left the Quins' play-off hopes hanging by a slender thread as they remained mired in a slump that had seen them winless in their last six games.

The Bulls were certain to finish at least in third place, but six sides were still vying for the final three positions in the top six as the race for the play-offs intensified.

Hull FC were now only a point ahead of Huddersfield Giants, but had a negative points difference and had still to face Leeds and Bradford in the final two weeks of the regular season. The Giants had games remaining against Wakefield and Hull KR and were coming off the back of a 34-22 victory at Warrington Wolves on the Friday night.

Brad Drew was in fine form again - his move to Wakefield at the end of the season confirmed. The final Huddersfield try by Kevin Brown put enough daylight between the teams to ensure Ben Westwood's hat-trick heroics came to nought. The RFL disciplinary committee that week found Paul Rauhihi guilty of a dangerous tackle and handed him a one-match suspension. Rauhihi had signed a new one-year deal, but the Wolves had announced that Chris Leikvoll, Brent Grose, and Henry Fa'afili would not be retained for the 2008 season. Warrington were still in sixth, but with seventh-placed Wigan only a point behind them,

After their 20-38 defeat in Perpignan, Wakefield were now eighth, with two more difficult away games to come at Huddersfield and Leeds. Harlequins were still an outside possibility of reaching the six with a home fixture against relegated Salford and a trip to the south of France awaiting them.

The Dragons players were presented to Barcelona soccer fans at the Nou Camp Stadium, in recognition of their Challenge Cup run, the night after their win over Wakefield. The game featured a rare eight-point try in the 53rd minute - effectively the gamebreaker as it gave the Dragons a 12-point lead - after Brett Ferres fouled Justin Murphy in the act of scoring.

The game exploded in the 75th minute when a flare-up at the scrum turned into a wholesale exchange of punches. Richard Moore and Alex Chan received one-match suspensions from the RFL.

The big news story of the week had been the success of Bulls' in-form forward Glenn Morrison's appeal against a three-match suspension after being found guilty of a deliberate high tackle on Keith Mason in the defeat at Huddersfield. The Appeal Committee changed the verdict of the original committee because it was presented with new evidence that suggested that Morrison did not make contact with Mason. Tame Tupou got a two-match suspension for his red card during the same match.

Round 25 established a new all-time high aggregate weekly crowd for the competition. The six matches which took place that weekend drew a total of 78,917 supporters at an average of over 13,000 per match.

Round 26

St Helens clinched their third successive League Leaders' Shield, the fifth time they had finished top of the league in 12 years of the summer era - with a round to spare. Leeds' 17-6 defeat to Hull FC at Headingley, coupled with their 36-16 win over Warrington meant they would take pole position into the play-offs.

Francis Meli's hat-trick, his second in the last three home games, helped Saints get over the loss of prop Nick Fozzard, who suffered a muscle injury in his arm inside the opening three minutes' play.

Despite taking a 4-0 lead through two Lee Briers penalties, the Wolves trailed 18-10 at the interval as Lee Gilmour, Meli, twice, and Ade Gardner scored tries, with just a Kevin Penny effort in reply. Second-half tries by James Roby, Meli and Leon Pryce, against a sparkling individual effort by Martin Gleeson confirmed Saints' superiority. The 7-2 try tally told the story. Warrington needed to win at Salford in their final league game to have a chance of the play-offs.

Injuries to Mark Gleeson and Rob Parker left the Wolves short of numbers ahead of the visit to Salford, after they had also lost Paul Wood - with a shoulder dislocation during the first half of the previous weekend's defeat to Huddersfield - for the rest of the campaign, and Adrian Morley through suspension. Morley said referee Ashley Klein had no other option but to dismiss him for a high tackle on Saints' Paul Clough. He got one match, and that was the end of a disappointing domestic season for him.

The Rhinos fell to a 17-6 home defeat to Hull FC, who bounced back in style from their derby humiliation the week before. From the beginning the game was played at a frenetic pace. Matt Diskin fell like a sack of spuds from Garreth Carvell's early challenge that went on report, although Carvell was later found not guilty.

September

Two players on their way out of the KC Stadium, Shaun Briscoe and Wayne Godwin, to Hull KR and Bradford respectively, were Hull's best on the night. Mathew Head's field goal with 15 minutes to go, allied to his tactical kicking, kept Hull one point ahead in fourth.

Huddersfield were guaranteed a play-off place in fifth, on the Sunday after they announced the signing of Salford City Reds scrum-half Luke Robinson, beating Wakefield for the fourth time that season 24-22. The Giants trailed 20-12 at half-time, and 22-12 shortly after the break. But tries from Jamahl Lolesi and Stephen Wild took the Giants home. The Wildcats were now out of the running, two points behind sixth-placed Wigan but with a vastly inferior points difference.

The Warriors kept their play-off hopes alive as Hull KR's home form let them down once again, Wigan winning 40-24. Rovers had beaten the Warriors twice already at the JJB Stadium but again it was the opening minutes of the match that proved to be Rovers' downfall as Liam Colbon and Darrell Goulding scored tries in the opening six minutes. That week Wigan announced the signing of Salford forward Andy Coley.

Bradford made sure they weren't going to fall at home for a second time to Catalans Dragons, winning 40-8 after going 8-0 behind after half an hour, scoring seven tries without reply. After Leeds' defeat to Hull, Bradford now needed to win at Hull on the following Friday night and hope Leeds lost at home against Wakefield Trinity Wildcats for the Bulls to finish in second place.

Bulls coach Steve McNamara was hoping to welcome back Paul Deacon after the scrum-half tweaked a hamstring again in the build up to the victory over the Dragons.

Former New Zealand international Henry Fa'afili was moving south to line up in Harlequins' colours in 2008, but pulled out at the last-minute to take up a huge offer to play union in France. Harlequins' 22-16 narrow home victory over Salford on the Saturday kept alive their faint play-off hopes for 24 hours until Wigan's win the following day. Rikki Sheriffe's second try with ten minutes to go put Quins ahead for good.

Off the field, current Doncaster coach John Stankevitch finally won a legal case brought against Wigan and their former player Craig Smith. The litigation followed an injury Stankevitch suffered during the Super League elimination semi-final match between Wigan and St Helens at the JJB Stadium on 3rd October 2003. A high court hearing in Manchester had been scheduled, but a meeting of lawyers representing the parties agreed a six-figure settlement out of court.

Round 27

After a two-year gap, Wigan won a place in the play-offs on the last Friday night of the regular Super League season. The crowd of 22,031 in the JJB Stadium created a great atmosphere as the Warriors conquered St Helens, who had already secured the League Leaders Trophy, 20-12. The bumper attendance meant Wigan finished with a crowd average in excess of 16,000, greater than any of their average crowds throughout their great years of the 'eighties and 'nineties.

The Warriors' seventh successive home league victory extended their season for at least another week as Saints' winning run of eight derby games came to an end. Pat Richards' penalty four minutes from time, his fourth successful goalkick, finally decided a pulsating encounter, after Saints had led 10-6 at the break.

Wigan's win meant that injury-hit Warrington's own 34-26 victory the same night at relegated Salford was not enough for them to make the play-offs. A workmanlike performance was enlivened by flashes of individual brilliance from halfbacks Chris Bridge and Lee Briers, with 18-year-old Lee Mitchell impressing in his first start and claiming a crucial try. The Wolves' form player of SLXII, Ben Westwood's second score on 49 minutes opened a ten-point gap.

Leeds made sure they finished second to go straight into the Qualifying Semi-final as they overwhelmed Wakefield at Headingley. Danny McGuire and Rob Burrow were magnificent and Brent Webb at his very best as the Rhinos produced their best attacking display of the season.

With an attendance just short of 20,000; Leeds compiled a Super League and post-war club record, season average of 17,516. And Keith Senior became the first player to play 300 regular season Super League games, eleven years after playing in the very first Super League game for Sheffield Eagles against Paris St Germain on 29th March 1996.

The Bulls were the only team who could have caught Leeds had Wakefield won, but they lost 20-10 at Hull, who secured fourth place themselves with the win. Mathew Head was an early casualty. 'He's got an ankle knock to go with his knee, his shoulder and his head,' Peter Sharp joked.

Bradford welcomed back Shontayne Hape, who suffered cruciate ligament damage in March. But they were again without Paul Deacon after he failed another late fitness check. Richard Whiting scored Hull's match-clinching try in the last minute.

The two remaining games were played on the Saturday evening. Hull Kingston Rovers had that week announced they had signed Chev Walker after a season out of Super League with Bath rugby union. And the Robins ended the campaign as they began it - with a stunning Saturday night win - only their third home win of the year - under the Craven Park lights, watched by a live TV audience. A dramatic 25-24 win over the Giants meant Rovers had won ten matches, and against all pre-season predictions had survived in the game's elite league.

Huddersfield had to avoid defeat by three points or more to ensure they'd finish in fifth place. When form winger Rod Jensen scored a quickfire try-double just before the hour mark, Sharp and just about everyone else must have thought the Giants would finish the regular season on a high. But Ben Fisher replied with two tries himself to tie the scores at 24-all before Paul Cooke's field goal five minutes from the end brought the house down.

In Perpignan, Stacey Jones was chaired around the pitch after ending his two-year Catalan Dragons career on a high with a 30-14 home win over Harlequins. Jones and Adam Mogg's kicking games proved too much for the battling Quins, who themselves were saying goodbye to Lee Hopkins in his last match before retiring. John Wilson's 44th minute try from Jones' kick opened up a 20-point margin that was always going to be too big for the Quins. The win meant the Dragons finished tenth and had beaten every other team in SLXII.

FINAL SUPER LEAGUE TABLE - *Saturday 15th September*

	P	W	D	L	F	A	D	PTS
St Helens	27	19	0	8	783	422	361	38
Leeds Rhinos	27	18	1	8	747	487	260	37
Bradford Bulls *	27	17	1	9	778	560	218	33
Hull FC	27	14	2	11	573	553	20	30
Huddersfield Giants	27	13	1	13	638	543	95	27
Wigan Warriors **	27	15	1	11	621	527	94	27
Warrington Wolves	27	13	0	14	693	736	-43	26
Wakefield T Wildcats	27	11	1	15	596	714	-118	23
Harlequins	27	10	3	14	495	636	-141	23
Catalans Dragons	27	10	1	16	570	685	-115	21
Hull Kingston Rovers	27	10	0	17	491	723	-232	20
Salford City Reds	27	6	1	20	475	874	-399	13

* 2 points deducted for 2006 salary cap breach
** 4 points deducted for 2006 salary cap breach

The average Super League attendance had risen to 10,264 per game, from 9,026 in 2006, beating the 10,000 barrier for the first time, although this involved the RFL counting the attendance in the stadium at the kick-off of each game on the Millennium weekend. Ten clubs had registered increased attendances this season, with promoted club Hull Kingston Rovers more than doubling their average crowd, while the Catalans Dragons, Huddersfield Giants, Hull FC and Wakefield Trinity Wildcats all experienced growth in excess of 20 per cent.

SUPER LEAGUE PLAY-OFFS
Top two to tango

Elimination Play-offs

Trent Barrett led Wigan to an astonishing 31-30 win at Bradford on the first Friday night of the play-offs, when they came back from 30-6 down after 55 minutes. It was the biggest comeback victory in the history of Super League. No team had turned around more than a 21-point deficit in a Super League play-off or regular round match.

Mark Calderwood's interception of an ill-judged Shontayne Hape pass and 85-metre sprint for a converted try levelled the scores at 30-all, before Wigan's astonishing fightback was completed by Pat Richards' match-winning field goal four minutes from time. It was the first he had ever kicked.

Calderwood's performance epitomised Wigan's, as it completed his second-half hat-trick after a disastrous start.

Third-placed Bradford's total collapse was difficult to understand. The loss of Chris Feather with a dislocated shoulder in the 25th minute was less of a major factor than the resting of Andy Lynch, Terry Newton and especially David Solomona for a spell midway through the second half. They had a chance to level with a field goal in the last seconds but, missing the still-injured Paul Deacon, they didn't have the composure to set up the position.

The other eliminator went with finishing position as fourth-placed Hull beat Huddersfield Giants 22-16 at the KC Stadium on the Saturday. Two tries from Gareth Raynor took Hull a step nearer their second consecutive Grand Final.

Huddersfield threatened an unlikely comeback late on, but they looked nervous in their first ever play-off game, and Hull's excellent start which put them 10-0 ahead contrasted to the Giants poor opening.

The second try had controversy about it. As Paul Reilly ran the ball out of the Giants '20', Garreth Carvell connected with a huge hit that dislodged the ball. Lee Radford scooped it up and sent Thomas Lee over by the posts as the Giants fans behind the woodwork appealed for a penalty for a high tackle. Referee Ashley Klein didn't agree with their assessment, awarded the score and Danny Tickle's conversion put the home side 10-0 ahead. By the time of Raynor's second try in the 67th minute, Hull led 22-6, although tries from Reilly and Kevin Brown created a tense last five minutes. Giants star Chris Nero broke his collar-bone in his last game for the Giants.

Qualifying Semi-final

St Helens went straight to Old Trafford after a magnificent Friday night 10-8 win over Leeds Rhinos at Knowsley Road.

The game was hailed as the most intense and brutal in history, and was Saints' first victory in three attempts over the Rhinos in 2007. Such was the defensive stranglehold that both sides could only manage a try apiece. Leeds' effort came early - Lee Smith, who had just failed with an earlier effort, intercepting a Jon Wilkin pass, wrestling the loose ball out of the arms of Willie Talau and racing clear down the touchline from five metres from his own line for a spectacular sixth-minute opener.

Leon Pryce replied with a brilliant opportunist effort on 16 minutes, selling a huge dummy that fooled at least four and probably six close-range Leeds defenders before cutting inside to score.

Leeds forced five goal-line drop-outs against the champions, with Saints not forcing one in reply. Matt Gidley, his nose bandaged after suffering a severe facial cut midway through the second half, somehow stopped Brent Webb in full flight for the line with just five minutes remaining to preserve his side's tenuous advantage.

Young scrum-half Matty Smith's 64th minute penalty eventually decided a titanic struggle.

Elimination Semi-final

Wigan's wonder-run from sixth continued after another tension-packed play-off victory, this time by 21-18. It was not quite the epic comeback that brought them a memorable victory after being 24 points down at Bradford a week earlier, but it still needed a massive effort to overturn Hull FC's 14-8 lead and then hold out against a late all-out assault on their line.

Once again Wigan owed much to Pat Richards, as for the second successive week they snatched victory despite only sharing the try-scoring with the opposition. He opened the try-scoring with a shock try inside two minutes, and the fullback went on to land four goals plus a field goal.

Richard Horne powered over for his 100th career try just after the half-hour mark to give Hull that six-point lead. But Wigan increased the tempo in the second half and virtually clinched victory with a quick two-try burst. Gareth Hock did well to break a tackle and go in from ten metres in the 49th minute and four minutes later Liam Colbon sauntered in off Trent Barrett's sweet cut-out pass. With Richards landing that goal from wide out Wigan were 20-14 ahead. But they sensed Hull were setting themselves for a desperate late challenge and Richards wisely pegged them back with his field goal that opened a vital seven-point gap with only nine minutes left.

Raynor's second try ensured Wigan had to do more desperate defending as Hull went within inches of grabbing a match-winning try.

Final Eliminator

Leeds Rhinos ended the Warriors' dreams the following Friday with an emphatic 36-6 win at Headingley Carnegie. Leeds looked very impressive, with an almost unheard of 100 per cent completion rate in the first half.

After a Kevin Sinfield penalty opened the scoring, Brent Webb tidied up superbly at the back and was on hand to support a monumental Jamie Peacock break as he ripped through to finish a stunning 65-metre move between the posts. Sinfield goaled and, following a mesmeric seven-man handling move, added another penalty after Kylie Leuluai had been taken high. A Danny McGuire drop off sent sub Ali Lauitiiti bludgeoning to the whitewash and Sinfield's goal made it 16-0 at the break.

Trent Barrett fashioned the Warriors' sole score. Thomas Leuluai chipped over from halfway on the last, Barrett brilliantly read and reacted to the bounce ahead of Webb and slipped the ball for Richards who trailed up the middle to the posts.

Jamie Jones-Buchanan produced a fine tackle on Sean O'Loughlin and then played a key role in the match-turning score. Sinfield was the architect, spotting and exploiting a gap out wide to arc clear before setting free JJB, sporting an infamous beard at the end of the season, his ball on the inside sending Rob Burrow scampering over. Webb got a second, Sinfield dropped a field goal and Gareth Hock's mounting frustrations saw him put on report for a dangerous, late tackle on Matt Diskin. Hock carried a two-match suspension into 2008.

O'Loughlin's long pass to ground was snaffled by Burrow and he rounded the last vestiges of the cover to go within one touchdown of a century for the club. Sinfield ended the match with a second one-pointer.

SUPER LEAGUE GRAND FINAL
Rhinos stampede

Leeds Rhinos earned their second Super League Grand Final success in four years under departing coach Tony Smith with an emphatic second-half display that ended in a 33-6 victory.

They led 8-6 at half-time but Ali Lauitiiti's powerhouse try ten minutes after the turnaround turned the tide the Rhinos' way, followed almost immediately by Scott Donald's superb winger's try from halfway, as Smith's side went on to post 25-unanswered points after the break.

Rob Burrow may have missed out on the try he needed to complete a career century, but he won the Harry Sunderland Trophy as man of the match. Burrow faced stiff competition, with fullback Brent Webb, wingers Lee Smith and Donald, forwards Jamie Peacock and Gareth Ellis and skipper Kevin Sinfield all ending the campaign in top form.

Huge crowds built up around Old Trafford long before kick-off, the postal strikes of the previous week meaning many supporters had to collect their tickets on the day.

Sean Long took his place in the Saints line-up after an injury-ravaged season and Maurie Fa'asavalu, who also missed the qualifying semi-final victory over Leeds, was back on the bench. Long lasted the 80 minutes without problem and was his side's most consistent performer, creating the break that led to Saints' only try, thrillingly finished off by James Roby - named Man of Steel earlier in the week - via Lee Gilmour.

Both sides settled well, and the tackling was fierce. Rhinos hooker Matt Diskin came up with the first error, obstructing Long as the Saints live-wire kicked ahead on the run. But Long unexpectedly was wide with the resulting 20-metre angled penalty attempt.

Rhinos skipper Kevin Sinfield got his side off the mark with a calmly potted 20-metre penalty on the angle - after Chris Flannery was penalised for offside on his own line.

The Rhinos were in the ascendancy and Kylie Leuluai, falling on Wilkin's charged-down kick on halfway, set up

ENGAGE SUPER LEAGUE GRAND FINAL

Saturday 13th October 2007

LEEDS RHINOS 33 ST HELENS 6

RHINOS: 1 Brent Webb; 5 Lee Smith; 3 Clinton Toopi; 4 Keith Senior; 2 Scott Donald; 6 Danny McGuire; 7 Rob Burrow; 8 Kylie Leuluai; 9 Matt Diskin; 10 Jamie Peacock; 11 Jamie Jones-Buchanan; 12 Gareth Ellis; 13 Kevin Sinfield (C). Subs (all used): 14 Ali Lauitiiti for Diskin (23); 16 Ryan Bailey for Leuluai (18); 18 Ian Kirke for Jones-Buchanan (33); 22 Carl Ablett for Kirke (57); Leuluai for Bailey (55); Jones-Buchanan for Lauitiiti (60); Diskin for Ablett (63); Kirke for Leuluai (65); Bailey for Kirke (76).
Tries: Webb (19), Lauitiiti (50), Donald (52), Smith (69), Jones-Buchanan (80); **Goals:** Sinfield 6/7;
Field goal: Burrow (55).
SAINTS: 1 Paul Wellens; 2 Ade Gardner; 3 Matt Gidley; 4 Willie Talau; 5 Francis Meli; 6 Leon Pryce; 7 Sean Long; 8 Nick Fozzard; 9 Keiron Cunningham (C); 10 Jason Cayless; 11 Lee Gilmour; 30 Chris Flannery; 12 Jon Wilkin. Subs (all used): 17 James Graham for Cayless (15); 14 James Roby for Cunningham (23); 23 Maurie Fa'asavalu for Fozzard (23); 15 Mike Bennett for Wilkin (31); Cayless for Fa'asavalu (34); Cunningham for Flannery (51); Wilkin for Bennett (55); Fa'asavalu for Cayless (55); Fozzard for Graham (57); Cayless for Fozzard (68); Graham for Fa'asavalu (68); Bennett for Gilmour (72).
Try: Roby (27); **Goals:** Long 1/2.
Rugby Leaguer & League Express Men of the Match:
Rhinos: Rob Burrow; *Saints:* Sean Long.
Penalty count: 4-5; **Half-time:** 8-6; **Referee:** Ashley Klein; **Attendance:** 71,352 *(at Old Trafford, Manchester).*

Leeds' Danny McGuire jumps for joy following Scott Donald's breathtaking second-half try

position for a brilliantly conceived try down the left. Sinfield was the pivot, Webb fed Keith Senior and Donald cleverly dodged inside two defenders. Webb then timed his angled run to perfection, keeping his body low to the ground, collecting the crisp pass and rounding Paul Wellens to score by the flag. Sinfield's touchline conversion was masterly and with it came an 8-0 lead.

After Roby's converted try made it 8-6, Danny McGuire's brilliant chip and chase from halfway followed by a measured kick to the left corner flag just eluded Donald's despairing dive before it ran into touch.

Saints forced the pace after half-time, Roby raising their game with his alertness at dummy-half. But the Rhinos survived a Donald error, after he conceded possession with a poor play-the-ball 20 metres from his own line, and another wave of attacks on the back of Clinton Toopi knocking-on attempting an interception to Roby's lofted pass to the left.

And when Willie Talau was unable to gather Roby's sharp pass 30 metres out, the Rhinos had the platform.

Burrow was denied after a scampering run but Sinfield re-gathered possession when his grubber-kick re-bounded off Jason Cayless. Smith, cleverly coming inside, kept the attack going and Lauitiiti took advantage, collecting his pass to the left and taking on Matt Gidley on a powerful, arcing run for the line, crossing in the left corner despite Wellens' late intervention. Though Sinfield was off-target with the conversion, Leeds held the initiative.

They built on that with a follow-up try from the re-start, Webb astutely shooting to the blind-side from dummy-half and, with Saints' defence caught out, Senior's sharp pass sending Donald streaking away from halfway down the left flank. Donald looked to be waiting for support on the inside but then a change of pace and swerve took him around Wellens for one of the best tries in Grand Final history. Sinfield converted and Burrow cleverly extended the lead with a well-struck field goal from in front of the posts at the end of the next set.

The body language of the players now told its own story - Saints looked weary and the Rhinos players full of vigour. With 11 minutes remaining McGuire's high, hanging kick to the right corner was brilliantly claimed by the on-rushing Smith ahead of Francis Meli, and the Leeds winger had the presence of mind to dart inside to make Sinfield's conversion easier. Sinfield then tagged on a sweetly struck 45-metre penalty goal for a high Leon Pryce tackle as the rampant Rhinos finished in control.

Just five seconds remained as the Rhinos applied the final act, Jamie Jones-Buchanan in support to collect Diskin's offload on the burst and bash his way over the line, despite last-man Wellens' tackle - confirmed by the under-worked video referee Ben Thaler. Sinfield - who had become the first Leeds player to play and score in every Cup and League match during a season - added his sixth goal to complete the Rhinos' glory night before jumping jubilantly into his teammates' arms.

The first cup final meeting of the two teams of the summer era, and the first time they had played one another in a final since the Regal Trophy Final of 1987/88, was Leeds' third win out of four over St Helens in 2007, wrecking Saints' hopes of maintaining their unbeaten record in their fifth Old Trafford appearance in ten years.

SUPER LEAGUE XII AWARDS
MAN OF STEEL: James Roby (St Helens)
PLAYERS' PLAYER OF THE YEAR: Trent Barrett (Wigan Warriors)
YOUNG PLAYER OF THE YEAR: Sam Burgess (Bradford Bulls)
COACH OF THE YEAR: Daniel Anderson (St Helens)
TOP TRYSCORER: Henry Fa'afili (Warrington Wolves) *for scoring 21 regular season tries*
TOP METRE-MAKER: James Roby (St Helens) *for making 3,303 regular season metres*
TOP TACKLER: Ben Fisher (Hull Kingston Rovers) *for making 841 regular season tackles*
REFEREE OF THE YEAR: Steve Ganson
SUPER LEAGUE DREAM TEAM 1 Paul Wellens (St Helens) 2 Kevin Penny (Warrington Wolves) 3 Adam Mogg (Catalans Dragons) 4 Jason Demetriou (Wakefield Trinity Wildcats) 5 Scott Donald (Leeds Rhinos) 6 Trent Barrett (Wigan Warriors) 7 Rob Burrow (Leeds Rhinos) 8 Nick Fozzard (St Helens) 9 James Roby (St Helens) 10 Jamie Peacock (Leeds Rhinos) 11 Gareth Ellis (Leeds Rhinos) 12 Glenn Morrison (Bradford Bulls) 13 Stephen Wild (Huddersfield Giants)

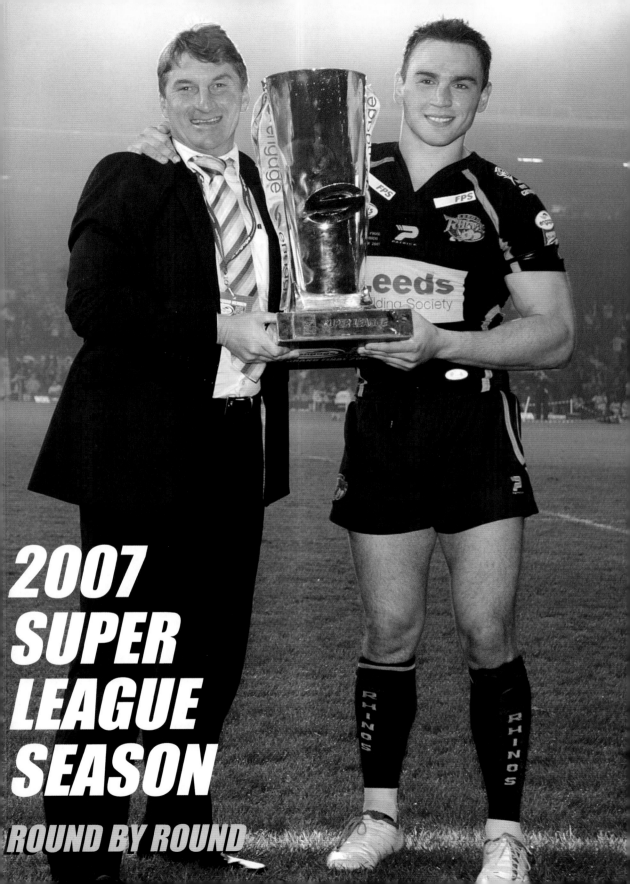

2007 SUPER LEAGUE SEASON

ROUND BY ROUND

LEFT: Lee Hopkins and Scott Hill celebrate at the final whistle after Harlequins' shock opening-round victory at St Helens
RIGHT: Stuart Reardon is held up by Bryan Fletcher as Warrington beat Wigan on a snowy night at the JJB Stadium

ROUND 1

Hull Kingston Rovers players go wild after making a winning return to Super League courtesy of victory over Wakefield

ABOVE: Mark Calderwood and a bevy of Catalans players enjoy an early bath as the Dragons lose at home to Wigan
RIGHT TOP: Peter Fox breaks in Wakefield's win over Saints
RIGHT BOTTOM: Jon Wilkin gives Bradford the run-around
BELOW: Lee Briers and Kirk Yeaman meet at the HJ Stadium

ROUND 2

ROUND 4

ROUND 3

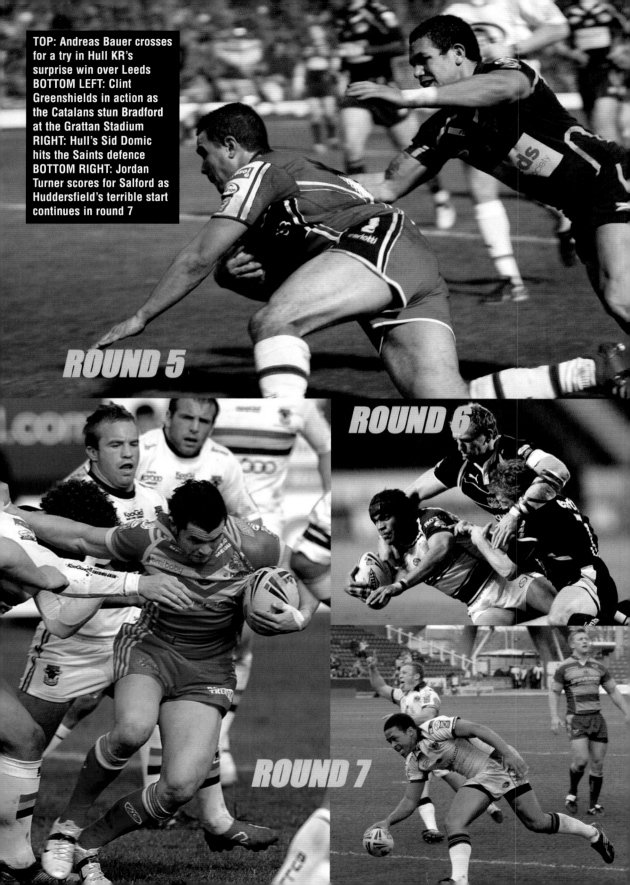

TOP: Andreas Bauer crosses for a try in Hull KR's surprise win over Leeds
BOTTOM LEFT: Clint Greenshields in action as the Catalans stun Bradford at the Grattan Stadium
RIGHT: Hull's Sid Domic hits the Saints defence
BOTTOM RIGHT: Jordan Turner scores for Salford as Huddersfield's terrible start continues in round 7

ROUND 5

ROUND 6

ROUND 7

ROUND 8

ROUND 9

TOP: Super League XII Man of Steel James Roby shows terrific early form as visitors St Helens win the annual Good Friday derby with Wigan
ABOVE: Scott Donald crosses for a breathtaking winning try for Leeds against Bradford in the first big local derby of the new season in round 8
LEFT: Danny Tickle is surrounded by Rovers tacklers as the Hull derby makes an Easter Monday return to top-flight British Rugby League

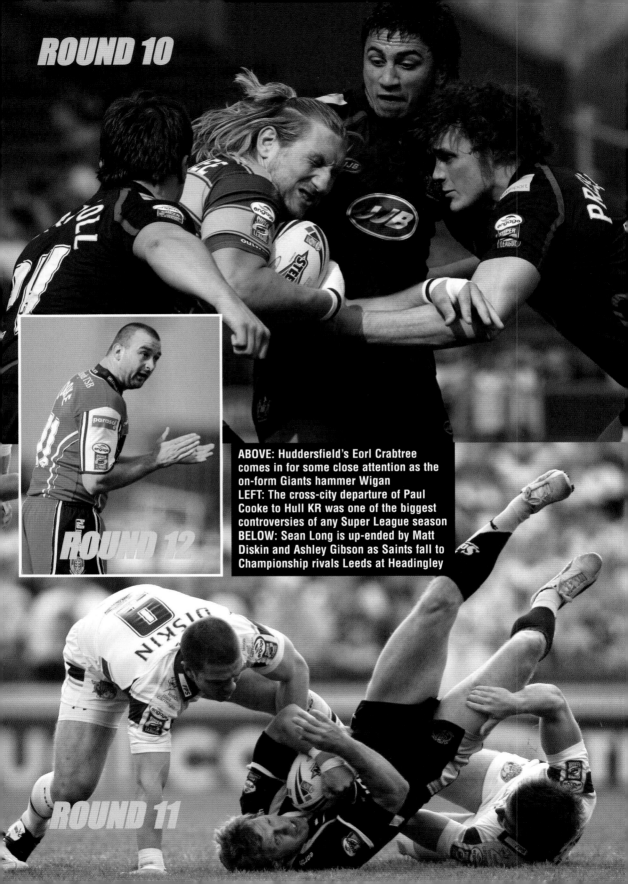

ROUND 10

ROUND 12

ROUND 11

ABOVE: Huddersfield's Eorl Crabtree comes in for some close attention as the on-form Giants hammer Wigan
LEFT: The cross-city departure of Paul Cooke to Hull KR was one of the biggest controversies of any Super League season
BELOW: Sean Long is up-ended by Matt Diskin and Ashley Gibson as Saints fall to Championship rivals Leeds at Headingley

Arguments and local derbies raged as a whole round of Super League was staged over two exciting days at the inaugural Millennium Magic weekend in Cardiff CLOCKWISE: Paul Sculthorpe is felled as Saints beat Wigan; Hull KR's Mark O'Neill is brought to ground against Hull; Jordan Tansey's controversial last-gasp try settles a season-defining encounter with Bradford Bulls

ROUND 13
MILLENNIUM MAGIC

ROUND 14

ABOVE INSET: Hull's Hutch Maiava releases the ball as Leeds defenders move in
ABOVE: Huddersfield's Martin Aspinwall escapes the clutches of Lesley Vainikolo as the Giants earn their first ever Super League victory over Bradford Bulls
BELOW: Hull's Shaun Briscoe howls in anguish as Trent Barrett touches down for a crucial Wigan try

ROUND 15

ROUND 17

ROUND 16

ROUND 18

TOP: Huddersfield's Robbie Paul and Hull's Paul King
wrestle as the clubs fight out a 9-9 draw in June
MAIN PIC: Bradford's James Evans leaps high under
pressure from Rob Burrow and Clinton Toopi to score,
as the Bulls gain revenge at Headingley Carnegie
RIGHT: Lesley Vainikolo bids farewell to Odsal

TOP: Rob Burrow darts away from St Helens fullback Paul Wellens as Leeds pull off an amazing win at Knowsley Road
BELOW LEFT: Bryan Fletcher in the thick of the action as struggling Wigan overcome Bradford
BELOW RIGHT: The Bulls bounced back with victory over Saints in the following round

ROUND 19

ROUND 20

ROUND 21

ABOVE: Andy Coley runs Paul Deacon and Iestyn Harris ragged as Salford play their game of the season at the Willows
LEFT INSET: Ben Jeffries and Ryan Atkins combine to halt Jamie Peacock as Wakefield stun Leeds at Headingley

James Webster leads Hull Kingston Rovers to Super League safety in a crucial away victory over Salford City Reds

ROUND 22

TOP: Super League leaders St Helens are humbled 21-0 as Catalans Dragons confirm their improvement
BELOW: Wakefield Frenchman Olivier Elima is felled as the Wildcats are put to the sword by Hull at Belle Vue

ROUND 25

ABOVE LEFT: Hull KR players take the plaudits as Rovers celebrate a devastating 42-6 win at the KC Stadium
ABOVE RIGHT: Sam Burgess & David Solomona meet Rob Burrow as Leeds & Bradford fight out a 16-16 draw
BELOW LEFT: Richard Horne & Danny Tickle get to grips with Kylie Leuluai as Hull give Leeds a wake-up call
BELOW RIGHT: Wigan claw their way into the play-offs with a surprise home victory over arch-rivals St Helens

ROUND 26

ROUND 27

ABOVE LEFT: Trent Barrett on song as unfancied Wigan complete one of the comebacks off all time against shell-shocked Bradford
LEFT: Field-goal hero Pat Richards & Odsal old boy Stuart Fielden
ABOVE RIGHT: Rod Jensen & Richard Whiting contest a high ball as Hull ensure Huddersfield's play-off debut ends in defeat

ELIMINATION PLAY-OFFS

LEFT: Wigan follow up their Odsal heroics with a well-earned 21-18 win at Hull

ELIMINATION SEMI-FINAL

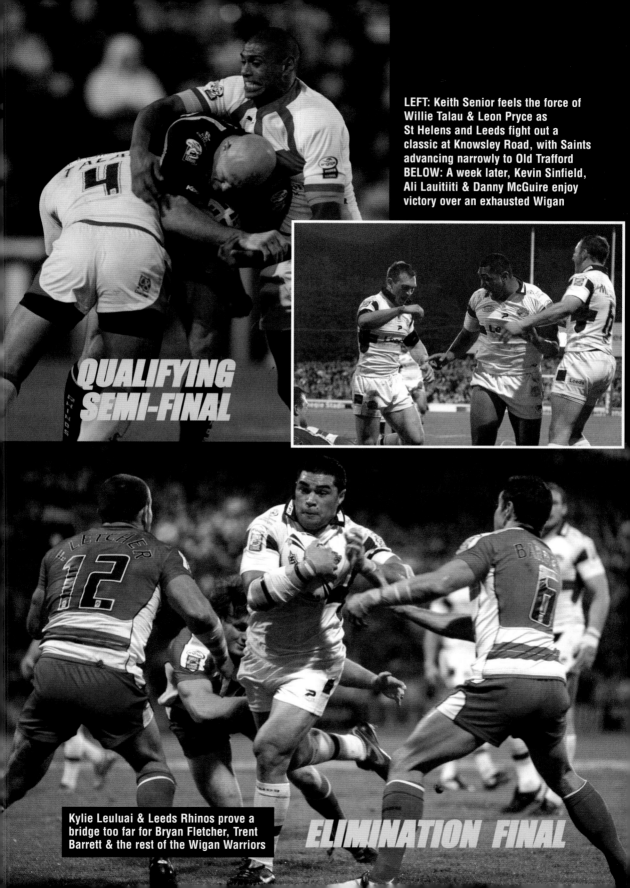

LEFT: Keith Senior feels the force of Willie Talau & Leon Pryce as St Helens and Leeds fight out a classic at Knowsley Road, with Saints advancing narrowly to Old Trafford BELOW: A week later, Kevin Sinfield, Ali Lauitiiti & Danny McGuire enjoy victory over an exhausted Wigan

QUALIFYING SEMI-FINAL

Kylie Leuluai & Leeds Rhinos prove a bridge too far for Bryan Fletcher, Trent Barrett & the rest of the Wigan Warriors

ELIMINATION FINAL

GRAND FINAL

CLOCKWISE: Saints' Maurie Fa'asavalu struggles to escape the attentions of Jamie Jones-Buchanan & Carl Ablett; Clinton Toopi gets the better of Willie Talau; Leeds players celebrate Jones-Buchanan's closing try; Jamie Peacock on a trademark barnstorming run

2
PERSONALITIES OF 2007

Rob Burrow

It was a dream 2007 for Rob Burrow. The Leeds scrum-half, who turned 25 in September, won a Super League Grand Final ring and represented Great Britain as they secured their first series win for 14 years. And to cap that he won the Harry Sunderland Award as the Grand Final's outstanding player, four weeks before collecting the George Smith medal as the man of the Gillette Fusion Series.

Burrow made his international debut as a substitute in the 42-26 Tri-Nations defeat by New Zealand at Loftus Road in 2005, and after that GB coach Brian Noble didn't pick him again in any of his last eight Tests in charge. Burrow went to Australia and New Zealand for six weeks last year but was never given a chance in the 2006 Gillette Tri-Nations, with Hull's Richard Horne getting the nod for the final game after Sean Long went home early. When Burrow's club coach Tony Smith took over as the Great Britain coach early in 2007, guess who was wearing the number 7 shirt for his first match in charge, the 42-14 win over France in June.

'I was just wanting a chance with GB to show what I could do but couldn't have written the script any better,' Burrow said after the third Test win over the Kiwis at Wigan, which featured one of his trademark solo specials three minutes after the half-time break - the 101st try of his career. It was the kind of score that only Burrow could conjure, and had been doing regularly for Leeds throughout their Championship year and before - in over 200 appearances for the Rhinos since making his debut in 2001. He was named the Rhinos Player of 2007.

After the Grand Final, his coach Tony Smith said: 'In the past Leeds have not had a general on the field. He was outstanding today, and has been all season. He has grown in stature in many respects. In the past he has been a very, very good individual player. Now he is a very, very good team player as well. He is also more of a general on the field.'

Burrow's masterly performance - his 55th minute field goal effectively killed off St Helens at Old Trafford - drew comparisons to another former Leeds and Great Britain scrum-half, Jeff Stevenson, who died on the morning of the Grand Final.

'You never think of winning individual awards,' said Burrow after the 33-6 win. 'It's all about doing it for the team. It makes me very proud to join the list of great players who have won it. It makes me truly grateful and thankful. I'm chuffed to bits.'

Jamie Peacock

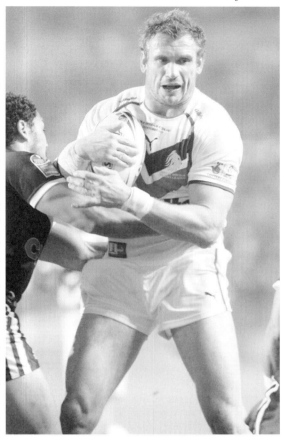

Jamie Peacock's standing in world Rugby League was already confirmed in 2006 when he was the only British player to be named in the World XIII by *Rugby League World* magazine.

But in 2007 things got even better for the inspirational Peacock as he led his club Leeds Rhinos to the Super League Championship. And not only did he retain the captaincy of Great Britain, he led the Lions to their first series victory in 14 years, as the side coached by his club mentor Tony Smith, beat New Zealand hands down in the Gillette Fusion Test Series.

Peacock's efforts in 2007 might not have reaped him the personal accolades that were showered on him in 2003 when he was named Man of Steel after leading from the front as his first professional club, Bradford Bulls won the Super League title and the Challenge Cup. But in all of Leeds' games in the SLXII season, and for his country as well, no-one would have argued if he had been given man of the match in every game. He's not the flashy, try-scoring type of player who hogs the headlines, just the most courageous and unrelenting player in the modern game. He has featured as one of this yearbook's personalities of the year no fewer than three times before - in 2000, 2003 and 2006.

Peacock, who turned 30 in December 2007, has certainly come a long way since being loaned out by the Bulls in 1998 and spending a year playing country football in Australia.

Remarkably, Peacock was still playing amateur football as a 19-year-old for Stanningley. Bradford's coach at the time, Matthew Elliott, recalled first seeing him play as a gangly youth. 'We went to watch him play a game and Jamie didn't have the best eyes. He started running in the wrong direction and we had no idea what he was chasing. There was a carrier bag blowing across the field and he thought it was the ball. So he didn't get off to the best of starts in front of me; I had no idea what he was doing!'

Nevertheless he was signed by Bradford and played for their Academy and Alliance in 1996 and '97 before a six-month spell down under. On his return he made four appearances at Featherstone (two off the bench), but the following year Peacock turned out 18 times (16 off the bench) for the Bulls.

The rest, as they say, is history. Even Matthew Elliott admits: 'Ten years ago, I couldn't have envisaged him leading his country in the future. But he hasn't left any stone unturned. When you meet people like that it's no coincidence that they end up being successful.'

Trent Barrett

It took a while for British fans to realise it, but Trent Barrett really is something special. The Wigan stand-off finished the season like a train, and on the back of that the Warriors stormed into the final eliminator at Leeds after securing sixth spot with a shock last-round victory over St Helens at the JJB Stadium.

Barrett got Wigan out of some holes during the 2007 season, no deeper than the one at Bradford in the first Elimination play-off, when Brian Noble's side trailed 30-6 after 55 minutes of a fairly-comprehensive towelling by the team that had finished third. Twenty-five minutes later Barrett's kicking, running and passing had conjured a stunning 31-30 win - the greatest comeback in Super League history. A week later he inspired a comeback of lesser proportions at the KC Stadium to knock out fourth-placed Hull, although the impossible dream was ended in conclusive fashion by Leeds in the final eliminator.

Wigan supporters and officials, and many outsiders were stunned when Barrett didn't collect the Man of Steel award at the end of the season, with St Helens' James Roby the recipient, although he was named Rugby League Writers' Association Player of the Year. But Warriors fans can console themselves with the fact that Barrett has two years remaining on the three-year contract he signed before the start of SLXII.

Wigan's faithful might think they have little to thank former coach Ian Millward for, but the arrival of Barrett is down to the Warriors coach who was sacked in the middle of the 2006 season. Barrett had two years left on his contract with St George Illawarra Dragons but exercised an opt-out clause in order to realise an ambition to play in England. He was the first player to play 100 games for St George Illawarra, was appointed captain in 2002, and played a total of 199 first-grade games for the joint venture, and Illawarra before that. In 2000 he won the Dally M as the best player in the NRL.

Millward's successor Brian Noble said: 'When I joined the club the first thing Maurice Lindsay asked me about was Trent Barrett. He wanted my view before the deal was concluded and it took me about one second to tell him to get the contract signed. Trent is all quality, as a man, a player and a teammate - he's a coach's dream.'

Trent Barrett is one of the most complete players in the modern game - strong in defence, with a great kicking game and wonderful handling skills. And there is plenty more to come.

Tony Smith

'An absolute perfectionist. Definitely the best coach I've ever worked with. Me and all the lads have really benefitted from his coaching skills.'

You couldn't get a better citation than the one that Rob Burrow gave to Leeds and Great Britain coach Tony Smith in the wake of the Lions 3-nil series win over New Zealand. Burrow was arguably the individual to benefit the most from the guidance of his mentor at club and international level as he ended 2007 as the outstanding player of the autumn.

In the Super League Grand Final, Smith, a great believer in hard work, discipline and a mastery of the game's basic skills, had produced another Rhinos performance to seal his place as Leeds' most successful coach ever. By beating Saints three times in four games in 2007, Rhinos were undisputed champions and had their second league championship in four years - a feat achieved by no other Leeds coach. And that only months after many Leeds fans were demanding his removal after a defeat at Hull KR.

The footballing style of Leeds' play produced a great Grand Final, and that was replicated in the displays of Great Britain in the following month. Smith's Lions played a less conservative game than many Great Britain sides before it, and proved an unstoppable force. Great Britain, from now on to be known as England, could look forward to the 2008 World Cup with some optimism.

As well as being an expert coach, Smith wasn't afraid to ruffle a few feathers.

He hit out at suggestions that Great Britain scored a whitewash against an understrength New Zealand Test side that was missing some of its big-name players. 'The series will be remembered as a Test series. I don't get it otherwise,' said Smith. 'Test football is all about getting players on the field. It's a test of the best available in your country against the best available for your rivals. Otherwise it is all hypothetical. All my boys want is to play and get out there. Injured players are not here, and we have had retirements too. It is just a test of what is available. If there is another way of doing it, let me know.' He also took a sideswipe at the match officials for the Test series: 'I thought the officiating made English officiating look good.'

Smith's appointment in a full-time capacity meant that he also took up the role of Technical Director to the RFL. 'We are heading in a good direction, but they want a little bit more technical input, and hopefully I can do that,' he said. 'I am very proud to be part of it.'

Maurie Fa'asavalu

At the start of 2007 no-one could have predicted that Samoan Maurie Fa'asavalu would emerge as one of the most talked about names in British Rugby League by the end of the year. A damn fine player, but just another big strong forward from the South Sea Islands earning his corn, albeit with one of the best club sides in the world.

But in late September the 27-year-old made the headlines by declaring himself available for Great Britain after fulfilling the current Rugby League International Federation qualification criterion of three years residency.

New Great Britain coach Tony Smith promised to consider the Samoan for his squad, even though Fa'asavalu had played for Samoa in the 2003 rugby union world cup. Fa'asavalu's eventual selection attracted no small amount of controversy. 'It was a big call and something I've thought long and hard about," Tony Smith said. 'He is a bit of a special case. For him only ever having played his Rugby League in this country is quite a unique situation.'

There were a few boos among the applause when he came into the game midway through the first half of the first Test with New Zealand at Huddersfield. Fa'asavalu immediately produced one of the runs that had endeared him to St Helens fans over the past four years, charging through tackle after tackle. 'That first carry was a very big one for his acceptance,' Smith said afterwards. A few minutes later he took a short pass from his Saints teammate James Roby and powered over the Kiwi line for Britain's first try. The Lions were 4-0 down at the time, and the score was key to Britain going onto win 20-14. Fa'asavalu's fumble set up a New Zealand try from Paul Whatuira shortly after, but he had done enough to dispel most of the grumbles about his selection.

'Before the game I felt really emotional and pumped up,' said Fa'asavalu. 'It was a great highlight of my career and an honour to play for this country, and I couldn't wait to get out there. Listening to the national anthem was really emotional.' GB captain Jamie Peacock pointed out that Fa'asavalu's selection was in line with every other sport. 'We've got some great traditions in this country but sometimes we fail to move on,' said Peacock. 'The rest of the world moves on but we don't. The fact is sport has changed and you don't always have to be born in the country you want to represent. That's just the way of life nowadays and it's about time we took advantage of it.'

Great Britain certainly took advantage by going on to win the series 3-0. Fa'asavalu was one of five uncapped players in the Great Britain squad, with the other great experiment, 18-year-old Bradford prop Sam Burgess, another great success.

3
NATIONAL LEAGUE 2007

NATIONAL LEAGUE ONE SEASON
High of the Tigers

CASTLEFORD TIGERS timed their season to perfection, peaking late in their Co-operative NL1 campaign before ultimately going onto Grand Final glory against Widnes.

Not that the Tigers cruised through 2007 without any doubts - in June there were few people backing Terry Matterson's side to go all the way. At that stage, Cas had lost both encounters with nearest rivals the Vikings, going down 20-44 at the Jungle in the league, and 12-18 at the Halton Stadium in the Northern Rail Cup semi-final.

But from that moment on, the Tigers would not lose again, and they racked up some massive scorelines in the process. That run culminated with a club-record 106-0 win at Rochdale Hornets on the final day of the league season, setting them up for their play-off double over Widnes.

Matterson had a host of heroes among his squad, with Danny Brough man of the match in the Grand Final and NL1 Players' Player of the Year. Stuart Donlan was a rock at fullback following his mid-season switch from the wing, while Andrew Henderson was as reliable as ever at hooker. And Awen Guttenbeil saved his biggest performance for the biggest matches.

Brough was joined in the NL1 All Stars team by Mark Leafa, Michael Shenton and Ryan Clayton. But arguably the most impressive aspect of all was the Tigers' latest batch of Academy products - NL1 Young Player of the Year Joe Westerman, prop Ryan Boyle and outside back Richard Owen should all prove terrific additions to Super League.

Andrew Henderson

Castleford's Awen Guttenbeil in action against Widnes during the National League One Grand Final

For the second consecutive season **WIDNES VIKINGS** fell at the final hurdle in their bid to return to Super League. But unlike the previous year, the 2007 campaign ended in near disaster for the club, as just two days after their Grand Final defeat to Castleford, they were forced into administration and an uncertain future.

It looked like it was going to be so different midway through the season, Having already beaten their nearest rivals Castleford twice, the Vikings then lifted the Northern Rail Cup with a complete demolition of Whitehaven, winning 54-6 in Blackpool.

But the grip that Steve McCormack's side had on top spot in the league was lost in an 18-24 loss to the Tigers at home in August. And two further defeats to Cas ended their hopes of a top-flight return.

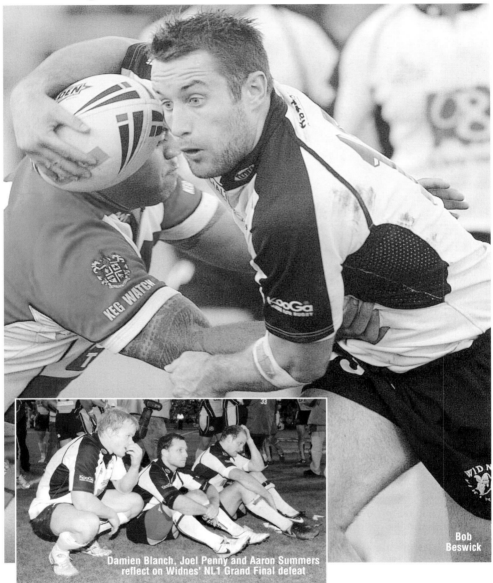

Bob
Beswick

Damien Blanch, Joel Penny and Aaron Summers
reflect on Widnes' NL1 Grand Final defeat

Still, there was much to be positive about on the field, with stand-off Dennis Moran named NL1 Player of the Year after an influential campaign. Joining him in the NL1 All Stars side were five other Vikings - Scott Grix, Damien Blanch, Mick Nanyn, Oliver Wilkes and Bob Beswick.

For many Widnes fans, the way the season ended will provide the over-riding memory of 2007. Long-standing financial problems hit a depressing low with the move into administration, and McCormack left the club along with the majority of their players, including the pick of the Vikings' impressive development work.

But, the purchase of the club by local businessman Steve O'Connor, and the return of McCormack after he had taken on an assistant coach's role at Hull KR, gave them hope for 2008.

Sean
Penkywicz

HALIFAX produced their best season for years under experienced National League coach Martin Hall, who continued his remarkable trend of guiding clubs to third place - the fifth time he has done so.

The fixture list provided Fax with a difficult start to the season - they played Cas and Widnes home and away in their first nine matches - and a shock home defeat to Dewsbury Rams put them further behind the front runners. But Hall's side regrouped superbly, and clinched third spot on the final day of the season with a win over Doncaster.

Star man for Fax was undoubtedly hooker or halfback Sean Penkywicz, who was nominated for the NL1 Player of the Year award and was also named at number nine in the All Stars team. But he had support all around him, with stand-off Graham Holroyd providing a tremendous impact on his mid-season return to his home-town club from Doncaster.

In the backs, Richard Varkulis, Lee Greenwood, Shad Royston and makeshift centre Mark Roberts caught the eye, while Frank Watene, Aaron Trinder, Paul Southern and Dave Larder were the pick of the forwards.

Fax almost went all the way to the Grand Final, only for a short turnaround between matches to hurt them in a gutsy final eliminator defeat at Widnes. Hall was set to move upstairs as director of football in 2008, with new coach Matt Calland looking to build on the progress made with a number of eye-catching signings.

Richard
Fletcher

WHITEHAVEN looked set for third place for much of the season, only for some late defeats to see them drop down to fourth. Ultimately that hurt Dave Rotheram's team, as they crashed out of the play-offs away at Halifax, who they had beaten three times at home earlier in the year.

What should have been the club's season high also turned into something of a low, as Haven made the Northern Rail Cup final only to be blown away 54-6 by Widnes Vikings at Bloomfield Road. Despite the disappointments, it was a surprise in some quarters when Rotheram was told his contract would not be renewed, and while he ended up with rivals Workington, former Barrow boss Paul Crarey took over at the Recreation Ground.

Rotheram's best signing during his time with Haven was second-rower Richard Fletcher, whose outstanding campaign saw him handed an All Stars place. Elsewhere, fullback Gary Broadbent was as reliable as ever at the back, Craig Calvert continued to threaten defences with his raw pace on the wing, and Carl Rudd enhanced his reputation with an excellent season.

In the forwards, Steve Trindall and David Fatialofa kept Haven rolling forward, and hookers Carl Sice and Graeme Mattinson caught the eye at different stages of the season.

But if Rotheram's departure from the club didn't signal the end of a new era for Whitehaven, then the retirement of legends David Seeds and Aaron Lester certainly did. Replacing those two stalwarts was vital for new coach Crarey in 2008.

The 2007 season provided something of a rollercoaster ride for **LEIGH CENTURIONS**, who will feel that they fell below expectations despite finishing fifth. Several high-profile signings after the end of the campaign ensured there was much to be positive about over the winter.

The campaign got off to a rocky start for Darren Shaw's side when they were beaten twice in the Northern Rail Cup group stages by NL2 side Celtic Crusaders, only to qualify for the knock-out stages as one of the best third-placed teams. A Challenge Cup exit at Dewsbury Rams was hardly ideal either, though the Centurions finally got their NL1 year going with five wins from six mid-summer.

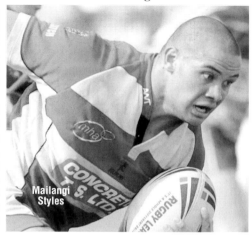

Mailangi Styles

They peaked with their best result of the season - a superb 28-12 win at Whitehaven. That match showcased the club's strong youth development system, with several home-grown players having a key role in the victory.

But the season fizzled out, with two defeats to Halifax ending any hopes of a top-three finish. The Centurions then crashed out of the play-offs at the first hurdle, this time losing at the Recreation Ground.

Arguably their most consistent player of 2007 was powerhouse Australian forward Mailangi Styles, who maintained his level of performance over the course of the year. Miles Greenwood, Aaron Heremaia and mid-season capture Sebastien Martins also had their moments, although with a superb new stadium on the horizon Leigh's thoughts are now very much focused on the future.

SHEFFIELD EAGLES surprised just about everybody - including most of their own supporters - in defying the odds to make the NL1 play-offs. Given the wretched past record of teams promoted from NL2, survival at the higher level would have constituted success for the Eagles, so to finish in the top six was a wonderful achievement.

Mark Aston was recognised for his considerable role in that by deservedly being named NL1 Coach of the Year, while pacy winger Danny Mills earned selection in the All Stars side. But if ever there was a shining example of a team effort, this was it.

Mitchell Stringer

Props Jack Howieson and Mitchell Stringer set the platform up front, and had willing and able forward allies in the likes of Ged Corcoran and Adam Hayes. Out wide, there was plenty of pace and cutting edge in the shape of Mills, Rob Worrincy, James Ford and Damien Reid, while Jonny Woodcock was outstanding at times from fullback.

Halfbacks Gavin Brown, Dominic Brambani and Brendon Lindsay also provided big contributions, and Aston's ethic of putting hard work before star names paid off.

Their home form played a big part in earning their sixth place, which was sealed with a televised Don Valley win over Whitehaven on the final weekend of the season. Their play-offs campaign lasted just one week, though again they emerged with great credit from a 30-26 defeat at Halifax.

National League One Season

For much of the year it looked as though **DEWSBURY RAMS** would be the newly-promoted team securing a play-off place at the first attempt. But five defeats from their final six games allowed Sheffield to leap-frog them on the final weekend, despite Andy Kelly's side having beaten the Eagles home and away.

Dominic Maloney

Still, there was much for Kelly to be positive about following an eye-catching return to NL1. Highlights included two home defeats of Leigh Centurions, one in the Challenge Cup, and a stirring away win at Halifax early in the league campaign. The Rams were looking to build on that progress in 2008.

They retained several young players after they impressed in 2007, including non-stop prop Dominic Maloney, who enhanced his growing reputation. Back-rower Martin Robinson also handled the step up in divisions well, as did Alex Bretherton, while Bryn Powell and Austin Buchanan provided pace on the wings.

Dean Lawford was typically influential from scrum-half, though he lost his halfback partner when Francis Maloney joined rivals Batley midway through the season. The form of the promising Pat Walker helped soften that blow.

Kelly had to battle against long-term injuries for much of the year, meaning that the influential Kane Epati, Josh Weeden and Richard Chapman missed massive chunks of the season. A little more luck should see the Rams improve again next time around.

BATLEY BULLDOGS fell below their own expectations for 2007, having made the NL1 play-offs the previous year. But by successfully avoiding relegation with two wins from their final four matches, the Bulldogs at least finished the year on a high.

Luke Menzies

Despite missing out on the top six, there were still plenty of good memories for the Bulldogs faithful, not least a league double over local rivals Dewsbury. The home match in particular was a terrific encounter, with hooker Kris Lythe's superb try sealing a stunning comeback up the Mount Pleasant hill for a 22-20 win in front of the television cameras.

Lythe was again Batley's most consistent performer, shouldering a tremendous workload in both attack and defence throughout the season. He had support in the forwards from the likes of Jonny Simpson, Luke Stenchion and Luke Menzies, the latter earning a move to Super League Hull KR.

In the backs, Ash Lindsay had his moments, while Craig Farrell and Chris Langley provided a try-scoring threat out wide. And the mid-season capture of Francis Maloney from the Rams provided Gary Thornton's side with some valuable experience in the middle of the field.

The Bulldogs started their recruitment for 2008 early, and the arrival of players such as Danny Maun, Kevin King and Ian Preece meant that a return to play-off contention was a realistic aim for Batley.

What had started out as a season of much promise for **ROCHDALE HORNETS** ended in disaster as they were relegated from NL1 after a disappointing year. Several well-known recruits suggested that Hornets were ready to kick on from their 2006 play-offs finish, but they simply never got going.

Tommy Goulden

They were hardly helped by a mid-season financial crisis that meant their players had to take pay cuts, and several departures ensued as defeat followed defeat. Coach Darren Abram paid for the slump with his job in July, though matters didn't get any better following his departure, and late-season defeats to Sheffield, Batley and Doncaster sealed Hornets' fate.

The campaign the ended on the lowest of lows when the club suffered a record 106-0 defeat at home to league leaders Castleford. But Hornets' supporters did have something to smile about soon after, when Bobbie Goulding returned to Spotland for his second spell as coach.

In a largely forgettable 2007, Kevin King, Tommy Goulden and Craig Robinson rarely let anyone down. But the vast majority of the squad headed for pastures new, and Goulding had a significant task on his hands to revive Hornets' fortunes in NL2, and spent the close season recruiting virtually a whole new team.

Few clubs in the professional game had as eventful a season as **DONCASTER**. They started the year under the moniker Lakers and, with a new Australian coach, full-time squad and brand new stadium, held hopes of a Super League franchise in 2009.

Alex Rowe

But things quickly started to go badly wrong. Results were disappointing under new boss Keiran Dempsey, and after a few promising early crowds, attendances fell below expectations as well. Dempsey was sacked - though even that wasn't clear cut as he took the club to court - and Gary Wilkinson briefly steadied the ship with a handful of good results. But chairman John Wright then announced that he could no longer financially support the club, and their difficulties were played out in a very public manner over several weeks.

At one stage, the very future of the club looked in danger, until local businessmen Craig Harrison and Shane Miller took over, ushering in a new era for the club. They dropped the Lakers title and appointed promising young coach John Stankevitch.

But despite signalling an improvement in performances, Stankevitch's hurriedly put together squad was always up against it due to the six league points deducted for the club entering administration. Leeds loanees Luke Gale and Luke Burgess certainly impressed, while Alex Rowe and club stalwarts Peter Green and Craig Lawton were among the best performers.

As such, the Dons had to start again in NL2 - though the signing of vastly-experienced Aussie Chris McKenna was a clear statement of intent by the new regime.

NATIONAL LEAGUE TWO SEASON
Celtic ray

CELTIC CRUSADERS' dream of securing a Super League franchise in 2009 meant that they needed to gain promotion to NL1 in 2007 - and after a rollercoaster of a year, they eventually achieved that on the final weekend of the season.

Favourites before the start of the campaign, John Dixon's side appeared to have blown their chance when a 23-16 defeat at Hunslet in June left them off the pace behind Featherstone. But they then put together a superb run that included a crucial 32-12 win at their nearest rivals in front of the television cameras in July. And the title was secured when Featherstone lost at Barrow on the last weekend, ensuring Crusaders could celebrate in style at Gateshead the following day.

Celtic's success was reflected in having six players named in the NL2 All Stars team, headed by free-scoring fullback Tony Duggan, who was named the competition's Player of the Year.

He was joined by Mark Dalle Court, Jace Van Dijk, Neil Budworth, Neale Wyatt and Damien Quinn, while Dixon was a nominee for the coaching award.

With some impressive crowds at Bridgend, including over 3,000 attending the home match with Oldham on Millennium Magic weekend, it was a season of considerable progression for the Welsh. And they made plenty of eye catching recruits for the next season as they aimed to push their top-flight claim further.

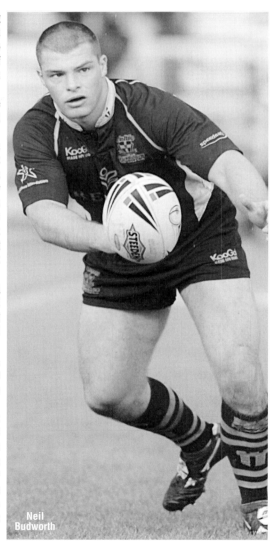

Neil Budworth

FEATHERSTONE ROVERS would have undoubtedly preferred to have finished top if asked at the start of the season - but earning promotion via the NL2 Grand Final could turn out to be a bigger plus in the long run for the club.

With Featherstone Lions also present and winning their showcase Rugby League Conference National grand final, Rovers' 24-6 triumph over Oldham at Headingley was a return to the Rugby League good times for the village.

Rovers' hopes of finishing top of NL2 all but vanished with a home defeat to Celtic in July, and Dave Hobbs' side stuttered for a few weeks after that. But they recovered to beat Barrow and Oldham in the play-offs, earning a return to NL1.

Scrum-half Paul Handforth was man of the match in the Grand Final and had an excellent year, while Stuart Dickens, Danny Kirmond and Tommy Haughey all made the All Stars line-up.

Paul Handforth

Ade Adebisi was one of a number of mid-season signings made by Hobbs, and added pace and excitement during the run-in, while the likes of Ian Tonks, Jamie Field and Andy Kain had their moments.

With so many experienced players in their squad, Rovers were well placed to survive and kick on at the higher level in 2008.

BARROW RAIDERS continued their progress under coach Paul Crarey in 2007, only for the season to end in disappointment and the coach's surprise departure.

Crarey had picked the club up from a major low point in late 2005, and a third place finish illustrated their development. But play-off defeats to Featherstone and Oldham ended their hopes of promotion, and Crarey resigned after learning that chief executive Des Johnston no longer had faith in him.

Crarey left to join Whitehaven soon after, and was replaced at Craven Park by former Australian hooker Dave Clark. Crarey's lasting legacy at the club will be to have got talented locals playing for Raiders again, and centre Liam Harrison was the club's sole representative in the All Stars

Dave Armistead

line-up. Arguably their most consistent player was outstanding Australian forward Dave Armistead, while fullback Khamal Ganley was among the tries again.

One downside was the long-term absence of experienced forward Brett McDermott, who missed much of the campaign with a torn bicep. Hooker Andy Ellis, halfback Liam Finch and back-rower Martin Ostler also stood out at times, and the ambitious club will want nothing short of promotion in 2008.

National League Two Season

The 2007 season signalled the return of **OLDHAM** as a major Rugby League force, as they picked themselves up from a winless league campaign the year before to make the NL2 Grand Final.

Neil Roden

They did so with the help of new investor Bill Quinn, whose arrival at the club to continue the work of long-standing directors Chris Hamilton and Sean Whitehead saw the club increase their prowess in the transfer market.

Mid-season signings James Coyle, Byron Ford and Rob Roberts - among others - all had an impact as the Roughyeds mounted a late-season charge.

That fell at the final hurdle as injuries hit them hard at Headingley against Featherstone - but more head-turning recruits since mean that Oldham will start the new season as one of the title favourites.

Stand-off Neil Roden was the club's key figure in 2007, providing Steve Deakin's side with experience and direction in the middle of the field, not least during their memorable televised win away at Celtic Crusaders.

They lost the return match in August, but it was another tremendous night for the club, as an innovative marketing push attracted a record NL2 crowd of over 4,000.

With Richard Mervill among the most consistent players in the division and Lucas Onyango one of the most dangerous, there was plenty to cheer for the Oldham faithful.

Nobody would have batted an eyelid if **WORKINGTON TOWN's** season had drifted towards obscurity after the messy early-season sacking of coach Ged Stokes.

The New Zealander was shown the door at Derwent Park amid a long-drawn out saga over an alleged act of misconduct, that an RFL panel cleared him of, and that eventually led to him taking action against the club.

But instead of hindering Town, the club's staff reacted superbly, with caretaker joint coaches Les Ashe and Craig Barker earning widespread praise for their work. They often had to battle with crippling injury lists as well, but won enough matches in a tough competition to finish fifth, and then knock York out of the play-offs.

Shaun Lunt

Oldham the following week was a bridge too far, and Workington certainly weren't helped by the absence of star player Shaun Lunt, banned after being sent off the previous week. But it was a rare blip on another outstanding season for Lunt, as he was named NL2 Young Player of the Year for the second season running. Other key performers included Australian Andrew Beattie, loan Widnes forward Adam Sidlow and halfback Carl Forber. With a new coach in place in the shape of ex-Whitehaven boss Dave Rotheram, Town could be set to rise again.

YORK CITY KNIGHTS were hit as much by injury and bad luck than anyone in NL2 - but will still feel that they should have done better in 2007. A heavy play-off defeat at 12-man Workington was a sad way to conclude the coaching reign of Mick Cook, who had already announced that he would be stepping down at the end of the campaign.

Cook's main problem in his final year in charge was the severe disruption to his main halfback pairing of Anthony Thackeray and Scott Rhodes. Thackeray was recalled to his club Hull after starting the season in fine style, while Rhodes missed big chunks through injury. The Knights still recorded enough wins to make the play-offs, but defeat in Cumbria ended the season on a low.

Prop Adam Sullivan was again a model of consistency and made the All Stars team, while Rob Spicer earned most of the club's own accolades at their awards night. Others to play their part included Aussie forward Dave Buckley, NL2 Young Player of the Year nominee Lee Mapals, and back-rower Ryan Esders.

The campaign finished with fears about the Knights' future following tales of doom from chief executive John Guilford, but they eased at the end of the season and the club had a new player-coach in Paul March.

SWINTON LIONS staged a stirring end-of-season charge to make the play-offs again - despite having been deducted six points for entering administration midway through the campaign.

Swinton's directors always insisted that the measure was taken to help them re-organise the club, not purely because of dire financial straits - and they were only in administration for a matter of days. But they were still docked the points by the Rugby Football League, and that was always going to impact on their year.

Paul Kidd's side reacted in the best way possible, beating play-off rivals York, Hunslet and Workington in a dramatic run-in. And although they exited the play-offs on the first weekend away at Oldham - failing to emulate 2006's Grand Final appearance - there was still much to be proud about.

Quicksilver hooker Phil Wood was the Lions' stand-out figure throughout, and deservedly cleaned up at the club's end of season presentation night. His former Widnes teammate Bruce Johnson was another player to impress in the front row. Winger Andy Saywell, fullback Wayne English, halfback Craig Ashall and the vastly experienced Martin Moana were also mainstays of Swinton's side.

99

HUNSLET HAWKS looked set to defy the odds and make the play-offs - until a late-season home defeat to Keighley cost them dear.

That provided tremendous disappointment for the Hawks and their coach Mark Cass, who had taken his side to the brink of the top seven, despite a much smaller budget than most rivals.

But further drama was to follow, as chairman Ian Johnson stepped down and the club was plunged into uncertainty, with Cass also resigning after being told he would have even less money to spend in 2008. The club held a crisis meeting chaired by former Batley and Leeds director Stephen Ball, where they asked 300 fans to pledge £5 a week to secure the

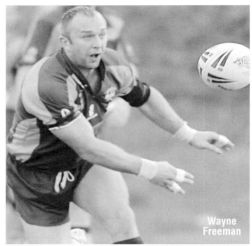

Wayne Freeman

future of the Hawks. Enough support was evident for Hunslet to continue, and they will be coached by former Great Britain centre Graeme Hallas in 2008.

Among the Hawks' best in 2007 were hooker Darren Robinson and experienced back rower Wayne Freeman. But equally impressive was the number of young players that made an impact at first-team level - such as Ben Jones and Ben Walkin - and they could well hold the keys to the club's future.

LONDON SKOLARS might have missed out on the play-offs - but the 2007 season will still go down as the best in the club's history. Eight wins and a draw constituted Skolars' best ever return - and deservedly resulted in Latham Tawhai being named NL2 Coach of the Year. Tawhai has been the key figure in the capital club becoming a competitive force in NL2.

Richard Louw

After a winless Northern Rail Cup group campaign, Skolars chalked up a number of impressive wins in the league - most notably away at Workington and Hunslet, and at home to Swinton.

Tawhai had plenty of players in his ranks who were little known before the start of the season, but ended it with big reputations. Heading that list was South

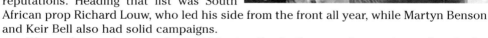

African prop Richard Louw, who led his side from the front all year, while Martyn Benson and Keir Bell also had solid campaigns.

Winger Austen Aggrey enhanced his standing in the game by earning a place in the NL2 All Stars team, and halfback Paul Thorman had a big impact after his switch from York.

KEIGHLEY COUGARS will look back on the 2007 season as a crucial one in their rebuilding under coach Barry Eaton - despite the disappointing tenth-placed finish.

Eaton placed his faith in plenty of promising young players, and the experience that they have gained should serve them well in coming years. And they will be joined by a host of more established figures in 2008, following an eye-catching winter recruitment campaign.

Among those to have impressed already, having been given their chance with Keighley, are hooker James Feather, centre Mick Fogerty and back-rower Richard Knight, a NL2 Young Player of the Year nominee.

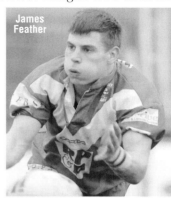
James Feather

Eaton himself proved that he could still turn it on at scrum-half, and had a willing ally in the experienced Chris Redfearn. Winger Alex Brown was voted the club's most improved player, though he left the club at the end of the season for Rochdale. Another departure is Matt Foster, who brought down the curtain on a long and illustrious Cougars career when he confirmed his retirement.

Highlights of his final season included impressive home wins over play-off sides Workington and Oldham during June.

GATESHEAD THUNDER are another club looking to the future after a below par season.

There were high hopes for the north-east club when former Castleford coach Dave Woods was appointed at the club, but despite a promising start to the league campaign, they faded towards the end.

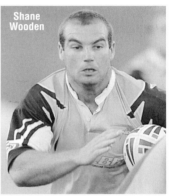
Shane Wooden

Woods certainly wasn't helped by a season-ending injury to his key halfback Jono Rolfe before NL2 had even started. And there were still plenty of positives to glean as they look to improve significantly next season. One was an impressive home win against York at Kingston Park, with another being the extensive community work that Woods oversaw.

With the club making a number of signings since the end of the year, Thunder were looking to make a big impact in 2008

The club's most consistent performers last season were Shane Wooden, Neil Thorman, Graham Stephenson and Nick Hyde. Local junior Ryan Clarke also hinted at the talent in the area by seeing plenty of action after earning promotion to the first team.

BLACKPOOL PANTHERS endured a generally miserable season, failing to win a single match all year.

They started the season with Simon Knox in charge and had hopes of pushing up the NL2 table. But Knox had to contend with a limited budget and injuries, and parted company with the club in June with them stranded at the bottom of the table.

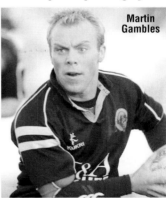
Martin Gambles

Succeeding him was former Wigan and Great Britain legend Andy Gregory, who was returning to the professional game after several seasons out. But he couldn't reverse the club's fortunes either, and left at the end of the campaign to be replaced by Martin Crompton. The ex-Warrington and Wigan halfback had a massive job on his hands to revive the Seasiders, but started the task full of enthusiasm.

The Panthers' best last season included vastly experienced hooker Phil Cantillon, who was an ever present and finished as the club's top try scorer. Halfback Martin Gambles and centre or second-rower Mike Stout were also willing contributors in an often lost cause.

NORTHERN RAIL
CUP FINAL
Viking glory

Widnes Vikings powered to victory in the Northern Rail Cup final, as Dennis Moran inspired a record-breaking win.

Of the Vikings' nine tries, stand-off Moran was influential in the build-up of six, and scored another himself. That ensured a final that was disappointingly one-sided for the neutral - but hugely impressive for a Widnes side laying down an early marker for the NL1 campaign.

Any hopes that Whitehaven had of continuing the trend of the underdog winning this final were effectively over by the 25th minute, by which time they trailed 20-0 after being blitzed by the Vikings attack.

Haven could point to the controversial sin-binning of fullback Gary Broadbent in the tenth minute, while two Vikings also

Gareth Price and Jordan James lift the Northern Rail Cup

involved in the incident, Scott Grix and Bob Beswick, were allowed to stay on the field.

Grix then played a significant role in the Vikings scoring 12-unanswered points in Broadbent's absence. But the Cumbrians could not dispute the clinical way in which Widnes took them apart - something that wasn't just restricted to that ten-minute spell.

'We started really well, and obviously the sin-binning helped us as well,' Vikings coach Steve McCormack said. 'I thought our discipline was superb, and I also felt we played the field superbly.'

The Vikings were 30-0 up at half-time, courtesy of tries to Toa Kohe-Love, Grix, Damien Blanch, Mick Nanyn and Lee Doran. Haven did find a brief response in the second half through Carl Rudd, but for the most part it was all Widnes and Moran. Mark Smith, Blanch again, Moran and Dean Gaskell completed the romp for the Vikings in front of over 8,000 supporters at Bloomfield Road.

'We had no ball,' Whitehaven coach Dave Rotheram admitted. 'In the first half, I think we had 13 goes with the ball, and Widnes had 22. Looking at that, there's no surprise the scoreline was what it was at half-time. It's pretty sombre in the dressing room, as you'd expect.

'You can't knock the players' effort. People will say 'they're not trying this, they're not doing that', but it's a cup final, and the players certainly tried their hardest.'

Damien Blanch shows his delight as he dives past Carl Rudd to score

NORTHERN RAIL CUP FINAL

Sunday 15th July 2007

WHITEHAVEN 6 WIDNES VIKINGS 54

WHITEHAVEN: 1 Gary Broadbent; 2 Craig Calvert; 3 Derry Eilbeck; 4 Rob Jackson; 5 Steve Maden; 13 Carl Rudd; 7 John Duffy; 8 Steve Trindall; 9 Aaron Smith; 10 David Fatialofa; 11 Spencer Miller; 12 Richard Fletcher; 6 Leroy Joe. Subs (all used): 14 Carl Sice; 15 Graeme Mattinson; 16 Marc Jackson; 17 Scott Teare.
Try: Rudd (62); **Goals:** Rudd 1/1.
Sin bin: Broadbent (10) - punching.
On report: Brawl (10).
VIKINGS: 1 Scott Grix; 2 Damien Blanch; 3 Toa Kohe-Love; 4 Mick Nanyn; 5 Dean Gaskell; 6 Dennis Moran; 7 Joel Penny; 8 Mick Cassidy; 9 Mark Smith; 10 Oliver Wilkes; 11 Lee Doran; 12 Paul Noone; 13 Bob Beswick. Subs (all used): 14 Aaron Summers; 15 Jordan James; 16 Ian Webster; 17 Gareth Price.
Tries: Kohe-Love (6), Grix (17), Blanch (21, 47), Nanyn (29), Doran (33), Smith (43), Moran (71), Gaskell (76);
Goals: Nanyn 9/12.
On report: Brawl (10).
Rugby Leaguer & League Express Men of the Match:
Whitehaven: Carl Rudd; *Vikings:* Dennis Moran.
Penalty count: 3-12; **Half-time:** 0-30; **Referee:** Jamie Leahy; **Attendance:** 8,236 *(at Bloomfield Road, Blackpool).*

NATIONAL LEAGUE PLAY-OFFS

NATIONAL LEAGUE ONE

Whitehaven started the 2007 play-offs campaign with an accomplished, if unspectacular, 19-6 televised win over Leigh. Carl Rudd, switched from stand-off to scrum-half to cover for the injured John Duffy, was Haven's key man, scoring a try in either half to end the Centurions' season.

Three days later Halifax extended their campaign with a hard-earned win over Sheffield Eagles. The Eagles opened up a 16-6 lead in the first half, only for two tries before the break to edge the home side ahead. But after looking as though they were cruising through at one point, Fax then conceded a 77th minute try to Rob Worrincy and were holding on in the desperate closing stags of an absorbing game.

The following week Castleford Tigers booked their place in the Grand Final courtesy of a 26-8 home win over second placed Widnes Vikings. The match was delicately poised when Mick Nanyn

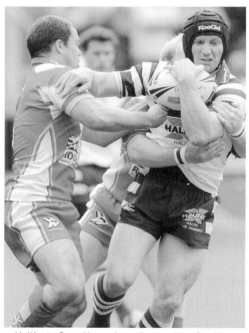

Halifax's Sam Hoare in action against Sheffield

powered over for the Vikings to give his side a narrow lead on 48 minutes. But tries to Michael Wainwright, Danny Williams and two to teenager Joe Westerman saw Cas home.

On the Sunday, Halifax were continuing their excellent run with another nail-biter at the Shay, this time against Whitehaven. Martin Hall's side held a commanding 18-6 half-time lead, only for quick tries to Rudd and Craig Calvert to level the scores. But Halifax held their nerve in the closing stages, with Damian Ball's try proving decisive.

That set up a final eliminator between Widnes and Fax - though crucially the Vikings held a significant advantage. With the play-off schedule adapted for televised games, Steve McCormack's team had three days extra preparation for the Halton Stadium showdown. How crucial that proved in the Vikings' 36-24 win is difficult to quantify - but Fax certainly emerged from the clash with plenty of credit after a gutsy display. In the end, though, Mark Smith's two tries proved central to Widnes's win.

Featherstone's Danny Kirmond beats Barrow's Nick Beach in the corner to score

NATIONAL LEAGUE TWO

There were no shocks on the opening weekend of the NL2 play-offs, as Oldham and Workington recorded impressive wins over Swinton and York respectively.

The Roughyeds had their clash with the Lions in the bag at half-time at Boundary Park, as Adam Hughes' first minute try set them on their way to a 26-0 interval lead. Lucas Onyango and Rob Roberts both finished with a brace of tries.

In West Cumbria, Town were arguably even more impressive in despatching the City Knights 42-4 at Derwent Park, despite having key man Shaun Lunt sent off after 28 minutes for biting. Stephen Dawes finished with a hat-trick and Carl Forber nine goals from as many attempts, as Mick Cook's tenure in charge of York ended in disappointment.

But Lunt's red card and subsequent ban had implications the following week for Workington, as Oldham brushed them aside 48-0 at Boundary Park. Hughes again start ed the romp early on and bagged a double, while Gareth Langley went one better to finish with a hat-trick.

At the same time, Featherstone Rovers were securing their Grand Final place with a 36-20 Qualifying Semi-final win over Barrow Raiders at the Chris Moyles Stadium. Dave Hobbs' side were in control by the tenth minute following early tries to wingers Danny Kirmond and Ade Adebisi, and never looked likely to lose.

That meant that Barrow would entertain Oldham for the remaining Grand Final place, and again Hughes was central to an excellent start. His opening try and another from scrum-half James Coyle saw Oldham 16-0 ahead at half-time. And though Raiders battled back well, Hughes completed a hat-trick in the closing stages to seal a 28-6 win.

NATIONAL LEAGUE GRAND FINALS
Tiger, tiger...

Danny Brough produced a fairytale finale for Castleford Tigers, guiding them back into Super League in his last game for the club.

Danny Brough celebrates Castleford's Grand Final win

Brough had already signed a three-year contract with Wakefield when he stepped onto the field against Widnes - but put all thoughts of that aside with a dazzling individual display as the Tigers brushed their opponents aside.

Brough directly created four Castleford tries, as Terry Matterson's side timed their peak to perfection. New Zealander Awen Guttenbeil provided powerful incisions throughout to go alongside his two tries, while teenage sensation Joe Westerman showed more of his considerable potential.

'We can put the demons of the last 12 months behind us now and move on,' Matterson said. 'We've worked bloody hard for 12 months for this performance. Danny Brough was outstanding, but he couldn't have done it without out our forwards. They laid the platform and they were magnificent.'

A poor performance in their biggest game of the year was hugely disappointing for the Vikings and their coach Steve McCormack, and to make matters worse, Widnes would enter administration just two days later.

'Castleford were far superior from the first second to the last second of the game,' said a magnanimous McCormack. 'It was a fantastic performance by them.'

The Vikings were still in the game, just, at half-time - as they trailed 13-4. A Brough kick had led to Michael Wainwright's opening try, and the scrum-half then booted a 40/20 to create the position for Ryan McGoldrick's effort.

Widnes gave themselves a glimmer of hope when Mick Nanyn forced his way over from close range. But it was Brough who ended that hope, brilliantly laying on Guttenbeil's first try on 44 minutes. He then gave Michael Shenton the space to step his way over out wide, and the Tigers' place back in the top flight was assured.

Cas scored further efforts through Westerman and Ryan Clayton, with the Vikings' only response being a powerful effort from prop Oliver Wilkes. But Guttenbeil brought the house down and had the final word with his second try in the closing minutes, leaving an emotional Brough to face the Rugby League media.

'A lot of people doubted my commitment to Castleford, but I'm chuffed to bits for the club,' a tearful Brough said.

Castleford's Michael Shenton touches down to score despite the attentions of Scott Grix

THE CO-OPERATIVE NATIONAL LEAGUE ONE GRAND FINAL

Sunday 7th October 2007

CASTLEFORD TIGERS 42 WIDNES VIKINGS 10

TIGERS: 1 Stuart Donlan; 2 Danny Williams; 3 Michael Shenton; 4 Ryan McGoldrick; 5 Kirk Dixon; 6 Anthony Thackeray; 7 Danny Brough; 8 Liam Higgins; 9 Andrew Henderson; 10 Awen Guttenbeil; 11 Joe Westerman; 12 Ryan Clayton; 13 Peter Lupton. Subs (all used): 14 Mark Leafa; 15 Chris Charles; 16 Michael Wainwright; 17 Ryan Boyle.
Tries: Wainwright (20), McGoldrick (29), Guttenbeil (44, 76), M Shenton (52), Westerman (62), Clayton (66);
Goals: Brough 6/9; **Field goals:** Brough (25, 55).
VIKINGS: 1 Scott Grix; 2 Damien Blanch; 3 Toa Kohe-Love; 4 Mick Nanyn; 5 Gavin Dodd; 6 Dennis Moran; 7 Joel Penny; 8 Mick Cassidy; 9 Mark Smith; 10 Oliver Wilkes; 11 Joel Tomkins; 12 Paul Noone; 13 Bob Beswick. Subs (all used): 14 Aaron Summers; 15 Jordan James; 16 Ian Webster; 17 Lee Doran.
Tries: Nanyn (35), Wilkes (69); **Goals:** Nanyn 1/2.
Rugby Leaguer & League Express Men of the Match:
Tigers: Danny Brough; *Vikings:* Scott Grix.
Penalty count: 7-2; **Half-time:** 13-4; **Referee:** Phil Bentham;
Attendance: 20,814 *(at Headingley Carnegie, Leeds).*

Featherstone's Ian Tonks, flanked by Jamie Field and Wayne McHugh, lifts the NL2 Grand Final trophy

Featherstone Rovers secured their return to Co-operative NL1 with an excellent Grand Final defeat of resurgent Oldham.

The Roughyeds had brushed aside all before them in the play-offs up until then, dismissing Swinton, Workington and Oldham en route to Headingley Carnegie. And the omens looked good for their coach Steve Deakin when centre Adam Hughes continued his remarkable run of scoring the first try in every play-off game, racing away for a 70-metre interception.

But his opposite number Wayne McHugh responded for Rovers right on half-time to hand them a 10-6 interval lead. And Dave Hobbs' side pulled away with converted tries to man of the match Paul Handforth and McHugh again.

Stuart Dickens' accurate kicking and two field goals from Loz Wildbore secured Rovers' victory, making it a memorable day for the thousands of fans from the village that made the trip to Leeds, following Featherstone Lions' win in the opening game of the day.

'It's the proudest day of my career,' said Dickens, sporting one of the flat caps which many of their supporters wore for the day. 'The lads have been fantastic, that's the best performance we've put together all year. I don't think we've defended like that for a long time. We were determined not to let them score and their only try came from an interception, which was a little disappointing.'

Defeat was a blow for an Oldham side that had come a long way during the course of the season. Their Grand Final was severely disrupted by injuries to Byron Ford, Tony Tonks and Geno Costin.

'Seventy-five per cent of the game was played out in Oldham's third of the field and when that happens you can't have complaints,' Roughyeds coach Steve Deakin admitted. 'To be honest, our one try was against the run of play.'

THE CO-OPERATIVE NATIONAL LEAGUE TWO GRAND FINAL

Sunday 7th October 2007

FEATHERSTONE ROVERS 24 OLDHAM 6

ROVERS: 1 Loz Wildbore; 2 Danny Kirmond; 3 Jon Whittle; 4 Wayne McHugh; 5 Ade Adebisi; 6 Andy Kain; 7 Paul Handforth; 8 Gareth Handford; 9 Joe McLocklan; 10 Stuart Dickens; 11 Jamie Field; 12 Richard Blakeway; 13 Tom Haughey. Subs (all used): 14 Jamie Benn; 15 Ian Tonks; 16 James Houston; 17 Gavin Swinson.
Tries: McHugh (39, 49), Handforth (46);
Goals: Dickens 5/6; **Field goals:** Wildbore (66, 70).
Dismissal: Blakeway (64) – head butt on Roberts.
OLDHAM: 1 Gareth Langley; 2 Byron Ford; 3 Craig Littler; 4 Adam Hughes; 5 Lucas Onyango; 6 Neil Roden; 7 James Coyle; 8 Anthony Tonks; 9 Simeon Hoyle; 10 Richard Mervill; 11 Ian Sinfield; 12 Robert Roberts; 13 Geno Costin. Subs (all used): 14 Ian Hodson; 15 Alex Wilkinson; 16 Said Tamghart; 17 Matty Brooks.
Try: Hughes (31); **Goals:** Langley 1/2.
Rugby Leaguer & League Express Men of the Match:
Rovers: Paul Handforth; *Oldham:* Robert Roberts.
Penalty count: 9-5; **Half-time:** 10-6;
Referee: Gareth Hewer. *(at Headingley Carnegie, Leeds).*

THE CO-OPERATIVE NATIONAL LEAGUE AWARDS

Castleford duo
Danny Brough and
Joe Westerman
(inset) show off
their awards

NATIONAL LEAGUE ONE

PLAYER OF THE YEAR
Dennis Moran (Widnes Vikings)

YOUNG PLAYER OF THE YEAR
Joe Westerman (Castleford Tigers)

COACH OF THE YEAR
Mark Aston (Sheffield Eagles)

RUGBY LEAGUE WORLD ALL STARS
1 Scott Grix (Widnes Vikings)
2 Damien Blanch (Widnes Vikings)
3 Michael Shenton (Castleford Tigers)
4 Mick Nanyn (Widnes Vikings)
5 Danny Mills (Sheffield Eagles)
6 Dennis Moran (Widnes Vikings)
7 Danny Brough (Castleford Tigers)
8 Oliver Wilkes (Widnes Vikings)
9 Sean Penkywicz (Halifax)
10 Mark Leafa (Castleford Tigers)
11 Richard Fletcher (Whitehaven)
12 Ryan Clayton (Castleford Tigers)
13 Bob Beswick (Widnes Vikings)

NATIONAL LEAGUE TWO

PLAYER OF THE YEAR
Tony Duggan (Celtic Crusaders)

YOUNG PLAYER OF THE YEAR
Shaun Lunt (Workington Town)

COACH OF THE YEAR
Latham Tawhai (London Skolars)

RUGBY LEAGUE WORLD ALL STARS
1 Tony Duggan (Celtic Crusaders)
2 Danny Kirmond (Featherstone Rovers)
3 Mark Dalle Cort (Celtic Crusaders)
4 Liam Harrison (Barrow Raiders)
5 Austen Aggrey (London Skolars)
6 Neil Roden (Oldham)
7 Jace Van Dijk (Celtic Crusaders)
8 Stuart Dickens (Featherstone Rovers)
9 Neil Budworth (Celtic Crusaders)
10 Adam Sullivan (York City Knights)
11 Neale Wyatt (Celtic Crusaders)
12 Tom Haughey (Featherstone Rovers)
13 Damien Quinn (Celtic Crusaders)

RUGBY LEAGUE CONFERENCE NATIONAL

PLAYER OF THE YEAR
Bart Thomsen (Featherstone Lions)

YOUNG PLAYER OF THE YEAR
Scott Green (Dewsbury Celtic)

COACH OF THE YEAR
Paul Cook (Bramley Buffaloes)

PLAYERS' PLAYER OF THE YEAR
Danny Brough (Castleford Tigers)

REFEREE OF THE YEAR
Gareth Hewer

CLUB OF THE YEAR
Widnes Vikings

BEST COMMUNITY PROGRAMME
Featherstone Rovers

The National League One All Stars

4
INTERNATIONAL YEAR

GILLETTE FUSION TEST SERIES
Great to be British

Great Britain completed their first series win since 1993 when they defeated New Zealand 3-0 to lift the Albert Baskerville Shield (they had done so in 2002, but only after a drawn series against the Kiwis).

The emphatic victory over the Kiwis in the Gillette Fusion Test Series capped a magnificent season for coach Tony Smith, who had been appointed as full-time coach to the national side earlier in the year. Smith guided the Lions to success only weeks after seeing his Leeds Rhinos side prove themselves the champion club in his last match in charge, the tenth Super League Grand Final.

The third Test at Wigan was the last Great Britain match for the foreseeable future, with the separate home nations due to compete in the 2008 World Cup in Australia and the Rugby Football League deciding that the national side to compete in future Tri-Nations would be known as England.

'We wanted to hang up the GB jersey in the right way, and that was important to all of us,' said Smith. 'We don t feel the jersey will be lost, but it is having a break for a little while, and we wanted to put it to bed on a good note. The GB job has been very enjoyable I have only had a short spell, but I have enjoyed it far more than I expected, and that has nothing to do with winning the series. Just working with these people on the field and off the field has been fantastic. There are things we can do better as a team, and there is always improvement in our players, but I think they are getting better and that is what I want to talk about.

'That is what we deserve. We are getting better, but we are not getting carried away and saying we are going to beat the Australians. But the Kiwis tested us and we came out on top. I am looking forward to my new role. There is a lot that can be influenced within the game. And I will have chance to do work with our officials too. I will get involved in shaping the game a little bit. It is a game I care a whole lot about.

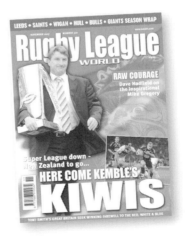

'I may miss the day-to-day coaching, but I am going into it with a very open mind. I am going as Technical Director to give advice on up-to-date International issues to our administrators. That is what they are after, and that is what I am going to do.

'We are heading in a good direction, but they want a little bit more technical input, and hopefully I can do that. I am very proud to be part of it, and to work with elite players and a national team is a great honour. I feel very grateful.'

Smith caused some controversy in the run-up to the series by promising to consider prop Maurie Fa'asavalu for selection after the Samoan - a former captain of his country's union team - declared he would like to be considered for England and Great Britain, after having satisfied the Rugby League International Federation's three-year residency rule since joining St Helens at the start of the 2004 season. 'St Helens and England is the birthplace of my Rugby League career and, having only ever played Rugby League in this country, both my family and I now feel extremely settled here,' Fa'asavalu said.

When Smith named his 25-man squad, Fa'asavalu, who had not looked 100 per cent fit in Saints' Grand Final defeat by

GREAT BRITAIN SQUAD: Sam Burgess (Bradford Bulls), Rob Burrow (Leeds Rhinos), Jon Clarke (Warrington Wolves), Gareth Ellis (Leeds Rhinos), Maurie Fa'asavalu (St Helens), Ade Gardner (St Helens), Martin Gleeson (Warrington Wolves), James Graham (St Helens), David Hodgson (Salford City Reds), Jamie Jones-Buchanan (Leeds Rhinos), Danny McGuire (Leeds Rhinos), Adrian Morley (Warrington Wolves), Terry Newton (Bradford Bulls), Sean O'Loughlin (Wigan Warriors), Jamie Peacock (Leeds Rhinos) (C), Michael Platt (Bradford Bulls), Leon Pryce (St Helens), Gareth Raynor (Hull FC), James Roby (St Helens), Keith Senior (Leeds Rhinos), Kevin Sinfield (Leeds Rhinos), Paul Wellens (St Helens), Stephen Wild (Huddersfield Giants), Jon Wilkin (St Helens), Kirk Yeaman (Hull FC).

Smith announced the names of players for his train-on squad as their clubs were eliminated from the Super League competition. Those players named but left out of the eventual 25-man squad were: Matt Blaymire (Wakefield Trinity Wildcats), Andy Coley (Salford City Reds), Andy Lynch (Bradford Bulls), Richard Moore (Wakefield Trinity Wildcats), Kevin Penny (Warrington Wolves), Jamie Rooney (Wakefield Trinity Wildcats), Paul Sykes (Harlequins), Danny Tickle (Hull FC) and Ben Westwood (Warrington Wolves)
Kevin Brown (Huddersfield Giants), Garreth Carvell (Hull FC), Paul Deacon (Bradford Bulls) and Richard Horne (Hull FC) all withdrew through injury.

Smith's Leeds Rhinos, was included. But Stuart Fielden - an ever-present in Great Britain squads since his debut in 2001 - was left out, Smith claiming that the Wigan prop would return better for the rest in time for the 2008 World Cup.

The squad included five uncapped players, with Bradford's Sam Burgess, the Super League Young Player of the Year at the age of 18, set to become the youngest Great Britain debutant since Andy Farrell in 1993. As well as Fa'asavalu, Bradford fullback Michael Platt, Warrington hooker Jon Clarke and Jamie Jones-Buchanan of Leeds Rhinos were also uncapped. There were 14 players in the squad who featured in the Grand Final, with both Leeds and St Helens providing seven players each. Jamie Peacock retained the captaincy.

Tony Smith's decision to leave Leeds Rhinos at the end on Super League XII had an indirect effect on New Zealand Rugby League, with Brian 'Bluey' McClennan being appointed new coach at Headingley. And though he wanted to retain the national coaching job - he guided the Kiwis to the 2005 Gillette Tri-Nations success and pushed the Aussies into extra-time the year after - the NZRL refused him on the grounds he was non-resident and appointed former Hull FC fullback and NZ international Gary Kemble as his successor.

Kemble - already missing retired Stacey Jones, Nigel Vagana and Ruben Wiki - was hit by a number of withdrawals and unavailability of star players. Back-rower Sonny Bill Williams suffered a fracture to his right forearm in the Bulldogs' NRL semi-final loss to Parramatta. Benji Marshall, Manu Vatuvei and Jerome Ropati had already suffered season-ending injuries. Back-rower David Fa alogo missed the tour through suspension. Former Test skipper Nathan Cayless sustained a torn bicep in the Eels' play-off defeat at Melbourne. Leeds' Brent Webb cited exhaustion to explain his unavailability.

Kemble had drafted seven uncapped players into his side to play Australia in the Centenary Test in Wellington before the tour of Britain and France.

They included Melbourne Storm interchange forwards Jeremy Smith and Jeff Lima, who learned of their inclusion immediately after their NRL Grand Final thrashing of Manly. The other newcomers were Cronulla's Australian-born winger Luke Covell, Parramatta prop Fuifui Moimoi, South Sydney scrum-half Jeremy Smith, Wests Tigers giant winger Taniela Tuiaki and St George-Illawarra threequarter Chase Stanley. The only British-based player in the original 19 was Bradford's Shontayne Hape.

The selection of Moimoi brought an end to a dispute over his international status. Australia's Test coach Ricky Stuart overlooked the Tongan-born star for his train-on squad for the clash with the Kiwis. But Moimoi needed clearance from the RLIF because he represented Tonga in World Cup qualifying games in 2006.

In the Kiwis 58-0 humbling by Australia, Kemble also lost winger Covell and utility back Krisnan Inu to injury. And allegations that members of the squad had sexually assaulted a woman in a Wellington hotel after the Test followed them to the northern hemisphere, although the accusations proved to be false.

Initially, the New Zealand selectors had planned to bring in one player from the All Golds to bolster the touring squad. But after the Centenary match at Warrington (see Other Internationals for details) second-rower David Kidwell returned home to be with his gravely ill mother, and Kemble sent an SOS to three members of the victorious All Golds side - Clinton Toopi, Tame Tupou and Ali Lauitiiti, though Lauitiiti had already decided to play for Samoa

NEW ZEALAND SQUAD: Louis Anderson (New Zealand Warriors), Roy Asotasi (South Sydney Rabbitohs) (C), Greg Eastwood (Brisbane Broncos), David Faiumu (North Queensland Cowboys), Dene Halatau (Wests Tigers), Shontayne Hape (Bradford Bulls), Lance Hohaia (New Zealand Warriors), Shaun Kenny-Dowall (Sydney Roosters), Epalahame Lauaki (New Zealand Warriors), Thomas Leuluai (Wigan Warriors), Jeff Lima (Melbourne Storm), Simon Mannering (New Zealand Warriors), Fuifui Moimoi (Parramatta Eels), Sam Perrett (Sydney Roosters), Frank Pritchard (Penrith Panthers), Sam Rapira (New Zealand Warriors), Ben Roberts (Bulldogs), Jeremy Smith (Melbourne Storm), Jeremy Smith (South Sydney Rabbitohs), Chase Stanley (St George-Illawarra Dragons), Clinton Toopi (Leeds Rhinos), Taniela Tuiaki (Wests Tigers), Tame Tupou (Bradford Bulls), Paul Whatuira (Wests Tigers).

After the series had concluded, Tony Smith hit out at suggestions that Great Britain had scored a whitewash against an understrength New Zealand side. 'The series will be remembered as a Test series. I don t get it otherwise,' said Smith. Why talk about what wasn't here or wasn t available. Do you just list your best seventeen down on paper and not play? Do you just cross them off and say mine is better than yours and never get to do battle on the field, so you just have a paper exercise?

'Test football is all about getting players on the field. It's a test of the best available in your country against the best available for your rivals. Otherwise it is all hypothetical. All my boys want is to play and get out there. Injured players are not here, and we have had retirements too. It is just a test of what is available. If there is another way of doing it, let me know. The talk about what has not been here has detracted from our boys' achievement, and nobody seems to be asking whether we have got a little bit better or not. That is what irks me.'

Kemble, despite his side suffering their first Test whitewash at the hands of Great Britain since 1993, held on to the Kiwi hot seat. 'I still want the job,' insisted Kemble, after the Kiwis' 28-22 third Test defeat. 'The New Zealand Rugby League are fully behind me. They know what is going on and what has been happening. The players have been a tight knit unit, and although we had a tough week leading up to this third Test the players have done themselves proud.'

'People have to remember that our major goal is the World Cup. New Zealand Rugby League have never won it, and that is our ultimate goal. My players did their country proud in this third Test and they will learn from the experience. I have told them that in the end they have only just missed out on winning a Test series.'

GILLETTE FUSION FIRST TEST

Three tries each was a fair indication of how close it was in Huddersfield, in what was a true Test match. The hits were ferocious, with 18-year-old debutant Sam Burgess and Kiwi Fuifui Moimoi conducting their own personal battle, mixed in with some fine football.

Britain had the major advantage at halfback where Leon Pryce and man of the match Rob Burrow produced most of the game's best individual moments. The Leeds scrum-half's quicksilver dashes were a constant threat to the opposition, although he spoiled one superb break when he sent out a poor pass to Maurie Fa'asavalu. Burrow's field kicking also repeatedly drove New Zealand back into their own quarter and it was his deep punt that Gareth Raynor chased and touched down inches from the dead-ball line. Add a 100 per cent success with his four goal kicks that made all the difference and

Maurie Fa'asavalu shows his delight after scoring on his Great Britain debut

Burrow's contribution to victory was clear. Pryce stepped in for the injured Danny McGuire and did enough to demonstrate stand-off was his best position. While the diminutive Burrow tended to buzz his way through, Pryce used a long stride and power. He added a subtle touch when slipping out a gem of a pass to send Burgess charging over for a try on his debut.

Burgess also had a big – and eventful - game, put on report and bringing off one shattering tackle that shook the crowd as much as Moimoi.

The head-high shot that put Burgess on report led to Moimoi being taken off badly shaken, and within two minutes the British prop had crashed over for his try. Burgess was found to have no case to answer. Following in the wake of New Zealand's official condemnation of Britain's other prop, Adrian Morley, escaping suspension after being put on report for a similar offence playing for the Northern Union against the All Golds a week earlier, there was some heated reaction to that decision from the Kiwi camp.

Maurie Fa'asavalu was a controversial choice because of his Samoan nationality, but he made his usual massive impact and scored a 27th minute debut try shortly after going on. On the debit side, his handling error led to New Zealand scoring six minutes later.

New Zealand could also have been acclaiming one of their Test debutants, but Sam Perrett marred an otherwise outstanding fullback display with a disastrous error that allowed Raynor to score his astonishing try. Perrett was under no pressure when Burrow put in a mighty 55-metre punt that was aimed at just gaining territory. Raynor was still 30 metres away when the ball entered the in-goal area, but as it bobbed up a few inches from the dead ball line Perrett dawdled and Britain's winger suddenly arrived to make a diving touchdown.

New Zealand's performance was a vast improvement on their record 58-0 defeat against Australia two weeks before, but they still looked like a side that had yet to come together. There was plenty of fire in the forwards, but little penetration from their halfbacks - Thomas Leuluai and Lance Hohaia selected ahead of NRL youngsters Ben Roberts and Jeremy Smith. Captain Roy Asotasi led by example in the front row.

Tony Smith's plans were disrupted shortly before the kick-off when Kevin Sinfield withdrew after being struck down by a bug and was replaced at loose forward by Sean O'Loughlin. The Kiwis had the best possible start when Leuluai put in a short kick and Shontayne Hape's touchdown was approved by the video referee. There seemed a lack of understanding as Hohaia had to come from the other end of the field to take the goal kick, which he missed.

Britain hit back with Fa'asavalu's short-range try, goaled by Burrow, who added a penalty soon after to put them 8-4 ahead. But within a couple of minutes Fa'asavalu had spoiled his effort with a dropped pass that resulted in New Zealand taking a two-point lead that they held up to the interval. Kiwi substitute Epalahame Lauaki booted the spilled ball 30 metres towards the home line where Paul Whatuira did well to scoop it up and touch down, eventually, after a great effort to get under him by O'Loughlin. Once again the video referee ruled in New Zealand's favour and Hohaia added the goal.

Early in the second half, the video referee ruled Raynor had pushed a defender out of the way in the scramble to touch down Burrow's kick. But the official could find no fault with Raynor's amazing touchdown two minutes later. With Burgess following up with his try and Burrow adding a couple of goals a British victory looked assured, although they had a late scare when Hape raced in for his second try after good work by Dene Halatau. A goal would have increased the pressure on Britain, but Hohaia missed once again.

GILLETTE FUSION FIRST TEST

Saturday 27th October 2007

GREAT BRITAIN 20 NEW ZEALAND 14

GREAT BRITAIN: 1 Paul Wellens (St Helens); 2 Ade Gardner (St Helens); 3 Martin Gleeson (Warrington Wolves); 4 Keith Senior (Leeds Rhinos); 5 Gareth Raynor (Hull FC); 6 Leon Pryce (St Helens); 7 Rob Burrow (Leeds Rhinos); 8 Adrian Morley (Warrington Wolves); 9 Terry Newton (Bradford Bulls) 10 Sam Burgess (Bradford Bulls) (D); 11 Jamie Peacock (Leeds Rhinos) (C); 12 Gareth Ellis (Leeds Rhinos); 13 Sean O'Loughlin (Wigan Warriors). Subs (all used): 14 Maurie Fa'asavalu (St Helens) (D); 15 James Roby (St Helens); 16 James Graham (St Helens); 17 Jon Wilkin (St Helens).
Tries: Fa'asavalu (27), Raynor (49), Burgess (61);
Goals: Burrow 4/4.
On report: Burgess (59) - high tackle on Moimoi.
NEW ZEALAND: 1 Sam Perrett (Sydney Roosters) (D); 2 Tame Tupou (Bradford Bulls); 3 Shontayne Hape (Bradford Bulls); 4 Paul Whatuira (Wests Tigers); 5 Taniela Tuiaki (Wests Tigers); 6 Lance Hohaia (New Zealand Warriors); 7 Thomas Leuluai (Wigan Warriors); 10 Roy Asotasi (South Sydney Rabbitohs) (C); 9 Dene Halatau (Wests Tigers); 18 Fuifui Moimoi (Parramatta Eels); 11 Simon Mannering (New Zealand Warriors); 12 Frank Pritchard (Penrith Panthers); 13 Jeremy Smith (Melbourne Storm). Subs (all used): 14 Greg Eastwood (Brisbane Broncos); 15 Louis Anderson (New Zealand Warriors); 16 Sam Rapira (New Zealand Warriors); 17 Epalahame Lauaki (New Zealand Warriors) (D).
Tries: Hape (3, 75), Whatuira (33); **Goals:** Hohaia 1/3.
Rugby Leaguer & League Express Men of the Match:
Great Britain: Rob Burrow; *New Zealand:* Roy Asotasi.
Penalty count: 6-8; **Half-time:** 8-10;
Referee: Tony Archer (Australia);
Attendance: 16,522 *(at Galpharm Stadium, Huddersfield).*

GILLETTE FUSION SECOND TEST

Great Britain claimed their first Test series win since 1993 with a clinical demolition of the Kiwis at the KC Stadium. It was a night of records - Great Britain's biggest win on home soil against New Zealand, and their highest winning margin against the Kiwis in Test matches, surpassing the 52-20 win in Auckland in 1910.

Inspirational leadership from Jamie Peacock, the official man of the match, great support from senior professionals Adrian Morley and Gareth Ellis in the pack, and a back-line orchestrated by a fine halfback partnership in Leon Pryce and Rob Burrow,

Jamie Peacock heads for the line to score the Lions' opening try in the second Test

underpinned by Paul Wellens' customary rock-solid contribution at fullback, were the highlights of an outstanding team display.

Smith made three changes from the Huddersfield Test, with only one enforced - James Roby, on parental leave. Terry Newton made way for debutant Jon Clarke, earning his reward for a highly consistent season with the Wolves. Kevin Sinfield had recovered from illness and was back in the starting XIII. Danny McGuire returned after injury, and Jon Wilkin was left out.

For the Kiwis, Clinton Toopi replaced the injured Tame Tupou, with Shontayne Hape switching to the wing. David Faiumu, impressive in the All Golds game, replaced the injured Epalahame Lauaki.

On a dry, still but increasingly chilly evening Great Britain made a magnificent start, with a try from skipper Peacock after only 75 seconds play. Peacock received on an arc from Clarke and showed great strength and elusiveness on a swerving run to the line, evading a six attempted tackles as Roy Asotasi and Dene Halatau initially went too high. The Kiwis responded by forcing a goal-line drop-out through Thomas Leuluai's kick, but the British defence was impressively solid. Taniela Tuiaki and Frank Pritchard were repelled close to the line, and Gareth Raynor cleared the danger with an impressive aerial take of Lance Hohaia's bomb. Ade Gardner then made a timely interception to Tuiaki's offload, after Sam Perrett's break and Pritchard's pass briefly opened up the home defence down the Kiwis' left-wing.

Raynor was just unable to take Burrow's high angled kick to the Kiwis' corner flag as Britain looked the more cohesive attacking side. But a harsh penalty for interference allowed the attack to continue and Pryce, taking Clarke's pass at first receiver, brilliantly side-stepped Hohaia's challenge and took two more defenders with him over the line, the grounding confirmed by the video referee. Sinfield's second conversion opened up a 12-0 lead.

Peacock had been rested after a fine opening 22 minutes, but Morley stayed on until the half-hour mark, blunting the Kiwis' defence with a series of strong charges. Maurie Fa'asavalu, James Graham and Sam Burgess added their contributions from the bench. Keith Senior, held up close to the line in a three-man tackle from Burrow's short pass, went closest to extending Britain's lead, before local Hull hero Raynor effectively took the game away from the Kiwis' grasp. Raynor had bombed a glorious chance, just unable to hang on to the ball by the line after the back-tracking Toopi was unable to collect Burrow's raking kick direct from a scrum. But, undaunted, he recovered to squeeze in the left corner flag and complete a flowing quick-passing move that involved Pryce, Wellens and Senior.

The Kiwis tested the home defence on both flanks after the half-time break, Senior wrapping up Toopi after Hape's sharp pass. Clarke took a breather to a round of warm applause, allowing McGuire a first taste of the action as Burrow assumed the dummy-half duties.

A sharp Paul Whatuira tackle denied Martin Gleeson after inter-passing by Burrow and Wellens made the opening, and the Huddersfield capture was equally vigilant to stop McGuire's burrowing run for the line. But the Kiwis were hanging on, and Pryce turned the screw with a precision angled steepling bomb. Toopi

GILLETTE FUSION SECOND TEST

Saturday 3rd November 2007

GREAT BRITAIN 44 NEW ZEALAND 0

GREAT BRITAIN: 1 Paul Wellens (St Helens); 2 Ade Gardner (St Helens); 3 Martin Gleeson (Warrington Wolves); 4 Keith Senior (Leeds Rhinos); 5 Gareth Raynor (Hull FC); 6 Leon Pryce (St Helens); 7 Rob Burrow (Leeds Rhinos); 8 Adrian Morley (Warrington Wolves); 9 Jon Clarke (Warrington Wolves) (D); 10 Jamie Peacock (Leeds Rhinos) (C); 11 Gareth Ellis (Leeds Rhinos); 12 Sean O'Loughlin (Wigan Warriors); 13 Kevin Sinfield (Leeds Rhinos). Subs (all used): 14 Maurie Fa'asavalu (St Helens); 15 James Graham (St Helens); 16 Sam Burgess (Bradford Bulls); 17 Danny McGuire (Leeds Rhinos).
Tries: Peacock (2), Pryce (14, 77), Raynor (39), Wellens (50), Gardner (56), Burrow (63), Senior (71);
Goals: Sinfield 5/5, Burrow 1/3.
NEW ZEALAND: 1 Sam Perrett (Sydney Roosters); 5 Shontayne Hape (Bradford Bulls); 3 Clinton Toopi (Leeds Rhinos); 4 Paul Whatuira (Wests Tigers); 2 Taniela Tuiaki (Wests Tigers); 6 Lance Hohaia (New Zealand Warriors); 7 Thomas Leuluai (Wigan Warriors); 17 Sam Rapira (New Zealand Warriors); 9 Dene Halatau (Wests Tigers); 10 Roy Asotasi (South Sydney Rabbitohs) (C); 11 Simon Mannering (New Zealand Warriors); 12 Frank Pritchard (Penrith Panthers); 13 Jeremy Smith (Melbourne Storm). Subs (all used): 14 David Faiumu (North Queensland Cowboys); 15 Louis Anderson (New Zealand Warriors); 16 Greg Eastwood (Brisbane Broncos); 8 Fuifui Moimoi (Parramatta Eels).
Rugby Leaguer & League Express Men of the Match:
Great Britain: Leon Pryce; *New Zealand:* Paul Whatuira.
Penalty count: 7-8; **Half-time:** 16-0;
Referee: Tony Archer (Australia); **Attendance:** 20,324
(at Kingston Communications Stadium, Hull).

and Hape failed to defuse it under pressure from Senior, who managed to palm the ball back, and Wellens, following up, jubilantly claimed the touchdown. Burrow converted, and that was effectively that.

Six minutes later, Gardner was over in the right corner for a wonderful try. McGuire had put in a short chip for the chasing Sean O'Loughlin which Toopi read well to collect. But O'Loughlin managed to rip the ball out of his grasp, and Burrow collected to embark on a dodging run to the right. He fed Martin Gleeson who turned the cover inside out to give Gardner enough space to squeeze in. Then Wellens took Raynor's inside pass and ushered the supporting Burrow over to complete a flowing move sparked by Morley's fine burst.

Senior compounded the Kiwis' misery by pouncing on Perrett's fumble from Wellens' kick in the corner after another sustained attack, and having the presence of mind to gallop under the posts. And Pryce completed what had become a rout, anticipating Hohaia's lofted pass and accelerating away from the tiring cover for a 70-metre solo try that brought the house down.

GILLETTE FUSION THIRD TEST

Great Britain completed a 3-0 whitewash after coming back from 12-0 behind to turn the game with a four-try burst inside eleven minutes either side of the interval.

James Graham's inspirational try, after he successfully took on six Kiwi defenders, sparked the revival, and further scores by Keith Senior, David Hodgson and Rob Burrow demonstrated the confidence flowing through the British side, confirmed by a majestic Danny McGuire clincher. Burrow, was voted Man of the Series. Sean O'Loughlin was an outstanding man of the match, with Gareth Ellis backing up superb contributions from the experienced quartet of Jamie Peacock, Keith Senior, Adrian Morley and Paul Wellens. Peacock, an inspirational leader, collected the Baskerville Shield as the curtain came down on what could have been the final home game to be played by a Great Britain side.

Great Britain coach Tony Smith rested Gareth Raynor and Leon Pryce and brought in David Hodgson on the wing and McGuire into the no 6 jersey. Jon Wilkin, James Roby and Jamie Jones-Buchanan, who became the fourth player to make his GB debut in the series, replaced Kevin Sinfield, Maurie Fa'asavalu and Sam Burgess. Pryce might have rivalled Burrow for the George Smith Medal had he played, but McGuire, Smith felt, deserved his chance and justified his selection. Huddersfield loose forward Stephen Wild missed out on the chance of a GB recall to be with his seriously ill mother.

For the Kiwis, coach Gary Kemble made a total of five changes to the seventeen from the thrashing at Hull, some of them injury enforced. Chase Stanley replaced the injured Shontayne Hape on the wing for his Test debut, and there was a new halfback pairing in Ben Roberts and Jeremy Smith, Thomas Leuluai missing out on his home ground through injury. Forwards Epalahame Lauaki and Jeff Lima came in on the bench.

On a mild though blustery evening the Kiwis made a decent start, Dene Halatau, Roberts and Clinton Toopi combining in a sweeping move to give Stanley a memorable start to his Test career. Forward Jeremy Smith converted from the touch-line. After the alert Paul Whatuira snaffled an intended Adrian Morley offload in heavy traffic to set up another Kiwi attack, the Giants capture was on hand to finish off superb approach play by the impressive Roberts and forward Smith for another converted try, this time on the left.

Ellis pulled off a superb diving tackle that just hauled down Louis Anderson short of the line from Halatau's offload. Then Hodgson tackled Stanley in the air after halfback Smith's chip-kick to the corner, and was perhaps fortunate to escape without a penalty try being awarded.

Substitute Graham made an immediate impact, receiving from Roby and targeting halfback Smith in the defensive line. Smith and Louis Anderson initially went too high, and though another four of their teammates came in to help, the Saints forward somehow managed to claim an opportunist touchdown as he twisted low for the line.

Within minutes Britain were just two points adrift, as O'Loughlin brilliantly committed the close-range defence before slipping out a fine pass for Senior to score in the corner.

And just before half-time the Kiwis crumbled. Stanley fumbled a McGuire kick to concede a close-range scrum, and O'Loughlin, Burrow and Senior combined superbly on the blind side from the scrum base for Hodgson to squeeze over with 37 seconds left on the clock. Burrow extended the home lead within three minutes of the re-start - a typically impudent effort as he received Graham's offload, then evaded Halatau's challenge before embarking on an elusive angled run to the line for a fine individual

Martin Gleeson looks to get the ball away under pressure from Paul Whatuira

effort. Burrow's conversion opened up an eight-point lead, with the Kiwis needing to re-group quickly as the enveloping drizzle turned into a sweeping downpour.

Cue a moment of magic, a rehearsed move, involving O'Loughlin and McGuire that effectively decided the issue. From a scrum midway inside their own half O'Loughlin, first receiver from Burrow's pass from the base, hit an inch-perfect kick downfield that was chased by McGuire. Showing an enviable turn of pace, the Rhinos stand-off burned off the cover, collected on the bounce and just reached the corner for a memorable score. Burrow's conversion looked to have left the Kiwis with too much to do.

Despite then forcing successive goal-line drop-outs, the Kiwis could not find away through until Stanley, diving bravely in the corner to connect with Roberts' raking kick, was awarded a try by the video referee on the benefit of the doubt ruling. Smith again converted, and suddenly the Kiwis spied a chance. But their hopes were ended as Stanley over-ran Sam Perrett's pass and the ball ended up over the side-line near the corner flag.

A Burrow penalty, after interference on Jon Clarke after he almost burrowed over the line, confirmed Britain's victory, though the Kiwis gained a late consolation when Taniela Tuiaki fastened onto the end of a sweeping attack to cross by the left corner flag with just 14 seconds remaining.

GILLETTE FUSION THIRD TEST

Saturday 10th November 2007

GREAT BRITAIN 28 NEW ZEALAND 22

GREAT BRITAIN: 1 Paul Wellens (St Helens); 5 Ade Gardner (St Helens); 3 Martin Gleeson (Warrington Wolves); 4 Keith Senior (Leeds Rhinos); 2 David Hodgson (Salford City Reds); 6 Danny McGuire (Leeds Rhinos); 7 Rob Burrow (Leeds Rhinos); 8 Adrian Morley (Warrington Wolves); 9 Jon Clarke (Warrington Wolves); 10 Jamie Peacock (Leeds Rhinos) (C); 11 Gareth Ellis (Leeds Rhinos); 12 Sean O'Loughlin (Wigan Warriors); 13 Jon Wilkin (St Helens). Subs (all used): 14 James Graham (St Helens); 15 Jamie Jones-Buchanan (Leeds Rhinos) (D); 16 James Roby (St Helens); 17 Kirk Yeaman (Hull FC).
Tries: Graham (33), Senior (37), Hodgson (40), Burrow (43), McGuire (55); **Goals:** Burrow 4/6.
NEW ZEALAND: 1 Sam Perrett (Sydney Roosters); 2 Chase Stanley (St George-Illawarra Dragons); 3 Clinton Toopi (Leeds Rhinos); 4 Paul Whatuira (Wests Tigers); 5 Taniela Tuiaki (Wests Tigers); 6 Ben Roberts (Bulldogs); 7 Jeremy Smith (South Sydney Rabbitohs); 8 Sam Rapira (New Zealand Warriors); 9 Dene Halatau (Wests Tigers); 10 Roy Asotasi (South Sydney Rabbitohs) (C); 11 Louis Anderson (New Zealand Warriors); 12 Jeremy Smith (Melbourne Storm); 13 Simon Mannering (New Zealand Warriors). Subs (all used): 14 Lance Hohaia (New Zealand Warriors); 15 Fuifui Moimoi (Parramatta Eels); 16 Epalahame Lauaki (New Zealand Warriors); 17 Jeff Lima (Melbourne Storm).
Tries: Stanley (7, 67), Whatuira (11), Tuiaki (80);
Goals: Smith (SR) 3/4.
Rugby Leaguer & League Express Men of the Match:
Great Britain: Sean O'Loughlin; *New Zealand:* Ben Roberts.
Penalty count: 7-7; **Half-time:** 14-12;
Referee: Tony Archer (Australia);
Attendance: 21,235 *(at JJB Stadium, Wigan).*

THE FRONTLINE TEST

France led 10-4 midway through the first half of the Frontline Test at Headingley in June. Tony Smith's first game in charge of Great Britain saw him rest several established Test players and Britain seemed to suffer a disruptive blow when Danny McGuire went off with concussion just after France had gone into their surprise 10-4 lead in the 24th minute. By then he had made a typical early break and scored a try. But McGuire's departure gave his club captain, Kevin Sinfield, the chance to prove a point after being left out of last year's Tri-Nations. His partnership with Burrow played a key role in Britain's revival. Sinfield took the official man of the match award, but there should have been at least a share for Burrow, who was an irritable nuisance to the French throughout. His great support play brought him two tries, and he was there again to send Stephen Wild over for the crucial early first touchdown after the interval.

Adrian Morley repaid coach Smith's faith in him as captain, blasting in for a try and flipping out a superb pass from a tackle to send in Burrow.

Although Britain's wingers did not get among the scorers, both sought to get involved in attack and defence. They combined to set up McGuire's try in a brilliant 80-metre raid. Ade Gardner began it with a powerful drive from a play-the-ball that took him curving through the middle before linking up with David Hodgson, who sent McGuire clear. Gardner also handed Paul Sykes a debut try when he leaped to take Sinfield's high kick to the corner and hooked out a brilliant pass to the centre.

Maxime Grésèque had an outstanding game for France, and scored the two tries that gave France their early lead. A neat little chip over the front line saw him combine with the impressive Julien Rinaldi, and, when the ball bounced around as the attack broke down, Grésèque came round to sweep it up and dive over in the corner in the 20th minute.

Four minutes later Grésèque's perseverance paid off again, after his field-goal attempt went astray. Scrambling play by both sides followed, before it ended with Cyril Gossard sending in the halfback for his second touchdown with another wonderful offload.

France started full of confidence, and with better finishing could have had tries on the left and right. But when McGuire put Britain ahead after nine minutes it looked like the start of the expected points avalanche.

It never came. France suddenly took the lead with Grésèque's two tries plus a Thomas Bosc conversion midway through the half. Burrow's first try, goaled by Sinfield, levelled the scores and Britain regained the lead when James Graham made a powerful midfield run to set up Jamie Langley to grab a Test debut try. Sinfield's goal made it 16-10.

France needed to contain Britain early in the second half, but they couldn't. In fact, they were blown apart by four tries in 12 minutes. Sinfield's growing influence was significant, and he was the central figure in a spectacular try by Wild. The stand-off then put Morley over, before Burrow scored his second try following good work by Jon Wilkin and Chris Melling. Two goals from Sinfield pushed up the score that became 36-10 when Sykes scored from his crossfield kick.

France came back with an Eric Anselme try off Greg Mounis's pass. But when James Roby powered in from close range off a superb Andy Lynch offload, and Sinfield added the goal, it looked certain that Britain would pass the half-century. They didn't due

Great Britain's Rob Burrow plunges through the French defence to score

to some spirited French resistance.

The Headingley attendance of 12,685 was the biggest for a Britain-France match since 13,173 saw a 37-0 home victory at The Boulevard, Hull, in 1981.

Former Great Britain and Wigan fullback Steve Hampson became the third ex-Lion to join Tony Smith's backroom staff, following the appointments of Steve McNamara and James Lowes. Iestyn Harris strongly criticised the RFL's decision to field an England team, instead of Great Britain, as its major representative team after the 2008 World Cup. The decision effectively meant that if a player wished to play in a future Tri-Nations series, he'd choose to play for England in the World Cup ahead of Wales, Scotland or Ireland. An irate Harris told Rugby League World magazine: 'Players shouldn't be held to ransom to play for England. It seems that they're saying that if you don't play for England then you can't play in the Tri-Nations from 2009 onwards. It's not good for the individuals, and it's not good for the sport. '

THE FRONTLINE TEST

Friday 22nd June 2007

GREAT BRITAIN 42 FRANCE 14

GREAT BRITAIN: 1 Chris Melling (Harlequins) (D); 2 David Hodgson (Salford City Reds); 3 Stephen Wild (Huddersfield Giants); 4 Paul Sykes (Harlequins) (D); 5 Ade Gardner (St Helens); 6 Danny McGuire (Leeds Rhinos); 7 Rob Burrow (Leeds Rhinos); 8 Adrian Morley (Warrington Wolves) (C); 9 James Roby (St Helens); 10 Andy Lynch (Bradford Bulls) (D); 11 Gareth Ellis (Leeds Rhinos); 12 Andy Coley (Salford City Reds) (D); 13 Jon Wilkin (St Helens). Subs (all used): 14 Sean O'Loughlin (Wigan Warriors); 15 James Graham (St Helens); 16 Kevin Sinfield (Leeds Rhinos); 17 Jamie Langley (Bradford Bulls) (D).
Tries: McGuire (9), Burrow (27, 50), Langley (35), Wild (42), Morley (47), Sykes (54), Roby (66);
Goals: Burrow 0/1, Sinfield 5/7.
FRANCE: 1 Thomas Bosc (Catalans Dragons) (D); 2 Sebastien Planas (Toulouse Olympique); 3 Sylvain Houles (Toulouse Olympique); 4 Cyril Stacul (Villeneuve) (D); 5 Constant Villegas (Toulouse Olympique) (D); 6 Maxime Greseque (Pia); 7 Christophe Moly (Carcassonne); 8 David Ferriol (Catalans Dragons); 9 Julien Rinaldi (Harlequins); 10 Jerome Guisset (Catalans Dragons) (C); 11 Olivier Elima (Wakefield Trinity Wildcats); 12 Eric Anselme (St Gaudens); 13 Aurelien Cologni (Catalans Dragons). Subs (all used): 14 James Wynne (Toulouse Olympique); 15 Jean-Christophe Borlin (St Gaudens); 16 Cyril Gossard (Catalans Dragons) (D); 17 Gregory Mounis (Catalans Dragons).
Tries: Greseque (20, 24), Anselme (60);
Goals: Bosc 1/2, Greseque 0/1.
Rugby Leaguer & League Express Men of the Match:
Great Britain: Rob Burrow; *France:* Maxime Greseque.
Penalty count: 4-4; **Half-time:** 16-10;
Referee: Steve Ganson (England);
Attendance: 12,685 *(at Headingley Carnegie, Leeds).*

WORLD CUP QUALIFIERS
Destination Australia

Ireland, Scotland and Samoa were the nations to qualify for the last three spots in the 2008 World Cup to be held in Australia.

That meant Wales failed to win a place in the 13th global tournament, despite having reached the semi-finals of the previous two World Cups in 1995 and 2000. Also eliminated in 2007 were the United States, Russia and Lebanon. England, Australia, New Zealand, Papua New Guinea and France were automatic entries and Tonga and Fiji had already qualified in 2006.

The draw for the tournament was announced in April, with England, Australia, New Zealand and Papua New Guinea placed in a 'super pool', the top three teams qualifying for the semi-finals, the fourth eliminated. The other two pools were to contain three nations each, one of those able to qualify for the semi-finals. The final was to take place at Brisbane's Suncorp Stadium on 22nd November 2008.

The draw created outrage in Papua New Guinea, with the formula making their chances of reaching the semi-finals remote. PNG great Marcus Bai said: 'I reckon it's crap. I am furious about this. It's really rubbish. Our guys will try very hard, but if you look at results over the past ten years you could say we've got no chance. They say anything can happen, but really...'

2007 QUALIFIERS

Irish eyes were smiling on a mild November evening in Dewsbury - the venue was switched because of the political situation in Lebanon - after a dramatic 16-all draw with the Cedars. Chris Bridge's easy penalty goal three minutes from time - harshly awarded by referee Ashley Klein for a high-tackle by Hassan Saleh on the Warrington stand-off - secured the point which was enough to take Ireland through on points difference due to their superior record against Russia.

Lebanon lamented the disallowing of a try to centre Hassan Saleh, controversially ruled offside after beating Scott Grix to the outstanding George Ndaira's kick. They now had to enter the repechage with Samoa, USA and Wales to decide the tenth place in the World Cup finals.

USA's chances - they had won the right to compete thanks to a 54-18 win over Japan at Aston, Pennsylvania 12 months before - of beating Samoa were rated at nil after a 70-0 defeat against Cumbria in a warm-up game in Barrow the Sunday before. With Nigel Vagana, Frank and Tony Puletua, Ali Lauitiiti and Harrison Hansen switching allegiances from New Zealand, John Ackland's Samoa were tipped to run up a century of points against the Tomahawks.

In the opening game of a double-header at Widnes, the Samoans went through, but the Americans made a lot of friends in their 42-10 defeat. US captain Matt Petersen was the man of the match and their coach Matthew Elliott admitted: "We've come a long way. Ten days ago when we had our first training session, I was frightened to death."

The second game of the double header pitted Wales against Lebanon, who were

Ali Lauitiiti battles through the Lebanon defence as Samoa secure the last World Cup place

weakened by the return down under of three players due to work commitments.

Wales were there after their elimination by Scotland, who they defeated 18-16 at Old Anniesland in Glasgow. Scotland went through on a 37-32 points aggregate because they defeated Wales 21-14 at Bridgend in 2006.

Scotland were behind 14-4 at half-time, but came back strongly in the second half through tries from hooker Ben Fisher and winger Jamie Benn to keep themselves in contention, with captain Danny Brough kicking four crucial goals from four attempts. Their coach, Steve McCormack, described World Cup qualification as the best achievement in his career.

Wales made their exit the following Friday as Lebanon produced a stunning second-half performance to win 50-26. It was an amazing turnaround that extended the Cedars' seven-year unbeaten run to 14 matches, with Damian Gibson's hat-trick try three minutes after the break having seemingly put Wales back in the driving seat at 20-10.

But Newtown Jets scrum-half Ndaira suddenly moved up a gear, and Wales couldn't handle his speed off the mark and clever ball work, with loose forward and captain Chris Salem the major beneficiary, his two second-half tries completing a hat-trick.

For much of the first half it looked like Wales were marching through to a rematch with Samoa that would have brought strong memories of the 1995 World Cup clash between the two at

QUALIFYING FINAL

Wednesday 14th November 2007

LEBANON 16 SAMOA 38

LEBANON: 1 Adnan Saleh (Sydney Bulls); 2 Adham El Zbaideh (Cessnock); 3 Frank Samia (St George-Illawarra Dragons); 4 Danny Chiha (Windsor); 5 Tom Joseph (Manly Sea Eagles); 6 Toufic Nicholas (Sydney Bulls); 7 George Ndaira (Newtown); 8 Ray Moujalli (Cronulla Sharks); 9 Jamie Clark (Bulldogs); 10 Khalid Deeb (Newtown); 11 Phillip Tatchi (Sydney Bulls); 12 Chris Saab (Cessnock); 13 Chris Salem (Sydney Bulls) (C). Subs (all used): 14 Ali Kourouche (LAU); 15 John Korbosi (Bulldogs); 16 Daniel Sayegh (LAU); 17 Robin Hachache (LAU). **Tries:** Tatchi (18), El Zbaideh (35), Chiha (50), Joseph (61); **Goals:** Nicholas 0/3, Clark 0/1.
SAMOA: 1 Tangi Ropati (Wynnum Manly); 2 Smith Samau (Gold Coast Titans); 3 Willie Talau (St Helens); 4 George Carmont (Newcastle Knights); 5 Andreas Bauer (Hull Kingston Rovers); 6 Nigel Vagana (South Sydney Rabbitohs) (C); 7 Joseph Paulo (Penrith Panthers); 8 Hutch Maiava (Hull FC); 9 Chris Vaefaga (Bulldogs); 10 Frank Puletua (Penrith Panthers); 11 Tony Puletua (Penrith Panthers); 12 Ali Lauitiiti (Leeds Rhinos); 13 Harrison Hansen (Wigan Warriors). Subs (all used): 14 Taualagi Lupupa (Marist); 15 Ponofasio Vasa (Marist); 16 Chris Leisham (Chanelle); 17 Phil Leuluai (Salford City Reds).
Tries: Vaefaga (7), Ropati (11), Vagana (26), F Puletua (30), Bauer (45), Maiava (74); **Goals:** Paulo 7/8.
Rugby Leaguer & League Express Men of the Match:
Lebanon: George Ndaira; *Samoa:* Joseph Paulo.
Penalty count: 6-7; **Half-time:** 8-28; **Referee:** Ashley Klein (Australia); **Attendance:** 1,323 *(at Chris Moyles Stadium, Featherstone).*

EUROPE - GROUP 1

Sunday 4th November 2007

SCOTLAND 16 WALES 18

SCOTLAND: 1 Wade Liddell (Brisbane Easts Tigers); 2 Jamie Benn (Featherstone Rovers); 3 Kevin Henderson (Wakefield Trinity Wildcats); 4 Mick Nanyn (Widnes Vikings); 5 Andy Todd (Edinburgh Eagles); 6 Lee Paterson (Batley Bulldogs); 7 Danny Brough (Castleford Tigers) (C); 8 Paul Jackson (Huddersfield Giants); 9 Ben Fisher (Hull Kingston Rovers); 10 Oliver Wilkes (Widnes Vikings); 11 Iain Morrison (Hull Kingston Rovers); 12 Duncan MacGillivray (Wakefield Trinity Wildcats); 13 Richard Fletcher (Whitehaven). Subs (all used): 14 David Lynn (Edinburgh Eagles); 15 Iain Marsh (Rochdale Hornets); 16 Neil Lowe (York City Knights); 17 Andrew Henderson (Castleford Tigers).
Tries: Fisher (53), Benn (74); **Goals:** Brough 4/4.
WALES: 1 Dave Halley (Bradford Bulls); 2 Anthony Blackwood (Celtic Crusaders); 3 Luke Dyer (Hull Kingston Rovers); 4 Adam Hughes (Oldham); 5 Damian Gibson (Halifax); 6 Iestyn Harris (Bradford Bulls) (C); 7 Lee Briers (Warrington Wolves); 8 Jordan James (Widnes Vikings); 9 Ian Webster (Widnes Vikings); 10 Gareth Dean (Celtic Crusaders); 11 Matt James (Bradford Bulls); 12 Robert Roberts (Oldham); 13 Phil Joseph (Halifax). Subs (all used): 14 Sean Penkywicz (Halifax); 15 Phil Cushion (Celtic Crusaders); 16 Andy Bracek (Warrington Wolves); 17 Craig Kopczak (Bradford Bulls).
Tries: Dyer (7), Hughes (36), Gibson (77); **Goals:** Harris 3/4.
Rugby Leaguer & League Express Men of the Match:
Scotland: Mick Nanyn; *Wales:* Dave Halley.
Penalty count: 9-5; **Half-time:** 4-14; **Referee:** Phil Bentham (England); **Attendance:** 911 *(at Old Anniesland, Glasgow).*

EUROPE - GROUP 2

Saturday 20th October 2007

IRELAND 58 RUSSIA 18

IRELAND: 1 Scott Grix (Widnes Vikings); 2 Damien Blanch (Widnes Vikings); 3 Stuart Littler (Salford City Reds) (C); 4 Sean Gleeson (Wakefield Trinity Wildcats); 5 Gavin Dodd (Widnes Vikings); 6 Paul Handforth (Featherstone Rovers); 7 Liam Finn (Dewsbury Rams); 8 Eamon O'Carroll (Wigan Warriors); 9 Bob Beswick (Widnes Vikings); 10 Dave Buckley (York City Knights); 11 Lee Doran (Widnes Vikings); 12 Ged Corcoran (Sheffield Eagles); 13 Anthony Stewart (Leigh Centurions). Subs (all used): 14 Steve Gibbons (Carlow Crusaders); 15 Billy Treacy (Treaty City Titans); 16 Wayne Kerr (Carlow Crusaders); 17 Clive Gee (Portlaoise Panthers).
Tries: Blanch (10, 39, 71), Gleeson (16, 24), Littler (31, 57, 63), Beswick (37, 60), Handforth (3/5.
RUSSIA: 1 Oleg Logunov; 2 Nikolay Zagoskin; 3 Sergey Dobrynin; 4 Vladimir Vlasiuk; 5 Valentin Baskakov; 6 Victor Nechaev; 7 Artem Grigoryan; 8 Evgeny Bozhukov; 9 Roman Ovchinnikov; 10 Azat Musin; 11 Sergey Matveev; 12 Marat Habibullin; 13 Oleg Smirnov. Subs (all used): 14 Andrey Zdobnikov; 15 Sergey Sidorov; 16 Andrey Medvedev; 17 Georgy Vinogradov.
Tries: Logunov (2), Baskakov (8), Zagoskin (48);
Goals: Grigoryan 2/3, Zdobvikov 1/1.
Rugby Leaguer & League Express Men of the Match:
Ireland: Bob Beswick; *Russia:* Roman Ovchinnikov.
Penalty count: 7-7; **Half-time:** 32-12; **Referee:** Phil Bentham (England); **Attendance:** 986 *(at Carlow).*

Saturday 27th October 2007

RUSSIA 0 LEBANON 48

RUSSIA: 1 Oleg Logunov; 2 Sergey Dobrynin; 3 Andrey Zdobnikov; 4 Vladimir Vlasiuk; 5 Valentin Baskakov; 6 Victor Nechaev; 7 Artem Grigoryan; 8 Evgeny Bozhukov; 9 Roman Ovchinnikov; 10 Azat Musin; 11 Sergey Matveev; 12 Marat Habibullin; 13 Oleg Smirnov. Subs (all used): 14 Andre Koltychov; 15 Sergey Sidorov; 16 Andrey Medvedev; 17 Alexandre Lysenkov.
LEBANON: 1 Toufic Nicholas; 2 Adnan Saleh; 3 Frank Samia; 4 Hassan Saleh; 5 Adham El Zbaideh; 6 Anthony Farah; 7 George Ndaira; 8 Charlie Nohra; 9 Jamie Clark; 10 Ray Moujalli; 11 John Korbosi; 12 Chris Saab; 13 Chris Salem. Subs (all used): 14 Allen Soultan; 15 Ali Kourouche; 16 Fred Khoussis; 17 Robin Hachache.
Tries: A Saleh (11, 23), El Zbaideh (29, 65), Nicholas (40), Samia (58, 62), Moujalli (64), Farah (69); **Goals:** Farah 2/5, Nicholas 4/4.
Rugby Leaguer & League Express Men of the Match:
Russia: Roman Ovchinnikov; *Lebanon:* George Ndaira.
Penalty count: 7-7; **Half-time:** 0-20; **Referee:** Richard Silverwood (England); **Attendance:** 1,426 *(at Naro Stadium, Narofominsk).*

Friday 2nd November 2007

IRELAND 16 LEBANON 16

IRELAND: 1 Scott Grix (Widnes Vikings); 2 Damien Blanch (Widnes Vikings); 3 Stuart Littler (Salford City Reds) (C); 4 Sean Gleeson (Wakefield Trinity Wildcats); 5 Anthony Stewart (Leigh Centurions); 6 Paul Handforth (Featherstone Rovers); 7 Liam Finn (Dewsbury Rams); 8 Mick Cassidy (Widnes Vikings); 9 Bob Beswick (Widnes Vikings); 10 Eamon O'Carroll (Wigan Warriors); 11 Paul Prescott (Wigan Warriors); 12 Ged Corcoran (Sheffield Eagles); 13 Lee Doran (Widnes Vikings). Subs: 14 Chris Bridge (Warrington Wolves); 15 Steve Gibbons (Carlow Crusaders); 16 Billy Treacy (Treaty City Titans) (not used); 17 Wayne Kerr (Carlow Crusaders).
Tries: Finn (2), Handforth (19); **Goals:** Finn 2/2, Bridge 2/2.
LEBANON: 1 Toufic Nicholas; 5 Adham El Zbaideh; 3 Frank Samia; 4 Hassan Saleh; 2 Adnan Saleh; 6 Anthony Farah; 7 George Ndaira; 8 Charlie Nohra; 9 Jamie Clark; 10 Ray Moujalli; 11 John Korbosi; 12 Chris Saab; 13 Chris Salem. Subs (all used): 14 Ali Kourouche; 15 Allen Soultan; 16 Robin Hachache; 17 Tom Joseph.
Tries: Ndaira (16), Salem (68); **Goals:** Nicholas 2/3.
Sin bin: Nohra (62) - high tackle on Cassidy.
On report: Clark (56) - alleged trip.
Rugby Leaguer & League Express Men of the Match:
Ireland: Damien Blanch; *Lebanon:* George Ndaira.
Penalty count: 16-12; **Half-time:** 12-4; **Referee:** Ashley Klein (Australia); **Attendance:** 803 *(at Tetley's Stadium, Dewsbury).*

EUROPE - GROUP TWO

	P	W	D	L	F	A	D	Pts
Ireland	4	2	2	0	142	64	78	6
Lebanon	4	2	2	0	104	42	62	6
Russia	4	0	0	4	38	178	-140	0

QUALIFYING SEMI-FINALS

Friday 9th November 2007

SAMOA 42 USA 10

SAMOA: 1 Tangi Ropati (Wynnum Manly); 2 Smith Samau (Gold Coast Titans); 3 Andreas Bauer (Hull Kingston Rovers); 4 George Carmont (Newcastle Knights); 5 Afa Lesa (Marist); 6 Nigel Vagana (South Sydney Rabbitohs) (C); 7 Joseph Paulo (Penrith Panthers); 8 Hutch Maiava (Hull FC); 9 Chris Vaefaga (Bulldogs); 10 Frank Puletua (Penrith Panthers); 11 Tony Puletua (Penrith Panthers); 12 Ali Lauitiiti (Leeds Rhinos); 13 Harrison Hansen (Wigan Warriors). Subs (all used): 14 Chris Leisham (Chanelle); 15 Ponofasio Vana (Marist); 16 Manulua Lafi (Nagenae); 17 Phil Leuluai (Salford City Reds).
Tries: Vagana (2), Maiava (5), T Puletua (30), Leisham (40), Samau (48), Hansen (64, 70), Ropati (79); **Goals:** Paulo 5/8.
USA: 1 Matt Petersen; 2 Tyrone Coppedge; 3 Ben Kelly; 4 Mark O'Halloran; 5 Eric Dortone; 6 Ryan McGoldrick; 7 David Myles; 8 Edward Woodbridge; 9 Dave Marando; 10 Ashley Laffranchi; 11 Mark Cantoni; 12 Curtis Kunz; 13 Marcus Vassilakopoulos. Subs (all used): 14 Louis Tulio; 15 Greg Stelutti; 16 Nick Isbrandtsen; 17 Bryan Confer.
Tries: McGoldrick (45); **Goals:** Vassilakopoulos 0/1, Marando 1/1.
Rugby Leaguer & League Express Men of the Match:
Samoa: Tony Puletua; *USA:* Matt Petersen.
Penalty count: 8-6; **Half-time:** 22-0; **Referee:** Ashley Klein (Australia).

LEBANON 50 WALES 26

LEBANON: 1 Toufic Nicholas; 2 Adham El Zbaideh; 3 Frank Samia; 4 Adnan Saleh; 5 Tom Joseph; 6 Anthony Farah; 7 George Ndaira; 8 Ray Moujalli; 9 Jamie Clark; 10 Khalid Deeb; 11 Phillip Tatchi; 12 Chris Saab; 13 Chris Salem. Subs (all used): 14 Ali Kourouche; 15 Robin Hachache; 16 Danny Chiha; 17 John Korbosi.
Tries: Samia (20), Salem (39, 46, 68), Ndaira (52), Moujalli (55), Kourouche (61), Saab (75), El Zbaideh (79); **Goals:** Nicholas 7/9.
WALES: 1 Dave Halley (Bradford Bulls); 2 Damian Gibson (Halifax); 3 Luke Dyer (Hull Kingston Rovers); 4 Adam Hughes (Oldham); 5 Anthony Blackwood (Celtic Crusaders); 6 Iestyn Harris (Bradford Bulls) (C); 7 Lee Briers (Warrington Wolves); 8 Craig Kopczak (Bradford Bulls); 9 Ian Webster (Widnes Vikings); 10 Jordan James (Widnes Vikings); 11 Matt James (Bradford Bulls); 12 Andy Bracek (Warrington Wolves); 13 Phil Joseph (Halifax). Subs (all used): 14 Sean Penkywicz (Halifax); 15 Mark Roberts (Halifax); 16 Gareth Dean (Celtic Crusaders); 12 Rob Roberts (Oldham).
Tries: Gibson (4, 24, 43), Bracek (9), Blackwood (72);
Goals: Harris 2/4, Briers 1/1.
Rugby Leaguer & League Express Men of the Match:
Lebanon: George Ndaira; *Wales:* Lee Briers.
Penalty count: 7-10; **Half-time:** 10-16; **Referee:** Thierry Alibert (France).

Attendance: 753 *(at Halton Stadium, Widnes).*

World Cup Qualifiers

Swansea that featured the teenaged Iestyn Harris. Harris announced his international retirement a week after the game.

Lebanon's hopes of beating Samoa at the tenth-place play-off at Featherstone the following Wednesday took a blow when Wests Tigers star Robbie Farah decided not to fly out for the showdown. The Australian Rugby League told him he had to choose between playing for his homeland or possible future representation for Australia.

After Samoa's 38-16 final victory, their coach John Ackland was talking about the World Cup semi-finals.

Lebanon overcame a poor start to provide a brave performance. From the 26th minute when Samoa led 20-4, the star-studded islanders were always going to win, but when the Cedars pulled back to 32-16 in the second half, despite not managing a single conversion, they were matching Samoa try for try. Among all the big names, Penrith junior Joseph Paulo was man of the match, setting up several tries and booting seven goals for Samoa.

2008 WORLD CUP

POOL 1	POOL 2	POOL 3
Australia	Fiji	Ireland
England	France	Samoa
New Zealand	Scotland	Tonga
Papua New Guinea		

GAME	DATE	VENUE	MATCH
1	Saturday 25th October	Dairy Farmers Stadium, Townsville	England v Papua New Guinea
2	Sunday 26th October	Canberra Stadium	Scotland v France
3	Sunday 26th October	Sydney Football Stadium *(Official Opening Ceremony)*	Australia v New Zealand
4	Monday 27th October	Parramatta Stadium	Tonga v Ireland
5	Friday 31st October	CUA Stadium, Penrith	Samoa v Tonga
6	Saturday 1st November	WIN Stadium, Wollongong	Fiji v France
7	Saturday 1st November	Skilled Park, Gold Coast	New Zealand v Papua New Guinea
8	Sunday 2nd November	Telstra Dome, Melbourne	Australia v England
9	Wednesday 5th November	Bluetongue Stadium, Central Coast	Scotland v Fiji
10	Wednesday 5th November	Parramatta Stadium	Ireland v Samoa
11	Saturday 8th November	Browne Park, Rockhampton	Pool 2, Team 2 v Pool 3, Team 2 *(ranking game)*
12	Saturday 8th November	Energy Australia Stadium, Newcastle	England v New Zealand
13	Sunday 9th November	CUA Stadium, Penrith	Pool 2, Team 3 v Pool 3, Team 3 *(ranking game)*
14	Sunday 9th November	Dairy Farmers Stadium, Townsville	Papua New Guinea v Australia
15	Monday 10th November	Skilled Stadium, Gold Coast	Semi-final Qualifier Pool 2, Team 1 v Pool 3, Team 1
16	Saturday 15th November	Suncorp Stadium, Brisbane	Semi Final (1)
17	Sunday 16th November	Sydney Football Stadium	Semi Final (2)
18	Saturday 22nd November	Suncorp Stadium, Brisbane	FINAL

● *Top three teams from Pool 1 qualify for Semi-finals*

OTHER INTERNATIONALS
Farewell Stacey

GILLETTE FUSION CENTENARY INTERNATIONAL

The celebration of one hundred years of international Rugby League at the Halliwell Jones Stadium, Warrington the week after the Super League Grand Final, drew a disappointing crowd thanks to a lacklustre promotional campaign.

The New Zealand All Golds, so named one hundred years ago as a play on the term 'All Blacks', in that these so-called mercenaries accepted gold to play for their country on the first professional tour, were up against the Northern Union, the original name for the Rugby Football League.

Risking their jobs, and receiving threats to their future livelihoods and their families, the pioneering tourists, organised by the visionary Bert Baskiville, blazed a trail that opened up the fledgling Northern Union game and took it onto the world stage. The first Kangaroos followed a year later, and international Rugby League was firmly entrenched in the calendar.

In the week leading up to the game, the All Golds were guests at Buckingham Palace and performed the haka for the Queen, the first side ever to have that honour.

For the five thousand or so people at Warrington the following Saturday, the occasion was memorable, and a fitting tribute to Baskiville's pioneers. The All Golds side - coached by Wayne Bennett - featured a blend of past, present and future Kiwi internationals, together with guest Australian prop Steve Price, who

GILLETTE FUSION CENTENARY INTERNATIONAL

Saturday 20th October 2007

NORTHERN UNION 18 NEW ZEALAND ALL GOLDS 25

NORTHERN UNION: 1 Michael Platt (Bradford Bulls); 2 David Hodgson (Salford City Reds); 3 Martin Gleeson (Warrington Wolves); 4 Kirk Yeaman (Hull FC); 5 Gareth Raynor (Hull FC); 6 Danny McGuire (Leeds Rhinos); 7 Jamie Rooney (Wakefield Trinity Wildcats); 8 Adrian Morley (Warrington Wolves) (C); 9 Terry Newton (Bradford Bulls); 10 Andy Lynch (Bradford Bulls); 11 Danny Tickle (Hull FC); 12 Stephen Wild (Huddersfield Giants); 13 Sam Burgess (Bradford Bulls). Subs (all used): 14 Jon Clarke (Warrington Wolves); 15 Richard Moore (Wakefield Trinity Wildcats); 16 Paul Sykes (Harlequins); 17 Andy Coley (Salford City Reds). **Coach:** Tony Smith.
Tries: McGuire (14, 50), Clarke (53), Yeaman (60); **Goals:** Rooney 3/4.
On report: Tickle (18) - high tackle on Vagana; Morley (42) - high tackle on Guttenbeil.
ALL GOLDS: 1 Sam Perrett (Sydney Roosters); 2 Shaun Kenny-Dowall (Sydney Roosters); 3 Nigel Vagana (South Sydney Rabbitohs); 4 Clinton Toopi (Leeds Rhinos); 5 Tame Tupou (Bradford Bulls); 6 Thomas Leuluai (Wigan Warriors); 7 Stacey Jones (Catalans Dragons); 8 Steve Price (New Zealand Warriors); 9 David Faiumu (North Queensland Cowboys); 10 Ruben Wiki (New Zealand Warriors) (C); 11 David Kidwell (South Sydney Rabbitohs); 12 Ali Lauitiiti (Leeds Rhinos); 13 Louis Anderson (New Zealand Warriors). Subs (all used): 14 Greg Eastwood (Brisbane Broncos); 15 Epalahame Lauaki (New Zealand Warriors); 16 Awen Guttenbeil (Castleford Tigers); 17 Chase Stanley (St George-Illawarra Dragons). **Coach:** Wayne Bennett.
Tries: Lauitiiti (26, 29), Eastwood (40), Anderson (66), Toopi (79); **Goals:** Jones 5/5.
Rugby Leaguer & League Express Men of the Match:
Northern Union: Sam Burgess; *New Zealand All Golds:* David Faiumu.
Penalty count: 6-6; **Half-time:** 5-15; **Referee:** Ashley Klein (Australia); **Attendance:** 5,500 *(at Halliwell Jones Stadium, Warrington).*

was retracing the steps of Dally Messenger one hundred years ago. Messenger was the sole Australian player in the All Golds ranks, and his knowledge gained of the game paid enormous dividends as he played a leading role in the establishment of the Rugby League game in Australia.

The All Golds included nine members of the Kiwi touring team after late call-ups to Shaun Kenny-Dowall and David Faiumu. Of those, fullback Sam Perrett, centre Chase Stanley and Kenny-Dowall had yet to make their Test debuts. To counteract that inexperience at international level coach Wayne Bennett was able to call upon the vastly experienced Ruben Wiki (a world record 55 caps), Stacey Jones (46), former Warrington

Nigel Vagana sent flying by a high Danny Tickle challenge during the Centenary International

centre Nigel Vagana (38) and David Kidwell (24). Jones was playing the final game of his illustrious career.

Tony Smith's selection included just one player - Leeds stand-off Danny McGuire - who had been involved in the previous week's Grand Final. Captained by Adrian Morley, his players had the ideal opportunity to stake their claims for a place in the first Test at Huddersfield the following Saturday. Ben Westwood, so outstanding for Warrington this season, missed the chance to press his Test claims when he was a late withdrawal through illness.

The 1907 scoring system of three points for a try and two points for any goal, including field goals, was adopted for the game. Jones missed with two attempts, which was the only flaw in a fine farewell performance.

It was an authentic international match, full of punishing defence and flair on attack, and it was taken seriously by all the participants, who were clearly proud to take part in such a landmark occasion. The All Golds looked the more cohesive side in the first half, and built a 15-5 interval lead, but they were pushed hard in the second before securing the spoils.

For the Northern Union, McGuire poached two class tries, Morley played a true captain's role with 80 minutes of toil in the engine room, and young Sam Burgess lifted the man of the match award ahead of a number candidates.

Jones was involved in everything for the All Golds, for whom hooker Faiumu was outstanding, with his distribution and control of the ruck, while Ali Lauitiiti scored two tries.

Though McGuire demonstrated his finishing skills to good effect, successfully juggling and catching the ball to complete a flowing move sparked by Terry Newton's slick pass and Burgess's searing break, the All Golds deserved their interval lead.

Lauitiiti showed his power close to the line by beating off the attentions of at least five defenders, and was then on the end of a flowing move involving Thomas Leuluai, Nigel Vagana and David Kidwell. When Greg Eastwood spun over the line just before half-time the All Golds, with the aid of three Jones conversions, held a sizeable advantage.

McGuire's second try was a glorious effort, completing a length-of-the-field counter-attack begun by Kirk Yeaman's break down the left, and Jon Clarke's close-range try from dummy-half restored parity. When Yeaman collected Newton's bullet pass to force his way over in the corner the Northern Union looked the likelier winners.

But Louis Anderson dived over from close range after Michael Platt's try-saving tackle on Tame Tupou, and Clinton Toopi clinched victory in the dying moments from Jones's piercing inside pass.

After the emotional moments before the game, with an impressive haka from the All Golds and Steve Prescott making the kick-off, the occasion was augmented by the memorable events after the final hooter. Wiki lifted the Centenary Shield before Jones was honoured with leading a final haka (with suited members of the Kiwi touring team joining in) before being given a guard of honour as he made his way off a field for a final time. 'I didn't expect anything like that,' Jones said afterwards. 'It's something I shall remember for the rest of my life.'

Northern Union captain Morley was put on report for a 42nd minute hit on All Golds substitute Awen Guttenbeil. He was found to have no case to answer. As was Danny Tickle, also put on report by referee Ashley Klein for his 19th minute challenge on Nigel Vagana, although Tickle hadn't been selected in the Great Britain squad

ANZAC TEST

The Brisbane Broncos' six internationals cocked a collective snoot at their critics as they starred in Australia's comprehensive victory over the Kiwis in the Anzac Test played at the club's home ground in April.

In the lead-up to the Test at the famous Lang Park arena there had been a rash of mutterings about the number of Broncos in the side – especially as the Premiers were languishing near the bottom of the NRL Premiership Ladder, with a solitary victory in their first five matches of the season.

Australia's Willie Mason closes down New Zealand's Benji Marshall during the Anzac Test

But captain Darren Lockyer contested man of the match honours with clubmate Karmichael Hunt. Winger Brent Tate played his best game of the season. Centre Justin Hodges danced as only he can, despite some close-marking by the Kiwis. Prop Petero Civoniceva was his usual reliable self. And Shaun Berrigan provided some spark when he came off the bench.

The Kiwis had none of their Super League stars. They were also missing Ruben Wiki, Stacey Jones and Nigel Vagana, who had all retired from the international ranks, and the injured David Kidwell. The quartet could boast 160 Test caps between them. Their line-up also included three debutants, including fullback Kris Inu, with just one senior game under his belt for Parramatta - a

ANZAC TEST

Friday 20th April 2007

AUSTRALIA 30 NEW ZEALAND 6

AUSTRALIA: 1 Karmichael Hunt (Brisbane Broncos); 2 Matt King (Melbourne Storm); 3 Jamie Lyon (Manly Sea Eagles); 4 Justin Hodges (Brisbane Broncos); 5 Brent Tate (Brisbane Broncos); 6 Darren Lockyer (Brisbane Broncos) (C); 7 Johnathan Thurston (North Queensland Cowboys); 8 Brent Kite (Manly Sea Eagles); 9 Cameron Smith (Melbourne Storm); 10 Petero Civoniceva (Brisbane Broncos); 11 Nathan Hindmarsh (Parramatta Eels); 12 Willie Mason (Bulldogs); 13 Andrew Ryan (Bulldogs). Subs (all used): 14 Luke Bailey (Gold Coast Titans); 15 Shaun Berrigan (Brisbane Broncos); 16 Steve Simpson (Newcastle Knights); 17 Anthony Tupou (Sydney Roosters).
Tries: Hindmarsh (19), King (45), Tate (57), Hunt (75), Lockyer (80);
Goals: Thurston 5/6.
NEW ZEALAND: 1 Kris Inu (Parramatta Eels) (D); 2 Jake Webster (Gold Coast Titans); 3 Iosia Soliola (Sydney Roosters); 4 Simon Mannering (New Zealand Warriors); 5 Manu Vatuvei (New Zealand Warriors); 6 Benji Marshall (Wests Tigers); 7 Ben Roberts (Bulldogs); 8 Nathan Cayless (Parramatta Eels) (C); 9 Dene Halatau (Wests Tigers); 10 Roy Asotasi (South Sydney Rabbitohs); 11 Sonny Bill Williams (Bulldogs); 12 Tony Puletua (Penrith Panthers); 13 David Fa'alogo (South Sydney Rabbitohs). Subs (all used): 14 David Faiumu (North Queensland Cowboys); 15 Sam Rapira (New Zealand Warriors) (D); 16 Greg Eastwood (Brisbane Broncos) (D); 17 Frank Pritchard (Penrith Panthers).
Try: Vatuvei (68); **Goals:** Marshall 1/1.
Rugby Leaguer & League Express Men of the Match:
Australia: Darren Lockyer; *New Zealand:* David Fa'alogo.
Penalty count: 7-7; **Half-time:** 6-0; **Referee:** Steve Ganson (England);
Attendance: 31,241 *(at Suncorp Stadium, Brisbane).*

record in the history of the game.

They were never expected to hold the Australians, but in a gutsy display they were still a part of the equation at half-time. But the Kiwis must have been pleased to find themselves only six points behind considering the huge amount of possession that the Australians had enjoyed.

Willie Mason took a superb inside pass from Lockyer to make a long run. From the next ruck, scrum-half Johnathan Thurston shot the ball quickly to second-rower Nathan Hindmarsh who was over within the blink of an eyelid. And Thurston's conversion attempt was spot on.

Three minutes into the second half, the Kiwis took the ball from ten metres inside their own half to near Australia's line where it was lost by Jake Webster. It proved to be a costly mistake. Within two minutes the play had moved to the other end of the pitch. New Zealand half Ben Roberts dropped a bomb. Australian threequarter Matt King kneed the ball ahead and pounced on it to touch down.

The sad night for the Kiwis continued when Lockyer and Hodges combined to send Tate over in the right corner. Twelve minutes from full-time the Kiwis finally got on the board thanks to a kick along the ground by Kiwi utility Simon Mannering. Manu Vatuvei dived on the ball to score.

Hunt sealed the victory with a try five minutes from full-time. Lockyer, who was magnificent all night, rubbed salt in the wound with his own try with just 23 seconds left on the clock.

CENTENARY TEST

The Kiwis got the worst possible warm-up for their centenary tour of Britain when they suffered a humiliating 58-0 thrashing at the hands of Australia in the New Zealand capital of Wellington. It was a record loss to their Trans-Tasman neighbours.

The Kiwis had no hope after Steve Matai was sent off by English referee Steve Ganson 23 minutes into the game. The Manly centre made a blatant late and high tackle on Mark Gasnier, who was taken from the pitch suffering from concussion and did not return. Matai was later banned for two matches next season for his misdemeanour.

The 11 tries to nil whitewash by the Australians was just the start – as two of the Kiwis left the pitch with injuries that brought an end to their tour aspirations. Winger Luke Covell was substituted after five minutes with a dislocated right elbow and exciting young fullback Kris Inu was replaced after a shoulder charge on Australia's hat-trick hero Greg Inglis went wrong 15 minutes from full-time.

The new-look Kiwis under rookie coach Gary Kemble had gone into the match full of hope, with six players making their Test debuts. But the Australians, with eight newcomers, made them look like amateurs.

The Test was a triumph for the Australian debutants, with Israel Folau (18) touching down twice and Jarryd Hayne (19), Brent Stewart (22) and Greg Bird (23) each snaring a try. Bird was also a stand-out man of the match.

After a week of consistent icy rain, match day dawned fine but cold. But Wellington's

CENTENARY TEST

Sunday 14th October 2007

NEW ZEALAND 0 AUSTRALIA 58

NEW ZEALAND: 1 Kris Inu (Parramatta Eels); 2 Luke Covell (Cronulla Sharks) (D); 3 Steve Matai (Manly Sea Eagles); 4 Paul Whatuira (Wests Tigers); 5 Taniela Tuiaki (Wests Tigers) (D); 6 Ben Roberts (Bulldogs); 7 Jeremy Smith (South Sydney Rabbitohs) (D); 8 Roy Asotasi (South Sydney Rabbitohs) (C); 9 Dene Halatau (Wests Tigers); 10 Fuifui Moimoi (Parramatta Eels) (D); 11 Simon Mannering (New Zealand Warriors); 12 Frank Pritchard (Penrith Panthers); 13 Jeremy Smith (Melbourne Storm) (D). Subs (all used): 14 David Faiumu (North Queensland Cowboys); 15 Shontayne Hape (Bradford Bulls); 16 Sam Rapira (New Zealand Warriors); 17 Jeff Lima (Melbourne Storm) (D). **Dismissal:** Matai (23) – high tackle on Gasnier.
AUSTRALIA: 1 Brett Stewart (Manly Sea Eagles) (D); 2 Israel Folau (Melbourne Storm) (D); 3 Mark Gasnier (St George-Illawarra Dragons); 4 Greg Inglis (Melbourne Storm) (D); 5 Jarryd Hayne (Parramatta Eels) (D); 6 Greg Bird (Cronulla Sharks) (D); 7 Cooper Cronk (Melbourne Storm) (D); 16 Steve Price (New Zealand Warriors); 9 Cameron Smith (Melbourne Storm) (C); 10 Petero Civoniceva (Brisbane Broncos); 11 Nathan Hindmarsh (Parramatta Eels); 12 Ryan Hoffman (Melbourne Storm) (D); 13 Dallas Johnson (Melbourne Storm) (D). Subs (all used): 8 Brent Kite (Manly Sea Eagles); 14 Kurt Gidley (Newcastle Knights) (D); 15 Willie Mason (Bulldogs); 17 Michael Crocker (Melbourne Storm) (D). **Tries:** Folau (14, 31), Price (21), Inglis (28, 47, 65), Hayne (34), Stewart (56), Bird (61), Mason (71), Smith (78).
Goals: Smith 6/10, Gidley 1/1.
Rugby Leaguer & League Express Men of the Match:
New Zealand: Roy Asotasi; *Australia:* Greg Bird.
Penalty count: 7-7; **Half-time:** 0-26; **Referee:** Steve Ganson (England); **Attendance:** 16,681 *(at Westpac Stadium, Wellington).*

Australia debutant Brett Stewart dives over during the Kangaroos' rout of the Kiwis

characteristic wind still swirled around the arena the locals call the 'Cake Tin' making playing conditions difficult.

The Kiwis almost pulled off an immediate try when the ball from the kick-off bounced back off an upright into the hands of Melbourne's Jeremy Smith, who was grassed less than a metre from the tryline by Cooper Cronk and Petero Civoniceva. There was only nine seconds on the clock. It was the only bright spot for the Kiwis all afternoon.

It wasn't long before the Australians started to show their dominance – despite having their youngest backline in the history of Rugby League Tests. NRL Rookie of the Year Folau bullocked his way past half-a-dozen would-be tacklers to score the first try. It was a sensational debut for the Melbourne Storm threequarter who at 18 years and 194 days had become the youngest Australian Test player in history.

From the youngest to the oldest. The 33-year-old prop Steve Price strolled out of weak tackles by Roy Asotasi and Jeff Lima to touch down next to the left-hand upright.

Then came the defining moment of the encounter – Matai's dismissal.

"It's a late hit, mate. It's not acceptable. Off!" said Ganson.

Within the space of six minutes the Australians ran in three tries. Inglis, Clive Churchill Medal winner in the grand final two weeks before, took a wonderful offload from Storm teammate Ryan Hoffman to score out wide on the left flank. Folau was across the stripe for his second try off a superb chip kick from scrum-half Cooper Cronk. And another debutant, Parramatta's Hayne, touched down after some great attacking passes from Cronk, Bird and Kurt Gidley.

It didn't take long for the Aussies to continue their tryfest in the second half. Fullback Stewart spun the ball back to Inglis for his second four-pointer of the match. Cronk and Gidley then combined to send Stewart across the whitewash in the left corner. Price made a strong burst, brushing off a couple of attempted tackles, popped the ball to Nathan Hindmarsh, who in turn swivelled and sent Bird away to score.

And when Kris Inu vainly tried to stop Inglis from scoring his hat-trick, Inu left the pitch with an injured right shoulder. The try was the seventh by Inglis in just six Test appearances.

Willie Mason and Smith grabbed late tries to ensure the slaughter was a record.

● New Zealand scored their first Test win under Gary Kemble in Paris, beating France 22-14 the week after losing the third Test against Great Britain at Wigan. It took late tries from centre Paul Whatuira and Thomas Leuluai to save the troubled Kiwis from their first loss to the Tricolours in 27 years.

With Maxime Grésèque and Eric Anselme starring, France led 6-0 and 8-0 for 24 minutes in the first half and 14-10 for 27 minutes in the second. The under-fire Kemble added: 'A relief? Sure it is. With all we've been through and the work the guys have put in - especially this week and last week - it's thoroughly deserved.'

The introduction of Leuluai to the game proved to be the difference. With eight minutes to go; his pass put Wests Tigers' Whatuira over and Ben Roberts converted from almost in front for 16-14. France had the chance to respond but found themselves too far out to mount a meaningful raid. Leuluai then took a pass a couple of men wide of the ruck and scored, Roberts' conversion completing a deceptive scoreline.

TEST MATCH

Sunday 18th November 2007

FRANCE 14 NEW ZEALAND 22

FRANCE: 1 Thomas Bosc (Catalans Dragons); 2 Justin Murphy (Catalans Dragons); 3 Sebastien Planas (Toulouse Olympique); 4 Sebastien Raguin (Catalans Dragons); 5 Cyril Stacul (Catalans Dragons); 6 Christophe Moly (Carcassonne); 7 Maxime Greseque (Pia); 8 David Ferriol (Catalans Dragons); 9 Julien Rinaldi (Harlequins) (C); 10 Adel Fellous (Catalans Dragons); 11 Cyril Gossard (Catalans Dragons); 12 Eric Anselme (Albi); 13 Laurent Carrasco (Toulouse Olympique). Subs (all used): 14 Jean-Christophe Borlin (St Gaudens); 15 Remi Casty (Catalans Dragons); 16 Teddy Sadaoui (Carcassonne); 17 James Wynne (Lezignan).
Tries: Anselme (1), Stacul (45); **Goals:** Greseque 3/3.
NEW ZEALAND: 1 Sam Perrett (Sydney Roosters); 2 Chase Stanley (St George-Illawarra Dragons); 3 Clinton Toopi (Leeds Rhinos); 4 Paul Whatuira (Wests Tigers); 5 Shaun Kenny-Dowall (Sydney Roosters); 6 Ben Roberts (Bulldogs); 7 Jeremy Smith (South Sydney Rabbitohs); 8 Sam Rapira (New Zealand Warriors); 9 Dene Halatau (Wests Tigers); 10 Roy Asotasi (South Sydney Rabbitohs) (C); 11 Louis Anderson (New Zealand Warriors); 12 Jeremy Smith (Melbourne Storm); 13 Simon Mannering (New Zealand Warriors). Subs (all used): 14 Thomas Leuluai (Wigan Warriors); 15 Jeff Lima (Melbourne Storm); 16 David Faiumu (North Queensland Cowboys); 17 Fuifui Moimoi (Parramatta Eels).
Tries: Anderson (25), Kenny-Dowall (33), Whatuira (73), Leuluai (80); **Goals:** Roberts 3/4.
Rugby Leaguer & League Express Men of the Match:
France: Eric Anselme; *New Zealand:* Roy Asotasi.
Penalty count: 5-7; **Half-time:** 8-10; **Referee:** Ashley Klein (Australia); **Attendance:** 6,781 *(at Stade Jean-Bouin, Paris).*

● Papua New Guinea embarked on a tour of Wales and France in the autumn and went home without a win in their three internationals.

They lost 50-10 to Wales in Bridgend, to France 38-26 in Avignon and 22-16 in Begles, near Bordeaux. They defeated France A 38-12 and a French President's XIII 20-6.

Before their tour, the Kumuls had produced one of their finest efforts since joining the international fraternity in 1974, when they stormed back from a 20-nil deficit at half-time to snatch a 24-all draw with a star-studded Australian Prime Minister's XIII in Port Moresby.

The Australian Prime Minister's XIII defence halts this Papua New Guinea attack

Other Internationals

Locals described the result, in what has become an annual clash, as the greatest for the Kumuls since they surprised the touring British Lions 20-18 in a Test at Goroka in 1990. All but two of the Kumuls were from the local PNG competition.

And also...

● Rugby League is played in Greece for the first time in late October 2006 as the Greeks beat Serbia 44-26.

● Dutch Rugby League announce they are pulling the plug on their international side because of lack of support from the European Federation.

● Souths Logan Magpies edge out Fiji 48-44 in the final of the Orara Valley Axemen Sevens tournament in January.

● Malta Knights produce a record breaking 82-0 scoreline over Japan at the Coffs Harbour International Stadium in January.

● In February, Fiji won the St Mary's international Sevens, beating Wests Tigers 8-4 in the final.

● West Yorkshire Police beat Jamaica 26-12 at the University of West Indies in Kingston in February.

● England win the European Student Championship, defeating Ireland 36-4 at the Halton Stadium in April.

● England win the European Nations under-16 championships held in Belgrade, beating France 14-12 in the final.

● In August, Germany defeat the Czech Republic 44-22.

● Auckland Lions win the last ever Bartercard Cup after 28-4 grand final victory over Harbour League at Mt Smart Stadium in September.

● In October, France beat Scotland 46-16 at Stade Gilbert Brutus. Scotland A also went down to defeat in Perpignan, conceding four late tries to lose 36-12 to France Federale.

PAPUA NEW GUINEA INTERNATIONALS

Sunday 23rd September 2007

PAPUA NEW GUINEA 24 AUSTRALIAN PRIME MINISTER'S XIII 24

PAPUA NEW GUINEA: 1 Menzie Yere (Kokopo Island Gurias); 2 Benjamin John (Port Moresby Bulldogs); 3 Charlie Wabo (Mendi Muruks); 4 Dusty Mockley (Lae Bombers); 5 Eki Ene (Lae Bombers); 6 Francis Ray (Mount Hagen Eagles); 7 George Moni (Mendi Muruks); 8 Gimapau Keimelo (Wri Vele Raiders); 9 Jesse Joe Parker (Port Moresby Bulldogs); 10 Johnson Kuike (Port Moresby Bulldogs); 11 Joseph Omae (Mendi Muruks); 12 Keith Peters (Penrith Panthers); 13 Larsen Marabe (Port Moresby Bulldogs). Subs (all used): 14 Michael Mark (Port Moresby Bulldogs); 15 Tu'u Maori (Cronulla Sharks); 16 Nickson Kolo (Wri Vele Raiders); 17 Nigel Hukula (Goroka Lahanis); 18 Nicko Slain (Goroka Lahanis); 19 Porian Bal (Kundiawa Warriors); 20 Rodney Pora (Kokopo Island Gurias); 21 Paul Aiton (Penrith Panthers).
Tries: Hukula (44), Aiton (52), Parker (56), Yere (72, 78); **Goals:** Keimelo 2/5.
PM XIII: 1 Kurt Gidley (Newcastle Knights); 2 Ben Pomeroy (Cronulla Sharks); 3 Mark Gasnier (St George-Illawarra Dragons) (C); 4 Joel Monaghan (Sydney Roosters); 5 Chris Lawrence (Wests Tigers); 6 Greg Bird (Cronulla Sharks); 7 Scott Prince (Gold Coast Titans); 8 David Shillington (Sydney Roosters); 9 Lincoln Withers (Canberra Raiders); 10 Luke Douglas (Cronulla Sharks); 11 Anthony Tupou (Sydney Roosters); 12 Paul Gallen (Cronulla Sharks); 13 Braith Anasta (Sydney Roosters). Subs (all used): 14 Dean Widders (South Sydney Rabbitohs); 15 Nate Myles (Sydney Roosters); 16 Sam Thaiday (Brisbane Broncos); 17 Brett Delaney (Gold Coast Titans).
Tries: Douglas (4), Monaghan (6), Lawrence (20, 26); **Goals:** Gidley 2/5.
Penalty count: 8-7; **Half-time:** 0-20; **Referee:** Gavin Badger (Australia);
Attendance: 10,500 *(at Lloyd Robson Oval, Port Moresby).*

Sunday 28th October 2007

WALES 50 PAPUA NEW GUINEA 10

WALES: 1 Mark Lennon (Hull Kingston Rovers); 2 Anthony Blackwood (Celtic Crusaders); 3 Luke Dyer (Hull Kingston Rovers); 4 Adam Hughes (Oldham); 5 Dave Halley (Bradford Bulls); 6 Iestyn Harris (Bradford Bulls) (C); 7 Lee Briers (Warrington Wolves); 8 Phil Cushion (Celtic Crusaders); 9 Ian Webster (Widnes Vikings); 10 Gareth Dean (Celtic Crusaders); 11 Matt James (Bradford Bulls); 12 Robert Roberts (Oldham); 13 Phil Joseph (Halifax). Subs (all used): 14 Steve Thomas (Celtic Crusaders); 15 Damian Gibson (Halifax); 16 Sean Penkywicz (Halifax); 17 Jordan James (Widnes Vikings); 18 Aaron Summers (Widnes Vikings); 19 Craig Kopczak (Bradford Bulls); 20 Byron Smith (Rochdale Hornets).
Tries: Joseph (15), Halley (18, 68), Gibson (30, 48), Roberts (54), M James (57), Penkywicz (75), Lennon (78); **Goals:** Harris 5/7, Lennon 1/1, Hughes 1/1.
PAPUA NEW GUINEA: 1 John Wilshere; 2 Tu'u Maori; 3 Gimapau Keimelo; 4 Steve Franciscus; 5 Michael Mark; 6 Jesse Joe Parker; 7 Keith Peters; 8 Nigel Hukula; 9 Paul Aiton; 10 Trevor Exton; 11 George Moni; 12 Joseph Omae; 13 Rod Griffin. Subs (all used): 14 Rodney Pora; 15 James Nightingale; 16 Nickson Kolo; 17 Charlie Wabo; 18 Kevin Prior; 19 Menzie Yere.
Tries: Moni (11), Kolo (65); **Goals:** Wilshere 1/2.
Rugby Leaguer & League Express Men of the Match:
Wales: Iestyn Harris; *Papua New Guinea:* Tu'u Maori.
Penalty count: 9-6; **Half-time:** 16-6; **Referee:** Thierry Alibert (France);
Attendance: 1,456 *(at Brewery Field, Bridgend).*

Saturday 3rd November 2007

FRANCE 38 PAPUA NEW GUINEA 26

FRANCE: 1 Thomas Bosc (Catalans Dragons); 2 Justin Murphy (Catalans Dragons); 3 Sebastien Planas (Toulouse Olympique); 4 Sylvain Houles (Toulouse Olympique); 5 Cyril Stacul (Catalans Dragons); 6 Christophe Moly (Carcassonne); 7 Maxime Greseque (Pia); 8 Remi Casty (Catalans Dragons); 9 Julien Rinaldi (Harlequins) (C); 10 Adel Fellous (Catalans Dragons); 11 Cyril Gossard (Catalans Dragons); 12 Eric Anselme (Albi); 13 Laurent Carrasco (Toulouse Olympique). Subs (all used): 14 David Ferriol (Catalans Dragons); 15 Jean-Christophe Borlin (St Gaudens); 16 Teddy Sadaoui (Carcassonne); 17 James Wynne (Lezignan).
Tries: Murphy (5, 70), Stacul (21, 76), Moly (49, 72), Bosc (56); **Goals:** Greseque 5/8.
PAPUA NEW GUINEA: 1 John Wilshere; 2 Michael Mark; 3 Tu'u Maori; 4 Menzie Yere; 5 George Keppa; 6 Jesse Joe Parker; 7 Benjamin John; 8 Rodney Pora; 9 Charlie Wabo; 10 Kevin Prior; 11 James Nightingale; 12 Nicko Slain; 13 Rod Griffin. Subs (all used): 14 Keith Peters; 15 Paul Aiton; 16 George Moni; 17 Trevor Exton.
Tries: Yere (14, 43), Aiton (33), Parker (41), Moni (79); **Goals:** Wilshere 3/5.
Rugby Leaguer & League Express Men of the Match:
France: Thomas Bosc; *Papua New Guinea:* Paul Aiton.
Penalty count: 7-7; **Half-time:** 10-10; **Referee:** Leon Williamson (New Zealand);
Attendance: 7,248 *(at Parc des Sports, Avignon).*

Saturday 10th November 2007

FRANCE 22 PAPUA NEW GUINEA 16

FRANCE: 1 Thomas Bosc (Catalans Dragons); 2 Justin Murphy (Catalans Dragons); 3 Sebastien Raguin (Catalans Dragons); 4 Sylvain Houles (Toulouse Olympique); 5 Cyril Stacul (Catalans Dragons); 6 Christophe Moly (Carcassonne); 7 Maxime Greseque (Pia); 8 Jean-Christophe Borlin (St Gaudens); 9 Julien Rinaldi (Harlequins) (C); 10 Mathieu Griffi (Catalans Dragons); 11 Cyril Gossard (Catalans Dragons); 12 Eric Anselme (Albi); 13 Laurent Carrasco (Toulouse Olympique). Subs (all used): 14 Adel Fellous (Catalans Dragons); 15 Remi Casty (Catalans Dragons); 16 Teddy Sadaoui (Carcassonne); 17 Gregory Mounis (Catalans Dragons).
Tries: Anselme (17), Stacul (41), Greseque (45, 51); **Goals:** Greseque 3/4.
On report: Casty (28) - high tackle.
PAPUA NEW GUINEA: 1 John Wilshere; 2 Michael Mark; 3 Tu'u Maori; 4 Menzie Yere; 5 George Keppa; 6 Jesse Joe Parker; 7 Keith Peters; 8 Rodney Pora; 9 Paul Aiton; 10 Kevin Prior; 11 James Nightingale; 12 Rod Griffin; 13 Charlie Wabo. Subs (all used): 14 Rodney Pora; 15 Joseph Omae; 16 George Moni; 17 Gimapau Keimelo.
Tries: Hukula (11), Maori (30), Wilshere (55); **Goals:** Wilshere 2/3.
Sin bin: Omae (39) - repeated infringements.
Rugby Leaguer & League Express Men of the Match:
France: Eric Anselme; *Papua New Guinea:* Keith Peters.
Penalty count: 10-10; **Half-time:** 6-12; **Referee:** Leon Williamson (New Zealand);
Attendance: 4,500 *(at Stade Andre Moga, Begles).*

SEASON DOWN UNDER
Joeygate and all that

Melbourne Storm may have stamped themselves as one of the great combinations of the modern era with their one-sided victory over Manly in the NRL grand final. The Australian Test side may have thrashed the Kiwis by a record margin, with exciting winger Israel Folau becoming the youngest Test debutant in the history of the game Down Under. But the story that truly dominated the headlines in 2007 was the retirement and subsequent drugs shame of the great scrum-half Andrew Johns. Caught by police in London with an ecstasy tablet in his possession, he was forced to confess to his fans that throughout his stellar career he had been plagued by depression and had turned to drugs and alcohol in a bid to fight it off.

His cruel season began soon after the opening whistle in Newcastle's first round clash with the Bulldogs. Kiwi Test star Sonny Bill Williams knocked Johns unconscious with a high tackle that smashed into his chin just 3min 23sec into the encounter. Williams was sent off and suspended for two weeks.

Johns came back for Newcastle's loss to Canberra three weeks later and suffered a neck injury. Scans revealed no problems from that injury. But the spinal specialists found a second problem. A bulging disc was pressing against his spinal cord. A blow to the neck could have severed the cord and left Johns a quadriplegic.

'I feel like I dodged a bullet,' Joey said as he announced his retirement. An avalanche of praise poured in. None was more succinct than that of coaching guru Wayne Bennett: 'He set the place alight because of his charisma and his great love of the game.'

Johns' long-time Newcastle and Test teammate Danny Buderus explained about a Knights team meeting at which the news had been broken: 'I told them [the Newcastle players] we've played with the best player that we'll probably ever get to play with – the best player of several generations.'

In late August the Johns legend was shattered. He was pulled aside and searched by police at Kings Cross underground station in London. They discovered an ecstasy pill in his pocket. At first Johns claimed a stranger had pushed the pill into his pocket at a nearby nightclub. But back in Australia he came clean. He admitted taking various drugs for years – but somehow managing to avoid detection by NRL drug testers.

'I took them throughout my career, mainly in the off-season,' Johns admitted. 'At times it was like playing Russian roulette when I took them during the season.' He also admitted he suffered from depression but said this was not an excuse. 'Only people close to me know of my volatile mood swings,' he said.

After his very public confession Johns took a low profile. He was missing from the spotlight at the Dally M Awards ceremony, where he had been due to figure prominently, and at the grand final, where he would normally have been given a special career farewell.

But his absence was soon forgotten after a packed Telstra Stadium witnessed one of the finest displays of recent years.

MELBOURNE STORM (Premiers)

If one word could describe Melbourne's 34-8 grand final success over the Manly Sea Eagles it was 'unbelievable'.

'How do I feel? Unbelievable,' said the Storm's captain Cameron Smith after the win. 'Unbelievable – the best feeling ever,' said fullback Billy Slater. 'I'm in shock. It's unbelievable,' said Matt King in his last Australian appearance before joining the Warrington Wolves in Super League. 'A grand final in my first year…it's unbelievable,' said rookie Folau. It was a reward for a season of hard work by the Storm after tasting disappointment 12 months earlier when beaten in the grand final by the Brisbane Broncos.

There was no indication in the first half of how one-sided the final score would be, with Melbourne going to the break with just a 10-4 lead. The Storm were first on the scoreboard after 12 minutes when three decoy runners fooled the Manly defence and some crisp passing saw the ball reach left-winger Anthony Quinn. 'Zorba' danced across the stripe and improved the position to make 2007 Rugby League World Golden Boot winner Cameron Smith's conversion a simple matter.

Some 18 minutes before half-time, after a sensational run from Slater, a kick sat up behind the Manly line, but the Sea Eagles were saved when fullback Brett Stewart swept the ball away over the dead-ball line. It didn't matter. Moments later Greg Inglis pushed aside both Anthony Watmough and Matt Orford to score close to the right upright. Right on half-time Manly finally broke through when Kiwi international centre Steve Matai stepped around Folau and crashed across the whitewash.

The second half started sensationally when Melbourne substitute Michael Crocker appeared to hit Brett Stewart with a forearm. It was defining moment of the encounter. A groggy Stewart was assisted from the pitch and the Sea Eagles seemed to capitulate.

Cameron Smith missed what should have been a simple attempt at a penalty goal for Melbourne. It mattered not. From the restart Crocker burst across the stripe to score. Then it was a case of the Storm players lining up looking for tries. King barrelled over the top of Jamie Lyon to score his 20th try of the season. Then Inglis gave a 'don't argue' fend to Michael Robertson, switched to fullback to cover for the injured Stewart, and extended the lead to 22-4. It would have been a lot more if Cameron Smith had been on target with his goal-kicking (He eventually finished with three goals from eight attempts).

Another Warrington signing, winger Chris Hicks, put a bit of respectability into the score, with a try for Manly 13 minutes from full-time as the match degenerated into a scrappy, fumbling affair. Melbourne forward Clint Newton, unwanted by coach Brian Smith at Newcastle but soon to sign for Hull KR, and winger Quinn scored late tries to put the icing on the cake.

Inglis was a stand-out man of the match. The Clive Churchill Medal hung around his neck wherever he went in the next few days. The pride was obvious. It came as no surprise that no less than eight Melbourne Storm players were involved in the Centenary Test between Australia and New Zealand two weeks later. Cameron Smith was Australia's captain. And among his Test teammates were winger Folau, stand-off (moved to centre for the Test) Inglis, scrum-half Cooper Cronk and back-rowers Dallas Johnson and Ryan Hoffman. King would also have been with them had he not been ineligible because of his signing to play Super League. Loose forward Jeremy Smith and substitute Jeff Lima were in the Kiwis line-up.

The Storm deserved their success through the consistent form they displayed all season. They lost only three matches, all away from home (beaten 30-12 by Wests Tigers, 13-12 by Manly and 26-16 by Sydney Roosters). In the final table after the season proper they were six points clear of their nearest rivals Manly and 12 points ahead of the third-placed Cowboys. And, in their three wins during the play-offs, Melbourne scored 100 points and conceded just 18. Craig Bellamy was justifiably the Dally M Coach of the Year.

MANLY SEA EAGLES (2nd)

It was the best season for the Sea Eagles since their return to the Premiership race in 2003 after the failure of the ill-conceived merger with North Sydney to form the Northern Eagles. Their attacking and defensive records were second only to those of Melbourne. It was the latter that won them so many of their matches, conceding an average of just 16 points per game. However, the Sea Eagles saved their worst performance for the grand final.

There were plenty of positives that will carry over into 2008. Fullback Brent Stewart continued his freakish tryscoring – with an incredible career strike-rate of almost one per match at Brookvale (40 tries in 42 appearances at the Sea Eagles' home ground).

Evergreen utility Steve Menzies continued to rewrite the record books. He had now scored 85 tries at Brookvale Oval, the most by any player at a single venue in the history of the Australian game. He took his Manly club record to 138 tries, which was also a record for any forward in the Premiership.

NORTH QUEENSLAND COWBOYS (3rd)

Critics described the Cowboys as a two-man team. Unfair? Maybe, but there were so many matches in which either halfback Johnathan Thurston or fullback Matt Bowen or both, pulled off a late win. And when either or both were missing the Cowboys usually struggled.

Thurston won his second Dally M Medal in three seasons as NRL Player of the Year. Yet he played for most of the year carrying injured shoulders and once the Cowboys' season finished he went under the surgeon's knife. The gifted talents of Bowen were on display every time he played. His 22 tries were the best of any NRL player.

The thing that really let the Cowboys down was their awful defence. They conceded 618 points in their 24 games during the home-and-away season (an average of 26). Only the Canberra Raiders (652) and Newcastle Knights (708) had worse defensive records.

PARRAMATTA EELS (4th)

It was another disappointing season for the Eels. For the sixth time in the past decade they reached at least the penultimate week and fell. But this time they ran up against the great Melbourne combination in the preliminary final, going down 26-10.

But there was plenty for new coach Michael Hagan to smile about, especially the emergence of several players as internationals stars. Teenage winger Jarryd Hayne, the 2006 Dally M Rookie of the Year, went from strength to strength. He was rewarded with a green and gold shirt in the Centenary Test against the Kiwis in October. Junior Kiwi utility star Kris Inu made his first-grade debut early in the season and after just one match in the senior ranks was chosen for the Anzac Test against Australia. He took over as first-choice goalkicker for Parramatta after a season-ending injury to Luke Burt and booted 37 at a success rate of more than 82 per cent. Nathan Hindmarsh continued to amaze. His 955 tackles were made at an average of 43.5 per appearance. Statistics vary from organisation to organisation. But against the Storm at 'The Graveyard' the Parramatta club attributed an incredible 75 tackles to Hindmarsh.

NEW ZEALAND WARRIORS (5th)

In 2006 the Warriors missed out on the play-offs only because they were penalised four competition points for a salary cap breach the previous year. This season they made amends. Inspired by consistently fine displays from skipper Steve Price, they finished in fourth spot on the table but were bundled out after successive losses in the play-offs (to the Eels and the Cowboys).

For his efforts Price received two gongs at the annual Dally M Awards – as Prop of the Year and Captain of the Year. And he found himself back in the Australian Test side and was seconded into the New Zealand All Golds side to play the Centenary International against the Northern Union at Warrington.

Young forwards such as Sam Rapira and Epalahame Lauaki learned a lot from Price and the most-capped player in history, Ruben Wiki. Both Rapira and Lauaki made their Test debuts. Stand-off Michael Witt, who took over the goalkicking duties midway through the season raised the flags 62 times. His success rate was an amazing 92 per cent.

BULLDOGS (6th)

With a side containing nine Test players the Bulldogs were certainly one of the underachievers of 2007. They made more line breaks than any other club and only the two grand final sides, Melbourne and Manly, scored more tries. But when the chips were down the Bulldogs could do no better than sixth.

They lost a narrow encounter to the Cowboys in their first game in the play-offs but then offered little more than a whimper when Parramatta ended their season. And with Willie Mason gone and no big-name signings it looked likely to be more of the same in 2008.

During the season Hazem El Masri became the first Bulldog to amass more than 2000 points in Premiership matches. His tally of 210 points was the best of any NRL player in 2007. His career total of 2,040 makes him the third highest pointscorer in history and, barring injury, he should overtake Jason Taylor (2107) and Andrew Johns (2170) in 2008.

SOUTH SYDNEY RABBITOHS (7th)

The purchase of Souths by Hollywood superstar Russell Crowe and millionaire businessman Peter Holmes a Court seemed to be bearing fruit. For the first time since 1989 (when the Rabbitohs were Minor Premiers) they didn't lose more than they won. And they made the play-offs for the first time since '89 although they were quickly bundled out by Manly.

Defence was the key to Souths' good season. The Rabbitohs missed fewer tackles than any of the Premiership teams – just under 27 per game. They conceded 70 tries. Only the two grand final teams, Manly (62) and Melbourne (47) had fewer scored against them. Their co-captains Roy Asotasi and Peter Cusack led by example, Asotasi taking over the New Zealand Test captaincy.

BRISBANE BRONCOS (8th)

What a come-down for the 2007 Premiers. The Broncos just scraped into the finals, only to suffer a humiliating 40-nil defeat at the hands of their eventual successors, Melbourne Storm.

After occupying the cellar with eight losses in their first 12 outings, Brisbane suddenly clicked. Five straight victories had them looking like the side from the previous season.

Then came one disaster after another as their stars fell like nine-pins, many to season-ending injuries – they included Test stars Darren Lockyer, Brent Tate, Shaun Berrigan and Karmichael Hunt.

Brisbane set a couple records. When the Broncos beat Newcastle 71-6 it was the biggest win in their history. But the 68-22 thrashing by the Eels in the final round was also their biggest defeat.

The Broncos were now in a rebuilding mode having lost five Test players for 2008 – Tate (to the New Zealand Warriors), Berrigan (Hull FC), Dane Carlaw (Catalans Dragons), Petero Civoniceva (Penrith Panthers) and Brad Thorn (rugby union).

WESTS TIGERS (9th)

The 'golden point' rule cost the Tigers a place in the finals. Had each of their matches that went to extra time been counted as a draw, they would have edged out the Broncos. But in the end Wests didn't deserve to be there.

With five rounds remaining they looked certainties to make the play-offs after humiliating North Queensland 54-10 at Leichhardt Oval and with each of their remaining five opponents sitting below them on the NRL Ladder. But they managed to win just one, against Cronulla, in extra time.

The Tigers were hardly helped by injuries to key players Brett Hodgson (who managed just 15 appearances) and Benji Marshall (13 games). The consistent hooker Robbie Farah, who narrowly missed out on the Dally M Medal as NRL Player of the Year, also played for the final month with injections killing the pain of a hip injury.

On the positive side Paul Whatuira, Taniela Tuiaki and Dene Halatau played Tests for the Kiwis. And young Junior Kangaroo Chris Lawrence continued his great form. He finished the season with 16 tries in 18 appearances for Wests.

SYDNEY ROOSTERS (10th)

Could the Roosters be at the dawn of a new era? The Freddy Fittler era? The former Test captain and Roosters' favourite son, stepped into the breach in mid-season when coach Chris Anderson quit for health reasons. A 56-0 thrashing by Manly had been the final straw. The Roosters had lost their first five matches and managed only five wins in their next 11.

The transformation was instantaneous, with the Roosters unbeaten in their first five matches under the tutelage of Fittler. But they couldn't go on with it. The absence of key players had played a part in the earlier slump, with 2005 Rugby League World Golden Boot winner Anthony Minichiello and Queensland Origin prop Nate Myles both missing.

But the future looks promising with the arrival of international prop Mark 'The Ogre' O'Meley from the Bulldogs and talented young hooker-cum-half James Aubusson from Melbourne.

CRONULLA SHARKS (11th)

If there was an unlucky side in 2007 it would have to have been Cronulla. The Sharks had the fifth best points-difference of the 16 Premiership sides, yet finished well down the ladder. Statistics show that seven of their 14 losses were by two points or less. Had they won those games they would have been in third spot on the opening weekend of the finals. Instead, their long Premiership drought continued – not having won the ultimate prize in the 41 years since they entered the big league back in 1967.

It didn't help that injuries kept their two halves, Brett Kimmorley and Adam Dykes, to just 13 matches each and in-form fullback Brett Kearney to only eight.

Stand-off Greg Bird and loose forward Paul Gallen were rewarded for their consistent form with spots in the Australian side for the Centenary Test in October, while Luke Covell played in the same match for New Zealand.

GOLD COAST TITANS (12th)

The new side on the Gold Coast, the Titans may have finished well down the ladder, but they showed enough to be seen as a future force, especially when they move into their new state-of-the-arts stadium Skilled Park at the start of the 2008 season.

Such was the local support that on seven occasions in 2007 they played in front of a virtual full house of around 18,000 at Carrara Stadium. And their two home games taken north to Brisbane's Suncorp Stadium drew attendances of 42,030 (versus Dragons) and 47,686 (Broncos). Indeed, the Titans average home crowd of 21,489 was second only to Brisbane's 32,868.

The importance of the home support was clearly evident. The Titans won eight of their 12 home games (the third best of any NRL side) but only two of their 12 away clashes (the worst record).

Critical to their failure to make the finals after being in fourth place on the ladder midway through the season, were injuries at vital times to internationals Scott Prince and Mat Rogers and consistent forward Anthony Laffranchi.

ST GEORGE-ILLAWARRA DRAGONS (13th)

Yet another season of unfulfilled hopes for the Dragons and coach Nathan Brown. Granted, they hoped for a lot from Mark Gasnier – and paid a lot of money to stop him from defecting to 'The Dark Side'. And when he went down in what appeared to be a season-ending injury in the pre-season Charity Shield friendly, it was a massive blow. He did make it back, but only for six appearances.

They also lost international prop Jason Ryles and Origin utility Ben Hornby at crucial stages and forward Dean Young for all but three matches. When half Jamie Soward arrived from the Roosters mid-season (and kicked a club record of nine goals against the Warriors) there was a mini-revival. But by then no one really believed they would challenge the top sides.

CANBERRA RAIDERS (14th)

Before a tackle was made in anger, critics had predicted the Raiders would finish with the wooden spoon. And they went close – just two competition points above Penrith.

Their unfashionable line-up had plenty of heart. But the ability wasn't there and when the inevitable injuries occurred there weren't sufficient replacements of first-grade standard. The six-week absence of playmaker Todd Carney after a driving incident involving the police didn't help either.

But the major problem was winning away from home. The Raiders won only twice in their 12 appearances on the road. And away from Canberra they haemorrhaged points – an average of 35 per match.

NEWCASTLE KNIGHTS (15th)

The Andrew Johns saga was not the only setback in Newcastle during the 2007 season. The club imploded from within as new coach Brian Smith began a wholesale clean-out of players, apparently acting on the orders of the Knights' board. And the internal rumblings spilled over onto the pitch, with only a surprise victory over Wests Tigers in the final round saving the Knights from their second straight wooden spoon.

Local boy made good Clint Newton left to join the Melbourne Storm midseason – and finished with a grand final winner's ring. Adam Woolnough and Brad Tighe agreed to join the Panthers in 2008 and Josh Perry put his signature to a Manly contract.

The worst came in Round 11 when the Knights were humiliated by a record score of 71-6 by Brisbane. And both the Warriors and Sea Eagles posted half-centuries against them.

PENRITH PANTHERS (16th)

Former Bradford Bulls coach Matt Elliott came up against a brick wall when he tried to change the 'laissez faire' attitude of players at his new club Penrith at the start of the season. Eventually midway through the season he had to go back to square one – and the Panthers paid the price by finishing stone motherless last.

In the meantime, the exciting half Peter Wallace was lost to the Broncos and former Test prop Joel Clinton followed him to Brisbane. Ironically, Test front-rower Petero Civoniceva switched to Penrith for 2008 because he could not be accommodated under the Broncos' salary cap and was expected to be the Panthers' new captain.

Despite the awful season Elliott must be feeling optimistic about the future. He unearthed a couple of super talents in 19-year-old threequarter Michael Jennings and fullback Jarrod Sammut, just one year older.

NRL SCOREBOARD

FINAL NRL PREMIERSHIP TABLE

	P	W	L	D	B	F	A	Pts
Melbourne Storm	24	21	3	0	1	627	277	44
Manly Sea Eagles	24	18	6	0	1	597	377	38
North Queensland Cowboys	24	15	9	0	1	547	618	32
New Zealand Warriors	24	13	10	1	1	593	434	29
Parramatta Eels	24	13	11	0	1	573	481	28
Bulldogs	24	12	12	0	1	575	528	26
South Sydney Rabbitohs	24	12	12	0	1	408	399	26
Brisbane Broncos	24	11	13	0	1	511	476	24
Wests Tigers	24	11	13	0	1	541	561	24
Sydney Roosters	24	10	13	1	1	445	610	23
Cronulla Sharks	24	10	14	0	1	463	403	22
Gold Coast Titans	24	10	14	0	1	409	559	22
St George-Illawarra Dragons	24	9	15	0	1	431	561	20
Canberra Raiders	24	9	15	0	1	522	652	20
Newcastle Knights	24	9	15	0	1	418	708	20
Penrith Panthers	24	8	16	0	1	539	607	18

QUALIFYING FINALS

Friday 7th September 2007

NEW ZEALAND WARRIORS 10 ....**PARRAMATTA EELS 12**
Warriors: Tries: Byrne (44), Witt (77, pen); Goals: Witt 1/2
Eels: Tries: Mateo (63), Hayne (70); Goals: Inu 2/2
Half-time: 0-0; Referee: Tony Archer; Attendance: 28,742

Saturday 8th September 2007

MANLY SEA EAGLES 30 ....**SOUTH SYDNEY RABBITOHS 6**
Sea Eagles: Tries: Menzies (16, 78), Watmough (50), B Stewart (60, 68); Goals: Orford 5/5
Rabbitohs: Try: Mellor (42); Goals: Williams 1/2
Half-time: 6-2; Referee: Shayne Hayne; Attendance: 19,785

NORTH QUEENSLAND COWBOYS 20 ....**BULLDOGS 18**
Cowboys: Tries: Thurston (10, 50), Bowman (18); Goals: Thurston 4/4
Bulldogs: Tries: Millard (22), Tonga (28), Patten (55); Goals: El Masri 3/4
Half-time: 14-14; Referee: Paul Simpkins; Attendance: 20,004

Sunday 9th September 2007

MELBOURNE STORM 40 ....**BRISBANE BRONCOS 0**
Storm: Tries: Quinn (5), Turner (14, 25, 40), C Smith (31), Geyer (34), Slater (57), King (72); Goals: C Smith 3/7, Folau 1/2
Half-time: 28-0; Referee: Steve Clark; Attendance: 15,522

SEMI-FINALS

Saturday 15th September 2007

BULLDOGS 6 ....**PARRAMATTA EELS 25**
Bulldogs: Try: Utai (4); Goals: El Masri 1/1
Eels: Tries: Riddell (19), Grothe (34), Tahu (73), Hayne (80); Goals: Inu 4/4; Field goal: Finch (51)
Half-time: 6-12; Referee: Shayne Hayne; Attendance: 50,621

Sunday 16th September 2007

NORTH QUEENSLAND COWBOYS 49 ......**NEW ZEALAND WARRIORS 12**
Cowboys: Tries: Henry (12), Farrar (21, 73), Williams (37), Graham (48), Bowen (61), Jason Smith (68), Cashmere (77); Goals: Thurston 7/7, Bowman 1/1; Field goal: Bowen (59)
Warriors: Tries: Crockett (5), Martin (15); Goals: Witt 2/2
Half-time: 18-12; Referee: Tony Archer; Attendance: 21,847

PRELIMINARY FINALS

Saturday 22nd September 2007

MANLY SEA EAGLES 28 ....**NORTH QUEENSLAND COWBOYS 6**
Sea Eagles: Tries: B Stewart (29), Watmough (43), Bell (52), Lyon (71), Williamson (74); Goals: Orford 4/7
Cowboys: Try: Lillyman (40); Goals: Thurston 1/1
Half-time: 6-6; Referee: Paul Simpkins; Attendance: 32,611 (at Sydney Football Stadium)

Sunday 23rd September 2007

MELBOURNE STORM 26 ....**PARRAMATTA EELS 10**
Storm: Tries: Turner (27), Cronk (31), King (53, 79); Goals: C Smith 5/6
Eels: Tries: Grothe (10), Reddy (42); Goals: Inu 1/2
Half-time: 10-4; Referee: Tony Archer; Attendance: 33,477 (at Telstra Dome, Melbourne)

GRAND FINAL

Sunday 30th September 2007

MANLY SEA EAGLES 8 MELBOURNE STORM 34

SEA EAGLES: 1 Brett Stewart; 2 Michael Robertson; 3 Steve Bell; 4 Steve Matai; 5 Chris Hicks; 6 Jamie Lyon; 7 Matt Orford (C); 8 Jason King; 9 Michael Monaghan; 10 Brent Kite; 11 Anthony Watmough; 12 Glenn Stewart; 13 Luke Williamson. Subs (all used): 16 Mark Bryant; 17 Steve Menzies; 19 Jack Afamasaga; 20 Adam Cuthbertson.
Tries: Matai (39), Hicks (67); **Goals:** Orford 0/2.
STORM: 1 Billy Slater; 2 Steve Turner; 3 Matt King; 4 Israel Folau; 5 Anthony Quinn; 6 Greg Inglis; 7 Cooper Cronk; 8 Ben Cross; 9 Cameron Smith (C); 10 Brett White; 11 Clint Newton; 12 Ryan Hoffman; 13 Dallas Johnson. Subs (all used): 14 Jeremy Smith; 15 Matt Geyer; 16 Michael Crocker; 17 Jeff Lima.
Tries: Quinn (12, 76), Inglis (23), Crocker (45), King (53), Inglis (55), Newton (72); **Goals:** C Smith 3/8.
Rugby Leaguer & League Express Men of the Match:
Sea Eagles: Jamie Lyon; *Storm:* Greg Inglis.
Half-time: 4-10; **Referee:** Tony Archer;
Attendance: 81,392 *(at Telstra Stadium, Sydney).*
Clive Churchill Medal: Greg Inglis (Melbourne Storm)

TOP POINTSCORERS

	T	G	FG	Pts
Hazem El Masri (Bulldogs)	10	85	0	210
Johnathan Thurston (North Queensland Cowboys)	10	78	0	196
Cameron Smith (Melbourne Storm)	4	88	0	192
Luke Covell (Cronulla Sharks)	10	68	0	176
Luke Burt (Parramatta Eels)	9	59	0	154

TOP TRYSCORERS

Matt Bowen (North Queensland Cowboys)	22
Israel Folau (Melbourne Storm)	21
Matt King (Melbourne Storm)	20
Brett Stewart (Manly Sea Eagles)	19
Ashley Graham (North Queensland Cowboys)	18

MINOR GRADES - GRAND FINALS

NSW PREMIER LEAGUE

NORTH SYDNEY BEARS 15 ....**PARRAMATTA EELS 20**
Bears: Tries: Gordon (4), Boston (47), Simmonds (64); Goals: Williams 1/4; Field goal: Williams (77)
Eels: Tries: Horo (8), I Hauraki (35), Reddy (69), W Hauaki (80); Goals: Williams 1/3, Wood 1/1
Half-time: 4-10; Referee: Jared Maxwell

JERSEY FLEGG TROPHY *(Under-20s)*

PARRAMATTA EELS 14 ....**PENRITH PANTHERS 19**
Eels: Tries: Wright (16), Russ (23), Hunt (42); Goals: Hodkinson 1/3
Panthers: Tries: Graham (20), McKendry (32), Sammut (64); Goals: Sammut 3/3; Field goal: Sammut (70)
Half-time: 10-12; Referee: Gerard Sutton

DALLY M AWARDS

Dally M Medal (Player of the Year):
Johnathan Thurston (North Queensland Cowboys)
Provan-Summons Medal (Fans Choice):
Nathan Hindmarsh (Parramatta Eels)
Coach of the Year: Craig Bellamy (Melbourne Storm)
Captain of the Year: Steve Price (New Zealand Warriors)
Rookie of the Year: Israel Folau (Melbourne Storm)
Representative Player of the Year: Cameron Smith (Melbourne Storm)

Fullback: Matt Bowen (North Queensland Cowboys)
Wing: Jarryd Hayne (Parramatta Eels)
Centre: Justin Hodges (Brisbane Broncos)
Stand-off: Darren Lockyer (Brisbane Broncos)
Scrum half: Johnathan Thurston (North Queensland Cowboys)
Prop: Steve Price (New Zealand Warriors)
Hooker: Robbie Farah (Wests Tigers)
Second row: Anthony Watmough (Manly Sea Eagles)
Loose forward: Dallas Johnson (Melbourne Storm)

HALL OF FAME *(2007 inductees)*

Pre-World War II era: Arthur 'Pony' Halloway (Test career: 1908-19); Sid 'Joe' Pearce (1932-37) and Tom Gorman (1924-30).

Post-World War II era: Harry Wells (1952-60), Keith Barnes (1959-66) and Mick Cronin (1973-82).

STATE OF ORIGIN

Queensland won the State of Origin series for the second straight year – and in doing so put paid to the so-called Homebush hoodoo. After 11 previous visits to Sydney's Olympic stadium at Homebush without a win, the Queensland side finally posted a victory. In the second Origin encounter they posted a 10-6 victory at Telstra Stadium to wrap up the series after winning the first clash at Lang Park.

New South Wales regained some pride by winning Origin III, but coach Graham Murray saw the writing on the wall and announced he would not be seeking the post in 2008. Instead the Dally M Coach of the Year, Melbourne Storm mentor Craig Bellamy will have hold of the reins.

ORIGIN I

The foundation for victory in the first Origin encounter was laid by two of the oldest players on the pitch. Steve Price, 33 years young, and his fellow prop Petero Civoniceva, two years his junior, ran rampant through the NSW pack as the Maroons overcame an 18-6 deficit at the break, to run in 19 unanswered points in the second half for a 25-18 victory. It was Queensland's biggest second-half haul in the history of the clashes.

Price made 24 tackles and 15 runs to net a total of 225 metres. Civoniceva finished with 32 tackles and 190 metres from 22 hit-ups. Their 415 metres was more than the combined total progress made by the entire NSW pack. It was a fairly even first half despite the big difference on the scoreboard. Three minutes into the game, Queensland winger Greg Inglis leaped high to take a cross-pitch bomb and touch down without a hand being placed on him. Johnathan Thurston's successful conversion from wide out on the left flank had the Maroons ahead 6-nil. But the visitors struck back. Stand-off Braith Anasta made a vital break and a trailing Nathan Hindmarsh forced his way across the stripe.

Some 18 minutes into the game, Queensland centre Steve Bell lost the ball when tackled as he crossed the tryline. Within two tackles Matt Cooper was in to score at the other end of the pitch. Jamie Lyon's conversion from near the sideline put the Blues ahead 12-6. With four minutes remaining in the half, Lyon stretched the lead with a penalty goal after Thurston was punished for obstruction.

A Queensland mistake right on the stroke of half-time handed the Blues another try. Tri-Nations winger Brent Tate put in an awful kick on the halfway line. It rebounded off the legs of Origin debutant Jarryd Hayne. He paused for a moment, picked up the ball and headed off down the pitch. As the defence came at him he kicked ahead. Hayne won the race for the ball and sent New South Wales to the interval with a handy 14-point lead.

The Maroons lifted in the second stanza. Captain Darren Lockyer sent a perfect pass to fullback Karmichael Hunt, who had chimed into the backline to make an extra man, to give Inglis his second try of the night (and his third in just two Origin appearances). And Price ran off a Thurston inside pass to score and make up for his disappointment of the first half. Thurston converted to level the scores at 18-all.

Then first-half hero Hayne made a terrible mistake. Chasing a kick near his own line he tried to throw a pass to Anthony Minichiello while lying on his stomach. The NSW fullback was caught on the wrong foot and Lockyer was on the spot to take the loose ball and score the simplest of tries. With 11 minutes left on the clock, Thurston snapped a field goal to give Queensland a seven-point buffer.

ORIGIN II

There was to be no compromise at Telstra Stadium as the Maroons wrapped up the series. 'At the end of the day, it came down to our guts and our defence,' Queensland captain Darren Lockyer said. 'It's just a great feeling. To go back-to-back [in series wins] is hard to do. I feel really proud.'

The Homebush encounter was a game for the purists with both sides stretching the rules. But the close scores kept everyone on the edges of their seats until Greg Inglis defused a bomb behind the Queensland line as the final siren sounded and handed the Maroons victory.

Like so many times in the past it was the incredible Queensland spirit that earned them victory. Eight minutes into the proceedings the Blues back-rower Steve Simpson made a superb break, only to be grassed a metre or so from the tryline. Debutant fullback Brett Stewart, only drafted into the side hours before the match to replace the injured Anthony Minichiello, jumped into dummy-half and dived his way past his opposite number, Karmichael Hunt, so score. Jamie Lyon's conversion had New South Wales ahead 6-nil.

That was as good as it got for the Blues. The momentum changed as the Queenslanders got more possession and with 20 minutes on the clock Cameron Smith made a dart from dummy-half before sending a low pass under the arms of would-be defenders for an unmarked Inglis on the left wing to touch down. This sent the two sides to the break locked at 6-all.

Shayne Hayne took a leaf out of the Bill Harrigan refereeing book – with the first penalty not coming until 50 minutes into the game. Most indiscretions went unchallenged by Hayne.

But midway through the half NSW substitute Luke Bailey gave away a stupid penalty by grabbing the leg of Steve Price to put him on his backside as the Queensland prop was about to play the ball. Bailey claimed Price had faked the fall. His pleas fell on deaf ears.

With field position the Queensland threequarter Steve Bell was able to pounce on a kick from Thurston to score and put his side ahead 10-6. It was a controversial try as the first pass in the move, from Carl Webb to Price, looked blatantly forward. Whatever the legality of the try, it swung the pendulum Queensland's way.

The Queensland pack laid the foundation for success, with none better than hooker Cameron Smith.

ORIGIN III

New South Wales restored some pride with a thrilling 18-4 victory in the final encounter – thus avoiding a whitewash. The result of the match hung in the balance until the Blues managed two tries in the final eight minutes against a side whose substitute bench had been decimated by injuries, and with those players still standing battling fatigue.

Having lost interchange forward Neville Costigan (with a broken hand) after a training mishap on the eve of Origin III, the Maroons then lost loose forward Dallas Johnson with concussion and internationals Brent Tate and Greg Inglis with serious knee problems. The Tate injury brought about an end to his season.

Johnson was replaced 20 seconds after kick-off. He suffered concussion in the first play of the evening after his head came into contact with teammate Tonie Carroll in a tackle. Incredibly Johnson returned to the fray five minutes into the second half, but then Nate Myles failed to finish the match after suffering a shoulder injury.

There was a surfeit of early unforced errors from both sides before the Blues eventually got a break. Centre Matt Cooper slipped a crisp pass to young winger Jarryd Hayne who danced past Justin Hodges before pushing off attempted tackles by Steve Price and Karmichael Hunt to score. Hazem El Masri's conversion from the sideline had the visitors in front 6-0.

But as Inglis left the pitch with an injured right knee, the Queenslanders struck back. A long pass from Cameron Smith found Hunt who quickly put Hodges in the clear and across the stripe for the Maroons to trail 4-6 at half-time.

Carl Webb and Cameron Smith celebrate Queensland's State of Origin win

Trysaving tackles stopped what had looked like two certain NSW tries to Matt Cooper. But, eventually, the lack of players on the bench to give the hard-tackling forwards a rest took its toll on the Queenslanders.

The mind was strong but the body was unable to react. With eight minutes remaining Warrington-bound Matt King was over. And El Masri's fine conversion gave the Blues an eight-point buffer.

Almost from the restart the result was sealed. Loose forward Paul Gallen, trapped on the Queensland tryline, managed to get away a freak pass to El Masri who scored. The Lebanese-born winger had waited a long time to make his Origin debut at the ripe old age of 31. But he certainly did it in style.

Gallen and Greg Bird, the Cronulla pair dubbed 'The Bash Brothers', played a major role in the NSW success, putting some 'mongrel' back into the Blues' ranks. Bird thoroughly deserved his man of the match award – although if the Queenslanders had won, the accolade would have undoubtedly gone to hooker Cameron Smith, who was rewarded with the Wally Lewis Medal as Man of the Series.

144

ORIGIN I

Wednesday 23rd May 2007

QUEENSLAND 25 NEW SOUTH WALES 18

QUEENSLAND: 1 Karmichael Hunt (Brisbane Broncos); 2 Brent Tate (Brisbane Broncos); 3 Steve Bell (Manly Sea Eagles); 4 Justin Hodges (Brisbane Broncos); 5 Greg Inglis (Melbourne Storm); 6 Darren Lockyer (Brisbane Broncos) (C); 7 Johnathan Thurston (North Queensland Cowboys); 8 Steve Price (New Zealand Warriors); 9 Cameron Smith (Melbourne Storm); 10 Petero Civoniceva (Brisbane Broncos); 11 Tonie Carroll (Brisbane Broncos); 16 Nate Myles (Sydney Roosters); 13 Dallas Johnson (Melbourne Storm). Subs (all used): 14 Shaun Berrigan (Brisbane Broncos); 15 Jacob Lillyman (North Queensland Cowboys); 17 Neville Costigan (Canberra Raiders); 18 Antonio Kaufusi (Melbourne Storm).
Tries: Inglis (3, 50), Price (57), Lockyer (60); **Goals:** Thurston 4/4;
Field goal: Thurston (69).
On report: Myles and Johnson (9) – dangerous tackle on White
NEW SOUTH WALES: 1 Anthony Minichiello (Sydney Roosters); 2 Matt King (Melbourne Storm); 3 Jamie Lyon (Manly Sea Eagles); 4 Matt Cooper (St George-Illawarra Dragons); 5 Jarryd Hayne (Parramatta Eels); 6 Braith Anasta (Sydney Roosters); 7 Jarrod Mullen (Newcastle Knights); 8 Brett White (Melbourne Storm); 9 Danny Buderus (Newcastle Knights) (C); 10 Brent Kite (Manly Sea Eagles); 11 Willie Mason (Bulldogs); 12 Nathan Hindmarsh (Parramatta Eels); 13 Andrew Ryan (Bulldogs). Subs (all used): 14 Luke Bailey (Gold Coast Titans); 15 Steve Simpson (Newcastle Knights); 16 Anthony Tupou (Sydney Roosters); 17 Kurt Gidley (Newcastle Knights).
Tries: Hindmarsh (10), Cooper (19), Hayne (40); **Goals:** Lyon 3/4.
Rugby Leaguer & League Express Men of the Match:
Queensland: Steve Price; *New South Wales:* Anthony Minichiello
Half-time: 6-18; **Referee:** Paul Simpkins;
Attendance: 53,498 *(at Suncorp Stadium, Brisbane).*

ORIGIN II

Wednesday 13th June 2007

NEW SOUTH WALES 6 QUEENSLAND 10

NEW SOUTH WALES: 19 Brett Stewart (Manly Sea Eagles); 2 Matt King (Melbourne Storm); 3 Jamie Lyon (Manly Sea Eagles); 4 Matt Cooper (St George-Illawarra Dragons); 5 Jarryd Hayne (Parramatta Eels); 6 Braith Anasta (Sydney Roosters); 7 Brett Kimmorley (Cronulla Sharks); 12 Willie Mason (Bulldogs); 9 Danny Buderus (Newcastle Knights) (C); 10 Brent Kite (Manly Sea Eagles); 11 Nathan Hindmarsh (Parramatta Eels); 15 Steve Simpson (Newcastle Knights); 13 Andrew Ryan (Bulldogs). Subs (all used): 8 Brett White (Melbourne Storm); 14 Luke Bailey (Gold Coast Titans); 16 Ryan Hoffman (Melbourne Storm); 17 Greg Bird (Cronulla Sharks).
Try: Stewart (8); **Goals:** Lyon 1/1.
QUEENSLAND: 1 Karmichael Hunt (Brisbane Broncos); 2 Brent Tate (Brisbane Broncos); 3 Steve Bell (Manly Sea Eagles); 4 Justin Hodges (Brisbane Broncos); 5 Greg Inglis (Melbourne Storm); 6 Darren Lockyer (Brisbane Broncos) (C); 7 Johnathan Thurston (North Queensland Cowboys); 8 Steve Price (New Zealand Warriors); 9 Cameron Smith (Melbourne Storm); 10 Petero Civoniceva (Brisbane Broncos); 11 Tonie Carroll (Brisbane Broncos); 12 Carl Webb (North Queensland Cowboys); 13 Dallas Johnson (Melbourne Storm). Subs (all used): 14 Shaun Berrigan (Brisbane Broncos); 15 Jacob Lillyman (North Queensland Cowboys); 16 Nate Myles (Sydney Roosters); 17 Neville Costigan (Canberra Raiders).
Tries: Inglis (20), Bell (63); **Goals:** Thurston 1/2.
Rugby Leaguer & League Express Men of the Match:
New South Wales: Andrew Ryan; *Queensland:* Cameron Smith.
Half-time: 6-6; **Referee:** Shayne Hayne;
Attendance: 76,924 *(at Telstra Stadium, Sydney).*

ORIGIN III

Wednesday 4th July 2007

QUEENSLAND 4 NEW SOUTH WALES 18

QUEENSLAND: 1 Karmichael Hunt (Brisbane Broncos); 2 Brent Tate (Brisbane Broncos); 3 Steve Bell (Manly Sea Eagles); 4 Justin Hodges (Brisbane Broncos); 5 Greg Inglis (Melbourne Storm); 6 Darren Lockyer (Brisbane Broncos) (C); 7 Johnathan Thurston (North Queensland Cowboys); 8 Steve Price (New Zealand Warriors); 9 Cameron Smith (Melbourne Storm); 10 Petero Civoniceva (Brisbane Broncos); 11 Tonie Carroll (Brisbane Broncos); 12 Carl Webb (North Queensland Cowboys); 13 Dallas Johnson (Melbourne Storm). Subs (all used): 14 Shaun Berrigan (Brisbane Broncos); 16 Nate Myles (Sydney Roosters); 18 Matt Bowen (North Queensland Cowboys); 19 Dane Carlaw (Brisbane Broncos).
Try: Hodges (25); **Goals:** Thurston 0/1.
NEW SOUTH WALES: 1 Brett Stewart (Manly Sea Eagles); 2 Hazem El Masri (Bulldogs); 3 Matt King (Melbourne Storm); 4 Matt Cooper (St George-Illawarra Dragons); 5 Jarryd Hayne (Parramatta Eels); 6 Greg Bird (Cronulla Sharks); 7 Brett Kimmorley (Cronulla Sharks); 8 Brent Kite (Manly Sea Eagles); 9 Danny Buderus (Newcastle Knights) (C); 10 Willie Mason (Bulldogs); 11 Nathan Hindmarsh (Parramatta Eels); 12 Andrew Ryan (Bulldogs); 13 Paul Gallen (Cronulla Sharks). Subs (all used): 14 Luke Bailey (Gold Coast Titans); 15 Steve Simpson (Newcastle Knights); 16 Ryan Hoffman (Melbourne Storm); 17 Kurt Gidley (Newcastle Knights).
Tries: Hayne (21), King (73), El Masri (78); **Goals:** El Masri 3/3.
Rugby Leaguer & League Express Men of the Match:
Queensland: Cameron Smith; *New South Wales:* Greg Bird.
Half-time: 4-6; **Referee:** Paul Simpkins;
Attendance: 52,469 *(at Suncorp Stadium, Brisbane).*

Wally Lewis Medal (Man of the Series): Cameron Smith (Queensland).

THIRD TEST

GREAT BRITAIN 28
NEW ZEALAND 22

MAIN PIC: Great Britain skipper Jamie Peacock lifts the Baskerville Shield at Wigan - after his side said farewell to the red, white & blue with a 3-0 Test whitewash
INSET: Rob Burrow's performances over the three games earned him the player of the series award

INTERNATIONAL
& CUP SEASONS

GREAT BRITAIN 44
NEW ZEALAND 0

ABOVE: Leon Pryce releases the ball under pressure at Hull
BELOW LEFT: Adrian Morley leads from the front against the Kiwis
BELOW RIGHT: Danny McGuire & Rob Burrow start the celebrations after the Lions win a first series victory in 14 years of trying

Gillette Fusion.
TEST SERIES

SECOND TEST

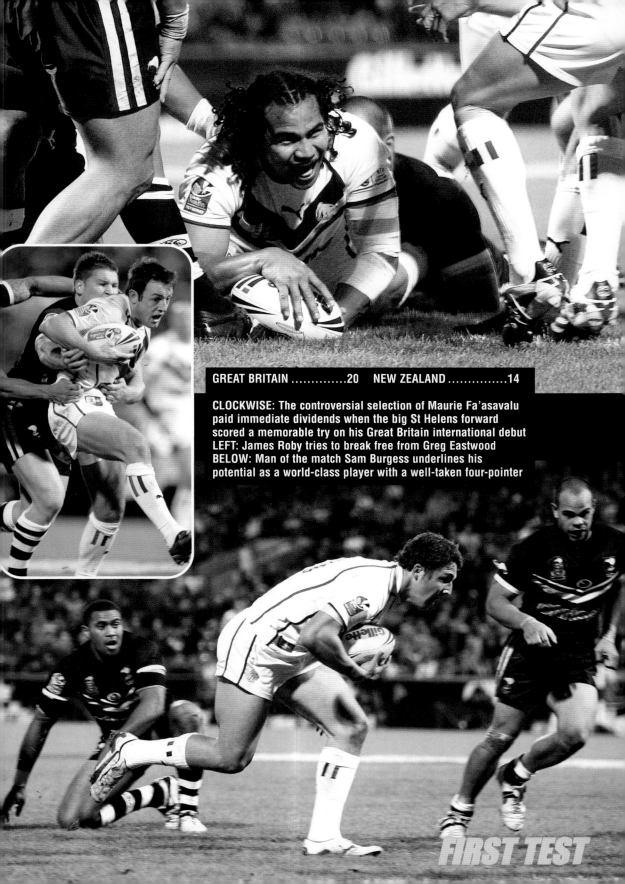

GREAT BRITAIN 20   NEW ZEALAND 14

CLOCKWISE: The controversial selection of Maurie Fa'asavalu paid immediate dividends when the big St Helens forward scored a memorable try on his Great Britain international debut
LEFT: James Roby tries to break free from Greg Eastwood
BELOW: Man of the match Sam Burgess underlines his potential as a world-class player with a well-taken four-pointer

FIRST TEST

ABOVE: Wales' Iestyn Harris gets a kick away under heavy pressure from the Scotland defence
LEFT: George Ndaira makes a break as Lebanon end Welsh World Cup hopes
BELOW: Samoa's Ali Lauitiiti looks for a gap in the USA defence

WORLD CUP 2008 QUALIFIERS

ABOVE: Samoa celebrate reaching the World Cup following victory over Lebanon
RIGHT: Samoa's Nigel Vagana closed down by the Lebanon defence
BELOW: Ireland stop this Lebanon attack
BELOW RIGHT: Mick Cassidy and Ged Corcoran show their delight at Irish qualification

FRONTLINE TEST

ABOVE: Skipper-for-the-night Adrian Morley shines bright at Headingley, as Test matches against France make a welcome return in June

LEFT: Kirk Yeaman darts away from Thomas Leuluai at Warrington
RIGHT: The great Stacey Jones leaves his boots on the HJ Stadium turf - signalling the end of a fabulous international Rugby League career
BELOW: A historic photo to celebrate 100 years of international RL

CENTENARY INTERNATIONAL

GILLETTE FUSION CENTENARY INTERNATIONAL
NORTHERN UNION v ALL GOLDS
20th October 2007
Celebrating 100 Years Of International Rugby League

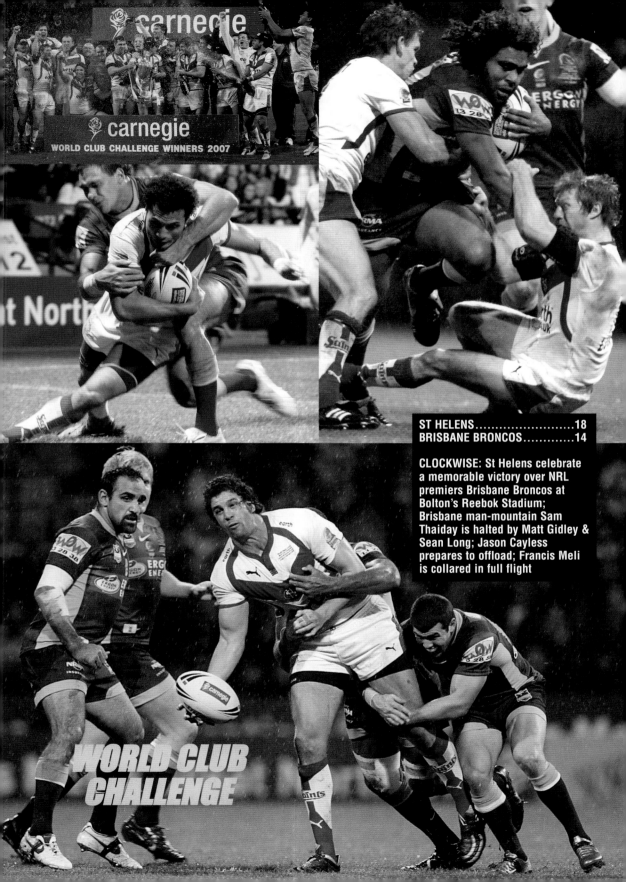

carnegie

carnegie
WORLD CLUB CHALLENGE WINNERS 2007

ST HELENS........................18
BRISBANE BRONCOS............14

CLOCKWISE: St Helens celebrate a memorable victory over NRL premiers Brisbane Broncos at Bolton's Reebok Stadium; Brisbane man-mountain Sam Thaiday is halted by Matt Gidley & Sean Long; Jason Cayless prepares to offload; Francis Meli is collared in full flight

WORLD CLUB CHALLENGE

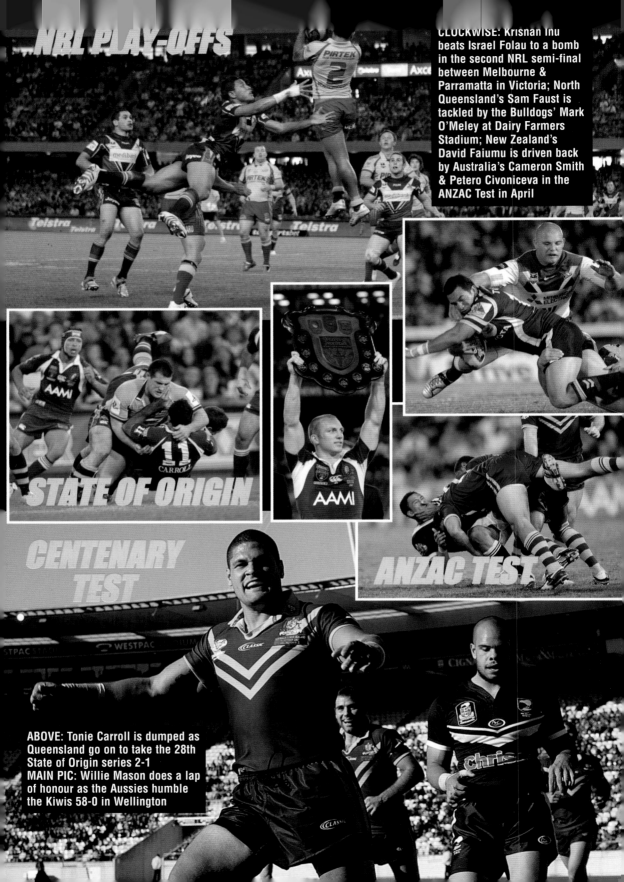

NRL PLAY-OFFS

CLOCKWISE: Krisnan Inu beats Israel Folau to a bomb in the second NRL semi-final between Melbourne & Parramatta in Victoria; North Queensland's Sam Faust is tackled by the Bulldogs' Mark O'Meley at Dairy Farmers Stadium; New Zealand's David Faiumu is driven back by Australia's Cameron Smith & Petero Civoniceva in the ANZAC Test in April

STATE OF ORIGIN

CENTENARY TEST

ANZAC TEST

ABOVE: Tonie Carroll is dumped as Queensland go on to take the 28th State of Origin series 2-1
MAIN PIC: Willie Mason does a lap of honour as the Aussies humble the Kiwis 58-0 in Wellington

MELBOURNE STORM 34   MANLY SEA EAGLES..........8

CLOCKWISE: Melbourne's Greg Inglis roars over for a try as the Storm put Manly to the sword at Telstra Stadium; coach Craig Bellamy & captain Cameron Smith are drowned in Gatorade; whizzkid Billy Slater is unceremoniously dumped

NRL GRAND FINAL

CATALANS DRAGONS 8
ST HELENS 30

CLOCKWISE: Keiron Cunningham holds the Challenge Cup aloft as the sport makes its long-awaited return to rebuilt Wembley Stadium; Leon Pryce & Cyril Gossard compete in the sunshine; Jason Croker leads from the front as the Catalans become the first French team to play in a Challenge Cup final; Sean Long tears away across the Wembley turf

CHALLENGE
CUP FINAL

CLOCKWISE: Ade Gardner in action as St Helens power past Bradford Bulls 35-14; Francis Meli & Chris McKenna contest a high ball in Huddersfield; Wigan's dejected players can't believe it as Catalans Dragons emerge 37-24 winners at the HJ Stadium

CHALLENGE CUP SEMI-FINALS

CHALLENGE CUP QUARTER-FINALS

CLOCKWISE:
Paul Rauhihi is tackled by Nick Fozzard & Jon Wilkin at Saints; Jerome Guisset helps Catalans shock Hull; Nathan McAvoy is stopped by the Castleford defence; Trent Barrett tears away from Jamie Jones-Buchanan

ROUND FOUR

ROUND FIVE

NL1 GRAND FINAL

CASTLEFORD TIGERS 42
WIDNES VIKINGS 10

CLOCKWISE: Awen Gutenbeil leads
the way for the Tigers; Andrew
Henderson lifts the Cup; Toa Kohe-
Love in a well-beaten Widnes team

NORTHERN RAIL CUP FINAL

WHITEHAVEN 6
WIDNES VIKINGS 54

ABOVE LEFT: Mark Smith lifts the
Northern Rail Cup after a one-sided
game in Blackpool
MAIN PIC: 'Haven's Marc Jackson
struggles to offload in the tackle

NL2 CHAMPIONS

CLOCKWISE: Celtic Crusaders celebrate promotion to NL1 after their final game of the season at Gateshead; Joel Penny leads the Widnes charge against Halifax; Oldham players & fans go wild against Barrow; Oldham's Geno Costin tries to break past Workington's defence; Halifax's Dave Larder bursts clear of Sheffield

NL1 PLAY-OFFS

NL2 PLAY-OFFS

NL2 GRAND FINAL

FEATHERSTONE ROVERS........24
OLDHAM 6

The 'flat-cappers' of Featherstone
celebrate promotion to NL1 after a
controlled demolition of Oldham
BELOW LEFT: Oldham's Alex
Wilkinson gets up close & personal

CONFERENCE NATIONAL GRAND FINAL

BRAMLEY 30
FEATHERSTONE LIONS 42

The Lions complete a first-class
day out at Headingley for
Featherstone with a comprehensive
victory over ambitious Bramley
RIGHT: Matt Hayes is tackled short

NATIONAL CONFERENCE GRAND FINAL

GMB CUP

RL CONFERENCE

CLOCKWISE: National Conference Grand Final winners Skirlaugh; Brett Waller in action against Leigh Miners Rangers; Widnes Saints won the RL Conference Grand Final; St Albans bagged the Regional title; Paul Hunt in action for GMB Cup winners Halton Simms Cross; Paul Roberts lifts the GMB Cup

5
STATISTICAL REVIEW

SUPER LEAGUE PLAYERS
1996-2007

Super League Players 1996-2007

PLAYER	CLUB	YEAR	APP	TRIES	GOALS	FG	PTS
Carl Ablett	Leeds	2004, 2006-07	(18)	1	0	0	4
	London	2005	3(2)	0	0	0	0
Darren Abram	Oldham	1996-97	25(2)	11	0	0	44
Darren Adams	Paris	1996	9(1)	1	0	0	4
Guy Adams	Huddersfield	1998	1(2)	0	0	0	0
Luke Adamson	Salford	2006-07	6(18)	1	0	0	4
Matt Adamson	Leeds	2002-04	54(8)	9	0	0	36
Phil Adamson	St Helens	1999	(1)	0	0	0	0
Ade Adebisi	London	2004	(1)	0	0	0	0
Jamie Ainscough	Wigan	2002-03	30(2)	18	0	0	72
Glen Air	London	1998-2001	57(13)	27	0	1	109
Makali Aizue	Hull KR	2007	11(8)	2	0	0	8
Darren Albert	St Helens	2002-05	105	77	0	0	308
Paul Alcock	Widnes	2003, 2005	1(7)	1	0	0	4
Neil Alexander	Salford	1998	(1)	0	0	0	0
Malcolm Alker	Salford	1997-2002, 2004-07	220(2)	39	0	1	157
Chris Allen	Castleford	1996	(1)	0	0	0	0
David Allen	Wigan	2003, 2005	6(15)	2	0	0	8
Gavin Allen	London	1996	10	0	0	0	0
John Allen	Workington	1996	20(1)	6	0	0	24
Ray Allen	London	1996	5(3)	3	0	0	12
Richard Allwood	Gateshead	1999	(4)	0	0	0	0
Sean Allwood	Gateshead	1999	3(17)	1	0	0	4
David Alstead	Warrington	2000-02	23(10)	3	0	0	12
Asa Amone	Halifax	1996-97	32(7)	10	0	0	40
Grant Anderson	Castleford	1996-97	15(6)	3	0	0	12
Paul Anderson	St Helens	2005-06	48(5)	7	1	0	30
	Bradford	1997-2004	74(104)	30	0	0	120
	Halifax	1996	5(1)	1	0	0	4
Paul Anderson	Sheffield	1999	3(7)	1	0	0	4
	St Helens	1996-98	2(28)	4	1	0	18
Vinnie Anderson	Warrington	2007	16	6	0	0	24
	St Helens	2005-06	28(14)	17	0	0	68
Phil Anderton	St Helens	2004	1	0	0	0	0
Eric Anselme	Halifax	1997	(2)	0	0	0	0
Mark Applegarth	Wakefield	2004-07	20(5)	3	0	0	12
Graham Appo	Warrington	2002-05	60(13)	35	80	0	300
	Huddersfield	2001	7	4	0	0	16
Anthony Armour	London	2005	11(7)	1	0	0	4
Colin Armstrong	Workington	1996	11(2)	1	0	0	4
Richard Armswood	Workington	1996	5(1)	1	0	0	4
Danny Arnold	Salford	2001-02	26(13)	13	0	0	52
	Huddersfield	1998-2000	55(7)	26	0	0	104
	Castleford	2000	(4)	0	0	0	0
	St Helens	1996-97	40(1)	33	0	0	132
Craig Ashall	St Helens	2006	1	1	0	0	4
Chris Ashton	Wigan	2005-07	44(2)	25	2	0	104
Martin Aspinwall	Huddersfield	2006-07	35	15	0	0	60
	Wigan	2001-05	85(13)	27	0	0	108
Mark Aston	Sheffield	1996-99	67(6)	6	243	6	516
Paul Atcheson	Widnes	2002-04	16(35)	4	0	0	16
	St Helens	1998-2000	58(4)	18	0	0	72
	Oldham	1996-97	40	21	0	0	84
David Atkins	Huddersfield	2001	26(1)	4	0	0	16
Ryan Atkins	Wakefield	2006-07	39(2)	23	0	0	92
Brad Attwood	Halifax	2003	(3)	0	0	0	0
Warren Ayres	Salford	1999	2(9)	1	2	0	8
Jerome Azema	Paris	1997	(1)	0	0	0	0
Marcus Bai	Bradford	2006	24	9	0	0	36
	Leeds	2004-05	57	42	0	0	168
David Baildon	Hull	1998-99	26(2)	4	0	0	16
Andy Bailey	Hull	2004-05	2(8)	1	0	0	4
Julian Bailey	Huddersfield	2003-04	47	13	0	0	52
Phil Bailey	Wigan	2007	30	6	0	0	24
Ryan Bailey	Leeds	2002-07	99(34)	8	0	0	32
Simon Baldwin	Salford	2004-06	20(29)	3	0	0	12
	Sheffield	1999	7(15)	2	0	0	8
	Halifax	1996-98	41(15)	16	0	1	65
Rob Ball	Wigan	1998-2000	3(4)	0	0	0	0
Paul Ballard	Widnes	2005	3(1)	2	0	0	8
Darren Bamford	Salford	2005	2(1)	0	0	0	0
Michael Banks	Bradford	1998	(1)	0	0	0	0
Steve Bannister	Harlequins	2007	(6)	0	0	0	0
	St Helens	2006-07	(3)	0	0	0	0
Frederic Banquet	Paris	1996	16(2)	7	4	0	36
Lee Bardauskas	Castleford	1996-97	(2)	0	0	0	0
Craig Barker	Workington	1996	(2)	0	0	0	0
Dwayne Barker	London	2004	3	1	0	0	4
	Hull	2003	(1)	0	0	0	0
Mark Barlow	Wakefield	2002	(1)	0	0	0	0
Danny Barnes	Halifax	1999	2	0	0	0	0
Richie Barnett	Salford	2007	7	4	0	0	16
	Warrington	2006-07	26(10)	15	0	0	60
	Hull	2004-05	21(5)	21	0	0	84
	Widnes	2005	4	2	0	0	8
Richie Barnett	Hull	2003-04	31(1)	17	0	0	68
	London	2001-02	31(4)	13	0	0	52
David Barnhill	Leeds	2000	20(8)	5	0	0	20
Trent Barrett	Wigan	2007	29	17	0	3	71
Paul Barrow	Warrington	1996-97	1(10)	1	0	0	4
Scott Barrow	St Helens	1997-2000	9(13)	1	0	0	4
Steve Barrow	London	2000	2	0	0	0	0
	Hull	1998-99	4(17)	1	0	0	4
	Wigan	1996	(8)	3	0	0	12
Ben Barton	Huddersfield	1998	1(6)	1	0	0	4
Danny Barton	Salford	2001	1	0	0	0	0
Wayne Bartrim	Castleford	2002-03	41(2)	9	157	0	350
Greg Barwick	London	1996-97	30(4)	21	110	2	306
David Bastian	Halifax	1996	(2)	0	0	0	0
David Bates	Castleford	2001-02	(4)	0	0	0	0
	Warrington	2001	1(2)	0	0	0	0
Nathan Batty	Wakefield	2001	1(1)	0	0	0	0
Andreas Bauer	Hull KR	2007	10(2)	5	0	0	20
Russell Bawden	London	1996-97, 2002-04	50(49)	15	0	0	60
Neil Baxter	Salford	2001	1	0	0	0	0
Neil Baynes	Salford	1999-2002, 2004	84(19)	10	0	0	40
	Wigan	1996-98	(10)	1	0	0	4
Chris Beattie	Catalans	2006	22(5)	3	0	0	12
Robbie Beazley	London	1997-99	48(15)	13	0	0	52
Robbie Beckett	Halifax	2002	27	15	0	0	60
Dean Bell	Leeds	1996	1	1	0	0	4
Ian Bell	Hull	2003	(1)	0	0	0	0
Mark Bell	Wigan	1998	22	12	0	0	48
Paul Bell	Leeds	2000	1	0	0	0	0
Troy Bellamy	Paris	1997	5(10)	0	0	0	0
Adrian Belle	Huddersfield	1998	10(2)	0	0	0	0
	Oldham	1996	19	8	0	0	32
Jamie Benn	Castleford	1998, 2000	3(8)	1	15	0	34
Andy Bennett	Warrington	1996	6(5)	1	0	0	4
Mike Bennett	St Helens	2000-07	70(60)	15	0	0	60
Andrew Bentley	Catalans	2007	9(4)	1	0	0	4
John Bentley	Huddersfield	1999	13(4)	3	0	0	12
	Halifax	1996, 1998	22(3)	24	0	0	96
Kane Bentley	Catalans	2007	1(5)	1	0	0	4
Phil Bergman	Paris	1997	20(1)	14	0	0	56
Joe Berry	Huddersfield	1998-99	25(14)	3	0	0	12
David Berthezene	Salford	2007	9(1)	0	0	0	0
	Catalans	2006-07	5(14)	0	0	0	0
Colin Best	Hull	2003-04	57	34	0	0	136
Roger Best	London	1997-98	1(5)	1	0	0	4
Bob Beswick	Wigan	2004-05	5(14)	2	0	0	8
Monty Betham	Wakefield	2006	26	2	0	0	8
Mike Bethwaite	Workington	1996	17(3)	1	0	0	4
Denis Betts	Wigan	1998-2001	82(24)	33	0	0	132
Cliff Beverley	Salford	2004-05	47(1)	14	0	0	56
Adam Bibey	Widnes	2004	(1)	0	0	0	0
Ricky Bibey	Wakefield	2007	11(6)	0	0	0	0
	St Helens	2004	4(14)	0	0	0	0
	Wigan	2001-03	5(29)	0	0	0	0
Chris Birchall	Halifax	2002-03	24(22)	4	0	0	16
	Bradford	2000	(1)	0	0	0	0
Deon Bird	Castleford	2006	17(6)	5	0	0	20
	Widnes	2003-04	39(6)	9	0	0	36
	Wakefield	2002	10(1)	1	0	0	4
	Hull	2000-02	37(22)	20	0	0	80
	Gateshead	1999	19(3)	13	0	0	52
	Paris	1996-97	30	12	2	0	52
Nathan Blacklock	Hull	2005-06	44(3)	33	0	0	132
Richie Blackmore	Leeds	1997-2000	63	25	0	0	100
Matthew Blake	Wakefield	2003-04	1(5)	0	0	0	0
Steve Blakeley	Salford	1997-2002	103(5)	26	241	2	588
	Warrington	2000	4(3)	1	9	0	22
Richard Blakeway	Castleford	2002-04	1(14)	1	0	0	4
Damien Blanch	Castleford	2006	3(2)	0	0	0	0
Matt Blaymire	Wakefield	2007	23	9	0	0	36
Ian Blease	Salford	1997	(1)	0	0	0	0
Jamie Bloem	Huddersfield	2003	18(4)	3	11	0	34
	Halifax	1998-2002	82(25)	25	100	2	302
Vea Bloomfield	Paris	1996	4(14)	3	0	0	12
Matty Blythe	Warrington	2007	(1)	0	0	0	0
Pascal Bomati	Paris	1996	17(1)	10	0	0	40
Simon Booth	Hull	1998-99	15(9)	2	0	0	8
	St Helens	1996-97	10(4)	1	0	0	4
Steve Booth	Huddersfield	1998-99	16(4)	2	3	0	14
Alan Boothroyd	Halifax	1997	2(3)	0	0	0	0
Thomas Bosc	Catalans	2006-07	28(3)	17	50	0	168
John Boslem	Paris	1996	(5)	0	0	0	0
Liam Bostock	St Helens	2004	1	0	0	0	0
Liam Botham	Wigan	2005	5	0	0	0	0
	Leeds	2003-05	2(11)	4	0	0	16
	London	2004	6(2)	3	6	0	24
Frano Botica	Castleford	1996	21	5	84	2	190
Matthew Bottom	Leigh	2005	(1)	0	0	0	0
Hadj Boudebza	Paris	1996	(2)	0	0	0	0
David Boughton	Huddersfield	1999	26(1)	4	0	0	16
David Bouveng	Halifax	1997-99	66(2)	19	0	0	76
Tony Bowes	Huddersfield	1998	3(2)	0	0	0	0
Radney Bowker	London	2004	3	1	0	0	4
	St Helens	2001	(1)	0	0	0	0
David Boyle	Bradford	1999-2000	36(13)	15	0	1	61
Ryan Boyle	Castleford	2006	(1)	0	0	0	0
Andy Bracek	Warrington	2005-07	5(29)	2	0	0	8
	St Helens	2004	(1)	0	0	0	0

PLAYER	CLUB	YEAR	APP	TRIES	GOALS	FG	PTS
David Bradbury	Hudds-Sheff	2000	21(2)	1	0	0	4
	Salford	1997-99	23(10)	6	0	0	24
	Oldham	1996-97	19(6)	9	0	0	36
John Braddish	St Helens	2001-02	1(1)	0	3	0	6
Graeme Bradley	Bradford	1996-98	62(1)	29	0	0	116
Nick Bradley-Qalilawa							
	Harlequins	2006	27	6	0	0	24
	London	2005	28	19	0	0	76
Darren Bradstreet	London	1999-2000	1(3)	0	0	0	0
Dominic Brambani							
	Castleford	2004	2(2)	0	0	0	0
Liam Bretherton	Wigan	1999	(5)	2	0	0	8
	Warrington	1997	(2)	0	0	0	0
Johnny Brewer	Halifax	1996	4(2)	2	0	0	8
Chris Bridge	Warrington	2005-07	51(6)	29	65	1	247
	Bradford	2003-04	2(14)	4	6	0	28
Lee Briers	Warrington	1997-2007	242(11)	81	714	55	1807
	St Helens	1997	3	0	11	0	22
Carl Briggs	Salford	1999	8(5)	3	0	1	13
	Halifax	1996	5(3)	1	0	0	4
Mike Briggs	Widnes	2002	1(2)	1	0	0	4
Shaun Briscoe	Hull	2004-07	83(9)	50	0	0	200
	Wigan	2002-03	23(5)	11	0	0	44
Darren Britt	St Helens	2002-03	41	3	0	0	12
Gary Broadbent	Salford	1997-2002	117(2)	22	0	0	88
Paul Broadbent	Wakefield	2002	16(5)	0	0	0	0
	Hull	2000-01	40(9)	3	0	0	12
	Halifax	1999	26(1)	2	0	0	8
	Sheffield	1996-98	63(1)	6	0	0	24
Andrew Brocklehurst							
	Salford	2004-07	34(23)	5	0	0	20
	London	2004	12(6)	2	0	0	8
	Halifax	2001-03	37(8)	2	0	0	8
Justin Brooker	Wakefield	2001	25	9	0	0	36
	Bradford	2000	17(4)	11	0	0	44
Danny Brough	Castleford	2006	10	1	31	2	68
	Hull	2005-06	25(12)	3	85	1	183
Darren Brown	Salford	1999-2001	47(9)	11	6	0	56
Gavin Brown	Leeds	1996-97	5(2)	1	2	0	8
Kevin Brown	Huddersfield	2006-07	37	12	0	0	48
	Wigan	2003-06	46(18)	27	0	0	108
Lee Brown	Hull	1999	(1)	0	0	0	0
Michael Brown	London	1996	(2)	0	0	0	0
Todd Brown	Paris	1996	8(1)	2	0	0	8
Adrian Brunker	Wakefield	1999	17	6	0	0	24
Justin Bryant	Paris	1996	4(1)	0	0	0	0
	London	1996	7(8)	1	0	0	4
Austin Buchanan	Wakefield	2005-06	6	2	0	0	8
	London	2003	3(1)	2	0	0	8
Neil Budworth	Harlequins	2006	2(19)	0	0	0	0
	London	2002-05	59(11)	4	1	0	18
James Bunyan	Huddersfield	1998-99	8(7)	2	0	0	8
Andy Burgess	Salford	1997	3(12)	0	0	0	0
Luke Burgess	Harlequins	2007	(3)	0	0	0	0
Sam Burgess	Bradford	2006-07	10(25)	4	5	0	26
Darren Burns	Warrington	2002-04	66(6)	19	0	0	76
Gary Burns	Oldham	1996	6	1	0	0	4
Paul Burns	Workington	1996	5(2)	1	0	0	4
Rob Burrow	Leeds	2001-07	121(66)	85	97	2	536
Dean Busby	Warrington	1999-2002	34(34)	7	0	0	28
	Hull	1998	8(6)	0	0	0	0
	St Helens	1996-98	1(7)	0	0	0	0
Ikram Butt	London	1996	5(1)	0	0	0	0
Shane Byrne	Huddersfield	1998-99	1(5)	0	0	0	0
Didier Cabestany	Paris	1996-97	20(6)	2	0	0	8
Joel Caine	Salford	2004	24	8	13	0	58
	London	2003	6	4	1	0	18
Mark Calderwood	Wigan	2006-07	47	18	0	0	72
	Leeds	2001-05	117(9)	88	0	0	352
Mike Callan	Warrington	2002	(4)	0	0	0	0
Matt Calland	Huddersfield	2003	2	0	0	0	0
	Hull	1999	1	0	0	0	0
	Bradford	1996-98	44(5)	24	0	0	96
Dean Callaway	London	1999-2000	26(24)	12	0	0	48
Laurent Cambres	Paris	1996	(1)	0	0	0	0
Chris Campbell	Warrington	2000	7(1)	2	0	0	8
Liam Campbell	Wakefield	2005	(1)	0	0	0	0
Logan Campbell	Hull	1998-99, 2001	70(13)	14	0	0	56
	Castleford	2000	14(2)	3	0	0	12
	Workington	1996	7(1)	1	0	0	4
Blake Cannova	Widnes	2002	(1)	0	0	0	0
Phil Cantillon	Widnes	2002-03	27(21)	18	0	0	72
	Leeds	1997	(1)	0	0	0	0
Daryl Cardiss	Warrington	2003-04	23(2)	3	4	0	20
	Halifax	1999-2003	91(8)	39	4	0	164
	Wigan	1996-98	12(6)	4	0	0	16
Dale Cardoza	Warrington	2002	5	1	0	0	4
	Halifax	2001	3	1	0	0	4
	Huddersfield	2000-01	20(9)	11	0	0	44
	Sheffield	1998-99	11(7)	3	0	0	12
Paul Carige	Salford	1999	24(1)	7	0	0	28

PLAYER	CLUB	YEAR	APP	TRIES	GOALS	FG	PTS
Jim Carlton	Huddersfield	1999	3(11)	2	0	0	8
Brian Carney	Wigan	2001-05	91(10)	42	1	0	170
	Hull	2000	13(3)	7	0	0	28
	Gateshead	1999	3(2)	2	0	0	8
Martin Carney	Warrington	1997	(1)	0	0	0	0
Paul Carr	Sheffield	1996-98	45(5)	15	0	0	60
Bernard Carroll	London	1996	2(1)	1	0	0	4
Mark Carroll	London	1998	15(3)	1	0	0	4
Tonie Carroll	Leeds	2001-02	42(2)	30	0	0	120
Darren Carter	Workington	1996	10(3)	0	1	0	2
Steve Carter	Widnes	2002	14(7)	4	0	0	16
John Cartwright	Salford	1997	9	0	0	0	0
Garreth Carvell	Hull	2001-07	61(82)	21	0	0	84
	Leeds	1997-2000	(4)	0	0	0	0
	Gateshead	1999	4(4)	1	0	0	4
Garen Casey	Salford	1999	13(5)	3	23	0	58
Mick Cassidy	Widnes	2005	24	0	0	0	0
	Wigan	1996-2004	184(36)	30	0	0	120
Remi Casty	Catalans	2006-07	3(14)	1	0	0	4
Ned Catic	Wakefield	2006-07	17(29)	4	0	0	16
Chris Causey	Warrington	1997-99	(18)	1	0	0	4
Jason Cayless	St Helens	2006-07	52(1)	6	0	0	24
Arnaud Cervello	Paris	1996	4	4	0	0	16
Gary Chambers	Warrington	1996-2000	65(28)	2	0	0	8
Pierre Chamorin	Paris	1996-97	27(3)	8	3	0	38
Alex Chan	Catalans	2006-07	34(17)	7	0	0	28
Chris Chapman	Leeds	1999	(1)	0	0	0	0
Damien Chapman	London	1998	6(2)	3	4	1	21
David Chapman	Castleford	1996-98	24(6)	8	0	0	32
Jaymes Chapman	Halifax	2002-03	5(8)	1	0	0	4
Richard Chapman							
	Sheffield	1996	1	2	0	0	8
Chris Charles	Salford	2004-06	59(16)	6	140	0	304
	Castleford	2001	1(4)	1	0	0	4
Olivier Charles	Catalans	2007	2	2	0	0	8
Andy Cheetham	Huddersfield	1998-99	30	11	0	0	44
Kris Chesney	London	1998	1(2)	0	0	0	0
Chris Chester	Hull KR	2007	19(2)	2	0	0	8
	Hull	2002-06	67(25)	13	0	0	52
	Wigan	1999-2001	21(22)	5	0	0	20
	Halifax	1996-99	47(14)	16	15	1	95
Lee Chilton	Workington	1996	10(3)	6	0	0	24
Gary Christie	Bradford	1996-97	4(7)	1	0	0	4
Dean Clark	Leeds	1996	11(2)	3	0	0	12
Des Clark	St Helens	1999	4	0	0	0	0
	Halifax	1998-99	35(13)	6	0	0	24
Greg Clarke	Halifax	1997	1(1)	0	0	0	0
John Clarke	Oldham	1996-97	27(4)	5	0	0	20
Jon Clarke	Warrington	2001-07	169(3)	42	2	0	172
	London	2000-01	19(11)	2	0	0	8
	Wigan	1997-99	13(10)	3	0	0	12
Ryan Clayton	Salford	2006	3(8)	2	0	0	8
	Huddersfield	2005	4(6)	0	0	0	0
	Castleford	2004	11(6)	3	0	0	12
	Halifax	2000, 2002-03	28(12)	6	0	0	24
Gavin Clinch	Salford	2004	21(1)	1	0	1	5
	Halifax	1998-99, 2001-02	88(2)	26	45	5	199
	Hudds-Sheff	2000	18(2)	5	0	1	21
	Wigan	1999	10(2)	4	12	0	40
John Clough	Salford	2004-06	1(16)	0	0	0	0
Paul Clough	St Helens	2005-07	6(17)	1	0	0	4
Tony Clubb	Harlequins	2006-07	10(2)	2	0	0	8
Bradley Clyde	Leeds	2001	7(5)	1	0	0	4
Evan Cochrane	London	1996	5(1)	1	0	0	4
Ben Cockayne	Hull KR	2007	20(1)	3	0	0	12
Liam Colbon	Wigan	2004-05, 2007	17(6)	7	0	0	28
Anthony Colella	Huddersfield	2003	5(1)	2	0	0	8
Liam Coleman	Leigh	2005	1(4)	0	0	0	0
Andy Coley	Salford	2001-02, 2004-07	112(34)	34	0	0	136
Richard Colley	Bradford	2004	1	0	0	0	0
Steve Collins	Hull	2000	28	17	0	0	68
	Gateshead	1999	20(4)	13	0	0	52
Wayne Collins	Leeds	1997	21	3	0	0	12
Aurelien Cologni	Catalans	2006	4(1)	3	0	0	12
Gary Connolly	Widnes	2005	20	4	1	0	18
	Wigan	1996-2002, 2004	168(10)	70	5	0	290
	Leeds	2003-04	27	6	0	0	24
Matt Cook	Bradford	2005-07	2(30)	0	0	0	0
Mick Cook	Sheffield	1996	9(10)	2	0	0	8
Paul Cook	Huddersfield	1998-99	11(6)	2	13	0	34
	Bradford	1996-97	14(8)	7	38	1	105
Peter Cook	St Helens	2004	(1)	0	0	0	0
Paul Cooke	Hull KR	2007	13(1)	1	36	2	78
	Hull	1999-2007	177(27)	32	333	4	798
Ben Cooper	Leigh	2005	25(1)	5	0	0	20
	Huddersfield	2000-01, 2003-04	28(12)	3	0	0	12
Michael Cooper	Warrington	2006-07	(7)	1	0	0	4
Ged Corcoran	Halifax	2003	1(11)	0	0	0	0

Super League Players 1996-2007

PLAYER	CLUB	YEAR	APP	TRIES	GOALS	FG	PTS
Wayne Corcoran	Halifax	2003	4(2)	0	0	0	0
Mark Corvo	Salford	2002	7(5)	0	0	0	0
Brandon Costin	Huddersfield	2001, 2003-04	69	42	93	3	357
	Bradford	2002	20(1)	8	0	0	32
Wes Cotton	London	1997-98	12	3	0	0	12
Phil Coussons	Salford	1997	7(2)	3	0	0	12
Alex Couttet	Paris	1997	1	0	0	0	0
Nick Couttet	Paris	1997	1	0	0	0	0
Jamie Coventry	Castleford	1996	1	0	0	0	0
Jimmy Cowan	Oldham	1996-97	2(8)	0	0	0	0
Will Cowell	Warrington	1998-2000	6(8)	1	0	0	4
Neil Cowie	Wigan	1996-2001	116(27)	10	0	1	41
Mark Cox	London	2003	(3)	0	0	0	0
James Coyle	Wigan	2005	2(3)	1	0	0	4
Eorl Crabtree	Huddersfield	2001, 2003-07	47(74)	15	0	0	60
Andy Craig	Halifax	1999	13(7)	1	3	0	10
	Wigan	1996	5(5)	2	0	0	8
Owen Craigie	Widnes	2005	15	7	0	2	30
Scott Cram	London	1999-2002	65(7)	4	0	0	16
Steve Craven	Hull	1998-2003	53(42)	4	0	0	16
Nicky Crellin	Workington	1996	(2)	0	0	0	0
Jason Critchley	Wakefield	2000	7(1)	4	0	0	16
	Castleford	1997-98	27(3)	11	0	0	44
Jason Croker	Catalans	2007	21	6	0	1	25
Martin Crompton	Salford	1998-2000	30(6)	11	6	2	58
	Oldham	1996-97	36(1)	16	0	3	67
Paul Crook	Widnes	2005	2(2)	0	5	1	11
Paul Crook	Oldham	1996	4(9)	0	3	0	6
Lee Crooks	Castleford	1996-97	27(2)	2	14	0	36
Alan Cross	St Helens	1997	(2)	0	0	0	0
Steve Crouch	Castleford	2004	4(1)	2	0	0	8
Kevin Crouthers	Warrington	2001-03	12(1)	4	0	0	16
	London	2000	6(4)	1	0	0	4
	Wakefield	1999	4(4)	1	0	0	4
	Bradford	1997-98	3(9)	2	0	0	8
Matt Crowther	Hull	2001-03	48	20	166	0	412
	Hudds-Sheff	2000	10(4)	5	22	0	64
	Sheffield	1996-99	43(4)	22	10	0	108
Heath Cruckshank	Halifax	2003	19(1)	0	0	0	0
	St Helens	2001	1(12)	0	0	0	0
Paul Cullen	Warrington	1996	19	3	0	0	12
Francis Cummins	Leeds	1996-2005	217(13)	120	26	2	534
Keiron Cunningham	St Helens	1996-2007	294(13)	120	0	0	480
Andy Currier	Warrington	1996-97	(2)	1	0	0	4
Joe Dakuitoga	Sheffield	1996	6(3)	0	0	0	0
Matty Dale	Hull	2006	(2)	1	0	0	4
Brett Dallas	Wigan	2000-06	156	89	0	0	356
Paul Darbyshire	Warrington	1997	(6)	0	0	0	0
Maea David	Hull	1998	1	0	0	0	0
Paul Davidson	Halifax	2001-03	22(30)	10	0	0	40
	London	2000	6(10)	4	0	0	16
	St Helens	1998-99	27(16)	7	0	0	28
	Oldham	1996-97	17(18)	14	0	1	57
Gareth Davies	Warrington	1996-97	1(6)	0	0	0	0
Wes Davies	Wigan	1998-2001	22(22)	11	0	0	44
Brad Davis	Castleford	1997-2000, 2004, 2006	102(3)	31	43	10	220
	Wakefield	2001-03	51(12)	15	22	5	109
	Gateshead	1999	30	25	0	0	100
Matt Daylight	Hull	2000	17(1)	7	0	0	28
Michael De Vere	Huddersfield	2005-06	36	6	74	0	172
Paul Deacon	Bradford	1998-2007	216(43)	66	861	19	2005
	Oldham	1997	(2)	0	0	0	0
Chris Dean	St Helens	2007	(1)	0	0	0	0
Craig Dean	Halifax	1996-97	25(11)	12	1	1	51
Gareth Dean	London	2002	(4)	0	0	0	0
Yacine Dekkiche	Hudds-Sheff	2000	11(3)	3	0	0	12
Jason Demetriou	Wakefield	2004-07	107(1)	41	2	0	168
	Widnes	2002-03	47(1)	15	1	0	62
Martin Dermott	Warrington	1997	1	0	0	0	0
David Despin	Paris	1996	(1)	0	0	0	0
Fabien Devecchi	Paris	1996-97	17(10)	2	0	0	8
Paul Devlin	Widnes	2002-04	32	16	0	0	64
Stuart Dickens	Salford	2005	4(5)	0	4	0	8
Matt Diskin	Leeds	2001-07	139(17)	31	0	0	124
Kirk Dixon	Hull	2004-06	13(4)	7	4	0	36
Paul Dixon	Sheffield	1997	5(9)	1	0	0	4
Gareth Dobson	Castleford	1998-2000	(10)	0	0	0	0
Michael Dobson	Wigan	2006	14	5	61	0	142
	Catalans	2006	10	4	31	1	79
Michael Docherty	Hull	2000-01	(6)	0	0	0	0
Sid Domic	Hull	2006-07	39(4)	15	0	0	60
	Wakefield	2004-05	48	30	0	0	120
	Warrington	2002-03	41(4)	17	0	0	68
Scott Donald	Leeds	2006-07	59	33	0	0	132
Glen Donkin	Hull	2002-03	(10)	1	0	0	4
Stuart Donlan	Huddersfield	2004-06	59(3)	15	0	0	60
	Halifax	2001-03	65(2)	22	0	0	88
Jason Donohue	Bradford	1996	(4)	0	0	0	0
Jeremy Donougher	Bradford	1996-99	40(21)	13	0	0	52
Justin Dooley	London	2000-01	37(18)	2	0	0	8
Dane Dorahy	Halifax	2003	20	7	45	0	118
	Wakefield	2000-01	16(2)	4	19	1	55
Luke Dorn	Salford	2007	19(8)	11	0	0	44
	Harlequins	2006	24	13	0	0	52
	London	2005	28	23	0	0	92
Ewan Dowes	Hull	2003-07	110(21)	8	0	0	32
	Leeds	2001-03	1(9)	0	0	0	0
Adam Doyle	Warrington	1998	9(3)	4	0	0	16
Rod Doyle	Sheffield	1997-99	52(10)	10	0	0	40
Brad Drew	Huddersfield	2005-07	74(8)	17	13	1	95
Damien Driscoll	Salford	2001	23(1)	1	0	0	4
Jason Duffy	Leigh	2005	3(1)	0	0	0	0
John Duffy	Leigh	2005	21	6	0	0	24
	Salford	2000	3(11)	0	1	1	3
	Warrington	1997-99	12(12)	0	0	0	0
Andrew Duncan	London	1997	2(4)	2	0	0	8
	Warrington	1997	(1)	0	0	0	0
Andrew Dunemann	Salford	2006	25	1	0	2	6
	Leeds	2003-05	76(4)	11	0	2	46
	Halifax	1999-2002	68	19	0	1	77
Matt Dunford	London	1997-98	18(20)	3	0	1	13
Vincent Duport	Catalans	2007	11(2)	3	0	0	12
Jamie Durbin	Widnes	2005	1	0	0	0	0
	Warrington	2003	(1)	0	0	0	0
James Durkin	Paris	1997	(5)	0	0	0	0
Bernard Dwyer	Bradford	1996-2000	65(10)	14	0	0	56
Luke Dyer	Hull KR	2007	26	13	0	0	52
	Castleford	2006	17(2)	5	0	0	20
Jim Dymock	London	2001-04	94(1)	15	0	1	61
Leo Dynevor	London	1996	8(11)	5	7	0	34
Jason Eade	Paris	1997	9	4	0	0	16
Michael Eagar	Hull	2004-05	12	4	0	0	16
	Castleford	1999-2003	130(2)	60	0	0	240
	Warrington	1998	21	6	0	0	24
Kyle Eastmond	St Helens	2007	2	0	0	0	0
Barry Eaton	Widnes	2002	25	2	49	4	110
	Castleford	2000	1(4)	0	3	0	6
Greg Ebrill	Salford	2002	15(6)	1	0	0	4
Cliff Eccles	Salford	1997-98	30(5)	1	0	0	4
Chris Eckersley	Warrington	1996	1	0	0	0	0
Steve Edmed	Sheffield	1997	15(1)	0	0	0	0
Mark Edmondson	Salford	2007	10(2)	0	0	0	0
	St Helens	1999-2005	27(75)	10	0	0	40
Diccon Edwards	Castleford	1996-97	10(5)	1	0	0	4
Grant Edwards	Castleford	2006	(2)	0	0	0	0
Peter Edwards	Salford	1997-98	35(2)	4	0	0	16
Shaun Edwards	London	1997-2000	32(8)	16	1	0	66
	Bradford	1998	8(2)	4	0	0	16
	Wigan	1996	17(3)	12	1	0	50
Danny Ekis	Halifax	2001	(1)	0	0	0	0
Abi Ekoku	Bradford	1997-98	21(4)	6	0	0	24
	Halifax	1996	15(1)	5	0	0	20
Shane Elford	Huddersfield	2007	9(1)	4	0	0	16
Olivier Elima	Wakefield	2003-07	40(47)	13	0	0	52
	Bradford	2002	(1)	1	0	0	4
Abderazak Elkhalouki	Paris	1997	(1)	0	0	0	0
Gareth Ellis	Leeds	2005-07	82	20	0	0	80
	Wakefield	1999-2004	86(17)	21	2	0	88
Danny Ellison	Castleford	1998-99	7(16)	6	0	0	24
	Wigan	1996-97	15(1)	13	0	0	52
Andrew Emelio	Widnes	2005	22(2)	8	0	0	32
Patrick Entat	Paris	1996	22	2	0	0	8
Jason Erba	Sheffield	1997	1(4)	0	0	0	0
James Evans	Bradford	2007	17(4)	12	0	0	48
	Wakefield	2006	6	3	0	0	12
	Huddersfield	2004-06	51	22	0	0	88
Paul Evans	Paris	1997	18	8	0	0	32
Wayne Evans	London	2002	11(6)	2	0	0	8
Richie Eyres	Warrington	1997	2(5)	0	0	0	0
	Sheffield	1997	2(3)	0	0	0	0
Henry Fa'afili	Warrington	2004-07	90(1)	70	0	0	280
Sala Fa'alogo	Widnes	2004-05	8(15)	2	0	0	8
Richard Fa'aoso	Castleford	2006	10(15)	5	0	0	20
Maurie Fa'asavalu	St Helens	2004-07	4(83)	18	0	0	72
Bolu Fagborun	Huddersfield	2004-06	4(2)	1	0	0	4
Esene Faimalo	Salford	1997-99	23(25)	2	0	0	8
	Leeds	1996	3(3)	0	0	0	0
Joe Faimalo	Salford	1998-2000	23(47)	7	0	0	28
	Oldham	1996-97	37(5)	7	0	0	28
Karl Fairbank	Bradford	1996	17(2)	4	0	0	16
David Fairleigh	St Helens	2001	26(1)	8	0	0	32
Jamel Fakir	Catalans	2006-07	21(8)	5	0	0	20
Jim Fallon	Leeds	1996	10	5	0	0	20
Danny Farrar	Warrington	1998-2000	76	13	0	0	52
Andy Farrell	Wigan	1996-2004	230	77	1026	16	2376

PLAYER	CLUB	YEAR	APP	TRIES	GOALS	FG	PTS
Anthony Farrell	Widnes	2002-03	24(22)	4	1	0	18
	Leeds	1997-2001	99(23)	18	0	0	72
	Sheffield	1996	14(5)	5	0	0	20
Craig Farrell	Hull	2000-01	1(3)	0	0	0	0
Abraham Fatnowna							
	London	1997-98	7(2)	2	0	0	8
	Workington	1996	5	2	0	0	8
Sione Faumuina	Hull	2005	3	1	0	0	4
Vince Fawcett	Wakefield	1999	13(1)	2	0	0	8
	Warrington	1998	4(7)	1	0	0	4
	Oldham	1997	5	3	0	0	12
Danny Fearon	Huddersfield	2001	(1)	0	0	0	0
	Halifax	1999-2000	5(6)	0	0	0	0
Chris Feather	Bradford	2007	5(11)	0	0	0	0
	Leeds	2003-04, 2006	16(35)	6	0	0	24
	Wakefield	2001-02, 2004-05	29(32)	9	0	0	36
Dom Feaunati	Leigh	2005	4	1	0	0	4
	St Helens	2004	10(7)	7	0	0	28
Adel Fellous	Catalans	2006-07	16(22)	4	0	0	16
Luke Felsch	Hull	2000-01	46(6)	7	0	0	28
	Gateshead	1999	28(1)	2	0	0	8
Leon Felton	Warrington	2002	4(2)	0	0	0	0
	St Helens	2001	1(1)	0	0	0	0
Dale Ferguson	Wakefield	2007	1(1)	0	0	0	0
Brett Ferres	Wakefield	2007	24(2)	2	5	0	18
	Bradford	2005-06	18(17)	11	2	0	48
David Ferriol	Catalans	2007	5(18)	3	0	0	12
Jason Ferris	Leigh	2005	4	1	0	0	4
Jamie Field	Wakefield	1999-2006	133(59)	19	0	0	76
	Huddersfield	1998	15(5)	0	0	0	0
	Leeds	1996-97	3(11)	0	0	0	0
Mark Field	Wakefield	2003-07	28(7)	3	0	0	12
Jamie Fielden	London	2003	(1)	0	0	0	0
	Huddersfield	1998-2000	4(8)	0	0	0	0
Stuart Fielden	Wigan	2006-07	39(2)	2	0	0	8
	Bradford	1998-2006	142(78)	41	0	0	164
Lafaele Filipo	Workington	1996	15(4)	3	0	0	12
Salesi Finau	Warrington	1996-97	16(15)	8	0	0	32
Liam Finn	Wakefield	2004	1(1)	0	1	0	2
	Halifax	2002-03	16(5)	2	30	1	69
Lee Finnerty	Halifax	2003	18(2)	5	2	0	24
Phil Finney	Warrington	1998	1	0	0	0	0
Simon Finnigan	Salford	2006-07	50	17	0	0	68
	Widnes	2003-05	51(19)	21	0	0	84
Matt Firth	Halifax	2000-01	12(2)	0	0	0	0
Andy Fisher	Wakefield	1999-2000	31(8)	4	0	0	16
Ben Fisher	Hull KR	2007	23(2)	5	0	0	20
Karl Fitzpatrick	Salford	2004-07	54(11)	22	2	0	92
Chris Flannery	St Helens	2007	8(1)	1	0	0	4
Darren Fleary	Leigh	2005	24	1	0	0	4
	Huddersfield	2003-04	43(8)	4	0	0	16
	Leeds	1997-2002	98(9)	3	0	0	12
Greg Fleming	London	1999-2001	64(1)	40	2	0	164
Adam Fletcher	Castleford	2006	10(3)	8	0	0	32
Bryan Fletcher	Wigan	2006-07	47(2)	14	0	0	56
Richard Fletcher	Castleford	2006	13(5)	3	4	0	20
	Hull	1999-2004	11(56)	5	0	0	20
Greg Florimo	Halifax	2000	26	6	4	0	32
	Wigan	1999	18(2)	7	1	0	30
Jason Flowers	Salford	2004	6(1)	0	0	0	0
	Halifax	2002	24(4)	4	0	0	16
	Castleford	1996-2001	119(19)	33	0	1	133
Stuart Flowers	Castleford	1996	(3)	0	0	0	0
Adrian Flynn	Castleford	1996-97	19(2)	10	0	0	40
Wayne Flynn	Sheffield	1997	3(5)	0	0	0	0
Adam Fogerty	Warrington	1998	4	0	0	0	0
	St Helens	1996	13	1	0	0	4
Carl Forber	Leigh	2005	4	1	0	0	4
	St Helens	2004	1(1)	0	6	0	12
Paul Forber	Salford	1997-98	19(12)	4	0	0	16
Byron Ford	Hull KR	2007	13	6	0	0	24
Mike Ford	Castleford	1997-98	25(12)	5	0	3	23
	Warrington	1996	3	0	0	0	0
Jim Forshaw	Salford	1999	(1)	0	0	0	0
Mike Forshaw	Warrington	2004	20(1)	5	0	0	20
	Bradford	1997-2003	162(7)	32	0	0	128
	Leeds	1996	11(3)	5	0	0	20
Mark Forster	Warrington	1996-2000	102(1)	40	0	0	160
David Foster	Halifax	2000-01	4(9)	0	0	0	0
Peter Fox	Wakefield	2007	23	11	0	0	44
Nick Fozzard	St Helens	2004-07	87(13)	6	0	0	24
	Warrington	2002-03	43(11)	2	0	0	8
	Huddersfield	1998-2000	24(8)	2	0	0	8
	Leeds	1996-97	6(16)	3	0	0	12
David Fraisse	Workington	1996	9	0	0	0	0
Daniel Frame	Widnes	2002-05	100(6)	24	0	0	96
Paul Franze	Castleford	2006	2(1)	0	0	0	0
Laurent Frayssinous							
	Catalans	2006	14(2)	3	32	0	76
Andrew Frew	Halifax	2003	17	5	0	0	20
	Wakefield	2002	21	8	0	0	32
	Huddersfield	2001	26	15	0	0	60
Dale Fritz	Castleford	1999-2003	120(4)	9	0	0	36
David Furner	Leeds	2003-04	45	8	23	0	78
	Wigan	2001-02	51(2)	21	13	0	110
David Furness	Castleford	1996	(1)	0	0	0	0
Matt Gafa	Harlequins	2006-07	45	9	12	0	60
Tommy Gallagher	Hull KR	2007	1(7)	0	0	0	0
	Widnes	2004	(6)	0	0	0	0
	London	2003	1(9)	1	0	0	4
Mark Gamson	Sheffield	1996	3	0	0	0	0
Jim Gannon	Hull KR	2007	7(16)	1	0	0	4
	Huddersfield	2003-06	79(14)	11	0	0	44
	Halifax	1999-2002	83(4)	14	0	0	56
Steve Garces	Salford	2001	(1)	0	0	0	0
Jean-Marc Garcia	Sheffield	1996-97	35(3)	22	0	0	88
Ade Gardner	St Helens	2002-07	130(11)	73	0	0	292
Matt Gardner	Huddersfield	2006-07	22(3)	7	0	0	28
	Castleford	2004	1	1	0	0	4
Steve Gartland	Oldham	1996	1(1)	0	1	0	2
Daniel Gartner	Bradford	2001-03	74(1)	26	0	0	104
Dean Gaskell	Warrington	2002-05	58(1)	10	0	0	40
Richard Gay	Castleford	1996-2002	94(16)	39	0	0	156
Andrew Gee	Warrington	2000-01	33(1)	4	0	0	16
Stanley Gene	Hull KR	2007	17(3)	5	0	0	20
	Bradford	2006	5(16)	8	0	0	32
	Huddersfield	2001, 2003-05	70(6)	27	0	0	108
	Hull	2000-01	5(23)	6	0	0	24
Steve Georgallis	Warrington	2001	5(1)	2	0	0	8
Luke George	Wakefield	2007	(2)	1	0	0	4
Shaun Geritas	Warrington	1997	(5)	1	0	0	4
Anthony Gibbons	Leeds	1996	9(4)	2	0	1	9
David Gibbons	Leeds	1996	3(4)	2	0	0	8
Scott Gibbs	St Helens	1996	9	3	0	0	12
Ashley Gibson	Leeds	2005-07	18(2)	10	8	0	56
Damian Gibson	Castleford	2003-04	40(3)	5	0	0	20
	Salford	2002	28	3	0	0	12
	Halifax	1998-2001	104(1)	39	0	0	156
	Leeds	1997	18	3	0	0	12
Matt Gidley	St Helens	2007	27	15	0	0	60
Ian Gildart	Oldham	1996-97	31(7)	0	0	0	0
Chris Giles	Widnes	2003-04	35	12	0	0	48
	St Helens	2002	(1)	0	0	0	0
Peter Gill	London	1996-99	75(6)	20	0	0	80
Carl Gillespie	Halifax	1996-99	47(36)	13	0	0	52
Michael Gillett	London	2001-02	23(21)	12	2	0	52
Simon Gillies	Warrington	1999	28	6	0	0	24
Lee Gilmour	St Helens	2004-07	95(3)	29	0	0	116
	Bradford	2001-03	44(31)	20	0	0	80
	Wigan	1997-2000	44(39)	22	0	0	88
Marc Glanville	Leeds	1998-99	43(3)	5	0	0	20
Eddie Glaze	Castleford	1996	1	0	0	0	0
Paul Gleadhill	Leeds	1996	4	0	0	0	0
Mark Gleeson	Warrington	2000-07	36(87)	11	0	0	44
Martin Gleeson	Warrington	2005-07	78	33	0	0	132
	St Helens	2002-04	56(1)	25	0	0	100
	Huddersfield	1999-2001	47(9)	18	0	0	72
Sean Gleeson	Wakefield	2007	4(4)	1	0	0	4
	Wigan	2005-06	3(3)	0	0	0	0
Jon Goddard	Hull KR	2007	20	2	0	0	8
	Castleford	2000-01	(2)	0	0	0	0
Richard Goddard	Castleford	1996-97	11(3)	2	10	0	28
Brad Godden	Leeds	1998-99	47	15	0	0	60
Wayne Godwin	Hull	2007	3(13)	1	0	0	4
	Wigan	2005-06	9(38)	6	0	0	24
	Castleford	2001-04	30(33)	18	56	0	184
Jason Golden	Wakefield	2007	8(4)	1	0	0	4
Marvin Golden	Widnes	2003	4	1	0	0	4
	London	2001	17(2)	1	0	0	4
	Halifax	2000	20(2)	5	0	0	20
	Leeds	1996-99	43(11)	19	0	0	76
Brett Goldspink	Halifax	2000-02	64(5)	2	0	0	8
	Wigan	1999	6(16)	1	0	0	4
	St Helens	1998	19(4)	2	0	0	8
	Oldham	1997	13(2)	0	0	0	0
Luke Goodwin	London	1998	9(2)	3	1	1	15
	Oldham	1997	16(4)	10	17	2	76
Aaron Gorrell	Catalans	2007	3	0	10	0	20
Andy Gorski	Salford	2001-02	(2)	0	0	0	0
Cyril Gossard	Catalans	2006-07	17(8)	3	0	0	12
Bobbie Goulding	Salford	2001-02	31(1)	2	56	4	124
	Wakefield	2000	12	3	25	3	65
	Huddersfield	1998-99	27(1)	3	65	4	146
	St Helens	1996-98	42(2)	9	210	4	460
Darrell Goulding	Wigan	2005-07	11(16)	9	0	0	36
Mick Govin	Leigh	2005	5(6)	4	0	0	16
David Gower	Salford	2006-07	(16)	0	0	0	0
James Graham	St Helens	2003-07	23(61)	18	0	0	72
Nathan Graham	Bradford	1996-98	17(28)	4	0	1	17
Nick Graham	Wigan	2003	13(1)	2	0	0	8
Jon Grayshon	Harlequins	2007	4(17)	2	0	0	8
	Huddersfield	2003-06	7(43)	5	0	0	20
Brett Green	Gateshead	1999	10(2)	0	0	0	0

PLAYER	CLUB	YEAR	APP	TRIES	GOALS	FG	PTS
Toby Green	Huddersfield	2001	3(1)	1	0	0	4
Craig Greenhill	Castleford	2004	21(4)	1	0	0	4
	Hull	2002-03	56	3	2	0	16
Clint Greenshields							
	Catalans	2007	27	12	0	0	48
Brandon Greenwood							
	Halifax	1996	1	0	0	0	0
Gareth Greenwood							
	Huddersfield	2003	(1)	0	0	0	0
	Halifax	2002	1	0	0	0	0
Lee Greenwood	Huddersfield	2005	7	3	0	0	12
	London	2004-05	30(2)	19	0	0	76
	Halifax	2000-03	38(2)	17	0	0	68
	Sheffield	1999	1(1)	0	0	0	0
Maxime Greseque							
	Wakefield	2007	2(1)	0	0	0	0
Mathieu Griffi	Catalans	2006-07	1(22)	0	0	0	0
Darrell Griffin	Huddersfield	2007	5(21)	1	0	0	4
	Wakefield	2003-06	55(37)	9	3	0	42
Jonathan Griffiths							
	Paris	1996	(4)	1	0	0	4
Andrew Grima	Workington	1996	2(9)	2	0	0	8
Tony Grimaldi	Hull	2000-01	56(1)	14	0	0	56
	Gateshead	1999	27(2)	10	0	0	40
Danny Grimley	Sheffield	1996	4(1)	1	0	0	4
Simon Grix	Warrington	2006-07	7(7)	6	0	0	24
	Halifax	2003	2(4)	0	0	0	0
Brett Grogan	Gateshead	1999	14(7)	3	0	0	12
Brent Grose	Warrington	2003-07	134(1)	55	0	0	220
Renaud Guigue	Catalans	2006	14(4)	3	0	0	12
Jerome Guisset	Catalans	2006-07	44(6)	3	0	0	12
	Wigan	2005	20(2)	3	0	0	12
	Warrington	2000-04	59(65)	21	0	0	84
Reece Guy	Oldham	1996	3(4)	0	0	0	0
Gareth Haggerty	Salford	2004-07	1(93)	15	0	0	60
	Widnes	2002	1(2)	1	0	0	4
Andy Haigh	St Helens	1996-98	20(16)	11	0	0	44
Carl Hall	Leeds	1996	7(2)	3	0	0	12
Craig Hall	Hull	2007	13	7	3	0	34
Martin Hall	Halifax	1998	2(10)	0	0	0	0
	Hull	1999	7	0	0	0	0
	Castleford	1998	4	0	0	0	0
	Wigan	1996-97	31(5)	7	6	0	40
Ryan Hall	Leeds	2007	8(1)	3	0	0	12
Steve Hall	Widnes	2004	1	0	0	0	0
	London	2002-03	35(3)	10	0	0	40
	St Helens	1999-2001	36(22)	19	0	0	76
Graeme Hallas	Huddersfield	2001	1	0	0	0	0
	Hull	1998-99	30(10)	6	39	1	103
	Halifax	1996	11(4)	5	0	0	20
Dave Halley	Bradford	2007	3(7)	3	0	0	12
Danny Halliwell	Salford	2007	2(3)	0	0	0	0
	Leigh	2005	5	3	0	0	12
	Halifax	2000-03	17(8)	4	0	0	16
	Warrington	2002	9(1)	8	0	0	32
	Wakefield	2002	3	0	0	0	0
Colum Halpenny	Wakefield	2003-06	103(1)	36	0	0	144
	Halifax	2002	22	12	0	0	48
Jon Hamer	Bradford	1996	(1)	0	0	0	0
Andrew Hamilton	London	1997, 2003	1(20)	3	0	0	12
John Hamilton	St Helens	1998	3	0	0	0	0
Karle Hammond	Halifax	2002	10(2)	2	14	0	36
	Salford	2001	2(3)	1	0	0	4
	London	1999-2000	47	23	2	3	99
	St Helens	1996-98	58(8)	28	0	4	116
Anthony Hancock	Paris	1997	8(6)	1	0	0	4
Michael Hancock	Salford	2001-02	12(24)	7	0	0	28
Gareth Handford	Castleford	2001	7(2)	0	0	0	0
	Bradford	2000	1(1)	0	0	0	0
Paul Handforth	Castleford	2006	2(15)	2	1	0	10
	Wakefield	2000-04	17(44)	10	13	0	66
Paddy Handley	Leeds	1996	1(1)	2	0	0	8
Dean Hanger	Warrington	1999	7(11)	3	0	0	12
	Huddersfield	1998	20(1)	5	0	0	20
Harrison Hansen	Wigan	2004-07	32(44)	10	0	0	40
Lee Hansen	Wigan	1997	10(5)	0	0	0	0
Shontayne Hape	Bradford	2003-07	105(2)	73	0	0	292
Lionel Harbin	Wakefield	2001	(1)	0	0	0	0
Ian Hardman	Hull KR	2007	18	4	0	0	16
	St Helens	2003-07	32(11)	9	5	0	46
Jeff Hardy	Hudds-Sheff	2000	20(5)	6	0	1	25
	Sheffield	1999	22(4)	7	0	0	28
Spencer Hargrave							
	Castleford	1996-99	(6)	0	0	0	0
Bryn Hargreaves	St Helens	2007	4(11)	0	0	0	0
	Wigan	2004-06	16(12)	1	0	0	4
Lee Harland	Castleford	1996-2004	148(35)	20	0	0	80
Neil Harmon	Halifax	2003	13(3)	0	0	0	0
	Salford	2001	6(5)	0	0	0	0
	Bradford	1998-2000	15(13)	2	0	0	8
	Huddersfield	1998	12	1	0	0	4
	Leeds	1996	10	1	0	0	4
Ben Harris	Bradford	2005-07	70(4)	24	0	0	96
Iestyn Harris	Bradford	2004-07	95(2)	32	57	2	244
	Leeds	1997-2001	111(7)	57	490	6	1214
	Warrington	1996	16	4	63	2	144
Ben Harrison	Warrington	2007	4(12)	0	0	0	0
Karl Harrison	Hull	1999	26	2	0	0	8
	Halifax	1996-98	60(2)	2	0	0	8
Andrew Hart	London	2004	12(1)	2	0	0	8
Tim Hartley	Harlequins	2006	2	1	0	0	4
	Salford	2004-05	6(7)	5	0	0	20
Carlos Hassan	Bradford	1996	6(4)	2	0	0	8
Phil Hassan	Wakefield	2002	9(1)	0	0	0	0
	Halifax	2000-01	25(4)	3	0	0	12
	Salford	1998	15	2	0	0	8
	Leeds	1996-97	38(4)	12	0	0	48
Tom Haughey	Castleford	2006	1(3)	1	0	0	4
	London	2003-04	10(8)	1	0	0	4
	Wakefield	2001-02	5(12)	0	0	0	0
Simon Haughton	Wigan	1996-2002	63(46)	32	0	0	128
Solomon Haumono							
	Harlequins	2006	10(9)	6	0	0	24
	London	2005	24(5)	8	0	0	32
Richie Hawkyard	Bradford	2007	1(2)	1	0	0	4
Andy Hay	Widnes	2003-04	50(2)	7	0	0	28
	Leeds	1997-2002	112(27)	43	0	0	172
	Sheffield	1996-97	17(3)	5	0	0	20
Adam Hayes	Hudds-Sheff	2000	2(1)	0	0	0	0
Joey Hayes	Salford	1999	9	2	0	0	8
	St Helens	1996-98	11(6)	7	0	0	28
Mathew Head	Hull	2007	9(1)	1	0	1	5
Mitch Healey	Castleford	2001-03	68(1)	10	16	0	72
Daniel Heckenberg							
	Harlequins	2006-07	27(9)	3	0	0	12
Ricky Helliwell	Salford	1997-99	(2)	0	0	0	0
Tom Hemingway	Huddersfield	2005-07	4(4)	0	2	0	4
Bryan Henare	St Helens	2000-01	4(12)	1	0	0	4
Richard Henare	Warrington	1996-97	28(2)	24	0	0	96
Andrew Henderson							
	Castleford	2006	28	2	0	0	8
Ian Henderson	Bradford	2005-07	33(37)	13	0	0	52
Kevin Henderson	Wakefield	2005-07	25(10)	5	0	0	20
	Leigh	2005	(1)	0	0	0	0
Brad Hepi	Castleford	1999, 2001	9(21)	3	0	0	12
	Salford	2000	3(5)	0	0	0	0
	Hull	1998	15(1)	3	0	0	12
Jon Hepworth	Castleford	2003-04	19(23)	7	8	0	44
	Leeds	2003	(1)	0	0	0	0
	London	2002	(2)	0	0	0	0
Ian Herron	Hull	2000	9	1	17	0	38
	Gateshead	1999	25	4	105	0	226
Jason Hetherington							
	London	2001-02	37	9	0	0	36
Gareth Hewitt	Salford	1999	2(1)	1	0	0	4
Andrew Hick	Hull	2000	9(9)	1	0	0	4
	Gateshead	1999	12(5)	2	0	0	8
Paul Hicks	Wakefield	1999	(1)	0	0	0	0
Darren Higgins	London	1998	5(6)	2	0	0	8
Iain Higgins	London	1997-98	1(7)	2	0	0	8
Liam Higgins	Hull	2003-06	1(34)	0	0	0	0
Mick Higham	Wigan	2006-07	36(23)	7	0	0	28
	St Helens	2001-05	43(56)	32	0	0	128
Chris Highton	Warrington	1997	1(1)	0	0	0	0
David Highton	London	2004-05	21(24)	2	0	0	8
	Salford	2002	4(5)	2	0	0	8
	Warrington	1998-2001	18(14)	2	0	0	8
Paul Highton	Salford	1998-2002, 2004-07	114(80)	14	0	0	56
	Halifax	1996-97	12(18)	2	0	0	8
Andy Hill	Huddersfield	1999	(4)	0	0	0	0
	Castleford	1999	4(4)	0	0	0	0
Chris Hill	Leigh	2005	(1)	0	0	0	0
Danny Hill	Wigan	2006-07	1(10)	0	0	0	0
	Hull KR	2007	2	0	0	0	0
	Hull	2004-06	4(6)	0	0	0	0
Howard Hill	Oldham	1996-97	22(12)	4	0	0	16
John Hill	St Helens	2003	(1)	0	0	0	0
	Halifax	2003	1(2)	0	0	0	0
	Warrington	2001-02	4	0	0	0	0
Scott Hill	Harlequins	2007	21(1)	6	0	0	24
Mark Hilton	Warrington	1996-2000, 2002-06	141(40)	7	0	0	28
Ian Hindmarsh	Catalans	2006	25	3	0	0	12
Andy Hobson	Widnes	2004	5(13)	0	0	0	0
	Halifax	1998-2003	51(85)	8	0	0	32
Gareth Hock	Wigan	2003-07	72(31)	14	0	0	56
Tommy Hodgkinson							
	St Helens	2006	(1)	0	0	0	0
Andy Hodgson	Wakefield	1999	14(2)	2	1	0	10
	Bradford	1997-98	8(2)	4	0	0	16
David Hodgson	Salford	2005-07	81	30	47	0	214
	Wigan	2000-04	90(19)	43	0	0	172
	Halifax	1999	10(3)	5	0	0	20
Darren Hogg	London	1996	(1)	0	0	0	0
Michael Hogue	Paris	1997	5(7)	0	0	0	0

PLAYER	CLUB	YEAR	APP	TRIES	GOALS	FG	PTS
Chris Holden	Warrington	1996-97	2(1)	0	0	0	0
Stephen Holgate	Halifax	2000	1(10)	0	0	0	0
	Hull	1999	1	0	0	0	0
	Wigan	1997-98	11(26)	2	0	0	8
	Workington	1996	19	3	0	0	12
Martyn Holland	Wakefield	2000-03	52(3)	6	0	0	24
Tim Holmes	Widnes	2004-05	15(4)	0	0	0	0
Graham Holroyd	Huddersfield	2003	3(5)	0	0	0	0
	Salford	2000-02	40(11)	8	75	5	187
	Halifax	1999	24(2)	3	74	5	165
	Leeds	1996-98	40(26)	22	101	8	298
Dallas Hood	Wakefield	2003-04	18(9)	1	0	0	4
Jason Hooper	St Helens	2003-07	89(6)	35	30	0	200
Lee Hopkins	Harlequins	2006-07	44(3)	11	0	0	44
	London	2005	29	6	0	0	24
Sean Hoppe	St Helens	1999-2002	69(16)	32	0	0	128
Graeme Horne	Hull	2003-07	17(64)	14	0	0	56
Richard Horne	Hull	1999-2007	221(9)	85	12	6	370
John Hough	Warrington	1996-97	9	2	0	0	8
Danny Houghton	Hull	2007	(4)	0	0	0	0
Sylvain Houles	Wakefield	2003, 2005	8(1)	1	0	0	4
	London	2001-02	17(10)	11	0	0	44
	Hudds-Sheff	2000	5(2)	1	0	0	4
Harvey Howard	Wigan	2001-02	25(27)	1	0	0	4
	Bradford	1998	4(2)	1	0	0	4
	Leeds	1996	8	0	0	0	0
Kim Howard	London	1997	4(5)	0	0	0	0
Stuart Howarth	Workington	1996	(2)	0	0	0	0
Phil Howlett	Bradford	1999	5(1)	2	0	0	8
Craig Huby	Castleford	2003-04, 2006	4(29)	2	19	0	46
Ryan Hudson	Huddersfield	1998-99, 2007	33(14)	6	0	0	24
	Castleford	2002-04	73(6)	21	0	0	84
	Wakefield	2000-01	42(9)	11	0	1	45
Adam Hughes	Widnes	2002-05	89(2)	45	51	0	282
	Halifax	2001	8(8)	8	0	0	32
	Wakefield	1999-2000	43(3)	21	34	0	152
	Leeds	1996-97	4(5)	4	0	0	16
Ian Hughes	Sheffield	1996	9(8)	4	0	0	16
Mark Hughes	Catalans	2006	23	9	0	0	36
Steffan Hughes	London	1999-2001	1(13)	1	0	0	4
David Hulme	Salford	1997-99	53(1)	5	0	0	20
	Leeds	1996	8(1)	2	0	0	8
Paul Hulme	Warrington	1996-97	23(1)	2	0	0	8
Gary Hulse	Widnes	2005	12(5)	2	0	0	8
	Warrington	2001-04	20(28)	8	0	1	33
Alan Hunte	Salford	2002	19(2)	9	0	0	36
	Warrington	1999-2001	83	49	0	0	196
	Hull	1998	21	7	0	0	28
	St Helens	1996-97	30(2)	28	0	0	112
Nick Hyde	Paris	1997	5(5)	1	0	0	4
Chaz I'Anson	Hull KR	2007	(1)	0	0	0	0
Andy Ireland	Hull	1998-99	22(15)	0	0	0	0
	Bradford	1996	1	0	0	0	0
Kevin Iro	St Helens	1999-2001	76	39	0	0	156
	Leeds	1996	16	9	0	0	36
Andrew Isherwood	Wigan	1998-99	(5)	0	0	0	0
Olu Iwenofu	London	2000-01	2(1)	0	0	0	0
Chico Jackson	Hull	1999	(4)	0	0	0	0
Lee Jackson	Hull	2001-02	37(9)	12	1	0	50
	Leeds	1999-2000	28(24)	7	0	0	28
Michael Jackson	Sheffield	1998-99	17(17)	2	0	0	8
	Halifax	1996-97	27(6)	11	0	0	44
Paul Jackson	Huddersfield	1998, 2005-07	35(43)	2	0	0	8
	Castleford	2003-04	7(21)	0	0	0	0
	Wakefield	1999-2002	57(41)	2	0	0	8
Rob Jackson	Leigh	2005	20(3)	5	0	0	20
	London	2002-04	26(14)	9	0	0	36
Wayne Jackson	Halifax	1996-97	17(5)	2	0	0	8
Aled James	Widnes	2003	3	0	0	0	0
Andy James	Halifax	1996	(4)	0	0	0	0
Jordan James	Wigan	2006	2(4)	3	0	0	12
Matt James	Bradford	2006-07	1(15)	0	0	0	0
Pascal Jampy	Catalans	2006	4(7)	0	0	0	0
	Paris	1996-97	3(2)	0	0	0	0
Ben Jeffries	Wakefield	2003-07	128(7)	62	14	4	280
Mick Jenkins	Hull	2000	24	2	0	0	8
	Gateshead	1999	16	3	0	0	12
Ed Jennings	London	1998-99	1(2)	0	0	0	0
Rod Jensen	Huddersfield	2007	12	5	0	0	20
Anthony Jerram	Warrington	2007	(2)	0	0	0	0
Lee Jewitt	Salford	2007	3(11)	0	0	0	0
	Wigan	2005	(2)	0	0	0	0
Andrew Johns	Warrington	2005	3	1	12	1	29
Matthew Johns	Wigan	2001	24	3	0	1	13
Andy Johnson	Salford	2004-05	8(26)	7	0	0	28
	Castleford	2002-03	32(16)	11	0	0	44
	London	2000-01	24(21)	12	0	0	48
	Huddersfield	1999	1	0	0	4	4
	Wigan	1996-99	24(20)	19	0	0	76
Bruce Johnson	Widnes	2004-05	(4)	0	0	0	0
Jason Johnson	St Helens	1997-99	2	0	0	0	0
Mark Johnson	Salford	1999-2000	22(9)	16	0	0	64
	Hull	1998	10(1)	4	0	0	16
	Workington	1996	12	4	0	0	16
Nick Johnson	London	2003	(1)	0	0	0	0
Paul Johnson	Warrington	2007	15	3	0	0	12
	Bradford	2004-06	46(8)	19	0	0	76
	Wigan	1996-2003	74(46)	54	0	0	216
Chris Jones	Leigh	2005	1(1)	0	0	0	0
Danny Jones	Halifax	2003	1	0	0	0	0
David Jones	Oldham	1997	14(1)	5	0	0	20
Mark Jones	Warrington	1996	8(11)	2	0	0	8
Phil Jones	Leigh	2005	16	8	31	0	94
	Wigan	1999-2001	14(7)	6	25	0	74
Stacey Jones	Catalans	2006-07	39	11	43	3	133
Stephen Jones	Huddersfield	2005	(1)	0	0	0	0
Stuart Jones	Huddersfield	2004-07	82(17)	14	0	0	56
	St Helens	2003	(18)	2	0	0	8
	Wigan	2002	5(3)	1	0	0	4
Jamie Jones-Buchanan	Leeds	1999-2007	79(52)	26	0	0	104
Tim Jonkers	Wigan	2006	3(1)	0	0	0	0
	Salford	2004-06	5(11)	0	0	0	0
	St Helens	1999-2004	41(64)	12	0	0	48
Darren Jordan	Wakefield	2003	(1)	0	0	0	0
Phil Joseph	Huddersfield	2004	7(6)	0	0	0	0
Warren Jowitt	Hull	2003	(2)	0	0	0	0
	Salford	2001-02	17(4)	2	0	0	8
	Wakefield	2000	19(3)	8	0	0	32
	Bradford	1996-99	13(25)	5	0	0	20
Chris Joynt	St Helens	1996-2004	201(14)	68	0	0	272
Gregory Kacala	Paris	1996	7	1	0	0	4
Andy Kain	Castleford	2004, 2006	9(7)	3	10	0	32
Mal Kaufusi	London	2004	1(3)	0	0	0	0
Stephen Kearney	Hull	2005	22(2)	5	0	0	20
Damon Keating	Wakefield	2002	7(17)	1	0	0	4
Shaun Keating	London	1996	1(3)	0	0	0	0
Mark Keenan	Workington	1996	3(4)	1	0	0	4
Tony Kemp	Wakefield	1999-2000	15(5)	2	0	1	9
	Leeds	1996-98	23(2)	5	0	2	22
Damien Kennedy	London	2003	5(11)	1	0	0	4
Ian Kenny	St Helens	2004	(1)	0	0	0	0
Jason Kent	Leigh	2005	23	1	0	0	4
Shane Kenward	Wakefield	1999	28	6	0	0	24
	Salford	1998	1	0	0	0	0
Jason Keough	Paris	1997	2	1	0	0	4
Keiran Kerr	Widnes	2005	6	2	0	0	8
Martin Ketteridge	Halifax	1996	7(5)	0	0	0	0
Ronnie Kettlewell	Warrington	1996	(1)	0	0	0	0
Younes Khattabi	Catalans	2006-07	11(3)	5	0	0	20
David Kidwell	Warrington	2001-02	14(12)	9	0	0	36
Andrew King	London	2003	23(1)	15	0	0	60
Dave King	Huddersfield	1998-99	11(17)	2	0	0	8
James King	Leigh	2005	5(7)	0	0	0	0
Kevin King	Wakefield	2005	8(1)	2	0	0	8
	Castleford	2004	(1)	0	0	0	0
Paul King	Hull	1999-2007	127(76)	20	0	1	81
Andy Kirk	Wakefield	2005	6(3)	1	0	0	4
	Salford	2004	20	5	0	0	20
	Leeds	2001-02	4(4)	0	0	0	0
Ian Kirke	Leeds	2006-07	9(29)	3	0	0	12
John Kirkpatrick	London	2004-05	18(1)	5	0	0	20
	St Helens	2001-03	10(11)	10	0	0	40
	Halifax	2003	4	1	0	0	4
Wayne Kitchin	Workington	1996	11(6)	3	17	1	47
Ian Knott	Leigh	2005	8(1)	2	0	0	8
	Wakefield	2002-03	34(5)	7	79	0	186
	Warrington	1996-2001	68(41)	24	18	0	132
Matt Knowles	Wigan	1996	(3)	0	0	0	0
Michael Knowles	Castleford	2006	(1)	0	0	0	0
Phil Knowles	Salford	1997	1	0	0	0	0
Simon Knox	Halifax	1999	(6)	0	0	0	0
	Salford	1998	1(1)	0	0	0	0
	Bradford	1996-98	9(19)	7	0	0	28
Toa Kohe-Love	Warrington	1996-2001, 2005-06	166(3)	90	0	0	360
	Bradford	2004	1(1)	0	0	0	0
	Hull	2002-03	42	19	0	0	76
Paul Koloi	Wigan	1997	1(2)	1	0	0	4
Craig Kopczak	Bradford	2006-07	(6)	0	0	0	0
Michael Korkidas	Salford	2007	26(1)	1	0	0	4
	Wakefield	2003-06	90(19)	11	0	0	44
David Krause	London	1996-97	22(1)	7	0	0	28
Ben Kusto	Huddersfield	2001	21(4)	9	0	1	37
Adrian Lam	Wigan	2001-04	105(2)	40	1	9	171
Mark Lane	Paris	1996	(2)	0	0	0	0
Allan Langer	Warrington	2000-01	47	13	4	0	60
Kevin Langer	London	1996	12(4)	2	0	0	8
Junior Langi	Salford	2005-06	27(7)	7	0	0	28
Chris Langley	Huddersfield	2000-01	18(1)	3	0	0	12
Gareth Langley	St Helens	2006	1	1	3	0	10
Jamie Langley	Bradford	2002-07	68(46)	28	0	0	112
Andy Last	Hull	1999-2005	16(10)	4	0	0	16

Super League Players 1996-2007

PLAYER	CLUB	YEAR	APP	TRIES	GOALS	FG	PTS
Dale Laughton	Warrington	2002	15(1)	0	0	0	0
	Huddersfield	2000-01	36(2)	4	0	0	16
	Sheffield	1996-99	48(22)	5	0	0	20
Ali Lauitiiti	Leeds	2004-07	40(54)	32	0	0	128
Jason Laurence	Salford	1997	1	0	0	0	0
Graham Law	Wakefield	1999-2002	34(30)	6	40	0	104
Neil Law	Wakefield	1999-2002	83	39	0	0	156
	Sheffield	1998	1(1)	1	0	0	4
Dean Lawford	Widnes	2003-04	17(1)	5	2	4	28
	Halifax	2001	1(1)	0	0	0	0
	Leeds	1997-2000	15(8)	2	3	0	14
	Huddersfield	1999	6(1)	0	6	1	13
	Sheffield	1996	9(5)	2	1	1	11
Johnny Lawless	Halifax	2001-03	73(1)	10	0	0	40
	Hudds-Sheff	2000	19(6)	3	0	0	12
	Sheffield	1996-99	76(4)	11	0	0	44
Michael Lawrence	Huddersfield	2007	(1)	0	0	0	0
Mark Leafa	Leigh	2005	28	2	0	0	8
Leroy Leapai	London	1996	2	0	0	0	0
Jim Leatham	Hull	1998-99	20(18)	4	0	0	16
	Leeds	1997	(1)	0	0	0	0
Andy Leathem	Warrington	1999	2(8)	0	0	0	0
	St Helens	1996-98	20(1)	1	0	0	4
Danny Lee	Gateshead	1999	16(2)	0	0	0	0
Jason Lee	Halifax	2001	10(1)	2	0	0	8
Mark Lee	Salford	1997-2000	25(11)	1	0	4	8
Robert Lee	Hull	1999	4(3)	0	0	0	0
Tommy Lee	Hull	2005-07	22(6)	4	0	0	16
Matthew Leigh	Salford	2000	(6)	0	0	0	0
Chris Leikvoll	Warrington	2004-07	72(18)	4	0	0	16
Jim Lenihan	Huddersfield	1999	19(1)	10	0	0	40
Mark Lennon	Hull KR	2007	11(4)	5	7	0	34
	Castleford	2001-03	30(21)	10	21	0	82
Tevita Leo-Latu	Wakefield	2006-07	3(19)	2	0	0	8
Gary Lester	Hull	1998-99	46	17	0	0	68
Stuart Lester	Wigan	1997	1(3)	0	0	0	0
Afi Leuila	Oldham	1996-97	17(3)	2	0	0	8
Kylie Leuluai	Leeds	2007	11(18)	1	0	0	4
Phil Leuluai	Salford	2007	3(2)	0	0	0	0
Thomas Leuluai	Wigan	2007	30	9	0	0	36
	Harlequins	2006	15(2)	6	0	0	24
	London	2005	20	13	0	0	52
Simon Lewis	Castleford	2001	4	3	0	0	12
Paul Leyland	St Helens	2006	1	0	0	0	0
Jon Liddell	Leeds	2001	1	0	0	0	0
Jason Lidden	Castleford	1997	15(1)	7	0	0	28
Danny Lima	Wakefield	2007	(3)	0	0	0	0
	Salford	2006	7(2)	0	0	0	0
	Warrington	2004-06	15(47)	9	0	0	36
Craig Littler	St Helens	2006	1	1	0	0	4
Stuart Littler	Salford	1998-2002, 2004-07	176(19)	56	0	0	224
Peter Livett	Workington	1996	3(1)	0	0	0	0
Scott Logan	Wigan	2006	10(11)	0	0	0	0
	Hull	2001-03	27(20)	5	0	0	20
Jamahl Lolesi	Huddersfield	2007	24(2)	10	0	0	40
Filimone Lolohea	Harlequins	2006	3(6)	0	0	0	0
	London	2005	8(15)	0	0	0	0
David Lomax	Huddersfield	2000-01	45(9)	4	0	0	16
	Paris	1997	19(2)	1	0	0	4
Dave Long	London	1999	(1)	0	0	0	0
Karl Long	London	2003	(1)	0	0	0	0
	Widnes	2002	4	1	0	0	4
Sean Long	St Helens	1997-2007	206(8)	114	673	15	1817
	Wigan	1996-97	1(5)	0	0	0	0
Davide Longo	Bradford	1996	1(3)	0	0	0	0
Gary Lord	Oldham	1996-97	28(12)	3	0	0	12
Paul Loughlin	Huddersfield	1998-99	34(2)	4	4	0	24
	Bradford	1996-97	36(4)	15	8	0	76
Rhys Lovegrove	Hull KR	2007	6(3)	5	0	0	20
Karl Lovell	Hudds-Sheff	2000	14	5	0	0	20
	Sheffield	1999	22(4)	8	0	0	32
James Lowes	Bradford	1996-2003	205	84	2	2	342
Laurent Lucchese	Paris	1996	13(5)	2	0	0	8
Zebastian Luisi	Harlequins	2006-07	23(2)	4	0	0	16
	London	2004-05	21(1)	7	0	0	28
Peter Lupton	Castleford	2006	15	4	0	0	16
	Hull	2003-06	19(26)	10	3	0	46
	London	2000-02	10(15)	2	2	0	12
Andy Lynch	Bradford	2005-07	56(29)	21	0	0	84
	Castleford	1999-2004	78(48)	15	0	0	60
Jamie Lyon	St Helens	2005-06	54(1)	39	172	0	500
Duncan MacGillivray	Wakefield	2004-07	55(15)	5	0	0	20
Brad Mackay	Bradford	2000	24(2)	8	0	0	32
Graham Mackay	Hull	2002	27	18	24	0	120
	Bradford	2001	16(3)	12	1	0	50
	Leeds	2000	12(8)	10	2	0	44
Keiron Maddocks	Leigh	2005	1(3)	0	0	0	0
Steve Maden	Leigh	2005	23	9	0	0	36
	Warrington	2002	3	0	0	0	0
Mateaki Mafi	Warrington	1996-97	7(8)	7	0	0	28
Brendan Magnus	London	2000	3	1	0	0	4
Mark Maguire	London	1996-97	11(4)	7	13	0	54
Adam Maher	Hull	2000-03	88(4)	24	0	0	96
	Gateshead	1999	21(5)	3	0	0	12
Lee Maher	Leeds	1996	4(1)	0	0	0	0
Shaun Mahony	Paris	1997	5	0	0	0	0
Hutch Maiava	Hull	2007	(19)	1	0	0	4
David Maiden	Hull	2000-01	32(10)	11	0	0	44
	Gateshead	1999	5(16)	8	0	0	32
Craig Makin	Salford	1999-2001	24(20)	2	0	0	8
Brady Malam	Wigan	2000	5(20)	1	0	0	4
Francis Maloney	Castleford	1998-99, 2003-04	71(7)	24	33	3	165
	Salford	2001-02	45(1)	26	5	0	114
	Wakefield	2000	11	1	1	0	6
	Oldham	1996-97	39(2)	12	91	2	232
George Mann	Warrington	1997	14(5)	1	0	0	4
	Leeds	1996	11(4)	2	0	0	8
Misili Manu	Widnes	2005	1	0	0	0	0
Willie Manu	Hull	2007	17(7)	6	0	0	24
	Castleford	2006	19(4)	9	0	0	36
David March	Wakefield	1999-2007	164(23)	34	126	0	388
Paul March	Wakefield	1999-2001, 2007	42(31)	17	23	0	114
	Huddersfield	2003-06	71(19)	17	36	1	141
Nick Mardon	London	1997-98	14	2	0	0	8
Oliver Marns	Halifax	1996-2002	54(19)	23	0	0	92
Paul Marquet	Warrington	2002	23(2)	0	0	0	0
Iain Marsh	Salford	1998-2001	1(4)	0	0	0	0
Lee Marsh	Salford	2001-02	3(4)	0	0	0	0
Richard Marshall	Leigh	2005	4(16)	0	0	0	0
	London	2002-03	33(11)	1	0	0	4
	Huddersfield	2000-01	35(14)	1	0	0	4
	Halifax	1996-99	38(34)	2	0	0	8
Jason Martin	Paris	1997	15(2)	3	0	0	12
Scott Martin	Salford	1997-99	32(18)	8	0	0	32
Tony Martin	London	1996-97, 2001-03	97(1)	36	170	1	485
Mick Martindale	Halifax	1996	(4)	0	0	0	0
Sebastien Martins	Catalans	2006	(1)	0	0	0	0
Tommy Martyn	St Helens	1996-2003	125(20)	87	63	12	486
Dean Marwood	Workington	1996	9(6)	0	22	0	44
Martin Masella	Warrington	2001	10(14)	5	0	0	20
	Wakefield	2000	14(8)	4	0	0	16
	Leeds	1997-1999	59(5)	1	0	0	4
Colin Maskill	Castleford	1996	8	1	1	0	6
Keith Mason	Huddersfield	2006-07	34(3)	1	0	0	4
	Castleford	2006	(2)	0	0	0	0
	St Helens	2003-05	33(23)	4	0	0	16
	Wakefield	2000-01	5(17)	0	0	0	0
Vila Matautia	St Helens	1996-2001	31(68)	9	0	0	36
Feleti Mateo	London	2005	4(10)	1	0	0	4
Barrie-Jon Mather	Castleford	1998, 2000-02	50(12)	21	0	0	84
Richard Mathers	Leeds	2002-06	85(2)	26	0	0	104
	Warrington	2002	4(3)	0	0	0	0
Jamie Mathiou	Leeds	1997-2001	31(82)	3	0	0	12
Terry Matterson	London	1996-98	46	15	90	6	246
Casey Mayberry	Halifax	2000	1(1)	0	0	0	0
Chris Maye	Halifax	2003	3(4)	0	0	0	0
Joe Mbu	Harlequins	2006-07	16(10)	1	0	0	4
	London	2003-05	29(19)	4	0	0	16
Danny McAllister	Gateshead	1999	3(3)	1	0	0	4
	Sheffield	1996-97	33(7)	10	0	0	40
John McAtee	St Helens	1996	2(1)	0	0	0	0
Nathan McAvoy	Bradford	1998-2002, 2007	83(31)	46	0	0	184
	Wigan	2006	15(2)	5	0	0	20
	Salford	1997-98, 2004-05	57(4)	18	0	0	72
Louie McCarthy-Scarsbrook	Harlequins	2006-07	9(16)	5	0	0	20
Dave McConnell	London	2003	1	0	0	0	0
	St Helens	2001-02	3(2)	4	0	0	16
Robbie McCormack	Wigan	1998	24	2	0	0	8
Steve McCurrie	Leigh	2005	7(3)	1	0	0	4
	Widnes	2002-04	55(22)	10	0	0	40
	Warrington	1998-2001	69(26)	31	0	0	124
Barrie McDermott	Leeds	1996-2005	163(69)	28	0	0	112
Brian McDermott	Bradford	1996-2002	138(32)	33	0	0	132
Ryan McDonald	Widnes	2002-03	6(4)	0	0	0	0
Wayne McDonald	Huddersfield	2005-06	11(23)	1	0	0	4
	Wigan	2005	(4)	0	0	0	0
	Leeds	2002-05	34(47)	14	0	0	56
	St Helens	2001	7(11)	4	0	0	16
	Hull	2000	5(8)	4	0	0	16
	Wakefield	1999	9(17)	8	0	0	32
Craig McDowell	Huddersfield	2003	(1)	0	0	0	0
	Warrington	2002	(1)	0	0	0	0
	Bradford	2000	(1)	0	0	0	0
Wes McGibbon	Halifax	1999	1	0	0	0	0

PLAYER	CLUB	YEAR	APP	TRIES	GOALS	FG	PTS
Dean McGilvray	St Helens	2006-07	4(1)	0	0	0	0
Billy McGinty	Workington	1996	1	0	0	0	0
Ryan McGoldrick	Castleford	2006	27	5	10	0	40
Kevin McGuinness							
	Salford	2004-07	63(3)	11	0	0	44
Casey McGuire	Catalans	2007	19(3)	7	0	0	28
Danny McGuire	Leeds	2001-07	110(32)	118	0	2	474
Gary McGuirk	Workington	1996	(4)	0	0	0	0
Michael McIlorum							
	Wigan	2007	(5)	0	0	0	0
Richard McKell	Castleford	1997-98	22(7)	2	0	0	8
Chris McKenna	Bradford	2006-07	40(7)	7	0	0	28
	Leeds	2003-05	65(4)	18	0	0	72
Phil McKenzie	Workington	1996	4	0	0	0	0
Chris McKinney	Oldham	1996-97	4(9)	2	0	0	8
Mark McLinden	Harlequins	2006-07	39(1)	19	0	1	77
	London	2005	22(3)	8	0	0	32
Shayne McMenemy							
	Hull	2003-07	80(8)	12	0	0	48
	Halifax	2001-03	63	11	0	0	44
Andy McNally	London	2004	5(3)	0	0	0	0
	Castleford	2001, 2003	2(5)	1	0	0	4
Steve McNamara	Huddersfield	2001, 2003	41(9)	3	134	1	281
	Wakefield	2000	15(2)	2	32	0	72
	Bradford	1996-99	90(3)	14	348	7	759
Paul McNicholas	Hull	2004-05	28(12)	4	0	0	16
Neil McPherson	Salford	1997	(1)	0	0	0	0
Duncan McRae	London	1996	11(2)	3	0	1	13
Derek McVey	St Helens	1996-97	28(4)	6	1	0	26
Dallas Mead	Warrington	1997	2	0	0	0	0
Robbie Mears	Leigh	2005	8(6)	0	0	0	0
	Leeds	2001	23	6	0	0	24
Paul Medley	Bradford	1996-98	6(35)	9	0	0	36
Francis Meli	St Helens	2006-07	45	28	0	0	112
Chris Melling	Harlequins	2007	14(2)	4	0	0	16
	Wigan	2004-05	8(2)	1	3	0	10
Paul Mellor	Castleford	2003-04	36(3)	18	0	0	72
Craig Menkins	Paris	1997	4(5)	0	0	0	0
Gary Mercer	Castleford	2002	(1)	0	0	0	0
	Leeds	1996-97, 2001	40(2)	9	0	0	36
	Warrington	2001	18	2	0	0	8
	Halifax	1998-2001	73(2)	16	0	0	64
Tony Mestrov	London	1996-97, 2001	59(8)	4	0	0	16
	Wigan	1998-2000	39(39)	3	0	0	12
Keiran Meyer	London	1996	4	1	0	0	4
Brad Meyers	Bradford	2005-06	40(11)	13	0	0	52
Gary Middlehurst	Widnes	2004	(2)	0	0	0	0
Simon Middleton	Castleford	1996-97	19(3)	8	0	0	32
Shane Millard	Wigan	2007	19(6)	3	0	0	12
	Leeds	2006	6(21)	3	0	0	12
	Widnes	2003-05	69	23	0	0	92
	London	1998-2001	72(14)	11	1	0	46
David Mills	Harlequins	2006-07	24(20)	2	0	0	8
	Widnes	2002-05	17(77)	8	0	0	32
Lee Milner	Halifax	1999	(1)	0	0	0	0
John Minto	London	1996	13	4	0	0	16
Lee Mitchell	Warrington	2007	1(3)	1	0	0	4
Martin Moana	Salford	2004	6(3)	1	0	0	4
	Halifax	1996-2001, 2003	126(22)	62	0	1	249
	Wakefield	2002	19(2)	10	0	0	40
	Huddersfield	2001	3(3)	2	0	0	8
Adam Mogg	Catalans	2007	26	8	0	0	32
Steve Molloy	Huddersfield	2000-01	26(20)	3	0	0	12
	Sheffield	1998-99	32(17)	3	0	0	12
Chris Molyneux	Huddersfield	2000-01	1(18)	0	0	0	0
	Sheffield	1999	1(2)	0	0	0	0
Adrian Moore	Huddersfield	1998-99	1(4)	0	0	0	0
Danny Moore	London	2000	7	0	0	0	0
	Wigan	1998-99	49(3)	18	0	0	72
Jason Moore	Workington	1996	(5)	0	0	0	0
Richard Moore	Wakefield	2007	14(12)	2	0	0	8
	Leigh	2005	2(5)	0	0	0	0
	Bradford	2002-04	1(26)	0	0	0	0
	London	2002, 2004	5(9)	2	0	0	8
Scott Moore	St Helens	2004-07	8(10)	2	0	0	8
Dennis Moran	Wigan	2005-06	39	17	1	1	71
	London	2001-04	107(2)	74	5	5	305
Willie Morganson	Sheffield	1997-98	18(12)	5	3	0	26
Paul Moriarty	Halifax	1996	3(2)	0	0	0	0
Adrian Morley	Warrington	2007	17	1	0	0	4
	Bradford	2005	2(4)	0	0	0	0
	Leeds	1996-2000	95(14)	25	0	0	100
Chris Morley	Salford	1999	3(5)	0	0	0	0
	Warrington	1998	2(8)	0	0	0	0
	St Helens	1996-97	21(16)	4	0	0	16
Glenn Morrison	Bradford	2007	24	10	0	0	40
Iain Morrison	Hull KR	2007	5(6)	1	0	0	4
	Huddersfield	2003-05	11(23)	0	0	0	0
	London	2001	(1)	0	0	0	0
Gareth Morton	Hull KR	2007	7(4)	3	23	0	58
	Leeds	2001-02	1(1)	0	0	0	0
Aaron Moule	Salford	2006-07	45	17	0	0	68
	Widnes	2004-05	29	12	0	0	48
Wilfried Moulinec	Paris	1996	1	0	0	0	0
Gregory Mounis	Catalans	2006-07	35(12)	5	0	0	20
Mark Moxon	Huddersfield	1998-2001	20(5)	1	0	1	5
Brett Mullins	Leeds	2001	5(3)	1	0	0	4
Damian Munro	Widnes	2002	8(2)	1	0	0	4
	Halifax	1996-99	9(6)	8	0	0	32
Matt Munro	Oldham	1996-97	26(5)	8	0	0	32
Craig Murdock	Salford	2000	(2)	0	0	0	0
	Hull	1998-99	21(6)	8	0	2	34
	Wigan	1996-98	18(17)	14	0	0	56
Justin Murphy	Catalans	2006-07	43	34	0	0	136
	Widnes	2004	5	1	0	0	4
Doc Murray	Warrington	1997	(2)	0	0	0	0
	Wigan	1997	6(2)	0	0	0	0
Scott Murrell	Hull KR	2007	19(4)	4	4	0	24
	Leeds	2005	(1)	0	0	0	0
	London	2004	3(3)	2	0	0	8
David Mycoe	Sheffield	1996-97	12(13)	1	0	0	4
Rob Myler	Oldham	1996-97	19(2)	6	0	0	24
Stephen Myler	Salford	2006	4(8)	1	15	0	34
	Widnes	2003-05	35(14)	8	74	0	180
Vinny Myler	Salford	2004	(4)	0	0	0	0
	Bradford	2003	(1)	0	0	0	0
Matt Nable	London	1997	2(2)	1	0	0	4
Brad Nairn	Workington	1996	14	4	0	0	16
Frank Napoli	London	2000	14(6)	2	0	0	8
Carlo Napolitano	Salford	2000	(3)	1	0	0	4
Stephen Nash	Salford	2007	2(7)	0	0	0	0
	Widnes	2005	4(1)	0	0	0	0
Jim Naylor	Halifax	2000	7(6)	2	0	0	8
Scott Naylor	Salford	1997-98, 2004	30(1)	9	0	0	36
	Bradford	1999-2003	127(1)	51	0	0	204
Mike Neal	Salford	1998	(1)	0	0	0	0
	Oldham	1996-97	6(4)	3	0	0	12
Jonathan Neill	Huddersfield	1998-99	20(11)	0	0	0	0
	St Helens	1996	1	0	0	0	0
Chris Nero	Huddersfield	2004-07	97(8)	38	0	0	152
Jason Netherton	Hull KR	2007	16(6)	3	0	0	12
	London	2003-04	6	0	0	0	0
	Halifax	2002	2(3)	0	0	0	0
	Leeds	2001	(3)	0	0	0	0
Kirk Netherton	Hull KR	2007	1(2)	0	0	0	0
Paul Newlove	Castleford	2004	5	1	0	0	4
	St Helens	1996-2003	162	106	0	0	424
Richard Newlove	Wakefield	2003	17(5)	8	0	0	32
Terry Newton	Bradford	2006-07	41(2)	14	0	0	56
	Wigan	2000-05	157(9)	62	0	0	248
	Leeds	1996-1999	55(14)	4	0	0	16
Gene Ngamu	Huddersfield	1999-2000	29(2)	9	67	0	170
Sonny Nickle	St Helens	1999-2002	86(18)	14	0	0	56
	Bradford	1996-98	25(16)	9	0	0	36
Jason Nicol	Salford	2000-02	52(7)	11	0	0	44
Tawera Nikau	Warrington	2000-01	51	7	0	0	28
Rob Nolan	Hull	1998-99	20(11)	6	0	0	24
Paul Noone	Harlequins	2006	5(2)	0	0	0	0
	Warrington	2000-06	60(59)	12	20	0	88
Chris Norman	Halifax	2003	13(3)	2	0	0	8
Paul Norman	Oldham	1996	(1)	0	0	0	0
Andy Northey	St Helens	1996-97	8(17)	2	0	0	8
Danny Nutley	Castleford	2006	28	3	0	0	12
	Warrington	1998-2001	94(1)	3	0	0	12
Tony Nuttall	Oldham	1996-97	1(7)	0	0	0	0
Clinton O'Brien	Wakefield	2003	(2)	0	0	0	0
Sam Obst	Wakefield	2005-07	43(20)	18	0	0	72
Eamon O'Carroll	Wigan	2006-07	(17)	0	0	0	0
Matt O'Connor	Paris	1997	11(4)	1	26	2	58
Terry O'Connor	Widnes	2005	25	1	2	0	8
	Wigan	1996-2004	177(45)	9	0	0	36
Jarrod O'Doherty	Huddersfield	2003	26	3	0	0	12
David O'Donnell	Paris	1997	21	3	0	0	12
Martin Offiah	Salford	2000-01	41	20	0	2	82
	London	1996-99	29(3)	21	0	0	84
	Wigan	1996	8	7	0	0	28
Mark O'Halloran	London	2004-05	34(3)	10	0	0	40
Hefin O'Hare	Huddersfield	2001, 2003-05	72(10)	27	0	0	108
Hitro Okesene	Hull	1998	21(1)	0	0	0	0
Anderson Okiwe	Sheffield	1997	1	0	0	0	0
Jamie Olejnik	Paris	1997	11	8	0	0	32
Kevin O'Loughlin	Halifax	1997-98	2(4)	0	0	0	0
	St Helens	1997	(3)	0	0	0	0
Sean O'Loughlin	Wigan	2002-07	127(18)	29	1	2	120
Jules O'Neill	Widnes	2003-05	57(3)	14	158	7	379
	Wakefield	2005	10(2)	2	4	0	16
	Wigan	2002-03	29(1)	12	72	0	192
Julian O'Neill	Widnes	2002-05	57(39)	3	0	0	12
	Wakefield	2001	24(1)	2	0	0	8
	St Helens	1997-2000	95(8)	5	0	0	20
Mark O'Neill	Hull KR	2007	17	5	0	0	20
	Leeds	2006	1(8)	0	0	0	0
Steve O'Neill	Gateshead	1999	1(1)	0	0	0	0

Super League Players 1996-2007

PLAYER	CLUB	YEAR	APP	TRIES	GOALS	FG	PTS
Tom O'Reilly	Warrington	2001-02	8(6)	1	0	0	4
Chris Orr	Huddersfield	1998	19(3)	2	0	0	8
Danny Orr	Harlequins	2007	25	3	1	0	14
	Wigan	2004-06	66(2)	18	11	0	94
	Castleford	1997-2003	150(18)	65	279	3	821
Nick Owen	Leigh	2005	8(1)	1	11	0	26
Iafeta Palea'aesina	Wigan	2006-07	46(7)	6	0	0	24
Jason Palmada	Workington	1996	12	2	0	0	8
Junior Paramore	Castleford	1996	5(5)	3	0	0	12
Paul Parker	Hull	1999-2002	23(18)	9	0	0	36
Rob Parker	Warrington	2006-07	7(33)	5	0	0	20
	Bradford	2000, 2002-05	19(76)	14	0	0	56
	London	2001	9	1	0	0	4
Wayne Parker	Halifax	1996-97	12(1)	0	0	0	0
Ian Parry	Warrington	2001	(1)	0	0	0	0
Jules Parry	Paris	1996	10(2)	0	0	0	0
Regis Pastre-Courtine	Paris	1996	4(3)	4	0	0	16
Andrew Patmore	Oldham	1996	8(5)	3	0	0	12
Henry Paul	Harlequins	2006-07	35(1)	3	59	1	131
	Bradford	1999-2001	81(5)	29	350	6	822
	Wigan	1996-98	60	37	23	0	194
Junior Paul	London	1996	3	1	0	0	4
Robbie Paul	Huddersfield	2006-07	44(8)	7	0	0	28
	Bradford	1996-2005	198(31)	121	3	0	490
Jason Payne	Castleford	2006	1(1)	0	0	0	0
Danny Peacock	Bradford	1997-99	32(2)	15	0	0	60
Jamie Peacock	Leeds	2006-07	53(1)	5	0	0	20
	Bradford	1999-2005	163(25)	38	0	0	152
Martin Pearson	Wakefield	2001	21(1)	3	60	3	135
	Halifax	1997-98, 2000	55(6)	24	181	0	458
	Sheffield	1999	17(6)	9	36	2	110
Jacques Pech	Paris	1996	16	0	0	0	0
Mike Pechey	Warrington	1998	6(3)	2	0	0	8
Bill Peden	London	2003	21(3)	7	0	0	28
Dimitri Pelo	Catalans	2007	12	4	0	0	16
Sean Penkywicz	Huddersfield	2004-05	21(11)	7	0	0	28
	Halifax	2000-03	29(27)	8	0	0	32
Julian Penni	Salford	1998-99	4	0	0	0	0
Kevin Penny	Warrington	2006-07	12(1)	12	0	0	48
Lee Penny	Warrington	1996-2003	140(5)	54	0	0	216
Paul Penrice	Workington	1996	11(2)	2	0	0	8
Chris Percival	Widnes	2002-03	26	6	0	0	24
Apollo Perelini	St Helens	1996-2000	103(16)	27	0	0	108
Mark Perrett	Halifax	1996-97	15(4)	4	0	0	16
Adam Peters	Paris	1997	16(3)	0	0	0	0
Dominic Peters	London	1998-2003	58(11)	12	0	0	48
Mike Peters	Warrington	2000	2(12)	1	0	0	4
	Halifax	2000	1	0	0	0	0
Willie Peters	Widnes	2004	9	3	0	2	14
	Wigan	2000	29	15	5	6	76
	Gateshead	1999	27	11	1	6	52
Adrian Petrie	Workington	1996	(1)	0	0	0	0
Rowland Phillips	Workington	1996	22	1	0	0	4
Nathan Picchi	Leeds	1996	(1)	0	0	0	0
Ian Pickavance	Hull	1999	4(2)	2	0	0	8
	Huddersfield	1999	3(14)	0	0	0	0
	St Helens	1996-98	12(44)	6	0	0	24
James Pickering	Castleford	1999	1(19)	0	0	0	0
Steve Pickersgill	Warrington	2005-07	1(25)	0	0	0	0
Nick Pinkney	Salford	2000-02	64	29	0	0	116
	Halifax	1999	26(2)	13	0	0	52
	Sheffield	1997-98	33	10	0	0	40
Mikhail Piskunov	Paris	1996	1(1)	1	0	0	4
Darryl Pitt	London	1996	2(16)	4	0	1	17
Andy Platt	Salford	1997-98	20(3)	1	0	0	4
Michael Platt	Bradford	2007	25	14	0	0	56
	Castleford	2006	26	7	0	0	28
	Salford	2001-02	3	1	0	0	4
Willie Poching	Leeds	2002-06	58(73)	44	0	0	176
	Wakefield	1999-2001	65(4)	20	0	0	80
Quentin Pongia	Wigan	2003-04	15(10)	0	0	0	0
Dan Potter	Widnes	2002-03	34(2)	6	0	0	24
	London	2001	1(3)	1	0	0	4
Craig Poucher	Hull	1999-2002	31(5)	5	0	0	20
Bryn Powell	Salford	2004	1(1)	0	0	0	0
Daio Powell	Sheffield	1999	13(1)	2	0	0	8
	Halifax	1997-98	30(3)	17	0	0	68
Daryl Powell	Leeds	1998-2000	49(30)	12	0	2	50
Karl Pratt	Bradford	2003-05	35(19)	18	0	0	72
	Leeds	1999-2002	62(12)	33	0	0	132
Paul Prescott	Wigan	2004-07	5(27)	1	0	0	4
Steve Prescott	Hull	1998-99, 2001-03	99	46	191	3	569
	Wakefield	2000	22(1)	3	13	0	38
	St Helens	1996-97	32	15	17	0	94
Lee Prest	Workington	1996	(1)	0	0	0	0
Gareth Price	Salford	2002	(2)	0	0	0	0
	London	2002	2(2)	3	0	0	12
	St Helens	1999	(11)	2	0	0	8
Gary Price	Wakefield	1999-2001	55(13)	11	0	0	44
Richard Price	Sheffield	1996	1(2)	0	0	0	0
Tony Priddle	Paris	1997	11(7)	3	0	0	12
Karl Pryce	Bradford	2003-06	28(19)	33	1	0	134
Leon Pryce	St Helens	2006-07	53(2)	28	0	0	112
	Bradford	1998-2005	159(29)	86	0	0	344
Waine Pryce	Wakefield	2007	10(2)	4	0	0	16
	Castleford	2000-06	97(12)	49	0	0	196
Andrew Purcell	Castleford	2000	15(5)	3	0	0	12
	Hull	1999	27	4	0	0	16
Rob Purdham	Harlequins	2006-07	41(1)	6	33	0	90
	London	2002-05	53(15)	16	2	1	69
Luke Quigley	Catalans	2007	16(1)	1	0	0	4
Scott Quinnell	Wigan	1996	6(3)	1	0	0	4
Lee Radford	Hull	1998, 2006-07	58(7)	9	0	0	36
	Bradford	1999-2005	79(65)	18	12	0	96
Kris Radlinski	Wigan	1996-2006	236(1)	134	1	0	538
Sebastien Raguin	Catalans	2007	11(5)	1	0	0	4
Adrian Rainey	Castleford	2002	4(7)	1	0	0	4
Andy Raleigh	Huddersfield	2006-07	31(18)	8	0	0	32
Jean-Luc Ramondou	Paris	1996	1(1)	1	0	0	4
Chad Randall	Harlequins	2006-07	47(2)	11	0	0	44
Craig Randall	Halifax	1999	8(11)	4	0	0	16
	Salford	1997-98	12(18)	4	0	0	16
Scott Ranson	Oldham	1996-97	19(2)	7	0	0	28
Aaron Raper	Castleford	1999-2001	48(4)	4	2	1	21
Stefan Ratchford	Salford	2007	4	1	0	0	4
Mike Ratu	Leeds	2007	(1)	0	0	0	0
Paul Rauhihi	Warrington	2006-07	34(6)	5	0	0	20
Ben Rauter	Wakefield	2001	15(6)	4	0	0	16
Gareth Raynor	Hull	2001-07	151	92	0	0	368
	Leeds	2000	(3)	0	0	0	0
Tony Rea	London	1996	22	4	0	0	16
Stuart Reardon	Warrington	2006-07	41	10	0	0	40
	Bradford	2003-05	62(11)	32	0	0	128
	Salford	2002	7(1)	3	0	0	12
Mark Reber	Wigan	1999-2000	9(9)	5	0	0	20
Alan Reddicliffe	Warrington	2001	1	0	0	0	0
Tahi Reihana	Bradford	1997-98	17(21)	0	0	0	0
Paul Reilly	Huddersfield	1999-2001, 2003-07	150(8)	35	1	0	142
Robert Relf	Widnes	2002-04	68(2)	5	0	0	20
Steve Renouf	Wigan	2000-01	55	40	0	0	160
Steele Retchless	London	1998-2004	177(6)	13	0	0	52
Scott Rhodes	Hull	2000	2	0	0	0	0
Phillipe Ricard	Paris	1996-97	2	0	0	0	0
Andy Rice	Huddersfield	2000-01	2(13)	1	0	0	4
Basil Richards	Huddersfield	1998-99	28(17)	1	0	0	4
Craig Richards	Oldham	1996	1	0	0	0	0
Pat Richards	Wigan	2006-07	51	25	121	2	344
Andy Richardson	Hudds-Sheff	2000	(2)	0	0	0	0
Sean Richardson	Widnes	2002	2(18)	1	0	0	4
	Wakefield	1999	5(1)	1	0	0	4
	Castleford	1996-97	3(8)	1	0	0	4
Neil Rigby	St Helens	2006	(1)	0	0	0	0
Shane Rigon	Bradford	2001	14(11)	12	0	0	48
Craig Rika	Halifax	1996	2	0	0	0	0
Chris Riley	Warrington	2005-07	8(8)	4	0	0	16
Peter Riley	Workington	1996	7(5)	0	0	0	0
Julien Rinaldi	Harlequins	2007	(26)	5	0	0	20
	Catalans	2006	16(6)	3	1	0	14
Dean Ripley	Castleford	2004	3(4)	1	0	0	4
Leroy Rivett	Warrington	2002	5(1)	1	0	0	4
	Hudds-Sheff	2000	5(1)	1	0	0	4
	Leeds	1996-2000	39(15)	21	0	0	84
Jason Roach	Warrington	1998-99	29(7)	15	0	0	60
	Castleford	1997	7	4	0	0	16
Ben Roarty	Castleford	2006	11(6)	2	0	0	8
	Huddersfield	2003-05	52	5	0	0	20
Mark Roberts	Wigan	2003	(3)	0	0	0	0
Robert Roberts	Huddersfield	2001	(1)	0	0	0	0
	Halifax	2000	(3)	0	0	0	0
	Hull	1999	24(2)	4	13	4	46
Craig Robinson	Wakefield	2005	(1)	0	0	0	0
Jason Robinson	Wigan	1996-2000	126(1)	87	0	1	349
Jeremy Robinson	Paris	1997	10(3)	1	21	0	46
John Robinson	Widnes	2003-04	7	1	0	0	4
Luke Robinson	Salford	2005-07	79	28	10	2	134
	Wigan	2002-04	17(25)	9	6	1	49
	Castleford	2004	9	4	3	0	22
Will Robinson	Hull	2000	22	4	0	0	16
	Gateshead	1999	28	9	0	0	36
James Roby	St Helens	2004-07	30(66)	22	0	0	88
Mike Roby	St Helens	2004	(1)	0	0	0	0
Carl Roden	Warrington	1997	1	0	0	0	0
Matt Rodwell	Warrington	2002	10	3	0	0	12
Darren Rogers	Castleford	1999-2004	162(1)	81	0	0	324
	Salford	1997-98	42	16	0	0	64
Jamie Rooney	Wakefield	2003-07	89(4)	49	309	21	835
	Castleford	2001	2(1)	0	6	0	12

PLAYER	CLUB	YEAR	APP	TRIES	GOALS	FG	PTS
Jonathan Roper	Castleford	2001	13	7	12	0	52
	Salford	2000	1(4)	1	3	0	10
	London	2000	4	0	0	0	0
	Warrington	1996-2000	75(8)	33	71	0	274
Scott Roskell	London	1996-97	30(2)	16	0	0	64
Steve Rosolen	London	1996-98	25(9)	10	0	0	40
Adam Ross	London	1996	(1)	0	0	0	0
Paul Round	Castleford	1996	(3)	0	0	0	0
Steve Rowlands	Widnes	2004-05	18(3)	2	15	0	38
	St Helens	2003	(1)	0	0	0	0
Paul Rowley	Leigh	2005	15(7)	3	0	0	12
	Huddersfield	2001	24	3	0	0	12
	Halifax	1996-2000	107(3)	27	1	3	113
Nigel Roy	London	2001-04	100	39	0	0	156
Nicky Royle	Widnes	2004	13	7	0	0	28
Chris Rudd	Warrington	1996-98	31(17)	10	16	0	72
Sean Rudder	Catalans	2006	22(1)	6	0	0	24
	Castleford	2004	9(3)	2	0	0	8
James Rushforth	Halifax	1997	(4)	0	0	0	0
Danny Russell	Huddersfield	1998-2000	50(13)	8	0	0	32
Ian Russell	Oldham	1997	1(3)	1	0	0	4
	Paris	1996	3	0	0	0	0
Richard Russell	Castleford	1996-98	37(4)	2	0	0	8
Robert Russell	Salford	1998-99	2(1)	0	1	0	2
Sean Rutgerson	Salford	2004-06	60(9)	4	0	0	16
Chris Ryan	London	1998-99	44(3)	17	10	0	88
Sean Ryan	Castleford	2004	11(5)	2	0	0	8
	Hull	2002-03	53	8	0	0	32
Justin Ryder	Wakefield	2004	19(3)	11	0	0	44
Teddy Sadaoui	Catalans	2006	7	0	0	0	0
Matt Salter	London	1997-99	14(34)	0	0	0	0
Ben Sammut	Hull	2000	20	4	67	0	150
	Gateshead	1999	26(2)	6	17	0	58
Dean Sampson	Castleford	1996-2003	124(28)	24	0	0	96
Paul Sampson	London	2004	1(2)	1	0	0	4
	Wakefield	2000	17	8	0	0	32
Lee Sanderson	London	2004	1(5)	1	7	0	18
Jason Sands	Paris	1996-97	28	0	0	0	0
Lokeni Savelio	Halifax	2000	2(11)	0	0	0	0
	Salford	1997-98	18(20)	0	0	0	0
Tom Saxton	Salford	2007	5	0	0	0	0
	Wakefield	2006	9(6)	2	0	0	8
	Hull	2005	19(8)	3	0	0	12
	Castleford	2002-04	37(12)	11	0	0	44
Jonathan Scales	Halifax	2000	1	0	0	0	0
	Bradford	1996-98	46(4)	24	0	0	96
Andrew Schick	Castleford	1996-98	45(13)	10	0	0	40
Garry Schofield	Huddersfield	1998	(2)	0	0	0	0
Gary Schubert	Workington	1996	(1)	0	0	0	0
Matt Schultz	Hull	1998-99	23(9)	2	0	0	8
	Leeds	1996	2(4)	0	0	0	0
John Schuster	Halifax	1996-97	31	9	127	3	293
Nick Scruton	Leeds	2002, 2004-07	4(35)	1	0	0	4
	Hull	2004	2(16)	3	0	0	12
Danny Sculthorpe							
	Wakefield	2007	(10)	0	0	0	0
	Castleford	2006	18(1)	4	0	1	17
	Wigan	2002-05	13(49)	7	0	0	28
Paul Sculthorpe	St Helens	1998-2007	211(3)	92	352	7	1079
	Warrington	1996-97	40	6	0	0	24
Mick Seaby	London	1997	3(2)	1	0	0	4
Danny Seal	Halifax	1996-99	8(17)	3	0	0	12
Matt Seers	Wakefield	2003	11(1)	2	0	0	8
Anthony Seibold	London	1999-2000	33(19)	5	0	0	20
Keith Senior	Leeds	1999-2007	223(1)	121	0	0	484
	Sheffield	1996-99	90(2)	40	0	0	160
Fili Seru	Hull	1998-99	37(1)	13	0	0	52
Anthony Seuseu	Halifax	2003	1(11)	1	0	0	4
Jerry Seuseu	Wigan	2005-06	29(9)	1	0	0	4
Darren Shaw	Salford	2002	5(9)	1	0	0	4
	London	1996, 2002	22(8)	3	0	0	12
	Castleford	2000-01	50(6)	1	0	0	4
	Sheffield	1998-99	51(1)	3	0	1	13
Mick Shaw	Halifax	1999	5	1	0	0	4
	Leeds	1996	12(2)	7	0	0	28
Phil Shead	Paris	1996	3(2)	0	0	0	0
Richard Sheil	St Helens	1997	(1)	0	0	0	0
Kelly Shelford	Warrington	1996-97	25(3)	4	0	2	18
Michael Shenton	Castleford	2004, 2006	27(2)	8	0	0	32
Ryan Sheridan	Castleford	2004	2	0	0	0	0
	Widnes	2003	14(3)	2	0	0	8
	Leeds	1997-2002	123(7)	46	0	1	185
	Sheffield	1996	9(3)	5	0	1	21
Rikki Sheriffe	Harlequins	2006-07	13(1)	8	0	0	32
	Halifax	2003	6(1)	3	0	0	12
Ian Sherratt	Oldham	1996	5(3)	1	0	0	4
Peter Shiels	St Helens	2001-02	44(3)	11	0	0	44
Gary Shillabeer	Huddersfield	1999	(2)	0	0	0	0
Mark Shipway	Salford	2004-05	30(12)	3	0	0	12
Ian Sibbit	Salford	2005-07	38(4)	9	0	0	36
	Warrington	1999-2001, 2003-04	63(18)	24	0	0	96
Mark Sibson	Huddersfield	1999	2	2	0	0	8

PLAYER	CLUB	YEAR	APP	TRIES	GOALS	FG	PTS
Jon Simms	St Helens	2002	(1)	0	0	0	0
Craig Simon	Hull	2000	23(2)	8	0	0	32
	Gateshead	1999	25(4)	6	0	0	24
Darren Simpson	Huddersfield	1998-99	17(1)	5	0	0	20
Robbie Simpson	London	1999	6(7)	0	0	0	0
Kevin Sinfield	Leeds	1997-2007	215(25)	39	675	11	1517
Matt Sing	Hull	2007	23	11	0	0	44
Wayne Sing	Paris	1997	18(1)	2	0	0	8
Fata Sini	Salford	1997	22	7	0	0	28
John Skandalis	Huddersfield	2007	23(4)	1	0	0	4
Ben Skerrett	Castleford	2003	(1)	0	0	0	0
Kelvin Skerrett	Halifax	1997-99	31(6)	2	0	0	8
	Wigan	1996	1(8)	0	0	0	0
Troy Slattery	Wakefield	2002-03	33(5)	4	0	0	16
	Huddersfield	1999	3	1	0	0	4
Mick Slicker	Huddersfield	2001, 2003-05	17(48)	2	0	0	8
	Sheffield	1999	(3)	1	0	0	4
	Halifax	1997	2(5)	0	0	0	0
Ian Smales	Castleford	1996-97	10(8)	5	0	0	20
Aaron Smith	Castleford	2006	(2)	0	0	0	0
	Bradford	2003-04	12(1)	3	0	0	12
Andy Smith	Harlequins	2007	6(3)	3	0	0	12
	Bradford	2004-06	9(9)	4	0	0	16
	Salford	2005	4	1	0	0	4
Byron Smith	Castleford	2004	(9)	0	0	0	0
	Halifax	2003	6(1)	0	0	0	0
Chris Smith	Hull	2001-02	12	3	0	0	12
	St Helens	1998-2000	62(9)	26	0	0	104
	Castleford	1996-97	36(1)	12	0	0	48
Craig Smith	Wigan	2002-04	77(3)	10	0	0	40
Damien Smith	St Helens	1998	21(1)	8	0	0	32
Danny Smith	Paris	1996	10(2)	1	15	0	34
	London	1996	2(1)	1	0	0	4
Darren Smith	St Helens	2003	25(1)	14	0	0	56
Gary Smith	Castleford	2001	(1)	0	0	0	0
Hudson Smith	Bradford	2000	8(22)	2	0	0	8
	Salford	1999	23(2)	5	0	0	20
James Smith	Salford	2000	23(3)	6	0	0	24
Jamie Smith	Hull	1998-99	24(6)	6	12	0	48
	Workington	1996	5(3)	0	1	0	2
Jason Smith	Hull	2001-04	61(3)	17	0	1	69
Kris Smith	London	2001	(1)	0	0	0	0
	Halifax	2001	(1)	0	0	0	0
Lee Smith	Leeds	2005-07	40(4)	21	5	0	94
Leigh Smith	Workington	1996	9	4	0	0	16
Mark Smith	Widnes	2005	12(15)	4	0	0	16
	Wigan	1999-2004	35(77)	8	0	0	32
Matty Smith	St Helens	2006-07	12(2)	2	4	1	17
Michael Smith	Hull KR	2007	(3)	1	0	0	4
	Castleford	1998, 2001-04	86(33)	32	0	0	128
	Hull	1999	12(6)	3	0	0	12
Paul Smith	Huddersfield	2004-06	52(17)	13	0	0	52
Paul Smith	Warrington	2001	(1)	0	0	0	0
	Castleford	1997-2000	6(37)	3	0	0	12
Paul Smith	London	1997	7(1)	2	0	0	8
Peter Smith	Oldham	1996	2	0	0	0	0
Richard Smith	Wakefield	2001	8(1)	1	0	0	4
	Salford	1997	(1)	1	0	0	4
Tony Smith	Hull	2001-03	43(5)	26	0	0	104
	Wigan	1997-2000	66(5)	46	0	0	184
	Castleford	1996-97	18(2)	10	0	0	40
Tony Smith	Workington	1996	9	1	0	0	4
Tyrone Smith	Harlequins	2006-07	49(3)	13	0	0	52
	London	2005	20(4)	11	0	0	44
Rob Smyth	Leigh	2005	15(1)	4	0	0	16
	Warrington	2000-03	65	35	20	0	180
	London	1998-2000	73(2)	9	15	0	66
	Wigan	1996	11(5)	16	0	0	64
Steve Snitch	Huddersfield	2006-07	9(30)	10	0	0	40
	Wakefield	2002-05	10(53)	4	0	0	16
Bright Sodje	Wakefield	2000	15	4	0	0	16
	Sheffield	1996-99	54	34	0	0	136
David Solomona	Bradford	2007	27(1)	12	0	0	48
	Wakefield	2004-06	73(3)	26	0	0	104
Alfred Songoro	Wakefield	1999	8(5)	4	0	0	16
Romain Sort	Paris	1997	(1)	0	0	0	0
Paul Southern	Salford	1997-2002	79(33)	6	13	0	50
	St Helens	2002	1(1)	0	0	0	0
Roy Southernwood							
	Wakefield	1999	1	0	0	0	0
	Halifax	1996	2	0	0	0	0
Jason Southwell	Huddersfield	2004	(1)	0	0	0	0
Waisale Sovatabua							
	Wakefield	2001-03	44(3)	19	0	0	76
	Hudds-Sheff	2000	23(1)	8	0	0	32
	Sheffield	1996-99	56(17)	19	0	1	77
Yusef Sozi	London	2000-01	(5)	0	0	0	0
Andy Speak	Castleford	2001	4(4)	0	0	0	0
	Wakefield	2000	6(5)	2	0	0	8
	Leeds	1999	4	1	0	0	4
Tim Spears	Castleford	2003	(3)	0	0	0	0
Ady Spencer	London	1996-99	8(36)	5	0	0	20

PLAYER	CLUB	YEAR	APP	TRIES	GOALS	FG	PTS
Rob Spicer	Wakefield	2002-05	28(18)	4	0	0	16
Stuart Spruce	Widnes	2002-03	45(4)	19	0	0	76
	Bradford	1996-2001	107(2)	57	0	0	228
Lee St Hilaire	Castleford	1997	4(2)	0	0	0	0
Marcus St Hilaire	Bradford	2006-07	34(1)	12	0	0	48
	Huddersfield	2003-05	72(2)	30	0	0	120
	Leeds	1996-2002	59(33)	31	0	0	124
Cyril Stacul	Catalans	2007	2	1	0	0	4
Dylan Stainton	Workington	1996	2(3)	0	0	0	0
Mark Stamper	Workington	1996	(1)	0	0	0	0
John Stankevitch	Widnes	2005	17(5)	0	0	0	0
	St Helens	2000-04	74(40)	25	0	0	100
Gareth Stanley	Bradford	2000	1	1	0	0	4
Craig Stapleton	Leigh	2005	27(1)	4	0	0	16
Graham Steadman							
	Castleford	1996-97	11(17)	5	0	0	20
Jon Steel	Hull KR	2007	4	2	0	0	8
Jamie Stenhouse	Warrington	2000-01	9(3)	3	0	0	12
Gareth Stephens	Sheffield	1997-99	23(6)	2	0	0	8
David Stephenson							
	Hull	1998	11(7)	3	0	0	12
	Oldham	1997	10(8)	2	0	0	8
Francis Stephenson							
	London	2002-05	42(34)	5	0	0	20
	Wigan	2001	2(9)	0	0	0	0
	Wakefield	1999-2000	50(1)	6	0	0	24
Paul Sterling	Leeds	1997-2000	79(12)	50	0	0	200
Paul Stevens	Oldham	1996	2(1)	0	0	0	0
	London	1996	(1)	0	0	0	0
Warren Stevens	Leigh	2005	4(14)	1	0	0	4
	Warrington	1996-99, 2002-05	17(66)	1	0	0	4
	Salford	2001	(8)	0	0	0	0
Anthony Stewart	Harlequins	2006	4	0	0	0	0
	Salford	2004-06	51(2)	15	0	0	60
	St Helens	1997-2003	93(23)	44	0	0	176
Troy Stone	Widnes	2002	18(6)	1	0	0	4
	Huddersfield	2001	12(1)	1	0	0	4
Lynton Stott	Wakefield	1999	21	4	6	1	29
	Sheffield	1996-98	40(4)	15	0	0	60
Mitchell Stringer	Salford	2005-06	12(4)	0	0	0	0
	London	2004-05	10(19)	0	0	0	0
Graham Strutton	London	1996	9(1)	2	0	0	8
Matt Sturm	Leigh	2005	8(19)	3	0	0	12
	Warrington	2002-04	1(18)	0	0	0	0
	Huddersfield	1998-99	46	8	0	0	32
Anthony Sullivan	St Helens	1996-2001	137(2)	105	0	0	420
Michael Sullivan	Warrington	2006-07	21(16)	8	1	0	34
Phil Sumner	Warrington	1996	(5)	0	0	0	0
Simon Svabic	Salford	1998-2000	13(5)	3	19	0	50
Richard Swain	Hull	2004-07	89	5	0	0	20
Anthony Swann	Warrington	2001	3	1	0	0	4
Logan Swann	Warrington	2005-06	49(1)	17	0	0	68
	Bradford	2004	25	6	0	0	24
Willie Swann	Warrington	1996-97	25(2)	6	0	0	24
Nathan Sykes	Castleford	1996-2004	158(52)	9	0	0	36
Paul Sykes	Harlequins	2006-07	31(2)	15	47	1	155
	London	2001-05	95(1)	26	220	3	547
	Bradford	1999-2002	5(4)	2	3	0	14
Wayne Sykes	London	1999	(2)	0	0	0	0
Semi Tadulala	Wakefield	2004-07	85	36	0	0	144
Whetu Taewa	Sheffield	1997-98	33(7)	8	0	0	32
Alan Tait	Leeds	1996	3(3)	1	0	0	4
Willie Talau	St Helens	2003-07	106(1)	39	0	0	156
Ian Talbot	Wakefield	1999	9(5)	2	31	0	70
	Wigan	1997	3	1	0	0	4
Albert Talipeau	Wakefield	2004	2(3)	0	0	0	0
Gael Tallec	Halifax	2000	5(19)	3	0	0	12
	Castleford	1998-99	19(21)	3	0	0	12
	Wigan	1996-97	8(12)	3	0	0	12
Joe Tamani	Bradford	1996	11(3)	4	0	0	16
Ryan Tandy	Hull KR	2007	8(4)	2	0	0	8
Andrew Tangata-Toa							
	Huddersfield	1999	15	2	0	0	8
David Tangata-Toa							
	Hull KR	2007	(17)	3	0	0	12
Jordan Tansey	Leeds	2006-07	12(19)	12	3	0	54
Kris Tassell	Wakefield	2002	24	10	0	0	40
	Salford	2000-01	35(10)	12	0	0	48
Shem Tatupu	Wigan	1996	(3)	0	0	0	0
Tony Tatupu	Wakefield	2000-01	20	2	0	0	8
	Warrington	1997	21(1)	6	0	0	24
James Taylor	Leigh	2005	(4)	0	0	0	0
Joe Taylor	Paris	1997	9(5)	2	0	0	8
Lawrence Taylor	Sheffield	1996	(1)	0	0	0	0
Frederic Teixido	Sheffield	1999	(4)	0	0	0	0
	Paris	1996-97	2(3)	1	0	0	4
Lionel Teixido	Catalans	2006-07	11(13)	3	0	0	12
Karl Temata	Harlequins	2006-07	30(7)	1	0	0	4
	London	2005	1(2)	1	0	0	4
Jason Temu	Hull	1998	13(2)	1	0	0	4
	Oldham	1996-97	25(3)	1	0	0	4
Paul Terry	London	1997	(1)	0	0	0	0

PLAYER	CLUB	YEAR	APP	TRIES	GOALS	FG	PTS
Anthony Thackeray							
	Hull	2007	2	0	0	0	0
Jamie Thackray	Leeds	2006-07	5(27)	7	0	0	28
	Hull	2005-06	25(20)	3	0	0	12
	Castleford	2003-04	7(11)	3	0	0	12
	Halifax	2000-02	10(38)	3	0	0	12
Adam Thaler	Castleford	2002	(1)	0	0	0	0
Giles Thomas	London	1997-99	1(2)	0	0	0	0
Steve Thomas	London	2004	4(2)	0	0	0	0
	Warrington	2001	2	0	0	0	0
Alex Thompson	Sheffield	1997	4(11)	0	0	0	0
Bobby Thompson	Salford	1999	28	5	2	0	24
Chris Thorman							
	Huddersfield	2000-01, 2005-07	107(18)	46	237	2	660
	London	2003	26(1)	7	81	1	191
	Sheffield	1999	5(13)	2	8	1	25
Tony Thorniley	Warrington	1997	(5)	0	0	0	0
Danny Tickle	Hull	2007	28	9	85	0	206
	Wigan	2002-06	94(36)	35	201	2	544
	Halifax	2000-02	25(17)	10	91	2	224
Kris Tickle	Warrington	2001	(1)	0	0	0	0
John Timu	London	1998-2000	57(3)	11	0	0	44
Kerrod Toby	London	1997	2(2)	0	0	0	0
Tulsen Tollett	London	1996-2001	105(5)	38	49	1	251
Joel Tomkins	Wigan	2005-07	6(16)	4	0	0	16
Glen Tomlinson	Wakefield	1999-2000	41(5)	8	0	0	32
	Hull	1998	5	1	0	0	4
	Bradford	1996-97	27(13)	12	0	0	48
Ian Tonks	Castleford	1996-2001	32(50)	11	13	0	70
Motu Tony	Hull	2005-07	57(20)	21	0	0	84
	Castleford	2004	8(1)	1	0	0	4
Mark Tookey	Harlequins	2006	12(14)	1	0	0	4
	London	2005	13(14)	5	0	0	20
	Castleford	2004	2(8)	1	0	0	4
Clinton Toopi	Leeds	2006-07	34(3)	9	0	0	36
Paul Topping	Oldham	1996-97	23(10)	1	19	0	42
Patrick Torreilles	Paris	1996	9(1)	1	25	0	54
Albert Torrens	Huddersfield	2006	7	5	0	0	20
Mat Toshack	London	1998-2004	120(21)	24	0	0	96
Julien Touxagas	Catalans	2006-07	10(13)	1	0	0	4
Darren Treacy	Salford	2002	24(1)	6	1	0	26
Dean Treister	Hull	2003	16(1)	3	0	0	12
Steve Trindall	London	2003-05	40(20)	3	0	0	12
George Truelove	Wakefield	2002	2	1	0	0	4
	London	2000	5	1	0	0	4
Va'aiga Tuigamala							
	Wigan	1996	21	10	3	0	46
Fereti Tuilagi	St Helens	1999-2000	43(15)	21	0	0	84
	Halifax	1996-98	55(3)	27	0	0	108
Sateki Tuipulotu	Leeds	1996	6(3)	1	2	0	8
Tame Tupou	Bradford	2007	8(2)	7	0	0	28
Neil Turley	Leigh	2005	6(3)	2	20	1	49
Darren Turner	Huddersfield	2000-01, 2003-04	42(13)	13	0	0	52
	Sheffield	1996-99	41(29)	15	0	0	60
Ian Turner	Paris	1996	1(1)	1	0	0	4
Jordan Turner	Salford	2006-07	7(10)	2	0	0	8
Gregory Tutard	Paris	1996	1(1)	0	0	0	0
Brendon Tuuta	Warrington	1998	18(2)	4	0	0	16
	Castleford	1996-97	41(1)	3	0	0	12
Stephen Tyrer	St Helens	2006-07	12(2)	7	36	0	100
Mike Umaga	Halifax	1996-97	38(1)	16	5	0	74
Kava Utoikamanu	Paris	1996	3(6)	0	0	0	0
David Vaealiki	Wigan	2005-07	67(1)	17	0	0	68
Joe Vagana	Bradford	2001-07	158(44)	16	0	0	64
Nigel Vagana	Warrington	1997	20	17	0	0	68
Tevita Vaikona	Bradford	1998-2004	145(2)	89	0	0	356
Lesley Vainikolo	Bradford	2002-07	132(4)	136	1	0	546
Eric Van Brussell	Paris	1996	2	0	0	0	0
Richard Varkulis	Warrington	2004	4(1)	3	0	0	12
Marcus Vassilakopoulos							
	Sheffield	1997-99	15(11)	3	10	2	34
	Leeds	1996-97	1(3)	0	0	0	0
Phil Veivers	Huddersfield	1998	7(6)	1	0	0	4
	St Helens	1996	(1)	1	0	0	4
Michael Vella	Hull KR	2007	22	1	0	0	4
Bruno Verges	Catalans	2006	25	6	0	0	24
Eric Vergniol	Paris	1996	14(1)	6	0	0	24
Gray Viane	Salford	2007	9	2	0	0	8
	Castleford	2006	20(7)	14	0	0	56
	Widnes	2005	20	13	0	0	52
	St Helens	2004	4	1	0	0	4
Adrian Vowles	Castleford	1997-2001, 2003	125(1)	29	1	1	119
	Wakefield	2002-03	24(3)	6	1	0	26
	Leeds	2002	14(3)	2	0	0	8
Michael Wainwright							
	Wakefield	2004-05	21(10)	8	0	0	32
Mike Wainwright	Salford	2000-02, 2007	75(3)	9	0	0	36
	Warrington	1996-99, 2003-07	168(14)	23	0	0	92
Ben Walker	Leeds	2002	23(1)	8	100	0	232

PLAYER	CLUB	YEAR	APP	TRIES	GOALS	FG	PTS
Chev Walker	Leeds	1999-2006	142(19)	77	0	0	308
Matt Walker	Huddersfield	2001	3(6)	0	0	0	0
Anthony Wall	Paris	1997	9	3	3	0	18
Mark Wallace	Workington	1996	14(1)	3	0	0	12
Joe Walsh	Harlequins	2007	1(2)	0	0	0	0
Kerrod Walters	Gateshead	1999	10(12)	2	1	0	10
Kevin Walters	Warrington	2001	1	0	0	0	0
Barry Ward	St Helens	2002-03	20(30)	4	0	0	16
Danny Ward	Hull KR	2007	11(9)	0	0	0	0
	Castleford	2006	18(7)	2	0	0	8
	Leeds	1999-2005	70(48)	9	0	1	37
Phil Waring	Salford	1997-99	6(8)	2	0	0	8
Brett Warton	London	1999-2001	49(7)	14	133	0	322
Kyle Warren	Castleford	2002	13(14)	3	0	0	12
Danny Washbrook							
	Hull	2005-07	37(12)	3	0	0	12
Adam Watene	Wakefield	2006-07	35(6)	3	0	0	12
	Bradford	2006	(4)	0	0	0	0
Frank Watene	Wakefield	1999-2001	24(37)	6	0	0	24
Dave Watson	Sheffield	1998-99	41(4)	4	0	0	16
Ian Watson	Salford	1997, 2002	24(17)	8	3	5	43
	Workington	1996	4(1)	1	15	0	34
Kris Watson	Warrington	1996	11(2)	2	0	0	8
Brad Watts	Widnes	2005	6	3	0	0	12
Michael Watts	Warrington	2002	3	0	0	0	0
Brent Webb	Leeds	2007	25	22	0	0	88
Jason Webber	Salford	2000	25(1)	10	0	0	40
Ian Webster	St Helens	2006	1	0	0	0	0
James Webster	Hull KR	2007	24	2	0	1	9
Pat Weisner	Hull KR	2007	(2)	0	0	0	0
	Harlequins	2006	10(6)	3	0	0	12
Kris Welham	Hull KR	2007	(1)	1	0	0	4
Paul Wellens	St Helens	1998-2007	230(23)	112	32	1	513
Jon Wells	Harlequins	2006-07	31	8	0	0	32
	London	2004-05	42(2)	19	0	0	76
	Wakefield	2003	22(1)	1	0	0	4
	Castleford	1996-2002	114(14)	49	0	0	196
Dwayne West	St Helens	2000-02	8(16)	6	0	0	24
	Wigan	1999	1(1)	0	0	0	0
Craig Weston	Widnes	2002, 2004	23(9)	2	1	2	12
	Huddersfield	1998-99	46(1)	15	15	0	90
Ben Westwood	Warrington	2002-07	128(5)	53	5	0	222
	Wakefield	1999-2002	31(7)	8	1	0	34
Andrew Whalley	Workington	1996	(2)	0	0	0	0
Scott Wheeldon	Hull	2006-07	1(40)	1	0	0	4
Matt Whitaker	Castleford	2006	8(2)	0	0	0	0
	Widnes	2004-05	10(20)	9	0	0	36
	Huddersfield	2003-04	3(14)	0	0	0	0
David White	Wakefield	2000	(1)	0	0	0	0
Josh White	Salford	1998	18(3)	5	5	1	31
	London	1997	14(2)	8	0	1	33
Paul White	Wakefield	2006-07	24(12)	12	0	0	48
	Huddersfield	2003-05	11(32)	17	16	0	100
Richard Whiting	Hull	2004-07	63(24)	29	3	2	124
Danny Whittle	Warrington	1998	(2)	0	0	0	0
David Whittle	St Helens	2002	1(2)	0	0	0	0
	Warrington	2001	1(2)	0	0	0	0
Jon Whittle	Wakefield	2006	8(2)	3	0	0	12
	Widnes	2005	13	2	0	0	8
	Wigan	2003	1	0	0	0	0
Stephen Wild	Huddersfield	2006-07	53(1)	23	0	0	92
	Wigan	2001-05	67(20)	24	0	0	96
Oliver Wilkes	Wigan	2006	1(5)	0	0	0	0
	Leigh	2005	13(1)	1	0	0	4
	Huddersfield	2000-01	1(6)	0	0	0	0
	Sheffield	1998	(1)	0	0	0	0
Jon Wilkin	St Helens	2003-07	82(22)	30	0	1	121
Alex Wilkinson	Hull	2003-04	11(4)	1	0	0	4
	Huddersfield	2003	8	4	0	0	16
	London	2002	5(1)	0	0	0	0
	Bradford	2000-01	3(3)	1	0	0	4
Bart Williams	London	1998	5(3)	1	0	0	4
Daley Williams	Salford	2006-07	9(2)	4	0	0	16
Danny Williams	Harlequins	2006	9(13)	4	0	0	16
	London	2005	1(16)	0	0	0	0
Danny Williams	Leeds	2006	13	7	0	0	28
Desi Williams	Wigan	2004	2	0	0	0	0
Jonny Williams	London	2004	(4)	0	0	0	0
John Wilshere	Salford	2006-07	47(2)	22	83	0	254
	Leigh	2005	26	8	6	0	44
	Warrington	2004	5	2	0	0	8
Craig Wilson	Hull	2000	2(16)	1	0	1	5
	Gateshead	1999	17(11)	5	0	1	21
George Wilson	Paris	1996	7(2)	3	0	0	12
John Wilson	Catalans	2006-07	45	16	0	0	64
Richard Wilson	Hull	1998-99	(13)	0	0	0	0
Scott Wilson	Warrington	1998-99	23(2)	6	0	0	24
Johan Windley	Hull	1999	2(2)	1	0	0	4
Paul Wingfield	Warrington	1997	5(3)	6	1	0	26
Michael Withers	Wigan	2007	6(1)	1	0	0	4
	Bradford	1999-2006	156(6)	94	15	4	410
Jeff Wittenberg	Huddersfield	1998	18(1)	1	0	0	4
	Bradford	1997	8(9)	4	0	0	16
Martin Wood	Sheffield	1997-98	24(11)	4	18	2	54

PLAYER	CLUB	YEAR	APP	TRIES	GOALS	FG	PTS
Nathan Wood	Warrington	2002-05	90	38	0	3	155
	Wakefield	2002	11	2	0	0	8
Paul Wood	Warrington	2000-07	85(85)	30	0	0	120
Phil Wood	Widnes	2004	2(1)	0	0	0	0
Darren Woods	Widnes	2005	(1)	0	0	0	0
David Woods	Halifax	2002	18(2)	8	0	0	32
Michael Worrincy	Harlequins	2006-07	7(9)	2	0	0	8
Rob Worrincy	Castleford	2004	1	0	0	0	0
Troy Wozniak	Widnes	2004	13(7)	1	0	0	4
Matthew Wray	Wakefield	2002-03	13(3)	2	0	0	8
David Wrench	Wakefield	2002-06	28(52)	6	0	0	24
	Leeds	1999-2001	7(17)	0	0	0	0
Craig Wright	Castleford	2000	1(9)	0	0	0	0
Nigel Wright	Huddersfield	1999	4(6)	1	0	0	4
	Wigan	1996-97	5(5)	2	0	1	9
Ricky Wright	Sheffield	1997-99	2(13)	1	0	0	4
Vincent Wulf	Paris	1996	13(4)	4	0	0	16
Andrew Wynyard	London	1999-2000	34(6)	4	0	0	16
Bagdad Yaha	Paris	1996	4(4)	2	4	0	16
Malakai Yasa	Sheffield	1996	1(3)	0	0	0	0
Kirk Yeaman	Hull	2001-07	121(17)	69	0	0	276
Grant Young	London	1998-99	22(2)	2	0	0	8
Ronel Zenon	Paris	1996	(4)	0	0	0	0
Nick Zisti	Bradford	1999	6(1)	0	0	0	0
Freddie Zitter	Catalans	2006	1	0	0	0	0

NEW FACES - Players making their Super League debuts in 2007

PLAYER	CLUB	DEBUT vs	ROUND	DATE
Makali Aizue	Hull KR	Wakefield (h)	1	10/2/07
Phil Bailey	Wigan	Warrington (h)	1	9/2/07
Trent Barrett	Wigan	Warrington (h)	1	9/2/07
Andreas Bauer	Hull KR	Leeds (h)	5	10/3/07
Andrew Bentley	Catalans	Hull KR (a)	8	6/4/07
(first team debut: Featherstone (h), CCR4, 31/3/07)				
Kane Bentley	Catalans	Hull KR (a)	8	6/4/07
(first team debut: Featherstone (h), CCR4, 31/3/07)				
Matt Blaymire	Wakefield	St Helens (h)	2	18/2/07
Matty Blythe	Warrington	Salford (a)	27	14/9/07
Luke Burgess	Harlequins	Catalans (MM)	13	5/5/07
Olivier Charles	Catalans	Warrington (h)	11	21/4/07
Ben Cockayne	Hull KR	Wakefield (h)	1	10/2/07
Jason Croker	Catalans	Hull (a)	1	11/2/07
Chris Dean	St Helens	Salford (a)	24	17/8/07
Vincent Duport	Catalans	Hull (a)	1	11/2/07
Kyle Eastmond	St Helens	Salford (a)	16	1/6/07
Shane Elford	Huddersfield	St Helens (h)	3	4/2/07
Dale Ferguson	Wakefield	Harlequins (a)	10	14/4/07
(first team debut: London Skolars (h), CCR4, 1/4/07)				
David Ferriol	Catalans	Hull (a)	1	11/2/07
Ben Fisher	Hull KR	Wakefield (h)	1	10/2/07
Chris Flannery	St Helens	Wigan (h)	21	20/7/07
Byron Ford	Hull KR	Wakefield (h)	1	10/2/07
Peter Fox	Wakefield	Hull KR (a)	1	10/2/07
Luke George	Wakefield	Leeds (a)	21	20/7/07
(first team debut: Bradford (h), CCR5, 13/5/07)				
Matt Gidley	St Helens	Huddersfield (a)	3	4/2/07
Jason Golden	Wakefield	Hull KR (a)	1	10/2/07
Aaron Gorrell	Catalans	Hull (a)	1	11/2/07
Clint Greenshields	Catalans	Hull (a)	1	11/2/07
Maxime Greseque	Wakefield	Bradford (a)	22	5/8/07
Craig Hall	Hull	Harlequins (a)	8	6/4/07
(first team debut: Hunslet (h), CCR4, 1/4/07)				
Ryan Hall	Leeds	Bradford (MM)	13	6/5/07
Dave Halley	Bradford	Hull KR (h)	10	15/4/07
Ben Harrison	Warrington	Salford (a)	8	6/4/07
(first team debut: London Skolars (h), CCR4, 2/4/06)				
Richie Hawkyard	Bradford	Huddersfield (a)	14	18/5/07
Mathew Head	Hull	Hull KR (a)	19	8/7/07
Scott Hill	Harlequins	St Helens (a)	1	9/2/07
Danny Houghton	Hull	Harlequins (h)	20	13/7/07
Chaz I'Anson	Hull KR	Huddersfield (h)	27	15/9/07
Rod Jensen	Huddersfield	Leeds (h)	17	17/6/07
(first team debut: Bradford (a), CCQF, 10/6/07)				
Anthony Jerram	Warrington	Leeds (h)	10	15/4/07
Michael Lawrence	Huddersfield	Warrington (a)	25	31/8/07
Kylie Leuluai	Leeds	Salford (a)	1	11/2/07
Phil Leuluai	Salford	Hull KR (h)	22	3/8/07
Jamahl Lolesi	Huddersfield	St Helens (h)	3	4/2/07
Rhys Lovegrove	Hull KR	Hull (h)	19	8/7/07
Hutch Maiava	Hull	Catalans (h)	1	11/2/07
Casey McGuire	Catalans	Hull (a)	1	11/2/07
Michael McIlorum	Wigan	Catalans (h)	1	16/6/07
(first team debut: Harlequins (h), CCQF, 8/6/07)				
Lee Mitchell	Warrington	Catalans (h)	24	19/8/07
Adam Mogg	Catalans	Hull (a)	1	11/2/07
Glenn Morrison	Bradford	Huddersfield (h)	1	11/2/07
Kirk Netherton	Hull KR	Catalans (h)	8	6/4/07
Dimitri Pelo	Catalans	Hull (a)	1	11/2/07
Luke Quigley	Catalans	Bradford (a)	7	25/3/07
Sebastien Raguin	Catalans	Hull (a)	1	11/2/07
Stefan Ratchford	Salford	St Helens (a)	16	1/6/07
(first team debut: Gateshead (h), CCR4, 30/3/07)				
Mike Ratu	Leeds	Salford (h)	23	10/8/07
Matt Sing	Hull	Catalans (h)	1	11/2/07
John Skandalis	Huddersfield	St Helens (h)	3	4/2/07
Cyril Stacul	Catalans	Bradford (a)	26	9/9/07
Jon Steel	Hull KR	St Helens (a)	7	23/3/07
Ryan Tandy	Hull KR	Leeds (h)	15	27/5/07
David Tangata-Toa	Hull KR	Huddersfield (a)	2	18/2/07
Anthony Thackeray	Hull	Wakefield (a)	12	28/4/07
Tame Tupou	Bradford	Hull (h)	17	17/6/07
(first team debut: Huddersfield (h), CCQF, 10/6/07)				
Michael Vella	Hull KR	Wakefield (h)	1	10/2/07
Joe Walsh	Harlequins	Catalans (MM)	13	5/5/07
Brent Webb	Leeds	Salford (h)	1	11/2/07
James Webster	Hull KR	Wakefield (h)	1	10/2/07
Kris Welham	Hull KR	Wigan (h)	26	9/9/07

OLD FACES - Players making their debuts for new clubs in 2007

PLAYER	CLUB	DEBUT vs	ROUND	DATE
Vinnie Anderson	Warrington	Wigan (a)	1	9/2/07
Steve Bannister	Harlequins	Salford (a)	17	15/6/07
(first team debut: Wigan (a), CCQF, 8/6/07)				
Richie Barnett	Salford	Bradford (h)	21	21/7/07
David Berthezene	Salford	Huddersfield (a)	7	25/3/07
Ricky Bibey	Wakefield	Harlequins (a)	10	14/4/07
Chris Chester	Hull KR	Wakefield (h)	1	10/2/07
Paul Cooke	Hull KR	Huddersfield (h)	12	27/4/07
Luke Dorn	Salford	Leeds (h)	1	11/2/07
Luke Dyer	Hull KR	Wakefield (h)	1	10/2/07
Mark Edmondson	Salford	Leeds (h)	1	11/2/07
James Evans	Bradford	Huddersfield (h)	1	11/2/07
Chris Feather	Bradford	Huddersfield (h)	1	11/2/07
Brett Ferres	Wakefield	Hull KR (a)	1	10/2/07
Tommy Gallagher	Hull KR	Wakefield (h)	1	10/2/07
Jim Gannon	Hull KR	Wakefield (h)	1	10/2/07
Stanley Gene	Hull KR	Wigan (a) (D2)	4	2/3/07
Sean Gleeson	Wakefield	St Helens (a)	14	18/5/07
Jon Goddard	Hull KR	Wakefield (h)	1	10/2/07
Wayne Godwin	Hull	Catalans (h)	1	11/2/07
Jon Grayshon	Harlequins	St Helens (a)	1	9/2/07
Darrell Griffin	Huddersfield	St Helens (h)	3	4/2/07
Danny Halliwell	Salford	Leeds (h)	1	11/2/07
Ian Hardman	Hull KR	Bradford (a)	10	15/4/07
Bryn Hargreaves	St Helens	Huddersfield (a)	3	4/2/07
Danny Hill	Hull KR	Bradford (a)	10	15/4/07
Ryan Hudson	Huddersfield	St Helens (h)	3	4/2/07
Lee Jewitt	Salford	Leeds (h)	1	11/2/07
Paul Johnson	Warrington	Wigan (a)	1	9/2/07
Michael Korkidas	Salford	Leeds (h)	1	11/2/07
Mark Lennon	Hull KR	Salford (h)	11	22/4/07
Thomas Leuluai	Wigan	Warrington (h)	1	9/2/07
Danny Lima	Wakefield	Hull KR (a)	1	10/2/07
Willie Manu	Hull	Warrington (a)	3	25/2/07
Paul March	Wakefield	Hull KR (a) (D2)	1	10/2/07
Joe Mbu	Harlequins	Wigan (h) (D2)	16	2/6/07
Nathan McAvoy	Bradford	Huddersfield (h) (D2)	1	11/2/07
Chris Melling	Harlequins	St Helens (h)	1	9/2/07
Shane Millard	Wigan	Warrington (h)	1	9/2/07
Richard Moore	Wakefield	Hull KR (a)	1	10/2/07
Adrian Morley	Warrington	Wigan (a)	1	9/2/07
Iain Morrison	Hull KR	Wakefield (h)	1	10/2/07
Gareth Morton	Hull KR	Wakefield (h)	1	10/2/07
Scott Murrell	Hull KR	Wakefield (h)	1	10/2/07
Stephen Nash	Salford	Huddersfield (h)	15	25/5/07
(first team debut: Gateshead (h), CCR4, 30/3/07)				
Jason Netherton	Hull KR	Wakefield (h)	1	10/2/07
Mark O'Neill	Hull KR	Harlequins (h)	3	25/2/07
Danny Orr	Harlequins	St Helens (a)	1	9/2/07
Michael Platt	Bradford	Huddersfield (h)	1	11/2/07
Waine Pryce	Wakefield	Hull (a)	4	4/3/07
Julien Rinaldi	Harlequins	St Helens (a)	1	9/2/07
Tom Saxton	Salford	Bradford (h)	21	21/7/07
Danny Sculthorpe	Wakefield	Hull (a)	4	4/3/07
Rikki Sheriffe	Harlequins	Hull KR (h) (D2)	18	30/6/07
Andy Smith	Harlequins	Warrington (h)	4	3/3/07
Michael Smith	Hull KR	Huddersfield (a)	2	18/2/07
David Solomona	Bradford	Huddersfield (h)	1	11/2/07
Danny Tickle	Hull	Catalans (h)	1	11/2/07
Gray Viane	Salford	Hull (h)	10	13/4/07
(first team debut: Gateshead (h), CCR4, 30/3/07)				
Mike Wainwright	Salford	Bradford (h) (D2)	21	21/7/07
Danny Ward	Hull KR	Wakefield (h)	1	10/2/07
Pat Weisner	Hull KR	Wakefield (h)	1	10/2/07
Michael Withers	Wigan	Warrington (h)	1	9/2/07

SUPER LEAGUE XII
Club by Club

20 November 2006 - Michael Platt's transfer from Castleford goes to tribunal. Academy starlet Taron Wildey joins Dewsbury.

25 November 2006 - Bulls sign New Zealand international David Solomona from Wakefield Trinity Wildcats on a three-year deal.

27 November 2006 - David Solomona to sue Wakefield for money still owed to him by the club.

5 December 2006 - Michael Withers ends speculation about his future by joining Wigan.

18 December 2006 - out-going chief executive Gareth Davies will not be replaced and his responsibilities will be shared by existing staff.

19 December 2006 - winger Marcus Bai announces his retirement from the game, despite having signed a new one-year deal.

22 December 2006 - Bulls pay Castleford a £10,000 transfer fee for Michael Platt.

4 January 2007 - Wigan announce the signing of 18-year-old stand-off Mark Flanagan from Bradford.

9 January 2007 - Paul Deacon is the new Bulls captain, taking over from Iestyn Harris. Glenn Morrison is vice-captain.

2 February 2007 - the Bulls announce the signing of Nathan McAvoy on a 12-month contract.

7 February 2007 - Harlequins sign Bulls winger Andy Smith.

24 February 2007 - Bradford beat Wigan 32-28 on Brian Noble's return to Odsal. Paul Deacon passes the 2,000-point mark for the club.

6 March 2007 - Terry Newton handed a two-match ban after being found guilty of striking Jon Wilkin in the Bulls' defeat at St Helens.

12 March 2007 - Bradford deny reports star winger Lesley Vainikolo is to leave to play rugby union.

17 March 2007 - Joe Vagana makes his 200th appearance for the club against Harlequins.

25 March 2007 - Shontayne Hape ruled out for six months after sustaining a knee injury in shock 29-22 home defeat by Catalans Dragons.

3 April 2007 - Jamie Langley signs a new three-year contract.

9 April 2007 - form back-rower Glenn Morrison breaks thumb in Easter Monday 36-24 win at Wakefield.

20 April 2007 - Steve McNamara celebrates his first year in charge with 32-22 victory at home-town Hull.

23 April 2007 - Bulls deny signing Matt King from Melbourne.

30 April 2007 - Steve McNamara appointed part-time assistant Great Britain coach.

2 May 2007 - Bulls sign Kiwi winger Tame Tupou, released by Brisbane, to replace outgoing Lesley Vainikolo.

KEY DATES - BRADFORD BULLS

6 May 2007 - Bulls suffer controversial last-second 42-38 defeat to Leeds in Millennium Magic weekend. Steve McNamara blasts Steve Ganson's refereeing performance.

8 May 2007 - Terry Newton gets three-match-ban for high tackle on Leeds prop Jamie Thackray.

10 May 2007 - Bulls threaten to serve legal papers in the pursuit of the two points they lost in Cardiff.

13 May 2007 - Bradford progress into the Carnegie Challenge Cup quarter-finals with a hard fought 14-4 victory over dogged Wildcats.

10 June 2007 - Iestyn Harris suffers hamstring injury in 52-20 Challenge Cup quarter-final win over the Giants, Tame Tupou scores twice on debut.

17 June 2007 - Lesley Vainikolo makes his final appearance at the Grattan Stadium as the Bulls brush past Hull 34-8. Terry Newton scores four tries.

23 June 2007 - hooker Ian Henderson announces he will join New Zealand Warriors at the end of the season.

27 June 2007 - Joe Vagana signs a new one-year contract to keep him at the Grattan Stadium until the end of the 2008 season.

29 June 2007 - Lesley Vainikolo signs off from the Super League in style with a brilliant individual try as Bradford land a 38-14 victory at Leeds.

5 July 2007 - Bradford Bulls are one of three clubs charged with breaching the 2006 salary cap.

7 July 2007 - Bulls suffer a 25-18 defeat at ex-coach Brian Noble's Wigan.

12 July 2007 - RFL tribunal finds Bulls guilty of breaching the 2006 salary cap by four per cent, and deducts two league points, effective immediately.

13 July 2007 - Bulls overcome St Helens 10-4 at a rain-soaked Grattan Stadium in a dress rehearsal for the Challenge Cup semi-final.

17 July 2007 - centre Ben Harris to leave the club at the end of the season to join North Queensland Cowboys.

21 July 2007 - Bulls slip to a shock 14-10 defeat at bottom side Salford.

23 July 2007 - Jamie Langley ruled out for the rest of the season after undergoing an operation to reconstruct his wrist.

28 July 2007 - 35-14 defeat by holders St Helens in Carnegie Challenge Cup semi-final.

2 August 2007 - fullback Michael Platt has his two-match suspension for punching St Helens' Maurie Fa'asavalu reduced to one.

5 August 2007 - Steve McNamara pays tribute to his side as they claim 38-24 home victory over Wakefield, despite having Joe Vagana sent off.

7 August 2007 - Vagana banned for two matches.

15 August 2007 - winger Dave Halley signs a new contract to end of 2008 season.

19 August 2007 - Bradford slump to 26-22 defeat in the derby at Huddersfield.

21 August 2007 - Glenn Morrison banned for three games for high tackle on Keith Mason and Tame Tupou two games for punching.

28 August 2007 - Nathan McAvoy not to be offered contract at end of the season.

29 August 2007 - Glenn Morrison has his ban overturned on appeal.

3 September 2007 - the Bradford club celebrates its centenary with a 16-16 draw at home to Leeds.

4 September 2007 - Harlequins centre Paul Sykes confirms his return to Bradford for 2008.

6 September 2007 - Chris McKenna and Marcus St Hilaire both to be released by the Bulls at the end of the season.

9 September 2007 - 40-8 victory over Challenge Cup runners up Catalans sets Bradford on course for a third-place finish.

11 September 2007 - Chris McKenna announces move to Doncaster, relegated to National League 2.

14 September 2007 - Bradford fall 20-10 at Hull FC in last round, meaning a home elimination play-off against Wigan.

21 September 2007 - Bulls surrender 30-6 lead to Wigan and lose 31-30.

22 September 2007 - Chris Nero joins from Huddersfield on a three-year contract; along with Ben Jeffries, two years, and winger Semi Tadulala, one year, from Wakefield Wildcats. Hull hooker Wayne Godwin and Salford's Simon Finnigan sign on one-year deals.

4 October 2007 - Paul Deacon withdraws from GB squad due to a hamstring injury.

16 October 2007 - Craig Kopczak signs a new 12-month contract.

BRADFORD BULLS

DATE	FIXTURE	RESULT	SCORERS	LGE	ATT
11/2/07	Huddersfield (h)	W18-14	t:Hape,Solomona,Morrison g:Deacon(3)	5th	12,130
18/2/07	Warrington (a)	W20-36	t:Platt(3),Morrison,Vainikolo,Evans g:Deacon(6)	1st	12,607
24/2/07	Wigan (h)	W32-28	t:Vainikolo(3),Morrison,Newton g:Deacon(6)	1st	12,798
2/3/07	St Helens (a)	L34-22	t:Hape(2),Langley,Solomona g:Deacon(3)	3rd	11,793
11/3/07	Salford (h)	W56-18	t:Platt(3),Solomona,Hape(2),St Hilaire,Henderson,McKenna(2) g:Deacon(8)	1st	10,640
17/3/07	Harlequins (a)	W22-36	t:Langley,Morrison(2),I Harris,Vainikolo,Platt g:Deacon(6)	1st	4,011
25/3/07	Catalans (h)	L22-29	t:Deacon,Evans(2),Platt g:Deacon(3)	1st	11,298
30/3/07	Castleford (h) (CCR4)	W24-16	t:Morrison,St Hilaire,Vainikolo,Solomona g:Deacon(4)	N/A	6,748
5/4/07	Leeds (h)	L14-18	t:St Hilaire,Vainikolo g:Deacon(3)	3rd	16,706
9/4/07	Wakefield (a)	W24-36	t:Vainikolo(2),Solomona,Henderson,Platt,McKenna g:Deacon(6)	2nd	9,106
15/4/07	Hull KR (h)	W52-22	t:Lynch(2),I Harris(2),Langley,Platt,B Harris,Halley,Solomona g:Deacon(8)	2nd	10,881
20/4/07	Hull (a)	W22-32	t:Evans(2),Newton,B Harris,Vagana,Lynch g:Deacon(4)	1st	12,767
29/4/07	Warrington (h)	W36-24	t:Deacon,Vainikolo,Platt(2),Langley,Evans g:Deacon(3),I Harris(3)	2nd	11,276
6/5/07	Leeds (MM) ●	L38-42	t:Platt(2),Vainikolo,Henderson,B Harris,Lynch g:Deacon(7)	3rd	N/A
13/5/07	Wakefield (a) (CCR5)	W4-14	t:Vainikolo(2),Cook g:Deacon	N/A	3,700
18/5/07	Huddersfield (a)	L36-12	t:Vainikolo,B Harris g:I Harris(2)	3rd	8,667
27/5/07	Harlequins (h)	W44-18	t:Vainikolo(3),Vagana,Deacon,Morrison,Henderson,Hawkyard g:Deacon(6)	3rd	10,418
2/6/07	Catalans (a)	W20-28	t:Vagana,Deacon,Vainikolo,Newton,Evans g:Deacon(4)	3rd	7,555
10/6/07	Huddersfield (h) (CCQF)	W52-20	t:B Harris(2),Solomona,Henderson,St Hilaire,Burgess,Tupou(2),Newton g:Deacon(8)	N/A	7,811
17/6/07	Hull (h)	W34-8	t:Newton(4),Tupou,Deacon g:Deacon(4),Vainikolo	3rd	11,557
29/6/07	Leeds (a)	W14-38	t:Vainikolo,Evans,Tupou,Lynch,Morrison,St Hilaire g:Deacon(7)	2nd	22,000
6/7/07	Wigan (a)	L25-18	t:Evans,B Harris g:Deacon(5)	3rd	15,107
13/7/07	St Helens (h)	W10-4	t:St Hilaire g:Deacon(3)	3rd	11,214
21/7/07	Salford (a)	L14-10	t:Tupou(2) g:Deacon	3rd	3,438
28/7/07	St Helens (CCSF) ●●	L14-35	t:Evans,Tupou,Vagana g:Deacon	N/A	14,316
5/8/07	Wakefield (h)	W38-24	t:Halley,Evans(2),Morrison,Tupou,Solomona,Burgess g:Burgess(5)	3rd	10,701
12/8/07	Hull KR (a)	W10-28	t:Burgess,Newton,Morrison,Henderson,St Hilaire g:I Harris(4)	3rd	6,695
19/8/07	Huddersfield (a)	L26-22	t:Solomona,Henderson,McKenna g:I Harris(5)	3rd	6,824
2/9/07	Leeds (h)	D16-16	t:Lynch,B Harris,Evans g:Deacon(2)	3rd	18,195
9/9/07	Catalans (h)	W40-8	t:Newton,Morrison,Solomona,McAvoy,Halley,I Harris,Vagana g:I Harris(6)	3rd	9,350
14/9/07	Hull (a)	L20-10	t:Tupou,Solomona g:I Harris	3rd	14,402
21/9/07	Wigan (h) (EPO)	L30-31	t:Solomona(3),Tupou,I Harris g:I Harris(5)	N/A	9,055

● Played at Millennium Stadium, Cardiff
●● Played at Galpharm Stadium, Huddersfield

	D.O.B.	APP		TRIES		GOALS		FG		PTS	
		ALL	SL	ALL	SL	ALL	SL	ALL	SL	ALL	SL
Sam Burgess	14/12/88	11(19)	10(16)	3	2	5	5	0	0	22	18
Matt Cook	14/11/86	1(16)	1(14)	1	0	0	0	0	0	4	0
Paul Deacon	13/2/79	25	21	5	5	112	98	0	0	244	216
James Evans	5/11/78	20(4)	17(4)	13	12	0	0	0	0	52	48
Chris Feather	7/12/81	5(13)	5(11)	0	0	0	0	0	0	0	0
Dave Halley	12/10/86	3(7)	3(7)	3	3	0	0	0	0	12	12
Shontayne Hape	30/1/82	9	9	5	5	0	0	0	0	20	20
Ben Harris	24/9/83	29(1)	25(1)	8	6	0	0	0	0	32	24
Iestyn Harris	25/6/76	26	22	5	5	26	26	0	0	72	72
Richie Hawkyard	21/1/86	1(2)	1(2)	1	1	0	0	0	0	4	4
Ian Henderson	23/4/83	10(21)	9(18)	7	6	0	0	0	0	28	24
Matt James	26/3/87	1(12)	1(11)	0	0	0	0	0	0	0	0
Craig Kopczak	20/12/86	(4)	(4)	0	0	0	0	0	0	0	0
Jamie Langley	21/12/83	17(1)	16	4	4	0	0	0	0	16	16
Andy Lynch	20/10/79	28(2)	24(2)	6	6	0	0	0	0	24	24
Nathan McAvoy	31/12/76	19(10)	16(9)	1	1	0	0	0	0	4	4
Chris McKenna	29/10/74	20(7)	17(6)	4	4	0	0	0	0	16	16
Glenn Morrison	28/5/76	28	24	11	10	0	0	0	0	44	40
Terry Newton	7/11/78	24(2)	21(2)	10	9	0	0	0	0	40	36
Michael Platt	23/3/84	28	25	14	14	0	0	0	0	56	56
David Solomona	26/1/78	31(1)	27(1)	14	12	0	0	0	0	56	48
Marcus St Hilaire	26/1/77	24(1)	21	7	5	0	0	0	0	28	20
Tame Tupou	22/10/82	9(3)	8(2)	10	7	0	0	0	0	40	28
Joe Vagana	21/1/75	27(2)	24(2)	5	4	0	0	0	0	20	16
Lesley Vainikolo	4/5/79	20	17	19	16	1	1	0	0	78	66

David Solomona

LEAGUE RECORD
P27-W17-D1-L9
(3rd, SL/Elimination Play-Off)
F778, A560, Diff+218
33 points. *(2 points deducted for 2006 salary cap breach)*

CHALLENGE CUP
Semi Finalists

ATTENDANCES
Best - v Leeds (SL - 18,195)
Worst - v Castleford (CC - 6,748)
Total (SL, inc play-offs) - 166,219
Average (SL, inc play-offs) - 11,873
(Up by 586 on 2006)

KEY DATES -
CATALANS DRAGONS

13 November 2006 - assistant coach Paul Donkin resigns.

5 December 2006 - former Canberra halfback Andrew McFadden joins as assistant coach on a two-year deal. Retired Laurent Frayssinous becomes kicking coach.

22 January 2007 - Stacey Jones ruled out for two months after knee surgery.

24 February 2007 - Aaron Gorrell ruled out for the season after damaging cruciate ligaments in stunning home round three win over Leeds.

11 March 2007 - Dragons sign Luke Quigley from Newcastle Knights to replace the injured Gorrell.

20 March 2007 - Salford sign David Berthezene on a months loan to cover for the injured Malcolm Alker.

25 March 2007 - Catalans' 29-22 victory at Bradford comes at a cost as Sebastien Raguin breaks an arm, and Gregory Mounis a finger, while Luke Quigley damages a hamstring.

29 March 2007 - Dragons refused fee for Ian Hindmarsh after he left the club for personal reasons and then signed for Parramatta.

31 March 2007 - Catalans win 70-12 against Featherstone Rovers in Challenge Cup.

20 April 2007 - Salford sign David Berthezene until the end of the season.

21 April 2007 - Catalans chief executive Nicolas Rayer steps down for personal reasons.

13 May 2007 - Dragons edge NL1 Whitehaven 24-14 to progress into quarter-finals of Carnegie Challenge Cup.

14 May 2007 - Catalans announce plans to play Challenge Cup tie in Barcelona.

19 May 2007 - Dragons post record club Super League victory with a 66-6 home demolition of Salford City Reds.

4 June 2007 - Jamel Fakir suffers injury to knee that sees him out for up to nine months.

5 June 2007 - Stacey Jones signs a one-year extension on his contract to keep him at the Dragons until end of 2008.

10 June 2007 - Catalans progress to the semi-finals of the Carnegie Challenge Cup with a scintillating 26-23 victory at Hull FC.

13 June 2007 - The draw pairs them with 17-time Cup winners Wigan.

Stacey Jones

15 June 2007 - Catalans are defeated 30-0 in Super League by their semi-final opponents Wigan.

6 July 2007 - Catalans capture Australian Test forward Dane Carlaw on a three-year deal from Brisbane Broncos.

7 July 2007 - third successive defeat 30-22 at Harlequins.

21 July 2007 - Leading scorer Thomas Bosc ruled out of the semi-final with a broken arm suffered in the 34-18 defeat by Hull.

24 July 2007 - Challenge Cup trophy visits France for the first time in 110 years as Catalans prepare for their semi-final against Wigan.

29 July 2007 - Catalans become first French side to reach the Challenge Cup Final in history with shock 37-24 win over Wigan.

5 August 2007 - coach Mick Potter slams his players for complacency after the 42-22 defeat by Huddersfield.

11 August 2007 - dress rehearsal for the cup final sees Catalans win 21-0 against league leaders St Helens.

24 August 2007 - stand-off Casey McGuire ruled out of Wembley showdown after failing a fitness test on a pectoral injury.

25 August 2007 - Catalans lose 30-8 to St Helens in the Challenge Cup Final at Wembley.

7 September 2007 - Catalans captain Stacey Jones announces his retirement despite signing a new 12-month contract earlier in the year.

9 September 2007 - Bradford demolish Catalans 40-8 in penultimate game of the season.

10 September 2007 - Stacey Jones wins August player of the month award.

15 September 2007 - Dragons finish season on a high with 30-14 home victory over Quins, as Stacey Jones kicks five goals out of five in his last club match.

16 September 2007 - Mick Potter admits interest in signing Hull FC halfback Mathew Head.

21 September 2007 - Marc Conesa appointed new chief executive

12 October 2007 - Wakefield prop Olivier Elima signs three-year contract; Adel Fellous leaves.

7 November 2007 - halfback Mathew Head in negotiations with the Dragons.

CATALANS DRAGONS

DATE	FIXTURE	RESULT	SCORERS	LGE	ATT
11/2/07	Hull (a)	D10-10	t:Mogg,Duport g:Gorrell	8th	12,673
17/2/07	Wigan (h)	L16-18	t:Chan,Murphy g:Gorrell(4)	9th	7,052
24/2/07	Leeds (h)	W30-22	t:Bosc,Chan,McGuire,Duport,Pelo g:Gorrell(5)	7th	7,630
3/3/07	Salford (a)	L10-0		8th	4,085
11/3/07	Wakefield (a)	L40-20	t:Murphy(2),Croker g:Bosc(4)	9th	5,332
17/3/07	Huddersfield (h)	W23-22	t:Bosc,Teixido,Greenshields,Mogg g:Bosc(3) fg:Jones	10th	8,300
25/3/07	Bradford (a)	W22-29	t:Bosc(2),Greenshields,Ferriol,Wilson g:Bosc(4) fg:Croker	8th	11,298
31/3/07	Featherstone (h) (CCR4)	W70-12	t:Duport,A Bentley,Ferriol,Fellous,Khattabi,Chan,Gossard(2),Bosc, Mogg(2),Casty g:Bosc(11)	N/A	1,545
6/4/07	Hull KR (a)	W20-34	t:Croker,Pelo,Duport,Greenshields,K Bentley,Jones g:Bosc(5)	6th	6,701
9/4/07	Harlequins (h)	L16-38	t:Bosc,Pelo,Fellous g:Bosc(2)	8th	9,300
13/4/07	St Helens (a)	L53-10	t:Touxagas,Pelo g:Bosc	9th	7,918
21/4/07	Warrington (h)	W27-16	t:Charles,McGuire,Chan,Bosc g:Bosc(5) fg:Jones	6th	9,050
27/4/07	Leeds (a)	L54-8	t:Charles,Mogg	7th	15,581
5/5/07	Harlequins (MM) ●	L28-32	t:Greenshields,Jones(2),Wilson,A Bentley g:Bosc(4)	10th	N/A
13/5/07	Whitehaven (a) (CCR5)	W14-24	t:Bosc,Duport,Touxagas,K Bentley g:Bosc(4)	N/A	3,008
19/5/07	Salford (h)	W66-6	t:Murphy(3),Mogg(2),Gossard,Bosc(2),McGuire(2),Guisset, Greenshields g:Bosc(9)	8th	8,820
27/5/07	Wakefield (a)	L18-12	t:Wilson(2) g:Bosc(2)	8th	4,023
2/6/07	Bradford (h)	L20-28	t:Gossard,Bosc,Wilson,McGuire g:Bosc(2)	9th	7,555
10/6/07	Hull (a) (CCQF)	W23-26	t:Mogg(2),Wilson,Greenshields g:Bosc(4) fg:Guisset,Bosc	N/A	7,441
15/6/07	Wigan (a)	L30-0		10th	12,641
30/6/07	Warrington (h)	W24-22	t:Khattabi,Ferriol,Wilson,McGuire,Croker g:Bosc(2)	8th	8,850
7/7/07	Harlequins (a)	L30-22	t:McGuire,Greenshields,Raguin,Bosc g:Bosc(3)	10th	2,346
14/7/07	Hull KR (h)	L20-22	t:Greenshields,Khattabi(2),Jones g:Bosc(2)	10th	7,830
21/7/07	Hull (h)	L18-34	t:Mogg,Quigley,Ferriol,Bosc g:Bosc	10th	7,560
29/7/07	Wigan (CCSF) ●●	W37-24	t:McGuire,Wilson,Mogg,Duport(2),Croker g:Jones(6) fg:Jones	N/A	10,218
5/8/07	Huddersfield (a)	L42-22	t:Croker,Chan,Mogg,Khattabi g:Jones(3)	11th	4,319
11/8/07	St Helens (h)	W21-0	t:Khattabi,Murphy,Croker,Greenshields g:Jones(2) fg:Jones	10th	8,655
19/8/07	Warrington (a)	L22-18	t:Greenshields,Jones,Murphy g:Jones(3)	10th	8,125
25/8/07	St Helens (CCF) ●●●	L8-30	t:Khattabi,Murphy	N/A	84,241
1/9/07	Wakefield (h)	W38-20	t:Gossard,Croker,Casty,Murphy,Greenshields,Mogg g:Jones(7)	10th	7,325
9/9/07	Bradford (a)	L40-8	t:Fellous g:Jones(2)	10th	9,350
15/9/07	Harlequins (h)	W30-14	t:Stacul,Wilson(2),Greenshields(2) g:Jones(5)	10th	8,420

● Played at Millennium Stadium, Cardiff
●● Played at Halliwell Jones Stadium, Warrington
●●● Played at Wembley Stadium

		APP		TRIES		GOALS		FG		PTS	
	D.O.B.	ALL	SL	ALL	SL	ALL	SL	ALL	SL	ALL	SL
Andrew Bentley	13/5/85	10(5)	9(4)	2	1	0	0	0	0	8	4
Kane Bentley	16/4/87	2(8)	1(5)	2	1	0	0	0	0	8	4
David Berthezene	27/10/80	(1)	(1)	0	0	0	0	0	0	0	0
Thomas Bosc	5/8/83	21(1)	18(1)	13	11	68	49	1	0	189	142
Remi Casty	5/2/85	4(8)	3(7)	2	1	0	0	0	0	8	4
Alex Chan	22/12/74	29(2)	25(1)	5	4	0	0	0	0	20	16
Olivier Charles	12/7/79	2	2	2	2	0	0	0	0	8	8
Jason Croker	10/3/73	23	21	7	6	0	0	1	1	29	25
Vincent Duport	15/12/87	14(3)	11(2)	7	3	0	0	0	0	28	12
Jamel Fakir	30/8/82	(2)	(2)	0	0	0	0	0	0	0	0
Adel Fellous	16/2/78	3(10)	3(9)	3	2	0	0	0	0	12	8
David Ferriol	24/4/79	6(22)	5(18)	4	3	0	0	0	0	16	12
Aaron Gorrell	31/3/81	3	3	0	0	10	10	0	0	20	20
Cyril Gossard	7/2/82	21(8)	17(7)	5	3	0	0	0	0	20	12
Clint Greenshields	11/1/82	31	27	13	12	0	0	0	0	52	48
Mathieu Griffi	2/3/83	1(18)	(16)	0	0	0	0	0	0	0	0
Jerome Guisset	29/8/78	24(5)	19(5)	1	1	0	0	1	0	5	4
Stacey Jones	7/5/76	28	23	5	5	28	22	4	3	80	67
Younes Khattabi	28/3/84	12(3)	8(3)	7	5	0	0	0	0	28	20
Casey McGuire	24/1/80	20(4)	19(3)	8	7	0	0	0	0	32	28
Adam Mogg	31/7/77	31	26	13	8	0	0	0	0	52	32
Gregory Mounis	18/1/85	22(2)	19(2)	0	0	0	0	0	0	0	0
Justin Murphy	14/2/78	18	15	10	9	0	0	0	0	40	36
Dimitri Pelo	17/4/85	13	12	4	4	0	0	0	0	16	16
Luke Quigley	20/7/81	19(1)	16(1)	1	1	0	0	0	0	4	4
Sebastien Raguin	14/2/79	13(5)	11(5)	1	1	0	0	0	0	4	4
Cyril Stacul	12/10/84	2	2	1	1	0	0	0	0	4	4
Lionel Teixido	1/9/79	8(11)	7(9)	1	1	0	0	0	0	4	4
Julien Touxagas	12/2/84	11(9)	9(7)	2	1	0	0	0	0	8	4
John Wilson	2/7/78	25	20	10	8	0	0	0	0	40	32

Adam Mogg

LEAGUE RECORD
P27-W10-D1-L16
(10th, SL)
F570, A685, Diff-115
21 points.

CHALLENGE CUP
Runners-Up

ATTENDANCES
Best - v Harlequins (SL - 9,300)
Worst - v Featherstone (CC - 1,545)
Total (SL only) - 106,347
Average (SL only) - 8,181
(Up by 1,639 on 2006)

KEY DATES - HARLEQUINS

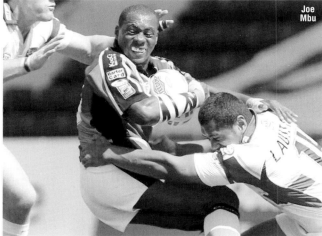

Joe Mbu

27 November 2006 - Pat Weisner joins promoted Hull KR after loan spell.

29 November 2006 - Mark Tookey retires after his release.

5 December 2006 - Thomas Leuluai is unveiled as a Wigan player.

8 December 2006 - Solomon Haumono returns to boxing and new recruit Sione Faumuina quits without playing a game for the club. Mark McLinden also to miss start of season.

11 December 2006 - Tim Hartley joins Halifax.

3 January 2007 - Sione Faumuina signs with North Queensland Cowboys after his release by Harlequins.

22 January 2007 - Rob Purdham named new captain, replacing Mark McLinden.

26 January 2007 - former South London Storm coach Rob Powell appointed assistant coach.

7 February 2007 - Quins sign Bradford winger Andy Smith. Tony Clubb signs new contract keeping him at the club until 2008.

15 February 2007 - Rob Purdham signs new deal until the end of 2009 season.

3 March 2007 - Richard Villasanti signs from Cronulla.

19 March 2007 - Quins attempt to sign former GB winger Brian Carney, who joins Munster RU.

2 May 2007 - Quins take 20-year-old Leeds Rhinos Academy prop Luke Burgess on loan.

5 May 2007 - Quins secure 32-28 victory in a thrilling encounter with Catalans at the Millennium Magic Weekend.

13 May 2007 - 66-6 victory over Oldham in the Challenge Cup fifth round.

28 May 2007 - Joe Mbu returns to the club after leaving nine months before to join Doncaster.

2 June 2007 - Quins record famous 18-8 victory at home to Wigan that relieves relegation pressure.

8 June 2007 - Wigan inflict the Quins' seventh loss of the season as they crash out of the Challenge Cup 25-6 at the JJB.

16 June 2007 - Quins suffer 5-2 defeat to Salford at the Willows.

19 June 2007 - Richard Villasanti retires at 27 after he fails to recover from knee surgery without playing a game for Quins.

4 August 2007 - Rob Purdham returns to action against Leeds for the first time since suffering a back injury in May.

4 August 2007 - Quins forward Lee Hopkins announces retirement at the end of the season.

7 August 2007 - Karl Temata and Matthew Gafa both sign 12-month contract extensions to keep them at Stoop until the end of 2008 season.

8 August 2007 - Rikki Sheriffe and Jon Grayshon sign new one-year deals.

12 August 2007 - 28-14 defeat at play-off rivals Wakefield.

13 August 2007 - Henry Paul signs one-year contract extension.

14 August 2007 - hooker Chad Randall signs two-year contract extension.

18 August 2007 - Quins throw away two-try lead to draw 16-16 at home to Wigan.

31 August 2007 - Rob Purdham suffers severe shoulder injury in Quins' 32-10 defeat by St Helens.

4 September 2007 - Paul Sykes announces his return to former club Bradford at end of season.

5 September 2007 - Quins announce signing of Henry Fa'afili on a two-year deal, after his release by Warrington.

7 September 2007 - Fa'afili pulls out and moves to French rugby union.

9 September 2007 - 22-16 victory over Salford keeps slim play-off hopes alive.

13 September 2007 - Gareth Haggerty signs from Salford on a two-year deal.

15 September 2007 - Quins defeated 30-14 at Catalans to end season in ninth position.

16 September 2007 - Quins chairman Ian Lenagan pledges his continued support to the club despite being linked with the purchase of Wigan Warriors.

20 September 2007 - David Mills joins Hull KR.

25 September 2007 - Danny Ward signs on two-year deal from Hull Kingston Rovers.

15 October 2007 - Joe Mbu agrees new deal that will see him stay at the Stoop until the end of 2008. Stephen Bannister joins Salford.

16 October 2007 - director of sport Tony Rea announces his resignation after 13 years with the club.

24 October 2007 - Quins owner Ian Lenagan takes over home-town Wigan.

26 October 2007 - back-row forward Dwayne Barker signs from Castleford on a 12-month deal.

29 October 2007 - Keith Hogg appointed chairman and Paul Brown as chief executive. Louie McCarthy-Scarsbrook agrees two-year contract extension until the end of 2010.

HARLEQUINS

DATE	FIXTURE	RESULT	SCORERS	LGE	ATT
9/2/07	St Helens (a)	W6-14	t:Orr,Hopkins,Wells g:Sykes	1st	7,515
17/2/07	Salford (h)	D18-18	t:T Smith,Melling,Sykes,Rinaldi g:Sykes	4th	3,515
25/2/07	Hull KR (a)	W10-26	t:Melling,Grayshon,McCarthy-Scarsbrook,Sykes(2) g:Sykes(3)	2nd	7,056
3/3/07	Warrington (h)	L12-19	t:Gafa,Hill g:Sykes(2)	6th	3,132
9/3/07	Wigan (a)	L16-12	t:Heckenberg,Hill g:Sykes(2)	7th	14,971
17/3/07	Bradford (h)	L22-36	t:Sykes(2),Purdham(2),Wells g:Purdham	8th	4,011
23/3/07	Leeds (a)	L28-16	t:Melling,Gafa,Sykes g:Paul,Purdham	9th	15,123
31/3/07	Pia (a) (CCR4)	W8-64	t:Hill,Randall,Gafa,Sykes(2),Hopkins,McCarthy-Scarsbrook(3), A Smith(2) g:Purdham(3),Paul(7)	N/A	300
6/4/07	Hull (h)	W30-28	t:Wells,Heckenberg,A Smith,Rinaldi,McLinden g:Paul(5)	9th	3,545
9/4/07	Catalans (a)	W16-38	t:Wells,Randall,Orr,McLinden(2),Rinaldi g:Paul(7)	7th	9,300
14/4/07	Wakefield (h)	D22-22	t:Hill,A Smith,Sykes,Hopkins g:Paul(2),Purdham	5th	2,532
22/4/07	Huddersfield (a)	L46-16	t:Randall,T Smith,Grayshon g:Purdham(2)	7th	4,894
29/4/07	St Helens (h)	L6-44	t:Melling g:Purdham	9th	4,362
5/5/07	Catalans (MM) ●	W28-32	t:A Smith,Wells,Randall(2),Sykes g:Purdham(6)	6th	N/A
13/5/07	Oldham (a) (CCR5) ●●	W6-66	t:Melling(2),Sykes(3),Temata(2),McLinden(2),Grayshon,A Smith(2) g:Purdham(9)	N/A	559
19/5/07	Warrington (a)	W4-17	t:Gafa,Purdham,Rinaldi g:Purdham(2) fg:Sykes	6th	7,818
27/5/07	Bradford (a)	L44-18	t:Wells,Randall,Sykes g:Sykes(3)	6th	10,418
2/6/07	Wigan (h)	W18-8	t:Sykes,Gafa g:Sykes(5)	5th	5,657
8/6/07	Wigan (a) (CCQF)	L25-6	t:Bannister g:Sykes	N/A	10,835
15/6/07	Salford (a)	L5-2	g:Sykes	5th	4,067
30/6/07	Hull KR (h)	W32-18	t:Worrincy,T Smith,Randall,Gafa,McCarthy-Scarsbrook g:Sykes(6)	5th	3,278
7/7/07	Catalans (h)	W30-22	t:Paul(2),Gafa,Sheriffe(2) g:Sykes(5)	5th	2,346
13/7/07	Hull (a)	L20-8	t:T Smith g:Sykes(2)	5th	12,270
21/7/07	Huddersfield (h)	L10-22	t:McCarthy-Scarsbrook,T Smith g:Sykes	8th	2,478
5/8/07	Leeds (h)	L20-54	t:Sykes,Hill,McLinden,Orr g:Sykes(2)	8th	3,734
12/8/07	Wakefield (a)	L28-14	t:Hill,Wells,T Smith g:Orr	9th	5,128
18/8/07	Wigan (h)	D16-16	t:Gafa,Hill,McLinden g:Paul(2)	9th	3,200
31/8/07	St Helens (a)	L32-10	t:Sheriffe(2) g:Paul	9th	7,939
8/9/07	Salford (h)	W22-16	t:Rinaldi,Sheriffe(2),McCarthy-Scarsbrook g:Sykes(3)	9th	2,347
15/9/07	Catalans (a)	L30-14	t:Sykes(2),Clubb g:Sykes	9th	8,420

● Played at Millennium Stadium, Cardiff
●● Played at Park Lane, Sedgley Park

	D.O.B.	APP ALL	APP SL	TRIES ALL	TRIES SL	GOALS ALL	GOALS SL	FG ALL	FG SL	PTS ALL	PTS SL
Steve Bannister	10/10/87	(7)	(6)	1	0	0	0	0	0	4	0
Luke Burgess	20/2/87	(3)	(3)	0	0	0	0	0	0	0	0
Tony Clubb	12/6/87	6	6	1	1	0	0	0	0	4	4
Matt Gafa	31/8/78	25	23	8	7	0	0	0	0	32	28
Jon Grayshon	10/5/83	4(19)	4(17)	3	2	0	0	0	0	12	8
Daniel Heckenberg	27/10/79	13(1)	11(1)	2	2	0	0	0	0	8	8
Scott Hill	30/5/77	23(1)	21(1)	7	6	0	0	0	0	28	24
Lee Hopkins	17/2/77	24(3)	21(3)	3	2	0	0	0	0	12	8
Zebastian Luisi	22/12/84	2(1)	2(1)	0	0	0	0	0	0	0	0
Joe Mbu	6/11/83	4(8)	4(8)	0	0	0	0	0	0	0	0
Louie McCarthy-Scarsbrook	14/1/86	10(13)	9(12)	7	4	0	0	0	0	28	16
Mark McLinden	8/7/79	25(1)	22(1)	7	5	0	0	0	0	28	20
Chris Melling	21/9/84	17(2)	14(2)	6	4	0	0	0	0	24	16
David Mills	1/6/81	11(9)	10(7)	0	0	0	0	0	0	0	0
Danny Orr	17/5/78	28	25	3	3	1	1	0	0	14	14
Henry Paul	10/2/74	21(1)	20	2	2	25	18	0	0	58	44
Rob Purdham	14/4/80	19(1)	17(1)	3	3	26	14	0	0	64	40
Chad Randall	30/12/80	30	27	7	6	0	0	0	0	28	24
Julien Rinaldi	27/4/79	(29)	(26)	5	5	0	0	0	0	20	20
Rikki Sheriffe	5/5/84	10	10	6	6	0	0	0	0	24	24
Andy Smith	6/7/84	9(3)	6(3)	7	3	0	0	0	0	28	12
Tyrone Smith	12/5/83	26(2)	23(2)	6	6	0	0	0	0	24	24
Paul Sykes	11/8/81	28	25	18	13	39	38	1	1	151	129
Karl Temata	12/7/82	21(6)	19(6)	2	0	0	0	0	0	8	0
Joe Walsh	13/1/86	1(3)	1(2)	0	0	0	0	0	0	0	0
Jon Wells	23/9/78	27	25	7	7	0	0	0	0	28	28
Michael Worrincy	16/2/86	6(7)	6(6)	1	1	0	0	0	0	4	4

Paul Sykes

LEAGUE RECORD
P27-W10-D3-L14
(9th, SL)
F495, A636, Diff-141
23 points.

CHALLENGE CUP
Quarter Finalists

ATTENDANCES
Best - v Wigan (SL - 5,657)
Worst - v Catalans (SL - 2,346)
Total (SL only) - 44,137
Average (SL only) - 3,395
(Down by 1,522 on 2006)

185

4 December 2006 - Wakefield sign young Giants threequarter Luke George.

20 December 2006 - 18-year-old Leroy Cudjoe signs a full-time contract.

11 January 2007 - Giants deny claims they have signed former St Helens winger Darren Albert after he walks out on Cronulla Sharks.

21 January 2007 - Ryan Hudson returns to action after two-year drugs ban.

29 January 2007 - Chris Thorman retains Giants captaincy, and Brad Drew the vice-captaincy.

30 January 2007 - Keith Mason suspended for one match after being found guilty of striking in Leeds friendly.

3 February 2007 - Sean Gleeson signs on loan from Wigan.

4 February 2007 - New sponsorship deal with Huddersfield University announced.

1 March 2007 - Giants sign Sam Barlow after impressive trials with the club.

13 March 2007 - Sean Gleeson returns to Wigan after loan spell ends.

23 March 2007 - Paul Jackson signs a new two-year deal.

25 March 2007 - 18-16 home defeat to Salford leaves Giants five points adrift at bottom of table after losing all seven games.

2 April 2007 - Eorl Crabtree opens talks over new contract.

6 April 2007 - 56-12 home Good Friday evening thrashing of Wakefield ends win drought.

22 April 2007 - Chris Thorman scores the 1,000th point of his career in 46-16 home win over Harlequins.

23 April 2007 - Paul Smith leaves to take up career in IT, and joins part-time National League side Halifax.

27 April 2007 - Giants complete fifth straight win with 28-16 win over Hull KR.

KEY DATES - HUDDERSFIELD GIANTS

6 May 2007 - Giants move into fifth place after another convincing victory over Wakefield, by 36-12, that sees their winning run extend to six matches.

11 May 2007 - Huddersfield brush past Salford 36-10 at the Willows to progress to round six of the Challenge Cup.

14 May 2007 - second-rower Andy Raleigh signs new deal for a further three years.

18 May 2007 - after 35 years, the Giants are finally victorious against the Bulls in the league after a 36-12 home win, moving them up to fourth place after seven straight victories.

25 May 2007 - seven-match winning run ends with shock 14-12 defeat against Salford at the Willows.

28 May 2007 - Eorl Crabtree declares desire to stay at Huddersfield after rumoured interest from other clubs.

3 June 2007 - Huddersfield held to 9-9 draw by Hull FC, coach Jon Sharp wrongly slams referee Ian Smith for not awarding kickable penalty in last second.

10 June 2007 - Giants exit Challenge Cup after 52-20 hammering at Bradford.

22 June 2007 - Giants centre Stephen Wild scores for Great Britain in 42-12 victory over France.

30 June 2007 - Chris Nero claims the only Huddersfield try as an understrength St Helens brush past them 54-4.

5 July 2007 - winger Martin Aspinwall signs three-year contract extension.

10 July 2007 - Aspinwall ruled out for the rest of the season after injury against Warrington requires reconstructive knee surgery.

12 July 2007 - Stephen Wild signs a new three-year contract.

13 July 2007 - promising prop Chris Lawson awarded full-time contract.

15 July 2007 - Giants bounce back from 13-0 down at half-time to win 24-23 at Wakefield, after five games without a win sees them drop from fourth to ninth.

25 July 2007 - second-row forward James Martin signs for the Giants on a full-time contract from 2008.

9 August 2007 - New Zealand international Paul Whatuira signs from Wests Tigers for the 2008 season on a three-year contract.

19 August 2007 - a hat-trick from Jamahl Lolesi helps the Giants triumph 26-22 over Bradford.

24 August 2007 - end-of-season departures of Paul Reilly, Brad Drew and Chris Nero confirmed.

28 August 2007 - New Zealand Warriors hooker George Gatis signs a two-year deal from the 2008 season.

31 August 2007 - 34-22 victory at Warrington gives Giants one foot in the play-offs.

5 September 2007 - Giants snap up scrum-half Luke Robinson from relegated Salford City Reds for 2008 on a three-year deal.

9 September 2007 - Huddersfield celebrate reaching play-offs for first time after nail-biting 24-22 home win over Wakefield.

12 September 2007 - halfback Tom Hemingway signs new two-year contract after loan spell at Batley.

15 September 2007 - final game of regular season sees Giants lose 25-24 at Hull KR, but remain fifth to set up elimination play-off at Hull FC.

22 September 2007 - 22-16 defeat at Hull ends campaign.

25 September 2007 - Giants sign GB international David Hodgson from Salford City Reds on a four-year contract.

HUDDERSFIELD GIANTS

DATE	FIXTURE	RESULT	SCORERS	LGE	ATT
4/2/07	St Helens (h)	L10-18	t:Gardner g:Thorman(3)	N/A	9,212
11/2/07	Bradford (a)	L18-14	t:Lolesi,Jones g:Thorman(3)	12th	12,130
18/2/07	Hull KR (h)	L10-17	t:Wild,Nero g:Thorman	12th	7,700
4/3/07	Leeds (a)	L16-12	t:Crabtree,Thorman g:Thorman(2)	12th	15,703
11/3/07	Hull (h)	L12-16	t:Thorman(2) g:Thorman(2)	12th	7,188
17/3/07	Catalans (a)	L23-22	t:Nero,Hudson,Jones,Wild g:Hemingway(2),Drew	12th	8,300
25/3/07	Salford (h)	L16-18	t:Gardner,Thorman,Raleigh g:Thorman(2)	12th	5,275
1/4/07	York (h) (CCR4)	W74-4	t:Skandalis,Snitch(3),Reilly(2),Aspinwall,Lolesi,Paul,Hudson, Elford(2),Nero g:Drew(11)	N/A	2,137
6/4/07	Wakefield (h)	W56-12	t:Wild,Drew,Paul,Brown(3),Aspinwall,Raleigh,Jones,Reilly g:Drew(4),Thorman(4)	12th	6,757
9/4/07	Warrington (a)	W18-26	t:Drew,Crabtree,Aspinwall g:Thorman(7)	12th	9,403
15/4/07	Wigan (h)	W41-16	t:Drew,Crabtree,Wild,Reilly,Hudson,Snitch g:Thorman(8) fg:Thorman	11th	7,117
22/4/07	Harlequins (h)	W46-16	t:Lolesi,Reilly(2),Snitch(2),Thorman,Nero,Wild g:Thorman(7)	10th	4,894
27/4/07	Hull KR (a)	W16-28	t:Jones,Raleigh,Wild,Lolesi g:Thorman(6)	8th	6,597
6/5/07	Wakefield (MM) ●	W36-12	t:Wild(2),Thorman,Paul,Lolesi,Aspinwall g:Thorman(6)	5th	N/A
11/5/07	Salford (a) (CCR5)	W10-36	t:Brown(2),Wild,Paul,Lolesi,Nero g:Thorman(6)	N/A	2,694
18/5/07	Bradford (h)	W36-12	t:Wild,Skandalis,Jones,Thorman(2),Brown g:Thorman(6)	4th	8,667
25/5/07	Salford (a)	L14-12	t:Wild,Reilly g:Thorman(2)	5th	3,379
3/6/07	Hull (a)	D9-9	t:Thorman g:Thorman(2) fg:Thorman	6th	12,094
10/6/07	Bradford (a) (CCQF)	L52-20	t:Nero,Lolesi,Paul,Hudson g:Drew(2)	N/A	7,811
17/6/07	Leeds (h)	L12-25	t:Jackson,Nero g:Drew(2)	6th	10,241
30/6/07	St Helens (a)	L54-4	t:Nero	7th	7,771
8/7/07	Warrington (h)	L28-47	t:Paul,Drew,Hudson(2),Elford g:Thorman(4)	9th	6,822
15/7/07	Wakefield (a)	W23-24	t:Thorman,Wild,Snitch,Elford g:Thorman(4)	9th	5,241
21/7/07	Harlequins (a)	W10-22	t:Nero(2),Snitch,Brown g:Thorman(3)	9th	2,478
5/8/07	Catalans (h)	W42-22	t:Jensen,Griffin,Elford(2),Wild(2),Thorman g:Thorman(7)	6th	4,319
10/8/07	Wigan (a)	L20-12	t:Wild,Nero g:Thorman(2)	7th	12,744
19/8/07	Bradford (h)	W26-22	t:Jensen,Lolesi(3) g:Drew(5)	6th	6,824
31/8/07	Warrington (a)	W22-34	t:Hudson,Drew,Jensen,Lolesi,Brown g:Thorman(7)	5th	8,843
9/9/07	Wakefield (h)	W24-22	t:Reilly,Lolesi(2),Wild g:Thorman(4)	5th	7,066
15/9/07	Hull KR (a)	L25-24	t:Reilly(2),Nero,Jensen(2) g:Thorman(2)	5th	6,700
22/9/07	Hull (a) (EPO)	L22-16	t:Hudson,Reilly,Brown g:Thorman(2)	N/A	12,140

● Played at Millennium Stadium, Cardiff

		APP		TRIES		GOALS		FG		PTS	
	D.O.B.	ALL	SL	ALL	SL	ALL	SL	ALL	SL	ALL	SL
Martin Aspinwall	21/10/81	15	12	4	3	0	0	0	0	16	12
Kevin Brown	2/10/84	30	27	9	7	0	0	0	0	36	28
Eorl Crabtree	2/10/82	7(23)	6(21)	3	3	0	0	0	0	12	12
Brad Drew	25/8/75	25(5)	22(5)	5	5	25	12	0	0	70	44
Shane Elford	28/12/87	10(1)	9(1)	6	4	0	0	0	0	24	16
Matt Gardner	24/8/84	11	11	2	2	0	0	0	0	8	8
Darrell Griffin	19/6/81	5(24)	5(21)	1	1	0	0	0	0	4	4
Tom Hemingway	6/12/86	1(1)	1(1)	0	0	2	2	0	0	4	4
Ryan Hudson	20/11/79	24(7)	21(7)	8	6	0	0	0	0	32	24
Paul Jackson	29/9/78	3(16)	3(14)	1	1	0	0	0	0	4	4
Rod Jensen	19/1/79	12(1)	12	5	5	0	0	0	0	20	20
Stuart Jones	7/12/81	17(7)	17(6)	5	5	0	0	0	0	20	20
Michael Lawrence	12/4/90	(1)	(1)	0	0	0	0	0	0	0	0
Jamahl Lolesi	20/3/81	27(2)	24(2)	13	10	0	0	0	0	52	40
Keith Mason	20/1/82	28(1)	25(1)	0	0	0	0	0	0	0	0
Chris Nero	14/2/81	31	28	12	9	0	0	0	0	48	36
Robbie Paul	3/2/76	17(10)	16(8)	6	3	0	0	0	0	24	12
Andy Raleigh	17/3/81	23(5)	21(5)	3	3	0	0	0	0	12	12
Paul Reilly	10/5/76	25(1)	22(1)	11	9	0	0	0	0	44	36
John Skandalis	16/6/76	26(4)	23(4)	2	1	0	0	0	0	8	4
Steve Snitch	22/2/83	10(13)	7(13)	8	5	0	0	0	0	32	20
Chris Thorman	26/9/80	26(1)	24(1)	11	11	102	96	2	2	250	238
Stephen Wild	26/4/81	30(1)	28	16	15	0	0	0	0	64	60

Stephen Wild

LEAGUE RECORD
P27-W13-D1-L13
(5th, SL/Elimination Play-Off)
F638, A543, Diff+95
27 points.

CHALLENGE CUP
Quarter Finalists

ATTENDANCES
Best - v Leeds (SL - 10,241)
Worst - v York (CC - 2,137)
Total (SL only) - 92,082
Average (SL only) - 7,083
(Up by 1,226 on 2006)

11 December 2006 - released Chris Chester signs for rivals Hull KR.

22 January 2007 - Lee Radford named Hull's new skipper, replacing Richard Swain.

2 February 2007 - Lee Radford beats former Bradford teammate Stuart Fielden in charity boxing match that raises £50,000 for Steve Prescott.

8 March 2007 - James Rule appointed new chief executive in management restructure.

20 March 2007 - Sid Domic suspended for two matches and fined after being found guilty of reckless high challenge against St Helens.

9 April 2007 - Hull FC beat Hull KR 22-14 in the first meeting between the clubs in Super League.

20 April 2007 - Hull FC coach Peter Sharp denies Paul Cooke is to join rivals Hull KR.

23 April 2007 - Paul Cooke hands in letter of resignation, claims he never signed a contract and leaves for Hull KR.

24 April 2007 - RFL block Paul Cooke's transfer to Hull KR, and tell the clubs to sort out the dispute themselves.

27 April 2007 - Paul Cooke makes Hull KR debut against Huddersfield, hours after RFL accepts his registration.

28 April 2007 - Anthony Thackeray makes his debut in 20-18 round 12 win at Wakefield.

30 April 2007 - Hull step up their search for a new halfback to replace departed Paul Cooke and are flooded with offers from Australian agents.

5 May 2007 - Hull FC defeated 14-10 by Hull KR in the Millennium Magic derby, with Paul Cooke the gamestar.

13 May 2007 - Hull cruise past Sheffield Eagles 44-10 to progress into round six of the Challenge Cup.

KEY DATES - HULL FC

14 May 2007 - Hull emerge as favourites to sign Manly utility star Michael Monaghan and sign 22-year-old Rob Worrincy from Doncaster.

4 June 2007 - Cronulla Sharks stand-off Adam Dykes joins for the 2008 season on two-year contract.

10 June 2007 - Hull crash out of the Challenge Cup with three-point defeat at home by Catalans Dragons.

14 June 2007 - Australian international Shaun Berrigan signed from Brisbane Broncos for 2008 on four-year contract.

17 June 2007 - Hull go down 34-8 at Bradford in Lesley Vainikolo's farewell appearance at Odsal, Shaun Briscoe breaks his jaw.

25 June 2007 - Mathew Head signs from St George Illawarra on a short-term deal until end of season, Sid Domic makes way and joins Dewsbury.

29 June 2007 - Hull's home match against Salford postponed as flooding hits the city.

6 July 2007 - Kirk Yeaman signs new three-year contract.

8 July 2007 - play-off hunt still on after 30-20 victory at local rivals Hull KR.

9 July 2007 - Hull confirm Wayne Goodwin will miss six weeks of action after breaking foot-bone in derby victory.

10 July 2007 - back injury forces Richard Swain to retire.

13 July 2007 - teenage hooker Danny Houghton handed two-year contract prior to making his debut in the 20-8 victory against Harlequins.

17 July 2007 - Anthony Thackeray leaves Hull to join the Castleford Tigers until the end of the season.

21 July 2007 - Hull beat the Dragons in France 34-18, giving them a third successive victory.

27 July 2007 - winger Gareth Raynor pledges to play out his career at the KC stadium and signs new three-year deal.

3 August 2007 - Hull release Australian back row Shayne McMenemy.

12 August 2007 - Hull easily dispose of fellow play-off contenders Warrington with a 46-14 win at the KC Stadium.

29 August 2007 - Shaun Briscoe not offered a new contract and joins arch rivals Hull KR for 2008.

30 August 2007 - 22-year-old utility player Richard Whiting given new two-year contract.

2 September 2007 - Hull thumped 42-6 at home by city rivals Hull KR to ensure Rovers' safety and send Salford down.

3 September 2007 - Paul Cooke charged by RFL with making an illegal approach to another club prior to the expiry of his contract.

5 September 2007 - Hull release teenage forward Ross Divorty.

7 September 2007 - Hull bounce back from derby defeat with 17-6 win at Leeds to secure play-off place. Hooker Wayne Goodwin to leave the club at end of season.

14 September 2007 - 20-10 win over third-place Bradford secures home play-off against Huddersfield.

22 September 2007 - Hull win 22-16 victory over the Giants.

29 September 2007 - Wigan Warriors end Hull's season with a 21-18 victory at the KC Stadium.

4 November 2007 - Hull make offer to Australian Test forward Willie Mason.

6 November 2007 - utility back Todd Byrne signs on a two-year contract from New Zealand Warriors.

14 November 2007 - Paul Cooke found guilty of misconduct in transfer saga and suspended until 17 March 2008.

HULL F C

HULL FC

DATE	FIXTURE	RESULT	SCORERS	LGE	ATT
11/2/07	Catalans (h)	D10-10	t:Sing g:Tickle(3)	7th	12,673
16/2/07	Leeds (a)	L18-4	t:Sing	11th	18,659
25/2/07	Warrington (a)	L25-24	t:Whiting,Radford,Raynor,Sing g:Cooke(4)	10th	11,097
4/3/07	Wakefield (h)	L6-19	t:Tickle g:Tickle	11th	13,229
11/3/07	Huddersfield (a)	W12-16	t:Briscoe,Sing,King g:Tickle(2)	10th	7,188
17/3/07	St Helens (h)	W24-12	t:Domic,Yeaman,Briscoe g:Tickle(6)	9th	12,678
23/3/07	Wigan (h)	L20-30	t:Maiava,Manu,R Horne g:Tickle(4)	10th	12,755
1/4/07	Hunslet (a) (CCR4) ●	W0-78	t:Yeaman(2),McMenemy,Hall(3),R Horne,Wheeldon,Sing,Manu(2), Dale,Godwin(2) g:Hall(11)	N/A	5,062
6/4/07	Harlequins (a)	L30-28	t:Domic,Yeaman,R Horne(2),Hall,Sing g:Hall(2)	10th	3,545
9/4/07	Hull KR (h)	W22-14	t:Tickle,Briscoe,Sing,Domic g:Cooke(3)	10th	23,002
13/4/07	Salford (a)	W18-35	t:Raynor(2),Cooke,Sing,Tickle,R Horne g:Cooke(5) fg:R Horne	8th	4,077
20/4/07	Bradford (h)	L22-32	t:Swain,Briscoe,Yeaman,Tony g:Cooke(3)	9th	12,767
28/4/07	Wakefield (a)	W18-20	t:McMenemy,Briscoe,Yeaman g:Tickle(4)	5th	7,142
5/5/07	Hull KR (MM) ●●	L10-14	t:Raynor,Domic g:Tickle	8th	N/A
13/5/07	Sheffield (h) (CCR5)	W44-6	t:Godwin,Hall(3),R Horne,Briscoe,Yeaman,Maiava g:Hall(6)	N/A	4,363
20/5/07	Leeds (h)	W16-12	t:Sing,Briscoe g:Tickle(4)	7th	14,256
26/5/07	Wigan (a)	L47-16	t:Radford,Hall,Manu g:Tickle(2)	7th	14,314
3/6/07	Huddersfield (h)	D9-9	t:Tickle g:Tickle(2) fg:R Horne	8th	12,094
10/6/07	Catalans (h) (CCQF)	L23-26	t:Briscoe,King,Domic g:Tickle(5) fg:R Horne	N/A	7,441
17/6/07	Bradford (a)	L34-8	t:Tony g:Tickle(2)	8th	11,557
8/7/07	Hull KR (a)	W20-30	t:Hall,Tickle,Wheeldon,Manu,Yeaman g:Tickle(5)	7th	9,035
13/7/07	Harlequins (h)	W20-8	t:R Horne,Hall g:Tickle(5),Hall	7th	12,270
21/7/07	Catalans (a)	W18-34	t:Tickle(2),Lee,Raynor,R Horne,Sing g:Tickle(5)	7th	7,560
29/7/07	Salford (h)	W48-26	t:Manu,R Horne(2),Hall(2),Sing,Radford,Whiting g:Tickle(8)	4th	13,338
3/8/07	St Helens (a)	L31-20	t:Tony,Sing,G Horne g:Tickle(4)	5th	10,005
12/8/07	Warrington (h)	W46-14	t:Manu,Raynor(2),Briscoe,Carvell,Tony(2),R Horne g:Tickle(7)	4th	13,404
17/8/07	Wakefield (a)	W24-42	t:Manu,Hall,Tickle,Raynor,Head,Whiting,Tony g:Tickle(7)	4th	8,115
2/9/07	Hull KR (h)	L6-42	t:Washbrook g:Tickle	4th	23,004
7/9/07	Leeds (a)	W6-17	t:Godwin,Raynor(2) g:Tickle(2) fg:Head	4th	17,424
14/9/07	Bradford (h)	W20-10	t:G Horne,Tickle,Whiting g:Tickle(4)	4th	14,402
22/9/07	Huddersfield (h) (EPO)	W22-16	t:Raynor(2),Lee,R Horne g:Tickle(3)	N/A	12,140
29/9/07	Wigan (h) (ESF)	L18-21	t:Raynor(2),R Horne g:Tickle(3)	N/A	16,291

● Played at Kingston Communications Stadium
●● Played at Millennium Stadium, Cardiff

	D.O.B.	APP ALL	APP SL	TRIES ALL	TRIES SL	GOALS ALL	GOALS SL	FG ALL	FG SL	PTS ALL	PTS SL
Shaun Briscoe	23/2/83	22(1)	19(1)	9	7	0	0	0	0	36	28
Garreth Carvell	21/4/80	16(5)	14(5)	1	1	0	0	0	0	4	4
Paul Cooke	17/4/81	4	4	1	1	15	15	0	0	34	34
Matty Dale	10/10/86	(2)	0	1	0	0	0	0	0	4	0
Sid Domic	8/2/75	11(4)	10(4)	5	4	0	0	0	0	20	16
Ewan Dowes	4/3/81	29(1)	27(1)	0	0	0	0	0	0	0	0
Wayne Godwin	13/3/82	6(13)	3(13)	4	1	0	0	0	0	16	4
Craig Hall	21/2/88	15	13	13	7	20	3	0	0	92	34
Mathew Head	9/5/82	9(1)	9(1)	1	1	0	0	1	1	5	5
Graeme Horne	22/3/85	2(12)	2(11)	2	2	0	0	0	0	8	8
Richard Horne	16/7/82	31	28	13	11	0	0	3	2	55	46
Danny Houghton	25/9/88	(4)	(4)	0	0	0	0	0	0	0	0
Paul King	28/6/79	16(9)	16(7)	2	1	0	0	0	0	8	4
Tommy Lee	1/2/88	21	19	2	2	0	0	0	0	8	8
Hutch Maiava	26/10/76	(22)	(19)	2	1	0	0	0	0	8	4
Willie Manu	20/3/80	20(7)	17(7)	8	6	0	0	0	0	32	24
Shayne McMenemy	19/7/76	3(1)	2(1)	2	1	0	0	0	0	8	4
Lee Radford	26/3/79	31	28	3	3	0	0	0	0	12	12
Gareth Raynor	24/2/78	28	27	14	14	0	0	0	0	56	56
Matt Sing	4/4/76	26	23	12	11	0	0	0	0	48	44
Richard Swain	2/7/75	16	16	1	1	0	0	0	0	4	4
Anthony Thackeray	19/2/86	2	2	0	0	0	0	0	0	0	0
Danny Tickle	10/3/83	29	28	9	9	90	85	0	0	216	206
Motu Tony	29/5/81	16(12)	14(11)	6	6	0	0	0	0	24	24
Danny Washbrook	18/9/85	18(10)	17(8)	1	1	0	0	0	0	4	4
Scott Wheeldon	23/2/86	3(18)	1(18)	2	1	0	0	0	0	8	4
Richard Whiting	20/12/84	13(6)	12(5)	4	4	0	0	0	0	16	16
Kirk Yeaman	15/9/83	29	26	8	5	0	0	0	0	32	20

Danny Tickle

LEAGUE RECORD
P27-W14-D2-L11
(4th, SL/Elimination Semi-Final)
F573, A553, Diff+20
30 points.

CHALLENGE CUP
Quarter Finalists

ATTENDANCES
Best - v Hull KR (SL - 23,004)
Worst - v Sheffield (CC - 4,363)
Total (SL, inc play-offs) - 218,303
Average (SL, inc play-offs) - 14,553
(Up by 3,342 on 2006)

8 October 2006 - Robins beat Widnes 29-16 in NL1 Grand Final to secure promotion.

24 October 2006 - released Dwayne Barker joins Castleford.

1 November 2006 - Stanley Gene re-signs for Rovers from Bradford on a two-year deal.

2 November 2006 - Jon Steel signs new one-year contract.

7 November 2006 - 20-year-old halfback Matty Brooks turns his loan spell from Bradford into permanent one-year deal. 21-year-old Academy prop Dave Wilson signs a one-year full-time contract.

16 November 2006 - Luke Dyer signs from Castleford.

20 November 2006 - Francis Stephenson retires due to an Achilles injury and joins the coaching staff at Craven Park.

27 November 2006 - Pat Weisner signs one-year deal with the Robins after loan spell from Harlequins.

29 November 2006 - Hull KR confirm new sponsorship deal with Lloyds TSB.

10 December 2006 - released winger Leroy Rivett joins Leigh Centurions.

11 December 2006 - Chris Chester joins from Hull FC. Damien Couturier signs for Leigh Centurions.

29 December 2006 - the Robins sign little-known Andreas Bauer from New Zealand.

9 January 2007 - Robins great Peter 'Flash' Flanagan dies aged 65.

16 January 2007 - James Webster retains the captaincy.

10 February 2007 - Hull KR beat Wakefield 14-9 in their first Super League match.

2 March 2007 - Stanley Gene makes delayed second 'debut' for KR in 26-16 win at Wigan.

16 March 2007 - Michael Smith's contract terminated and he joins Barrow.

9 April 2007 - Hull KR lose first Super League meeting against rival Hull FC 22-14. Barrow sign Pat Weisner.

11 April 2007 - Hull KR sign St Helens back Ian Hardman on a month's loan.

12 April 2007 - former Hull FC forward Danny Hill joins on loan from Wigan.

15 April 2007 - Jon Steel ruled out for the season after he breaks leg in collision with Bradford's Lesley Vainikolo.

18 April 2007 - Justin Morgan signs new deal at Hull KR which will keep him in charge until end of 2010.

19 April 2007 - Hull KR sign former Castleford halfback Mark Lennon until end of season.

23 April 2007 - Robins sign 'free agent' Paul Cooke from neighbours Hull FC on three-and-a-half year deal.

24 April 2007 - The RFL block Paul Cooke's transfer from Hull FC to Hull KR, but tell the clubs to sort out the situation themselves.

KEY DATES - HULL KINGSTON ROVERS

Last-gasp Robins gamble and win in Super League debut

27 April 2007 - Paul Cooke makes debut in 28-16 home defeat by Huddersfield.

5 May 2007 - Rovers record famous 14-10 win over derby rivals Hull FC on the Millennium Magic Weekend, with Paul Cooke the gamestar against his old club.

7 May 2007 - Australian prop Ryan Tandy joins from Doncaster.

3 June 2007 - Rovers defeated 30-15 at Wakefield and have Makali Aizue dismissed, the first player in Super League XII to be sent off.

4 June 2007 - Makali Aizue gets three-match ban, upheld on appeal.

9 June 2007 - Ian Hardman's loan is extended to rest of the season.

17 June 2007 - Justin Morgan is left looking for more consistency from his team as his side is hammered 40-0 at home by St Helens.

30 June 2007 - St George Illawarra 20-year-old utility player Rhys Lovegrove added to the squad.

3 July 2007 - Hull KR make offer to Melbourne Storm centre Matt King.

8 July 2007 - 30-20 defeat at home to arch rivals Hull leaves Hull KR facing a tough relegation battle.

14 July 2007 - Justin Morgan salutes Ben Cockayne for two try-saving tackles in a crucial 22-20 win over Catalans.

22 July 2007 - Robins suffer 60-20 home humiliation at the hands of Warrington.

24 July 2007 - Ben Cockayne and Iain Morrison handed one-match bans for high tackles ahead of the crunch relegation battle against Salford.

3 August 2007 - Hull KR come out on top in a tight game at Salford with a 30-24 victory.

21 August 2007 - former Leeds Rhinos junior Chaz I'Anson signs on one-year deal for 2008.

25 August 2007 - Scott Murrell and Jason Netherton both sign new two-year contracts.

30 August 2007 - Hull KR sign 23-year-old New Zealand Test centre Jake Webster on a three-year deal.

2 September 2007 - superb 42-6 victory over rivals Hull at the KC Stadium ensures the Robins' Super League survival as Salford are relegated.

3 September 2007 - Paul Cooke charged with making an illegal approach to Hull KR prior to the expiry of his contract.

4 September 2007 - Hull KR land 23-year-old winger Peter Fox from Wakefield.

5 September 2007 - Shaun Briscoe joins from neighbours Hull FC on a two-year deal.

6 September 2007 - Michael Vella sweeps the board at Hull KR's player of the year awards.

10 September 2007 - 29-year-old Ben Galea signs from NRL side Wests Tigers on three-year deal.

13 September 2007 - Hull KR confirm signing of former Leeds favourite Chev Walker on three-year contract less than a year after he switched codes to play for Bath.

14 September 2007 - 27-year-old Daniel Fitzhenry signs on two-year deal from Wests Tigers.

15 September 2007 - Justin Morgan expresses his pride after 25-24 victory over Huddersfield in final game of SLXII.

16 September 2007 - Andreas Bauer, Matty Brooks, Luke Dyer, Byron Ford, Tommy Gallagher, Jon Goddard, Mark Lennon, Iain Morrison, Gareth Morton, Ryan Tandy, David Tangata-Toa, Danny Ward all released.

20 September 2007 - Welsh international prop forward David Mills signs from Harlequins on 12-month deal.

21 September 2007 - winger Jon Steel signs new 12-month deal.

9 October 2007 - Rhys Lovegrove signs a new two-year contract until the end of 2009.

16 October 2007 - NRL Grand Final winner Clint Newton joins till end of 2009 with option for another year.

18 October 2007 - former deputy prime minister John Prescott joins the board as unpaid associate director.

24 October 2007 - Steve McCormack appointed new assistant coach, but returns days later to continue as head coach of Widnes.

25 October 2007 - Melbourne Storm prop Garret Crossman joins on two-year deal.

14 November 2007 - Paul Cooke found guilty of misconduct in transfer saga and suspended until 17 March 2008.

HULL KINGSTON ROVERS

DATE	FIXTURE	RESULT	SCORERS	LGE	ATT
10/2/07	Wakefield (h)	W14-9	t:Murrell,Cockayne g:Morton(3)	3rd	7,154
18/2/07	Huddersfield (a)	W10-17	t:Murrell,Cockayne g:Morton(4) fg:Webster	3rd	7,700
25/2/07	Harlequins (h)	L10-26	t:Dyer,Smith g:Morton	5th	7,056
2/3/07	Wigan (a)	W16-26	t:Ford(2),Fisher,Dyer,Morton g:Morton(3)	4th	15,178
10/3/07	Leeds (h)	W22-20	t:Webster,Dyer,Bauer g:Morton(5)	3rd	8,086
18/3/07	Warrington (a)	L30-12	t:J Netherton,Ford g:Morton(2)	4th	10,030
23/3/07	St Helens (a)	L42-14	t:Steel,Ford,Morton g:Morton	7th	10,523
31/3/07	Warrington (a) (CCR4)	L38-10	t:Tangata-Toa,K Netherton g:Morton	N/A	4,523
6/4/07	Catalans (h)	L20-34	t:Gene,Ford,Murrell,Dyer g:Morton(2)	8th	6,701
9/4/07	Hull (a)	L22-14	t:Dyer,Tangata-Toa,Bauer g:Murrell	9th	23,002
15/4/07	Bradford (a)	L52-22	t:Steel,Gene,Tangata-Toa,Dyer g:Murrell(3)	10th	10,881
22/4/07	Salford (h)	L24-28	t:Gannon,O'Neill,Lennon,Goddard,Bauer g:Morton(2)	11th	6,299
27/4/07	Huddersfield (h)	L16-28	t:Bauer,Gene g:Cooke(4)	11th	6,597
5/5/07	Hull (MM) ●	W10-14	t:Aizue,Cockayne g:Cooke(3)	11th	N/A
18/5/07	Wigan (a)	W10-12	t:Dyer,Hardman g:Cooke(2)	10th	13,538
27/5/07	Leeds (h)	L10-18	t:J Netherton g:Cooke(3)	11th	7,731
3/6/07	Wakefield (a)	L30-15	t:Dyer,Ford,Hardman g:Cooke fg:Cooke	11th	6,107
17/6/07	St Helens (h)	L0-40		11th	7,011
30/6/07	Harlequins (a)	L32-18	t:Tandy,Lennon,Chester g:Cooke(3)	11th	3,278
8/7/07	Hull (h)	L20-30	t:Dyer,Tangata-Toa,O'Neill,Lovegrove g:Cooke(2)	11th	9,035
14/7/07	Catalans (a)	W20-22	t:Lennon,Gene,Hardman,O'Neill g:Lennon(3)	11th	7,830
22/7/07	Warrington (h)	L20-60	t:Hardman,Fisher,Aizue,Morton g:Lennon(2)	11th	6,640
3/8/07	Salford (a)	W24-30	t:O'Neill(2),Cooke,Lennon,Dyer g:Cooke(5)	10th	7,165
12/8/07	Bradford (h)	L10-28	t:Goddard,Fisher g:Cooke	11th	6,695
17/8/07	Leeds (a)	L34-18	t:Lovegrove,Dyer,Tandy g:Cooke(3)	11th	17,389
2/9/07	Hull (a)	W6-42	t:J Netherton,Dyer(2),Lennon,Lovegrove(2),Webster,Gene g:Cooke(5)	11th	23,004
9/9/07	Wigan (h)	L24-40	t:Murrell,Bauer,Morrison,Welham,Lovegrove g:Lennon(2)	11th	7,370
15/9/07	Huddersfield (h)	W25-24	t:Vella,Chester,Fisher(2) g:Cooke(4) fg:Cooke	11th	6,700

● Played at Millennium Stadium, Cardiff

		APP		TRIES		GOALS		FG		PTS	
	D.O.B.	ALL	SL	ALL	SL	ALL	SL	ALL	SL	ALL	SL
Makali Aizue	30/12/77	12(8)	11(8)	2	2	0	0	0	0	8	8
Andreas Bauer	26/9/82	11(2)	10(2)	5	5	0	0	0	0	20	20
Matty Brooks	9/10/86	1	0	0	0	0	0	0	0	0	0
Chris Chester	8/10/78	19(2)	19(2)	2	2	0	0	0	0	8	8
Ben Cockayne	20/7/83	21(1)	20(1)	3	3	0	0	0	0	12	12
Paul Cooke	17/4/81	13(1)	13(1)	1	1	36	36	2	2	78	78
Luke Dyer	15/8/81	27	26	13	13	0	0	0	0	52	52
Ben Fisher	4/2/81	24(2)	23(2)	5	5	0	0	0	0	20	20
Byron Ford	21/8/81	14	13	6	6	0	0	0	0	24	24
Tommy Gallagher	10/9/83	2(7)	1(7)	0	0	0	0	0	0	0	0
Jim Gannon	16/6/77	8(16)	7(16)	1	1	0	0	0	0	4	4
Stanley Gene	11/5/74	17(3)	17(3)	5	5	0	0	0	0	20	20
Jon Goddard	21/6/82	20	20	2	2	0	0	0	0	8	8
Ian Hardman	8/12/84	18	18	4	4	0	0	0	0	16	16
Danny Hill	31/10/84	2	2	0	0	0	0	0	0	0	0
Chaz I'Anson	30/11/86	(1)	(1)	0	0	0	0	0	0	0	0
Mark Lennon	17/8/80	11(4)	11(4)	5	5	7	7	0	0	34	34
Rhys Lovegrove	11/3/87	6(3)	6(3)	5	5	0	0	0	0	20	20
Iain Morrison	6/5/83	5(6)	5(6)	1	1	0	0	0	0	4	4
Gareth Morton	21/10/82	7(5)	7(4)	3	3	24	23	0	0	60	58
Scott Murrell	5/9/85	20(4)	19(4)	4	4	4	4	0	0	24	24
Jason Netherton	5/10/82	17(6)	16(6)	3	3	0	0	0	0	12	12
Kirk Netherton	10/5/85	1(3)	1(2)	1	0	0	0	0	0	4	0
Mark O'Neill	19/6/75	17	17	5	5	0	0	0	0	20	20
Michael Smith	10/5/76	(3)	(3)	1	1	0	0	0	0	4	4
Jon Steel	14/3/80	5	4	2	2	0	0	0	0	8	8
Ryan Tandy	20/9/81	8(4)	8(4)	2	2	0	0	0	0	8	8
David Tangata-Toa	15/7/81	(18)	(17)	4	3	0	0	0	0	16	12
Michael Vella	19/2/80	22	22	1	1	0	0	0	0	4	4
Danny Ward	15/6/80	12(9)	11(9)	0	0	0	0	0	0	0	0
James Webster	11/7/79	24	24	2	2	0	0	1	1	9	9
Pat Weisner	17/3/82	(2)	(2)	0	0	0	0	0	0	0	0
Kris Welham	12/5/87	(1)	(1)	1	1	0	0	0	0	4	4
Dave Wilson	30/9/84	(1)	(1)	0	0	0	0	0	0	0	0

Michael Vella

LEAGUE RECORD
P27-W10-D0-L17
(11th, SL)
F491, A723, Diff-232
20 points.

CHALLENGE CUP
Round Four

ATTENDANCES
Best - v Hull (SL - 9,035)
Worst - v Salford (SL - 6,299)
Total (SL only) - 93,075
Average (SL only) - 7,160
(Up by 3,830 on 2006, NL1)

KEY DATES - LEEDS RHINOS

1 December 2006 - Keith Senior signs new deal at Headingley Carnegie until end of 2008.

5 December 2006 - Shane Millard joins Wigan.

19 December 2006 - Academy products Ben Kaye, Luke Burgess and Ryan Hall promoted to first-team squad.

26 December 2006 - retired Willie Poching plays his final game for Leeds in 22-14 friendly win against Wakefield.

12 January 2007 - England international Ashley Gibson agrees new three-year contract to end of 2009.

21 February 2007 - prop Nick Scruton ruled out for four months with stress fracture to his foot.

10 March 2007 - Leeds shocked by Hull KR 22-20 at Craven Park.

26 March 2007 - Leeds boss Tony Smith appointed GB boss and set to leave the Rhinos at the end of the season.

5 April 2007 - Leeds beat Bradford 18-14 at Odsal, following winger Scott Donald's late try.

10 April 2007 - fullback Brent Webb told he has no case to answer after being placed on report for a high tackle against Bradford.

15 April 2007 - Keith Senior scores his 200th career try against Warrington.

6 May 2007 - Rhinos beat Bradford 42-38 in a Millennium Magic encounter surrounded by controversy.

12 May 2007 - Leeds defeated at home by Wigan 22-18, to crash out of the Challenge Cup.

18 May 2007 - Ali Lauitiiti undergoes keyhole surgery on posterior cruciate ligament.

21 May 2007 - Brian Noble rumoured to be new Rhinos coach.

27 May 2007 - Leeds grind out 18-10 victory away at Hull KR to go top of the league.

17 June 2007 - a stunning late flurry of scoring gives Leeds a 25-12 victory at Huddersfield.

29 June 2007 - Bulls thump Rhinos 38-14 at Headingley in Lesley Vainikolo's last game.

6 July 2007 - Tony Smith praises Rob Burrow as he inspires them to a 22-10 victory at St Helens, Matt Diskin ruled out for at least four weeks after fracturing a bone in his hand.

11 July 2007 - Leeds appoint New Zealand coach Brian McClennan to succeed Tony Smith at end of season.

12 July 2007 - Rhinos miss chance to go top as they go down 18-2 at Wigan.

20 July 2007 - Leeds lose 23-16 at home to Wakefield.

8 August 2007 - Brent Webb banned for four matches for two high tackles in the 54-20 victory at Harlequins.

15 August 2007 - Brent Webb's four-match ban reduced to three after appeal. A double fracture of the hand rules prop Nick Scruton out for rest of season.

2 September 2007 - Rhinos spoil Bradford's centenary celebrations by grabbing a 16-16 draw at Odsal.

7 September 2007 - Leeds go down 17-6 at home to Hull to end chances of League Leaders trophy.

14 September 2007 - Rhinos consolidate second place with 46-4 home victory over Wakefield. Keith Senior becomes first ever to play 300 regular league games.

17 September 2007 - Rob Burrow named player of the year at the Rhinos annual awards dinner.

28 September 2007 - Rhinos edged 10-8 in Qualifying Semi-final at St Helens..

5 October 2007 - final eliminator 36-6 victory over Wigan Warriors at Headingley secures Grand Final place.

12 October 2007 - Kevin Sinfield, 27, agrees new four-year contract until the end of the 2011 season.

13 October 2007 - Leeds Rhinos crowned champions after 33-6 win over St Helens at Old Trafford.

1 November 2007 - 21 year-old Carl Ablett signs a one-year extension to his contract.

7 November 2007 - new Rhinos boss Brian McClennan arrives at Headingley and declares himself 'luckiest coach in the world'.

10 November 2007 - Tony Smith guides Great Britain to 3-0 series win over New Zealand.

10 November 2007 - Rob Burrow awarded George Smith Medal as man of the Gillette Fusion Test series.

LEEDS RHINOS

DATE	FIXTURE	RESULT	SCORERS	LGE	ATT
11/2/07	Salford (a)	W26-30	t:Webb(2),McGuire,Burrow,Tansey g:Sinfield(5)	4th	8,070
16/2/07	Hull (h)	W18-4	t:Smith,Sinfield,Bailey g:Sinfield(3)	2nd	18,659
24/2/07	Catalans (a)	L30-22	t:Jones-Buchanan,Thackray,Donald,Smith g:Sinfield(3)	4th	7,630
4/3/07	Huddersfield (h)	W16-12	t:Toopi,Jones-Buchanan,Smith g:Sinfield(2)	2nd	15,703
10/3/07	Hull KR (a)	L22-20	t:Gibson(3),Smith g:Sinfield(2)	5th	8,086
16/3/07	Wakefield (a)	W26-32	t:Donald,Senior,Tansey,McGuire,Bailey g:Sinfield(5),Burrow	3rd	9,973
23/3/07	Harlequins (h)	W28-16	t:McGuire(2),Webb(2) g:Sinfield(6)	3rd	15,123
30/3/07	Workington (h) (CCR4)	W72-10	t:Donald(4),Tansey(2),Sinfield,Burrow(3),Lauitiiti,Ablett,Diskin g:Sinfield(8),Burrow(2)	N/A	3,576
5/4/07	Bradford (a)	W14-18	t:Donald(2),Ellis g:Sinfield(3)	1st	16,706
10/4/07	Wigan (h)	L18-20	t:Senior,Burrow,Ellis g:Sinfield(3)	3rd	16,465
15/4/07	Warrington (a)	W10-52	t:Ellis,Toopi,Donald,Senior,Burrow(2),Thackray,Webb,McGuire g:Sinfield(8)	3rd	10,155
21/4/07	St Helens (h)	W38-19	t:Donald,McGuire,Toopi,Peacock,Webb,Burrow g:Sinfield(6),Burrow	2nd	21,975
27/4/07	Catalans (h)	W54-8	t:Webb(3),Toopi,Sinfield(2),Ellis,Donald,Burrow g:Sinfield(9)	1st	15,581
6/5/07	Bradford (MM) ●	W38-42	t:Jones-Buchanan,Webb(3),Senior,Burrow,Tansey g:Sinfield(7)	1st	N/A
12/5/07	Wigan (h) (CCR5)	L18-22	t:Toopi,Webb(2) g:Sinfield(3)	N/A	9,612
20/5/07	Hull (a)	L16-12	t:Jones-Buchanan,Webb g:Sinfield,Burrow	2nd	14,256
27/5/07	Hull KR (a)	W10-18	t:McGuire,Toopi,Tansey g:Sinfield(3)	2nd	7,731
1/6/07	Warrington (h)	W42-26	t:Senior(2),Webb(2),McGuire,Toopi,Kirke g:Sinfield(7)	2nd	15,873
17/6/07	Huddersfield (a)	W12-25	t:McGuire(2),Tansey,Donald g:Sinfield(4) fg:Sinfield	2nd	10,241
29/6/07	Bradford (h)	L14-38	t:Diskin,Smith,Webb g:Sinfield	3rd	22,000
6/7/07	St Helens (a)	W10-22	t:McGuire,Burrow,Hall,Tansey g:Sinfield(3)	2nd	10,074
12/7/07	Wigan (a)	L18-2	g:Sinfield	2nd	14,554
20/7/07	Wakefield (h)	L16-23	t:Bailey,Burrow,Donald g:Sinfield(2)	2nd	16,654
5/8/07	Harlequins (a)	W20-54	t:Thackray,Webb(2),Tansey,Sinfield,Ellis,Donald,Peacock,McGuire g:Sinfield(7),Tansey(2)	2nd	3,734
10/8/07	Salford (h)	W52-14	t:Hall,Thackray(2),Leuluai,Senior,McGuire(2),Donald,Lauitiiti g:Sinfield(7),Tansey	2nd	15,637
17/8/07	Hull KR (h)	W34-18	t:Donald(2),Hall,Diskin,Toopi,McGuire g:Sinfield(5)	2nd	17,389
2/9/07	Bradford (a)	D16-16	t:Diskin,Donald(2) g:Sinfield(2)	2nd	18,195
7/9/07	Hull (h)	L6-17	t:Ablett g:Sinfield	2nd	17,424
14/9/07	Wakefield (h)	W46-4	t:McGuire(2),Sinfield,Burrow(2),Toopi,Webb,Smith g:Sinfield(7)	2nd	19,226
28/9/07	St Helens (a) (QSF)	L10-8	t:Smith g:Sinfield(2)	N/A	12,064
5/10/07	Wigan (h) (FE) ●●	W36-6	t:Webb(2),Lauitiiti,Burrow(2) g:Sinfield(7) fg:Sinfield(2)	N/A	16,112
13/10/07	St Helens (GF) ●●	W33-6	t:Webb,Lauitiiti,Donald,Smith,Jones-Buchanan g:Sinfield(6) fg:Burrow	N/A	71,352

● Played at Millennium Stadium, Cardiff
●● Played at Old Trafford, Manchester

	D.O.B.	APP ALL	APP SL	TRIES ALL	TRIES SL	GOALS ALL	GOALS SL	FG ALL	FG SL	PTS ALL	PTS SL
Carl Ablett	19/12/85	(13)	(12)	2	1	0	0	0	0	8	4
Ryan Bailey	11/11/83	25(3)	24(2)	3	3	0	0	0	0	12	12
Rob Burrow	26/9/82	30	28	16	13	5	3	1	1	75	59
Matt Diskin	27/1/82	24	22	4	3	0	0	0	0	16	12
Scott Donald	14/2/80	32	30	20	16	0	0	0	0	80	64
Gareth Ellis	3/5/81	31	30	5	5	0	0	0	0	20	20
Ashley Gibson	25/9/86	10	9	3	3	0	0	0	0	12	12
Ryan Hall	27/11/87	8(1)	8(1)	3	3	0	0	0	0	12	12
Jamie Jones-Buchanan	1/8/81	30(2)	29(1)	5	5	0	0	0	0	20	20
Ian Kirke	26/12/80	6(20)	5(19)	1	1	0	0	0	0	4	4
Ali Lauitiiti	13/7/79	2(21)	1(20)	4	3	0	0	0	0	16	12
Kylie Leuluai	29/3/78	12(19)	11(18)	1	1	0	0	0	0	4	4
Danny McGuire	6/12/82	32	30	17	17	0	0	0	0	68	68
Jamie Peacock	14/12/77	28(1)	27(1)	2	2	0	0	0	0	8	8
Mike Ratu	16/10/87	(1)	(1)	0	0	0	0	0	0	0	0
Nick Scruton	24/12/84	(2)	(2)	0	0	0	0	0	0	0	0
Keith Senior	24/4/76	30	29	7	7	0	0	0	0	28	28
Kevin Sinfield	12/9/80	32	30	6	5	139	128	3	3	305	279
Lee Smith	8/8/86	20	18	8	8	0	0	0	0	32	32
Jordan Tansey	9/9/86	6(17)	5(17)	9	7	3	3	0	0	42	34
Jamie Thackray	30/9/79	3(24)	2(23)	5	5	0	0	0	0	20	20
Clinton Toopi	29/2/80	29(3)	27(3)	9	8	0	0	0	0	36	32
Brent Webb	8/11/80	26	25	24	22	0	0	0	0	96	88

Kevin Sinfield

LEAGUE RECORD
P27-W18-D1-L8
(2nd, SL/Grand Final Winners,
Champions)
F747, A487, Diff+260
37 points.

CHALLENGE CUP
Round Five

ATTENDANCES
Best - v Bradford (SL - 22,000)
Worst - v Workington (CC - 3,576)
Total (SL, inc play-offs) - 243,821
Average (SL, inc play-offs) - 17.416
(Up by 2,078 on 2006)

KEY DATES -
SALFORD CITY REDS

27 November 2006 - Salford announce £200,000 shirt sponsorship deal with the Trafford Centre.

12 December 2006 - Gray Viane joins from relegated Castleford.

15 December 2006 - former chairman Keith Snape dies, aged 78.

3 January 2007 - chairman John Wilkinson OBE celebrates 25 years in charge.

5 March 2007 - Sydney reports claim that Salford have bid for Hazem El Masri.

5 March 2007 - Karl Harrison rules himself out of the running for the GB job, for the time being.

9 April 2007 - Salford confirm interest in New Zealand Test centre Paul Whatuira.

9 April 2007 - 35-18 round 10 home defeat to Hull sends Reds to bottom of table

13 April 2007 - Danny Halliwell, signed from Leigh at the start of the season, goes back to Hilton Park on a month's loan.

20 April 2007 - Salford sign David Berthezene from Catalans Dragons until the end of the season as cover for the injured Malcolm Alker.

27 April 2007 - Salford are hammered 50-24 by Wigan at home.

30 April 2007 - the Reds facing a battle to keep the services of Andy Coley.

11 May 2007 - Reds crash out of the Challenge Cup with a 36-10 defeat to the Giants.

19 May 2007 - Reds hammered 66-6 by Catalans in Perpignan. Malcolm Alker breaks hand.

21 May 2007 - 'Karl Harrison's job is secure,' claims director Dave Tarry, who sacks him days later.

25 May 2007 - Shaun McRae spotted in crowd at 14-12 home win over in-form Huddersfield.

1 June 2007 - gallant Salford defeated away at Saints 27-26 by a 79th minute Matty Smith field goal.

4 June 2007 - Reds board still unsure of coaching position after meeting with McRae. James Lowes also a candidate for the post.

11 June 2007 - Shaun McRae named as Salford City Reds coach, on a four-and-a-half year contract.

16 June 2007 - Salford win first game under Shaun McRae by 5-2 over Harlequins.

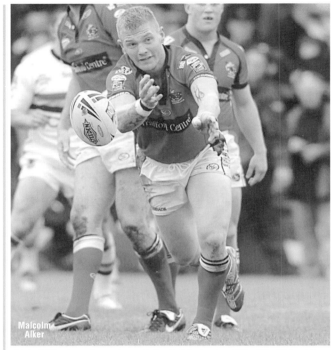

Malcolm Alker

6 July 2007 - James Lowes leaves Reds to take up assistant coaching position at Warrington.

15 July 2007 - Salford three points adrift at the bottom of the table after 42-6 defeat at Warrington.

17 July 2007 - Mike Wainwright signs from Warrington for the second time and the Reds also bring in Tom Saxton from Castleford.

18 July 2007 - Salford make their third signing in 24 hours by securing winger Richie Barnett from Warrington.

21 July 2007 - Salford stun Bradford with a 14-10 victory at the Willows.

27 July 2007 - Reds announce signing of New Zealand prop Phillip Leuluai on two-and-a-half year deal.

3 August 2007 - Salford suffer 30-24 home defeat to fellow strugglers Hull KR.

10 August 2007 - Salford slide closer to relegation after a 52-14 defeat by Leeds.

13 August 2007 - Australian prop forward Craig Stapleton signs two-year contract from 2008 season.

31 August 2007 - Wigan thump Salford 40-16 at the JJB Stadium.

2 September 2007 - Salford relegated as Hull KR thrash rivals Hull FC 42-6 to condemn the Reds.

4 September 2007 - Mike Wainwright leaves Salford to join Leigh after three appearances since returning from Warrington.

5 September 2007 - scrum-half Luke Robinson joins Huddersfield Giants.

6 September 2007 - Wigan Warriors confirm signing of Andy Coley.

9 September 2007 - Salford go down 22-16 at Harlequins.

14 September 2007 - final-round 34-26 home defeat to Warrington sees the Reds bow out of Super League.

25 September 2007 - Huddersfield sign David Hodgson.

28 September 2007 - Robbie Paul released by Huddersfield and signs two-year contract with the City Reds.

5 October 2007 - Matt Gardner joins from Huddersfield on 12-month deal.

15 October 2007 - former St Helens second row forward Stephen Bannister signs from Harlequins on 12-month contract.

22 October 2007 - Michael Korkidas leaves for Castleford Tigers.

30 October 2007 - Mark Edmondson also joins Castleford.

6 November 2007 - long-serving prop forward Paul Highton signs a new 12-month contract to keep him at the Willows for his testimonial year.

SALFORD CITY REDS

DATE	FIXTURE	RESULT	SCORERS	LGE	ATT
11/2/07	Leeds (h)	L26-30	t:Wilshere(2),Moule(2),Haggerty g:Robinson(3)	9th	8,070
17/2/07	Harlequins (a)	D18-18	t:Wilshere,Robinson,Coley,Korkidas g:Hodgson	10th	3,515
25/2/07	Wakefield (a)	L36-24	t:Finnigan,Adamson,Haggerty,Williams g:Wilshere(4)	11th	6,385
3/3/07	Catalans (h)	W10-0	t:Dorn,Alker g:Wilshere	9th	4,085
11/3/07	Bradford (a)	L56-18	t:Coley,Dorn,Williams g:Wilshere(3)	11th	10,640
16/3/07	Wigan (h)	L6-25	t:McGuinness g:Wilshere	11th	6,025
25/3/07	Huddersfield (a)	W16-18	t:Robinson(2),Turner g:Wilshere(3)	11th	5,275
30/3/07	Gateshead (a) (CCR4) ●	W4-64	t:Coley,Hodgson(2),Halliwell,Highton,Finnigan,Robinson(4),Brocklehurst g:Wilshere(10)	N/A	1,283
6/4/07	Warrington (h)	L32-34	t:Wilshere,Robinson,Dorn,Littler,Williams,Hodgson g:Wilshere(4)	11th	6,177
9/4/07	St Helens (a)	L48-4	t:Coley	11th	9,409
13/4/07	Hull (h)	L18-35	t:Moule,Dorn,Wilshere g:Wilshere(3)	12th	4,077
22/4/07	Hull KR (a)	W24-28	t:Wilshere,Dorn,Moule,Robinson,Hodgson g:Wilshere(4)	12th	6,299
27/4/07	Wigan (h)	L24-50	t:Coley(2),Finnigan,Moule g:Wilshere(4)	12th	6,603
6/5/07	Warrington (MM) ●●	L18-50	t:Dorn,McGuinness,Brocklehurst g:Wilshere(3)	12th	N/A
11/5/07	Huddersfield (h) (CCR5)	L10-36	t:Dorn,Littler g:Wilshere	N/A	2,694
19/5/07	Catalans (a)	L66-6	t:Dorn g:Wilshere	12th	8,820
25/5/07	Huddersfield (h)	W14-12	t:McGuinness,Hodgson,Viane g:Wilshere	12th	3,379
1/6/07	St Helens (a)	L27-26	t:Ratchford,Wilshere(2),Hodgson,Coley g:Wilshere(2),Hodgson	12th	7,801
15/6/07	Harlequins (h)	W5-2	g:Wilshere(2) fg:Robinson	12th	4,067
6/7/07	Wakefield (h)	L18-35	t:Robinson,Hodgson,Finnigan g:Wilshere(3)	12th	4,178
15/7/07	Warrington (a)	L42-6	t:Dorn g:Wilshere	12th	9,634
21/7/07	Bradford (h)	W14-10	t:Viane,Robinson g:Wilshere(3)	12th	3,438
29/7/07	Hull (a)	L48-26	t:Wilshere,Moule(2),Dorn,Finnigan g:Wilshere(3)	12th	13,338
3/8/07	Hull KR (h)	L24-30	t:Barnett,Finnigan,Moule,Hodgson g:Wilshere(4)	12th	7,165
10/8/07	Leeds (a)	L52-14	t:Littler,Dorn,Coley g:Wilshere	12th	15,637
17/8/07	St Helens (h)	L20-32	t:Littler,Wilshere(2) g:Wilshere(4)	12th	5,031
31/8/07	Wigan (a)	L40-16	t:Fitzpatrick,Highton,McGuinness g:Wilshere(2)	12th	13,611
8/9/07	Harlequins (a)	L22-16	t:Barnett,Dorn,Wilshere g:Wilshere,Hodgson	12th	2,347
14/9/07	Warrington (h)	L26-34	t:Barnett(2),Turner,McGuinness(2) g:Wilshere(3)	12th	5,152

● Played at The Willows
●● Played at Millennium Stadium, Cardiff

	D.O.B.	APP ALL	APP SL	TRIES ALL	TRIES SL	GOALS ALL	GOALS SL	FG ALL	FG SL	PTS ALL	PTS SL
Luke Adamson	17/11/87	6(10)	6(10)	1	1	0	0	0	0	4	4
Malcolm Alker	4/11/78	19(1)	18(1)	1	1	0	0	0	0	4	4
Richie Barnett	26/4/81	7	7	4	4	0	0	0	0	16	16
David Berthezene	27/10/80	9(1)	9(1)	0	0	0	0	0	0	0	0
Andrew Brocklehurst	6/3/83	9(10)	8(9)	2	1	0	0	0	0	8	4
Andy Coley	7/7/78	25	23	8	7	0	0	0	0	32	28
Luke Dorn	2/7/82	21(8)	19(8)	12	11	0	0	0	0	48	44
Mark Edmondson	3/11/79	10(3)	10(2)	0	0	0	0	0	0	0	0
Simon Finnigan	8/12/81	27	25	6	5	0	0	0	0	24	20
Karl Fitzpatrick	13/9/80	3	3	1	1	0	0	0	0	4	4
David Gower	30/9/85	(14)	(12)	0	0	0	0	0	0	0	0
Gareth Haggerty	8/9/81	(20)	(18)	2	2	0	0	0	0	8	8
Danny Halliwell	23/3/81	3(3)	2(3)	1	0	0	0	0	0	4	0
Paul Highton	10/11/76	9(5)	8(5)	2	1	0	0	0	0	8	4
David Hodgson	8/8/81	26	24	8	6	3	3	0	0	38	30
Lee Jewitt	14/2/87	4(11)	3(11)	0	0	0	0	0	0	0	0
Michael Korkidas	12/1/81	28(1)	26(1)	1	1	0	0	0	0	4	4
Phil Leuluai	16/7/77	3(2)	3(2)	0	0	0	0	0	0	0	0
Stuart Littler	19/2/79	22(7)	20(7)	4	3	0	0	0	0	16	12
Kevin McGuinness	10/11/76	25	24	6	6	0	0	0	0	24	24
Aaron Moule	20/6/77	16	16	8	8	0	0	0	0	32	32
Stephen Nash	14/1/86	2(8)	2(7)	0	0	0	0	0	0	0	0
Stefan Ratchford	19/7/88	5(1)	4	1	1	0	0	0	0	4	4
Luke Robinson	25/7/84	27	25	11	7	3	3	1	1	51	35
Tom Saxton	3/10/83	5	5	0	0	0	0	0	0	0	0
Ian Sibbit	15/10/80	8(1)	8(1)	0	0	0	0	0	0	0	0
Jordan Turner	9/1/89	8(9)	7(9)	2	2	0	0	0	0	8	8
Gray Viane	19/2/82	11	9	2	2	0	0	0	0	8	8
Mike Wainwright	25/2/75	3	3	0	0	0	0	0	0	0	0
Daley Williams	15/5/86	7(1)	7(1)	3	3	0	0	0	0	12	12
John Wilshere	5/5/78	29	27	12	12	72	61	0	0	192	170

John Wilshere

LEAGUE RECORD
P27-W6-D1-L20
(12th, SL)
F475, A874, Diff-399
13 points.

CHALLENGE CUP
Round Five

ATTENDANCES
Best - v Leeds (SL - 8,070)
Worst - v Gateshead (CC - 1,283)
Total (SL only) - 67,447
Average (SL only) - 5,188
(Up by 368 on 2006)

9 December 2006 - St Helens win BBC 'Team of the Year' and Daniel Anderson wins 'Coach of the Year' at the Sports Personality of the Year Awards.

2 January 2007 - Paul Wellens scoops 'Rugby Leaguer & League Express' Super League Player of the Year 2006.

16 January 2007 - former Saints player Tommy Martyn auctions his Challenge Cup winners medal to raise funds for Steve Prescott who is battling cancer.

18 January 2007 - Daniel Anderson signs an extension to his contract until the end of 2008.

26 January 2007 - Jason Hooper sent home from training camp in Dubai with a shoulder injury.

7 February 2007 - Jon Wilkin banned for two matches after being found guilty of striking in opening night 18-10 win at Huddersfield.

10 February 2007 - St Helens beaten at home 14-4 by Harlequins in SLXII round one.

23 February 2007 - Paul Sculthorpe returns from injury to inspire Saints as they beat Brisbane Broncos 18-14 to win the World Club Challenge.

11 April 2007 - Ian Hardman goes on loan to Hull KR.

16 April 2007 - Sean Long tells Rugby League World he has retired from international rugby.

20 April 2007 - Take-over bid from an Irish-based consortium turned down.

21 April 2007 - Ade Gardner misses Leeds game after being attacked on a night out in Barrow.

23 April 2007 - chief executive Sean McGuire quits.

7 May 2007 - Sean Long sustains calf injury in 34-18 win over Wigan in Cardiff.

11 May 2007 - Saints beat Rochdale Hornets 70-10 to progress into the sixth round of the Challenge Cup.

28 May 2007 - Jason Cayless agrees a contract extension that will keep him at Knowsley Road until the end of 2009.

1 June 2007 - Saints edge home thriller against Salford, a 79th minute Matty Smith drop goal the difference between the teams.

KEY DATES -
ST HELENS

8 June 2007 - Achilles training injury ends Paul Sculthorpe's season.

11 June 2007 - Saints 11/8 favourites to win Challenge Cup for second year running.

12 June 2007 - Donal McGuire, Paul Barrow and Chris Green all retire from the board, as local businessman Andy Bell buys a 16.4 per cent stake in the club.

14 June 2007 - Saints swoop to sign Sydney Roosters back-row forward Chris Flannery on a three-and-a-half year deal.

17 June 2007 - Saints hammer Hull KR 40-0 at Craven Park.

28 June 2007 - Plans for a new 18,000 capacity stadium unveiled.

30 June 2007 - Jon Wilkin, James Graham and Ade Gardner all sign new deals. Wilkin commits for another five years with Graham and Gardner extending by four.

5 July 2007 - St Helens charged along with Bradford and Wigan with breaching 2006 salary cap.

6 July 2007 - Saints lose 22-10 to Leeds as the Rhinos go level on points.

12 July 2007 - Saints found guilty of breaching 2006 salary cap by 0.8 per cent and fined £22,000.

15 July 2007 - Jon Wilkin sent off as 12-man Saints go down 10-4 at Bradford.

17 July 2007 - Saints announce scrum-half Sean Long will make comeback against Wigan but Jon Wilkin misses due to his two-game suspension.

20 July 2007 - Saints avoid a hat-trick of consecutive defeats with a 19-12 victory over Wigan. Winger Francis Meli signs three-year extension to his contract.

24 July 2007 - rising stars Stephen Tyrer, Paul Clough, Gary Wheeler and Gareth Frodsham all sign long-term contracts until the end of the 2010 season. Keiron Cunningham cleared to play in Challenge Cup semi-final despite being found guilty of a swinging arm against Wigan.

25 July 2007 - Saints forward Paul Sculthorpe resigns as Great Britain captain and retires from international Rugby League.

26 July 2007 - Jason Cayless flies home to Australia and misses Challenge Cup semi-final against Bradford after the sudden death of his mother.

28 July 2007 - 35-14 victory over Bradford sees the Saints through to the Challenge Cup final at the new Wembley.

31 July 2007 - Lyon Pryce banned for three matches after being found guilty of ungentlemanly misconduct - grabbing Sam Burgess's testicles.

3 August 2007 - St Helens go four points clear at the top of Super League after 31-20 home victory over Hull FC.

21 August 2007 - Keiron Cunningham, the only survivor from Saints' last Wembley triumph in 1997, made captain for this year's final.

25 August 2007 - Saints beat Catalans 30-8 at Wembley to secure their 11th Challenge Cup win.

28 August 2007 - Daniel Anderson insists he still intends to quit the Saints at the end of the 2008 season.

31 August 2007 - Saints beat Harlequins 32-10 as they set their sights on another double.

4 September 2007 - Matty Smith agrees a one-year contract extension.

7 September 2007 - Saints beat Warrington 36-16 and secure the League Leaders Shield as Hull win at Leeds.

14 September 2007 - Saints go down 20-12 at rivals Wigan in the final round, but made odds on 8/15 favourites to retain their Super League title.

27 September 2007 - Paul Sculthorpe signs a new one-year contract.

28 September 2007 - Saints edge Qualifying Semi-final with Leeds at Knowsley Road by 10-8.

13 October 2007 - Leeds Rhinos crowned champions after 33-6 win over St Helens at Old Trafford.

ST HELENS

DATE	FIXTURE	RESULT	SCORERS	LGE	ATT
4/2/07	Huddersfield (a)	W10-18	t:Gilmour(2),Pryce,Gardner g:Long	N/A	9,212
9/2/07	Harlequins (h)	L6-14	t:Gidley g:Long	6th	7,515
18/2/07	Wakefield (a)	L29-22	t:Bennett,Graham,Pryce,Gardner g:Long(3)	7th	7,385
23/2/07	Brisbane (WCC) ●	W18-14	t:Gardner(2),Sculthorpe g:Sculthorpe(3)	N/A	23,207
2/3/07	Bradford (h)	W34-22	t:Fozzard,Gardner,Wilkin,Talau,Gilmour,Tyrer g:Tyrer(5)	7th	11,793
9/3/07	Warrington (a)	W12-48	t:Gidley(3),Gardner,Meli,Bennett,Pryce(2),Wellens g:Long(6)	4th	13,024
17/3/07	Hull (a)	L24-12	t:Graham,Wellens g:Tyrer(2)	6th	12,678
23/3/07	Hull KR (h)	W42-14	t:Meli(2),Graham,Fa'asavalu,Pryce,Sculthorpe,Gidley,Gilmour g:Tyrer,Sculthorpe(4)	4th	10,523
30/3/07	Batley (h) (CCR4)	W78-14	t:Gardner,Wellens(2),Meli(2),Gilmour(2),Gidley,Cunningham,Fa'asavalu(2),Graham,Clough,Wilkin g:Tyrer(11)	N/A	4,335
6/4/07	Wigan (a)	W14-32	t:Meli,Talau,Roby,Fa'asavalu,Gidley,Bennett g:Sculthorpe(3),Long	2nd	24,028
9/4/07	Salford (h)	W48-4	t:Long,Gidley,Meli,Wellens,Gardner,Fa'asavalu,Bennett(2),Roby g:Long(2),Wellens(4)	1st	9,409
13/4/07	Catalans (h)	W53-10	t:Cayless,Pryce,Cunningham,Gidley,Wellens(4),Fa'asavalu,Meli g:Sculthorpe(6) fg:Long	1st	7,918
21/4/07	Leeds (a)	L38-19	t:Tyrer,Roby,Wellens g:Sculthorpe(2),Tyrer fg:Long	3rd	21,975
29/4/07	Harlequins (a)	W6-44	t:Pryce,Cunningham,Gidley(2),Meli,Tyrer,Wellens(2),Talau g:Sculthorpe(3),Wellens	3rd	4,362
5/5/07	Wigan (MM) ●●	W34-18	t:Meli,Wellens(4),Gidley g:Sculthorpe(5)	2nd	N/A
11/5/07	Rochdale (h) (CCR5)	W70-10	t:Meli(2),Wilkin(3),Graham,Wellens(2),Gardner(2),Sculthorpe,Fa'asavalu g:Sculthorpe(11)	N/A	3,586
18/5/07	Wakefield (h)	W34-14	t:Gidley(2),Pryce,Gardner,Wellens(2) g:Sculthorpe(5)	1st	8,529
28/5/07	Warrington (a)	W12-40	t:Wilkin,Smith,Pryce(3),Gardner,Fa'asavalu g:Sculthorpe(4),Smith,Tyrer	1st	13,024
1/6/07	Salford (h)	W27-26	t:Talau,Pryce,Meli,Cunningham,Gilmour g:Sculthorpe(3) fg:Smith	1st	7,801
9/6/07	Warrington (h) (CCQF)	W25-14	t:Gilmour(2),Talau,Gardner,Roby g:Wellens(2) fg:Long	N/A	8,503
17/6/07	Hull KR (a)	W0-40	t:Talau,Pryce,Cunningham,Gidley,Wellens,Tyrer,Graham g:Tyrer(6)	1st	7,011
30/6/07	Huddersfield (h)	W54-4	t:Wilkin(2),Pryce,Talau,Fa'asavalu,Tyrer(2),Gardner,Gilmour,Wellens g:Tyrer(7)	1st	7,771
6/7/07	Leeds (h)	L10-22	t:Roby,Tyrer g:Tyrer	1st	10,074
13/7/07	Bradford (a)	L10-4	t:Talau	1st	11,214
20/7/07	Wigan (h)	W19-12	t:Cayless,Meli,Pryce g:Long(2),Wellens fg:Long	1st	14,293
28/7/07	Bradford (CCSF) ●●●	W14-35	t:Talau,Meli,Gidley,Clough,Pryce,Bennett g:Long(4),Wellens fg:Long	N/A	14,316
3/8/07	Hull (h)	W31-20	t:Long,Clough,Gardner,Meli(3) g:Long(3) fg:Long	1st	10,005
11/8/07	Catalans (a)	L21-0		1st	8,655
17/8/07	Salford (a)	W20-32	t:Gardner(2),Gidley,Graham,Cunningham g:Tyrer(6)	1st	5,031
25/8/07	Catalans (CCF) ●●●●	W8-30	t:Roby,Gardner(2),Wellens,Clough g:Long(5)	N/A	84,241
31/8/07	Harlequins (h)	W32-10	t:Cayless,Graham,Wellens,Flannery,Gilmour g:Tyrer(6)	1st	7,939
7/9/07	Warrington (h)	W36-16	t:Gilmour,Meli(3),Gardner,Roby,Pryce g:Wellens(4)	1st	11,746
14/9/07	Wigan (a)	L20-12	t:Talau,Gardner g:Wellens(2)	1st	22,031
28/9/07	Leeds (h) (QSF)	W10-8	t:Pryce g:Smith(3)	N/A	12,064
13/10/07	Leeds (GF) ●●●●●	L33-6	t:Roby g:Long	N/A	71,352

● Played at Reebok Stadium, Bolton; ●● Played at Millennium Stadium, Cardiff; ●●● Played at Galpharm Stadium, Huddersfield; ●●●● Played at Wembley Stadium, London; ●●●●● Played at Old Trafford, Manchester

		APP		TRIES		GOALS		FG		PTS	
	D.O.B.	ALL	SL	ALL	SL	ALL	SL	ALL	SL	ALL	SL
Steve Bannister	10/10/87	(2)	(2)	0	0	0	0	0	0	0	0
Mike Bennett	9/5/80	23(4)	19(4)	6	5	0	0	0	0	24	20
Jason Cayless	15/1/80	31	27	3	3	0	0	0	0	12	12
Paul Clough	27/9/87	6(19)	5(15)	4	1	0	0	0	0	16	4
Keiron Cunningham	28/10/76	30(5)	26(3)	5	4	0	0	0	0	20	16
Chris Dean	17/1/88	(1)	(1)	0	0	0	0	0	0	0	0
Kyle Eastmond	17/7/89	2	2	0	0	0	0	0	0	0	0
Maurie Fa'asavalu	12/1/80	(30)	(25)	9	6	0	0	0	0	36	24
Chris Flannery	5/6/80	8(1)	8(1)	1	1	0	0	0	0	4	4
Nick Fozzard	22/7/77	29(3)	24(2)	1	1	0	0	0	0	4	4
Ade Gardner	24/6/83	32	26	21	13	0	0	0	0	84	52
Matt Gidley	1/7/77	33	27	17	15	0	0	0	0	68	60
Lee Gilmour	12/3/78	27	22	12	8	0	0	0	0	48	32
James Graham	10/9/85	11(23)	9(19)	8	6	0	0	0	0	32	24
Ian Hardman	8/12/84	1(1)	1(1)	0	0	0	0	0	0	0	0
Bryn Hargreaves	14/11/85	6(14)	4(11)	0	0	0	0	0	0	0	0
Jason Hooper	14/10/77	(2)	(2)	0	0	0	0	0	0	0	0
Sean Long	24/9/76	22(1)	17(1)	2	2	29	20	6	4	72	52
Dean McGilvray	24/4/88	3(1)	3(1)	0	0	0	0	0	0	0	0
Francis Meli	20/8/80	29	23	21	16	0	0	0	0	84	64
Scott Moore	23/1/88	(8)	(7)	0	0	0	0	0	0	0	0
Leon Pryce	9/10/81	32	26	18	17	0	0	0	0	72	68
James Roby	22/11/85	12(21)	10(18)	8	6	0	0	0	0	32	24
Paul Sculthorpe	22/9/77	9(3)	8(2)	4	2	49	35	0	0	114	78
Matty Smith	23/7/87	10	9	1	1	4	4	1	1	13	13
Willie Talau	25/1/76	29	24	10	8	0	0	0	0	40	32
Steve Tyrer	16/3/89	13(1)	12(1)	7	7	47	36	0	0	122	100
Paul Wellens	27/2/80	31	25	24	19	15	12	0	0	126	100
Jon Wilkin	11/1/83	26	20	8	4	0	0	0	0	32	16

Leon Pryce

LEAGUE RECORD
P27-W19-D0-L8
(1st, SL/Grand Final Runners-Up)
F783, A422, Diff+361
38 points.

CHALLENGE CUP
Winners

ATTENDANCES
Best - v Wigan (SL - 14,293)
Worst - v Rochdale (CC - 3,586)
Total (SL, inc play-offs) - 137,380
Average (SL, inc play-offs) - 9,813
(Down by 1,209 on 2006)

25 November 2006 - David Solomona leaves for Bradford. Wakefield receive cash plus Brett Ferres who signs on a three-year deal.

1 December 2006 - Monty Betham quits rugby for a career in boxing.

4 December 2006 - Wakefield sign Luke George from Huddersfield and rumoured to be targeting a move for Michael Withers.

13 December 2006 - new signing Waine Pryce given all clear to resume training after recovering from broken leg.

10 February 2007 - Wildcats suffer 14-9 reverse at unfancied promoted side Hull KR in round one.

4 March 2007 - Trinity top table after 19-6 round four win at Hull.

17 March 2007 - Semi Tadulala out for up to three months with broken forearm.

26 March 2007 - Paul White joins Halifax on one-month's loan.

20 April 2007 - Danny Lima joins Widnes after being released.

27 April 2007 - prop Richard Moore (rto end of 2008) and hooker Tevita Leo-Latu (three years) sign new contracts.

28 April 2007 - Coach John Kear signs new two-year contract.

13 May 2007 - Wakefield knocked out of the Challenge Cup by Bradford 14-4 at home.

18 May 2007 - 34-14 away defeat by Saints leaves Wildcats sitting second bottom of the table.

27 May 2007 - Wakefield alleviate relegation problems with 18-12 victory over Catalans.

3 June 2007 - Wakefield win second consecutive game with a 30-15 victory at home over Hull KR and progress to seventh spot.

KEY DATES - WAKEFIELD T WILDCATS

15 June 2007 - Adam Watene handed new contract to keep him at Belle Vue until the end of 2009 season; Jason Golden gets 12-month extension.

17 June 2007 - Wakefield go down 31-12 away at struggling Warrington.

1 July 2007 - Wakefield secure impressive 32-6 home victory over Wigan and confirm signing of French halfback Maxime Grésèque until end of the season.

6 July 2007 - Wildcats move up to fifth following 38-18 victory at Salford.

13 July 2007 - captain Jason Demetriou signs a 12-month contract extension.

15 July 2007 - Wildcats throw away 13-0 half-time lead to lose 24-23 at home to Huddersfield.

20 July 2007 - Wakefield bounce back with impressive 23-16 victory at Leeds.

23 July 2007 - Scrum-half Ben Jeffries to be released by Wakefield at end of season with 12 months left on his contract.

31 July 2007 - Tony Martin signs for the Wildcats from New Zealand Warriors on a two-year deal from 2008.

7 August 2007 - Tevita Leo-Latu suspended for six games after making a racist remark to Kevin Penny in 31-12 defeat at Warrington on 17 June.

8 August 2007 - Kevin Henderson and Ricky Bibey both sign two-year contract extensions.

17 August 2007 - Wildcats defeated 42-24 at Belle Vue by Hull FC.

22 August 2007 - Wakefield decide not to appeal against the six-match ban handed to Leo-Latu. Fans favourite Semi Tadulala set to leave Wakefield at the end of the season.

23 August 2007 - Matt Blaymire, Sean Gleeson and Aaron Murphy all sign contract extensions at the club. Blaymire and Murphy both sign two-year deals while Gleeson earns a one-year extension.

4 September 2007 - Peter Fox to leave Wakefield for Hull KR as the Wildcats sign Danny Brough from Castleford on three-year deal.

7 September 2007 - Wakefield announce capture of Huddersfield duo Brad Drew and Paul Reilly on two-year and one-year deals respectively.

9 September 2007 - Wakefield lose 24-22 to Huddersfield at the Galpharm Stadium to end play-off hopes.

14 September 2007 - final-round 46-4 thumping at Leeds gives Trinity an eighth-place finish.

16 September 2007 - Hooker Sam Obst agrees two-year contract extension.

18 September 2007 - Jason Demetriou named club Man of Steel for the third time in four seasons.

19 September 2007 - chief executive Steve Ferres announces he is to leave the club.

4 October 2007 - Wildcats release French international forward Olivier Elima, who joins Catalan Dragons.

10 October 2007 - Widnes Vikings' Damien Blanch joins the Wildcats on a two-year deal.

1 November 2007 - Oliver Wilkes and Scott Grix sign from Widnes Vikings on two-year deals.

1 November 2007 - former stand-off Nigel Wright joins coaching staff while ex-prop forward Francis Stephenson becomes the club's general manager.

7 November 2007 - Wildcats linked with USA captain and Gold Coast winger Matt Petersen.

WAKEFIELD T WILDCATS

DATE	FIXTURE	RESULT	SCORERS	LGE	ATT
10/2/07	Hull KR (a)	L14-9	t:Obst g:Rooney(2) fg:Rooney	10th	7,154
18/2/07	St Helens (h)	W29-22	t:Ferres,Catic,Atkins,Rooney,Blaymire g:Rooney(4) fg:Rooney	5th	7,385
25/2/07	Salford (h)	W36-24	t:Atkins,MacGillivray,Henderson,Leo-Latu,Rooney g:Rooney(8)	3rd	6,385
4/3/07	Hull (a)	W6-19	t:Demetriou,P March,Ferres g:Rooney(3) fg:Rooney	1st	13,229
11/3/07	Catalans (h)	W40-20	t:Tadulala,Demetriou(2),Jeffries,Blaymire,Fox,Rooney g:Rooney(6)	2nd	5,332
16/3/07	Leeds (h)	L26-32	t:Jeffries,Fox(2),Atkins(2) g:Rooney(3)	2nd	9,973
25/3/07	Warrington (h)	W30-24	t:Fox,Atkins,P March,Pryce,Jeffries,Leo-Latu g:Rooney(3)	2nd	6,119
1/4/07	London Skolars (a) (CCR4) ●	W4-52	t:Fox,Pryce,Golden,P March,Catic,Ferres,Henderson(2),Murphy, Jeffries,Buchanan g:P March(3),Ferres	N/A	2,427
6/4/07	Huddersfield (a)	L56-12	t:Moore,Blaymire g:Rooney(2)	4th	6,757
9/4/07	Bradford (h)	L24-36	t:Blaymire,Henderson,Fox(2),Rooney g:Rooney(2)	5th	9,106
14/4/07	Harlequins (a)	D22-22	t:P March,Blaymire(2),Pryce g:Rooney(3)	4th	2,532
20/4/07	Wigan (a)	L44-10	t:Jeffries,Demetriou g:Rooney	4th	14,108
28/4/07	Hull (h)	L18-20	t:Jeffries,Golden,Atkins(2) g:Rooney	6th	7,142
6/5/07	Huddersfield (MM) ●●	L36-12	t:White,Rooney g:Rooney(2)	9th	N/A
13/5/07	Bradford (h) (CCR5)	L4-14	t:White	N/A	3,700
18/5/07	St Helens (a)	L34-14	t:Gleeson,Elima g:Rooney(3)	11th	8,529
27/5/07	Catalans (h)	W18-12	t:Demetriou,Pryce,Rooney g:Rooney(3)	9th	4,023
3/6/07	Hull KR (h)	W30-15	t:Jeffries,Blaymire(2),White,Watene g:P March(5)	7th	6,107
17/6/07	Warrington (a)	L31-12	t:Catic,Pryce g:Ferres(2)	7th	10,324
1/7/07	Wigan (h)	W32-6	t:Demetriou,Jeffries(2),Blaymire,Fox,Moore g:Ferres(3),Jeffries	6th	8,126
6/7/07	Salford (a)	W18-35	t:Rooney,MacGillivray,Jeffries,Atkins(2),Fox g:Rooney(5) fg:Rooney	6th	4,178
15/7/07	Huddersfield (h)	L23-24	t:Fox(2),Obst(2) g:Rooney(3) fg:Rooney	6th	5,241
20/7/07	Leeds (a)	W16-23	t:Elima,Atkins,George g:Rooney(5) fg:Rooney	5th	16,654
5/8/07	Bradford (a)	L38-24	t:Atkins,Fox,Demetriou,Henderson g:Rooney(4)	7th	10,701
12/8/07	Harlequins (h)	W28-14	t:Rooney,Atkins(2),White,Catic g:Rooney(4)	5th	5,128
17/8/07	Hull (h)	L24-42	t:Atkins,Demetriou,Rooney g:Rooney(6)	7th	8,115
1/9/07	Catalans (a)	L38-20	t:Rooney(2),Obst g:Rooney(4)	8th	7,325
9/9/07	Huddersfield (a)	L24-22	t:White,Demetriou(2) g:Rooney(5)	8th	7,066
14/9/07	Leeds (a)	L46-4	t:Jeffries	8th	19,226

● Played at Belle Vue
●● Played at Millennium Stadium, Cardiff

	D.O.B.	APP ALL	APP SL	TRIES ALL	TRIES SL	GOALS ALL	GOALS SL	FG ALL	FG SL	PTS ALL	PTS SL
Mark Applegarth	10/12/84	(1)	(1)	0	0	0	0	0	0	0	0
Ryan Atkins	7/10/85	22(2)	20(2)	14	14	0	0	0	0	56	56
Ricky Bibey	22/9/81	11(7)	11(6)	0	0	0	0	0	0	0	0
Matt Blaymire	10/6/82	24(1)	23	9	9	0	0	0	0	36	36
Austin Buchanan	22/5/84	(1)	0	1	0	0	0	0	0	4	0
Ned Catic	2/8/78	8(20)	6(20)	4	3	0	0	0	0	16	12
Jason Demetriou	13/1/76	28	27	10	10	0	0	0	0	40	40
Olivier Elima	19/5/83	17(4)	17(4)	2	2	0	0	0	0	8	8
Dale Ferguson	13/4/88	1(2)	1(1)	0	0	0	0	0	0	0	0
Brett Ferres	17/4/86	26(2)	24(2)	3	2	6	5	0	0	24	18
Mark Field	21/3/84	2	1	0	0	0	0	0	0	0	0
Peter Fox	5/11/83	24	23	12	11	0	0	0	0	48	44
Luke George	30/10/87	1(2)	(2)	1	1	0	0	0	0	4	4
Sean Gleeson	29/11/87	4(4)	4(4)	1	1	0	0	0	0	4	4
Jason Golden	6/11/85	9(5)	8(4)	2	1	0	0	0	0	8	4
Maxime Greseque	18/3/81	2(1)	2(1)	0	0	0	0	0	0	0	0
Kevin Henderson	1/10/81	15(6)	13(6)	5	3	0	0	0	0	20	12
Ben Jeffries	4/9/80	27(2)	26(1)	11	10	1	1	0	0	46	42
Tevita Leo-Latu	3/7/81	3(16)	3(16)	2	2	0	0	0	0	8	8
Danny Lima	27/7/75	1(3)	(3)	0	0	0	0	0	0	0	0
Duncan MacGillivray	25/10/76	21(1)	20(1)	2	2	0	0	0	0	8	8
David March	25/7/79	5(1)	4(1)	0	0	0	0	0	0	0	0
Paul March	25/7/79	12(8)	10(8)	4	3	8	5	0	0	32	22
Richard Moore	2/2/81	15(13)	14(12)	2	2	0	0	0	0	8	8
Aaron Murphy	26/11/88	(1)	0	1	0	0	0	0	0	4	0
Sam Obst	26/11/80	14(1)	13(1)	4	4	0	0	0	0	16	16
Waine Pryce	3/10/81	11(2)	10(2)	5	4	0	0	0	0	20	16
Jamie Rooney	17/3/80	25	24	11	11	82	82	6	6	214	214
Danny Sculthorpe	8/9/79	1(10)	(10)	0	0	0	0	0	0	0	0
Semi Tadulala	3/3/81	6	6	1	1	0	0	0	0	4	4
Adam Watene	7/10/77	26	26	1	1	0	0	0	0	4	4
Paul White	7/12/82	16	15	5	4	0	0	0	0	20	16

Jamie Rooney

LEAGUE RECORD
P27-W11-D1-L15
(8th, SL)
F596, A714, Diff-118
23 points.

CHALLENGE CUP
Round Five

ATTENDANCES
Best - v Leeds (SL - 9,973)
Worst - v London Skolars
(CC - 2,427)
Total (SL only) - 88,182
Average (SL only) - 6,783
(Up by 1,334 on 2006)

KEY DATES - WARRINGTON WOLVES

17 June 2007 - Wolves bounce back with 31-12 win against Wakefield.

20 June 2007 - conditioner Paul Darbyshire joins Munster as head of fitness and conditioning.

21 June 2007 - Utility back Chris Hicks completes move to Warrington in 2008 from NRL side Manly Sea Eagles on a two-year deal.

22 June 2007 - Adrian Morley captains Britain to a 42-14 victory over France.

6 July 2007 - James Lowes takes up coaching role with the Wolves after leaving Salford.

8 July 2007 - Paul Cullen praises Adrian Morley after an emphatic 47-28 victory at Huddersfield.

10 July 2007 - Matt King joins the Wolves from Melbourne Storm on a four-year deal from 2008.

15 July 2007 - Paul Cullen salutes hat-trick hero Kevin Penny as Warrington thrash Salford 42-6.

17 July 2007 - Mike Wainwright leaves to join Salford for second time.

18 July 2007 - Richie Barnett follows Wainwright to Salford the following day.

19 July 2007 - teenage winger Kevin Penny earns a new contract to keep him at the Halliwell Jones Stadium until the end of the 2011 season.

20 July 2007 - Wolves hooker or halfback Michael Sullivan announces he will return home at the end of the season to play with Canterbury.

22 July 2007 - Warrington inflict 60-20 demolition of Hull KR at Craven Park.

26 July 2007 - Andrew Bracek lands a new contract until the end of the 2010 season.

30 July 2007 - Paul Cullen agrees two-year contract extension.

5 August 2007 - 43-24 derby win over Wigan keeps play-off hopes alive.

6 August 2007 - Paul Cullen is coach of the month and Kevin Penny player of the month for July.

14 August 2007 - Paul Wood avoids suspension but is fined £300 when found guilty of a high tackle in 46-14 defeat at Hull.

15 August 2007 - Stuart Reardon misses the rest of the season after needing a full shoulder re-construction.

19 August 2007 - Play-offs still a target for Wolves as they defeat Challenge Cup finalists Catalans 22-18.

23 August 2007 - Overseas trio Chris Leikvoll, Brent Grose and Henry Fa'afili to be released.

30 August 2007 - Ben Harrison, Steve Pickersgill, Chris Riley and Mike Cooper all sign contract extensions. Harrison signs a three-year deal whilst Pickersgill, Riley and Cooper all earn one-year deals.

31 August 2007 - Wolves lose crucial home match with Huddersfield 34-22.

3 September 2007 - dislocated shoulder rules Paul Wood out for the rest of the season.

4 September 2007 - Paul Rauhihi handed a 12-month contract extension, and suspended for one game for a dangerous tackle against the Giants.

7 September 2007 - 36-16 defeat at leaders Saints means Wolves must win at Salford in final round to stand any chance of making play-offs.

7 September 2007 - Rob Parker (fractured cheekbone) and Mark Gleeson (dislocated shoulder) added to injury list for Warrington's must win game at relegated Salford.

11 September 2007 - Adrian Morley banned for one match after being found guilty of reckless high tackle in defeat to St Helens.

14 September 2007 - Wolves miss out on the play-offs despite last-day 34-26 win at Salford.

14 November 2007 - Martin Gleeson, 27, signs contract extension until the end of 2010.

19 November 2007 - former Warrington great Mike Gregory dies, aged 43.

10 November 2006 - Paul Noone joins Widnes.

4 December 2006 - Paul Cullen refuses to be drawn on reports in Australia that Andrew Johns is to join the Wolves in 2008.

26 December 2006 - Simon Grix suffers serious shoulder injury during Boxing Day friendly at Widnes.

9 January 2007 - Andy Bracek and Ben Harrison go to Widnes on rolling one-month loans.

12 January 2007 - Warrington announce the capture of Louis Anderson, brother of Vinnie, for 2008.

9 February 2007 - Adrian Morley fractures eye socket on his Warrington debut, a 16-10 win at Wigan.

18 March 2007 - Adrian Morley breaks a cheekbone for the second time in his comeback game, a home round 6 win over Hull KR.

26 March 2007 - Paul Johnson suffers spiral fracture of the index finger in the round 7 defeat at Wakefield.

10 April 2007 - Andrew Johns retires due to injury, ruling out a move to the Wolves.

10 June 2007 - Warrington crash out of Challenge Cup with their second defeat to St Helens in two weeks.

WARRINGTON WOLVES

DATE	FIXTURE	RESULT	SCORERS	LGE	ATT
9/2/07	Wigan (a)	W10-16	t:Barnett,Anderson g:Briers(4)	2nd	21,693
18/2/07	Bradford (h)	L20-36	t:Westwood(2),Leikvoll g:Briers(4)	8th	12,607
25/2/07	Hull (h)	W25-24	t:Sullivan,Briers,Clarke,Anderson g:Briers(4) fg:Briers	6th	11,097
3/3/07	Harlequins (a)	W12-19	t:Martin Gleeson,Fa'afili(2),Reardon g:Bridge fg:Briers	5th	3,132
9/3/07	St Helens (h)	L12-48	t:Briers,Fa'afili g:Briers(2)	6th	13,024
18/3/07	Hull KR (h)	W30-12	t:Fa'afili,Johnson(2),Westwood,Clarke(2) g:Sullivan,Clarke,Westwood	4th	10,030
25/3/07	Wakefield (a)	L30-24	t:Wood,Fa'afili,Bridge,Clarke g:Bridge(4)	6th	6,119
31/3/07	Hull KR (h) (CCR4)	W38-10	t:Grose(2),Reardon,Anderson(2),Bridge,Rauhihi g:Bridge(5)	N/A	4,523
6/4/07	Salford (a)	W32-34	t:Rauhihi(2),Grose,Fa'afili,Wainwright,Bracek g:Briers(5)	5th	6,177
9/4/07	Huddersfield (h)	L18-26	t:Fa'afili(2),Martin Gleeson g:Briers(3)	6th	9,403
15/4/07	Leeds (h)	L10-52	t:Westwood,Grose g:Westwood	7th	10,155
21/4/07	Catalans (a)	L27-16	t:Westwood(2),Fa'afili g:Briers(2)	8th	9,050
29/4/07	Bradford (a)	L36-24	t:Grose,Anderson,Briers(2) g:Briers(4)	10th	11,276
6/5/07	Salford (MM) ●	W18-50	t:Johnson,Briers,Anderson(2),Fa'afili,Reardon,Martin Gleeson(2),Barnett,Clarke g:Briers(3),Westwood(2)	7th	N/A
13/5/07	Barrow (h) (CCR5)	W48-16	t:Anderson(3),Martin Gleeson(2),Mark Gleeson,Grose,Barnett(2) g:Briers(6)	N/A	4,184
19/5/07	Harlequins (h)	L4-17	t:Martin Gleeson	9th	7,818
28/5/07	St Helens (h)	L12-40	t:Anderson,Fa'afili g:Briers(2)	10th	13,024
1/6/07	Leeds (a)	L42-26	t:Fa'afili(3),Penny(2) g:Briers(3)	10th	15,873
9/6/07	St Helens (a) (CCQF)	L25-14	t:Penny,Fa'afili g:Briers(3)	N/A	8,503
17/6/07	Wakefield (h)	W31-12	t:Clarke,Leikvoll,Riley(2),Grose g:Briers(5) fg:Briers	9th	10,324
30/6/07	Catalans (a)	L24-22	t:Penny,Briers(2) g:Briers(5)	10th	8,850
8/7/07	Huddersfield (a)	W28-47	t:Bridge(3),Reardon,Penny(2),Sullivan g:Briers(9) fg:Briers	8th	6,822
15/7/07	Salford (h)	W42-6	t:Clarke(2),Westwood,Fa'afili,Briers,Martin Gleeson,Penny(3) g:Briers(3)	8th	9,634
22/7/07	Hull KR (a)	W20-60	t:Reardon(2),Morley,Mark Gleeson,Clarke(2),Briers(3),Bridge,Fa'afili g:Briers(8)	6th	6,640
5/8/07	Wigan (h)	W43-24	t:Reardon,Penny,Briers,Grose,Clarke,Fa'afili,Bridge g:Briers(7) fg:Briers	4th	12,552
12/8/07	Hull (a)	L46-14	t:Martin Gleeson,Fa'afili(2) g:Briers	6th	13,404
19/8/07	Catalans (h)	W22-18	t:Riley,Penny,Grose(2),Parker g:Briers	5th	8,125
31/8/07	Huddersfield (h)	L22-34	t:Fa'afili,Westwood(3),Penny g:Westwood	6th	8,843
7/9/07	St Helens (a)	L36-16	t:Penny,Martin Gleeson g:Briers(4)	7th	11,746
14/9/07	Salford (a)	W26-34	t:Fa'afili,Bridge,Westwood(2),Mitchell,Rauhihi g:Briers(5)	7th	5,152

● Played at Millennium Stadium, Cardiff

		APP		TRIES		GOALS		FG		PTS	
	D.O.B.	ALL	SL	ALL	SL	ALL	SL	ALL	SL	ALL	SL
Vinnie Anderson	14/2/79	18	16	11	6	0	0	0	0	44	24
Richie Barnett	26/4/81	9(4)	7(4)	4	2	0	0	0	0	16	8
Matty Blythe	20/11/88	(1)	(1)	0	0	0	0	0	0	0	0
Andy Bracek	21/3/84	5(12)	5(11)	1	1	0	0	0	0	4	4
Chris Bridge	5/7/84	15(1)	14(1)	8	7	10	5	0	0	52	38
Lee Briers	14/6/78	26	24	12	12	93	84	5	5	239	221
Jon Clarke	4/4/79	30	27	11	11	1	1	0	0	46	46
Michael Cooper	15/9/88	(4)	(4)	0	0	0	0	0	0	0	0
Henry Fa'afili	30/5/80	28(1)	25(1)	22	21	0	0	0	0	88	84
Mark Gleeson	16/6/82	16(9)	14(8)	2	1	0	0	0	0	8	4
Martin Gleeson	28/5/80	24	22	10	8	0	0	0	0	40	32
Simon Grix	28/9/85	(3)	(3)	0	0	0	0	0	0	0	0
Brent Grose	11/9/79	29	26	10	7	0	0	0	0	40	28
Ben Harrison	24/2/88	4(13)	4(12)	0	0	0	0	0	0	0	0
Anthony Jerram	11/10/85	(2)	(2)	0	0	0	0	0	0	0	0
Paul Johnson	25/11/78	17	15	3	3	0	0	0	0	12	12
Chris Leikvoll	4/12/75	11(11)	10(10)	2	2	0	0	0	0	8	8
Lee Mitchell	8/9/88	1(3)	1(3)	1	1	0	0	0	0	4	4
Adrian Morley	10/5/77	19	17	1	1	0	0	0	0	4	4
Rob Parker	5/9/81	4(19)	3(17)	1	1	0	0	0	0	4	4
Kevin Penny	3/10/87	13	12	13	12	0	0	0	0	52	48
Steve Pickersgill	28/11/85	1(13)	1(11)	0	0	0	0	0	0	0	0
Paul Rauhihi	3/7/73	24(4)	23(2)	4	3	0	0	0	0	16	12
Stuart Reardon	13/10/81	21	19	7	6	0	0	0	0	28	24
Chris Riley	22/2/88	7(3)	6(3)	3	3	0	0	0	0	12	12
Michael Sullivan	18/6/80	5(9)	5(7)	2	2	1	1	0	0	10	10
Mike Wainwright	25/2/75	20(1)	17(1)	1	1	0	0	0	0	4	4
Ben Westwood	25/7/81	28	25	12	12	5	5	0	0	58	58
Paul Wood	10/10/81	15(6)	13(6)	1	1	0	0	0	0	4	4

Henry Fa'afili

LEAGUE RECORD
P27-W13-D0-L14
(7th, SL)
F693, A736, Diff-43
26 points.

CHALLENGE CUP
Quarter Finalists

ATTENDANCES
Best - v St Helens (SL - 13,024)
Worst - v Barrow (CC - 4,184)
Total (SL only) - 136,636
Average (SL only) - 10,510
(Up by 104 on 2006)

13 November 2006 - captain Sean O'Loughlin signs new two-year deal.

14 November 2006 - Harrison Hansoen and Iafeta Palea'aesina sign new four-year deals to keep them at the JJB until 2010.

20 November 2006 - Brian Noble expresses desire to stay on as GB coach.

5 December 2006 - Wigan announce capture of Thomas Leuluai, Michael Withers and Shane Millard for 2007.

4 January 2007 - Wigan raid Bradford for young stand-off Mark Flanagan.

11 January 2007 - released Brett Dallas retires.

17 January 2007 - RFL announce that Brian Noble will not be offered new contract as GB coach.

3 February 2007 - Stuart Fielden loses to former Bulls teammate Lee Radford in charity boxing match in aid of former St Helens player Steve Prescott who is battling cancer.

12 February 2007 - Dean Bell is inducted into Wigan Hall of Fame.

20 February 2007 - Gareth Hock fined £600 after being found guilty of making a dangerous tackle in 18-16 victory at Catalans Dragons.

24 February 2007 - Brian Noble, Stuart Fielden and Michael Withers make their first return to Odsal as the Warriors lose 32-28.

13 March 2007 - Sean Gleeson returns to Wigan after a loan spell with Huddersfield.

19 March 2007 - Chris Ashton signs with Northampton RU and will leave the Warriors at the end of the season.

20 March 2007 - Dean Bell returns to New Zealand to take up a community and development manager's role at the New Zealand Warriors.

6 April 2007 - Eric Ashton inducted into Wigan Hall of Fame.

12 April 2007 - Danny Hill goes on loan to Hull KR.

20 April 2007 - Brian Noble celebrates one year in charge with 44-10 victory at home over Wakefield.

24 April 2007 - Darrell Goulding, Eamon O'Carroll and Michael McIlorum all extend their contracts for 18 months to keep them at the club until the end of the 2008 season.

12 May 2007 - Wigan edge the Rhinos 22-18 at Headingley.

14 May 2007 - Wigan linked with St George prop forward Jason Ryles.

21 May 2007 - Brian Noble rumoured to be set to leave Wigan for Leeds Rhinos.

27 May 2007 - Wigan hammer Hull FC 47-16 at home.

8 June 2007 - Wigan go through to Challenge Cup semis with a convincing 25-6 win over Harlequins.

KEY DATES - WIGAN WARRIORS

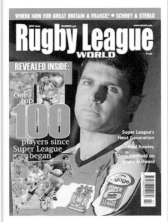

13 June 2007 - Warriors avoid Saints and Bradford in semi-final draw to land tie with Catalans.

16 June 2007 - former Warriors fullback Kris Radlinski receives MBE in Queen's Birthday honours.

16 June 2007 - Wigan thrash Catalans 30-0 in dress rehearsal for the Cup semi-final.

27 June 2007 - Michael Withers retires from game after persistent knee problems.

1 July 2007 - Wigan crash 32-6 at Wakefield.

5 July 2007 - Wigan charged, alongside Bradford and St Helens, with breaching 2006 salary cap.

12 July 2007 - 18-2 victory over Leeds follows thrilling 25-18 victory over Bradford.

20 July 2007 - Wigan go down 19-12 to Saints.

25 July 2007 - Wigan drop from fourth to ninth after being found guilty of being six per cent over the salary cap in 2006. The Warriors are docked four points.

27 July 2007 - Joel Tomkins joins Widnes on loan.

29 July 2007 - Catalans stun Wigan in the Challenge Cup semi-final, winning 37-24, to cap a miserable week on and off the field for the Warriors.

30 July 2007 - Wigan club chairman Maurice Lindsay announces he is stepping down at the end of the season.

31 July 2007 - Wigan owner Dave Whelan reveals he is considering his own position.

5 August 2007 - Wigan on the wrong end of 43-24 scoreline in derby at Warrington.

10 August 2007 - Brian Noble delighted to get back to winning ways against Huddersfield in a 20-12 home triumph.

20 August 2007 - Chris Ashton released by Warriors.

4 September 2007 - Stuart Fielden cleared of any wrongdoing after investigation of racial abuse accusation in 20-12 home victory against Huddersfield.

5 September 2007 - Iafeta Palea'aesina cleared to play in crucial match at Hull KR after having one-match ban overturned.

6 September 2007 - Wigan confirm signing of Salford prop Andy Coley on two-year deal.

9 September 2007 - 40-24 success at Hull KR leaves Warriors in sixth position with only a home tie against league leaders St Helens left.

14 September 2007 - Brian Noble backs his side to win Super League after 20-12 win at home over leaders St Helens secures sixth place. An attendance of 22,031 breaks 19-year old record for seasonal averages.

14 September 2007 - Ellery Hanley inducted into Wigan Hall of Fame.

21 September 2007 - Wigan snatch 31-30 victory in Elimination play-off at Odsal, after trailing 30-6.

29 September 2007 - 21-18 Elimination semi-final win at Hull FC keeps season alive, but Mark Calderwood breaks an ankle.

5 October 2007 - 36-6 defeat by Leeds Rhinos in final eliminator.

6 October 2007 - former Australian Test forward Bryan Fletcher confirms retirement

9 October 2007 - Gareth Hock to miss opening of 2008 season after being handed two-match ban for a dangerous tackle on Matt Diskin.

5 November 2007 - Warriors sign Richie Mathers from Gold Coast on three-year contract, with the second and third seasons subject to him playing a minimum number of Super League games in 2008.

11 November 2007 - new owner and chairman Ian Lenagan maintains the club has not made an offer to Australian Willie Mason.

1 December 2007 - Wigan RLFC officially changes hands as new owner Ian Lenagan takes control.

WIGAN WARRIORS

DATE	FIXTURE	RESULT	SCORERS	LGE	ATT
9/2/07	Warrington (h)	L10-16	t:Calderwood,Vaealiki g:Richards	11th	21,693
17/2/07	Catalans (a)	W16-18	t:Ashton,Bailey,O'Loughlin g:Richards(3)	6th	7,052
24/2/07	Bradford (a)	L32-28	t:Fletcher,Ashton,Fielden(2),Leuluai g:Richards(4)	9th	12,798
2/3/07	Hull KR (h)	L16-26	t:Calderwood,Millard,O'Loughlin g:Richards(2)	10th	15,178
9/3/07	Harlequins (h)	W16-12	t:Withers,Vaealiki g:Richards(4)	8th	14,971
16/3/07	Salford (a)	W6-25	t:Ashton,O'Loughlin,Calderwood g:Richards(6) fg:Barrett	7th	6,025
23/3/07	Hull (a)	W20-30	t:Barrett(2),Richards(2),Ashton g:Richards(5)	5th	12,755
1/4/07	Widnes (a) (CCR4)	W24-34	t:O'Loughlin,Leuluai,Richards(2),Goulding,Barrett g:Richards(5)	N/A	6,006
6/4/07	St Helens (h)	L14-32	t:Richards,Leuluai g:Richards(3)	7th	24,028
10/4/07	Leeds (a)	W18-20	t:Fletcher,Calderwood,Bailey g:Richards(4)	4th	16,465
15/4/07	Huddersfield (a)	L41-16	t:Leuluai,Vaealiki(2) g:Richards(2)	6th	7,117
20/4/07	Wakefield (h)	W44-10	t:Vaealiki,Richards,Barrett(2),Goulding,Ashton(2) g:Richards(8)	4th	14,108
27/4/07	Salford (a)	W24-50	t:Bailey,Barrett(3),Leuluai,Hansen,Millard(2),Goulding g:Richards(7)	4th	6,603
5/5/07	St Helens (MM) ●	L34-18	t:Fletcher,Ashton,Goulding g:Richards(3)	4th	N/A
12/5/07	Leeds (a) (CCR5)	W18-22	t:Ashton,O'Loughlin,Calderwood g:Richards(5)	N/A	9,612
18/5/07	Hull KR (h)	L10-12	t:Barrett,Richards g:Richards	5th	13,538
26/5/07	Hull (h)	W47-16	t:Barrett(2),Richards(3),Higham,Ashton g:Richards(9) fg:Barrett	4th	14,314
2/6/07	Harlequins (a)	L18-8	t:Ashton,Barrett	4th	5,657
8/6/07	Harlequins (h) (CCQF)	W25-6	t:Ashton,Richards,Calderwood,O'Loughlin g:Richards(4) fg:Barrett	N/A	10,835
15/6/07	Catalans (h)	W30-0	t:Bailey,Barrett,Ashton,Richards,Calderwood g:Richards(5)	4th	12,641
1/7/07	Wakefield (a)	L32-6	t:Barrett g:Richards	4th	8,126
6/7/07	Bradford (h)	W25-18	t:Barrett,Bailey(2),Calderwood,Vaealiki g:Ashton(2) fg:Barrett	4th	15,107
12/7/07	Leeds (h)	W18-2	t:Colbon,Fletcher g:Richards(5)	4th	14,554
20/7/07	St Helens (a)	L19-12	t:Richards,Goulding g:Richards,O'Loughlin	4th	14,293
29/7/07	Catalans (CCSF) ●●	L37-24	t:Leuluai,Higham,Calderwood,Goulding g:Richards(4)	N/A	10,218
5/8/07	Warrington (a)	L43-24	t:Colbon,Leuluai,Goulding(2) g:Richards(4)	9th	12,552
10/8/07	Huddersfield (h)	W20-12	t:Goulding,Higham g:Richards(6)	8th	12,744
18/8/07	Harlequins (a)	D16-16	t:Leuluai,Barrett(2) g:Richards(2)	8th	3,200
31/8/07	Salford (h)	W40-16	t:Barrett,Calderwood(2),Vaealiki,Palea'aesina,Richards,O'Loughlin g:Richards(6)	7th	13,611
9/9/07	Hull KR (a)	W24-40	t:Colbon(2),Goulding,Vaealiki,Prescott,Leuluai,Calderwood g:Richards(6)	6th	7,370
14/9/07	St Helens (h)	W20-12	t:Vaealiki,Leuluai,Colbon g:Richards(4)	6th	22,031
21/9/07	Bradford (a) (EPO)	W30-31	t:Leuluai,Calderwood(3),Hansen g:Richards(5) fg:Richards	N/A	9,055
29/9/07	Hull (a) (ESF)	W18-21	t:Richards,Hock,Colbon g:Richards(4) fg:Richards	N/A	16,291
5/10/07	Leeds (a) (FE)	L36-6	t:Richards g:Richards	N/A	16,112

● Played at Millennium Stadium, Cardiff
●● Played at Halliwell Jones Stadium, Warrington

		APP		TRIES		GOALS		FG		PTS	
	D.O.B.	ALL	SL	ALL	SL	ALL	SL	ALL	SL	ALL	SL
Chris Ashton	29/3/87	20(2)	17(2)	12	10	2	2	0	0	52	44
Phil Bailey	25/5/80	34	30	6	6	0	0	0	0	24	24
Trent Barrett	18/11/77	33	29	18	17	0	0	4	3	76	71
Mark Calderwood	25/10/81	31	27	15	12	0	0	0	0	60	48
Liam Colbon	30/9/84	13	12	6	6	0	0	0	0	24	24
Stuart Fielden	14/9/79	32(2)	28(2)	2	2	0	0	0	0	8	8
Bryan Fletcher	12/4/74	32	28	4	4	0	0	0	0	16	16
Darrell Goulding	3/3/88	4(18)	3(15)	10	8	0	0	0	0	40	32
Harrison Hansen	26/10/85	8(24)	8(20)	2	2	0	0	0	0	8	8
Mick Higham	18/9/80	14(20)	11(19)	3	2	0	0	0	0	12	8
Danny Hill	31/10/84	(8)	(7)	0	0	0	0	0	0	0	0
Gareth Hock	5/9/83	28(3)	24(3)	1	1	0	0	0	0	4	4
Thomas Leuluai	22/6/85	34	30	11	9	0	0	0	0	44	36
Michael McIlorum	10/1/88	(7)	(5)	0	0	0	0	0	0	0	0
Shane Millard	30/7/75	20(7)	19(6)	3	3	0	0	0	0	12	12
Eamon O'Carroll	13/6/87	(14)	(13)	0	0	0	0	0	0	0	0
Sean O'Loughlin	24/11/82	34	30	7	4	1	1	0	0	30	18
Iafeta Palea'aesina	10/2/82	32(1)	28(1)	1	1	0	0	0	0	4	4
Paul Prescott	1/1/86	2(25)	2(22)	1	1	0	0	0	0	4	4
Pat Richards	27/2/82	33	29	16	13	130	112	2	2	326	278
Joel Tomkins	21/3/87	(3)	(3)	0	0	0	0	0	0	0	0
David Vaealiki	13/11/80	32(1)	29(1)	9	9	0	0	0	0	36	36
Michael Withers	16/5/76	6(1)	6(1)	1	1	0	0	0	0	4	4

Trent Barrett

LEAGUE RECORD
P27-W15-D1-L11
(6th, SL/Final Eliminator)
F621, A527, Diff+94
27 points. *(4 points deducted for 2006 salary cap breach)*

CHALLENGE CUP
Semi Finalists

ATTENDANCES
Best - v St Helens (SL - 24,028)
Worst - v Harlequins (CC - 10,835)
Total (SL only) - 208,518
Average (SL only) - 16,040
(Up by 1,576 on 2006)

SUPER LEAGUE XII
Round by Round

ROUND 3

Sunday 4th February 2007

HUDDERSFIELD GIANTS 10 ST HELENS 18

GIANTS: 6 Chris Thorman (C); 5 Shane Elford (D); 3 Jamahl Lolesi (D); 11 Chris Nero; 21 Matt Gardner; 4 Kevin Brown; 7 Robbie Paul; 10 John Skandalis (D); 9 Brad Drew; 15 Paul Jackson; 14 Stuart Jones; 13 Stephen Wild; 8 Eorl Crabtree. Subs (all used): 12 Andy Raleigh; 18 Darrell Griffin (D); 19 Ryan Hudson (D); 20 Steve Snitch.
Try: Gardner (23); **Goals:** Thorman 3/3.
SAINTS: 14 James Roby; 2 Ade Gardner; 3 Matt Gidley (D); 11 Lee Gilmour; 5 Francis Meli; 6 Leon Pryce; 7 Sean Long (C); 8 Nick Fozzard; 9 Keiron Cunningham; 10 Jason Cayless; 15 Mike Bennett; 12 Jon Wilkin; 17 James Graham. Subs (all used): 20 Scott Moore; 16 Jason Hooper; 18 Bryn Hargreaves (D); 23 Maurie Fa'asavalu.
Tries: Gilmour (7, 50), Pryce (14), Gardner (20);
Goals: Long 1/3, Hooper 0/1.
Sin bin: Wilkin (57) - late challenge on Thorman.
On report: Wilkin (57) - late challenge on Thorman.
Rugby Leaguer & League Express Men of the Match:
Giants: Eorl Crabtree; *Saints:* Leon Pryce.
Penalty count: 14-13; **Half-time:** 10-14;
Referee: Ashley Klein; **Attendance:** 9,212.

ROUND 1

Friday 9th February 2007

ST HELENS 6 HARLEQUINS 14

SAINTS: 19 Ian Hardman; 2 Ade Gardner; 3 Matt Gidley; 4 Willie Talau; 5 Francis Meli; 6 Leon Pryce; 7 Sean Long (C); 8 Nick Fozzard; 9 Keiron Cunningham; 10 Jason Cayless; 15 Mike Bennett; 17 James Graham; 14 James Roby. Subs (all used): 16 Jason Hooper; 18 Bryn Hargreaves; 20 Scott Moore; 23 Maurie Fa'asavalu.
Try: Gidley (13); **Goals:** Long 1/2.
HARLEQUINS: 16 Chris Melling (D); 2 Jon Wells; 3 Paul Sykes; 4 Tyrone Smith; 18 Matt Gafa; 6 Scott Hill (D); 7 Danny Orr (D); 8 Karl Temata; 9 Chad Randall; 15 David Mills; 13 Rob Purdham (C); 12 Lee Hopkins; 23 Henry Paul. Subs (all used): 14 Julien Rinaldi (D); 17 Louie McCarthy-Scarsbrook; 20 Jon Grayshon (D); 22 Michael Worrincy.
Tries: Orr (7), Hopkins (25), Wells (58); **Goals:** Sykes 1/3.
Sin bin: Rinaldi (39) - interference.
Rugby Leaguer & League Express Men of the Match:
Saints: Leon Pryce; *Harlequins:* Danny Orr.
Penalty count: 9-7; **Half-time:** 6-10;
Referee: Phil Bentham; **Attendance:** 7,515.

WIGAN WARRIORS 10 WARRINGTON WOLVES 16

WARRIORS: 1 Chris Ashton; 2 Mark Calderwood; 3 Phil Bailey (D); 4 Michael Withers (D); 5 Pat Richards; 6 Trent Barrett (D); 7 Thomas Leuluai (D); 8 Stuart Fielden; 16 Shane Millard (D); 10 Iafeta Palea'aesina; 11 Gareth Hock; 12 Bryan Fletcher; 13 Sean O'Loughlin (C). Subs (all used): 9 Mick Higham; 14 David Vaealiki; 19 Harrison Hansen; 24 Eamon O'Carroll.
Tries: Calderwood (48), Vaealiki (74);
Goals: Richards 1/3.
WOLVES: 1 Stuart Reardon; 2 Henry Fa'afili; 3 Martin Gleeson; 4 Paul Johnson (D); 18 Richie Barnett; 6 Chris Bridge; 7 Lee Briers (C); 8 Chris Leikvoll; 9 Jon Clarke; 10 Paul Rauhihi; 11 Adrian Morley (D); 12 Ben Westwood; 13 Vinnie Anderson (D). Subs (all used): 23 Mike Wainwright; 16 Paul Wood; 15 Rob Parker; 17 Michael Sullivan.
Tries: Barnett (28), Anderson (38); **Goals:** Briers 4/6.
Rugby Leaguer & League Express Men of the Match:
Warriors: Bryan Fletcher; *Wolves:* Jon Clarke.
Penalty count: 13-10; **Half-time:** 2-12;
Referee: Steve Ganson; **Attendance:** 21,693.

Saturday 10th February 2007

HULL KINGSTON ROVERS 14
WAKEFIELD TRINITY WILDCATS 9

ROVERS: 1 Ben Cockayne; 21 Luke Dyer (D); 3 Jon Goddard; 4 Gareth Morton; 5 Byron Ford; 6 Scott Murrell; 7 James Webster (C); 18 Danny Ward (D); 9 Ben Fisher; 20 Michael Vella (D); 16 Jason Netherton; 11 Iain Morrison; 28 Chris Chester (D). Subs (all used): 8 Makali Aizue; 13 Tommy Gallagher; 15 Jim Gannon (D); 23 Pat Weisner.
Tries: Murrell (3), Cockayne (78); **Goals:** Morton 3/4.
Sin bin: Cockayne (40) - fighting.
WILDCATS: 1 Mark Field; 22 Peter Fox (D); 3 Jason Demetriou (C); 4 Ryan Atkins; 5 Semi Tadulala; 6 Jamie Rooney; 7 Ben Jeffries; 8 Adam Watene; 9 Sam Obst; 25 Richard Moore (D); 18 Olivier Elima; 23 Jason Golden (D); 13 Brett Ferres (D). Subs (all used): 14 Paul March (D2); 20 Tevita Leo-Latu; 11 Ned Catic; 19 Danny Lima (D).
Try: Obst (14); **Goals:** Rooney 2/2;
Field goal: Rooney (72).
Sin bin: Leo-Latu (32) - high tackle on Gannon; Moore (40) - fighting.
On report: Moore (2) - alleged dangerous tackle.
Rugby Leaguer & League Express Men of the Match:
Rovers: Chris Chester; *Wildcats:* Jamie Rooney.
Penalty count: 14-11; **Half-time:** 8-6;
Referee: Ashley Klein; **Attendance:** 7,154.

Sunday 11th February 2007

BRADFORD BULLS 18 HUDDERSFIELD GIANTS 14

BULLS: 19 Michael Platt (D); 1 Marcus St Hilaire; 17 James Evans (D); 4 Shontayne Hape; 5 Lesley Vainikolo; 26 David Solomona (D); 7 Paul Deacon (C); 8 Joe Vagana; 9 Terry Newton; 14 Chris Feather (D); 13 Jamie Langley; 3 Ben Harris; 12 Glenn Morrison (D). Subs (all used): 15 Matt Cook; 16 Ian Henderson; 2 Nathan McAvoy (D2); 18 Sam Burgess.
Tries: Hape (15), Solomona (36), Morrison (71);
Goals: Deacon 3/4.
Sin bin: Platt (39) - obstruction.
On report: Cook (46) - alleged dangerous throw.
GIANTS: 1 Paul Reilly; 3 Jamahl Lolesi; 11 Chris Nero; 4 Kevin Brown; 21 Matt Gardner; 6 Chris Thorman (C); 7 Robbie Paul; 16 Keith Mason; 19 Ryan Hudson; 10 John Skandalis; 14 Stuart Jones; 13 Stephen Wild; 8 Eorl Crabtree. Subs (all used): 9 Brad Drew; 18 Darrell Griffin; 15 Paul Jackson; 20 Steve Snitch.
Tries: Lolesi (9), Jones (47); **Goals:** Thorman 3/3.
Rugby Leaguer & League Express Men of the Match:
Bulls: David Solomona; *Giants:* John Skandalis.
Penalty count: 14-15; **Half-time:** 12-8;
Referee: Richard Silverwood; **Attendance:** 12,130.

SALFORD CITY REDS 26 LEEDS RHINOS 30

CITY REDS: 2 David Hodgson; 22 Danny Halliwell (D); 3 Kevin McGuinness; 4 Aaron Moule; 5 John Wilshere; 6 Luke Dorn (D); 7 Luke Robinson; 8 Andy Coley; 9 Malcolm Alker (C); 24 Lee Jewitt (D); 11 Mark Edmondson (D); 19 Stuart Littler; 13 Simon Finnigan. Subs (all used): 10 Michael Korkidas (D); 16 Andrew Brocklehurst; 17 Gareth Haggerty; 18 Luke Adamson.
Tries: Wilshere (9, 43), Moule (50, 76), Haggerty (71);
Goals: Robinson 3/5, Wilshere 0/1.
RHINOS: 1 Brent Webb (D); 20 Ashley Gibson; 3 Clinton Toopi; 4 Keith Senior; 2 Scott Donald; 6 Danny McGuire; 7 Rob Burrow; 16 Ryan Bailey; 9 Matt Diskin; 8 Kylie Leuluai (D); 14 Ali Lauitiiti; 12 Gareth Ellis; 13 Kevin Sinfield (C). Subs (all used): 11 Jamie Jones-Buchanan; 15 Jamie Thackray; 17 Nick Scruton; 23 Jordan Tansey.
Tries: Webb (3, 38), McGuire (6), Burrow (34), Tansey (67); **Goals:** Sinfield 5/6.
Sin bin: Senior (45) - professional foul.
Rugby Leaguer & League Express Men of the Match:
City Reds: David Hodgson; *Rhinos:* Brent Webb.
Penalty count: 12-8; **Half-time:** 6-22;
Referee: Ian Smith; **Attendance:** 8,070.

HULL FC 10 CATALANS DRAGONS 10

HULL: 1 Shaun Briscoe; 2 Matt Sing (D); 3 Kirk Yeaman; 4 Sid Domic; 5 Gareth Raynor; 23 Tommy Lee; 7 Richard Horne; 8 Ewan Dowes; 9 Richard Swain; 10 Garreth Carvell; 11 Lee Radford (C); 16 Danny Tickle (D); 13 Danny Washbrook. Subs (all used): 21 Hutch Maiava (D); 18 Wayne Godwin (D); 26 Scott Wheeldon; 12 Shayne McMenemy.
Try: Sing (55); **Goals:** Tickle 3/4.
DRAGONS: 1 Clint Greenshields (D); 2 Justin Murphy; 4 Adam Mogg (D); 18 Vincent Duport (D); 5 Dimitri Pelo (D); 6 Casey McGuire (D); 3 John Wilson; 10 Jerome Guisset (C); 23 Aaron Gorrell (D); 19 Alex Chan; 12 Jason Croker (D); 11 Sebastien Raguin (D); 13 Gregory Mounis. Subs (all used): 20 Adel Fellous; 16 Lionel Teixido; 17 Cyril Gossard; 8 David Ferriol (D).
Tries: Mogg (11), Duport (51); **Goals:** Gorrell 1/2.
Sin bin: Chan (64) - holding down.
Rugby Leaguer & League Express Men Of the Match:
Hull: Danny Tickle; *Dragons:* Casey McGuire.
Penalty count: 14-10; **Half-time:** 0-6;
Referee: Ben Thaler; **Attendance:** 12,673.

ROUND 2

Friday 16th February 2007

LEEDS RHINOS 18 HULL FC 4

RHINOS: 1 Brent Webb; 2 Scott Donald; 3 Clinton Toopi; 4 Keith Senior; 5 Lee Smith; 6 Danny McGuire; 7 Rob Burrow; 8 Kylie Leuluai; 9 Matt Diskin; 16 Ryan Bailey; 11 Jamie Jones-Buchanan; 12 Gareth Ellis; 13 Kevin Sinfield (C). Subs (all used): 10 Jamie Peacock; 14 Ali Lauitiiti; 15 Jamie Thackray; 23 Jordan Tansey.
Tries: Smith (16), Sinfield (46), Bailey (69);
Goals: Sinfield 3/4.
HULL: 1 Shaun Briscoe; 2 Matt Sing; 20 Richard Whiting; 3 Kirk Yeaman; 5 Gareth Raynor; 7 Richard Horne; 23 Tommy Lee; 8 Ewan Dowes; 9 Richard Swain (C); 10 Garreth Carvell; 16 Danny Tickle; 12 Shayne McMenemy; 13 Danny Washbrook. Subs (all used): 21 Hutch Maiava; 26 Scott Wheeldon; 19 Graeme Horne; 18 Wayne Godwin.
Try: Sing (57); **Goals:** Tickle 0/1.
Rugby Leaguer & League Express Men of the Match:
Rhinos: Danny McGuire; *Hull:* Danny Tickle.
Penalty count: 7-6; **Half-time:** 6-0;
Referee: Steve Ganson; **Attendance:** 18,659.

Saturday 17th February 2007

CATALANS DRAGONS 16 WIGAN WARRIORS 18

DRAGONS: 1 Clint Greenshields; 2 Justin Murphy; 4 Adam Mogg; 18 Vincent Duport; 5 Dimitri Pelo; 6 Casey McGuire; 3 John Wilson; 10 Jerome Guisset (C); 23 Aaron Gorrell; 20 Adel Fellous; 19 Alex Chan; 12 Jason Croker; 13 Gregory Mounis. Subs (all used): 16 Lionel Teixido; 17 Cyril Gossard; 8 David Ferriol; 24 Remi Casty.
Tries: Chan (4), Murphy (57); **Goals:** Gorrell 4/5.
WARRIORS: 1 Chris Ashton; 2 Mark Calderwood; 3 Phil Bailey; 14 David Vaealiki; 5 Pat Richards; 6 Trent Barrett; 7 Thomas Leuluai; 8 Stuart Fielden; 16 Shane Millard; 10 Iafeta Palea'aesina; 11 Gareth Hock; 12 Bryan Fletcher; 13 Sean O'Loughlin (C). Subs (all used): 9 Mick Higham; 4 Michael Withers; 19 Harrison Hansen; 24 Eamon O'Carroll.
Tries: Ashton (37), Bailey (63), O'Loughlin (79);
Goals: Richards 3/3.
Sin bin: Hock (72) - dissent.
On report: Hock (62) - alleged spear tackle on Croker.
Rugby Leaguer & League Express Men of the Match:
Dragons: Alex Chan; *Warriors:* Sean O'Loughlin.
Penalty count: 14-8; **Half-time:** 10-6;
Referee: Ian Smith; **Attendance:** 7,052.

HARLEQUINS 18 SALFORD CITY REDS 18

HARLEQUINS: 16 Chris Melling; 2 Jon Wells; 3 Paul Sykes; 4 Tyrone Smith; 18 Matt Gafa; 6 Scott Hill; 7 Danny Orr; 8 Karl Temata; 9 Chad Randall; 15 David Mills; 13 Rob Purdham (C); 12 Lee Hopkins; 23 Henry Paul. Subs (all used): 14 Julien Rinaldi; 17 Louie McCarthy-Scarsbrook; 20 Jon Grayshon; 22 Michael Worrincy.
Tries: T Smith (7), Melling (11), Sykes (17), Rinaldi (43); **Goals:** Sykes 1/4.
CITY REDS: 2 David Hodgson; 22 Danny Halliwell; 3 Kevin McGuinness; 19 Stuart Littler; 5 John Wilshere; 6 Luke Dorn; 7 Luke Robinson; 8 Andy Coley; 9 Malcolm Alker (C); 10 Michael Korkidas; 11 Mark Edmondson; 18 Luke Adamson; 13 Simon Finnigan. Subs (all used): 17 Gareth Haggerty; 24 Lee Jewitt; 25 Daley Williams; 16 Andrew Brocklehurst.
Tries: Wilshere (30), Robinson (40), Coley (74), Korkidas (78); **Goals:** Hodgson 1/4.
Rugby Leaguer & League Express Men of the Match:
Harlequins: Rob Purdham; *City Reds:* David Hodgson.
Penalty count: 7-9; **Half-time:** 14-10;
Referee: Phil Bentham; **Attendance:** 3,515.

Sunday 18th February 2007

HUDDERSFIELD GIANTS 10
HULL KINGSTON ROVERS 17

GIANTS: 1 Paul Reilly; 21 Matt Gardner; 13 Stephen Wild; 4 Kevin Brown; 3 Jamahl Lolesi; 6 Chris Thorman (C); 7 Robbie Paul; 16 Keith Mason; 9 Brad Drew; 10 John Skandalis; 11 Chris Nero; 8 Eorl Crabtree; 14 Stuart Jones. Subs (all used): 15 Paul Jackson; 18 Darrell Griffin; 19 Ryan Hudson; 20 Steve Snitch.
Tries: Wild (39), Nero (66); **Goals:** Thorman 1/2.
Sin bin: Jones (57) - fighting.
ROVERS: 1 Ben Cockayne; 21 Luke Dyer; 3 Jon Goddard; 4 Gareth Morton; 5 Byron Ford; 6 Scott Murrell; 7 James Webster (C); 18 Danny Ward; 9 Ben Fisher; 20 Michael Vella; 11 Iain Morrison; 16 Jason Netherton; 28 Chris Chester. Subs (all used): 12 Michael Smith; 15 Jim Gannon; 10 David Tangata-Toa; 13 Tommy Gallagher.
Tries: Murrell (11), Cockayne (35); **Goals:** Morton 4/4;
Field goal: Webster (76).
Sin bin: Morrison (57) - fighting.
Rugby Leaguer & League Express Men of the Match:
Giants: Eorl Crabtree; *Rovers:* James Webster.
Penalty count: 10-8; **Half-time:** 4-16;
Referee: Ben Thaler; **Attendance:** 7,700.

WARRINGTON WOLVES 20 BRADFORD BULLS 36

WOLVES: 1 Stuart Reardon; 2 Henry Fa'afili; 5 Brent Grose; 4 Paul Johnson; 18 Richie Barnett; 17 Michael Sullivan; 7 Lee Briers (C); 8 Chris Leikvoll; 9 Jon Clarke; 10 Paul Rauhihi; 23 Mike Wainwright; 12 Ben Westwood; 15 Rob Parker. Subs (all used): 14 Mark Gleeson; 16 Paul Wood; 19 Steve Pickersgill; 24 Chris Riley.
Tries: Westwood (18, 34), Leikvoll (68); **Goals:** Briers 4/4.
BULLS: 19 Michael Platt; 1 Marcus St Hilaire; 3 Ben Harris; 4 Shontayne Hape; 5 Lesley Vainikolo; 6 Iestyn Harris; 7 Paul Deacon (C); 8 Joe Vagana; 9 Terry Newton; 14 Chris Feather; 26 David Solomona; 13 Jamie Langley; 12 Glenn Morrison. Subs (all used): 17 James Evans; 15 Matt Cook; 18 Sam Burgess; 2 Nathan McAvoy.
Tries: Platt (22, 58, 75), Morrison (40), Vainikolo (51), Evans (56); **Goals:** Deacon 6/7.
Sin bin: Burgess (67) - interference.
Rugby Leaguer & League Express Men of the Match:
Wolves: Rob Parker; *Bulls:* Glenn Morrison.
Penalty count: 6-6; **Half-time:** 14-12;
Referee: Ashley Klein; **Attendance:** 12,607.

WAKEFIELD TRINITY WILDCATS 29 ST HELENS 22

WILDCATS: 21 Matt Blaymire (D); 22 Peter Fox; 3 Jason Demetriou (C); 4 Ryan Atkins; 5 Semi Tadulala; 6 Jamie Rooney; 7 Ben Jeffries; 8 Adam Watene; 9 Sam Obst; 25 Richard Moore; 18 Olivier Elima; 12 Duncan MacGillivray; 13 Brett Ferres. Subs (all used): 14 Paul March; 20 Tevita Leo-Latu; 19 Danny Lima; 11 Ned Catic.
Tries: Ferres (29), Catic (45), Atkins (61), Rooney (66), Blaymire (76); **Goals:** Rooney 4/6;
Field goal: Rooney (76).
SAINTS: 1 Paul Wellens; 2 Ade Gardner; 3 Matt Gidley; 4 Willie Talau; 5 Francis Meli; 6 Leon Pryce; 7 Sean Long (C); 8 Nick Fozzard; 9 Keiron Cunningham; 17 James Graham; 11 Lee Gilmour; 15 Mike Bennett; 14 James Roby. Subs (all used): 18 Bryn Hargreaves; 19 Ian Hardman; 20 Scott Moore; 23 Maurie Fa'asavalu.
Tries: Bennett (15), Graham (23), Pryce (36), Gardner (80); **Goals:** Long 3/4.
Rugby Leaguer & League Express Men of the Match:
Wildcats: Jamie Rooney; *Saints:* James Roby.
Penalty count: 6-5; **Half-time:** 6-18;
Referee: Richard Silverwood; **Attendance:** 7,385.

Catalans' Jason Croker looks for support under pressure from Leeds' Kevin Sinfield during a stunning win for the Dragons

ROUND 3

Saturday 24th February 2007

BRADFORD BULLS 32 WIGAN WARRIORS 28

BULLS: 19 Michael Platt; 1 Marcus St Hilaire; 3 Ben Harris; 4 Shontayne Hape; 5 Lesley Vainikolo; 6 Iestyn Harris; 7 Paul Deacon (C); 8 Joe Vagana; 9 Terry Newton; 14 Chris Feather; 26 David Solomona; 18 Sam Burgess; 12 Glenn Morrison. Subs (all used): 17 James Evans; 15 Matt Cook; 16 Ian Henderson; 10 Andy Lynch. **Tries:** Vainikolo (16, 20, 48), Morrison (29), Newton (44); **Goals:** Deacon 6/6.
WARRIORS: 4 Michael Withers; 1 Chris Ashton; 3 Phil Bailey; 14 David Vaealiki; 5 Pat Richards; 6 Trent Barrett; 7 Thomas Leuluai; 8 Stuart Fielden; 9 Mick Higham; 10 Iafeta Palea'aesina; 11 Gareth Hock; 12 Bryan Fletcher; 13 Sean O'Loughlin (C). Subs (all used): 16 Shane Millard; 18 Paul Prescott; 19 Harrison Hansen; 24 Eamon O'Carroll.
Tries: Fletcher (3), Ashton (13), Fielden (54, 59), Leuluai (77); **Goals:** Richards 4/5.
Sin bin: Ashton (69) - interference
Rugby Leaguer & League Express Men of the Match: *Bulls:* Terry Newton; *Warriors:* Michael Withers.
Penalty count: 11-8; **Half-time:** 18-10;
Referee: Ashley Klein; **Attendance:** 12,798.

CATALANS DRAGONS 30 LEEDS RHINOS 22

DRAGONS: 1 Clint Greenshields; 2 Justin Murphy; 18 Vincent Duport; 4 Adam Mogg; 5 Dimitri Pelo; 14 Thomas Bosc; 6 Casey McGuire; 19 Alex Chan; 23 Aaron Gorrell; 20 Adel Fellous; 11 Sebastien Raguin; 12 Jason Croker; 13 Gregory Mounis. Subs (all used): 10 Jerome Guisset (C); 17 Cyril Gossard; 8 David Ferriol; 16 Lionel Teixido.
Tries: Bosc (5), Chan (19), McGuire (46), Duport (57), Pelo (66); **Goals:** Gorrell 5/6.
RHINOS: 1 Brent Webb; 2 Scott Donald; 3 Clinton Toopi; 4 Keith Senior; 5 Lee Smith; 6 Danny McGuire; 7 Rob Burrow; 16 Ryan Bailey; 13 Kevin Sinfield (C); 8 Kylie Leuluai; 11 Jamie Jones-Buchanan; 10 Jamie Peacock; 12 Gareth Ellis. Subs (all used): 14 Ali Lauitiiti; 15 Jamie Thackray; 18 Ian Kirke; 23 Jordan Tansey.
Tries: Jones-Buchanan (9), Thackray (27), Donald (29), Smith (37); **Goals:** Sinfield 3/4.
Rugby Leaguer & League Express Men of the Match: *Dragons:* Casey McGuire; *Rhinos:* Rob Burrow.
Penalty count: 10-7; **Half-time:** 12-22;
Referee: Richard Silverwood; **Attendance:** 7,630.

Sunday 25th February 2007

HULL KINGSTON ROVERS 10 HARLEQUINS 26

ROVERS: 1 Ben Cockayne; 21 Luke Dyer; 3 Jon Goddard; 4 Gareth Morton; 5 Byron Ford; 6 Scott Murrell; 7 James Webster (C); 15 Jim Gannon; 9 Ben Fisher; 20 Michael Vella; 11 Iain Morrison; 16 Jason Netherton; 17 Mark O'Neill (D). Subs (all used): 12 Michael Smith; 18 Danny Ward; 10 David Tangata-Toa; 13 Tommy Gallagher.
Tries: Dyer (28), Smith (43); **Goals:** Morton 1/2.
HARLEQUINS: 16 Chris Melling; 2 Jon Wells; 3 Paul Sykes; 4 Tyrone Smith; 18 Matt Gafa; 6 Scott Hill; 7 Danny Orr; 22 Michael Worrincy; 9 Chad Randall; 15 David Mills; 13 Rob Purdham (C); 12 Lee Hopkins; 23 Henry Paul. Subs (all used): 14 Julien Rinaldi; 20 Jon Grayshon; 17 Louie McCarthy-Scarsbrook; 1 Mark McLinden.
Tries: Melling (2), Grayshon (17), McCarthy-Scarsbrook (23), Sykes (38, 72); **Goals:** Sykes 3/5.
Rugby Leaguer & League Express Men of the Match: *Rovers:* Ben Fisher; *Harlequins:* Danny Orr.
Penalty count: 15-8; **Half-time:** 4-22;
Referee: Ben Thaler; **Attendance:** 7,056.

WARRINGTON WOLVES 25 HULL FC 24

WOLVES: 1 Stuart Reardon; 2 Henry Fa'afili; 3 Martin Gleeson; 4 Paul Johnson; 5 Brent Grose; 17 Michael Sullivan; 7 Lee Briers (C); 8 Chris Leikvoll; 9 Jon Clarke; 10 Paul Rauhihi; 23 Mike Wainwright; 12 Ben Westwood; 13 Vinnie Anderson. Subs (all used): 14 Mark Gleeson; 15 Rob Parker; 16 Paul Wood; 19 Steve Pickersgill.
Tries: Sullivan (24), Briers (30), Clarke (44), Anderson (58); **Goals:** Briers 4/6; **Field goal:** Briers (77).
Sin bin: Rauhihi (14) - dissent.
HULL: 14 Motu Tony; 2 Matt Sing; 20 Richard Whiting; 3 Kirk Yeaman; 5 Gareth Raynor; 6 Paul Cooke; 7 Richard Horne; 8 Ewan Dowes; 9 Richard Swain; 10 Garreth Carvell; 11 Lee Radford (C); 16 Danny Tickle; 13 Danny Washbrook. Subs (all used): 18 Wayne Godwin; 17 Willie Manu (D); 15 Paul King; 21 Hutch Maiava.
Tries: Whiting (16), Radford (18), Raynor (64), Sing (75); **Goals:** Cooke 4/4.
Rugby Leaguer & League Express Men of the Match: *Wolves:* Lee Briers; *Hull:* Paul Cooke.
Penalty count: 11-8; **Half-time:** 12-12;
Referee: Steve Ganson; **Attendance:** 11,097.

WAKEFIELD TRINITY WILDCATS 36 SALFORD CITY REDS 24

WILDCATS: 21 Matt Blaymire; 22 Peter Fox; 3 Jason Demetriou (C); 4 Ryan Atkins; 5 Semi Tadulala; 6 Jamie Rooney; 7 Ben Jeffries; 8 Adam Watene; 14 Paul March; 25 Richard Moore; 18 Olivier Elima; 12 Duncan MacGillivray; 13 Brett Ferres. Subs (all used): 17 Kevin Henderson; 20 Tevita Leo-Latu; 19 Danny Lima; 11 Ned Catic.
Tries: Atkins (26), MacGillivray (31), Henderson (49), Leo-Latu (59), Rooney (79); **Goals:** Rooney 8/8.

CITY REDS: 2 David Hodgson; 25 Daley Williams; 19 Stuart Littler; 3 Kevin McGuinness; 5 John Wilshere; 6 Luke Dorn; 7 Luke Robinson; 8 Andy Coley; 9 Malcolm Alker (C); 10 Michael Korkidas; 11 Mark Edmondson; 18 Luke Adamson; 13 Simon Finnigan. Subs (all used): 17 Gareth Haggerty; 24 Lee Jewitt; 22 Danny Halliwell; 16 Andrew Brocklehurst.
Tries: Finnigan (12), Adamson (35), Haggerty (68), Williams (76); **Goals:** Wilshere 4/5.
Rugby Leaguer & League Express Men of the Match: *Wildcats:* Jamie Rooney; *City Reds:* Malcolm Alker.
Penalty count: 11-9; **Half-time:** 16-14;
Referee: Ian Smith; **Attendance:** 6,385.

ROUND 4

Friday 2nd March 2007

ST HELENS 34 BRADFORD BULLS 22

SAINTS: 1 Paul Wellens; 2 Ade Gardner; 3 Matt Gidley; 4 Willie Talau; 5 Francis Meli; 6 Leon Pryce; 7 Sean Long (C); 8 Nick Fozzard; 14 James Roby; 10 Jason Cayless; 11 Lee Gilmour; 12 Jon Wilkin; 24 Steve Tyrer. Subs (all used): 9 Keiron Cunningham; 17 James Graham; 18 Bryn Hargreaves; 25 Steve Bannister.
Tries: Fozzard (3), Gardner (7), Wilkin (14), Talau (18), Gilmour (21), Tyrer (47); **Goals:** Tyrer 5/6.
BULLS: 19 Michael Platt; 2 Nathan McAvoy; 3 Ben Harris; 4 Shontayne Hape; 5 Lesley Vainikolo; 6 Iestyn Harris; 7 Paul Deacon (C); 8 Joe Vagana; 9 Terry Newton; 14 Chris Feather; 13 Jamie Langley; 26 David Solomona; 12 Glenn Morrison. Subs (all used): 10 Andy Lynch; 16 Ian Henderson; 11 Chris McKenna; 18 Sam Burgess.
Tries: Hape (35, 79), Langley (38), Solomona (50); **Goals:** Deacon 3/4.
On report: Newton (74) - late challenge on Wilkin.
Rugby Leaguer & League Express Men of the Match: *Saints:* James Roby; *Bulls:* Ian Henderson.
Penalty count: 8-9; **Half-time:** 28-12;
Referee: Richard Silverwood; **Attendance:** 11,793.

WIGAN WARRIORS 16 HULL KINGSTON ROVERS 26

WARRIORS: 1 Chris Ashton; 2 Mark Calderwood; 3 Phil Bailey; 14 David Vaealiki; 5 Pat Richards; 4 Michael Withers; 7 Thomas Leuluai; 8 Stuart Fielden; 9 Mick Higham; 10 Iafeta Palea'aesina; 11 Gareth Hock; 12 Bryan Fletcher; 13 Sean O'Loughlin (C). Subs (all used): 16 Shane Millard; 18 Paul Prescott; 19 Harrison Hansen; 21 Danny Hill.
Tries: Calderwood (49), Millard (52), O'Loughlin (58); **Goals:** Richards 2/3.
ROVERS: 1 Ben Cockayne; 21 Luke Dyer; 4 Gareth

Morton; 3 Jon Goddard; 5 Byron Ford; 6 Scott Murrell; 7 James Webster (C); 20 Michael Vella; 9 Ben Fisher; 8 Makali Aizue; 16 Jason Netherton; 28 Chris Chester; 14 Stanley Gene (D2). Subs (all used): 15 Jim Gannon; 18 Danny Ward; 12 Michael Smith; 13 Tommy Gallagher.
Tries: Ford (2, 16), Fisher (26), Dyer (34), Morton (39);
Goals: Morton 3/6.
Sin bin: J Netherton (30) - late tackle on Leuluai; Chester (51) - obstruction.
Rugby Leaguer & League Express Men of the Match: *Warriors:* Sean O'Loughlin; *Rovers:* Ben Fisher.
Penalty count: 10-7; **Half-time:** 16-26;
Referee: Phil Bentham; **Attendance:** 15,178.

Saturday 3rd March 2007

HARLEQUINS 12 WARRINGTON WOLVES 19

HARLEQUINS: 1 Mark McLinden; 2 Jon Wells; 3 Paul Sykes; 16 Chris Melling; 18 Matt Gafa; 6 Scott Hill; 7 Danny Orr; 8 Karl Temata; 9 Chad Randall; 15 David Mills; 20 Jon Grayshon; 13 Rob Purdham (C); 23 Henry Paul. Subs (all used): 14 Julien Rinaldi; 17 Louie McCarthy-Scarsbrook; 10 Daniel Heckenberg; 24 Andy Smith (D).
Tries: Gafa (7), Hill (15); **Goals:** Sykes 2/2.
WOLVES: 1 Stuart Reardon; 2 Henry Fa'afili; 3 Martin Gleeson; 4 Paul Johnson; 5 Brent Grose; 17 Michael Sullivan; 7 Lee Briers (C); 16 Paul Wood; 9 Jon Clarke; 10 Paul Rauhihi; 23 Mike Wainwright; 12 Ben Westwood; 13 Vinnie Anderson. Subs (all used): 14 Mark Gleeson; 15 Rob Parker; 6 Chris Bridge; 19 Steve Pickersgill.
Tries: Martin Gleeson (18), Fa'afili (30, 48), Reardon (61); **Goals:** Bridge 1/1, Briers 0/3;
Field goal: Briers (74).
Rugby Leaguer & League Express Men of the Match: *Harlequins:* Danny Orr; *Wolves:* Martin Gleeson.
Penalty count: 4-7; **Half-time:** 12-8;
Referee: Ben Thaler; **Attendance:** 3,132.

SALFORD CITY REDS 10 CATALANS DRAGONS 0

CITY REDS: 2 David Hodgson; 25 Daley Williams; 19 Stuart Littler; 3 Kevin McGuinness; 5 John Wilshere; 6 Luke Dorn; 7 Luke Robinson; 8 Andy Coley; 9 Malcolm Alker (C); 10 Michael Korkidas; 18 Luke Adamson; 11 Mark Edmondson; 13 Simon Finnigan. Subs (all used): 17 Gareth Haggerty; 20 David Gower; 22 Danny Halliwell; 24 Lee Jewitt.
Tries: Dorn (12), Alker (71); **Goals:** Wilshere 1/2.
DRAGONS: 1 Clint Greenshields; 2 Justin Murphy; 3 John Wilson; 4 Adam Mogg; 5 Dimitri Pelo; 14 Thomas Bosc; 6 Casey McGuire; 20 Adel Fellous; 16 Lionel Teixido; 10 Jerome Guisset (C); 11 Sebastien Raguin; 12 Jason Croker; 13 Gregory Mounis. Subs (all used): 8 David Ferriol; 9 David Berthezene; 17 Cyril Gossard; 19 Alex Chan.
Rugby Leaguer & League Express Men of the Match: *City Reds:* Malcolm Alker; *Dragons:* Alex Chan.
Penalty count: 13-8; **Half-time:** 6-0;
Referee: Steve Ganson; **Attendance:** 4,085.

Sunday 4th March 2007

LEEDS RHINOS 16 HUDDERSFIELD GIANTS 12

RHINOS: 1 Brent Webb; 2 Scott Donald; 3 Clinton Toopi; 4 Keith Senior; 5 Lee Smith; 6 Danny McGuire; 7 Rob Burrow; 10 Jamie Peacock; 9 Matt Diskin; 16 Ryan Bailey; 11 Jamie Jones-Buchanan; 12 Gareth Ellis; 13 Kevin Sinfield (C). Subs (all used): 8 Kylie Leuluai; 15 Jamie Thackray; 14 Ali Lauitiiti; 23 Jordan Tansey.
Tries: Toopi (17), Jones-Buchanan (25), Smith (32);
Goals: Sinfield 2/4.
Sin bin: Webb (32) - fighting, (76) - dissent.
GIANTS: 6 Chris Thorman (C); 21 Matt Gardner; 3 Jamahl Lolesi; 11 Chris Nero; 1 Paul Reilly; 4 Kevin Brown; 7 Robbie Paul; 16 Keith Mason; 9 Brad Drew; 10 John Skandalis; 14 Stuart Jones; 8 Eorl Crabtree; 13 Stephen Wild. Subs (all used): 18 Darrell Griffin; 12 Andy Raleigh; 19 Ryan Hudson; 20 Steve Snitch.
Tries: Crabtree (22), Thorman (79); **Goals:** Thorman 2/3.
Sin bin: Reilly (32) - late challenge on Smith; Lolesi (57) - late challenge on Burrow.
Rugby Leaguer & League Express Men of the Match: *Rhinos:* Gareth Ellis; *Giants:* Brad Drew.
Penalty count: 8-11; **Half-time:** 14-8;
Referee: Ian Smith; **Attendance:** 15,703.

HULL FC 6 WAKEFIELD TRINITY WILDCATS 19

HULL: 14 Motu Tony; 2 Matt Sing; 20 Richard Whiting; 3 Kirk Yeaman; 5 Gareth Raynor; 23 Tommy Lee; 7 Richard Horne; 8 Ewan Dowes; 9 Richard Swain; 10 Garreth Carvell; 11 Lee Radford (C); 16 Danny Tickle; 13 Danny Washbrook. Subs (all used): 4 Sid Domic; 17 Willie Manu; 26 Scott Wheeldon; 15 Paul King.
Try: Tickle (7); **Goals:** Tickle 1/1.
WILDCATS: 21 Matt Blaymire; 22 Peter Fox; 3 Jason Demetriou (C); 17 Kevin Henderson; 5 Semi Tadulala; 6 Jamie Rooney; 7 Ben Jeffries; 8 Adam Watene; 14 Paul March; 25 Richard Moore; 18 Olivier Elima; 12 Duncan MacGillivray; 13 Brett Ferres. Subs (all used): 10 Danny Sculthorpe (D); 11 Ned Catic; 20 Tevita Leo-Latu; 2 Waine Pryce (D).
Tries: Demetriou (3), P March (16), Ferres (69);
Goals: Rooney 3/4; **Field goal:** Rooney (75).
Sin bin: Ferres (33) - obstruction.
On report: Sculthorpe (36) - late tackle on R Horne.
Rugby Leaguer & League Express Men of the Match: *Hull:* Danny Tickle; *Wildcats:* Jamie Rooney.
Penalty count: 9-7; **Half-time:** 6-12;
Referee: Ashley Klein; **Attendance:** 13,229.

ROUND 5

Friday 9th March 2007

WARRINGTON WOLVES 12 ST HELENS 48

WOLVES: 1 Stuart Reardon; 2 Henry Fa'afili; 3 Martin Gleeson; 4 Paul Johnson; 5 Brent Grose; 6 Chris Bridge; 7 Lee Briers (C); 10 Paul Rauhihi; 9 Jon Clarke; 16 Paul Wood; 23 Mike Wainwright; 12 Ben Westwood; 13 Vinnie Anderson. Subs (all used): 8 Chris Leikvoll; 14 Mark Gleeson; 15 Rob Parker; 17 Michael Sullivan.
Tries: Briers (36), Fa'afili (39); **Goals:** Briers 2/2.
SAINTS: 1 Paul Wellens; 2 Ade Gardner; 3 Matt Gidley; 4 Willie Talau; 5 Francis Meli; 6 Leon Pryce; 7 Sean Long (C); 8 Nick Fozzard; 9 Keiron Cunningham; 10 Jason Cayless; 11 Lee Gilmour; 15 Mike Bennett; 12 Jon Wilkin. Subs (all used): 14 James Roby; 17 James Graham; 23 Maurie Fa'asavalu; 25 Steve Bannister.
Tries: Gidley (13, 32, 51), Gardner (32), Meli (42), Bennett (58), Pryce (70, 72), Wellens (79);
Goals: Long 6/9.
Rugby Leaguer & League Express Men of the Match: *Wolves:* Lee Briers; *Saints:* Matt Gidley.
Penalty count: 10-8; **Half-time:** 12-16;
Referee: Ashley Klein; **Attendance:** 13,024.

WIGAN WARRIORS 16 HARLEQUINS 12

WARRIORS: 4 Michael Withers; 2 Mark Calderwood; 3 Phil Bailey; 14 David Vaealiki; 5 Pat Richards; 6 Trent Barrett; 7 Thomas Leuluai; 8 Stuart Fielden; 16 Shane Millard; 10 Iafeta Palea'aesina; 11 Gareth Hock; 12 Bryan Fletcher; 13 Sean O'Loughlin (C). Subs (all used): 9 Mick Higham; 18 Paul Prescott; 19 Harrison Hansen; 21 Danny Hill.
Tries: Withers (21), Vaealiki (65); **Goals:** Richards 4/4.
HARLEQUINS: 1 Mark McLinden; 18 Matt Gafa; 3 Paul Sykes; 4 Tyrone Smith; 2 Jon Wells; 6 Scott Hill; 7 Danny Orr; 10 Daniel Heckenberg; 9 Chad Randall; 15 David Mills; 20 Jon Grayshon; 13 Rob Purdham (C); 23 Henry Paul. Subs (all used): 14 Julien Rinaldi; 17 Louie McCarthy-Scarsbrook; 8 Karl Temata; 16 Chris Melling.
Tries: Heckenberg (15), Hill (38); **Goals:** Sykes 2/2.
On report: T Smith (77) - alleged dangerous tackle.
Rugby Leaguer & League Express Men of the Match: *Warriors:* Trent Barrett; *Harlequins:* Scott Hill.
Penalty count: 6-4; **Half-time:** 10-12;
Referee: Ian Smith; **Attendance:** 14,971.

Saturday 10th March 2007

HULL KINGSTON ROVERS 22 LEEDS RHINOS 20

ROVERS: 1 Ben Cockayne; 21 Luke Dyer; 4 Gareth Morton; 22 Andreas Bauer (D); 5 Byron Ford; 6 Scott Murrell; 7 James Webster (C); 8 Makali Aizue; 9 Ben Fisher; 20 Michael Vella; 16 Jason Netherton; 28 Chris Chester; 14 Stanley Gene. Subs (all used): 10 David Tangata-Toa; 13 Tommy Gallagher; 15 Jim Gannon; 11 Iain Morrison.
Tries: Webster (31), Dyer (45), Bauer (56);
Goals: Morton 5/5.
RHINOS: 1 Brent Webb; 2 Scott Donald; 3 Clinton Toopi; 20 Ashley Gibson; 5 Lee Smith; 6 Danny McGuire; 7 Rob Burrow; 10 Jamie Peacock; 9 Matt Diskin; 16 Ryan Bailey; 11 Jamie Jones-Buchanan; 12 Gareth Ellis; 13 Kevin Sinfield (C). Subs (all used): 8 Kylie Leuluai; 15 Jamie Thackray; 14 Ali Lauitiiti; 23 Jordan Tansey.
Tries: Gibson (11, 65, 79), Smith (35);
Goals: Sinfield 2/4.
Rugby Leaguer & League Express Men of the Match: *Rovers:* James Webster; *Rhinos:* Ashley Gibson.
Penalty count: 10-11; **Half-time:** 8-10;
Referee: Richard Silverwood; **Attendance:** 8,086.

Sunday 11th March 2007

BRADFORD BULLS 56 SALFORD CITY REDS 18

BULLS: 19 Michael Platt; 1 Marcus St Hilaire; 3 Ben Harris; 4 Shontayne Hape; 5 Lesley Vainikolo; 6 Iestyn Harris; 7 Paul Deacon (C); 8 Joe Vagana; 16 Ian Henderson; 10 Andy Lynch; 26 David Solomona; 12 Glenn Morrison; 13 Jamie Langley. Subs (all used): 11 Chris McKenna; 18 Sam Burgess; 14 Chris Feather; 2 Nathan McAvoy.
Tries: Platt (7, 61, 70), Solomona (11), Hape (14, 46), St Hilaire (27), Henderson (50), McKenna (64, 74);
Goals: Deacon 8/10.
CITY REDS: 2 David Hodgson; 25 Daley Williams; 19 Stuart Littler; 3 Kevin McGuinness; 5 John Wilshere; 6 Luke Dorn; 7 Luke Robinson; 8 Andy Coley; 9 Malcolm Alker (C); 10 Michael Korkidas; 18 Luke Adamson; 11 Mark Edmondson; 13 Simon Finnigan. Subs (all used): 17 Gareth Haggerty; 24 Lee Jewitt; 22 Danny Halliwell; 20 David Gower.
Tries: Coley (19), Dorn (40), Williams (79, pen);
Goals: Wilshere 3/3.
Rugby Leaguer & League Express Men of the Match: *Bulls:* Michael Platt; *City Reds:* Malcolm Alker.
Penalty count: 8-7; **Half-time:** 22-12;
Referee: Ben Thaler; **Attendance:** 10,640.

HUDDERSFIELD GIANTS 12 HULL FC 16

GIANTS: 1 Paul Reilly; 21 Matt Gardner; 4 Kevin Brown; 11 Chris Nero; 3 Jamahl Lolesi; 6 Chris Thorman (C); 7 Robbie Paul; 16 Keith Mason; 9 Brad Drew; 10 John Skandalis; 13 Stephen Wild; 8 Eorl Crabtree; 14 Stuart Jones. Subs (all used): 5 Shane Elford; 12 Andy Raleigh; 18 Darrell Griffin; 19 Ryan Hudson.
Tries: Thorman (9, 80); **Goals:** Thorman 2/2.
HULL: 1 Shaun Briscoe; 2 Matt Sing; 3 Kirk Yeaman; 4 Sid Domic; 5 Gareth Raynor; 7 Richard Horne; 23 Tommy Lee; 8 Ewan Dowes; 9 Richard Swain; 10 Garreth Carvell; 11 Lee Radford (C); 16 Danny Tickle; 13 Danny Washbrook. Subs (all used): 14 Motu Tony; 15 Paul King; 17 Willie Manu; 18 Wayne Godwin.
Tries: Briscoe (27), Sing (54), King (64);
Goals: Tickle 2/3.
Rugby Leaguer & League Express Men of the Match: *Giants:* Robbie Paul; *Hull:* Shaun Briscoe.
Penalty count: 3-7; **Half-time:** 6-6;
Referee: Steve Ganson; **Attendance:** 7,188.

WAKEFIELD TRINITY WILDCATS 40 CATALANS DRAGONS 20

WILDCATS: 21 Matt Blaymire; 22 Peter Fox; 3 Jason Demetriou (C); 17 Kevin Henderson; 5 Semi Tadulala; 6 Jamie Rooney; 7 Ben Jeffries; 8 Adam Watene; 14 Paul March; 25 Richard Moore; 18 Olivier Elima; 12 Duncan MacGillivray; 13 Brett Ferres. Subs (all used): 10 Danny Sculthorpe; 11 Ned Catic; 20 Tevita Leo-Latu; 2 Waine Pryce.
Tries: Tadulala (4), Demetriou (22, 78), Jeffries (49), Blaymire (62), Fox (70), Rooney (75); **Goals:** Rooney 6/7.
DRAGONS: 1 Clint Greenshields; 2 Justin Murphy; 18 Vincent Duport; 4 Adam Mogg; 5 Dimitri Pelo; 6 Casey McGuire; 7 Stacey Jones (C); 19 Alex Chan; 16 Lionel Teixido; 8 David Ferriol; 11 Sebastien Raguin; 12 Jason Croker; 13 Gregory Mounis. Subs (all used): 10 Jerome Guisset; 14 Thomas Bosc; 17 Cyril Gossard; 20 Adel Fellous.
Tries: Murphy (15, 40), Croker (37);
Goals: Jones 0/1, Bosc 4/4.
Rugby Leaguer & League Express Men of the Match: *Wildcats:* Jamie Rooney; *Dragons:* Jason Croker.
Penalty count: 7-7; **Half-time:** 10-16;
Referee: Phil Bentham; **Attendance:** 5,332.

ROUND 6

Friday 16th March 2007

SALFORD CITY REDS 6 WIGAN WARRIORS 25

CITY REDS: 2 David Hodgson; 25 Daley Williams; 19 Stuart Littler; 3 Kevin McGuinness; 5 John Wilshere; 6 Luke Dorn; 7 Luke Robinson; 14 Paul Highton; 9 Malcolm Alker (C); 10 Michael Korkidas; 11 Mark Edmondson; 8 Andy Coley; 13 Simon Finnigan. Subs (all used): 23 Jordan Turner; 24 Lee Jewitt; 17 Gareth Haggerty; 16 Andrew Brocklehurst.
Try: McGuinness (78); **Goals:** Wilshere 1/2.
On report:
Coley (62) - alleged high tackle on Calderwood.
WARRIORS: 1 Chris Ashton; 2 Mark Calderwood; 3 Phil Bailey; 14 David Vaealiki; 5 Pat Richards; 6 Trent Barrett; 7 Thomas Leuluai; 8 Stuart Fielden; 9 Mick Higham; 10 Iafeta Palea'aesina; 11 Gareth Hock; 12 Bryan Fletcher; 13 Sean O'Loughlin (C). Subs (all used): 16 Shane Millard; 18 Paul Prescott; 19 Harrison Hansen; 21 Danny Hill.
Tries: Ashton (38), O'Loughlin (53), Calderwood (57);
Goals: Richards 6/6; Field goal: Barrett (74).
Sin bin: Ashton (69) - flopping on Robinson.
Rugby Leaguer & League Express Men of the Match: *City Reds:* Luke Robinson; *Warriors:* Sean O'Loughlin.
Penalty count: 12-10; **Half-time:** 2-8;
Referee: Steve Ganson; **Attendance:** 6,025.

WAKEFIELD TRINITY WILDCATS 26 LEEDS RHINOS 32

WILDCATS: 21 Matt Blaymire; 22 Peter Fox; 3 Jason Demetriou (C); 17 Kevin Henderson; 5 Semi Tadulala; 6 Jamie Rooney; 7 Ben Jeffries; 8 Adam Watene; 14 Paul March; 25 Richard Moore; 18 Olivier Elima; 12 Duncan MacGillivray; 13 Brett Ferres. Subs (all used): 4 Ryan Atkins; 11 Ned Catic; 20 Tevita Leo-Latu; 23 Jason Golden.
Tries: Jeffries (39), Fox (42, 47), Atkins (53, 78);
Goals: Rooney 3/5.
Sin bin: Elima (22) - fighting; P March (25) - interference; Moore (68) - late challenge on McGuire.
On report: Moore (68) - late challenge on McGuire.
RHINOS: 23 Jordan Tansey; 2 Scott Donald; 3 Clinton Toopi; 4 Keith Senior; 20 Ashley Gibson; 6 Danny McGuire; 7 Rob Burrow; 10 Jamie Peacock; 9 Matt Diskin; 16 Ryan Bailey; 11 Jamie Jones-Buchanan; 12 Gareth Ellis; 13 Kevin Sinfield (C). Subs (all used): 8 Kylie Leuluai; 15 Jamie Thackray; 14 Ali Lauitiiti; 18 Ian Kirke.
Tries: Donald (5), Senior (13), Tansey (29), McGuire (35), Bailey (65); **Goals:** Sinfield 5/6, Burrow 1/2.
Sin bin: Senior (22) - fighting.
Rugby Leaguer & League Express Men of the Match: *Wildcats:* Jamie Rooney; *Rhinos:* Jordan Tansey.
Penalty count: 8-18; **Half-time:** 6-24;
Referee: Ashley Klein; **Attendance:** 9,973.

Saturday 17th March 2007

HARLEQUINS 22 BRADFORD BULLS 36

HARLEQUINS: 1 Mark McLinden; 2 Jon Wells; 3 Paul Sykes; 4 Tyrone Smith; 18 Matt Gafa; 6 Scott Hill; 7 Danny Orr; 10 Daniel Heckenberg; 9 Chad Randall; 8 Karl Temata; 13 Rob Purdham (C); 12 Lee Hopkins; 23 Henry Paul. Subs (all used): 14 Julien Rinaldi; 17 Louie McCarthy-Scarsbrook; 20 Jon Grayshon; 16 Chris Melling.
Tries: Sykes (28, 58), Purdham (31, 44), Wells (48);
Goals: Purdham 1/1, Sykes 0/4.
BULLS: 19 Michael Platt; 1 Marcus St Hilaire; 3 Ben Harris; 4 Shontayne Hape; 5 Lesley Vainikolo; 6 Iestyn Harris; 7 Paul Deacon (C); 8 Joe Vagana; 16 Ian Henderson; 10 Andy Lynch; 26 David Solomona; 12

Glenn Morrison; 13 Jamie Langley. Subs (all used): 11 Chris McKenna; 18 Sam Burgess; 14 Chris Feather; 2 Nathan McAvoy.
Tries: Langley (8), Morrison (18, 53), I Harris (62), Vainikolo (66), Platt (72); **Goals:** Deacon 6/6.
Rugby Leaguer & League Express Men of the Match: *Harlequins:* Rob Purdham; *Bulls:* Glenn Morrison.
Penalty count: 5-10; **Half-time:** 8-12;
Referee: Phil Bentham; **Attendance:** 4,011.

HULL FC 24 ST HELENS 12

HULL: 1 Shaun Briscoe; 2 Matt Sing; 4 Sid Domic; 3 Kirk Yeaman; 5 Gareth Raynor; 23 Tommy Lee; 7 Richard Horne; 8 Ewan Dowes; 9 Richard Swain; 15 Paul King; 11 Lee Radford (C); 16 Danny Tickle; 13 Danny Washbrook. Subs (all used): 14 Motu Tony; 17 Willie Manu; 18 Wayne Godwin; 21 Hutch Maiava.
Tries: Domic (34), Yeaman (59), Briscoe (61);
Goals: Tickle 6/7.
On report:
Domic (27) - alleged swinging arm on Gilmour.
SAINTS: 1 Paul Wellens; 2 Ade Gardner; 3 Matt Gidley; 24 Steve Tyrer; 5 Francis Meli; 6 Leon Pryce; 7 Sean Long (C); 8 Nick Fozzard; 9 Keiron Cunningham; 10 Jason Cayless; 11 Lee Gilmour; 15 Mike Bennett; 12 Jon Wilkin. Subs (all used): 14 James Roby; 17 James Graham; 23 Maurie Fa'asavalu; 13 Paul Sculthorpe.
Tries: Graham (20), Wellens (71); **Goals:** Tyrer 2/2.
Sin bin: Pryce (56) - holding down.
Rugby Leaguer & League Express Men of the Match: *Hull:* Shaun Briscoe; *Saints:* Paul Wellens.
Penalty count: 9-7; **Half-time:** 10-6;
Referee: Richard Silverwood; **Attendance:** 12,678.

CATALANS DRAGONS 23 HUDDERSFIELD GIANTS 22

DRAGONS: 1 Clint Greenshields; 14 Thomas Bosc; 18 Vincent Duport; 4 Adam Mogg; 5 Dimitri Pelo; 6 Casey McGuire; 7 Stacey Jones (C); 19 Alex Chan; 16 Lionel Teixido; 8 David Ferriol; 17 Cyril Gossard; 12 Jason Croker; 13 Gregory Mounis. Subs (all used): 10 Jerome Guisset; 11 Sebastien Raguin; 15 Mathieu Griffi; 20 Adel Fellous.
Tries: Bosc (7), Teixido (20), Greenshields (45), Mogg (53); **Goals:** Bosc 3/4; **Field goal:** Jones (39).
GIANTS: 1 Paul Reilly; 21 Matt Gardner; 11 Chris Nero; 4 Kevin Brown; 3 Jamahl Lolesi; 22 Tom Hemingway; 7 Robbie Paul; 16 Keith Mason; 9 Brad Drew (C); 10 John Skandalis; 8 Eorl Crabtree; 14 Stuart Jones; 13 Stephen Wild. Subs (all used): 12 Andy Raleigh; 15 Paul Jackson; 18 Darrell Griffin; 19 Ryan Hudson.
Tries: Nero (23), Hudson (35), Jones (69), Wild (74);
Goals: Hemingway 2/2, Drew 1/2.
Rugby Leaguer & League Express Men of the Match: *Dragons:* Gregory Mounis; *Giants:* Ryan Hudson.
Penalty count: 7-9; **Half-time:** 13-12;
Referee: Ben Thaler; **Attendance:** 8,300.

Sunday 18th March 2007

WARRINGTON WOLVES 30
HULL KINGSTON ROVERS 12

WOLVES: 1 Stuart Reardon; 2 Henry Fa'afili; 3 Martin Gleeson; 4 Paul Johnson; 5 Brent Grose; 13 Vinnie Anderson; 9 Jon Clarke; 10 Paul Rauhihi (C); 17 Michael Sullivan; 8 Chris Leikvoll; 12 Ben Westwood; 11 Adrian Morley; 23 Mike Wainwright. Subs (all used): 14 Mark Gleeson; 15 Rob Parker; 16 Paul Wood; 18 Richie Barnett.
Tries: Fa'afili (7), Johnson (28, 42), Westwood (34), Clarke (56, 65);
Goals: Sullivan 1/1, Clarke 1/3, Westwood 1/2.
ROVERS: 1 Ben Cockayne; 21 Luke Dyer; 4 Gareth Morton; 3 Jon Goddard; 5 Byron Ford; 6 Scott Murrell; 7 James Webster (C); 8 Makali Aizue; 9 Ben Fisher; 20 Michael Vella; 16 Jason Netherton; 28 Chris Chester; 13 Tommy Gallagher. Subs (all used): 10 David Tangata-Toa; 11 Iain Morrison; 14 Stanley Gene; 15 Jim Gannon.
Tries: J Netherton (34), Ford (79); **Goals:** Morton 2/2.
Rugby Leaguer & League Express Men of the Match: *Wolves:* Paul Wood; *Rovers:* Chris Chester.
Penalty count: 10-9; **Half-time:** 16-6;
Referee: Ian Smith; **Attendance:** 10,030.

ROUND 7

Friday 23rd March 2007

HULL FC 20 WIGAN WARRIORS 30

HULL: 1 Shaun Briscoe; 2 Matt Sing; 20 Richard Whiting; 3 Kirk Yeaman; 5 Gareth Raynor; 23 Tommy Lee; 7 Richard Horne; 8 Ewan Dowes; 9 Richard Swain; 15 Paul King; 11 Lee Radford (C); 16 Danny Tickle; 13 Danny Washbrook. Subs (all used): 14 Motu Tony; 17 Willie Manu; 18 Wayne Godwin; 21 Hutch Maiava.
Tries: Maiava (45), Manu (73), R Horne (76);
Goals: Tickle 4/4.
WARRIORS: 1 Chris Ashton; 2 Mark Calderwood; 3 Phil Bailey; 14 David Vaealiki; 5 Pat Richards; 6 Trent Barrett; 7 Thomas Leuluai; 8 Stuart Fielden; 9 Mick Higham; 10 Iafeta Palea'aesina; 11 Gareth Hock; 12 Bryan Fletcher; 13 Sean O'Loughlin (C). Subs (all used): 16 Shane Millard; 18 Paul Prescott; 19 Harrison Hansen; 21 Danny Hill.
Tries: Barrett (31, 58), Richards (34, 63), Ashton (70);
Goals: Richards 5/6.
Rugby Leaguer & League Express Men of the Match: *Hull:* Willie Manu; *Warriors:* Trent Barrett.
Penalty count: 8-7; **Half-time:** 2-12;
Referee: Ashley Klein; **Attendance:** 12,755.

LEEDS RHINOS 28 HARLEQUINS 16

RHINOS: 1 Brent Webb; 2 Scott Donald; 3 Clinton Toopi; 4 Keith Senior; 20 Ashley Gibson; 6 Danny McGuire; 7 Rob Burrow; 10 Jamie Peacock; 9 Matt Diskin; 16 Ryan Bailey; 11 Jamie Jones-Buchanan; 12 Gareth Ellis; 13 Kevin Sinfield (C). Subs (all used): 15 Jamie Thackray; 18 Ian Kirke; 14 Ali Lauitiiti; 23 Jordan Tansey.
Tries: McGuire (7, 33), Webb (10, 43);
Goals: Sinfield 6/6.
HARLEQUINS: 16 Chris Melling; 24 Andy Smith; 3 Paul Sykes; 4 Tyrone Smith; 18 Matt Gafa; 7 Danny Orr; 1 Mark McLinden; 20 Jon Grayshon; 9 Chad Randall; 10 Daniel Heckenberg; 13 Rob Purdham (C); 12 Lee Hopkins; 23 Henry Paul. Subs (all used): 8 Karl Temata; 15 David Mills; 14 Julien Rinaldi; 17 Louie McCarthy-Scarsbrook.
Tries: Melling (23), Gafa (51), Sykes (78);
Goals: Paul 1/2, Purdham 1/1.
Rugby Leaguer & League Express Men of the Match: *Rhinos:* Brent Webb; *Harlequins:* Chad Randall.
Penalty count: 9-5; **Half-time:** 20-4;
Referee: Ben Thaler; **Attendance:** 15,123.

ST HELENS 42 HULL KINGSTON ROVERS 14

SAINTS: 1 Paul Wellens; 2 Ade Gardner; 3 Matt Gidley; 24 Steve Tyrer; 5 Francis Meli; 6 Leon Pryce; 7 Sean Long (C); 8 Nick Fozzard; 9 Keiron Cunningham; 10 Jason Cayless; 11 Lee Gilmour; 15 Mike Bennett; 12 Jon Wilkin. Subs (all used): 14 James Roby; 13 Paul Sculthorpe; 17 James Graham; 23 Maurie Fa'asavalu.
Tries: Meli (14, 77), Graham (24), Fa'asavalu (36), Pryce (43), Sculthorpe (55), Gidley (57), Gilmour (66);
Goals: Tyrer 1/3, Sculthorpe 4/5.
ROVERS: 1 Ben Cockayne; 2 Jon Steel; 3 Jon Goddard; 21 Luke Dyer; 5 Byron Ford; 28 Chris Chester; 6 Scott Murrell; 8 Makali Aizue; 9 Ben Fisher; 20 Michael Vella; 18 Danny Ward (C); 16 Jason Netherton; 14 Stanley Gene. Subs (all used): 4 Gareth Morton; 11 Iain Morrison; 15 Jim Gannon; 23 Pat Weisner.
Tries: Steel (11), Ford (53), Morton (72);
Goals: Murrell 0/1, Morton 1/2.
Rugby Leaguer & League Express Men of the Match: *Saints:* James Graham; *Rovers:* Chris Chester.
Penalty count: 5-10; **Half-time:** 16-4;
Referee: Phil Bentham; **Attendance:** 10,523.

Sunday 25th March 2007

BRADFORD BULLS 22 CATALANS DRAGONS 29

BULLS: 19 Michael Platt; 2 Nathan McAvoy; 3 Ben Harris; 4 Shontayne Hape; 5 Lesley Vainikolo; 6 Iestyn Harris; 7 Paul Deacon (C); 8 Joe Vagana; 16 Ian Henderson; 10 Andy Lynch; 26 David Solomona; 12 Glenn Morrison; 13 Jamie Langley. Subs (all used): 11 Chris McKenna; 9 Terry Newton; 14 Chris Feather; 17 James Evans.
Tries: Deacon (34), Evans (40, 75), Platt (68);
Goals: Deacon 3/4.
Sin bin: Morrison (56) - holding down.
DRAGONS: 1 Clint Greenshields; 14 Thomas Bosc; 3 John Wilson; 4 Adam Mogg; 5 Dimitri Pelo; 6 Casey McGuire; 7 Stacey Jones (C); 19 Alex Chan; 16 Lionel Teixido; 10 Jerome Guisset; 17 Cyril Gossard; 12 Jason Croker; 13 Gregory Mounis. Subs (all used): 8 David Ferriol; 11 Sebastien Raguin; 15 Mathieu Griffi; 26 Luke Quigley (D).
Tries: Bosc (5, 24), Greenshields (45), Ferriol (48), Wilson (79); **Goals:** Bosc 4/6; **Field goal:** Croker (65).
Sin bin: Chan (67) - holding down.
Rugby Leaguer & League Express Men of the Match: *Bulls:* Ian Henderson; *Dragons:* Casey McGuire.
Penalty count: 9-7; **Half-time:** 10-10;
Referee: Ian Smith; **Attendance:** 11,298.

HUDDERSFIELD GIANTS 16 SALFORD CITY REDS 18

GIANTS: 1 Paul Reilly; 2 Martin Aspinwall; 3 Jamahl Lolesi; 11 Chris Nero; 21 Matt Gardner; 6 Chris Thorman (C); 7 Robbie Paul; 16 Keith Mason; 9 Brad Drew; 10 John Skandalis; 14 Stuart Jones; 12 Andy Raleigh; 13 Stephen Wild. Subs (all used): 8 Eorl Crabtree; 15 Paul Jackson; 18 Darrell Griffin; 19 Ryan Hudson.
Tries: Gardner (16), Thorman (40), Raleigh (77);
Goals: Thorman 2/4.
CITY REDS: 2 David Hodgson; 25 Daley Williams; 3 Kevin McGuinness; 23 Jordan Turner; 5 John Wilshere; 6 Luke Dorn; 7 Luke Robinson (C); 10 Michael Korkidas; 27 David Berthezene (D); 14 Paul Highton; 8 Andy Coley; 18 Luke Adamson; 13 Simon Finnigan. Subs (all used): 19 Stuart Littler; 17 Gareth Haggerty; 24 Lee Jewitt; 16 Andrew Brocklehurst.
Tries: Robinson (7, 31), Turner (55); **Goals:** Wilshere 3/3.
Sin bin: Berthezene (26) - interference.
Rugby Leaguer & League Express Men of the Match: *Giants:* Chris Nero; *City Reds:* Luke Robinson.
Penalty count: 9-6; **Half-time:** 10-12;
Referee: Richard Silverwood; **Attendance:** 5,275.

WAKEFIELD TRINITY WILDCATS 30
WARRINGTON WOLVES 24

WILDCATS: 21 Matt Blaymire; 22 Peter Fox; 3 Jason Demetriou (C); 4 Ryan Atkins; 2 Waine Pryce; 6 Jamie Rooney; 7 Ben Jeffries; 8 Adam Watene; 20 Tevita Leo-Latu; 25 Richard Moore; 18 Olivier Elima; 12 Duncan MacGillivray; 13 Brett Ferres. Subs (all used): 17 Kevin Henderson; 11 Ned Catic; 14 Paul March; 23 Jason Golden.
Tries: Fox (3), Atkins (8), P March (35), Pryce (55), Jeffries (58), Leo-Latu (63);
Goals: Rooney 3/5, Jeffries 0/1.
WOLVES: 1 Stuart Reardon; 2 Henry Fa'afili; 3 Martin Gleeson; 4 Paul Johnson; 5 Brent Grose; 6 Chris Bridge; 9 Jon Clarke; 10 Paul Rauhihi (C); 14 Mark Gleeson; 8 Chris Leikvoll; 12 Ben Westwood; 23 Mike Wainwright; 13 Vinnie Anderson. Subs (all used): 17 Michael Sullivan; 15 Rob Parker; 16 Paul Wood; 18 Richie Barnett.
Tries: Wood (22), Fa'afili (40), Bridge (46), Clarke (53);
Goals: Bridge 4/4.
Rugby Leaguer & League Express Men of the Match: *Wildcats:* Ben Jeffries; *Wolves:* Jon Clarke.
Penalty count: 4-10; **Half-time:** 16-12;
Referee: Steve Ganson; **Attendance:** 6,119.

ROUND 8

Thursday 5th April 2007

BRADFORD BULLS 14 LEEDS RHINOS 18

BULLS: 19 Michael Platt; 1 Marcus St Hilaire; 3 Ben Harris; 17 James Evans; 5 Lesley Vainikolo; 6 Iestyn Harris; 7 Paul Deacon (C); 18 Sam Burgess; 9 Terry Newton; 10 Andy Lynch; 11 Chris McKenna; 12 Glenn Morrison; 13 Jamie Langley. Subs (all used): 14 Chris Feather; 8 Joe Vagana; 16 Ian Henderson; 26 David Solomona.
Tries: St Hilaire (28), Vainikolo (45); **Goals:** Deacon 3/5.
RHINOS: 1 Brent Webb; 2 Scott Donald; 3 Clinton Toopi; 4 Keith Senior; 20 Ashley Gibson; 6 Danny McGuire; 7 Rob Burrow; 16 Ryan Bailey; 9 Matt Diskin; 10 Jamie Peacock; 11 Jamie Jones-Buchanan; 12 Gareth Ellis; 13 Kevin Sinfield (C). Subs (all used): 8 Kylie Leuluai; 14 Ali Lauitiiti; 15 Jamie Thackray; 23 Jordan Tansey.
Tries: Donald (12, 77), Ellis (65); **Goals:** Sinfield 3/4.
Sin bin: Webb (22) - high tackle on Evans.
On report: Webb (10) - alleged high tackle on I Harris.
Rugby Leaguer & League Express Men of the Match: *Bulls:* Iestyn Harris; *Rhinos:* Danny McGuire.
Penalty count: 5-4; **Half-time:** 10-6;
Referee: Steve Ganson; **Attendance:** 16,706.

Friday 6th April 2007

HARLEQUINS 30 HULL FC 28

HARLEQUINS: 16 Chris Melling; 2 Jon Wells; 3 Paul Sykes; 18 Matt Gafa; 24 Andy Smith; 1 Mark McLinden; 7 Danny Orr; 10 Daniel Heckenberg; 9 Chad Randall; 17 Louie McCarthy-Scarsbrook; 13 Rob Purdham (C); 23 Henry Paul; 6 Scott Hill. Subs (all used): 14 Julien Rinaldi; 8 Karl Temata; 15 David Mills; 4 Tyrone Smith.
Tries: Wells (12), Heckenberg (17), A Smith (39), Rinaldi (44), McLinden (57); **Goals:** Paul 5/6.
HULL: 1 Shaun Briscoe; 2 Matt Sing; 22 Craig Hall; 3 Kirk Yeaman; 5 Gareth Raynor; 13 Danny Washbrook; 7 Richard Horne; 8 Ewan Dowes; 9 Richard Swain; 26 Scott Wheeldon; 11 Lee Radford (C); 17 Willie Manu; 4 Sid Domic. Subs (all used): 14 Motu Tony; 18 Wayne Godwin; 19 Graeme Horne; 21 Hutch Maiava.
Tries: Domic (5), Yeaman (20), R Horne (49, 69), Hall (71), Sing (74); **Goals:** Hall 2/6.
Rugby Leaguer & League Express Men of the Match: *Harlequins:* Paul Sykes; *Hull:* Sid Domic.
Penalty count: 3-4; **Half-time:** 18-8;
Referee: Ian Smith; **Attendance:** 3,545.

HULL KINGSTON ROVERS 20 CATALANS DRAGONS 34

ROVERS: 1 Ben Cockayne; 2 Jon Steel; 21 Luke Dyer; 3 Jon Goddard; 5 Byron Ford; 28 Chris Chester; 6 Scott Murrell; 15 Jim Gannon; 9 Ben Fisher; 20 Michael Vella; 16 Jason Netherton; 18 Danny Ward (C); 14 Stanley Gene. Subs (all used): 10 David Tangata-Toa; 4 Gareth Morton; 27 Kirk Netherton; 8 Makali Aizue.
Tries: Gene (35), Ford (39), Murrell (68), Dyer (76);
Goals: Morton 2/4.
DRAGONS: 1 Clint Greenshields; 14 Thomas Bosc; 18 Vincent Duport; 4 Adam Mogg; 5 Dimitri Pelo; 6 Casey McGuire; 7 Stacey Jones (C); 19 Alex Chan; 16 Lionel Teixido; 10 Jerome Guisset; 17 Cyril Gossard; 28 Andrew Bentley; 12 Jason Croker. Subs (all used): 8 David Ferriol; 21 Julien Touxagas; 24 Remi Casty; 27 Kane Bentley.
Tries: Croker (4), Pelo (20), Duport (46), Greenshields (53), K Bentley (57), Jones (64); **Goals:** Bosc 5/6.
Rugby Leaguer & League Express Men of the Match: *Rovers:* Stanley Gene; *Dragons:* Stacey Jones.
Penalty count: 7-4; **Half-time:** 10-10;
Referee: Phil Bentham; **Attendance:** 6,701.

SALFORD CITY REDS 32 WARRINGTON WOLVES 34

CITY REDS: 2 David Hodgson; 25 Daley Williams; 5 John Wilshere; 4 Aaron Moule; 23 Jordan Turner; 6 Luke Dorn; 7 Luke Robinson (C); 10 Michael Korkidas; 27 David Berthezene; 14 Paul Highton; 19 Stuart Littler; 8 Andy Coley; 13 Simon Finnigan. Subs (all used): 18 Luke Adamson; 16 Andrew Brocklehurst; 24 Lee Jewitt; 17 Gareth Haggerty.
Tries: Wilshere (8), Robinson (22), Dorn (56), Littler (76), Williams (78), Hodgson (79); **Goals:** Wilshere 4/6.
Sin bin: Williams (44) – obstruction.
WOLVES: 1 Stuart Reardon; 2 Henry Fa'afili; 3 Martin Gleeson; 6 Chris Bridge; 5 Brent Grose; 7 Lee Briers (C); 9 Jon Clarke; 8 Chris Leikvoll; 14 Mark Gleeson; 10 Paul Rauhihi; 23 Mike Wainwright; 22 Ben Harrison; 13 Vinnie Anderson. Subs (all used): 18 Richie Barnett; 19 Steve Pickersgill; 21 Andy Bracek; 25 Michael Cooper.
Tries: Rauhihi (11, 64), Grose (38), Fa'afili (45), Wainwright (71), Bracek (74);
Goals: Briers 5/6, Bridge 0/1.
Sin bin: Leikvoll (25) – late challenge on Robinson.

Huddersfield's Darrell Griffin on the charge against former club Wakefield, as the Giants pick up their first Super League win of 2007

Rugby Leaguer & League Express Men of the Match:
City Reds: Luke Robinson; *Wolves:* Paul Rauhihi.
Penalty count: 8-7; **Half-time:** 12-10;
Referee: Ben Thaler; **Attendance:** 6,177.

WIGAN WARRIORS 14 ST HELENS 32

WARRIORS: 4 Michael Withers; 2 Mark Calderwood; 3 Phil Bailey; 14 David Vaealiki; 5 Pat Richards; 6 Trent Barrett; 7 Thomas Leuluai; 8 Stuart Fielden; 9 Mick Higham; 10 Iafeta Palea'aesina; 11 Gareth Hock; 12 Bryan Fletcher; 13 Sean O'Loughlin (C). Subs (all used): 1 Chris Ashton; 16 Shane Millard; 24 Eamon O'Carroll; 19 Harrison Hansen.
Tries: Richards (6), Leuluai (49); **Goals:** Richards 3/3.
Sin bin: Withers (19) - interference.
SAINTS: 1 Paul Wellens; 2 Ade Gardner; 3 Matt Gidley; 4 Willie Talau; 5 Francis Meli; 6 Leon Pryce; 7 Sean Long; 8 Nick Fozzard; 9 Keiron Cunningham; 10 Jason Cayless; 11 Lee Gilmour; 13 Paul Sculthorpe (C); 12 Jon Wilkin. Subs (all used): 15 Mike Bennett; 14 James Roby; 17 James Graham; 23 Maurie Fa'asavalu.
Tries: Meli (11), Talau (22), Roby (34), Fa'asavalu (43), Gidley (64), Bennett (79);
Goals: Sculthorpe 3/4, Long 1/3.
Rugby Leaguer & League Express Men of the Match:
Warriors: Thomas Leuluai; *Saints:* James Roby.
Penalty count: 10-12; **Half-time:** 8-16;
Referee: Ashley Klein; **Attendance:** 24,028.

HUDDERSFIELD GIANTS 56
WAKEFIELD TRINITY WILDCATS 12

GIANTS: 1 Paul Reilly; 2 Martin Aspinwall; 4 Kevin Brown; 11 Chris Nero; 5 Shane Elford; 9 Brad Drew (C); 7 Robbie Paul; 16 Keith Mason; 19 Ryan Hudson; 10 John Skandalis; 20 Steve Snitch; 12 Andy Raleigh; 13 Stephen Wild. Subs (all used): 6 Chris Thorman; 8 Eorl Crabtree; 14 Stuart Jones; 18 Darrell Griffin.
Tries: Wild (3), Drew (9), Paul (17), Brown (27, 47, 51), Aspinwall (34), Raleigh (44), Jones (52), Reilly (68);
Goals: Drew 4/5, Thorman 4/5.
Sin bin: Brown (65) - obstruction.
WILDCATS: 21 Matt Blaymire; 2 Waine Pryce; 3 Jason Demetriou; 4 Ryan Atkins; 22 Peter Fox; 6 Jamie Rooney; 7 Ben Jeffries; 8 Adam Watene; 20 Tevita Leo-Latu; 25 Richard Moore; 18 Olivier Elima; 12 Duncan MacGillivray; 13 Brett Ferres. Subs (all used): 14 Paul March; 17 Kevin Henderson; 10 Danny Sculthorpe; 11 Ned Catic.
Tries: Moore (39), Blaymire (74); **Goals:** Rooney 2/2.
Rugby Leaguer & League Express Men of the Match:
Giants: Kevin Brown; *Wildcats:* Waine Pryce.
Penalty count: 9-6; **Half-time:** 28-6;
Referee: Richard Silverwood; **Attendance:** 6,757.

ROUND 9

Monday 9th April 2007

HULL FC 22 HULL KINGSTON ROVERS 14

HULL: 1 Shaun Briscoe; 2 Matt Sing; 4 Sid Domic; 3 Kirk Yeaman; 5 Gareth Raynor; 6 Paul Cooke; 7 Richard Horne; 8 Ewan Dowes; 9 Richard Swain; 15 Paul King; 11 Lee Radford (C); 17 Willie Manu; 16 Danny Tickle. Subs (all used): 14 Motu Tony; 13 Danny Washbrook; 21 Hutch Maiava; 26 Scott Wheeldon.
Tries: Tickle (6), Briscoe (18), Sing (49), Domic (80);
Goals: Cooke 3/4.
ROVERS: 3 Jon Goddard; 2 Jon Steel; 21 Luke Dyer; 22 Andreas Bauer; 5 Byron Ford; 6 Scott Murrell; 7 James Webster (C); 8 Makali Aizue; 9 Ben Fisher; 20 Michael Vella; 16 Jason Netherton; 28 Chris Chester; 14 Stanley Gene. Subs (all used): 10 David Tangata-Toa; 13 Tommy Gallagher; 15 Jim Gannon; 18 Danny Ward.
Tries: Dyer (34), Tangata-Toa (54), Bauer (60);
Goals: Murrell 1/3.
Rugby Leaguer & League Express Men of the Match:
Hull: Paul Cooke; *Rovers:* Jon Goddard.
Penalty count: 2-10; **Half-time:** 12-4;
Referee: Steve Ganson; **Attendance:** 23,002.

ST HELENS 48 SALFORD CITY REDS 4

SAINTS: 1 Paul Wellens; 2 Ade Gardner; 3 Matt Gidley; 4 Willie Talau; 5 Francis Meli; 6 Leon Pryce; 7 Sean Long (C); 8 Nick Fozzard; 9 Keiron Cunningham; 10 Jason Cayless; 11 Lee Gilmour; 15 Mike Bennett; 14 James Roby. Subs (all used): 17 James Graham; 20 Scott Moore; 22 Paul Clough; 23 Maurie Fa'asavalu.
Tries: Long (7), Gidley (11), Meli (15), Wellens (25), Gardner (29), Fa'asavalu (41), Bennett (49, 59), Roby (56); **Goals:** Long 2/4, Wellens 4/5.
CITY REDS: 2 David Hodgson; 25 Daley Williams; 3 Kevin McGuinness; 4 Aaron Moule; 5 John Wilshere; 6 Luke Dorn; 7 Luke Robinson (C); 14 Paul Highton; 27 David Berthezene; 10 Michael Korkidas; 8 Andy Coley; 16 Andrew Brocklehurst; 13 Simon Finnigan. Subs (all used): 12 Ian Sibbit; 17 Gareth Haggerty; 18 Luke Adamson; 19 Stuart Littler.
Try: Coley (72); **Goals:** Wilshere 0/1.
Rugby Leaguer & League Express Men of the Match:
Saints: Paul Wellens; *City Reds:* Andy Coley.
Penalty count: 10-7; **Half-time:** 26-0;
Referee: Ian Smith; **Attendance:** 9,409.

WARRINGTON WOLVES 18 HUDDERSFIELD GIANTS 26

WOLVES: 1 Stuart Reardon; 18 Richie Barnett; 3 Martin Gleeson; 6 Chris Bridge; 5 Brent Grose; 9 Jon Clarke; 7

Lee Briers (C); 19 Steve Pickersgill; 14 Mark Gleeson; 10 Paul Rauhihi; 2 Henry Fa'afili; 23 Mike Wainwright; 13 Vinnie Anderson. Subs (all used): 24 Chris Riley; 22 Ben Harrison; 25 Michael Cooper; 21 Andy Bracek.
Tries: Fa'afili (17, 63), Martin Gleeson (45);
Goals: Briers 3/4.
GIANTS: 1 Paul Reilly; 2 Martin Aspinwall; 13 Stephen Wild; 11 Chris Nero; 5 Shane Elford; 4 Kevin Brown; 6 Chris Thorman (C); 16 Keith Mason; 9 Brad Drew; 15 Paul Jackson; 20 Steve Snitch; 12 Andy Raleigh; 19 Ryan Hudson. Subs (all used): 3 Jamahl Lolesi; 8 Eorl Crabtree; 14 Stuart Jones; 18 Darrell Griffin.
Tries: Drew (9), Crabtree (26), Aspinwall (32);
Goals: Thorman 7/7.
Rugby Leaguer & League Express Men of the Match:
Wolves: Lee Briers; *Giants:* Brad Drew.
Penalty count: 14-6; **Half-time:** 8-22;
Referee: Ashley Klein; **Attendance:** 9,403.

WAKEFIELD TRINITY WILDCATS 24
BRADFORD BULLS 36

WILDCATS: 21 Matt Blaymire; 22 Peter Fox; 3 Jason Demetriou; 2 Waine Pryce; 6 Jamie Rooney; 7 Ben Jeffries; 8 Adam Watene; 20 Tevita Leo-Latu; 25 Richard Moore; 18 Olivier Elima; 12 Duncan MacGillivray; 13 Brett Ferres. Subs (all used): 10 Danny Sculthorpe; 11 Ned Catic; 14 Paul March; 23 Jason Golden.
Tries: Blaymire (20), Henderson (47), Fox (55, 69), Rooney (78); **Goals:** Rooney 2/5.
BULLS: 19 Michael Platt; 2 Nathan McAvoy; 3 Ben Harris; 17 James Evans; 5 Lesley Vainikolo; 6 Iestyn Harris; 7 Paul Deacon (C); 8 Joe Vagana; 16 Ian Henderson; 10 Andy Lynch; 26 David Solomona; 12 Glenn Morrison; 13 Jamie Langley. Subs (all used): 11 Chris McKenna; 14 Chris Feather; 15 Matt Cook; 18 Sam Burgess.
Tries: Vainikolo (14, 39), Solomona (17), Henderson (24), Platt (63), McKenna (73); **Goals:** Deacon 6/7.
Rugby Leaguer & League Express Men of the Match:
Wildcats: Matt Blaymire; *Bulls:* Lesley Vainikolo.
Penalty count: 12-10; **Half-time:** 6-24;
Referee: Phil Bentham; **Attendance:** 9,106.

CATALANS DRAGONS 16 HARLEQUINS 38

DRAGONS: 1 Clint Greenshields; 14 Thomas Bosc; 4 Adam Mogg; 18 Vincent Duport; 5 Dimitri Pelo; 6 Casey McGuire; 7 Stacey Jones (C); 19 Alex Chan; 16 Lionel Teixido; 10 Jerome Guisset; 28 Andrew Bentley; 12 Jason Croker; 21 Julien Touxagas. Subs (all used): 8 David Ferriol; 27 Kane Bentley; 15 Mathieu Griffi; 20 Adel Fellous.
Tries: Bosc (6), Pelo (45), Fellous (70); **Goals:** Bosc 2/3.
On report: Chan (79) - alleged elbow on Paul.
HARLEQUINS: 16 Chris Melling; 2 Jon Wells; 3 Paul

Wigan's Shane Millard halted against Leeds as the Warriors pull off a last-gasp win at Headingley

Sykes; 4 Tyrone Smith; 24 Andy Smith; 7 Danny Orr; 1 Mark McLinden; 17 Louie McCarthy-Scarsbrook; 9 Chad Randall; 10 Daniel Heckenberg; 13 Rob Purdham (C); 12 Lee Hopkins; 23 Henry Paul. Subs (all used): 14 Julien Rinaldi; 15 David Mills; 8 Karl Temata; 6 Scott Hill. **Tries:** Wells (2), Randall (15), Orr (22), McLinden (36, 75), Rinaldi (48); **Goals:** Paul 7/8, Purdham 0/1.
Rugby Leaguer & League Express Men of the Match: *Dragons:* Adel Fellous; *Harlequins:* Mark McLinden.
Penalty count: 10-8; **Half-time:** 6-24;
Referee: Ben Thaler; **Attendance:** 9,300.

Tuesday 10th April 2007

LEEDS RHINOS 18 WIGAN WARRIORS 20

RHINOS: 1 Brent Webb; 2 Scott Donald; 3 Clinton Toopi; 4 Keith Senior; 20 Ashley Gibson; 6 Danny McGuire; 7 Rob Burrow; 10 Jamie Peacock; 9 Matt Diskin; 16 Ryan Bailey; 11 Jamie Jones-Buchanan; 12 Gareth Ellis; 13 Kevin Sinfield (C). Subs (all used): 15 Jamie Thackray; 8 Kylie Leuluai; 14 Ali Lauitiiti; 18 Ian Kirke.
Tries: Senior (11), Burrow (59), Ellis (61);
Goals: Sinfield 3/4.
On report: Bailey (22) - alleged high tackle on Fielden.
WARRIORS: 4 Michael Withers; 2 Mark Calderwood; 3 Phil Bailey; 14 David Vaealiki; 5 Pat Richards; 6 Trent Barrett; 7 Thomas Leuluai; 8 Stuart Fielden; 16 Shane Millard; 18 Paul Prescott; 11 Gareth Hock; 12 Bryan Fletcher; 13 Sean O'Loughlin (C). Subs (all used): 10 Iafeta Palea'aesina; 9 Mick Higham; 24 Eamon O'Carroll; 1 Chris Ashton.
Tries: Fletcher (24), Calderwood (45), Bailey (79);
Goals: Richards 4/5.
Sin bin: Fielden (38) - interference;
Hock (67) - interference.
Rugby Leaguer & League Express Men of the Match: *Rhinos:* Jamie Peacock; *Warriors:* Trent Barrett.
Penalty count: 14-11; **Half-time:** 4-8;
Referee: Richard Silverwood; **Attendance:** 16,465.

ROUND 10

Friday 13th April 2007

SALFORD CITY REDS 18 HULL FC 35

CITY REDS: 2 David Hodgson; 15 Gray Viane; 3 Kevin McGuinness; 4 Aaron Moule; 5 John Wilshere; 6 Luke Dorn; 7 Luke Robinson; 8 Andy Coley; 27 David Berthezene; 10 Michael Korkidas; 18 Luke Adamson; 12 Ian Sibbit; 13 Simon Finnigan. Subs (all used): 9 Malcolm Alker (C); 14 Paul Highton; 19 Stuart Littler; 17 Gareth Haggerty.

Tries: Moule (4), Dorn (6), Wilshere (46);
Goals: Wilshere 3/3.
On report: Korkidas (14) - alleged use of the elbow; Haggerty (62) - alleged high tackle on Wheeldon.
HULL: 1 Shaun Briscoe; 2 Matt Sing; 4 Sid Domic; 3 Kirk Yeaman; 5 Gareth Raynor; 6 Paul Cooke; 7 Richard Horne; 8 Ewan Dowes; 9 Richard Swain; 15 Paul King; 11 Lee Radford (C); 17 Willie Manu; 16 Danny Tickle. Subs (all used): 14 Motu Tony; 19 Graeme Horne; 21 Hutch Maiava; 26 Scott Wheeldon.
Tries: Raynor (12, 80), Cooke (16), Sing (23), Tickle (34), R Horne (79); **Goals:** Cooke 5/7;
Field goal: R Horne (76).
Rugby Leaguer & League Express Men of the Match: *City Reds:* Luke Robinson; *Hull:* Paul Cooke.
Penalty count: 11-9; **Half-time:** 12-22;
Referee: Ashley Klein; **Attendance:** 4,077.

ST HELENS 53 CATALANS DRAGONS 10

SAINTS: 1 Paul Wellens; 2 Ade Gardner; 3 Matt Gidley; 4 Willie Talau; 5 Francis Meli; 6 Leon Pryce; 7 Sean Long; 8 Nick Fozzard; 9 Keiron Cunningham; 10 Jason Cayless; 11 Lee Gilmour; 15 Mike Bennett; 13 Paul Sculthorpe (C). Subs (all used): 14 James Roby; 18 Bryn Hargreaves; 22 Paul Clough; 23 Maurie Fa'asavalu.
Tries: Cayless (14), Pryce (19), Cunningham (26), Gidley (33), Wellens (42, 56, 62, 67), Fa'asavalu (74), Meli (77); **Goals:** Sculthorpe 6/10; **Field goal:** Long (39).
DRAGONS: 1 Clint Greenshields; 14 Thomas Bosc; 4 Adam Mogg; 3 John Wilson; 5 Dimitri Pelo; 6 Casey McGuire; 7 Stacey Jones (C); 19 Alex Chan; 16 Lionel Teixido; 10 Jerome Guisset; 12 Jason Croker; 28 Andrew Bentley; 21 Julien Touxagas. Subs (all used): 15 Mathieu Griffi; 8 David Ferriol; 27 Kane Bentley; 20 Adel Fellous.
Tries: Touxagas (7), Pelo (50); **Goals:** Bosc 1/2.
Rugby Leaguer & League Express Men of the Match: *Saints:* Paul Wellens; *Dragons:* Stacey Jones.
Penalty count: 8-3; **Half-time:** 19-6;
Referee: Phil Bentham; **Attendance:** 7,918.

Saturday 14th April 2007

HARLEQUINS 22 WAKEFIELD TRINITY WILDCATS 22

HARLEQUINS: 1 Mark McLinden; 2 Jon Wells; 3 Paul Sykes; 18 Matt Gafa; 24 Andy Smith; 6 Scott Hill; 7 Danny Orr; 17 Louie McCarthy-Scarsbrook; 9 Chad Randall; 10 Daniel Heckenberg; 13 Rob Purdham (C); 12 Lee Hopkins; 23 Henry Paul. Subs (all used): 14 Julien Rinaldi; 8 Karl Temata; 15 David Mills; 4 Tyrone Smith.
Tries: Hill (20), A Smith (33), Sykes (40), Hopkins (62); **Goals:** Paul 2/3, Purdham 1/1.
WILDCATS: 21 Matt Blaymire; 22 Peter Fox; 3 Jason Demetriou; 17 Kevin Henderson; 2 Waine Pryce; 6 Jamie Rooney; 7 Ben Jeffries; 8 Adam Watene; 14 Paul

March; 25 Richard Moore; 11 Ned Catic; 18 Olivier Elima; 12 Duncan MacGillivray. Subs (all used): 16 Ricky Bibey (D); 20 Tevita Leo-Latu; 13 Brett Ferres; 24 Dale Ferguson.
Tries: P March (8), Blaymire (14, 64), Pryce (46); **Goals:** Rooney 3/4.
Rugby Leaguer & League Express Men of the Match: *Harlequins:* Rob Purdham; *Wildcats:* Jamie Rooney.
Penalty count: 3-5; **Half-time:** 16-10;
Referee: Ian Smith; **Attendance:** 2,532.

Sunday 15th April 2007

BRADFORD BULLS 52 HULL KINGSTON ROVERS 22

BULLS: 19 Michael Platt; 2 Nathan McAvoy; 3 Ben Harris; 11 Chris McKenna; 5 Lesley Vainikolo; 6 Iestyn Harris; 7 Paul Deacon (C); 8 Joe Vagana; 16 Ian Henderson; 10 Andy Lynch; 18 Sam Burgess; 26 David Solomona; 13 Jamie Langley. Subs (all used): 24 Dave Halley (D); 9 Terry Newton; 14 Chris Feather; 15 Matt Cook.
Tries: Lynch (9, 48), I Harris (30, 38), Langley (59), Platt (60), B Harris (63), Halley (65), Solomona (72); **Goals:** Deacon 8/9.
ROVERS: 3 Jon Goddard; 2 Jon Steel; 21 Luke Dyer; 22 Andreas Bauer; 24 Ian Hardman (D); 6 Scott Murrell; 14 Stanley Gene; 8 Makali Aizue; 27 Kirk Netherton; 20 Michael Vella; 25 Danny Hill (D); 17 Mark O'Neill. Subs (all used): 10 David Tangata-Toa; 1 Ben Cockayne; 13 Tommy Gallagher; 15 Jim Gannon.
Tries: Steel (17), Gene (33), Tangata-Toa (45), Dyer (79); **Goals:** Murrell 3/4.
Rugby Leaguer & League Express Men of the Match: *Bulls:* Terry Newton; *Rovers:* Luke Dyer.
Penalty count: 5-8; **Half-time:** 18-10;
Referee: Richard Silverwood; **Attendance:** 10,881.

HUDDERSFIELD GIANTS 41 WIGAN WARRIORS 16

GIANTS: 1 Paul Reilly; 2 Martin Aspinwall; 4 Kevin Brown; 11 Chris Nero; 3 Jamahl Lolesi; 6 Chris Thorman (C); 9 Brad Drew; 16 Keith Mason; 19 Ryan Hudson; 10 John Skandalis; 13 Stephen Wild; 12 Andy Raleigh; 20 Steve Snitch. Subs (all used): 15 Paul Jackson; 8 Eorl Crabtree; 14 Stuart Jones; 18 Darrell Griffin.
Tries: Drew (9), Crabtree (33), Wild (38), Reilly (51), Hudson (56), Snitch (73); **Goals:** Thorman 8/10;
Field goal: Thorman (70).
WARRIORS: 1 Chris Ashton; 2 Mark Calderwood; 3 Phil Bailey; 14 David Vaealiki; 5 Pat Richards; 6 Trent Barrett; 7 Thomas Leuluai; 8 Stuart Fielden; 16 Shane Millard; 10 Iafeta Palea'aesina; 11 Gareth Hock; 19 Harrison Hansen; 13 Sean O'Loughlin (C). Subs (all used): 9 Mick Higham; 18 Paul Prescott; 20 Darrell Goulding; 24 Eamon O'Carroll.
Tries: Leuluai (13), Vaealiki (29, 61); **Goals:** Richards 2/3.

Sin bin: Calderwood (47) - holding down.
Rugby Leaguer & League Express Men of the Match: *Giants:* Chris Thorman; *Warriors:* Harrison Hansen.
Penalty count: 7-4; **Half-time:** 18-10;
Referee: Steve Ganson; **Attendance:** 7,117.

WARRINGTON WOLVES 10 LEEDS RHINOS 52

WOLVES: 1 Stuart Reardon; 2 Henry Fa'afili; 3 Martin Gleeson; 5 Brent Grose; 18 Richie Barnett; 13 Vinnie Anderson; 9 Jon Clarke; 10 Paul Rauhihi (C); 14 Mark Gleeson; 21 Andy Bracek; 12 Ben Westwood; 23 Mike Wainwright; 22 Ben Harrison. Subs (all used): 24 Chris Riley; 28 Anthony Jerram (D); 25 Michael Cooper; 19 Steve Pickersgill.
Tries: Westwood (16), Grose (38); **Goals:** Westwood 1/2.
RHINOS: 1 Brent Webb; 5 Lee Smith; 20 Ashley Gibson; 4 Keith Senior; 2 Scott Donald; 6 Danny McGuire; 7 Rob Burrow; 10 Jamie Peacock; 9 Matt Diskin; 16 Ryan Bailey; 11 Jamie Jones-Buchanan; 12 Gareth Ellis; 13 Kevin Sinfield (C). Subs (all used): 15 Jamie Thackray; 18 Ian Kirke; 3 Clinton Toopi; 8 Kylie Leuluai.
Tries: Ellis (31), Toopi (35), Donald (40), Senior (42), Burrow (46, 76), Thackray (55), Webb (66), McGuire (70); **Goals:** Sinfield 8/9.
Rugby Leaguer & League Express Men of the Match: *Wolves:* Vinnie Anderson; *Rhinos:* Danny McGuire.
Penalty count: 2-3; **Half-time:** 10-18;
Referee: Ben Thaler; **Attendance:** 10,155.

ROUND 11

Friday 20th April 2007

HULL FC 22 BRADFORD BULLS 32

HULL: 1 Shaun Briscoe; 2 Matt Sing; 4 Sid Domic; 3 Kirk Yeaman; 5 Gareth Raynor; 6 Paul Cooke; 7 Richard Horne; 8 Ewan Dowes; 9 Richard Swain; 15 Paul King; 16 Danny Tickle; 11 Lee Radford (C); 13 Danny Washbrook. Subs (all used): 14 Motu Tony; 19 Graeme Horne; 10 Garreth Carvell; 21 Hutch Maiava.
Tries: Swain (5), Briscoe (8), Yeaman (43), Tony (69); **Goals:** Cooke 3/5.
BULLS: 19 Michael Platt; 2 Nathan McAvoy; 3 Ben Harris; 17 James Evans; 24 Dave Halley; 6 Iestyn Harris; 7 Paul Deacon (C); 18 Sam Burgess; 9 Terry Newton; 10 Andy Lynch; 11 Chris McKenna; 26 David Solomona; 13 Jamie Langley. Subs (all used): 15 Matt Cook; 16 Ian Henderson; 22 Craig Kopczak; 8 Joe Vagana.
Tries: Evans (25, 74), Newton (28), B Harris (46), Vagana (53), Lynch (78); **Goals:** Deacon 4/6.
Sin bin: Solomona (39) - interference.
Rugby Leaguer & League Express Men of the Match: *Hull:* Richard Swain; *Bulls:* David Solomona.
Penalty count: 9-3; **Half-time:** 12-10;
Referee: Ben Thaler; **Attendance:** 12,767.

WIGAN WARRIORS 44 WAKEFIELD TRINITY WILDCATS 10

WARRIORS: 1 Chris Ashton; 2 Mark Calderwood; 3 Phil Bailey; 14 David Vaealiki; 5 Pat Richards; 6 Trent Barrett; 7 Thomas Leuluai; 8 Stuart Fielden; 16 Shane Millard; 10 Iafeta Palea'aesina; 11 Gareth Hock; 12 Bryan Fletcher; 13 Sean O'Loughlin (C). Subs (all used): 9 Mick Higham; 18 Paul Prescott; 19 Harrison Hansen; 20 Darrell Goulding.
Tries: Vaealiki (15), Richards (22), Barrett (42, 48), Goulding (63), Ashton (68, 80); **Goals:** Richards 8/8.
Sin bin: Fletcher (80) - holding down.
WILDCATS: 21 Matt Blaymire; 2 Waine Pryce; 3 Jason Demetriou (C); 17 Kevin Henderson; 22 Peter Fox; 6 Jamie Rooney; 7 Ben Jeffries; 8 Adam Watene; 14 Paul March; 25 Richard Moore; 11 Ned Catic; 18 Olivier Elima; 12 Duncan MacGillivray. Subs (all used): 4 Ryan Atkins; 16 Ricky Bibey; 20 Tevita Leo-Latu; 13 Brett Ferres.
Tries: Jeffries (24), Demetriou (75); **Goals:** Rooney 1/2.
Rugby Leaguer & League Express Men of the Match: *Warriors:* Trent Barrett; *Wildcats:* Richard Moore.
Penalty count: 9-13; **Half-time:** 14-4;
Referee: Phil Bentham; **Attendance:** 14,108.

Saturday 21st April 2007

LEEDS RHINOS 38 ST HELENS 19

RHINOS: 1 Brent Webb; 2 Scott Donald; 4 Keith Senior; 20 Ashley Gibson; 5 Lee Smith; 6 Danny McGuire; 7 Rob Burrow; 10 Jamie Peacock; 9 Matt Diskin; 16 Ryan Bailey; 11 Jamie Jones-Buchanan; 12 Gareth Ellis; 13 Kevin Sinfield (C). Subs (all used): 15 Jamie Thackray; 3 Clinton Toopi; 8 Kylie Leuluai; 18 Ian Kirke.
Tries: Donald (13), McGuire (23), Toopi (41), Peacock (56), Webb (67), Burrow (78);
Goals: Sinfield 6/7, Burrow 1/1.
SAINTS: 1 Paul Wellens; 24 Steve Tyrer; 28 Dean McGilvray; 4 Willie Talau; 5 Francis Meli; 6 Leon Pryce; 7 Sean Long; 8 Nick Fozzard; 9 Keiron Cunningham; 10 Jason Cayless; 15 Mike Bennett; 13 Paul Sculthorpe (C); 14 James Roby. Subs (all used): 17 James Graham; 23 Maurie Fa'asavalu; 20 Scott Moore; 22 Paul Clough.
Tries: Tyrer (2), Roby (27), Wellens (37);
Goals: Sculthorpe 2/2, Tyrer 1/1; **Field goal:** Long (39).
Rugby Leaguer & League Express Men of the Match: *Rhinos:* Kevin Sinfield; *Saints:* Paul Wellens.
Penalty count: 5-4; **Half-time:** 14-19;
Referee: Ashley Klein; **Attendance:** 21,975.

CATALANS DRAGONS 27 WARRINGTON WOLVES 16

DRAGONS: 1 Clint Greenshields; 29 Olivier Charles (D); 3 John Wilson; 4 Adam Mogg; 5 Dimitri Pelo; 14 Thomas Bosc; 7 Stacey Jones (C); 19 Alex Chan; 27 Kane Bentley; 10 Jerome Guisset; 28 Andrew Bentley; 12 Jason Croker; 21 Julien Touxagas. Subs (all used): 6 Casey McGuire; 8 David Ferriol; 24 Remi Casty; 25 Younes Khattabi.
Tries: Charles (19), McGuire (45), Chan (61), Bosc (78); **Goals:** Bosc 5/5; **Field goal:** Jones (66).
WOLVES: 1 Stuart Reardon; 2 Henry Fa'afili; 3 Martin Gleeson; 5 Brent Grose; 18 Richard Barnett; 9 Jon Clarke; 7 Lee Briers (C); 10 Paul Rauhihi; 14 Mark Gleeson; 21 Andy Bracek; 12 Ben Westwood; 23 Mike Wainwright; 13 Vinnie Anderson. Subs: 24 Chris Riley (not used); 28 Anthony Jerram; 22 Ben Harrison; 25 Michael Cooper.
Tries: Westwood (31, 52), Fa'afili (39); **Goals:** Briers 2/4.
Rugby Leaguer & League Express Men of the Match: *Dragons:* Thomas Bosc; *Wolves:* Martin Gleeson.
Penalty count: 10-7; **Half-time:** 8-10;
Referee: Ian Smith; **Attendance:** 9,050.

Sunday 22nd April 2007

HUDDERSFIELD GIANTS 46 HARLEQUINS 16

GIANTS: 6 Chris Thorman (C); 2 Martin Aspinwall; 11 Chris Nero; 3 Jamahl Lolesi; 1 Paul Reilly; 4 Kevin Brown; 9 Brad Drew; 16 Keith Mason; 19 Ryan Hudson; 10 John Skandalis; 13 Stephen Wild; 12 Andy Raleigh; 14 Stuart Jones. Subs (all used): 15 Paul Jackson; 8 Eorl Crabtree; 20 Steve Snitch; 18 Darrell Griffin.
Tries: Lolesi (7), Reilly (32, 60), Snitch (37, 47), Thorman (49), Nero (57), Wild (71); **Goals:** Thorman 7/10.
HARLEQUINS: 16 Chris Melling; 2 Jon Wells; 3 Paul Sykes; 4 Tyrone Smith; 24 Andy Smith; 7 Danny Orr; 1 Mark McLinden; 15 David Mills; 9 Chad Randall; 10 Daniel Heckenberg; 13 Rob Purdham (C); 12 Lee Hopkins; 6 Scott Hill. Subs (all used): 22 Michael Worrincy; 8 Karl Temata; 20 Jon Grayshon; 25 Zebastian Luisi.
Tries: Randall (20), T Smith (28), Grayshon (77);
Goals: Purdham 2/3.
Sin bin: Hopkins (40) - time wasting.
Rugby Leaguer & League Express Men of the Match: *Giants:* Chris Thorman; *Harlequins:* Rob Purdham.
Penalty count: 9-9; **Half-time:** 20-10;
Referee: Richard Silverwood; **Attendance:** 4,894.

HULL KINGSTON ROVERS 24 SALFORD CITY REDS 28

ROVERS: 1 Ben Cockayne; 22 Andreas Bauer; 3 Jon Goddard; 4 Gareth Morton; 24 Ian Hardman; 28 Chris Chester; 7 James Webster (C); 18 Danny Ward; 9 Ben Fisher; 20 Michael Vella; 25 Danny Hill; 16 Jason Netherton; 17 Mark O'Neill. Subs (all used): 14 Stanley Gene; 15 Jim Gannon; 8 Makali Aizue; 30 Mark Lennon (D).
Tries: Gannon (25), O'Neill (29), Lennon (41), Goddard (62), Bauer (79); **Goals:** Morton 2/5.
CITY REDS: 2 David Hodgson; 15 Gray Viane; 3 Kevin McGuinness; 4 Aaron Moule; 5 John Wilshere; 6 Luke Dorn; 7 Luke Robinson (C); 8 Andy Coley; 27 David Berthezene; 10 Michael Korkidas; 19 Stuart Littler; 12 Ian Sibbit; 13 Simon Finnigan. Subs (all used): 23 Jordan Turner; 18 Luke Adamson; 17 Gareth Haggerty; 11 Mark Edmondson.
Tries: Wilshere (1), Dorn (4), Moule (8), Robinson (47), Hodgson (74); **Goals:** Wilshere 4/5.
Rugby Leaguer & League Express Men of the Match: *Rovers:* Makali Aizue; *City Reds:* Luke Robinson.
Penalty count: 13-3; **Half-time:** 10-16;
Referee: Gareth Hewer; **Attendance:** 6,299.

ROUND 12

Friday 27th April 2007

HULL KINGSTON ROVERS 16 HUDDERSFIELD GIANTS 28

ROVERS: 1 Ben Cockayne; 24 Ian Hardman; 21 Luke Dyer; 3 Jon Goddard; 22 Andreas Bauer; 31 Paul Cooke (D); 7 James Webster (C); 8 Makali Aizue; 9 Ben Fisher; 20 Michael Vella; 28 Chris Chester; 17 Mark O'Neill; 14 Stanley Gene. Subs (all used): 18 Danny Ward; 15 Jim Gannon; 16 Jason Netherton; 30 Mark Lennon.
Tries: Bauer (20), Gene (52); **Goals:** Cooke 4/4.
Sin bin: O'Neill (70) - alleged late challenge on Hudson.
On report: O'Neill (70) - alleged late challenge on Hudson.
GIANTS: 6 Chris Thorman (C); 1 Paul Reilly; 3 Jamahl Lolesi; 13 Stephen Wild; 2 Martin Aspinwall; 9 Brad Drew; 4 Kevin Brown; 16 Keith Mason; 19 Ryan Hudson; 10 John Skandalis; 11 Chris Nero; 12 Andy Raleigh; 14 Stuart Jones. Subs (all used): 8 Eorl Crabtree; 15 Paul Jackson; 18 Darrell Griffin; 20 Steve Snitch.
Tries: Jones (10), Raleigh (14), Wild (65), Lolesi (75);
Goals: Thorman 6/6.
Rugby Leaguer & League Express Men of the Match: *Rovers:* Paul Cooke; *Giants:* Brad Drew.
Penalty count: 6-7; **Half-time:** 8-12;
Referee: Phil Bentham; **Attendance:** 6,597.

LEEDS RHINOS 54 CATALANS DRAGONS 8

RHINOS: 1 Brent Webb; 2 Scott Donald; 20 Ashley Gibson; 4 Keith Senior; 5 Lee Smith; 6 Danny McGuire; 7 Rob Burrow; 10 Jamie Peacock; 9 Matt Diskin; 16 Ryan Bailey; 11 Jamie Jones-Buchanan; 12 Gareth Ellis; 13 Kevin Sinfield (C). Subs (all used): 15 Jamie Thackray; 8 Kylie Leuluai; 3 Clinton Toopi; 18 Ian Kirke.
Tries: Webb (9, 21, 64), Toopi (33), Sinfield (41, 79), Ellis (45), Donald (72), Burrow (74); **Goals:** Sinfield 9/9.
DRAGONS: 1 Clint Greenshields; 5 Dimitri Pelo; 4 Adam Mogg; 3 John Wilson; 29 Olivier Charles; 14 Thomas Bosc; 7 Stacey Jones (C); 19 Alex Chan; 26 Luke Quigley; 10 Jerome Guisset; 28 Andrew Bentley; 17 Cyril Gossard; 21 Julien Touxagas. Subs (all used): 24 Remi Casty; 6 Casey McGuire; 8 David Ferriol; 25 Younes Khattabi.
Tries: Charles (5), Mogg (53); **Goals:** Bosc 0/2.
Sin bin: Mogg (25) - interference.
Rugby Leaguer & League Express Men of the Match: *Rhinos:* Gareth Ellis; *Dragons:* Cyril Gossard.
Penalty count: 12-5; **Half-time:** 18-4;
Referee: Ben Thaler; **Attendance:** 15,581.

SALFORD CITY REDS 24 WIGAN WARRIORS 50

CITY REDS: 2 David Hodgson; 15 Gray Viane; 3 Kevin McGuinness; 4 Aaron Moule; 5 John Wilshere; 6 Luke Dorn; 7 Luke Robinson (C); 8 Andy Coley; 27 David Berthezene; 10 Michael Korkidas; 19 Stuart Littler; 12 Ian Sibbit; 13 Simon Finnigan. Subs (all used): 18 Luke Adamson; 11 Mark Edmondson; 23 Jordan Turner; 24 Lee Jewitt.
Tries: Coley (7, 17), Finnigan (29), Moule (58);
Goals: Wilshere 4/4.
WARRIORS: 1 Chris Ashton; 2 Mark Calderwood; 3 Phil Bailey; 14 David Vaealiki; 5 Pat Richards; 6 Trent Barrett; 7 Thomas Leuluai; 8 Stuart Fielden; 16 Shane Millard; 10 Iafeta Palea'aesina; 11 Gareth Hock; 12 Bryan Fletcher; 13 Sean O'Loughlin (C). Subs (all used): 9 Mick Higham; 18 Paul Prescott; 19 Harrison Hansen; 20 Darrell Goulding.
Tries: Bailey (1), Barrett (12, 25, 53), Leuluai (39), Hansen (42), Millard (61, 65), Goulding (75);
Goals: Richards 7/9.
Rugby Leaguer & League Express Men of the Match: *City Reds:* Andy Coley; *Warriors:* Trent Barrett.
Penalty count: 9-6; **Half-time:** 18-24;
Referee: Richard Silverwood; **Attendance:** 6,603.

Saturday 28th April 2007

WAKEFIELD TRINITY WILDCATS 18 HULL FC 20

WILDCATS: 21 Matt Blaymire; 2 Waine Pryce; 3 Jason Demetriou (C); 4 Ryan Atkins; 22 Peter Fox; 6 Jamie Rooney; 7 Ben Jeffries; 8 Adam Watene; 13 Brett Ferres; 25 Richard Moore; 17 Kevin Henderson; 12 Duncan MacGillivray; 23 Jason Golden. Subs (all used): 11 Ned Catic; 16 Ricky Bibey; 20 Tevita Leo-Latu; 29 Mark Applegarth.
Tries: Jeffries (7), Golden (28), Atkins (44, 77);
Goals: Rooney 1/4.
HULL: 1 Shaun Briscoe; 2 Matt Sing; 4 Sid Domic; 3 Kirk Yeaman; 5 Gareth Raynor; 13 Danny Washbrook; 24 Anthony Thackeray (D); 8 Ewan Dowes; 9 Richard Swain; 15 Paul King; 11 Lee Radford (C); 16 Danny Tickle; 12 Shayne McMenemy. Subs (all used): 14 Motu Tony; 19 Graeme Horne; 18 Wayne Godwin; 10 Garreth Carvell.
Tries: McMenemy (13), Briscoe (24), Yeaman (61);
Goals: Tickle 4/5.
Rugby Leaguer & League Express Men of the Match: *Wildcats:* Jason Demetriou; *Hull:* Anthony Thackeray.
Penalty count: 5-9; **Half-time:** 10-14;
Referee: Steve Ganson; **Attendance:** 7,142.

Sunday 29th April 2007

BRADFORD BULLS 36 WARRINGTON WOLVES 24

BULLS: 19 Michael Platt; 2 Nathan McAvoy; 3 Ben Harris; 17 James Evans; 5 Lesley Vainikolo; 6 Iestyn Harris; 7 Paul Deacon (C); 8 Joe Vagana; 9 Terry Newton; 10 Andy Lynch; 11 Chris McKenna; 26 David Solomona; 13 Jamie Langley. Subs (all used): 24 Dave Halley; 15 Matt Cook; 16 Ian Henderson; 18 Sam Burgess.
Tries: Deacon (3), Vainikolo (21), Platt (27, 60), Langley (66), Evans (71); **Goals:** Deacon 3/3, I Harris 3/5.
WOLVES: 1 Stuart Reardon; 2 Henry Fa'afili; 3 Martin Gleeson; 4 Paul Johnson; 5 Brent Grose; 6 Chris Bridge; 7 Lee Briers (C); 10 Paul Rauhihi; 9 Jon Clarke; 11 Adrian Morley; 12 Ben Westwood; 23 Mike Wainwright; 13 Vinnie Anderson. Subs (all used): 8 Chris Leikvoll; 19 Steve Pickersgill; 22 Ben Harrison; 18 Richie Barnett.
Tries: Grose (7), Anderson (32), Briers (37, 79);
Goals: Briers 4/4.
On report: Morley (25) - alleged late challenge on I Harris.
Rugby Leaguer & League Express Men of the Match: *Bulls:* Iestyn Harris; *Wolves:* Lee Briers.
Penalty count: 17-7; **Half-time:** 18-18;
Referee: Ashley Klein; **Attendance:** 11,276.

HARLEQUINS 6 ST HELENS 44

HARLEQUINS: 1 Mark McLinden; 2 Jon Wells; 4 Tyrone Smith; 25 Zebastian Luisi; 16 Chris Melling; 6 Scott Hill; 7 Danny Orr; 8 Karl Temata; 9 Chad Randall; 10 Daniel Heckenberg; 12 Lee Hopkins; 20 Jon Grayshon; 13 Rob Purdham (C). Subs (all used): 14 Julien Rinaldi; 22 Michael Worrincy; 17 Louie McCarthy-Scarsbrook; 24 Andy Smith.
Try: Melling (24); **Goals:** Purdham 1/1.
SAINTS: 1 Paul Wellens; 24 Steve Tyrer; 3 Matt Gidley; 4 Willie Talau; 5 Francis Meli; 6 Leon Pryce; 7 Sean Long; 8 Nick Fozzard; 9 Keiron Cunningham; 10 Jason Cayless; 13 Paul Sculthorpe (C); 15 Mike Bennett; 18 Bryn Hargreaves. Subs (all used): 14 James Roby; 17 James Graham; 22 Paul Clough; 23 Maurie Fa'asavalu.
Tries: Pryce (11), Sculthorpe (17), Gidley (36, 78), Meli (40), Tyrer (51), Wellens (55, 64), Talau (57);
Goals: Sculthorpe 3/8, Wellens 1/1.
Rugby Leaguer & League Express Men of the Match: *Harlequins:* Mark McLinden; *Saints:* Willie Talau.
Penalty count: 10-3; **Half-time:** 6-20;
Referee: Ian Smith; **Attendance:** 4,362.

ROUND 13 - MILLENNIUM MAGIC

Saturday 5th May 2007

CATALANS DRAGONS 28 HARLEQUINS 32

DRAGONS: 1 Clint Greenshields; 2 Justin Murphy; 3 John Wilson; 4 Adam Mogg; 18 Vincent Duport; 14 Thomas Bosc; 7 Stacey Jones (C); 24 Remi Casty; 26 Luke Quigley; 19 Alex Chan; 28 Andrew Bentley; 21 Julien Touxagas; 17 Cyril Gossard. Subs (all used): 6 Casey McGuire; 8 David Ferriol; 10 Jerome Guisset; 16 Lionel Teixido.
Tries: Greenshields (23), Jones (26, 55), Wilson (48), A Bentley (60); **Goals:** Bosc 4/5.
HARLEQUINS: 16 Chris Melling; 2 Jon Wells; 3 Paul Sykes; 4 Tyrone Smith; 24 Andy Smith; 7 Danny Orr; 1 Mark McLinden; 8 Karl Temata; 9 Chad Randall; 10 Daniel Heckenberg; 13 Rob Purdham (C); 12 Lee Hopkins; 6 Scott Hill. Subs (all used): 14 Julien Rinaldi; 20 Jon Grayshon; 26 Joe Walsh (D); 27 Luke Burgess (D).
Tries: A Smith (3), Wells (8), Randall (32, 74), Sykes (64); **Goals:** Purdham 6/6.
Rugby Leaguer & League Express Men of the Match: *Dragons:* Stacey Jones; *Harlequins:* Rob Purdham.
Penalty count: 1-6; **Half-time:** 12-18;
Referee: Phil Bentham.

HULL FC 10 HULL KINGSTON ROVERS 14

HULL: 1 Shaun Briscoe; 2 Matt Sing; 4 Sid Domic; 3 Kirk Yeaman; 5 Gareth Raynor; 13 Danny Washbrook; 7 Richard Horne; 8 Ewan Dowes; 9 Richard Swain; 15 Paul King; 11 Lee Radford (C); 17 Willie Manu; 16 Danny Tickle. Subs (all used): 14 Motu Tony; 19 Graeme Horne; 18 Wayne Godwin; 10 Garreth Carvell.
Tries: Raynor (40), Domic (48); **Goals:** Tickle 1/2.
ROVERS: 1 Ben Cockayne; 24 Ian Hardman; 21 Luke Dyer; 3 Jon Goddard; 5 Byron Ford; 31 Paul Cooke; 7 James Webster (C); 8 Makali Aizue; 9 Ben Fisher; 15 Jim Gannon; 28 Chris Chester; 17 Mark O'Neill; 14 Stanley Gene. Subs (all used): 18 Danny Ward; 10 David Tangata-Toa; 16 Jason Netherton; 30 Mark Lennon.
Tries: Aizue (4), Cockayne (24); **Goals:** Cooke 3/3.
Rugby Leaguer & League Express Men of the Match: *Hull:* Richard Swain; *Rovers:* Paul Cooke.
Penalty count: 9-4; **Half-time:** 6-14;
Referee: Richard Silverwood.

ST HELENS 34 WIGAN WARRIORS 18

SAINTS: 1 Paul Wellens; 24 Steve Tyrer; 3 Matt Gidley; 4 Willie Talau; 5 Francis Meli; 6 Leon Pryce; 7 Sean Long; 8 Nick Fozzard; 9 Keiron Cunningham; 10 Jason Cayless; 12 Jon Wilkin; 13 Paul Sculthorpe (C); 18 Bryn Hargreaves. Subs (all used): 14 James Roby; 17 James Graham; 22 Paul Clough; 23 Maurie Fa'asavalu.
Tries: Meli (7), Wellens (16, 25, 45, 61), Gidley (22); **Goals:** Sculthorpe 5/7.
WARRIORS: 1 Chris Ashton; 2 Mark Calderwood; 3 Phil Bailey; 14 David Vaealiki; 5 Pat Richards; 6 Trent Barrett; 7 Thomas Leuluai; 8 Stuart Fielden; 16 Shane Millard; 10 Iafeta Palea'aesina; 11 Gareth Hock; 12 Bryan Fletcher; 13 Sean O'Loughlin (C). Subs (all used): 9 Mick Higham; 18 Paul Prescott; 19 Harrison Hansen; 20 Darrell Goulding.
Tries: Fletcher (12), Ashton (54), Goulding (66); **Goals:** Richards 3/3.
Rugby Leaguer & League Express Men of the Match: *Saints:* Paul Wellens; *Warriors:* Trent Barrett.
Penalty count: 7-4; **Half-time:** 22-6;
Referee: Ashley Klein.

Attendance: 32,384 *(at Millennium Stadium, Cardiff).*

Sunday 6th May 2007

HUDDERSFIELD GIANTS 36
WAKEFIELD TRINITY WILDCATS 12

GIANTS: 6 Chris Thorman (C); 1 Paul Reilly; 11 Chris Nero; 3 Jamahl Lolesi; 2 Martin Aspinwall; 4 Kevin Brown; 9 Brad Drew; 16 Keith Mason; 19 Ryan Hudson; 10 John Skandalis; 20 Steve Snitch; 12 Andy Raleigh; 13 Stephen Wild. Subs (all used): 15 Paul Jackson; 18 Darrell Griffin; 7 Robbie Paul; 8 Eorl Crabtree.
Tries: Wild (21, 36), Thorman (33), Paul (43), Lolesi (48), Aspinwall (73); **Goals:** Thorman 6/9.
Sin bin: Lolesi (66) - professional foul.
On report: Raleigh (26) - alleged high tackle on Jeffries.
WILDCATS: 21 Matt Blaymire; 22 Peter Fox; 3 Jason Demetriou (C); 4 Ryan Atkins; 28 Paul White; 6 Jamie Rooney; 7 Ben Jeffries; 8 Adam Watene; 9 Sam Obst; 12 Duncan MacGillivray; 13 Brett Ferres; 17 Kevin Henderson; 23 Jason Golden. Subs (all used): 25 Richard Moore; 11 Ned Catic; 16 Ricky Bibey; 18 Olivier Elima.
Tries: White (39), Rooney (79); **Goals:** Rooney 2/3.
Rugby Leaguer & League Express Men of the Match: *Giants:* Brad Drew; *Wildcats:* Richard Moore.
Penalty count: 8-8; **Half-time:** 20-6; **Referee:** Ian Smith.

SALFORD CITY REDS 18 WARRINGTON WOLVES 50

CITY REDS: 2 David Hodgson; 15 Gray Viane; 3 Kevin McGuinness; 23 Jordan Turner; 5 John Wilshere; 6 Luke Dorn; 7 Luke Robinson (C); 11 Mark Edmondson; 27 David Berthezene; 10 Michael Korkidas; 19 Stuart Littler; 12 Ian Sibbit; 13 Simon Finnigan. Subs (all used): 17 Gareth Haggerty; 18 Luke Adamson; 24 Lee Jewitt; 16 Andrew Brocklehurst.
Tries: Dorn (28), McGuinness (68), Brocklehurst (70); **Goals:** Wilshere 3/3.
WOLVES: 1 Stuart Reardon; 2 Henry Fa'afili; 3 Martin Gleeson; 5 Brent Grose; 18 Richie Barnett; 7 Lee Briers (C); 13 Vinnie Anderson; 10 Paul Rauhihi; 9 Jon Clarke; 11 Adrian Morley; 4 Paul Johnson; 23 Mike Wainwright; 12 Ben Westwood. Subs (all used): 8 Chris Leikvoll; 14 Mark Gleeson; 15 Rob Parker; 22 Ben Harrison.
Tries: Johnson (9), Briers (13), Anderson (22, 60), Fa'afili (36), Reardon (43), Martin Gleeson (52, 55), Barnett (58), Clarke (76);
Goals: Briers 3/7, Westwood 2/3.
Rugby Leaguer & League Express Men of the Match: *City Reds:* Kevin McGuinness; *Wolves:* Vinnie Anderson.
Penalty count: 2-3; **Half-time:** 6-18; **Referee:** Ben Thaler.

BRADFORD BULLS 38 LEEDS RHINOS 42

BULLS: 19 Michael Platt; 2 Nathan McAvoy; 3 Ben Harris; 17 James Evans; 5 Lesley Vainikolo; 6 Iestyn Harris; 7 Paul Deacon (C); 8 Joe Vagana; 9 Terry Newton; 10 Andy Lynch; 15 Matt Cook; 26 David Solomona; 13 Jamie Langley. Subs (all used): 24 Dave Halley; 16 Ian Henderson; 22 Craig Kopczak; 18 Sam Burgess.
Tries: Platt (7, 23), Vainikolo (32), Henderson (38), B Harris (49), Lynch (62); **Goals:** Deacon 7/7.
On report: Newton (8) - alleged high tackle on Thackray.
RHINOS: 1 Brent Webb; 2 Scott Donald; 3 Clinton Toopi; 4 Keith Senior; 5 Lee Smith; 6 Danny McGuire; 7 Rob Burrow; 15 Jamie Thackray; 13 Kevin Sinfield (C); 8 Kylie Leuluai; 11 Jamie Jones-Buchanan; 18 Ian Kirke; 12 Gareth Ellis. Subs (all used): 25 Ryan Hall (D); 14 Ali Lauitiiti; 22 Carl Ablett; 23 Jordan Tansey.
Tries: Jones-Buchanan (11), Webb (14, 43, 67), Senior (37), Burrow (53), Tansey (80); **Goals:** Sinfield 7/8.
Sin bin: Webb (45) - dissent.
Rugby Leaguer & League Express Men of the Match: *Bulls:* Michael Platt; *Rhinos:* Kevin Sinfield.
Penalty count: 5-5; **Half-time:** 26-18;
Referee: Steve Ganson.

Attendance: 26,447 *(at Millennium Stadium, Cardiff).*

ROUND 14

Friday 18th May 2007

HUDDERSFIELD GIANTS 36 BRADFORD BULLS 12

GIANTS: 6 Chris Thorman (C); 2 Martin Aspinwall; 11 Chris Nero; 3 Jamahl Lolesi; 1 Paul Reilly; 4 Kevin Brown; 9 Brad Drew; 16 Keith Mason; 19 Ryan Hudson; 10 John Skandalis; 14 Stuart Jones; 12 Andy Raleigh; 13 Stephen Wild. Subs (all used): 7 Robbie Paul; 8 Eorl Crabtree; 15 Paul Jackson; 18 Darrell Griffin.
Tries: Wild (9), Skandalis (18), Jones (33), Thorman (36, 80), Brown (62); **Goals:** Thorman 6/7.
BULLS: 1 Marcus St Hilaire; 2 Nathan McAvoy; 3 Ben Harris; 17 James Evans; 5 Lesley Vainikolo; 6 Iestyn Harris; 27 Richie Hawkyard (D); 8 Joe Vagana; 16 Ian Henderson; 10 Andy Lynch; 26 David Solomona; 12 Glenn Morrison (C); 18 Sam Burgess. Subs (all used): 11 Chris McKenna; 22 Craig Kopczak; 23 Matt James; 24 Dave Halley.
Tries: Vainikolo (46), B Harris (74); **Goals:** I Harris 2/2.
Rugby Leaguer & League Express Men of the Match: *Giants:* Chris Thorman; *Bulls:* Marcus St Hilaire.
Penalty count: 5-4; **Half-time:** 24-0;
Referee: Phil Bentham; **Attendance:** 8,667.

ST HELENS 34 WAKEFIELD TRINITY WILDCATS 14

SAINTS: 1 Paul Wellens; 2 Ade Gardner; 3 Matt Gidley; 4 Willie Talau; 28 Dean McGilvray; 6 Leon Pryce; 21 Matty Smith; 8 Nick Fozzard; 9 Keiron Cunningham; 10 Jason Cayless; 12 Jon Wilkin; 13 Paul Sculthorpe (C); 18 Bryn Hargreaves. Subs (all used): 14 James Roby; 17 James Graham; 22 Paul Clough; 23 Maurie Fa'asavalu.
Tries: Gidley (5, 52), Pryce (20), Gardner (35), Wellens (56, 71); **Goals:** Sculthorpe 5/7.
WILDCATS: 6 Jamie Rooney; 2 Waine Pryce; 33 Sean Gleeson (D); 3 Jason Demetriou (C); 28 Paul White; 9 Sam Obst; 14 Paul March; 25 Richard Moore; 15 David March; 12 Duncan MacGillivray; 11 Ned Catic; 13 Brett Ferres; 17 Kevin Henderson. Subs (all used): 7 Ben Jeffries; 16 Ricky Bibey; 23 Jason Golden; 18 Olivier Elima.
Tries: Gleeson (2), Elima (74); **Goals:** Rooney 3/3.
Sin bin: D March (65) – dissent.
Rugby Leaguer & League Express Men of the Match: *Saints:* Paul Sculthorpe; *Wildcats:* David March.
Penalty count: 7-3; **Half-time:** 16-8;
Referee: Gareth Hewer; **Attendance:** 8,529.

WIGAN WARRIORS 10 HULL KINGSTON ROVERS 12

WARRIORS: 1 Chris Ashton; 2 Mark Calderwood; 3 Phil Bailey; 14 David Vaealiki; 5 Pat Richards; 6 Trent Barrett; 7 Thomas Leuluai; 8 Stuart Fielden; 16 Shane Millard; 10 Iafeta Palea'aesina; 11 Gareth Hock; 19 Harrison Hansen; 13 Sean O'Loughlin (C). Subs (all used): 9 Mick Higham; 24 Eamon O'Carroll; 22 Joel Tomkins; 20 Darrell Goulding.
Tries: Barrett (48), Richards (69); **Goals:** Richards 1/2.
ROVERS: 1 Ben Cockayne; 24 Ian Hardman; 21 Luke Dyer; 3 Jon Goddard; 5 Byron Ford; 31 Paul Cooke; 7 James Webster (C); 20 Michael Vella; 9 Ben Fisher; 15 Jim Gannon; 17 Mark O'Neill; 28 Chris Chester; 14 Stanley Gene. Subs (all used): 30 Mark Lennon; 16 Jason Netherton; 18 Danny Ward; 10 David Tangata-Toa.
Tries: Dyer (28), Hardman (35); **Goals:** Cooke 2/4.
Rugby Leaguer & League Express Men of the Match: *Warriors:* Iafeta Palea'aesina; *Rovers:* Luke Dyer.
Penalty count: 9-9; **Half-time:** 0-10;
Referee: Ronnie Laughton; **Attendance:** 13,538.

Saturday 19th May 2007

CATALANS DRAGONS 66 SALFORD CITY REDS 6

DRAGONS: 1 Clint Greenshields; 2 Justin Murphy; 3 John Wilson; 4 Adam Mogg; 14 Thomas Bosc; 6 Casey McGuire; 7 Stacey Jones (C); 19 Alex Chan; 26 Luke Quigley; 10 Jerome Guisset; 17 Cyril Gossard; 21 Julien Touxagas; 13 Gregory Mounis. Subs (all used): 8 David Ferriol; 15 Mathieu Griffi; 22 Jamel Fakir; 28 Andrew Bentley.
Tries: Murphy (7, 66, 67), Mogg (11, 41), Gossard (15), Bosc (18, 21), McGuire (27, 31), Guisset (63), Greenshields (78); **Goals:** Bosc 9/13.
CITY REDS: 2 David Hodgson; 5 John Wilshere; 3 Kevin McGuinness; 23 Jordan Turner; 15 Gray Viane; 6 Luke Dorn; 7 Luke Robinson; 24 Lee Jewitt; 9 Malcolm Alker (C); 10 Michael Korkidas; 8 Andy Coley; 16 Andrew Brocklehurst; 13 Simon Finnigan. Subs (all used): 18 Luke Adamson; 19 Stuart Littler; 20 David Gower; 27 David Berthezene.
Try: Dorn (53); **Goals:** Wilshere 1/1.
Rugby Leaguer & League Express Men of the Match: *Dragons:* Adam Mogg; *City Reds:* Kevin McGuinness.
Penalty count: 12-5; **Half-time:** 38-0;
Referee: Richard Silverwood; **Attendance:** 8,820.

WARRINGTON WOLVES 4 HARLEQUINS 17

WOLVES: 1 Stuart Reardon; 2 Henry Fa'afili; 3 Martin Gleeson; 4 Paul Johnson; 5 Brent Grose; 7 Lee Briers (C); 13 Vinnie Anderson; 10 Paul Rauhihi; 9 Jon Clarke; 8 Chris Leikvoll; 12 Ben Westwood; 11 Adrian Morley; 23 Mike Wainwright. Subs (all used): 14 Mark Gleeson; 15 Rob Parker; 16 Paul Wood; 22 Ben Harrison.
Try: Martin Gleeson (22); **Goals:** Briers 0/1.
On report: Morley (60) - alleged high tackle.
HARLEQUINS: 16 Chris Melling; 18 Matt Gafa; 3 Paul Sykes; 4 Tyrone Smith; 19 Tony Clubb; 1 Mark McLinden; 7 Danny Orr; 8 Karl Temata; 9 Chad Randall; 10 Daniel Heckenberg; 13 Rob Purdham (C); 12 Lee Hopkins; 26 Joe Walsh. Subs (all used): 14 Julien Rinaldi; 15 David Mills; 20 Jon Grayshon; 27 Luke Burgess.
Tries: Gafa (18), Purdham (33), Rinaldi (37);
Goals: Purdham 2/4; **Field goal:** Sykes (78).
Rugby Leaguer & League Express Men of the Match: *Wolves:* Stuart Reardon; *Harlequins:* Rob Purdham.
Penalty count: 6-8; **Half-time:** 4-14;
Referee: Ben Thaler; **Attendance:** 7,818.

Sunday 20th May 2007

HULL FC 16 LEEDS RHINOS 12

HULL: 1 Shaun Briscoe; 2 Matt Sing; 22 Craig Hall; 3 Kirk Yeaman; 5 Gareth Raynor; 7 Richard Horne; 23 Tommy Lee; 8 Ewan Dowes; 9 Richard Swain; 10 Garreth Carvell; 11 Lee Radford (C); 17 Willie Manu; 16 Danny Tickle. Subs (all used): 14 Motu Tony; 4 Sid Domic; 15 Paul King; 21 Hutch Maiava.
Tries: Sing (14), Briscoe (34); **Goals:** Tickle 4/4.
RHINOS: 1 Brent Webb; 2 Scott Donald; 3 Clinton Toopi; 4 Keith Senior; 25 Ryan Hall; 6 Danny McGuire; 7 Rob Burrow; 16 Ryan Bailey; 18 Ian Kirke; 10 Jamie Peacock; 11 Jamie Jones-Buchanan; 12 Gareth Ellis; 13 Kevin Sinfield (C). Subs (all used): 23 Jordan Tansey; 15 Jamie Thackray; 22 Carl Ablett; 8 Kylie Leuluai.
Tries: Jones-Buchanan (18), Webb (67);
Goals: Sinfield 1/1, Burrow 1/1.
Sin bin: McGuire (20) - delaying restart.
Rugby Leaguer & League Express Men of the Match: *Hull:* Richard Swain; *Rhinos:* Rob Burrow.
Penalty count: 5-3; **Half-time:** 14-6;
Referee: Ian Smith; **Attendance:** 14,256.

ROUND 15

Friday 25th May 2007

SALFORD CITY REDS 14 HUDDERSFIELD GIANTS 12

CITY REDS: 5 John Wilshere; 15 Gray Viane; 3 Kevin McGuinness; 19 Stuart Littler; 2 David Hodgson; 6 Luke Dorn; 7 Luke Robinson (C); 24 Lee Jewitt; 27 David Berthezene; 10 Michael Korkidas; 8 Andy Coley; 16 Andrew Brocklehurst; 13 Simon Finnigan. Subs (all used): 21 Stephen Nash; 20 David Gower; 23 Jordan Turner; 18 Luke Adamson.
Tries: McGuinness (34), Hodgson (57), Viane (65);
Goals: Wilshere 1/3.
GIANTS: 6 Chris Thorman (C); 2 Martin Aspinwall; 13 Stephen Wild; 11 Chris Nero; 1 Paul Reilly; 4 Kevin Brown; 9 Brad Drew; 16 Keith Mason; 19 Ryan Hudson; 10 John Skandalis; 14 Stuart Jones; 12 Andy Raleigh; 20 Steve Snitch. Subs (all used): 7 Robbie Paul; 8 Eorl Crabtree; 15 Paul Jackson; 18 Darrell Griffin.
Tries: Wild (43), Reilly (73); **Goals:** Thorman 2/3.
Rugby Leaguer & League Express Men of the Match: *City Reds:* John Wilshere; *Giants:* Brad Drew.
Penalty count: 4-9; **Half-time:** 4-0;
Referee: Ben Thaler; **Attendance:** 3,379.

Saturday 26th May 2007

WIGAN WARRIORS 47 HULL FC 16

WARRIORS: 1 Chris Ashton; 2 Mark Calderwood; 3 Phil Bailey; 14 David Vaealiki; 5 Pat Richards; 6 Trent Barrett; 7 Thomas Leuluai; 8 Stuart Fielden; 16 Shane Millard; 10 Iafeta Palea'aesina; 11 Gareth Hock; 12 Bryan Fletcher; 13 Sean O'Loughlin (C). Subs (all used): 9 Mick Higham; 18 Paul Prescott; 19 Harrison Hansen; 24 Eamon O'Carroll.
Tries: Barrett (36, 39), Richards (42, 49, 79),

Debutant Kyle Eastmond tackled by Salford duo David Hodgson and Michael Korkidas, as St Helens edge a thriller

Higham (59), Ashton (78); **Goals:** Richards 9/11; **Field goal:** Barrett (72).
HULL: 1 Shaun Briscoe; 2 Matt Sing; 22 Craig Hall; 3 Kirk Yeaman; 5 Gareth Raynor; 7 Richard Horne; 23 Tommy Lee; 8 Ewan Dowes; 9 Richard Swain; 10 Garreth Carvell; 11 Lee Radford (C); 17 Willie Manu; 16 Danny Tickle. Subs (all used): 14 Motu Tony; 4 Sid Domic; 26 Scott Wheeldon; 21 Hutch Maiava.
Tries: Radford (14), Hall (22), Manu (32);
Goals: Tickle 2/3.
Rugby Leaguer & League Express Men of the Match:
Warriors: Iafeta Palea'aesina; *Hull:* Willie Manu.
Penalty count: 8-4; **Half-time:** 22-0.
Referee: Gareth Hewer; **Attendance:** 10,418.

HULL KINGSTON ROVERS 10 LEEDS RHINOS 18

ROVERS: 1 Ben Cockayne; 24 Ian Hardman; 21 Luke Dyer; 3 Jon Goddard; 5 Byron Ford; 31 Paul Cooke; 7 James Webster (C); 32 Ryan Tandy (D); 9 Ben Fisher; 15 Jim Gannon; 17 Mark O'Neill; 16 Jason Netherton; 14 Stanley Gene. Subs (all used): 10 David Tangata-Toa; 8 Makali Aizue; 11 Iain Morrison; 6 Scott Murrell.
Tries: J Netherton (70); **Goals:** Cooke 3/3.
RHINOS: 1 Brent Webb; 2 Scott Donald; 3 Clinton Toopi; 4 Keith Senior; 25 Ryan Hall; 6 Danny McGuire; 7 Rob Burrow; 10 Kylie McGuire; 18 Ian Kirke; 10 Jamie Peacock; 11 Jamie Jones-Buchanan; 12 Gareth Ellis; 13 Kevin Sinfield (C). Subs (all used): 23 Jordan Tansey; 15 Jamie

Thackray; 22 Carl Ablett; 8 Kylie Leuluai.
Tries: McGuire (24), Toopi (45), Tansey (66);
Goals: Sinfield 3/3.
Rugby Leaguer & League Express Men of the Match:
Rovers: Jason Netherton; *Rhinos:* Kevin Sinfield.
Penalty count: 9-3; **Half-time:** 4-6;
Referee: Ashley Klein; **Attendance:** 7,731.

WAKEFIELD TRINITY WILDCATS 18 CATALANS DRAGONS 12

WILDCATS: 21 Matt Blaymire; 2 Waine Pryce; 3 Jason Demetriou (C); 4 Ryan Atkins; 28 Paul White; 6 Jamie Rooney; 7 Ben Jeffries; 16 Ricky Bibey; 14 Paul March; 8 Adam Watene; 23 Jason Golden; 13 Brett Ferres. Subs (all used): 11 Ned Catic; 18 Olivier Elima; 20 Tevita Leo-Latu; 25 Richard Moore.
Tries: Demetriou (26), Pryce (33), Rooney (50);
Goals: Rooney 3/4.
DRAGONS: 1 Clint Greenshields; 2 Justin Murphy; 4 Adam Mogg; 3 John Wilson; 14 Thomas Bosc; 6 Casey McGuire; 7 Stacey Jones (C); 19 Alex Chan; 26 Luke Quigley; 10 Jerome Guisset; 17 Cyril Gossard; 21 Julien Touxagas; 13 Gregory Mounis. Subs (all used): 15 Mathieu Griffi; 16 Lionel Teixido; 22 Jamel Fakir; 28 Andrew Bentley.
Tries: Wilson (4, 71); **Goals:** Bosc 2/2.
Rugby Leaguer & League Express Men of the Match:
Wildcats: Paul March; *Dragons:* Clint Greenshields.
Penalty count: 6-7; **Half-time:** 10-6.
Referee: Ian Smith; **Attendance:** 4,023.

Monday 28th May 2007

WARRINGTON WOLVES 12 ST HELENS 40

WOLVES: 5 Brent Grose; 2 Henry Fa'afili; 3 Martin Gleeson; 4 Paul Johnson; 18 Richie Barnett; 13 Vinnie Anderson; 7 Lee Briers (C); 16 Paul Wood; 9 Jon Clarke; 8 Chris Leikvoll; 12 Ben Westwood; 11 Adrian Morley; 23 Mike Wainwright. Subs (all used): 14 Mike Gleeson; 15 Rob Parker; 21 Andy Bracek; 22 Ben Harrison.
Tries: Anderson (9), Fa'afili (33); **Goals:** Briers 2/2.
Sin bin: Wainwright (28) - fighting.
SAINTS: 1 Paul Wellens; 28 Dean McGilvray; 11 Lee Gilmour; 3 Matt Gidley; 2 Ade Gardner; 6 Leon Pryce; 21 Matty Smith; 17 James Graham; 14 James Roby; 10 Jason Cayless; 12 Jon Wilkin; 13 Paul Sculthorpe (C); 22 Paul Clough. Subs (all used): 9 Keiron Cunningham; 18 Bryn Hargreaves; 24 Steve Tyrer; 23 Maurie Fa'asavalu.
Tries: Wilkin (20), Smith (43), Pryce (48, 58, 68), Gardner (65), Fa'asavalu (72);
Goals: Sculthorpe 4/4, Smith 1/1, Tyrer 1/2.
Sin bin: Fa'asavalu (28) - fighting.
Rugby Leaguer & League Express Men of the Match:
Wolves: Henry Fa'afili; *Saints:* Jon Wilkin.

Penalty count: 5-4; **Half-time:** 12-6;
Referee: Richard Silverwood; **Attendance:** 13,024.

ROUND 16

Friday 1st June 2007

LEEDS RHINOS 42 WARRINGTON WOLVES 26

RHINOS: 1 Brent Webb; 2 Scott Donald; 3 Clinton Toopi; 4 Keith Senior; 5 Lee Smith; 6 Danny McGuire; 7 Rob Burrow; 10 Jamie Peacock; 13 Kevin Sinfield (C); 16 Ryan Bailey; 11 Jamie Jones-Buchanan; 18 Ian Kirke; 12 Gareth Ellis. Subs (all used): 15 Jamie Thackray; 8 Kylie Leuluai; 22 Carl Ablett; 23 Jordan Tansey.
Tries: Senior (16, 30), Webb (21, 62), McGuire (36), Toopi (47), Kirke (70); **Goals:** Sinfield 7/7.
WOLVES: 5 Brent Grose; 24 Chris Riley; 2 Henry Fa'afili; 4 Paul Johnson; 26 Kevin Penny; 9 Jon Clarke; 7 Lee Briers (C); 16 Paul Wood; 14 Mark Gleeson; 11 Adrian Morley; 12 Ben Westwood; 23 Mike Wainwright; 15 Rob Parker. Subs (all used): 21 Andy Bracek; 17 Michael Sullivan; 10 Paul Rauhihi; 19 Steve Pickersgill.
Tries: Fa'afili (3, 39, 58), Penny (27, 79);
Goals: Briers 3/5.
Rugby Leaguer & League Express Men of the Match:
Rhinos: Danny McGuire; *Wolves:* Michael Sullivan.
Penalty count: 7-3; **Half-time:** 24-14;
Referee: Ben Thaler; **Attendance:** 15,873.

ST HELENS 27 SALFORD CITY REDS 26

SAINTS: 6 Leon Pryce; 2 Ade Gardner; 24 Steve Tyrer; 4 Willie Talau; 5 Francis Meli; 26 Kyle Eastmond (D); 21 Matty Smith; 17 James Graham; 9 Keiron Cunningham; 10 Jason Cayless; 13 Paul Sculthorpe (C); 11 Lee Gilmour; 22 Paul Clough. Subs (all used): 20 Scott Moore; 18 Bryn Hargreaves; 8 Nick Fozzard; 28 Dean McGilvray.
Tries: Talau (4), Pryce (19), Meli (39), Cunningham (61), Gilmour (73); **Goals:** Sculthorpe 3/5.
Field goal: Smith (79).
On report:
Incident (49) - resulting in head injury to Littler.
CITY REDS: 5 John Wilshere; 2 David Hodgson; 19 Stuart Littler; 3 Kevin McGuinness; 26 Stefan Ratchford; 6 Luke Dorn; 7 Luke Robinson (C); 14 Paul Highton; 27 David Berthezene; 10 Michael Korkidas; 8 Andy Coley; 16 Andrew Brocklehurst; 13 Simon Finnigan. Subs (all used): 20 David Gower; 23 Jordan Turner; 21 Stephen Nash; 18 Luke Adamson.
Tries: Ratchford (15), Wilshere (28, 55), Hodgson (33), Coley (40); **Goals:** Wilshere 2/4, Hodgson 1/1.
Rugby Leaguer & League Express Men of the Match:
Saints: Leon Pryce; *City Reds:* Simon Finnigan.

Salford's Luke Dorn bursts through the Harlequins defence, as the City Reds come out on top in a try-less Round 17 fixture

Penalty count: 9-4; **Half-time:** 14-22;
Referee: Thierry Alibert; **Attendance:** 7,801.

Saturday 2nd June 2007

HARLEQUINS 18 WIGAN WARRIORS 8

HARLEQUINS: 16 Chris Melling; 2 Jon Wells; 3 Paul Sykes; 4 Tyrone Smith; 19 Tony Clubb; 7 Danny Orr; 1 Mark McLinden (C); 8 Karl Temata; 9 Chad Randall; 15 David Mills; 18 Matt Gafa; 12 Lee Hopkins; 6 Scott Hill. Subs (all used): 14 Julien Rinaldi; 22 Michael Worrincy; 29 Joe Mbu (D2); 26 Joe Walsh.
Tries: Sykes (27), Gafa (48); **Goals:** Sykes 5/5.
WARRIORS: 1 Chris Ashton; 2 Mark Calderwood; 3 Phil Bailey; 14 David Vaealiki; 5 Pat Richards; 6 Trent Barrett; 7 Thomas Leuluai; 8 Stuart Fielden; 16 Shane Millard; 10 Iafeta Palea'aesina; 11 Gareth Hock; 12 Bryan Fletcher; 13 Sean O'Loughlin (C). Subs (all used): 9 Mick Higham; 19 Harrison Hansen; 24 Eamon O'Carroll; 18 Paul Prescott.
Tries: Ashton (7), Barrett (61); **Goals:** Richards 0/3.
Sin bin: Hock (74) − dissent.
On report: Hock (25) − alleged high tackle.
Rugby Leaguer & League Express Men of the Match: *Harlequins:* Danny Orr; *Warriors:* Trent Barrett.
Penalty count: 13-6; **Half-time:** 8-4;
Referee: Ashley Klein; **Attendance:** 5,657.

CATALANS DRAGONS 20 BRADFORD BULLS 28

DRAGONS: 1 Clint Greenshields; 2 Justin Murphy; 3 John Wilson; 4 Adam Mogg; 14 Thomas Bosc; 6 Casey McGuire; 7 Stacey Jones (C); 10 Jerome Guisset; 26 Luke Quigley; 19 Alex Chan; 21 Julien Touxagas; 17 Cyril Gossard; 13 Gregory Mounis. Subs (all used): 15 Mathieu Griffi; 28 Andrew Bentley; 8 David Ferriol; 16 Lionel Teixido.
Tries: Gossard (2), Bosc (15), Wilson (19); **Goals:** Bosc 2/4.
BULLS: 1 Marcus St Hilaire; 24 Dave Halley; 5 Lesley Vainikolo; 3 Ben Harris; 17 James Evans; 6 Iestyn Harris; 7 Paul Deacon (C); 10 Andy Lynch; 9 Terry Newton; 8 Joe Vagana; 26 David Solomona; 11 Chris McKenna; 12 Glenn Morrison. Subs (all used): 16 Ian Henderson; 18 Sam Burgess; 23 Matt James; 22 Craig Kopczak.
Tries: Vagana (48), Deacon (24), Vainikolo (35), Newton (52), Evans (79); **Goals:** Deacon 4/6.
Rugby Leaguer & League Express Men of the Match: *Dragons:* Luke Quigley; *Bulls:* Ian Henderson.
Penalty count: 6-8; **Half-time:** 14-20;
Referee: Phil Bentham; **Attendance:** 7,555.

Sunday 3rd June 2007

HULL FC 9 HUDDERSFIELD GIANTS 9

HULL: 1 Shaun Briscoe; 14 Motu Tony; 4 Sid Domic; 3

Kirk Yeaman; 5 Gareth Raynor; 7 Richard Horne; 23 Tommy Lee; 8 Ewan Dowes; 9 Richard Swain; 10 Garreth Carvell; 11 Lee Radford (C); 17 Willie Manu; 16 Danny Tickle. Subs (all used): 13 Danny Washbrook; 19 Graeme Horne; 15 Paul King; 21 Hutch Maiava.
Try: Tickle (47); **Goals:** Tickle 2/2.
Field goal: R Horne (78).
On report:
Manu (75) - alleged dangerous tackle on Drew.
GIANTS: 6 Chris Thorman (C); 1 Paul Reilly; 3 Jamahl Lolesi; 11 Chris Nero; 2 Martin Aspinwall; 4 Kevin Brown; 9 Brad Drew; 16 Keith Mason; 19 Ryan Hudson; 10 John Skandalis; 20 Steve Snitch. 12 Andy Raleigh; 13 Stephen Wild. Subs (all used): 7 Robbie Paul; 8 Eorl Crabtree; 14 Stuart Jones; 18 Darrell Griffin.
Try: Thorman (15); **Goals:** Thorman 2/2.
Field goal: Thorman (75).
Rugby Leaguer & League Express Men of the Match: *Hull:* Gareth Raynor; *Giants:* Chris Thorman.
Penalty count: 8-4; **Half-time:** 0-6;
Referee: Ian Smith; **Attendance:** 12,094.

WAKEFIELD TRINITY WILDCATS 30 HULL KINGSTON ROVERS 15

WILDCATS: 21 Matt Blaymire; 2 Waine Pryce; 3 Jason Demetriou (C); 4 Ryan Atkins; 28 Paul White; 14 Paul March; 7 Ben Jeffries; 16 Ricky Bibey; 9 Sam Obst; 8 Adam Watene; 12 Duncan MacGillivray; 23 Jason Golden; 13 Brett Ferres. Subs (all used): 11 Ned Catic; 18 Olivier Elima; 20 Tevita Leo-Latu; 25 Richard Moore.
Tries: Jeffries (43), Blaymire (47, 66), White (51), Watene (70); **Goals:** P March 5/6.
ROVERS: 1 Ben Cockayne; 24 Ian Hardman; 21 Luke Dyer; 3 Jon Goddard; 5 Byron Ford; 31 Paul Cooke; 7 James Webster (C); 20 Michael Vella; 9 Ben Fisher; 18 Danny Ward; 16 Jason Netherton; 17 Mark O'Neill; 14 Stanley Gene. Subs (all used): 6 Scott Murrell; 8 Makali Aizue; 15 Jim Gannon; 28 Chris Chester.
Tries: Dyer (9), Ford (30), Hardman (58); **Goals:** Cooke 1/3; **Field goal:** Cooke (36).
Dismissal: Aizue (33) - high tackle on White.
Rugby Leaguer & League Express Men of the Match: *Wildcats:* Paul White; *Rovers:* Michael Vella.
Penalty count: 7-4; **Half-time:** 2-9;
Referee: Richard Silverwood; **Attendance:** 6,107.

ROUND 17

Friday 15th June 2007

SALFORD CITY REDS 5 HARLEQUINS 2

CITY REDS: 5 John Wilshere; 2 David Hodgson; 3 Kevin McGuinness; 4 Aaron Moule; 19 Stuart Littler; 6 Luke

Dorn; 7 Luke Robinson; 10 Michael Korkidas; 9 Malcolm Alker (C); 14 Paul Highton; 8 Andy Coley; 11 Mark Edmondson; 13 Simon Finnigan. Subs (all used): 16 Andrew Brocklehurst; 20 David Gower; 23 Jordan Turner; 24 Lee Jewitt.
Goals: Wilshere 2/2; **Field goal:** Robinson (69).
HARLEQUINS: 16 Chris Melling; 2 Jon Wells; 3 Paul Sykes; 4 Tyrone Smith; 18 Matt Gafa; 1 Mark McLinden (C); 7 Danny Orr; 8 Karl Temata; 9 Chad Randall; 15 David Mills; 12 Lee Hopkins; 22 Michael Worrincy; 23 Henry Paul. Subs (all used): 14 Julien Rinaldi; 29 Joe Mbu; 30 Steve Bannister; 20 Jon Grayshon.
Goals: Sykes 1/1.
On report: Unspecified player
(23) - alleged late tackle on Robinson.
Rugby Leaguer & League Express Men of the Match: *City Reds:* Michael Korkidas; *Harlequins:* Danny Orr.
Penalty count: 11-10; **Half-time:** 2-0;
Referee: Richard Silverwood; **Attendance:** 4,067.

WIGAN WARRIORS 30 CATALANS DRAGONS 0

WARRIORS: 1 Chris Ashton; 2 Mark Calderwood; 3 Phil Bailey; 14 David Vaealiki; 5 Pat Richards; 6 Trent Barrett; 7 Thomas Leuluai; 8 Stuart Fielden; 9 Mick Higham; 18 Paul Prescott; 19 Harrison Hansen; 12 Bryan Fletcher; 13 Sean O'Loughlin (C). Subs (all used): 22 Joel Tomkins; 24 Eamon O'Carroll; 20 Darrell Goulding; 25 Michael McIlorum.
Tries: Bailey (24), Barrett (26), Ashton (52), Richards (61), Calderwood (63); **Goals:** Richards 5/8.
DRAGONS: 1 Clint Greenshields; 2 Justin Murphy; 4 Adam Mogg; 3 John Wilson; 14 Thomas Bosc; 6 Casey McGuire; 7 Stacey Jones (C); 19 Alex Chan; 26 Luke Quigley; 10 Jerome Guisset; 21 Julien Touxagas; 17 Cyril Gossard; 13 Gregory Mounis. Subs (all used): 28 Andrew Bentley; 15 Mathieu Griffi; 8 David Ferriol; 25 Younes Khattabi.
Sin bin: Mogg (23) - holding down.
Rugby Leaguer & League Express Men of the Match: *Warriors:* Stuart Fielden; *Dragons:* Gregory Mounis.
Penalty count: 9-4; **Half-time:** 14-0;
Referee: Steve Ganson; **Attendance:** 12,641.

Sunday 17th June 2007

HUDDERSFIELD GIANTS 12 LEEDS RHINOS 25

GIANTS: 7 Robbie Paul; 2 Martin Aspinwall; 11 Chris Nero; 3 Jamahl Lolesi; 1 Paul Reilly; 4 Kevin Brown; 9 Brad Drew (C); 15 Paul Jackson; 19 Ryan Hudson; 10 John Skandalis; 24 Rod Jensen; 12 Andy Raleigh; 13 Stephen Wild. Subs (all used): 8 Eorl Crabtree; 16 Keith Mason; 18 Darrell Griffin; 20 Steve Snitch.
Tries: Jackson (10), Nero (47); **Goals:** Drew 2/2.
RHINOS: 23 Jordan Tansey; 2 Scott Donald; 3 Clinton Toopi; 4 Keith Senior; 5 Lee Smith; 6 Danny McGuire; 7

Rob Burrow; 16 Ryan Bailey; 9 Matt Diskin; 10 Jamie Peacock; 11 Jamie Jones-Buchanan; 12 Gareth Ellis; 13 Kevin Sinfield (C). Subs (all used): 8 Kylie Leuluai; 18 Ian Kirke; 15 Jamie Thackray; 22 Carl Ablett.
Tries: McGuire (1, 4), Tansey (77), Donald (79);
Goals: Sinfield 4/6; **Field goal:** Sinfield (75).
Rugby Leaguer & League Express Men of the Match:
Giants: Kevin Brown; *Rhinos:* Danny McGuire.
Penalty count: 12-5; **Half-time:** 6-12;
Referee: Ashley Klein; **Attendance:** 10,241.

HULL KINGSTON ROVERS 0 ST HELENS 40

ROVERS: 30 Mark Lennon; 1 Ben Cockayne; 3 Jon Goddard; 21 Luke Dyer; 24 Ian Hardman; 31 Paul Cooke; 7 James Webster (C); 20 Michael Vella; 9 Ben Fisher; 15 Jim Gannon; 17 Mark O'Neill; 16 Jason Netherton; 14 Stanley Gene. Subs (all used): 10 David Tangata-Toa; 32 Ryan Tandy; 6 Scott Murrell; 28 Chris Chester.
SAINTS: 1 Paul Wellens (C); 2 Ade Gardner; 3 Matt Gidley; 4 Willie Talau; 24 Steve Tyrer; 6 Leon Pryce; 21 Matty Smith; 8 Nick Fozzard; 14 James Roby; 10 Jason Cayless; 11 Lee Gilmour; 22 Paul Clough; 12 Jon Wilkin. Subs (all used): 17 James Graham; 9 Keiron Cunningham; 23 Maurie Fa'asavalu; 15 Mike Bennett.
Tries: Talau (3), Pryce (6), Cunningham (45), Gidley (56), Wellens (59), Tyrer (65), Graham (76); **Goals:** Tyrer 6/7.
Rugby Leaguer & League Express Men of the Match:
Rovers: Jason Netherton; *Saints:* Paul Wellens.
Penalty count: 4-5; **Half-time:** 0-12;
Referee: Phil Bentham; **Attendance:** 7,011.

WARRINGTON WOLVES 31
WAKEFIELD TRINITY WILDCATS 12

WOLVES: 5 Brent Grose; 24 Chris Riley; 4 Paul Johnson; 2 Henry Fa'afili; 26 Kevin Penny; 9 Jon Clarke; 7 Lee Briers (C); 16 Paul Wood; 14 Mark Gleeson; 11 Adrian Morley; 23 Mike Wainwright; 15 Rob Parker; 12 Ben Westwood. Subs (all used): 17 Michael Sullivan; 21 Andy Bracek; 10 Paul Rauhihi; 8 Chris Leikvoll.
Tries: Clarke (21), Leikvoll (31), Riley (43, 76), Grose (60); **Goals:** Briers 5/6; **Field goal:** Briers (64).
WILDCATS: 21 Matt Blaymire; 2 Waine Pryce; 3 Jason Demetriou (C); 4 Ryan Atkins; 28 Paul White; 7 Ben Jeffries; 14 Paul March; 16 Ricky Bibey; 9 Sam Obst; 8 Adam Watene; 18 Olivier Elima; 23 Jason Golden; 13 Brett Ferres. Subs (all used): 10 Danny Sculthorpe; 11 Ned Catic; 20 Tevita Leo-Latu; 25 Richard Moore.
Tries: Catic (36), Pryce (79); **Goals:** Ferres 2/3.
Rugby Leaguer & League Express Men of the Match:
Wolves: Ben Westwood; *Wildcats:* Tevita Leo-Latu.
Penalty count: 8-9; **Half-time:** 12-6;
Referee: Ian Smith; **Attendance:** 10,324.

BRADFORD BULLS 34 HULL FC 8

BULLS: 19 Michael Platt; 1 Marcus St Hilaire; 2 Nathan McAvoy; 17 James Evans; 5 Lesley Vainikolo; 26 David Solomona; 7 Paul Deacon (C); 8 Joe Vagana; 9 Terry Newton; 10 Andy Lynch; 11 Chris McKenna; 13 Jamie Langley; 12 Glenn Morrison. Subs (all used): 20 Tame Tupou; 23 Matt James; 16 Ian Henderson; 18 Sam Burgess.
Tries: Newton (8, 64, 70, 76), Tupou (53), Deacon (79);
Goals: Deacon 4/5, Vainikolo 1/1.
HULL: 14 Motu Tony; 2 Matt Sing; 20 Richard Whiting; 3 Kirk Yeaman; 5 Gareth Raynor; 7 Richard Horne; 24 Anthony Thackeray; 8 Ewan Dowes; 18 Wayne Godwin; 10 Garreth Carvell; 11 Lee Radford (C); 17 Willie Manu; 16 Danny Tickle. Subs (all used): 4 Sid Domic; 1 Shaun Briscoe; 15 Paul King; 21 Hutch Maiava.
Try: Tony (5); **Goals:** Tickle 2/2.
Rugby Leaguer & League Express Men of the Match:
Bulls: Terry Newton; *Hull:* Anthony Thackeray.
Penalty count: 4-3; **Half-time:** 6-8;
Referee: Ben Thaler; **Attendance:** 11,557.

ROUND 18

Friday 29th June 2007

LEEDS RHINOS 14 BRADFORD BULLS 38

RHINOS: 1 Brent Webb; 2 Scott Donald; 3 Clinton Toopi; 4 Keith Senior; 5 Lee Smith; 6 Danny McGuire; 7 Rob Burrow; 16 Ryan Bailey; 9 Matt Diskin; 10 Jamie Peacock; 11 Jamie Jones-Buchanan; 12 Gareth Ellis; 13 Kevin Sinfield (C). Subs (all used): 15 Jamie Thackray; 8 Kylie Leuluai; 18 Ian Kirke; 23 Jordan Tansey.
Tries: Diskin (25), Smith (38), Webb (57);
Goals: Sinfield 1/3.
BULLS: 19 Michael Platt; 1 Marcus St Hilaire; 2 Nathan McAvoy; 17 James Evans; 5 Lesley Vainikolo; 26 David Solomona; 7 Paul Deacon (C); 8 Joe Vagana; 9 Terry Newton; 10 Andy Lynch; 11 Chris McKenna; 13 Jamie Langley; 12 Glenn Morrison. Subs (all used): 18 Sam Burgess; 16 Ian Henderson; 20 Tame Tupou; 23 Matt James.
Tries: Vainikolo (10), Evans (35), Tupou (50), Lynch (60), Morrison (62), St Hilaire (76); **Goals:** Deacon 7/7.
Rugby Leaguer & League Express Men of the Match:
Rhinos: Matt Diskin; *Bulls:* Jamie Langley.
Penalty count: 7-7; **Half-time:** 8-14;
Referee: Phil Bentham; **Attendance:** 22,000.

Saturday 30th June 2007

HARLEQUINS 32 HULL KINGSTON ROVERS 18

HARLEQUINS: 1 Mark McLinden (C); 2 Jon Wells; 4 Tyrone Smith; 3 Paul Sykes; 28 Rikki Sheriffe (D2); 23 Henry Paul; 25 Zebastian Luisi; 8 Karl Temata; 9 Chad Randall; 22 Michael Worrincy; 29 Joe Mbu; 12 Lee Hopkins; 18 Matt Gafa. Subs (all used): 14 Julien Rinaldi; 17 Louie McCarthy-Scarsbrook; 30 Steve Bannister; 20 Jon Grayshon.
Tries: Worrincy (10), T Smith (17), Randall (27), Gafa (64), McCarthy-Scarsbrook (80); **Goals:** Sykes 6/6.
ROVERS: 30 Mark Lennon; 1 Ben Cockayne; 3 Jon Goddard; 21 Luke Dyer; 24 Ian Hardman; 31 Paul Cooke; 7 James Webster (C); 20 Michael Vella; 18 Danny Ward; 32 Ryan Tandy; 11 Iain Morrison; 17 Mark O'Neill; 28 Chris Chester. Subs (all used): 6 Scott Murrell; 16 Jason Netherton; 10 David Tangata-Toa; 15 Jim Gannon.
Tries: Tandy (13), Lennon (19), Chester (61);
Goals: Cooke 3/4.
Rugby Leaguer & League Express Men of the Match:
Harlequins: Paul Sykes; *Rovers:* Chris Chester.
Penalty count: 6-7; **Half-time:** 18-12;
Referee: Steve Ganson; **Attendance:** 3,278.

ST HELENS 54 HUDDERSFIELD GIANTS 4

SAINTS: 1 Paul Wellens; 2 Ade Gardner; 3 Matt Gidley; 4 Willie Talau; 24 Steve Tyrer; 6 Leon Pryce; 21 Matty Smith; 8 Nick Fozzard; 9 Keiron Cunningham (C); 10 Jason Cayless; 11 Lee Gilmour; 15 Mike Bennett; 12 Jon Wilkin. Subs (all used): 14 James Roby; 17 James Graham; 22 Paul Clough; 23 Maurie Fa'asavalu.
Tries: Wilkin (6, 50), Pryce (17), Talau (20), Fa'asavalu (31), Tyrer (39, 74), Gardner (45), Gilmour (66), Wellens (79); **Goals:** Tyrer 7/10.
GIANTS: 6 Chris Thorman (C); 1 Paul Reilly; 3 Jamahl Lolesi; 11 Chris Nero; 24 Rod Jensen; 4 Kevin Brown; 9 Brad Drew; 16 Keith Mason; 7 Robbie Paul; 10 John Skandalis; 14 Stuart Jones; 12 Andy Raleigh; 13 Stephen Wild. Subs (all used): 15 Paul Jackson; 18 Darrell Griffin; 19 Ryan Hudson; 20 Steve Snitch.
Try: Nero (13); **Goals:** Thorman 0/1.
Rugby Leaguer & League Express Men of the Match:
Saints: Steve Tyrer; *Giants:* Chris Thorman.
Penalty count: 8-4; **Half-time:** 28-4;
Referee: Ben Thaler; **Attendance:** 7,771.

CATALANS DRAGONS 24 WARRINGTON WOLVES 22

DRAGONS: 1 Clint Greenshields; 25 Younes Khattabi; 3 John Wilson; 4 Adam Mogg; 14 Thomas Bosc; 6 Casey McGuire; 7 Stacey Jones (C); 19 Alex Chan; 26 Luke Quigley; 10 Jerome Guisset; 17 Cyril Gossard; 12 Jason Croker; 13 Gregory Mounis. Subs (all used): 8 David Ferriol; 11 Sebastien Raguin; 15 Mathieu Griffi; 21 Julien Touxagas.
Tries: Khattabi (13), Ferriol (33), Wilson (51), McGuire (54), Croker (62); **Goals:** Bosc 2/5.
WOLVES: 5 Brent Grose; 26 Kevin Penny; 2 Henry Fa'afili; 6 Chris Bridge; 24 Chris Riley; 9 Jon Clarke; 7 Lee Briers (C); 10 Paul Rauhihi; 14 Mark Gleeson; 16 Paul Wood; 11 Adrian Morley; 23 Mike Wainwright; 12 Ben Westwood. Subs (all used): 8 Chris Leikvoll; 15 Rob Parker; 17 Michael Sullivan; 21 Andy Bracek.
Tries: Penny (25), Briers (39, 68); **Goals:** Briers 5/5.
On report: Westwood (11) - alleged high tackle.
Rugby Leaguer & League Express Men of the Match:
Dragons: Luke Quigley; *Wolves:* Lee Briers.
Penalty count: 7-7; **Half-time:** 10-12;
Referee: Ashley Klein; **Attendance:** 8,850.

Sunday 1st July 2007

WAKEFIELD TRINITY WILDCATS 32
WIGAN WARRIORS 6

WILDCATS: 33 Sean Gleeson; 22 Peter Fox; 3 Jason Demetriou (C); 4 Ryan Atkins; 28 Paul White; 21 Matt Blaymire; 7 Ben Jeffries; 8 Adam Watene; 9 Sam Obst; 16 Ricky Bibey; 12 Duncan MacGillivray; 18 Olivier Elima; 13 Brett Ferres. Subs (all used): 10 Danny Sculthorpe; 11 Ned Catic; 20 Tevita Leo-Latu; 25 Richard Moore.
Tries: Demetriou (10), Jeffries (25, 72), Blaymire (35), Fox (40), Moore (78); **Goals:** Ferres 3/5, Jeffries 1/2.
On report: Incident (72) - after Jeffries try.
WARRIORS: 1 Chris Ashton; 2 Mark Calderwood; 3 Phil Bailey; 14 David Vaealiki; 5 Pat Richards; 6 Trent Barrett; 7 Thomas Leuluai; 8 Stuart Fielden; 9 Mick Higham; 10 Iafeta Palea'aesina; 11 Gareth Hock; 12 Bryan Fletcher; 13 Sean O'Loughlin (C). Subs (all used): 16 Shane Millard; 18 Paul Prescott; 19 Harrison Hansen; 22 Joel Tomkins.
Try: Barrett (6); **Goals:** Richards 1/1.
Sin bin: Barrett (70) - high tackle on Watene.
On report: Barrett (69) - alleged high tackle;
Incident (72) - after Jeffries try.
Rugby Leaguer & League Express Men of the Match:
Wildcats: Ben Jeffries; *Warriors:* Sean O'Loughlin.
Penalty count: 11-10; **Half-time:** 22-6;
Referee: Richard Silverwood; **Attendance:** 8,126.

ROUND 19

Friday 6th July 2007

SALFORD CITY REDS 18
WAKEFIELD TRINITY WILDCATS 35

CITY REDS: 5 John Wilshere; 2 David Hodgson; 3 Kevin McGuinness; 4 Aaron Moule; 19 Stuart Littler; 6 Luke Dorn; 7 Luke Robinson; 8 Andy Coley; 9 Malcolm Alker (C); 10 Michael Korkidas; 11 Mark Edmondson; 12 Ian Sibbit; 13 Simon Finnigan. Subs (all used): 23 Jordan Tuner; 17 Gareth Haggerty; 20 David Gower; 24 Lee Jewitt.
Tries: Robinson (12), Hodgson (32), Finnigan (79);
Goals: Wilshere 3/4.
WILDCATS: 21 Matt Blaymire; 22 Peter Fox; 33 Sean Gleeson; 4 Ryan Atkins; 28 Paul White; 6 Jamie Rooney; 7 Ben Jeffries; 8 Adam Watene; 9 Sam Obst; 16 Ricky Bibey; 3 Jason Demetriou (C); 12 Duncan MacGillivray; 13 Brett Ferres. Subs (all used): 25 Richard Moore; 20 Tevita Leo-Latu; 10 Danny Sculthorpe; 11 Ned Catic.
Tries: Rooney (6), MacGillivray (15), Jeffries (20), Atkins (28, 75), Fox (67); **Goals:** Rooney 5/8;
Field goal: Rooney (73).
Rugby Leaguer & League Express Men of the Match:
City Reds: Andy Coley; *Wildcats:* Ben Jeffries.
Penalty count: 12-6; **Half-time:** 12-20;
Referee: Phil Bentham; **Attendance:** 4,178.

ST HELENS 10 LEEDS RHINOS 22

SAINTS: 1 Paul Wellens; 2 Ade Gardner; 3 Matt Gidley; 4 Willie Talau; 24 Steve Tyrer; 6 Leon Pryce; 21 Matty Smith; 8 Nick Fozzard; 9 Keiron Cunningham (C); 10 Jason Cayless; 11 Lee Gilmour; 15 Mike Bennett; 12 Jon Wilkin. Subs (all used): 14 James Roby; 17 James Graham; 22 Paul Clough; 23 Maurie Fa'asavalu.
Tries: Roby (27), Tyrer (39); **Goals:** Tyrer 1/2.
RHINOS: 1 Brent Webb; 2 Scott Donald; 3 Clinton Toopi; 4 Keith Senior; 25 Ryan Hall; 6 Danny McGuire; 7 Rob Burrow; 16 Ryan Bailey; 9 Matt Diskin; 10 Jamie Peacock; 12 Gareth Ellis; 11 Jamie Jones-Buchanan; 13 Kevin Sinfield (C). Subs (all used): 23 Jordan Tansey; 14 Ali Lauitiiti; 8 Kylie Leuluai; 18 Ian Kirke.
Tries: McGuire (33), Burrow (48), Hall (74), Tansey (77);
Goals: Sinfield 3/5.
Rugby Leaguer & League Express Men of the Match:
Saints: Matty Smith; *Rhinos:* Rob Burrow.
Penalty count: 6-8; **Half-time:** 10-8;
Referee: Richard Silverwood; **Attendance:** 10,074.

WIGAN WARRIORS 25 BRADFORD BULLS 18

WARRIORS: 1 Chris Ashton; 2 Mark Calderwood; 3 Phil Bailey; 14 David Vaealiki; 23 Liam Colbon; 6 Trent Barrett; 7 Thomas Leuluai; 8 Stuart Fielden; 9 Mick Higham; 10 Iafeta Palea'aesina; 11 Gareth Hock; 12 Bryan Fletcher; 13 Sean O'Loughlin (C). Subs (all used): 18 Paul Prescott; 19 Harrison Hansen; 20 Darrell Goulding; 25 Michael McIlorum.
Tries: Barrett (17), Bailey (27, 37), Calderwood (65), Vaealiki (75); **Goals:** Ashton 2/5; **Field goal:** Barrett (79).
BULLS: 19 Michael Platt; 1 Marcus St Hilaire; 2 Nathan McAvoy; 17 James Evans; 20 Tame Tupou; 12 Glenn Morrison; 7 Paul Deacon (C); 8 Joe Vagana; 9 Terry Newton; 10 Andy Lynch; 11 Chris McKenna; 26 David Solomona; 13 Jamie Langley. Subs (all used): 16 Ian Henderson; 3 Ben Harris; 18 Sam Burgess; 23 Matt James.
Tries: Evans (1), B Harris (52); **Goals:** Deacon 5/5.
Rugby Leaguer & League Express Men of the Match:
Warriors: Bryan Fletcher; *Bulls:* Terry Newton.
Penalty count: 9-6; **Half-time:** 14-10;
Referee: Steve Ganson; **Attendance:** 15,107.

Saturday 7th July 2007

HARLEQUINS 30 CATALANS DRAGONS 22

HARLEQUINS: 1 Mark McLinden (C); 2 Jon Wells; 4 Tyrone Smith; 3 Paul Sykes; 28 Rikki Sheriffe; 6 Scott Hill; 23 Henry Paul; 8 Karl Temata; 9 Chad Randall; 22 Michael Worrincy; 29 Joe Mbu; 12 Lee Hopkins; 18 Matt Gafa. Subs (all used): 14 Julien Rinaldi; 17 Louie McCarthy-Scarsbrook; 30 Steve Bannister; 15 David Mills.
Tries: Paul (21, 31), Gafa (36), Sheriffe (41, 74);
Goals: Sykes 5/7.
DRAGONS: 1 Clint Greenshields; 25 Younes Khattabi; 3 John Wilson; 4 Adam Mogg; 14 Thomas Bosc; 6 Casey McGuire; 7 Stacey Jones (C); 19 Alex Chan; 26 Luke Quigley; 10 Jerome Guisset; 17 Cyril Gossard; 12 Jason Croker; 13 Gregory Mounis. Subs (all used): 20 Adel Fellous; 15 Mathieu Griffi; 11 Sebastien Raguin; 21 Julien Touxagas.
Tries: McGuire (8), Greenshields (27), Raguin (48), Bosc (57); **Goals:** Bosc 3/4.
Rugby Leaguer & League Express Men of the Match:
Harlequins: Rikki Sheriffe; *Dragons:* Clint Greenshields.
Penalty count: 7-3; **Half-time:** 18-12;
Referee: Ashley Klein; **Attendance:** 2,346.

Sunday 8th July 2007

HULL KINGSTON ROVERS 20 HULL FC 30

ROVERS: 1 Ben Cockayne; 30 Mark Lennon; 33 Rhys Lovegrove (D); 21 Luke Dyer; 24 Ian Hardman; 6 Scott Murrell; 7 James Webster (C); 32 Ryan Tandy; 9 Ben Fisher; 18 Danny Ward; 17 Mark O'Neill; 28 Chris Chester; 14 Stanley Gene. Subs (all used): 10 David Tangata-Toa; 11 Iain Morrison; 31 Paul Cooke; 15 Jim Gannon.
Tries: Dyer (7), Tangata-Toa (28), O'Neill (40), Lovegrove (57); **Goals:** Lennon 0/1, Cooke 2/3.
HULL: 14 Motu Tony; 2 Matt Sing; 22 Craig Hall; 3 Kirk Yeaman; 5 Gareth Raynor; 7 Richard Horne; 32 Mathew Head (D); 8 Ewan Dowes; 18 Wayne Godwin; 10 Garreth Carvell; 11 Lee Radford (C); 16 Danny Tickle; 13 Danny Washbrook. Subs (all used): 20 Richard Whiting; 17 Willie Manu; 21 Hutch Maiava; 26 Scott Wheeldon.
Tries: Hall (4), Tickle (21), Wheeldon (41), Manu (45), Yeaman (51); **Goals:** Tickle 5/6.
Rugby Leaguer & League Express Men of the Match:
Rovers: James Webster; *Hull:* Danny Tickle.
Penalty count: 7-4; **Half-time:** 14-12;
Referee: Ben Thaler; **Attendance:** 9,035.

HUDDERSFIELD GIANTS 28 WARRINGTON WOLVES 47

GIANTS: 6 Chris Thorman (C); 24 Rod Jensen; 5 Shane Elford; 11 Chris Nero; 2 Martin Aspinwall; 4 Kevin Brown; 7 Robbie Paul; 16 Keith Mason; 19 Ryan

Hudson; 10 John Skandalis; 14 Stuart Jones; 20 Steve Snitch; 13 Stephen Wild. Subs (all used): 3 Jamahl Lolesi; 8 Eorl Crabtree; 9 Brad Drew; 12 Andy Raleigh.
Tries: Paul (4), Drew (49), Hudson (67, 76), Elford (79); **Goals:** Thorman 4/5.
WOLVES: 5 Brent Grose; 1 Stuart Reardon; 2 Henry Fa'afili; 4 Paul Johnson; 26 Kevin Penny; 6 Chris Bridge; 7 Lee Briers (C); 16 Paul Wood; 17 Michael Sullivan; 10 Paul Rauhihi; 11 Adrian Morley; 12 Ben Westwood; 9 Jon Clarke. Subs (all used): 15 Rob Parker; 8 Chris Leikvoll; 21 Andy Bracek; 22 Ben Harrison.
Tries: Bridge (7, 17, 64), Reardon (32), Penny (45, 80), Sullivan (61); **Goals:** Briers 9/9; **Field goal:** Briers (72).
Rugby Leaguer & League Express Men of the Match: *Giants:* Rod Jensen; *Wolves:* Chris Bridge.
Penalty count: 6-5; **Half-time:** 6-20; **Referee:** Ian Smith; **Attendance:** 6,822.

ROUND 20

Thursday 12th July 2007

WIGAN WARRIORS 18 LEEDS RHINOS 2

WARRIORS: 5 Pat Richards; 2 Mark Calderwood; 3 Phil Bailey; 14 David Vaealiki; 23 Liam Colbon; 6 Trent Barrett; 7 Thomas Leuluai; 8 Stuart Fielden; 9 Mick Higham; 10 Iafeta Palea'aesina; 11 Gareth Hock; 12 Bryan Fletcher; 13 Sean O'Loughlin (C). Subs (all used): 18 Paul Prescott; 19 Harrison Hansen; 20 Darrell Goulding; 25 Michael McIlorum.
Tries: Colbon (60), Fletcher (70); **Goals:** Richards 5/5.
RHINOS: 1 Brent Webb; 25 Ryan Hall; 3 Clinton Toopi; 4 Keith Senior; 2 Scott Donald; 6 Danny McGuire; 7 Rob Burrow; 16 Ryan Bailey; 13 Kevin Sinfield (C); 10 Jamie Peacock; 18 Ian Kirke; 11 Jamie Jones-Buchanan; 12 Gareth Ellis. Subs (all used): 23 Jordan Tansey; 8 Kylie Leuluai; 15 Jamie Thackray; 14 Ali Lauitiiti.
Goals: Sinfield 1/1.
Sin bin: Ellis (79) - professional foul.
Rugby Leaguer & League Express Men of the Match: *Warriors:* Bryan Fletcher; *Rhinos:* Ian Kirke.
Penalty count: 9-5; **Half-time:** 4-0; **Referee:** Ben Thaler; **Attendance:** 14,554.

Friday 13th July 2007

BRADFORD BULLS 10 ST HELENS 4

BULLS: 19 Michael Platt; 1 Marcus St Hilaire; 2 Nathan McAvoy; 3 Ben Harris; 20 Tame Tupou; 12 Glenn Morrison; 7 Paul Deacon (C); 8 Joe Vagana; 9 Terry Newton; 10 Andy Lynch; 26 David Solomona; 11 Chris McKenna; 13 Jamie Langley. Subs (all used): 24 Dave Halley; 16 Ian Henderson; 18 Sam Burgess; 23 Matt James.
Try: St Hilaire (29); **Goals:** Deacon 3/3.
SAINTS: 1 Paul Wellens; 2 Ade Gardner; 3 Matt Gidley; 4 Willie Talau; 5 Francis Meli; 6 Leon Pryce; 21 Matty Smith; 17 James Graham; 9 Keiron Cunningham (C); 10 Jason Cayless; 11 Lee Gilmour; 15 Mike Bennett; 12 Jon Wilkin. Subs (all used): 14 James Roby; 8 Nick Fozzard; 22 Paul Clough; 23 Maurie Fa'asavalu.
Try: Talau (52); **Goals:** Wellens 0/1.
Dismissal: Wilkin (59) - high tackle on James.
Rugby Leaguer & League Express Men of the Match: *Bulls:* David Solomona; *Saints:* Paul Wellens.
Penalty count: 6-7; **Half-time:** 8-0; **Referee:** Phil Bentham; **Attendance:** 11,214.

HULL FC 20 HARLEQUINS 8

HULL: 14 Motu Tony; 2 Matt Sing; 22 Craig Hall; 3 Kirk Yeaman; 5 Gareth Raynor; 7 Richard Horne; 23 Tommy Lee; 8 Ewan Dowes; 13 Danny Washbrook; 15 Paul King; 11 Lee Radford (C); 17 Willie Manu; 16 Danny Tickle. Subs (all used): 26 Scott Wheeldon; 20 Richard Whiting; 21 Hutch Maiava; 27 Danny Houghton (D).
Tries: R Horne (56), Hall (66); **Goals:** Tickle 5/5, Hall 1/1.
HARLEQUINS: 1 Mark McLinden (C); 2 Jon Wells; 3 Paul Sykes; 4 Tyrone Smith; 28 Rikki Sheriffe; 7 Danny Orr; 6 Scott Hill; 8 Karl Temata; 9 Chad Randall; 15 David Mills; 18 Matt Gafa; 12 Lee Hopkins; 23 Henry Paul. Subs (all used): 14 Julien Rinaldi; 29 Joe Mbu; 20 Jon Grayshon; 17 Louie McCarthy-Scarsbrook.
Try: T Smith (10); **Goals:** Sykes 2/2.
Rugby Leaguer & League Express Men of the Match: *Hull:* Paul King; *Harlequins:* Mark McLinden.
Penalty count: 8-7; **Half-time:** 8-8; **Referee:** Ashley Klein; **Attendance:** 12,270.

Saturday 14th July 2007

CATALANS DRAGONS 20 HULL KINGSTON ROVERS 22

DRAGONS: 1 Clint Greenshields; 25 Younes Khattabi; 3 John Wilson; 4 Adam Mogg; 14 Thomas Bosc; 6 Casey McGuire; 7 Stacey Jones (C); 19 Alex Chan; 26 Luke Quigley; 10 Jerome Guisset; 17 Cyril Gossard; 12 Jason Croker; 13 Gregory Mounis. Subs (all used): 11 Sebastien Raguin; 15 Mathieu Griffi; 18 Vincent Duport; 20 Adel Fellous.
Tries: Greenshields (3), Khattabi (48, 58), Jones (64); **Goals:** Bosc 2/4.
ROVERS: 1 Ben Cockayne; 24 Ian Hardman; 21 Luke Dyer; 33 Rhys Lovegrove; 30 Mark Lennon; 6 Scott Murrell; 7 James Webster (C); 32 Ryan Tandy; 9 Ben Fisher; 18 Danny Ward; 17 Mark O'Neill; 16 Jason Netherton; 14 Stanley Gene. Subs (all used): 4 Gareth Morton; 8 Makali Aizue; 10 David Tangata-Toa; 22 Andreas Bauer.
Tries: Lennon (18), Gene (22), Hardman (24), O'Neill (29); **Goals:** Lennon 3/4.
Rugby Leaguer & League Express Men of the Match: *Dragons:* Clint Greenshields; *Rovers:* Ryan Tandy.
Penalty count: 6-8; **Half-time:** 6-22; **Referee:** Ian Smith; **Attendance:** 7,830.

Sunday 15th July 2007

WARRINGTON WOLVES 42 SALFORD CITY REDS 6

WOLVES: 5 Brent Grose; 1 Stuart Reardon; 3 Martin Gleeson; 4 Paul Johnson; 26 Kevin Penny; 6 Chris Bridge; 7 Lee Briers (C); 16 Paul Wood; 9 Jon Clarke; 10 Paul Rauhihi; 12 Ben Westwood; 11 Adrian Morley; 13 Vinnie Anderson. Subs (all used): 2 Henry Fa'afili; 8 Chris Leikvoll; 15 Rob Parker; 17 Michael Sullivan.
Tries: Clarke (1, 76), Westwood (22), Fa'afili (34), Briers (39), Martin Gleeson (57), Penny (64, 69, 74); **Goals:** Briers 3/10, Bridge 0/1.
CITY REDS: 5 John Wilshere; 19 Stuart Littler; 3 Kevin McGuinness; 4 Aaron Moule; 15 Gray Viane; 6 Luke Dorn; 7 Luke Robinson; 8 Andy Coley; 9 Malcolm Alker (C); 10 Michael Korkidas; 11 Mark Edmondson; 12 Ian Sibbit; 13 Simon Finnigan. Subs (all used): 16 Andrew Brocklehurst; 17 Gareth Haggerty; 20 David Gower; 23 Jordan Turner.
Try: Dorn (8); **Goals:** Wilshere 1/1.
Rugby Leaguer & League Express Men of the Match: *Wolves:* Chris Bridge; *City Reds:* Michael Korkidas.
Penalty count: 12-8; **Half-time:** 22-6; **Referee:** Richard Silverwood; **Attendance:** 9,634.

WAKEFIELD TRINITY WILDCATS 23 HUDDERSFIELD GIANTS 24

WILDCATS: 21 Matt Blaymire; 22 Peter Fox; 3 Jason Demetriou (C); 4 Ryan Atkins; 28 Paul White; 6 Jamie Rooney; 7 Ben Jeffries; 8 Adam Watene; 9 Sam Obst; 16 Ricky Bibey; 11 Ned Catic; 12 Duncan MacGillivray; 13 Brett Ferres. Subs (all used): 10 Danny Sculthorpe; 17 Kevin Henderson; 20 Tevita Leo-Latu; 25 Richard Moore.
Tries: Fox (5, 15), Obst (63, 79); **Goals:** Rooney 3/5; **Field goal:** Rooney (22).
On report: Sculthorpe (71) - alleged swinging arm on Snitch.
GIANTS: 6 Chris Thorman (C); 1 Paul Reilly; 11 Chris Nero; 5 Shane Elford; 24 Rod Jensen; 4 Kevin Brown; 7 Robbie Paul; 18 Darrell Griffin; 19 Ryan Hudson; 16 Keith Mason; 3 Jamahl Lolesi; 12 Andy Raleigh; 13 Stephen Wild. Subs (all used): 8 Eorl Crabtree; 9 Brad Drew; 10 John Skandalis; 20 Steve Snitch.
Tries: Thorman (44), Wild (48), Snitch (52), Elford (58); **Goals:** Thorman 4/5.
Rugby Leaguer & League Express Men of the Match: *Wildcats:* Ben Jeffries; *Giants:* Steve Snitch.
Penalty count: 11-6; **Half-time:** 13-0; **Referee:** Steve Ganson; **Attendance:** 5,241.

ROUND 21

Friday 20th July 2007

LEEDS RHINOS 16 WAKEFIELD TRINITY WILDCATS 23

RHINOS: 1 Brent Webb; 2 Scott Donald; 3 Clinton Toopi; 4 Keith Senior; 25 Ryan Hall; 6 Danny McGuire; 7 Rob Burrow; 16 Ryan Bailey; 23 Jordan Tansey; 10 Jamie Peacock; 11 Jamie Jones-Buchanan; 12 Gareth Ellis; 13 Kevin Sinfield (C). Subs (all used): 8 Kylie Leuluai; 15 Jamie Thackray; 14 Ali Lauitiiti; 18 Ian Kirke.
Tries: Bailey (16), Burrow (47), Donald (67); **Goals:** Sinfield 2/3.
WILDCATS: 21 Matt Blaymire; 22 Peter Fox; 17 Kevin Henderson; 4 Ryan Atkins; 28 Paul White; 6 Jamie Rooney; 7 Ben Jeffries; 8 Adam Watene; 9 Sam Obst; 16 Ricky Bibey; 13 Brett Ferres; 18 Olivier Elima; 3 Jason Demetriou (C). Subs (all used): 25 Richard Moore; 11 Ned Catic; 26 Luke George; 20 Tevita Leo-Latu.
Tries: Elima (62), Atkins (71), George (78); **Goals:** Rooney 5/6; **Field goal:** Rooney (75).
Rugby Leaguer & League Express Men of the Match: *Rhinos:* Brent Webb; *Wildcats:* Adam Watene.
Penalty count: 9-10; **Half-time:** 6-4; **Referee:** Richard Silverwood; **Attendance:** 16,654.

ST HELENS 19 WIGAN WARRIORS 12

SAINTS: 1 Paul Wellens; 2 Ade Gardner; 3 Matt Gidley; 4 Willie Talau; 5 Francis Meli; 6 Leon Pryce; 14 James Roby; 8 Nick Fozzard; 9 Keiron Cunningham (C); 10 Jason Cayless; 15 Mike Bennett; 22 Paul Clough; 18 Bryn Hargreaves. Subs (all used): 7 Sean Long; 17 James Graham; 23 Maurie Fa'asavalu; 30 Chris Flannery (D).
Tries: Cayless (7), Meli (12), Pryce (51); **Goals:** Long 2/3, Wellens 1/2; **Field goal:** Long (77).
On report: Cunningham (59) - alleged swinging arm on Richards.
WARRIORS: 5 Pat Richards; 2 Mark Calderwood; 3 Phil Bailey; 14 David Vaealiki; 23 Liam Colbon; 6 Trent Barrett; 7 Thomas Leuluai; 8 Stuart Fielden; 9 Mick Higham; 10 Iafeta Palea'aesina; 11 Gareth Hock; 12 Bryan Fletcher; 13 Sean O'Loughlin (C). Subs (all used): 18 Paul Prescott; 25 Michael McIlorum; 19 Harrison Hansen; 20 Darrell Goulding.
Tries: Richards (40), Goulding (66); **Goals:** Richards 1/1, O'Loughlin 1/1.
Rugby Leaguer & League Express Men of the Match: *Saints:* Nick Fozzard; *Warriors:* Phil Bailey.
Penalty count: 11-9; **Half-time:** 10-6; **Referee:** Ashley Klein; **Attendance:** 14,293.

Saturday 21st July 2007

HARLEQUINS 10 HUDDERSFIELD GIANTS 22

HARLEQUINS: 1 Mark McLinden (C); 2 Jon Wells; 4 Tyrone Smith; 3 Paul Sykes; 28 Rikki Sheriffe; 7 Danny Orr; 6 Scott Hill; 8 Karl Temata; 9 Chad Randall; 15 David Mills; 18 Matt Gafa; 12 Lee Hopkins; 29 Joe Mbu. Subs (all used): 14 Julien Rinaldi; 20 Jon Grayshon; 17 Louie McCarthy-Scarsbrook; 22 Michael Worrincy.
Tries: McCarthy-Scarsbrook (35), T Smith (62); **Goals:** Sykes 1/2.
GIANTS: 6 Chris Thorman (C); 21 Matt Gardner; 11 Chris Nero; 5 Shane Elford; 24 Rod Jensen; 4 Kevin Brown; 7 Robbie Paul; 18 Darrell Griffin; 19 Ryan Hudson; 16 Keith Mason; 3 Jamahl Lolesi; 12 Andy Raleigh; 13 Stephen Wild. Subs (all used): 8 Eorl Crabtree; 9 Brad Drew; 10 John Skandalis; 20 Steve Snitch.
Tries: Nero (10, 43), Snitch (51), Brown (68); **Goals:** Thorman 3/4.
Rugby Leaguer & League Express Men of the Match: *Harlequins:* Danny Orr; *Giants:* Robbie Paul.
Penalty count: 4-3; **Half-time:** 6-6; **Referee:** Phil Bentham; **Attendance:** 2,478.

SALFORD CITY REDS 14 BRADFORD BULLS 10

CITY REDS: 29 Tom Saxton (D); 30 Richie Barnett (D); 3 Kevin McGuinness; 4 Aaron Moule; 15 Gray Viane; 5 John Wilshere; 7 Luke Robinson; 8 Andy Coley; 9 Malcolm Alker (C); 10 Michael Korkidas; 28 Mike Wainwright (D2); 16 Andrew Brocklehurst; 13 Simon Finnigan. Subs (all used): 6 Luke Dorn; 17 Gareth Haggerty; 19 Stuart Littler; 21 Stephen Nash.
Tries: Viane (22), Robinson (66); **Goals:** Wilshere 3/4.
BULLS: 19 Michael Platt; 1 Marcus St Hilaire; 3 Ben Harris; 2 Nathan McAvoy; 20 Tame Tupou; 6 Iestyn Harris; 7 Paul Deacon (C); 8 Joe Vagana; 9 Terry Newton; 10 Andy Lynch; 11 Chris McKenna; 26 David Solomona; 12 Glenn Morrison. Subs (all used): 17 James Evans; 16 Ian Henderson; 18 Sam Burgess; 23 Matt James.
Tries: Tupou (50, 59); **Goals:** Deacon 1/2.
Rugby Leaguer & League Express Men of the Match: *City Reds:* Luke Robinson; *Bulls:* Michael Platt.
Penalty count: 10-7; **Half-time:** 8-0; **Referee:** Ian Smith; **Attendance:** 3,438.

CATALANS DRAGONS 18 HULL FC 34

DRAGONS: 1 Clint Greenshields; 25 Younes Khattabi; 3 John Wilson; 4 Adam Mogg; 14 Thomas Bosc; 6 Casey McGuire; 7 Stacey Jones (C); 19 Alex Chan; 26 Luke Quigley; 10 Jerome Guisset; 11 Sebastien Raguin; 12 Jason Croker; 13 Gregory Mounis. Subs (all used): 15 Mathieu Griffi; 18 Vincent Duport; 8 David Ferriol; 17 Cyril Gossard.
Tries: Mogg (6), Quigley (26), Ferriol (36), Bosc (70); **Goals:** Bosc 1/4.
Sin bin: Greenshields (52) - interference.
HULL: 14 Motu Tony; 2 Matt Sing; 22 Craig Hall; 3 Kirk Yeaman; 5 Gareth Raynor; 7 Richard Horne; 23 Tommy Lee; 8 Ewan Dowes; 13 Danny Washbrook; 15 Paul King; 11 Lee Radford (C); 17 Willie Manu; 16 Danny Tickle. Subs (all used): 20 Richard Whiting; 21 Hutch Maiava; 26 Scott Wheeldon; 27 Danny Houghton.
Tries: Tickle (16, 75), Lee (18), Raynor (30), R Horne (43), Sing (63); **Goals:** Tickle 5/6.
Sin bin: Raynor (54) - interference.
Rugby Leaguer & League Express Men of the Match: *Dragons:* Adam Mogg; *Hull:* Danny Tickle.
Penalty count: 8-5; **Half-time:** 14-18; **Referee:** Steve Ganson; **Attendance:** 7,560.

Sunday 22nd July 2007

HULL KINGSTON ROVERS 20 WARRINGTON WOLVES 60

ROVERS: 1 Ben Cockayne; 30 Mark Lennon; 33 Rhys Lovegrove; 21 Luke Dyer; 24 Ian Hardman; 6 Scott Murrell; 7 James Webster (C); 32 Ryan Tandy; 9 Ben Fisher; 18 Danny Ward; 11 Iain Morrison; 16 Jason Netherton; 14 Stanley Gene. Subs (all used): 8 Makali Aizue; 10 David Tangata-Toa; 4 Gareth Morton; 22 Andreas Bauer.
Tries: Hardman (15), Fisher (47), Aizue (71), Morton (79); **Goals:** Lennon 2/4.
WOLVES: 5 Brent Grose; 1 Stuart Reardon; 3 Martin Gleeson; 2 Henry Fa'afili; 26 Kevin Penny; 6 Chris Bridge; 7 Lee Briers (C); 16 Paul Wood; 14 Mark Gleeson; 10 Paul Rauhihi; 12 Ben Westwood; 11 Adrian Morley; 9 Jon Clarke. Subs (all used): 15 Rob Parker; 8 Chris Leikvoll; 21 Andy Bracek; 22 Ben Harrison.
Tries: Reardon (2, 41), Morley (17), Mark Gleeson (26), Clarke (28, 77), Briers (38, 57, 63), Bridge (39), Fa'afili (74); **Goals:** Briers 8/11.
Rugby Leaguer & League Express Men of the Match: *Rovers:* Ben Cockayne; *Wolves:* Lee Briers.
Penalty count: 8-4; **Half-time:** 4-32; **Referee:** Ben Thaler; **Attendance:** 6,640.

ROUND 18

Sunday 29th July 2007

HULL FC 48 SALFORD CITY REDS 26

HULL: 14 Motu Tony; 2 Matt Sing; 20 Richard Whiting; 19 Graeme Horne; 22 Craig Hall; 7 Richard Horne; 32 Mathew Head; 8 Ewan Dowes; 23 Tommy Lee; 15 Paul King; 11 Lee Radford (C); 17 Willie Manu; 16 Danny

Warrington's Kevin Penny crashes past Chris Ashton to score during the Wolves' home win over Wigan

Tickle. Subs (all used): 26 Scott Wheeldon; 13 Danny Washbrook; 21 Hutch Maiava; 27 Danny Houghton.
Tries: Manu (5), R Horne (15, 23), Hall (21, 60), Sing (49), Radford (53), Whiting (78); **Goals:** Tickle 8/9.
CITY REDS: 29 Tom Saxton; 30 Richie Barnett; 3 Kevin McGuinness; 4 Aaron Moule; 15 Gray Viane; 5 John Wilshere; 7 Luke Robinson; 8 Andy Coley; 9 Malcolm Alker (C); 10 Michael Korkidas; 28 Mike Wainwright; 16 Andrew Brocklehurst; 13 Simon Finnigan. Subs (all used): 6 Luke Dorn; 17 Gareth Haggerty; 19 Stuart Littler; 21 Stephen Nash.
Tries: Wilshere (34), Moule (38, 45), Dorn (65), Finnigan (70); **Goals:** Wilshere 3/5.
Rugby Leaguer & League Express Men of the Match:
Hull: Willie Manu; *City Reds:* Aaron Moule.
Penalty count: 8-7; **Half-time:** 26-10;
Referee: Phil Bentham; **Attendance:** 13,338.

ROUND 22

Friday 3rd August 2007

SALFORD CITY REDS 24 HULL KINGSTON ROVERS 30

CITY REDS: 29 Tom Saxton; 2 David Hodgson; 19 Stuart Littler; 4 Aaron Moule; 30 Richie Barnett; 5 John Wilshere; 7 Luke Robinson; 14 Paul Highton; 9 Malcolm Alker (C); 10 Michael Korkidas; 8 Andy Coley; 28 Mike Wainwright; 13 Simon Finnigan. Subs (all used): 6 Luke Dorn; 17 Gareth Haggerty; 31 Phil Leuluai (D); 21 Stephen Nash.
Tries: Barnett (9), Finnigan (31), Moule (64), Hodgson (79); **Goals:** Wilshere 4/4.
Sin bin: Coley (17) - delaying restart.
ROVERS: 24 Ian Hardman; 30 Mark Lennon; 3 Jon Goddard; 21 Luke Dyer; 22 Andreas Bauer; 31 Paul Cooke; 7 James Webster (C); 8 Makali Aizue; 6 Scott Murrell; 20 Michael Vella; 28 Chris Chester; 17 Mark O'Neill; 14 Stanley Gene. Subs (all used): 18 Danny Ward; 32 Ryan Tandy; 33 Rhys Lovegrove; 9 Ben Fisher.
Tries: O'Neill (18, 44), Cooke (25), Lennon (58), Dyer (60); **Goals:** Cooke 5/7.
Sin bin: Ward (77) - high tackle.
Rugby Leaguer & League Express Men of the Match:
City Reds: Simon Finnigan; *Rovers:* James Webster.
Penalty count: 8-6; **Half-time:** 12-10;
Referee: Ashley Klein; **Attendance:** 7,165.

ST HELENS 31 HULL FC 20

SAINTS: 1 Paul Wellens; 2 Ade Gardner; 3 Matt Gidley; 4 Willie Talau; 5 Francis Meli; 12 Jon Wilkin; 7 Sean Long (C); 8 Nick Fozzard; 9 Keiron Cunningham; 17 James Graham; 11 Lee Gilmour; 15 Mike Bennett; 30 Chris

Flannery. Subs (all used): 14 James Roby; 18 Bryn Hargreaves; 22 Paul Clough; 23 Maurie Fa'asavalu.
Tries: Long (24), Clough (28), Gardner (30), Meli (49, 67, 80); **Goals:** Long 3/7; Fa'asavalu 0/1;
Field goal: Long (79).
On report:
Cunningham (70) - alleged leading with the elbow.
HULL: 14 Motu Tony; 2 Matt Sing; 20 Richard Whiting; 19 Graeme Horne; 22 Craig Hall; 7 Richard Horne; 32 Mathew Head; 8 Ewan Dowes; 23 Tommy Lee; 15 Paul King; 11 Lee Radford (C); 17 Willie Manu; 16 Danny Tickle. Subs (all used): 27 Danny Houghton; 13 Danny Washbrook; 26 Scott Wheeldon; 21 Hutch Maiava.
Tries: Tony (18), Sing (60), G Horne (75);
Goals: Tickle 4/5.
Sin bin: Head (39) - high tackle on Gardner.
Rugby Leaguer & League Express Men of the Match:
Saints: Francis Meli; *Hull:* Lee Radford.
Penalty count: 12-8; **Half-time:** 16-8;
Referee: Ben Thaler; **Attendance:** 10,005.

Sunday 5th August 2007

HARLEQUINS 20 LEEDS RHINOS 54

HARLEQUINS: 1 Mark McLinden (C); 2 Jon Wells; 4 Tyrone Smith; 3 Paul Sykes; 28 Rikki Sheriffe; 7 Danny Orr; 6 Scott Hill; 8 Karl Temata; 9 Chad Randall; 17 Louie McCarthy-Scarsbrook; 18 Matt Gafa; 12 Lee Hopkins; 23 Henry Paul. Subs (all used): 14 Julien Rinaldi; 13 Rob Purdham; 29 Joe Mbu; 20 Jon Grayshon.
Tries: Sykes (10), Hill (22), McLinden (31), Orr (73);
Goals: Sykes 2/4.
RHINOS: 1 Brent Webb; 2 Scott Donald; 3 Clinton Toopi; 4 Keith Senior; 25 Ryan Hall; 6 Danny McGuire; 7 Rob Burrow; 16 Ryan Bailey; 13 Kevin Sinfield (C); 8 Kylie Leuluai; 11 Jamie Jones-Buchanan; 10 Jamie Peacock; 12 Gareth Ellis. Subs (all used): 15 Jamie Thackray; 23 Jordan Tansey; 14 Ali Lauitiiti; 18 Ian Kirke.
Tries: Thackray (20), Webb (47, 78), Tansey (52), Sinfield (54), Ellis (60), Donald (65), Peacock (68), McGuire (75); **Goals:** Sinfield 7/7; Tansey 2/2.
Sin bin: Webb (21) - high tackle on T Smith.
On report: Webb (8) - alleged high tackle on Orr, alleged high tackle on Randall.
Rugby Leaguer & League Express Men of the Match:
Harlequins: Danny Orr; *Rhinos:* Danny McGuire.
Penalty count: 11-10; **Half-time:** 16-6;
Referee: Phil Bentham; **Attendance:** 3,734.

**BRADFORD BULLS 38
WAKEFIELD TRINITY WILDCATS 24**

BULLS: 1 Marcus St Hilaire; 24 Dave Halley; 3 Ben Harris; 17 James Evans; 20 Tame Tupou; 12 Glenn Morrison (C); 16 Ian Henderson; 8 Joe Vagana; 9 Terry Newton; 10

Andy Lynch; 11 Chris McKenna; 26 David Solomona; 18 Sam Burgess. Subs (all used): 2 Nathan McAvoy; 23 Matt James; 15 Matt Cook; 27 Richie Hawkyard.
Tries: Halley (15), Evans (28, 66), Morrison (37), Tupou (41), Solomona (45), Burgess (71); **Goals:** Burgess 5/8.
Dismissal: Vagana (39) – leading with the elbow.
WILDCATS: 21 Matt Blaymire; 22 Peter Fox; 3 Jason Demetriou (C); 4 Ryan Atkins; 28 Paul White; 6 Jamie Rooney; 7 Ben Jeffries; 8 Adam Watene; 9 Sam Obst; 11 Ned Catic; 13 Brett Ferres; 18 Olivier Elima; 17 Kevin Henderson. Subs (all used): 36 Maxime Greseque (D); 25 Richard Moore; 26 Luke George; 12 Duncan MacGillivray.
Tries: Atkins (19), Fox (33), Demetriou (58), Henderson (62); **Goals:** Rooney 4/5.
Rugby Leaguer & League Express Men of the Match:
Bulls: Sam Burgess; *Wildcats:* Adam Watene.
Penalty count: 6-4; **Half-time:** 16-12;
Referee: Steve Ganson; **Attendance:** 10,701.

HUDDERSFIELD GIANTS 42 CATALANS DRAGONS 22

GIANTS: 6 Chris Thorman (C); 21 Matt Gardner; 11 Chris Nero; 5 Shane Elford; 24 Rod Jensen; 4 Kevin Brown; 7 Robbie Paul; 16 Keith Mason; 19 Ryan Hudson; 18 Darrell Griffin; 3 Jamahl Lolesi; 12 Andy Raleigh; 13 Stephen Wild. Subs (all used): 8 Eorl Crabtree; 9 Brad Drew; 10 John Skandalis; 20 Steve Snitch.
Tries: Jensen (4), Griffin (9), Elford (20, 33), Wild (30, 42), Thorman (72); **Goals:** Thorman 7/8.
DRAGONS: 1 Clint Greenshields; 18 Vincent Duport; 3 John Wilson; 4 Adam Mogg; 25 Younes Khattabi; 6 Casey McGuire; 7 Stacey Jones (C); 19 Alex Chan; 26 Luke Quigley; 10 Jerome Guisset; 11 Sebastien Raguin; 12 Jason Croker; 13 Gregory Mounis. Subs (all used): 8 David Ferriol; 15 Mathieu Griffi; 17 Cyril Gossard; 21 Julien Touxagas.
Tries: Croker (16), Chan (56), Mogg (59), Khattabi (75);
Goals: Jones 3/4.
Sin bin: Greenshields (22) – holding down, (69) – interference.
Rugby Leaguer & League Express Men of the Match:
Giants: Rod Jensen; *Dragons:* Stacey Jones.
Penalty count: 28-6;
Referee: Richard Silverwood; **Attendance:** 4,319.

WARRINGTON WOLVES 43 WIGAN WARRIORS 24

WOLVES: 5 Brent Grose; 1 Stuart Reardon; 3 Martin Gleeson; 2 Henry Fa'afili; 26 Kevin Penny; 6 Chris Bridge; 7 Lee Briers (C); 16 Paul Wood; 14 Mark Gleeson; 10 Paul Rauhihi; 12 Ben Westwood; 11 Adrian Morley; 9 Jon Clarke. Subs (all used): 19 Rob Parker; 20 Simon Grix; 21 Andy Bracek; 22 Ben Harrison.
Tries: Reardon (4), Penny (9), Briers (22), Grose (25), Clarke (57), Fa'afili (70), Bridge (74); **Goals:** Briers 7/7;
Field goal: Briers (39).

Paul Wellens feels the force of the Catalans defence, as the Dragons nil St Helens in Perpignan

WARRIORS: 1 Chris Ashton; 23 Liam Colbon; 3 Phil Bailey; 14 David Vaealiki; 5 Pat Richards; 6 Trent Barrett; 7 Thomas Leuluai; 8 Stuart Fielden; 9 Mick Higham; 10 Iafeta Palea'aesina; 12 Bryan Fletcher; 11 Gareth Hock; 13 Sean O'Loughlin (C). Subs (all used): 24 Eamon O'Carroll; 19 Harrison Hansen; 20 Darrell Goulding; 25 Michael McIlorum.
Tries: Colbon (13), Leuluai (42), Goulding (66, 79);
Goals: Richards 4/4.
Sin bin: Fielden (56) - late challenge on Briers.
Rugby Leaguer & League Express Men of the Match: *Wolves:* Lee Briers; *Warriors:* Darrell Goulding.
Penalty count: 9-8; **Half-time:** 25-6;
Referee: Ian Smith; **Attendance:** 12,552.

ROUND 23

Friday 10th August 2007

LEEDS RHINOS 52 SALFORD CITY REDS 14

RHINOS: 23 Jordan Tansey; 2 Scott Donald; 3 Clinton Toopi; 4 Keith Senior; 25 Ryan Hall; 13 Kevin Sinfield (C); 6 Danny McGuire; 15 Jamie Thackray; 9 Matt Diskin; 8 Kylie Leuluai; 10 Jamie Peacock; 11 Jamie Jones-Buchanan; 12 Gareth Ellis. Subs (all used): 17 Nick Scruton; 18 Ian Kirke; 14 Ali Lauititi; 27 Mike Ratu (D).
Tries: Hall (3), Thackray (9, 65), Leuluai (11), Senior (21), McGuire (39, 67), Donald (41), Lauititi (79);
Goals: Sinfield 7/8, Tansey 1/1.
CITY REDS: 29 Tom Saxton; 2 David Hodgson; 19 Stuart Littler; 4 Aaron Moule; 30 Richie Barnett; 5 John Wilshere; 7 Luke Robinson; 14 Paul Highton; 9 Malcolm Alker (C); 10 Michael Korkidas; 8 Andy Coley; 31 Phil Leuluai; 13 Simon Finnigan. Subs (all used): 21 Stephen Nash; 17 Gareth Haggerty; 23 Jordan Turner; 6 Luke Dorn.
Tries: Littler (28), Dorn (47), Coley (72);
Goals: Wilshere 1/3.
Sin bin: Korkidas (64) - interference.
Rugby Leaguer & League Express Men of the Match: *Rhinos:* Matt Diskin; *City Reds:* Simon Finnigan.
Penalty count: 13-6; **Half-time:** 28-4;
Referee: Ben Thaler; **Attendance:** 15,637.

WIGAN WARRIORS 20 HUDDERSFIELD GIANTS 12

WARRIORS: 5 Pat Richards; 2 Mark Calderwood; 20 Darrell Goulding; 14 David Vaealiki; 23 Liam Colbon; 6 Trent Barrett; 7 Thomas Leuluai; 16 Shane Millard; 10 Iafeta Palea'aesina; 3 Phil Bailey; 11 Gareth Hock; 13 Sean O'Loughlin (C). Subs (all used): 8 Stuart Fielden; 9 Mick Higham; 18 Paul Prescott; 19 Harrison Hansen.

Tries: Goulding (5), Higham (37); **Goals:** Richards 6/6.
On report: Fielden (67) - incident in back-play.
GIANTS: 6 Chris Thorman (C); 24 Rod Jensen; 5 Shane Elford; 11 Chris Nero; 21 Matt Gardner; 4 Kevin Brown; 7 Robbie Paul; 16 Keith Mason; 19 Ryan Hudson; 18 Darrell Griffin; 3 Jamahl Lolesi; 12 Andy Raleigh; 13 Stephen Wild. Subs (all used): 8 Eorl Crabtree; 14 Stuart Jones; 10 John Skandalis; 22 Tom Hemingway.
Tries: Wild (9), Nero (48); **Goals:** Thorman 2/3.
Sin bin: Wild (76) - late challenge on Barrett.
On report: Lolesi (67) - incident in back-play.
Rugby Leaguer & League Express Men of the Match: *Warriors:* Pat Richards; *Giants:* Stephen Wild.
Penalty count: 12-5; **Half-time:** 14-6;
Referee: Steve Ganson; **Attendance:** 12,744.

Saturday 11th August 2007

CATALANS DRAGONS 21 ST HELENS 0

DRAGONS: 1 Clint Greenshields; 2 Justin Murphy; 3 John Wilson; 11 Sebastien Raguin; 25 Younes Khattabi; 4 Adam Mogg; 7 Stacey Jones (C); 19 Alex Chan; 26 Luke Quigley; 10 Jerome Guisset; 17 Cyril Gossard; 12 Jason Croker; 13 Gregory Mounis. Subs (all used): 8 David Ferriol; 21 Julien Touxagas; 27 Kane Bentley; 24 Remi Casty.
Tries: Khattabi (33), Murphy (46), Croker (56), Greenshields (71); **Goals:** Jones 2/4.
Field goal: Jones (75).
SAINTS: 1 Paul Wellens; 2 Ade Gardner; 3 Matt Gidley; 4 Willie Talau; 5 Francis Meli; 26 Kyle Eastmond; 7 Sean Long (C); 17 James Graham; 9 Keiron Cunningham; 10 Jason Cayless; 15 Mike Bennett; 30 Chris Flannery; 12 Jon Wilkin. Subs (all used): 18 Bryn Hargreaves; 14 James Roby; 23 Maurie Fa'asavalu; 22 Paul Clough.
Rugby Leaguer & League Express Men of the Match: *Dragons:* Clint Greenshields; *Saints:* Jon Wilkin.
Penalty count: 7-9; **Half-time:** 4-0;
Referee: Phil Bentham; **Attendance:** 8,655.

Sunday 12th August 2007

HULL KINGSTON ROVERS 10 BRADFORD BULLS 28

ROVERS: 1 Ben Cockayne; 24 Ian Hardman; 21 Luke Dyer; 3 Jon Goddard; 30 Mark Lennon; 31 Paul Cooke; 7 James Webster (C); 20 Michael Vella; 6 Scott Murrell; 15 Jim Gannon; 17 Mark O'Neill; 28 Chris Chester; 14 Stanley Gene. Subs (all used): 32 Ryan Tandy; 18 Danny Ward; 9 Ben Fisher; 33 Rhys Lovegrove.
Tries: Goddard (3), Fisher (60); **Goals:** Cooke 1/2.
BULLS: 19 Michael Platt; 1 Marcus St Hilaire; 3 Ben Harris; 12 James Evans; 20 Tame Tupou; 2 Glenn Morrison (C); 6 Iestyn Harris; 10 Andy Lynch; 9 Terry Newton; 23 Matt James; 26 David Solomona; 11 Chris

McKenna; 18 Sam Burgess. Subs (all used): 14 Chris Feather; 16 Ian Henderson; 2 Nathan McAvoy; 15 Matt Cook.
Tries: Burgess (3), Newton (16), Morrison (20), Henderson (24), St Hilaire (33); **Goals:** I Harris 4/5.
Rugby Leaguer & League Express Men of the Match: *Rovers:* James Webster; *Bulls:* Glenn Morrison.
Penalty count: 10-6; **Half-time:** 4-28;
Referee: Ian Smith; **Attendance:** 6,695.

HULL FC 46 WARRINGTON WOLVES 14

HULL: 14 Motu Tony; 1 Shaun Briscoe; 20 Richard Whiting; 22 Craig Hall; 5 Gareth Raynor; 7 Richard Horne; 32 Mathew Head; 8 Ewan Dowes; 23 Tommy Lee; 15 Paul King; 11 Lee Radford (C); 17 Willie Manu; 16 Danny Tickle. Subs (all used): 26 Scott Wheeldon; 13 Danny Washbrook; 19 Graeme Horne; 10 Garreth Carvell.
Tries: Manu (22), Raynor (28, 42), Carvell (46), Tony (50, 64), R Horne (66); **Goals:** Tickle 7/9.
WOLVES: 5 Brent Grose; 1 Stuart Reardon; 3 Martin Gleeson; 2 Henry Fa'afili; 26 Kevin Penny; 6 Chris Bridge; 7 Lee Briers (C); 16 Paul Wood; 14 Mark Gleeson; 10 Paul Rauhihi; 12 Ben Westwood; 11 Adrian Morley; 9 Jon Clarke. Subs (all used): 19 Steve Pickersgill; 20 Simon Grix; 21 Andy Bracek; 22 Ben Harrison.
Tries: Martin Gleeson (13), Fa'afili (33, 36);
Goals: Briers 1/2, Westwood 0/1.
Dismissal: Wood (62) - high tackle on Wheeldon.
Rugby Leaguer & League Express Men of the Match: *Hull:* Motu Tony; *Wolves:* Henry Fa'afili.
Penalty count: 14-9; **Half-time:** 18-14;
Referee: Ashley Klein; **Attendance:** 13,404.

WAKEFIELD TRINITY WILDCATS 28 HARLEQUINS 14

WILDCATS: 21 Matt Blaymire; 22 Peter Fox; 3 Jason Demetriou (C); 4 Ryan Atkins; 28 Paul White; 6 Jamie Rooney; 7 Ben Jeffries; 8 Adam Watene; 15 David March; 16 Ricky Bibey; 18 Olivier Elima; 13 Brett Ferres; 17 Kevin Henderson. Subs (all used): 14 Ned Catic; 14 Paul March; 25 Richard Moore; 33 Sean Gleeson.
Tries: Rooney (6), Atkins (22, 76), White (33), Catic (52); **Goals:** Rooney 4/7.
HARLEQUINS: 1 Mark McLinden; 2 Jon Wells; 3 Paul Sykes; 4 Tyrone Smith; 28 Rikki Sheriffe; 6 Scott Hill; 7 Danny Orr; 8 Karl Temata; 9 Chad Randall; 17 Louie McCarthy-Scarsbrook; 18 Matt Gafa; 13 Rob Purdham (C); 23 Henry Paul. Subs (all used): 14 Julien Rinaldi; 12 Lee Hopkins; 20 Jon Grayshon; 29 Joe Mbu.
Tries: Hill (40), Wells (63), T Smith (80);
Goals: Sykes 0/2, Orr 1/1.
Rugby Leaguer & League Express Men of the Match: *Wildcats:* Richard Moore; *Harlequins:* Mark McLinden.
Penalty count: 9-6; **Half-time:** 14-4;
Referee: Richard Silverwood; **Attendance:** 5,128.

ROUND 24

Friday 17th August 2007

LEEDS RHINOS 34 HULL KINGSTON ROVERS 18

RHINOS: 5 Lee Smith; 2 Scott Donald; 3 Clinton Toopi; 4 Keith Senior; 25 Ryan Hall; 13 Kevin Sinfield (C); 6 Danny McGuire; 16 Ryan Bailey; 9 Matt Diskin; 8 Kylie Leuluai; 10 Jamie Peacock; 11 Jamie Jones-Buchanan; 12 Gareth Ellis. Subs (all used): 15 Jamie Thackray; 14 Ali Lauitiiti; 18 Ian Kirke; 22 Carl Ablett.
Tries: Donald (13, 64), Hall (24), Diskin (29), Toopi (55), McGuire (79); **Goals:** Sinfield 5/6.
ROVERS: 24 Ian Hardman; 22 Andreas Bauer; 3 Jon Goddard; 21 Luke Dyer; 30 Mark Lennon; 31 Paul Cooke; 7 James Webster (C); 20 Michael Vella; 9 Ben Fisher; 8 Makali Aizue; 28 Chris Chester; 17 Mark O'Neill; 6 Scott Murrell. Subs (all used): 18 Danny Ward; 32 Ryan Tandy; 16 Jason Netherton; 33 Rhys Lovegrove.
Tries: Lovegrove (42), Dyer (49), Tandy (70);
Goals: Cooke 3/3.
Sin bin: Chester (16) - interference.
Rugby Leaguer & League Express Men of the Match:
Rhinos: Jamie Peacock; *Rovers:* Michael Vella.
Penalty count: 8-7; **Half-time:** 16-0;
Referee: Richard Silverwood; **Attendance:** 17,389.

SALFORD CITY REDS 20 ST HELENS 32

CITY REDS: 1 Karl Fitzpatrick; 2 David Hodgson; 3 Kevin McGuinness; 4 Aaron Moule; 30 Richie Barnett; 5 John Wilshere; 7 Luke Robinson; 31 Phil Leuluai; 9 Malcolm Alker (C); 10 Michael Korkidas; 19 Stuart Littler; 12 Ian Sibbit; 23 Jordan Turner. Subs (all used): 6 Luke Dorn; 20 David Gower; 14 Paul Highton; 21 Stephen Nash.
Tries: Littler (8), Wilshere (35, 71); **Goals:** Wilshere 4/4.
SAINTS: 3 Matt Gidley; 2 Ade Gardner; 24 Steve Tyrer; 11 Lee Gilmour; 5 Francis Meli; 14 James Roby; 21 Matty Smith; 8 Nick Fozzard; 9 Keiron Cunningham (C); 10 Jason Cayless; 15 Mike Bennett; 22 Paul Clough; 30 Chris Flannery. Subs (all used): 17 James Graham; 18 Bryn Hargreaves; 20 Scott Moore; 31 Chris Dean (D).
Tries: Gardner (4, 77), Gidley (21), Graham (63), Cunningham (66); **Goals:** Tyrer 6/6.
Rugby Leaguer & League Express Men of the Match:
City Reds: John Wilshere; *Saints:* Matt Gidley.
Penalty count: 8-9; **Half-time:** 12-12;
Referee: Ian Smith; **Attendance:** 5,031.

WAKEFIELD TRINITY WILDCATS 24 HULL FC 42

WILDCATS: 6 Jamie Rooney; 22 Peter Fox; 3 Jason Demetriou (C); 4 Ryan Atkins; 28 Paul White; 36 Maxime Greseque; 7 Ben Jeffries; 8 Adam Watene; 15 David March; 16 Ricky Bibey; 18 Olivier Elima; 13 Brett Ferres; 24 Dale Ferguson. Subs (all used): 11 Ned Catic; 14 Paul March; 25 Richard Moore; 33 Sean Gleeson.
Tries: Atkins (18), Demetriou (23), Rooney (38);
Goals: Rooney 6/6.
Sin bin: Bibey (20) - holding down;
Elima (66) - obstruction; Watene (67) - high tackle.
On report: Moore (45) - alleged high tackle.
HULL: 14 Motu Tony; 1 Shaun Briscoe; 22 Craig Hall; 3 Kirk Yeaman; 5 Gareth Raynor; 7 Richard Horne; 32 Mathew Head; 8 Ewan Dowes; 23 Tommy Lee; 15 Paul King; 11 Lee Radford (C); 17 Willie Manu; 16 Danny Tickle. Subs (all used): 10 Garreth Carvell; 20 Richard Whiting; 13 Danny Washbrook; 26 Scott Wheeldon.
Tries: Manu (4), Hall (20), Tickle (46), Raynor (54), Head (68), Whiting (73), Tony (74); **Goals:** Tickle 7/9.
Sin bin: R Horne (9) - holding down.
On report: King (60) - alleged leading with the forearm.
Rugby Leaguer & League Express Men of the Match:
Wildcats: Olivier Elima; *Hull:* Willie Manu.
Penalty count: 8-16; **Half-time:** 24-16;
Referee: Phil Bentham; **Attendance:** 8,115.

Saturday 18th August 2007

HARLEQUINS 16 WIGAN WARRIORS 16

HARLEQUINS: 1 Mark McLinden; 2 Jon Wells; 19 Tony Clubb; 4 Tyrone Smith; 28 Rikki Sheriffe; 6 Scott Hill; 7 Danny Orr; 17 Louie McCarthy-Scarsbrook; 9 Chad Randall; 29 Joe Mbu; 18 Matt Gafa; 13 Rob Purdham (C); 23 Henry Paul. Subs (all used): 14 Julien Rinaldi; 20 Jon Grayshon; 30 Steve Bannister; 12 Lee Hopkins.
Tries: Gafa (15), Hill (18), McLinden (29);
Goals: Paul 2/3.
WARRIORS: 5 Pat Richards; 2 Mark Calderwood; 3 Phil Bailey; 14 David Vaealiki; 23 Liam Colbon; 6 Trent Barrett; 7 Thomas Leuluai; 12 Bryan Fletcher; 16 Shane Millard; 10 Iafeta Palea'aesina; 11 Gareth Hock; 19 Harrison Hansen; 13 Sean O'Loughlin (C). Subs (all used): 8 Stuart Fielden; 9 Mick Higham; 18 Paul Prescott; 20 Darrell Goulding.
Tries: Leuluai (22), Barrett (46, 64); **Goals:** Richards 2/4.
Rugby Leaguer & League Express Men of the Match:
Harlequins: Mark McLinden; *Warriors:* Trent Barrett.
Penalty count: 7-8; **Half-time:** 16-8;
Referee: Ben Thaler; **Attendance:** 3,200.

Sunday 19th August 2007

HUDDERSFIELD GIANTS 26 BRADFORD BULLS 22

GIANTS: 7 Robbie Paul; 24 Rod Jensen; 11 Chris Nero; 5 Shane Elford; 21 Matt Gardner; 4 Kevin Brown; 9 Brad Drew (C); 16 Keith Mason; 19 Ryan Hudson; 10 John Skandalis; 3 Jamahl Lolesi; 12 Andy Raleigh; 13 Stephen Wild. Subs (all used): 1 Paul Reilly; 8 Eorl Crabtree; 14 Stuart Jones; 18 Darrell Griffin.
Tries: Jensen (3), Lolesi (39, 55, 69); **Goals:** Drew 5/5.
Dismissal: Mason (63) - head butt on Solomona.
BULLS: 19 Michael Platt; 20 Tame Tupou; 2 Nathan McAvoy; 3 Ben Harris; 1 Marcus St Hilaire; 12 Glenn Morrison (C); 6 Iestyn Harris; 14 Chris Feather; 9 Terry Newton; 10 Andy Lynch; 11 Chris McKenna; 26 David Solomona; 18 Sam Burgess. Subs (all used): 23 Matt James; 15 Matt Cook; 16 Ian Henderson; 24 Dave Halley.
Tries: Solomona (5), Henderson (28), McKenna (77);
Goals: I Harris 5/5.
Dismissal: Tupou (61) - punching.
Rugby Leaguer & League Express Men of the Match:
Giants: Jamahl Lolesi; *Bulls:* Terry Newton.
Penalty count: 13-12; **Half-time:** 12-16;
Referee: Ashley Klein; **Attendance:** 6,824.

WARRINGTON WOLVES 22 CATALANS DRAGONS 18

WOLVES: 5 Brent Grose; 24 Chris Riley; 3 Martin Gleeson; 12 Ben Westwood; 26 Kevin Penny; 9 Jon Clarke; 7 Lee Briers (C); 16 Paul Wood; 14 Mark Gleeson; 10 Paul Rauhihi; 11 Adrian Morley; 21 Andy Bracek; 22 Ben Harrison. Subs (all used): 8 Chris Leikvoll; 15 Rob Parker; 19 Steve Pickersgill; 29 Lee Mitchell (D).
Tries: Riley (14), Penny (26), Grose (33, 47), Parker (59); **Goals:** Briers 1/4, Westwood 0/1.
Sin bin: Briers (33) - dissent.
DRAGONS: 1 Clint Greenshields; 2 Justin Murphy; 3 John Wilson; 11 Sebastien Raguin; 25 Younes Khattabi; 4 Adam Mogg; 7 Stacey Jones (C); 8 David Ferriol; 26 Luke Quigley; 19 Alex Chan; 17 Cyril Gossard; 12 Jason Croker; 13 Gregory Mounis. Subs (all used): 20 Adel Fellous; 21 Julien Touxagas; 24 Remi Casty; 27 Kane Bentley.
Tries: Greenshields (23), Jones (44), Murphy (80);
Goals: Jones 3/3.
Sin bin: Greenshields (56) - flop;
Wilson (73) - interference.
On report: Ferriol (38) - alleged leading with the elbow.
Rugby Leaguer & League Express Men of the Match:
Wolves: Brent Grose; *Dragons:* Clint Greenshields.
Penalty count: 7-3; **Half-time:** 12-6;
Referee: Steve Ganson; **Attendance:** 8,125.

ROUND 25

Friday 31st August 2007

ST HELENS 32 HARLEQUINS 10

SAINTS: 1 Paul Wellens; 2 Ade Gardner; 3 Matt Gidley; 4 Willie Talau; 24 Steve Tyrer; 6 Leon Pryce; 7 Sean Long; 8 Nick Fozzard; 9 Keiron Cunningham (C); 10 Jason Cayless; 11 Lee Gilmour; 12 Jon Wilkin; 30 Chris Flannery. Subs (all used): 14 James Roby; 17 James Graham; 22 Paul Clough; 23 Maurie Fa'asavalu.
Tries: Cayless (3), Graham (32), Wellens (54), Flannery (66), Gilmour (76); **Goals:** Tyrer 6/6.
HARLEQUINS: 1 Mark McLinden; 2 Jon Wells; 3 Paul Sykes; 4 Tyrone Smith; 28 Rikki Sheriffe; 6 Scott Hill; 7 Danny Orr; 8 Karl Temata; 9 Chad Randall; 17 Louie McCarthy-Scarsbrook; 18 Matt Gafa; 13 Rob Purdham (C); 23 Henry Paul. Subs (all used): 12 Lee Hopkins; 14 Julien Rinaldi; 20 Jon Grayshon; 29 Joe Mbu.
Tries: Sheriffe (7, 20); **Goals:** Paul 1/2.
Sin bin: Hill (64) - interference;
T Smith (73) - interference.
Rugby Leaguer & League Express Men of the Match:
Saints: James Graham; *Harlequins:* Rikki Sheriffe.
Penalty count: 9-4; **Half-time:** 12-10;
Referee: Ben Thaler; **Attendance:** 7,939.

WARRINGTON WOLVES 22 HUDDERSFIELD GIANTS 34

WOLVES: 5 Brent Grose; 2 Henry Fa'afili; 3 Martin Gleeson; 12 Ben Westwood; 26 Kevin Penny; 9 Jon Clarke; 7 Lee Briers (C); 16 Paul Wood; 14 Mark Gleeson; 10 Paul Rauhihi; 11 Adrian Morley; 21 Andy Bracek; 22 Ben Harrison. Subs (all used): 8 Chris Leikvoll; 19 Steve Pickersgill; 15 Rob Parker; 29 Lee Mitchell.
Tries: Fa'afili (3), Westwood (11, 66, 72), Penny (36);
Goals: Briers 0/3, Westwood 1/2.
On report: Morley (53) - alleged high tackle;
Rauhihi (56) - alleged dangerous throw.
GIANTS: 6 Chris Thorman (C); 24 Rod Jensen; 3 Jamahl Lolesi; 11 Chris Nero; 1 Paul Reilly; 4 Kevin Brown; 9 Brad Drew; 18 Darrell Griffin; 19 Ryan Hudson; 10 John Skandalis; 14 Stuart Jones; 12 Andy Raleigh; 13 Stephen Wild. Subs (all used): 7 Robbie Paul; 8 Eorl Crabtree; 15 Paul Jackson; 27 Michael Lawrence (D).
Tries: Hudson (6), Drew (24), Jensen (47), Lolesi (60), Brown (69); **Goals:** Thorman 7/8.
Rugby Leaguer & League Express Men of the Match:
Wolves: Ben Westwood; *Giants:* Brad Drew.
Penalty count: 6-9; **Half-time:** 12-12;
Referee: Richard Silverwood; **Attendance:** 8,843.

WIGAN WARRIORS 40 SALFORD CITY REDS 16

WARRIORS: 5 Pat Richards; 2 Mark Calderwood; 3 Phil Bailey; 14 David Vaealiki; 23 Liam Colbon; 6 Trent Barrett; 7 Thomas Leuluai; 8 Stuart Fielden; 16 Shane Millard; 10 Iafeta Palea'aesina; 19 Harrison Hansen; 12 Bryan Fletcher; 13 Sean O'Loughlin (C). Subs (all used): 9 Mick Higham; 24 Eamon O'Carroll; 20 Darrell Goulding; 21 Danny Hill.
Tries: Barrett (3), Calderwood (46, 79), Vaealiki (49), Palea'aesina (59), Richards (63), O'Loughlin (66);
Goals: Richards 6/8.
Sin bin: Vaealiki (34) - fighting;
Palea'aesina (34) - fighting.
On report: Brawl (34);
Higham (55) - alleged dangerous tackle.
CITY REDS: 1 Karl Fitzpatrick; 2 David Hodgson; 3 Kevin McGuinness; 4 Aaron Moule; 5 John Wilshere; 26 Stefan Ratchford; 7 Luke Robinson; 31 Phil Leuluai; 9 Malcolm Alker (C); 10 Michael Korkidas; 8 Andy Coley; 12 Ian Sibbit; 13 Simon Finnigan. Subs (all used): 6 Luke Dorn; 20 David Gower; 14 Paul Highton; 19 Stuart Littler.
Tries: Fitzpatrick (18), Highton (39), McGuinness (53);
Goals: Wilshere 2/3.
Sin bin: Littler (34) - fighting.
On report: Brawl (34).
Rugby Leaguer & League Express Men of the Match:
Warriors: Trent Barrett; *City Reds:* Kevin McGuinness.
Penalty count: 8-6; **Half-time:** 6-10;
Referee: Ashley Klein; **Attendance:** 13,611.

Saturday 1st September 2007

CATALANS DRAGONS 38 WAKEFIELD TRINITY WILDCATS 20

DRAGONS: 1 Clint Greenshields; 2 Justin Murphy; 18 Vincent Duport; 11 Sebastien Raguin; 25 Younes Khattabi; 4 Adam Mogg; 7 Stacey Jones (C); 19 Alex Chan; 26 Luke Quigley; 8 David Ferriol; 17 Cyril Gossard; 12 Jason Croker; 28 Andrew Bentley. Subs (all used): 13 Gregory Mounis; 16 Lionel Teixido; 15 Mathieu Griffi; 24 Remi Casty.
Tries: Gossard (10), Croker (17), Casty (44), Murphy (53), Greenshields (64), Mogg (78); **Goals:** Jones 7/7.
Dismissal: Chan (75) - fighting.
Sin bin: Quigley (75) - fighting.
WILDCATS: 6 Jamie Rooney; 22 Peter Fox; 4 Ryan Atkins; 33 Sean Gleeson; 28 Paul White; 36 Maxime Greseque; 7 Ben Jeffries; 8 Adam Watene; 15 David March; 16 Ricky Bibey; 13 Brett Ferres; 11 Ned Catic; 3 Jason Demetriou (C). Subs (all used): 9 Sam Obst; 25 Richard Moore; 10 Danny Sculthorpe; 17 Kevin Henderson.
Tries: Rooney (37, 68), Obst (48); **Goals:** Rooney 4/4.
Dismissal: Moore (75) - fighting.
Rugby Leaguer & League Express Men of the Match:
Dragons: Adam Mogg; *Wildcats:* Jamie Rooney.
Penalty count: 11-14; **Half-time:** 12-8;
Referee: Ian Smith; **Attendance:** 7,325.

Sunday 2nd September 2007

HULL FC 6 HULL KINGSTON ROVERS 42

HULL: 14 Motu Tony; 1 Shaun Briscoe; 22 Craig Hall; 3 Kirk Yeaman; 5 Gareth Raynor; 7 Richard Horne; 32 Mathew Head; 8 Ewan Dowes; 18 Wayne Godwin; 15 Paul King; 11 Lee Radford (C); 17 Willie Manu; 16 Danny Tickle. Subs (all used): 20 Richard Whiting; 21 Hutch Maiava; 26 Scott Wheeldon; 13 Danny Washbrook.
Try: Washbrook (56); **Goals:** Tickle 1/1.
ROVERS: 24 Ian Hardman; 30 Mark Lennon; 33 Rhys Lovegrove; 21 Luke Dyer; 22 Andreas Bauer; 31 Paul Cooke; 7 James Webster (C); 20 Michael Vella; 9 Ben Fisher; 32 Ryan Tandy; 17 Mark O'Neill; 28 Chris Chester; 6 Scott Murrell. Subs (all used): 14 Stanley Gene; 16 Jason Netherton; 15 Jim Gannon; 10 David Tangata-Toa.
Tries: J Netherton (12), Dyer (27, 39), Lennon (53), Lovegrove (63, 78), Webster (66), Gene (73);
Goals: Cooke 5/8.
Rugby Leaguer & League Express Men of the Match:
Hull: Motu Tony; *Rovers:* James Webster.
Penalty count: 5-3; **Half-time:** 0-16;
Referee: Steve Ganson; **Attendance:** 23,004.

BRADFORD BULLS 16 LEEDS RHINOS 16

BULLS: 19 Michael Platt; 1 Marcus St Hilaire; 3 Ben Harris; 17 James Evans; 2 Nathan McAvoy; 6 Iestyn Harris; 7 Paul Deacon (C); 8 Joe Vagana; 9 Terry Newton; 10 Andy Lynch; 11 Chris McKenna; 26 David Solomona; 12 Glenn Morrison. Subs (all used): 18 Sam Burgess; 14 Chris Feather; 16 Ian Henderson; 15 Matt Cook.
Tries: Lynch (15), B Harris (48), Evans (78);
Goals: Deacon 2/4.
RHINOS: 23 Jordan Tansey; 2 Scott Donald; 3 Clinton Toopi; 4 Keith Senior; 5 Lee Smith; 6 Danny McGuire; 7 Rob Burrow; 10 Jamie Peacock; 9 Matt Diskin; 16 Ryan Bailey; 11 Jamie Jones-Buchanan; 12 Gareth Ellis; 13 Kevin Sinfield (C). Subs (all used): 15 Jamie Thackray; 14 Ali Lauitiiti; 22 Carl Ablett; 8 Kylie Leuluai.
Tries: Diskin (46, pen), Donald (54, 71);
Goals: Sinfield 2/4.
Rugby Leaguer & League Express Men of the Match:
Bulls: Glenn Morrison; *Rhinos:* Jamie Peacock.
Penalty count: 8-5; **Half-time:** 8-0;
Referee: Phil Bentham; **Attendance:** 18,195.

ROUND 26

Friday 7th September 2007

LEEDS RHINOS 6 HULL FC 17

RHINOS: 1 Brent Webb; 2 Scott Donald; 3 Clinton Toopi; 4 Keith Senior; 5 Lee Smith; 6 Danny McGuire; 7 Rob Burrow; 16 Ryan Bailey; 9 Matt Diskin; 10 Jamie Peacock; 11 Jamie Jones-Buchanan; 12 Gareth Ellis; 13 Kevin Sinfield (C). Subs (all used): 8 Kylie Leuluai; 15 Jamie Thackray; 22 Carl Ablett; 18 Ian Kirke.
Try: Ablett (28); **Goals:** Sinfield 1/1.
HULL: 1 Shaun Briscoe; 22 Craig Hall; 20 Richard Whiting; 3 Kirk Yeaman; 5 Gareth Raynor; 7 Richard Horne; 32 Mathew Head; 15 Paul King; 23 Tommy Lee; 10 Garreth Carvell; 11 Lee Radford (C); 16 Danny Tickle; 13 Danny Washbrook. Subs (all used): 26 Scott Wheeldon; 17 Willie Manu; 18 Wayne Godwin; 19 Graeme Horne.
Tries: Godwin (32), Raynor (35, 78); **Goals:** Tickle 2/4;

Huddersfield's Chris Nero swamped by the Wakefield defence, as a narrow Giants win earns a play-off place

Bradford's Michael Platt halted by Catalans' Luke Quigley as the Bulls down the Dragons at Odsal

Field goal: Head (65).
On report: Carvell (2) - alleged late challenge on Diskin.
Rugby Leaguer & League Express Men of the Match:
Rhinos: Brent Webb; *Hull:* Mathew Head.
Penalty count: 9-6; **Half-time:** 6-10;
Referee: Richard Silverwood; **Attendance:** 17,424.

ST HELENS 36 WARRINGTON WOLVES 16

SAINTS: 1 Paul Wellens; 2 Ade Gardner; 3 Matt Gidley; 4 Willie Talau; 5 Francis Meli; 6 Leon Pryce; 12 Jon Wilkin; 8 Nick Fozzard; 9 Keiron Cunningham (C); 10 Jason Cayless; 11 Lee Gilmour; 15 Mike Bennett; 30 Chris Flannery. Subs (all used): 14 James Roby; 17 James Graham; 22 Paul Clough; 23 Maurie Fa'asavalu.
Tries: Gilmour (19), Meli (24, 35, 56), Gardner (26), Roby (43), Pryce (72); **Goals:** Wellens 4/8.
On report: Fozzard (1) - alleged high tackle.
WOLVES: 5 Brent Grose; 26 Kevin Penny; 3 Martin Gleeson; 2 Henry Fa'afili; 24 Chris Riley; 6 Chris Bridge; 7 Lee Briers (C); 8 Chris Leikvoll; 14 Mark Gleeson; 11 Adrian Morley; 12 Ben Westwood; 21 Andy Bracek; 9 Jon Clarke. Subs (all used): 29 Lee Mitchell; 22 Ben Harrison; 15 Rob Parker; 19 Steve Pickersgill.
Tries: Penny (32), Martin Gleeson (61); **Goals:** Briers 4/4.
Dismissal: Morley (68) - high tackle on Clough.
Rugby Leaguer & League Express Men of the Match:
Saints: Francis Meli; *Wolves:* Rob Parker.
Penalty count: 11-8; **Half-time:** 18-10;
Referee: Ashley Klein; **Attendance:** 11,746.

Saturday 8th September 2007

HARLEQUINS 22 SALFORD CITY REDS 16

HARLEQUINS: 2 Jon Wells; 28 Rikki Sheriffe; 3 Paul Sykes; 4 Tyrone Smith; 19 Tony Clubb; 7 Danny Orr; 6 Scott Hill; 8 Karl Temata; 9 Chad Randall; 17 Louie McCarthy-Scarsbrook; 18 Matt Gafa; 12 Lee Hopkins (C); 23 Henry Paul. Subs (all used): 14 Julien Rinaldi; 29 Joe Mbu; 20 Jon Grayshon; 30 Steve Bannister.
Tries: Rinaldi (17), Sheriffe (21, 70), McCarthy-Scarsbrook (51); **Goals:** Sykes 3/4.
CITY REDS: 1 Karl Fitzpatrick; 2 David Hodgson; 3 Kevin McGuinness; 4 Aaron Moule; 30 Richie Barnett; 5 John Wilshere; 26 Stefan Ratchford; 10 Michael Korkidas; 9 Malcolm Alker (C); 21 Stephen Nash; 19 Stuart Littler; 16 Andrew Brocklehurst; 23 Jordan Turner. Subs (all used): 14 Paul Highton; 31 Phil Leuluai; 20 David Gower; 6 Luke Dorn.
Tries: Barnett (11), Dorn (36), Wilshere (44); **Goals:** Wilshere 1/2, Hodgson 1/1.
Rugby Leaguer & League Express Men of the Match:
Harlequins: Rikki Sheriffe; *City Reds:* Malcolm Alker.
Penalty count: 10-11; **Half-time:** 10-10;
Referee: Phil Bentham; **Attendance:** 2,347.

Sunday 9th September 2007

BRADFORD BULLS 40 CATALANS DRAGONS 8

BULLS: 19 Michael Platt; 1 Marcus St Hilaire; 3 Ben Harris; 17 James Evans; 2 Nathan McAvoy; 6 Iestyn Harris; 16 Ian Henderson; 8 Joe Vagana; 9 Terry Newton; 10 Andy Lynch; 26 David Solomona; 11 Chris McKenna; 12 Glenn Morrison (C). Subs (all used): 14 Chris Feather; 15 Matt Cook; 24 Dave Halley; 23 Matt James.
Tries: Newton (32), Morrison (38), Solomona (43), McAvoy (48), Halley (66), I Harris (69), Vagana (74); **Goals:** I Harris 6/7.
DRAGONS: 1 Clint Greenshields; 2 Justin Murphy; 18 Vincent Duport; 11 Sebastien Raguin; 30 Cyril Stacul (D); 12 Jason Croker; 7 Stacey Jones (C); 24 Remi Casty; 26 Luke Quigley; 8 David Ferriol; 13 Gregory Mounis; 17 Cyril Gossard; 28 Andrew Bentley. Subs (all used): 20 Adel Fellous; 15 Mathieu Griffi; 16 Lionel Teixido; 21 Julien Touxagas.
Try: Fellous (27); **Goals:** Jones 2/2.
On report: Ferriol (66) - alleged high tackle.
Rugby Leaguer & League Express Men of the Match:
Bulls: David Solomona; *Dragons:* Luke Quigley.
Penalty count: 14-7; **Half-time:** 12-8;
Referee: Ben Thaler; **Attendance:** 9,350.

HULL KINGSTON ROVERS 24 WIGAN WARRIORS 40

ROVERS: 24 Ian Hardman; 30 Mark Lennon; 33 Rhys Lovegrove; 21 Luke Dyer; 22 Andreas Bauer; 31 Paul Cooke; 7 James Webster (C); 20 Michael Vella; 9 Ben Fisher; 32 Ryan Tandy; 8 Makali Aizue; 17 Mark O'Neill; 6 Scott Murrell. Subs (all used): 15 Jim Gannon; 10 David Tangata-Toa; 11 Iain Morrison; 34 Kris Welham.
Tries: Murrell (21), Bauer (29), Morrison (43), Welham (68), Lovegrove (76); **Goals:** Lennon 2/2, Cooke 0/3.
WARRIORS: 5 Pat Richards; 2 Mark Calderwood; 14 David Vaealiki; 20 Darrell Goulding; 23 Liam Colbon; 6 Trent Barrett; 7 Thomas Leuluai; 8 Stuart Fielden; 16 Shane Millard; 10 Iafeta Palea'aesina; 3 Phil Bailey; 12 Bryan Fletcher; 13 Sean O'Loughlin (C). Subs (all used): 9 Mick Higham; 18 Paul Prescott; 21 Danny Hill; 24 Eamon O'Carroll.
Tries: Colbon (2, 37), Goulding (5), Vaealiki (23), Prescott (39), Leuluai (49), Calderwood (79); **Goals:** Richards 6/7.
Rugby Leaguer & League Express Men of the Match:
Rovers: Ben Fisher; *Warriors:* Pat Richards.
Penalty count: 9-4; **Half-time:** 8-28;
Referee: Ian Smith; **Attendance:** 7,370.

HUDDERSFIELD GIANTS 24 WAKEFIELD TRINITY WILDCATS 22

GIANTS: 6 Chris Thorman (C); 24 Rod Jensen; 11 Chris

Hull KR's Michael Vella stretches out to score against Huddersfield, as a Robins win crowns a fine debut Super League season

Nero; 3 Jamahl Lolesi; 1 Paul Reilly; 4 Kevin Brown; 9 Brad Drew; 16 Keith Mason; 19 Ryan Hudson; 10 John Skandalis; 14 Stuart Jones; 12 Andy Raleigh; 13 Stephen Wild. Subs (all used): 7 Robbie Paul; 8 Eorl Crabtree; 15 Paul Jackson; 20 Steve Snitch.
Tries: Reilly (20), Lolesi (31, 53), Wild (56);
Goals: Thorman 4/5.
WILDCATS: 21 Matt Blaymire; 28 Paul White; 4 Ryan Atkins; 3 Jason Demetriou (C); 22 Peter Fox; 6 Jamie Rooney; 7 Ben Jeffries; 8 Adam Watene; 9 Sam Obst; 16 Ricky Bibey; 12 Duncan MacGillivray; 23 Jason Golden; 13 Brett Ferres. Subs (all used): 14 Paul March; 11 Ned Catic; 33 Sean Gleeson; 17 Kevin Henderson.
Tries: White (5); Demetriou (33, 39); **Goals:** Rooney 5/5.
Rugby Leaguer & League Express Men of the Match:
Giants: Jamahl Lolesi; *Wildcats:* Jason Demetriou.
Penalty count: 12-9; **Half-time:** 12-20;
Referee: Steve Ganson; **Attendance:** 7,066.

ROUND 27

Friday 14th September 2007

HULL FC 20 BRADFORD BULLS 10

HULL: 1 Shaun Briscoe; 22 Craig Hall; 20 Richard Whiting; 3 Kirk Yeaman; 5 Gareth Raynor; 7 Richard Horne; 32 Mathew Head; 10 Garreth Carvell; 23 Tommy Lee; 15 Paul King; 11 Lee Radford (C); 16 Danny Tickle; 13 Danny Washbrook. Subs (all used): 18 Wayne Godwin; 19 Graeme Horne; 8 Ewan Dowes; 26 Scott Wheeldon.
Tries: G Horne (47), Tickle (52), Whiting (79);
Goals: Tickle 4/5.
Sin bin: Whiting (43) - holding down.
BULLS: 19 Michael Platt; 1 Marcus St Hilaire; 4 Shontayne Hape; 17 James Evans; 20 Tame Tupou; 12 Glenn Morrison (C); 6 Iestyn Harris; 8 Joe Vagana; 9 Terry Newton; 10 Andy Lynch; 26 David Solomona; 3 Ben Harris; 18 Sam Burgess. Subs (all used): 14 Chris Feather; 15 Matt Cook; 2 Nathan McAvoy; 16 Ian Henderson.
Tries: Tupou (19), Solomona (52); **Goals:** I Harris 1/2.
Rugby Leaguer & League Express Men of the Match:
Hull: Lee Radford; *Bulls:* David Solomona.
Penalty count: 6-6; **Half-time:** 4-4;
Referee: Richard Silverwood; **Attendance:** 14,402.

LEEDS RHINOS 46 WAKEFIELD TRINITY WILDCATS 4

RHINOS: 1 Brent Webb; 2 Scott Donald; 3 Clinton Toopi; 4 Keith Senior; 5 Lee Smith; 6 Danny McGuire; 7 Rob Burrow; 8 Kylie Leuluai; 9 Matt Diskin; 10 Jamie Peacock; 11 Jamie Jones-Buchanan; 12 Gareth Ellis; 13 Kevin Sinfield (C). Subs (all used): 14 Ali Lauitiiti; 22

Carl Ablett; 18 Ian Kirke; 23 Jordan Tansey.
Tries: McGuire (3, 30), Sinfield (24), Burrow (43, 53), Toopi (48), Webb (60), Smith (73); **Goals:** Sinfield 7/8.
WILDCATS: 21 Matt Blaymire; 22 Peter Fox; 3 Jason Demetriou (C); 4 Ryan Atkins; 28 Paul White; 6 Jamie Rooney; 7 Ben Jeffries; 8 Adam Watene; 9 Sam Obst; 25 Richard Moore; 23 Jason Golden; 12 Duncan MacGillivray; 17 Kevin Henderson. Subs (all used): 10 Danny Sculthorpe; 16 Ricky Bibey; 33 Sean Gleeson; 15 David March.
Try: Jeffries (63); **Goals:** Rooney 0/1.
Sin bin: Jeffries (70) - professional foul.
Rugby Leaguer & League Express Men of the Match:
Rhinos: Danny McGuire; *Wildcats:* Kevin Henderson.
Penalty count: 5-5; **Half-time:** 18-0;
Referee: Steve Ganson; **Attendance:** 19,226.

SALFORD CITY REDS 26 WARRINGTON WOLVES 34

CITY REDS: 29 Tom Saxton; 2 David Hodgson; 3 Kevin McGuinness; 19 Stuart Littler; 30 Richie Barnett; 5 John Wilshere; 26 Stefan Ratchford; 10 Michael Korkidas; 9 Malcolm Alker (C); 21 Stephen Nash; 16 Andrew Brocklehurst; 13 Simon Finnigan; 23 Jordan Turner. Subs (all used): 6 Luke Dorn; 14 Paul Highton; 18 Luke Adamson; 20 David Gower.
Tries: Barnett (14, 34), Turner (25), McGuinness (74, 78); **Goals:** Wilshere 3/4, Korkidas 0/1.
WOLVES: 5 Brent Grose; 24 Chris Riley; 3 Martin Gleeson; 2 Henry Fa'afili; 26 Kevin Penny; 6 Chris Bridge; 7 Lee Briers (C); 10 Paul Rauhihi; 9 Jon Clarke; 8 Chris Leikvoll; 12 Ben Westwood; 29 Lee Mitchell; 13 Vinnie Anderson. Subs (all used): 20 Simon Grix; 21 Andy Bracek; 22 Ben Harrison; 27 Matty Blythe (D).
Tries: Fa'afili (2), Bridge (21), Westwood (28, 49), Mitchell (37), Rauhihi (64); **Goals:** Briers 5/7.
Rugby Leaguer & League Express Men of the Match:
City Reds: Malcolm Alker; *Wolves:* Chris Bridge.
Penalty count: 3-6; **Half-time:** 16-20;
Referee: Ben Thaler; **Attendance:** 5,152.

WIGAN WARRIORS 20 ST HELENS 12

WARRIORS: 5 Pat Richards; 2 Mark Calderwood; 3 Phil Bailey; 14 David Vaealiki; 23 Liam Colbon; 6 Trent Barrett; 7 Thomas Leuluai; 8 Stuart Fielden; 16 Shane Millard; 10 Iafeta Palea'aesina; 19 Harrison Hansen; 12 Bryan Fletcher; 13 Sean O'Loughlin (C). Subs (all used): 9 Mick Higham; 11 Gareth Hock; 20 Darrell Goulding; 18 Paul Prescott.
Tries: Vaealiki (19), Leuluai (44), Colbon (61);
Goals: Richards 4/5.
SAINTS: 1 Paul Wellens; 2 Ade Gardner; 3 Matt Gidley; 4 Willie Talau; 5 Francis Meli; 6 Leon Pryce; 12 Jon Wilkin; 17 James Graham; 9 Keiron Cunningham (C); 10 Jason Cayless; 11 Lee Gilmour; 15 Mike Bennett; 30 Chris

Flannery. Subs (all used): 14 James Roby; 18 Bryn Hargreaves; 22 Paul Clough; 23 Maurie Fa'asavalu.
Tries: Talau (14), Gardner (28); **Goals:** Wellens 2/3.
Rugby Leaguer & League Express Men of the Match:
Warriors: Pat Richards; *Saints:* Paul Wellens.
Penalty count: 6-12; **Half-time:** 6-10;
Referee: Ashley Klein; **Attendance:** 22,031.

Saturday 15th September 2007

HULL KINGSTON ROVERS 25 HUDDERSFIELD GIANTS 24

ROVERS: 24 Ian Hardman; 30 Mark Lennon; 33 Rhys Lovegrove; 21 Luke Dyer; 22 Andreas Bauer; 31 Paul Cooke; 7 James Webster (C); 20 Michael Vella; 9 Ben Fisher; 32 Ryan Tandy; 28 Chris Chester; 16 Jason Netherton; 6 Scott Murrell. Subs (all used): 8 Makali Aizue; 15 Jim Gannon; 27 Kirk Netherton; 35 Chaz I'Anson (D).
Tries: Vella (18), Chester (37), Fisher (64, 68);
Goals: Cooke 4/4. **Field goal:** Cooke (75).
GIANTS: 6 Chris Thorman (C); 1 Paul Reilly; 3 Jamahl Lolesi; 11 Chris Nero; 24 Rod Jensen; 4 Kevin Brown; 9 Brad Drew; 16 Keith Mason; 19 Ryan Hudson; 10 John Skandalis; 14 Stuart Jones; 12 Andy Raleigh; 13 Stephen Wild. Subs (all used): 7 Robbie Paul; 8 Eorl Crabtree; 15 Paul Jackson; 20 Steve Snitch.
Tries: Reilly (8, 27), Nero (32), Jensen (56, 60);
Goals: Thorman 2/5.
Rugby Leaguer & League Express Men of the Match:
Rovers: Ben Fisher; *Giants:* Rod Jensen.
Penalty count: 9-3; **Half-time:** 12-14;
Referee: Phil Bentham; **Attendance:** 6,700.

CATALANS DRAGONS 30 HARLEQUINS 14

DRAGONS: 1 Clint Greenshields; 2 Justin Murphy; 3 John Wilson; 11 Sebastien Raguin; 30 Cyril Stacul; 4 Adam Mogg; 7 Stacey Jones (C); 24 Remi Casty; 26 Luke Quigley; 19 Alex Chan; 12 Jason Croker; 17 Cyril Gossard; 28 Andrew Bentley. Subs (all used): 10 Jerome Guisset; 15 Mathieu Griffi; 16 Lionel Teixido; 13 Gregory Mounis.
Tries: Stacul (11), Wilson (16, 44), Greenshields (26, 37, 80); **Goals:** Greenshields 5/5.
HARLEQUINS: 2 Jon Wells; 19 Tony Clubb; 3 Paul Sykes; 18 Matt Gafa; 28 Rikki Sheriffe; 6 Scott Hill; 7 Danny Orr; 8 Karl Temata; 9 Chad Randall; 17 Louie McCarthy-Scarsbrook; 12 Lee Hopkins (C); 22 Michael Worrincy; 23 Henry Paul. Subs (all used): 14 Julien Rinaldi; 20 Jon Grayshon; 29 Joe Mbu; 30 Steve Bannister.
Tries: Sykes (26, 52), Clubb (62); **Goals:** Sykes 1/3.
Rugby Leaguer & League Express Men of the Match:
Dragons: Stacey Jones; *Harlequins:* Danny Orr.
Penalty count: 6-5; **Half-time:** 18-4;
Referee: Gareth Hewer; **Attendance:** 8,420.

Mark Calderwood scores to set Wigan on the comeback trail during an amazing Elimination Play-off at Odsal

PLAY-OFFS

ELIMINATION PLAY-OFFS

Friday 21st September 2007

BRADFORD BULLS 30 WIGAN WARRIORS 31

BULLS: 19 Michael Platt; 1 Marcus St Hilaire; 3 Ben Harris; 4 Shontayne Hape; 20 Tame Tupou; 12 Glenn Morrison (C); 6 Iestyn Harris; 8 Joe Vagana; 9 Terry Newton; 10 Andy Lynch; 26 David Solomona; 11 Chris McKenna; 18 Sam Burgess. Subs (all used): 14 Chris Feather; 15 Matt Cook; 2 Nathan McAvoy; 16 Ian Henderson.
Tries: Solomona (3, 32, 37), Tupou (22), I Harris (42);
Goals: I Harris 5/6.
WARRIORS: 5 Pat Richards; 2 Mark Calderwood; 3 Phil Bailey; 14 David Vaealiki; 23 Liam Colbon; 6 Trent Barrett; 7 Thomas Leuluai; 8 Stuart Fielden; 16 Shane Millard; 10 Iafeta Palea'aesina; 19 Harrison Hansen; 12 Bryan Fletcher; 13 Sean O'Loughlin (C). Subs (all used): 9 Mick Higham; 18 Paul Prescott; 11 Gareth Hock; 20 Darrell Goulding.
Tries: Leuluai (26), Calderwood (55, 62, 71), Hansen (65); **Goals:** Richards 5/5; **Field goal:** Richards (76).
On report: O'Loughlin (47) - alleged high tackle.
Rugby Leaguer & League Express Men of the Match:
Bulls: David Solomona; *Warriors:* Trent Barrett.
Penalty count: 5-6; **Half-time:** 22-6;
Referee: Steve Ganson; **Attendance:** 9,055.

Saturday 22nd September 2007

HULL FC 22 HUDDERSFIELD GIANTS 16

HULL: 14 Motu Tony; 2 Matt Sing; 20 Richard Whiting; 3 Kirk Yeaman; 5 Gareth Raynor; 7 Richard Horne; 32 Mathew Head; 8 Ewan Dowes; 23 Tommy Lee; 10 Garreth Carvell; 11 Lee Radford (C); 17 Willie Manu; 16 Danny Tickle. Subs (all used): 18 Wayne Godwin; 13 Danny Washbrook; 26 Scott Wheeldon; 15 Paul King.
Tries: Raynor (7, 67), Lee (11), R Horne (60);
Goals: Tickle 3/5.
GIANTS: 6 Chris Thorman (C); 1 Paul Reilly; 3 Jamahl Lolesi; 11 Chris Nero; 24 Rod Jensen; 4 Kevin Brown; 9 Brad Drew; 16 Keith Mason; 19 Ryan Hudson; 10 John Skandalis; 12 Andy Raleigh; 14 Stuart Jones; 13 Stephen Wild. Subs (all used): 7 Robbie Paul; 18 Darrell Griffin; 20 Steve Snitch; 8 Eorl Crabtree.
Tries: Hudson (50), Reilly (73), Brown (75);
Goals: Thorman 2/3.
Rugby Leaguer & League Express Men of the Match:
Hull: Motu Tony; *Giants:* Stephen Wild.
Penalty count: 4-4; **Half-time:** 10-0;
Referee: Ashley Klein; **Attendance:** 12,140.

QUALIFYING SEMI-FINAL

Friday 28th September 2007

ST HELENS 10 LEEDS RHINOS 8

SAINTS: 1 Paul Wellens; 2 Ade Gardner; 3 Matt Gidley; 4 Willie Talau; 5 Francis Meli; 6 Leon Pryce; 21 Matty Smith; 8 Nick Fozzard; 9 Keiron Cunningham (C); 10 Jason Cayless; 11 Lee Gilmour; 12 Jon Wilkin; 30 Chris Flannery. Subs (all used): 14 James Roby; 17 James Graham; 22 Paul Clough; 15 Mike Bennett.
Try: Pryce (16); **Goals:** Smith 3/3.
RHINOS: 1 Brent Webb; 5 Lee Smith; 4 Keith Senior; 3 Clinton Toopi; 2 Scott Donald; 6 Danny McGuire; 7 Rob Burrow; 8 Kylie Leuluai; 9 Matt Diskin; 10 Jamie Peacock; 11 Jamie Jones-Buchanan; 12 Gareth Ellis; 13 Kevin Sinfield (C). Subs (all used): 14 Ali Lauitiiti; 18 Ian Kirke; 23 Jordan Tansey; 22 Carl Ablett.
Try: Smith (6); **Goals:** Sinfield 2/3.
Rugby Leaguer & League Express Men of the Match:
Saints: Paul Wellens; *Rhinos:* Jamie Peacock.
Penalty count: 9-7; **Half-time:** 8-6;
Referee: Ashley Klein; **Attendance:** 12,064.

ELIMINATION SEMI-FINAL

Saturday 29th September 2007

HULL FC 18 WIGAN WARRIORS 21

HULL: 14 Motu Tony; 2 Matt Sing; 20 Richard Whiting; 3 Kirk Yeaman; 5 Gareth Raynor; 13 Danny Washbrook; 7 Richard Horne; 10 Garreth Carvell; 23 Tommy Lee; 8 Ewan Dowes; 11 Lee Radford (C); 17 Willie Manu; 16 Danny Tickle. Subs (all used): 32 Mathew Head; 18 Wayne Godwin; 19 Graeme Horne; 26 Scott Wheeldon.
Tries: Raynor (28, 76), R Horne (31); **Goals:** Tickle 3/4.
WARRIORS: 5 Pat Richards; 2 Mark Calderwood; 3 Phil Bailey; 14 David Vaealiki; 23 Liam Colbon; 6 Trent Barrett; 7 Thomas Leuluai; 8 Stuart Fielden; 16 Shane Millard; 10 Iafeta Palea'aesina; 19 Harrison Hansen; 12 Bryan Fletcher; 13 Sean O'Loughlin (C). Subs (all used): 9 Mick Higham; 18 Paul Prescott; 11 Gareth Hock; 20 Darrell Goulding.
Tries: Richards (2), Hock (49), Colbon (53);
Goals: Richards 4/5; **Field goal:** Richards (71).
Sin bin: Calderwood (28) - holding down.
On report: Millard (59) – alleged late tackle on Head.
Rugby Leaguer & League Express Men of the Match:
Hull: Richard Horne; *Warriors:* Thomas Leuluai.
Penalty count: 11-7; **Half-time:** 14-10;
Referee: Steve Ganson; **Attendance:** 16,291.

FINAL ELIMINATOR

Friday 5th October 2007

LEEDS RHINOS 36 WIGAN WARRIORS 6

RHINOS: 1 Brent Webb; 2 Scott Donald; 3 Clinton Toopi; 4 Keith Senior; 5 Lee Smith; 6 Danny McGuire; 7 Rob Burrow; 8 Kylie Leuluai; 9 Matt Diskin; 10 Jamie Peacock; 11 Jamie Jones-Buchanan; 12 Gareth Ellis; 13 Kevin Sinfield (C). Subs (all used): 16 Ryan Bailey; 14 Ali Lauitiiti; 18 Ian Kirke; 22 Carl Ablett.
Tries: Webb (14, 66), Lauitiiti (36), Burrow (64, 75);
Goals: Sinfield 7/7; **Field goals:** Sinfield (72, 78).
WARRIORS: 5 Pat Richards; 23 Liam Colbon; 3 Phil Bailey; 20 Darrell Goulding; 14 David Vaealiki; 6 Trent Barrett; 7 Thomas Leuluai; 8 Stuart Fielden; 16 Shane Millard; 10 Iafeta Palea'aesina; 11 Gareth Hock; 12 Bryan Fletcher; 13 Sean O'Loughlin (C). Subs (all used): 18 Paul Prescott; 9 Mick Higham; 19 Harrison Hansen; 21 Danny Hill.
Try: Richards (56); **Goals:** Richards 1/1.
On report: Hock (73) - dangerous tackle on Diskin.
Rugby Leaguer & League Express Men of the Match:
Rhinos: Jamie Peacock; *Warriors:* Shane Millard.
Penalty count: 9-7; **Half-time:** 16-0;
Referee: Steve Ganson; **Attendance:** 16,112.

GRAND FINAL

Saturday 13th October 2007

LEEDS RHINOS 33 ST HELENS 6

RHINOS: 1 Brent Webb; 5 Lee Smith; 3 Clinton Toopi; 4 Keith Senior; 2 Scott Donald; 6 Danny McGuire; 7 Rob Burrow; 8 Kylie Leuluai; 9 Matt Diskin; 10 Jamie Peacock; 11 Jamie Jones-Buchanan; 12 Gareth Ellis; 13 Kevin Sinfield (C). Subs (all used): 16 Ryan Bailey for Leuluai (18); 18 Ian Kirke for Jones-Buchanan (33); 22 Carl Ablett for Kirke (57); Leuluai for Bailey (55); Jones-Buchanan for Lauitiiti (60); Diskin for Ablett (63); Kirke for Leuluai (65); Bailey for Kirke (76).
Tries: Webb (19), Lauitiiti (50), Donald (52), Smith (69), Jones-Buchanan (80); **Goals:** Sinfield 6/7;
Field goal: Burrow (55).
SAINTS: 1 Paul Wellens; 2 Ade Gardner; 3 Matt Gidley; 4 Willie Talau; 5 Francis Meli; 6 Leon Pryce; 7 Sean Long; 8 Nick Fozzard; 9 Keiron Cunningham (C); 10 Jason Cayless; 11 Lee Gilmour; 30 Chris Flannery; 12 Jon Wilkin. Subs (all used): 17 James Graham for Cayless (15); 14 James Roby for Cunningham (23); 23 Maurie Fa'asavalu for Fozzard (23); 15 Mike Bennett for Wilkin (31); Cayless for Fa'asavalu (34); Cunningham for Flannery (51); Wilkin for Bennett (55); Fa'asavalu for Cayless (55); Fozzard for Graham (57); Cayless for Fozzard (68); Graham for Fa'asavalu (68); Bennett for Gilmour (72).
Try: Roby (27); **Goals:** Long 1/2.
Rugby Leaguer & League Express Men of the Match:
Rhinos: Rob Burrow; *Saints:* Sean Long.
Penalty count: 4-5; **Half-time:** 8-6;
Referee: Ashley Klein;
Attendance: 71,352 *(at Old Trafford, Manchester).*

Leeds' Lee Smith beats St Helens' Francis Meli to a high ball on the way to his try, during a stunning Grand Final win for the Rhinos

SUPER LEAGUE XII
Opta Index Analysis

SUPER LEAGUE XII
TOP PERFORMERS

TACKLES
Ben Fisher	Hull KR	841
Sean O'Loughlin		
	Wigan	836
Kevin Sinfield	Leeds	817
Simon Finnigan	Salford	770
Stephen Wild	Huddersfield	736
Glenn Morrison	Bradford	733
Jamie Jones-Buchanan		
	Leeds	708
Chad Randall	Harlequins	706
Brett Ferres	Wakefield	695
Ewan Dowes	Hull	685

TACKLES MADE *(% Success)*
Aaron Gorrell	Catalans	99.04
Chris Flannery	St Helens	98.65
Wayne Godwin	Hull	98.05
Andy Lynch	Bradford	97.26
Mark O'Neill	Hull KR	97.13
Rob Purdham	Harlequins	96.98
Mike Bennett	St Helens	96.94
Paul Wood	Warrington	96.73
Glenn Morrison	Bradford	96.68
Danny Washbrook		
	Hull	96.58

OFFLOADS
Gareth Raynor	Hull	60
Kevin Sinfield	Leeds	60
David Solomona		
	Bradford	59
Gareth Hock	Wigan	58
Richard Moore	Wakefield	54
Leon Pryce	St Helens	53
Jason Cayless	St Helens	52
Danny McGuire	Leeds	51
Paul Rauhihi	Warrington	50
Sean O'Loughlin		
	Wigan	48

CLEAN BREAKS
Jason Demetriou		
	Wakefield	31
Paul Wellens	St Helens	29
Lee Briers	Warrington	27
Martin Gleeson	Warrington	27
Clint Greenshields		
	Catalans	27
Kevin McGuinness		
	Salford	26
Danny McGuire	Leeds	26
Lesley Vainikolo	Bradford	26
Scott Donald	Leeds	25
Willie Manu	Hull	25

TRY ASSISTS
Lee Briers	Warrington	23
Danny McGuire	Leeds	22
Stacey Jones	Catalans	20
Ben Jeffries	Wakefield	19
Trent Barrett	Wigan	17
Brad Drew	Huddersfield	17
Kevin Sinfield	Leeds	17
Danny Orr	Harlequins	16
Leon Pryce	St Helens	16
Adam Mogg	Catalans	15

MARKER TACKLES
Sean O'Loughlin		
	Wigan	93
Glenn Morrison	Bradford	89
Chad Randall	Harlequins	86
Ben Fisher	Hull KR	85
Danny Washbrook		
	Hull	83
Jamie Jones-Buchanan		
	Leeds	82
Julien Rinaldi	Harlequins	81
James Roby	St Helens	81
Richard Swain	Hull	81
Kevin Sinfield	Leeds	79

METRES
James Roby	St Helens	3303
Clint Greenshields		
	Catalans	3284
Jamie Peacock	Leeds	3248
Michael Korkidas		
	Salford	3189
Pat Richards	Wigan	3119
Michael Platt	Bradford	3018
Mark McLinden	Harlequins	3000
Brent Webb	Leeds	2964
John Skandalis	Huddersfield	2958
Andy Lynch	Bradford	2905

CARRIES
Clint Greenshields		
	Catalans	513
Trent Barrett	Wigan	456
Mark McLinden	Harlequins	453
James Roby	St Helens	444
Jamie Peacock	Leeds	431
John Skandalis	Huddersfield	420
Michael Korkidas		
	Salford	413
Paul Wellens	St Helens	412
Andy Lynch	Bradford	406
Chris Thorman	Huddersfield	405

Trent Barrett

AVERAGE GAIN PER CARRY *(Metres)*
Rod Jensen	Huddersfield	10.05
Lesley Vainikolo	Bradford	9.15
Darrell Griffin	Huddersfield	8.90
Iafeta Palea'aesina		
	Wigan	8.83
Willie Manu	Hull	8.81
Dimitri Pelo	Catalans	8.78
Ryan Atkins	Wakefield	8.76
Kylie Leuluai	Leeds	8.71
Paul White	Wakefield	8.71
Hutch Maiava	Hull	8.65

TACKLE BUSTS
Clint Greenshields		
	Catalans	105
Ian Henderson	Bradford	91
Willie Manu	Hull	91
Maurie Fa'asavalu		
	St Helens	86
Paul Wellens	St Helens	82
James Roby	St Helens	80
Gareth Raynor	Hull	74
Jamie Thackray	Leeds	73
Rob Burrow	Leeds	72
Stuart Reardon	Warrington	72

40/20's
Paul Deacon	Bradford	5
Trent Barrett	Wigan	4
Luke Robinson	Salford	4
Lee Briers	Warrington	3
Brad Drew	Huddersfield	3
Sean Long	St Helens	3
Jamie Rooney	Wakefield	3
Jordan Tansey	Leeds	3
Stacey Jones	Catalans	2
Scott Murrell	Hull KR	2

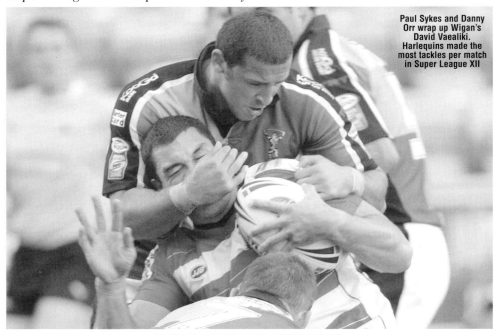

Paul Sykes and Danny Orr wrap up Wigan's David Vaealiki. Harlequins made the most tackles per match in Super League XII

SUPER LEAGUE XII AVERAGES PER MATCH

TACKLES		OFFLOADS		METRES		ERRORS	
Harlequins	286.1	Leeds Rhinos	16.6	Bradford Bulls	1425.9	Bradford Bulls	12.9
St Helens	281.3	St Helens	15.9	St Helens	1411.1	St Helens	12.6
Hull FC	278.8	Bradford Bulls	14.7	Huddersfield Giants	1340.3	Harlequins	11.6
Leeds Rhinos	278.6	Warrington Wolves	14.0	Leeds Rhinos	1309.1	Wigan Warriors	11.5
Catalans Dragons	274.9	Wigan Warriors	13.5	Hull FC	1297.3	Catalans Dragons	11.4
Salford City Reds	274.8	Hull FC	13.3	Wigan Warriors	1293.9	Warrington Wolves	11.3
Wakefield T Wildcats	273.0	Huddersfield Giants	12.6	Warrington Wolves	1283.1	Leeds Rhinos	11.0
Hull Kingston Rovers	266.7	Catalans Dragons	12.4	Harlequins	1262.1	Huddersfield Giants	10.9
Huddersfield Giants	264.0	Hull Kingston Rovers	10.2	Wakefield T Wildcats	1206.2	Wakefield T Wildcats	10.3
Wigan Warriors	263.7	Salford City Reds	9.9	Catalans Dragons	1202.2	Hull FC	10.1
Bradford Bulls	258.9	Wakefield T Wildcats	9.4	Hull Kingston Rovers	1184.1	Salford City Reds	10.1
Warrington Wolves	248.0	Harlequins	9.3	Salford City Reds	1102.3	Hull Kingston Rovers	9.9

MISSED TACKLES		CLEAN BREAKS		CARRIES		KICKS IN GENERAL PLAY	
Wakefield T Wildcats	29.5	Bradford Bulls	8.5	Bradford Bulls	205.8	Hull Kingston Rovers	21.1
Hull Kingston Rovers	28.7	St Helens	8.1	St Helens	205.7	Hull FC	20.2
Harlequins	26.4	Leeds Rhinos	7.8	Hull FC	193.6	Harlequins	19.3
Warrington Wolves	25.1	Warrington Wolves	7.8	Leeds Rhinos	193.5	Leeds Rhinos	18.8
Salford City Reds	24.9	Huddersfield Giants	7.7	Hull Kingston Rovers	192.0	Huddersfield Giants	18.6
Hull FC	22.1	Hull FC	6.8	Wigan Warriors	189.9	Catalans Dragons	18.5
Catalans Dragons	21.6	Salford City Reds	6.6	Harlequins	189.8	Wakefield T Wildcats	18.4
Huddersfield Giants	21.2	Harlequins	6.5	Huddersfield Giants	189.3	Wigan Warriors	18.0
Bradford Bulls	21.1	Catalans Dragons	6.3	Catalans Dragons	185.7	Bradford Bulls	17.5
Wigan Warriors	20.4	Wigan Warriors	6.2	Warrington Wolves	180.6	Salford City Reds	17.1
Leeds Rhinos	19.6	Wakefield T Wildcats	6.1	Wakefield T Wildcats	172.8	Warrington Wolves	16.6
St Helens	18.1	Hull Kingston Rovers	5.3	Salford City Reds	165.8	St Helens	16.3

SUPER LEAGUE XII TRIES SCORED/CONCEDED

TOTAL TRIES SCORED		TOTAL TRIES CONCEDED		SCORED FROM KICKS		CONCEDED FROM KICKS	
St Helens	143	Salford City Reds	155	Wakefield T Wildcats	28	Bradford Bulls	26
Bradford Bulls	132	Hull Kingston Rovers	129	Catalans Dragons	27	Warrington Wolves	25
Leeds Rhinos	127	Warrington Wolves	128	Leeds Rhinos	26	Leeds Rhinos	24
Warrington Wolves	124	Wakefield T Wildcats	121	Huddersfield Giants	24	Catalans Dragons	22
Huddersfield Giants	105	Catalans Dragons	119	Wigan Warriors	20	Huddersfield Giants	21
Wigan Warriors	102	Harlequins	112	Warrington Wolves	18	Salford City Reds	18
Catalans Dragons	101	Bradford Bulls	98	Hull FC	17	Wakefield T Wildcats	18
Wakefield T Wildcats	101	Hull FC	97	Salford City Reds	17	St Helens	17
Hull FC	94	Huddersfield Giants	91	Harlequins	16	Hull FC	16
Harlequins	88	Wigan Warriors	87	Bradford Bulls	15	Wigan Warriors	16
Hull Kingston Rovers	87	Leeds Rhinos	82	Hull Kingston Rovers	15	Hull Kingston Rovers	15
Salford City Reds	85	St Helens	70	St Helens	9	Harlequins	14

SUPER LEAGUE XII TRIES SCORED/CONCEDED

TRIES SCORED FROM OWN HALF

Huddersfield Giants 24
St Helens 24
Leeds Rhinos 22
Salford City Reds 19
Wigan Warriors 19
Hull FC 16
Warrington Wolves...........16
Bradford Bulls 15
Wakefield T Wildcats 12
Catalans Dragons 8
Harlequins 7
Hull Kingston Rovers 3

TRIES CONCEDED FROM OVER 50M

Salford City Reds 24
Hull Kingston Rovers 21
Bradford Bulls 19
Warrington Wolves...........19
Wakefield T Wildcats 19
Catalans Dragons 18
Harlequins 18
St Helens 11
Huddersfield Giants 10
Hull FC 9
Leeds Rhinos 9
Wigan Warriors 8

TRIES SCORED FROM UNDER 10M

St Helens 67
Bradford Bulls 61
Leeds Rhinos 61
Catalans Dragons 58
Warrington Wolves...........48
Wakefield T Wildcats 46
Hull FC 45
Wigan Warriors 44
Huddersfield Giants 42
Harlequins 39
Hull Kingston Rovers 39
Salford City Reds 38

TRIES CONCEDED FROM UNDER 10M

Salford City Reds 72
Warrington Wolves...........61
Hull Kingston Rovers 57
Wakefield T Wildcats 54
Harlequins 50
Catalans Dragons 49
Bradford Bulls 44
Hull FC 43
Leeds Rhinos 43
Wigan Warriors 43
Huddersfield Giants 41
St Helens 31

SUPER LEAGUE XII PENALTIES

TOTAL PENALTIES AWARDED

St Helens 242
Wigan Warriors 239
Huddersfield Giants 231
Bradford Bulls 229
Leeds Rhinos 228
Salford City Reds 220
Hull Kingston Rovers 218
Hull FC 217
Wakefield T Wildcats 217
Warrington Wolves..........196
Harlequins 192
Catalans Dragons 189

TOTAL PENALTIES CONCEDED

Wigan Warriors 260
Wakefield T Wildcats 257
Catalans Dragons 236
Salford City Reds 233
Huddersfield Giants 224
Leeds Rhinos 219
Warrington Wolves..........211
Harlequins 210
Bradford Bulls 207
St Helens 198
Hull FC 188
Hull Kingston Rovers 175

FOUL PLAY - AWARDED

Huddersfield Giants 71
St Helens 65
Wigan Warriors 64
Hull Kingston Rovers 59
Bradford Bulls 58
Harlequins 58
Hull FC 58
Leeds Rhinos 58
Salford City Reds 53
Catalans Dragons 49
Wakefield T Wildcats 49
Warrington Wolves...........48

FOUL PLAY - CONCEDED

Catalans Dragons 71
Wakefield T Wildcats 68
Warrington Wolves...........64
Leeds Rhinos 63
Wigan Warriors 63
Salford City Reds 62
Huddersfield Giants 53
Harlequins 52
Bradford Bulls 51
Hull FC 49
Hull Kingston Rovers 49
St Helens 45

OFFSIDE - AWARDED

Hull Kingston Rovers 54
Salford City Reds 51
Wigan Warriors 46
Leeds Rhinos 45
Bradford Bulls 43
Catalans Dragons 43
Hull FC 43
St Helens 43
Huddersfield Giants 42
Wakefield T Wildcats 42
Warrington Wolves...........32
Harlequins 31

OFFSIDE - CONCEDED

St Helens 55
Wigan Warriors 54
Warrington Wolves...........50
Wakefield T Wildcats 46
Salford City Reds 44
Harlequins 42
Huddersfield Giants 42
Leeds Rhinos 42
Bradford Bulls 40
Hull FC 38
Hull Kingston Rovers 38
Catalans Dragons 24

INTERFERENCE - AWARDED

St Helens 86
Leeds Rhinos 80
Bradford Bulls 76
Salford City Reds 75
Wigan Warriors 71
Hull FC 70
Huddersfield Giants 67
Wakefield T Wildcats 65
Warrington Wolves...........63
Harlequins 55
Hull Kingston Rovers 52
Catalans Dragons 49

INTERFERENCE - CONCEDED

Catalans Dragons 87
Wakefield T Wildcats 86
Wigan Warriors 83
Harlequins 79
Hull FC 77
Huddersfield Giants 67
Salford City Reds 67
Bradford Bulls 63
Hull Kingston Rovers 56
St Helens 52
Leeds Rhinos 50
Warrington Wolves...........42

OBSTRUCTION - AWARDED

Wigan Warriors 18
Wakefield T Wildcats 14
Catalans Dragons 12
Harlequins 11
Hull FC 11
Hull Kingston Rovers 11
Warrington Wolves...........11
Leeds Rhinos 10
Salford City Reds 10
Huddersfield Giants 9
St Helens 9
Bradford Bulls 7

OBSTRUCTION - CONCEDED

Huddersfield Giants 16
St Helens 16
Wigan Warriors 16
Bradford Bulls 14
Warrington Wolves...........13
Catalans Dragons 11
Wakefield T Wildcats 10
Harlequins 9
Leeds Rhinos 9
Hull Kingston Rovers 7
Hull FC 6
Salford City Reds 6

BALL STEALING - AWARDED

Wakefield T Wildcats 23
Huddersfield Giants 21
Hull Kingston Rovers 19
Harlequins 16
Wigan Warriors 16
Catalans Dragons 14
Salford City Reds 13
Leeds Rhinos 12
St Helens 12
Bradford Bulls 11
Warrington Wolves...........11
Hull FC 10

BALL STEALING - CONCEDED

Salford City Reds 22
Leeds Rhinos 20
Catalans Dragons 19
Warrington Wolves...........19
Bradford Bulls 17
Wakefield T Wildcats 16
Harlequins 14
Wigan Warriors 12
Huddersfield Giants 12
Hull Kingston Rovers 12
Hull FC 9
St Helens 5

OFFSIDE MARKERS - AWARDED

Leeds Rhinos 23
Catalans Dragons 20
Salford City Reds 16
Bradford Bulls 14
Hull Kingston Rovers 13
Huddersfield Giants 12
Wakefield T Wildcats 12
Warrington Wolves...........12
St Helens 10
Hull FC 8
Wigan Warriors 8
Harlequins 6

OFFSIDE MARKERS - CONCEDED

St Helens 18
Harlequins 16
Hull FC 15
Hull Kingston Rovers 15
Bradford Bulls 13
Leeds Rhinos 13
Catalans Dragons 12
Wigan Warriors 12
Huddersfield Giants 11
Wakefield T Wildcats 10
Warrington Wolves...........10
Salford City Reds 9

NOT PLAYING BALL CORRECTLY - AWARDED

Wakefield T Wildcats 12
Huddersfield Giants 8
Salford City Reds 8
Leeds Rhinos 7
Bradford Bulls 6
Warrington Wolves.............6
Wigan Warriors 6
Hull FC 5
Hull Kingston Rovers 5
St Helens 5
Catalans Dragons 4
Harlequins 3

NOT PLAYING BALL CORRECTLY - CONCEDED

Wigan Warriors 11
Catalans Dragons 10
Bradford Bulls 8
Huddersfield Giants 8
St Helens 7
Wakefield T Wildcats 7
Leeds Rhinos 6
Harlequins 4
Hull FC 4
Salford City Reds 4
Warrington Wolves.............4
Hull Kingston Rovers 2

DISSENT - AWARDED

Bradford Bulls 7
Harlequins 5
Hull FC 5
Hull Kingston Rovers 4
Leeds Rhinos 3
St Helens 3
Catalans Dragons 2
Huddersfield Giants 2
Salford City Reds 2
Wakefield T Wildcats 2
Warrington Wolves.............2
Wigan Warriors 2

DISSENT - CONCEDED

Huddersfield Giants 8
Leeds Rhinos 7
St Helens 6
Wakefield T Wildcats 4
Warrington Wolves.............4
Salford City Reds 3
Wigan Warriors 3
Catalans Dragons 2
Bradford Bulls 1
Harlequins 1
Hull FC 0
Hull Kingston Rovers 0

BRADFORD BULLS

Michael Platt

Glenn Morrison

TACKLES
Glenn Morrison	757
Andy Lynch	639
Ian Henderson	576
Terry Newton	566
Chris McKenna	522

OFFLOADS
David Solomona	59
Andy Lynch	45
Glenn Morrison	40
Michael Platt	39
Terry Newton	36

CLEAN BREAKS
Lesley Vainikolo	26
David Solomona	22
James Evans	19
Michael Platt	18
Ben Harris	16

TRY ASSISTS
Iestyn Harris	14
David Solomona	14
Paul Deacon	11
Glenn Morrison	10
Terry Newton	8

METRES
Michael Platt	3098
Andy Lynch	3031
Joe Vagana	2626
David Solomona	2551
Ben Harris	2400

TACKLE BUSTS
Ian Henderson	91
Michael Platt	69
Lesley Vainikolo	59
Ben Harris	43
David Solomona	43

MARKER TACKLES
Glenn Morrison	89
Chris McKenna	63
Terry Newton	62
Ian Henderson	60
Jamie Langley	58

CARRIES
Andy Lynch	425
Michael Platt	415
Terry Newton	396
David Solomona	377
Iestyn Harris	349

TOTAL OPTA INDEX
Glenn Morrison	17733
Michael Platt	17079
Andy Lynch	16735
Ian Henderson	15916
David Solomona	14932

CATALANS DRAGONS

Adam Mogg

Clint Greenshields

TACKLES
Jason Croker	619
Luke Quigley	563
Alex Chan	556
Gregory Mounis	521
Jerome Guisset	476

OFFLOADS
Adam Mogg	43
David Ferriol	32
Jerome Guisset	27
Stacey Jones	23
Clint Greenshields	22

CLEAN BREAKS
Clint Greenshields	27
Thomas Bosc	16
Adam Mogg	15
Justin Murphy	14
John Wilson	12

TRY ASSISTS
Stacey Jones	20
Adam Mogg	15
Casey McGuire	8
Clint Greenshields	4
Jason Croker	3

METRES
Clint Greenshields	3284
Alex Chan	2696
Adam Mogg	2562
Jerome Guisset	2533
David Ferriol	2113

TACKLE BUSTS
Clint Greenshields	105
Adam Mogg	64
Alex Chan	32
John Wilson	32
Jerome Guisset	27

MARKER TACKLES
Jason Croker	74
Luke Quigley	65
Adam Mogg	63
Alex Chan	60
Gregory Mounis	50

CARRIES
Clint Greenshields	513
Adam Mogg	391
Alex Chan	385
Jerome Guisset	347
Stacey Jones	342

TOTAL OPTA INDEX
Clint Greenshields	18483
Adam Mogg	17840
Alex Chan	13615
Stacey Jones	13563
Jerome Guisset	12655

HARLEQUINS

Mark McLinden

Chad Randall

MARKER TACKLES
Chad Randall	86
Julien Rinaldi	81
Rob Purdham	70
Karl Temata	70
Lee Hopkins	52

METRES
Mark McLinden	3000
Jon Wells	2354
Karl Temata	2314
Tyrone Smith	2296
Paul Sykes	1842

CARRIES
Mark McLinden	453
Scott Hill	352
Tyrone Smith	336
Karl Temata	314
Danny Orr	313

TACKLE BUSTS
Mark McLinden	68
Jon Wells	45
Lee Hopkins	44
Tyrone Smith	40
Paul Sykes	39

TACKLES
Chad Randall	706
Karl Temata	599
Julien Rinaldi	556
Rob Purdham	546
Lee Hopkins	542

CLEAN BREAKS
Paul Sykes	25
Mark McLinden	22
Tyrone Smith	16
Jon Wells	16
Danny Orr	14

OFFLOADS
Scott Hill	37
Lee Hopkins	26
Danny Orr	23
Tyrone Smith	23
Mark McLinden	17

TRY ASSISTS
Danny Orr	16
Mark McLinden	14
Scott Hill	9
Tyrone Smith	5
Paul Sykes	4

TOTAL OPTA INDEX
Mark McLinden	17196
Chad Randall	14448
Scott Hill	13323
Danny Orr	12558
Karl Temata	12014

HUDDERSFIELD GIANTS

Brad Drew

Chris Thorman

MARKER TACKLES
Stephen Wild	77
Andy Raleigh	57
Eorl Crabtree	48
Keith Mason	48
Chris Nero	46

METRES
John Skandalis	3064
Chris Thorman	2934
Keith Mason	2704
Darrell Griffin	2295
Eorl Crabtree	2272

CARRIES
John Skandalis	435
Chris Thorman	427
Brad Drew	400
Kevin Brown	340
Keith Mason	333

TACKLES
Stephen Wild	765
Andy Raleigh	646
Ryan Hudson	594
Eorl Crabtree	561
Keith Mason	518

CLEAN BREAKS
Stephen Wild	24
Chris Nero	23
Brad Drew	21
Ryan Hudson	19
Kevin Brown	17

TACKLE BUSTS
Paul Reilly	49
Chris Nero	48
Chris Thorman	47
Ryan Hudson	44
Brad Drew	43

OFFLOADS
Robbie Paul	39
Kevin Brown	37
Eorl Crabtree	31
Chris Nero	31
Ryan Hudson	30

TRY ASSISTS
Brad Drew	20
Kevin Brown	10
Robbie Paul	10
Chris Thorman	9
Ryan Hudson	6

TOTAL OPTA INDEX
Brad Drew	16431
Chris Thorman	15925
Stephen Wild	15205
Ryan Hudson	14993
Chris Nero	14740

HULL FC

Ewan Dowes

TACKLES
Ewan Dowes 730
Danny Washbrook 707
Lee Radford 703
Danny Tickle 658
Richard Swain 590

OFFLOADS
Gareth Raynor 61
Lee Radford 37
Danny Washbrook 33
Paul King 26
Danny Tickle 26

CLEAN BREAKS
Willie Manu 25
Kirk Yeaman 23
Richard Horne 16
Gareth Raynor 15
Danny Tickle 12

TRY ASSISTS
Richard Horne 14
Mathew Head......................6
Tommy Lee 5
Danny Washbrook 5
Craig Hall...........................4

MARKER TACKLES
Danny Washbrook 89
Richard Swain 81
Lee Radford 78
Danny Tickle 67
Ewan Dowes 65

Danny Tickle

METRES
Ewan Dowes 2686
Danny Tickle 2573
Willie Manu 2273
Motu Tony 2257
Gareth Raynor 2216

CARRIES
Ewan Dowes 390
Danny Tickle 382
Richard Horne 367
Motu Tony 334
Gareth Raynor 320

TACKLE BUSTS
Willie Manu 93
Gareth Raynor 80
Richard Horne 55
Kirk Yeaman 45
Shaun Briscoe 43

TOTAL OPTA INDEX
Danny Tickle 14248
Ewan Dowes 13670
Richard Horne 13636
Gareth Raynor 13568
Lee Radford...............13217

HULL KINGSTON ROVERS

Stanley Gene

TACKLES
Ben Fisher 841
Jason Netherton 560
Jim Gannon 476
Michael Vella 458
Scott Murrell 431

OFFLOADS
Ben Cockayne 28
Michael Vella 26
Jim Gannon 24
Stanley Gene 19
David Tangata-Toa 19

CLEAN BREAKS
Luke Dyer 15
Ben Cockayne 12
Stanley Gene 10
Jon Goddard 10
Rhys Lovegrove...............10

TRY ASSISTS
James Webster 11
Paul Cooke 9
Ben Cockayne 7
Chris Chester 7
Scott Murrell 7

MARKER TACKLES
Ben Fisher 85
Jason Netherton 58
Jim Gannon 43
Scott Murrell 42
Paul Cooke 40

Ben Fisher

METRES
Luke Dyer 2358
Michael Vella 2229
Stanley Gene 2212
Ben Cockayne 2186
Jon Goddard 1826

CARRIES
Stanley Gene 394
Ben Cockayne 340
Luke Dyer 324
Michael Vella 322
Jim Gannon 300

TACKLE BUSTS
Stanley Gene 70
Ben Cockayne 51
Ben Fisher 33
Michael Vella 30
Luke Dyer 27

TOTAL OPTA INDEX
Ben Fisher 14761
Stanley Gene 12884
Michael Vella 12381
Ben Cockayne 12282
James Webster 11002

LEEDS RHINOS

Kevin
Sinfield

MARKER TACKLES

Jamie Jones-Buchanan	92
Kevin Sinfield	88
Jamie Peacock	73
Gareth Ellis	69
Clinton Toopi	67

METRES

Jamie Peacock	3933
Brent Webb	3366
Scott Donald	2469
Gareth Ellis	2417
Danny McGuire	2394

CARRIES

Jamie Peacock	515
Danny McGuire	456
Kevin Sinfield	450
Brent Webb	434
Gareth Ellis	374

TACKLES

Kevin Sinfield	913
Jamie Jones-Buchanan	787
Gareth Ellis	767
Jamie Peacock	749
Matt Diskin	623

CLEAN BREAKS

Danny McGuire	30
Scott Donald	28
Brent Webb	23
Rob Burrow	20
Keith Senior	15

TACKLE BUSTS

Rob Burrow	84
Jamie Peacock	73
Jamie Thackray	73
Brent Webb	71
Keith Senior	57

OFFLOADS

Kevin Sinfield	66
Danny McGuire	60
Clinton Toopi	51
Jamie Peacock	50
Keith Senior	47

TRY ASSISTS

Danny McGuire	24
Kevin Sinfield	18
Brent Webb	11
Rob Burrow	7
Jamie Jones-Buchanan	7

TOTAL OPTA INDEX

Kevin Sinfield	19967
Jamie Peacock	19624
Danny McGuire	18679
Brent Webb	18219
Keith Senior	16058

Jamie
Peacock

SALFORD CITY REDS

Luke
Robinson

MARKER TACKLES

Michael Korkidas	52
Stuart Littler	52
Malcolm Alker	44
Simon Finnigan	42
Andy Coley	35

METRES

Michael Korkidas	3189
John Wilshere	2362
David Hodgson	2302
Andy Coley	2207
Stuart Littler	1731

CARRIES

Michael Korkidas	413
John Wilshere	327
David Hodgson	320
Andy Coley	312
Luke Robinson	276

TACKLES

Simon Finnigan	770
Andy Coley	596
Michael Korkidas	554
Malcolm Alker	518
Stuart Littler	513

CLEAN BREAKS

Kevin McGuinness	26
John Wilshere	22
Luke Robinson	17
Luke Dorn	15
David Hodgson	14

TACKLE BUSTS

Kevin McGuinness	69
John Wilshere	67
Luke Robinson	65
David Hodgson	58
Andy Coley	48

OFFLOADS

Andy Coley	37
John Wilshere	21
Gareth Haggerty	19
Kevin McGuinness	17
Michael Korkidas	15

TRY ASSISTS

Luke Robinson	13
Luke Dorn	12
Andy Coley	4
Aaron Moule	4
John Wilshere	4

TOTAL OPTA INDEX

Luke Robinson	15448
Michael Korkidas	14108
Andy Coley	14107
John Wilshere	14087
Kevin McGuinness	12289

Michael
Korkidas

ST HELENS

Leon Pryce

TACKLES
James Roby 739
James Graham 650
Mike Bennett 601
Keiron Cunningham 594
Jon Wilkin 562

OFFLOADS
Jason Cayless 56
Leon Pryce 53
James Roby 43
Maurie Fa'asavalu 40
James Graham 39

CLEAN BREAKS
Paul Wellens 29
Leon Pryce 21
Ade Gardner 19
James Roby 19
Willie Talau 19

TRY ASSISTS
Leon Pryce 16
Sean Long 12
Matt Gidley 8
Jon Wilkin 8
Keiron Cunningham 7

MARKER TACKLES
James Roby 90
Paul Clough 64
James Graham 64
Mike Bennett 61
Keiron Cunningham 56

James Roby

METRES
James Roby 3524
James Graham 3003
Paul Wellens 2966
Jason Cayless 2715
Nick Fozzard 2630

CARRIES
James Roby 472
Paul Wellens 453
James Graham 414
Keiron Cunningham 395
Nick Fozzard 370

TACKLE BUSTS
Maurie Fa'asavalu 87
James Roby 85
Paul Wellens 85
Leon Pryce 73
Willie Talau 65

TOTAL OPTA INDEX
James Roby 20389
Leon Pryce 18074
Paul Wellens 17347
James Graham 16112
Jason Cayless 14059

WAKEFIELD T WILDCATS

Ben Jeffries

TACKLES
Brett Ferres 695
Ned Catic 612
Jason Demetriou 536
Adam Watene 515
Duncan MacGillivray 513

OFFLOADS
Richard Moore 54
Jason Demetriou 21
Danny Sculthorpe 20
Olivier Elima 16
Kevin Henderson 15

CLEAN BREAKS
Jason Demetriou 31
Jamie Rooney 20
Ryan Atkins 15
Matt Blaymire 13
Ben Jeffries 11

TRY ASSISTS
Ben Jeffries 19
Jamie Rooney 12
Jason Demetriou 9
Tevita Leo-Latu 6
Olivier Elima 5

MARKER TACKLES
Ned Catic 74
Duncan MacGillivray 72
Brett Ferres 64
Olivier Elima 59
Jason Demetriou 54

Jason Demetriou

METRES
Jason Demetriou 2768
Adam Watene 2531
Matt Blaymire 2234
Richard Moore 2144
Jamie Rooney 1907

CARRIES
Ben Jeffries 360
Adam Watene 351
Jason Demetriou 336
Matt Blaymire 325
Jamie Rooney 309

TACKLE BUSTS
Jason Demetriou 68
Ryan Atkins 48
Peter Fox 42
Richard Moore 37
Kevin Henderson 36

TOTAL OPTA INDEX
Jason Demetriou 17716
Ben Jeffries 13453
Jamie Rooney 12905
Brett Ferres 11484
Matt Blaymire 11409

232

WARRINGTON WOLVES

Lee Briers

Ben Westwood

MARKER TACKLES
Ben Westwood	72
Mark Gleeson	62
Jon Clarke	47
Chris Leikvoll	45
Mike Wainwright	45

METRES
Paul Rauhihi	2794
Brent Grose	2359
Ben Westwood	2089
Henry Fa'afili	2033
Stuart Reardon	1973

CARRIES
Brent Grose	332
Paul Rauhihi	327
Lee Briers	324
Ben Westwood	294
Stuart Reardon	284

TACKLES
Ben Westwood	653
Jon Clarke	599
Mark Gleeson	503
Mike Wainwright	449
Paul Rauhihi	395

CLEAN BREAKS
Lee Briers	27
Martin Gleeson	27
Brent Grose	19
Stuart Reardon	17
Henry Fa'afili	16

TACKLE BUSTS
Stuart Reardon	72
Brent Grose	57
Martin Gleeson	56
Lee Briers	54
Henry Fa'afili	54

OFFLOADS
Paul Rauhihi	50
Mike Wainwright	41
Martin Gleeson	39
Henry Fa'afili	31
Adrian Morley	27

TRY ASSISTS
Lee Briers	23
Martin Gleeson	15
Brent Grose	8
Chris Bridge	7
Jon Clarke	6

TOTAL OPTA INDEX
Lee Briers	14780
Ben Westwood	14666
Martin Gleeson	13720
Jon Clarke	13458
Paul Rauhihi	13356

WIGAN WARRIORS

Trent Barrett

Sean O'Loughlin

MARKER TACKLES
Sean O'Loughlin	101
Harrison Hansen	85
Mick Higham	69
David Vaealiki	65
Phil Bailey	60

METRES
Pat Richards	3495
Iafeta Palea'aesina	3073
Bryan Fletcher	2801
Stuart Fielden	2771
Trent Barrett	2742

CARRIES
Trent Barrett	510
Pat Richards	433
Bryan Fletcher	413
Stuart Fielden	389
Thomas Leuluai	361

TACKLES
Sean O'Loughlin	959
Stuart Fielden	756
Mick Higham	706
Harrison Hansen	627
Bryan Fletcher	598

CLEAN BREAKS
David Vaealiki	23
Trent Barrett	22
Pat Richards	19
Chris Ashton	14
Thomas Leuluai	14

TACKLE BUSTS
Thomas Leuluai	75
Stuart Fielden	70
Iafeta Palea'aesina	69
David Vaealiki	65
Gareth Hock	57

OFFLOADS
Gareth Hock	69
Sean O'Loughlin	49
Bryan Fletcher	39
Iafeta Palea'aesina	33
Mick Higham	25

TRY ASSISTS
Trent Barrett	22
Thomas Leuluai	16
Sean O'Loughlin	12
David Vaealiki	6
Chris Ashton	5

TOTAL OPTA INDEX
Trent Barrett	21920
Sean O'Loughlin	15629
David Vaealiki	15602
Pat Richards	15144
Iafeta Palea'aesina	14950

NATIONAL LEAGUE ONE 2007
Club by Club

BATLEY BULLDOGS

DATE	FIXTURE	RESULT	SCORERS	LGE	ATT
11/2/07	Dewsbury (h) (NLC)	L6-49	t:Clemie g:Paterson	3rd(NLC-G3)	1,169
18/2/07	Rochdale (a) (NLC)	W29-30	t:Langley,Stokes,Clemie(2),Menzies,J Gallagher g:Gordon(3)	3rd(NLC-G3)	971
25/2/07	Hunslet (h) (NLC)	L16-18	t:Lindsay,Marns,Lythe g:Paterson,Gordon	3rd(NLC-G3)	540
4/3/07	Dewsbury (a) (NLC)	L24-6	t:Lythe g:Gordon	3rd(NLC-G3)	1,032
11/3/07	Widnes St Maries (h) (CCR3)	W60-6	t:D Rourke,Spears,J Gallagher,Murray,Mossop(2),Simpson,Lindsay(2),Marns,Henderson g:Gordon(8)	N/A	407
18/3/07	Hunslet (a) (NLC)	W4-32	t:Lindsay,Simpson,J Gallagher(2),Lythe g:Gordon(6)	3rd(NLC-G3)	438
25/3/07	Rochdale (h) (NLC)	L10-13	t:Langley,Watson g:Gordon	2nd(NLC-G3)	489
30/3/07	St Helens (a) (CCR4)	L78-14	t:Spears,Lythe,Mossop g:Gordon	N/A	4,335
6/4/07	Dewsbury (a)	W16-24	t:Lythe(3),McLoughlin g:Gordon(4)	4th	1,566
9/4/07	Sheffield (h)	D22-22	t:Lindsay,Clemie,Simpson,Paterson g:Gordon(3)	4th	667
15/4/07	Castleford (a)	L75-12	t:Lingard,Clemie g:Gordon(2)	4th	5,223
22/4/07	Widnes (a) (NLCQFQ)	L62-6	t:Lythe g:Gordon	N/A	2,140
29/4/07	Whitehaven (h)	L18-34	t:McLoughlin,J Gallagher,Menzies,Lingard g:Gordon	7th	682
6/5/07	Widnes (a)	L66-14	t:Lindsay,P Farrell g:Duffy(3)	8th	2,753
20/5/07	Leigh (h)	L30-44	t:Langley,J Gallagher,Paterson,Lythe,Stokes,Duffy g:Duffy(3)	9th	841
3/6/07	Doncaster (a)	W14-48	t:Stokes(2),Paterson(2),Langley,Lythe,Watson,Laurie g:Duffy(8)	7th	970
10/6/07	Halifax (h)	L8-58	t:Lindsay,Stokes	8th	898
17/6/07	Rochdale (a)	L38-14	t:McLoughlin,Henderson(2) g:Hemingway	8th	644
28/6/07	Dewsbury (h)	W22-20	t:Hemingway,Speakman,Lindsay,Lythe g:Hemingway(3)	7th	2,208
8/7/07	Leigh (a)	L26-22	t:Langley(2),Stokes,Lythe g:Hemingway(3)	7th	1,469
22/7/07	Castleford (a)	L6-42	t:T Gallagher g:Hemingway	8th	2,378
27/7/07	Sheffield (a)	L56-24	t:Lindsay,Barlow,Stokes,Simpson g:Hemingway(2),Maloney(2)	8th	916
5/8/07	Whitehaven (a)	L24-14	t:Stenchion,Stokes,Marns g:Maloney	8th	1,556
12/8/07	Doncaster (h)	W26-12	t:Lythe,C Farrell,Menzies,Colley g:Maloney(5)	8th	732
19/8/07	Halifax (a)	L48-20	t:Langley(3),Marns g:Maloney,Langley	8th	1,550
2/9/07	Rochdale (h)	W30-16	t:Langley(2),Stokes,Toohey,Stenchion g:Maloney(5)	8th	532
9/9/07	Widnes (h)	L18-34	t:C Farrell,Lingard,Lindsay,Paterson g:C Farrell	8th	1,139

		APP		TRIES		GOALS		FG		PTS	
	D.O.B.	ALL	NL1	ALL	NL1	ALL	NL1	ALL	NL1	ALL	NL1
Mark Barlow	16/2/84	6(3)	4(2)	1	1	0	0	0	0	4	4
David Best	1/5/79	9	4	0	0	0	0	0	0	0	0
Daryl Cardiss	13/7/77	2	2	0	0	0	0	0	0	0	0
Alex Clemie	15/3/83	11	3	5	2	0	0	0	0	20	8
Richard Colley	9/1/84	7(1)	7(1)	1	1	0	0	0	0	4	4
Leigh Cooke	26/2/86	2	1	0	0	0	0	0	0	0	0
Kevin Doyle	6/8/85	2	2	0	0	0	0	0	0	0	0
Jay Duffy	16/4/87	11(1)	7	1	1	14	14	0	0	32	32
Craig Farrell	8/10/81	11(2)	11(2)	2	2	1	1	0	0	10	10
Phil Farrell	14/2/80	11(1)	7	1	1	0	0	0	0	4	4
John Gallagher	25/9/85	15	8	6	2	0	0	0	0	24	8
Tommy Gallagher	10/9/83	7	7	1	1	0	0	0	0	4	4
Ian Gordon	2/9/85	13	5	0	0	32	10	0	0	64	20
Tom Hemingway	6/12/86	5	5	1	1	10	10	0	0	24	24
Anthony Henderson	9/12/82	8(9)	8(4)	3	2	0	0	0	0	12	8
Andy Jarrett	26/4/83	2(4)	2(4)	0	0	0	0	0	0	0	0
Lee Kerr	12/12/84	(3)	(1)	0	0	0	0	0	0	0	0
Chris Langley	11/10/80	21(1)	13(1)	11	9	1	1	0	0	46	38
Steve Laurie	1/11/80	4	4	1	1	0	0	0	0	4	4
Ashley Lindsay	31/7/83	21(5)	15(3)	10	6	0	0	0	0	40	24
Craig Lingard	11/12/77	9(1)	5(1)	3	3	0	0	0	0	12	12
Kris Lythe	29/3/83	27	18	13	8	0	0	0	0	52	32
Francis Maloney	26/5/73	5	5	0	0	14	14	0	0	28	28
Oliver Marns	10/10/78	26	17	4	2	0	0	0	0	16	8
Martin McLoughlin	2/8/80	12(6)	9(5)	3	3	0	0	0	0	12	12
Luke Menzies	29/6/88	3(12)	3(7)	3	2	0	0	0	0	12	8
Jason Mossop	12/9/85	9	4	3	0	0	0	0	0	12	0
Anthony Murray	25/5/77	(3)	0	1	0	0	0	0	0	4	0
Lee Paterson	5/7/81	14(6)	8(6)	5	5	2	0	0	0	24	20
Sean Richardson	20/8/73	3	0	0	0	0	0	0	0	0	0
David Rourke	12/3/81	12	4	1	0	0	0	0	0	4	0
John Rourke	17/7/85	(2)	(1)	0	0	0	0	0	0	0	0
Jon Simpson	16/7/83	(24)	(17)	4	2	0	0	0	0	16	8
Danny Speakman	5/12/85	3	3	1	1	0	0	0	0	4	4
Tim Spears	27/7/84	19(2)	10(2)	2	0	0	0	0	0	8	0
Luke Stenchion	15/2/86	14(8)	13(5)	2	2	0	0	0	0	8	8
Jamie Stokes	13/8/79	16	12	9	8	0	0	0	0	36	32
Anthony Thewliss	22/6/85	(2)	(2)	0	0	0	0	0	0	0	0
Mark Toohey	16/6/82	6(4)	6(4)	1	1	0	0	0	0	4	4
Jack Watson	29/9/86	5(8)	2(4)	2	1	0	0	0	0	8	4

Kris Lythe

LEAGUE RECORD
P18-W5-D1-L12-BP2
(8th, NL1)
F372, A645, Diff-273
19 points.

CHALLENGE CUP
Round Four

NATIONAL LEAGUE CUP
Quarter Final Qualifying Round/
2nd, Group 3

ATTENDANCES
Best - v Castleford (NL1 - 2,378)
Worst - v Widnes St Maries (CC - 407)
Total (excluding Challenge Cup) - 12,275
Average (excluding Challenge Cup) - 1,023
(Up by 96 on 2006)

CASTLEFORD TIGERS

DATE	FIXTURE	RESULT	SCORERS	LGE	ATT
11/2/07	Doncaster (a) (NLC)	W6-30	t:Saxton,Henderson(2),Donlan,Owen,Huby g:Brough(3)	2nd(NLC-G1)	4,180
18/2/07	Featherstone (h) (NLC)	W48-10	t:Saxton,Donlan(3),Dixon,Wainwright(2),Charles(2) g:Brough(5),Huby	1st(NLC-G1)	6,871
25/2/07	Sheffield (h) (NLC)	W38-12	t:Saxton,Owen,Donlan,Henderson,Brough,McGoldrick,Boyle g:Brough(5)	1st(NLC-G1)	5,108
4/3/07	Featherstone (a) (NLC)	W16-22	t:Dixon(2),Henderson,Charles g:Brough(3)	1st(NLC-G1)	3,229
11/3/07	Castleford Lock Lane (h) (CCR3)	W88-10	t:A Shenton(2),Westerman,Owen,Barker,Clayton,Johnson,Croft(2),Jones(2),Watts,Knowles,Duckworth,Boyle(2) g:Westerman(12)	N/A	3,948
16/3/07	Sheffield (a) (NLC)	W6-44	t:Donlan(2),Leafa,M Shenton(2),Brough,Barker,Lupton g:Brough(6)	1st(NLC-G1)	1,897
25/3/07	Doncaster (h) (NLC)	W64-8	t:Saxton,Wainwright(2),Clayton,Barker,Guttenbeil(2),Lupton,Dixon,Owen(2),Brough g:Brough(6),Dixon(2)	1st(NLC-G1)	4,613
30/3/07	Bradford (a) (CCR4)	L24-16	t:Wainwright,M Shenton,Lupton g:Brough(2)	N/A	6,748
6/4/07	Halifax (h)	W46-22	t:Saxton,Clayton,Donlan,Wainwright,McGoldrick,Henderson,Huby(2) g:Brough(7)	3rd	6,284
12/4/07	Doncaster (a)	W4-66	t:Charles,Henderson,McGoldrick,Barker,Dixon(3),Wainwright,Brough(2),Huby,Donlan(2) g:Brough(7)	1st	6,528
15/4/07	Batley (h)	W75-12	t:Brough,Glassie,Saxton(2),Donlan(3),Leafa,McGoldrick,Owen(2),Dixon,Huby g:Brough(11),fg:McGoldrick	1st	5,223
22/4/07	Workington (h) (NLCQFQ)	W50-24	t:Dixon,Saxton(2),Barker,Knowles(2),McGoldrick,Owen,Leafa g:Brough(7)	N/A	3,610
29/4/07	Rochdale (h)	W56-6	t:Higgins,M Shenton(3),Donlan(2),Dixon(2),Guttenbeil,Barker,Saxton g:Brough(6)	1st	4,645
6/5/07	Leigh (a)	W24-32	t:Brough,Lupton(2),Owen,McGoldrick,Dixon g:Brough(4)	1st	2,683
17/5/07	Widnes (h)	L20-44	t:Owen,Donlan(2),Brough g:Brough(2)	3rd	6,007
27/5/07	Leigh (h) (NLCQF)	W42-6	t:Wainwright,M Shenton,Barker(2),Leafa,McGoldrick,Clayton,Donlan g:Dixon(5)	N/A	3,205
3/6/07	Halifax (a)	W14-30	t:M Shenton,Leafa,Guttenbeil,Dixon,Huby,Wainwright g:Dixon,Brough,Charles	3rd	2,990
10/6/07	Dewsbury (h)	W56-8	t:McGoldrick(3),Wainwright(2),Brough,Dixon(2),Saxton,Barker,Knowles g:Dixon(3),Brough,Westerman(2)	2nd	4,739
15/6/07	Sheffield (a)	W15-27	t:Wainwright,Dixon,Henderson,Huby(2) g:Westerman(3) fg:Saxton	2nd	1,333
24/6/07	Widnes (a) (NLCSF)	L18-12	t:Boyle(2) g:Brough(2)	N/A	5,388
1/7/07	Whitehaven (h)	W44-12	t:Barker,Leafa,M Shenton,Boyle,Dixon,Westerman(2),Owen g:Brough(3),Westerman(2),Dixon	2nd	4,902
8/7/07	Doncaster (h)	W66-4	t:Leafa(2),Wainwright(2),McGoldrick,Clayton,Barker(3),Westerman(2),Glassie g:Dixon(8),Westerman	2nd	4,109
22/7/07	Batley (a)	W6-42	t:Williams(3),Dixon(2),Lupton,M Shenton,Guttenbeil g:Dixon(5)	2nd	2,378
29/7/07	Dewsbury (a)	W10-36	t:M Shenton(3),Henderson,Thackeray,Lupton,Clayton g:Dixon(4)	2nd	3,010
5/8/07	Sheffield (h)	W52-26	t:Thackeray(2),Westerman,Williams,Barker(2),M Shenton(2),Dixon g:Dixon(6),Brough(2)	2nd	4,538
9/8/07	Whitehaven (a)	W12-20	t:Clayton,Dixon,Barker g:Brough(4)	2nd	3,366
16/8/07	Widnes (a)	W18-24	t:Williams,Wainwright,Dixon g:Brough(6)	1st	4,598
2/9/07	Leigh (h)	W62-10	t:Dixon,Glassie,Thackeray(4),Donlan,Westerman(2),Williams,Wainwright g:Brough(8),Dixon	1st	5,525
9/9/07	Rochdale (a)	W0-106	t:M Shenton(3),Brough(2),Henderson(3),Leafa(2),Guttenbeil,Williams(3),Donlan,Boyle,Thackeray,Westerman,Clayton g:Dixon(3),Brough(11),Charles	1st	2,506
20/9/07	Widnes (h) (QSF)	W26-8	t:Wainwright,Williams,Westerman(2) g:Brough(5)	N/A	6,179
7/10/07	Widnes (GF) ●	W42-10	t:Wainwright,McGoldrick,Guttenbeil(2),M Shenton,Westerman,Clayton g:Brough(6) fg:Brough(2)	N/A	20,814

● Played at Headingley Carnegie, Leeds

	D.O.B.	APP		TRIES		GOALS		FG		PTS	
		ALL	NL1	ALL	NL1	ALL	NL1	ALL	NL1	ALL	NL1
Dwayne Barker	21/9/83	16(10)	9(7)	16	10	0	0	0	0	64	40
Jake Bassinder	15/7/90	(1)	(1)	0	0	0	0	0	0	0	0
Ryan Boyle	17/10/87	6(18)	3(13)	7	2	0	0	0	0	28	8
Danny Brough	15/1/83	25	16	11	8	123	84	2	2	292	202
Chris Charles	7/3/76	21(6)	14(5)	4	1	2	2	0	0	20	8
Ryan Clayton	22/11/82	23(5)	17(1)	9	6	0	0	0	0	36	24
Eddie Croft	14/6/87	1	0	2	0	0	0	0	0	8	0
Kirk Dixon	19/7/84	29	20	23	18	39	32	0	0	170	136
Stuart Donlan	29/8/78	28(1)	19(1)	20	12	0	0	0	0	80	48
Matthew Duckworth	26/7/89	1	0	1	0	0	0	0	0	4	0
Tere Glassie	1/12/77	9(10)	7(6)	3	3	0	0	0	0	12	12
Awen Guttenbeil	14/3/76	23	16	8	6	0	0	0	0	32	24
Andrew Henderson	17/6/79	27	18	11	7	0	0	0	0	44	28
Liam Higgins	19/7/83	22(5)	15(3)	1	1	0	0	0	0	4	4
Craig Huby	21/5/86	10(8)	3(7)	8	7	1	0	0	0	34	28
Sean Johnson	12/4/88	3(2)	1(1)	1	0	0	0	0	0	4	0
Adam Jones	31/5/90	1	0	2	0	0	0	0	0	8	0
Michael Knowles	2/5/87	1(9)	(3)	4	1	0	0	0	0	16	4
Mark Leafa	4/12/80	16(10)	10(7)	10	7	0	0	0	0	40	28
Peter Lupton	7/3/82	14(2)	9(2)	7	4	0	0	0	0	28	16
Nathan Massey	11/7/89	(1)	0	0	0	0	0	0	0	0	0
Ryan McGoldrick	12/1/81	25(1)	14(1)	12	9	0	0	1	1	49	37
Richard Owen	25/4/90	9(11)	2(10)	11	5	0	0	0	0	44	20
Jason Payne	20/1/88	1(2)	0	0	0	0	0	0	0	0	0
Craig Potter	17/12/80	(1)	0	0	0	0	0	0	0	0	0
Tom Saxton	3/10/83	17(1)	8(1)	11	5	0	0	1	1	45	21
Alex Shenton	8/3/90	1	0	2	0	0	0	0	0	8	0
Michael Shenton	22/7/86	20	16	19	15	0	0	0	0	76	60
Anthony Thackeray	19/2/86	8(1)	8(1)	8	8	0	0	0	0	32	32
Michael Wainwright	4/11/80	29(1)	19(1)	18	12	0	0	0	0	72	48
Liam Watts	8/7/90	(1)	0	1	0	0	0	0	0	4	0
Joe Westerman	15/11/89	9(15)	7(8)	12	11	20	8	0	0	88	60
Danny Williams	26/9/86	9	9	10	10	0	0	0	0	40	40

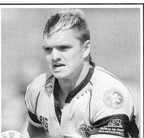

Danny Brough

LEAGUE RECORD
P18-W17-D0-L1-BP0
(1st, NL1/Grand Final Winners, Champions)
F860, A247, Diff+613
51 points.

CHALLENGE CUP
Round Four

NATIONAL LEAGUE CUP
Semi Finalists/1st, Group 1

ATTENDANCES
Best - v Featherstone (NLC - 6,871)
Worst - v Leigh (NLCQF - 3,205)
Total (excluding Challenge Cup) - 75,558
Average (excluding Challenge Cup) - 5,037
(Down by 2,059 on 2006, SL)

DEWSBURY RAMS

DATE	FIXTURE	RESULT	SCORERS	LGE	ATT
11/2/07	Batley (a) (NLC)	W6-49	t:Haigh,Preece(2),Epati,Finn,Crouthers,Bostock,Close g:F Maloney(5),Finn(3) fg:Lawford	1st(NLC-G3)	1,169
18/2/07	Hunslet (a) (NLC)	L16-8	t:Crouthers,Ratcliffe	1st(NLC-G3)	756
25/2/07	Oldham (h) (NLC)	W32-22	t:Bostock,Weeden,Epati(2),Crouthers,Haigh g:F Maloney(3),Lawford	1st(NLC-G3)	819
4/3/07	Batley (h) (NLC)	W24-6	t:Maun(2),Crouthers,F Maloney(2) g:F Maloney(2)	1st(NLC-G3)	1,032
11/3/07	Leigh (h) (CCR3)	W36-34	t:F Maloney,Bretherton,Lawford,Bostock,Weeden,Crouthers g:F Maloney(6)	N/A	1,131
18/3/07	Oldham (a) (NLC)	W8-32	t:Maun,Bostock,Oakes,F Maloney,Close,Robinson g:F Maloney(4)	1st(NLC-G3)	622
25/3/07	Hunslet (h) (NLC)	W83-6	t:Bostock(2),Preece,Crouthers,Epati,Lawford(2),Robinson,Bates,Powell(2),Maun,Weeden,Waters g:F Maloney(13) fg:Crouthers	1st(NLC-G3)	824
1/4/07	Sheffield (h) (CCR4)	L28-46	t:Crouthers,Bretherton,Weeden,Maun,Close,Preece g:F Maloney(2)	N/A	1,038
6/4/07	Batley (h)	L16-24	t:Epati(2),Maun g:F Maloney(2)	7th	1,566
9/4/07	Halifax (a)	W24-27	t:Crouthers,Hall,Bretherton,Finn,F Maloney g:F Maloney(3) fg:Lawford	5th	1,889
15/4/07	Whitehaven (a)	L28-12	t:Preece,Weeden g:Lawford(2)	7th	2,008
22/4/07	Leigh (h) (NLCQFQ)	L30-46	t:Crouthers,Powell,Preece,Kelly,Walker g:Finn(5)	N/A	1,070
29/4/07	Doncaster (a)	L26-33	t:Weeden,Powell,F Maloney,Maun,Crawley g:F Maloney,Finn(2)	6th	1,021
6/5/07	Rochdale (h)	L24-36	t:Preece(2),F Maloney,Crawley g:F Maloney(4)	7th	754
18/5/07	Sheffield (a)	W12-26	t:Hirst,Powell,Buchanan,Bostock g:F Maloney(5)	5th	881
31/5/07	Whitehaven (h)	L22-32	t:F Maloney,Hall,Bostock g:F Maloney(4),Finn	5th	2,010
10/6/07	Castleford (a)	L56-8	t:Maun,Buchanan	6th	4,739
17/6/07	Leigh (h)	W27-18	t:F Maloney,Maun,Bretherton,Buchanan g:F Maloney(3),Finn(2) fg:Finn	6th	1,611
28/6/07	Batley (a)	L22-20	t:Buchanan(2),Bostock,Kelly g:F Maloney(2)	6th	2,208
5/7/07	Widnes (h)	L10-50	t:F Maloney,Lawford g:Finn	6th	1,885
19/7/07	Rochdale (a)	W12-36	t:D Maloney,Hall,Bretherton,Domic,Robinson(2) g:Finn(6)	6th	1,093
29/7/07	Castleford (h)	L10-36	t:Hobson,Buchanan g:Finn	6th	3,010
5/8/07	Halifax (h)	L36-38	t:Robinson,Helme,Hobson,Powell,Walker,Maun g:Finn(4),Walker(2)	6th	1,183
12/8/07	Widnes (a)	L48-12	t:Robinson,Crouthers g:Finn,Lawford	7th	2,853
19/8/07	Sheffield (h)	W16-10	t:Finn,Maun g:Finn(4)	6th	1,009
2/9/07	Doncaster (a)	L51-18	t:Powell(2),Hall g:Finn(3)	7th	1,130
9/9/07	Leigh (a)	L42-0		7th	1,359

		APP		TRIES		GOALS		FG		PTS	
	D.O.B.	ALL	NL1	ALL	NL1	ALL	NL1	ALL	NL1	ALL	NL1
David Bates	23/10/80	1(10)	(2)	1	0	0	0	0	0	4	0
Andrew Bostock	25/2/85	12(1)	4(1)	9	3	0	0	0	0	36	12
Alex Bretherton	5/12/82	26	18	5	3	0	0	0	0	20	12
Austin Buchanan	22/5/84	14	14	6	6	0	0	0	0	24	24
Richard Chapman	5/9/75	1	1	0	0	0	0	0	0	0	0
Lee Close	1/5/86	7	0	3	0	0	0	0	0	12	0
Liam Crawley	18/4/87	(12)	(10)	2	2	0	0	0	0	8	8
Kevin Crouthers	3/1/76	22(3)	13(3)	10	2	0	0	1	0	41	8
Sid Domic	8/2/75	2	2	1	1	0	0	0	0	4	4
Kane Epati	13/8/81	3	3	6	2	0	0	0	0	24	8
Liam Finn	2/11/83	14(13)	11(7)	3	2	33	25	1	1	79	59
Ryan Glynn	3/9/87	3(1)	1(1)	0	0	0	0	0	0	0	0
Luke Haigh	24/7/87	13(8)	6(7)	2	0	0	0	0	0	8	0
Chris Hall	12/12/82	13	12	4	4	0	0	0	0	16	16
Joe Helme	1/4/84	4(7)	4(7)	1	1	0	0	0	0	4	4
Keegan Hirst	13/12/88	3(7)	2(7)	1	1	0	0	0	0	4	4
Andy Hobson	26/12/78	23	15	2	2	0	0	0	0	8	8
Rob Kelly	1/3/86	1(19)	1(12)	2	1	0	0	0	0	8	4
Dean Lawford	9/5/77	25	17	4	1	4	3	2	1	26	11
Dominic Maloney	12/3/87	23	15	1	1	0	0	0	0	4	4
Francis Maloney	26/5/73	18(1)	10(1)	10	6	59	24	0	0	158	72
Danny Maun	5/1/81	25	17	11	6	0	0	0	0	44	24
John Oakes	12/2/88	1(1)	0	1	0	0	0	0	0	4	0
Bryn Powell	5/9/79	20	17	8	5	0	0	0	0	32	20
Ian Preece	13/6/85	22	15	8	3	0	0	0	0	32	12
Danny Ratcliffe	14/3/87	1	0	1	0	0	0	0	0	4	0
Martin Robinson	9/4/81	15(11)	13(4)	6	4	0	0	0	0	24	16
Jason Southwell	14/7/86	(5)	(5)	0	0	0	0	0	0	0	0
Andy Spink	12/1/79	1(5)	1(2)	0	0	0	0	0	0	0	0
Pat Walker	24/3/86	12(2)	11(1)	2	1	2	2	0	0	12	8
Joe Waters	15/6/87	1	0	1	0	0	0	0	0	4	0
Josh Weeden	10/11/83	20	11	6	2	0	0	0	0	24	8
Taron Wildey	11/9/87	(1)	(1)	0	0	0	0	0	0	0	0
Jake Wilson	23/3/89	(1)	(1)	0	0	0	0	0	0	0	0

Danny Maun

LEAGUE RECORD
P18-W5-D0-L13-BP6
(7th, NL1)
F346, A572, Diff-226
21 points.

CHALLENGE CUP
Round Four

NATIONAL LEAGUE CUP
Quarter Final Qualifying Round/
1st, Group 3

ATTENDANCES
Best - v Castleford (NL1 - 3,010)
Worst - v Rochdale (NL1 - 754)
Total (excluding Challenge Cup) - 17,794
Average (excluding Challenge Cup) - 1,369
(Up by 491 on 2006, NL2)

DONCASTER

DATE	FIXTURE	RESULT	SCORERS	LGE	ATT
11/2/07	Castleford (h) (NLC)	L6-30	t:Wildbore g:Holroyd	3rd(NLC-G1)	4,180
16/2/07	Sheffield (a) (NLC)	W18-20	t:Leaf,Wildbore,P Green g:Holroyd(4)	3rd(NLC-G1)	1,043
25/2/07	Featherstone (a) (NLC)	L24-22	t:Lynn,Leaf,Gorton,Sheriffe g:Wildbore(3)	2nd(NLC-G1)	1,335
4/3/07	Sheffield (h) (NLC)	L12-20	t:Lowe,Leaf g:Wildbore(2)	3rd(NLC-G1)	2,753
11/3/07	Whitehaven (a) (CCR3)	L24-10	t:D Mills,Mbu g:Wildbore	N/A	1,268
18/3/07	Featherstone (h) (NLC)	D18-18	t:D Mills,Sheriffe,Buttery(2) g:McLocklan	3rd(NLC-G1)	1,775
25/3/07	Castleford (a) (NLC)	L64-8	t:McLocklan g:Wildbore(2)	4th(NLC-G1)	4,613
6/4/07	Sheffield (a)	W20-24	t:Garmston,Andrews(2),Mbu g:Wildbore(4)	5th	1,142
12/4/07	Castleford (h)	L4-66	t:Lowe	7th	6,528
15/4/07	Leigh (h)	L18-52	t:Wildbore,Penny(2) g:Wildbore(3)	9th	1,339
29/4/07	Dewsbury (a)	W26-33	t:Sheriffe(3),Penny(2),Tandy g:Holroyd(4) fg:Penny	5th	1,021
6/5/07	Whitehaven (h)	W26-16	t:P Green,Wildbore,Buttery,D Mills g:Holroyd(4) fg:Buttery,Holroyd	4th	831
20/5/07	Rochdale (a)	L58-12	t:Close,Adebisi g:McLocklan(2)	6th	904
3/6/07	Batley (h)	L14-48	t:Adebisi(3) g:McLocklan	6th	970
10/6/07	Widnes (h)	L4-90	t:Adebisi	7th	1,248
15/6/07	Whitehaven (a)	L60-6	t:Close g:McLocklan	10th	1,410
1/7/07	Sheffield (h)	L20-32	t:Rowe,Munro(2),Woods g:Skelton(2)	10th	1,038
8/7/07	Castleford (a)	L66-4	t:Munro	10th	4,109
22/7/07	Halifax (h)	L30-44	t:Gale,P Green,Woods,Castle,Forster g:Gale(5)	10th	1,202
29/7/07	Widnes (a)	L40-18	t:Burgess,Gale,Forster g:Gale(3)	10th	2,607
5/8/07	Rochdale (h)	W34-30	t:Woods(2),Hodgkinson,Benson,W Green,Rowe g:Gale(4),W Green	10th	838
12/8/07	Batley (a)	L26-12	t:Woods(2) g:Gale(2)	10th	732
19/8/07	Leigh (a)	L34-14	t:Munro,Forster,Woods g:Forster	10th	1,093
2/9/07	Dewsbury (h)	W51-18	t:Woods,Lawton,Munro,Buttery,Hodgkinson,Forster,Johnson,Gale g:Gale(8),Castle fg:Gale	10th	1,130
9/9/07	Halifax (a)	L52-24	t:Benson,Lythe,W Green,Munro g:Forster(3),Speake	10th	1,905

● 'Lakers' dropped from club's name, end of June

		APP		TRIES		GOALS		FG		PTS	
	D.O.B.	ALL	NL1	ALL	NL1	ALL	NL1	ALL	NL1	ALL	NL1
Ade Adebisi	7/1/86	7(2)	6(2)	5	5	0	0	0	0	20	20
Paul Anderson	2/4/77	3(1)	3(1)	0	0	0	0	0	0	0	0
Dean Andrews	1/7/79	4(3)	4(3)	2	2	0	0	0	0	8	8
Alex Benson	22/5/85	9(9)	6(8)	2	2	0	0	0	0	8	8
Lee Bettinson	22/7/81	3	3	0	0	0	0	0	0	0	0
Joe Brown	24/4/87	7	7	0	0	0	0	0	0	0	0
Luke Burgess	20/2/87	7(2)	7(2)	1	1	0	0	0	0	4	4
Chris Buttery	23/12/85	16(2)	10(2)	4	2	0	0	1	1	17	9
Gareth Carey	17/10/86	(1)	(1)	0	0	0	0	0	0	0	0
Mark Castle	19/2/86	8(9)	8(6)	1	1	1	1	0	0	6	6
Lee Close	1/5/86	7	7	2	2	0	0	0	0	8	8
Phil Crosby	19/3/87	(1)	(1)	0	0	0	0	0	0	0	0
James Endersby	26/9/86	2(1)	1	0	0	0	0	0	0	0	0
Ayden Faal	12/12/86	1(1)	1(1)	0	0	0	0	0	0	0	0
Chris Forster	3/5/88	5(1)	5(1)	4	4	4	4	0	0	24	24
Lee Forth	20/1/86	2(1)	2(1)	0	0	0	0	0	0	0	0
Luke Gale	22/6/88	9	9	3	3	22	22	1	1	57	57
James Garmston	6/8/86	8(3)	5(2)	1	1	0	0	0	0	4	4
Dean Gorton	16/1/84	12	5	1	0	0	0	0	0	4	0
Peter Green	2/12/81	22(3)	17(1)	3	2	0	0	0	0	12	8
Wayne Green	1/1/83	3(1)	3(1)	2	2	1	1	0	0	10	10
Shaun Hesketh	17/8/86	3(2)	3(2)	0	0	0	0	0	0	0	0
Tommy Hodgkinson	15/4/70	6	6	2	2	0	0	0	0	8	8
Graham Holroyd	25/10/75	4	2	0	0	13	8	1	1	27	17
Sean Johnson	12/4/88	(4)	(4)	1	1	0	0	0	0	4	4
Craig Lawton	17/2/81	21(3)	17(1)	1	1	0	0	0	0	4	4
Shaun Leaf	10/2/84	14(1)	11	3	0	0	0	0	0	12	0
Lewis Lilley	12/10/87	(1)	(1)	0	0	0	0	0	0	0	0
Neil Lowe	20/12/78	9(2)	3(2)	2	1	0	0	0	0	8	4
Terry Lynn	12/1/78	2(1)	0	1	0	0	0	0	0	4	0
Chris Lythe	1/9/87	(4)	(4)	1	1	0	0	0	0	4	4
Joe Mbu	6/11/83	10	3	2	1	0	0	0	0	8	4
Joe McLocklan	2/10/86	15	8	1	0	5	4	0	0	14	8
Danny Mills	10/8/82	11	5	3	1	0	0	0	0	12	4
Karl Mills	7/2/84	(5)	(5)	0	0	0	0	0	0	0	0
Damian Munro	6/10/76	8	8	6	6	0	0	0	0	24	24
Adam Myers	3/2/89	(1)	(1)	0	0	0	0	0	0	0	0
John Okul	24/11/72	(1)	0	0	0	0	0	0	0	0	0
Joel Penny	22/1/80	8	4	4	4	0	0	1	1	17	17
Craig Potter	17/12/80	5(2)	5(2)	0	0	0	0	0	0	0	0
Gary Richardson	3/11/76	6(1)	6(1)	0	0	0	0	0	0	0	0
Adam Robinson	8/4/87	4(5)	3(1)	0	0	0	0	0	0	0	0
Alex Rowe	11/3/85	2(17)	2(11)	2	2	0	0	0	0	8	8
Adam Scott	1/1/85	1(5)	0	0	0	0	0	0	0	0	0
Rikki Sheriffe	5/5/84	12	5	5	3	0	0	0	0	20	12
Craig Skelton	3/1/88	6	6	0	0	2	2	0	0	4	4
Andy Speake	28/9/86	6(2)	6(2)	0	0	1	1	0	0	2	2
Ryan Tandy	20/9/81	8	4	1	1	0	0	0	0	4	4
Andy Taylor	15/12/82	1(1)	1(1)	0	0	0	0	0	0	0	0
Brett Turner	1/12/87	4	0	0	0	0	0	0	0	0	0
Loz Wildbore	23/9/84	12	5	4	2	15	7	0	0	46	22
Darren Woods	24/3/84	9	9	8	8	0	0	0	0	32	32
Simon Worrall	10/10/84	3(1)	3(1)	0	0	0	0	0	0	0	0

Craig Lawton

LEAGUE RECORD
P18-W5-D0-L13-BP1
(10th, NL1)
F348, A778, Diff-430
10 points *(6 points deducted)*.

CHALLENGE CUP
Round Three

NATIONAL LEAGUE CUP
4th, Group 1

ATTENDANCES
Best - v Castleford (NL1 - 6,528)
Worst - v Whitehaven (NL1 - 831)
Total (excluding Challenge Cup) - 23,832
Average (excluding Challenge Cup) - 1,986
(Up by 980 on 2006)

HALIFAX

DATE	FIXTURE	RESULT	SCORERS	LGE	ATT
11/2/07	Keighley (a) (NLC)	W18-44	t:Roberts,Watene,Gibson,Royston,Govin(2),Ball g:Hartley(2),Govin,Jones(5)	2nd(NLC-G2)	1,352
18/2/07	York (h) (NLC)	W34-14	t:Royston(2),Roberts,Trinder,Greenwood(2),Varkulis g:Jones(2),Govin	1st(NLC-G2)	2,113
25/2/07	Gateshead (a) (NLC)	W6-22	t:Ball(2),Hoare(2) g:Haley(3)	1st(NLC-G2)	403
4/3/07	Keighley (h) (NLC)	W52-4	t:Haley,Larder,Ball,Roberts(2),Watene,Royston(2),Watson g:Haley(8)	1st(NLC-G2)	1,676
11/3/07	Eccles & Salford (h) (CCR3)	W86-12	t:George(3),Greenwood(4),Larder(4),Attwood,Roberts(2),Hoare,Haley g:Haley(11)	N/A	825
18/3/07	Gateshead (h) (NLC)	W30-8	t:Southern,George(2),Royston,Gibson,Jones g:Jones(3)	1st(NLC-G2)	1,504
25/3/07	York (a) (NLC)	W20-60	t:White,Penkywicz,Royston(2),Watson,Gibson,Roberts,Larder,Ball(2),White g:Watson(3),Hartley(5)	1st(NLC-G2)	1,729
1/4/07	Whitehaven (a) (CCR4)	L36-8	t:Wrench g:Hartley(2)	N/A	2,128
6/4/07	Castleford (a)	L46-22	t:Greenwood,Jones(2),Penkywicz g:Hartley(3)	8th	6,284
9/4/07	Dewsbury (h)	L24-27	t:Hartley,Ball,White,George,Larder g:Hartley(2)	8th	1,889
15/4/07	Rochdale (h)	L20-38	t:Penkywicz,Varkulis(2),Heaton(2),Trinder(2) g:Hartley(5)	6th	820
22/4/07	Featherstone (h) (NLCQFQ)	W76-16	t:Penkywicz,Joseph(2),Heaton,Varkulis(2),Hartley,Trinder,Greenwood(2),Law,White,Jones g:Hartley(12)	N/A	1,318
26/4/07	Widnes (a)	L48-12	t:Gibson(2) g:Hartley(2)	8th	3,042
6/5/07	Sheffield (h)	W46-8	t:Wrench,Larder,Smith,Greenwood,Hartley,George(2),Gibson g:Hartley(7)	6th	1,519
20/5/07	Whitehaven (a)	L40-24	t:George,Hartley,Roberts,Smith g:Hartley(4)	7th	1,729
26/5/07	Celtic Crusaders (h) (NLCQF)	W30-18	t:Varkulis,Penkywicz,Greenwood(2),Hartley,Joseph g:Hartley,Holroyd(2)	N/A	1,086
3/6/07	Castleford (h)	L14-30	t:George,Greenwood,Gibson g:Holroyd	8th	2,990
10/6/07	Batley (a)	W8-58	t:George(2),Heaton,Greenwood(2),Joseph(2),Holroyd,Penkywicz,Hoare g:Holroyd(6),Watson(3)	5th	898
14/6/07	Widnes (h)	W12-6	t:Ball,Larder g:Holroyd(2)	5th	2,412
24/6/07	Whitehaven (a) (NLCSF)	L34-19	t:Varkulis,Greenwood,Smith g:Holroyd(3) fg:Watson	N/A	2,246
1/7/07	Leigh (a)	W6-18	t:Varkulis,Patterson,Watene g:Holroyd(3)	5th	1,803
8/7/07	Rochdale (h)	W54-8	t:Smith,Gibson(2),Southern,Hoare,Greenwood,Royston(2),Penkywicz g:Holroyd(7),Watson(2)	5th	1,733
22/7/07	Doncaster (a)	W30-44	t:Royston,Smith,Ball,Patterson,Larder,Penkywicz,Greenwood,Joseph g:Holroyd(6)	4th	1,202
29/7/07	Whitehaven (h)	L20-26	t:Greenwood,Ball(2),Holroyd g:Holroyd(2)	5th	1,745
5/8/07	Dewsbury (a)	W36-38	t:Ball,Joseph,Royston,Hoare,Gibson,Larder,Watene g:Holroyd(5)	4th	1,183
12/8/07	Leigh (h)	W68-22	t:Larder(2),Ball,Hoare,Joseph,Watene,Smith(2),Royston(2),Greenwood(2) g:Holroyd(10)	4th	1,816
19/8/07	Batley (h)	W48-20	t:Gibson,Greenwood(2),Varkulis(2),Haley,Holroyd(2),Royston g:Holroyd(6)	4th	1,550
31/8/07	Sheffield (a)	W16-24	t:Varkulis(2),Penkywicz,Trinder g:Holroyd(4)	4th	864
9/9/07	Doncaster (h)	W52-24	t:Larder,Holroyd(2),Varkulis,Penkywicz,Haley,Joseph,Watson,Royston g:Holroyd(7),Watson	3rd	1,905
16/9/07	Sheffield (h) (EPO)	W30-26	t:Royston(2),Penkywicz,Trinder,Smith g:Holroyd(5)	N/A	1,711
23/9/07	Whitehaven (h) (ESF)	W32-24	t:Larder,Royston,Trinder,Varkulis,Ball g:Holroyd(6)	N/A	2,184
27/9/07	Widnes (a) (FE)	L36-24	t:Roberts,Royston,Watene,Varkulis,Hoare g:Holroyd(2)	N/A	3,347

		APP		TRIES		GOALS		FG		PTS	
	D.O.B.	ALL	NL1	ALL	NL1	ALL	NL1	ALL	NL1	ALL	NL1
Brad Attwood	24/11/84	2	0	1	0	0	0	0	0	4	0
Damian Ball	14/7/75	17(10)	9(9)	14	8	0	0	0	0	56	32
Matthew Bottom	2/1/86	(2)	0	0	0	0	0	0	0	0	0
Jamie Bovill	21/3/83	(1)	(1)	0	0	0	0	0	0	0	0
Marcus George	28/2/86	13	8	12	7	0	0	0	0	48	28
Damian Gibson	14/5/75	27	19	11	8	0	0	0	0	44	32
Mick Govin	5/11/84	3(1)	(1)	2	0	2	0	0	0	12	0
Lee Greenwood	28/9/80	29	20	23	12	0	0	0	0	92	48
James Haley	2/7/85	7	3	4	2	22	0	0	0	60	8
Tim Hartley	2/1/86	10(2)	6	5	3	45	23	0	0	110	58
Danny Heaton	19/4/81	7(8)	4(4)	4	3	0	0	0	0	16	12
Sam Hoare	24/8/85	13(9)	8(8)	8	5	0	0	0	0	32	20
Graham Holroyd	25/10/75	18	16	6	6	77	72	0	0	178	168
Danny Jones	6/3/86	4(8)	(5)	4	2	10	0	0	0	36	8
Phil Joseph	10/1/85	23(5)	15(4)	9	6	0	0	0	0	36	24
David Larder	5/6/76	24(5)	18(3)	15	9	0	0	0	0	60	36
Scott Law	19/2/85	3(3)	0	1	0	0	0	0	0	4	0
Damian Munro	6/10/76	2(1)	0	0	0	0	0	0	0	0	0
Lee Patterson	20/7/82	7	7	2	2	0	0	0	0	8	8
Sean Penkywicz	18/5/82	23(5)	18(3)	11	8	0	0	0	0	44	32
Mark Roberts	9/11/82	21(5)	12(4)	9	2	0	0	0	0	36	8
Shad Royston	29/11/82	19	12	20	12	0	0	0	0	80	48
Andy Shickell	9/5/81	8(6)	4(4)	0	0	0	0	0	0	0	0
Luke Simeunovich	28/9/85	1(1)	0	0	0	0	0	0	0	0	0
Paul Smith	17/5/77	17(2)	15(2)	8	7	0	0	0	0	32	28
Paul Southern	18/3/76	28(2)	20	2	1	0	0	0	0	8	4
Aaron Trinder	6/11/80	4(16)	(12)	7	5	0	0	0	0	28	20
Richard Varkulis	21/5/82	30	21	15	10	0	0	0	0	60	40
Frank Watene	15/2/77	4(26)	2(18)	6	4	0	0	0	0	24	16
Ian Watson	27/10/76	25(5)	16(5)	3	1	9	6	1	0	31	16
Paul White	7/12/82	6	4	4	1	0	0	0	0	16	4
David Wrench	3/1/79	21(5)	16(1)	2	1	0	0	0	0	8	4

Lee Greenwood

LEAGUE RECORD
P18-W12-D0-L6-BP2
(3rd, NL1/Final Eliminator)
F616, A421, Diff+195
38 points.

CHALLENGE CUP
Round Four

NATIONAL LEAGUE CUP
Semi Finalists/1st, Group 2

ATTENDANCES
Best - v Castleford (NL1 - 2,990)
Worst - v Eccles & Salford (CC - 825)
Total (excluding Challenge Cup) - 29,151
Average (excluding Challenge Cup) - 1,822
(Up by 229 on 2006)

LEIGH CENTURIONS

DATE	FIXTURE	RESULT	SCORERS	LGE	ATT
11/2/07	London Skolars (a) (NLC)	W8-52	t:Alstead(2),Couturier,Greenwood(3),Stewart,J Hill,Heremaia		
			g:Couturier(7),Heremaia	2nd(NLC-G6)	379
18/2/07	Widnes (a) (NLC)	L34-20	t:Ainscough,Clough,Rivett,Rudd g:Heremaia(2)	2nd(NLC-G6)	4,133
25/2/07	Celtic Crusaders (h) (NLC)	L22-26	t:Greenwood,Speakman,Stewart,Clough g:Heremaia(3)	3rd(NLC-G6)	1,637
4/3/07	Widnes (h) (NLC)	W24-8	t:Roberts,Greenwood,Grundy,Rivett,Cookson g:Heremaia(2)	3rd(NLC-G6)	2,291
11/3/07	Dewsbury (a) (CCR3)	L36-34	t:Grundy,Hughes,Cookson,Styles,Jonkers,Greenwood g:Heremaia(4),Hughes	N/A	1,131
18/3/07	Celtic Crusaders (a) (NLC)	L22-14	t:Ainscough(2),Smyth g:Hughes	3rd(NLC-G6)	440
25/3/07	London Skolars (h) (NLC)	W60-22	t:C Hill,Rivett,Ainscough(2),Greenwood(2),Alstead(3),Grundy(2) g:Hughes(8)	3rd(NLC-G6)	1,277
5/4/07	Widnes (a)	L46-12	t:Heremaia(2) g:Hughes(2)	9th	3,792
9/4/07	Whitehaven (h)	L12-18	t:C Hill,Alstead g:Couturier(2)	9th	1,825
15/4/07	Doncaster (a)	W18-52	t:Couturier,Heremaia,Butterworth(2),Halliwell(3),Ainscough,Hughes g:Couturier(8)	5th	1,339
22/4/07	Dewsbury (a) (NLCQFQ)	W30-46	t:Greenwood,Heremaia(2),Taylor,Roberts,Ainscough,Wilson,Couturier		
			g:Couturier(7)	N/A	1,070
29/4/07	Sheffield (h)	W38-22	t:Couturier,C Hill,Hughes,Ainscough,Heremaia(2),Halliwell g:Couturier(5)	4th	1,810
6/5/07	Castleford (h)	L24-32	t:Ainscough(2),Greenwood,Heremaia g:Couturier(4)	5th	2,683
20/5/07	Batley (a)	W30-44	t:Halliwell(2),Couturier,Rudd,Heremaia(2),Rivett,Alstead g:Couturier(6)	4th	841
27/5/07	Castleford (a) (NLCQF)	L42-6	t:Couturier g:Couturier	N/A	3,205
3/6/07	Rochdale (h)	W32-4	t:Couturier,Heremaia,Butterworth,Cookson,Stewart g:Couturier(6)	4th	1,669
10/6/07	Whitehaven (a)	W12-28	t:Rudd,Heremaia,Alstead(2),Rivett g:Couturier(4)	4th	2,065
17/6/07	Dewsbury (a)	L27-18	t:Cookson,Rivett,Thomas g:Couturier,Heremaia(2)	4th	1,611
1/7/07	Halifax (h)	L6-18	t:Heremaia g:Heremaia	4th	1,803
8/7/07	Batley (h)	W26-22	t:Halliwell,Martins(2),Grundy,C Hill g:Halliwell(3)	4th	1,469
20/7/07	Sheffield (a)	L39-12	t:Greenwood(2),Alstead	5th	870
29/7/07	Rochdale (a)	W4-42	t:Halliwell(3),McConnell,Rivett,Couturier(2),Wilson g:Couturier(4),Halliwell	4th	650
2/8/07	Widnes (h)	L0-38		5th	3,095
12/8/07	Halifax (a)	L68-22	t:Halliwell,Styles,Richardson,Greenwood g:Heremaia(3)	5th	1,816
19/8/07	Doncaster (h)	W34-14	t:Stewart,Greenwood(2),Styles,Alstead(3) g:Couturier(2),Halliwell	5th	1,093
2/9/07	Castleford (a)	L62-10	t:Halliwell,Alstead g:Halliwell	5th	5,525
9/9/07	Dewsbury (h)	W42-0	t:Rivett(2),Greenwood,Kay,Giles(2),Stewart,Martins g:Couturier(4),Heremaia	5th	1,359
13/9/07	Whitehaven (a) (EPO)	L19-6	t:Hough g:Heremaia	N/A	1,761

		APP		TRIES		GOALS		FG		PTS	
	D.O.B.	ALL	NL1	ALL	NL1	ALL	NL1	ALL	NL1	ALL	NL1
Martin Ainscough	23/10/85	16(2)	9(2)	10	4	0	0	0	0	40	16
David Alstead	18/2/82	26	18	14	9	0	0	0	0	56	36
Matt Astley	26/9/86	5(4)	4(4)	0	0	0	0	0	0	0	0
John Boland	7/1/86	(1)	(1)	0	0	0	0	0	0	0	0
John Braddish	25/1/81	1	0	0	0	0	0	0	0	0	0
Sam Butterworth	12/2/78	8(13)	6(6)	3	3	0	0	0	0	12	12
John Clough	13/9/84	11(5)	6(4)	2	0	0	0	0	0	8	0
John Cookson	12/12/84	5(14)	5(6)	4	2	0	0	0	0	16	8
Damien Couturier	9/7/81	16	13	9	6	61	46	0	0	158	116
Chris Giles	26/12/81	6	6	2	2	0	0	0	0	8	8
Miles Greenwood	30/7/87	26	17	16	7	0	0	0	0	64	28
Tommy Grundy	17/4/85	16	8	5	1	0	0	0	0	20	4
Danny Halliwell	23/3/81	13(2)	11(2)	12	12	6	6	0	0	60	60
Aaron Heremaia	19/9/82	26	17	14	11	20	8	0	0	96	60
Chris Hill	3/11/87	6(13)	3(8)	4	3	0	0	0	0	16	12
John Hill	7/10/81	5	0	1	0	0	0	0	0	4	0
Chris Hough	30/8/81	7	7	1	1	0	0	0	0	4	4
Adam Hughes	1/10/77	5(3)	2(2)	3	2	12	2	0	0	36	12
Chad Isles	7/2/87	1(2)	1(2)	0	0	0	0	0	0	0	0
Tim Jonkers	3/7/81	6(3)	1(1)	1	0	0	0	0	0	4	0
Daryl Kay	6/11/87	(8)	(5)	1	1	0	0	0	0	4	4
Sebastien Martins	18/11/84	3(8)	3(8)	3	3	0	0	0	0	12	12
Dave McConnell	25/3/81	8	8	1	1	0	0	0	0	4	4
Gareth Pemberton	8/7/85	(6)	(6)	0	0	0	0	0	0	0	0
Sean Richardson	20/8/73	2(8)	1(8)	1	1	0	0	0	0	4	4
Leroy Rivett	17/12/76	27	19	9	6	0	0	0	0	36	24
Robert Roberts	21/6/82	8(1)	5	2	0	0	0	0	0	8	0
Paul Rowley	12/3/75	3	1	0	0	0	0	0	0	0	0
Adam Rudd	29/7/86	9(3)	6(3)	3	2	0	0	0	0	12	8
Rob Smyth	22/2/77	6	3	1	0	0	0	0	0	4	0
Danny Speakman	5/12/85	2(2)	0	1	0	0	0	0	0	4	0
Warren Stevens	4/10/78	13	6	0	0	0	0	0	0	0	0
Anthony Stewart	5/3/79	23	15	5	3	0	0	0	0	20	12
Mailangi Styles	6/6/84	18(6)	13(4)	3	2	0	0	0	0	12	8
James Taylor	11/9/84	16(2)	14	1	0	0	0	0	0	4	0
Adam Thomas	4/11/87	4(2)	4(1)	1	1	0	0	0	0	4	4
Dana Wilson	22/5/83	17(3)	15(2)	2	1	0	0	0	0	8	4
Tom Woodcock	21/5/87	(1)	(1)	0	0	0	0	0	0	0	0

David Alstead

LEAGUE RECORD
P18-W9-D0-L9-BP4
(5th, NL1/Elimination Play-Off)
F454, A474, Diff-20
31 points.

CHALLENGE CUP
Round Three

NATIONAL LEAGUE CUP
Quarter Finalists/3rd, Group 6

ATTENDANCES
Best - v Widnes (NL1 - 3,095)
Worst - v Doncaster (NL1 - 1,093)
Total (excluding Challenge Cup) - 22,011
Average (excluding Challenge Cup) - 1,834
(Down by 404 on 2006)

ROCHDALE HORNETS

DATE	FIXTURE	RESULT	SCORERS	LGE	ATT
11/2/07	Oldham (a) (NLC)	W8-24	t:Goulden,Blanchard,Andrews,McConnell g:King(3) fg:Svabic(2)	2nd(NLC-G4)	1,145
18/2/07	Batley (h) (NLC)	L29-38	t:Blanchard,Andrews,Fagborun(3) g:King(4) fg:Svabic	2nd(NLC-G4)	971
25/2/07	Swinton (a) (NLC)	W14-40	t:Goulden(2),McConnell,Patterson(2),Hasty(2) g:King(6)	1st(NLC-G4)	572
4/3/07	Oldham (h) (NLC)	W16-6	t:McConnell,Goulden g:King(4)	1st(NLC-G4)	816
11/3/07	Saddleworth (h) (CCR3)	W48-6	t:Hulse,Hasty(2),Anderson,Andrews,King(2),Corcoran,Gledhill g:King(6)	N/A	552
18/3/07	Swinton (h) (NLC)	W42-10	t:Anderson(2),King(3),Fagborun,Hulse,Goulden g:King(5)	1st(NLC-G4)	556
25/3/07	Batley (a) (NLC)	W10-13	t:Giles g:King(4) fg:Svabic	1st(NLC-G4)	489
1/4/07	Celtic Crusaders (h) (CCR4)	W20-16	t:Giles,Patterson,Hulse,Andrews g:King(2)	N/A	482
6/4/07	Whitehaven (a)	L42-4	t:Fagborun	10th	2,071
9/4/07	Widnes (h)	L18-40	t:King,McConnell,Fagborun g:King(3)	10th	1,485
15/4/07	Halifax (h)	L20-38	t:McConnell,Goulden(2) g:King(2)	10th	820
22/4/07	Swinton (h) (NLCQFQ)	W30-16	t:Andrews,Hasty,Hulse,Robinson,Gledhill g:King(5)	N/A	501
29/4/07	Castleford (a)	L56-6	t:Hasty g:King	10th	4,645
6/5/07	Dewsbury (a)	W24-36	t:Corcoran(2),Svabic,Goulden,King(3) g:King(4)	10th	754
11/5/07	St Helens (a) (CCR5)	L70-10	t:Fagborun,Andrews g:King	N/A	3,586
20/5/07	Doncaster (h)	W58-12	t:Hasty(2),Gorski,Hulse,Svabic,Andrews(2),Baldwin,Patterson,King g:King(9)	8th	904
27/5/07	Widnes (h) (NLCQF) ●	L0-24		N/A	2,362
3/6/07	Leigh (a)	L32-4	t:Baldwin	9th	1,669
7/6/07	Sheffield (a)	L24-0		9th	1,463
17/6/07	Batley (h)	W38-14	t:Hasty(2),King,Fagborun(2),Baldwin,Smith g:King(5)	7th	644
1/7/07	Widnes (a)	L32-0		9th	4,879
8/7/07	Halifax (a)	L54-8	t:Hulse,Marsh	9th	1,733
19/7/07	Dewsbury (h)	L12-36	t:Hasty,Robinson g:McCully(2)	9th	1,093
29/7/07	Leigh (h)	L4-42	t:Gorski	9th	650
5/8/07	Doncaster (a)	L34-30	t:Goulden,Hulse,Hasty,Robinson(2),McCully g:McCully(3)	9th	838
12/8/07	Sheffield (h)	L36-56	t:Goulden(2),McCully(2),Hasty,Andrews g:McCully(6)	9th	503
19/8/07	Whitehaven (h)	L12-28	t:McCully,Andrews g:McCully(2)	9th	555
2/9/07	Batley (a)	L30-16	t:Campbell,McCully,Hasty g:McCully(2)	9th	532
9/9/07	Castleford (h)	L0-106		9th	2,506

● Played at Halton Stadium, Widnes

	D.O.B.	APP ALL	APP NL1	TRIES ALL	TRIES NL1	GOALS ALL	GOALS NL1	FG ALL	FG NL1	PTS ALL	PTS NL1
Paul Anderson	2/4/77	6(3)	3(1)	3	0	0	0	0	0	12	0
Eric Andrews	11/2/82	28	18	10	4	0	0	0	0	40	16
Brad Attwood	24/11/84	4	4	0	0	0	0	0	0	0	0
Andy Bailey	15/10/82	10(4)	8(3)	0	0	0	0	0	0	0	0
Simon Baldwin	31/3/75	20	11	3	3	0	0	0	0	12	12
Rob Ball	22/3/76	9(5)	7(3)	0	0	0	0	0	0	0	0
Gareth Barber	15/12/80	4(1)	4(1)	0	0	0	0	0	0	0	0
Ryan Benjafield	3/8/82	6(12)	4(8)	0	0	0	0	0	0	0	0
Mark Blanchard	11/7/82	15(6)	7(6)	2	0	0	0	0	0	8	0
Chris Campbell	2/12/80	6	6	1	1	0	0	0	0	4	4
Wayne Corcoran	10/7/85	11(12)	10(5)	3	2	0	0	0	0	12	8
Dave Cunliffe	15/1/80	3(2)	3(2)	0	0	0	0	0	0	0	0
Bolu Fagborun	28/3/86	22	12	9	4	0	0	0	0	36	16
Chris Giles	26/12/81	12(1)	5	2	0	0	0	0	0	8	0
John Gledhill	23/1/85	3(6)	1(2)	2	0	0	0	0	0	8	0
Andy Gorski	31/3/81	20(3)	13(2)	2	2	0	0	0	0	8	8
Tommy Goulden	30/6/81	26	16	11	6	0	0	0	0	44	24
Phil Hasty	28/5/80	24(4)	17	14	9	0	0	0	0	56	36
Gary Hulse	20/1/81	18(7)	8(7)	7	3	0	0	0	0	28	12
Eric Johnson	14/3/87	(2)	(2)	0	0	0	0	0	0	0	0
Nick Johnson	16/4/83	5	3	0	0	0	0	0	0	0	0
Kevin King	18/1/85	21	10	11	6	66	26	0	0	176	76
Scott Law	19/2/85	6	6	0	0	0	0	0	0	0	0
Iain Marsh	6/10/80	10(6)	9(4)	1	1	0	0	0	0	4	4
Dave McConnell	25/3/81	17(1)	9	5	2	0	0	0	0	20	8
Mark McCully	24/10/79	6(1)	6(1)	5	5	15	15	0	0	50	50
Paul Norman	25/3/74	(16)	(10)	0	0	0	0	0	0	0	0
Todd O'Brien	5/10/84	1(2)	1(2)	0	0	0	0	0	0	0	0
Lee Patterson	20/7/82	18	8	4	1	0	0	0	0	16	4
Craig Robinson	30/7/85	(15)	(8)	4	3	0	0	0	0	16	12
Jode Sheriffe	4/7/86	(2)	(2)	0	0	0	0	0	0	0	0
Byron Smith	5/3/84	24(3)	15(2)	1	1	0	0	0	0	4	4
Simon Svabic	18/1/80	21(1)	10(1)	2	2	0	0	4	0	12	8
Matt Whitaker	6/3/82	1(1)	0	0	0	0	0	0	0	0	0

Phil Hasty

LEAGUE RECORD
P18-W3-D0-L15-BP1
(9th, NL1)
F302, A700, Diff-398
10 points.

CHALLENGE CUP
Round Five

NATIONAL LEAGUE CUP
Quarter Finalists/1st, Group 4

ATTENDANCES
Best - v Castleford (NL1 - 2,506)
Worst - v Celtic Crusaders (CC - 482)
Total (excluding Challenge Cup) - 12,004
Average (excluding Challenge Cup) - 923
(Up by 3 on 2006)

SHEFFIELD EAGLES

DATE	FIXTURE	RESULT	SCORERS	LGE	ATT
11/2/07	Featherstone (a) (NLC)	L54-22	t:Hepworth,Presley,Crawford,Bravo g:Brambani(3)	4th(NLC-G1)	1,209
16/2/07	Doncaster (h) (NLC)	L18-20	t:Farrow,Law,Presley g:Brambani(3)	4th(NLC-G1)	1,043
25/2/07	Castleford (a) (NLC)	L38-12	t:Hurst,Corcoran g:Brambani(2)	4th(NLC-G1)	5,108
4/3/07	Doncaster (a) (NLC)	W12-20	t:Newlove(2),Law g:Woodcock(4)	4th(NLC-G1)	2,753
11/3/07	Leigh Miners Rangers (a) (CCR3)	W18-46	t:Hayes(2),Law(2),Woodcock,Bravo,Newlove,Hurst g:Woodcock(7)	N/A	499
16/3/07	Castleford (h) (NLC)	L6-44	t:Lindsay g:Woodcock	4th(NLC-G1)	1,897
23/3/07	Featherstone (h) (NLC)	W32-8	t:Newlove,Reid,Lindsay,Woodcock(2) g:Woodcock(6)	3rd(NLC-G1)	1,196
1/4/07	Dewsbury (a) (CCR4)	W28-46	t:Hurst(2),Pickering,Holdstock(2),Woodcock(2) g:Woodcock(9)	N/A	1,038
6/4/07	Doncaster (h)	L20-24	t:Pickering,Lindsay,Hurst(2) g:Woodcock(2)	6th	1,142
9/4/07	Batley (a)	D22-22	t:Cook,Newlove g:Woodcock(7)	6th	667
13/4/07	Widnes (h)	L4-46	t:Farrow	8th	1,211
29/4/07	Leigh (a)	L38-22	t:Newlove,Ford,Cook,Woodcock g:Woodcock,Brambani(2)	9th	1,810
6/5/07	Halifax (a)	L46-8	t:Crawford,Ford	9th	1,519
13/5/07	Hull (a) (CCR5)	L44-6	t:Buckenham g:Woodcock	N/A	4,363
18/5/07	Dewsbury (h)	L12-26	t:Corcoran,Brambani g:Woodcock(2)	10th	881
3/6/07	Widnes (a)	L56-10	t:Ford(2) g:Woodcock	10th	2,837
7/6/07	Rochdale (h)	W24-0	t:Reid,Ford,Woodcock,Lindsay g:Brambani(4)	10th	1,463
15/6/07	Castleford (h)	L15-27	t:Hurst,Ford g:Woodcock(3) fg:Lindsay	9th	1,333
1/7/07	Doncaster (a)	W20-32	t:Ford,Woodcock,Mills,Trayler,Reid(2) g:Woodcock,Brambani(3)	8th	1,038
8/7/07	Whitehaven (a)	L44-16	t:Reid,Hayes,Edwards g:Woodcock(2)	8th	1,473
20/7/07	Leigh (h)	W39-12	t:Ford(4),Woodcock,Worrincy g:Woodcock(7) fg:G Brown	7th	870
27/7/07	Batley (h)	W56-24	t:Brambani,Mills(4),Lindsay,G Brown,Worrincy,Newlove g:Brambani(10)	7th	916
5/8/07	Castleford (a)	L52-26	t:Ford(2),G Brown,Worrincy g:Brambani(5)	7th	4,538
12/8/07	Rochdale (a)	W36-56	t:Howieson,Reid,Lindsay,Worrincy(3),Woodcock(2),Stringer,Newlove g:Woodcock(8)	6th	503
19/8/07	Dewsbury (a)	L16-10	t:Ford,Worrincy g:Woodcock	7th	1,009
31/8/07	Halifax (h)	L16-24	t:Stringer,Woodcock g:Woodcock(4)	6th	864
6/9/07	Whitehaven (h)	W26-14	t:Corcoran,G Brown,Reid,Mills g:Woodcock(5)	6th	1,045
16/9/07	Halifax (a) (EPO)	L30-26	t:Ford(2),Brambani,Newlove,Worrincy g:Woodcock(3)	N/A	1,711

		APP		TRIES		GOALS		FG		PTS	
	D.O.B.	ALL	NL1	ALL	NL1	ALL	NL1	ALL	NL1	ALL	NL1
Jon Aston	5/6/76	3(7)	(4)	0	0	0	0	0	0	0	0
Dominic Brambani	10/5/85	16(9)	10(8)	3	3	32	24	0	0	76	60
Caldon Bravo	22/5/85	5(4)	3	2	0	0	0	0	0	8	0
Craig Brown	2/12/80	11(2)	10(2)	0	0	0	0	0	0	0	0
Gavin Brown	18/9/77	19(2)	14	3	3	0	0	1	1	13	13
Tom Buckenham	15/8/84	10(9)	3(7)	1	0	0	0	0	0	4	0
Craig Cook	26/5/83	12(1)	8(1)	2	2	0	0	0	0	8	8
Ged Corcoran	28/3/83	18(5)	10(5)	3	2	0	0	0	0	12	8
John Crawford	12/8/85	2(2)	(2)	2	1	0	0	0	0	8	4
Grant Edwards	22/3/87	4(8)	2(6)	1	1	0	0	0	0	4	4
Grant Farrow	10/4/85	2(1)	(1)	2	1	0	0	0	0	8	4
James Ford	29/9/82	24	19	16	16	0	0	0	0	64	64
Adam Hayes	30/11/81	23(3)	16(2)	3	1	0	0	0	0	12	4
Brad Hepi	11/2/68	2(2)	2(2)	0	0	0	0	0	0	0	0
Ryan Hepworth	16/1/81	2(7)	1(3)	1	0	0	0	0	0	4	0
Zac Hill	5/8/86	3	0	0	0	0	0	0	0	0	0
Dale Holdstock	2/8/79	10(7)	8(5)	2	0	0	0	0	0	8	0
Jack Howieson	28/7/81	23	17	1	1	0	0	0	0	4	4
Greg Hurst	22/6/80	18	10	7	3	0	0	0	0	28	12
Neil Law	23/10/74	5(4)	1(1)	4	0	0	0	0	0	16	0
Brendon Lindsay	21/9/77	20(4)	15(3)	6	4	0	0	1	1	25	17
Danny Mills	10/8/82	14	14	6	6	0	0	0	0	24	24
James Morrow	8/3/83	(3)	(3)	0	0	0	0	0	0	0	0
Simon Morton	4/10/82	1	1	0	0	0	0	0	0	0	0
Richard Newlove	18/7/78	12(8)	6(7)	9	5	0	0	0	0	36	20
Paul Pickering	16/12/82	16(3)	11(1)	2	1	0	0	0	0	8	4
Jon Presley	8/7/84	1(3)	0	2	0	0	0	0	0	8	0
Damien Reid	14/3/84	21	15	7	6	0	0	0	0	28	24
Mitchell Stringer	1/11/83	18(8)	15(4)	2	2	0	0	0	0	8	8
Tommy Trayler	27/4/83	16(7)	11(6)	1	1	0	0	0	0	4	4
Nick Turnbull	22/11/82	(3)	(3)	0	0	0	0	0	0	0	0
Johnny Woodcock	5/2/81	25	17	12	7	75	47	0	0	198	122
Rob Worrincy	9/7/85	8	8	8	8	0	0	0	0	32	32

Johnny Woodcock

LEAGUE RECORD
P18-W6-D1-L11-BP4
(6th, NL1/Elimination Play-Off)
F414, A527, Diff-113
24 points.

CHALLENGE CUP
Round Five

NATIONAL LEAGUE CUP
3rd, Group 1

ATTENDANCES
Best - v Castleford (NLC - 1,897)
Worst - v Halifax (NL1 - 864)
Total (excluding Challenge Cup) - 13,861
Average (excluding Challenge Cup) - 1,155
(Up by 263 on 2006, NL2)

WHITEHAVEN

DATE	FIXTURE	RESULT	SCORERS	LGE	ATT
11/2/07	Workington (a) (NLC)	W18-44	t:Miller,S McAvoy,Calvert,Joe,Duffy,Sice(2) g:Rudd(8)	2nd(NLC-G5)	2,368
18/2/07	Blackpool (a) (NLC)	W18-32	t:R Jackson,Broadbent(3),Calvert,Teare g:Rudd(4)	1st(NLC-G5)	449
25/2/07	Barrow (h) (NLC)	D22-22	t:S McAvoy,Lester,Calvert,Eilbeck g:Rudd(3)	1st(NLC-G5)	1,537
4/3/07	Blackpool (h) (NLC)	W62-0	t:S McAvoy,Maden(2),Calvert(3),A Smith,Rudd(3),Trindall,Sice g:Rudd(7)	1st(NLC-G5)	1,004
11/3/07	Doncaster (h) (CCR3)	W24-10	t:Fletcher(2),Sice,S McAvoy g:Rudd(4)	N/A	1,268
16/3/07	Barrow (a) (NLC)	W6-16	t:M Jackson,Joe,S McAvoy g:Rudd(2)	1st(NLC-G5)	1,669
25/3/07	Workington (h) (NLC)	W58-12	t:Broadbent,Rudd(2),Hill,S McAvoy(2),Fletcher(3),Bainbridge g:Rudd(9)	1st(NLC-G5)	2,636
1/4/07	Halifax (h) (CCR4)	W36-8	t:Fletcher(2),Rudd,S McAvoy,Sice g:Rudd(8)	N/A	2,128
6/4/07	Rochdale (h)	W42-4	t:Eilbeck,Broadbent(2),Maden,Fletcher,Sice(2) g:Rudd(7)	1st	2,071
9/4/07	Leigh (a)	W12-18	t:Maden,Rudd,Fletcher,Hill g:Rudd	3rd	1,825
15/4/07	Dewsbury (h)	W28-12	t:Eilbeck,Calvert(2),Maden,Duffy g:Rudd,Fletcher,M Jackson(2)	3rd	2,008
22/4/07	Bramley (h) (NLCQFQ)	W52-4	t:Calvert(3),Eilbeck(2),Duffy(2),Broadbent,A Smith g:Rudd(5),M Jackson,Ford(2)	N/A	858
29/4/07	Batley (a)	W18-34	t:Broadbent,Calvert(3),Eilbeck,Rudd g:Rudd(5)	3rd	682
6/5/07	Doncaster (a)	L26-16	t:Maden,Calvert,Miller g:Rudd,Fletcher	3rd	831
13/5/07	Catalans (h) (CCR5)	L14-24	t:Calvert,R Jackson,Maden g:Rudd	N/A	3,008
20/5/07	Halifax (h)	W40-24	t:Fletcher(2),Broadbent,Eilbeck(2),R Jackson,Sice g:Rudd(6)	2nd	1,729
27/5/07	Barrow (h) (NLCQF)	W34-14	t:Fletcher(3),Duffy(2),Seeds(2) g:Fletcher(2),Rudd	N/A	1,484
31/5/07	Dewsbury (a)	W22-32	t:Seeds,Maden,Mattinson,Duffy,Fatialofa,Calvert g:Bainbridge(3),Fletcher	2nd	2,010
10/6/07	Leigh (h)	L12-28	t:Calvert,Dale g:Rudd(2)	3rd	2,065
15/6/07	Doncaster (h)	W60-6	t:Trindall,Fletcher(2),Dale,C McAvoy,Sice(2),Duffy,Calvert,Mattinson,Teare g:Rudd(8)	3rd	1,410
24/6/07	Halifax (h) (NLCSF)	W34-19	t:Joe,Sice,Duffy,Rudd,Eilbeck,A Smith g:Rudd(4),Fletcher	N/A	2,246
1/7/07	Castleford (a)	L44-12	t:Duffy,Calvert g:Rudd(2)	3rd	4,902
8/7/07	Sheffield (h)	W44-16	t:Calvert(2),Miller,Broadbent,Mattinson,M Jackson,Sice,Fatialofa g:Rudd(6)	3rd	1,473
15/7/07	Widnes (NLCF) ●	L6-54	t:Rudd g:Rudd	N/A	8,236
22/7/07	Widnes (a)	L16-14	t:M Jackson,Eilbeck g:Rudd(3)	3rd	3,299
29/7/07	Halifax (a)	W20-26	t:Rudd,Calvert,Hill,Seeds g:Rudd(5)	3rd	1,745
5/8/07	Batley (h)	W24-14	t:Seeds(2),Sice,Miller g:Rudd(4)	3rd	1,556
9/8/07	Castleford (h)	L12-20	t:Fletcher,Baldwin g:Rudd(2)	3rd	3,366
19/8/07	Rochdale (a)	W12-28	t:Rudd,Fletcher,Calvert,S McAvoy,Sice g:Rudd(4)	3rd	555
2/9/07	Widnes (h)	L18-22	t:Maden,Rudd,Calvert g:Rudd(3)	3rd	2,360
6/9/07	Sheffield (a)	L26-14	t:Rudd,Broadbent g:Rudd(3)	4th	1,045
13/9/07	Leigh (h) (EPO)	W19-6	t:Calvert,Rudd(2),Seeds g:Rudd fg:Rudd	N/A	1,761
23/9/07	Halifax (a) (ESF)	L32-24	t:Calvert(2),Rudd,Fatialofa g:Rudd(4)	N/A	2,184

● Played at Bloomfield Road, Blackpool

		APP		TRIES		GOALS		FG		PTS	
	D.O.B.	ALL	NL1	ALL	NL1	ALL	NL1	ALL	NL1	ALL	NL1
Marc Bainbridge	22/12/87	3	1	1	0	3	3	0	0	10	6
Simon Baldwin	31/3/75	7(1)	7(1)	1	1	0	0	0	0	4	4
Steve Bannister	10/10/87	4	3	0	0	0	0	0	0	0	0
Craig Benson	19/8/85	4	3	0	0	0	0	0	0	0	0
Gary Broadbent	31/10/76	33	20	11	6	0	0	0	0	44	24
Craig Calvert	10/2/84	33	20	28	18	0	0	0	0	112	72
Matty Dale	10/10/86	2(1)	2(1)	2	2	0	0	0	0	8	8
John Duffy	2/7/80	24	14	10	4	0	0	0	0	40	16
Derry Eilbeck	1/6/84	24	13	10	6	0	0	0	0	40	24
Scott Farmer	13/1/85	(1)	0	0	0	0	0	0	0	0	0
David Fatialofa	11/6/74	18	14	3	3	0	0	0	0	12	12
Richard Fletcher	17/5/81	29	18	18	8	6	3	0	0	84	38
David Ford	29/5/87	1(3)	1(2)	0	0	2	0	0	0	4	0
Howard Hill	16/1/75	2(18)	1(11)	3	2	0	0	0	0	12	8
Marc Jackson	21/8/79	7(14)	4(8)	3	2	3	2	0	0	18	12
Rob Jackson	4/9/81	23	13	3	1	0	0	0	0	12	4
Leroy Joe	31/12/74	16(13)	12(5)	3	0	0	0	0	0	12	0
Andrew Jones	21/10/87	(1)	(1)	0	0	0	0	0	0	0	0
Aaron Lester	16/5/73	13	8	1	0	0	0	0	0	4	0
Steve Maden	13/9/82	24	15	9	6	0	0	0	0	36	24
Graeme Mattinson	24/4/85	12(17)	9(9)	3	3	0	0	0	0	12	12
Craig McAvoy	16/4/83	1	1	1	1	0	0	0	0	4	4
Scott McAvoy	9/4/86	13(2)	5(1)	9	1	0	0	0	0	36	4
Spencer Miller	27/2/80	29	17	4	3	0	0	0	0	16	12
Carl Rudd	10/10/82	32	19	17	9	125	68	1	1	319	173
David Seeds	23/6/74	12(2)	11(2)	7	5	0	0	0	0	28	20
Carl Sice	13/4/80	5(21)	2(15)	14	8	0	0	0	0	56	32
Aaron Smith	10/9/82	23(5)	11(4)	3	0	0	0	0	0	12	0
Daniel Smith	29/11/87	(1)	0	0	0	0	0	0	0	0	0
Scott Teare	22/12/78	5(18)	(10)	2	1	0	0	0	0	8	4
Steve Trindall	23/4/77	28(2)	16(1)	2	1	0	0	0	0	8	4
Ricky Wright	15/3/77	2(13)	(9)	0	0	0	0	0	0	0	0

Craig Calvert

LEAGUE RECORD
P18-W11-D0-L7-BP5
(4th, NL1/Elimination Semi-Final)
F474, A342, Diff+132
38 points.

CHALLENGE CUP
Round Five

NATIONAL LEAGUE CUP
Runners-Up/1st, Group 5

ATTENDANCES
Best - v Castleford (NL1 - 3,366)
Worst - v Bramley (NLCQFQ - 858)
Total (excluding Challenge Cup) - 29,564
Average (excluding Challenge Cup) - 1,848
(Down by 113 on 2006)

WIDNES VIKINGS

DATE	FIXTURE	RESULT	SCORERS	LGE	ATT
9/2/07	Celtic Crusaders (a) (NLC)	W6-56	t:Nanyn,Grix(3),Beswick,Moran(2),Smith,Kohe-Love,Blanch g:Nanyn(8)	1st(NLC-G6)	452
18/2/07	Leigh (h) (NLC)	W34-20	t:Dodd(2),Kohe-Love,Kain,Smith,Bracek g:Nanyn(5)	1st(NLC-G6)	4,133
25/2/07	London Skolars (h) (NLC)	W60-10	t:Kohe-Love(4),Grix(2),Nanyn,Draper,Smith,Kirk,Doran g:Nanyn(6),Dodd(2)	1st(NLC-G6)	2,700
4/3/07	Leigh (a) (NLC)	L24-8	t:Cardiss,Beswick	1st(NLC-G6)	2,291
11/3/07	Normanton (a) (CCR3) ●	W10-78	t:Gaskell(2),Wilkes,Noone,Webster(2),Smith(2),Kirk(2),Moran(4) g:Nanyn(11)	N/A	1,606
18/3/07	London Skolars (a) (NLC)	W0-66	t:Wilkes(2),Moran(3),Webster(3),Kohe-Love(2),Nanyn,Kirk g:Nanyn(7),Noone(2)	1st(NLC-G6)	789
25/3/07	Celtic Crusaders (h) (NLC)	W32-10	t:Bowman,Draper,Grix(3),Cardiss g:Dodd(4)	1st(NLC-G6)	2,540
1/4/07	Wigan (h) (CCR4)	L24-34	t:Kohe-Love,Grix,James,Noone g:Nanyn(4)	N/A	6,006
5/4/07	Leigh (h)	W46-12	t:Grix(2),Blanch,Kohe-Love,Moran(3),Dodd g:Nanyn(7)	2nd	3,792
9/4/07	Rochdale (a)	W18-40	t:Blanch,Moran,Nanyn(3),Webster,Dodd g:Nanyn(6)	2nd	1,485
13/4/07	Sheffield (a)	W4-46	t:Beswick,Nanyn(2),Dodd,Moran,Smith,James,Blanch g:Nanyn(7)	2nd	1,211
22/4/07	Batley (h) (NLCQFQ)	W62-6	t:Kain(2),Cassidy,Gaskell(2),Moran,Smith,Beswick,Wilkes,Noone,Kirk g:Dodd(9)	N/A	2,140
26/4/07	Halifax (h)	W48-12	t:Nanyn(3),Grix,Smith,Moran,Kohe-Love,Blanch,James g:Nanyn(6)	2nd	3,042
6/5/07	Batley (h)	W66-14	t:Moran(3),Noone,Dodd,Grix(2),Nanyn,Kirk,Wilkes,Smith g:Nanyn(11)	2nd	2,753
17/5/07	Castleford (a)	W20-44	t:Dodd,Smith(2),James,Webster,Blanch(2),Beswick g:Nanyn(6)	1st	6,007
27/5/07	Rochdale (a) (NLCQF) ●	W0-24	t:Blanch(2),Kirk,Webster g:Nanyn(4)	N/A	2,362
3/6/07	Sheffield (h)	W56-10	t:Wilkes(3),James,Nanyn(3),Moran,Dodd,Penny g:Nanyn(8)	1st	2,837
10/6/07	Doncaster (a)	W4-90	t:Dodd(3),Blanch(3),Wilkes(2),Penny(3),Kirk,Summers(2),Gaskell,Grix g:Dodd(13)	1st	1,248
14/6/07	Halifax (a)	L12-6	t:Webster g:Nanyn	1st	2,412
24/6/07	Castleford (h) (NLCSF)	W18-12	t:Wilkes,Nanyn g:Nanyn(5)	N/A	5,388
1/7/07	Rochdale (h)	W32-0	t:Dodd,Gaskell,Wilkes,Grix,Penny,Webster g:Nanyn(4)	1st	4,879
5/7/07	Dewsbury (a)	W10-50	t:Gaskell(3),Penny,James,Grix,Nanyn,Kohe-Love,Summers g:Nanyn(5)	1st	1,885
15/7/07	Whitehaven (NLCF) ●●	W6-54	t:Kohe-Love,Grix,Blanch(2),Nanyn,Doran,Smith,Moran,Gaskell g:Nanyn(9)	N/A	8,236
22/7/07	Whitehaven (h)	W16-14	t:Moran,Blanch,Nanyn g:Nanyn(2)	1st	3,299
29/7/07	Doncaster (h)	W40-18	t:Doran(2),Nanyn,Blanch,Kohe-Love(2),Wilkes,Dodd g:Nanyn(4)	1st	2,607
2/8/07	Leigh (a)	W0-38	t:Tomkins,Nanyn(3),Beswick,Gaskell,Grix g:Nanyn(5)	1st	3,095
12/8/07	Dewsbury (h)	W48-12	t:Blanch(2),Nanyn,Penny(2),Noone,Dodd,Kohe-Love g:Nanyn(8)	1st	2,853
16/8/07	Castleford (h)	L18-24	t:Nanyn,Kohe-Love,Dodd g:Nanyn(3)	2nd	4,598
2/9/07	Whitehaven (a)	W18-22	t:Grix,Blanch,Dodd(2) g:Nanyn(3)	2nd	2,360
9/9/07	Batley (h)	W18-34	t:Nanyn,Tomkins,Penny(2),Doran,Wilkes g:Nanyn(5)	2nd	1,139
20/9/07	Castleford (a) (QSF)	L26-8	t:Nanyn g:Nanyn(2)	N/A	6,179
27/9/07	Halifax (h) (FE)	W36-24	t:Noone,Smith(2),Grix,Beswick g:Nanyn(8)	N/A	3,347
7/10/07	Castleford (GF) ●●●	L42-10	t:Nanyn,Wilkes g:Nanyn	N/A	20,814

● Played at Halton Stadium
●● Played at Bloomfield Road, Blackpool
●●● Played at Headingley Carnegie, Leeds

		APP		TRIES		GOALS		FG		PTS	
	D.O.B.	ALL	NL1	ALL	NL1	ALL	NL1	ALL	NL1	ALL	NL1
Bob Beswick	8/12/84	32	20	7	4	0	0	0	0	28	16
Damien Blanch	24/5/83	26(1)	18	19	14	0	0	0	0	76	56
Adam Bowman	12/11/87	(2)	0	1	0	0	0	0	0	4	0
Andy Bracek	21/3/84	3		1		0		0		4	
Daryl Cardiss	13/7/77	2(4)	(1)	2	0	0	0	0	0	8	0
Mick Cassidy	8/7/73	17(11)	11(9)	1	0	0	0	0	0	4	0
Gavin Dodd	28/2/81	27(3)	18(2)	17	15	28	13	0	0	124	86
Lee Doran	23/3/81	23(9)	14(6)	5	3	0	0	0	0	20	12
Rob Draper	30/11/87	1(2)	0	2	0	0	0	0	0	8	0
Dean Gaskell	12/4/83	16(4)	10(2)	11	6	0	0	0	0	44	24
Scott Grix	1/5/84	32	20	21	11	0	0	0	0	84	44
Ben Harrison	24/2/88	1(2)	0	0	0	0	0	0	0	0	0
Jordan James	24/5/80	13(20)	7(14)	6	5	0	0	0	0	24	20
Andy Kain	1/9/85	9	2	3	0	0	0	0	0	12	0
Andy Kirk	2/8/82	12(5)	5(5)	8	2	0	0	0	0	32	8
Toa Kohe-Love	2/12/76	25	16	17	7	0	0	0	0	68	28
Danny Lima	27/7/75	(5)	(3)	0	0	0	0	0	0	0	0
Dennis Moran	22/1/77	28	19	23	12	0	0	0	0	92	48
Mike Morrison	9/9/87	(3)	0	0	0	0	0	0	0	0	0
Richard Myler	21/5/90	(2)	(2)	0	0	0	0	0	0	0	0
Mick Nanyn	3/6/82	29	20	28	23	161	102	0	0	434	296
Paul Noone	22/4/81	29(1)	18	6	3	0	0	0	0	28	12
Joel Penny	22/1/80	14(1)	12(1)	10	10	0	0	0	0	40	40
Gareth Price	28/6/80	2(16)	1(12)	0	0	0	0	0	0	0	0
Adam Sidlow	25/10/87	(4)	(1)	0	0	0	0	0	0	0	0
Mark Smith	18/8/81	31	20	14	7	0	0	0	0	56	28
Aaron Summers	11/8/81	7(17)	6(13)	3	3	0	0	0	0	12	12
Joel Tomkins	21/3/87	8	8	2	2	0	0	0	0	8	8
Ian Webster	16/11/86	12(15)	8(11)	10	4	0	0	0	0	40	16
Oliver Wilkes	2/5/80	30(3)	20(1)	15	10	0	0	0	0	60	40

Dennis Moran

LEAGUE RECORD
P18-W16-D0-L2-BP2
(2nd, NL1/Grand Final Runners-Up)
F740, A220, Diff+520
50 points.

CHALLENGE CUP
Round Four

NATIONAL LEAGUE CUP
Winners/1st, Group 6

ATTENDANCES
Best - v Wigan (CC - 6,006)
Worst - v Normanton (CC - 1,606)
Total (excluding Challenge Cup) - 53,270
Average (excluding Challenge Cup) - 3,329
(Down by 316 on 2006)

NATIONAL LEAGUE ONE 2007
Round by Round

WEEK 1

Thursday 5th April 2007

WIDNES VIKINGS 46 LEIGH CENTURIONS 12

VIKINGS: 1 Scott Grix; 2 Damien Blanch; 3 Toa Kohe-Love; 4 Mick Nanyn; 5 Gavin Dodd; 6 Dennis Moran; 7 Andy Kain; 8 Jordan James; 9 Mark Smith; 10 Oliver Wilkes; 11 Lee Doran; 12 Paul Noone; 13 Bob Beswick. Subs (all used): 14 Aaron Summers; 15 Mick Cassidy; 16 Daryl Cardiss; 17 Gareth Price.
Tries: Grix (2, 65), Blanch (16), Kohe-Love (29), Moran (39, 61, 74), Dodd (45); **Goals:** Nanyn 7/9.
CENTURIONS: 1 Miles Greenwood; 2 Rob Smyth; 3 David Alstead; 4 Adam Hughes; 5 Leroy Rivett; 6 Martin Ainscough; 7 Aaron Heremaia; 8 Warren Stevens; 9 John Clough; 10 Dana Wilson; 11 Chris Hill; 12 Tommy Grundy; 13 Robert Roberts. Subs (all used): 14 Sam Butterworth; 15 Tim Jonkers; 16 Sean Richardson; 17 John Cookson.
Tries: Heremaia (72, 78); **Goals:** Hughes 2/2.
Sin bin: Greenwood (38) – holding down; Butterworth (67) - interference.
Rugby Leaguer & League Express Men of the Match: *Vikings:* Dennis Moran; *Centurions:* Aaron Heremaia.
Penalty count: 10-3; **Half-time:** 24-0;
Referee: Gareth Hewer; **Attendance:** 3,792.

Friday 6th April 2007

WHITEHAVEN 42 ROCHDALE HORNETS 4

WHITEHAVEN: 1 Gary Broadbent; 2 Craig Calvert; 3 Scott McAvoy; 4 Derry Eilbeck; 5 Steve Maden; 6 Carl Rudd; 7 John Duffy; 8 Steve Trindall; 9 Aaron Smith; 10 David Ford; 11 Spencer Miller; 12 Richard Fletcher; 13 Aaron Lester. Subs (all used): 14 Carl Sice; 15 Graeme Mattinson; 16 Howard Hill; 17 Scott Teare.
Tries: Eilbeck (15), Broadbent (18, 63), Maden (40), Fletcher (44), Sice (63, 78); **Goals:** Rudd 7/7.
HORNETS: 1 Chris Giles; 2 Eric Andrews; 3 Lee Patterson; 4 Kevin King; 5 Bolu Fagborun; 6 Simon Svabic; 7 Phil Hasty; 8 Simon Baldwin; 9 Dave McConnell; 10 Byron Smith; 11 Paul Anderson; 12 Mark Blanchard; 13 Tommy Goulden. Subs (all used): 14 Wayne Corcoran; 15 Paul Norman; 16 Andy Bailey; 17 Rob Ball.
Try: Fagborun (33); **Goals:** King 0/1.
Sin bin: Patterson (43) - holding down.
Rugby Leaguer & League Express Men of the Match: *Whitehaven:* Gary Broadbent; *Hornets:* Bolu Fagborun.
Penalty count: 6-7; **Half-time:** 18-4;
Referee: Craig Halloran; **Attendance:** 2,071.

SHEFFIELD EAGLES 20 DONCASTER LAKERS 24

EAGLES: 1 Johnny Woodcock; 2 James Ford; 3 Damien Reid; 4 Richard Newlove; 5 Greg Hurst; 6 Brendon Lindsay; 7 Gavin Brown; 8 Jack Howieson; 9 Paul Pickering; 10 Tom Buckenham; 11 Dale Holdstock; 12 Ged Corcoran; 13 Adam Hayes. Subs (all used): 14 Neil Law; 15 Craig Brown; 16 Tommy Trayler; 17 Mitchell Stringer.
Tries: Pickering (20), Lindsay (32), Hurst (52, 76); **Goals:** Woodcock 2/4.
Sin bin: Stringer (69) – late challenge.
LAKERS: 1 Loz Wildbore; 2 Rikki Sheriffe; 3 Dean Gorton; 4 Chris Buttery; 5 Danny Mills; 6 Joe McLocklan; 7 Joel Penny; 8 James Garmston; 9 Peter Green; 10 Ryan Tandy; 11 Joe Mbu; 12 Adam Robinson; 13 Craig Lawton. Subs (all used): 14 Mark Castle; 15 Neil Lowe; 16 Dean Andrews; 17 Alex Rowe.
Tries: Garmston (7), Andrews (35, 60), Mbu (70); **Goals:** Wildbore 4/6.
Sin bin: Sheriffe (52) – dissent.
Rugby Leaguer & League Express Men of the Match: *Eagles:* Tommy Trayler; *Lakers:* Ryan Tandy.
Penalty count: 8-12; **Half-time:** 8-12;
Referee: Jamie Leahy; **Attendance:** 1,142.

DEWSBURY RAMS 16 BATLEY BULLDOGS 24

RAMS: 1 Ian Preece; 2 Bryn Powell; 3 Alex Bretherton; 4 Danny Maun; 5 Kane Epati; 6 Francis Maloney; 7 Dean Lawford; 8 Andy Hobson; 9 Richard Chapman; 10 Dominic Maloney; 11 Kevin Crouthers; 12 Andy Spink; 13 Josh Weeden. Subs (all used): 14 Liam Finn; 15 Rob Kelly; 16 Martin Robinson; 17 Liam Crawley.
Tries: Epati (9, 17), Maun (55); **Goals:** F Maloney 2/3.
BULLDOGS: 1 Ashley Lindsay; 2 Alex Clemie; 3 Jason Mossop; 4 Chris Langley; 5 Oliver Marns; 6 Ian Gordon; 7 Jay Duffy; 8 David Best; 9 Kris Lythe; 10 Luke Stenchion; 11 Phil Farrell; 12 Tim Spears; 13 John Gallagher. Subs (all used): 14 Lee Paterson; 15 Jon Simpson; 16 Martin McLoughlin; 17 Anthony Henderson.
Tries: Lythe (24, 32, 77), McLoughlin (42); **Goals:** Gordon 4/4.
Rugby Leaguer & League Express Men of the Match: *Rams:* Ian Preece; *Bulldogs:* Kris Lythe.
Penalty count: 6-5; **Half-time:** 12-12;
Referee: Ronnie Laughton; **Attendance:** 1,566.

CASTLEFORD TIGERS 46 HALIFAX 22

TIGERS: 1 Tom Saxton; 2 Stuart Donlan; 3 Ryan Clayton; 4 Kirk Dixon; 5 Michael Wainwright; 6 Ryan McGoldrick; 7 Danny Brough; 8 Liam Higgins; 9 Andrew Henderson; 10 Mark Leafa; 11 Awen Guttenbeil; 12 Dwayne Barker; 13 Chris Charles. Subs (all used): 14 Tere Glassie; 15 Craig Huby; 16 Michael Knowles; 17 Richard Owen.
Tries: Saxton (5), Clayton (18), Donlan (28), Wainwright (31), McGoldrick (33), Henderson (43), Huby (47, 57); **Goals:** Brough 7/8.
Sin bin: McGoldrick (72) – dissent.
HALIFAX: 1 Damian Gibson; 2 Marcus George; 3 Tim Hartley; 4 Richard Varkulis; 5 Lee Greenwood; 6 Paul White; 7 Ian Watson; 8 Paul Southern; 9 Sean Penkywicz; 10 David Wrench; 11 David Larder; 12 Mark Roberts; 13 Damian Ball. Subs (all used): 14 Danny Jones; 15 Aaron Trinder; 16 Phil Joseph; 17 Frank Watene.
Tries: Greenwood (14), Jones (66, 76), Penkywicz (72); **Goals:** Hartley 3/4.
Sin bin: Gibson (42) – professional foul.
On report: Watene (35) – alleged high tackle.
Rugby Leaguer & League Express Men of the Match: *Tigers:* Andrew Henderson; *Halifax:* Sean Penkywicz.
Penalty count: 12-11; **Half-time:** 28-6;
Referee: Robert Hicks; **Attendance:** 6,284.

WEEK 2

Monday 9th April 2007

BATLEY BULLDOGS 22 SHEFFIELD EAGLES 22

BULLDOGS: 1 Ashley Lindsay; 2 Alex Clemie; 3 Jason Mossop; 4 Chris Langley; 5 Oliver Marns; 6 Ian Gordon; 7 Jay Duffy; 8 David Rourke; 9 Kris Lythe; 10 Luke Stenchion; 11 Phil Farrell; 12 Tim Spears; 13 John Gallagher. Subs (all used): 14 Lee Paterson; 15 Jon Simpson; 16 Martin McLoughlin; 17 Anthony Henderson.
Tries: Lindsay (7), Clemie (17), Simpson (25), Paterson (77); **Goals:** Gordon 3/5.
EAGLES: 1 Johnny Woodcock; 2 James Ford; 3 Neil Law; 4 Richard Newlove; 5 Greg Hurst; 6 Brendon Lindsay; 7 Dominic Brambani; 8 Jack Howieson; 9 Craig Cook; 10 Tom Buckenham; 11 Craig Brown; 12 Ged Corcoran; 13 Adam Hayes. Subs (all used): 14 Paul Pickering; 15 Jon Aston; 16 Tommy Trayler; 17 Mitchell Stringer.
Tries: Cook (22), Newlove (40); **Goals:** Woodcock 7/7.
Sin bin: Brambani (50) - late challenge.
Rugby Leaguer & League Express Men of the Match: *Bulldogs:* Oliver Marns; *Eagles:* Dominic Brambani.
Penalty count: 6-9; **Half-time:** 18-14;
Referee: Gareth Hewer; **Attendance:** 667.

HALIFAX 24 DEWSBURY RAMS 27

HALIFAX: 1 Damian Gibson; 2 Marcus George; 3 Tim Hartley; 4 Richard Varkulis; 5 Lee Greenwood; 6 Paul White; 7 Ian Watson; 8 Paul Southern; 9 Sean Penkywicz; 10 David Wrench; 11 David Larder; 12 Damian Ball; 13 Phil Joseph. Subs (all used): 14 Mark Roberts; 15 Andy Shickell; 16 Danny Jones; 17 Frank Watene.
Tries: Hartley (4), Ball (38), White (44), George (68), Larder (79); **Goals:** Hartley 2/5.
RAMS: 1 Ian Preece; 2 Bryn Powell; 3 Chris Hall; 4 Danny Maun; 5 Kane Epati; 6 Francis Maloney; 7 Dean Lawford; 8 Andy Hobson; 9 Luke Haigh; 10 Dominic Maloney; 11 Kevin Crouthers; 12 Alex Bretherton; 13 Josh Weeden. Subs (all used): 14 Liam Finn; 15 Andy Spink; 16 Martin Robinson; 17 David Bates.
Tries: Crouthers (6), Hall (10), Bretherton (21), Finn (32), F Maloney (76); **Goals:** F Maloney 3/6;
Field goal: Lawford (72).
On report: Maun (3) - alleged dangerous tackle.
Rugby Leaguer & League Express Men of the Match: *Halifax:* Sean Penkywicz; *Rams:* Chris Hall.
Penalty count: 5-8; **Half-time:** 12-18;
Referee: Robert Hicks; **Attendance:** 1,889.

LEIGH CENTURIONS 12 WHITEHAVEN 18

CENTURIONS: 1 Miles Greenwood; 2 Rob Smyth; 3 David Alstead; 4 Damien Couturier; 5 Leroy Rivett; 6 Martin Ainscough; 7 Aaron Heremaia; 8 Warren Stevens; 9 Sam Butterworth; 10 Chris Hill; 11 Tim Jonkers; 12 Tommy Grundy; 13 Robert Roberts. Subs (all used): 14 John Clough; 15 Daryl Kay; 16 Sean Richardson; 17 Dana Wilson.
Tries: C Hill (8), Alstead (25); **Goals:** Couturier 2/2.
On report: Roberts (15) - alleged high tackle on Teare.
WHITEHAVEN: 1 Gary Broadbent; 2 Craig Calvert; 3 Steve Maden; 4 Derry Eilbeck; 5 Craig Benson; 6 Carl Rudd; 7 John Duffy; 8 Steve Trindall; 9 Aaron Smith; 10 Marc Jackson; 11 Spencer Miller; 12 Richard Fletcher; 13 Aaron Lester. Subs (all used): 14 Carl Sice; 15 Graeme Mattinson; 16 Howard Hill; 17 Scott Teare.
Tries: Maden (16), Rudd (27), Fletcher (53), Hill (75); **Goals:** Rudd 1/4.
Rugby Leaguer & League Express Men of the Match: *Centurions:* Martin Ainscough; *Whitehaven:* Gary Broadbent.
Penalty count: 2-4; **Half-time:** 12-10;
Referee: Ronnie Laughton; **Attendance:** 1,825.

ROCHDALE HORNETS 18 WIDNES VIKINGS 40

HORNETS: 1 Eric Andrews; 2 Nick Johnson; 3 Lee Patterson; 4 Kevin King; 5 Bolu Fagborun; 6 Simon Svabic; 7 Phil Hasty; 8 Simon Baldwin; 9 Dave McConnell; 10 Byron Smith; 11 Paul Anderson; 12 Mark Blanchard; 13 Tommy Goulden. Subs (all used): 14 Wayne Corcoran; 15 Paul Norman; 16 Andy Gorski; 17 Rob Ball.
Tries: King (13), McConnell (18), Fagborun (39); **Goals:** King 3/3.
VIKINGS: 1 Scott Grix; 2 Damien Blanch; 3 Toa Kohe-Love; 4 Mick Nanyn; 5 Gavin Dodd; 6 Dennis Moran; 7 Andy Kain; 8 Jordan James; 9 Mark Smith; 10 Oliver Wilkes; 11 Lee Doran; 12 Paul Noone; 13 Bob Beswick. Subs: 14 Aaron Summers; 15 Ian Webster; 16 Andy Kirk (not used); 17 Gareth Price.
Tries: Blanch (6), Moran (25), Nanyn (36, 76, 80), Webster (48), Dodd (52); **Goals:** Nanyn 6/9.
Rugby Leaguer & League Express Men of the Match: *Hornets:* Byron Smith; *Vikings:* Dennis Moran.
Penalty count: 7-13; **Half-time:** 18-14;
Referee: Craig Halloran; **Attendance:** 1,485.

Thursday 12th April 2007

DONCASTER LAKERS 4 CASTLEFORD TIGERS 66

LAKERS: 1 Loz Wildbore; 2 Danny Mills; 3 Dean Gorton; 4 Dean Andrews; 5 Rikki Sheriffe; 6 Joe McLocklan; 7 Joel Penny; 8 Joe Mbu; 9 Peter Green; 10 Ryan Tandy; 11 Adam Robinson; 12 Neil Lowe; 13 Craig Lawton. Subs (all used): 14 Ade Adebisi; 15 Alex Rowe; 16 Mark Castle; 17 James Garmston.
Try: Lowe (74); **Goals:** Wildbore 0/1.
TIGERS: 1 Tom Saxton; 2 Stuart Donlan; 3 Dwayne Barker; 4 Kirk Dixon; 5 Michael Wainwright; 6 Ryan McGoldrick; 7 Danny Brough; 8 Mark Leafa; 9 Andrew Henderson; 10 Craig Huby; 11 Awen Guttenbeil; 12 Ryan Clayton; 13 Chris Charles. Subs (all used): 14 Liam Higgins; 15 Tere Glassie; 16 Joe Westerman; 17 Richard Owen.
Tries: Charles (2), Henderson (6), McGoldrick (21), Barker (23), Dixon (36, 48, 56), Wainwright (38), Brough (51, 61), Huby (59), Donlan (65, 79); **Goals:** Brough 7/13.
Rugby Leaguer & League Express Men of the Match: *Lakers:* Ryan Tandy; *Tigers:* Danny Brough.
Penalty count: 6-9; **Half-time:** 0-30;
Referee: Jamie Leahy; **Attendance:** 6,528.

WEEK 3

Friday 13th April 2007

SHEFFIELD EAGLES 4 WIDNES VIKINGS 46

EAGLES: 1 Johnny Woodcock; 2 James Ford; 3 Caldon Bravo; 4 Richard Newlove; 5 Greg Hurst; 6 Brendon Lindsay; 7 Dominic Brambani; 8 Jack Howieson; 9 Craig Cook; 10 Simon Morton; 11 Craig Brown; 12 Dale Holdstock; 13 Grant Edwards. Subs (all used): 14 Grant Farrow; 15 Ged Corcoran; 16 Tommy Trayler; 17 Mitchell Stringer.
Try: Farrow (77); **Goals:** Woodcock 0/1.
VIKINGS: 1 Scott Grix; 2 Damien Blanch; 3 Toa Kohe-Love; 4 Mick Nanyn; 5 Gavin Dodd; 6 Dennis Moran; 7 Ian Webster; 8 Jordan James; 9 Mark Smith; 10 Oliver Wilkes; 11 Lee Doran; 12 Paul Noone; 13 Bob Beswick. Subs (all used): 14 Aaron Summers; 15 Mick Cassidy; 16 Andy Kirk; 17 Gareth Price.
Tries: Beswick (1), Nanyn (20, 70), Dodd (26), Moran (29), Smith (34), James (58), Blanch (63); **Goals:** Nanyn 7/8.
Rugby Leaguer & League Express Men of the Match: *Eagles:* Grant Edwards; *Vikings:* Bob Beswick.
Penalty count: 6-6; **Half-time:** 0-30;
Referee: Robert Hicks; **Attendance:** 1,211.

Sunday 15th April 2007

DONCASTER LAKERS 18 LEIGH CENTURIONS 52

LAKERS: 1 Rikki Sheriffe; 2 James Endersby; 3 Dean Gorton; 4 Dean Andrews; 5 Danny Mills; 6 Loz Wildbore; 7 Joel Penny; 8 James Garmston; 9 Joe McLocklan; 10 Ryan Tandy; 11 Joe Mbu; 12 Peter Green; 13 Craig Lawton. Subs (all used): 14 Adam Robinson; 15 Ade Adebisi; 16 Mark Castle; 17 Craig Potter.
Tries: Wildbore (30), Penny (61, 74); **Goals:** Wildbore 3/4.
Sin bin: Andrews (23) - professional foul.
CENTURIONS: 1 Miles Greenwood; 2 Leroy Rivett; 3 Damien Couturier; 4 Danny Halliwell; 5 David Alstead; 6 Robert Roberts; 7 Aaron Heremaia; 8 Warren Stevens; 9 Sam Butterworth; 10 Dana Wilson; 11 Adam Hughes; 12 Tommy Grundy; 13 Anthony Stewart. Subs (all used): 14 Martin Ainscough; 15 Mailangi Styles; 16 Chris Hill; 17 Sean Richardson.
Tries: Couturier (11), Heremaia (14), Butterworth (36, 68), Halliwell (39, 49, 71), Ainscough (42), Hughes (77); **Goals:** Couturier 8/9.
Rugby Leaguer & League Express Men of the Match: *Lakers:* Loz Wildbore; *Centurions:* Sam Butterworth.
Penalty count: 6-5; **Half-time:** 6-24;
Referee: Gareth Hewer; **Attendance:** 1,339.

ROCHDALE HORNETS 20 HALIFAX 38

HORNETS: 1 Eric Andrews; 2 Nick Johnson; 3 Lee Patterson; 4 Kevin King; 5 Bolu Fagborun; 6 Simon Svabic; 7 Phil Hasty; 8 Simon Baldwin; 9 Dave McConnell; 10 Byron Smith; 11 Paul Anderson; 12 Mark Blanchard; 13 Tommy Goulden. Subs (all used): 14 Gary Hulse; 15 Paul Norman; 16 Andy Gorski; 17 Ryan Benjafield.
Tries: McConnell (8), Goulden (11, 23); **Goals:** King 4/4.
HALIFAX: 1 Damian Gibson; 2 Marcus George; 3 Richard Varkulis; 4 Tim Hartley; 5 Lee Greenwood; 6 Paul White; 7 Ian Watson; 8 Paul Southern; 9 Sean Penkywicz; 10 Andy Shickell; 11 David Larder; 12 Danny Heaton; 13 Mark Roberts. Subs (all used): 14 Phil Joseph; 15 Aaron Trinder; 16 Danny Jones; 17 Frank Watene.
Tries: Penkywicz (4), Varkulis (5, 65), Heaton (19, 54), Trinder (45, 50); **Goals:** Hartley 5/7.
Rugby Leaguer & League Express Men of the Match: *Hornets:* Tommy Goulden; *Halifax:* Richard Varkulis.
Penalty count: 7-6; **Half-time:** 20-18;
Referee: Mike Dawber; **Attendance:** 820.

WHITEHAVEN 28 DEWSBURY RAMS 12

WHITEHAVEN: 1 Gary Broadbent; 2 Craig Calvert; 3

Leigh's Paul Rowley, in his last game before retirement, takes on Sheffield's Johnny Woodcock

Steve Maden; 4 Derry Eilbeck; 5 Craig Benson; 6 Carl Rudd; 7 John Duffy; 8 Steve Trindall; 9 Aaron Smith; 10 Marc Jackson; 11 Spencer Miller; 12 Richard Fletcher; 13 Aaron Lester. Subs (all used): 14 Graeme Mattinson; 15 David Ford; 16 Howard Hill; 17 Scott Teare.
Tries: Eilbeck (5), Calvert (31, 63), Maden (55), Duffy (71); **Goals:** Rudd 1/2, Fletcher 1/1, M Jackson 2/3.
RAMS: 1 Ian Preece; 2 Bryn Powell; 3 Danny Maun; 4 Chris Hall; 5 Kane Epati; 6 Josh Weeden; 7 Dean Lawford; 8 Andy Hobson; 9 Luke Haigh; 10 Dominic Maloney; 11 Kevin Crouthers; 12 Martin Robinson; 13 Alex Bretherton. Subs (all used): 14 Liam Finn; 15 Rob Kelly; 16 Liam Crawley; 17 David Bates.
Tries: Preece (21), Weeden (78); **Goals:** Lawford 2/2.
Dismissal: Hobson (17) - late tackle on Rudd.
Rugby Leaguer & League Express Men of the Match:
Whitehaven: Craig Calvert; *Rams:* Ian Preece.
Penalty count: 6-8; **Half-time:** 12-6;
Referee: Peter Taberner; **Attendance:** 2,008.

CASTLEFORD TIGERS 75 BATLEY BULLDOGS 12

TIGERS: 1 Tom Saxton; 2 Stuart Donlan; 3 Ryan Clayton; 4 Kirk Dixon; 5 Michael Wainwright; 6 Ryan McGoldrick; 7 Danny Brough; 8 Liam Higgins; 9 Sean Johnson; 10 Tere Glassie; 11 Awen Guttenbeil; 12 Dwayne Barker; 13 Chris Charles. Subs (all used): 14 Joe Westerman; 15 Richard Owen; 16 Craig Huby; 17 Mark Leafa.
Tries: Brough (9), Glassie (12), Saxton (17, 59), Donlan (20, 33, 55), Leafa (25), McGoldrick (29), Owen (37, 67), Dixon (48), Huby (52);
Goals: Brough 11/13; **Field goal:** McGoldrick (31).
BULLDOGS: 1 Craig Lingard; 2 Alex Clemie; 3 Jason Mossop; 4 Chris Langley; 5 Oliver Marns; 6 Lee Paterson; 7 Ian Gordon; 8 David Rourke; 9 Kris Lythe; 10 Luke Stenchion; 11 Leigh Cooke; 12 Tim Spears; 13 Martin McLoughlin. Subs (all used): 14 Ashley Lindsay; 15 Anthony Henderson; 16 Luke Menzies; 17 Jon Simpson.
Tries: Lingard (74), Clemie (77); **Goals:** Gordon 2/2.
Rugby Leaguer & League Express Men of the Match:
Tigers: Craig Huby; *Bulldogs:* Ian Gordon.
Penalty count: 9-4; **Half-time:** 45-0;
Referee: Ronnie Laughton; **Attendance:** 5,223.

WEEK 4

Thursday 26th April 2007

WIDNES VIKINGS 48 HALIFAX 12

VIKINGS: 1 Scott Grix; 2 Damien Blanch; 3 Toa Kohe-Love; 4 Mick Nanyn; 5 Gavin Dodd; 6 Dennis Moran; 7 Ian Webster; 8 Jordan James; 9 Mark Smith; 10 Oliver Wilkes; 11 Lee Doran; 12 Paul Noone; 13 Bob Beswick. Subs (all used): 14 Aaron Summers; 15 Mick Cassidy;

16 Andy Kirk; 17 Gareth Price.
Tries: Nanyn (2, 48, 75), Grix (37), Smith (44), Moran (60), Kohe-Love (64), Blanch (70), James (78);
Goals: Nanyn 6/10.
On report: Moran (11) – alleged dangerous tackle; Brawl (70).
HALIFAX: 1 Paul White; 2 Damian Gibson; 3 Mark Roberts; 4 Richard Varkulis; 5 Lee Greenwood; 6 Tim Hartley; 7 Ian Watson; 8 Paul Southern; 9 Sean Penkywicz; 10 Frank Watene; 11 David Larder; 12 Paul Smith; 13 Phil Joseph. Subs (all used): 14 Danny Jones; 15 Damian Ball; 16 Aaron Trinder; 17 David Wrench.
Tries: Gibson (14, 28); **Goals:** Hartley 2/2.
Sin bin: Roberts (44) - holding down;
Watson (78) - high tackle.
On report: Brawl (70).
Rugby Leaguer & League Express Men of the Match:
Vikings: Dennis Moran; *Halifax:* Ian Watson.
Penalty count: 11-11; **Half-time:** 12-12;
Referee: Robert Hicks; **Attendance:** 3,042.

Sunday 29th April 2007

BATLEY BULLDOGS 18 WHITEHAVEN 34

BULLDOGS: 1 Craig Lingard; 2 Jason Mossop; 3 Ian Gordon; 4 Chris Langley; 5 Oliver Marns; 6 John Gallagher; 7 Jay Duffy; 8 Martin McLoughlin; 9 Kris Lythe; 10 Luke Stenchion; 11 Phil Farrell; 12 Tim Spears; 13 Mark Toohey. Subs (all used): 14 Ashley Lindsay; 15 Lee Paterson; 16 Luke Menzies; 17 Jon Simpson.
Tries: McLoughlin (2), J Gallagher (20), Menzies (32), Lingard (35); **Goals:** Gordon 1/5.
WHITEHAVEN: 1 Gary Broadbent; 2 Craig Calvert; 3 Derry Eilbeck; 4 Rob Jackson; 5 Steve Maden; 6 Carl Rudd; 7 Leroy Joe; 8 Marc Jackson; 9 Aaron Smith; 10 Steve Trindall; 11 Spencer Miller; 12 Richard Fletcher; 13 Aaron Lester. Subs (all used): 14 Carl Sice; 15 Graeme Mattinson; 16 Ricky Wright; 17 Scott Teare.
Tries: Broadbent (5), Calvert (9, 46, 79), Eilbeck (18), Rudd (50); **Goals:** Rudd 5/7.
Rugby Leaguer & League Express Men of the Match:
Bulldogs: Ashley Lindsay; *Whitehaven:* Carl Rudd.
Penalty count: 10-10; **Half-time:** 18-18;
Referee: Ronnie Laughton; **Attendance:** 682.

DEWSBURY RAMS 26 DONCASTER LAKERS 33

RAMS: 1 Ian Preece; 2 Bryn Powell; 3 Francis Maloney; 4 Chris Hall; 5 Danny Maun; 6 Pat Walker; 7 Dean Lawford; 8 Keegan Hirst; 9 Liam Finn; 10 Dominic Maloney; 11 Kevin Crouthers; 12 Alex Bretherton; 13 Josh Weeden. Subs (all used): 14 Ryan Glynn; 15 Rob Kelly; 16 Martin Robinson; 17 Liam Crawley.
Tries: Weeden (8), Powell (22), F Maloney (26), Maun (34), Crawley (38); **Goals:** F Maloney 1/3, Finn 2/3.

LAKERS: 1 Loz Wildbore; 2 Ade Adebisi; 3 Rikki Sheriffe; 4 Dean Gorton; 5 Danny Mills; 6 Graham Holroyd; 7 Joel Penny; 8 Craig Potter; 9 Chris Buttery; 10 Ryan Tandy; 11 Adam Robinson; 12 Craig Lawton; 13 Peter Green. Subs (all used): 14 Dean Andrews; 15 Neil Lowe; 16 Mark Castle; 17 Alex Rowe.
Tries: Sheriffe (3, 59, 78), Penny (18, 70), Tandy (53);
Goals: Holroyd 4/7; **Field goal:** Penny (79).
Rugby Leaguer & League Express Men of the Match:
Rams: Dominic Maloney; *Lakers:* Joel Penny.
Penalty count: 8-9; **Half-time:** 26-10;
Referee: Thierry Alibert; **Attendance:** 1,021.

LEIGH CENTURIONS 38 SHEFFIELD EAGLES 22

CENTURIONS: 1 Miles Greenwood; 2 Leroy Rivett; 3 Damien Couturier; 4 Danny Halliwell; 5 David Alstead; 6 Martin Ainscough; 7 Aaron Heremaia; 8 Warren Stevens; 9 Paul Rowley; 10 Dana Wilson; 11 James Taylor; 12 Tommy Grundy; 13 Robert Roberts. Subs (all used): 14 Sam Butterworth; 15 Adam Hughes; 16 Mailangi Styles; 17 Chris Hill.
Tries: Couturier (4), C Hill (37), Hughes (40), Ainscough (47), Heremaia (54, 80), Halliwell (70);
Goals: Couturier 5/7.
Sin bin: Greenwood (29) - interference.
EAGLES: 1 Johnny Woodcock; 2 James Ford; 3 Brad Hepi; 4 Richard Newlove; 5 Greg Hurst; 6 Brendon Lindsay; 7 Dominic Brambani; 8 Jack Howieson; 9 Craig Cook; 10 Ryan Hepworth; 11 Tommy Trayler; 12 Ged Corcoran; 13 Grant Edwards. Subs (all used): 14 John Crawford; 15 Jon Aston; 16 Adam Hayes; 17 Mitchell Stringer.
Tries: Newlove (12), Ford (17), Cook (27), Woodcock (62); **Goals:** Woodcock 1/3, Brambani 2/2.
Sin bin: Hurst (77) - dissent;
Hepi (79) - use of the forearm.
Rugby Leaguer & League Express Men of the Match:
Centurions: Robert Roberts; *Eagles:* Craig Cook.
Penalty count: 15-7; **Half-time:** 16-16;
Referee: Jamie Leahy; **Attendance:** 1,810.

CASTLEFORD TIGERS 56 ROCHDALE HORNETS 6

TIGERS: 1 Tom Saxton; 2 Stuart Donlan; 3 Michael Shenton; 4 Kirk Dixon; 5 Michael Wainwright; 6 Ryan McGoldrick; 7 Danny Brough; 8 Liam Higgins; 9 Chris Charles; 10 Mark Leafa; 11 Awen Guttenbeil; 12 Ryan Clayton; 13 Peter Lupton. Subs (all used): 14 Dwayne Barker; 15 Sean Johnson; 16 Tere Glassie; 17 Ryan Boyle.
Tries: Higgins (17), M Shenton (20, 53, 77), Donlan (33, 37), Dixon (47, 75), Guttenbeil (50), Barker (60), Saxton (62); **Goals:** Brough 6/11.
HORNETS: 1 Eric Andrews; 2 Nick Johnson; 3 Lee Patterson; 4 Kevin King; 5 Bolu Fagborun; 6 Phil Hasty; 7 Gary Hulse; 8 Simon Baldwin; 9 Dave McConnell; 10

Andy Bailey; 11 Andy Gorski; 12 John Gledhill; 13 Tommy Goulden. Subs (all used): 14 Craig Robinson; 15 Mark Blanchard; 16 Paul Anderson; 17 Paul Norman.
Try: Hasty (67); **Goals:** King 1/1.
Rugby Leaguer & League Express Men of the Match: *Tigers:* Michael Shenton; *Hornets:* Phil Hasty.
Penalty count: 9-5; **Half-time:** 20-0;
Referee: Gareth Hewer; **Attendance:** 4,645.

WEEK 5

Sunday 6th May 2007

DEWSBURY RAMS 24 ROCHDALE HORNETS 36

RAMS: 1 Ian Preece; 2 Bryn Powell; 3 Chris Hall; 4 Danny Maun; 5 Austin Buchanan; 6 Francis Maloney; 7 Ryan Glynn; 8 Joe Helme; 9 Liam Finn; 10 Dominic Maloney; 11 Kevin Crouthers; 12 Martin Robinson; 13 Alex Bretherton. Subs (all used): 14 Pat Walker; 15 Taron Wildey; 16 Liam Crawley; 17 Keegan Hirst.
Tries: Preece (21, 42), F Maloney (26), Crawley (48);
Goals: F Maloney 4/5.
HORNETS: 1 Gary Hulse; 2 Eric Andrews; 3 Lee Patterson; 4 Kevin King; 5 Bolu Fagborun; 6 Simon Svabic; 7 Phil Hasty; 8 Andy Bailey; 9 Wayne Corcoran; 10 Byron Smith; 11 Andy Gorski; 12 Simon Baldwin; 13 Tommy Goulden. Subs (all used): 14 Iain Marsh; 15 Mark Blanchard; 16 Craig Robinson; 17 Paul Norman.
Tries: Corcoran (9, 77), Svabic (28), Goulden (32), King (53, 58, 69); **Goals:** King 4/7.
Rugby Leaguer & League Express Men of the Match: *Rams:* Francis Maloney; *Hornets:* Kevin King.
Penalty count: 7-10; **Half-time:** 10-18;
Referee: Gareth Hewer; **Attendance:** 754.

DONCASTER LAKERS 26 WHITEHAVEN 16

LAKERS: 1 Loz Wildbore; 2 Ade Adebisi; 3 Rikki Sheriffe; 4 Dean Gorton; 5 Danny Mills; 6 Graham Holroyd; 7 Joe McLocklan; 8 Craig Potter; 9 Chris Buttery; 10 Mark Castle; 11 Neil Lowe; 12 Craig Lawton; 13 Peter Green. Subs (all used): 14 Adam Myers; 15 Alex Benson; 16 Dean Andrews; 17 Alex Rowe.
Tries: P Green (11), Wildbore (14), Buttery (23), D Mills (62); **Goals:** Holroyd 4/6;
Field goals: Buttery (77), Holroyd (79).
WHITEHAVEN: 1 Gary Broadbent; 2 Craig Calvert; 3 Derry Eilbeck; 4 Rob Jackson; 5 Steve Maden; 6 Carl Rudd; 7 John Duffy; 8 Richard Fletcher; 9 Carl Sice; 10 Steve Trindall; 11 Spencer Miller; 12 Steve Bannister; 13 Aaron Lester. Subs (all used): 14 Graeme Mattinson; 15 Leroy Joe; 16 David Ford; 17 Andrew Jones.
Tries: Maden (30), Calvert (39), Miller (58);
Goals: Rudd 1/2, Fletcher 1/1.
Sin bin: Maden (70) – dissent.
Rugby Leaguer & League Express Men of the Match: *Lakers:* Alex Rowe; *Whitehaven:* Spencer Miller.
Penalty count: 10-6; **Half-time:** 16-10;
Referee: Peter Taberner; **Attendance:** 831.

HALIFAX 46 SHEFFIELD EAGLES 8

HALIFAX: 1 Damian Gibson; 2 Marcus George; 3 Mark Roberts; 4 Richard Varkulis; 5 Lee Greenwood; 6 Tim Hartley; 7 Ian Watson; 8 Paul Southern; 9 Sam Hoare; 10 David Wrench; 11 David Larder; 12 Paul Smith; 13 Damian Ball. Subs (all used): 14 Sean Penkywicz; 15 Phil Joseph; 16 Aaron Trinder; 17 Frank Watene.
Tries: Wrench (7), Larder (15), Smith (24), Greenwood (31), Hartley (36), George (54, 79), Gibson (63); **Goals:** Hartley 7/8.
EAGLES: 1 Johnny Woodcock; 2 James Ford; 3 Brendon Lindsay; 4 Damien Reid; 5 Caldon Bravo; 6 Gavin Brown; 7 Dominic Brambani; 8 Jack Howieson; 9 Craig Cook; 10 Mitchell Stringer; 11 Tommy Trayler; 12 Ged Corcoran; 13 Adam Hayes. Subs (all used): 14 John Crawford; 15 Tom Buckenham; 16 Grant Edwards; 17 Jon Aston.
Tries: Crawford (69), Ford (73); **Goals:** Brambani 0/2.
Rugby Leaguer & League Express Men of the Match: *Halifax:* Tim Hartley; *Eagles:* James Ford.
Penalty count: 7-7; **Half-time:** 30-0;
Referee: Thierry Alibert; **Attendance:** 1,519.

LEIGH CENTURIONS 24 CASTLEFORD TIGERS 32

CENTURIONS: 1 Miles Greenwood; 2 Leroy Rivett; 3 Damien Couturier; 4 Danny Halliwell; 5 David Alstead; 6 Martin Ainscough; 7 Aaron Heremaia; 8 Dana Wilson; 9 Sam Butterworth; 10 Warren Stevens; 11 James Taylor; 12 Robert Roberts; 13 Anthony Stewart. Subs (all used): 14 Adam Hughes; 15 Gareth Pemberton; 16 Mailangi Styles; 17 Matt Astley.
Tries: Ainscough (10, 68), Greenwood (21), Heremaia (45); **Goals:** Couturier 4/5.
Sin bin: Butterworth (64) - interference.
TIGERS: 1 Tom Saxton; 2 Stuart Donlan; 3 Michael Shenton; 4 Kirk Dixon; 5 Michael Wainwright; 6 Ryan McGoldrick; 7 Danny Brough; 8 Liam Higgins; 9 Andrew Henderson; 10 Awen Guttenbeil; 11 Dwayne Barker; 12 Chris Charles; 13 Peter Lupton. Subs (all used): 14 Richard Owen; 15 Tere Glassie; 16 Mark Leafa; 17 Ryan Boyle.
Tries: Brough (6), Lupton (58, 80), Owen (66), McGoldrick (72), Dixon (77); **Goals:** Brough 4/6.
Rugby Leaguer & League Express Men of the Match: *Centurions:* Mailangi Styles; *Tigers:* Peter Lupton.
Penalty count: 5-15; **Half-time:** 12-6;
Referee: Mike Dawber; **Attendance:** 2,683.

WIDNES VIKINGS 66 BATLEY BULLDOGS 14

VIKINGS: 1 Scott Grix; 2 Damien Blanch; 3 Andy Kirk; 4 Mick Nanyn; 5 Gavin Dodd; 6 Dennis Moran; 7 Ian Webster; 8 Jordan James; 9 Mark Smith; 10 Oliver Wilkes; 11 Lee Doran; 12 Paul Noone; 13 Bob Beswick. Subs (all used): 14 Aaron Summers; 15 Gareth Price; 16 Dean Gaskell; 17 Mick Cassidy.
Tries: Moran (5, 40, 73), Noone (29), Dodd (35), Grix (39, 65), Nanyn (42), Kirk (48), Wilkes (58), Smith (62); **Goals:** Nanyn 11/11.
BULLDOGS: 1 Craig Lingard; 2 Ashley Lindsay; 3 Steve Laurie; 4 Chris Langley; 5 Oliver Marns; 6 John Gallagher; 7 Jay Duffy; 8 Martin McLoughlin; 9 Kris Lythe; 10 Luke Stenchion; 11 Anthony Henderson; 12 Tim Spears; 13 Phil Farrell. Subs (all used): 14 Lee Paterson; 15 Craig Farrell; 16 Luke Menzies; 17 Jon Simpson.
Tries: Lindsay (8), P Farrell (56); **Goals:** Duffy 3/3.
Rugby Leaguer & League Express Men of the Match: *Vikings:* Dennis Moran; *Bulldogs:* Jay Duffy.
Penalty count: 5-5; **Half-time:** 30-8;
Referee: Dave Merrick; **Attendance:** 2,753.

WEEK 6

Thursday 17th May 2007

CASTLEFORD TIGERS 20 WIDNES VIKINGS 44

TIGERS: 1 Stuart Donlan; 2 Richard Owen; 3 Michael Shenton; 4 Kirk Dixon; 5 Michael Wainwright; 6 Ryan McGoldrick; 7 Danny Brough; 8 Liam Higgins; 9 Andrew Henderson; 10 Tere Glassie; 11 Awen Guttenbeil; 12 Dwayne Barker; 13 Chris Charles. Subs (all used): 14 Ryan Boyle; 15 Tom Saxton; 16 Peter Lupton; 17 Mark Leafa.
Tries: Owen (14), Donlan (66, 80), Brough (73);
Goals: Brough 2/4.
VIKINGS: 1 Scott Grix; 2 Damien Blanch; 3 Andy Kirk; 4 Mick Nanyn; 5 Gavin Dodd; 6 Dennis Moran; 7 Ian Webster; 8 Mick Cassidy; 9 Mark Smith; 10 Oliver Wilkes; 11 Lee Doran; 12 Paul Noone; 13 Bob Beswick. Subs (all used): 14 Aaron Summers; 15 Jordan James; 16 Dean Gaskell; 17 Gareth Price.
Tries: Dodd (5), Smith (11, 59), James (51), Webster (53), Blanch (64, 79), Beswick (76); **Goals:** Nanyn 6/9.
Rugby Leaguer & League Express Men of the Match: *Tigers:* Ryan Boyle; *Vikings:* Mark Smith.
Penalty count: 7-4; **Half-time:** 4-12;
Referee: Peter Taberner; **Attendance:** 6,007.

Friday 18th May 2007

SHEFFIELD EAGLES 12 DEWSBURY RAMS 26

EAGLES: 1 Johnny Woodcock; 2 James Ford; 3 Damien Reid; 4 Caldon Bravo; 5 Danny Mills; 6 Brendon Lindsay; 7 Dominic Brambani; 8 Tom Buckenham; 9 Paul Pickering; 10 Mitchell Stringer; 11 Tommy Trayler; 12 Ged Corcoran; 13 Adam Hayes. Subs (all used): 14 Craig Cook; 15 Brad Hepi; 16 Grant Edwards; 17 Jon Aston.
Tries: Corcoran (16), Brambani (63);
Goals: Woodcock 2/2.
RAMS: 1 Ian Preece; 2 Bryn Powell; 3 Andrew Bostock; 4 Danny Maun; 5 Austin Buchanan; 6 Francis Maloney; 7 Dean Lawford; 8 Keegan Hirst; 9 Luke Haigh; 10 Dominic Maloney; 11 Kevin Crouthers; 12 Martin Robinson; 13 Alex Bretherton. Subs (all used): 14 Liam Finn; 15 Rob Kelly; 16 Liam Crawley; 17 Jason Southwell.
Tries: Hirst (3), Powell (39), Buchanan (48), Bostock (68); **Goals:** F Maloney 5/6.
Rugby Leaguer & League Express Men of the Match: *Eagles:* Ged Corcoran; *Rams:* Dominic Maloney.
Penalty count: 12-11; **Half-time:** 6-12;
Referee: Ashley Klein; **Attendance:** 881.

Sunday 20th May 2007

BATLEY BULLDOGS 30 LEIGH CENTURIONS 44

BULLDOGS: 1 Jamie Stokes; 2 Steve Laurie; 3 Craig Farrell; 4 Chris Langley; 5 Oliver Marns; 6 John Gallagher; 7 Jay Duffy; 8 Luke Stenchion; 9 Kris Lythe; 10 Martin McLoughlin; 11 Phil Farrell; 12 Anthony Henderson; 13 Ashley Lindsay. Subs (all used): 14 Lee Paterson; 15 Andy Jarrett; 16 Lee Kerr; 17 Jon Simpson.
Tries: Langley (38), J Gallagher (55), Paterson (58), Lythe (72), Stokes (74), Duffy (79);
Goals: Duffy 3/5, Paterson 0/1.
CENTURIONS: 1 Miles Greenwood; 2 Leroy Rivett; 3 Damien Couturier; 4 Danny Halliwell; 5 David Alstead; 6 Martin Ainscough; 7 Aaron Heremaia; 8 Warren Stevens; 9 Sam Butterworth; 10 Dana Wilson; 11 James Taylor; 12 Mailangi Styles; 13 Anthony Stewart. Subs (all used): 14 Adam Rudd; 15 Matt Astley; 16 John Cookson; 17 Sean Richardson.
Tries: Halliwell (2, 32), Couturier (11), Rudd (27), Heremaia (35, 68), Rivett (45), Alstead (65);
Goals: Couturier 6/8.
Rugby Leaguer & League Express Men of the Match: *Bulldogs:* Jamie Stokes; *Centurions:* Aaron Heremaia.
Penalty count: 11-6; **Half-time:** 4-30;
Referee: Thierry Alibert; **Attendance:** 841.

ROCHDALE HORNETS 58 DONCASTER LAKERS 12

HORNETS: 1 Gary Hulse; 2 Eric Andrews; 3 Lee Patterson; 4 Kevin King; 5 Bolu Fagborun; 6 Simon Svabic; 7 Phil Hasty; 8 Andy Bailey; 9 Dave McConnell; 10 Byron Smith; 11 Andy Gorski; 12 Simon Baldwin; 13 Tommy Goulden. Subs (all used): 14 Wayne Corcoran; 15 Mark Blanchard; 16 Iain Marsh; 17 Ryan Benjafield.
Tries: Hasty (7, 54), Gorski (20), Hulse (23), Svabic (33), Andrews (37, 42), Baldwin (56), Patterson (62), King (75); **Goals:** King 9/10.
LAKERS: 1 Andy Taylor; 2 Ade Adebisi; 3 Craig Lawton; 4 Dean Andrews; 5 Lee Close; 6 Shaun Leaf; 7 Joe McLocklan; 8 Craig Potter; 9 Chris Buttery; 10 Alex Benson; 11 Neil Lowe; 12 James Garmston; 13 Peter Green. Subs (all used): 14 Shaun Hesketh; 15 Karl Mills; 16 Phil Crosby; 17 Alex Rowe.
Tries: Close (1), Adebisi (40); **Goals:** McLocklan 2/2.
Rugby Leaguer & League Express Men of the Match: *Hornets:* Phil Hasty; *Lakers:* Lee Close.
Penalty count: 5-7; **Half-time:** 28-12;
Referee: Jamie Leahy; **Attendance:** 904.

WHITEHAVEN 40 HALIFAX 24

WHITEHAVEN: 1 Gary Broadbent; 2 Craig Calvert; 3 David Seeds; 4 Rob Jackson; 5 Derry Eilbeck; 6 Carl Rudd; 7 John Duffy; 8 Steve Trindall; 9 Graeme Mattinson; 10 David Fatialofa; 11 Steve Bannister; 12 Richard Fletcher; 13 Aaron Smith. Subs (all used): 14 Carl Sice; 15 Leroy Joe; 16 Ricky Wright; 17 Scott Teare.
Tries: Fletcher (16, 34), Broadbent (19), Eilbeck (44, 60), R Jackson (66), Sice (79); **Goals:** Rudd 6/7.
HALIFAX: 1 Damian Gibson; 2 Marcus George; 3 Richard Varkulis; 4 Tim Hartley; 5 Lee Greenwood; 6 Graham Holroyd; 7 Ian Watson; 8 Paul Southern; 9 Sam Hoare; 10 David Wrench; 11 David Larder; 12 Paul Smith; 13 Damian Ball. Subs (all used): 14 Sean Penkywicz; 15 Mark Roberts; 16 Aaron Trinder; 17 Frank Watene.
Tries: George (4), Hartley (11), Roberts (26), Smith (42);
Goals: Hartley 4/4.
Rugby Leaguer & League Express Men of the Match: *Whitehaven:* Richard Fletcher; *Halifax:* Graham Holroyd.
Penalty count: 5-5; **Half-time:** 18-18;
Referee: Mike Dawber; **Attendance:** 1,729.

WEEK 7

Thursday 31st May 2007

DEWSBURY RAMS 22 WHITEHAVEN 32

RAMS: 1 Ian Preece; 2 Bryn Powell; 3 Chris Hall; 4 Danny Maun; 5 Austin Buchanan; 6 Francis Maloney; 7 Dean Lawford; 8 Andy Hobson; 9 Luke Haigh; 10 Dominic Maloney; 11 Kevin Crouthers; 12 Martin Robinson; 13 Alex Bretherton. Subs (all used): 14 Liam Finn; 15 Andrew Bostock; 16 Jason Southwell; 17 Keegan Hirst.
Tries: F Maloney (23), Hall (54), Bostock (79);
Goals: F Maloney 4/4, Finn 1/1.
Sin bin: Preece (69) - dissent.
WHITEHAVEN: 1 Gary Broadbent; 2 Craig Calvert; 3 David Seeds; 4 Derry Eilbeck; 5 Steve Maden; 6 Marc Bainbridge; 7 John Duffy; 8 Steve Trindall; 9 Aaron Smith; 10 David Fatialofa; 11 Steve Bannister; 12 Richard Fletcher; 13 Aaron Lester. Subs (all used): 14 Graeme Mattinson; 15 Leroy Joe; 16 Ricky Wright; 17 Marc Jackson.
Tries: Seeds (10), Maden (15), Mattinson (39), Duffy (58), Fatialofa (73), Calvert (77);
Goals: Bainbridge 3/5, Fletcher 1/2.
Rugby Leaguer & League Express Men of the Match: *Rams:* Francis Maloney; *Whitehaven:* Gary Broadbent.
Penalty count: 9-7; **Half-time:** 10-16;
Referee: Dave Merrick; **Attendance:** 2,010.

Sunday 3rd June 2007

DONCASTER LAKERS 14 BATLEY BULLDOGS 48

LAKERS: 1 Craig Skelton; 2 Lee Close; 3 Chris Buttery; 4 Dean Andrews; 5 Ade Adebisi; 6 Shaun Leaf; 7 Joe McLocklan; 8 Craig Potter; 9 Lee Bettinson; 10 James Garmston; 11 Craig Lawton; 12 Shaun Hesketh; 13 Peter Green. Subs (all used): 14 Alex Benson; 15 Karl Mills; 16 Andy Taylor; 17 Alex Rowe.
Tries: Adebisi (9, 29, 32); **Goals:** McLocklan 1/3.
BULLDOGS: 1 Jamie Stokes; 2 Oliver Marns; 3 Danny Speakman; 4 Chris Langley; 5 Steve Laurie; 6 Lee Paterson; 7 Jay Duffy; 8 Martin McLoughlin; 9 Kris Lythe; 10 David Best; 11 Anthony Henderson; 12 Phil Farrell; 13 Ashley Lindsay. Subs (all used): 14 Luke Stenchion; 15 Craig Farrell; 16 Jack Watson; 17 Jon Simpson.
Tries: Stokes (3, 41), Paterson (16, 24), Langley (36), Lythe (49), Watson (57), Laurie (77); **Goals:** Duffy 8/8.
Rugby Leaguer & League Express Men of the Match: *Lakers:* Lee Bettinson; *Bulldogs:* Jamie Stokes.
Penalty count: 5-6; **Half-time:** 14-24;
Referee: Gareth Hewer; **Attendance:** 970.

HALIFAX 14 CASTLEFORD TIGERS 30

HALIFAX: 1 Damian Gibson; 2 Marcus George; 3 Mark Roberts; 4 Richard Varkulis; 5 Lee Greenwood; 6 Graham Holroyd; 7 Ian Watson; 8 Paul Southern; 9 Sean Penkywicz; 10 Andy Shickell; 11 Phil Joseph; 12 Paul Smith; 13 Damian Ball. Subs (all used): 14 Sam Hoare; 15 David Larder; 16 Danny Heaton; 17 Frank Watene.
Tries: George (65), Greenwood (69), Gibson (70);
Goals: Holroyd 1/3.
TIGERS: 1 Tom Saxton; 2 Stuart Donlan; 3 Michael Shenton; 4 Kirk Dixon; 5 Michael Wainwright; 6 Ryan McGoldrick; 7 Danny Brough; 8 Ryan Boyle; 9 Andrew Henderson; 10 Mark Leafa; 11 Awen Guttenbeil; 12 Dwayne Barker; 13 Ryan Clayton. Subs (all used): 14 Chris Charles; 15 Joe Westerman; 16 Craig Huby; 17 Richard Owen.
Tries: M Shenton (7), Leafa (9), Guttenbeil (17), Dixon (25), Huby (52), Wainwright (73);
Goals: Dixon 1/3, Brough 1/1, Charles 1/2.
Rugby Leaguer & League Express Men of the Match: *Halifax:* Marcus George; *Tigers:* Michael Wainwright.
Penalty count: 6-6; **Half-time:** 0-20;
Referee: Peter Taberner; **Attendance:** 2,990.

LEIGH CENTURIONS 32 ROCHDALE HORNETS 4

CENTURIONS: 1 Miles Greenwood; 2 Leroy Rivett; 3 Damien Couturier; 4 Anthony Stewart; 5 David Alstead; 6 Martin Ainscough; 7 Aaron Heremaia; 8 Dana Wilson; 9 Sam Butterworth; 10 John Cookson; 11 Adam Rudd; 12 James Taylor; 13 Mailangi Styles. Subs (all used): 14 Chad Isles; 15 Adam Thomas; 16 John Boland; 17 Matt Astley.
Tries: Couturier (5), Heremaia (13), Butterworth (54), Cookson (75), Stewart (80); **Goals:** Couturier 6/7.
HORNETS: 1 Chris Giles; 2 Eric Andrews; 3 Lee Patterson; 4 Kevin King; 5 Bolu Fagborun; 6 Simon Svabic; 7 Phil Hasty; 8 Andy Bailey; 9 Wayne Corcoran; 10 Byron Smith; 11 Andy Gorski; 12 Simon Baldwin; 13 Tommy Goulden. Subs (all used): 14 Gary Hulse; 15 Iain Marsh; 16 Mark Blanchard; 17 Ryan Benjafield.
Try: Baldwin (77); **Goals:** King 0/1.
Rugby Leaguer & League Express Men of the Match: *Centurions:* Miles Greenwood; *Hornets:* Eric Andrews.
Penalty count: 5-4; **Half-time:** 12-0;
Referee: Ronnie Laughton; **Attendance:** 1,669.

WIDNES VIKINGS 56 SHEFFIELD EAGLES 10

VIKINGS: 1 Gavin Dodd; 2 Damien Blanch; 3 Andy Kirk; 4 Mick Nanyn; 5 Dean Gaskell; 6 Dennis Moran; 7 Ian Webster; 8 Mick Cassidy; 9 Mark Smith; 10 Oliver Wilkes; 11 Lee Doran; 12 Aaron Summers; 13 Bob Beswick. Subs (all used): 14 Joel Penny; 15 Danny Lima; 16 Jordan James; 17 Gareth Price.
Tries: Wilkes (22, 45, 55), James (30), Nanyn (40, 65, 76), Moran (47), Dodd (60), Penny (71); **Goals:** Nanyn 8/10.
EAGLES: 1 Johnny Woodcock; 2 Danny Mills; 3 James Ford; 4 Damien Reid; 5 Greg Hurst; 6 Brendon Lindsay; 7 Gavin Brown; 8 Mitchell Stringer; 9 Craig Cook; 10 Ged Corcoran; 11 Craig Brown; 12 Tommy Trayler; 13 Adam Hayes. Subs (all used): 14 Dominic Brambani; 15 Ryan Hepworth; 16 Dale Holdstock; 17 Tom Buckenham.
Tries: Ford (5, 52); **Goals:** Woodcock 1/2.
Rugby Leaguer & League Express Men of the Match: *Vikings:* Oliver Wilkes; *Eagles:* James Ford.
Penalty count: 10-5; **Half-time:** 18-4;
Referee: Jamie Leahy; **Attendance:** 2,837.

WEEK 8

Thursday 7th June 2007

SHEFFIELD EAGLES 24 ROCHDALE HORNETS 0

EAGLES: 1 Johnny Woodcock; 2 Danny Mills; 3 James Ford; 4 Damien Reid; 5 Greg Hurst; 6 Brendon Lindsay; 7 Gavin Brown; 8 Jack Howieson; 9 Paul Pickering; 10 Mitchell Stringer; 11 Craig Brown; 12 Dale Holdstock; 13 Brad Hepi. Subs (all used): 14 Dominic Brambani; 15 James Morrow; 16 Adam Hayes; 17 Ryan Hepworth.
Tries: Reid (36), Ford (68), Woodcock (71), Lindsay (74); **Goals:** Woodcock 0/1, Brambani 4/5.
HORNETS: 1 Chris Giles; 2 Eric Andrews; 3 Lee Patterson; 4 Kevin King; 5 Bolu Fagborun; 6 Simon Svabic; 7 Phil Hasty; 8 Rob Ball; 9 Dave McConnell; 10 Byron Smith; 11 Andy Gorski; 12 Simon Baldwin; 13 Tommy Goulden. Subs (all used): 14 Gary Hulse; 15 Iain Marsh; 16 Wayne Corcoran; 17 Paul Norman.
Goals: King 0/1.
Rugby Leaguer & League Express Men of the Match: *Eagles:* Jack Howieson; *Hornets:* Simon Baldwin.
Penalty count: 9-10; **Half-time:** 4-0;
Referee: Jamie Leahy; **Attendance:** 1,463.

Sunday 10th June 2007

BATLEY BULLDOGS 8 HALIFAX 58

BULLDOGS: 1 Jamie Stokes; 2 Oliver Marns; 3 Ian Gordon; 4 Chris Langley; 5 Steve Laurie; 6 Lee Paterson; 7 Jay Duffy; 8 Martin McLoughlin; 9 Kris Lythe; 10 David Best; 11 Anthony Henderson; 12 Craig Farrell; 13 Ashley Lindsay. Subs (all used): 14 John Rourke; 15 Luke Stenchion; 16 Jack Watson; 17 Jon Simpson.
Tries: Lindsay (25), Stokes (67); **Goals:** Duffy 0/2.
Sin bin: Duffy (28) - dissent.
HALIFAX: 1 Damian Gibson; 2 Marcus George; 3 Mark Roberts; 4 Richard Varkulis; 5 Lee Greenwood; 6 Graham Holroyd; 7 Ian Watson; 8 Andy Shickell; 9 Sean Penkywicz; 10 David Wrench; 11 Danny Heaton; 12 Paul Smith; 13 Phil Joseph. Subs (all used): 14 Sam Hoare; 15 Damian Ball; 16 David Larder; 17 Frank Watene.
Tries: George (6, 43), Heaton (7), Greenwood (28, 52), Joseph (35, 79), Holroyd (55), Penkywicz (70), Hoare (76); **Goals:** Holroyd 6/7, Watson 3/3.
Rugby Leaguer & League Express Men of the Match: *Bulldogs:* David Best; *Halifax:* Graham Holroyd.
Penalty count: 9-7; **Half-time:** 4-22;
Referee: Mike Dawber; **Attendance:** 898.

DONCASTER LAKERS 4 WIDNES VIKINGS 90

LAKERS: 1 Craig Skelton; 2 Lee Close; 3 Chris Buttery; 4 Shaun Leaf; 5 Ade Adebisi; 6 Joe McLocklan; 7 Andy Speake; 8 James Garmston; 9 Lee Bettinson; 10 Alex Benson; 11 Craig Lawton; 12 Shaun Hesketh; 13 Peter Green. Subs (all used): 14 Gareth Carey; 15 Karl Mills; 16 Mark Castle; 17 Alex Rowe.
Try: Adebisi (34); **Goals:** McLocklan 0/1.
VIKINGS: 1 Scott Grix; 2 Dean Gaskell; 3 Andy Kirk; 4 Damien Blanch; 5 Gavin Dodd; 6 Dennis Moran; 7 Joel Penny; 8 Mick Cassidy; 9 Mark Smith; 10 Oliver Wilkes; 11 Lee Doran; 12 Aaron Summers; 13 Bob Beswick. Subs (all used): 14 Ian Webster; 15 Danny Lima; 16 Jordan James; 17 Gareth Price.
Tries: Dodd (1, 18, 44), Blanch (6, 54, 67), Wilkes (19, 74), Penny (27, 51, 71), Kirk (39), Summers (46, 50), Gaskell (56), Grix (62); **Goals:** Dodd 13/16.
Rugby Leaguer & League Express Men of the Match: *Lakers:* Andy Speake; *Vikings:* Gavin Dodd.
Penalty count: 1-2; **Half-time:** 4-34;
Referee: Steve Ganson; **Attendance:** 1,248.

WHITEHAVEN 12 LEIGH CENTURIONS 28

WHITEHAVEN: 1 Gary Broadbent; 2 Craig Calvert; 3 Spencer Miller; 4 Derry Eilbeck; 5 Craig Benson; 6 Carl Rudd; 7 John Duffy; 8 Steve Trindall; 9 Aaron Smith; 10 David Fatialofa; 11 Matty Dale; 12 Richard Fletcher; 13 Aaron Lester. Subs (all used): 14 Graeme Mattinson; 15 Leroy Joe; 16 Marc Jackson; 17 Scott Teare.
Tries: Calvert (5), Dale (77); **Goals:** Rudd 2/2.
CENTURIONS: 1 Miles Greenwood; 2 Leroy Rivett; 3 Damien Couturier; 4 Anthony Stewart; 5 David Alstead; 6 Martin Ainscough; 7 Aaron Heremaia; 8 John Cookson; 9 John Clough; 10 Mailangi Styles; 11 Adam Rudd; 12 Adam Thomas; 13 James Taylor. Subs (all used): 14 Chad Isles; 15 Matt Astley; 16 Chris Hill; 17 Sean Richardson.
Tries: Rudd (11), Heremaia (34), Alstead (47, 67), Rivett (79); **Goals:** Couturier 4/5.
Rugby Leaguer & League Express Men of the Match: *Whitehaven:* Gary Broadbent; *Centurions:* Mailangi Styles.
Penalty count: 4-8; **Half-time:** 6-12;
Referee: Ian Smith; **Attendance:** 2,065.

CASTLEFORD TIGERS 56 DEWSBURY RAMS 8

TIGERS: 1 Tom Saxton; 2 Stuart Donlan; 3 Michael Shenton; 4 Kirk Dixon; 5 Michael Wainwright; 6 Ryan McGoldrick; 7 Danny Brough; 8 Ryan Boyle; 9 Andrew Henderson; 10 Mark Leafa; 11 Chris Charles; 12 Joe Westerman; 13 Ryan Clayton. Subs (all used): 14 Michael Knowles; 15 Dwayne Barker; 16 Craig Huby; 17 Richard Owen.
Tries: McGoldrick (3, 46, 69), Wainwright (9, 27), Brough (12), Dixon (19, 26), Saxton (47), Barker (55), Knowles (71); **Goals:** Dixon 3/4, Brough 1/5, Westerman 2/2.
RAMS: 1 Ian Preece; 2 Austin Buchanan; 3 Pat Walker; 4 Andrew Bostock; 5 Danny Maun; 6 Francis Maloney; 7 Dean Lawford; 8 Andy Hobson; 9 Liam Finn; 10 Dominic Maloney; 11 Kevin Crouthers; 12 Martin Robinson; 13 Alex Bretherton. Subs (all used): 14 Luke Haigh; 15 Rob Kelly; 16 Jason Southwell; 17 Keegan Hirst.
Tries: Maun (55), Buchanan (60); **Goals:** F Maloney 0/2.
Rugby Leaguer & League Express Men of the Match: *Tigers:* Mark Leafa; *Rams:* Alex Bretherton.
Penalty count: 10-6; **Half-time:** 28-0;
Referee: Gareth Hewer; **Attendance:** 4,739.

WEEK 9

Thursday 14th June 2007

HALIFAX 12 WIDNES VIKINGS 6

HALIFAX: 1 Damian Gibson; 2 Marcus George; 3 Mark Roberts; 4 Richard Varkulis; 5 Lee Greenwood; 6 Graham Holroyd; 7 Ian Watson; 8 Paul Southern; 9 Sean Penkywicz; 10 Frank Watene; 11 Danny Heaton; 12 Paul Smith; 13 Phil Joseph. Subs (all used): 14 Sam Hoare; 15 David Larder; 16 Damian Ball; 17 Andy Shickell.
Tries: Ball (21), Larder (45); **Goals:** Holroyd 2/3.
Sin bin: Shickell (26) - late challenge.
VIKINGS: 1 Scott Grix; 2 Damien Blanch; 3 Toa Kohe-Love; 4 Mick Nanyn; 5 Gavin Dodd; 6 Dennis Moran; 7 Joel Penny; 8 Mick Cassidy; 9 Mark Smith; 10 Oliver Wilkes; 11 Lee Doran; 12 Paul Noone; 13 Bob Beswick. Subs (all used): 14 Aaron Summers; 15 Jordan James; 16 Andy Kirk; 17 Ian Webster.
Tries: Webster (73); **Goals:** Nanyn 1/1.
Rugby Leaguer & League Express Men of the Match: *Halifax:* Graham Holroyd; *Vikings:* Dennis Moran.
Penalty count: 8-10; **Half-time:** 6-0;
Referee: Jamie Leahy; **Attendance:** 2,412.

Friday 15th June 2007

WHITEHAVEN 60 DONCASTER LAKERS 6

WHITEHAVEN: 1 Gary Broadbent; 2 Craig Calvert; 3 Spencer Miller; 4 Derry Eilbeck; 5 Craig McAvoy; 6 Carl Rudd; 7 John Duffy; 8 Steve Trindall; 9 Aaron Smith; 10 David Fatialofa; 11 Matty Dale; 12 Richard Fletcher; 13 Aaron Lester. Subs (all used): 14 Carl Sice; 15 Leroy Joe; 16 Scott Teare; 17 Graeme Mattinson.
Tries: Trindall (2), Fletcher (14, 22), Dale (17), C McAvoy (25), Sice (33, 56), Duffy (39), Calvert (54), Mattinson (64), Teare (74); **Goals:** Rudd 8/11.
LAKERS: 1 Craig Skelton; 2 Lee Close; 3 Chris Buttery; 4 Shaun Leaf; 5 Ade Adebisi; 6 Joe McLocklan; 7 Andy Speake; 8 Alex Rowe; 9 Lee Bettinson; 10 Alex Benson; 11 Craig Lawton; 12 Shaun Hesketh; 13 Peter Green. Subs (all used): 14 Mark Castle; 15 James Garmston; 16 Chris Lythe; 17 Wayne Green.
Try: Close (45); **Goals:** McLocklan 1/1.
Sin bin: P Green (43) - holding down.
Rugby Leaguer & League Express Men of the Match: *Whitehaven:* Carl Sice; *Lakers:* Alex Rowe.
Penalty count: 11-9; **Half-time:** 38-0;
Referee: Mike Dawber; **Attendance:** 1,410.

SHEFFIELD EAGLES 15 CASTLEFORD TIGERS 27

EAGLES: 1 Johnny Woodcock; 2 Danny Mills; 3 James Ford; 4 Damien Reid; 5 Greg Hurst; 6 Brendon Lindsay; 7 Gavin Brown; 8 Jack Howieson; 9 Paul Pickering; 10 Mitchell Stringer; 11 Craig Brown; 12 Tommy Trayler; 13 Adam Hayes. Subs (all used): 14 Dominic Brambani; 15 James Morrow; 16 Brad Hepi; 17 Tom Buckenham.
Tries: Hurst (12), Ford (67); **Goals:** Woodcock 3/4;
Field goal: Lindsay (80).
TIGERS: 1 Tom Saxton; 2 Stuart Donlan; 3 Richard Owen; 4 Kirk Dixon; 5 Michael Wainwright; 6 Ryan McGoldrick; 7 Joe Westerman; 8 Ryan Boyle; 9 Andrew Henderson; 10 Mark Leafa; 11 Craig Huby; 12 Chris Charles; 13 Ryan Clayton. Subs (all used): 14 Michael Knowles; 15 Dwayne Barker; 16 Liam Higgins; 17 Jake Bassinder.
Tries: Wainwright (3), Dixon (50), Henderson (61), Huby (75, 77); **Goals:** Dixon 0/2, Westerman 3/3;
Field goal: Saxton (73).
Rugby Leaguer & League Express Men of the Match: *Eagles:* James Ford; *Tigers:* Joe Westerman.
Penalty count: 4-4; **Half-time:** 6-4;
Referee: Peter Taberner; **Attendance:** 1,333.

Sunday 17th June 2007

DEWSBURY RAMS 27 LEIGH CENTURIONS 18

RAMS: 1 Ian Preece; 2 Bryn Powell; 3 Andrew Bostock; 4 Danny Maun; 5 Austin Buchanan; 6 Francis Maloney; 7 Dean Lawford; 8 Andy Hobson; 9 Luke Haigh; 10 Dominic Maloney; 11 Martin Robinson; 12 Alex Bretherton; 13 Pat Walker. Subs (all used): 14 Liam Finn; 15 Rob Kelly; 16 Joe Helme; 17 Keegan Hirst.
Tries: F Maloney (10), Maun (32), Bretherton (43), Buchanan (60); **Goals:** F Maloney 3/3, Finn 2/2;
Field goal: Finn (75).
CENTURIONS: 1 Rob Smyth; 2 Leroy Rivett; 3 Damien Couturier; 4 Anthony Stewart; 5 David Alstead; 6 Martin Ainscough; 7 Aaron Heremaia; 8 John Cookson; 9 John Clough; 10 Mailangi Styles; 11 Adam Rudd; 12 Adam Thomas; 13 James Taylor. Subs (all used): 14 Chris Hill; 15 Sean Richardson; 16 Sebastien Martins; 17 Dana Wilson.
Tries: Cookson (38), Rivett (56), Thomas (63);
Goals: Couturier 1/1, Heremaia 2/2.
Rugby Leaguer & League Express Men of the Match: *Rams:* Alex Bretherton; *Centurions:* Damien Couturier.
Penalty count: 5-3; **Half-time:** 14-6;
Referee: Gareth Hewer; **Attendance:** 1,611.

ROCHDALE HORNETS 38 BATLEY BULLDOGS 14

HORNETS: 1 Chris Giles; 2 Eric Andrews; 3 Iain Marsh; 4 Kevin King; 5 Bolu Fagborun; 6 Simon Svabic; 7 Phil Hasty; 8 Andy Bailey; 9 Dave McConnell; 10 Byron Smith; 11 Andy Gorski; 12 Simon Baldwin; 13 Tommy Goulden. Subs (all used): 14 Gary Hulse; 15 John Gledhill; 16 Wayne Corcoran; 17 Paul Norman.
Tries: Hasty (2, 16), King (5), Fagborun (33, 77), Baldwin (47), Smith (63); **Goals:** King 5/8.
BULLDOGS: 1 Craig Lingard; 2 Oliver Marns; 3 Danny Speakman; 4 Chris Langley; 5 Jamie Stokes; 6 Lee Paterson; 7 Tom Hemingway; 8 David Best; 9 Kris Lythe; 10 Jack Watson; 11 Anthony Henderson; 12 Craig Farrell; 13 Martin McLoughlin. Subs (all used): 14 Mark Barlow; 15 Ashley Lindsay; 16 Luke Stenchion; 17 Jon Simpson.
Tries: McLoughlin (10), Henderson (70, 79);
Goals: Hemingway 1/3.
Rugby Leaguer & League Express Men of the Match: *Hornets:* Simon Baldwin; *Bulldogs:* Tom Hemingway.
Penalty count: 9-7; **Half-time:** 24-4;
Referee: Ronnie Laughton; **Attendance:** 644.

WEEK 10

Thursday 28th June 2007

BATLEY BULLDOGS 22 DEWSBURY RAMS 20

BULLDOGS: 1 Craig Lingard; 2 Ashley Lindsay; 3 Chris Langley; 4 Danny Speakman; 5 Oliver Marns; 6 Richard Colley; 7 Tom Hemingway; 8 David Rourke; 9 Kris Lythe; 10 Martin McLoughlin; 11 Anthony Henderson; 12 Craig Farrell; 13 John Gallagher. Subs (all used): 14 Luke Stenchion; 15 Mark Toohey; 16 Luke Menzies; 17 Jon Simpson.
Tries: Hemingway (3), Speakman (7), Lindsay (64), Lythe (76); **Goals:** Hemingway 3/4.
RAMS: 1 Ian Preece; 2 Bryn Powell; 3 Andrew Bostock; 4 Danny Maun; 5 Austin Buchanan; 6 Francis Maloney; 7 Dean Lawford; 8 Andy Hobson; 9 Luke Haigh; 10 Dominic Maloney; 11 Martin Robinson; 12 Alex Bretherton; 13 Pat Walker. Subs (all used): 14 Liam Finn; 15 Rob Kelly; 16 Kevin Crouthers; 17 Joe Helme.
Tries: Buchanan (12, 42), Bostock (23), Kelly (34);
Goals: F Maloney 2/4.
Sin bin: Lawford (73) - high tackle.
Rugby Leaguer & League Express Men of the Match: *Bulldogs:* Richard Colley; *Rams:* Dominic Maloney.
Penalty count: 9-6; **Half-time:** 10-16;
Referee: Gareth Hewer; **Attendance:** 2,208.

Sunday 1st July 2007

DONCASTER 20 SHEFFIELD EAGLES 32

DONCASTER: 1 Craig Skelton; 2 Lee Close; 3 Damian Munro; 4 Shaun Leaf; 5 Darren Woods; 6 Luke Gale; 7 Andy Speake; 8 Craig Potter; 9 Gary Richardson; 10 Luke Burgess; 11 Craig Lawton; 12 Mark Castle; 13 Peter Green. Subs (all used): 14 Alex Benson; 15 Alex Rowe; 16 Karl Mills; 17 Shaun Hesketh.
Tries: Rowe (21), Munro (39, 57), Woods (75);
Goals: Skelton 2/4.
Sin bin: Close (9) - high tackle.
EAGLES: 1 Johnny Woodcock; 2 Danny Mills; 3 James Ford; 4 Damien Reid; 5 Greg Hurst; 6 Brendon Lindsay;

Jubilation at Mount Pleasant, as Batley's Kris Lythe scores a late try to secure victory over local rivals Dewsbury

7 Gavin Brown; 8 Jack Howieson; 9 Paul Pickering; 10 Mitchell Stringer; 11 Craig Brown; 12 Tommy Trayler; 13 Adam Hayes. Subs (all used): 14 Dominic Brambani; 15 Dale Holdstock; 16 Richard Newlove; 17 James Morrow.
Tries: Ford (15), Woodcock (24), Mills (41), Trayler (45), Reid (53, 62); **Goals:** Woodcock 1/4, Brambani 3/3.
Rugby Leaguer & League Express Men of the Match: *Doncaster:* Gary Richardson; *Eagles:* James Ford.
Penalty count: 11-7; **Half-time:** 12-10;
Referee: Robert Hicks; **Attendance:** 1,038.

LEIGH CENTURIONS 6 HALIFAX 18

CENTURIONS: 1 Miles Greenwood; 2 Leroy Rivett; 3 Adam Rudd; 4 Anthony Stewart; 5 Danny Halliwell; 6 Sam Butterworth; 7 Aaron Heremaia; 8 Dana Wilson; 9 John Clough; 10 John Cookson; 11 Mailangi Styles; 12 Adam Thomas; 13 James Taylor. Subs (all used): 14 Martin Ainscough; 15 Gareth Pemberton; 16 Chris Hill; 17 Sebastien Martins.
Try: Heremaia (4); **Goals:** Heremaia 1/1.
HALIFAX: 1 Damian Gibson; 2 Lee Patterson; 3 Shad Royston; 4 Richard Varkulis; 5 Lee Greenwood; 6 Graham Holroyd; 7 Ian Watson; 8 Paul Southern; 9 Sean Penkywicz; 10 David Wrench; 11 David Larder; 12 Paul Smith; 13 Phil Joseph. Subs (all used): 14 Sam Hoare; 15 Andy Shickell; 16 Danny Jones; 17 Frank Watene.
Tries: Varkulis (36), Patterson (38), Watene (67);
Goals: Holroyd 3/4.
Rugby Leaguer & League Express Men of the Match: *Centurions:* John Clough; *Halifax:* Phil Joseph.
Penalty count: 9-4; **Half-time:** 6-10;
Referee: Dave Merrick; **Attendance:** 1,803.

WIDNES VIKINGS 32 ROCHDALE HORNETS 0

VIKINGS: 1 Scott Grix; 2 Dean Gaskell; 3 Toa Kohe-Love; 4 Mick Nanyn; 5 Gavin Dodd; 6 Dennis Moran; 7 Joel Penny; 8 Jordan James; 9 Mark Smith; 10 Gareth Price; 11 Lee Doran; 12 Oliver Wilkes; 13 Bob Beswick. Subs (all used): 14 Ian Webster; 15 Mick Cassidy; 16 Andy Kirk; 17 Danny Lima.
Tries: Dodd (6), Gaskell (14), Wilkes (17), Grix (24), Penny (52), Webster (55); **Goals:** Nanyn 4/6.
HORNETS: 1 Chris Giles; 2 Eric Andrews; 3 Iain Marsh; 4 Kevin King; 5 Bolu Fagborun; 6 Phil Hasty; 7 Gary Hulse; 8 Andy Bailey; 9 Dave McConnell; 10 Byron Smith; 11 Andy Gorski; 12 Simon Baldwin; 13 Tommy Goulden. Subs (all used): 14 John Gledhill; 15 Ryan Benjafield; 16 Mark Blanchard; 17 Paul Norman.
Rugby Leaguer & League Express Men of the Match: *Vikings:* Dean Gaskell; *Hornets:* Phil Hasty.
Penalty count: 4-5; **Half-time:** 20-0;
Referee: Craig Halloran; **Attendance:** 4,879.

CASTLEFORD TIGERS 44 WHITEHAVEN 12

TIGERS: 1 Stuart Donlan; 2 Michael Shenton; 3 Ryan

Clayton; 4 Kirk Dixon; 5 Michael Wainwright; 6 Ryan McGoldrick; 7 Danny Brough; 8 Mark Leafa; 9 Andrew Henderson; 10 Craig Huby; 11 Awen Guttenbeil; 12 Chris Charles; 13 Dwayne Barker. Subs (all used): 14 Richard Owen; 15 Joe Westerman; 16 Ryan Boyle; 17 Liam Higgins.
Tries: Barker (4), Leafa (8), M Shenton (35), Boyle (42), Dixon (54), Westerman (57, 73), Owen (69);
Goals: Brough 3/4, Westerman 2/4, Dixon 1/1.
WHITEHAVEN: 1 Gary Broadbent; 2 Craig Calvert; 3 David Seeds; 4 Derry Eilbeck; 5 Rob Jackson; 6 Leroy Joe; 7 John Duffy; 8 Marc Jackson; 9 Aaron Smith; 10 Steve Trindall; 11 Spencer Miller; 12 Richard Fletcher; 13 Carl Rudd. Subs (all used): 14 Carl Sice; 15 Graeme Mattinson; 16 Matty Dale; 17 Scott Teare.
Tries: Duffy (13), Calvert (15); **Goals:** Rudd 2/2.
Rugby Leaguer & League Express Men of the Match: *Tigers:* Ryan Boyle; *Whitehaven:* John Duffy.
Penalty count: 14-7; **Half-time:** 16-12;
Referee: Jamie Leahy; **Attendance:** 4,902.

WEEK 11

Thursday 5th July 2007

DEWSBURY RAMS 10 WIDNES VIKINGS 50

RAMS: 1 Ian Preece; 2 Bryn Powell; 3 Francis Maloney; 4 Danny Maun; 5 Austin Buchanan; 6 Pat Walker; 7 Dean Lawford; 8 Andy Hobson; 9 Liam Finn; 10 Dominic Maloney; 11 Kevin Crouthers; 12 Martin Robinson; 13 Alex Bretherton. Subs (all used): 14 Luke Haigh; 15 Rob Kelly; 16 Joe Helme; 17 Jason Southwell.
Tries: F Maloney (4), Lawford (63);
Goals: F Maloney 0/1, Finn 1/1.
VIKINGS: 1 Scott Grix; 2 Dean Gaskell; 3 Toa Kohe-Love; 4 Mick Nanyn; 5 Gavin Dodd; 6 Dennis Moran; 7 Joel Penny; 8 Mick Cassidy; 9 Mark Smith; 10 Oliver Wilkes; 11 Lee Doran; 12 Paul Noone; 13 Bob Beswick. Subs (all used): 14 Aaron Summers; 15 Jordan James; 16 Ian Webster; 17 Gareth Price.
Tries: Gaskell (14, 42, 78), Penny (18), James (29), Grix (34), Moran (50), Nanyn (55), Kohe-Love (71), Summers (74); **Goals:** Nanyn 5/10.
Rugby Leaguer & League Express Men of the Match: *Rams:* Dean Lawford; *Vikings:* Dennis Moran.
Penalty count: 4-5; **Half-time:** 4-20;
Referee: Gareth Hewer; **Attendance:** 1,885.

Sunday 8th July 2007

HALIFAX 54 ROCHDALE HORNETS 8

HALIFAX: 1 Damian Gibson; 2 Lee Patterson; 3 Shad Royston; 4 Richard Varkulis; 5 Lee Greenwood; 6 Graham Holroyd; 7 Ian Watson; 8 Paul Southern; 9 Sean

Penkywicz; 10 Andy Shickell; 11 David Larder; 12 Paul Smith; 13 Phil Joseph. Subs (all used): 14 Sam Hoare; 15 Jamie Bovill; 16 Damian Ball; 17 Frank Watene.
Tries: Smith (22), Gibson (24, 33), Southern (44), Hoare (49), Greenwood (52), Royston (58, 78), Penkywicz (73); **Goals:** Holroyd 7/8, Watson 2/2.
HORNETS: 1 Gary Hulse; 2 Eric Andrews; 3 Iain Marsh; 4 Mark Blanchard; 5 Bolu Fagborun; 6 Wayne Corcoran; 7 Phil Hasty; 8 Andy Bailey; 9 Dave McConnell; 10 Byron Smith; 11 Andy Gorski; 12 Simon Baldwin; 13 Tommy Goulden. Subs (all used): 14 Todd O'Brien; 15 Ryan Benjafield; 16 Paul Norman; 17 Rob Ball.
Tries: Hulse (12), Marsh (55); **Goals:** Corcoran 0/2.
Sin bin: McConnell (64) – high tackle.
Rugby Leaguer & League Express Men of the Match: *Halifax:* Sean Penkywicz; *Hornets:* Gary Hulse.
Penalty count: 11-5; **Half-time:** 20-4;
Referee: Jamie Leahy; **Attendance:** 1,733.

LEIGH CENTURIONS 26 BATLEY BULLDOGS 22

CENTURIONS: 1 Miles Greenwood; 2 Leroy Rivett; 3 Adam Rudd; 4 Danny Halliwell; 5 David Alstead; 6 Chad Isles; 7 Aaron Heremaia; 8 Dana Wilson; 9 John Clough; 10 Sebastien Martins; 11 Tommy Grundy; 12 Mailangi Styles; 13 Anthony Stewart. Subs (all used): 14 Sam Butterworth; 15 Gareth Pemberton; 16 Chris Hill; 17 John Cookson.
Tries: Halliwell (9), Martins (17, 59), Grundy (23), C Hill (75); **Goals:** Heremaia 0/1, Halliwell 3/4.
BULLDOGS: 1 Jamie Stokes; 2 Ashley Lindsay; 3 Daryl Cardiss; 4 Chris Langley; 5 Oliver Marns; 6 Richard Colley; 7 Tom Hemingway; 8 David Rourke; 9 Kris Lythe; 10 Martin McLoughlin; 11 Anthony Henderson; 12 Craig Farrell; 13 John Gallagher. Subs (all used): 14 Luke Stenchion; 15 Mark Toohey; 16 Luke Menzies; 17 Jon Simpson.
Tries: Langley (27, 64), Stokes (32), Lythe (52);
Goals: Hemingway 3/4.
Rugby Leaguer & League Express Men of the Match: *Centurions:* Mailangi Styles; *Bulldogs:* Mark Toohey.
Penalty count: 8-7; **Half-time:** 16-10;
Referee: Mike Dawber; **Attendance:** 1,469.

WHITEHAVEN 44 SHEFFIELD EAGLES 16

WHITEHAVEN: 1 Gary Broadbent; 2 Craig Calvert; 3 Rob Jackson; 4 Derry Eilbeck; 5 Steve Maden; 6 Carl Rudd; 7 Leroy Joe; 8 Steve Trindall; 9 Aaron Smith; 10 David Fatialofa; 11 Spencer Miller; 12 Richard Fletcher; 13 Graeme Mattinson. Subs (all used): 14 Carl Sice; 15 David Seeds; 16 Marc Jackson; 17 Scott Teare.
Tries: Calvert (7, 45), Miller (11), Broadbent (27), Mattinson (35), M Jackson (50), Sice (56), Fatialofa (79); **Goals:** Rudd 6/8.
EAGLES: 1 Johnny Woodcock; 2 Danny Mills; 3 James Ford; 4 Damien Reid; 5 Rob Worrincy; 6 Brendon Lindsay; 7 Gavin Brown; 8 Jack Howieson; 9

Phil Joseph tries to break free during Halifax's win at Doncaster

Pickering; 10 Mitchell Stringer; 11 Dale Holdstock; 12 Tommy Trayler; 13 Adam Hayes. Subs (all used): 14 Dominic Brambani; 15 Ryan Hepworth; 16 Grant Edwards; 17 Tom Buckenham.
Tries: Reid (18), Hayes (40), Edwards (64);
Goals: Woodcock 2/3.
Sin bin: Pickering (53) - late tackle on Joe.
Rugby Leaguer & League Express Men of the Match:
Whitehaven: Carl Sice; *Eagles:* Brendon Lindsay.
Penalty count: 7-7; **Half-time:** 20-12;
Referee: Robert Hicks; **Attendance:** 1,473.

CASTLEFORD TIGERS 66 DONCASTER 4

TIGERS: 1 Stuart Donlan; 2 Michael Shenton; 3 Dwayne Barker; 4 Kirk Dixon; 5 Michael Wainwright; 6 Ryan McGoldrick; 7 Peter Lupton; 8 Liam Higgins; 9 Andrew Henderson; 10 Mark Leafa; 11 Awen Guttenbeil; 12 Ryan Clayton; 13 Joe Westerman. Subs (all used): 14 Richard Owen; 15 Chris Charles; 16 Craig Huby; 17 Tere Glassie.
Tries: Leafa (11, 74), Wainwright (17, 51), McGoldrick (23), Clayton (36), Barker (39, 51, 68), Westerman (46, 66), Glassie (62); **Goals:** Dixon 8/11, Westerman 1/1.
DONCASTER: 1 Craig Skelton; 2 Lee Close; 3 Damian Munro; 4 Darren Woods; 5 Joe Brown; 6 Luke Gale; 7 Andy Speake; 8 Alex Rowe; 9 Gary Richardson; 10 Mark Castle; 11 Peter Green; 12 Shaun Leaf; 13 Alex Benson. Subs (all used): 14 Karl Mills; 15 Craig Potter; 16 Luke Burgess; 17 Craig Lawton.
Try: Munro (6); **Goals:** Skelton 0/1.
Sin bin: Richardson (53) – dangerous play.
Rugby Leaguer & League Express Men of the Match:
Tigers: Mark Leafa; *Doncaster:* Craig Skelton.
Penalty count: 13-5; **Half-time:** 28-4;
Referee: Dave Merrick; **Attendance:** 4,109.

WEEK 12

Thursday 19th July 2007

ROCHDALE HORNETS 12 DEWSBURY RAMS 36

HORNETS: 1 Gary Hulse; 2 Eric Andrews; 3 Iain Marsh; 4 Mark Blanchard; 5 Bolu Fagborun; 6 Wayne Corcoran; 7 Phil Hasty; 8 Rob Ball; 9 Todd O'Brien; 10 Byron Smith; 11 Ryan Benjafield; 12 Andy Bailey; 13 Andy Gorski. Subs (all used): 14 Eric Johnson; 15 Mark McCully; 16 Craig Robinson; 17 Paul Norman.
Tries: Hasty (54), Robinson (77); **Goals:** McCully 2/2.
RAMS: 1 Chris Hall; 2 Bryn Powell; 3 Sid Domic; 4 Danny Maun; 5 Austin Buchanan; 6 Pat Walker; 7 Dean Lawford; 8 Andy Hobson; 9 Liam Finn; 10 Dominic Maloney; 11 Martin Robinson; 12 Alex Bretherton; 13 Josh Weeden. Subs (all used): 14 Francis Maloney; 15

Kevin Crouthers; 16 Joe Helme; 17 Jason Southwell.
Tries: D Maloney (4), Hall (8), Bretherton (13), Domic (21), Robinson (27, 67); **Goals:** Finn 6/6.
Rugby Leaguer & League Express Men of the Match:
Hornets: Rob Ball; *Rams:* Dominic Maloney.
Penalty count: 5-10; **Half-time:** 0-30;
Referee: Dave Merrick; **Attendance:** 1,093.

Friday 20th July 2007

SHEFFIELD EAGLES 39 LEIGH CENTURIONS 12

EAGLES: 1 Johnny Woodcock; 2 Danny Mills; 3 James Ford; 4 Damien Reid; 5 Rob Worrincy; 6 Gavin Brown; 7 Dominic Brambani; 8 Jack Howieson; 9 Paul Pickering; 10 Mitchell Stringer; 11 Craig Brown; 12 Tommy Trayler; 13 Adam Hayes. Subs (all used): 14 Grant Edwards; 15 Dale Holdstock; 16 Richard Newlove; 17 Ged Corcoran.
Tries: Ford (8, 12, 21, 62), Woodcock (27), Worrincy (56); **Goals:** Woodcock 7/7; **Field goal:** G Brown (35).
CENTURIONS: 1 Miles Greenwood; 2 Leroy Rivett; 3 Danny Halliwell; 4 Anthony Stewart; 5 David Alstead; 6 Dave McConnell; 7 Chris Hough; 8 Dana Wilson; 9 John Clough; 10 John Cookson; 11 Chris Hill; 12 Tommy Grundy; 13 Mailangi Styles. Subs (all used): 14 Sam Butterworth; 15 Gareth Pemberton; 16 Sean Richardson; 17 Sebastien Martins.
Tries: Greenwood (18, 59), Alstead (73);
Goals: Hough 0/3.
Rugby Leaguer & League Express Men of the Match:
Eagles: Dominic Brambani; *Centurions:* Sam Butterworth.
Penalty count: 6-6; **Half-time:** 27-4;
Referee: Jamie Leahy; **Attendance:** 870.

Sunday 22nd July 2007

BATLEY BULLDOGS 6 CASTLEFORD TIGERS 42

BULLDOGS: 1 Jamie Stokes; 2 Kevin Doyle; 3 Daryl Cardiss; 4 Oliver Marns; 5 Ashley Lindsay; 6 Richard Colley; 7 Tom Hemingway; 8 Anthony Henderson; 9 Kris Lythe; 10 Luke Stenchion; 11 Mark Toohey; 12 Tommy Gallagher; 13 John Gallagher. Subs (all used): 14 Tim Spears; 15 Luke Menzies; 16 Jack Watson; 17 Jon Simpson.
Try: T Gallagher (36); **Goals:** Hemingway 1/1.
Sin bin: Hemingway (60) - holding down.
TIGERS: 1 Stuart Donlan; 2 Danny Williams; 3 Michael Shenton; 4 Kirk Dixon; 5 Michael Wainwright; 6 Peter Lupton; 7 Ryan McGoldrick; 8 Liam Higgins; 9 Andrew Henderson; 10 Tere Glassie; 11 Awen Guttenbeil; 12 Chris Charles; 13 Ryan Clayton. Subs (all used): 14 Dwayne Barker; 15 Anthony Thackeray; 16 Craig Huby; 17 Ryan Boyle.
Tries: Williams (10, 68, 79), Dixon (21, 54), Lupton (46), M Shenton (64), Guttenbeil (76); **Goals:** Dixon 5/8.

Dismissal: McGoldrick (34) - punching.
Rugby Leaguer & League Express Men of the Match:
Bulldogs: Luke Menzies; *Tigers:* Danny Williams.
Penalty count: 5-6; **Half-time:** 6-12;
Referee: Gareth Hewer; **Attendance:** 2,378.

DONCASTER 30 HALIFAX 44

DONCASTER: 1 Damian Munro; 2 Lee Close; 3 Chris Buttery; 4 Darren Woods; 5 Joe Brown; 6 Shaun Leaf; 7 Luke Gale; 8 Craig Lawton; 9 Gary Richardson; 10 Luke Benson. Subs (all used): 14 Ayden Faal; 15 Chris Lythe; 16 Lewis Lilley; 17 Chris Forster.
Tries: Gale (12), P Green (17), Woods (20), Castle (66), Forster (72); **Goals:** Gale 5/5.
Dismissal: Buttery (79) – dissent.
Sin bin: Munro (63) – dissent.
HALIFAX: 1 Damian Gibson; 2 Lee Patterson; 3 Shad Royston; 4 Richard Varkulis; 5 Lee Greenwood; 6 Graham Holroyd; 7 Ian Watson; 8 Paul Southern; 9 Sean Penkywicz; 10 David Wrench; 11 David Larder; 12 Paul Smith; 13 Phil Joseph. Subs (all used): 14 Sam Hoare; 15 Damian Ball; 16 Danny Heaton; 17 Andy Shickell.
Tries: Royston (3), Smith (29), Ball (45), Patterson (53), Larder (55), Penkywicz (57), Greenwood (69), Joseph (79); **Goals:** Holroyd 6/8.
Sin bin: Southern (65) - professional foul.
Rugby Leaguer & League Express Men of the Match:
Doncaster: Luke Gale; *Halifax:* Paul Smith.
Penalty count: 9-11; **Half-time:** 18-10;
Referee: Paul Carr; **Attendance:** 1,202.

WIDNES VIKINGS 16 WHITEHAVEN 14

VIKINGS: 1 Scott Grix; 2 Damien Blanch; 3 Toa Kohe-Love; 4 Mick Nanyn; 5 Dean Gaskell; 6 Dennis Moran; 7 Ian Webster; 8 Mick Cassidy; 9 Mark Smith; 10 Oliver Wilkes; 11 Lee Doran; 12 Paul Noone; 13 Bob Beswick. Subs (all used): 14 Aaron Summers; 15 Jordan James; 16 Andy Kirk; 17 Gareth Price.
Tries: Moran (11), Blanch (70), Nanyn (75);
Goals: Nanyn 2/3.
WHITEHAVEN: 1 Gary Broadbent; 2 Craig Calvert; 3 Derry Eilbeck; 4 Rob Jackson; 5 Steve Maden; 6 Leroy Joe; 7 John Duffy; 8 Steve Trindall; 9 Graeme Mattinson; 10 David Fatialofa; 11 Spencer Miller; 12 Howard Hill; 13 Carl Rudd. Subs (all used): 14 Carl Sice; 15 David Seeds; 16 Marc Jackson; 17 Ricky Wright.
Tries: M Jackson (34), Eilbeck (44); **Goals:** Rudd 3/3.
Rugby Leaguer & League Express Men of the Match:
Vikings: Mick Nanyn; *Whitehaven:* Gary Broadbent.
Penalty count: 9-5; **Half-time:** 6-8;
Referee: Mike Dawber; **Attendance:** 3,299.

WEEK 13

Friday 27th July 2007

SHEFFIELD EAGLES 56 BATLEY BULLDOGS 24

EAGLES: 1 Rob Worrincy; 2 Danny Mills; 3 James Ford; 4 Richard Newlove; 5 Greg Hurst; 6 Gavin Brown; 7 Dominic Brambani; 8 Jack Howieson; 9 Paul Pickering; 10 Mitchell Stringer; 11 Craig Brown; 12 Tommy Trayler; 13 Adam Hayes. Subs (all used): 14 Brendon Lindsay; 15 Dale Holdstock; 16 Grant Edwards; 17 Ged Corcoran.
Tries: Brambani (1), Mills (9, 48, 59, 76), Lindsay (25), G Brown (34), Worrincy (41), Newlove (55);
Goals: Brambani 10/12.
BULLDOGS: 1 Jamie Stokes; 2 Ashley Lindsay; 3 Craig Farrell; 4 Mark Barlow; 5 Kevin Doyle; 6 Francis Maloney; 7 Tom Hemingway; 8 Jack Watson; 9 Kris Lythe; 10 Luke Stenchion; 11 Tommy Gallagher; 12 Phil Farrell; 13 Mark Toohey. Subs (all used): 14 Tim Spears; 15 Martin McLoughlin; 16 Luke Menzies; 17 Jon Simpson.
Tries: Lindsay (44), Barlow (51), Stokes (69), Simpson (72); **Goals:** Hemingway 2/2, Maloney 2/2.
Sin bin: Toohey (20) - use of the knee; Lythe (38) - interference.
Rugby Leaguer & League Express Men of the Match: *Eagles:* Dominic Brambani; *Bulldogs:* Ashley Lindsay.
Penalty count: 10-10; **Half-time:** 30-0;
Referee: Leon Williamson; **Attendance:** 916.

Sunday 29th July 2007

DEWSBURY RAMS 10 CASTLEFORD TIGERS 36

RAMS: 1 Chris Hall; 2 Bryn Powell; 3 Sid Domic; 4 Danny Maun; 5 Austin Buchanan; 6 Pat Walker; 7 Dean Lawford; 8 Andy Hobson; 9 Liam Finn; 10 Dominic Maloney; 11 Martin Robinson; 12 Alex Bretherton; 13 Josh Weeden. Subs (all used): 14 Rob Kelly; 15 Kevin Crouthers; 16 Joe Helme; 17 Liam Crawley.
Tries: Hobson (71), Buchanan (75); **Goals:** Finn 1/2.
TIGERS: 1 Kirk Dixon; 2 Danny Williams; 3 Michael Shenton; 4 Ryan McGoldrick; 5 Michael Wainwright; 6 Peter Lupton; 7 Anthony Thackeray; 8 Liam Higgins; 9 Andrew Henderson; 10 Tere Glassie; 11 Awen Guttenbeil; 12 Chris Charles; 13 Ryan Clayton. Subs (all used): 14 Stuart Donlan; 15 Joe Westerman; 16 Ryan Boyle; 17 Craig Huby.
Tries: M Shenton (4, 12, 58), Henderson (21), Thackeray (32), Lupton (38), Clayton (53);
Goals: Dixon 4/7.
Rugby Leaguer & League Express Men of the Match: *Rams:* Martin Robinson; *Tigers:* Anthony Thackeray.
Penalty count: 5-10; **Half-time:** 0-26;
Referee: Mike Dawber; **Attendance:** 3,010.

HALIFAX 20 WHITEHAVEN 26

HALIFAX: 1 Damian Gibson; 2 Lee Patterson; 3 Shad Royston; 4 Richard Varkulis; 5 Lee Greenwood; 6 Graham Holroyd; 7 Ian Watson; 8 Paul Southern; 9 Sean Penkywicz; 10 David Wrench; 11 David Larder; 12 Paul Smith; 13 Phil Joseph. Subs (all used): 14 Sam Hoare; 15 Damian Ball; 16 Danny Heaton; 17 Frank Watene.
Tries: Greenwood (27), Ball (36, 38), Holroyd (79);
Goals: Holroyd 2/4.
WHITEHAVEN: 1 Gary Broadbent; 2 Craig Calvert; 3 David Seeds; 4 Rob Jackson; 5 Steve Maden; 6 Leroy Joe; 7 John Duffy; 8 Steve Trindall; 9 Graeme Mattinson; 10 David Fatialofa; 11 Spencer Miller; 12 Simon Baldwin; 13 Carl Rudd. Subs (all used): 14 Carl Sice; 15 Aaron Smith; 16 Howard Hill; 17 Ricky Wright.
Tries: Rudd (2), Calvert (9), Hill (55), Seeds (67);
Goals: Rudd 5/5.
Rugby Leaguer & League Express Men of the Match: *Halifax:* Sean Penkywicz; *Whitehaven:* Gary Broadbent.
Penalty count: 6-3; **Half-time:** 16-12;
Referee: Ian Smith; **Attendance:** 1,745.

ROCHDALE HORNETS 4 LEIGH CENTURIONS 42

HORNETS: 1 Brad Attwood; 2 Eric Andrews; 3 Mark McCully; 4 Mark Blanchard; 5 Chris Campbell; 6 Phil Hasty; 7 Gary Hulse; 8 Rob Ball; 9 Wayne Corcoran; 10 Ryan Benjafield; 11 Andy Gorski; 12 Scott Law; 13 Tommy Goulden. Subs (all used): 14 Todd O'Brien; 15 Byron Smith; 16 Craig Robinson; 17 Jode Sheriffe.
Try: Gorski (21); **Goals:** McCully 0/1.
CENTURIONS: 1 Chris Giles; 2 Leroy Rivett; 3 Damien Couturier; 4 Tommy Grundy; 5 David Alstead; 6 Chris Hough; 7 Aaron Heremaia; 8 Dana Wilson; 9 Dave McConnell; 10 Sebastien Martins; 11 Adam Thomas; 12 James Taylor; 13 Anthony Stewart. Subs (all used): 14 Sam Butterworth; 15 Danny Halliwell; 16 John Cookson; 17 Mailangi Styles.
Tries: Halliwell (24, 50, 72), McConnell (29), Rivett (47), Couturier (60, 77), Wilson (67);
Goals: Couturier 4/7, Halliwell 1/1.
Rugby Leaguer & League Express Men of the Match: *Hornets:* Scott Law; *Centurions:* Dave McConnell.
Penalty count: 12-6; **Half-time:** 4-8;
Referee: Gareth Hewer; **Attendance:** 650.

WIDNES VIKINGS 40 DONCASTER 18

VIKINGS: 1 Scott Grix; 2 Damien Blanch; 3 Toa Kohe-Love; 4 Mick Nanyn; 5 Dean Gaskell; 6 Dennis Moran; 7 Joel Penny; 8 Jordan James; 9 Ian Webster; 10 Aaron Summers; 11 Lee Doran; 12 Joel Tomkins; 13 Paul Noone. Subs (all used): 14 Mick Cassidy; 15 Oliver Wilkes; 16 Gavin Dodd; 17 Gareth Price.
Tries: Doran (17, 38), Nanyn (28), Blanch (45), Kohe-Love (58, 61), Wilkes (67), Dodd (69);
Goals: Nanyn 4/8.
DONCASTER: 1 Shaun Leaf; 2 Craig Skelton; 3 Damian Munro; 4 Darren Woods; 5 Joe Brown; 6 Chris Forster; 7 Luke Gale; 8 Tommy Hodgkinson; 9 Gary Richardson; 10 Luke Burgess; 11 Craig Lawton; 12 Peter Green; 13 Alex Benson. Subs (all used): 14 Chris Buttery; 15 Simon Worrall; 16 Paul Anderson; 17 Alex Rowe.
Tries: Burgess (19), Gale (51), Forster (77);
Goals: Gale 3/3.
Rugby Leaguer & League Express Men of the Match: *Vikings:* Toa Kohe-Love; *Doncaster:* Luke Burgess.
Penalty count: 12-8; **Half-time:** 16-6;
Referee: Thierry Alibert; **Attendance:** 2,607.

WEEK 14

Thursday 2nd August 2007

LEIGH CENTURIONS 0 WIDNES VIKINGS 38

CENTURIONS: 1 Chris Giles; 2 Leroy Rivett; 3 Damien Couturier; 4 Danny Halliwell; 5 David Alstead; 6 Miles Greenwood; 7 Chris Hough; 8 Dana Wilson; 9 Dave McConnell; 10 Mailangi Styles; 11 Tommy Grundy; 12 James Taylor; 13 Anthony Stewart. Subs (all used): 14 Sam Butterworth; 15 Gareth Pemberton; 16 John Cookson; 17 Sebastien Martins.
VIKINGS: 1 Scott Grix; 2 Dean Gaskell; 3 Toa Kohe-Love; 4 Mick Nanyn; 5 Gavin Dodd; 6 Dennis Moran; 7 Joel Penny; 8 Mick Cassidy; 9 Mark Smith; 10 Oliver Wilkes; 11 Joel Tomkins; 12 Paul Noone; 13 Bob Beswick. Subs (all used): 14 Aaron Summers; 15 Jordan James; 16 Ian Webster; 17 Gareth Price.
Tries: Tomkins (8), Nanyn (14, 22, 24), Beswick (47), Gaskell (60), Grix (80); **Goals:** Nanyn 5/8.
Rugby Leaguer & League Express Men of the Match: *Centurions:* Miles Greenwood; *Vikings:* Mark Smith.
Penalty count: 7-7; **Half-time:** 0-22;
Referee: Gareth Hewer; **Attendance:** 3,095.

Sunday 5th August 2007

DEWSBURY RAMS 36 HALIFAX 38

RAMS: 1 Chris Hall; 2 Bryn Powell; 3 Alex Bretherton; 4 Danny Maun; 5 Austin Buchanan; 6 Pat Walker; 7 Dean Lawford; 8 Andy Hobson; 9 Liam Finn; 10 Dominic Maloney; 11 Rob Kelly; 12 Martin Robinson; 13 Josh Weeden. Subs (all used): 14 Luke Haigh; 15 Andy Spink; 16 Joe Helme; 17 Liam Crawley.
Tries: Robinson (23), Helme (26), Hobson (38), Powell (45), Walker (62), Maun (79);
Goals: Finn 4/4, Walker 2/2.
HALIFAX: 1 Shad Royston; 2 Damian Gibson; 3 Mark Roberts; 4 Richard Varkulis; 5 Lee Patterson; 6 Graham Holroyd; 7 Sean Penkywicz; 8 Paul Southern; 9 Sam Hoare; 10 David Wrench; 11 David Larder; 12 Damian Ball; 13 Phil Joseph. Subs (all used): 14 Ian Watson; 15 Paul Smith; 16 Danny Heaton; 17 Frank Watene.
Tries: Ball (5), Joseph (18), Royston (36), Hoare (48), Gibson (69), Larder (73), Watene (79);
Goals: Holroyd 5/7.
Rugby Leaguer & League Express Men of the Match: *Rams:* Pat Walker; *Halifax:* Sean Penkywicz.
Penalty count: 7-8; **Half-time:** 18-16;
Referee: Robert Hicks; **Attendance:** 1,183.

DONCASTER 34 ROCHDALE HORNETS 30

DONCASTER: 1 Wayne Green; 2 Darren Woods; 3 Paul Anderson; 4 Simon Worrall; 5 Joe Brown; 6 Chris Forster; 7 Luke Gale; 8 Tommy Hodgkinson; 9 Gary Richardson; 10 Luke Burgess; 11 Craig Lawton; 12 Mark Castle; 13 Peter Green. Subs (all used): 14 Lee Forth; 15 Sean Johnson; 16 Alex Benson; 17 Alex Rowe.
Tries: Woods (7, 57), Hodgkinson (16), Benson (39), W Green (52), Rowe (75); **Goals:** Gale 4/6, W Green 1/1.
Dismissal: Castle (60) – fighting.
Sin bin: P Green (60) – fighting.
HORNETS: 1 Brad Attwood; 2 Eric Andrews; 3 Iain Marsh; 4 Mark McCully; 5 Chris Campbell; 6 Gareth Barber; 7 Phil Hasty; 8 Rob Ball; 9 Wayne Corcoran; 10 Byron Smith; 11 Andy Gorski; 12 Scott Law; 13 Tommy Goulden. Subs (all used): 14 Gary Hulse; 15 Craig Robinson; 16 Dave Cunliffe; 17 Ryan Benjafield.
Tries: Goulden (22), Hulse (28), Hasty (34), Robinson (42, 77), McCully (80); **Goals:** McCully 3/6.
Dismissal: Hulse (72) – dissent.
Sin bin: McCully (60) – fighting; Hulse (72) - incident in tackle.
Rugby Leaguer & League Express Men of the Match: *Doncaster:* Paul Anderson; *Hornets:* Craig Robinson.
Penalty count: 13-7; **Half-time:** 18-12;
Referee: Jamie Leahy; **Attendance:** 838.

WHITEHAVEN 24 BATLEY BULLDOGS 14

WHITEHAVEN: 1 Gary Broadbent; 2 Craig Calvert; 3 David Seeds; 4 Rob Jackson; 5 Steve Maden; 6 Leroy Joe; 7 John Duffy; 8 Simon Baldwin; 9 Graeme Mattinson; 10 David Fatialofa; 11 Spencer Miller; 12 Richard Fletcher; 13 Carl Rudd. Subs (all used): 14 Carl Sice; 15 Aaron Smith; 16 Howard Hill; 17 Ricky Wright.
Tries: Seeds (19, 65), Sice (26), Miller (76);
Goals: Rudd 4/4.
Sin bin: Broadbent (34) - holding down.
BULLDOGS: 1 Jamie Stokes; 2 Ashley Lindsay; 3 Craig Farrell; 4 Mark Barlow; 5 Oliver Marns; 6 Richard Colley; 7 Francis Maloney; 8 Luke Menzies; 9 Kris Lythe; 10 Luke Stenchion; 11 Tim Spears; 12 Tommy Gallagher; 13 Mark Toohey. Subs (all used): 14 Andy Jarrett; 15 Lee Paterson; 16 Martin McLoughlin; 17 Jon Simpson.
Tries: Stenchion (38), Stokes (60), Marns (79);
Goals: Paterson 0/1, Maloney 1/2.
Rugby Leaguer & League Express Men of the Match: *Whitehaven:* David Seeds; *Bulldogs:* Francis Maloney.
Penalty count: 6-5; **Half-time:** 12-4;
Referee: Mike Dawber; **Attendance:** 1,556.

CASTLEFORD TIGERS 52 SHEFFIELD EAGLES 26

TIGERS: 1 Stuart Donlan; 2 Danny Williams; 3 Michael Shenton; 4 Kirk Dixon; 5 Michael Wainwright; 6 Anthony Thackeray; 7 Danny Brough; 8 Liam Higgins; 9 Andrew Henderson; 10 Tere Glassie; 11 Awen Guttenbeil; 12 Dwayne Barker; 13 Joe Westerman. Subs (all used): 14 Ryan Clayton; 15 Richard Owen; 16 Chris Charles; 17 Ryan Boyle.
Tries: Thackeray (13, 41), Westerman (20), Williams (31), Barker (44, 69), M Shenton (60, 74), Dixon (66); **Goals:** Dixon 6/7, Brough 2/2.
EAGLES: 1 Rob Worrincy; 2 Danny Mills; 3 James Ford; 4 Damien Reid; 5 Greg Hurst; 6 Gavin Brown; 7 Dominic Brambani; 8 Jack Howieson; 9 Paul Pickering; 10 Mitchell Stringer; 11 Craig Brown; 12 Tommy Trayler; 13 Adam Hayes. Subs (all used): 14 Brendon Lindsay; 15 Grant Edwards; 16 Richard Newlove; 17 Ged Corcoran.
Tries: Ford (26, 48), G Brown (39), Worrincy (79);
Goals: Brambani 5/6.
Rugby Leaguer & League Express Men of the Match: *Tigers:* Anthony Thackeray; *Eagles:* Dominic Brambani.
Penalty count: 13-6; **Half-time:** 18-14;
Referee: James Child; **Attendance:** 4,538.

WEEK 15

Thursday 9th August 2007

WHITEHAVEN 12 CASTLEFORD TIGERS 20

WHITEHAVEN: 1 Gary Broadbent; 2 Craig Calvert; 3 David Seeds; 4 Rob Jackson; 5 Steve Maden; 6 Leroy Joe; 7 John Duffy; 8 Simon Baldwin; 9 Graeme Mattinson; 10 David Fatialofa; 11 Spencer Miller; 12 Richard Fletcher; 13 Carl Rudd. Subs (all used): 14 Carl Sice; 15 Aaron Smith; 16 Marc Jackson; 17 Howard Hill.
Tries: Fletcher (5), Baldwin (63); **Goals:** Rudd 2/2.
TIGERS: 1 Stuart Donlan; 2 Danny Williams; 3 Michael Shenton; 4 Kirk Dixon; 5 Michael Wainwright; 6 Anthony Thackeray; 7 Danny Brough; 8 Liam Higgins; 9 Andrew Henderson; 10 Tere Glassie; 11 Chris Charles; 12 Ryan Clayton; 13 Joe Westerman. Subs (all used): 14 Richard Owen; 15 Dwayne Barker; 16 Ryan Boyle; 17 Mark Leafa.
Tries: Clayton (15), Dixon (33), Barker (35);
Goals: Brough 4/4.
Rugby Leaguer & League Express Men of the Match: *Whitehaven:* Marc Jackson; *Tigers:* Danny Brough.
Penalty count: 5-8; **Half-time:** 6-18;
Referee: Ian Smith; **Attendance:** 3,366.

Sunday 12th August 2007

BATLEY BULLDOGS 26 DONCASTER 12

BULLDOGS: 1 Jamie Stokes; 2 Ashley Lindsay; 3 Craig Farrell; 4 Mark Barlow; 5 Oliver Marns; 6 Richard Colley; 7 Francis Maloney; 8 Luke Menzies; 9 Kris Lythe; 10 Luke Stenchion; 11 Tim Spears; 12 Tommy Gallagher; 13 Lee Paterson. Subs (all used): 14 Mark Toohey; 15 Andy Jarrett; 16 Martin McLoughlin; 17 Jon Simpson.
Tries: Lythe (29), C Farrell (46), Menzies (55), Colley (66); **Goals:** Maloney 5/5.
DONCASTER: 1 Wayne Green; 2 Darren Woods; 3 Damian Munro; 4 Paul Anderson; 5 Joe Brown; 6 Luke Gale; 7 Andy Speake; 8 Tommy Hodgkinson; 9 Gary Richardson; 10 Luke Burgess; 11 Craig Lawton; 12 Simon Worrall; 13 Peter Green. Subs (all used): 14 Chris Buttery; 15 Sean Johnson; 16 Alex Benson; 17 Alex Rowe.
Tries: Woods (25, 38); **Goals:** Gale 2/3.
Dismissal: Lawton (76) – punching.
Sin bin: Munro (37) - holding down; Burgess (55) - ball steal, (75) - high tackle.
On report: Rowe (72) – incident in tackle.
Rugby Leaguer & League Express Men of the Match: *Bulldogs:* Craig Farrell; *Doncaster:* Darren Woods.
Penalty count: 14-8; **Half-time:** 6-12;
Referee: James Child; **Attendance:** 732.

HALIFAX 68 LEIGH CENTURIONS 22

HALIFAX: 1 Shad Royston; 2 Lee Patterson; 3 Mark Roberts; 4 Richard Varkulis; 5 Lee Greenwood; 6 Graham Holroyd; 7 Sean Penkywicz; 8 Paul Southern; 9 Sam Hoare; 10 David Wrench; 11 David Larder; 12 Damian Ball; 13 Phil Joseph. Subs (all used): 14 Ian Watson; 15 Paul Smith; 16 Aaron Trinder; 17 Frank Watene.
Tries: Larder (9, 43), Ball (13), Hoare (16), Joseph (18), Watene (27), Smith (31, 53), Royston (40, 71), Greenwood (49, 77); **Goals:** Holroyd 10/12.
CENTURIONS: 1 Chris Giles; 2 Leroy Rivett; 3 David Alstead; 4 Danny Halliwell; 5 Miles Greenwood; 6 Chris Hough; 7 Aaron Heremaia; 8 Sean Richardson; 9 Dave McConnell; 10 Sebastien Martins; 11 Mailangi Styles; 12 James Taylor; 13 Anthony Stewart. Subs (all used): 14 John Clough; 15 Tom Woodcock; 16 Gareth Pemberton; 17 John Cookson.
Tries: Halliwell (6), Styles (33), Richardson (57), Greenwood (65); **Goals:** Heremaia 3/4.
Sin bin: Stewart (52) - holding down.
Rugby Leaguer & League Express Men of the Match: *Halifax:* Graham Holroyd; *Centurions:* Miles Greenwood.
Penalty count: 13-5; **Half-time:** 42-12;
Referee: Jamie Leahy; **Attendance:** 1,816.

ROCHDALE HORNETS 36 SHEFFIELD EAGLES 56

HORNETS: 1 Mark McCully; 2 Eric Andrews; 3 Iain

Marsh; 4 Dave Cunliffe; 5 Chris Campbell; 6 Gareth Barber; 7 Phil Hasty; 8 Rob Ball; 9 Wayne Corcoran; 10 Byron Smith; 11 Andy Gorski; 12 Scott Law; 13 Tommy Goulden. Subs (all used): 14 Gary Hulse; 15 Craig Robinson; 16 Simon Svabic; 17 Ryan Benjafield.
Tries: Goulden (3, 71), McCully (8, 75), Hasty (15), Andrews (65); **Goals:** McCully 6/6.
EAGLES: 1 Johnny Woodcock; 2 Danny Mills; 3 James Ford; 4 Damien Reid; 5 Rob Worrincy; 6 Gavin Brown; 7 Dominic Brambani; 8 Jack Howieson; 9 Paul Pickering; 10 Mitchell Stringer; 11 Craig Brown; 12 Tommy Trayler; 13 Adam Hayes. Subs (all used): 14 Brendon Lindsay; 15 Dale Holdstock; 16 Richard Newlove; 17 Ged Corcoran.
Tries: Howieson (25), Reid (37), Lindsay (40), Worrincy (45, 61, 80), Woodcock (48, 79), Stringer (55), Newlove (69); **Goals:** Woodcock 8/10.
Rugby Leaguer & League Express Men of the Match:
Hornets: Tommy Goulden; *Eagles:* Mitchell Stringer.
Penalty count: 7-6; **Half-time:** 18-18;
Referee: Gareth Hewer; **Attendance:** 503.

WIDNES VIKINGS 48 DEWSBURY RAMS 12

VIKINGS: 1 Gavin Dodd; 2 Damien Blanch; 3 Toa Kohe-Love; 4 Mick Nanyn; 5 Dean Gaskell; 6 Scott Grix; 7 Joel Penny; 8 Mick Cassidy; 9 Mark Smith; 10 Oliver Wilkes; 11 Joel Tomkins; 12 Paul Noone; 13 Bob Beswick. Subs (all used): 14 Aaron Summers; 15 Jordan James; 16 Ian Webster; 17 Lee Doran.
Tries: Blanch (10, 58), Nanyn (22), Penny (29, 40), Noone (56), Dodd (68), Kohe-Love (79);
Goals: Nanyn 8/9.
RAMS: 1 Ian Preece; 2 Bryn Powell; 3 Chris Hall; 4 Kevin Crouthers; 5 Austin Buchanan; 6 Pat Walker; 7 Dean Lawford; 8 Andy Hobson; 9 Liam Finn; 10 Dominic Maloney; 11 Martin Robinson; 12 Alex Bretherton; 13 Josh Weeden. Subs (all used): 14 Luke Haigh; 15 Rob Kelly; 16 Joe Helme; 17 Liam Crawley.
Tries: Buchanan (37), Crouthers (44);
Goals: Finn 1/1, Lawford 1/1.
Rugby Leaguer & League Express Men of the Match:
Vikings: Joel Penny; *Rams:* Ian Preece.
Penalty count: 9-13; **Half-time:** 24-6;
Referee: Leon Williamson; **Attendance:** 2,853.

WEEK 16

Thursday 16th August 2007

WIDNES VIKINGS 18 CASTLEFORD TIGERS 24

VIKINGS: 1 Scott Grix; 2 Damien Blanch; 3 Toa Kohe-Love; 4 Mick Nanyn; 5 Dean Gaskell; 6 Dennis Moran; 7 Joel Penny; 8 Mick Cassidy; 9 Mark Smith; 10 Oliver Wilkes; 11 Lee Doran; 12 Paul Noone; 13 Bob Beswick. Subs (all used): 14 Aaron Summers; 15 Jordan James; 16 Ian Webster; 17 Gavin Dodd.
Tries: Nanyn (5), Kohe-Love (40), Dodd (77);
Goals: Nanyn 3/4.
Sin bin: Moran (41) - late challenge on Brough.
TIGERS: 1 Stuart Donlan; 5 Michael Wainwright; 4 Kirk Dixon; 3 Michael Shenton; 2 Danny Williams; 6 Anthony Thackeray; 7 Danny Brough; 8 Liam Higgins; 9 Andrew Henderson; 10 Mark Leafa; 11 Awen Guttenbeil; 12 Chris Charles; 13 Ryan Clayton. Subs (all used): 14 Joe Westerman; 15 Ryan Boyle; 16 Tere Glassie; 17 Peter Lupton.
Tries: Williams (27), Wainwright (37), Dixon (57);
Goals: Brough 6/7.
Sin bin: Higgins (72) - holding down.
Rugby Leaguer & League Express Men of the Match:
Vikings: Paul Noone; *Tigers:* Danny Brough.
Penalty count: 11-9; **Half-time:** 10-14;
Referee: Ashley Klein; **Attendance:** 4,598.

Sunday 19th August 2007

DEWSBURY RAMS 16 SHEFFIELD EAGLES 10

RAMS: 1 Ian Preece; 2 Bryn Powell; 3 Chris Hall; 4 Danny Maun; 5 Austin Buchanan; 6 Pat Walker; 7 Dean Lawford; 8 Andy Hobson; 9 Liam Finn; 10 Joe Helme; 11 Kevin Crouthers; 12 Alex Bretherton; 13 Josh Weeden. Subs (all used): 14 Luke Haigh; 15 Rob Kelly; 16 Liam Crawley; 17 Keegan Hirst.
Tries: Finn (57), Maun (69); **Goals:** Finn 4/5.
EAGLES: 1 Johnny Woodcock; 2 Danny Mills; 3 James Ford; 4 Damien Reid; 5 Rob Worrincy; 6 Brendon Lindsay; 7 Gavin Brown; 8 Jack Howieson; 9 Paul Pickering; 10 Mitchell Stringer; 11 Dale Holdstock; 12 Ged Corcoran; 13 Adam Hayes. Subs (all used): 14 Dominic Brambani; 15 Tommy Trayler; 16 Richard Newlove; 17 Craig Brown.
Tries: Ford (36), Worrincy (43); **Goals:** Woodcock 1/2.
Rugby Leaguer & League Express Men of the Match:
Rams: Liam Finn; *Eagles:* Ged Corcoran.
Penalty count: 10-8; **Half-time:** 4-4;
Referee: Mike Dawber; **Attendance:** 1,009.

HALIFAX 48 BATLEY BULLDOGS 20

HALIFAX: 1 Shad Royston; 2 Damian Gibson; 3 James Haley; 4 Richard Varkulis; 5 Lee Greenwood; 6 Graham Holroyd; 7 Sean Penkywicz; 8 Paul Southern; 9 Sam Hoare; 10 David Wrench; 11 David Larder; 12 Damian Ball; 13 Paul Smith. Subs (all used): 14 Ian Watson; 15 Mark Roberts; 16 Aaron Trinder; 17 Frank Watene.
Tries: Gibson (7), Greenwood (16, 22), Varkulis (39, 56), Haley (45), Holroyd (64, 73), Royston (79); **Goals:** Holroyd 6/9.
BULLDOGS: 1 Jamie Stokes; 2 Ashley Lindsay; 3 Craig Farrell; 4 Mark Barlow; 5 Oliver Marns; 6 Richard Colley; 7 Francis Maloney; 8 Andy Jarrett; 9 Kris Lythe; 10 Luke

Stenchion; 11 Tommy Gallagher; 12 Tim Spears; 13 Lee Paterson. Subs (all used): 14 Mark Toohey; 15 Chris Langley; 16 Jack Watson; 17 Anthony Thewliss.
Tries: Langley (33, 48, 76), Marns (59);
Goals: Maloney 1/3, Langley 1/1.
Rugby Leaguer & League Express Men of the Match:
Halifax: Shad Royston; *Bulldogs:* Chris Langley.
Penalty count: 10-9; **Half-time:** 18-4;
Referee: Gareth Hewer; **Attendance:** 1,550.

LEIGH CENTURIONS 34 DONCASTER 14

CENTURIONS: 1 Miles Greenwood; 2 Leroy Rivett; 3 David Alstead; 4 Anthony Stewart; 5 Danny Halliwell; 6 Martin Ainscough; 7 Aaron Heremaia; 8 Matt Astley; 9 Dave McConnell; 10 Dana Wilson; 11 Damien Couturier; 12 Mailangi Styles; 13 James Taylor. Subs (all used): 16 John Clough; 15 Daryl Kay; 16 Sean Richardson; 17 Sebastien Martins.
Tries: Stewart (4), Greenwood (8, 47), Styles (24), Alstead (40, 50, 57);
Goals: Couturier 2/4, Halliwell 1/2, Heremaia 0/1.
DONCASTER: 1 Damian Munro; 2 Joe Brown; 3 Paul Anderson; 4 Lee Forth; 5 Darren Woods; 6 Chris Forster; 7 Andy Speake; 8 Tommy Hodgkinson; 9 Luke Gale; 10 Ayden Faal; 11 Mark Castle; 12 Craig Lawton; 13 Shaun Leaf. Subs (all used): 14 Luke Burgess; 15 Peter Green; 16 Gary Richardson; 17 Alex Benson.
Tries: Munro (32), Forster (70), Woods (80);
Goals: Gale 0/2, Forster 1/1.
Dismissal: Richardson (66) - dissent.
Sin bin: Munro (12) - holding down;
Richardson (66) - interference.
Rugby Leaguer & League Express Men of the Match:
Centurions: Mailangi Styles; *Doncaster:* Chris Forster.
Penalty count: 15-8; **Half-time:** 20-4;
Referee: Jamie Leahy; **Attendance:** 1,093.

ROCHDALE HORNETS 12 WHITEHAVEN 28

HORNETS: 1 Brad Attwood; 2 Eric Andrews; 3 Iain Marsh; 4 Mark McCully; 5 Chris Campbell; 6 Simon Svabic; 7 Gareth Barber; 8 Ryan Benjafield; 9 Wayne Corcoran; 10 Byron Smith; 11 Andy Gorski; 12 Scott Law; 13 Tommy Goulden. Subs (all used): 14 Eric Johnson; 15 Mark Blanchard; 16 Dave Cunliffe; 17 Jode Sheriffe.
Tries: McCully (12), Andrews (36); **Goals:** McCully 2/2.
WHITEHAVEN: 1 Gary Broadbent; 2 Craig Calvert; 3 David Seeds; 4 Rob Jackson; 5 Steve Maden; 6 Leroy Joe; 7 John Duffy; 8 Steve Trindall; 9 Carl Sice; 10 David Fatialofa; 11 Spencer Miller; 12 Richard Fletcher; 13 Carl Rudd. Subs (all used): 14 Scott McAvoy; 15 Aaron Smith; 16 Howard Hill; 17 Steve Trindall.
Tries: Rudd (2), Fletcher (17), Calvert (28),
S McAvoy (60), Sice (64); **Goals:** Rudd 4/5.
Rugby Leaguer & League Express Men of the Match:
Hornets: Tommy Goulden; *Whitehaven:* Craig Calvert.
Penalty count: 5-7; **Half-time:** 12-16;
Referee: Robert Hicks; **Attendance:** 555.

WEEK 17

Friday 31st August 2007

SHEFFIELD EAGLES 16 HALIFAX 24

EAGLES: 1 Johnny Woodcock; 2 Danny Mills; 3 James Ford; 4 Damien Reid; 5 Rob Worrincy; 6 Brendon Lindsay; 7 Gavin Brown; 8 Jack Howieson; 9 Craig Cook; 10 Mitchell Stringer; 11 Dale Holdstock; 12 Ged Corcoran; 13 Adam Hayes. Subs (all used): 14 Dominic Brambani; 15 Nick Turnbull; 16 Richard Newlove; 17 Tom Buckenham.
Tries: Stringer (8), Woodcock (65); **Goals:** Woodcock 4/4.
HALIFAX: 1 Shad Royston; 2 Damian Gibson; 3 James Haley; 4 Richard Varkulis; 5 Lee Greenwood; 6 Graham Holroyd; 7 Sean Penkywicz; 8 Paul Southern; 9 Sam

Hoare; 10 David Wrench; 11 David Larder; 12 Paul Smith; 13 Phil Joseph. Subs (all used): 14 Ian Watson; 15 Mark Roberts; 16 Aaron Trinder; 17 Frank Watene.
Tries: Varkulis (31, 72), Penkywicz (75), Trinder (80);
Goals: Holroyd 4/4.
Sin bin: Southern (58) – punching.
Rugby Leaguer & League Express Men of the Match:
Eagles: Mitchell Stringer; *Halifax:* Richard Varkulis.
Penalty count: 7-9; **Half-time:** 6-6;
Referee: James Child; **Attendance:** 864.

Sunday 2nd September 2007

BATLEY BULLDOGS 30 ROCHDALE HORNETS 16

BULLDOGS: 1 Ashley Lindsay; 2 Jamie Stokes; 3 Craig Farrell; 4 Chris Langley; 5 Oliver Marns; 6 Mark Toohey; 7 Francis Maloney; 8 Luke Menzies; 9 Kris Lythe; 10 Luke Stenchion; 11 Tommy Gallagher; 12 Tim Spears; 13 Lee Paterson. Subs (all used): 14 Richard Colley; 15 Andy Jarrett; 16 Anthony Henderson; 17 Jon Simpson.
Tries: Langley (28, 54), Stokes (43), Toohey (67), Stenchion (72); **Goals:** Maloney 5/5.
Sin bin: T Gallagher (62) - fighting.
HORNETS: 1 Gary Hulse; 2 Eric Andrews; 3 Iain Marsh; 4 Mark McCully; 5 Chris Campbell; 6 Simon Svabic; 7 Phil Hasty; 8 Rob Ball; 9 Wayne Corcoran; 10 Ryan Benjafield; 11 Dave Cunliffe; 12 Scott Law; 13 Tommy Goulden. Subs (all used): 14 Gareth Barber; 15 Byron Smith; 16 Craig Robinson; 17 Andy Bailey.
Tries: Campbell (64), McCully (78), Hasty (80);
Goals: McCully 2/3.
Sin bin: Hasty (34) - high tackle;
Benjafield (61) - fighting.
Rugby Leaguer & League Express Men of the Match:
Bulldogs: Mark Toohey; *Hornets:* Mark McCully.
Penalty count: 10-6; **Half-time:** 6-0;
Referee: Gareth Hewer; **Attendance:** 532.

DONCASTER 51 DEWSBURY RAMS 18

DONCASTER: 1 Damian Munro; 2 Darren Woods; 3 Shaun Leaf; 4 Lee Forth; 5 Joe Brown; 6 Chris Forster; 7 Luke Gale; 8 Tommy Hodgkinson; 9 Chris Buttery; 10 Luke Burgess; 11 Mark Castle; 12 Craig Lawton; 13 Peter Green. Subs (all used): 14 Andy Speake; 15 Sean Johnson; 16 Alex Benson; 17 Chris Lythe.
Tries: Woods (3), Lawton (8), Munro (30), Buttery (34), Hodgkinson (50), Forster (65), Johnson (70), Gale (75);
Goals: Gale 8/9, Castle 1/1; **Field goal:** Gale (69).
RAMS: 1 Ian Preece; 2 Bryn Powell; 3 Chris Hall; 4 Danny Maun; 5 Austin Buchanan; 6 Pat Walker; 7 Dean Lawford; 8 Andy Hobson; 9 Liam Finn; 10 Joe Helme; 11 Kevin Crouthers; 12 Alex Bretherton; 13 Josh Weeden. Subs (all used): 14 Luke Haigh; 15 Martin Robinson; 16 Liam Crawley; 17 Keegan Hirst.
Tries: Powell (9, 42), Hall (37); **Goals:** Finn 3/4.
Rugby Leaguer & League Express Men of the Match:
Doncaster: Shaun Leaf; *Rams:* Bryn Powell.
Penalty count: 10-9; **Half-time:** 26-12;
Referee: Robert Hicks; **Attendance:** 1,130.

WHITEHAVEN 18 WIDNES VIKINGS 22

WHITEHAVEN: 1 Gary Broadbent; 2 Craig Calvert; 3 David Seeds; 4 Rob Jackson; 5 Steve Maden; 6 Leroy Joe; 7 Carl Rudd; 8 Steve Trindall; 9 Aaron Smith; 10 David Fatialofa; 11 Simon Baldwin; 12 Richard Fletcher; 13 Scott McAvoy. Subs (all used): 14 Carl Sice; 15 Howard Hill; 16 Marc Jackson; 17 Ricky Wright.
Tries: Maden (12), Rudd (44), Calvert (55);
Goals: Rudd 3/3.
Sin bin: Fletcher (63) - holding down.
VIKINGS: 1 Scott Grix; 2 Damien Blanch; 3 Toa Kohe-Love; 4 Mick Nanyn; 5 Gavin Dodd; 6 Dennis Moran; 7 Joel Penny; 8 Aaron Summers; 9 Mark Smith; 10 Oliver Wilkes; 11 Joel Tomkins; 12 Paul Noone; 13 Bob Beswick. Subs (all used): 14 Mick Cassidy; 15 Jordan

Whitehaven's Craig Calvert beats Widnes' Toa Kohe-Love and Damien Blanch to score

Sheffield's Damien Reid crashes over for a try, as the Eagles secure a play-off place with victory against Whitehaven

James; 16 Ian Webster; 17 Lee Doran.
Tries: Grix (3), Blanch (6), Dodd (31, 49);
Goals: Nanyn 3/5.
Sin bin: Summers (65) - holding down;
Beswick (74) - late tackle on Rudd.
Rugby Leaguer & League Express Men of the Match:
Whitehaven: Aaron Smith; *Vikings:* Dennis Moran.
Penalty count: 13-12; **Half-time:** 6-16;
Referee: Peter Taberner; **Attendance:** 2,360.

CASTLEFORD TIGERS 62 LEIGH CENTURIONS 10

TIGERS: 1 Stuart Donlan; 2 Danny Williams; 3 Michael
Shenton; 4 Kirk Dixon; 5 Michael Wainwright; 6 Anthony
Thackeray; 7 Danny Brough; 8 Liam Higgins; 9 Andrew
Henderson; 10 Mark Leafa; 11 Tere Glassie; 12 Ryan
Clayton; 13 Peter Lupton. Subs: 14 Joe Westerman; 15
Dwayne Barker; 16 Awen Guttenbeil (not used); 17 Ryan
Boyle.
Tries: Dixon (2), Glassie (14), Thackeray (22, 53, 60, 76),
Donlan (44), Westerman (58, 64), Williams (71),
Wainwright (79); **Goals:** Brough 8/10, Dixon 1/1.
CENTURIONS: 1 Chris Giles; 2 Leroy Rivett; 3 Danny
Halliwell; 4 David Alstead; 5 Miles Greenwood; 6 Chris
Hough; 7 Aaron Heremaia; 8 Matt Astley; 9 Dave
McConnell; 10 Damien Couturier; 11 Damien Couturier; 12
Mailangi Styles; 13 James Taylor. Subs (all used): 14
John Clough; 15 Adam Rudd; 16 Daryl Kay; 17
Sebastien Martins.
Tries: Halliwell (31), Alstead (39); **Goals:** Halliwell 1/2.
Rugby Leaguer & League Express Men of the Match:
Tigers: Anthony Thackeray; *Centurions:* Aaron Heremaia.
Penalty count: 11-2; **Half-time:** 16-10;
Referee: Jamie Leahy; **Attendance:** 5,525.

WEEK 18

Thursday 6th September 2007

SHEFFIELD EAGLES 26 WHITEHAVEN 14

EAGLES: 1 Johnny Woodcock; 2 Richard Newlove; 3
James Ford; 4 Damien Reid; 5 Danny Mills; 6 Brendon
Lindsay; 7 Gavin Brown; 8 Jack Howieson; 9 Craig Cook;
10 Mitchell Stringer; 11 Dale Holdstock; 12 Ged
Corcoran; 13 Adam Hayes. Subs (all used): 14 Dominic
Brambani; 15 Nick Turnbull; 16 Tommy Trayler; 17 Tom
Buckenham.
Tries: Corcoran (21), G Brown (43), Reid (51),
Mills (79); **Goals:** Woodcock 5/6.
WHITEHAVEN: 1 Gary Broadbent; 2 Craig Calvert; 3
David Seeds; 4 Scott McAvoy; 5 Derry Eilbeck; 6 Leroy
Joe; 7 Carl Rudd; 8 Steve Trindall; 9 Graeme Mattinson;
10 David Fatialofa; 11 Simon Baldwin; 12 Richard

Fletcher; 13 Spencer Miller. Subs (all used): 14 Carl
Sice; 15 Howard Hill; 16 Scott Teare; 17 Ricky Wright.
Tries: Rudd (13), Broadbent (70); **Goals:** Rudd 3/3.
Rugby Leaguer & League Express Men of the Match:
Eagles: Johnny Woodcock; *Whitehaven:* Carl Rudd.
Penalty count: 5-3; **Half-time:** 8-8;
Referee: Ronnie Laughton; **Attendance:** 1,045.

Sunday 9th September 2007

BATLEY BULLDOGS 18 WIDNES VIKINGS 34

BULLDOGS: 1 Jamie Stokes; 2 Ashley Lindsay; 3 Craig
Farrell; 4 Chris Langley; 5 Oliver Marns; 6 Mark Toohey;
7 Richard Colley; 8 Andy Jarrett; 9 Kris Lythe; 10 Luke
Stenchion; 11 Tommy Gallagher; 12 Tim Spears; 13 Lee
Paterson. Subs (all used): 14 Mark Barlow; 15 Craig
Lingard; 16 Anthony Thewliss; 17 Jon Simpson.
Tries: C Farrell (11), Lingard (42), Lindsay (72),
Paterson (80); **Goals:** C Farrell 1/1, Paterson 0/3.
VIKINGS: 1 Gavin Dodd; 2 Damien Blanch; 3 Andy Kirk;
4 Mick Nanyn; 5 Dean Gaskell; 6 Scott Grix; 7 Joel
Penny; 8 Aaron Summers; 9 Mark Smith; 10 Oliver
Wilkes; 11 Joel Tomkins; 12 Paul Noone; 13 Bob
Beswick. Subs (all used): 14 Mick Cassidy; 15 Jordan
James; 16 Richard Myler; 17 Lee Doran.
Tries: Nanyn (14), Tomkins (24), Penny (34, 65).
Doran (51), Wilkes (56); **Goals:** Nanyn 5/6.
Rugby Leaguer & League Express Men of the Match:
Bulldogs: Ashley Lindsay; *Vikings:* Joel Penny.
Penalty count: 3-6; **Half-time:** 4-16;
Referee: Mike Dawber; **Attendance:** 1,139.

HALIFAX 52 DONCASTER 24

HALIFAX: 1 Shad Royston; 2 Lee Patterson; 3 James
Haley; 4 Richard Varkulis; 5 Lee Greenwood; 6 Graham
Holroyd; 7 Ian Watson; 8 Paul Southern; 9 Sean
Penkywicz; 10 David Wrench; 11 David Larder; 12 Danny
Heaton; 13 Damian Ball. Subs (all used): 14 Mick Govin;
15 Aaron Trinder; 16 Phil Joseph; 17 Frank Watene.
Tries: Larder (9), Holroyd (11, 41), Varkulis (26),
Penkywicz (34), Haley (54), Joseph (55), Watson (56),
Royston (76); **Goals:** Holroyd 7/8, Watson 1/1.
DONCASTER: 1 Damian Munro; 2 Darren Woods; 3
Shaun Leaf; 4 Simon Worrall; 5 Wayne Green; 6 Chris
Forster; 7 Luke Gale; 8 Tommy Hodgkinson; 9 Chris
Buttery; 10 Luke Burgess; 11 Mark Castle; 12 Craig
Lawton; 13 Peter Green. Subs (all used): 14 Andy Speake;
15 Sean Johnson; 16 Alex Benson; 17 Chris Lythe.
Tries: Benson (28), Lythe (32), W Green (51),
Munro (65); **Goals:** Forster 3/3, Speake 1/1.
Rugby Leaguer & League Express Men of the Match:
Halifax: Lee Greenwood; *Doncaster:* Damian Munro.
Penalty count: 7-4; **Half-time:** 22-12;
Referee: Peter Taberner; **Attendance:** 1,905.

LEIGH CENTURIONS 42 DEWSBURY RAMS 0

CENTURIONS: 1 Chris Giles; 2 Leroy Rivett; 3 David
Alstead; 4 Anthony Stewart; 5 Miles Greenwood; 6 Chris
Hough; 7 Aaron Heremaia; 8 Matt Astley; 9 Dave
McConnell; 10 Dana Wilson; 11 Damien Couturier; 12
Mailangi Styles; 13 James Taylor. Subs (all used): 14
Adam Rudd; 15 Daryl Kay; 16 Chris Hill; 17 Sebastien
Martins.
Tries: Rivett (3, 71), Greenwood (6), Kay (21),
Giles (39, 58), Stewart (62), Martins (80);
Goals: Couturier 4/5, Heremaia 1/2, Hough 0/2.
Sin bin: Styles (67) - fighting.
On report: Brawl (67).
RAMS: 1 Ian Preece; 2 Bryn Powell; 3 Chris Hall; 4
Danny Maun; 5 Austin Buchanan; 6 Josh Weeden; 7
Dean Lawford; 8 Andy Hobson; 9 Liam Finn; 10 Joe
Helme; 11 Kevin Crouthers; 12 Martin Robinson; 13 Alex
Bretherton. Subs (all used): 14 Luke Haigh; 15 Rob
Kelly; 16 Jake Wilson; 17 Keegan Hirst.
Dismissal: Helme (79) - high tackle on Martins.
Sin bin: Hobson (64) - high tackle;
Crouthers (67) - fighting.
On report: Brawl (67).
Rugby Leaguer & League Express Men of the Match:
Centurions: Anthony Stewart; *Rams:* Kevin Crouthers.
Penalty count: 10-6; **Half-time:** 24-0;
Referee: Ronnie Laughton; **Attendance:** 1,359.

ROCHDALE HORNETS 0 CASTLEFORD TIGERS 106

HORNETS: 1 Brad Attwood; 2 Eric Andrews; 3 Iain
Marsh; 4 Mark McCully; 5 Chris Campbell; 6 Gareth
Barber; 7 Phil Hasty; 8 Rob Ball; 9 Wayne Corcoran; 10
Byron Smith; 11 Mark Blanchard; 12 Scott Law; 13 Dave
Cunliffe. Subs (all used): 14 Gary Hulse; 15 Andy Bailey;
16 Craig Robinson; 17 Ryan Benjafield.
Sin bin: Hasty (20) - holding down;
Smith (44) - holding down.
TIGERS: 1 Stuart Donlan; 2 Danny Williams; 3 Michael
Shenton; 4 Kirk Dixon; 5 Michael Wainwright; 6 Anthony
Thackeray; 7 Danny Brough; 8 Liam Higgins; 9 Andrew
Henderson; 10 Chris Charles; 11 Awen Guttenbeil; 12
Ryan Clayton; 13 Peter Lupton. Subs (all used): 14 Joe
Westerman; 15 Dwayne Barker; 16 Mark Leafa; 17 Ryan
Boyle.
Tries: M Shenton (3, 18, 32), Brough (9, 36),
Henderson (16, 51, 80), Leafa (23, 25), Guttenbeil (30),
Williams (41, 53, 76), Donlan (43), Boyle (46),
Thackeray (62), Westerman (67), Clayton (80);
Goals: Dixon 3/5, Brough 11/12, Charles 1/2.
Rugby Leaguer & League Express Men of the Match:
Hornets: Wayne Corcoran; *Tigers:* Andrew Henderson.
Penalty count: 1-7; **Half-time:** 0-50;
Referee: Craig Halloran; **Attendance:** 2,506.

No stopping Shad Royston as Halifax defeat Whitehaven in the Elimination Semi-final

PLAY-OFFS

ELIMINATION PLAY-OFFS

Thursday 13th September 2007

WHITEHAVEN 19 LEIGH CENTURIONS 6

WHITEHAVEN: 1 Gary Broadbent; 2 Craig Calvert; 3 David Seeds; 4 Rob Jackson; 5 Steve Maden; 6 Leroy Joe; 7 Carl Rudd; 8 Steve Trindall; 9 Graeme Mattinson; 10 David Fatialofa; 11 Richard Fletcher; 12 Spencer Miller; 13 Scott McAvoy. Subs (all used): 14 Carl Sice; 15 Howard Hill; 16 Marc Jackson; 17 Simon Baldwin.
Tries: Calvert (7), Rudd (34, 54), Seeds (40);
Goals: Rudd 1/5; **Field goal:** Rudd (70).
On report: Trindall (67) - high tackle on McConnell.
CENTURIONS: 1 Chris Giles; 2 Leroy Rivett; 3 David Alstead; 4 Anthony Stewart; 5 Miles Greenwood; 6 Chris Hough; 7 Aaron Heremaia; 8 Matt Astley; 9 Dave McConnell; 10 Dana Wilson; 11 Adam Rudd; 12 Mailangi Styles; 13 James Taylor. Subs (all used): 14 Danny Halliwell; 15 Daryl Kay; 16 Chris Hill; 17 Sebastien Martins.
Try: Hough (27); **Goals:** Heremaia 1/1.
On report: Rivett (51) - punching.
Rugby Leaguer & League Express Men of the Match:
Whitehaven: David Seeds; *Centurions:* Sebastien Martins.
Penalty count: 7-6; **Half-time:** 14-6.
Referee: Ian Smith; **Attendance:** 1,761.

Sunday 16th September 2007

HALIFAX 30 SHEFFIELD EAGLES 26

HALIFAX: 1 Shad Royston; 2 Damian Gibson; 3 Mark Roberts; 4 Richard Varkulis; 5 Lee Greenwood; 6 Graham Holroyd; 7 Sean Penkywicz; 8 Paul Southern; 9 Sam Hoare; 10 David Wrench; 11 David Larder; 12 Paul Smith; 13 Phil Joseph. Subs (all used): 14 Ian Watson; 15 Damian Ball; 16 Aaron Trinder; 17 Frank Watene.
Tries: Royston (2, 61), Penkywicz (32), Trinder (36), Smith (42); **Goals:** Holroyd 5/6.
EAGLES: 1 Johnny Woodcock; 2 Danny Mills; 3 James Ford; 4 Damien Reid; 5 Rob Worrincy; 6 Brendon Lindsay; 7 Dominic Brambani; 8 Jack Howieson; 9 Craig Cook; 10 Mitchell Stringer; 11 Dale Holdstock; 12 Ged Corcoran; 13 Adam Hayes. Subs (all used): 14 Richard Newlove; 15 Nick Turnbull; 16 Tommy Trayler; 17 Tom Buckenham.
Tries: Ford (7, 54), Brambani (20), Newlove (24), Worrincy (77); **Goals:** Woodcock 3/6.
On report: Newlove (31) - alleged high tackle on Royston.
Rugby Leaguer & League Express Men of the Match:
Halifax: Sean Penkywicz; *Eagles:* Rob Worrincy.
Penalty count: 9-6; **Half-time:** 18-16.
Referee: Mike Dawber; **Attendance:** 1,711.

QUALIFYING SEMI-FINAL

Thursday 20th September 2007

CASTLEFORD TIGERS 26 WIDNES VIKING 8

TIGERS: 1 Stuart Donlan; 5 Michael Wainwright; 4 Kirk Dixon; 3 Michael Shenton; 2 Danny Williams; 6 Anthony Thackeray; 7 Danny Brough; 8 Liam Higgins; 9 Andrew Henderson; 10 Ryan Clayton; 11 Awen Guttenbeil; 12 Joe Westerman; 13 Peter Lupton. Subs (all used): 14 Ryan McGoldrick; 15 Chris Charles; 16 Ryan Boyle; 17 Mark Leafa.
Tries: Wainwright (54), Williams (61).
Westerman (64, 68), **Goals:** Brough 5/5, Dixon 0/1.
VIKINGS: 1 Scott Grix; 2 Damien Blanch; 3 Toa Kohe-Love; 4 Mick Nanyn; 5 Gavin Dodd; 6 Dennis Moran; 7 Ian Webster; 8 Aaron Summers; 9 Mark Smith; 10 Oliver Wilkes; 11 Joel Tomkins; 12 Paul Noone; 13 Bob Beswick. Subs (all used): 14 Mick Cassidy; 15 Jordan James; 16 Adam Sidlow; 17 Lee Doran.
Try: Nanyn (48); **Goals:** Nanyn 2/3.
Rugby Leaguer & League Express Men of the Match:
Tigers: Stuart Donlan; *Vikings:* Mark Smith.
Penalty count: 8-6; **Half-time:** 4-4;
Referee: Richard Silverwood; **Attendance:** 6,179.

ELIMINATION SEMI-FINAL

Sunday 23rd September 2007

HALIFAX 32 WHITEHAVEN 24

HALIFAX: 1 Shad Royston; 2 Damian Gibson; 3 Mark Roberts; 4 Richard Varkulis; 5 Lee Greenwood; 6 Graham Holroyd; 7 Ian Watson; 8 Paul Southern; 9 Sam Hoare; 10 David Wrench; 11 David Larder; 12 Paul Smith; 13 Phil Joseph. Subs (all used): 14 Sean Penkywicz; 15 Damian Ball; 16 Aaron Trinder; 17 Frank Watene.
Tries: Larder (29), Royston (32), Trinder (39), Varkulis (54), Ball (63); **Goals:** Holroyd 6/7.
WHITEHAVEN: 1 Gary Broadbent; 2 Craig Calvert; 3 David Seeds; 4 Rob Jackson; 5 Steve Maden; 6 Leroy Joe; 7 Carl Rudd; 8 Steve Trindall; 9 Graeme Mattinson; 10 David Fatialofa; 11 Spencer Miller; 12 Richard Fletcher; 13 Scott McAvoy. Subs (all used): 14 Carl Sice; 15 Howard Hill; 16 Marc Jackson; 17 Ricky Wright.
Tries: Calvert (35, 48), Rudd (42), Fatialofa (71);
Goals: Rudd 4/5.
Rugby Leaguer & League Express Men of the Match:
Halifax: Graham Holroyd; *Whitehaven:* Carl Rudd.
Penalty count: 9-4; **Half-time:** 18-6.
Referee: Phil Bentham; **Attendance:** 2,184.

FINAL ELIMINATOR

Thursday 27th September 2007

WIDNES VIKINGS 36 HALIFAX 24

VIKINGS: 1 Scott Grix; 2 Damien Blanch; 3 Toa Kohe-Love; 4 Mick Nanyn; 5 Gavin Dodd; 6 Dennis Moran; 7 Joel Penny; 8 Mick Cassidy; 9 Mark Smith; 10 Oliver Wilkes; 11 Joel Tomkins; 12 Paul Noone; 13 Bob Beswick. Subs (all used): 14 Ian Webster; 15 Jordan James; 16 Adam Sidlow; 17 Lee Doran.
Tries: Noone (27), Smith (46, 50), Grix (66), Beswick (77); **Goals:** Nanyn 8/8.
HALIFAX: 1 Shad Royston; 2 Damian Gibson; 3 Mark Roberts; 4 Richard Varkulis; 5 Lee Greenwood; 6 Graham Holroyd; 7 Ian Watson; 8 Paul Southern; 9 Sean Penkywicz; 10 David Wrench; 11 David Larder; 12 Paul Smith; 13 Phil Joseph. Subs (all used): 14 Sam Hoare; 15 Damian Ball; 16 Aaron Trinder; 17 Frank Watene.
Tries: Roberts (15), Royston (62), Watene (71), Varkulis (73), Hoare (79); **Goals:** Holroyd 2/5.
Rugby Leaguer & League Express Men of the Match:
Vikings: Scott Grix; *Halifax:* Sean Penkywicz.
Penalty count: 6-3; **Half-time:** 12-4.
Referee: Phil Bentham; **Attendance:** 3,347.

GRAND FINAL

Sunday 7th October 2007

CASTLEFORD TIGERS 42 WIDNES VIKINGS 10

TIGERS: 1 Stuart Donlan; 2 Danny Williams; 3 Michael Shenton; 4 Ryan McGoldrick; 5 Kirk Dixon; 6 Anthony Thackeray; 7 Danny Brough; 8 Liam Higgins; 9 Andrew Henderson; 10 Awen Guttenbeil; 11 Joe Westerman; 12 Ryan Clayton; 13 Peter Lupton. Subs (all used): 14 Mark Leafa; 15 Chris Charles; 16 Michael Wainwright; 17 Ryan Boyle.
Tries: Wainwright (20), McGoldrick (29), Guttenbeil (44, 76), M Shenton (52), Westerman (62), Clayton (66);
Goals: Brough 6/9; **Field goals:** Brough (25, 55).
VIKINGS: 1 Scott Grix; 2 Damien Blanch; 3 Toa Kohe-Love; 4 Mick Nanyn; 5 Gavin Dodd; 6 Dennis Moran; 7 Joel Penny; 8 Mick Cassidy; 9 Mark Smith; 10 Oliver Wilkes; 11 Joel Tomkins; 12 Paul Noone; 13 Bob Beswick. Subs (all used): 14 Aaron Summers; 15 Jordan James; 16 Ian Webster; 17 Lee Doran.
Tries: Nanyn (35), Wilkes (69); **Goals:** Nanyn 1/2.
Rugby Leaguer & League Express Men of the Match:
Tigers: Danny Brough; *Vikings:* Scott Grix.
Penalty count: 7-2; **Half-time:** 13-4;
Referee: Phil Bentham;
Attendance: 20,814 *(at Headingley Carnegie, Leeds).*

Castleford's Ryan McGoldrick and Widnes' Scott Grix meet head on, as the Tigers clinch a return to Super League

257

NATIONAL LEAGUE TWO 2007
Club by Club

BARROW RAIDERS

DATE	FIXTURE	RESULT	SCORERS	LGE	ATT
9/2/07	Blackpool (h) (NLC)	W44-4	t:Beach(3),Nixon(2),Sanderson,Ganley,Ellis g:Holt(4),Sanderson(2)	1st(NLC-G5)	975
18/2/07	Workington (a) (NLC)	L32-24	t:Ellis,Wilcock,McDermott,Harrison g:Sanderson(4)	2nd(NLC-G5)	927
25/2/07	Whitehaven (a) (NLC)	D22-22	t:Atkinson,Marshall,L Finch,Nixon g:Atkinson(2),Beach	2nd(NLC-G5)	1,537
2/3/07	Workington (h) (NLC)	W36-12	t:Harrison(3),L Finch,Ellis,Atkinson,Nixon,Ganley g:Holt(2)	2nd(NLC-G5)	1,230
11/3/07	West Hull (a) (CCR3)	W18-70	t:McDermott,Holt,Ganley(3),Ellis,Atkinson,Nixon(2),J Finch,Marshall(2) g:Holt(11)	N/A	450
16/3/07	Whitehaven (h) (NLC)	L6-16	t:Atkinson g:Holt	2nd(NLC-G5)	1,669
25/3/07	Blackpool (a) (NLC)	W22-78	t:McDermott(2),Ostler,Ellis,Beach(3),Marshall(4),L Finch(2),Raftrey g:Holt(4),Atkinson(3),Beach(4)	2nd(NLC-G5)	358
1/4/07	Swinton (a) (CCR4)	W14-47	t:Nixon(2),Wilcock,Atkinson,Holt,Ostler,Marshall,Ganley g:Holt(7) fg:Holt	N/A	596
6/4/07	Workington (h)	W46-10	t:Atkinson,McDermott,Ostler,Ellis(2),Ganley(2),Beach g:Holt(7)	1st	1,714
9/4/07	Swinton (a)	W30-35	t:Ganley(2),Atkinson,Basan,Ellis g:Holt(7) fg:Holt	2nd	416
15/4/07	Gateshead (a)	W10-65	t:Atkinson(2),Ellis,Beach(4),Ganley(3),Nixon,Smith g:Holt(8) fg:Weisner	2nd	305
22/4/07	York (a) (NLCQFQ)	W16-18	t:Holt,Basan g:Holt(4) fg:Holt,Weisner	N/A	658
29/4/07	York (h)	W30-10	t:Harrison,Nixon,Beach,Rawlinson,L Finch g:Holt(5)	2nd	1,404
6/5/07	Hunslet (a)	W4-32	t:Ellis,Ganley,Rawlinson,Basan,Harrison,Nixon g:Holt(2),Weisner(2)	1st	393
13/5/07	Warrington (a) (CCR5)	L48-16	t:McDermott,Ganley,Beach g:Beach(2)	N/A	4,184
16/5/07	London Skolars (h)	W38-8	t:Ganley,J Finch,Basan(2),Smith,L Finch,Marshall,Irabor g:Beach(3)	1st	1,045
20/5/07	Oldham (a)	L50-18	t:Nixon,McDermott,Rawlinson g:Weisner(3)	2nd	848
27/5/07	Whitehaven (a) (NLCQF)	L34-14	t:Nixon,J Finch(2) g:Holt	N/A	1,484
3/6/07	Swinton (h)	W52-24	t:Marshall(2),Harrison,Ganley,Whitehead(2),J Finch(2),L Finch g:Holt(8)	3rd	1,188
9/6/07	Celtic Crusaders (a)	L26-14	t:L Finch,Ganley g:Holt(3)	4th	903
13/6/07	Keighley (h)	W30-0	t:Ellis,Weisner,Larkin,Raftrey,Dutton g:Holt(5)	2nd	1,058
17/6/07	Gateshead (h)	W60-22	t:L Finch(3),Atkinson,Harrison(3),Nixon(2),Raftrey,J Finch g:Holt(7),Atkinson	2nd	1,040
24/6/07	Blackpool (a)	W14-28	t:Holt,Smith,Nixon,Weisner,Whitehead g:Holt(4)	2nd	425
1/7/07	Hunslet (h)	W32-22	t:J Finch(2),Holt,Atkinson,Harrison,Ganley g:Holt(4)	2nd	1,252
8/7/07	York (a)	L14-4	g:Holt(2)	2nd	846
15/7/07	Oldham (h)	W34-26	t:Ganley,Rawlinson,J Finch,Whitehead,Smith,Ellis g:Holt(5)	2nd	1,348
21/7/07	Featherstone (a)	L37-28	t:Atkinson,Ganley(3),Weisner g:Holt(4)	3rd	1,557
29/7/07	London Skolars (a)	W18-31	t:Weisner(2),Archer,Ellis(2) g:Holt(5) fg:Weisner	3rd	467
5/8/07	Celtic Crusaders (h)	L24-26	t:J Finch,Whitehead(2),Basan g:Holt(4)	3rd	1,806
12/8/07	Keighley (a)	W4-54	t:Beach(3),Ellis,J Finch,Weisner,Ganley(2),Basan g:Holt(5),Weisner(3),Beach	3rd	658
19/8/07	Workington (a)	W16-28	t:L Finch,Beach(2),Smith,Holt g:Holt(4)	3rd	857
31/8/07	Blackpool (h)	W56-12	t:L Finch,Ganley,Beach(2),Ellis,Marshall(2),J Finch,Raftrey,Harrison g:Holt(8)	3rd	1,065
8/9/07	Featherstone (h)	W30-4	t:Harrison,Beach,Ganley,Weisner,Basan g:Holt(4),Weisner	3rd	1,901
23/9/07	Featherstone (a) (QSF)	L36-20	t:Harrison,Ellis,Dutton,Basan g:Holt(2)	N/A	1,792
30/9/07	Oldham (h) (FE)	L6-28	t:Basan g:Holt	N/A	2,771

	D.O.B.	APP ALL	APP NL2	TRIES ALL	TRIES NL2	GOALS ALL	GOALS NL2	FG ALL	FG NL2	PTS ALL	PTS NL2
Chris Archer	18/9/83	1(11)	1(11)	1	1	0	0	0	0	4	4
Dave Armistead	15/1/84	34	24	0	0	0	0	0	0	0	0
Phil Atkinson	25/9/74	22(3)	13(3)	12	7	6	1	0	0	60	30
Mike Basan	4/9/85	20	16	10	9	0	0	0	0	40	36
Nick Beach	22/1/85	25	14	21	14	11	4	0	0	106	64
Adam Bibey	30/4/86	1(1)	0	0	0	0	0	0	0	0	0
Jamie Butler	29/8/80	2(3)	1(3)	0	0	0	0	0	0	0	0
Lee Dutton	3/11/80	8(24)	7(16)	2	2	0	0	0	0	8	8
Andy Ellis	15/12/84	34	23	17	12	0	0	0	0	68	48
James Finch	9/7/83	21(6)	19(2)	13	10	0	0	0	0	52	40
Liam Finch	19/3/85	28(1)	18(1)	13	9	0	0	0	0	52	36
Khamal Ganley	1/3/80	29	21	27	20	0	0	0	0	108	80
James Gordon	26/6/86	(2)	(2)	0	0	0	0	0	0	0	0
Liam Harrison	3/12/82	35	24	14	10	0	0	0	0	56	40
Darren Holt	21/9/76	31	22	6	3	138	104	3	1	303	221
Anthony Horton	11/9/79	(1)	0	0	0	0	0	0	0	0	0
Shane Irabor	14/1/82	1(5)	1(3)	1	1	0	0	0	0	4	4
Chris Larkin	20/6/86	1	1	1	1	0	0	0	0	4	4
Geoff Luxon	2/6/71	(6)	(2)	0	0	0	0	0	0	0	0
Jamie Marshall	17/7/78	4(20)	4(11)	13	5	0	0	0	0	52	20
Brett McDermott	10/9/78	14(1)	5	7	2	0	0	0	0	28	8
Joe McKenna	21/8/87	(1)	(1)	0	0	0	0	0	0	0	0
James Nixon	10/8/85	25	14	16	7	0	0	0	0	64	28
Lee Norman	13/3/84	1	0	0	0	0	0	0	0	0	0
Martin Ostler	21/6/80	20(3)	12(3)	3	1	0	0	0	0	12	4
Paul Raftrey	26/1/78	25(8)	15(7)	4	3	0	0	0	0	16	12
Ian Rawlinson	22/2/76	(8)	(6)	4	4	0	0	0	0	16	16
Lee Sanderson	16/12/81	1(2)	0	1	0	6	0	0	0	16	0
Michael Smith	10/5/76	21(1)	20(1)	5	5	0	0	0	0	20	20
Pat Weisner	17/3/82	22	20	7	7	9	9	3	2	49	48
Mike Whitehead	25/8/78	26(3)	16(3)	6	6	0	0	0	0	24	24
Paul Wilcock	9/12/79	3(30)	1(21)	2	0	0	0	0	0	8	0

Andy Ellis

LEAGUE RECORD
P22-W17-D0-L5-BP4
(3rd, NL2/Final Eliminator)
F769, A387, Diff+382
55 points.

CHALLENGE CUP
Round Five

NATIONAL LEAGUE CUP
Quarter Finalists/2nd, Group 5

ATTENDANCES
Best - v Oldham (FE - 2,771)
Worst - v Blackpool (NLC - 975)
Total (excluding Challenge Cup) - 21,466
Average (excluding Challenge Cup) - 1,431
(Up by 389 on 2006)

BLACKPOOL PANTHERS

DATE	FIXTURE	RESULT	SCORERS	LGE	ATT
9/2/07	Barrow (a) (NLC)	L44-4	t:Parry	4th(NLC-G5)	975
18/2/07	Whitehaven (h) (NLC)	L18-32	t:Parry,Maye,Patel g:Brand(3)	4th(NLC-G5)	449
25/2/07	Workington (h) (NLC)	L28-34	t:Cantillon(3),Patel,Leigh g:Brand(4)	4th(NLC-G5)	335
4/3/07	Whitehaven (a) (NLC)	L62-0		4th(NLC-G5)	1,004
10/3/07	Pia (h) (CCR3)	L18-42	t:Leigh,Ramsdale,Cantillon(2) g:Brand	N/A	327
18/3/07	Workington (a) (NLC)	L28-20	t:Maye,Cantillon(2),Brown g:Brand(2)	4th(NLC-G5)	464
25/3/07	Barrow (h) (NLC)	L22-78	t:Brown(2),Ratcliffe,Maye g:Brand(3)	4th(NLC-G5)	358
6/4/07	Swinton (h)	L34-40	t:Ramsdale,Patel,Leigh(2),Cantillon,Gambles g:Ramsdale(3),Gambles(2)	7th	332
9/4/07	Celtic Crusaders (a)	L68-0		11th	2,805
15/4/07	Oldham (h)	L20-40	t:Ratcliffe,Hayden,Bannister g:Brand(4)	12th	501
29/4/07	Featherstone (a)	L70-24	t:Gambles(3),Cantillon(2) g:Gambles(2)	12th	754
6/5/07	Keighley (a)	L30-10	t:Maye,Chamberlain g:Brand	12th	628
13/5/07	Workington (h)	L10-52	t:Kilgannon,Barton g:Brand	12th	309
20/5/07	Hunslet (a)	L30-18	t:Gambles,Chamberlain,Cantillon g:Brand(3)	12th	291
27/5/07	York (h)	L12-24	t:Stout g:Brand(2)	12th	306
3/6/07	Gateshead (h)	L18-28	t:Cantillon(2),Maye g:Brand(2),Gambles	12th	275
10/6/07	Featherstone (h)	L0-58		12th	485
16/6/07	London Skolars (a)	L28-14	t:Gambles,Cantillon g:Brand(3)	12th	413
24/6/07	Barrow (h)	L14-28	t:Duell,Barton,Chamberlain g:Brand	12th	425
1/7/07	Keighley (h)	L10-26	t:C Jones,Cantillon g:Campbell	12th	372
7/7/07	Gateshead (a)	L28-26	t:Alker(2),C Jones,Cantillon g:Campbell(5)	12th	145
15/7/07	Workington (a)	L86-6	t:Smith g:Brand	12th	624
22/7/07	Celtic Crusaders (h)	L8-54	t:C Jones,Barton	12th	276
29/7/07	Hunslet (h)	L22-32	t:Seeds,Dootson,Ratcliffe,Lever g:Gambles(3)	12th	302
5/8/07	Oldham (a)	L46-12	t:Gambles,C Jones g:Gambles(2)	12th	858
12/8/07	Swinton (a)	L70-20	t:Dootson(2),C Jones,Stout g:Gambles(2)	12th	349
19/8/07	London Skolars (h)	L20-34	t:Sloman,Stout(3) g:Gambles(2)	12th	263
31/8/07	Barrow (a)	L56-12	t:Cantillon,Kilgannon g:Gambles(2)	12th	1,065
9/9/07	York (a)	L56-22	t:Stout,Seeds,Kilgannon,C Jones g:Gambles(3)	12th	825

		APP		TRIES		GOALS		FG		PTS	
	D.O.B.	ALL	NL2	ALL	NL2	ALL	NL2	ALL	NL2	ALL	NL2
Melvin Alker	6/3/80	9	9	2	2	0	0	0	0	8	8
Steve Bannister	6/9/88	3	3	1	1	0	0	0	0	4	4
Danny Barton	7/9/83	10(13)	8(10)	3	3	0	0	0	0	12	12
Neil Baynes	14/9/77	(1)	(1)	0	0	0	0	0	0	0	0
Chris Brand	24/11/82	19(1)	12(1)	0	0	31	18	0	0	62	36
Steven Brown	15/10/82	9	3	3	0	0	0	0	0	12	0
Craig Campbell	4/1/77	2	2	0	0	6	6	0	0	12	12
Phil Cantillon	2/6/76	29	22	17	10	0	0	0	0	68	40
Jon Chamberlain	1/5/82	5(15)	3(12)	3	3	0	0	0	0	12	12
Sean Conway	18/3/83	2	2	0	0	0	0	0	0	0	0
Adrian Dootson	22/9/86	7(2)	7(2)	3	3	0	0	0	0	12	12
Deon Duell	3/12/78	26(1)	20	1	1	0	0	0	0	4	4
Martin Gambles	8/3/80	28	21	7	7	19	19	0	0	66	66
Anton Garcia	7/9/79	4	0	0	0	0	0	0	0	0	0
Neil Hayden	25/11/82	7	7	1	1	0	0	0	0	4	4
Simon Holden	12/6/86	4	4	0	0	0	0	0	0	0	0
Carl Jones	20/11/82	11	11	6	6	0	0	0	0	24	24
Gareth Jones	14/10/82	14(9)	13(3)	0	0	0	0	0	0	0	0
Eddie Kilgannon	4/12/77	20(4)	13(4)	3	3	0	0	0	0	12	12
Simon Knox	14/10/72	(2)	(2)	0	0	0	0	0	0	0	0
Rob Lamb	5/2/86	4(12)	2(11)	0	0	0	0	0	0	0	0
Mark Leigh	23/3/84	18	11	4	2	0	0	0	0	16	8
Tom Lever	18/8/86	2	2	1	1	0	0	0	0	4	4
Chris Maye	28/2/84	13(3)	7(2)	5	2	0	0	0	0	20	8
Ryan Millington	14/1/87	(1)	0	0	0	0	0	0	0	0	0
Danny Morton	20/4/79	(1)	(1)	0	0	0	0	0	0	0	0
Luke Murfin	12/2/87	6(5)	6(1)	0	0	0	0	0	0	0	0
Daniel Palmer	22/3/82	4(9)	(9)	0	0	0	0	0	0	0	0
Ian Parry	2/4/81	3(2)	1(2)	2	0	0	0	0	0	8	0
Safraz Patel	20/10/76	11(7)	5(6)	3	1	0	0	0	0	12	4
Richard Rafferty	12/8/84	1(9)	1(6)	0	0	0	0	0	0	0	0
Chris Ramsdale	25/4/82	6(3)	2	2	1	3	3	0	0	14	10
Kris Ratcliffe	28/5/81	26	21	3	2	0	0	0	0	12	8
Martin Roden	26/12/79	8(2)	8(2)	0	0	0	0	0	0	0	0
Lee Rowley	3/2/83	23(2)	17(1)	0	0	0	0	0	0	0	0
Kieron Seeds	14/5/86	15(1)	15(1)	2	2	0	0	0	0	8	8
James Simon	20/1/87	2(2)	2(2)	0	0	0	0	0	0	0	0
Rob Sloman	10/7/86	3(2)	3(2)	1	1	0	0	0	0	4	4
Gus Smith	21/8/81	(2)	(2)	1	1	0	0	0	0	4	4
Warren Stevens	4/10/78	(1)	(1)	0	0	0	0	0	0	0	0
Mike Stout	6/4/84	17(1)	17(1)	7	7	0	0	0	0	28	28
Tim Street	29/6/68	(1)	(1)	0	0	0	0	0	0	0	0
Matt Strong	17/2/87	3(1)	3(1)	0	0	0	0	0	0	0	0
Craig Waia	10/2/80	3(1)	3(1)	0	0	0	0	0	0	0	0

Phil Cantillon

LEAGUE RECORD
P22-W0-D0-L22-BP6
(12th, NL2)
F332, A984, Diff-652
6 points.

CHALLENGE CUP
Round Three

NATIONAL LEAGUE CUP
4th, Group 5

ATTENDANCES
Best - v Oldham (NL2 - 501)
Worst - v London Skolars (NL2 - 263)
Total (excluding Challenge Cup) - 4,988
Average (excluding Challenge Cup) - 356
(Down by 125 on 2006)

CELTIC CRUSADERS

DATE	FIXTURE	RESULT	SCORERS	LGE	ATT
9/2/07	Widnes (h) (NLC)	L6-56	t:Johnston g:Quinn	4th(NLC-G6)	452
17/2/07	London Skolars (h) (NLC)	W44-28	t:Blackwood(2),Quinn,Duggan(3),Budworth,Van Dijk,Johnston g:Quinn(4)	3rd(NLC-G6)	301
25/2/07	Leigh (a) (NLC)	W22-26	t:Blackwood,Cushion,Duggan(2),Johnston g:Quinn(3)	2nd(NLC-G6)	1,637
4/3/07	London Skolars (a) (NLC)	W4-28	t:G Davies,Quinn,Ballard(2),Richards g:Quinn(4)	2nd(NLC-G6)	289
10/3/07	Eastmoor (h) (CCR3)	W50-10	t:Cale,Ballard(2),Young,Dean,Duggan(2),Richards(2) g:Young(7)	N/A	300
18/3/07	Leigh (h) (NLC)	W22-14	t:Dalle Cort,Toshack,Epton,Ballard g:Quinn(3)	2nd(NLC-G6)	440
25/3/07	Widnes (a) (NLC)	L32-10	t:Duggan(2) g:Quinn	2nd(NLC-G6)	2,540
1/4/07	Rochdale (a) (CCR4)	L20-16	t:Richards,Quinn,Cushion g:Quinn(2)	N/A	482
6/4/07	London Skolars (a)	W18-42	t:Martin,Dean,Richards(2),Ballard,Johnston(2),Fitzgerald g:Quinn(5)	2nd	211
9/4/07	Blackpool (h)	W68-0	t:Toshack(2),Van Dijk,Budworth,Dalle Cort,Richards(4),Johnston(2),Quinn g:Quinn(10)	1st	2,805
15/4/07	Keighley (a)	W12-62	t:Mapp,Fitzgerald,Richards,Duggan(2),Johnston,Toshack(3),Ballard,Budworth g:Quinn(9)	1st	672
21/4/07	Hunslet (a) (NLCQFQ) ●	W14-28	t:Johnston,I'Anson,Duggan(2),Blackwood g:Williams(4)	N/A	222
28/4/07	Swinton (h)	W82-4	t:Dalle Cort(2),Toshack,Martin,Duggan(3),Quinn(4),Richards(2),Blackwood, Van Dijk g:Quinn(11)	1st	823
4/5/07	Oldham (h)	L26-34	t:Van Dijk,Duggan,Blackwood,Quinn,Richards g:Quinn(3)	2nd	3,441
13/5/07	York (a)	W4-26	t:Duggan,Johnston,Dalle Cort,Van Dijk,Blackwood g:Quinn(3)	1st	1,444
20/5/07	Workington (a)	L28-16	t:H Davies,Dalle Cort,Epton g:Quinn(2)	4th	896
26/5/07	Halifax (a) (NLCQF)	L30-18	t:Boothroyd,Epton,Fitzgerald g:Quinn(3)	N/A	1,086
2/6/07	Featherstone (h)	W36-28	t:Cushion,Duggan,Quinn(2),Blackwood,Young g:Quinn(6)	4th	931
9/6/07	Barrow (h)	W26-14	t:Mapp,Budworth,Duggan,Van Dijk,Ballard g:Quinn(3)	2nd	903
17/6/07	Hunslet (a)	L23-16	t:Blackwood,Ballard g:Quinn(4)	4th	324
23/6/07	Workington (h)	W26-12	t:Cale,Ballard(2),Quinn,Duggan g:Quinn(3)	3rd	945
30/6/07	York (h)	W30-16	t:Quinn,Duggan(2),Blackwood(2),Ballard g:Quinn(2),Van Dijk	3rd	702
7/7/07	London Skolars (h)	W50-6	t:Ballard(4),Wyatt,Mapp(2),Duggan,Dalle Cort,Van Dijk g:Van Dijk(5)	3rd	807
15/7/07	Swinton (a)	W20-26	t:Epton,Duggan,Quinn,Wyatt,Dalle Cort g:Van Dijk(3)	3rd	488
22/7/07	Blackpool (a)	W8-54	t:Duggan(3),Johnston(2),Ballard(2),Epton,Quinn g:Van Dijk(9)	2nd	276
26/7/07	Featherstone (a)	W12-32	t:Ballard(2),Quinn,Epton(2) g:Van Dijk(6)	2nd	2,993
5/8/07	Barrow (a)	W24-26	t:Duggan(2),Toshack,Dalle Cort g:Van Dijk(5)	2nd	1,806
11/8/07	Hunslet (h)	W84-10	t:Ballard(3),Dalle Cort(2),Duggan(3),Quinn,Epton,Toshack,I'Anson,Cologni, Young,Mapp g:Van Dijk(10),Quinn(2)	2nd	795
18/8/07	Keighley (h)	W34-12	t:Hannay,Duggan(2),Dalle Cort,Blackwood,Wyatt g:Van Dijk(5)	2nd	801
26/8/07	Gateshead (h)	W64-26	t:Toshack(2),Quinn,Mapp,Duggan,Hannay,Dalle Cort,Budworth(2),Blackwood(2), Young g:Van Dijk(5),Quinn(2),Hannay	1st	827
30/8/07	Oldham (a)	W18-32	t:Ballard(2),Dalle Cort(2),Duggan g:Van Dijk(6)	1st	4,327
9/9/07	Gateshead (a)	W16-60	t:Ballard,Toshack,Quinn(2),Duggan(3),Mapp,Wyatt,Epton,Van Dijk g:Van Dijk(7),Beasley	1st	473

● Played at Tetley's Stadium, Dewsbury

		APP		TRIES		GOALS		FG		PTS	
	D.O.B.	ALL	NL2	ALL	NL2	ALL	NL2	ALL	NL2	ALL	NL2
Paul Ballard	4/9/84	22(4)	16(2)	26	21	0	0	0	0	104	84
Chris Beasley	17/10/83	13(6)	11(6)	0	0	1	1	0	0	2	2
Anthony Blackwood	13/9/82	20	15	14	10	0	0	0	0	56	40
Andy Boothroyd	7/1/85	5(6)	1(5)	1	0	0	0	0	0	4	0
Neil Budworth	10/3/82	26(1)	20	6	5	0	0	0	0	24	20
Tom Burnell	7/3/88	(2)	0	0	0	0	0	0	0	0	0
Josh Cale	4/3/82	17(4)	9(3)	2	1	0	0	0	0	8	4
Aurelien Cologni	11/2/78	(5)	(5)	1	1	0	0	0	0	4	4
Phil Cushion	15/6/78	7(14)	7(7)	3	1	0	0	0	0	12	4
Mark Dalle Cort	19/5/82	30	21	15	14	0	0	0	0	60	56
Geraint Davies	7/3/86	3(2)	(1)	1	0	0	0	0	0	4	0
Hywel Davies	19/12/81	7(23)	4(17)	1	1	0	0	0	0	4	4
Gareth Dean	31/3/81	21(2)	14(1)	2	1	0	0	0	0	8	4
Tony Duggan	29/8/78	28	21	40	29	0	0	0	0	160	116
Grant Epton	5/1/82	15(6)	8(6)	9	7	0	0	0	0	36	28
Dean Fitzgerald	20/12/81	10(8)	2(6)	3	2	0	0	0	0	12	8
Josh Hannay	11/1/80	4	4	2	2	1	1	0	0	10	10
Jamie I'Anson	19/6/87	4(24)	1(18)	2	1	0	0	0	0	8	4
Richard Johnston	26/2/80	15(2)	15(2)	9	8	0	0	0	0	48	32
Lee Jones	10/11/78	(4)	(1)	0	0	0	0	0	0	0	0
Owen Lewis	1/10/80	1(1)	0	0	0	0	0	0	0	0	0
Darren Mapp	8/10/80	24	20	7	7	0	0	0	0	28	28
Terry Martin	25/5/80	16(3)	12(3)	2	2	0	0	0	0	8	8
Damien Quinn	24/8/81	30	22	20	17	86	65	0	0	252	198
Craig Richards	10/10/78	10	5	14	10	0	0	0	0	56	40
Rob Toshack	8/2/80	23(1)	18	12	11	0	0	0	0	48	44
Jace Van Dijk	25/2/81	29	22	8	7	62	62	0	0	156	152
Chris Vitalini	5/5/87	(2)	0	0	0	0	0	0	0	0	0
Lee Williams	19/2/88	2(1)	(1)	0	0	4	0	0	0	8	0
Neale Wyatt	2/2/81	16(2)	14(1)	4	4	0	0	0	0	16	16
Luke Young	31/8/80	18(5)	10(5)	4	3	7	0	0	0	30	12

Tony Duggan

LEAGUE RECORD
P22-W19-D0-L3-BP3
(1st, NL2/Champions)
F918, A345, Diff+573
60 points.

CHALLENGE CUP
Round Four

NATIONAL LEAGUE CUP
Quarter Finalists/2nd, Group 6

ATTENDANCES
Best - v Oldham (NL2 - 3,441)
Worst - v Eastmoor (CC - 300)
Total (excluding Challenge Cup) - 14,973
Average (excluding Challenge Cup) - 1,070
(Up by 399 on 2006)

FEATHERSTONE ROVERS

DATE	FIXTURE	RESULT	SCORERS	LGE	ATT
11/2/07	Sheffield (h) (NLC)	W54-22	t:P Hughes(2),Haughey,Kirmond(2),Ross,Cardoza,McHugh,Whittle,Handforth g:Dickens(6),Handford	1st(NLC-G1)	1,209
18/2/07	Castleford (a) (NLC)	L48-10	t:Ross g:Dickens(3)	2nd(NLC-G1)	6,871
25/2/07	Doncaster (h) (NLC)	W24-22	t:Whittle(2),Bower,McHugh g:Dickens(4)	2nd(NLC-G1)	1,335
4/3/07	Castleford (h) (NLC)	L16-22	t:P Hughes,McHugh,Handforth g:Dickens(2)	2nd(NLC-G1)	3,229
11/3/07	Drighlington (h) (CCR3)	W52-10	t:Field(2),McHugh(2),Dickens,Dooler,Cardoza,Haughey,Ross,Handford g:Dickens(5),Speake	N/A	1,161
18/3/07	Doncaster (a) (NLC)	D18-18	t:Handford,Blakeway,Swinson g:Dickens(2),Ross	2nd(NLC-G1)	1,775
23/3/07	Sheffield (a) (NLC)	L32-8	t:McHugh,Larvin	2nd(NLC-G1)	1,196
31/3/07	Catalans (a) (CCR4)	L70-12	t:Glassell,Dooler g:Dickens,Glassell	N/A	1,545
4/4/07	Oldham (a)	W12-23	t:McHugh,Ross,Haughey(2) g:Ross,Dickens(2) fg:Handford	4th	1,162
9/4/07	Keighley (h)	W36-22	t:Blakeway,Handford,Ward,McHugh,Handforth,Haughey,Larvin g:Glassell(4)	3rd	1,237
15/4/07	Workington (a)	L16-13	t:McHugh,Whittle g:Dickens,Ross fg:P Hughes	3rd	846
22/4/07	Halifax (a) (NLCQFQ)	L76-16	t:Ross,Field,Colton g:Dickens(2)	N/A	1,318
29/4/07	Blackpool (h)	W70-24	t:Kirmond(3),Handforth(2),Cardoza(2),Field,Blakeway,McHugh(2),Whittle,Colton g:Dickens(9)	3rd	754
6/5/07	London Skolars (a)	W6-62	t:Dickens,Whittle,McHugh(2),Handforth,C Hughes,Dooler,Blakeway,Cardoza, Kirmond,Haughey g:Dickens(5),Ross(4)	3rd	382
13/5/07	Hunslet (h)	W36-12	t:Field,Haughey,Whittle,Kirmond,Swinson,Colton,Handforth g:Dickens(4)	2nd	1,008
20/5/07	Gateshead (a)	W16-74	t:Whittle,Colton,Dickens,Tonks,Kirmond(4),Houston,Handforth,Wildbore,Ross, C Hughes g:Dickens(11)	1st	385
27/5/07	Swinton (h)	W42-4	t:Dooler(2),Field,Haughey,Colton(2),Kirmond,P Hughes g:Dickens(5)	1st	1,014
2/6/07	Celtic Crusaders (a)	L36-28	t:Kain(2),Handforth,C Hughes,Haughey g:Dickens(4)	1st	931
10/6/07	Blackpool (a)	W0-58	t:Whittle,McHugh(3),Haughey,Handforth(3),Kain,C Hughes g:Dickens(5),Handforth,Ross(3)	1st	485
17/6/07	Oldham (h)	W24-18	t:Handford,Dickens,C Hughes(2) g:Dickens(4)	1st	1,587
24/6/07	York (a)	W12-46	t:Kain(3),Haughey(2),Handford,Kirmond,Dickens g:Dickens(6),Blakeway	1st	1,924
1/7/07	London Skolars (h)	W30-10	t:Dickens(2),Whittle,Handforth,Kirmond,McHugh g:Dickens(3)	1st	1,160
8/7/07	Keighley (a)	W6-68	t:Kain,Whittle,Wildbore(3),Kirmond(4),C Hughes,Handford,Blakeway,Handforth g:Dickens(7),Handforth	1st	1,101
15/7/07	Gateshead (h)	W30-4	t:Kirmond,Tonks,Blakeway,Adebisi(3) g:Dickens(2),Handforth	1st	1,030
21/7/07	Barrow (h)	W37-28	t:Haughey(2),McHugh(2),Kirmond,Field g:Dickens(6) fg:Handforth	1st	1,557
26/7/07	Celtic Crusaders (h)	L12-32	t:Kirmond,Wildbore g:Dickens,Handforth	1st	2,993
5/8/07	Swinton (a)	W22-28	t:Blakeway(2),C Hughes,Field,McHugh g:Dickens(3),Handforth	1st	603
12/8/07	York (h)	W38-12	t:Kain,Whittle,Haughey,McLocklan,Dickens,Kirmond,Wildbore g:Dickens(5)	1st	1,314
19/8/07	Hunslet (a)	W10-20	t:Haughey,Kain,Blakeway g:Wildbore,Dickens(3)	1st	773
2/9/07	Workington (h)	W40-34	t:Wildbore,Haughey(2),Kirmond,Handforth,Whittle,Adebisi g:Dickens(6)	2nd	1,346
8/9/07	Barrow (a)	L30-4	t:McHugh	2nd	1,901
23/9/07	Barrow (h) (QSF)	W36-20	t:Kirmond(2),Adebisi,Handford,McHugh,Field g:Dickens(6)	N/A	1,792
7/10/07	Oldham (GF) ●	W24-6	t:McHugh(2),Handforth g:Dickens(5) fg:Wildbore(2)	N/A	N/A

● Played at Headingley Carnegie, Leeds

		APP		TRIES		GOALS		FG		PTS	
	D.O.B.	ALL	NL2	ALL	NL2	ALL	NL2	ALL	NL2	ALL	NL2
Ade Adebisi	7/1/86	11	11	5	5	0	0	0	0	20	20
Jamie Benn	4/5/77	2(7)	1(7)	0	0	0	0	0	0	0	0
Richard Blakeway	22/7/83	27(3)	21(2)	9	8	1	1	0	0	38	34
Craig Bower	1/5/80	4(2)	1	1	0	0	0	0	0	4	0
Dale Cardoza	13/7/79	12(1)	6	5	3	0	0	0	0	20	12
Craig Cawthray	19/2/85	(2)	0	0	0	0	0	0	0	0	0
Dean Colton	18/2/83	18(1)	14(1)	6	5	0	0	0	0	24	20
Matty Dale	10/10/86	(4)	(4)	0	0	0	0	0	0	0	0
Stuart Dickens	23/3/80	32(1)	23(1)	8	7	128	103	0	0	288	234
Steve Dooler	31/12/77	15(8)	8(6)	5	3	0	0	0	0	20	12
Gary Ellery	29/6/85	(2)	(1)	0	0	0	0	0	0	0	0
Jamie Field	12/12/76	27	22	9	6	0	0	0	0	36	24
Scott Glassell	14/8/88	3	2	1	0	5	4	0	0	14	8
Gareth Handford	22/4/80	24(5)	17(4)	7	5	0	0	0	0	28	20
Paul Handforth	6/10/81	29	21	16	14	6	5	2	2	78	68
Tom Haughey	30/1/82	29(2)	21(2)	18	16	0	0	0	0	72	64
James Houston	28/12/82	4(23)	2(18)	1	1	0	0	0	0	4	4
Carl Hughes	30/11/82	1(15)	1(14)	8	8	0	0	0	0	32	32
Paul Hughes	28/12/84	22(3)	13(3)	4	1	0	0	1	1	17	5
Andy Kain	1/9/85	16	16	9	9	0	0	0	0	36	36
Danny Kirmond	11/11/85	32	24	25	23	0	0	0	0	100	92
Nathan Larvin	25/7/85	8	3	2	1	0	0	0	0	8	4
Wayne McHugh	1/2/80	25(4)	19(3)	24	18	0	0	0	0	96	72
Joe McLocklan	2/10/86	7(2)	7(2)	1	1	0	0	0	0	4	4
Craig Moss	4/8/84	5(1)	0	0	0	0	0	0	0	0	0
Danny Richardson	25/6/88	1	1	0	0	0	0	0	0	0	0
Chris Ross	23/8/78	12(7)	6(5)	6	2	10	9	0	0	44	26
Andy Speake	28/9/86	1	0	0	1	0	0	0	0	2	0
Brian Sutton	7/3/85	(1)	0	0	0	0	0	0	0	0	0
Gavin Swinson	21/3/78	6(9)	6(5)	2	1	0	0	0	0	8	4
Ian Tonks	13/2/76	10(19)	7(14)	2	2	0	0	0	0	8	8
James Ward	22/1/78	(7)	(3)	1	1	0	0	0	0	4	4
Jon Whittle	9/9/82	28	21	13	10	0	0	0	0	52	40
Loz Wildbore	23/9/84	18	18	7	7	1	1	2	2	32	32
Scott Wilson	21/9/88	(1)	(1)	0	0	0	0	0	0	0	0
Dale Wynne	23/2/88	(1)	0	0	0	0	0	0	0	0	0

Danny Kirmond

LEAGUE RECORD
P22-W18-D0-L4-BP2
(2nd, NL2/Grand Final Winners)
F819, A366, Diff+453
56 points.

CHALLENGE CUP
Round Four

NATIONAL LEAGUE CUP
Quarter Final Qualifying Round/
2nd, Group 1

ATTENDANCES
Best - v Castleford (NLC - 3,229)
Worst - v Blackpool (NL2 - 754)
Total (excluding Challenge Cup) - 22,565
Average (excluding Challenge Cup) - 1,504
(Up by 435 on 2006)

GATESHEAD THUNDER

DATE	FIXTURE	RESULT	SCORERS	LGE	ATT
11/2/07	York (h) (NLC)	L12-58	t:Till,Rutherford g:Thorman(2)	4th(NLC-G2)	503
18/2/07	Keighley (a) (NLC)	L50-12	t:Rolfe,Nash g:Rolfe(2)	4th(NLC-G2)	628
25/2/07	Halifax (h) (NLC)	L6-22	t:Nash g:Rolfe	4th(NLC-G2)	403
4/3/07	York (a) (NLC)	L46-4	t:Martin	4th(NLC-G2)	1,033
10/3/07	Limoux (h) (CCR3)	W38-22	t:Stephenson,Rolfe(2),Williamson(2),Till,Clarke g:Rolfe(5)	N/A	211
18/3/07	Halifax (a) (NLC)	L30-8	t:Rolfe g:Rolfe(2)	4th(NLC-G2)	1,504
25/3/07	Keighley (h) (NLC)	L26-30	t:Williamson(2),Stephenson,Wilson,Scott g:Rolfe,Clarke(2)	4th(NLC-G2)	389
30/3/07	Salford (h) (CCR4) ●	L4-64	t:Clarke	N/A	1,283
6/4/07	York (h) ●●	W26-18	t:Hyde,Wilson,Scott,Walton,Clarke g:Clarke(3)	5th	557
9/4/07	Workington (a)	L68-0		8th	679
15/4/07	Barrow (h)	L10-65	t:Clarke,Till g:Clarke	9th	305
7/5/07	Swinton (a)	L58-12	t:Frazer,Thorman,Nash	11th	403
20/5/07	Featherstone (h)	L16-74	t:Wooden,Martin,Williamson g:Thorman(2)	11th	385
27/5/07	Keighley (h)	W32-12	t:Thorman,Till(2),Christensen(2) g:Thorman(6)	9th	277
3/6/07	Blackpool (a)	W18-28	t:Williamson,Nash,Hyde,Thorman,Stephenson g:Thorman(4)	9th	275
10/6/07	London Skolars (h)	L20-28	t:Harris,Christensen,Martin,Thorman(2)	10th	278
17/6/07	Barrow (a)	L60-22	t:Martin(2),Nash,Hyde g:Christensen(3)	11th	1,040
23/6/07	Hunslet (h)	W18-6	t:Martin(2),Christensen g:Clarke(3)	10th	276
1/7/07	Oldham (a) ●●●	L36-12	t:Clarke,Sanderson g:Sanderson(2)	10th	847
7/7/07	Blackpool (h)	W28-26	t:Harris,Williamson,Knowles,Nash,Thorman g:Clarke,Knowles(3)	9th	145
15/7/07	Featherstone (a)	L30-4	t:Knowles	11th	1,030
21/7/07	Swinton (h)	L8-34	t:Payne g:Knowles(2)	11th	219
29/7/07	Workington (a)	L32-36	t:Williamson,Thorman,Knowles(2),Wooden,Bradley g:Knowles(4)	11th	275
5/8/07	York (a)	L38-26	t:Knowles,Stephenson,Wooden,Martin,Williamson g:Knowles(2),Clarke	11th	825
11/8/07	London Skolars (a) ●●●●	L32-12	t:Peers,Stephenson(2)	11th	326
19/8/07	Oldham (h)	L14-28	t:Martin(2) g:Knowles(3)	11th	407
26/8/07	Celtic Crusaders (a)	L64-26	t:Partis,Thorman,Peers,Stephenson,Wooden g:Knowles(3)	11th	827
2/9/07	Keighley (a)	W18-19	t:Wilson,Nash,Wooden g:Knowles(3) fg:Martin	11th	636
5/9/07	Hunslet (a)	L13-0		11th	307
9/9/07	Celtic Crusaders (h)	L16-60	t:Peers,Knowles(2) g:Knowles(2)	11th	473

● Played at The Willows, Salford
●● Played at Kingston Park, Newcastle
●●● Played at Park Lane, Sedgley Park
●●●● Played at Summers Lane, Finchley

		APP		TRIES		GOALS		FG		PTS	
	D.O.B.	ALL	NL2	ALL	NL2	ALL	NL2	ALL	NL2	ALL	NL2
Matt Barron	17/11/86	1(17)	1(12)	0	0	0	0	0	0	0	0
Steven Bradley	27/7/81	15(7)	7(7)	1	1	0	0	0	0	4	4
Tabua Cakacaka	8/3/77	12(2)	12(2)	0	0	0	0	0	0	0	0
Mark Christensen	19/4/82	10	10	4	4	3	3	0	0	22	22
Ryan Clarke	8/9/85	15(13)	12(9)	5	3	11	9	0	0	42	30
Tony Doherty	3/8/83	5(17)	4(12)	0	0	0	0	0	0	0	0
Clint Frazer	25/2/83	5(9)	5(9)	1	1	0	0	0	0	4	4
Odell Harris	21/3/79	20	13	2	2	0	0	0	0	8	8
Nick Hyde	10/12/75	28	20	3	3	0	0	0	0	12	12
Michael Knowles	2/5/87	11	11	7	7	22	22	0	0	72	72
Michael Land	16/4/83	(2)	(1)	0	0	0	0	0	0	0	0
Tim Martin	5/4/78	28(1)	21(1)	10	9	0	0	1	1	41	37
Damian Martinez	13/8/78	(3)	(1)	0	0	0	0	0	0	0	0
Mark McKinley	16/9/85	2(1)	2(1)	0	0	0	0	0	0	0	0
Richie Metcalfe	4/3/86	2(6)	(2)	0	0	0	0	0	0	0	0
Dylan Nash	28/12/86	18(5)	16(3)	7	5	0	0	0	0	28	20
Chris Parker	9/9/78	1(9)	1(9)	0	0	0	0	0	0	0	0
Scott Partis	14/8/83	2(1)	2(1)	1	1	0	0	0	0	4	4
Jason Payne	20/1/88	11	11	1	1	0	0	0	0	4	4
Robin Peers	18/1/82	20(6)	14(6)	3	3	0	0	0	0	12	12
Andrew Pybus	21/9/86	(4)	(4)	0	0	0	0	0	0	0	0
Jono Rolfe	21/9/82	6	0	4	0	11	0	0	0	38	0
Steve Rutherford	24/8/81	6(6)	3(2)	1	0	0	0	0	0	4	0
Stuart Sanderson	10/4/85	7	7	1	1	2	2	0	0	8	8
Jonny Scott	13/3/87	9(4)	5(2)	2	1	0	0	0	0	8	4
Dan Smith	16/6/81	8(1)	8(1)	0	0	0	0	0	0	0	0
Graham Stephenson	10/5/84	30	22	7	5	0	0	0	0	28	20
Neil Thorman	4/6/84	27(1)	20	8	8	14	12	0	0	60	56
Kevin Till	3/10/82	15(4)	9(3)	5	3	0	0	0	0	20	12
Matt Walton	1/10/84	6	2	1	1	0	0	0	0	4	4
Pat Williamson	29/9/81	27	19	9	5	0	0	0	0	36	20
Danny Wilson	3/6/82	14	8	3	2	0	0	0	0	12	8
Shane Wooden	28/1/80	29	21	5	5	0	0	0	0	20	20

Tim Martin

LEAGUE RECORD
P22-W6-D0-L16-BP3
(11th, NL2)
F381, A822, Diff-441
21 points.

CHALLENGE CUP
Round Four

NATIONAL LEAGUE CUP
4th, Group 2

ATTENDANCES
Best - v York (NL2 - 557)
Worst - v Blackpool (NL2 - 145)
Total (excluding Challenge Cup) - 4,892
Average (excluding Challenge Cup) - 349
(Down by 3 on 2006)

HUNSLET HAWKS

DATE	FIXTURE	RESULT	SCORERS	LGE	ATT
11/2/07	Swinton (a) (NLC)	L38-20	t:Murgatroyd,Mack,Bramald,Foster g:D Robinson,Williams	2nd(NLC-G3)	432
18/2/07	Dewsbury (h) (NLC)	W16-8	t:Foster,Cook g:D Robinson,Bramald(3)	2nd(NLC-G3)	756
25/2/07	Batley (a) (NLC)	W16-18	t:D Robinson,Morton g:D Robinson(3),Bramald(2)	2nd(NLC-G3)	540
4/3/07	Swinton (h) (NLC)	D10-10	t:Morton g:D Robinson(3)	2nd(NLC-G3)	403
11/3/07	Rochdale Mayfield (h) (CCR3)	W40-22	t:D Robinson,Freeman,Cook,A Robinson,Mack(2),Bramald g:D Robinson(3),Bramald(3)	N/A	282
18/3/07	Batley (h) (NLC)	L4-32	t:Morton	2nd(NLC-G3)	438
25/3/07	Dewsbury (a) (NLC)	L83-6	t:Murgatroyd g:Bramald	3rd(NLC-G3)	824
1/4/07	Hull (h) (CCR4) ●	L0-78		N/A	5,062
6/4/07	Keighley (a)	W26-38	t:Mack(3),Firth(2),Morton,Moxon g:D Robinson(5)	3rd	806
15/4/07	York (a)	W14-19	t:Bramald(2),Holmes g:D Robinson(3) fg:D Robinson	6th	1,036
21/4/07	Celtic Crusaders (h) (NLCQFQ) ●●	L14-28	t:Morton,Ekis,D Robinson g:D Robinson	N/A	222
6/5/07	Barrow (h)	L4-32	t:Morton	7th	393
13/5/07	Featherstone (a)	L36-12	t:A Robinson,Cass g:D Robinson(2)	7th	1,008
20/5/07	Blackpool (h)	W30-18	t:Bramald,A Robinson,Morton,Cook,D Robinson g:D Robinson(5)	7th	291
27/5/07	Workington (a)	L30-18	t:A Robinson,P Smith(2) g:Bramald(2),D Robinson	8th	741
3/6/07	London Skolars (a)	W20-21	t:Cook,P Smith,A Robinson,Cunningham g:Bramald,D Robinson fg:Bramald	7th	413
10/6/07	Swinton (h)	L10-17	t:Morton,Firth g:D Robinson	7th	364
17/6/07	Celtic Crusaders (h)	W23-16	t:D Robinson,Cartledge,Jones(2) g:D Robinson(2),Bramald fg:D Robinson	6th	324
23/6/07	Gateshead (a)	L18-6	t:Morton g:D Robinson	6th	276
1/7/07	Barrow (a)	L32-22	t:Cartledge,Freeman,Seal,Moxon g:D Robinson(3)	6th	1,252
8/7/07	Workington (h)	W28-24	t:Jones,B Walkin,Bramald,Cook,Morton g:Bramald,D Robinson(3)	6th	409
15/7/07	York (h)	L14-16	t:A Robinson,Jones,Cartledge g:Ross	6th	462
22/7/07	Oldham (a)	L52-22	t:Ross(2),Morton,Bramald g:Bramald(2),D Robinson	7th	1,024
29/7/07	Blackpool (a)	W22-32	t:A Robinson,Bramald,Ross(2),Freeman g:D Robinson(6)	7th	302
5/8/07	London Skolars (h)	L6-32	t:Bravo g:D Robinson	7th	273
11/8/07	Celtic Crusaders (a)	L84-10	t:Moxon,Bravo g:D Robinson	8th	795
19/8/07	Featherstone (h)	L10-20	t:Cook g:Bramald,D Robinson(2)	8th	773
22/8/07	Oldham (h)	L6-42	t:Cook g:D Robinson	8th	538
2/9/07	Swinton (a)	L14-12	t:Moxon,Jones g:Bramald,D Robinson	9th	447
5/9/07	Gateshead (h)	W13-0	t:D Robinson,Freeman g:D Robinson(2) fg:D Robinson	7th	307
9/9/07	Keighley (h)	L12-26	t:Greenwood,D Robinson g:D Robinson,Bramald	8th	400

● Played at Kingston Communications Stadium, Hull
●● Played at Tetley's Stadium, Dewsbury

	D.O.B.	APP		TRIES		GOALS		FG		PTS	
		ALL	NL2	ALL	NL2	ALL	NL2	ALL	NL2	ALL	NL2
Luke Blake	10/8/89	1	0	0	0	0	0	0	0	0	0
Craig Bower	1/5/80	4	4	0	0	0	0	0	0	0	0
Matt Bramald	6/2/73	30	21	8	6	19	10	1	1	71	45
Caldon Bravo	22/5/85	3	3	2	2	0	0	0	0	8	8
Matt Carbutt	3/10/85	2(19)	1(12)	0	0	0	0	0	0	0	0
Will Cartledge	11/9/79	29	20	3	3	0	0	0	0	12	12
Mark Cass	17/11/71	(3)	(1)	1	1	0	0	0	0	4	4
Danny Cook	14/10/81	19(9)	15(5)	7	5	0	0	0	0	28	20
Mark Cunningham	24/9/81	12(2)	11(2)	1	1	0	0	0	0	4	4
Aaron Dobek	10/9/87	(1)	0	0	0	0	0	0	0	0	0
Danny Ekis	17/1/82	23	14	1	0	0	0	0	0	4	0
Matt Firth	19/2/81	29	21	3	3	0	0	0	0	12	12
David Foster	8/4/81	18	11	2	0	0	0	0	0	8	0
Wayne Freeman	30/4/74	30	22	4	3	0	0	0	0	16	12
David Gibbons	18/1/76	(2)	(1)	0	0	0	0	0	0	0	0
Gareth Greenwood	14/1/83	23(8)	14(8)	1	1	0	0	0	0	4	4
Karl Gunney	18/1/87	(4)	0	0	0	0	0	0	0	0	0
Dale Harris	15/12/86	2(1)	1(1)	0	0	0	0	0	0	0	0
Mark Holmes	3/11/80	(4)	(3)	1	1	0	0	0	0	4	4
Scott Houston	27/1/84	7(5)	5(2)	0	0	0	0	0	0	0	0
Ben Jones	30/10/83	11(2)	11(2)	5	5	0	0	0	0	20	20
Eddie Mack	5/8/84	8	2	6	3	0	0	0	0	24	12
Gary McClelland	30/12/84	1(1)	1(1)	0	0	0	0	0	0	0	0
Steve Morton	10/5/69	28(1)	20(1)	11	7	0	0	0	0	44	28
Mark Moxon	22/8/80	31	22	4	4	0	0	0	0	16	16
Danny Murgatroyd	23/10/80	6(8)	1(6)	2	0	0	0	0	0	8	0
Gareth Naylor	18/12/80	4(1)	3	0	0	0	0	0	0	0	0
Glen Pennington	7/8/84	3(5)	3(5)	0	0	0	0	0	0	0	0
Luke Pennington	29/6/88	1	1	0	0	0	0	0	0	0	0
Andy Robinson	15/11/78	30	22	7	6	0	0	0	0	28	24
Darren Robinson	28/5/79	23(8)	14(8)	7	4	55	43	3	3	141	105
Paul Robinson	3/7/82	1(1)	1(1)	0	0	0	0	0	0	0	0
Chris Ross	23/8/78	3(1)	3(1)	4	4	1	1	0	0	18	18
Danny Samuels	8/8/85	(2)	(2)	0	0	0	0	0	0	0	0
Paul Seal	21/4/78	3(8)	3(8)	1	1	0	0	0	0	4	4
Daniel Smith	10/9/82	(1)	(1)	0	0	0	0	0	0	0	0
Paul Smith	31/5/84	6(3)	6(3)	3	3	0	0	0	0	12	12
Jonny Wainhouse	12/1/84	1(2)	1(1)	0	0	0	0	0	0	0	0
Nick Walker	21/4/84	1(2)	0	0	0	0	0	0	0	0	0
Ben Walkin	7/5/86	9(13)	8(7)	1	1	0	0	0	0	4	4
Joey Walkin	22/8/90	(6)	(6)	0	0	0	0	0	0	0	0
Tony Williams	30/6/84	(1)	0	0	0	1	0	0	0	2	0
Stuart Young	7/5/88	1	1	0	0	0	0	0	0	0	0

Darren Robinson

LEAGUE RECORD
P22-W8-D0-L14-BP7
(8th, NL2)
F368, A591, Diff-223
31 points.

CHALLENGE CUP
Round Four

NATIONAL LEAGUE CUP
Quarter Final Qualifying Round/
3rd, Group 3

ATTENDANCES
Best - v Featherstone (NL2 - 773)
Worst - v Celtic Crusaders
(NLCQFQ - 222)
Total (excluding Challenge Cup) - 6,353
Average (excluding Challenge Cup) - 423
(Down by 3 on 2006)

KEIGHLEY COUGARS

DATE	FIXTURE	RESULT	SCORERS	LGE	ATT
11/2/07	Halifax (h) (NLC)	L18-44	t:Fogerty,Foster,Redfearn g:Eaton(3)	3rd(NLC-G2)	1,352
18/2/07	Gateshead (h) (NLC)	W50-12	t:Fogerty(3),Fawcett(2),R Smith,Redfearn,Foster,Nicholson g:Eaton(7)	3rd(NLC-G2)	628
25/2/07	York (a) (NLC)	L24-22	t:Palmer,Gardner(2),Fawcett g:Eaton(3)	3rd(NLC-G2)	1,182
4/3/07	Halifax (a) (NLC)	L52-4	g:Eaton(2)	3rd(NLC-G2)	1,676
11/3/07	Thornhill (h) (CCR3)	W34-6	t:Knight,Foster(2),Sutcliffe,Gardner,Hastings,R Smith g:Eaton,Knight(2)	N/A	868
18/3/07	York (h) (NLC)	L12-26	t:Hastings(2) g:Eaton(2)	3rd(NLC-G2)	758
25/3/07	Gateshead (a) (NLC)	W26-30	t:Hastings,Bissell,Redfearn,Duffy,Fogerty g:Eaton(5)	3rd(NLC-G2)	389
1/4/07	Oldham (h) (CCR4)	L16-26	t:Duffy,Nicholson,Knight g:Eaton(2)	N/A	1,039
6/4/07	Hunslet (h)	L26-38	t:Knight(2),Nicholson,Fogerty,B Sutton g:Eaton(3)	10th	806
9/4/07	Featherstone (a)	L36-22	t:Fawcett,Sutcliffe,Redfearn,Eaton g:Eaton(3)	10th	1,237
15/4/07	Celtic Crusaders (h)	L12-62	t:K Smith,Redfearn g:Eaton(2)	11th	672
29/4/07	Oldham (a)	L32-20	t:Eaton,Redfearn,Duffy g:Eaton(4)	11th	847
6/5/07	Blackpool (h)	W30-10	t:Nicholson(2),R Smith,J Feather,Duffy g:Eaton(5)	9th	628
20/5/07	London Skolars (h)	D16-16	t:Duffy,Knight g:Eaton(2),Knight(2)	9th	643
27/5/07	Gateshead (a)	L32-12	t:Knight,Fogerty g:Eaton(2)	9th	277
3/6/07	York (a)	L34-8	t:Redfearn g:Eaton(2)	10th	938
10/6/07	Workington (h)	W33-22	t:Gardner,Fogerty(2),J Feather,L Sutton g:Knight(6) fg:Fawcett	9th	613
13/6/07	Barrow (a)	L30-0		9th	1,058
17/6/07	Swinton (a)	L44-18	t:Knight(2),Gardner g:Knight(3)	10th	426
24/6/07	Oldham (h)	W26-18	t:B Sutton,Knight(2),Gardner g:Knight(5)	9th	969
1/7/07	Blackpool (a)	W10-26	t:Fawcett,Duffy(2),R Smith,B Sutton g:Knight(3)	8th	372
8/7/07	Featherstone (h)	L6-68	t:Duffy g:Knight	8th	1,101
14/7/07	London Skolars (a)	L39-20	t:Sutcliffe,Knight,B Sutton,Eaton g:Knight,Eaton	10th	406
22/7/07	York (h)	L10-42	t:Brown,Foster g:Knight	10th	787
29/7/07	Swinton (h)	W52-22	t:Brown(2),Hill(2),Purseglove,Bissell,Palmer,Rawlins,Sutcliffe,Hastings g:Knight(5),Eaton	10th	471
5/8/07	Workington (a)	L18-10	t:Crawford,Hill g:Knight	10th	721
12/8/07	Barrow (h)	L4-54	t:Sutcliffe	10th	658
18/8/07	Celtic Crusaders (a)	L34-12	t:Palmer,Bissell,Knight	10th	801
2/9/07	Gateshead (h)	L18-19	t:Duffy(2),Brown g:Knight(3)	10th	636
9/9/07	Hunslet (a)	W12-26	t:Gardner,Purseglove,Eaton,Brown(2) g:Knight(3)	10th	400

		APP		TRIES		GOALS		FG		PTS	
	D.O.B.	ALL	NL2	ALL	NL2	ALL	NL2	ALL	NL2	ALL	NL2
Simon Bissell	25/12/85	25(4)	18(4)	3	2	0	0	0	0	12	8
Alex Brown	28/8/87	14(3)	13	6	6	0	0	0	0	24	24
John Crawford	12/8/85	4	4	1	1	0	0	0	0	4	4
Jason Dubas-Fisher	1/8/86	1(1)	(1)	0	0	0	0	0	0	0	0
Gavin Duffy	9/4/87	27(2)	21	10	8	0	0	0	0	40	32
Barry Eaton	30/9/73	23(5)	15(5)	4	4	50	25	0	0	116	66
Gareth English	7/3/83	11(7)	5(7)	0	0	0	0	0	0	0	0
Craig Fawcett	8/11/85	28(1)	20(1)	5	2	0	0	1	1	21	9
Andy Feather	3/11/84	(2)	0	0	0	0	0	0	0	0	0
James Feather	15/4/84	30	22	2	2	0	0	0	0	8	8
Mick Fogerty	19/2/81	18	13	9	4	0	0	0	0	36	16
Matt Foster	10/6/76	18(4)	10(4)	5	1	0	0	0	0	20	4
Sam Gardner	28/8/77	21(1)	13(1)	7	4	0	0	0	0	28	16
Michael Hastings	16/1/86	13(5)	7(3)	5	1	0	0	0	0	20	4
Zac Hill	5/8/86	4	4	3	3	0	0	0	0	12	12
Gareth Holmes	18/9/85	1	1	0	0	0	0	0	0	0	0
Gary Keegan	25/7/80	(1)	(1)	0	0	0	0	0	0	0	0
Richard Knight	6/10/85	27(1)	20(1)	12	10	36	34	0	0	120	108
Adam Mitchell	7/8/81	4(5)	4(5)	0	0	0	0	0	0	0	0
Greg Nicholson	24/9/85	21(4)	13(4)	5	3	0	0	0	0	20	12
Tom Palmer	8/4/86	9(14)	7(9)	3	2	0	0	0	0	12	8
Oliver Purseglove	18/1/86	7	7	2	2	0	0	0	0	8	8
Brendan Rawlins	28/1/86	11(12)	11(9)	1	1	0	0	0	0	4	4
Chris Redfearn	4/12/80	27(1)	19(1)	7	4	0	0	0	0	28	16
Chris Roe	13/7/84	(1)	0	0	0	0	0	0	0	0	0
Karl Smith	28/5/77	2(1)	2(1)	1	1	0	0	0	0	4	4
Ryan Smith	19/9/87	15	9	4	2	0	0	0	0	16	8
Wayne Sutcliffe	6/5/83	7(19)	7(12)	5	4	0	0	0	0	20	16
Brian Sutton	7/3/85	10(7)	10(7)	4	4	0	0	0	0	16	16
Luke Sutton	25/2/86	7(14)	6(8)	1	1	0	0	0	0	4	4
Gareth Walker	23/8/82	(2)	(1)	0	0	0	0	0	0	0	0
Craig Weston	20/12/73	5(3)	5(3)	0	0	0	0	0	0	0	0

Richard Knight

LEAGUE RECORD
P22-W6-D1-L15-BP4
(10th, NL2)
F407, A692, Diff-285
24 points.

CHALLENGE CUP
Round Four

NATIONAL LEAGUE CUP
3rd, Group 2

ATTENDANCES
Best - v Halifax (NLC - 1,352)
Worst - v Swinton (NL2 - 471)
Total (excluding Challenge Cup) - 10,722
Average (excluding Challenge Cup) - 766
(Down by 79 on 2006)

LONDON SKOLARS

DATE	FIXTURE	RESULT	SCORERS	LGE	ATT
11/2/07	Leigh (h) (NLC)	L8-52	t:Maitua(2)	3rd(NLC-G6)	379
17/2/07	Celtic Crusaders (a) (NLC)	L44-28	t:Tozer(3),Aggrey,Williams g:Thorman(4)	4th(NLC-G6)	301
25/2/07	Widnes (a) (NLC)	L60-10	t:Maitua,Ellison g:Thorman	4th(NLC-G6)	2,700
4/3/07	Celtic Crusaders (h) (NLC)	L4-28	t:Simms	4th(NLC-G6)	289
10/3/07	West Bowling (a) (CCR3)	W8-24	t:Brown,Tozer(2),Reid,Aggrey g:Thorman(2)	N/A	230
18/3/07	Widnes (h) (NLC)	L0-66		4th(NLC-G6)	789
25/3/07	Leigh (h) (NLC)	L60-22	t:Thorman,Green,Brown,Honor g:Nowland(3)	4th(NLC-G6)	1,277
1/4/07	Wakefield (h) (CCR4) ●	L4-52	t:Shears	N/A	2,427
6/4/07	Celtic Crusaders (h)	L18-42	t:Coleman(2),Shears,Pittman g:Coleman	11th	211
9/4/07	York (a)	L40-18	t:Miller(2),Barker,Simms g:Thorman	12th	1,074
15/4/07	Swinton (a)	L34-26	t:Jonker,Maitua(2),Webster,Hodgkinson g:Webster(3)	10th	352
28/4/07	Workington (h)	L12-22	t:Hodgkinson,Reid g:Webster(2)	10th	329
6/5/07	Featherstone (h)	L6-62	t:Simms g:Webster	10th	382
16/5/07	Barrow (h)	L38-8	t:Benson,Webster	11th	1,045
20/5/07	Keighley (a)	D16-16	t:Simms,Kerr g:Nowland(3) fg:Nowland(2)	10th	643
26/5/07	Oldham (h)	L6-34	t:Aggrey g:Nowland	11th	635
3/6/07	Hunslet (h)	L20-21	t:Hodgkinson(2),Maitua g:Nowland(4)	11th	413
10/6/07	Gateshead (a)	W20-28	t:Honor,Nowland(2),Hodgkinson,Tozer g:Nowland(4)	11th	278
16/6/07	Blackpool (h)	W28-14	t:Aggrey,Hodgkinson(2),Tozer,Price g:Thorman(4)	9th	413
24/6/07	Swinton (h)	W34-12	t:Hodgkinson(2),Benson,Lynton,Thorman,Tozer g:Thorman(5)	8th	379
1/7/07	Featherstone (a)	L30-10	t:Hodgkinson,Coleman g:Thorman	9th	1,160
7/7/07	Celtic Crusaders (a)	L50-6	t:Lynton g:Thorman	11th	807
14/7/07	Keighley (h)	W39-20	t:Tozer,Honor(2),Benson,Hodgkinson,Lynton g:Thorman(7) fg:Thorman	8th	406
22/7/07	Workington (a)	W24-31	t:Hodgkinson(2),Coleman,Maitua,Nowland g:Thorman(5) fg:Thorman	8th	697
29/7/07	Barrow (h)	L18-31	t:Simms,Barker,Aggrey g:Thorman(3)	8th	467
5/8/07	Hunslet (a)	W6-32	t:Hodgkinson,Webster,Nowland(3) g:Thorman(6)	8th	273
11/8/07	Gateshead (h) ●●	W32-12	t:Simms,Lynton,Tozer,Shears,Aggrey g:Thorman(6)	7th	326
19/8/07	Blackpool (a)	W20-34	t:Hodgkinson,Louw,Aggrey,Shears,Barker,Thorman g:Thorman(5)	7th	263
24/8/07	York (h)	L0-34		7th	1,288
9/9/07	Oldham (a)	L28-26	t:Nowland,Simms(2),Tozer,Maitua g:Thorman(3)	9th	918

● Played at Belle Vue, Wakefield
●● Played at Summers Lane, Finchley

		APP		TRIES		GOALS		FG		PTS	
	D.O.B.	ALL	NL2	ALL	NL2	ALL	NL2	ALL	NL2	ALL	NL2
Dave Afrey	13/6/85	(1)	(1)	0	0	0	0	0	0	0	0
Austen Aggrey	12/5/79	18(2)	14(1)	7	5	0	0	0	0	28	20
Craig Anderson	25/6/85	(4)	(4)	0	0	0	0	0	0	0	0
Alan Barker	10/12/78	11(12)	7(9)	3	3	0	0	0	0	12	12
Keir Bell	14/6/85	3(6)	2(6)	0	0	0	0	0	0	0	0
Martyn Benson	5/6/82	22(4)	17(4)	3	3	0	0	0	0	12	12
Powhiri Bidois	23/2/74	1	0	0	0	0	0	0	0	0	0
Mark Brenton	19/3/84	1	1	0	0	0	0	0	0	0	0
Dave Brown	17/10/81	3(4)	(2)	2	0	0	0	0	0	8	0
Mike Castle	21/5/85	14(7)	10(5)	0	0	0	0	0	0	0	0
Jermaine Coleman	17/6/82	27(1)	20(1)	4	4	1	1	0	0	18	18
Tryfan Edwards	21/1/82	2	2	0	0	0	0	0	0	0	0
Dave Ellison	2/4/82	2(2)	0	1	0	0	0	0	0	4	0
Steve Green	13/6/78	3(1)	(1)	1	0	0	0	0	0	4	0
Douglas Hann	30/10/89	(1)	(1)	0	0	0	0	0	0	0	0
Warren Heilig	25/5/79	(7)	(5)	0	0	0	0	0	0	0	0
Pete Hodgkinson	26/2/85	26	20	15	15	0	0	0	0	60	60
Gareth Honor	1/10/81	22(4)	18(1)	4	3	0	0	0	0	16	12
Rubert Jonker	7/1/79	(3)	(3)	1	1	0	0	0	0	4	4
Jake Kerr	30/12/82	10	9	1	1	0	0	0	0	4	4
Richard Louw	8/6/79	23(5)	19(2)	1	1	0	0	0	0	4	4
Chris Lynton	6/2/85	12(3)	12(3)	4	4	0	0	0	0	16	16
Lydan Maitua	23/2/84	26	19	8	5	0	0	0	0	32	20
Dene Miller	14/12/81	6(1)	5	2	2	0	0	0	0	8	8
Jamie Nowland	18/9/84	14(1)	11(1)	7	7	15	12	2	2	60	54
Kurt Pittman	11/10/77	10(3)	3(2)	1	1	0	0	0	0	4	4
Joe Price	7/10/85	11(6)	10(4)	1	1	0	0	0	0	4	4
Frank Reid	1/11/78	9(18)	6(13)	2	1	0	0	0	0	8	4
Dave Roberson	17/1/74	(1)	(1)	0	0	0	0	0	0	0	0
Chris Shears	15/4/78	20(9)	14(8)	4	3	0	0	0	0	16	12
Corey Simms	18/2/80	21(3)	16(2)	8	7	0	0	0	0	32	28
Callan Sipthorp	7/11/81	1	0	0	0	0	0	0	0	0	0
Mitchell Stone	3/5/87	(1)	(1)	0	0	0	0	0	0	0	0
Tane Taitoko	21/11/78	5(6)	5(6)	0	0	0	0	0	0	0	0
Paul Thorman	28/9/82	30	22	3	2	54	47	2	2	122	104
Ashley Tozer	19/8/78	21(1)	15	11	6	0	0	0	0	44	24
Scott Unwin	12/9/77	(1)	(1)	0	0	0	0	0	0	0	0
William Webster	3/3/87	9(1)	8	3	3	6	6	0	0	24	24
Johnny Williams	23/8/85	7	1	1	0	0	0	0	0	4	0

Pete Hodgkinson

LEAGUE RECORD
P22-W8-D1-L13-BP4
(9th, NL2)
F448, A610, Diff-162
30 points.

CHALLENGE CUP
Round Four

NATIONAL LEAGUE CUP
4th, Group 6

ATTENDANCES
Best - v York (NL2 - 1,288)
Worst - v Celtic Crusaders (NL2 - 211)
Total (excluding Challenge Cup) - 6,706
Average (excluding Challenge Cup) - 479
(Up by 24 on 2006)

OLDHAM

DATE	FIXTURE	RESULT	SCORERS	LGE	ATT
11/2/07	Rochdale (h) (NLC)	L8-24	t:Wilkinson,Smith	3rd(NLC-G4)	1,145
18/2/07	Swinton (h) (NLC)	L18-28	t:Roden,Baines,Costin g:Ashton(3)	3rd(NLC-G4)	1,017
25/2/07	Dewsbury (a) (NLC)	L32-22	t:Wilkinson,O'Connor,Wingfield,Tamghart g:Ashton(3)	3rd(NLC-G4)	819
4/3/07	Rochdale (a) (NLC)	L16-6	t:Langley g:Ashton	3rd(NLC-G4)	816
10/3/07	East Hull (a) (CCR3)	W10-26	t:Ogden,Roden,Stout,Wilkinson(2) g:Ogden(3)	N/A	300
18/3/07	Dewsbury (h) (NLC)	L8-32	t:O'Connor,Langley	3rd(NLC-G4)	622
25/3/07	Swinton (a) (NLC)	W18-42	t:Hoyle,Roden,Sinfield,O'Connor,Smith,Wilkinson(2) g:Ogden(7)	3rd(NLC-G4)	555
1/4/07	Keighley (a) (CCR4)	W16-26	t:Langley(2),Ashton,Smith(2) g:Ashton(3)	N/A	1,039
4/4/07	Featherstone (a)	L12-23	t:Langley,Tamghart g:Sanderson,Ashton	9th	1,162
15/4/07	Blackpool (a)	W20-40	t:Smith,Wilkinson,Crabtree,Onyango,Mervill,Hodson,Littler g:Ashton(6)	8th	501
29/4/07	Keighley (h)	W32-20	t:O'Connor,Roden,Langley,Ashton,Wilkinson g:Ashton(6)	5th	847
4/5/07	Celtic Crusaders (a)	W26-34	t:Onyango,Tonks,Langley,Wilkinson(2),Littler g:Sanderson(3),Langley(2)	5th	3,441
13/5/07	Harlequins (h) (CCR5) ●	L6-66	t:Ashton g:Ashton	N/A	559
20/5/07	Barrow (h)	W50-18	t:Hughes(2),Roden(3),Sanderson,Wilkinson,Robinson g:Sanderson(6),Langley(3)	5th	848
26/5/07	London Skolars (a)	W6-34	t:Houston(2),Wilkinson,Hodson,Costin,Hughes,Onyango g:Sanderson(3)	5th	635
3/6/07	Workington (a)	W18-27	t:Hughes,Onyango,Hodson,Baines g:Sanderson(5) fg:Roden	5th	1,213
10/6/07	York (h) ●	W21-10	t:Tonks,Robinson,Onyango,Gorey g:Sanderson(2) fg:Roden	5th	1,024
17/6/07	Featherstone (a)	L24-18	t:Hughes(2),Onyango g:Langley(3)	5th	1,587
24/6/07	Keighley (a)	L26-18	t:Roden,Hodson,Robinson g:Ashton(3)	5th	969
1/7/07	Gateshead (h) ●	W36-12	t:Onyango(2),Littler(2),Costin,Langley,Roden g:Langley(4)	5th	847
8/7/07	Swinton (a)	L17-10	t:Hughes,Langley g:Langley	5th	757
15/7/07	Barrow (a)	L34-26	t:Hughes(2),Costin,Onyango g:Langley(5)	5th	1,348
22/7/07	Hunslet (h)	W52-22	t:Hughes(4),Sinfield,Costin,Onyango,Littler,Coyle g:Langley(8)	5th	1,024
29/7/07	York (a)	W14-15	t:Coyle,Onyango,Houston g:Langley fg:Roberts	5th	1,064
5/8/07	Blackpool (h)	W46-12	t:Onyango,Hughes,Tamghart(2),Mervill,Houston,Roberts(2) g:Hughes(7)	5th	858
12/8/07	Workington (h)	W44-18	t:Hughes,Costin,Coyle,Brooks,Onyango(2),Morton,Ford(2) g:Hughes(2),Morton(2)	4th	1,034
19/8/07	Gateshead (a)	W14-28	t:Houston,Mervill,Roden,Ford,Gorey g:Morton(4)	4th	407
22/8/07	Hunslet (a)	W6-42	t:Morton,Onyango,Houston,Tonks,Roberts,Ford(2) g:Morton(7)	4th	538
30/8/07	Celtic Crusaders (h)	L18-32	t:Morton,Ford g:Morton(5)	4th	4,327
5/9/07	Swinton (h)	W30-22	t:Langley,Coyle,Littler,Ford(3) g:Morton(3)	4th	950
9/9/07	London Skolars (h)	W28-26	t:Ford(2),Hoyle,Hodson,Morton g:Morton(4)	4th	918
16/9/07	Swinton (h) (EPO)	W36-6	t:Hughes,Ford,Onyango(2),Costin,Roberts(2) g:Morton(4)	N/A	1,120
23/9/07	Workington (h) (ESF)	W48-0	t:Hughes(2),Onyango,Hodson,Langley(3),Coyle,Brooks,Costin g:Langley,Hughes(3)	N/A	1,128
30/9/07	Barrow (a) (FE)	W6-28	t:Hughes(3),Coyle g:Langley(6)	N/A	2,771
7/10/07	Featherstone (GF) ●●	L24-6	t:Hughes g:Langley	N/A	N/A

● Played at Park Lane, Sedgley Park
●● Played at Headingley Carnegie, Leeds

		APP		TRIES		GOALS		FG		PTS	
	D.O.B.	ALL	NL2	ALL	NL2	ALL	NL2	ALL	NL2	ALL	NL2
Paul Ashton	17/6/79	7(4)	3(1)	3	1	27	16	0	0	66	36
Chris Baines	25/9/84	15(7)	9(7)	2	1	0	0	0	0	8	4
Jason Boults	7/9/83	21(4)	13(4)	0	0	0	0	0	0	0	0
Matty Brooks	9/10/86	3(14)	3(14)	2	2	0	0	0	0	8	8
Geno Costin	16/3/84	23(2)	20(1)	8	7	0	0	0	0	32	28
James Coyle	28/12/85	13(1)	13(1)	6	6	0	0	0	0	24	24
Andy Crabtree	7/12/82	9(15)	8(8)	1	1	0	0	0	0	4	4
Byron Ford	21/8/81	10	10	12	12	0	0	0	0	48	48
Ian Gordon	2/9/85	5	5	0	0	0	0	0	0	0	0
Andy Gorey	31/10/85	7(3)	5	2	2	0	0	0	0	8	8
Ian Hodson	23/10/81	18(5)	17(4)	6	6	0	0	0	0	24	24
John Hough	14/4/76	(2)	(1)	0	0	0	0	0	0	0	0
Drew Houston	21/1/83	20(5)	11(5)	6	6	0	0	0	0	24	24
Simeon Hoyle	18/9/79	27(1)	18(1)	2	1	0	0	0	0	8	4
Adam Hughes	1/10/77	16	16	22	22	12	12	0	0	112	112
Gareth Langley	24/10/84	29(1)	21	13	9	35	35	0	0	122	106
Craig Littler	4/9/85	26(1)	19	6	6	0	0	0	0	24	24
Richard Mervill	24/6/81	29(2)	26	3	3	0	0	0	0	12	12
Gareth Morton	21/10/82	6(1)	6(1)	4	4	29	29	0	0	74	74
Paul O'Connor	3/6/84	14	5	4	1	0	0	0	0	16	4
Mark Ogden	10/2/83	5	0	1	0	10	0	0	0	24	0
Stuart Oldham	8/3/83	1	0	0	0	0	0	0	0	0	0
Lucas Onyango	12/4/81	23	23	18	18	0	0	0	0	72	72
Robert Roberts	21/6/78	11(1)	11(1)	5	5	0	0	1	1	21	21
Adam Robinson	8/4/87	2(8)	2(8)	3	3	0	0	0	0	12	12
Neil Roden	9/4/80	34	26	10	7	0	0	2	2	42	30
Wes Rogers	3/11/77	5(5)	1(1)	0	0	0	0	0	0	0	0
Lee Sanderson	16/12/81	6(2)	6(1)	1	1	20	20	0	0	44	44
Ian Sinfield	7/4/77	22(2)	14(2)	2	1	0	0	0	0	8	4
Kris Smith	20/8/78	8(2)	3	5	1	0	0	0	0	20	4
Warren Stevens	4/10/78	3(2)	3(2)	0	0	0	0	0	0	0	0
Mike Stout	6/4/84	1(3)	0	1	0	0	0	0	0	4	0
Said Tamghart	13/5/80	3(26)	(20)	4	3	0	0	0	0	16	12
Anthony Tonks	27/4/85	8(12)	8(12)	3	3	0	0	0	0	12	12
Alex Wilkinson	9/10/82	21(9)	13(9)	12	6	0	0	0	0	48	24
Lee Wingfield	9/6/81	4	0	1	0	0	0	0	0	4	0

Lucas Onyango

LEAGUE RECORD
P22-W16-D0-L6-BP5
(4th, NL2/Grand Final Runners-Up)
F661, A420, Diff+241
53 points.

CHALLENGE CUP
Round Five

NATIONAL LEAGUE CUP
3rd, Group 4

ATTENDANCES
Best - v Celtic Crusaders (NL2 - 4,327)
Worst - v Harlequins (CC - 559)
Total (excluding Challenge Cup) - 18,871
Average (excluding Challenge Cup) - 1,179
(Up by 237 on 2006, NL1)

SWINTON LIONS

DATE	FIXTURE	RESULT	SCORERS	LGE	ATT
11/2/07	Hunslet (h) (NLC)	W38-20	t:Newton(2),Morley,Line,English,Saywell,Walker g:McGovern(5)	1st(NLC-G4)	432
18/2/07	Oldham (a) (NLC)	W18-28	t:D Woods(4),P Wood,Saywell g:McGovern,Hough	1st(NLC-G4)	1,017
25/2/07	Rochdale (h) (NLC)	L14-40	t:Billy(2),Brocklehurst g:Ashall	2nd(NLC-G4)	572
4/3/07	Hunslet (a) (NLC)	D10-10	t:Walker,D Woods g:McGovern	2nd(NLC-G4)	403
11/3/07	Lokomotiv Moscow (h) (CCR3)	W60-20	t:Saywell(3),Ashall(2),P Wood,D Woods(2),English,Johnson,McGovern g:McGovern(8)	N/A	331
18/3/07	Rochdale (a) (NLC)	L42-10	t:P Wood,Ashton g:McGovern	2nd(NLC-G4)	556
25/3/07	Oldham (h) (NLC)	L18-42	t:Saywell(2),English g:McGovern(3)	2nd(NLC-G4)	555
1/4/07	Barrow (h) (CCR4)	L14-47	t:D Woods,Morley,Smith g:McGovern	N/A	596
6/4/07	Blackpool (a)	W34-40	t:Williams(3),P Wood,Line,Saywell,Moana,McGovern g:McGovern,Marsh(3)	6th	332
9/4/07	Barrow (h)	L30-35	t:Saywell,English(2),Alcock,Hayes g:Marsh(5)	5th	416
15/4/07	London Skolars (h)	W34-26	t:Billy,Johnson,Williams(3),Brocklehurst,D Woods g:Marsh(3)	4th	352
22/4/07	Rochdale (a) (NLCQFQ)	L30-16	t:Billy,P Wood,Moana g:Ogden(2)	N/A	501
28/4/07	Celtic Crusaders (a)	L82-4	t:Johnson	6th	823
7/5/07	Gateshead (h)	W58-12	t:Line,D Woods(3),Billy(2),Moana,Ogden,Williamson,P Wood g:Marsh(9)	6th	403
20/5/07	York (h)	L26-38	t:Alcock,Billy,Williams,Marsh,Watkins g:Marsh(3)	6th	541
27/5/07	Featherstone (a)	L42-4	t:Gorton	7th	1,014
3/6/07	Barrow (a)	L52-24	t:Johnson,Morley,Saywell(2),Ashall g:Hough(2)	8th	1,188
10/6/07	Hunslet (a)	W10-17	t:Bates,Billy g:McGovern(4) fg:McGovern	8th	364
17/6/07	Keighley (h)	W44-18	t:McGovern,Gorton,Line,Saywell,Hough,Ashton,Hull,Marsh g:McGovern(6)	8th	426
24/6/07	London Skolars (a)	L34-12	t:Ashall,Bates g:Marsh(2)	11th	379
1/7/07	Workington (a)	L38-33	t:Gorton,Hayes,Moana,Smith,P Wood g:McGovern(6) fg:McGovern	11th	734
8/7/07	Oldham (h)	W17-10	t:English,Saywell,Ashall g:McGovern(2) fg:McGovern	10th	757
15/7/07	Celtic Crusaders (h)	L20-26	t:Gorton,Smith,Saywell,Hough g:Marsh(2)	9th	488
21/7/07	Gateshead (a)	W8-34	t:Hull(2),Bates,P Wood,Marsh,Alcock g:Marsh(5)	9th	219
29/7/07	Keighley (a)	L52-22	t:Moana,Hull,Marsh,Billy g:Marsh(3)	9th	471
5/8/07	Featherstone (h)	L22-28	t:Saywell(2),Gorton,Duffy g:Marsh,McGovern(2)	9th	603
12/8/07	Blackpool (h)	W70-20	t:Billy,Bates,English(2),Brocklehurst,Alcock,Line(2),P Wood(2),Saywell(2) g:Marsh(9),McGovern(2)	9th	349
19/8/07	York (a)	W16-22	t:Moana,Marsh,Saywell g:Marsh(5)	9th	806
2/9/07	Hunslet (a)	W14-12	t:Moana(2),Brocklehurst g:Marsh	7th	447
5/9/07	Oldham (a)	L30-22	t:P Wood,Duffy,Marsh(2) g:Marsh(3)	8th	950
9/9/07	Workington (a)	W36-26	t:Saywell(2),Moana(2),Billy(2) g:Marsh(6)	7th	557
16/9/07	Oldham (a) (EPO)	L36-6	t:Ashall g:Marsh	N/A	1,120

		APP		TRIES		GOALS		FG		PTS	
	D.O.B.	ALL	NL2	ALL	NL2	ALL	NL2	ALL	NL2	ALL	NL2
Danny Aboushakra	9/12/86	2(4)	2(2)	0	0	0	0	0	0	0	0
Paul Alcock	12/11/82	15(2)	13(1)	4	4	0	0	0	0	16	16
Craig Ashall	26/9/85	20(3)	15(1)	6	4	1	0	0	0	26	16
Dave Ashton	20/4/84	9(1)	6	2	1	0	0	0	0	8	4
David Bates	23/10/80	9(4)	9(4)	4	4	0	0	0	0	16	16
Marlon Billy	22/11/73	25	19	12	9	0	0	0	0	48	36
Adam Bowman	12/11/87	4	4	0	0	0	0	0	0	0	0
Mark Brocklehurst	27/9/86	14	9	4	3	0	0	0	0	16	12
Matt Bryers	28/11/85	3(10)	2(8)	0	0	0	0	0	0	0	0
Sean Conway	18/3/83	2	0	0	0	0	0	0	0	0	0
Rob Draper	30/11/87	4(1)	4(1)	0	0	0	0	0	0	0	0
Jay Duffy	16/4/87	5(3)	5(3)	2	2	0	0	0	0	8	8
Wayne English	8/3/80	28(1)	19(1)	8	5	0	0	0	0	32	20
Craig Farrimond	20/11/82	4(7)	3(2)	0	0	0	0	0	0	0	0
Dean Gorton	16/1/84	14(1)	14(1)	5	5	0	0	0	0	20	20
Gareth Hayes	15/6/85	14(15)	6(14)	2	2	0	0	0	0	8	8
Chris Hough	30/8/81	8(9)	4(7)	2	2	3	2	0	0	14	12
Chris Hull	4/12/86	8	8	4	4	0	0	0	0	16	16
Bruce Johnson	26/1/84	18(3)	11(3)	4	3	0	0	0	0	16	12
Rob Line	13/10/82	16(8)	15(5)	6	5	0	0	0	0	24	20
Lee Marsh	5/3/83	19(4)	17(3)	7	7	61	61	0	0	150	150
Richard Marshall	9/10/75	1(4)	1(4)	0	0	0	0	0	0	0	0
Steve McCurrie	1/6/73	(4)	(4)	0	0	0	0	0	0	0	0
Liam McGovern	6/10/84	25(2)	17(2)	3	2	43	23	3	3	101	57
Martin Moana	13/8/73	22(8)	15(6)	10	9	0	0	0	0	40	36
Chris Morley	22/9/73	11(10)	6(6)	3	1	0	0	0	0	12	4
Dave Newton	22/12/81	10(10)	5(8)	2	0	0	0	0	0	8	0
Mark Ogden	10/2/83	5	4	1	1	2	0	0	0	8	4
Andy Saywell	1/1/79	22	15	21	14	0	0	0	0	84	56
Adam Sharples	19/4/85	(2)	0	0	0	0	0	0	0	0	0
Mike Smith	28/11/86	19(4)	15(1)	3	2	0	0	0	0	12	8
John Walker	28/7/87	2(1)	0	2	0	0	0	0	0	8	0
Kash Watkins	20/6/88	3	3	1	1	0	0	0	0	4	4
Desi Williams	24/9/85	13	8	7	7	0	0	0	0	28	28
Ben Williamson	10/4/83	3(3)	3(2)	1	1	0	0	0	0	4	4
Phil Wood	25/10/83	26(2)	18(2)	11	7	0	0	0	0	44	28
Darren Woods	24/3/84	12(1)	4(1)	12	4	0	0	0	0	48	16

Marlon Billy

LEAGUE RECORD
P22-W11-D0-L11-BP6
(7th, NL2/Elimination Play-Off)
F605, A649, Diff-44
33 points *(6 points deducted)*

CHALLENGE CUP
Round Four

NATIONAL LEAGUE CUP
Quarter Final Qualifying Round/
2nd, Group 4

ATTENDANCES
Best - v Oldham (NL2 - 757)
Worst - v Lokomotiv Moscow (CC - 331)
Total (excluding Challenge Cup) - 6,898
Average (excluding Challenge Cup) - 493
(Down by 76 on 2006)

WORKINGTON TOWN

DATE	FIXTURE	RESULT	SCORERS	LGE	ATT
11/2/07	Whitehaven (h) (NLC)	L18-44	t:Dawes,R Lunt,Whitworth g:Forber,Kirkbride(2)	3rd(NLC-G5)	2,368
18/2/07	Barrow (h) (NLC)	W32-24	t:Whitworth,Walsh,Dawes,Campbell,Burgess g:Forber(6)	3rd(NLC-G5)	927
25/2/07	Blackpool (a) (NLC)	W28-34	t:S Lunt(4),Campbell,Forber g:Forber(5)	3rd(NLC-G5)	335
2/3/07	Barrow (a) (NLC)	L36-12	t:Dawes,Beattie g:Forber(2)	3rd(NLC-G5)	1,230
11/3/07	Oulton (h) (CCR3)	W18-10	t:Walsh,Campbell,Whitworth g:Forber(3)	N/A	529
18/3/07	Blackpool (h) (NLC)	W28-20	t:Walsh(3),Dawes(2),Forber g:Forber(2)	3rd(NLC-G5)	464
25/3/07	Whitehaven (a) (NLC)	L58-12	t:Campbell,Wilson g:Kirkbride(2)	3rd(NLC-G5)	2,636
30/3/07	Leeds (a) (CCR4)	L72-10	t:Dawes,King g:Kirkbride	N/A	3,576
6/4/07	Barrow (a)	L46-10	t:Ormesher,Walsh g:Kirkbride	12th	1,714
9/4/07	Gateshead (h)	W68-0	t:Beattie(3),R Lunt(2),Walsh(2),Wilson,Beaumont,Woodcock,Frazer,Campbell g:Forber(10)	6th	679
15/4/07	Featherstone (h)	W16-13	t:Burgess,Campbell,Wilson g:Forber(2)	5th	846
22/4/07	Castleford (a) (NLCQFQ)	L50-24	t:Forber(2),Kmet,Beattie g:Forber(4)	N/A	3,610
28/4/07	London Skolars (a)	W12-22	t:King(2),Campbell(2) g:Forber(3)	4th	329
6/5/07	York (h)	W31-8	t:Walsh,Dawes,Campbell,Beattie,Purdham g:Forber(5) fg:S Lunt	4th	1,151
13/5/07	Blackpool (a)	W10-52	t:Campbell(2),Kmet(2),Frazer(2),R Lunt(2),S Lunt g:Forber(8)	4th	309
20/5/07	Celtic Crusaders (h)	W28-16	t:Forber,Dawes,S Lunt,Wilson g:Forber(6)	3rd	896
27/5/07	Hunslet (h)	W30-18	t:Dawes,Kmet(2),Sidlow,Ormesher g:Forber(5)	2nd	741
3/6/07	Oldham (h)	L18-27	t:Beattie,R Lunt,Keavney g:Forber(3)	2nd	1,213
10/6/07	Keighley (a)	L33-22	t:Sidlow,King,S Lunt,R Lunt g:Forber(3)	3rd	613
17/6/07	York (a)	W18-26	t:Beattie,Wilson,R Lunt,Keavney g:Forber(5)	3rd	1,402
23/6/07	Celtic Crusaders (a)	L26-12	t:Miller,Sidlow g:Forber(2)	4th	945
1/7/07	Swinton (h)	W38-33	t:Sidlow(2),Beaumont,Beattie,S Lunt,Lavulavu g:Forber(7)	4th	734
8/7/07	Hunslet (a)	L28-24	t:S Lunt(2),Miller,Keavney g:Forber(4)	4th	409
15/7/07	Blackpool (h)	W86-6	t:S Lunt(2),Sidlow,Forber(3),Blair(2),Keavney(2),Frazer,Mossop,Kmet(2),R Lunt g:Forber(13)	4th	624
22/7/07	London Skolars (h)	L24-31	t:Lavulavu,Sidlow,R Lunt,Blair g:Forber(4)	4th	697
29/7/07	Gateshead (a)	W32-36	t:S Lunt,Frazer,Ormesher,Kmet(2),King g:Forber(6)	4th	275
5/8/07	Keighley (h)	W18-10	t:Keavney,Mossop,Sidlow g:Forber(3)	4th	721
12/8/07	Oldham (a)	L44-18	t:McDonald,Miller,S Lunt g:Forber(3)	5th	1,034
19/8/07	Barrow (h)	L16-28	t:Frazer,S Lunt(2) g:Forber(2)	5th	857
2/9/07	Featherstone (a)	L40-34	t:Blair,S Lunt(3),Keavney,Sidlow g:Kmet,Forber(4)	5th	1,346
9/9/07	Swinton (a)	L36-26	t:Kmet,Mossop,Wilson(2),Dawes g:Forber(3)	5th	557
16/9/07	York (h) (EPO)	W42-4	t:Miller(2),Dawes(3),Wilson g:Forber(9)	N/A	669
23/9/07	Oldham (a) (ESF)	L48-0		N/A	1,128

		APP		TRIES		GOALS		FG		PTS	
	D.O.B.	ALL	NL2	ALL	NL2	ALL	NL2	ALL	NL2	ALL	NL2
Tom Armstrong	29/10/81	2(1)	0	0	0	0	0	0	0	0	0
Andrew Beattie	12/1/81	22	14	9	7	0	0	0	0	36	28
Jamie Beaumont	22/1/75	24(3)	16(3)	2	2	0	0	0	0	8	8
Ryan Blair	19/12/83	10	10	4	4	0	0	0	0	16	16
Liam Bretherton	20/6/79	5	0	0	0	0	0	0	0	0	0
Dean Burgess	11/10/84	9(15)	8(10)	2	1	0	0	0	0	8	4
Liam Campbell	5/6/86	13(1)	6	11	7	0	0	0	0	44	28
Kris Coward	1/10/81	1(1)	1(1)	0	0	0	0	0	0	0	0
Mark Cox	22/1/78	(6)	(6)	0	0	0	0	0	0	0	0
Tyrone Dalton	7/1/89	(2)	(2)	0	0	0	0	0	0	0	0
Stephen Dawes	14/1/85	22(1)	14(1)	13	7	0	0	0	0	52	28
Peter Dobson	23/11/85	(2)	(2)	0	0	0	0	0	0	0	0
Carl Forber	17/3/85	32(1)	24	8	4	133	110	0	0	298	236
Neil Frazer	7/3/76	28	23	6	6	0	0	0	0	24	24
Scott Gorman	27/4/83	1(4)	1(4)	0	0	0	0	0	0	0	0
Martin Keavney	5/12/87	16	16	7	7	0	0	0	0	28	28
Darren King	9/3/82	19(9)	16(7)	5	4	0	0	0	0	20	16
Steve Kirkbride	10/1/81	4(4)	1	0	0	6	1	0	0	12	2
Franco Kmet	29/1/85	20(7)	18(6)	10	9	1	1	0	0	42	38
Taani Lavulavu	22/3/76	17(11)	10(10)	2	2	0	0	0	0	8	8
Rob Lunt	8/2/85	22	19	10	9	0	0	0	0	40	36
Shaun Lunt	15/4/86	22(4)	14(4)	19	15	0	0	1	1	77	61
Tane Manihera	6/8/74	(1)	(1)	0	0	0	0	0	0	0	0
Ashley McDonald	21/1/89	2	2	1	1	0	0	0	0	4	4
Allan McGuiness	30/6/82	1(10)	(4)	0	0	0	0	0	0	0	0
Dexter Miller	3/6/82	17(5)	14(4)	5	5	0	0	0	0	20	20
Jason Mossop	12/9/85	11	11	3	3	0	0	0	0	12	12
Steve Ormesher	5/4/78	9(7)	7(6)	3	3	0	0	0	0	12	12
Garry Purdham	20/10/78	11(7)	9(4)	1	1	0	0	0	0	4	4
James Robinson	4/3/79	(4)	(2)	0	0	0	0	0	0	0	0
Jon Roper	5/5/76	5(1)	0	0	0	0	0	0	0	0	0
Weldon Saayman	24/10/74	(2)	(2)	0	0	0	0	0	0	0	0
Adam Sidlow	25/10/87	15(3)	15(3)	9	9	0	0	0	0	36	36
Matthew Tunstall	7/9/77	1(11)	1(7)	0	0	0	0	0	0	0	0
Dean Vaughan	9/2/78	23(4)	15(4)	0	0	0	0	0	0	0	0
Craig Walsh	19/9/78	10(1)	4(1)	9	4	0	0	0	0	36	16
David Whitworth	6/1/85	5(1)	0	3	0	0	0	0	0	12	0
Martyn Wilson	22/10/82	23(3)	18(2)	8	7	0	0	0	0	32	28
Matthew Woodcock	26/10/77	7	5	1	1	0	0	0	0	4	4

Carl Forber

LEAGUE RECORD
P22-W12-D0-L10-BP7
(5th, NL2/Elimination Semi-Final)
F655, A515, Diff+140
43 points.

CHALLENGE CUP
Round Four

NATIONAL LEAGUE CUP
Quarter Final Qualifying Round/
3rd, Group 5

ATTENDANCES
Best - v Whitehaven (NLC - 2,368)
Worst - v Blackpool (NLC - 464)
Total (excluding Challenge Cup) - 13,587
Average (excluding Challenge Cup) - 906
(Up by 52 on 2006)

YORK CITY KNIGHTS

DATE	FIXTURE	RESULT	SCORERS	LGE	ATT
11/2/07	Gateshead (a) (NLC)	W12-58	t:Priestley,Brown,Rhodes,Rayner,Helme(2),Esders,Cakacaka,Thackeray,Mapals g:Wray(9)	1st(NLC-G2)	503
18/2/07	Halifax (a) (NLC)	L34-14	t:Rayner,Mapals,Buckley g:Wray	2nd(NLC-G2)	2,113
25/2/07	Keighley (h) (NLC)	W24-22	t:Smith,Brown,Liddell,Thackeray,Buckley g:Wray,Liddell	2nd(NLC-G2)	1,182
4/3/07	Gateshead (h) (NLC)	W46-4	t:Mapals(2),C Spurr,Elston(2),Rhodes,Buckley,Potter g:Gargan(7)	2nd(NLC-G2)	1,033
11/3/07	Toulouse (h) (CCR3)	W54-28	t:Buckley,Brown(4),Mapals(2),C Spurr(2),Thackeray g:Thackeray(7)	N/A	701
18/3/07	Keighley (a) (NLC)	W12-26	t:Sullivan,Thackeray,Smith,Wray g:Wray(4),Gargan	2nd(NLC-G2)	758
25/3/07	Halifax (h) (NLC)	L20-60	t:Grundy,Lingard,Thackeray,Elston g:Wray(2)	2nd(NLC-G2)	1,729
1/4/07	Huddersfield (a) (CCR4)	L74-4	t:C Spurr	N/A	2,137
6/4/07	Gateshead (a) ●	L26-18	t:Rayner(3),Elston g:Wray	8th	557
9/4/07	London Skolars (h)	W40-18	t:Mapals,Buckley,Rayner,Spicer,Potter,Cakacaka,Esders g:Lingard(6)	4th	1,074
15/4/07	Hunslet (h)	L14-19	t:Potter,Dunmore(2) g:Liddell	7th	1,036
22/4/07	Barrow (h) (NLCQFQ)	L16-18	t:Rhodes,Brown,Dunmore g:Wray,Dunmore	N/A	658
29/4/07	Barrow (a)	L30-10	t:Wray,C Spurr g:Wray	8th	1,404
6/5/07	Workington (a)	L31-8	t:Mapals g:Gargan(2)	8th	1,151
13/5/07	Celtic Crusaders (h)	L4-26	t:Potter	8th	1,444
20/5/07	Swinton (a)	W26-38	t:C Spurr,Spicer,Godfrey(2),Esders,Potter,Mapals(2) g:Wray,Brooks,Liddell	8th	541
27/5/07	Blackpool (a)	W12-24	t:Brooks,Godfrey,C Spurr,Elston,Mapals,Lowe	6th	306
3/6/07	Keighley (h)	W34-8	t:Mapals,Grimshaw,Lowe,Spicer,Godfrey,Rhodes g:Grimshaw(4),Liddell	6th	938
10/6/07	Oldham (a) ●●	L21-10	t:Mapals(2) g:Grimshaw	6th	1,024
17/6/07	Workington (h)	L18-26	t:C Spurr,Brown,Liddell g:Grimshaw(3)	7th	1,402
24/6/07	Featherstone (h)	L12-46	t:Spicer,Buckley g:Grimshaw(2)	7th	1,924
30/6/07	Celtic Crusaders (a)	L30-16	t:Elston,Mapals(2) g:Grimshaw(2)	7th	702
8/7/07	Barrow (a)	W14-4	t:Rhodes,Grundy g:Grimshaw(2),Liddell	7th	846
15/7/07	Hunslet (a)	W14-16	t:Waldron,Palmer g:Esders(3),Liddell	7th	462
22/7/07	Keighley (a)	W10-42	t:Lingard(4),Potter,Esders,Williams,McDonald g:Esders(4),Lingard	6th	787
29/7/07	Oldham (h)	L14-15	t:Lingard,C Spurr g:Esders(2),Lingard	6th	1,064
5/8/07	Gateshead (h)	W38-26	t:Lingard,C Spurr(2),Esders(2),M Spurr,Buckley,Potter g:Lingard(3)	6th	825
12/8/07	Featherstone (a)	L38-12	t:Lowe(2) g:Esders(2)	6th	1,314
19/8/07	Swinton (h)	L16-22	t:C Spurr,Priestley,Wray g:Esders(2)	6th	806
24/8/07	London Skolars (a)	W0-34	t:Godfrey,Lowe(3),Sullivan g:Esders(5),Liddell,McDonald	6th	1,288
9/9/07	Blackpool (h)	W56-22	t:Palmer(2),Burton,Lowe,Rhodes,Mapals(3),Godfrey,Buckley g:Esders(8)	6th	825
16/9/07	Workington (a) (EPO)	L42-4	g:Esders(2)	N/A	669

● Played at Kingston Park, Newcastle
●● Played at Park Lane, Sedgley Park

		APP		TRIES		GOALS		FG		PTS	
	D.O.B.	ALL	NL2	ALL	NL2	ALL	NL2	ALL	NL2	ALL	NL2
Matty Brooks	9/10/86	3	3	1	1	1	1	0	0	6	6
Ian Brown	27/1/74	19(1)	12(1)	8	1	0	0	0	0	32	4
Dave Buckley	14/10/81	28(3)	21(2)	8	4	0	0	0	0	32	16
Tom Burton	5/11/87	11	11	1	1	0	0	0	0	4	4
Tabua Cakacaka	8/3/77	9(1)	3(1)	2	1	0	0	0	0	8	4
Tom Dunmore	11/10/86	4	3	3	2	1	0	0	0	14	8
Jimmy Elston	8/12/79	12(17)	10(13)	6	3	0	0	0	0	24	12
Adam Endersby	7/1/82	(1)	(1)	0	0	0	0	0	0	0	0
Ryan Esders	20/10/86	22(6)	16(4)	6	5	28	28	0	0	80	76
Andy Gargan	21/3/87	7	4	0	0	10	2	0	0	20	4
Alex Godfrey	2/12/78	10	9	6	6	0	0	0	0	24	24
Danny Grimshaw	25/2/86	8	8	1	1	14	14	0	0	32	32
Stephen Grundy	2/12/85	5(7)	4(7)	2	1	0	0	0	0	8	4
Joe Helme	1/4/84	(8)	(3)	2	0	0	0	0	0	8	0
Jon Liddell	25/8/82	23(8)	22(1)	2	1	7	6	0	0	22	16
Lee Lingard	21/10/83	16(1)	10(1)	7	6	11	11	0	0	50	46
Neil Lowe	20/12/78	9(7)	9(7)	8	8	0	0	0	0	32	32
Lee Mapals	17/7/85	31	22	19	13	0	0	0	0	76	52
Ryan McDonald	24/2/78	(17)	(11)	1	1	1	1	0	0	6	6
Kyle Palmer	7/1/85	6(3)	5(3)	3	3	0	0	0	0	12	12
Dan Potter	8/11/78	20	15	7	6	0	0	0	0	28	24
Nathan Priestley	21/8/87	14(11)	10(8)	2	1	0	0	0	0	8	4
George Rayner	19/9/80	19	11	6	4	0	0	0	0	24	16
Scott Rhodes	21/6/80	23	15	6	3	0	0	0	0	24	12
John Smith	14/8/80	6(4)	3(1)	2	0	0	0	0	0	8	0
Rob Spicer	22/9/84	17	13	4	4	0	0	0	0	16	16
Chris Spurr	7/7/80	28	20	12	8	0	0	0	0	48	32
Mark Spurr	8/11/83	6(5)	6(5)	1	1	0	0	0	0	4	4
Adam Sullivan	14/11/82	27(1)	18(1)	2	1	0	0	0	0	8	4
Anthony Thackeray	19/2/86	6	0	5	0	7	0	0	0	34	0
Jonny Waldron	22/10/82	1	1	1	1	0	0	0	0	4	4
Liam Watling	28/6/87	(1)	0	0	0	0	0	0	0	0	0
Toby Williams	15/5/86	5(18)	2(14)	1	1	0	0	0	0	4	4
Jamaine Wray	15/3/84	21(8)	13(8)	3	2	21	3	0	0	54	14

Lee Mapals

LEAGUE RECORD
P22-W10-D0-L12-BP6
(6th, NL2/Elimination Play-Off)
F488, A470, Diff+18
36 points.

CHALLENGE CUP
Round Four

NATIONAL LEAGUE CUP
Quarter Final Qualifying Round/
2nd, Group 2

ATTENDANCES
Best - v Featherstone (NL2 - 1,924)
Worst - v Barrow (NLCQFQ - 658)
Total (excluding Challenge Cup) - 16,786
Average (excluding Challenge Cup) - 1,119
(Down by 563 on 2006, NL1)

NATIONAL LEAGUE TWO 2007
Round by Round

WEEK 1

Wednesday 4th April 2007

OLDHAM 12 FEATHERSTONE ROVERS 23

OLDHAM: 1 Paul O'Connor; 2 Gareth Langley; 3 Craig Littler; 4 Drew Houston; 5 Alex Wilkinson; 6 Neil Roden; 7 Lee Sanderson; 8 Jason Boults; 9 Simeon Hoyle; 10 Richard Mervill; 11 Ian Hodson; 12 Ian Sinfield; 13 Kris Smith. Subs (all used): 14 Wes Rogers; 15 Said Tamghart; 16 Chris Baines; 17 Paul Ashton.
Tries: Langley (23), Tamghart (40);
Goals: Sanderson 1/3, Ashton 1/1.
ROVERS: 1 Nathan Larvin; 2 Danny Kirmond; 3 Wayne McHugh; 4 Jon Whittle; 5 Dean Colton; 6 Chris Ross; 7 Paul Handforth; 8 Gareth Handford; 9 Paul Hughes; 10 Stuart Dickens; 11 Jamie Field; 12 Steve Dooler; 13 Richard Blakeway. Subs (all used): 14 Tom Haughey; 15 Ian Tonks; 16 James Houston; 17 James Ward.
Tries: McHugh (16), Ross (65), Haughey (68, 79);
Goals: Ross 1/2, Dickens 2/2; **Field goal:** Handforth (74).
Rugby Leaguer & League Express Men of the Match:
Oldham: Kris Smith; *Rovers:* Jamie Field.
Penalty count: 6-6; **Half-time:** 10-6;
Referee: Peter Taberner; **Attendance:** 1,162.

Friday 6th April 2007

BLACKPOOL PANTHERS 34 SWINTON LIONS 40

PANTHERS: 1 Mark Leigh; 2 Chris Ramsdale; 3 Steven Brown; 4 Chris Maye; 5 Matt Strong; 6 Safraz Patel; 7 Martin Gambles; 8 Lee Rowley; 9 Phil Cantillon; 10 Gareth Jones; 11 Luke Murfin; 12 Kris Ratcliffe; 13 Deon Duell. Subs (all used): 14 Jon Chamberlain; 15 Eddie Kilgannon; 16 Danny Barton; 17 Richard Rafferty.
Tries: Ramsdale (4), Patel (12), Leigh (48, 67), Cantillon (58), Gambles (62); **Goals:** Ramsdale 3/5, Gambles 2/2.
Sin bin: Duell (11) - fighting.
LIONS: 1 Wayne English; 2 Andy Saywell; 3 Ben Williamson; 4 Mark Brocklehurst; 5 Desi Williams; 6 Lee Marsh; 7 Liam McGovern; 8 Bruce Johnson; 9 Phil Wood; 10 Matt Bryers; 11 Chris Morley; 12 Mike Smith; 13 Craig Farrimond. Subs (all used): 14 Darren Woods; 15 Martin Moana; 16 Gareth Hayes; 17 Rob Line.
Tries: Williams (18, 45, 72), P Wood (21), Line (34), Saywell (54), Moana (70), McGovern (80);
Goals: McGovern 1/5, Marsh 3/3.
Sin bin: Bryers (11) - fighting.
Rugby Leaguer & League Express Men of the Match:
Panthers: Phil Cantillon; *Lions:* Desi Williams.
Penalty count: 5-9; **Half-time:** 14-14;
Referee: Peter Taberner; **Attendance:** 332.

BARROW RAIDERS 46 WORKINGTON TOWN 10

RAIDERS: 1 Khamal Ganley; 2 Nick Beach; 3 Phil Atkinson; 4 Liam Harrison; 5 James Nixon; 6 Mike Basan; 7 Darren Holt; 8 Paul Raftrey; 9 Andy Ellis; 10 Brett McDermott; 11 Michael Smith; 12 Dave Armistead; 13 Martin Ostler. Subs (all used): 14 Jamie Marshall; 15 Paul Wilcock; 16 Geoff Luxon; 17 Lee Dutton.
Tries: Atkinson (6), McDermott (12), Ostler (24), Ellis (40, 75), Ganley (58, 67), Beach (69); **Goals:** Holt 7/10.
TOWN: 1 Rob Lunt; 2 Stephen Dawes; 3 Franco Kmet; 4 Andrew Beattie; 5 Martyn Wilson; 6 Carl Forber; 7 Steve Kirkbride; 8 Dean Vaughan; 9 Darren King; 10 Taani Lavulavu; 11 Steve Ormesher; 12 Jamie Beaumont; 13 Craig Walsh. Subs (all used): 14 James Robinson; 15 Allan McGuiness; 16 Garry Purdham; 17 Dean Burgess.
Tries: Ormesher (9), Walsh (48); **Goals:** Kirkbride 1/2.
Rugby Leaguer & League Express Men of the Match:
Raiders: Martin Ostler; *Town:* Andrew Beattie.
Penalty count: 5-7; **Half-time:** 18-6;
Referee: Mike Dawber; **Attendance:** 1,714.

GATESHEAD THUNDER 26 YORK CITY KNIGHTS 18

THUNDER: 1 Neil Thorman; 2 Matt Walton; 3 Graham Stephenson; 4 Steve Rutherford; 5 Danny Wilson; 6 Tim Martin; 7 Kevin Till; 8 Jonny Scott; 9 Ryan Clarke; 10 Steven Bradley; 11 Shane Wooden; 12 Nick Hyde; 13 Odell Harris. Subs (all used): 14 Robin Peers; 15 Richie Metcalfe; 16 Matt Barron; 17 Tony Doherty.
Tries: Hyde (34), Wilson (44), Scott (56), Walton (68), Clarke (75); **Goals:** Clarke 3/5.
CITY KNIGHTS: 1 George Rayner; 2 Lee Mapals; 3 Ian Brown; 4 Chris Spurr; 5 Lee Lingard; 6 Scott Rhodes; 7 Andy Gargan; 8 Toby Williams; 9 Jamaine Wray; 10 Adam Sullivan; 11 Dave Buckley; 12 Nathan Priestley; 13 Jon Liddell. Subs (all used): 14 Jimmy Elston; 15 John Smith; 16 Tabua Cakacaka; 17 Joe Helme.
Tries: Rayner (21, 65, 78), Elston (49); **Goals:** Wray 1/4.
Rugby Leaguer & League Express Men of the Match:
Thunder: Neil Thorman; *City Knights:* George Rayner.
Penalty count: 8-6; **Half-time:** 6-4; **Referee:** Paul Carr;
Attendance: 557 *(at Kingston Park, Newcastle).*

LONDON SKOLARS 18 CELTIC CRUSADERS 42

SKOLARS: 1 Pete Hodgkinson; 2 Corey Simms; 3 Chris Shears; 4 Jake Kerr; 5 William Webster; 6 Chris Lynton; 7 Paul Thorman; 8 Alan Barker; 9 Gareth Honor; 10 Richard Louw; 11 Kurt Pittman; 12 Lydan Maitua; 13 Jermaine Coleman. Subs (all used): 14 Steve Green; 15 Joe Price; 16 Dave Brown; 17 Rubert Jonker.
Tries: Coleman (12, 80), Shears (16), Pittman (73);
Goals: Coleman 1/4.
CRUSADERS: 1 Richard Johnston; 2 Paul Ballard; 3 Rob Toshack; 4 Mark Dalle Cort; 5 Craig Richards; 6 Luke Young; 7 Jace Van Dijk; 8 Hywel Davies; 9 Neil Budworth; 10 Gareth Dean; 11 Terry Martin; 12 Dean Fitzgerald; 13 Damien Quinn. Subs (all used): 14 Chris Beasley; 15 Jamie I'Anson; 16 Phil Cushion; 17 Lee Williams.
Tries: Martin (2), Dean (5), Richards (21, 35), Ballard (27), Johnston (39, 46), Fitzgerald (67);
Goals: Quinn 5/8.
Rugby Leaguer & League Express Men of the Match:
Skolars: Jermaine Coleman; *Crusaders:* Luke Young.
Penalty count: 7-6; **Half-time:** 10-32;
Referee: Dave Merrick; **Attendance:** 211.

KEIGHLEY COUGARS 26 HUNSLET HAWKS 38

COUGARS: 1 Matt Foster; 2 Brian Sutton; 3 Michael Hastings; 4 Mick Fogerty; 5 Gavin Duffy; 6 Craig Fawcett; 7 Barry Eaton; 8 Simon Bissell; 9 James Feather; 10 Tom Palmer; 11 Greg Nicholson; 12 Richard Knight; 13 Chris Redfearn. Subs (all used): 14 Adam Mitchell; 15 Wayne Sutcliffe; 16 Brendan Rawlins; 17 Luke Sutton.
Tries: Knight (11, 19), Nicholson (48), Fogerty (64), B Sutton (73); **Goals:** Eaton 3/5.
HAWKS: 1 Matt Bramald; 2 Andy Robinson; 3 David Foster; 4 Eddie Mack; 5 Steve Morton; 6 Mark Moxon; 7 Matt Firth; 8 Danny Ekis; 9 Gareth Greenwood; 10 Wayne Freeman; 11 Gareth Naylor; 12 Will Cartledge; 13 Darren Robinson. Subs (all used): 14 Danny Cook; 15 Matt Carbutt; 16 Danny Murgatroyd; 17 Scott Houston.
Tries: Mack (25, 31, 70), Firth (39, 42), Morton (76), Moxon (79); **Goals:** D Robinson 5/7.
Rugby Leaguer & League Express Men of the Match:
Cougars: Chris Redfearn; *Hawks:* Eddie Mack.
Penalty count: 2-4; **Half-time:** 12-18;
Referee: Thierry Alibert; **Attendance:** 806.

WEEK 2

Monday 9th April 2007

CELTIC CRUSADERS 68 BLACKPOOL PANTHERS 0

CRUSADERS: 1 Tony Duggan; 2 Richard Johnston; 3 Rob Toshack; 4 Mark Dalle Cort; 5 Craig Richards; 6 Luke Young; 7 Jace Van Dijk; 8 Phil Cushion; 9 Neil Budworth; 10 Hywel Davies; 11 Terry Martin; 12 Dean Fitzgerald; 13 Damien Quinn. Subs (all used): 14 Andy Boothroyd; 15 Jamie I'Anson; 16 Chris Beasley; 17 Lee Jones.
Tries: Toshack (1, 66), Van Dijk (19), Budworth (21), Dalle Cort (25), Richards (30, 51, 55, 73), Johnston (46, 53), Quinn (71); **Goals:** Quinn 10/12.
PANTHERS: 1 Mark Leigh; 2 Chris Brand; 3 Steven Brown; 4 Chris Maye; 5 Jon Chamberlain; 6 Deon Duell; 7 Martin Gambles; 8 Lee Rowley; 9 Phil Cantillon; 10 Gareth Jones; 11 Luke Murfin; 12 Kris Ratcliffe; 13 Chris Ramsdale. Subs (all used): 14 Matt Strong; 15 Eddie Kilgannon; 16 Danny Barton; 17 Ian Parry.
Rugby Leaguer & League Express Men of the Match:
Crusaders: Craig Richards; *Panthers:* Jon Chamberlain.
Penalty count: 7-7; **Half-time:** 28-0;
Referee: Mike Dawber; **Attendance:** 2,805.

SWINTON LIONS 30 BARROW RAIDERS 35

LIONS: 1 Wayne English; 2 Andy Saywell; 3 Ben Williamson; 4 Mark Brocklehurst; 5 Desi Williams; 6 Lee Marsh; 7 Liam McGovern; 8 Bruce Johnson; 9 Chris Hough; 10 Rob Line; 11 Paul Alcock; 12 Chris Morley; 13 Mike Smith. Subs (all used): 14 Martin Moana; 15 Dave Newton; 16 Matt Bryers; 17 Gareth Hayes.
Tries: Saywell (10), English (48, 70), Alcock (58), Hayes (67); **Goals:** Marsh 5/5.
Dismissal: Morley (63) - head butt.
Sin bin: Hough (61) - fighting.
RAIDERS: 1 Khamal Ganley; 2 Nick Beach; 3 Phil Atkinson; 4 Liam Harrison; 5 James Nixon; 6 Mike Basan; 7 Darren Holt; 8 Paul Raftrey; 9 Andy Ellis; 10 Lee Dutton; 11 Michael Smith; 12 Dave Armistead; 13 Brett McDermott. Subs (all used): 14 Jamie Marshall; 15 Paul Wilcock; 16 Geoff Luxon; 17 Shane Irabor.
Tries: Ganley (5, 13), Atkinson (8), Basan (37), Ellis (64); **Goals:** Holt 7/7; **Field goal:** Holt (73).
Rugby Leaguer & League Express Men of the Match:
Lions: Gareth Hayes; *Raiders:* Darren Holt.
Penalty count: 8-6; **Half-time:** 6-28;
Referee: Paul Carr; **Attendance:** 416.

WORKINGTON TOWN 68 GATESHEAD THUNDER 0

TOWN: 1 Rob Lunt; 2 Matthew Woodcock; 3 Andrew Beattie; 4 Neil Frazer; 5 Martyn Wilson; 6 Carl Forber; 7 Liam Campbell; 8 Dean Vaughan; 9 Darren King; 10 Taani Lavulavu; 11 Jamie Beaumont; 12 Steve Ormesher; 13 Craig Walsh. Subs (all used): 14 Franco Kmet; 15 Garry Purdham; 16 Allan McGuiness; 17 Dean Burgess.
Tries: Beattie (10, 28, 71), R Lunt (16, 51), Walsh (19, 39), Wilson (31), Beaumont (36), Woodcock (44), Frazer (62), Campbell (77); **Goals:** Forber 10/12.
THUNDER: 1 Neil Thorman; 2 Robin Peers; 3 Graham Stephenson; 4 Matt Walton; 5 Danny Wilson; 6 Tim Martin; 7 Kevin Till; 8 Jonny Scott; 9 Ryan Clarke; 10 Steven Bradley; 11 Steve Rutherford; 12 Nick Hyde; 13 Odell Harris. Subs (all used): 14 Andrew Pybus; 15 Richie Metcalfe; 16 Dylan Nash; 17 Tony Doherty.
Rugby Leaguer & League Express Men of the Match:
Town: Liam Campbell; *Thunder:* Kevin Till.
Penalty count: 7-5; **Half-time:** 40-0;
Referee: Peter Taberner; **Attendance:** 679.

YORK CITY KNIGHTS 40 LONDON SKOLARS 18

CITY KNIGHTS: 1 George Rayner; 2 Lee Mapals; 3 Dan Potter; 4 Ian Brown; 5 Lee Lingard; 6 Jon Liddell; 7 Scott Rhodes; 8 Tabua Cakacaka; 9 Jimmy Elston; 10 Adam Sullivan; 11 Dave Buckley; 12 Ryan Esders; 13 Rob Spicer. Subs (all used): 14 Mark Spurr; 15 Nathan Priestley; 16 Toby Williams; 17 Joe Helme.
Tries: Mapals (17), Buckley (20), Rayner (27), Spicer (35), Potter (44), Cakacaka (66), Esders (78);
Goals: Lingard 6/7.
SKOLARS: 1 William Webster; 2 Dene Miller; 3 Chris Shears; 4 Jake Kerr; 5 Johnny Williams; 6 Kurt Pittman; 7 Paul Thorman; 8 Alan Barker; 9 Gareth Honor; 10 Richard Louw; 11 Joe Price; 12 Mike Castle; 13 Jermaine Coleman. Subs (all used): 14 Frank Reid; 15 Corey Simms; 16 Martyn Benson; 17 Scott Unwin.
Tries: Miller (37, 62), Barker (51), Simms (73);
Goals: Thorman 1/3, Coleman 0/1.
Rugby Leaguer & League Express Men of the Match:
City Knights: Ryan Esders; *Skolars:* Frank Reid.
Penalty count: 4-11; **Half-time:** 24-4;
Referee: Thierry Alibert; **Attendance:** 1,074.

FEATHERSTONE ROVERS 36 KEIGHLEY COUGARS 22

ROVERS: 1 Nathan Larvin; 2 Danny Kirmond; 3 Jon Whittle; 4 Steve Dooler; 5 Dean Colton; 6 Scott Glassell; 7 Paul Handforth; 8 Gareth Handford; 9 Paul Hughes; 10 Ian Tonks; 11 Jamie Field; 12 Tom Haughey; 13 Richard Blakeway. Subs (all used): 14 Wayne McHugh; 15 Stuart Dickens; 16 James Houston; 17 James Ward.
Tries: Blakeway (6), Handford (12), Ward (37), McHugh (44), Handforth (47), Haughey (56), Larvin (78); **Goals:** Glassell 4/4, Dickens 0/3.
COUGARS: 1 Gavin Duffy; 2 Michael Hastings; 3 Richard Knight; 4 Mick Fogerty; 5 Karl Smith; 6 Craig Fawcett; 7 Barry Eaton; 8 Simon Bissell; 9 James Feather; 10 Tom Palmer; 11 Greg Nicholson; 12 Wayne Sutcliffe; 13 Chris Redfearn. Subs (all used): 14 Adam Mitchell; 15 Gary Keegan; 16 Brendan Rawlins; 17 Luke Sutton.
Tries: Fawcett (24), Sutcliffe (34), Redfearn (60), Eaton (69); **Goals:** Eaton 3/4.
Rugby Leaguer & League Express Men of the Match:
Rovers: Tom Haughey; *Cougars:* Barry Eaton.
Penalty count: 4-8; **Half-time:** 16-12;
Referee: James Child; **Attendance:** 1,237.

WEEK 3

Sunday 15th April 2007

BLACKPOOL PANTHERS 20 OLDHAM 40

PANTHERS: 1 Chris Brand; 2 Neil Hayden; 3 Eddie Kilgannon; 4 Chris Maye; 5 Steve Bannister; 6 Safraz Patel; 7 Martin Gambles; 8 Ian Parry; 9 Phil Cantillon; 10 Lee Rowley; 11 Luke Murfin; 12 Kris Ratcliffe; 13 Deon Duell. Subs (all used): 14 Jon Chamberlain; 15 Danny Barton; 16 Gareth Jones; 17 Rob Lamb.
Tries: Ratcliffe (18), Hayden (31), Bannister (59);
Goals: Brand 4/5.
Sin bin: Maye (37) – high tackle;
Rowley (75) – swinging arm.
OLDHAM: 1 Paul O'Connor; 2 Gareth Langley; 3 Craig Littler; 4 Alex Wilkinson; 5 Lucas Onyango; 6 Neil Roden; 7 Paul Ashton; 8 Richard Mervill; 9 Andy Crabtree; 10 Geno Costin; 11 Chris Baines; 12 Ian Hodson; 13 Kris Smith. Subs (all used): 14 John Hough; 15 Said Tamghart; 16 Anthony Tonks; 17 Drew Houston.
Tries: Smith (5), Wilkinson (23), Crabtree (33), Onyango (46), Mervill (54), Hodson (61), Littler (69);
Goals: Ashton 6/8.
On report: Roden (76) - alleged swinging arm.
Rugby Leaguer & League Express Men of the Match:
Panthers: Phil Cantillon; *Oldham:* Lucas Onyango.
Penalty count: 8-19; **Half-time:** 12-18;
Referee: Thierry Alibert; **Attendance:** 501.

GATESHEAD THUNDER 10 BARROW RAIDERS 65

THUNDER: 1 Neil Thorman; 2 Danny Wilson; 3 Graham Stephenson; 4 Dylan Nash; 5 Robin Peers; 6 Tim Martin; 7 Kevin Till; 8 Jonny Scott; 9 Ryan Clarke; 10 Steven Bradley; 11 Shane Wooden; 12 Nick Hyde; 13 Odell Harris. Subs (all used): 14 Andrew Pybus; 15 Matt Barron; 16 Chris Parker; 17 Damian Martinez.
Tries: Clarke (31), Till (69); **Goals:** Clarke 1/2.
RAIDERS: 1 Khamal Ganley; 2 Nick Beach; 3 Phil Atkinson; 4 Liam Harrison; 5 James Nixon; 6 Mike Basan; 7 Darren Holt; 8 Michael Smith; 9 Andy Ellis; 10 Brett McDermott; 11 Martin Ostler; 12 Dave Armistead; 13 Pat Weisner. Subs (all used): 14 Jamie Marshall; 15 Paul Wilcock; 16 Paul Raftrey; 17 Lee Dutton.
Tries: Atkinson (6, 25), Ellis (12), Beach (16, 65, 72, 74), Ganley (22, 42, 59), Nixon (47), Smith (61); **Goals:** Holt 8/12; **Field goal:** Weisner (55).
Rugby Leaguer & League Express Men of the Match:
Thunder: Nick Hyde; *Raiders:* Khamal Ganley.
Penalty count: 12-5; **Half-time:** 6-28;
Referee: Dave Merrick; **Attendance:** 305.

KEIGHLEY COUGARS 12 CELTIC CRUSADERS 62

COUGARS: 1 Gavin Duffy; 2 Gareth Holmes; 3 Matt Foster; 4 Mick Fogerty; 5 Karl Smith; 6 Craig Fawcett; 7 Barry Eaton; 8 Simon Bissell; 9 James Feather; 10 Tom Palmer; 11 Wayne Sutcliffe; 12 Brian Sutton; 13 Chris Redfearn. Subs (all used): 14 Adam Mitchell; 15 Jason Dubas-Fisher; 16 Brendan Rawlins; 17 Luke Sutton.
Tries: K Smith (4), Redfearn (19); **Goals:** Eaton 2/2.
Sin bin: Rawlins (25) - fighting.
CRUSADERS: 1 Tony Duggan; 2 Richard Johnston; 3 Anthony Blackwood; 4 Mark Dalle Cort; 5 Craig Richards; 6 Damien Quinn; 7 Jace Van Dijk; 8 Darren Mapp; 9 Neil Budworth; 10 Jamie I'Anson; 11 Terry Martin; 12 Chris Beasley; 13 Rob Toshack. Subs (all used): 14 Paul Ballard; 15 Dean Fitzgerald; 16 Andy Boothroyd; 17 Hywel Davies.
Tries: Mapp (14), Fitzgerald (26), Richards (29),

Simeon Hoyle closes down Jamie I'Anson during Oldham's thrilling comeback win over Celtic Crusaders

Duggan (39, 47), Johnston (42), Toshack (52, 75, 77), Ballard (59), Budworth (79); **Goals:** Quinn 9/11.
Sin bin: Beasley (25) - fighting.
Rugby Leaguer & League Express Men of the Match:
Cougars: Brian Sutton; *Crusaders:* Rob Toshack.
Penalty count: 9-18; **Half-time:** 12-24;
Referee: Craig Halloran; **Attendance:** 672.

SWINTON LIONS 34 LONDON SKOLARS 26

LIONS: 1 Wayne English; 2 Desi Williams; 3 Darren Woods; 4 Mark Brocklehurst; 5 Marlon Billy; 6 Lee Marsh; 7 Liam McGovern; 8 Bruce Johnson; 9 Chris Hough; 10 Rob Line; 11 Matt Bryers; 12 Paul Alcock; 13 Mike Smith. Subs (all used): 14 Phil Wood; 15 Martin Moana; 16 Chris Morley; 17 Gareth Hayes.
Tries: Billy (3), Johnson (14), Williams (20, 36, 69), Brocklehurst (38), D Woods (64);
Goals: Marsh 3/5, Hough 0/2.
On report: Brocklehurst (43) - alleged use of the elbow.
SKOLARS: 1 Pete Hodgkinson; 2 Dene Miller; 3 Jake Kerr; 4 Joe Price; 5 William Webster; 6 Chris Shears; 7 Paul Thorman; 8 Alan Barker; 9 Gareth Honor; 10 Richard Louw; 11 Mike Castle; 12 Lydan Maitua; 13 Jermaine Coleman. Subs (all used): 14 Frank Reid; 15 Dave Brown; 16 Martyn Benson; 17 Rubert Jonker.
Tries: Jonker (23), Maitua (32, 51), Webster (73), Hodgkinson (78);
Goals: Webster 3/3, Coleman 0/1, Hodgkinson 0/1.
Rugby Leaguer & League Express Men of the Match:
Lions: Liam McGovern; *Skolars:* Rubert Jonker.
Penalty count: 5-7; **Half-time:** 26-8;
Referee: James Child; **Attendance:** 352.

WORKINGTON TOWN 16 FEATHERSTONE ROVERS 13

TOWN: 1 Rob Lunt; 2 Matthew Woodcock; 3 Andrew Beattie; 4 Neil Frazer; 5 Martyn Wilson; 6 Carl Forber; 7 Liam Campbell; 8 Dean Vaughan; 9 Darren King; 10 Dean Burgess; 11 Jamie Beaumont; 12 Garry Purdham; 13 Craig Walsh. Subs (all used): 14 Franco Kmet; 15 Allan McGuiness; 16 Dexter Miller; 17 James Robinson.
Tries: Burgess (26), Campbell (39), Wilson (69);
Goals: Forber 2/3.
ROVERS: 1 Nathan Larvin; 2 Danny Kirmond; 3 Jon Whittle; 4 Wayne McHugh; 5 Dean Colton; 6 Richard Blakeway; 7 Scott Glassell; 8 Gareth Handford; 9 Paul Hughes; 10 Stuart Dickens; 11 Jamie Field; 12 Steve Dooler; 13 Tom Haughey. Subs (all used): 14 Chris Ross; 15 Ian Tonks; 16 James Houston; 17 James Ward.
Tries: McHugh (30), Whittle (47);
Goals: Dickens 0/2, Ross 1/1; **Field goal:** P Hughes (65).
Rugby Leaguer & League Express Men of the Match:
Town: Liam Campbell; *Rovers:* Ian Tonks.
Penalty count: 7-9; **Half-time:** 12-6;
Referee: Jamie Leahy; **Attendance:** 846.

YORK CITY KNIGHTS 14 HUNSLET HAWKS 19

CITY KNIGHTS: 1 George Rayner; 2 Lee Mapals; 3 Dan Potter; 4 Ian Brown; 5 Tom Dunmore; 6 Jon Liddell; 7 Scott Rhodes; 8 Tabua Cakacaka; 9 Jamaine Wray; 10 Dave Buckley; 11 John Smith; 12 Ryan Esders; 13 Rob Spicer. Subs (all used): 14 Jimmy Elston; 15 Nathan Priestley; 16 Toby Williams; 17 Joe Helme.
Tries: Potter (34), Dunmore (41, 44);
Goals: Dunmore 0/1, Liddell 1/2.
HAWKS: 1 Matt Bramald; 2 Andy Robinson; 3 David Foster; 4 Gareth Naylor; 5 Steve Morton; 6 Mark Moxon; 7 Matt Firth; 8 Danny Ekis; 9 Gareth Greenwood; 10 Wayne Freeman; 11 Danny Cook; 12 Will Cartledge; 13 Darren Robinson. Subs (all used): 14 Gary McClelland; 15 Mark Holmes; 16 Matt Carbutt; 17 Danny Murgatroyd.
Tries: Bramald (47, 62), Holmes (58);
Goals: D Robinson 3/3; **Field goal:** D Robinson (67).
Rugby Leaguer & League Express Men of the Match:
City Knights: Jon Liddell; *Hawks:* Danny Cook.
Penalty count: 7-5; **Half-time:** 4-0;
Referee: Paul Carr; **Attendance:** 1,036.

WEEK 4

Saturday 28th April 2007

LONDON SKOLARS 12 WORKINGTON TOWN 22

SKOLARS: 1 Pete Hodgkinson; 2 Corey Simms; 3 Jake Kerr; 4 Ashley Tozer; 5 William Webster; 6 Chris Shears; 7 Paul Thorman; 8 Alan Barker; 9 Gareth Honor; 10 Martyn Benson; 11 Joe Price; 12 Lydan Maitua; 13 Jermaine Coleman. Subs (all used): 14 Frank Reid; 15 Mike Castle; 16 Richard Louw; 17 Rubert Jonker.
Tries: Hodgkinson (24), Reid (67); **Goals:** Webster 2/3.
TOWN: 1 Rob Lunt; 2 Matthew Woodcock; 3 Andrew Beattie; 4 Neil Frazer; 5 Martyn Wilson; 6 Carl Forber; 7 Liam Campbell; 8 Dean Vaughan; 9 Darren King; 10 Dean Burgess; 11 Steve Ormesher; 12 Dexter Miller; 13 Garry Purdham. Subs (all used): 14 Franco Kmet; 15 Allan McGuiness; 16 Craig Walsh; 17 Jamie Beaumont.
Tries: King (18, 74), Campbell (28, 34); **Goals:** Forber 3/4.
Rugby Leaguer & League Express Men of the Match:
Skolars: Lydan Maitua; *Town:* Steve Ormesher.
Penalty count: 12-4; **Half-time:** 8-16;
Referee: Matthew Thomasson; **Attendance:** 329.

CELTIC CRUSADERS 82 SWINTON LIONS 4

CRUSADERS: 1 Tony Duggan; 2 Richard Johnston; 3 Anthony Blackwood; 4 Mark Dalle Cort; 5 Craig Richards; 6 Damien Quinn; 7 Jace Van Dijk; 8 Josh Cale; 9 Neil Budworth; 10 Gareth Dean; 11 Terry Martin; 12 Darren

Mapp; 13 Rob Toshack. Subs (all used): 14 Luke Young; 15 Jamie I'Anson; 16 Chris Beasley; 17 Hywel Davies.
Tries: Dalle Cort (4, 66), Toshack (7), Martin (10), Duggan (14, 63, 70), Quinn (26, 38, 51, 78), Richards (40, 48), Blackwood (74), Van Dijk (76);
Goals: Quinn 11/15.
LIONS: 1 Wayne English; 2 Desi Williams; 3 Darren Woods; 4 Ben Williamson; 5 Marlon Billy; 6 Mark Ogden; 7 Chris Hough; 8 Bruce Johnson; 9 Phil Wood; 10 Rob Line; 11 Paul Alcock; 12 Mike Smith; 13 Martin Moana. Subs (all used): 14 Liam McGovern; 15 Lee Marsh; 16 Matt Bryers; 17 Gareth Hayes.
Try: Johnson (55); **Goals:** Marsh 0/1.
Rugby Leaguer & League Express Men of the Match:
Crusaders: Damien Quinn; *Lions:* Marlon Billy.
Penalty count: 5-5; **Half-time:** 38-0;
Referee: Paul Carr; **Attendance:** 823.

Sunday 29th April 2007

BARROW RAIDERS 30 YORK CITY KNIGHTS 10

RAIDERS: 1 Khamal Ganley; 2 Nick Beach; 3 James Finch; 4 Liam Harrison; 5 James Nixon; 6 Mike Basan; 7 Darren Holt; 8 Paul Raftrey; 9 Andy Ellis; 10 Lee Dutton; 11 Dave Armistead; 12 Paul Wilcock; 13 Phil Atkinson. Subs (all used): 14 Jamie Marshall; 15 Liam Finch; 16 Shane Irabor; 17 Ian Rawlinson.
Tries: Harrison (33), Nixon (42), Beach (47), Rawlinson (67), L Finch (73); **Goals:** Holt 5/6.
CITY KNIGHTS: 1 George Rayner; 2 Chris Spurr; 3 Dan Potter; 4 Lee Mapals; 5 James Nixon; 6 Scott Rhodes; 7 Jimmy Elston; 8 Tabua Cakacaka; 9 Jamaine Wray; 10 Adam Sullivan; 11 John Smith; 12 Ryan Esders; 13 Mark Spurr. Subs (all used): 14 Jon Liddell; 15 Stephen Grundy; 16 Toby Williams; 17 Dave Buckley.
Tries: Wray (23), C Spurr (78); **Goals:** Wray 1/2.
Sin bin: Elston (35) – holding down.
Rugby Leaguer & League Express Men of the Match:
Raiders: Lee Dutton; *City Knights:* Scott Rhodes.
Penalty count: 8-7; **Half-time:** 6-6;
Referee: Peter Taberner; **Attendance:** 1,404.

FEATHERSTONE ROVERS 70 BLACKPOOL PANTHERS 24

ROVERS: 1 Craig Bower; 2 Danny Kirmond; 3 Jon Whittle; 4 Dale Cardoza; 5 Dean Colton; 6 Chris Ross; 7 Paul Handforth; 8 Gareth Handford; 9 Paul Hughes; 10 Stuart Dickens; 11 Jamie Field; 12 Steve Dooler; 13 Tom Haughey. Subs (all used): 14 Carl Hughes; 15 Richard Blakeway; 16 James Houston; 17 Wayne McHugh.
Tries: Kirmond (1, 35, 64), Handforth (16, 28), Cardoza (32, 50), Field (39), Blakeway (41), McHugh (46, 80), Whittle (55), Colton (79); **Goals:** Dickens 9/13.
PANTHERS: 1 Mark Leigh; 2 Steve Bannister; 3 Sean

Conway; 4 Eddie Kilgannon; 5 Matt Strong; 6 Steven Brown; 7 Martin Gambles; 8 Lee Rowley; 9 Phil Cantillon; 10 Gareth Jones; 11 Luke Murfin; 12 Kris Ratcliffe; 13 Deon Duell. Subs (all used): 14 Safraz Patel; 15 Chris Maye; 16 James Simon; 17 Mike Stout.
Tries: Gambles (9, 22, 68), Cantillon (75, 77);
Goals: Gambles 2/5.
Sin bin: Ratcliffe (39) – interference.
Rugby Leaguer & League Express Men of the Match: *Rovers:* Paul Handforth; *Panthers:* Martin Gambles.
Penalty count: 12-5; **Half-time:** 36-10;
Referee: Mike Dawber; **Attendance:** 754.

OLDHAM 32 KEIGHLEY COUGARS 20

OLDHAM: 1 Paul O'Connor; 2 Gareth Langley; 3 Craig Littler; 4 Alex Wilkinson; 5 Lucas Onyango; 6 Neil Roden; 7 Paul Ashton; 8 Wes Rogers; 9 Andy Crabtree; 10 Richard Mervill; 11 Geno Costin; 12 Drew Houston; 13 Kris Smith. Subs (all used): 14 Chris Baines; 15 Said Tamghart; 16 Anthony Tonks; 17 Simeon Hoyle.
Tries: O'Connor (13), Roden (20), Langley (37), Ashton (55), Wilkinson (60); **Goals:** Ashton 6/6.
Sin bin: Langley (42) – fighting.
COUGARS: 1 Gavin Duffy; 2 Sam Gardner; 3 Matt Foster; 4 Mick Fogerty; 5 Ryan Smith; 6 Craig Fawcett; 7 Barry Eaton; 8 Brendan Rawlins; 9 James Feather; 10 Tom Palmer; 11 Brian Sutton; 12 Wayne Sutcliffe; 13 Chris Redfearn. Subs (all used): 14 Adam Mitchell; 15 Richard Knight; 16 Simon Bissell; 17 Luke Sutton.
Tries: Eaton (10), Redfearn (74), Duffy (79);
Goals: Eaton 4/4.
Sin bin: Sutcliffe (50) – high tackle.
Rugby Leaguer & League Express Men of the Match: *Oldham:* Neil Roden; *Cougars:* Craig Fawcett.
Penalty count: 6-8; **Half-time:** 18-8;
Referee: Dave Merrick; **Attendance:** 847.

WEEK 5

Friday 4th May 2007

CELTIC CRUSADERS 26 OLDHAM 34

CRUSADERS: 1 Tony Duggan; 2 Richard Johnston; 3 Anthony Blackwood; 4 Mark Dalle Cort; 5 Craig Richards; 6 Luke Young; 7 Jace Van Dijk; 8 Josh Cale; 9 Rob Toshack; 10 Hywel Davies; 11 Terry Martin; 12 Darren Mapp; 13 Damien Quinn. Subs (all used): 14 Dean Fitzgerald; 15 Jamie I'Anson; 16 Chris Beasley; 17 Phil Cushion.
Tries: Van Dijk (18), Duggan (25), Blackwood (33), Quinn (37), Richards (46); **Goals:** Quinn 3/5.
Sin bin: Young (51) - fighting.
OLDHAM: 1 Paul O'Connor; 2 Gareth Langley; 3 Craig Littler; 4 Drew Houston; 5 Lucas Onyango; 6 Neil Roden; 7 Lee Sanderson; 8 Anthony Tonks; 9 Simeon Hoyle; 10 Richard Mervill; 11 Geno Costin; 12 Ian Hodson; 13 Chris Baines. Subs (all used): 14 Andy Crabtree; 15 Said Tamghart; 16 Jason Boults; 17 Alex Wilkinson.
Tries: Onyango (14), Tonks (53), Langley (55), Wilkinson (62, 77), Littler (66);
Goals: Sanderson 3/4, Langley 2/2.
Sin bin: Boults (51) - fighting.
Rugby Leaguer & League Express Men of the Match: *Crusaders:* Jace Van Dijk; *Oldham:* Gareth Langley.
Penalty count: 2-4; **Half-time:** 22-6;
Referee: Gareth Hewer; **Attendance:** 3,441.

Sunday 6th May 2007

KEIGHLEY COUGARS 30 BLACKPOOL PANTHERS 10

COUGARS: 1 Gavin Duffy; 2 Ryan Smith; 3 Michael Hastings; 4 Mick Fogerty; 5 Alex Brown; 6 Craig Fawcett; 7 Barry Eaton; 8 Brendan Rawlins; 9 James Feather; 10 Tom Palmer; 11 Brian Sutton; 12 Richard Knight; 13 Greg Nicholson. Subs (all used): 14 Adam Mitchell; 15 Karl Smith; 16 Simon Bissell; 17 Luke Sutton.
Tries: Nicholson (17, 54), R Smith (29), J Feather (35), Duffy (39); **Goals:** Eaton 5/6.
Sin bin: Bissell (52) – fighting; Brown (78) - dissent.
PANTHERS: 1 Chris Brand; 2 Matt Strong; 3 Chris Maye; 4 Sean Conway; 5 Steve Bannister; 6 Deon Duell; 7 Martin Gambles; 8 Lee Rowley; 9 Phil Cantillon; 10 Kris Ratcliffe; 11 Luke Murfin; 12 Mike Stout; 13 Martin Roden. Subs (all used): 14 Jon Chamberlain; 15 Danny Barton; 16 James Simon; 17 Simon Knox.
Tries: Maye (60), Chamberlain (65); **Goals:** Brand 1/2.
Sin bin: Chamberlain (52) – fighting, (74) – fighting.
Rugby Leaguer & League Express Men of the Match: *Cougars:* Greg Nicholson; *Panthers:* Kris Ratcliffe.
Penalty count: 10-7; **Half-time:** 22-0;
Referee: Paul Carr; **Attendance:** 628.

LONDON SKOLARS 6 FEATHERSTONE ROVERS 62

SKOLARS: 1 Pete Hodgkinson; 2 Corey Simms; 3 Jake Kerr; 4 Ashley Tozer; 5 William Webster; 6 Kurt Pittman; 7 Paul Thorman; 8 Mike Castle; 9 Chris Lynton; 10 Martyn Benson; 11 Joe Price; 12 Lydan Maitua; 13 Jermaine Coleman. Subs (all used): 14 Frank Reid; 15 Austen Aggrey; 16 Tane Taitoko; 17 Richard Louw.
Try: Simms (15); **Goals:** Webster 1/1.
Sin bin: Pittman (54) - dissent.
ROVERS: 1 Wayne McHugh; 2 Danny Kirmond; 3 Jon Whittle; 4 Dale Cardoza; 5 Dean Colton; 6 Chris Ross; 7 Paul Handforth; 8 James Houston; 9 Gavin Swinson; 10 Stuart Dickens; 11 Jamie Field; 12 Richard Blakeway; 13 Tom Haughey. Subs (all used): 14 Paul Hughes; 15 Ian Tonks; 16 Steve Dooler; 17 Carl Hughes.
Tries: Dickens (10), Whittle (19), McHugh (24, 63), Handforth (27), C Hughes (46), Dooler (48), Blakeway (52), Cardoza (57), Kirmond (66), Haughey (72);
Goals: Dickens 5/5, Ross 4/6.
Rugby Leaguer & League Express Men of the Match: *Skolars:* Ashley Tozer; *Rovers:* Paul Handforth.
Penalty count: 13-11; **Half-time:** 6-24;
Referee: Andrew Grundy; **Attendance:** 382.

WORKINGTON TOWN 31 YORK CITY KNIGHTS 8

TOWN: 1 Rob Lunt; 2 Matthew Woodcock; 3 Andrew Beattie; 4 Neil Frazer; 5 Stephen Dawes; 6 Carl Forber; 7 Liam Campbell; 8 Dean Vaughan; 9 Darren King; 10 Dean Burgess; 11 Jamie Beaumont; 12 Franco Kmet; 13 Craig Walsh. Subs (all used): 14 Shaun Lunt; 15 Garry Purdham; 16 Steve Ormesher; 17 Taani Lavulavu.
Tries: Walsh (14), Dawes (38), Campbell (60), Beattie (65), Purdham (69); **Goals:** Forber 5/6;
Field goal: S Lunt (77).
CITY KNIGHTS: 1 George Rayner; 2 Chris Spurr; 3 Dan Potter; 4 Ian Brown; 5 Lee Mapals; 6 Jon Liddell; 7 Andy Gargan; 8 Dave Buckley; 9 Jamaine Wray; 10 Adam Sullivan; 11 Stephen Grundy; 12 Ryan Esders; 13 Rob Spicer. Subs (all used): 14 Jimmy Elston; 15 Mark Spurr; 16 Toby Williams; 17 Adam Endersby.
Try: Mapals (21); **Goals:** Gargan 2/3.
Sin bin: Buckley (77) – dissent.
Rugby Leaguer & League Express Men of the Match: *Town:* Dean Vaughan; *City Knights:* Adam Sullivan.
Penalty count: 11-3; **Half-time:** 10-8;
Referee: Craig Halloran; **Attendance:** 1,151.

HUNSLET HAWKS 4 BARROW RAIDERS 32

HAWKS: 1 Matt Bramald; 2 Mark Cunningham; 3 Andy Robinson; 4 Gareth Naylor; 5 Steve Morton; 6 Mark Moxon; 7 Matt Firth; 8 Danny Ekis; 9 Gareth Greenwood; 10 Wayne Freeman; 11 Danny Cook; 12 Will Cartledge; 13 Darren Robinson. Subs (all used): 14 David Gibbons; 15 Mark Holmes; 16 Danny Murgatroyd; 17 Matt Carbutt.
Try: Morton (58); **Goals:** D Robinson 0/1.
Sin bin: D Robinson (23) - fighting.
RAIDERS: 1 Khamal Ganley; 2 Nick Beach; 3 Mike Basan; 4 Liam Harrison; 5 James Nixon; 6 Liam Finch; 7 Darren Holt; 8 Paul Raftrey; 9 Andy Ellis; 10 Lee Dutton; 11 Michael Smith; 12 Dave Armistead; 13 Pat Weisner. Subs (all used): 14 Jamie Marshall; 15 James Finch; 16 Paul Wilcock; 17 Ian Rawlinson.
Tries: Ellis (27), Ganley (41), Rawlinson (52), Basan (72), Harrison (78), Nixon (80);
Goals: Holt 2/4, Weisner 2/2.
Sin bin: Dutton (23) - fighting.
Rugby Leaguer & League Express Men of the Match: *Hawks:* Gareth Greenwood; *Raiders:* Andy Ellis.
Penalty count: 8-9; **Half-time:** 0-4;
Referee: Ronnie Laughton; **Attendance:** 393.

Monday 7th May 2007

SWINTON LIONS 58 GATESHEAD THUNDER 12

LIONS: 1 Wayne English; 2 Desi Williams; 3 Darren Woods; 4 Kash Watkins; 5 Marlon Billy; 6 Mark Ogden; 7 Liam McGovern; 8 Bruce Johnson; 9 Phil Wood; 10 Rob Line; 11 Paul Alcock; 12 Martin Moana; 13 Lee Marsh. Subs (all used): 14 Ben Williamson; 15 Richard Marshall; 16 Chris Morley; 17 Gareth Hayes.
Tries: Line (5), D Woods (7, 10, 18), Billy (14, 41), Moana (36), Ogden (50), Williamson (63), P Wood (70);
Goals: Marsh 9/10.
THUNDER: 1 Neil Thorman; 2 Robin Peers; 3 Graham Stephenson; 4 Pat Williamson; 5 Mark Christensen; 6 Tim Martin; 7 Kevin Till; 8 Jonny Scott; 9 Ryan Clarke; 10 Steven Bradley; 11 Shane Wooden; 12 Nick Hyde; 13 Odell Harris. Subs (all used): 14 Dylan Nash; 15 Matt Barron; 16 Tony Doherty; 17 Clint Frazer.
Tries: Frazer (24), Thorman (30), Nash (54);
Goals: Clarke 0/2, Christensen 0/1.
Rugby Leaguer & League Express Men of the Match: *Lions:* Martin Moana; *Thunder:* Neil Thorman.
Penalty count: 8-7; **Half-time:** 34-8;
Referee: Matthew Thomasson; **Attendance:** 403.

WEEK 6

Sunday 13th May 2007

BLACKPOOL PANTHERS 10 WORKINGTON TOWN 52

PANTHERS: 1 Mark Leigh; 2 Neil Hayden; 3 Chris Maye; 4 Eddie Kilgannon; 5 Chris Brand; 6 Martin Roden; 7 Martin Gambles; 8 Kris Ratcliffe; 9 Phil Cantillon; 10 James Simon; 11 Danny Barton; 12 Mike Stout; 13 Deon Duell. Subs (all used): 14 Jon Chamberlain; 15 Luke Murfin; 16 Lee Rowley; 17 Rob Lamb.
Tries: Kilgannon (20), Barton (58); **Goals:** Brand 1/3.
TOWN: 1 Rob Lunt; 2 Stephen Dawes; 3 Andrew Beattie; 4 Neil Frazer; 5 Martyn Wilson; 6 Carl Forber; 7 Liam Campbell; 8 Dean Vaughan; 9 Darren King; 10 Dean Burgess; 11 Jamie Beaumont; 12 Franco Kmet; 13 Garry Purdham. Subs (all used): 14 Shaun Lunt; 15 Scott Gorman; 16 Steve Ormesher; 17 Taani Lavulavu.
Tries: Campbell (14, 76), Kmet (30, 37), Frazer (32, 74), R Lunt (53, 80), S Lunt (68); **Goals:** Forber 8/9.
Sin bin: Purdham (64) - holding down.
Rugby Leaguer & League Express Men of the Match: *Panthers:* Eddie Kilgannon; *Town:* Franco Kmet.
Penalty count: 8-8; **Half-time:** 6-24;
Referee: Dave Merrick; **Attendance:** 309.

YORK CITY KNIGHTS 4 CELTIC CRUSADERS 26

CITY KNIGHTS: 1 George Rayner; 2 Tom Dunmore; 3 Dan Potter; 4 Chris Spurr; 5 Lee Mapals; 6 Jon Liddell; 7 Matty Brooks; 8 Dave Buckley; 9 Jamaine Wray; 10 Adam Sullivan; 11 Ian Brown; 12 Ryan Esders; 13 Rob Spicer. Subs (all used): 14 Jimmy Elston; 15 Stephen Grundy; 16 Toby Williams; 17 Nathan Priestley.
Try: Potter (36); **Goals:** Dunmore 0/1.
CRUSADERS: 1 Tony Duggan; 2 Richard Johnston; 3 Anthony Blackwood; 4 Mark Dalle Cort; 5 Paul Ballard; 6 Luke Young; 7 Jace Van Dijk; 8 Josh Cale; 9 Andy Boothroyd; 10 Phil Cushion; 11 Chris Beasley; 12 Darren Mapp; 13 Damien Quinn. Subs (all used): 14 Geraint Davies; 15 Jamie I'Anson; 16 Dean Fitzgerald; 17 Hywel Davies.
Tries: Duggan (5), Johnston (15), Dalle Cort (21), Van Dijk (39), Blackwood (52); **Goals:** Quinn 3/5.
Rugby Leaguer & League Express Men of the Match: *City Knights:* Dave Buckley; *Crusaders:* Tony Duggan.
Penalty count: 7-6; **Half-time:** 4-22;
Referee: Jamie Leahy; **Attendance:** 1,444.

FEATHERSTONE ROVERS 36 HUNSLET HAWKS 12

ROVERS: 1 Wayne McHugh; 2 Danny Kirmond; 3 Jon Whittle; 4 Dale Cardoza; 5 Dean Colton; 6 Chris Ross; 7 Paul Handforth; 8 Ian Tonks; 9 Gavin Swinson; 10 Stuart Dickens; 11 Jamie Field; 12 Richard Blakeway; 13 Tom Haughey. Subs (all used): 14 Paul Hughes; 15 Carl Hughes; 16 Steve Dooler; 17 James Houston.
Tries: Field (3), Haughey (18), Whittle (30), Kirmond (37), Swinson (56), Colton (64), Handforth (66);
Goals: Dickens 4/5, Ross 0/2.
Dismissal: Tonks (14) - high tackle on D Robinson.
HAWKS: 1 Matt Bramald; 2 Mark Cunningham; 3 Andy Robinson; 4 Danny Cook; 5 Steve Morton; 6 Mark Moxon; 7 Stuart Young; 8 Danny Murgatroyd; 9 Gareth Greenwood; 10 Matt Carbutt; 11 Wayne Freeman; 12 Will Cartledge; 13 Darren Robinson. Subs (all used): 14 Mark Cass; 15 Mark Holmes; 16 Ben Walkin; 17 Paul Smith.
Tries: A Robinson (39), Cass (79);
Goals: D Robinson 2/2.
Sin bin: Moxon (55) - interference;
Young (60) – punching.
Rugby Leaguer & League Express Men of the Match: *Rovers:* Paul Handforth; *Hawks:* Darren Robinson.
Penalty count: 15-5; **Half-time:** 20-6;
Referee: Mike Dawber; **Attendance:** 1,008.

Wednesday 16th May 2007

BARROW RAIDERS 38 LONDON SKOLARS 8

RAIDERS: 1 Khamal Ganley; 2 Nick Beach; 3 James Finch; 4 Liam Harrison; 5 Shane Irabor; 6 Mike Basan; 7 Liam Finch; 8 Michael Smith; 9 Andy Ellis; 10 Jamie Butler; 11 Mike Whitehead; 12 Dave Armistead; 13 Pat Weisner. Subs (all used): 14 Jamie Marshall; 15 Paul Wilcock; 16 Lee Dutton; 17 Ian Rawlinson.
Tries: Ganley (8), J Finch (20), Basan (22, 53), Smith (39), L Finch (44), Marshall (63), Irabor (68);
Goals: Beach 3/8.
SKOLARS: 1 Pete Hodgkinson; 2 Corey Simms; 3 Tryfan Edwards; 4 Dene Miller; 5 William Webster; 6 Mark Brenton; 7 Paul Thorman; 8 Martyn Benson; 9 Chris Lynton; 10 Richard Louw; 11 Keir Bell; 12 Tane Taitoko; 13 Chris Shears. Subs (all used): 14 Douglas Hann; 15 Mitchell Stone; 16 Dave Afrey; 17 Dave Robinson.
Tries: Benson (48), Webster (75); **Goals:** Webster 0/2.
Rugby Leaguer & League Express Men of the Match: *Raiders:* Mike Basan; *Skolars:* Dene Miller.
Penalty count: 8-12; **Half-time:** 20-0;
Referee: Paul Carr; **Attendance:** 1,045.

WEEK 7

Sunday 20th May 2007

GATESHEAD THUNDER 16 FEATHERSTONE ROVERS 74

THUNDER: 1 Neil Thorman; 2 Robin Peers; 3 Graham Stephenson; 4 Pat Williamson; 5 Odell Harris; 6 Mark Christensen; 7 Kevin Till; 8 Jonny Scott; 9 Nick Hyde; 10 Clint Frazer; 11 Steven Bradley; 12 Dylan Nash; 13 Shane Wooden. Subs (all used): 14 Tim Martin; 15 Ryan Clarke; 16 Andrew Pybus; 17 Chris Parker.
Tries: Wooden (21), Martin (48), Williamson (55);
Goals: Thorman 2/3.
Sin bin: Nash (38) - persistent offending.
ROVERS: 1 Loz Wildbore; 2 Danny Kirmond; 3 Jon Whittle; 4 Dale Cardoza; 5 Dean Colton; 6 Chris Ross; 7 Paul Handforth; 8 Ian Tonks; 9 Paul Hughes; 10 Stuart Dickens; 11 Jamie Field; 12 Richard Blakeway; 13 Tom Haughey. Subs (all used): 14 Gavin Swinson; 15 Carl Hughes; 16 Steve Dooler; 17 James Houston.
Tries: Whittle (5), Colton (10), Dickens (15), Tonks (19), Kirmond (25, 28, 65, 77), Houston (41), Handforth (43), Wildbore (58), Ross (60), C Hughes (62);
Goals: Dickens 11/13.
Dismissal: Haughey (53) - punching.
Rugby Leaguer & League Express Men of the Match: *Thunder:* Pat Williamson; *Rovers:* Danny Kirmond.
Penalty count: 5-9; **Half-time:** 6-34;
Referee: Robert Hicks; **Attendance:** 385.

KEIGHLEY COUGARS 16 LONDON SKOLARS 16

COUGARS: 1 Gavin Duffy; 2 Ryan Smith; 3 Michael Hastings; 4 Mick Fogerty; 5 Alex Brown; 6 Craig Fawcett; 7 Barry Eaton; 8 Brendan Rawlins; 9 James Feather; 10 Tom Palmer; 11 Brian Sutton; 12 Richard Knight; 13 Greg Nicholson. Subs (all used): 14 Chris Redfearn; 15 Matt Foster; 16 Simon Bissell; 17 Luke Sutton.
Tries: Duffy (65), Knight (67);
Goals: Eaton 2/2, Knight 2/2.
SKOLARS: 1 Pete Hodgkinson; 2 Corey Simms; 3 Jake

Kerr; 4 Ashley Tozer; 5 Austen Aggrey; 6 Jermaine Coleman; 7 Paul Thorman; 8 Martyn Benson; 9 Gareth Honor; 10 Richard Louw; 11 Tane Taitoko; 12 Lydan Maitua; 13 Chris Shears. Subs (all used): 14 Frank Reid; 15 Jamie Nowland; 16 Joe Price; 17 Alan Barker.
Tries: Simms (43), Kerr (50); **Goals:** Nowland 3/4;
Field goals: Nowland (57, 79).
Dismissal: Barker (65) - late challenge on Eaton.
Rugby Leaguer & League Express Men of the Match:
Cougars: Richard Knight; *Skolars:* Corey Simms.
Penalty count: 5-11; **Half-time:** 4-2;
Referee: Peter Taberner; **Attendance:** 643.

OLDHAM 50 BARROW RAIDERS 18

OLDHAM: 1 Paul O'Connor; 2 Gareth Langley; 3 Drew Houston; 4 Adam Hughes; 5 Lucas Onyango; 6 Neil Roden; 7 Lee Sanderson; 8 Jason Boults; 9 Simeon Hoyle; 10 Richard Mervill; 11 Geno Costin; 12 Ian Sinfield; 13 Ian Hodson. Subs (all used): 14 Andy Crabtree; 15 Anthony Tonks; 16 Adam Robinson; 17 Alex Wilkinson.
Tries: Hughes (17, 48), Roden (20, 38, 78), Sanderson (44), Wilkinson (67), Robinson (80);
Goals: Sanderson 6/6, Langley 3/3.
RAIDERS: 1 Khamal Ganley; 2 Nick Beach; 3 Mike Basan; 4 Liam Harrison; 5 James Nixon; 6 Liam Finch; 7 Pat Weisner; 8 Lee Dutton; 9 Andy Ellis; 10 Brett McDermott; 11 Michael Smith; 12 Dave Armistead; 13 Mike Whitehead. Subs (all used): 14 Shane Irabor; 15 James Finch; 16 Paul Wilcock; 17 Ian Rawlinson.
Tries: Nixon (30), McDermott (56), Rawlinson (71);
Goals: Weisner 3/3.
Rugby Leaguer & League Express Men of the Match:
Oldham: Lee Sanderson; *Raiders:* Dave Armistead.
Penalty count: 10-3; **Half-time:** 20-6;
Referee: James Child; **Attendance:** 848.

SWINTON LIONS 26 YORK CITY KNIGHTS 38

LIONS: 1 Wayne English; 2 Desi Williams; 3 Darren Woods; 4 Kash Watkins; 5 Marlon Billy; 6 Mark Ogden; 7 Liam McGovern; 8 Bruce Johnson; 9 Phil Wood; 10 Rob Line; 11 Paul Alcock; 12 Martin Moana; 13 Lee Marsh. Subs (all used): 14 Mike Smith; 15 Richard Marshall; 16 Chris Morley; 17 Gareth Hayes.
Tries: Alcock (2), Billy (26), Williams (58), Marsh (71), Watkins (75); **Goals:** Marsh 3/5.
Sin bin: Alcock (74) - fighting.
CITY KNIGHTS: 1 George Rayner; 2 Lee Mapals; 3 Dan Potter; 4 Chris Spurr; 5 Alex Godfrey; 6 Scott Rhodes; 7 Matty Brooks; 8 Dave Buckley; 9 Jamaine Wray; 10 Adam Sullivan; 11 Rob Spicer; 12 Ryan Esders; 13 Jon Liddell. Subs (all used): 14 Jimmy Elston; 15 Stephen Grundy; 16 Toby Williams; 17 Nathan Priestley.
Tries: C Spurr (12), Spicer (17), Godfrey (31, 46), Esders (37), Potter (50), Mapals (55, 80);
Goals: Wray 1/2, Brooks 1/3, Liddell 1/2, Mapals 0/1.
Sin bin: Godfrey (53) – dissent; Wray (74) - fighting.
Rugby Leaguer & League Express Men of the Match:
Lions: Phil Wood; *City Knights:* Scott Rhodes.
Penalty count: 4-7; **Half-time:** 10-18;
Referee: Dave Merrick; **Attendance:** 541.

WORKINGTON TOWN 28 CELTIC CRUSADERS 16

TOWN: 1 Rob Lunt; 2 Stephen Dawes; 3 Andrew Beattie; 4 Neil Frazer; 5 Martyn Wilson; 6 Carl Forber; 7 Liam Campbell; 8 Dean Vaughan; 9 Darren King; 10 Dean Burgess; 11 Jamie Beaumont; 12 Franco Kmet; 13 Garry Purdham. Subs (all used): 14 Shaun Lunt; 15 Adam Sidlow; 16 Steve Ormesher; 17 Taani Lavulavu.
Tries: Forber (26), Dawes (38), S Lunt (68), Wilson (80); **Goals:** Forber 6/7.
CRUSADERS: 1 Tony Duggan; 2 Richard Johnston; 3 Anthony Blackwood; 4 Mark Dalle Cort; 5 Paul Ballard; 6 Luke Young; 7 Jace Van Dijk; 8 Josh Cale; 9 Neil Budworth; 10 Phil Cushion; 11 Chris Beasley; 12 Darren Mapp; 13 Damien Quinn. Subs (all used): 14 Andy Boothroyd; 15 Jamie I'Anson; 16 Grant Epton; 17 Hywel Davies.
Tries: H Davies (34), Dalle Cort (74), Epton (76);
Goals: Quinn 2/3.
Rugby Leaguer & League Express Men of the Match:
Town: Carl Forber; *Crusaders:* Andy Boothroyd.
Penalty count: 9-11; **Half-time:** 14-6;
Referee: Craig Halloran; **Attendance:** 896.

HUNSLET HAWKS 30 BLACKPOOL PANTHERS 18

HAWKS: 1 Matt Bramald; 2 Andy Robinson; 3 Ben Jones; 4 Danny Cook; 5 Steve Morton; 6 Mark Moxon; 7 Matt Firth; 8 Danny Ekis; 9 Darren Robinson; 10 Paul Smith; 11 Wayne Freeman; 12 Mark Cunningham; 13 Will Cartledge. Subs (all used): 14 Gareth Greenwood; 15 Matt Carbutt; 16 Ben Walkin; 17 Scott Houston.
Tries: Bramald (23), A Robinson (43), Morton (48), Cook (55), D Robinson (74); **Goals:** D Robinson 5/7.
PANTHERS: 1 Chris Brand; 2 Kieron Seeds; 3 Chris Maye; 4 Eddie Kilgannon; 5 Mark Leigh; 6 Neil Hayden; 7 Martin Gambles; 8 Lee Rowley; 9 Phil Cantillon; 10 James Simon; 11 Kris Ratcliffe; 12 Mike Stout; 13 Deon Duell. Subs (all used): 14 Safraz Patel; 15 Jon Chamberlain; 16 Simon Knox; 17 Rob Lamb.
Tries: Gambles (19), Chamberlain (39), Cantillon (60);
Goals: Brand 3/4.
Rugby Leaguer & League Express Men of the Match:
Hawks: Wayne Freeman; *Panthers:* Martin Gambles.
Penalty count: 9-11; **Half-time:** 6-12;
Referee: Paul Carr; **Attendance:** 291.

WEEK 8

Saturday 26th May 2007

LONDON SKOLARS 6 OLDHAM 34

SKOLARS: 1 Pete Hodgkinson; 2 William Webster; 3 Jake Kerr; 4 Dene Miller; 5 Austen Aggrey; 6 Paul Thorman; 7 Jamie Nowland; 8 Alan Barker; 9 Gareth Honor; 10 Richard Louw; 11 Keir Bell; 12 Joe Price; 13 Chris Shears. Subs (all used): 14 Frank Reid; 15 Jermaine Coleman; 16 Chris Lynton; 17 Martyn Benson.
Try: Aggrey (61); **Goals:** Nowland 1/1.
Sin bin: Lynton (67) - fighting.
OLDHAM: 1 Gareth Langley; 2 Alex Wilkinson; 3 Drew Houston; 4 Adam Hughes; 5 Lucas Onyango; 6 Neil Roden; 7 Lee Sanderson; 8 Jason Boults; 9 Simeon Hoyle; 10 Richard Mervill; 11 Geno Costin; 12 Ian Sinfield; 13 Ian Hodson. Subs (all used): 14 Andy Crabtree; 15 Anthony Tonks; 16 Chris Baines; 17 Adam Robinson.
Tries: Houston (9, 51), Wilkinson (21), Hodson (24), Costin (25), Hughes (38), Onyango (71);
Goals: Sanderson 3/7.
Sin bin: Hughes (67) - fighting.
Rugby Leaguer & League Express Men of the Match:
Skolars: Jamie Nowland; *Oldham:* Neil Roden.
Penalty count: 13-12; **Half-time:** 0-26;
Referee: Paul Carr; **Attendance:** 635.

Sunday 27th May 2007

BLACKPOOL PANTHERS 12 YORK CITY KNIGHTS 24

PANTHERS: 1 Chris Brand; 2 Kieron Seeds; 3 Mike Stout; 4 Eddie Kilgannon; 5 Mark Leigh; 6 Neil Hayden; 7 Martin Gambles; 8 Lee Rowley; 9 Phil Cantillon; 10 Rob Lamb; 11 Kris Ratcliffe; 12 Danny Barton; 13 Deon Duell. Subs (all used): 14 Safraz Patel; 15 Jon Chamberlain; 16 Gareth Jones; 17 Daniel Palmer.
Tries: Stout (43, 80); **Goals:** Brand 2/2.
CITY KNIGHTS: 1 George Rayner; 2 Lee Mapals; 3 Dan Potter; 4 Chris Spurr; 5 Alex Godfrey; 6 Scott Rhodes; 7 Matty Brooks; 8 Dave Buckley; 9 Jamaine Wray; 10 Adam Sullivan; 11 Rob Spicer; 12 Nathan Priestley; 13 Jon Liddell. Subs (all used): 14 Jimmy Elston; 15 Ian Brown; 16 Toby Williams; 17 Neil Lowe.
Tries: Brooks (2), Godfrey (13), C Spurr (32), Elston (54), Mapals (59), Lowe (80);
Goals: Wray 0/3, Godfrey 0/1, Liddell 0/1, Lowe 0/1.
Rugby Leaguer & League Express Men of the Match:
Panthers: Phil Cantillon; *City Knights:* Jamaine Wray.
Penalty count: 8-6; **Half-time:** 0-12;
Referee: Dave Merrick; **Attendance:** 306.

FEATHERSTONE ROVERS 42 SWINTON LIONS 4

ROVERS: 1 Loz Wildbore; 2 Danny Kirmond; 3 Jon Whittle; 4 Dale Cardoza; 5 Dean Colton; 6 Chris Ross; 7 Paul Handforth; 8 Gareth Handford; 9 Paul Hughes; 10 Stuart Dickens; 11 Jamie Field; 12 Steve Dooler; 13 Tom Haughey. Subs (all used): 14 Wayne McHugh; 15 Gavin Swinson; 16 James Houston; 17 Carl Hughes.
Tries: Dooler (2, 29), Field (6), Haughey (13), Colton (20, 37), Kirmond (55), P Hughes (66);
Goals: Dickens 5/7, Ross 0/1.
LIONS: 1 Wayne English; 2 Desi Williams; 3 Dean Gorton; 4 Dave Ashton; 5 Marlon Billy; 6 Mark Ogden; 7 Phil Wood; 8 Bruce Johnson; 9 Craig Ashall; 10 Rob Line; 11 Chris Morley; 12 Mike Smith; 13 Kash Watkins. Subs (all used): 14 Chris Hough; 15 Richard Marshall; 16 David Bates; 17 Danny Aboushakra.
Try: Gorton (75); **Goals:** P Wood 0/1.
Rugby Leaguer & League Express Men of the Match:
Rovers: Jamie Field; *Lions:* Phil Wood.
Penalty count: 7-4; **Half-time:** 32-0;
Referee: Peter Taberner; **Attendance:** 1,014.

GATESHEAD THUNDER 32 KEIGHLEY COUGARS 12

THUNDER: 1 Neil Thorman; 2 Stuart Sanderson; 3 Graham Stephenson; 4 Mark Christensen; 5 Odell Harris; 6 Tim Martin; 7 Kevin Till; 8 Clint Frazer; 9 Nick Hyde; 10 Tabua Cakacaka; 11 Shane Wooden; 12 Dylan Nash; 13 Pat Williamson. Subs (all used): 14 Ryan Clarke; 15 Robin Peers; 16 Steve Rutherford; 17 Matt Barron.
Tries: Thorman (18), Till (30, 68), Christensen (36, 61);
Goals: Thorman 6/8.
COUGARS: 1 Gavin Duffy; 2 Ryan Smith; 3 Matt Foster; 4 Mick Fogerty; 5 Alex Brown; 6 Craig Fawcett; 7 Barry Eaton; 8 Simon Bissell; 9 James Feather; 10 Tom Palmer; 11 Greg Nicholson; 12 Richard Knight; 13 Chris Redfearn. Subs (all used): 14 Brian Sutton; 15 Sam Gardner; 16 Wayne Sutcliffe; 17 Luke Sutton.
Tries: Knight (46), Fogerty (50); **Goals:** Eaton 2/2.
Sin bin: Sutcliffe (71) - off the ball incident;
Fogerty (80) - dissent.
Rugby Leaguer & League Express Men of the Match:
Thunder: Neil Thorman; *Cougars:* Richard Knight.
Penalty count: 14-5; **Half-time:** 18-0;
Referee: Jamie Leahy; **Attendance:** 277.

WORKINGTON TOWN 30 HUNSLET HAWKS 18

TOWN: 1 Rob Lunt; 2 Stephen Dawes; 3 Andrew Beattie; 4 Neil Frazer; 5 Martyn Wilson; 6 Carl Forber; 7 Shaun Lunt; 8 Dean Vaughan; 9 Darren King; 10 Adam Sidlow; 11 Steve Ormesher; 12 Franco Kmet; 13 Garry Purdham. Subs (all used): 14 Jamie Beaumont; 15 Weldon Saayman; 16 Dean Burgess; 17 Taani Lavulavu.
Tries: Dawes (3), Kmet (13, 77), Sidlow (58), Ormesher (61); **Goals:** Forber 5/5.
HAWKS: 1 Matt Bramald; 2 Andy Robinson; 3 Ben Jones; 4 Danny Cook; 5 Steve Morton; 6 Mark Moxon; 7 Matt Firth; 8 Danny Ekis; 9 Darren Robinson; 10 Scott Houston; 11 Wayne Freeman; 12 Mark Cunningham; 13 Will Cartledge. Subs (all used): 14 Gareth Greenwood; 15 Matt Carbutt; 16 Ben Walkin; 17 Paul Smith.
Tries: A Robinson (29), P Smith (34, 48);
Goals: Bramald 2/2, D Robinson 1/3.
Rugby Leaguer & League Express Men of the Match:
Town: Darren King; *Hawks:* Wayne Freeman.
Penalty count: 6-11; **Half-time:** 12-12;
Referee: Robert Hicks; **Attendance:** 741.

WEEK 9

Saturday 2nd June 2007

CELTIC CRUSADERS 36 FEATHERSTONE ROVERS 28

CRUSADERS: 1 Tony Duggan; 2 Anthony Blackwood; 3 Rob Toshack; 4 Mark Dalle Cort; 5 Grant Epton; 6 Luke Young; 7 Jace Van Dijk; 8 Josh Cale; 9 Neil Budworth; 10 Phil Cushion; 11 Chris Beasley; 12 Darren Mapp; 13 Damien Quinn. Subs (all used): 14 Andy Boothroyd; 15 Jamie I'Anson; 16 Neale Wyatt; 17 Hywel Davies.
Tries: Cushion (21), Duggan (36), Quinn (38, 63), Blackwood (71), Young (80); **Goals:** Quinn 6/7.
ROVERS: 1 Loz Wildbore; 2 Danny Kirmond; 3 Wayne McHugh; 4 Steve Dooler; 5 Dale Cardoza; 6 Andy Kain; 7 Paul Handforth; 8 Ian Tonks; 9 Paul Hughes; 10 Stuart Dickens; 11 Jamie Field; 12 Richard Blakeway; 13 Tom Haughey. Subs (all used): 14 Chris Ross; 15 Carl Hughes; 16 James Houston; 17 Gareth Handford.
Tries: Kain (11, 51), Handforth (57), C Hughes (67), Haughey (73); **Goals:** Dickens 4/5.
Rugby Leaguer & League Express Men of the Match:
Crusaders: Anthony Blackwood; *Rovers:* Paul Handforth.
Penalty count: 5-4; **Half-time:** 18-6;
Referee: Robert Hicks; **Attendance:** 931.

Sunday 3rd June 2007

BARROW RAIDERS 52 SWINTON LIONS 24

RAIDERS: 1 Khamal Ganley; 2 Nick Beach; 3 James Finch; 4 Liam Harrison; 5 Jamie Marshall; 6 Liam Finch; 7 Darren Holt; 8 Paul Raftrey; 9 Andy Ellis; 10 Lee Dutton; 11 Mike Whitehead; 12 Dave Armistead; 13 Pat Weisner. Subs (all used): 14 Chris Archer; 15 Paul Wilcock; 16 Michael Smith; 17 Ian Rawlinson.
Tries: Marshall (4, 65), Harrison (7), Ganley (9), Whitehead (26, 37), J Finch (52, 58), L Finch (75);
Goals: Holt 8/9.
LIONS: 1 Wayne English; 2 Andy Saywell; 3 Dean Gorton; 4 Dave Ashton; 5 Marlon Billy; 6 Martin Moana; 7 Chris Hough; 8 David Bates; 9 Phil Wood; 10 Richard Marshall; 11 Chris Morley; 12 Bruce Johnson; 13 Mike Smith. Subs (all used): 14 Craig Ashall; 15 Paul Alcock; 16 Rob Line; 17 Danny Aboushakra.
Tries: Johnson (15), Morley (31), Saywell (47, 80), Ashall (70); **Goals:** Hough 2/5.
Rugby Leaguer & League Express Men of the Match:
Raiders: Dave Armistead; *Lions:* Wayne English.
Penalty count: 8-5; **Half-time:** 30-10;
Referee: James Child; **Attendance:** 1,188.

BLACKPOOL PANTHERS 18 GATESHEAD THUNDER 28

PANTHERS: 1 Chris Brand; 2 Kieron Seeds; 3 Mike Stout; 4 Eddie Kilgannon; 5 Mark Leigh; 6 Neil Hayden; 7 Martin Gambles; 8 Lee Rowley; 9 Phil Cantillon; 10 Rob Lamb; 11 Danny Barton; 12 Kris Ratcliffe; 13 Deon Duell. Subs (all used): 14 Safraz Patel; 15 Jon Chamberlain; 16 Chris Maye; 17 Gareth Jones.
Tries: Cantillon (24, 71), Maye (37);
Goals: Brand 2/2, Gambles 1/1.
THUNDER: 1 Neil Thorman; 2 Stuart Sanderson; 3 Graham Stephenson; 4 Mark Christensen; 5 Odell Harris; 6 Tim Martin; 7 Kevin Till; 8 Tabua Cakacaka; 9 Nick Hyde; 10 Clint Frazer; 11 Shane Wooden; 12 Dylan Nash; 13 Pat Williamson. Subs (all used): 14 Robin Peers; 15 Ryan Clarke; 16 Steve Rutherford; 17 Steven Bradley.
Tries: Williamson (3), Nash (13), Hyde (18), Thorman (56), Stephenson (66); **Goals:** Thorman 4/5.
Rugby Leaguer & League Express Men of the Match:
Panthers: Phil Cantillon; *Thunder:* Neil Thorman.
Penalty count: 7-5; **Half-time:** 12-18;
Referee: Mike Dawber; **Attendance:** 275.

LONDON SKOLARS 20 HUNSLET HAWKS 21

SKOLARS: 1 Jermaine Coleman; 2 Jake Kerr; 3 Pete Hodgkinson; 4 Joe Price; 5 Austen Aggrey; 6 Paul Thorman; 7 Jamie Nowland; 8 Martyn Benson; 9 Gareth Honor; 10 Richard Louw; 11 Tane Taitoko; 12 Lydan Maitua; 13 Chris Shears. Subs (all used): 14 Frank Reid; 15 Kurt Pittman; 16 Chris Lynton; 17 Keir Bell.
Tries: Hodgkinson (14, 21), Maitua (19);
Goals: Nowland 4/5.
HAWKS: 1 Matt Bramald; 2 Andy Robinson; 3 David Foster; 4 Danny Cook; 5 Steve Morton; 6 Mark Moxon; 7 Matt Firth; 8 Paul Smith; 9 Darren Robinson; 10 Scott Houston; 11 Wayne Freeman; 12 Mark Cunningham; 13 Will Cartledge. Subs (all used): 14 Gareth Greenwood; 15 Matt Carbutt; 16 Paul Seal; 17 Danny Murgatroyd.
Tries: Cook (33), P Smith (60), A Robinson (68), Cunningham (71); **Goals:** Bramald 1/3, D Robinson 1/2;
Field goal: Bramald (74).
Rugby Leaguer & League Express Men of the Match:
Skolars: Pete Hodgkinson; *Hawks:* Mark Cunningham.
Penalty count: 10-11; **Half-time:** 18-4;
Referee: Matthew Thomasson; **Attendance:** 413.

WORKINGTON TOWN 18 OLDHAM 27

TOWN: 1 Rob Lunt; 2 Stephen Dawes; 3 Andrew Beattie;

4 Neil Frazer; 5 Dexter Miller; 6 Carl Forber; 7 Martin Keavney; 8 Dean Vaughan; 9 Darren King; 10 Adam Sidlow; 11 Jamie Beaumont; 12 Franco Kmet; 13 Garry Purdham. Subs (all used): 14 Shaun Lunt; 15 Weldon Saayman; 16 Dean Burgess; 17 Taani Lavulavu.
Tries: Beattie (25), R Lunt (64), Keavney (78);
Goals: Forber 3/3.
OLDHAM: 1 Gareth Langley; 2 Alex Wilkinson; 3 Drew Houston; 4 Adam Hughes; 5 Lucas Onyango; 6 Neil Roden; 7 Lee Sanderson; 8 Jason Boults; 9 Simeon Hoyle; 10 Richard Mervill; 11 Geno Costin; 12 Ian Sinfield; 13 Ian Hodson. Subs (all used): 14 Andy Crabtree; 15 Said Tamghart; 16 Adam Robinson; 17 Chris Baines.
Tries: Hughes (15), Onyango (19), Hodson (31), Baines (73); **Goals:** Sanderson 5/6; **Field goal:** Roden (70).
Rugby Leaguer & League Express Men of the Match: *Town:* Rob Lunt; *Oldham:* Neil Roden.
Penalty count: 5-8; **Half-time:** 6-18;
Referee: Craig Halloran; **Attendance:** 1,213.

YORK CITY KNIGHTS 34 KEIGHLEY COUGARS 8

CITY KNIGHTS: 1 George Rayner; 2 Alex Godfrey; 3 Ian Brown; 4 Chris Spurr; 5 Lee Mapals; 6 Scott Rhodes; 7 Danny Grimshaw; 8 Dave Buckley; 9 Jamaine Wray; 10 Neil Lowe; 11 Rob Spicer; 12 Nathan Priestley; 13 Jon Liddell. Subs (all used): 14 Jimmy Elston; 15 Ryan Esders; 16 Toby Williams; 17 Adam Sullivan.
Tries: Mapals (22), Grimshaw (36), Lowe (55), Spicer (61), Godfrey (72), Rhodes (80);
Goals: Grimshaw 4/5, Liddell 1/2.
Sin bin: Buckley (13) – late tackle on Eaton.
COUGARS: 1 Gavin Duffy; 2 Sam Gardner; 3 Matt Foster; 4 Mick Fogerty; 5 Alex Brown; 6 Adam Mitchell; 7 Barry Eaton; 8 Simon Bissell; 9 James Feather; 10 Luke Sutton; 11 Greg Nicholson; 12 Richard Knight; 13 Chris Redfearn. Subs (all used): 14 Craig Weston; 15 Brian Sutton; 16 Wayne Sutcliffe; 17 Tom Palmer.
Try: Redfearn (67); **Goals:** Eaton 2/3.
Sin bin: Eaton (80) - professional foul.
Rugby Leaguer & League Express Men of the Match: *City Knights:* Danny Grimshaw; *Cougars:* Gavin Duffy.
Penalty count: 13-9; **Half-time:** 12-2;
Referee: Paul Carr; **Attendance:** 938.

WEEK 10

Saturday 9th June 2007

CELTIC CRUSADERS 26 BARROW RAIDERS 14

CRUSADERS: 1 Tony Duggan; 2 Anthony Blackwood; 3 Rob Toshack; 4 Mark Dalle Cort; 5 Grant Epton; 6 Luke Young; 7 Jace Van Dijk; 8 Josh Cale; 9 Neil Budworth; 10 Phil Cushion; 11 Neale Wyatt; 12 Darren Mapp; 13 Damien Quinn. Subs (all used): 14 Paul Ballard; 15 Jamie I'Anson; 16 Dean Fitzgerald; 17 Hywel Davies.
Tries: Mapp (9), Budworth (21), Duggan (24), Van Dijk (48), Ballard (77); **Goals:** Quinn 3/5.
RAIDERS: 1 Khamal Ganley; 2 James Finch; 3 Mike Whitehead; 4 Liam Harrison; 5 Jamie Marshall; 6 Liam Finch; 7 Darren Holt; 8 Michael Smith; 9 Andy Ellis; 10 Paul Raftrey; 11 Martin Ostler; 12 Dave Armistead; 13 Pat Weisner. Subs (all used): 14 Chris Archer; 15 Paul Wilcock; 16 Phil Atkinson; 17 Lee Dutton.
Tries: L Finch (34), Ganley (43); **Goals:** Holt 3/3.
Rugby Leaguer & League Express Men of the Match: *Crusaders:* Darren Mapp; *Raiders:* Liam Finch.
Penalty count: 5-3; **Half-time:** 16-6;
Referee: Dave Merrick; **Attendance:** 903.

Sunday 10th June 2007

BLACKPOOL PANTHERS 0 FEATHERSTONE ROVERS 58

PANTHERS: 1 Chris Maye; 2 Kieron Seeds; 3 Mike Stout; 4 Eddie Kilgannon; 5 Mark Leigh; 6 Deon Duell; 7 Martin Gambles; 8 Lee Rowley; 9 Phil Cantillon; 10 Gareth Jones; 11 Jon Chamberlain; 12 Kris Ratcliffe; 13 Danny Barton. Subs (all used): 14 Chris Brand; 15 Daniel Palmer; 16 Ian Parry; 17 Rob Lamb.
Sin bin: Palmer (40) – dissent.
ROVERS: 1 Loz Wildbore; 2 Wayne McHugh; 3 Jon Whittle; 4 Danny Kirmond; 5 Dean Colton; 6 Andy Kain; 7 Paul Handforth; 8 Ian Tonks; 9 Gavin Swinson; 10 Stuart Dickens; 11 Jamie Field; 12 Richard Blakeway; 13 Tom Haughey. Subs (all used): 14 Chris Ross; 15 Carl Hughes; 16 Steve Dooler; 17 Gareth Handford.
Tries: Whittle (2), McHugh (8, 17, 66), Haughey (28), Handforth (43, 62, 73), Kain (54), C Hughes (78);
Goals: Dickens 5/6, Handforth 1/1, Ross 3/3.
Rugby Leaguer & League Express Men of the Match: *Panthers:* Eddie Kilgannon; *Rovers:* Paul Handforth.
Penalty count: 13-7; **Half-time:** 0-22;
Referee: Craig Halloran; **Attendance:** 485.

GATESHEAD THUNDER 20 LONDON SKOLARS 28

THUNDER: 1 Neil Thorman; 2 Stuart Sanderson; 3 Graham Stephenson; 4 Mark Christensen; 5 Odell Harris; 6 Tim Martin; 7 Kevin Till; 8 Tabua Cakacaka; 9 Nick Hyde; 10 Clint Frazer; 11 Shane Wooden; 12 Dylan Nash; 13 Pat Williamson. Subs (all used): 14 Ryan Clarke; 15 Robin Peers; 16 Mark McKinley; 17 Chris Parker.
Tries: Harris (6), Christensen (18), Martin (29), Thorman (46, 54); **Goals:** Thorman 0/5.
SKOLARS: 1 Jermaine Coleman; 2 Jake Kerr; 3 Pete Hodgkinson; 4 Ashley Tozer; 5 Austen Aggrey; 6 Paul Thorman; 7 Jamie Nowland; 8 Martyn Benson; 9 Gareth Honor; 10 Richard Louw; 11 Tane Taitoko; 12 Lydan Maitua; 13 Chris Shears. Subs (all used): 14 Frank Reid; 15 Joe Price; 16 Craig Anderson; 17 Alan Barker.
Tries: Honor (15), Nowland (21, 59), Hodgkinson (38), Tozer (75); **Goals:** Nowland 4/6.
Rugby Leaguer & League Express Men of the Match: *Thunder:* Neil Thorman; *Skolars:* Martyn Benson.
Penalty count: 5-7; **Half-time:** 12-16;
Referee: Paul Carr; **Attendance:** 278.

KEIGHLEY COUGARS 33 WORKINGTON TOWN 22

COUGARS: 1 Gavin Duffy; 2 Sam Gardner; 3 Matt Foster; 4 Mick Fogerty; 5 Alex Brown; 6 Adam Mitchell; 7 Craig Fawcett; 8 Simon Bissell; 9 James Feather; 10 Luke Sutton; 11 Greg Nicholson; 12 Richard Knight; 13 Chris Redfearn. Subs (all used): 14 Barry Eaton; 15 Brian Sutton; 16 Wayne Sutcliffe; 17 Brendan Rawlins.
Tries: Gardner (28), Fogerty (33, 37), J Feather (59), L Sutton (79); **Goals:** Knight 6/7; **Field goal:** Fawcett (55).
TOWN: 1 Rob Lunt; 2 Stephen Dawes; 3 Andrew Beattie; 4 Neil Frazer; 5 Martyn Wilson; 6 Carl Forber; 7 Martin Keavney; 8 Taani Lavulavu; 9 Shaun Lunt; 10 Adam Sidlow; 11 Franco Kmet; 12 Steve Ormesher; 13 Garry Purdham. Subs (all used): 14 Darren King; 15 Dexter Miller; 16 Jamie Beaumont; 17 Mark Cox.
Tries: Sidlow (10), King (43), S Lunt (72), R Lunt (75);
Goals: Forber 3/4.
Sin bin: Lavulavu (59) - dissent.
Rugby Leaguer & League Express Men of the Match: *Cougars:* James Feather; *Town:* Shaun Lunt.
Penalty count: 8-3; **Half-time:** 18-6;
Referee: Peter Taberner; **Attendance:** 613.

OLDHAM 21 YORK CITY KNIGHTS 10

OLDHAM: 1 Andy Gorey; 2 Gareth Langley; 3 Craig Littler; 4 Alex Wilkinson; 5 Lucas Onyango; 6 Neil Roden; 7 Lee Sanderson; 8 Jason Boults; 9 Simeon Hoyle; 10 Richard Mervill; 11 Ian Hodson; 12 Ian Sinfield; 13 Chris Baines. Subs (all used): 14 Andy Crabtree; 15 Anthony Tonks; 16 Said Tamghart; 17 Adam Robinson.
Tries: Tonks (34), Robinson (36), Onyango (40), Gorey (74); **Goals:** Sanderson 2/3, Langley 0/1;
Field goal: Roden (79).
CITY KNIGHTS: 1 George Rayner; 2 Lee Mapals; 3 Ian Brown; 4 Chris Spurr; 5 Alex Godfrey; 6 Scott Rhodes; 7 Danny Grimshaw; 8 Neil Lowe; 9 Jamaine Wray; 10 Adam Sullivan; 11 Rob Spicer; 12 Nathan Priestley; 13 Jon Liddell. Subs (all used): 14 Jimmy Elston; 15 Ryan Esders; 16 Toby Williams; 17 Dave Buckley.
Tries: Mapals (11, 55); **Goals:** Grimshaw 1/3.
Rugby Leaguer & League Express Men of the Match: *Oldham:* Anthony Tonks; *City Knights:* Lee Mapals.
Penalty count: 10-12; **Half-time:** 16-4; **Referee:** Jamie Leahy; **Attendance:** 1,024 *(at Park Lane, Sedgley Park).*

HUNSLET HAWKS 10 SWINTON LIONS 17

HAWKS: 1 Matt Bramald; 2 Andy Robinson; 3 David Foster; 4 Danny Cook; 5 Steve Morton; 6 Mark Moxon; 7 Matt Firth; 8 Paul Smith; 9 Gareth Greenwood; 10 Scott Houston; 11 Wayne Freeman; 12 Will Cartledge; 13 Darren Robinson. Subs (all used): 14 Ben Jones; 15 Paul Seal; 16 Paul Robinson; 17 Matt Carbutt.
Tries: Morton (6), Firth (52); **Goals:** D Robinson 1/2.
LIONS: 1 Chris Hull; 2 Andy Saywell; 3 Dean Gorton; 4 Dave Ashton; 5 Marlon Billy; 6 Craig Ashall; 7 Liam McGovern; 8 David Bates; 9 Phil Wood; 10 Danny Aboushakra; 11 Paul Alcock; 12 Mike Smith; 13 Martin Moana. Subs (all used): 14 Chris Hough; 15 Chris Morley; 16 Rob Line; 17 Gareth Hayes.
Tries: Bates (17), Billy (38); **Goals:** McGovern 4/5;
Field goal: McGovern (67).
Rugby Leaguer & League Express Men of the Match: *Hawks:* Wayne Freeman; *Lions:* Liam McGovern.
Penalty count: 7-6; **Half-time:** 6-14;
Referee: Robert Hicks; **Attendance:** 364.

Wednesday 13th June 2007

BARROW RAIDERS 30 KEIGHLEY COUGARS 0

RAIDERS: 1 Jamie Marshall; 2 James Finch; 3 Phil Atkinson; 4 Liam Harrison; 5 Chris Larkin; 6 Liam Finch; 7 Darren Holt; 8 Paul Raftrey; 9 Andy Ellis; 10 Michael Smith; 11 Mike Whitehead; 12 Dave Armistead; 13 Pat Weisner. Subs (all used): 14 Chris Archer; 15 Paul Wilcock; 16 Martin Ostler; 17 Lee Dutton.
Tries: Ellis (7), Weisner (36), Larkin (61), Raftrey (66), Dutton (78); **Goals:** Holt 5/5.
COUGARS: 1 Gavin Duffy; 2 Sam Gardner; 3 Matt Foster; 4 Mick Fogerty; 5 Ryan Smith; 6 Adam Mitchell; 7 Craig Fawcett; 8 Simon Bissell; 9 James Feather; 10 Gareth English; 11 Greg Nicholson; 12 Richard Knight; 13 Chris Redfearn. Subs (all used): 14 Craig Weston; 15 Brian Sutton; 16 Wayne Sutcliffe; 17 Brendan Rawlins.
Rugby Leaguer & League Express Men of the Match: *Raiders:* Michael Smith; *Cougars:* Mick Fogerty.
Penalty count: 5-4; **Half-time:** 12-0;
Referee: Gareth Hewer; **Attendance:** 1,058.

WEEK 11

Saturday 16th June 2007

LONDON SKOLARS 28 BLACKPOOL PANTHERS 14

SKOLARS: 1 Jermaine Coleman; 2 Corey Simms; 3 Pete Hodgkinson; 4 Ashley Tozer; 5 Austen Aggrey; 6 Paul Thorman; 7 Gareth Honor; 8 Martyn Benson; 9 Frank Reid; 10 Richard Louw; 11 Tane Taitoko; 12 Lydan Maitua; 13 Chris Shears. Subs (all used): 14 Kurt Pittman; 15 Joe Price; 16 Craig Anderson; 17 Keir Bell.
Tries: Aggrey (50), Hodgkinson (57, 65), Tozer (68), Price (70); **Goals:** Thorman 4/5.
On report: Louw (20) – alleged late tackle.
PANTHERS: 1 Mark Leigh; 2 Simon Holden; 3 Mike Stout; 4 Chris Brand; 5 Kieron Seeds; 6 Neil Hayden; 7 Martin Gambles; 8 Lee Rowley; 9 Phil Cantillon; 10 Gareth Jones; 11 Jon Chamberlain; 12 Kris Ratcliffe; 13 Deon Duell. Subs (all used): 14 Eddie Kilgannon; 15 Danny Barton; 16 Daniel Palmer; 17 Rob Lamb.
Tries: Gambles (7), Cantillon (77); **Goals:** Brand 3/4.
Rugby Leaguer & League Express Men of the Match: *Skolars:* Pete Hodgkinson; *Panthers:* Lee Rowley.
Penalty count: 6-10; **Half-time:** 0-8;
Referee: Robert Hicks; **Attendance:** 413.

Sunday 17th June 2007

BARROW RAIDERS 60 GATESHEAD THUNDER 22

RAIDERS: 1 Jamie Marshall; 2 James Finch; 3 Phil Atkinson; 4 Liam Harrison; 5 James Nixon; 6 Liam Finch; 7 Darren Holt; 8 Paul Raftrey; 9 Andy Ellis; 10 Michael Smith; 11 Mike Whitehead; 12 Dave Armistead; 13 Pat Weisner. Subs (all used): 14 Chris Archer; 15 James Gordon; 16 Martin Ostler; 17 Lee Dutton.
Tries: L Finch (7, 20, 80), Atkinson (12), Harrison (35, 39, 50), Nixon (37, 75), Raftrey (59), J Finch (61); **Goals:** Holt 7/9, Atkinson 1/2.
THUNDER: 1 Stuart Sanderson; 2 Robin Peers; 3 Graham Stephenson; 4 Mark McKinley; 5 Odell Harris; 6 Mark Christensen; 7 Tim Martin; 8 Clint Frazer; 9 Nick Hyde; 10 Matt Barron; 11 Shane Wooden; 12 Dylan Nash; 13 Pat Williamson. Subs: 14 Ryan Clarke (not used); 15 Andrew Pybus; 16 Chris Parker; 17 Tony Doherty.
Tries: Martin (3, 43), Nash (55), Hyde (69);
Goals: Christensen 3/4.
Rugby Leaguer & League Express Men of the Match: *Raiders:* Liam Harrison; *Thunder:* Tim Martin.
Penalty count: 11-10; **Half-time:** 32-6;
Referee: Matthew Thomasson; **Attendance:** 1,040.

FEATHERSTONE ROVERS 24 OLDHAM 18

ROVERS: 1 Loz Wildbore; 2 Wayne McHugh; 3 Jon Whittle; 4 Danny Kirmond; 5 Dean Colton; 6 Andy Kain; 7 Paul Handforth; 8 Ian Tonks; 9 Paul Hughes; 10 Stuart Dickens; 11 Jamie Field; 12 Steve Dooler; 13 Tom Haughey. Subs (all used): 14 Carl Hughes; 15 Richard Blakeway; 16 Gavin Swinson; 17 Gareth Handford.
Tries: Handford (43), Dickens (65), C Hughes (75, 78);
Goals: Dickens 4/4.
Sin bin: Handforth (39) - punching;
Swinson (47) - retaliation.
OLDHAM: 1 Andy Gorey; 2 Gareth Langley; 3 Craig Littler; 4 Adam Hughes; 5 Lucas Onyango; 6 Ian Hodson; 7 Neil Roden; 8 Anthony Tonks; 9 Simeon Hoyle; 10 Richard Mervill; 11 Geno Costin; 12 Ian Sinfield; 13 Chris Baines. Subs (all used): 14 Andy Crabtree; 15 Jason Boults; 16 Said Tamghart; 17 Adam Robinson.
Tries: Hughes (3, 70), Onyango (19); **Goals:** Langley 3/5.
Dismissal: Tonks (47) - punching.
Sin bin: Tonks (14) - punching.
Rugby Leaguer & League Express Men of the Match: *Rovers:* Jamie Field; *Oldham:* Neil Roden.
Penalty count: 12-12; **Half-time:** 0-12;
Referee: Craig Halloran; **Attendance:** 1,587.

SWINTON LIONS 44 KEIGHLEY COUGARS 18

LIONS: 1 Chris Hull; 2 Andy Saywell; 3 Dean Gorton; 4 Dave Ashton; 5 Marlon Billy; 6 Craig Ashall; 7 Liam McGovern; 8 David Bates; 9 Phil Wood; 10 Danny Aboushakra; 11 Chris Morley; 12 Mike Smith; 13 Martin Moana. Subs (all used): 14 Chris Hough; 15 Lee Marsh; 16 Rob Line; 17 Gareth Hayes.
Tries: McGovern (16), Gorton (25), Line (43), Saywell (61), Hough (65), Ashton (68), Hull (73), Marsh (77); **Goals:** McGovern 6/8.
COUGARS: 1 Gavin Duffy; 2 Sam Gardner; 3 Matt Foster; 4 Mick Fogerty; 5 Alex Brown; 6 Adam Mitchell; 7 Craig Fawcett; 8 Simon Bissell; 9 James Feather; 10 Luke Sutton; 11 Greg Nicholson; 12 Richard Knight; 13 Chris Redfearn. Subs (all used): 14 Craig Weston; 15 Brian Sutton; 16 Gareth English; 17 Brendan Rawlins.
Tries: Knight (4, 32), Gardner (38); **Goals:** Knight 3/5.
Rugby Leaguer & League Express Men of the Match: *Lions:* Liam McGovern; *Cougars:* Richard Knight.
Penalty count: 5-9; **Half-time:** 10-18;
Referee: James Child; **Attendance:** 426.

YORK CITY KNIGHTS 18 WORKINGTON TOWN 26

CITY KNIGHTS: 1 Alex Godfrey; 2 Lee Mapals; 3 Ian Brown; 4 Chris Spurr; 5 Tom Dunmore; 6 Scott Rhodes; 7 Danny Grimshaw; 8 Dave Buckley; 9 Jimmy Elston; 10 Adam Sullivan; 11 Rob Spicer; 12 Nathan Priestley; 13 Jon Liddell. Subs (all used): 14 Jamaine Wray; 15 Ryan Esders; 16 Toby Williams; 17 Neil Lowe.
Tries: C Spurr (17), Brown (54), Liddell (65);
Goals: Grimshaw 3/4.
TOWN: 1 Rob Lunt; 2 Stephen Dawes; 3 Andrew Beattie; 4 Neil Frazer; 5 Martyn Wilson; 6 Carl Forber; 7 Martin Keavney; 8 Taani Lavulavu; 9 Shaun Lunt; 10 Adam Sidlow; 11 Franco Kmet; 12 Dexter Miller; 13 Garry Purdham. Subs (all used): 14 Darren King; 15 Steve Ormesher; 16 Dean Vaughan; 17 Mark Cox.
Tries: Beattie (29), Wilson (42), R Lunt (58), Keavney (78); **Goals:** Forber 5/6.
Dismissal: Ormesher (34) – head butt on Lowe.
Sin bin: Kmet (65) - dissent.
Rugby Leaguer & League Express Men of the Match: *City Knights:* Lee Mapals; *Town:* Shaun Lunt.
Penalty count: 9-9; **Half-time:** 8-4;
Referee: Dave Merrick; **Attendance:** 1,402.

HUNSLET HAWKS 23 CELTIC CRUSADERS 16

HAWKS: 1 Matt Bramald; 2 Andy Robinson; 3 David Foster; 4 Ben Jones; 5 Steve Morton; 6 Mark Moxon; 7 Matt Firth; 8 Paul Smith; 9 Darren Robinson; 10 Scott Houston; 11 Wayne Freeman; 12 Paul Seal; 13 Will Cartledge. Subs (all used): 14 Gareth Greenwood; 15 Danny Cook; 16 Danny Samuels; 17 Matt Carbutt.
Tries: D Robinson (22), Cartledge (39), Jones (62, 64);
Goals: D Robinson 2/4, Bramald 1/3;
Field goal: D Robinson (78).
CRUSADERS: 1 Tony Duggan; 2 Paul Ballard; 3 Rob Toshack; 4 Anthony Blackwood; 5 Grant Epton; 6 Luke Young; 7 Jace Van Dijk; 8 Josh Cale; 9 Neil Budworth; 10 Hywel Davies; 11 Neale Wyatt; 12 Darren Mapp; 13 Damien Quinn. Subs (all used): 14 Andy Boothroyd; 15 Jamie I'Anson; 16 Dean Fitzgerald; 17 Gareth Dean.
Tries: Blackwood (9), Ballard (57); **Goals:** Quinn 4/4.
Sin bin: Fitzgerald (52) - ball steal.
Rugby Leaguer & League Express Men of the Match: *Hawks:* Ben Jones; *Crusaders:* Anthony Blackwood.
Penalty count: 11-7; **Half-time:** 12-8;
Referee: Paul Carr; **Attendance:** 324.

WEEK 12

Saturday 23rd June 2007

CELTIC CRUSADERS 26 WORKINGTON TOWN 12

CRUSADERS: 1 Tony Duggan; 2 Anthony Blackwood; 3 Rob Toshack; 4 Mark Dalle Cort; 5 Paul Ballard; 6 Damien Quinn; 7 Jace Van Dijk; 8 Josh Cale; 9 Neil Budworth; 10 Gareth Dean; 11 Chris Beasley; 12 Darren Mapp; 13 Neale Wyatt. Subs (all used): 14 Grant Epton; 15 Terry Martin; 16 Hywel Davies; 17 Phil Cushion.
Tries: Cale (34), Ballard (52, 71), Quinn (56), Duggan (58); **Goals:** Quinn 3/6.
TOWN: 1 Rob Lunt; 2 Stephen Dawes; 3 Andrew Beattie; 4 Neil Frazer; 5 Martyn Wilson; 6 Carl Forber; 7 Martin Keavney; 8 Dean Vaughan; 9 Shaun Lunt; 10 Adam Sidlow; 11 Jamie Beaumont; 12 Dexter Miller; 13 Garry Purdham. Subs (all used): 14 Franco Kmet; 15 Mark Cox; 16 Matthew Tunstall; 17 Taani Lavulavu.
Tries: Miller (45), Sidlow (62); **Goals:** Forber 2/3.
Rugby Leaguer & League Express Men of the Match: *Crusaders:* Paul Ballard; *Town:* Franco Kmet.
Penalty count: 8-5; **Half-time:** 6-2;
Referee: Craig Halloran; **Attendance:** 945.

GATESHEAD THUNDER 18 HUNSLET HAWKS 6

THUNDER: 1 Neil Thorman; 2 Robin Peers; 3 Graham Stephenson; 4 Mark McKinley; 5 Odell Harris; 6 Mark Christensen; 7 Tim Martin; 8 Tony Doherty; 9 Nick Hyde; 10 Tabua Cakacaka; 11 Shane Wooden; 12 Dylan Nash; 13 Pat Williamson. Subs (all used): 14 Ryan Clarke; 15 Clint Frazer; 16 Chris Parker; 17 Steven Bradley.
Tries: Martin (45, 49), Christensen (77);
Goals: Clarke 3/3.
Sin bin: McKinley (15) - holding down.
HAWKS: 1 Matt Bramald; 2 Andy Robinson; 3 David Foster; 4 Ben Jones; 5 Steve Morton; 6 Mark Moxon; 7 Matt Firth; 8 Wayne Freeman; 9 Darren Robinson; 10 Scott Houston; 11 Mark Cunningham; 12 Paul Seal; 13 Will Cartledge. Subs (all used): 14 Gareth Greenwood; 15 Danny Samuels; 16 Ben Walkin; 17 Matt Carbutt.
Try: Morton (24); **Goals:** D Robinson 1/2.
Rugby Leaguer & League Express Men of the Match: *Thunder:* Tim Martin; *Hawks:* Matt Firth.
Penalty count: 7-6; **Half-time:** 0-6;
Referee: Mike Dawber; **Attendance:** 276.

Sunday 24th June 2007

BLACKPOOL PANTHERS 14 BARROW RAIDERS 28

PANTHERS: 1 Mark Leigh; 2 Kieron Seeds; 3 Mike Stout; 4 Carl Jones; 5 Chris Brand; 6 Neil Hayden; 7 Martin Gambles; 8 Lee Rowley; 9 Phil Cantillon; 10 Gareth Jones; 11 Melvin Alker; 12 Kris Ratcliffe; 13 Deon Duell. Subs (all used): 14 Jon Chamberlain; 15 Danny Barton; 16 Daniel Palmer; 17 Rob Lamb.
Tries: Duell (7), Barton (54), Chamberlain (75);
Goals: Brand 1/3.
RAIDERS: 1 Mike Basan; 2 James Finch; 3 Phil Atkinson; 4 Liam Harrison; 5 James Nixon; 6 Liam Finch; 7 Darren Holt; 8 Paul Raftrey; 9 Chris Archer; 10 Martin Ostler; 11 Michael Smith; 12 Dave Armistead; 13 Pat Weisner. Subs (all used): 14 Jamie Marshall; 15 Paul Wilcock; 16 Mike Whitehead; 17 Lee Dutton.
Tries: Holt (21), Smith (27), Nixon (35), Weisner (63), Whitehead (67); **Goals:** Holt 4/5.
Rugby Leaguer & League Express Men of the Match: *Panthers:* Melvin Alker; *Raiders:* Michael Smith.
Penalty count: 5-8; **Half-time:** 4-16;
Referee: Robert Hicks; **Attendance:** 425.

KEIGHLEY COUGARS 26 OLDHAM 18

COUGARS: 1 Gavin Duffy; 2 Sam Gardner; 3 Oliver Purseglove; 4 Brian Sutton; 5 Ryan Smith; 6 Craig Weston; 7 Craig Fawcett; 8 Simon Bissell; 9 James Feather; 10 Luke Sutton; 11 Greg Nicholson; 12 Richard Knight; 13 Chris Redfearn. Subs (all used): 14 Barry Eaton; 15 Wayne Sutcliffe; 16 Gareth English; 17 Brendan Rawlins.
Tries: B Sutton (11), Knight (51, 68), Gardner (56);
Goals: Knight 5/8.
Sin bin: Fawcett (25) – fighting.
OLDHAM: 1 Andy Gorey; 2 Craig Littler; 3 Drew Houston; 4 Adam Hughes; 5 Lucas Onyango; 6 Neil Roden; 7 Paul Ashton; 8 Anthony Tonks; 9 Simeon Hoyle; 10 Richard Mervill; 11 Geno Costin; 12 Ian Sinfield; 13 Ian Hodson. Subs (all used): 14 Andy Crabtree; 15 Adam Robinson; 16 Jason Boults; 17 Matty Brooks.
Tries: Roden (3), Hodson (35), Robinson (42);
Goals: Ashton 3/3.
Sin bin: Littler (18) – late tackle on Weston; Roden (25) – fighting.
Rugby Leaguer & League Express Men of the Match: *Cougars:* Simon Bissell; *Oldham:* Anthony Tonks.
Penalty count: 6-4; **Half-time:** 8-12;
Referee: Dave Merrick; **Attendance:** 969.

LONDON SKOLARS 34 SWINTON LIONS 12

SKOLARS: 1 Jermaine Coleman; 2 Corey Simms; 3 Pete Hodgkinson; 4 Ashley Tozer; 5 Austen Aggrey; 6 Paul Thorman; 7 Gareth Honor; 8 Martyn Benson; 9 Frank Reid; 10 Richard Louw; 11 Joe Price; 12 Lydan Maitua; 13 Chris Lynton. Subs (all used): 14 Chris Shears; 15 Mike Castle; 16 Craig Anderson; 17 Alan Barker.
Tries: Hodgkinson (5, 80), Benson (11), Lynton (13), Thorman (38), Tozer (67); **Goals:** Thorman 5/7.
LIONS: 1 Wayne English; 2 Andy Saywell; 3 Dean Gorton; 4 Mark Brocklehurst; 5 Marlon Billy; 6 Craig Ashall; 7 Liam McGovern; 8 David Bates; 9 Phil Wood; 10 Rob Line; 11 Chris Morley; 12 Mike Smith; 13 Martin Moana. Subs (all used): 14 Chris Hough; 15 Lee Marsh; 16 Dave Newton; 17 Gareth Hayes.
Tries: Ashall (53), Bates (59); **Goals:** Marsh 2/2.
Rugby Leaguer & League Express Men of the Match: *Skolars:* Austen Aggrey; *Lions:* Phil Wood.
Penalty count: 7-8; **Half-time:** 24-0;
Referee: Paul Carr; **Attendance:** 379.

YORK CITY KNIGHTS 12 FEATHERSTONE ROVERS 46

CITY KNIGHTS: 1 Jon Liddell; 2 Lee Mapals; 3 Mark Spurr; 4 Chris Spurr; 5 Kyle Palmer; 6 Scott Rhodes; 7 Danny Grimshaw; 8 Neil Lowe; 9 Jimmy Elston; 10 Adam Sullivan; 11 Dave Buckley; 12 Nathan Priestley; 13 Rob Spicer. Subs (all used): 14 Jamaine Wray; 15 Ryan Esders; 16 Toby Williams; 17 Stephen Grundy.
Tries: Spicer (34), Buckley (71); **Goals:** Grimshaw 2/3.
ROVERS: 1 Loz Wildbore; 2 Danny Kirmond; 3 Wayne McHugh; 4 Steve Dooler; 5 Dean Colton; 6 Andy Kain; 7 Paul Handforth; 8 Gareth Handford; 9 Paul Hughes; 10 Stuart Dickens; 11 Jamie Field; 12 Richard Blakeway; 13 Tom Haughey. Subs (all used): 14 Carl Hughes; 15 Ian Tonks; 16 Scott Wilson; 17 James Houston.
Tries: Kain (8, 21, 24), Haughey (27, 39), Handford (62), Kirmond (69), Dickens (76);
Goals: Dickens 6/7, Blakeway 1/1.
Rugby Leaguer & League Express Men of the Match: *City Knights:* Rob Spicer; *Rovers:* Andy Kain.
Penalty count: 8-9; **Half-time:** 8-28;
Referee: Peter Taberner; **Attendance:** 1,924.

WEEK 13

Saturday 30th June 2007

CELTIC CRUSADERS 30 YORK CITY KNIGHTS 16

CRUSADERS: 1 Tony Duggan; 2 Anthony Blackwood; 3 Rob Toshack; 4 Mark Dalle Cort; 5 Paul Ballard; 6 Damien Quinn; 7 Jace Van Dijk; 8 Josh Cale; 9 Neil Budworth; 10 Gareth Dean; 11 Chris Beasley; 12 Darren Mapp; 13 Neale Wyatt. Subs (all used): 14 Grant Epton; 15 Terry Martin; 16 Hywel Davies; 17 Phil Cushion.
Tries: Quinn (6), Duggan (17, 50), Blackwood (30, 54), Ballard (69); **Goals:** Quinn 2/5, Van Dijk 1/1.
CITY KNIGHTS: 1 Jon Liddell; 2 Lee Mapals; 3 Mark Spurr; 4 Chris Spurr; 5 Tom Burton; 6 Scott Rhodes; 7 Danny Grimshaw; 8 Neil Lowe; 9 Jamaine Wray; 10 Adam Sullivan; 11 Dave Buckley; 12 Nathan Priestley; 13 Rob Spicer. Subs (all used): 14 Jimmy Elston; 15 Stephen Grundy; 16 Ryan McDonald; 17 Toby Williams.
Tries: Elston (36), Mapals (45, 57); **Goals:** Grimshaw 2/3.
Rugby Leaguer & League Express Men of the Match: *Crusaders:* Anthony Blackwood; *City Knights:* Lee Mapals.
Penalty count: 3-3; **Half-time:** 16-6;
Referee: Mike Dawber; **Attendance:** 702.

Sunday 1st July 2007

BARROW RAIDERS 32 HUNSLET HAWKS 22

RAIDERS: 1 Khamal Ganley; 2 James Finch; 3 Phil Atkinson; 4 Liam Harrison; 5 James Nixon; 6 Liam Finch; 7 Darren Holt; 8 Michael Smith; 9 Andy Ellis; 10 Paul Raftrey; 11 Martin Ostler; 12 Dave Armistead; 13 Pat Weisner. Subs (all used): 14 Chris Archer; 15 Paul Wilcock; 16 Mike Whitehead; 17 Lee Dutton.
Tries: J Finch (3, 50), Holt (22), Atkinson (31), Harrison (54), Ganley (65); **Goals:** Holt 4/6.
Sin bin: Armistead (74) - dissent.
HAWKS: 1 Matt Bramald; 2 Andy Robinson; 3 David Foster; 4 Ben Jones; 5 Steve Morton; 6 Mark Moxon; 7 Matt Firth; 8 Paul Smith; 9 Darren Robinson; 10 Danny Cook; 11 Wayne Freeman; 12 Mark Cunningham; 13 Will Cartledge. Subs (all used): 14 Gareth Greenwood; 15 Daniel Smith; 16 Ben Walkin; 17 Paul Seal.
Tries: Cartledge (10), Freeman (36), Seal (78), Moxon (80); **Goals:** D Robinson 3/4.
Rugby Leaguer & League Express Men of the Match: *Raiders:* Liam Harrison; *Hawks:* Wayne Freeman.
Penalty count: 6-8; **Half-time:** 16-10;
Referee: Gareth Hewer; **Attendance:** 1,252.

BLACKPOOL PANTHERS 10 KEIGHLEY COUGARS 26

PANTHERS: 1 Mark Leigh; 2 Kieron Seeds; 3 Mike Stout; 4 Carl Jones; 5 Craig Campbell; 6 Safraz Patel; 7 Martin Gambles; 8 Richard Rafferty; 9 Phil Cantillon; 10 Gareth Jones; 11 Melvin Alker; 12 Kris Ratcliffe; 13 Deon Duell. Subs (all used): 14 Adrian Dootson; 15 Jon Chamberlain; 16 Daniel Palmer; 17 Neil Baynes.
Tries: C Jones (68), Cantillon (80); **Goals:** Campbell 1/2.
Sin bin: Rafferty (3) – late tackle on Weston.
COUGARS: 1 Gavin Duffy; 2 Sam Gardner; 3 Brian Sutton; 4 Mick Fogerty; 5 Ryan Smith; 6 Craig Weston; 7 Craig Fawcett; 8 Simon Bissell; 9 James Feather; 10 Luke Sutton; 11 Greg Nicholson; 12 Richard Knight; 13 Chris Redfearn. Subs (all used): 14 Barry Eaton; 15 Wayne Sutcliffe; 16 Gareth English; 17 Brendan Rawlins.
Tries: Fawcett (3), Duffy (11, 50), R Smith (41), B Sutton (60); **Goals:** Knight 3/6.
Rugby Leaguer & League Express Men of the Match: *Panthers:* Carl Jones; *Cougars:* Gavin Duffy.
Penalty count: 8-2; **Half-time:** 0-10;
Referee: Paul Carr; **Attendance:** 372.

FEATHERSTONE ROVERS 30 LONDON SKOLARS 10

ROVERS: 1 Loz Wildbore; 2 Danny Kirmond; 3 Jon Whittle; 4 Wayne McHugh; 5 Dean Colton; 6 Andy Kain; 7 Paul Handforth; 8 Gareth Handford; 9 Paul Hughes; 10 Stuart Dickens; 11 Jamie Field; 12 Richard Blakeway; 13 Tom Haughey. Subs (all used): 14 Chris Ross; 15 Ian Tonks; 16 Jamie Benn; 17 Carl Hughes.
Tries: Dickens (14, 62), Whittle (16), Handforth (20), Kirmond (39), McHugh (76); **Goals:** Dickens 3/6.
SKOLARS: 1 Jermaine Coleman; 2 Corey Simms; 3 Pete Hodgkinson; 4 Ashley Tozer; 5 Austen Aggrey; 6 Paul Thorman; 7 Gareth Honor; 8 Martyn Benson; 9 Frank Reid; 10 Richard Louw; 11 Joe Price; 12 Lydan Maitua; 13 Chris Shears. Subs (all used): 14 Chris Lynton; 15 Mike Castle; 16 Craig Anderson; 17 Alan Barker.
Tries: Hodgkinson (43), Coleman (71);
Goals: Thorman 1/2.
Sin bin: Anderson (28) – holding down.
Rugby Leaguer & League Express Men of the Match: *Rovers:* Stuart Dickens; *Skolars:* Paul Thorman.
Penalty count: 11-14; **Half-time:** 20-0;
Referee: Matthew Thomasson; **Attendance:** 1,160.

OLDHAM 36 GATESHEAD THUNDER 12

OLDHAM: 1 Gareth Langley; 2 Alex Wilkinson; 3 Craig Littler; 4 Adam Hughes; 5 Lucas Onyango; 6 Neil Roden; 7 Matty Brooks; 8 Jason Boults; 9 Andy Crabtree; 10 Richard Mervill; 11 Geno Costin; 12 Adam Robinson; 13 Chris Baines. Subs (all used): 14 Drew Houston; 15 Said Tamghart; 16 Lee Sanderson; 17 Ian Sinfield.
Tries: Onyango (4, 12), Littler (9, 70), Costin (22), Langley (42), Roden (75); **Goals:** Langley 4/7.
THUNDER: 1 Stuart Sanderson; 2 Robin Peers; 3 Graham Stephenson; 4 Steve Rutherford; 5 Odell Harris; 6 Pat Williamson; 7 Tim Martin; 8 Jason Payne; 9 Nick Hyde; 10 Tabua Cakacaka; 11 Shane Wooden; 12 Steven Bradley; 13 Dylan Nash. Subs (all used): 14 Ryan Clarke; 15 Tony Doherty; 16 Matt Barron; 17 Clint Frazer.
Tries: Clarke (35), Sanderson (57); **Goals:** Sanderson 2/2.
Rugby Leaguer & League Express Men of the Match: *Oldham:* Chris Baines; *Thunder:* Stuart Sanderson.
Penalty count: 9-3; **Half-time:** 20-6; **Referee:** James Child; **Attendance:** 847 *(at Park Lane, Sedgley Park)*.

WORKINGTON TOWN 38 SWINTON LIONS 33

TOWN: 1 Andrew Beattie; 2 Matthew Woodcock; 3 Stephen Dawes; 4 Neil Frazer; 5 Martyn Wilson; 6 Carl Forber; 7 Martin Keavney; 8 Dean Vaughan; 9 Shaun Lunt; 10 Adam Sidlow; 11 Jamie Beaumont; 12 Dexter Miller; 13 Franco Kmet. Subs (all used): 14 Darren King; 15 Tane Manihera; 16 Mark Cox; 17 Taani Lavulavu.
Tries: Sidlow (6, 79), Beaumont (26), Beattie (50), S Lunt (66), Lavulavu (78); **Goals:** Forber 7/7.
On report: Lavulavu (76) – alleged high tackle.
LIONS: 1 Chris Hull; 2 Andy Saywell; 3 Paul Alcock; 4 Dean Gorton; 5 Dave Ashton; 6 Craig Ashall; 7 Liam McGovern; 8 David Bates; 9 Phil Wood; 10 Rob Line; 11 Mike Smith; 12 Martin Moana; 13 Lee Marsh. Subs: 14 Wayne English (not used); 15 Dave Newton; 16 Matt Bryers; 17 Gareth Hayes.
Tries: Gorton (2), Hayes (30), Moana (37), Smith (47), P Wood (70); **Goals:** McGovern 6/7;
Field goal: McGovern (77).
Sin bin: Hull (79) – dissent.
Rugby Leaguer & League Express Men of the Match: *Town:* Adam Sidlow; *Lions:* Phil Wood.
Penalty count: 8-8; **Half-time:** 14-20;
Referee: Peter Taberner; **Attendance:** 734.

WEEK 14

Saturday 7th July 2007

CELTIC CRUSADERS 50 LONDON SKOLARS 6

CRUSADERS: 1 Tony Duggan; 2 Anthony Blackwood; 3 Rob Toshack; 4 Mark Dalle Cort; 5 Paul Ballard; 6 Luke Young; 7 Jace Van Dijk; 8 Terry Martin; 9 Neil Budworth; 10 Gareth Dean; 11 Neale Wyatt; 12 Darren Mapp; 13 Damien Quinn. Subs (all used): 14 Grant Epton; 15 Dean Fitzgerald; 16 Jamie I'Anson; 17 Hywel Davies.
Tries: Ballard (4, 32, 45, 68), Wyatt (39), Mapp (42, 52), Duggan (55), Dalle Cort (57), Van Dijk (60);
Goals: Van Dijk 5/10.
SKOLARS: 1 Jermaine Coleman; 2 Ashley Tozer; 3 Pete Hodgkinson; 4 Tryfan Edwards; 5 Dene Miller; 6 Paul Thorman; 7 Gareth Honor; 8 Martyn Benson; 9 Frank Reid; 10 Richard Louw; 11 Joe Price; 12 Lydan Maitua; 13 Chris Lynton. Subs (all used): 14 Corey Simms; 15 Chris Shears; 16 Mike Castle; 17 Alan Barker.

Blackpool's Kris Ratcliffe swamped by the Gateshead defence, as the Thunder edge out the Panthers

Try: Lynton (73); **Goals:** Thorman 1/1.
Rugby Leaguer & League Express Men of the Match:
Crusaders: Paul Ballard; *Skolars:* Jermaine Coleman.
Penalty count: 5-3; **Half-time:** 14-0;
Referee: Chris Dean; **Attendance:** 807.

GATESHEAD THUNDER 28 BLACKPOOL PANTHERS 26

THUNDER: 1 Neil Thorman; 2 Robin Peers; 3 Graham Stephenson; 4 Pat Williamson; 5 Odell Harris; 6 Mark Christensen; 7 Tim Martin; 8 Jason Payne; 9 Ryan Clarke; 10 Tabua Cakacaka; 11 Shane Wooden; 12 Michael Knowles; 13 Nick Hyde. Subs (all used): 14 Dylan Nash; 15 Tony Doherty; 16 Steven Bradley; 17 Clint Frazer.
Tries: Harris (2), Williamson (41), Knowles (54), Nash (59), Thorman (66); **Goals:** Clarke 1/3, Knowles 3/4.
PANTHERS: 1 Craig Campbell; 2 Chris Brand; 3 Carl Jones; 4 Kieron Seeds; 5 Simon Holden; 6 Deon Duell; 7 Martin Gambles; 8 Lee Rowley; 9 Adrian Dootson; 10 Gareth Jones; 11 Melvin Alker; 12 Kris Ratcliffe; 13 Phil Cantillon. Subs (all used): 14 Jon Chamberlain; 15 Martin Roden; 16 Danny Morton; 17 Daniel Palmer.
Tries: Alker (10, 63), C Jones (21), Cantillon (32);
Goals: Campbell 5/5, Brand 0/1.
Rugby Leaguer & League Express Men of the Match:
Thunder: Michael Knowles; *Panthers:* Melvin Alker.
Penalty count: 8-8; **Half-time:** 4-22;
Referee: Peter Brooke; **Attendance:** 145.

Sunday 8th July 2007

KEIGHLEY COUGARS 6 FEATHERSTONE ROVERS 68

COUGARS: 1 Gavin Duffy; 2 Sam Gardner; 3 Brian Sutton; 4 Mick Fogerty; 5 Ryan Smith; 6 Craig Weston; 7 Craig Fawcett; 8 Simon Bissell; 9 James Feather; 10 Luke Sutton; 11 Greg Nicholson; 12 Richard Knight; 13 Chris Redfearn. Subs (all used): 14 Barry Eaton; 15 Wayne Sutcliffe; 16 Gareth English; 17 Brendan Rawlins.
Try: Duffy (21); **Goals:** Knight 1/1.
Sin bin: English (38) - holding down;
Rawlins (64) - punching.
ROVERS: 1 Loz Wildbore; 2 Danny Kirmond; 3 Jon Whittle; 4 Wayne McHugh; 5 Ade Adebisi; 6 Andy Kain; 7 Paul Handforth; 8 Gareth Handford; 9 Paul Hughes; 10 Stuart Dickens; 11 Jamie Field; 12 Richard Blakeway; 13 Tom Haughey. Subs (all used): 14 Jamie Benn; 15 Ian Tonks; 16 James Houston; 17 Carl Hughes.
Tries: Kain (5), Whittle (13), Wildbore (15, 36, 80), Kirmond (30, 47, 54, 70), C Hughes (39), Handford (60), Blakeway (68), Handforth (78);
Goals: Dickens 7/9, Handforth 1/2, Field 0/2.
Rugby Leaguer & League Express Men of the Match:
Cougars: Simon Bissell; *Rovers:* Andy Kain.
Penalty count: 10-8; **Half-time:** 6-32;
Referee: Gareth Hewer; **Attendance:** 1,101.

SWINTON LIONS 17 OLDHAM 10

LIONS: 1 Chris Hull; 2 Andy Saywell; 3 Dean Gorton; 4 Paul Alcock; 5 Wayne English; 6 Craig Ashall; 7 Liam McGovern; 8 Rob Line; 9 Phil Wood; 10 Gareth Hayes; 11 Mike Smith; 12 Martin Moana; 13 Lee Marsh. Subs (all used): 14 Chris Hough; 15 Richard Marshall; 16 Matt Bryers; 17 Dave Newton.
Tries: English (6), Saywell (16), Ashall (66);
Goals: McGovern 2/4; **Field goal:** McGovern (74).
Sin bin: McGovern (78) - fighting.
OLDHAM: 1 Gareth Langley; 2 Lucas Onyango; 3 Craig Littler; 4 Adam Hughes; 5 Alex Wilkinson; 6 Neil Roden; 7 Matty Brooks; 8 Jason Boults; 9 Andy Crabtree; 10 Richard Mervill; 11 Geno Costin; 12 Adam Robinson; 13 Chris Baines. Subs (all used): 14 Anthony Tonks; 15 Drew Houston; 16 Said Tamghart; 17 James Coyle.
Tries: Hughes (40), Langley (43); **Goals:** Langley 1/2.
Sin bin: Baines (78) - fighting.
Rugby Leaguer & League Express Men of the Match:
Lions: Phil Wood; *Oldham:* Gareth Langley.
Penalty count: 9-10; **Half-time:** 12-4;
Referee: James Child; **Attendance:** 757.

YORK CITY KNIGHTS 14 BARROW RAIDERS 4

CITY KNIGHTS: 1 Jon Liddell; 2 Lee Mapals; 3 Ryan Esders; 4 Chris Spurr; 5 Tom Burton; 6 Scott Rhodes; 7 Danny Grimshaw; 8 Neil Lowe; 9 Jamaine Wray; 10 Adam Sullivan; 11 Dave Buckley; 12 Nathan Priestley; 13 Rob Spicer. Subs (all used): 14 Jimmy Elston; 15 Stephen Grundy; 16 Ryan McDonald; 17 Toby Williams.
Tries: Rhodes (23), Grundy (67);
Goals: Grimshaw 2/2, Liddell 1/1.
Sin bin: Wray (63) - fighting.
RAIDERS: 1 Khamal Ganley; 2 James Finch; 3 Phil Atkinson; 4 Liam Harrison; 5 James Nixon; 6 Liam Finch; 7 Darren Holt; 8 Paul Raftrey; 9 Andy Ellis; 10 Michael Smith; 11 Martin Ostler; 12 Dave Armistead; 13 Pat Weisner. Subs (all used): 14 Chris Archer; 15 Paul Wilcock; 16 Mike Whitehead; 17 Lee Dutton.
Goals: Holt 2/2.
Sin bin: L Finch (63) - fighting.
Rugby Leaguer & League Express Men of the Match:
City Knights: Rob Spicer; *Raiders:* Dave Armistead.
Penalty count: 9-6; **Half-time:** 6-4;
Referee: Paul Carr; **Attendance:** 846.

HUNSLET HAWKS 28 WORKINGTON TOWN 24

HAWKS: 1 Matt Bramald; 2 Andy Robinson; 3 David Foster; 4 Ben Jones; 5 Steve Morton; 6 Mark Moxon; 7 Matt Firth; 8 Danny Ekis; 9 Gareth Greenwood; 10 Danny Cook; 11 Wayne Freeman; 12 Mark Cunningham; 13 Will Cartledge. Subs (all used): 14 Darren Robinson; 15 Ben

Walkin; 16 Glen Pennington; 17 Paul Seal.
Tries: Jones (5), B Walkin (31), Bramald (33), Cook (60), Morton (74); **Goals:** Bramald 1/2, D Robinson 3/4.
TOWN: 1 Rob Lunt; 2 Martyn Wilson; 3 Andrew Beattie; 4 Jason Mossop; 5 Neil Frazer; 6 Carl Forber; 7 Martin Keavney; 8 Taani Lavulavu; 9 Darren King; 10 Adam Sidlow; 11 Dexter Miller; 12 Franco Kmet; 13 Shaun Lunt. Subs (all used): 14 Stephen Dawes; 15 Garry Purdham; 16 Mark Cox; 17 Dean Burgess.
Tries: S Lunt (9, 22), Miller (17), Keavney (57);
Goals: Forber 4/6.
Rugby Leaguer & League Express Men of the Match:
Hawks: Will Cartledge; *Town:* Neil Frazer.
Penalty count: 9-7; **Half-time:** 16-14;
Referee: Matthew Kidd; **Attendance:** 409.

WEEK 15

Saturday 14th July 2007

LONDON SKOLARS 39 KEIGHLEY COUGARS 20

SKOLARS: 1 Jermaine Coleman; 2 Corey Simms; 3 Pete Hodgkinson; 4 Ashley Tozer; 5 Austen Aggrey; 6 Paul Thorman; 7 Jamie Nowland; 8 Martyn Benson; 9 Gareth Honor; 10 Richard Louw; 11 Joe Price; 12 Lydan Maitua; 13 Chris Lynton. Subs (all used): 14 Frank Reid; 15 Chris Shears; 16 Mike Castle; 17 Tane Taitoko.
Tries: Tozer (9), Honor (12, 65), Benson (31), Hodgkinson (35), Lynton (54); **Goals:** Thorman 7/7, Honor 0/1; **Field goal:** Thorman (79).
COUGARS: 1 Gavin Duffy; 2 Sam Gardner; 3 Brian Sutton; 4 Matt Foster; 5 Ryan Smith; 6 Craig Weston; 7 Craig Fawcett; 8 Simon Bissell; 9 James Feather; 10 Brendan Rawlins; 11 Greg Nicholson; 12 Richard Knight; 13 Chris Redfearn. Subs (all used): 14 Barry Eaton; 15 Wayne Sutcliffe; 16 Gareth English; 17 Tom Palmer.
Tries: Sutcliffe (39), Knight (43), B Sutton (62), Eaton (72); **Goals:** Knight 1/3, Eaton 1/1.
Sin bin: Fawcett (79) - obstruction.
Rugby Leaguer & League Express Men of the Match:
Skolars: Martyn Benson; *Cougars:* Richard Knight.
Penalty count: 7-9; **Half-time:** 26-4;
Referee: Matthew Kidd; **Attendance:** 406.

Sunday 15th July 2007

BARROW RAIDERS 34 OLDHAM 26

RAIDERS: 1 Khamal Ganley; 2 James Finch; 3 Phil Atkinson; 4 Liam Harrison; 5 James Nixon; 6 Liam Finch; 7 Darren Holt; 8 Michael Smith; 9 Andy Ellis; 10 Dave Armistead; 11 Martin Ostler; 12 Mike Whitehead; 13 Pat Weisner. Subs (all used): 14 Chris Archer; 15

Paul Wilcock; 16 Paul Raftrey; 17 Ian Rawlinson.
Tries: Ganley (25), Rawlinson (37), J Finch (43), Whitehead (62), Smith (66), Ellis (75); **Goals:** Holt 5/6.
Sin bin: L Finch (17) - late challenge on Roden.
OLDHAM: 1 Gareth Langley; 2 Lucas Onyango; 3 Craig Littler; 4 Adam Hughes; 5 Alex Wilkinson; 6 Neil Roden; 7 James Coyle; 8 Anthony Tonks; 9 Andy Crabtree; 10 Richard Mervill; 11 Ian Hodson; 12 Ian Sinfield; 13 Chris Baines. Subs (all used): 14 Geno Costin; 15 Adam Robinson; 16 Jason Boults; 17 Matty Brooks.
Tries: Hughes (8, 15), Costin (34), Onyango (56);
Goals: Langley 5/5.
Rugby Leaguer & League Express Men of the Match: *Raiders:* Dave Armistead; *Oldham:* Neil Roden.
Penalty count: 6-4; **Half-time:** 12-20;
Referee: Mike Dawber; **Attendance:** 1,348.

FEATHERSTONE ROVERS 30 GATESHEAD THUNDER 4

ROVERS: 1 Loz Wildbore; 2 Ade Adebisi; 3 Danny Kirmond; 4 Wayne McHugh; 5 Dean Colton; 6 Andy Kain; 7 Paul Handforth; 8 Gareth Handford; 9 Paul Hughes; 10 Stuart Dickens; 11 Jamie Field; 12 Richard Blakeway; 13 Tom Haughey. Subs (all used): 14 Jamie Benn; 15 Ian Tonks; 16 James Houston; 17 Matty Dale.
Tries: Kirmond (17), Tonks (48), Blakeway (58), Adebisi (65, 76, 79);
Goals: Dickens 2/2, Benn 0/2, Handforth 1/2.
Sin bin: Handford (70) - fighting.
THUNDER: 1 Neil Thorman; 2 Graham Stephenson; 3 Pat Williamson; 4 Mark Christensen; 5 Odell Harris; 6 Nick Hyde; 7 Tim Martin; 8 Jason Payne; 9 Ryan Clarke; 10 Tabua Cakacaka; 11 Shane Wooden; 12 Dylan Nash; 13 Michael Knowles. Subs (all used): 14 Tony Doherty; 15 Matt Barron; 16 Steven Bradley; 17 Clint Frazer.
Try: Knowles (4); **Goals:** Knowles 0/2.
Sin bin: Payne (55) - interference;
Cakacaka (70) - fighting.
Rugby Leaguer & League Express Men of the Match: *Rovers:* Ade Adebisi; *Thunder:* Tim Martin.
Penalty count: 8-6; **Half-time:** 6-4;
Referee: Paul Carr; **Attendance:** 1,030.

SWINTON LIONS 20 CELTIC CRUSADERS 26

LIONS: 1 Chris Hull; 2 Andy Saywell; 3 Dean Gorton; 4 Marlon Billy; 5 Wayne English; 6 Craig Ashall; 7 Liam McGovern; 8 Rob Line; 9 Phil Wood; 10 Gareth Hayes; 11 Mike Smith; 12 Martin Moana; 13 Lee Marsh. Subs (all used): 14 Chris Hough; 15 Chris Morley; 16 Bruce Johnson; 17 Dave Newton.
Tries: Gorton (5), Smith (68), Saywell (76), Hough (78);
Goals: Marsh 2/4.
Sin bin: Morley (44) - punching, (55) - high tackle.
CRUSADERS: 1 Tony Duggan; 2 Richard Johnston; 3 Paul Ballard; 4 Mark Dalle Cort; 5 Grant Epton; 6 Damien Quinn; 7 Jace Van Dijk; 8 Terry Martin; 9 Neil Budworth; 10 Gareth Dean; 11 Neale Wyatt; 12 Darren Mapp; 13 Chris Beasley. Subs (all used): 14 Aurelien Cologni; 15 Jamie I'Anson; 16 Josh Cale; 17 Hywel Davies.
Tries: Epton (23), Duggan (28), Quinn (33), Wyatt (54), Dalle Cort (57); **Goals:** Van Dijk 3/6.
Rugby Leaguer & League Express Men of the Match: *Lions:* Lee Marsh; *Crusaders:* Grant Epton.
Penalty count: 11-6; **Half-time:** 6-16;
Referee: Robert Hicks; **Attendance:** 488.

WORKINGTON TOWN 86 BLACKPOOL PANTHERS 6

TOWN: 1 Rob Lunt; 2 Ryan Blair; 3 Dexter Miller; 4 Jason Mossop; 5 Neil Frazer; 6 Carl Forber; 7 Martin Keavney; 8 Adam Sidlow; 9 Shaun Lunt; 10 Taani Lavulavu; 11 Jamie Beaumont; 12 Kris Coward; 13 Franco Kmet. Subs (all used): 14 Darren King; 15 Mark Cox; 16 Dean Burgess; 17 Steve Ormesher.
Tries: S Lunt (6, 78), Sidlow (10), Forber (14, 28, 54), Blair (19, 30), Keavney (22, 73), Frazer (34), Mossop (43), Kmet (58, 68), R Lunt (61); **Goals:** Forber 13/15.
PANTHERS: 1 Chris Brand; 2 Kieron Seeds; 3 Mike Stout; 4 Carl Jones; 5 Simon Holden; 6 Safraz Patel; 7 Phil Cantillon; 8 Lee Rowley; 9 Adrian Dootson; 10 Luke Murfin; 11 Melvin Alker; 12 Kris Ratcliffe; 13 Danny Barton. Subs (all used): 14 Jon Chamberlain; 15 Eddie Kilgannon; 16 Daniel Palmer; 17 Gus Smith.
Try: Smith (76); **Goals:** Brand 1/1.
Rugby Leaguer & League Express Men of the Match: *Town:* Carl Forber; *Panthers:* Danny Barton.
Penalty count: 6-9; **Half-time:** 44-0;
Referee: Matthew Thomasson; **Attendance:** 624.

HUNSLET HAWKS 14 YORK CITY KNIGHTS 16

HAWKS: 1 Matt Bramald; 2 Andy Robinson; 3 Danny Cook; 4 Ben Jones; 5 Steve Morton; 6 Mark Moxon; 7 Matt Firth; 8 Danny Ekis; 9 Gareth Greenwood; 10 Paul Smith; 11 Wayne Freeman; 12 Mark Cunningham; 13 Will Cartledge. Subs (all used): 14 Darren Robinson; 15 Glen Pennington; 16 Chris Ross; 17 Paul Seal.
Tries: A Robinson (3), Jones (54), Cartledge (58);
Goals: Bramald 0/1, D Robinson 0/1, Ross 1/2.
Sin bin: Seal (36) - persistent infringements.
CITY KNIGHTS: 1 Lee Mapals; 2 Jonny Waldron; 3 Kyle Palmer; 4 Chris Spurr; 5 Tom Burton; 6 Rob Spicer; 7 Jon Liddell; 8 Dave Buckley; 9 Jimmy Elston; 10 Neil Lowe; 11 Stephen Grundy; 12 Nathan Priestley; 13 Ryan Esders. Subs (all used): 14 Jamaine Wray; 15 Lee Lingard; 16 Ryan McDonald; 17 Toby Williams.
Tries: Waldron (13), Palmer (25);
Goals: Esders 3/6, Liddell 1/1.
Rugby Leaguer & League Express Men of the Match: *Hawks:* Wayne Freeman; *City Knights:* Neil Lowe.
Penalty count: 13-16; **Half-time:** 4-14;
Referee: Craig Halloran; **Attendance:** 462.

WEEK 16

Saturday 21st July 2007

FEATHERSTONE ROVERS 37 BARROW RAIDERS 28

ROVERS: 1 Loz Wildbore; 2 Danny Kirmond; 3 Jon Whittle; 4 Wayne McHugh; 5 Ade Adebisi; 6 Andy Kain; 7 Paul Handforth; 8 Gareth Handford; 9 Gavin Swinson; 10 Stuart Dickens; 11 Jamie Field; 12 Richard Blakeway; 13 Tom Haughey. Subs (all used): 14 Joe McLocklan; 15 Ian Tonks; 16 James Houston; 17 Matty Dale.
Tries: Haughey (13, 23), McHugh (35, 79), Kirmond (43), Field (52); **Goals:** Dickens 6/7;
Field goal: Handforth (71).
RAIDERS: 1 Khamal Ganley; 2 James Finch; 3 Phil Atkinson; 4 Liam Harrison; 5 James Nixon; 6 Liam Finch; 7 Darren Holt; 8 Michael Smith; 9 Andy Ellis; 10 Dave Armistead; 11 Martin Ostler; 12 Mike Whitehead; 13 Pat Weisner. Subs (all used): 14 Chris Archer; 15 Paul Wilcock; 16 Paul Raftrey; 17 Lee Dutton.
Tries: Atkinson (18), Ganley (20, 38, 75), Weisner (68);
Goals: Holt 4/6.
Sin bin: Smith (29) - holding down;
Raftrey (34) - obstruction.
Rugby Leaguer & League Express Men of the Match: *Rovers:* Paul Handforth; *Raiders:* Khamal Ganley.
Penalty count: 10-8; **Half-time:** 18-18;
Referee: Robert Hicks; **Attendance:** 1,557.

GATESHEAD THUNDER 8 SWINTON LIONS 34

THUNDER: 1 Neil Thorman; 2 Graham Stephenson; 3 Mark Christensen; 4 Pat Williamson; 5 Stuart Sanderson; 6 Nick Hyde; 7 Tim Martin; 8 Jason Payne; 9 Ryan Clarke; 10 Tabua Cakacaka; 11 Shane Wooden; 12 Dylan Nash; 13 Michael Knowles. Subs (all used): 14 Dan Smith; 15 Tony Doherty; 16 Steven Bradley; 17 Clint Frazer.
Try: Payne (7); **Goals:** Knowles 2/3.
LIONS: 1 Chris Hull; 2 Wayne English; 3 Dean Gorton; 4 Paul Alcock; 5 Marlon Billy; 6 Craig Ashall; 7 Liam McGovern; 8 David Bates; 9 Phil Wood; 10 Dave Newton; 11 Mike Smith; 12 Martin Moana; 13 Lee Marsh. Subs (all used): 14 Jay Duffy; 15 Craig Farrimond; 16 Steve McCurrie; 17 Chris Morley.
Tries: Hull (34, 65), Bates (54), P Wood (62), Marsh (69), Alcock (76); **Goals:** Marsh 5/6.
Sin bin: P Wood (26) - persistent fouling.
Rugby Leaguer & League Express Men of the Match: *Thunder:* Neil Thorman; *Lions:* Phil Wood.
Penalty count: 11-8; **Half-time:** 8-6;
Referee: Matthew Thomasson; **Attendance:** 219.

Sunday 22nd July 2007

BLACKPOOL PANTHERS 8 CELTIC CRUSADERS 54

PANTHERS: 1 Chris Brand; 2 Kieron Seeds; 3 Eddie Kilgannon; 4 Carl Jones; 5 Tom Lever; 6 Safraz Patel; 7 Martin Gambles; 8 Kris Ratcliffe; 9 Martin Roden; 10 Danny Barton; 11 Melvin Alker; 12 Mike Stout; 13 Phil Cantillon. Subs (all used): 14 Gus Smith; 15 Rob Sloman; 16 Daniel Palmer; 17 Tim Street.
Tries: C Jones (5), Barton (62);
Goals: Brand 0/1, Seeds 0/1.
Sin bin: Patel (53) - fighting.
CRUSADERS: 1 Tony Duggan; 2 Grant Epton; 3 Paul Ballard; 4 Mark Dalle Cort; 5 Richard Johnston; 6 Luke Young; 7 Jace Van Dijk; 8 Terry Martin; 9 Neil Budworth; 10 Gareth Dean; 11 Neale Wyatt; 12 Darren Mapp; 13 Damien Quinn. Subs (all used): 14 Aurelien Cologni; 15 Jamie I'Anson; 16 Josh Cale; 17 Hywel Davies.
Tries: Duggan (12, 43, 76), Johnston (22, 31), Ballard (28, 71), Epton (48), Quinn (74); **Goals:** Van Dijk 9/9.
Sin bin: Johnston (53) - fighting.
Rugby Leaguer & League Express Men of the Match: *Panthers:* Carl Jones; *Crusaders:* Tony Duggan.
Penalty count: 6-6; **Half-time:** 4-24;
Referee: Craig Halloran; **Attendance:** 276.

KEIGHLEY COUGARS 10 YORK CITY KNIGHTS 42

COUGARS: 1 John Crawford; 2 Sam Gardner; 3 Zac Hill; 4 Matt Foster; 5 Alex Brown; 6 Craig Weston; 7 Barry Eaton; 8 Gareth English; 9 James Feather; 10 Brendan Rawlins; 11 Brian Sutton; 12 Wayne Sutcliffe; 13 Richard Knight. Subs (all used): 14 Craig Fawcett; 15 Gareth Walker; 16 Simon Bissell; 17 Tom Palmer.
Tries: Brown (15), Foster (73); **Goals:** Knight 1/2.
Sin bin: Sutcliffe (30) – fighting;
Crawford (37) – professional foul.
CITY KNIGHTS: 1 Lee Lingard; 2 Lee Mapals; 3 Dan Potter; 4 Chris Spurr; 5 Tom Burton; 6 Jon Liddell; 7 Andy Gargan; 8 Toby Williams; 9 Jimmy Elston; 10 Neil Lowe; 11 Stephen Grundy; 12 Dave Buckley; 13 Ryan Esders. Subs (all used): 14 Jamaine Wray; 15 Mark Spurr; 16 Ryan McDonald; 17 Kyle Palmer.
Tries: Lingard (5, 21, 66, 79), Potter (39), Esders (51), Williams (70), McDonald (77);
Goals: Esders 4/6, Lingard 1/1, Liddell 0/1.
Sin bin: Wray (30) - fighting.
Rugby Leaguer & League Express Men of the Match: *Cougars:* James Feather; *City Knights:* Lee Lingard.
Penalty count: 6-10; **Half-time:** 4-18; **Referee:** Dave Merrick *(replaced by Michael Haigh, 60)*; **Attendance:** 787.

OLDHAM 52 HUNSLET HAWKS 22

OLDHAM: 1 Gareth Langley; 2 Lucas Onyango; 3 Craig Littler; 4 Adam Hughes; 5 Alex Wilkinson; 6 Neil Roden; 7 James Coyle; 8 Jason Boults; 9 Simeon Hoyle; 10 Richard Mervill; 11 Geno Costin; 12 Ian Sinfield; 13 Ian Hodson. Subs (all used): 14 Drew Houston; 15 Anthony Tonks; 16 Chris Baines; 17 Matty Brooks.
Tries: Hughes (8, 36, 75, 78), Sinfield (14), Costin (25), Onyango (40), Littler (47), Coyle (66);
Goals: Langley 8/10.
HAWKS: 1 Matt Bramald; 2 Andy Robinson; 3 Craig Bower; 4 Ben Jones; 5 Steve Morton; 6 Mark Moxon; 7 Matt Firth; 8 Danny Ekis; 9 Gareth Greenwood; 10 Wayne Freeman; 11 Mark Cunningham; 12 Will Cartledge; 13 Chris Ross. Subs (all used): 14 Darren Robinson; 15 Danny Cook; 16 Ben Walkin; 17 Paul Seal.
Tries: Ross (4, 71), Morton (21), Bramald (32);
Goals: Bramald 2/3, D Robinson 1/1.
Rugby Leaguer & League Express Men of the Match: *Oldham:* Gareth Langley; *Hawks:* Wayne Freeman.
Penalty count: 8-5; **Half-time:** 30-16;
Referee: James Child; **Attendance:** 1,024.

WORKINGTON TOWN 24 LONDON SKOLARS 31

TOWN: 1 Rob Lunt; 2 Ryan Blair; 3 Dexter Miller; 4 Jason Mossop; 5 Neil Frazer; 6 Carl Forber; 7 Martin Keavney; 8 Adam Sidlow; 9 Shaun Lunt; 10 Taani Lavulavu; 11 Jamie Beaumont; 12 Steve Ormesher; 13 Franco Kmet. Subs (all used): 14 Darren King; 15 Dean Vaughan; 16 Dean Burgess; 17 Kris Coward.
Tries: Lavulavu (19), Sidlow (21), R Lunt (42), Blair (54); **Goals:** Forber 4/4.
SKOLARS: 1 Jermaine Coleman; 2 Corey Simms; 3 Pete Hodgkinson; 4 Ashley Tozer; 5 Austin Aggrey; 6 Paul Thorman; 7 Jamie Nowland; 8 Martyn Benson; 9 Frank Reid; 10 Richard Louw; 11 Mike Castle; 12 Lydan Maitua; 13 Chris Lynton. Subs (all used): 14 Chris Shears; 15 Keir Bell; 16 Warren Heilig; 17 Tane Taitoko.
Tries: Hodgkinson (14, 49), Coleman (61), Maitua (63), Nowland (73); **Goals:** Thorman 5/7;
Field goal: Thorman (76).
Sin bin: Coleman (38) – holding down.
Rugby Leaguer & League Express Men of the Match: *Town:* Taani Lavulavu; *Skolars:* Frank Reid.
Penalty count: 4-7; **Half-time:** 12-6;
Referee: Leon Williamson; **Attendance:** 697.

WEEK 17

Thursday 26th July 2007

FEATHERSTONE ROVERS 12 CELTIC CRUSADERS 32

ROVERS: 1 Loz Wildbore; 2 Danny Kirmond; 3 Jon Whittle; 4 Wayne McHugh; 5 Ade Adebisi; 6 Andy Kain; 7 Paul Handforth; 8 Gareth Handford; 9 Gavin Swinson; 10 Stuart Dickens; 11 Jamie Field; 12 Richard Blakeway; 13 Tom Haughey. Subs (all used): 14 Joe McLocklan; 15 Ian Tonks; 16 James Houston; 17 Matty Dale.
Tries: Kirmond (29), Wildbore (71);
Goals: Dickens 1/2, Wildbore 0/1, Handforth 1/1.
CRUSADERS: 1 Tony Duggan; 2 Paul Ballard; 3 Rob Toshack; 4 Mark Dalle Cort; 5 Grant Epton; 6 Damien Quinn; 7 Jace Van Dijk; 8 Terry Martin; 9 Neil Budworth; 10 Gareth Dean; 11 Neale Wyatt; 12 Darren Mapp; 13 Chris Beasley. Subs (all used): 14 Luke Young; 15 Jamie I'Anson; 16 Phil Cushion; 17 Hywel Davies.
Tries: Ballard (21, 72), Quinn (26), Epton (49, 66);
Goals: Van Dijk 6/8.
Rugby Leaguer & League Express Men of the Match: *Rovers:* Jamie Field; *Crusaders:* Jace Van Dijk.
Penalty count: 7-12; **Half-time:** 6-14;
Referee: Ashley Klein; **Attendance:** 2,993.

Sunday 29th July 2007

BLACKPOOL PANTHERS 22 HUNSLET HAWKS 32

PANTHERS: 1 Kieron Seeds; 2 Mike Stout; 3 Eddie Kilgannon; 4 Carl Jones; 5 Tom Lever; 6 Deon Duell; 7 Martin Gambles; 8 Kris Ratcliffe; 9 Adrian Dootson; 10 Danny Barton; 11 Melvin Alker; 12 Martin Roden; 13 Phil Cantillon. Subs (all used): 14 Safraz Patel; 15 Rob Sloman; 16 Daniel Palmer; 17 Rob Lamb.
Tries: Seeds (20), Dootson (26), Ratcliffe (56), Lever (74); **Goals:** Gambles 3/4.
Sin bin: Duell (18) - interference.
HAWKS: 1 Matt Bramald; 2 Caldon Bravo; 3 Craig Bower; 4 Ben Jones; 5 Andy Robinson; 6 Darren Robinson; 7 Matt Firth; 8 Danny Ekis; 9 Mark Moxon; 10 Wayne Freeman; 11 Ben Walkin; 12 Will Cartledge; 13 Chris Ross. Subs (all used): 14 Gareth Greenwood; 15 Danny Cook; 16 Mark Cunningham; 17 Paul Seal.
Tries: A Robinson (4), Bramald (10), Ross (14, 59), Freeman (68); **Goals:** D Robinson 6/7.
Dismissal: Jones (30) - high tackle.
Sin bin: Cartledge (35) - late tackle.
Rugby Leaguer & League Express Men of the Match: *Panthers:* Martin Gambles; *Hawks:* Chris Ross.
Penalty count: 5-8; **Half-time:** 10-18;
Referee: Peter Brooke; **Attendance:** 302.

GATESHEAD THUNDER 32 WORKINGTON TOWN 36

THUNDER: 1 Neil Thorman; 2 Graham Stephenson; 3 Dylan Nash; 4 Pat Williamson; 5 Stuart Sanderson; 6 Ryan Clarke; 7 Tim Martin; 8 Jason Payne; 9 Dan Smith; 10 Steven Bradley; 11 Shane Wooden; 12 Michael Knowles; 13 Nick Hyde. Subs (all used): 14 Robin Peers; 15 Tony Doherty; 16 Matt Barron; 17 Clint Frazer.
Tries: Williamson (1), Thorman (34), Knowles (52, 71), Wooden (68), Bradley (75); **Goals:** Knowles 4/6.
TOWN: 1 Rob Lunt; 2 Ryan Blair; 3 Jason Mossop; 4 Neil Frazer; 5 Martyn Wilson; 6 Carl Forber; 7 Martin Keavney; 8 Adam Sidlow; 9 Shaun Lunt; 10 Taani Lavulavu; 11 Jamie Beaumont; 12 Steve Ormesher; 13 Franco Kmet. Subs (all used): 14 Darren King; 15 Dexter Miller; 16 Dean Burgess; 17 Dean Vaughan.
Tries: S Lunt (18), Frazer (27), Ormesher (48),

Kmet (56, 59), King (63); **Goals:** Forber 6/7.
Dismissal: Mossop (16) - trip on Hyde.
Rugby Leaguer & League Express Men of the Match: *Thunder:* Neil Thorman; *Town:* Franco Kmet.
Penalty count: 9-11; **Half-time:** 10-14;
Referee: Paul Carr; **Attendance:** 275.

KEIGHLEY COUGARS 52 SWINTON LIONS 22

COUGARS: 1 Gavin Duffy; 2 Zac Hill; 3 John Crawford; 4 Oliver Purseglove; 5 Alex Brown; 6 Craig Fawcett; 7 Barry Eaton; 8 Gareth English; 9 James Feather; 10 Brendan Rawlins; 11 Simon Bissell; 12 Richard Knight; 13 Chris Redfearn. Subs (all used): 14 Michael Hastings; 15 Greg Nicholson; 16 Wayne Sutcliffe; 17 Tom Palmer.
Tries: Brown (10, 25), Hill (14, 79), Purseglove (18), Bissell (28), Palmer (49), Rawlins (58), Sutcliffe (61), Hastings (75); **Goals:** Knight 5/8, Eaton 1/2.
LIONS: 1 Chris Hull; 2 Wayne English; 3 Dean Gorton; 4 Paul Alcock; 5 Marlon Billy; 6 Craig Ashall; 7 Liam McGovern; 8 David Bates; 9 Phil Wood; 10 Dave Newton; 11 Mike Smith; 12 Martin Moana; 13 Lee Marsh. Subs (all used): 14 Jay Duffy; 15 Craig Farrimond; 16 Steve McCurrie; 17 Gareth Hayes.
Tries: Moana (3), Hull (21), Marsh (40), Billy (68);
Goals: Marsh 3/4.
Rugby Leaguer & League Express Men of the Match: *Cougars:* Barry Eaton; *Lions:* Craig Ashall.
Penalty count: 8-8; **Half-time:** 24-16;
Referee: Robert Hicks; **Attendance:** 471.

LONDON SKOLARS 18 BARROW RAIDERS 31

SKOLARS: 1 Jermaine Coleman; 2 Corey Simms; 3 Pete Hodgkinson; 4 Chris Shears; 5 Austen Aggrey; 6 Paul Thorman; 7 Jamie Nowland; 8 Alan Barker; 9 Frank Reid; 10 Richard Louw; 11 Mike Castle; 12 Lydan Maitua; 13 Chris Shears. Subs (all used): 14 Gareth Honor; 15 Keir Bell; 16 Tane Taitoko; 17 Martyn Benson.
Tries: Simms (3), Barker (9), Aggrey (56);
Goals: Thorman 3/4.
RAIDERS: 1 Khamal Ganley; 2 James Finch; 3 Mike Basan; 4 Liam Harrison; 5 James Nixon; 6 Liam Finch; 7 Darren Holt; 8 Michael Smith; 9 Andy Ellis; 10 Dave Armistead; 11 Martin Ostler; 12 Mike Whitehead; 13 Pat Weisner. Subs (all used): 14 Chris Archer; 15 Joe McKenna; 16 Paul Raftrey; 17 Lee Dutton.
Tries: Weisner (17, 38), Archer (36), Ellis (64, 68);
Goals: Holt 5/5; **Field goal:** Weisner (40).
Rugby Leaguer & League Express Men of the Match: *Skolars:* Corey Simms; *Raiders:* Dave Armistead.
Penalty count: 10-4; **Half-time:** 12-19;
Referee: Charlie Nielson; **Attendance:** 467.

YORK CITY KNIGHTS 14 OLDHAM 15

CITY KNIGHTS: 1 Lee Lingard; 2 Lee Mapals; 3 Dan Potter; 4 Chris Spurr; 5 Tom Burton; 6 Jon Liddell; 7 Andy Gargan; 8 Dave Buckley; 9 Jimmy Elston; 10 Neil Lowe; 11 Ian Brown; 12 Stephen Grundy; 13 Ryan Esders. Subs (all used): 14 Jamaine Wray; 15 Mark Spurr; 16 Ryan McDonald; 17 Kyle Palmer.
Tries: Lingard (6), C Spurr (66);
Goals: Esders 2/3, Lingard 1/1.
OLDHAM: 1 Gareth Langley; 2 Lucas Onyango; 3 Craig Littler; 4 Adam Hughes; 5 Alex Wilkinson; 6 Neil Roden; 7 James Coyle; 8 Jason Boults; 9 Simeon Hoyle; 10 Richard Mervill; 11 Geno Costin; 12 Ian Sinfield; 13 Chris Baines. Subs (all used): 14 Robert Roberts; 15 Adam Robinson; 16 Drew Houston; 17 Matty Brooks.
Tries: Coyle (12), Onyango (50), Houston (78);
Goals: Langley 1/3; **Field goal:** Roberts (80).
Rugby Leaguer & League Express Men of the Match: *City Knights:* Neil Lowe; *Oldham:* Neil Roden.
Penalty count: 11-3; **Half-time:** 10-6;
Referee: Leon Williamson; **Attendance:** 1,064.

WEEK 18

Sunday 5th August 2007

BARROW RAIDERS 24 CELTIC CRUSADERS 26

RAIDERS: 1 Khamal Ganley; 2 James Finch; 3 Mike Basan; 4 Liam Harrison; 5 James Nixon; 6 Liam Finch; 7 Darren Holt; 8 Michael Smith; 9 Andy Ellis; 10 Dave Armistead; 11 Mike Whitehead; 12 Phil Atkinson; 13 Pat Weisner. Subs (all used): 14 Chris Archer; 15 Paul Wilcock; 16 Paul Raftrey; 17 Lee Dutton.
Tries: J Finch (8), Whitehead (24, 38), Basan (45);
Goals: Holt 4/5.
CRUSADERS: 1 Tony Duggan; 2 Paul Ballard; 3 Rob Toshack; 4 Mark Dalle Cort; 5 Grant Epton; 6 Damien Quinn; 7 Jace Van Dijk; 8 Terry Martin; 9 Neil Budworth; 10 Gareth Dean; 11 Neale Wyatt; 12 Darren Mapp; 13 Chris Beasley. Subs (all used): 14 Luke Young; 15 Jamie I'Anson; 16 Phil Cushion; 17 Hywel Davies.
Tries: Duggan (19, 27), Toshack (35), Dalle Cort (40);
Goals: Van Dijk 5/5.
Rugby Leaguer & League Express Men of the Match: *Raiders:* Michael Smith; *Crusaders:* Jace Van Dijk.
Penalty count: 7-8; **Half-time:** 16-26;
Referee: Gareth Hewer; **Attendance:** 1,806.

OLDHAM 46 BLACKPOOL PANTHERS 12

OLDHAM: 1 Ian Gordon; 2 Andy Gorey; 3 Drew Houston; 4 Adam Hughes; 5 Lucas Onyango; 6 Neil Roden; 7 James Coyle; 8 Jason Boults; 9 Simeon Hoyle; 10 Richard Mervill; 11 Robert Roberts; 12 Ian Hodson; 13 Geno Costin. Subs (all used): 14 Anthony Tonks; 15 Alex Wilkinson; 16 Said Tamghart; 17 Matty Brooks.
Tries: Onyango (25), Hughes (30), Tamghart (32, 76), Mervill (54), Houston (65), Roberts (67, 79);
Goals: Hughes 7/8.
PANTHERS: 1 Kieron Seeds; 2 Eddie Kilgannon; 3 Danny Barton; 4 Carl Jones; 5 Mike Stout; 6 Deon Duell; 7 Martin Gambles; 8 Gareth Jones; 9 Phil Cantillon; 10 Kris Ratcliffe; 11 Melvin Alker; 12 Martin Roden; 13 Adrian Dootson. Subs (all used): 14 Safraz Patel; 15 Rob Lamb; 16 Richard Rafferty; 17 Warren Stevens.
Tries: Gambles (4), C Jones (38); **Goals:** Gambles 2/2.
Rugby Leaguer & League Express Men of the Match: *Oldham:* Lucas Onyango; *Panthers:* Martin Gambles.
Penalty count: 7-7; **Half-time:** 18-12;
Referee: Clint Sharrad; **Attendance:** 858.

SWINTON LIONS 22 FEATHERSTONE ROVERS 28

LIONS: 1 Chris Hull; 2 Andy Saywell; 3 Dean Gorton; 4 Dave Ashton; 5 Marlon Billy; 6 Jay Duffy; 7 Liam McGovern; 8 David Bates; 9 Craig Ashall; 10 Dave Newton; 11 Craig Farrimond; 12 Paul Alcock; 13 Lee Marsh. Subs (all used): 14 Ben Williamson; 15 Matt Bryers; 16 Steve McCurrie; 17 Gareth Hayes.
Tries: Saywell (11, 50), Gorton (36), Duffy (54);
Goals: Marsh 1/2, McGovern 2/2.
ROVERS: 1 Loz Wildbore; 2 Danny Kirmond; 3 Jon Whittle; 4 Wayne McHugh; 5 Ade Adebisi; 6 Andy Kain; 7 Paul Handforth; 8 Gareth Handford; 9 Joe McLocklan; 10 Stuart Dickens; 11 Jamie Field; 12 Richard Blakeway; 13 Carl Hughes. Subs (all used): 14 Dean Colton; 15 Tom Haughey; 16 James Houston; 17 Matty Dale.
Tries: Blakeway (3, 28), C Hughes (23), Field (39), McHugh (78); **Goals:** Dickens 3/4, Handforth 1/2.
Sin bin: Kirmond (33) - ball steal.
Rugby Leaguer & League Express Men of the Match: *Lions:* Liam McGovern; *Rovers:* Paul Handforth.
Penalty count: 8-7; **Half-time:** 10-22;
Referee: Paul Carr; **Attendance:** 603.

WORKINGTON TOWN 18 KEIGHLEY COUGARS 10

TOWN: 1 Rob Lunt; 2 Ryan Blair; 3 Neil Frazer; 4 Jason Mossop; 5 Martyn Wilson; 6 Carl Forber; 7 Martin Keavney; 8 Dean Burgess; 9 Darren King; 10 Taani Lavulavu; 11 Jamie Beaumont; 12 Adam Sidlow; 13 Shaun Lunt. Subs (all used): 14 Franco Kmet; 15 Dexter Miller; 16 Dean Vaughan; 17 Matthew Tunstall.
Tries: Keavney (30), Mossop (36), Sidlow (54);
Goals: Forber 3/3.
Sin bin: S Lunt (59) – obstruction.
COUGARS: 1 Gavin Duffy; 2 Zac Hill; 3 John Crawford; 4 Oliver Purseglove; 5 Alex Brown; 6 Craig Fawcett; 7 Barry Eaton; 8 Gareth English; 9 James Feather; 10 Brendan Rawlins; 11 Simon Bissell; 12 Richard Knight; 13 Chris Redfearn. Subs (all used): 14 Michael Hastings; 15 Brian Sutton; 16 Wayne Sutcliffe; 17 Tom Palmer.
Tries: Crawford (23), Hill (56); **Goals:** Knight 1/2.
Rugby Leaguer & League Express Men of the Match: *Town:* Martin Keavney; *Cougars:* Barry Eaton.
Penalty count: 7-8; **Half-time:** 12-4;
Referee: Chris Dean; **Attendance:** 721.

YORK CITY KNIGHTS 38 GATESHEAD THUNDER 26

CITY KNIGHTS: 1 Lee Lingard; 2 Lee Mapals; 3 Dan Potter; 4 Chris Spurr; 5 Tom Burton; 6 George Rayner; 7 Jon Liddell; 8 Dave Buckley; 9 Jimmy Elston; 10 Adam Sullivan; 11 Ian Brown; 12 Ryan Esders; 13 Mark Spurr. Subs (all used): 14 Jamaine Wray; 15 Stephen Grundy; 16 Ryan McDonald; 17 Neil Lowe.
Tries: Lingard (8), C Spurr (17, 30), Esders (25, 66), M Spurr (30), Buckley (56), Potter (74);
Goals: Esders 0/3, Lingard 3/5.
THUNDER: 1 Neil Thorman; 2 Robin Peers; 3 Dylan Nash; 4 Pat Williamson; 5 Graham Stephenson; 6 Ryan Clarke; 7 Tim Martin; 8 Jason Payne; 9 Dan Smith; 10 Tabua Cakacaka; 11 Shane Wooden; 12 Michael Knowles; 13 Nick Hyde. Subs (all used): 14 Kevin Till; 15 Tony Doherty; 16 Steven Bradley; 17 Clint Frazer.
Tries: Knowles (2), Stephenson (20), Wooden (39), Martin (50), Williamson (63);
Goals: Knowles 2/3, Clarke 1/2.
Rugby Leaguer & League Express Men of the Match: *City Knights:* Jimmy Elston; *Thunder:* Dan Smith.
Penalty count: 8-10; **Half-time:** 22-14;
Referee: Charlie Nielson; **Attendance:** 825.

HUNSLET HAWKS 6 LONDON SKOLARS 32

HAWKS: 1 Matt Bramald; 2 Andy Robinson; 3 Craig Bower; 4 Caldon Bravo; 5 Steve Morton; 6 Darren Robinson; 7 Matt Firth; 8 Danny Ekis; 9 Mark Moxon; 10 Paul Seal; 11 Wayne Freeman; 12 Ben Walkin; 13 Chris Ross. Subs (all used): 14 Gareth Greenwood; 15 Danny Cook; 16 Mark Cunningham; 17 Paul Smith.
Try: Bravo (22); **Goals:** D Robinson 1/1.
Sin bin: Ekis (70) - fighting.
SKOLARS: 1 Jermaine Coleman; 2 Corey Simms; 3 Pete Hodgkinson; 4 Ashley Tozer; 5 William Webster; 6 Paul Thorman; 7 Jamie Nowland; 8 Martyn Benson; 9 Gareth Honor; 10 Richard Louw; 11 Mike Castle; 12 Lydan Maitua; 13 Chris Lynton. Subs (all used): 14 Chris Shears; 15 Keir Bell; 16 Warren Heilig; 17 Alan Barker.
Tries: Hodgkinson (33), Webster (44), Nowland (47, 55, 76); **Goals:** Thorman 6/8.
Sin bin: Louw (70) - fighting.
Rugby Leaguer & League Express Men of the Match: *Hawks:* Chris Ross; *Skolars:* Jamie Nowland.
Penalty count: 10-8; **Half-time:** 6-10;
Referee: Leon Williamson; **Attendance:** 273.

WEEK 19

Saturday 11th August 2007

LONDON SKOLARS 32 GATESHEAD THUNDER 12

SKOLARS: 1 Jermaine Coleman; 2 Corey Simms; 3 Pete Hodgkinson; 4 Ashley Tozer; 5 Austen Aggrey; 6 Paul Thorman; 7 Jamie Nowland; 8 Martyn Benson; 9 Gareth Honor; 10 Richard Louw; 11 Mike Castle; 12 Lydan Maitua; 13 Chris Lynton. Subs (all used): 14 Frank Reid; 15 Chris Shears; 16 Warren Heilig; 17 Alan Barker.
Tries: Simms (16), Lynton (52), Tozer (59), Shears (77), Aggrey (80); **Goals:** Thorman 6/6.
THUNDER: 1 Neil Thorman; 2 Robin Peers; 3 Dylan Nash; 4 Pat Williamson; 5 Graham Stephenson; 6 Ryan Clarke; 7 Tim Martin; 8 Jason Payne; 9 Dan Smith; 10 Tabua Cakacaka; 11 Shane Wooden; 12 Michael Knowles; 13 Nick Hyde. Subs (all used): 14 Kevin Till; 15 Tony Doherty; 16 Steven Bradley; 17 Chris Parker.
Tries: Peers (5), Stephenson (27, 47);
Goals: Knowles 0/3.
Rugby Leaguer & League Express Men of the Match: *Skolars:* Chris Lynton; *Thunder:* Graham Stephenson.
Penalty count: 7-8; **Half-time:** 6-8; **Referee:** Paul Carr;
Attendance: 326 *(at Summers Lane, Finchley)*.

CELTIC CRUSADERS 84 HUNSLET HAWKS 10

CRUSADERS: 1 Tony Duggan; 2 Paul Ballard; 3 Rob Toshack; 4 Mark Dalle Cort; 5 Grant Epton; 6 Damien Quinn; 7 Jace Van Dijk; 8 Phil Cushion; 9 Neil Budworth; 10 Gareth Dean; 11 Neale Wyatt; 12 Darren Mapp; 13 Terry Martin. Subs (all used): 14 Luke Young; 15 Jamie I'Anson; 16 Hywel Davies; 17 Aurelien Cologni.
Tries: Ballard (2, 19, 60), Dalle Cort (8, 65), Duggan (10, 58, 78), Quinn (13), Epton (17), Toshack (30), I'Anson (34), Cologni (53), Young (56), Mapp (72); **Goals:** Van Dijk 10/13, Quinn 2/2.
HAWKS: 1 Matt Bramald; 2 Mark Cunningham; 3 Craig Bower; 4 Caldon Bravo; 5 Steve Morton; 6 Mark Moxon; 7 Matt Firth; 8 Danny Cook; 9 Jonny Wainhouse; 10 Wayne Freeman; 11 Ben Walkin; 12 Andy Robinson; 13 Gareth Greenwood. Subs (all used): 14 Darren Robinson; 15 Joey Walkin; 16 Glen Pennington; 17 Paul Seal.
Tries: Moxon (25), Bravo (46); **Goals:** D Robinson 1/2.
Rugby Leaguer & League Express Men of the Match: *Crusaders:* Darren Mapp; *Hawks:* Mark Moxon.
Penalty count: 4-4; **Half-time:** 44-4;
Referee: Mike Dawber; **Attendance:** 795.

Sunday 12th August 2007

FEATHERSTONE ROVERS 38 YORK CITY KNIGHTS 12

ROVERS: 1 Loz Wildbore; 2 Ade Adebisi; 3 Jon Whittle; 4 Danny Kirmond; 5 Dean Colton; 6 Joe McLocklan; 7 Andy Kain; 8 Gareth Handford; 9 Gavin Swinson; 10 Stuart Dickens; 11 Jamie Field; 12 Richard Blakeway; 13 Tom Haughey. Subs (all used): 14 Jamie Benn; 15 Ian Tonks; 16 James Houston; 17 Gary Ellery.
Tries: Kain (4), Whittle (8), Haughey (48), McLocklan (52), Dickens (64), Kirmond (73), Wildbore (75); **Goals:** Dickens 5/7.
Sin bin: Haughey (38) – grapple tackle.
CITY KNIGHTS: 1 Lee Lingard; 2 Lee Mapals; 3 Dan Potter; 4 Chris Spurr; 5 Tom Burton; 6 Danny Grimshaw; 7 Jon Liddell; 8 Dave Buckley; 9 Jimmy Elston; 10 Adam Sullivan; 11 Ian Brown; 12 Ryan Esders; 13 Mark Spurr. Subs (all used): 14 Jamaine Wray; 15 Nathan Priestley; 16 Ryan McDonald; 17 Neil Lowe.
Tries: Lowe (19, 58); **Goals:** Esders 2/2.
Rugby Leaguer & League Express Men of the Match: *Rovers:* Tom Haughey; *City Knights:* Neil Lowe.
Penalty count: 10-14; **Half-time:** 10-6;
Referee: Craig Halloran; **Attendance:** 1,314.

KEIGHLEY COUGARS 4 BARROW RAIDERS 54

COUGARS: 1 Gavin Duffy; 2 Zac Hill; 3 John Crawford; 4 Oliver Purseglove; 5 Alex Brown; 6 Craig Fawcett; 7 Barry Eaton; 8 Gareth English; 9 James Feather; 10 Brendan Rawlins; 11 Simon Bissell; 12 Richard Knight; 13 Chris Redfearn. Subs (all used): 14 Michael Hastings; 15 Wayne Sutcliffe; 16 Brian Sutton; 17 Tom Palmer.
Try: Sutcliffe (39); **Goals:** Knight 0/1.
RAIDERS: 1 Khamal Ganley; 2 James Finch; 3 Mike Basan; 4 Liam Harrison; 5 Nick Beach; 6 Liam Finch; 7 Darren Holt; 8 Michael Smith; 9 Andy Ellis; 10 Dave Armistead; 11 Mike Whitehead; 12 Phil Atkinson; 13 Pat Weisner. Subs (all used): 14 Chris Archer; 15 Paul Wilcock; 16 Paul Raftrey; 17 Lee Dutton.
Tries: Beach (3, 67, 74), Ellis (28), J Finch (47), Weisner (57), Ganley (64, 65), Basan (66);
Goals: Holt 5/6, Weisner 3/3, Beach 1/2.
Rugby Leaguer & League Express Men of the Match: *Cougars:* Brendan Rawlins; *Raiders:* Nick Beach.
Penalty count: 13-7; **Half-time:** 4-14;
Referee: Charlie Nielson; **Attendance:** 658.

OLDHAM 44 WORKINGTON TOWN 18

OLDHAM: 1 Ian Gordon; 2 Byron Ford; 3 Craig Littler; 4 Adam Hughes; 5 Lucas Onyango; 6 Neil Roden; 7 James Coyle; 8 Jason Boults; 9 Simeon Hoyle; 10 Richard Mervill; 11 Ian Hodson; 12 Robert Roberts; 13 Geno Costin. Subs (all used): 14 Anthony Tonks; 15 Gareth Morton; 16 Said Tamghart; 17 Matty Brooks.
Tries: Hughes (2), Costin (12), Coyle (18), Brooks (29), Onyango (42, 68), Morton (56), Ford (72, 75);
Goals: Hughes 2/5, Morton 2/5.
Sin bin: Mervill (49) - interference.
TOWN: 1 Ashley McDonald; 2 Neil Frazer; 3 Dexter Miller; 4 Jason Mossop; 5 Ryan Blair; 6 Carl Forber; 7

Martin Keavney; 8 Dean Vaughan; 9 Darren King; 10 Adam Sidlow; 11 Jamie Beaumont; 12 Franco Kmet; 13 Shaun Lunt. Subs (all used): 14 Martyn Wilson; 15 Matthew Tunstall; 16 Dean Burgess; 17 Taani Lavulavu.
Tries: McDonald (15), Miller (38), S Lunt (60);
Goals: Forber 3/3.
Rugby Leaguer & League Express Men of the Match:
Oldham: James Coyle; *Town:* Shaun Lunt.
Penalty count: 5-8; **Half-time:** 20-12;
Referee: Ronnie Laughton; **Attendance:** 1,034.

SWINTON LIONS 70 BLACKPOOL PANTHERS 20

LIONS: 1 Wayne English; 2 Andy Saywell; 3 Dean Gorton; 4 Mark Brocklehurst; 5 Marlon Billy; 6 Jay Duffy; 7 Liam McGovern; 8 Bruce Johnson; 9 Phil Wood; 10 David Bates; 11 Craig Farrimond; 12 Paul Alcock; 13 Lee Marsh. Subs (all used): 14 Martin Moana; 15 Rob Line; 16 Steve McCurrie; 17 Gareth Hayes.
Tries: Billy (4), Bates (15), English (22, 35), Brocklehurst (39), Alcock (41), Line (44, 54), P Wood (50, 76), Saywell (67, 69);
Goals: Marsh 9/10, McGovern 2/2.
PANTHERS: 1 Kieron Seeds; 2 Eddie Kilgannon; 3 Adrian Dootson; 4 Carl Jones; 5 Mike Stout; 6 Craig Waia; 7 Martin Gambles; 8 Lee Rowley; 9 Phil Cantillon; 10 Gareth Jones; 11 Melvin Alker; 12 Kris Ratcliffe; 13 Deon Duell. Subs (all used): 14 Jon Chamberlain; 15 Danny Barton; 16 Martin Roden; 17 Richard Rafferty.
Tries: Dootson (20, 58), C Jones (61), Stout (65);
Goals: Gambles 2/4.
Dismissal: Alker (75) - punching.
Rugby Leaguer & League Express Men of the Match:
Lions: Wayne English; *Panthers:* Martin Gambles.
Penalty count: 5-8; **Half-time:** 28-4;
Referee: Robert Hicks; **Attendance:** 349.

WEEK 20

Saturday 18th August 2007

CELTIC CRUSADERS 34 KEIGHLEY COUGARS 12

CRUSADERS: 1 Tony Duggan; 2 Paul Ballard; 3 Rob Toshack; 4 Mark Dalle Cort; 5 Anthony Blackwood; 6 Josh Hannay; 7 Jace Van Dijk; 8 Chris Beasley; 9 Neil Budworth; 10 Gareth Dean; 11 Neale Wyatt; 12 Darren Mapp; 13 Damien Quinn. Subs (all used): 14 Aurelien Cologni; 15 Phil Cushion; 16 Josh Cale; 17 Hywel Davies.
Tries: Hannay (8), Duggan (11, 79), Dalle Cort (18), Blackwood (23), Wyatt (43); **Goals:** Van Dijk 5/6.
Sin bin: Mapp (56) - late challenge on Eaton.
COUGARS: 1 Gavin Duffy; 2 Sam Gardner; 3 Michael Hastings; 4 Oliver Purseglove; 5 Alex Brown; 6 Craig Fawcett; 7 Barry Eaton; 8 Simon Bissell; 9 James Feather; 10 Brendan Rawlins; 11 Wayne Sutcliffe; 12 Richard Knight; 13 Chris Redfearn. Subs (all used): 14 Matt Foster; 15 Greg Nicholson; 16 Gareth English; 17 Tom Palmer.
Tries: Palmer (27), Bissell (54), Knight (58);
Goals: Knight 0/3.
Rugby Leaguer & League Express Men of the Match:
Crusaders: Tony Duggan; *Cougars:* Barry Eaton.
Penalty count: 3-6; **Half-time:** 22-4;
Referee: Craig Halloran; **Attendance:** 801.

Sunday 19th August 2007

BLACKPOOL PANTHERS 20 LONDON SKOLARS 34

PANTHERS: 1 Kieron Seeds; 2 Simon Holden; 3 Carl Jones; 4 Rob Sloman; 5 Mike Stout; 6 Deon Duell; 7 Martin Gambles; 8 Lee Rowley; 9 Adrian Dootson; 10 Gareth Jones; 11 Melvin Alker; 12 Martin Roden; 13 Phil Cantillon. Subs (all used): 14 Craig Waia; 15 Rob Lamb; 16 Danny Barton; 17 Richard Rafferty.
Tries: Sloman (39), Stout (58, 71, 80);
Goals: Gambles 2/4.
SKOLARS: 1 Jermaine Coleman; 2 Corey Simms; 3 Pete Hodgkinson; 4 Ashley Tozer; 5 Austen Aggrey; 6 Paul Thorman; 7 Jamie Nowland; 8 Martyn Benson; 9 Gareth Honor; 10 Richard Louw; 11 Mike Castle; 12 Lydan Maitua; 13 Chris Lynton. Subs (all used): 14 Frank Reid; 15 Chris Shears; 16 Warren Heilig; 17 Alan Barker.
Tries: Hodgkinson (10), Louw (15), Aggrey (24), Shears (32), Barker (75), Thorman (78); **Goals:** Thorman 5/6.
Rugby Leaguer & League Express Men of the Match:
Panthers: Mike Stout; *Skolars:* Austen Aggrey.
Penalty count: 7-9; **Half-time:** 4-22;
Referee: Matthew Thomasson; **Attendance:** 263.

GATESHEAD THUNDER 14 OLDHAM 28

THUNDER: 1 Neil Thorman; 2 Graham Stephenson; 3 Dylan Nash; 4 Pat Williamson; 5 Danny Wilson; 6 Tim Martin; 7 Scott Partis; 8 Jason Payne; 9 Dan Smith; 10 Tabua Cakacaka; 11 Shane Wooden; 12 Michael Knowles; 13 Nick Hyde. Subs (all used): 14 Ryan Clarke; 15 Robin Peers; 16 Tony Doherty; 17 Matt Barron.
Tries: Martin (24, 55); **Goals:** Knowles 3/3.
OLDHAM: 1 Ian Gordon; 2 Byron Ford; 3 Craig Littler; 4 Alex Wilkinson; 5 Andy Gorey; 6 Neil Roden; 7 James Coyle; 8 Jason Boults; 9 Andy Crabtree; 10 Richard Mervill; 11 Drew Houston; 12 Robert Roberts; 13 Gareth Morton. Subs (all used): 14 Chris Baines; 15 Warren Stevens; 16 Said Tamghart; 17 Matty Brooks.
Tries: Houston (10), Mervill (17), Roden (25), Ford (33), Gorey (42); **Goals:** Morton 4/5.
Sin bin: Mervill (60) - interference.
Rugby Leaguer & League Express Men of the Match:
Thunder: Michael Knowles; *Oldham:* Matty Brooks.
Penalty count: 12-7; **Half-time:** 8-22;
Referee: Charlie Nielson; **Attendance:** 407.

Featherstone's Jon Whittle halts the progress of Barrow's Lee Dutton

WORKINGTON TOWN 16 BARROW RAIDERS 28

TOWN: 1 Ashley McDonald; 2 Neil Frazer; 3 Dexter Miller; 4 Jason Mossop; 5 Ryan Blair; 6 Carl Forber; 7 Martin Keavney; 8 Dean Vaughan; 9 Darren King; 10 Adam Sidlow; 11 Jamie Beaumont; 12 Franco Kmet; 13 Shaun Lunt. Subs: 14 Martyn Wilson; 15 Peter Dobson (not used); 16 Matthew Tunstall; 17 Dean Burgess.
Tries: Frazer (27), S Lunt (50, 60); **Goals:** Forber 2/4.
RAIDERS: 1 Khamal Ganley; 2 James Houston; 3 Mike Basan; 4 Liam Harrison; 5 Nick Beach; 6 Liam Finch; 7 Darren Holt; 8 Paul Raftrey; 9 Andy Ellis; 10 Lee Dutton; 11 Michael Smith; 12 Mike Whitehead; 13 Dave Armistead. Subs (all used): 14 Jamie Marshall; 15 Paul Wilcock; 16 James Gordon; 17 Jamie Butler.
Tries: L Finch (15), Beach (31, 76), Smith (47), Holt (72); **Goals:** Holt 4/6.
Rugby Leaguer & League Express Men of the Match:
Town: Shaun Lunt; *Raiders:* Dave Armistead.
Penalty count: 9-7; **Half-time:** 6-10;
Referee: Paul Carr; **Attendance:** 857.

YORK CITY KNIGHTS 16 SWINTON LIONS 22

CITY KNIGHTS: 1 Lee Lingard; 2 Alex Godfrey; 3 Dan Potter; 4 Chris Spurr; 5 Tom Burton; 6 Danny Grimshaw; 7 Jon Liddell; 8 Dave Buckley; 9 Jimmy Elston; 10 Adam Sullivan; 11 Nathan Priestley; 12 Ryan Esders; 13 Mark Spurr. Subs (all used): 14 Jamaine Wray; 15 Kyle Palmer; 16 Ryan McDonald; 17 Neil Lowe.
Tries: C Spurr (42), Priestley (45), Wray (60);
Goals: Esders 2/3.
Sin bin: Esders (32) - dissent.
On report: Alleged late tackle (40) - on P Wood.
LIONS: 1 Wayne English; 2 Andy Saywell; 3 Dean Gorton; 4 Mark Brocklehurst; 5 Marlon Billy; 6 Craig Ashall; 7 Liam McGovern; 8 Rob Line; 9 Phil Wood; 10 Gareth Hayes; 11 Bruce Johnson; 12 Paul Alcock; 13 Lee Marsh. Subs (all used): 14 Martin Moana; 15 Rob Draper; 16 Matt Bryers; 17 Dave Newton.
Tries: Moana (26), Marsh (40), Saywell (67);
Goals: Marsh 5/6.
Sin bin: Billy (34) - interference.
On report: Alleged spear tackle (11) - on C Spurr.
Rugby Leaguer & League Express Men of the Match:
City Knights: Ryan Esders; *Lions:* Craig Ashall.
Penalty count: 8-9; **Half-time:** 0-14;
Referee: Peter Taberner; **Attendance:** 806.

HUNSLET HAWKS 10 FEATHERSTONE ROVERS 20

HAWKS: 1 Matt Bramald; 2 Andy Robinson; 3 David Foster; 4 Danny Cook; 5 Steve Morton; 6 Mark Moxon; 7 Matt Firth; 8 Danny Ekis; 9 Darren Robinson; 10 Wayne Freeman; 11 Ben Walkin; 12 Will Cartledge; 13 Gareth Greenwood. Subs (all used): 14 Jonny Wainhouse; 15 Joey Walkin; 16 Glen Pennington; 17 Danny Murgatroyd.
Try: Cook (44); **Goals:** Bramald 1/2, D Robinson 2/4.
ROVERS: 1 Loz Wildbore; 2 Danny Kirmond; 3 Jon Whittle; 4 Wayne McHugh; 5 Ade Adebisi; 6 Joe McLocklan; 7 Andy Kain; 8 Ian Tonks; 9 Paul Hughes; 10 Stuart Dickens; 11 Jamie Field; 12 Richard Blakeway; 13 Tom Haughey. Subs (all used): 14 Chris Ross; 15 Carl Hughes; 16 James Houston; 17 Gareth Handford.
Tries: Haughey (16), Kain (27), Blakeway (77);
Goals: Wildbore 1/1, Dickens 3/4.
Sin bin: Dickens (21) - interference;
McHugh (58) - interference.
Rugby Leaguer & League Express Men of the Match:

Hawks: Jonny Wainhouse; *Rovers:* Tom Haughey.
Penalty count: 13-11; **Half-time:** 2-10;
Referee: Ronnie Laughton; **Attendance:** 773.

Wednesday 22nd August 2007

HUNSLET HAWKS 6 OLDHAM 42

HAWKS: 1 Gary McClelland; 2 Andy Robinson; 3 David Foster; 4 Danny Cook; 5 Steve Morton; 6 Mark Moxon; 7 Matt Firth; 8 Danny Ekis; 9 Gareth Greenwood; 10 Wayne Freeman; 11 Ben Walkin; 12 Glen Pennington; 13 Will Cartledge. Subs (all used): 14 Darren Robinson; 15 Danny Murgatroyd; 16 Ben Jones; 17 Joey Walkin.
Try: Cook (53); **Goals:** McClelland 0/1, D Robinson 1/1.
Sin bin: Freeman (32) - holding down.
OLDHAM: 1 Gareth Langley; 2 Byron Ford; 3 Gareth Morton; 4 Drew Houston; 5 Lucas Onyango; 6 Neil Roden; 7 Matty Brooks; 8 Warren Stevens; 9 Simeon Hoyle; 10 Richard Mervill; 11 Ian Hodson; 12 Robert Roberts; 13 Chris Baines. Subs (all used): 14 Alex Wilkinson; 15 Anthony Tonks; 16 Said Tamghart; 17 Andy Crabtree.
Tries: Morton (40), Onyango (48), Houston (50), Tonks (60), Roberts (64), Ford (70, 75); **Goals:** Morton 7/7.
Rugby Leaguer & League Express Men of the Match:
Hawks: Danny Ekis; *Oldham:* Byron Ford.
Penalty count: 6-9; **Half-time:** 0-6;
Referee: Jamie Leahy; **Attendance:** 538.

Friday 24th August 2007

LONDON SKOLARS 0 YORK CITY KNIGHTS 34

SKOLARS: 1 Jermaine Coleman; 2 Corey Simms; 3 Pete Hodgkinson; 4 Ashley Tozer; 5 Austen Aggrey; 6 Paul Thorman; 7 Jamie Nowland; 8 Martyn Benson; 9 Gareth Honor; 10 Richard Louw; 11 Mike Castle; 12 Lydan Maitua; 13 Chris Lynton. Subs (all used): 14 Frank Reid; 15 Chris Shears; 16 Tane Taitoko; 17 Alan Barker.
Sin bin: Lynton (67) - obstruction.
CITY KNIGHTS: 1 Lee Lingard; 2 Lee Mapals; 3 Dan Potter; 4 Tom Burton; 5 Alex Godfrey; 6 Scott Rhodes; 7 Jon Liddell; 8 Kyle Palmer; 9 John Smith; 10 Adam Sullivan; 11 Dave Buckley; 12 Chris Spurr; 13 Ryan Esders. Subs (all used): 14 Jimmy Elston; 15 Nathan Priestley; 16 Ryan McDonald; 17 Neil Lowe.
Tries: Godfrey (8), Lowe (25, 77, 80), Sullivan (59);
Goals: Esders 5/5, Liddell 1/1, McDonald 1/1.
Rugby Leaguer & League Express Men of the Match:
Skolars: Chris Shears; *City Knights:* Neil Lowe.
Penalty count: 5-8; **Half-time:** 0-16;
Referee: Gareth Hewer; **Attendance:** 1,288.

Sunday 26th August 2007

CELTIC CRUSADERS 64 GATESHEAD THUNDER 26

CRUSADERS: 1 Tony Duggan; 2 Paul Ballard; 3 Rob Toshack; 4 Mark Dalle Cort; 5 Anthony Blackwood; 6 Josh Hannay; 7 Jace Van Dijk; 8 Chris Beasley; 9 Neil Budworth; 10 Gareth Dean; 11 Neale Wyatt; 12 Darren Mapp; 13 Damien Quinn. Subs (all used): 14 Luke Young; 15 Aurelien Cologni; 16 Jamie I'Anson; 17 Hywel Davies.
Tries: Toshack (8, 54), Quinn (12), Mapp (16), Duggan (19), Hannay (40), Dalle Cort (46), Budworth (51, 77), Blackwood (57, 75), Young (72); **Goals:** Van Dijk 5/7, Quinn 2/2, Hannay 1/3.
THUNDER: 1 Neil Thorman; 2 Robin Peers; 3 Graham

Stephenson; 4 Dylan Nash; 5 Danny Wilson; 6 Tim Martin; 7 Scott Partis; 8 Jason Payne; 9 Dan Smith; 10 Tony Doherty; 11 Shane Wooden; 12 Michael Knowles; 13 Pat Williamson. Subs (all used): 14 Ryan Clarke; 15 Matt Barron; 16 Chris Parker; 17 Jonny Scott.
Tries: Partis (23), Thorman (33), Peers (42), Stephenson (60), Wooden (63); **Goals:** Knowles 3/5.
Dismissal: Nash (45) - spear tackle on Duggan.
Rugby Leaguer & League Express Men of the Match: *Crusaders:* Neale Wyatt; *Thunder:* Jason Payne.
Penalty count: 5-4; **Half-time:** 26-10;
Referee: Jamie Leahy; **Attendance:** 827.

WEEK 21

Thursday 30th August 2007

OLDHAM 18 CELTIC CRUSADERS 32

OLDHAM: 1 Ian Gordon; 2 Byron Ford; 3 Gareth Morton; 4 Alex Wilkinson; 5 Lucas Onyango; 6 Neil Roden; 7 James Coyle; 8 Warren Stevens; 9 Andy Crabtree; 10 Richard Mervill; 11 Ian Hodson; 12 Robert Roberts; 13 Geno Costin. Subs (all used): 14 Chris Baines; 15 Anthony Tonks; 16 Said Tamghart; 17 Matty Brooks.
Tries: Morton (15), Ford (79); **Goals:** Morton 5/6.
CRUSADERS: 1 Tony Duggan; 2 Paul Ballard; 3 Rob Toshack; 4 Mark Dalle Cort; 5 Anthony Blackwood; 6 Josh Hannay; 7 Jace Van Dijk; 8 Phil Cushion; 9 Neil Budworth; 10 Gareth Dean; 11 Neale Wyatt; 12 Darren Mapp; 13 Damien Quinn. Subs (all used): 14 Grant Epton; 15 Jamie I'Anson; 16 Terry Martin; 17 Chris Beasley.
Tries: Ballard (34, 41), Dalle Cort (48, 77), Duggan (75);
Goals: Van Dijk 6/8.
Sin bin: Dean (52) - interference.
Rugby Leaguer & League Express Men of the Match: *Oldham:* James Coyle; *Crusaders:* Damien Quinn.
Penalty count: 8-9; **Half-time:** 12-6;
Referee: Gareth Hewer; **Attendance:** 4,327.

Friday 31st August 2007

BARROW RAIDERS 56 BLACKPOOL PANTHERS 12

RAIDERS: 1 Khamal Ganley; 2 James Finch; 3 Mike Basan; 4 Liam Harrison; 5 Nick Beach; 6 Liam Finch; 7 Darren Holt; 8 Paul Raftrey; 9 Andy Ellis; 10 Lee Dutton; 11 Dave Armistead; 12 Mike Whitehead; 13 Pat Weisner. Subs (all used): 14 Jamie Marshall; 15 Paul Wilcock; 16 Martin Ostler; 17 Jamie Butler.
Tries: L Finch (3), Ganley (8), Beach (20, 40), Ellis (23), Marshall (42, 74), J Finch (51), Raftrey (70), Harrison (78); **Goals:** Holt 8/10.
PANTHERS: 1 Adrian Dootson; 2 Eddie Kilgannon; 3 Carl Jones; 4 Rob Sloman; 5 Mike Stout; 6 Craig Waia; 7 Martin Gambles; 8 Lee Rowley; 9 Phil Cantillon; 10 Gareth Jones; 11 Martin Roden; 12 Kris Ratcliffe; 13 Deon Duell. Subs (all used): 14 Kieron Seeds; 15 Rob Lamb; 16 Danny Barton; 17 Richard Rafferty.
Tries: Cantillon (32), Kilgannon (63); **Goals:** Gambles 2/2.
Rugby Leaguer & League Express Men of the Match: *Raiders:* Andy Ellis; *Panthers:* Martin Gambles.
Penalty count: 4-4; **Half-time:** 26-6;
Referee: Charlie Nielson; **Attendance:** 1,065.

Sunday 2nd September 2007

FEATHERSTONE ROVERS 40 WORKINGTON TOWN 34

ROVERS: 1 Loz Wildbore; 2 Danny Kirmond; 3 Jon Whittle; 4 Wayne McHugh; 5 Ade Adebisi; 6 Andy Kain; 7 Paul Handforth; 8 Gareth Handford; 9 Joe McLocklan; 10 Stuart Dickens; 11 James Houston; 12 Richard Blakeway; 13 Tom Haughey. Subs (all used): 14 Jamie Benn; 15 Ian Tonks; 16 Gavin Swinson; 17 Carl Hughes.
Tries: Wildbore (5), Haughey (36, 47), Kirmond (43), Handforth (45), Whittle (57), Adebisi (77);
Goals: Dickens 6/7.
TOWN: 1 Martyn Wilson; 2 Ryan Blair; 3 Neil Frazer; 4 Jason Mossop; 5 Stephen Dawes; 6 Carl Forber; 7 Martin Keavney; 8 Dean Vaughan; 9 Darren King; 10 Dean Burgess; 11 Dexter Miller; 12 Franco Kmet; 13 Shaun Lunt. Subs (all used): 14 Tyrone Dalton; 15 Scott Gorman; 16 Matthew Tunstall; 17 Adam Sidlow.
Tries: Blair (10), S Lunt (12, 25, 80), Keavney (29), Sidlow (71); **Goals:** Kmet 1/2, Forber 4/5.
Rugby Leaguer & League Express Men of the Match: *Rovers:* Tom Haughey; *Town:* Shaun Lunt.
Penalty count: 2-9; **Half-time:** 12-24;
Referee: Ronnie Laughton; **Attendance:** 1,346.

KEIGHLEY COUGARS 18 GATESHEAD THUNDER 19

COUGARS: 1 Gavin Duffy; 2 Sam Gardner; 3 Michael Hastings; 4 Oliver Purseglove; 5 Alex Brown; 6 Craig Fawcett; 7 Barry Eaton; 8 Simon Bissell; 9 James Feather; 10 Brendan Rawlins; 11 Wayne Sutcliffe; 12 Richard Knight; 13 Chris Redfearn. Subs (all used): 14 Matt Foster; 15 Greg Nicholson; 16 Gareth English; 17 Tom Palmer.
Tries: Duffy (9, 52), Brown (54); **Goals:** Knight 3/4.
THUNDER: 1 Neil Thorman; 2 Robin Peers; 3 Graham Stephenson; 4 Dylan Nash; 5 Danny Wilson; 6 Ryan Clarke; 7 Tim Martin; 8 Jason Payne; 9 Dan Smith; 10 Tony Doherty; 11 Shane Wooden; 12 Michael Knowles; 13 Pat Williamson. Subs (all used): 14 Scott Partis; 15 Matt Barron; 16 Tabua Cakacaka; 17 Chris Parker.
Tries: Wilson (30), Nash (31), Wooden (48);
Goals: Knowles 3/4; **Field goal:** Martin (70).
Rugby Leaguer & League Express Men of the Match: *Cougars:* Gavin Duffy; *Thunder:* Jason Payne.
Penalty count: 7-7; **Half-time:** 8-12;
Referee: Paul Carr; **Attendance:** 636.

SWINTON LIONS 14 HUNSLET HAWKS 12

LIONS: 1 Wayne English; 2 Andy Saywell; 3 Adam Bowman; 4 Mark Brocklehurst; 5 Marlon Billy; 6 Craig Ashall; 7 Liam McGovern; 8 Bruce Johnson; 9 Phil Wood; 10 Rob Line; 11 Rob Draper; 12 Martin Moana; 13 Lee Marsh. Subs (all used): 14 Jay Duffy; 15 Matt Bryers; 16 Dave Newton; 17 Gareth Hayes.
Tries: Moana (46, 77), Brocklehurst (62);
Goals: Marsh 1/4.
HAWKS: 1 Matt Bramald; 2 Andy Robinson; 3 David Foster; 4 Ben Jones; 5 Steve Morton; 6 Mark Moxon; 7 Matt Firth; 8 Danny Ekis; 9 Gareth Greenwood; 10 Wayne Freeman; 11 Ben Walkin; 12 Danny Cook; 13 Will Cartledge. Subs (all used): 14 Darren Robinson; 15 Matt Carbutt; 16 Glen Pennington; 17 Joey Walkin.
Tries: Moxon (3), Jones (43);
Goals: Bramald 1/2, D Robinson 1/1.
Rugby Leaguer & League Express Men of the Match: *Lions:* Craig Ashall; *Hawks:* Mark Moxon.
Penalty count: 4-6; **Half-time:** 0-6;
Referee: Craig Halloran; **Attendance:** 447.

Wednesday 5th September 2007

HUNSLET HAWKS 13 GATESHEAD THUNDER 0

HAWKS: 1 Matt Bramald; 2 Andy Robinson; 3 Luke Pennington; 4 Danny Cook; 5 Steve Morton; 6 Mark Moxon; 7 Matt Firth; 8 Danny Ekis; 9 Gareth Greenwood; 10 Wayne Freeman; 11 Ben Walkin; 12 Glen Pennington; 13 Will Cartledge. Subs (all used): 14 Darren Robinson; 15 Matt Carbutt; 16 Dale Harris; 17 Joey Walkin.
Tries: D Robinson (28), Freeman (80);
Goals: D Robinson 2/2; **Field goal:** D Robinson (54).
THUNDER: 1 Neil Thorman; 2 Danny Wilson; 3 Pat Williamson; 4 Graham Stephenson; 5 Robin Peers; 6 Tim Martin; 7 Ryan Clarke; 8 Tony Doherty; 9 Dan Smith; 10 Jason Payne; 11 Shane Wooden; 12 Nick Hyde; 13 Michael Knowles. Subs (all used): 14 Kevin Till; 15 Matt Barron; 16 Chris Parker; 17 Tabua Cakacaka.
Goals: Knowles 0/1.
Sin bin: Cakacaka (27) - use of the elbow.
Rugby Leaguer & League Express Men of the Match: *Hawks:* Ben Walkin; *Thunder:* Michael Knowles.
Penalty count: 12-9; **Half-time:** 6-0;
Referee: Peter Taberner; **Attendance:** 307.

OLDHAM 30 SWINTON LIONS 22

OLDHAM: 1 Ian Gordon; 2 Gareth Langley; 3 Craig Littler; 4 Gareth Morton; 5 Byron Ford; 6 Neil Roden; 7 James Coyle; 8 Warren Stevens; 9 Andy Crabtree; 10 Richard Mervill; 11 Ian Hodson; 12 Robert Roberts; 13 Geno Costin. Subs (all used): 14 Alex Wilkinson; 15 Anthony Tonks; 16 Said Tamghart; 17 Matty Brooks.
Tries: Langley (3), Coyle (26), Littler (32), Ford (36, 47, 70); **Goals:** Morton 3/6.
LIONS: 1 Wayne English; 2 Desi Williams; 3 Adam Bowman; 4 Mark Brocklehurst; 5 Marlon Billy; 6 Craig Ashall; 7 Jay Duffy; 8 Rob Line; 9 Phil Wood; 10 Gareth Hayes; 11 Rob Draper; 12 Mike Smith; 13 Lee Marsh. Subs (all used): 14 Liam McGovern; 15 Martin Moana; 16 Dave Newton; 17 David Bates.
Tries: P Wood (17), Duffy (39), Marsh (61, 77);
Goals: Marsh 3/4.
Dismissal: Newton (51) - fighting.
Sin bin: Ashall (24) - holding down.
Rugby Leaguer & League Express Men of the Match: *Oldham:* Alex Wilkinson; *Lions:* Lee Marsh.
Penalty count: 11-10; **Half-time:** 20-12;
Referee: Jamie Leahy; **Attendance:** 950.

WEEK 22

Saturday 8th September 2007

BARROW RAIDERS 30 FEATHERSTONE ROVERS 4

RAIDERS: 1 Khamal Ganley; 2 James Finch; 3 Mike Basan; 4 Liam Harrison; 5 Nick Beach; 6 Liam Finch; 7 Darren Holt; 8 Paul Raftrey; 9 Andy Ellis; 10 Dave Armistead; 11 Martin Ostler; 12 Mike Whitehead; 13 Pat Weisner. Subs (all used): 14 Jamie Marshall; 15 Paul Wilcock; 16 Lee Dutton; 17 Jamie Butler.
Tries: Harrison (4), Beach (32), Ganley (44), Weisner (72), Basan (77); **Goals:** Holt 4/6, Weisner 1/1.
Sin bin: Holt (57) - fighting.
ROVERS: 1 Loz Wildbore; 2 Danny Kirmond; 3 Jon Whittle; 4 Wayne McHugh; 5 Ade Adebisi; 6 Andy Kain; 7 Paul Handforth; 8 Gareth Handford; 9 Joe McLocklan; 10 Stuart Dickens; 11 Richard Blakeway; 12 Danny Richardson; 13 Jamie Benn. Subs (all used): 14 Paul Hughes; 15 Ian Tonks; 16 Carl Hughes; 17 Steve Dooler.
Try: McHugh (17); **Goals:** Dickens 0/1.
Sin bin: Tonks (57) - fighting;
Adebisi (70) - holding down.
Rugby Leaguer & League Express Men of the Match: *Raiders:* Liam Harrison; *Rovers:* Wayne McHugh.
Penalty count: 11-8; **Half-time:** 12-4;
Referee: Gareth Hewer; **Attendance:** 1,901.

Sunday 9th September 2007

GATESHEAD THUNDER 16 CELTIC CRUSADERS 60

THUNDER: 1 Neil Thorman; 2 Robin Peers; 3 Graham Stephenson; 4 Pat Williamson; 5 Danny Wilson; 6 Tim Martin; 7 Kevin Till; 8 Chris Parker; 9 Dan Smith; 10 Tabua Cakacaka; 11 Shane Wooden; 12 Nick Hyde; 13 Michael Knowles. Subs (all used): 14 Ryan Clarke; 15 Clint Frazer; 16 Matt Barron; 17 Jonny Scott.
Tries: Peers (3), Knowles (45, 64); **Goals:** Knowles 2/3.
CRUSADERS: 1 Tony Duggan; 2 Paul Ballard; 3 Rob Toshack; 4 Mark Dalle Cort; 5 Anthony Blackwood; 6 Josh Hannay; 7 Jace Van Dijk; 8 Terry Martin; 9 Neil Budworth; 10 Gareth Dean; 11 Neale Wyatt; 12 Darren Mapp; 13 Damien Quinn. Subs (all used): 14 Grant Epton; 15 Jamie I'Anson; 16 Chris Beasley; 17 Hywel Davies.
Tries: Ballard (6), Toshack (13), Quinn (15, 48), Duggan (19, 33, 68), Mapp (23), Wyatt (29), Epton (51), Van Dijk (74); **Goals:** Van Dijk 7/10, Beasley 1/1.
Rugby Leaguer & League Express Men of the Match: *Thunder:* Michael Knowles; *Crusaders:* Tony Duggan.
Penalty count: 5-4; **Half-time:** 4-38;
Referee: Robert Hicks; **Attendance:** 473.

OLDHAM 28 LONDON SKOLARS 26

OLDHAM: 1 Byron Ford; 2 Gareth Langley; 3 Craig Littler; 4 Gareth Morton; 5 Lucas Onyango; 6 Neil Roden; 7 James Coyle; 8 Jason Boults; 9 Simeon Hoyle; 10 Richard Mervill; 11 Ian Hodson; 12 Robert Roberts; 13 Drew Houston. Subs (all used): 14 Warren Stevens; 15 Ian Sinfield; 16 Said Tamghart; 17 Matty Brooks.
Tries: Ford (7, 37), Hoyle (14), Hodson (28), Morton (60); **Goals:** Morton 4/6.
SKOLARS: 1 Jermaine Coleman; 2 Corey Simms; 3 Chris Shears; 4 Ashley Tozer; 5 Austen Aggrey; 6 Paul Thorman; 7 Jamie Nowland; 8 Martyn Benson; 9 Gareth Honor; 10 Alan Barker; 11 Mike Castle; 12 Lydan Maitua; 13 Chris Lynton. Subs (all used): 14 Frank Reid; 15 Keir Bell; 16 Tane Taitoko; 17 Warren Heilig.
Tries: Nowland (33), Simms (47, 74), Tozer (63), Maitua (70); **Goals:** Thorman 3/5.
Rugby Leaguer & League Express Men of the Match: *Oldham:* Said Tamghart; *Skolars:* Jamie Nowland.
Penalty count: 5-10; **Half-time:** 22-6;
Referee: Charlie Nielson; **Attendance:** 918.

SWINTON LIONS 36 WORKINGTON TOWN 26

LIONS: 1 Wayne English; 2 Andy Saywell; 3 Adam Bowman; 4 Mark Brocklehurst; 5 Marlon Billy; 6 Martin Moana; 7 Jay Duffy; 8 Rob Line; 9 Craig Ashall; 10 Gareth Hayes; 11 Rob Draper; 12 Dave Newton; 13 Lee Marsh. Subs (all used): 14 Phil Wood; 15 Dean Gorton; 16 Bruce Johnson; 17 David Bates.
Tries: Saywell (14, 57), Moana (27, 35), Billy (30, 62);
Goals: Marsh 6/7.
Sin bin: Duffy (20) - fighting.
TOWN: 1 Martyn Wilson; 2 Ryan Blair; 3 Neil Frazer; 4 Jason Mossop; 5 Stephen Dawes; 6 Carl Forber; 7 Martin Keavney; 8 Matthew Tunstall; 9 Darren King; 10 Dean Burgess; 11 Dexter Miller; 12 Scott Gorman; 13 Franco Kmet. Subs (all used): 14 Tyrone Dalton; 15 Peter Dobson; 16 Adam Sidlow; 17 Taani Lavulavu.
Tries: Kmet (9), Mossop (44), Wilson (28, 74), Dawes (77); **Goals:** Forber 3/5.
Dismissal: Lavulavu (51) - high tackle on Line.
Sin bin: Forber (20) – fighting; Miller (21) – dissent; Lavulavu (26) - high tackle on Johnson.
Rugby Leaguer & League Express Men of the Match: *Lions:* Martin Moana; *Town:* Carl Forber.
Penalty count: 4-6; **Half-time:** 22-4;
Referee: Jamie Leahy; **Attendance:** 557.

YORK CITY KNIGHTS 56 BLACKPOOL PANTHERS 22

CITY KNIGHTS: 1 Lee Lingard; 2 Lee Mapals; 3 Dan Potter; 4 Tom Burton; 5 Alex Godfrey; 6 Jon Liddell; 7 Scott Rhodes; 8 Kyle Palmer; 9 Jamaine Wray; 10 Adam Sullivan; 11 Dave Buckley; 12 Chris Spurr; 13 Ryan Esders. Subs (all used): 14 Jimmy Elston; 15 Nathan Priestley; 16 Ryan McDonald; 17 Neil Lowe.
Tries: Palmer (5, 79), Burton (29), Lowe (32), Rhodes (35), Mapals (37, 45, 50), Godfrey (39), Buckley (76); **Goals:** Esders 8/10, Lingard 0/1.
PANTHERS: 1 Kieron Seeds; 2 Mike Stout; 3 Carl Jones; 4 Eddie Kilgannon; 5 Rob Sloman; 6 Craig Waia; 7 Martin Gambles; 8 Lee Rowley; 9 Phil Cantillon; 10 Gareth Jones; 11 Martin Roden; 12 Kris Ratcliffe; 13 Deon Duell. Subs (all used): 14 Adrian Dootson; 15 Danny Barton; 16 Richard Rafferty; 17 Rob Lamb.
Tries: Stout (63), Seeds (67), Kilgannon (73), C Jones (80); **Goals:** Gambles 3/4.
Rugby Leaguer & League Express Men of the Match: *City Knights:* Ryan Esders; *Panthers:* Martin Gambles.
Penalty count: 8-5; **Half-time:** 36-0;
Referee: Paul Carr; **Attendance:** 825.

HUNSLET HAWKS 12 KEIGHLEY COUGARS 26

HAWKS: 1 Matt Bramald; 2 Andy Robinson; 3 Ben Jones; 4 Eddie Mack; 5 Dale Harris; 6 Mark Moxon; 7 Matt Firth; 8 Glen Pennington; 9 Gareth Greenwood; 10 Wayne Freeman; 11 Ben Walkin; 12 Paul Robinson; 13 Will Cartledge. Subs (all used): 14 Darren Robinson; 15 Matt Carbutt; 16 Steve Morton; 17 Joey Walkin.
Tries: Greenwood (9), D Robinson (75);
Goals: D Robinson 1/1, Bramald 1/1.
COUGARS: 1 Gavin Duffy; 2 Sam Gardner; 3 Michael Hastings; 4 Oliver Purseglove; 5 Alex Brown; 6 Craig Fawcett; 7 Barry Eaton; 8 Simon Bissell; 9 James Feather; 10 Brendan Rawlins; 11 Wayne Sutcliffe; 12 Richard Knight; 13 Chris Redfearn. Subs (all used): 14 Matt Foster; 15 Greg Nicholson; 16 Tom Palmer; 17 Luke Sutton.
Tries: Gardner (21), Purseglove (39), Eaton (53), Brown (65, 70); **Goals:** Knight 3/6.
Sin bin: Fawcett (9) – holding down.
Rugby Leaguer & League Express Men of the Match: *Hawks:* Gareth Greenwood; *Cougars:* Barry Eaton.
Penalty count: 9-11; **Half-time:** 6-10;
Referee: Peter Brooke; **Attendance:** 400.

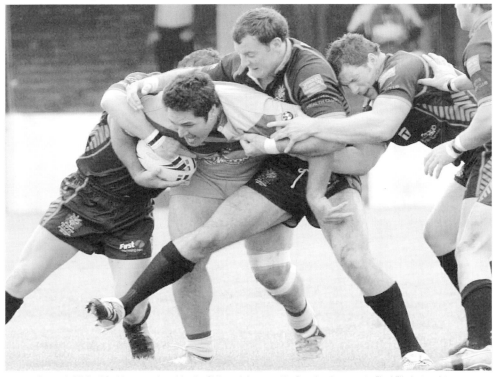

Barrow's Michael Smith outnumbered by the Oldham defence, as the Roughyeds sweep to Final Eliminator victory

PLAY-OFFS

ELIMINATION PLAY-OFFS

Sunday 16th September 2007

OLDHAM 36 SWINTON LIONS 6

OLDHAM: 1 Gareth Langley; 2 Byron Ford; 3 Gareth Morton; 4 Adam Hughes; 5 Lucas Onyango; 6 Neil Roden; 7 James Coyle; 8 Anthony Tonks; 9 Simeon Hoyle; 10 Richard Mervill; 11 Ian Sinfield; 12 Robert Roberts; 13 Geno Costin. Subs (all used): 14 Alex Wilkinson; 15 Ian Hodson; 16 Said Tamghart; 17 Matty Brooks.
Tries: Hughes (1), Ford (7), Onyango (12, 53), Costin (18), Roberts (28, 69); **Goals:** Morton 4/8.
LIONS: 1 Wayne English; 2 Andy Saywell; 3 Adam Bowman; 4 Dean Gorton; 5 Marlon Billy; 6 Martin Moana; 7 Jay Duffy; 8 Rob Line; 9 Craig Ashall; 10 Gareth Hayes; 11 Rob Draper; 12 Dave Newton; 13 Lee Marsh. Subs (all used): 14 Chris Hough; 15 Matt Bryers; 16 Bruce Johnson; 17 David Bates.
Try: Ashall (68); **Goals:** Marsh 1/1.
Rugby Leaguer & League Express Men of the Match:
Oldham: Robert Roberts; *Lions:* David Bates.
Penalty count: 12-5; **Half-time:** 26-0;
Referee: Craig Halloran; **Attendance:** 1,120.

WORKINGTON TOWN 42 YORK CITY KNIGHTS 4

TOWN: 1 Martyn Wilson; 2 Ryan Blair; 3 Neil Frazer; 4 Jason Mossop; 5 Stephen Dawes; 6 Carl Forber; 7 Martin Keavney; 8 Adam Sidlow; 9 Shaun Lunt; 10 Dean Vaughan; 11 Dexter Miller; 12 Franco Kmet; 13 Rob Lunt. Subs (all used): 14 Darren King; 15 Scott Gorman; 16 Matthew Tunstall; 17 Taani Lavulavu.
Tries: Miller (13, 45), Dawes (59, 70, 80), Wilson (73);
Goals: Forber 9/9.
Dismissal: S Lunt (28) - biting.
Sin bin: Lavulavu (51) - punching.
CITY KNIGHTS: 1 Lee Lingard; 2 Lee Mapals; 3 Dan Potter; 4 Tom Burton; 5 Alex Godfrey; 6 Jon Liddell; 7 Scott Rhodes; 8 Kyle Palmer; 9 Jamaine Wray; 10 Adam Sullivan; 11 Dave Buckley; 12 Neil Lowe; 13 Ryan Esders. Subs (all used): 14 Jimmy Elston; 15 Nathan Priestley; 16 Ryan McDonald; 17 Mark Spurr.
Goals: Esders 2/2.
Sin bin: McDonald (40) - punching.
Rugby Leaguer & League Express Men of the Match:
Town: Carl Forber; *City Knights:* Jamaine Wray.
Penalty count: 13-10; **Half-time:** 10-4;
Referee: Jamie Leahy; **Attendance:** 669.

QUALIFYING SEMI-FINAL

Sunday 23rd September 2007

FEATHERSTONE ROVERS 36 BARROW RAIDERS 20

ROVERS: 1 Loz Wildbore; 2 Danny Kirmond; 3 Jon Whittle; 4 Wayne McHugh; 5 Ade Adebisi; 6 Andy Kain; 7 Paul Handforth; 8 Gareth Handford; 9 Joe McLocklan; 10 Stuart Dickens; 11 Jamie Field; 12 Richard Blakeway; 13 Tom Haughey. Subs (all used): 14 Jamie Benn; 15 Ian Tonks; 16 James Houston; 17 Steve Dooler.
Tries: Kirmond (7, 45), Adebisi (9), Handford (18), McHugh (38), Field (75); **Goals:** Dickens 6/8.
RAIDERS: 1 Khamal Ganley; 2 James Finch; 3 Mike Basan; 4 Liam Harrison; 5 Nick Beach; 6 Pat Weisner; 7 Darren Holt; 8 Michael Smith; 9 Andy Ellis; 10 Paul Raftrey; 11 Martin Ostler; 12 Mike Whitehead; 13 Dave Armistead. Subs (all used): 14 Jamie Marshall; 15 Phil Atkinson; 16 Paul Wilcock; 17 Lee Dutton.
Tries: Harrison (27), Ellis (42), Dutton (50), Basan (71);
Goals: Holt 2/4.
Rugby Leaguer & League Express Men of the Match:
Rovers: Paul Handforth; *Raiders:* Pat Weisner.
Penalty count: 7-7; **Half-time:** 20-6;
Referee: Gareth Hewer; **Attendance:** 1,792.

ELIMINATION SEMI-FINAL

Sunday 23rd September 2007

OLDHAM 48 WORKINGTON TOWN 0

OLDHAM: 1 Gareth Langley; 2 Byron Ford; 3 Craig Littler; 4 Adam Hughes; 5 Lucas Onyango; 6 Neil Roden; 7 James Coyle; 8 Anthony Tonks; 9 Simeon Hoyle; 10 Richard Mervill; 11 Ian Sinfield; 12 Robert Roberts; 13 Geno Costin. Subs (all used): 14 Alex Wilkinson; 15 Ian Hodson; 16 Said Tamghart; 17 Matty Brooks.
Tries: Hughes (3, 58), Onyango (7), Hodson (28), Langley (35, 72, 80), Coyle (45), Brooks (48), Costin (76); **Goals:** Langley 1/5, Hughes 3/6.
TOWN: 1 Martyn Wilson; 2 Ryan Blair; 3 Neil Frazer; 4 Jason Mossop; 5 Stephen Dawes; 6 Carl Forber; 7 Martin Keavney; 8 Adam Sidlow; 9 Darren King; 10 Taani Lavulavu; 11 Dexter Miller; 12 Jamie Beaumont; 13 Rob Lunt. Subs (all used): 14 Scott Gorman; 15 Franco Kmet; 16 Matthew Tunstall; 17 Steve Ormesher.
Sin bin: Kmet (43) - obstruction.
Rugby Leaguer & League Express Men of the Match:
Oldham: James Coyle; *Town:* Dexter Miller.
Penalty count: 7-6; **Half-time:** 18-0;
Referee: Mike Dawber; **Attendance:** 1,128.

FINAL ELIMINATOR

Sunday 30th September 2007

BARROW RAIDERS 6 OLDHAM 28

RAIDERS: 1 Khamal Ganley; 2 James Finch; 3 Mike Basan; 4 Liam Harrison; 5 Nick Beach; 6 Pat Weisner; 7 Darren Holt; 8 Michael Smith; 9 Andy Ellis; 10 Brett McDermott; 11 Martin Ostler; 12 Mike Whitehead; 13 Dave Armistead. Subs (all used): 14 Phil Atkinson; 15 Paul Wilcock; 16 Paul Raftrey; 17 Lee Dutton.
Try: Basan (47); **Goals:** Holt 1/1.
OLDHAM: 1 Gareth Langley; 2 Byron Ford; 3 Craig Littler; 4 Adam Hughes; 5 Lucas Onyango; 6 Neil Roden; 7 James Coyle; 8 Anthony Tonks; 9 Simeon Hoyle; 10 Richard Mervill; 11 Ian Sinfield; 12 Robert Roberts; 13 Geno Costin. Subs (all used): 14 Alex Wilkinson; 15 Ian Hodson; 16 Said Tamghart; 17 Matty Brooks.
Tries: Hughes (25, 72, 75), Coyle (30);
Goals: Langley 6/6.
Rugby Leaguer & League Express Men of the Match:
Raiders: Andy Ellis; *Oldham:* Adam Hughes.
Penalty count: 9-13; **Half-time:** 0-16;
Referee: Richard Silverwood; **Attendance:** 2,771.

GRAND FINAL

Sunday 7th October 2007

FEATHERSTONE ROVERS 24 OLDHAM 6

ROVERS: 1 Loz Wildbore; 2 Danny Kirmond; 3 Jon Whittle; 4 Wayne McHugh; 5 Ade Adebisi; 6 Andy Kain; 7 Paul Handforth; 8 Gareth Handford; 9 Joe McLocklan; 10 Stuart Dickens; 11 Jamie Field; 12 Richard Blakeway; 13 Tom Haughey. Subs (all used): 14 Jamie Benn; 15 Ian Tonks; 16 James Houston; 17 Gavin Swinson.
Tries: McHugh (39, 49), Handforth (46);
Goals: Dickens 5/6; **Field goals:** Wildbore (66, 70).
Dismissal: Blakeway (64) – head butt on Roberts.
OLDHAM: 1 Gareth Langley; 2 Byron Ford; 3 Craig Littler; 4 Adam Hughes; 5 Lucas Onyango; 6 Neil Roden; 7 James Coyle; 8 Anthony Tonks; 9 Simeon Hoyle; 10 Richard Mervill; 11 Ian Sinfield; 12 Robert Roberts; 13 Geno Costin. Subs (all used): 14 Ian Hodson; 15 Alex Wilkinson; 16 Said Tamghart; 17 Matty Brooks.
Try: Hughes (31); **Goals:** Langley 1/2.
Rugby Leaguer & League Express Men of the Match:
Rovers: Paul Handforth; *Oldham:* Robert Roberts.
Penalty count: 9-5; **Half-time:** 10-6;
Referee: Gareth Hewer. *(at Headingley Carnegie, Leeds).*

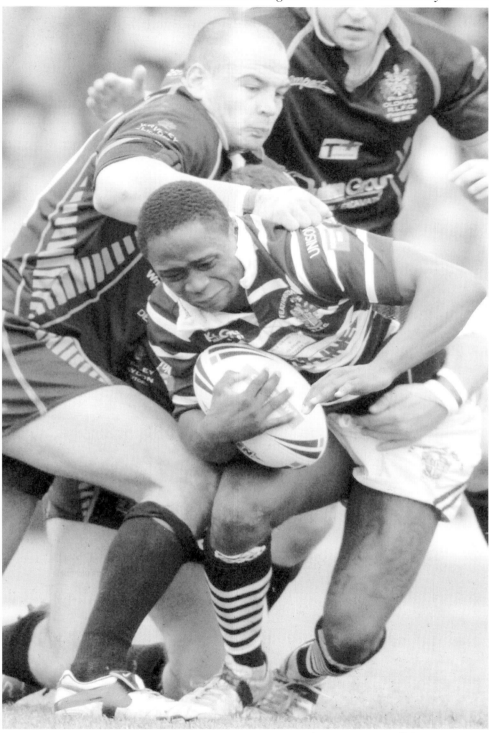

Featherstone's Ade Adebisi collared by Ian Sinfield during Rovers' Grand Final win against Oldham

NATIONAL LEAGUE CUP 2007
Round by Round

WEEK 1

Friday 9th February 2007

GROUP 5

BARROW RAIDERS 44 BLACKPOOL PANTHERS 4

RAIDERS: 1 Khamal Ganley; 2 Nick Beach; 3 Phil Atkinson; 4 Liam Harrison; 5 James Nixon; 6 Darren Holt; 7 Liam Finch; 8 Paul Raftrey; 9 Andy Ellis; 10 Brett McDermott; 11 Martin Ostler; 12 Dave Armistead; 13 Mike Whitehead. Subs (all used): 14 Lee Sanderson; 15 Paul Wilcock; 16 Adam Bibey; 17 Lee Dutton.
Tries: Beach (5, 30, 35), Nixon (10, 66), Sanderson (51), Ganley (71), Ellis (80); **Goals:** Holt 4/5, Sanderson 2/3.
PANTHERS: 1 Mark Leigh; 2 Chris Brand; 3 Chris Ramsdale; 4 Chris Maye; 5 Anton Garcia; 6 Safraz Patel; 7 Martin Gambles; 8 Ian Parry; 9 Phil Cantillon; 10 Lee Rowley; 11 Eddie Kilgannon; 12 Daniel Palmer; 13 Deon Duell. Subs (all used): 14 Ryan Millington; 15 Gareth Jones; 16 Danny Barton; 17 Luke Murfin.
Try: Parry (20); **Goals:** Brand 0/1.
Rugby Leaguer & League Express Men of the Match: *Raiders:* Nick Beach; *Panthers:* Martin Gambles.
Penalty count: 10-9; **Half-time:** 22-4;
Referee: Gareth Hewer; **Attendance:** 975.

GROUP 6

CELTIC CRUSADERS 6 WIDNES VIKINGS 56

CRUSADERS: 1 Tony Duggan; 2 Richard Johnston; 3 Mark Dalle Cort; 4 Anthony Blackwood; 5 Paul Ballard; 6 Luke Young; 7 Jace Van Dijk; 8 Josh Cale; 9 Neil Budworth; 10 Gareth Dean; 11 Neale Wyatt; 12 Darren Mapp; 13 Damien Quinn. Subs (all used): 14 Rob Toshack; 15 Dean Fitzgerald; 16 Jamie I'Anson; 17 Hywel Davies.
Try: Johnston (56); **Goals:** Quinn 1/1.
VIKINGS: 1 Scott Grix; 2 Damien Blanch; 3 Toa Kohe-Love; 4 Mick Nanyn; 5 Gavin Dodd; 6 Dennis Moran; 7 Andy Kain; 8 Mick Cassidy; 9 Mark Smith; 10 Andy Bracek; 11 Lee Doran; 12 Paul Noone; 13 Bob Beswick. Subs (all used): 14 Ian Webster; 15 Oliver Wilkes; 16 Jordan James; 17 Ben Harrison.
Tries: Nanyn (18), Grix (26, 61, 80), Beswick (31), Moran (44, 64), Smith (50), Kohe-Love (69), Blanch (76); **Goals:** Nanyn 8/9, Moran 0/1.
Rugby Leaguer & League Express Men of the Match: *Crusaders:* Neil Budworth; *Vikings:* Bob Beswick.
Penalty count: 5-10; **Half-time:** 0-18;
Referee: Ian Smith; **Attendance:** 452.

Sunday 11th February 2007

GROUP 1

DONCASTER LAKERS 6 CASTLEFORD TIGERS 30

LAKERS: 1 Loz Wildbore; 2 Rikki Sheriffe; 3 Dean Gorton; 4 Chris Buttery; 5 Danny Mills; 6 Graham Holroyd; 7 Brett Turner; 8 James Garmston; 9 Peter Green; 10 Alex Benson; 11 Joe Mbu; 12 Neil Lowe; 13 Joe McLocklan. Subs (all used): 14 Alex Rowe; 15 Craig Lawton; 16 Adam Scott; 17 Shaun Leaf.
Try: Wildbore (67); **Goals:** Holroyd 1/1.
Sin bin: Gorton (54) – punching.
TIGERS: 1 Tom Saxton; 2 Michael Wainwright; 3 Stuart Donlan; 4 Ryan McGoldrick; 5 Richard Owen; 6 Peter Lupton; 7 Danny Brough; 8 Liam Higgins; 9 Andrew Henderson; 10 Tere Glassie; 11 Awen Guttenbeil; 12 Dwayne Barker; 13 Chris Charles. Subs (all used): 14 Craig Huby; 15 Mark Leafa; 16 Ryan Clayton; 17 Joe Westerman.
Tries: Saxton (6), Henderson (13, 63), Donlan (19), Owen (29), Huby (52); **Goals:** Brough 3/6.
Rugby Leaguer & League Express Men of the Match: *Lakers:* Loz Wildbore; *Tigers:* Andrew Henderson.
Penalty count: 15-11; **Half-time:** 0-20;
Referee: Steve Ganson; **Attendance:** 4,180.

FEATHERSTONE ROVERS 54 SHEFFIELD EAGLES 22

ROVERS: 1 Wayne McHugh; 2 Danny Kirmond; 3 Jon Whittle; 4 Dale Cardoza; 5 Craig Moss; 6 Chris Ross; 7 Paul Handforth; 8 Gareth Handford; 9 Paul Hughes; 10 Stuart Dickens; 11 Tom Haughey; 12 Ian Tonks; 13 Richard Blakeway. Subs (all used): 14 Craig Bower; 15 Steve Dooler; 16 James Houston; 17 James Ward.
Tries: P Hughes (4, 9), Haughey (6), Kirmond (15, 74), Ross (32), Cardoza (48), McHugh (50), Whittle (53), Handforth (56); **Goals:** Dickens 6/10, Handforth 1/1.
EAGLES: 1 John Crawford; 2 Greg Hurst; 3 Caldon Bravo; 4 Richard Newlove; 5 Zac Hill; 6 Gavin Brown; 7 Dominic Brambani; 8 Tom Buckenham; 9 Paul Pickering; 10 Jon Aston; 11 Ged Corcoran; 12 Tommy Trayler; 13 Adam Hayes. Subs (all used): 14 Jon Presley; 15 Neil Law; 16 Grant Edwards; 17 Ryan Hepworth.
Tries: Hepworth (24), Presley (35), Crawford (61), Bravo (66); **Goals:** Brambani 3/3, G Brown 0/1.
Sin bin: Hepworth (27) - holding down;
Crawford (39) - holding down.
Rugby Leaguer & League Express Men of the Match: *Rovers:* Paul Handforth; *Eagles:* Ged Corcoran.
Penalty count: 10-7; **Half-time:** 28-10;
Referee: Jamie Leahy; **Attendance:** 1,209.

GROUP 2

GATESHEAD THUNDER 12 YORK CITY KNIGHTS 58

THUNDER: 1 Graham Stephenson; 2 Robin Peers; 3 Odell Harris; 4 Pat Williamson; 5 Matt Walton; 6 Neil Thorman; 7 Kevin Till; 8 Shane Wooden; 9 Steve Rutherford; 10 Richie Metcalfe; 11 Tony Doherty; 12 Steven Bradley; 13 Nick Hyde. Subs (all used): 14 Ryan Clarke; 15 Jonny Scott; 16 Dylan Nash; 17 Matt Barron.
Tries: Till (6), Rutherford (32); **Goals:** Thorman 2/2.
Sin bin: Metcalfe (63) - holding down.
CITY KNIGHTS: 1 George Rayner; 2 Chris Spurr; 3 Dan Potter; 4 Ian Brown; 5 Lee Mapals; 6 Scott Rhodes; 7 Anthony Thackeray; 8 Tabua Cakacaka; 9 Jamaine Wray; 10 Adam Sullivan; 11 Nathan Priestley; 12 Dave Buckley; 13 Ryan Esders. Subs (all used): 14 Jon Liddell; 15 Toby Williams; 16 Ryan McDonald; 17 Joe Helme.
Tries: Priestley (21), Brown (34), Rhodes (46), Rayner (48), Helme (60, 62), Esders (66), Cakacaka (70), Thackeray (73), Mapals (78); **Goals:** Wray 9/10.
Rugby Leaguer & League Express Men of the Match: *Thunder:* Kevin Till; *City Knights:* Jamaine Wray.
Penalty count: 9-8; **Half-time:** 12-12;
Referee: Andrew Grundy; **Attendance:** 503.

KEIGHLEY COUGARS 18 HALIFAX 44

COUGARS: 1 Gavin Duffy; 2 Sam Gardner; 3 Matt Foster; 4 Mick Fogerty; 5 Ryan Smith; 6 Craig Fawcett; 7 Barry Eaton; 8 Simon Bissell; 9 James Feather; 10 Gareth English; 11 Greg Nicholson; 12 Richard Knight; 13 Chris Redfearn. Subs (all used): 14 Michael Hastings; 15 Wayne Sutcliffe; 16 Brendan Rawlins; 17 Tom Palmer.
Tries: Fogerty (12), Foster (42), Redfearn (54);
Goals: Eaton 3/4.
Sin bin: Redfearn (64) – professional foul.
HALIFAX: 1 Shad Royston; 2 Damian Gibson; 3 James Haley; 4 Richard Varkulis; 5 Lee Greenwood; 6 Tim Hartley; 7 Ian Watson; 8 Paul Southern; 9 Mick Govin; 10 David Wrench; 11 David Larder; 12 Mark Roberts; 13 Damian Ball. Subs (all used): 14 Danny Jones; 15 Frank Watene; 16 Aaron Trinder; 17 Scott Law.
Tries: Roberts (7), Watene (33), Gibson (37), Royston (48), Govin (59, 71), Ball (77);
Goals: Hartley 2/2, Govin 1/1, Jones 5/5.
Sin bin: Watson (41) – professional foul.
Rugby Leaguer & League Express Men of the Match: *Cougars:* Mick Fogerty; *Halifax:* Mick Govin.
Penalty count: 15-9; **Half-time:** 8-18;
Referee: Dave Merrick; **Attendance:** 1,352.

GROUP 3

BATLEY BULLDOGS 6 DEWSBURY RAMS 49

BULLDOGS: 1 Craig Lingard; 2 Alex Clemie; 3 Chris Langley; 4 Oliver Marns; 5 Jamie Stokes; 6 Lee Paterson; 7 Jay Duffy; 8 David Rourke; 9 Kris Lythe; 10 David Best; 11 Martin McLoughlin; 12 Tim Spears; 13 John Gallagher. Subs (all used): 14 Ashley Lindsay; 15 Jon Simpson; 16 Luke Menzies; 17 Lee Kerr.
Try: Clemie (30); **Goals:** Paterson 1/1.
RAMS: 1 Ian Preece; 2 Lee Close; 3 Andrew Bostock; 4 Danny Maun; 5 Kane Epati; 6 Francis Maloney; 7 Dean Lawford; 8 Andy Hobson; 9 Luke Haigh; 10 David Bates; 11 Kevin Crouthers; 12 Alex Bretherton; 13 Josh Weeden. Subs (all used): 14 Liam Finn; 15 Rob Kelly; 16 Martin Robinson; 17 Liam Crawley.
Tries: Haigh (22), Preece (34, 51), Epati (36), Finn (49), Crouthers (56), Bostock (58), Close (67);
Goals: F Maloney 5/6, Finn 3/3; **Field goal:** Lawford (47).
Sin bin: Haigh (9) - holding down.
Rugby Leaguer & League Express Men of the Match: *Bulldogs:* David Rourke; *Rams:* Dean Lawford.
Penalty count: 14-12; **Half-time:** 6-20;
Referee: Gareth Hewer; **Attendance:** 1,169.

GROUP 4

OLDHAM 8 ROCHDALE HORNETS 24

OLDHAM: 1 Paul O'Connor; 2 Gareth Langley; 3 Craig Littler; 4 Drew Houston; 5 Alex Wilkinson; 6 Kris Smith; 7 Neil Roden; 8 Jason Boults; 9 Simeon Hoyle; 10 Richard Mervill; 11 Lee Wingfield; 12 Said Tamghart; 13 Ian Sinfield. Subs (all used): 14 Geno Costin; 15 Wes Rogers; 16 Andy Crabtree; 17 Mike Stout.
Tries: Wilkinson (32), Smith (40); **Goals:** Smith 0/2.
HORNETS: 1 Chris Giles; 2 Eric Andrews; 3 Lee Patterson; 4 Kevin King; 5 Bolu Fagborun; 6 Simon Svabic; 7 Gary Hulse; 8 Simon Baldwin; 9 Dave McConnell; 10 Byron Smith; 11 Andy Gorski; 12 Mark Blanchard; 13 Tommy Goulden. Subs (all used): 14 Phil Hasty; 15 Craig Robinson; 16 Wayne Corcoran; 17 Rob Ball.
Tries: Goulden (7), Blanchard (19), Andrews (50), McConnell (76);
Goals: King 3/4; **Field goals:** Svabic (22, 75).
Rugby Leaguer & League Express Men of the Match: *Oldham:* Said Tamghart; *Hornets:* Tommy Goulden.
Penalty count: 7-5; **Half-time:** 8-11;
Referee: Phil Bentham; **Attendance:** 1,145.

GROUP 4 v GROUP 3

SWINTON LIONS 38 HUNSLET HAWKS 20

LIONS: 1 Wayne English; 2 Andy Saywell; 3 Darren Woods; 4 Sean Conway; 5 Marlon Billy; 6 Martin Moana; 7 Liam McGovern; 8 Bruce Johnson; 9 Phil Wood; 10 Gareth Hayes; 11 Dave Newton; 12 Chris Morley; 13 Craig Ashall. Subs (all used): 14 Chris Hough; 15 John Walker; 16 Mike Smith; 17 Rob Line.
Tries: Newton (4, 73), Morley (17), Line (31), English (40), Saywell (70), Walker (76);
Goals: McGovern 5/6, Hough 0/2.
HAWKS: 1 Matt Bramald; 2 Dale Harris; 3 David Foster; 4 Eddie Mack; 5 Steve Morton; 6 Mark Moxon; 7 Matt Firth; 8 Danny Ekis; 9 Darren Robinson; 10 Danny Murgatroyd; 11 Wayne Freeman; 12 Will Cartledge; 13 Gareth Greenwood. Subs (all used): 14 Tony Williams; 15 Matt Carbutt; 16 Danny Cook; 17 Scott Houston.
Tries: Murgatroyd (23), Mack (36), Bramald (65), Foster (80); **Goals:** D Robinson 1/3, Williams 1/1.
Sin bin: Bramald (31) - dissent.
Rugby Leaguer & League Express Men of the Match: *Lions:* Martin Moana; *Hawks:* Eddie Mack.
Penalty count: 12-10; **Half-time:** 26-10;
Referee: Peter Brooke; **Attendance:** 432.

GROUP 5

WORKINGTON TOWN 18 WHITEHAVEN 44

TOWN: 1 Martyn Wilson; 2 Stephen Dawes; 3 Rob Lunt; 4 Neil Frazer; 5 David Whitworth; 6 Carl Forber; 7 Liam Campbell; 8 Dean Vaughan; 9 Shaun Lunt; 10 Jamie Beaumont; 11 Darren King; 12 Dexter Miller; 13 Garry Purdham. Subs (all used): 14 Steve Kirkbride; 15 Allan McGuiness; 16 Dean Burgess; 17 Taani Lavulavu.
Tries: Dawes (53), R Lunt (70), Whitworth (79);
Goals: Forber 1/2, Kirkbride 2/2.
On report:
McGuiness (75) – alleged leading with the forearm.
WHITEHAVEN: 1 Gary Broadbent; 2 Craig Calvert; 3 Scott McAvoy; 4 Rob Jackson; 5 Derry Eilbeck; 6 Carl Rudd; 7 John Duffy; 8 Steve Trindall; 9 Carl Sice; 10 Scott Teare; 11 Spencer Miller; 12 Ricky Wright; 13 Aaron Lester. Subs (all used): 14 Marc Jackson; 15 Graeme Mattinson; 16 Leroy Joe; 17 Howard Hill.
Tries: Miller (19), S McAvoy (38), Calvert (42), Joe (45), Duffy (61), Sice (63, 76); **Goals:** Rudd 8/10.
Sin bin: Lester (30) – interference.
Rugby Leaguer & League Express Men of the Match: *Town:* Rob Lunt; *Whitehaven:* John Duffy.
Penalty count: 13-15; **Half-time:** 2-18;
Referee: Robert Hicks; **Attendance:** 2,368.

GROUP 6

LONDON SKOLARS 8 LEIGH CENTURIONS 52

SKOLARS: 1 Ashley Tozer; 2 Johnny Williams; 3 Chris Shears; 4 Dene Miller; 5 Austen Aggrey; 6 Jermaine Coleman; 7 Paul Thorman; 8 Richard Louw; 9 Frank Reid; 10 Powhiri Bidois; 11 Kurt Pittman; 12 Mike Castle; 13 Lydan Maitua. Subs (all used): 14 Corey Simms; 15 Gareth Honor; 16 Alan Barker; 17 Dave Ellison.
Tries: Maitua (72, 78); **Goals:** Thorman 0/2.
CENTURIONS: 1 Miles Greenwood; 2 David Alstead; 3 Damien Couturier; 4 Anthony Stewart; 5 Leroy Rivett; 6 John Braddish; 7 Aaron Heremaia; 8 Chris Hill; 9 John Clough; 10 John Hill; 11 James Taylor; 12 Mailangi Styles; 13 Tommy Grundy. Subs (all used): 14 Sam Butterworth; 15 Tim Jonkers; 16 Robert Roberts; 17 John Cookson.
Tries: Alstead (8, 63), Couturier (12), Greenwood (31, 40, 74), Stewart (44), J Hill (53), Heremaia (61);
Goals: Couturier 7/8, Heremaia 1/1.
Rugby Leaguer & League Express Men of the Match: *Skolars:* Lydan Maitua; *Centurions:* Miles Greenwood.
Penalty count: 12-11; **Half-time:** 0-24;
Referee: James Child; **Attendance:** 379.

GROUP 7

HEMEL STAGS 6 BRAMLEY BUFFALOES 42

WARRINGTON WIZARDS 42 DEWSBURY CELTIC 12

WEEK 2

Friday 16th February 2007

GROUP 1

SHEFFIELD EAGLES 18 DONCASTER LAKERS 20

EAGLES: 1 Johnny Woodcock; 2 Greg Hurst; 3 Neil Law; 4 Damien Reid; 5 Grant Farrow; 6 Gavin Brown; 7 Dominic Brambani; 8 Jack Howieson; 9 Craig Cook; 10 Mitchell Stringer; 11 Ged Corcoran; 12 Craig Brown; 13 Adam Hayes. Subs (all used): 14 Jon Presley; 15 Jon Aston; 16 Richard Newlove; 17 Tom Buckenham.
Tries: Farrow (30), Law (57), Presley (74);
Goals: Brambani 3/3.
LAKERS: 1 Loz Wildbore; 2 Rikki Sheriffe; 3 Chris Buttery; 4 Dean Gorton; 5 Danny Mills; 6 Graham Holroyd; 7 Joe McLocklan; 8 Alex Benson; 9 Peter Green; 10 Craig Lawton; 11 Joe Mbu; 12 Neil Lowe; 13 Shaun Leaf. Subs (all used): 14 Alex Rowe; 15 Adam Scott; 16 Adam Robinson; 17 Terry Lynn.
Tries: Leaf (26), Wildbore (67), P Green (71);
Goals: Holroyd 4/4.
Rugby Leaguer & League Express Men of the Match: *Eagles:* Dominic Brambani; *Lakers:* Alex Rowe.
Penalty count: 10-14; **Half-time:** 6-8;
Referee: Robert Hicks; **Attendance:** 1,043.

Saturday 17th February 2007

GROUP 6

CELTIC CRUSADERS 44 LONDON SKOLARS 28

CRUSADERS: 1 Tony Duggan; 2 Grant Epton; 3 Rob Toshack; 4 Anthony Blackwood; 5 Craig Richards; 6 Luke Young; 7 Jace Van Dijk; 8 Josh Cale; 9 Neil Budworth; 10 Jamie I'Anson; 11 Neale Wyatt; 12 Mark Dalle Cort; 13 Damien Quinn. Subs (all used): 14 Richard Johnston; 15 Dean Fitzgerald; 16 Hywel Davies; 17 Phil Cushion.
Tries: Blackwood (4, 16), Quinn (24), Duggan (43, 52,

72), Budworth (63), Van Dijk (74), Johnston (79);
Goals: Quinn 4/9.
SKOLARS: 1 Pete Hodgkinson; 2 Corey Simms; 3 Chris Shears; 4 Ashley Tozer; 5 Johnny Williams; 6 Kurt Pittman; 7 Paul Thorman; 8 Martyn Benson; 9 Gareth Honor; 10 Dave Ellison; 11 Mike Castle; 12 Lydan Maitua; 13 Jermaine Coleman. Subs: 14 Frank Reid; 15 Austen Aggrey; 16 Alan Barker; 17 Warren Heilig (not used).
Tries: Tozer (21, 58, 65), Aggrey (32), Williams (40);
Goals: Thorman 4/6.
Rugby Leaguer & League Express Men of the Match: *Crusaders:* Tony Duggan; *Skolars:* Ashley Tozer.
Penalty count: 5-9; **Half-time:** 16-18;
Referee: Chris Dean; **Attendance:** 301.

GROUP 7

WARRINGTON WIZARDS 52 HEMEL STAGS 12

Sunday 18th February 2007

GROUP 1

CASTLEFORD TIGERS 48 FEATHERSTONE ROVERS 10

TIGERS: 1 Tom Saxton; 2 Michael Wainwright; 3 Richard Owen; 4 Kirk Dixon; 5 Stuart Donlan; 6 Ryan McGoldrick; 7 Danny Brough; 8 Liam Higgins; 9 Andrew Henderson; 10 Craig Huby; 11 Awen Guttenbeil; 12 Mark Leafa; 13 Chris Charles. Subs (all used): 14 Ryan Clayton; 15 Dwayne Barker; 16 Ryan Boyle; 17 Joe Westerman.
Tries: Saxton (9), Donlan (32, 66, 78), Dixon (45), Wainwright (47, 69), Charles (52, 74);
Goals: Brough 5/8, Huby 1/1.
ROVERS: 1 Jamie Benn; 2 Danny Kirmond; 3 Wayne McHugh; 4 Jon Whittle; 5 Craig Moss; 6 Chris Ross; 7 Paul Handforth; 8 Gareth Handford; 9 Paul Hughes; 10 Stuart Dickens; 11 Tom Haughey; 12 Steve Dooler; 13 Richard Blakeway. Subs (all used): 14 Craig Bower; 15 James Ward; 16 James Houston; 17 Ian Tonks.
Try: Ross (6); **Goals:** Dickens 3/3.
Rugby Leaguer & League Express Men of the Match: *Tigers:* Danny Brough; *Rovers:* Chris Ross.
Penalty count: 12-14; **Half-time:** 10-8;
Referee: Karl Kirkpatrick; **Attendance:** 6,871.

GROUP 2

HALIFAX 34 YORK CITY KNIGHTS 14

HALIFAX: 1 Shad Royston; 2 Damian Gibson; 3 Mark Roberts; 4 Richard Varkulis; 5 Lee Greenwood; 6 Danny Jones; 7 Ian Watson; 8 Paul Southern; 9 Mick Govin; 10 Aaron Trinder; 11 David Larder; 12 Scott Law; 13 Damian Ball. Subs (all used): 14 David Wrench; 15 Frank Watene; 16 Damian Munro; 17 Danny Heaton.
Tries: Royston (34, 42), Roberts (37), Trinder (46), Greenwood (49, 59), Varkulis (77);
Goals: Jones 2/5, Govin 1/2.
CITY KNIGHTS: 1 George Rayner; 2 Chris Spurr; 3 Nathan Priestley; 4 Ian Brown; 5 Lee Mapals; 6 Scott Rhodes; 7 Anthony Thackeray; 8 Tabua Cakacaka; 9 Jamaine Wray; 10 Adam Sullivan; 11 John Smith; 12 Dave Buckley; 13 Ryan Esders. Subs (all used): 14 Jon Liddell; 15 Toby Williams; 16 Ryan McDonald; 17 Joe Helme.
Tries: Rayner (6), Mapals (20), Buckley (79);
Goals: Wray 1/3.
Rugby Leaguer & League Express Men of the Match: *Halifax:* Danny Heaton; *City Knights:* George Rayner.
Penalty count: 9-11; **Half-time:** 10-10;
Referee: Gareth Hewer; **Attendance:** 2,113.

KEIGHLEY COUGARS 50 GATESHEAD THUNDER 12

COUGARS: 1 Gavin Duffy; 2 Sam Gardner; 3 Matt Foster; 4 Mick Fogerty; 5 Ryan Smith; 6 Craig Fawcett; 7 Barry Eaton; 8 Simon Bissell; 9 James Feather; 10 Gareth English; 11 Greg Nicholson; 12 Richard Knight; 13 Chris Redfearn. Subs (all used): 14 Michael Hastings; 15 Wayne Sutcliffe; 16 Tom Palmer; 17 Luke Sutton.
Tries: Fogerty (5, 30, 61), Fawcett (10, 69), R Smith (12), Redfearn (35), Foster (48), Nicholson (58);
Goals: Eaton 7/9.
THUNDER: 1 Graham Stephenson; 2 Robin Peers; 3 Odell Harris; 4 Pat Williamson; 5 Matt Walton; 6 Jono Rolfe; 7 Kevin Till; 8 Shane Wooden; 9 Tim Martin; 10 Richie Metcalfe; 11 Steve Rutherford; 12 Steven Bradley; 13 Nick Hyde. Subs (all used): 14 Neil Thorman; 15 Dylan Nash; 16 Matt Barron; 17 Damian Martinez.
Tries: Rolfe (3), Nash (78); **Goals:** Rolfe 2/2.
Rugby Leaguer & League Express Men of the Match: *Cougars:* Richard Knight; *Thunder:* Kevin Till.
Penalty count: 12-9; **Half-time:** 28-6;
Referee: James Child; **Attendance:** 628.

GROUP 3

HUNSLET HAWKS 16 DEWSBURY RAMS 8

HAWKS: 1 Matt Bramald; 2 Andy Robinson; 3 David Foster; 4 Eddie Mack; 5 Steve Morton; 6 Mark Moxon; 7 Matt Firth; 8 Danny Ekis; 9 Gareth Greenwood; 10 Danny Murgatroyd; 11 Wayne Freeman; 12 Will Cartledge; 13 Darren Robinson. Subs (all used): 14 Jonny Wainhouse; 15 Ben Walkin; 16 Danny Cook; 17 Matt Carbutt.
Tries: Foster (23), Cook (74);
Goals: D Robinson 1/2, Bramald 3/3.
Sin bin: Firth (16) - interference.
RAMS: 1 Ian Preece; 2 Danny Ratcliffe; 3 Andrew Bostock; 4 Kane Epati; 5 Danny Maun; 6 Francis Maloney; 7 Dean Lawford; 8 Andy Hobson; 9 Luke Haigh; 10 Dominic Maloney; 11 Kevin Crouthers; 12 Alex Bretherton; 13 Josh Weeden. Subs (all used): 14 Liam Finn; 15 Rob Kelly; 16 Martin Robinson; 17 David Bates.
Tries: Crouthers (10), Ratcliffe (17); **Goals:** F Maloney 0/2.
Sin bin: Preece (22) - holding down;
D Maloney (76) - high tackle; F Maloney (78) - dissent.
Rugby Leaguer & League Express Men of the Match: *Hawks:* Danny Ekis; *Rams:* Kevin Crouthers.
Penalty count: 19-13; **Half-time:** 6-8;
Referee: Robert Hicks; **Attendance:** 756.

GROUP 4

OLDHAM 18 SWINTON LIONS 28

OLDHAM: 1 Paul O'Connor; 2 Andy Gorey; 3 Craig Littler; 4 Mike Stout; 5 Stuart Oldham; 6 Neil Roden; 7 Paul Ashton; 8 Geno Costin; 9 Simeon Hoyle; 10 Said Tamghart; 11 Chris Baines; 12 Drew Houston; 13 Ian Sinfield. Subs (all used): 14 Wes Rogers; 15 Kris Smith; 16 Andy Crabtree; 17 Gareth Langley.
Tries: Roden (8), Baines (14), Costin (49);
Goals: Ashton 3/3.
Dismissal: Tamghart (76) - high tackle.
Sin bin: Rogers (67) - interference.
LIONS: 1 Wayne English; 2 Andy Saywell; 3 Darren Woods; 4 Sean Conway; 5 Desi Williams; 6 Martin Moana; 7 Liam McGovern; 8 Bruce Johnson; 9 Phil Wood; 10 Gareth Hayes; 11 Dave Newton; 12 Chris Morley; 13 Paul Alcock. Subs (all used): 14 Chris Hough; 15 Mike Smith; 16 Adam Sharples; 17 Rob Line.
Tries: D Woods (4, 22, 55, 63), P Wood (60), Saywell (69); **Goals:** McGovern 1/2, Hough 1/4.
Rugby Leaguer & League Express Men of the Match: *Oldham:* Paul Ashton; *Lions:* Darren Woods.
Penalty count: 13-13; **Half-time:** 12-10;
Referee: Dave Merrick; **Attendance:** 1,017.

GROUP 4 v GROUP 3

ROCHDALE HORNETS 29 BATLEY BULLDOGS 30

HORNETS: 1 Chris Giles; 2 Eric Andrews; 3 Iain Marsh; 4 Kevin King; 5 Bolu Fagborun; 6 Simon Svabic; 7 Gary Hulse; 8 Simon Baldwin; 9 Dave McConnell; 10 Byron Smith; 11 Andy Gorski; 12 Mark Blanchard; 13 Tommy Goulden. Subs (all used): 14 Phil Hasty; 15 John Gledhill; 16 Matt Whitaker; 17 Rob Ball.
Tries: Blanchard (4), Andrews (12), Fagborun (28, 47, 73); **Goals:** King 4/6; **Field goal:** Svabic (58).
Dismissal: Ball (50) - punching.
Sin bin: Svabic (75) - dissent.
BULLDOGS: 1 Craig Lingard; 2 Alex Clemie; 3 Oliver Marns; 4 Chris Langley; 5 Jamie Stokes; 6 Ian Gordon; 7 John Gallagher; 8 David Rourke; 9 Kris Lythe; 10 David Best; 11 Sean Richardson; 12 Tim Spears; 13 Lee Paterson. Subs (all used): 14 Luke Stenchion; 15 Jack Watson; 16 Luke Menzies; 17 Lee Kerr.
Tries: Langley (38), Stokes (51), Clemie (65, 69), Menzies (76), J Gallagher (79); **Goals:** Gordon 3/6.
Rugby Leaguer & League Express Men of the Match: *Hornets:* Gary Hulse; *Bulldogs:* Kris Lythe.
Penalty count: 7-7; **Half-time:** 16-4;
Referee: Jamie Leahy; **Attendance:** 971.

GROUP 5

BLACKPOOL PANTHERS 18 WHITEHAVEN 32

PANTHERS: 1 Chris Brand; 2 Anton Garcia; 3 Chris Maye; 4 Steven Brown; 5 Mark Leigh; 6 Safraz Patel; 7 Martin Gambles; 8 Ian Parry; 9 Phil Cantillon; 10 Daniel Palmer; 11 Eddie Kilgannon; 12 Gareth Jones; 13 Deon Duell. Subs (all used): 14 Chris Ramsdale; 15 Jon Chamberlain; 16 Lee Rowley; 17 Richard Rafferty.
Tries: Parry (14), Maye (18), Patel (42); **Goals:** Brand 3/4.
WHITEHAVEN: 1 Carl Sice; 2 Craig Calvert; 3 Gary Broadbent; 4 Rob Jackson; 5 Derry Eilbeck; 6 Carl Rudd; 7 John Duffy; 8 Steve Trindall; 9 Aaron Smith; 10 Richard Fletcher; 11 Spencer Miller; 12 Scott McAvoy; 13 Aaron Lester. Subs (all used): 14 Graeme Mattinson; 15 Scott Teare; 16 Howard Hill; 17 Ricky Wright.
Tries: R Jackson (21), Broadbent (31, 35, 52), Calvert (62), Teare (76); **Goals:** Rudd 4/6.
Rugby Leaguer & League Express Men of the Match: *Panthers:* Chris Brand; *Whitehaven:* Gary Broadbent.
Penalty count: 7-6; **Half-time:** 14-14;
Referee: Andrew Grundy; **Attendance:** 449.

WORKINGTON TOWN 32 BARROW RAIDERS 24

TOWN: 1 Andrew Beattie; 2 Stephen Dawes; 3 Neil Frazer; 4 David Whitworth; 5 Tom Armstrong; 6 Carl Forber; 7 Liam Campbell; 8 Dean Vaughan; 9 Shaun Lunt; 10 Taani Lavulavu; 11 Jamie Beaumont; 12 Jon Roper; 13 Craig Walsh. Subs (all used): 14 Dexter Miller; 15 Allan McGuiness; 16 Dean Burgess; 17 Matthew Tunstall.
Tries: Whitworth (12), Walsh (30), Dawes (42), Campbell (53), Burgess (57); **Goals:** Forber 6/8.
Sin bin: Campbell (38) – dissent, (63) – holding down.
On report: Brawl (74).
RAIDERS: 1 Khamal Ganley; 2 Nick Beach; 3 Phil Atkinson; 4 Liam Harrison; 5 James Nixon; 6 Liam Finch; 7 Darren Holt; 8 Adam Bibey; 9 Andy Ellis; 10 Brett McDermott; 11 Martin Ostler; 12 Dave Armistead; 13 Mike Whitehead. Subs (all used): 14 Lee Sanderson; 15 Paul Wilcock; 16 Paul Raftrey; 17 Lee Dutton.
Tries: Ellis (38), Wilcock (48), McDermott (68), Harrison (74); **Goals:** Sanderson 4/4.
Sin bin: Ellis (64) – swinging arm.
On report: Brawl (74).
Rugby Leaguer & League Express Men of the Match: *Town:* Carl Forber; *Raiders:* Andy Ellis.
Penalty count: 15-13; **Half-time:** 14-6;
Referee: Peter Brooke; **Attendance:** 927.

GROUP 6

WIDNES VIKINGS 34 LEIGH CENTURIONS 20

VIKINGS: 1 Scott Grix; 2 Damien Blanch; 3 Toa Kohe-Love; 4 Mick Nanyn; 5 Gavin Dodd; 6 Dennis Moran; 7 Andy Kain; 8 Mick Cassidy; 9 Mark Smith; 10 Andy Bracek; 11 Paul Noone; 12 Oliver Wilkes; 13 Bob Beswick. Subs (all used): 14 Ian Webster; 15 Lee Doran; 16 Jordan James; 17 Ben Harrison.
Tries: Dodd (18, 38), Kohe-Love (53), Kain (58), Smith (63), Bracek (76); **Goals:** Nanyn 5/6.
On report: Smith (32) - alleged punching.
CENTURIONS: 1 Miles Greenwood; 2 Adam Rudd; 3 Anthony Stewart; 4 David Alstead; 5 Leroy Rivett; 6 Martin Ainscough; 7 Aaron Heremaia; 8 Warren Stevens; 9 John Clough; 10 John Hill; 11 Mailangi Styles; 12 Tommy Grundy; 13 Tim Jonkers. Subs (all used): 14 Sam Butterworth; 15 Danny Speakman; 16 John Cookson; 17 Chris Hill.
Tries: Ainscough (5), Clough (9), Rivett (43), Rudd (70);
Goals: Heremaia 2/3, Ainscough 0/1.
On report: Grundy (45) - alleged high tackle on Noone.
Rugby Leaguer & League Express Men of the Match: *Vikings:* Andy Kain; *Centurions:* Martin Ainscough.
Penalty count: 13-9; **Half-time:** 10-12;
Referee: Steve Clark; **Attendance:** 4,133.

GROUP 7

BRAMLEY BUFFALOES 32 DEWSBURY CELTIC 12

WEEK 3

Sunday 25th February 2007

GROUP 1

FEATHERSTONE ROVERS 24 DONCASTER LAKERS 22

ROVERS: 1 Craig Bower; 2 Danny Kirmond; 3 Jon Whittle; 4 Dale Cardoza; 5 Craig Moss; 6 Chris Ross; 7 Paul Handforth; 8 Gareth Handford; 9 Paul Hughes; 10 Stuart Dickens; 11 Steve Dooler; 12 Ian Tonks; 13 Tom Haughey. Subs (all used): 14 Gavin Swinson; 15 Dale Wynne; 16 James Houston; 17 Wayne McHugh.
Tries: Whittle (12, 17), Bower (24), McHugh (49);
Goals: Dickens 4/6.
LAKERS: 1 Loz Wildbore; 2 Rikki Sheriffe; 3 Dean Gorton; 4 James Endersby; 5 Ade Adebisi; 6 Joe McLocklan; 7 Joel Penny; 8 James Garmston; 9 Terry Lynn; 10 Ryan Tandy; 11 Joe Mbu; 12 Neil Lowe; 13 Shaun Leaf. Subs (all used): 14 Alex Rowe; 15 Alex Benson; 16 Adam Scott; 17 Peter Green.
Tries: Lynn (6), Leaf (26), Gorton (34), Sheriffe (63);
Goals: Wildbore 3/4.
Rugby Leaguer & League Express Men of the Match: *Rovers:* Tom Haughey; *Lakers:* Joel Penny.
Penalty count: 14-10; **Half-time:** 16-16;
Referee: Peter Brooke; **Attendance:** 1,335.

CASTLEFORD TIGERS 38 SHEFFIELD EAGLES 12

TIGERS: 1 Tom Saxton; 2 Richard Owen; 3 Stuart Donlan; 4 Kirk Dixon; 5 Michael Wainwright; 6 Ryan McGoldrick; 7 Danny Brough; 10 Craig Huby; 9 Andrew Henderson; 15 Mark Leafa; 11 Ryan Clayton; 12 Dwayne Barker; 13 Joe Westerman. Subs (all used): 14 Chris Charles; 8 Liam Higgins; 16 Ryan Boyle; 17 Michael Knowles.
Tries: Saxton (5), Owen (10), Donlan (22), Henderson (48), Brough (51), McGoldrick (69), Boyle (74);
Goals: Brough 5/7.
EAGLES: 1 Johnny Woodcock; 2 Greg Hurst; 3 Damien Reid; 4 Richard Newlove; 5 Grant Farrow; 6 John Crawford; 7 Dominic Brambani; 8 Jack Howieson; 9 Craig Cook; 10 Tom Buckenham; 11 Jon Aston; 12 Ged Corcoran; 13 Grant Edwards. Subs (all used): 14 Jon Presley; 15 Caldon Bravo; 16 Neil Law; 17 Ryan Hepworth.
Tries: Hurst (65), Corcoran (79); **Goals:** Brambani 2/2.
Rugby Leaguer & League Express Men of the Match: *Tigers:* Danny Brough; *Eagles:* Ged Corcoran.
Penalty count: 12-9; **Half-time:** 16-0;
Referee: Jamie Leahy; **Attendance:** 5,108.

GROUP 2

GATESHEAD THUNDER 6 HALIFAX 22

THUNDER: 1 Neil Thorman; 2 Robin Peers; 3 Graham Stephenson; 4 Pat Williamson; 5 Danny Wilson; 6 Jono Rolfe; 7 Tim Martin; 8 Shane Wooden; 9 Ryan Clarke; 10 Steven Bradley; 11 Dylan Nash; 12 Nick Hyde; 13 Odell Harris. Subs (all used): 14 Richie Metcalfe; 15 Matt Barron; 16 Tony Doherty; 17 Jonny Scott.
Try: Nash (60); **Goals:** Rolfe 1/1.
Sin bin: Nash (79) - persistent fouling.
HALIFAX: 1 Shad Royston; 2 Damian Munro; 3 James Haley; 4 Richard Varkulis; 5 Lee Greenwood; 6 Phil Joseph; 7 Danny Jones; 8 Andy Shickell; 9 Sam Hoare; 10 David Wrench; 11 Scott Law; 12 Mark Roberts; 13 Damian Ball. Subs (all used): 14 Luke Simeunovich; 15 Aaron Trinder; 16 Matthew Bottom; 17 Danny Heaton.
Tries: Ball (36, 56), Hoare (68, 79); **Goals:** Haley 3/4.
Sin bin: Joseph (31) - persistent fouling.
Rugby Leaguer & League Express Men of the Match: *Thunder:* Jono Rolfe; *Halifax:* James Haley.
Penalty count: 14-7; **Half-time:** 0-6;
Referee: Chris Dean; **Attendance:** 403.

YORK CITY KNIGHTS 24 KEIGHLEY COUGARS 22

CITY KNIGHTS: 1 George Rayner; 2 Lee Lingard; 3 Chris Spurr; 4 Ian Brown; 5 Lee Mapals; 6 Scott Rhodes; 7

Doncaster duo Graham Holroyd and Neil Lowe halt Sheffield's Ged Corcoran

Anthony Thackeray; 8 Tabua Cakacaka; 9 Jamaine Wray; 10 Adam Sullivan; 11 John Smith; 12 Dave Buckley; 13 Ryan Esders. Subs (all used): 14 Jon Liddell; 15 Toby Williams; 16 Nathan Priestley; 17 Joe Helme.
Tries: Smith (2), Brown (13), Liddell (27), Thackeray (42), Buckley (63);
Goals: Wray 1/3, Rayner 0/1, Liddell 1/2.
COUGARS: 1 Gavin Duffy; 2 Sam Gardner; 3 Matt Foster; 4 Michael Hastings; 5 Ryan Smith; 6 Craig Fawcett; 7 Barry Eaton; 8 Simon Bissell; 9 James Feather; 10 Gareth English; 11 Greg Nicholson; 12 Richard Knight; 13 Chris Redfearn. Subs (all used): 14 Alex Brown; 15 Wayne Sutcliffe; 16 Tom Palmer; 17 Luke Sutton.
Tries: Palmer (36), Gardner (55, 58), Fawcett (77);
Goals: Eaton 3/6.
Sin bin: Duffy (40) – holding down.
Rugby Leaguer & League Express Men of the Match:
City Knights: Anthony Thackeray; *Cougars:* Barry Eaton.
Penalty count: 11-10; **Half-time:** 16-10;
Referee: Robert Hicks; **Attendance:** 1,182.

GROUP 3

BATLEY BULLDOGS 16 HUNSLET HAWKS 18

BULLDOGS: 1 Craig Lingard; 2 Alex Clemie; 3 Oliver Marns; 4 Chris Langley; 5 Jamie Stokes; 6 Ian Gordon; 7 John Gallagher; 8 David Rourke; 9 Kris Lythe; 10 David Best; 11 Sean Richardson; 12 Tim Spears; 13 Lee Paterson. Subs (all used): 14 Ashley Lindsay; 15 Luke Stenchion; 16 Luke Menzies; 17 Jack Watson.
Tries: Lindsay (38), Marns (57), Lythe (79);
Goals: Paterson 1/1, Gordon 1/2.
HAWKS: 1 Matt Bramald; 2 Andy Robinson; 3 David Foster; 4 Eddie Mack; 5 Steve Morton; 6 Mark Moxon; 7 Matt Firth; 8 Danny Ekis; 9 Gareth Greenwood; 10 Scott Houston; 11 Wayne Freeman; 12 Will Cartledge; 13 Darren Robinson. Subs (all used): 14 Nick Walker; 15 Danny Murgatroyd; 16 Ben Walkin; 17 Matt Carbutt.
Tries: D Robinson (21), Morton (63);
Goals: Dodd 3/3, Bramald 2/4.
Rugby Leaguer & League Express Men of the Match:
Bulldogs: Kris Lythe; *Hawks:* Danny Ekis.
Penalty count: 5-11; **Half-time:** 6-10;
Referee: Andrew Grundy; **Attendance:** 540.

GROUP 3 v GROUP 4

DEWSBURY RAMS 32 OLDHAM 22

RAMS: 1 Ian Preece; 2 Lee Close; 3 Andrew Bostock; 4 Danny Maun; 5 Kane Epati; 6 Francis Maloney; 7 Dean Lawford; 8 Keegan Hirst; 9 Luke Haigh; 10 Dominic Maloney; 11 Kevin Crouthers; 12 Alex Bretherton; 13 Josh Weeden. Subs (all used): 14 Liam Finn; 15 Rob Kelly; 16 Martin Robinson; 17 David Bates.
Tries: Bostock (14), Weeden (31), Epati (33, 67), Crouthers (46), Haigh (79);
Goals: F Maloney 3/6, Lawford 1/1.
Sin bin: Bostock (54) - fighting.
OLDHAM: 1 Paul O'Connor; 2 Gareth Langley; 3 Craig Littler; 4 Drew Houston; 5 Alex Wilkinson; 6 Neil Roden; 7 Paul Ashton; 8 Jason Boults; 9 Simeon Hoyle; 10 Geno Costin; 11 Lee Wingfield; 12 Ian Sinfield; 13 Chris Baines. Subs (all used): 14 Andy Gorey; 15 Andy Crabtree; 16 Mike Stout; 17 Said Tamghart.
Tries: Wilkinson (6), O'Connor (24), Wingfield (59), Tamghart (75); **Goals:** Ashton 3/4.
Sin bin: Langley (54) - fighting.

On report: Langley (54) – alleged head butt.
Rugby Leaguer & League Express Men of the Match:
Rams: Danny Maun; *Oldham:* Paul Ashton.
Penalty count: 11-12; **Half-time:** 14-10;
Referee: Andrew Smith; **Attendance:** 819.

GROUP 4

SWINTON LIONS 14 ROCHDALE HORNETS 40

LIONS: 1 Wayne English; 2 Desi Williams; 3 Mark Brocklehurst; 4 Dave Ashton; 5 Marlon Billy; 6 Martin Moana; 7 Chris Hough; 8 Bruce Johnson; 9 Phil Wood; 10 Gareth Hayes; 11 Dave Newton; 12 Chris Morley; 13 Craig Ashall. Subs (all used): 14 Craig Farrimond; 15 Danny Aboushakra; 16 Adam Sharples; 17 Matt Bryers.
Tries: Billy (57, 68), Brocklehurst (78); **Goals:** Ashall 1/3.
HORNETS: 1 Chris Giles; 2 Eric Andrews; 3 Lee Patterson; 4 Kevin King; 5 Bolu Fagborun; 6 Simon Svabic; 7 Phil Hasty; 8 Simon Baldwin; 9 Dave McConnell; 10 Byron Smith; 11 Andy Gotski; 12 Mark Blanchard; 13 Tommy Goulden. Subs (all used): 14 Wayne Corcoran; 15 Ryan Benjafield; 16 Paul Anderson; 17 Paul Norman.
Tries: Goulden (2, 19), McConnell (35), Patterson (39, 65), Hasty (45, 48); **Goals:** King 6/7.
Rugby Leaguer & League Express Men of the Match:
Lions: Marlon Billy; *Hornets:* Tommy Goulden.
Penalty count: 6-9; **Half-time:** 0-22;
Referee: Phil Bentham; **Attendance:** 572.

GROUP 5

BLACKPOOL PANTHERS 28 WORKINGTON TOWN 34

PANTHERS: 1 Chris Brand; 2 Anton Garcia; 3 Chris Maye; 4 Steven Brown; 5 Mark Leigh; 6 Safraz Patel; 7 Martin Gambles; 8 Lee Rowley; 9 Phil Cantillon; 10 Daniel Palmer; 11 Eddie Kilgannon; 12 Kris Ratcliffe; 13 Danny Barton. Subs (all used): 14 Deon Duell; 15 Chris Ramsdale; 16 David Jones; 17 Rob Lamb.
Tries: Cantillon (22, 39, 79), Patel (26), Leigh (54);
Goals: Forber 4/5.
TOWN: 1 Liam Bretherton; 2 Neil Frazer; 3 Andrew Beattie; 4 David Whitworth; 5 Stephen Dawes; 6 Carl Forber; 7 Liam Campbell; 8 Dean Vaughan; 9 Shaun Lunt; 10 Taani Lavulavu; 11 Jamie Beaumont; 12 Jon Roper; 13 Craig Walsh. Subs (all used): 14 Steve Kirkbride; 15 Darren King; 16 Dean Burgess; 17 Matthew Tunstall.
Tries: S Lunt (3, 31, 56, 61), Campbell (4), Forber (9);
Goals: Forber 5/6.
Rugby Leaguer & League Express Men of the Match:
Panthers: Phil Cantillon; *Town:* Shaun Lunt.
Penalty count: 13-9; **Half-time:** 18-24;
Referee: Charlie Neilson; **Attendance:** 335.

WHITEHAVEN 22 BARROW RAIDERS 22

WHITEHAVEN: 1 Gary Broadbent; 2 Craig Calvert; 3 Rob Jackson; 4 Scott McAvoy; 5 Derry Eilbeck; 6 Leroy Joe; 7 Carl Rudd; 8 Steve Trindall; 9 Aaron Smith; 10 Scott Teare; 11 Spencer Miller; 12 Richard Fletcher; 13 Aaron Lester. Subs (all used): 14 Marc Jackson; 15 Graeme Mattinson; 16 Ricky Wright; 17 Howard Hill.
Tries: S McAvoy (7), Lester (36), Calvert (58), Eilbeck (72); **Goals:** Rudd 3/5.
RAIDERS: 1 Khamal Ganley; 2 Nick Beach; 3 Phil Atkinson; 4 Liam Harrison; 5 James Nixon; 6 Liam Finch; 7 Lee Sanderson; 8 Paul Raftrey; 9 Andy Ellis; 10

Brett McDermott; 11 Martin Ostler; 12 Dave Armistead; 13 Mike Whitehead. Subs (all used): 14 Jamie Marshall; 15 James Finch; 16 Paul Wilcock; 17 Lee Dutton.
Tries: Atkinson (14), Marshall (39), L Finch (43), Nixon (64). **Goals:** Atkinson 2/4, Beach 1/1.
Sin bin: L Finch (56) - dissent.
Rugby Leaguer & League Express Men of the Match:
Whitehaven: Richard Fletcher; *Raiders:* Martin Ostler.
Penalty count: 13-9; **Half-time:** 12-10;
Referee: Dave Merrick; **Attendance:** 1,537.

GROUP 6

LEIGH CENTURIONS 22 CELTIC CRUSADERS 26

CENTURIONS: 1 Miles Greenwood; 2 Adam Rudd; 3 Anthony Stewart; 4 Danny Speakman; 5 Leroy Rivett; 6 Martin Ainscough; 7 Aaron Heremaia; 8 Warren Stevens; 9 John Clough; 10 Chris Hill; 11 Mailangi Styles; 12 Tommy Grundy; 13 Tim Jonkers. Subs (all used): 14 Sam Butterworth; 15 James Taylor; 16 Daryl Kay; 17 John Cookson.
Tries: Greenwood (11), Speakman (29), Stewart (37), Clough (80); **Goals:** Heremaia 3/4.
CRUSADERS: 1 Paul Ballard; 2 Grant Epton; 3 Anthony Blackwood; 4 Tony Duggan; 5 Richard Johnston; 6 Luke Young; 7 Jace Van Dijk; 8 Gareth Dean; 9 Neil Budworth; 10 Hywel Davies; 11 Dean Fitzgerald; 12 Mark Dalle Cort; 13 Damien Quinn. Subs (all used): 14 Andy Boothroyd; 15 Jamie I'Anson; 16 Josh Cale; 17 Phil Cushion.
Tries: Blackwood (26), Cushion (46), Duggan (51, 73), Johnston (66); **Goals:** Quinn 3/5.
Rugby Leaguer & League Express Men of the Match:
Centurions: Danny Speakman; *Crusaders:* Jace Van Dijk.
Penalty count: 7-9; **Half-time:** 18-4;
Referee: Karl Kirkpatrick; **Attendance:** 1,637.

WIDNES VIKINGS 60 LONDON SKOLARS 10

VIKINGS: 1 Gavin Dodd; 2 Andy Kirk; 3 Toa Kohe-Love; 4 Mick Nanyn; 5 Dean Gaskell; 6 Scott Grix; 7 Andy Kain; 8 Jordan James; 9 Mark Smith; 10 Ben Harrison; 11 Lee Doran; 12 Oliver Wilkes; 13 Bob Beswick. Subs (all used): 14 Adam Bowman; 15 Rob Draper; 16 Paul Noone; 17 Gareth Price.
Tries: Kohe-Love (8, 14, 30, 40), Grix (21, 61), Nanyn (26), Draper (35), Smith (60), Kirk (67), Doran (70); **Goals:** Nanyn 6/7, Dodd 2/3.
Dismissal: Wilkes (76) - retaliation.
Sin bin: Doran (47) – holding down.
SKOLARS: 1 Pete Hodgkinson; 2 Johnny Williams; 3 Callan Sipthorp; 4 Ashley Tozer; 5 Austen Aggrey; 6 Frank Reid; 7 Paul Thorman; 8 Alan Barker; 9 Kurt Pittman; 10 Martyn Benson; 11 Keir Bell; 12 Lydan Maitua; 13 Jermaine Coleman. Subs (all used): 14 Gareth Honor; 15 Mike Castle; 16 Richard Louw; 17 Dave Ellison.
Tries: Maitua (3), Ellison (50); **Goals:** Thorman 1/2.
Dismissal: Louw (76) - use of the elbow.
Sin bin: Barker (20) – holding down;
Reid (55) – holding down.
Rugby Leaguer & League Express Men of the Match:
Vikings: Scott Grix; *Skolars:* Pete Hodgkinson.
Penalty count: 14-10; **Half-time:** 40-4;
Referee: Matthew Thomasson; **Attendance:** 2,700.

GROUP 7

BRAMLEY BUFFALOES 24 WARRINGTON WIZARDS 20

WEEK 4

Friday 2nd March 2007

GROUP 5

BARROW RAIDERS 36 WORKINGTON TOWN 12

RAIDERS: 1 Khamal Ganley; 2 Nick Beach; 3 Phil Atkinson; 4 Liam Harrison; 5 James Nixon; 6 Liam Finch; 7 Darren Holt; 8 Paul Raftrey; 9 Andy Ellis; 10 Brett McDermott; 11 Martin Ostler; 12 Dave Armistead; 13 Mike Whitehead. Subs (all used): 14 Jamie Marshall; 15 James Finch; 16 Paul Wilcock; 17 Lee Dutton.
Tries: Harrison (6, 66, 78), L Finch (18), Ellis (22), Atkinson (24), Nixon (27), Ganley (41); **Goals:** Holt 2/8.
TOWN: 1 Liam Bretherton; 2 Stephen Dawes; 3 Neil Frazer; 4 Andrew Beattie; 5 Tom Armstrong; 6 Carl Forber; 7 Steve Kirkbride; 8 Dean Vaughan; 9 Shaun Lunt; 10 Taani Lavulavu; 11 Jamie Beaumont; 12 Dexter Miller; 13 Jon Roper. Subs (all used): 14 Liam Campbell; 15 Garry Purdham; 16 Allan McGuiness; 17 Matthew Tunstall.
Tries: Dawes (9), Beattie (48); **Goals:** Forber 2/2.
Rugby Leaguer & League Express Men of the Match: *Raiders:* Dave Armistead; *Town:* Taani Lavulavu.
Penalty count: 6-11; **Half-time:** 22-6;
Referee: Ashley Klein; **Attendance:** 1,230.

Sunday 4th March 2007

GROUP 1

DONCASTER LAKERS 12 SHEFFIELD EAGLES 20

LAKERS: 1 Loz Wildbore; 2 Rikki Sheriffe; 3 Dean Gorton; 4 Chris Buttery; 5 Danny Mills; 6 Joe McLocklan; 7 Joel Penny; 8 James Garmston; 9 Terry Lynn; 10 Ryan Tandy; 11 Joe Mbu; 12 Neil Lowe; 13 Shaun Leaf. Subs (all used): 14 Alex Rowe; 15 Craig Lawton; 16 Adam Robinson; 17 Peter Green.
Tries: Lowe (23), Leaf (63); **Goals:** Wildbore 2/2.
EAGLES: 1 Johnny Woodcock; 2 Greg Hurst; 3 Neil Law; 4 Richard Newlove; 5 Zac Hill; 6 Gavin Brown; 7 Jon Presley; 8 Tom Buckenham; 9 Paul Pickering; 10 Mitchell Stringer; 11 Ged Corcoran; 12 Dale Holdstock; 13 Grant Edwards. Subs (all used): 14 Brendon Lindsay; 15 Adam Hayes; 16 Caldon Bravo; 17 Ryan Hepworth.
Tries: Newlove (19, 27), Law (52); **Goals:** Woodcock 4/5.
Rugby Leaguer & League Express Men of the Match: *Lakers:* Loz Wildbore; *Eagles:* Richard Newlove.
Penalty count: 11-8; **Half-time:** 6-14;
Referee: Dave Merrick; **Attendance:** 2,753.

FEATHERSTONE ROVERS 16 CASTLEFORD TIGERS 22

ROVERS: 1 Nathan Larvin; 2 Danny Kirmond; 3 Wayne McHugh; 4 Dale Cardoza; 5 Craig Moss; 6 Chris Ross; 7 Paul Handforth; 8 Gareth Handford; 9 Paul Hughes; 10 Stuart Dickens; 11 Steve Dooler; 12 Richard Blakeway; 13 Tom Haughey. Subs: 14 Gavin Swinson; 15 Ian Tonks; 16 Brian Sutton (not used); 17 James Houston.
Tries: P Hughes (16), McHugh (22), Handforth (38);
Goals: Dickens 2/3.
Sin bin: Handford (57) - high tackle on Guttenbeil.
TIGERS: 1 Richard Owen; 2 Stuart Donlan; 3 Ryan Clayton; 4 Kirk Dixon; 5 Michael Wainwright; 6 Ryan McGoldrick; 7 Danny Brough; 8 Ryan Boyle; 9 Andrew Henderson; 10 Craig Huby; 11 Awen Guttenbeil; 12 Dwayne Barker; 13 Chris Charles. Subs (all used): 14 Mark Leafa; 15 Joe Westerman; 16 Jason Payne; 17 Michael Knowles.
Tries: Dixon (4, 28), Henderson (7), Charles (32);
Goals: Brough 3/6.
Sin bin: Henderson (53) - late challenge on Handforth.
Rugby Leaguer & League Express Men of the Match: *Rovers:* Paul Handforth; *Tigers:* Danny Brough.
Penalty count: 12-13; **Half-time:** 16-20;
Referee: Gareth Hewer; **Attendance:** 3,229.

GROUP 2

HALIFAX 52 KEIGHLEY COUGARS 4

HALIFAX: 1 Shad Royston; 2 Damian Gibson; 3 Mark Roberts; 4 James Haley; 5 Lee Greenwood; 6 Mick Govin; 7 Ian Watson; 8 Paul Southern; 9 Sam Hoare; 10 David Wrench; 11 David Larder; 12 Damian Ball; 13 Phil Joseph. Subs (all used): 14 Danny Jones; 15 Andy Shickell; 16 Aaron Trinder; 17 Frank Watene.
Tries: Haley (9), Larder (22), Ball (25), Roberts (33, 47), Watene (41), Royston (50, 64), Watson (79);
Goals: Haley 8/9.
COUGARS: 1 Gavin Duffy; 2 Sam Gardner; 3 Matt Foster; 4 Michael Hastings; 5 Ryan Smith; 6 Craig Fawcett; 7 Barry Eaton; 8 Luke Sutton; 9 James Feather; 10 Gareth English; 11 Greg Nicholson; 12 Jason Dubas-Fisher; 13 Chris Redfearn. Subs (all used): 14 Andy Feather; 15 Alex Brown; 16 Gareth Walker; 17 Chris Roe.
Goals: Eaton 2/2.
Rugby Leaguer & League Express Men of the Match: *Halifax:* Phil Joseph; *Cougars:* Barry Eaton.
Penalty count: 10-6; **Half-time:** 22-4;
Referee: Craig Halloran; **Attendance:** 1,676.

YORK CITY KNIGHTS 46 GATESHEAD THUNDER 4

CITY KNIGHTS: 1 George Rayner; 2 Lee Lingard; 3 Dan Potter; 4 Chris Spurr; 5 Lee Mapals; 6 Scott Rhodes; 7 Andy Gargan; 8 Tabua Cakacaka; 9 Jimmy Elston; 10 Adam Sullivan; 11 Ian Brown; 12 Dave Buckley; 13 Rob Spicer. Subs (all used): 14 Jon Liddell; 15 Ryan Esders; 16 Ryan McDonald; 17 Joe Helme.
Tries: Mapals (3, 60), C Spurr (6), Elston (29, 80), Rhodes (39), Buckley (54), Potter (71);
Goals: Gargan 7/8.
THUNDER: 1 Neil Thorman; 2 Robin Peers; 3 Graham Stephenson; 4 Pat Williamson; 5 Danny Wilson; 6 Jono Rolfe; 7 Tim Martin; 8 Shane Wooden; 9 Ryan Clarke; 10 Steven Bradley; 11 Dylan Nash; 12 Nick Hyde; 13 Odell Harris. Subs (all used): 14 Kevin Till; 15 Tony Doherty; 16 Steve Rutherford; 17 Michael Land.
Try: Martin (19); **Goals:** Rolfe 0/1.
Sin bin: Wooden (70) – interference.
Rugby Leaguer & League Express Men of the Match: *City Knights:* Joe Helme; *Thunder:* Tim Martin.
Penalty count: 9-7; **Half-time:** 22-4;
Referee: James Child; **Attendance:** 1,033.

GROUP 3

DEWSBURY RAMS 24 BATLEY BULLDOGS 6

RAMS: 1 Ian Preece; 2 Lee Close; 3 Andrew Bostock; 4 Danny Maun; 5 Kane Epati; 6 Francis Maloney; 7 Dean Lawford; 8 Andy Hobson; 9 Luke Haigh; 10 Dominic Maloney; 11 Kevin Crouthers; 12 Alex Bretherton; 13 Josh Weeden. Subs (all used): 14 Liam Finn; 15 Rob Kelly; 16 Martin Robinson; 17 David Bates.
Tries: Maun (36, 67), Crouthers (39), F Maloney (42, 76); **Goals:** F Maloney 2/5.
BULLDOGS: 1 Ashley Lindsay; 2 Alex Clemie; 3 Oliver Marns; 4 Chris Langley; 5 Jamie Stokes; 6 Ian Gordon; 7 John Gallagher; 8 David Rourke; 9 Kris Lythe; 10 Jack Watson; 11 Sean Richardson; 12 Tim Spears; 13 Lee Paterson. Subs (all used): 14 Jay Duffy; 15 Martin McLoughlin; 16 Phil Farrell; 17 Jon Simpson.
Try: Lythe (16); **Goals:** Gordon 1/1.
Rugby Leaguer & League Express Men of the Match: *Rams:* Kevin Crouthers; *Bulldogs:* Oliver Marns.
Penalty count: 7-8; **Half-time:** 10-6;
Referee: Mike Dawber; **Attendance:** 1,032.

GROUP 3 v GROUP 4

HUNSLET HAWKS 10 SWINTON LIONS 10

HAWKS: 1 Matt Bramald; 2 Andy Robinson; 3 David Foster; 4 Danny Cook; 5 Steve Morton; 6 Mark Moxon; 7 Matt Firth; 8 Danny Ekis; 9 Gareth Greenwood; 10 Danny Murgatroyd; 11 Wayne Freeman; 12 Will Cartledge; 13 Darren Robinson. Subs (all used): 14 Mark Cass; 15 Ben Walkin; 16 Karl Gunney; 17 Scott Houston.
Try: Morton (19); **Goals:** D Robinson 3/5, Bramald 0/1.
LIONS: 1 Wayne English; 2 Andy Saywell; 3 Darren Woods; 4 Mark Brocklehurst; 5 Marlon Billy; 6 Liam McGovern; 7 Chris Hough; 8 Bruce Johnson; 9 Phil Wood; 10 Gareth Hayes; 11 John Walker; 12 Chris Morley; 13 Craig Ashall. Subs (all used): 14 Martin Moana; 15 Craig Farrimond; 16 Dave Newton; 17 Mike Smith.
Tries: Walker (52), D Woods (79); **Goals:** McGovern 1/2.
Rugby Leaguer & League Express Men of the Match: *Hawks:* Matt Bramald; *Lions:* Craig Farrimond.
Penalty count: 10-7; **Half-time:** 10-0;
Referee: Matthew Thomasson; **Attendance:** 403.

GROUP 4

ROCHDALE HORNETS 16 OLDHAM 6

HORNETS: 1 Chris Giles; 2 Nick Johnson; 3 Lee Patterson; 4 Kevin King; 5 Bolu Fagborun; 6 Simon Svabic; 7 Gary Hulse; 8 Simon Baldwin; 9 Dave McConnell; 10 Byron Smith; 11 Andy Gorski; 12 Mark Blanchard; 13 Tommy Goulden. Subs (all used): 14 Phil Hasty; 15 Ryan Benjafield; 16 Paul Anderson; 17 Paul Norman.
Tries: McConnell (45), Goulden (78); **Goals:** King 4/4.
Sin bin: Norman (42) - dissent.
OLDHAM: 1 Paul O'Connor; 2 Gareth Langley; 3 Craig Littler; 4 Drew Houston; 5 Alex Wilkinson; 6 Mark Ogden; 7 Paul Ashton; 8 Jason Boults; 9 Simeon Hoyle; 10 Wes Rogers; 11 Lee Wingfield; 12 Ian Sinfield; 13 Chris Baines. Subs (all used): 14 Said Tamghart; 15 Kris Smith; 16 Andy Crabtree; 17 Andy Gorey.
Try: Langley (6); **Goals:** Ashton 1/3.
Dismissal: O'Connor (58) – head butt.
Sin bin: Ogden (5) - holding down.
Rugby Leaguer & League Express Men of the Match: *Hornets:* Chris Giles; *Oldham:* Paul O'Connor.
Penalty count: 9-9; **Half-time:** 2-4;
Referee: Karl Kirkpatrick; **Attendance:** 816.

GROUP 5

WHITEHAVEN 62 BLACKPOOL PANTHERS 0

WHITEHAVEN: 1 Gary Broadbent; 2 Craig Calvert; 3 Scott McAvoy; 4 Rob Jackson; 5 Steve Maden; 6 Carl Rudd; 7 John Duffy; 8 Steve Trindall; 9 Graeme Mattinson; 10 Scott Teare; 11 Spencer Miller; 12 Richard Fletcher; 13 Aaron Smith. Subs (all used): 14 Carl Sice; 15 Leroy Joe; 16 Marc Jackson; 17 Howard Hill.
Tries: S McAvoy (2), Maden (4, 49), Calvert (9, 12, 44), A Smith (19), Rudd (26, 55, 69), Trindall (30), Sice (52);
Goals: Rudd 7/12.
PANTHERS: 1 Chris Brand; 2 Anton Garcia; 3 Chris Maye; 4 Steven Brown; 5 Mark Leigh; 6 Safraz Patel; 7 Martin Gambles; 8 Lee Rowley; 9 Phil Cantillon; 10 Kris Ratcliffe; 11 Eddie Kilgannon; 12 Deon Duell; 13 Danny Barton. Subs (all used): 14 Chris Ramsdale; 15 Jon Chamberlain; 16 Gareth Jones; 17 Richard Rafferty.
Sin bin: Chamberlain (48) - interference.
Rugby Leaguer & League Express Men of the Match: *Whitehaven:* Scott Teare; *Panthers:* Eddie Kilgannon.
Penalty count: 10-6; **Half-time:** 36-0;
Referee: Robert Hicks; **Attendance:** 1,004.

GROUP 6

LEIGH CENTURIONS 24 WIDNES VIKINGS 8

CENTURIONS: 1 Miles Greenwood; 2 David Alstead; 3 Tommy Grundy; 4 Anthony Stewart; 5 Leroy Rivett; 6 Martin Ainscough; 7 Aaron Heremaia; 8 Warren Stevens; 9 Paul Rowley; 10 John Hill; 11 Mailangi Styles; 12 Robert Roberts; 13 Tim Jonkers. Subs (all used): 14 Sam Butterworth; 15 Daryl Kay; 16 Chris Hill; 17 John Cookson.
Tries: Roberts (1), Greenwood (23), Grundy (34), Rivett (41), Cookson (78); **Goals:** Heremaia 2/5.
Sin bin: Rowley (66) - fighting.
On report: Brawl (66).
VIKINGS: 1 Gavin Dodd; 2 Daryl Cardiss; 3 Toa Kohe-Love; 4 Andy Kirk; 5 Dean Gaskell; 6 Scott Grix; 7 Andy Kain; 8 Mick Cassidy; 9 Mark Smith; 10 Andy Bracek; 11 Lee Doran; 12 Paul Noone; 13 Bob Beswick. Subs: 14 Adam Bowman (not used); 15 Oliver Wilkes; 16 Jordan James; 17 Gareth Price.
Tries: Cardiss (55), Beswick (70); **Goals:** Dodd 0/2.
Sin bin: Price (66) - fighting
On report: Brawl (66).
Rugby Leaguer & League Express Men of the Match: *Centurions:* John Cookson; *Vikings:* Bob Beswick.
Penalty count: 10-10; **Half-time:** 16-0;
Referee: Jamie Leahy; **Attendance:** 2,291.

LONDON SKOLARS 4 CELTIC CRUSADERS 28

SKOLARS: 1 Pete Hodgkinson; 2 Corey Simms; 3 Chris Shears; 4 Steve Green; 5 Austen Aggrey; 6 Kurt Pittman; 7 Paul Thorman; 8 Alan Barker; 9 Frank Reid; 10 Martyn Benson; 11 Mike Castle; 12 Dave Brown; 13 Jermaine Coleman. Subs (all used): 14 Gareth Honor; 15 Joe Price; 16 Richard Louw; 17 Ashley Tozer.
Try: Simms (51); **Goals:** Thorman 0/1.
CRUSADERS: 1 Richard Johnston; 2 Grant Epton; 3 Paul Ballard; 4 Mark Dalle Cort; 5 Craig Richards; 6 Rob Toshack; 7 Jace Van Dijk; 8 Josh Cale; 9 Andy Boothroyd; 10 Gareth Dean; 11 Dean Fitzgerald; 12 Geraint Davies; 13 Damien Quinn. Subs (all used): 14 Neil Budworth; 15 Lee Jones; 16 Owen Lewis; 17 Hywel Davies.
Tries: G Davies (13), Quinn (19), Ballard (25, 64), Richards (36); **Goals:** Quinn 4/5.
Rugby Leaguer & League Express Men of the Match: *Skolars:* Paul Thorman; *Crusaders:* Damien Quinn.
Penalty count: 6-3; **Half-time:** 0-22;
Referee: Ben Thaler; **Attendance:** 289.

GROUP 7

DEWSBURY CELTIC 24 BRAMLEY BUFFALOES 26

HEMEL STAGS 22 WARRINGTON WIZARDS 10

WEEK 5

Friday 16th March 2007

GROUP 1

SHEFFIELD EAGLES 6 CASTLEFORD TIGERS 44

EAGLES: 1 Johnny Woodcock; 2 Greg Hurst; 3 Neil Law; 4 Damien Reid; 5 James Ford; 6 Brendon Lindsay; 7 Dominic Brambani; 8 Jack Howieson; 9 Craig Cook; 10 Jon Aston; 11 Ryan Hepworth; 12 Tommy Trayler; 13 Adam Hayes. Subs (all used): 14 Caldon Bravo; 15 Tom Buckenham; 16 Paul Pickering; 17 Mitchell Stringer.
Try: Lindsay (14); **Goals:** Woodcock 1/1.
Sin bin: Aston (35) – holding down; Cook (75) - dissent.
TIGERS: 1 Tom Saxton; 2 Stuart Donlan; 3 Michael Shenton; 4 Kirk Dixon; 5 Michael Wainwright; 6 Ryan McGoldrick; 7 Danny Brough; 8 Liam Higgins; 9 Andrew Henderson; 10 Mark Leafa; 11 Ryan Clayton; 12 Chris Charles; 13 Peter Lupton. Subs (all used): 14 Ryan Boyle; 15 Dwayne Barker; 16 Michael Knowles; 17 Tere Glassie.
Tries: Donlan (2, 54), Leafa (5), M Shenton (11, 47), Brough (21), Barker (58), Lupton (73);
Goals: Brough 6/8.
Sin bin: Higgins (45) - late challenge on Lindsay.
On report: Higgins (45) – late challenge on Lindsay.
Rugby Leaguer & League Express Men of the Match: *Eagles:* Johnny Woodcock; *Tigers:* Mark Leafa.
Penalty count: 13-7; **Half-time:** 6-22;
Referee: Gareth Hewer; **Attendance:** 1,897.

GROUP 5

BARROW RAIDERS 6 WHITEHAVEN 16

RAIDERS: 1 Khamal Ganley; 2 Nick Beach; 3 Phil Atkinson; 4 Liam Harrison; 5 James Nixon; 6 Liam Finch; 7 Darren Holt; 8 Paul Raftrey; 9 Andy Ellis; 10 Brett McDermott; 11 Martin Ostler; 12 Dave Armistead; 13 Mike Whitehead. Subs (all used): 14 Jamie Marshall; 15 Paul Wilcock; 16 Geoff Luxon; 17 Lee Dutton.
Try: Atkinson (5); **Goals:** Holt 1/1.
WHITEHAVEN: 1 Gary Broadbent; 2 Craig Calvert; 3 Derry Eilbeck; 4 Rob Jackson; 5 Steve Maden; 6 Carl Rudd; 7 John Duffy; 8 Marc Jackson; 9 Carl Sice; 10 Howard Hill; 11 Scott McAvoy; 12 Richard Fletcher; 13 Spencer Miller. Subs (all used): 14 Aaron Smith; 15 Leroy Joe; 16 Steve Trindall; 17 Scott Teare.
Tries: M Jackson (31), Joe (52), S McAvoy (63);
Goals: Rudd 2/3.
Rugby Leaguer & League Express Men of the Match: *Raiders:* Brett McDermott; *Whitehaven:* Gary Broadbent.
Penalty count: 6-8; **Half-time:** 6-6;
Referee: Mike Dawber; **Attendance:** 1,669.

Castleford's Jason Payne feels the force of the Featherstone defence

Saturday 17th March 2007

GROUP 7

DEWSBURY CELTIC 44 WARRINGTON WIZARDS 22

Sunday 18th March 2007

GROUP 1

DONCASTER LAKERS 18 FEATHERSTONE ROVERS 18

LAKERS: 1 Loz Wildbore; 2 Rikki Sheriffe; 3 Dean Gorton; 4 Chris Buttery; 5 Danny Mills; 6 Joe McLocklan; 7 Joel Penny; 8 Craig Lawton; 9 Brett Turner; 10 Ryan Tandy; 11 Joe Mbu; 12 Neil Lowe; 13 Peter Green. Subs (all used): 14 Alex Rowe; 15 Adam Robinson; 16 Mark Castle; 17 Adam Scott. **Tries:** D Mills (17), Sheriffe (20), Buttery (34, 56); **Goals:** Wildbore 0/3, McLocklan 1/1. **Sin bin:** Scott (50) – persistent offside. **ROVERS:** 1 Nathan Larvin; 2 Danny Kirmond; 3 Jon Whittle; 4 Dale Cardoza; 5 Dean Colton; 6 Chris Ross; 7 Paul Handforth; 8 Gareth Handford; 9 Paul Hughes; 10 Stuart Dickens; 11 Jamie Field; 12 Steve Dooler; 13 Tom Haughey. Subs (all used): 14 Craig Moss; 15 Ian Tonks; 16 Richard Blakeway; 17 Gavin Swinson. **Tries:** Handford (7), Blakeway (59), Swinson (68); **Goals:** Dickens 2/3, Ross 1/1. **Dismissal:** Cardoza (20) – dissent. **On report:** Blakeway (76) - late challenge on Lowe. **Rugby Leaguer & League Express Men of the Match:** *Lakers:* Brett Turner; *Rovers:* Paul Handforth. **Penalty count:** 5-9; **Half-time:** 12-6; **Referee:** Jamie Leahy; **Attendance:** 1,775.

GROUP 2

HALIFAX 30 GATESHEAD THUNDER 8

HALIFAX: 1 Brad Attwood; 2 Damian Gibson; 3 Shad Royston; 4 Richard Varkulis; 5 Marcus George; 6 Danny Jones; 7 Sean Penkywicz; 8 Paul Southern; 9 Sam Hoare; 10 David Wrench; 11 Scott Law; 12 Danny Heaton; 13 Luke Simeunovich. Subs (all used): 14 Phil Joseph; 15 Matthew Bottom; 16 Tim Hartley; 17 Frank Watene. **Tries:** Southern (11), George (14, 50), Royston (57), Gibson (59), Jones (72); **Goals:** Jones 3/6. **THUNDER:** 1 Neil Thorman; 2 Robin Peers; 3 Graham Stephenson; 4 Pat Williamson; 5 Danny Wilson; 6 Jono Rolfe; 7 Kevin Till; 8 Jonny Scott; 9 Tim Martin; 10 Steven Bradley; 11 Nick Hyde; 12 Shane Wooden; 13 Michael Land; 16 Tony Doherty; 17 Richie Metcalfe. **Try:** Rolfe (61); **Goals:** Rolfe 2/2. **Rugby Leaguer & League Express Men of the Match:** *Halifax:* Danny Jones; *Thunder:* Jono Rolfe. **Penalty count:** 11-11; **Half-time:** 10-2; **Referee:** Peter Brooke; **Attendance:** 1,504.

KEIGHLEY COUGARS 12 YORK CITY KNIGHTS 26

COUGARS: 1 Matt Foster; 2 Sam Gardner; 3 Michael Hastings; 4 Mick Fogerty; 5 Ryan Smith; 6 Craig Fawcett;

7 Barry Eaton; 8 Simon Bissell; 9 James Feather; 10 Gareth English; 11 Greg Nicholson; 12 Richard Knight; 13 Chris Redfearn. Subs (all used): 14 Gavin Duffy; 15 Wayne Sutcliffe; 16 Tom Palmer; 17 Luke Sutton. **Tries:** Hastings (57, 62); **Goals:** Eaton 2/3. **CITY KNIGHTS:** 1 George Rayner; 2 Lee Mapals; 3 Dan Potter; 4 Chris Spurr; 5 Lee Lingard; 6 Andy Gargan; 7 Anthony Thackeray; 8 Toby Williams; 9 Jamaine Wray; 10 Adam Sullivan; 11 John Smith; 12 Nathan Priestley; 13 Rob Spicer. Subs (all used): 14 Jon Liddell; 15 Jimmy Elston; 16 Ryan McDonald; 17 Ryan Esders. **Tries:** Sullivan (10), Thackeray (13), Smith (42), Wray (80); **Goals:** Wray 4/4, Gargan 1/1. **Rugby Leaguer & League Express Men of the Match:** *Cougars:* Simon Bissell; *City Knights:* Toby Williams. **Penalty count:** 10-14; **Half-time:** 2-12; **Referee:** James Child; **Attendance:** 758.

GROUP 3

HUNSLET HAWKS 4 BATLEY BULLDOGS 32

HAWKS: 1 Matt Bramald; 2 Andy Robinson; 3 David Foster; 4 Eddie Mack; 5 Steve Morton; 6 Mark Moxon; 7 Matt Firth; 8 Danny Ekis; 9 Gareth Greenwood; 10 Matt Carbutt; 11 Wayne Freeman; 12 Will Cartledge; 13 Darren Robinson. Subs (all used): 14 Mark Cass; 15 Karl Gunney; 16 Ben Walkin; 17 Danny Cook. **Try:** Morton (13); **Goals:** D Robinson 0/1. **BULLDOGS:** 1 Ashley Lindsay; 2 Alex Clemie; 3 Mark Barlow; 4 Jason Mossop; 5 Oliver Marns; 6 Ian Gordon; 7 Jay Duffy; 8 David Rourke; 9 Kris Lythe; 10 Martin McLoughlin; 11 Phil Farrell; 12 Tim Spears; 13 John Gallagher. Subs (all used): 14 Anthony Murray; 15 Anthony Henderson; 16 Jon Simpson; 17 Jack Watson. **Tries:** Lindsay (21), Simpson (43), J Gallagher (48, 74), Lythe (70); **Goals:** Gordon 6/6. **Rugby Leaguer & League Express Men of the Match:** *Hawks:* Steve Morton; *Bulldogs:* David Rourke. **Penalty count:** 8-8; **Half-time:** 4-8; **Referee:** Robert Hicks; **Attendance:** 438.

GROUP 4

ROCHDALE HORNETS 42 SWINTON LIONS 10

HORNETS: 1 Chris Giles; 2 Eric Andrews; 3 Lee Patterson; 4 Kevin King; 5 Bolu Fagborun; 6 Simon Svabic; 7 Phil Hasty; 8 Simon Baldwin; 9 Gary Hulse; 10 Byron Smith; 11 Paul Anderson; 12 Mark Blanchard; 13 Tommy Goulden. Subs (all used): 14 Wayne Corcoran; 15 Craig Robinson; 16 John Gledhill; 17 Paul Norman. **Tries:** Anderson (5, 35), King (24, 46, 48), Fagborun (52), Hulse (76), Goulden (80); **Goals:** King 5/8. **LIONS:** 1 Wayne English; 2 Andy Saywell; 3 Darren Woods; 4 Dave Ashton; 5 Marlon Billy; 6 Martin Moana; 7 Liam McGovern; 8 Gareth Hayes; 9 Phil Wood; 10 Dave Newton; 11 Paul Alcock; 12 Mike Smith; 13 Craig Ashall. Subs (all used): 14 Lee Marsh; 15 Craig Farrimond; 16 Danny Aboushakra; 17 Chris Morley. **Tries:** P Wood (27), Ashton (64); **Goals:** McGovern 1/3. **Rugby Leaguer & League Express Men of the Match:** *Hornets:* Kevin King; *Lions:* Phil Wood. **Penalty count:** 11-12; **Half-time:** 14-6;

Referee: Dave Merrick; **Attendance:** 556.

GROUP 4 v GROUP 3

OLDHAM 8 DEWSBURY RAMS 32

OLDHAM: 1 Paul O'Connor; 2 Gareth Langley; 3 Drew Houston; 4 Alex Wilkinson; 5 Andy Gorey; 6 Mark Ogden; 7 Neil Roden; 8 Jason Boults; 9 Simeon Hoyle; 10 Wes Rogers; 11 Kris Smith; 12 Ian Sinfield; 13 Chris Baines. Subs (all used): 14 Said Tamghart; 15 Richard Mervill; 16 Andy Crabtree; 17 Paul Ashton. **Tries:** O'Connor (65); Langley (67); **Goals:** Ashton 0/2. **Sin bin:** Ogden (18) - holding down. **RAMS:** 1 Alex Bretherton; 2 Lee Close; 3 Andrew Bostock; 4 Danny Maun; 5 John Oakes; 6 Francis Maloney; 7 Liam Finn; 8 Andy Hobson; 9 Luke Haigh; 10 Dominic Maloney; 11 Kevin Crouthers; 12 Martin Robinson; 13 Josh Weeden. Subs (all used): 14 Pat Walker; 15 Rob Kelly; 16 Andy Spink; 17 David Bates. **Tries:** Maun (15), Bostock (19), Oakes (27), F Maloney (47), Close (56), Robinson (77); **Goals:** F Maloney 4/6. **Rugby Leaguer & League Express Men of the Match:** *Oldham:* Paul O'Connor; *Rams:* Francis Maloney. **Penalty count:** 7-6; **Half-time:** 0-14; **Referee:** Mike Dawber; **Attendance:** 622.

GROUP 5

WORKINGTON TOWN 28 BLACKPOOL PANTHERS 20

TOWN: 1 Liam Bretherton; 2 Stephen Dawes; 3 Andrew Beattie; 4 David Whitworth; 5 Martyn Wilson; 6 Carl Forber; 7 Liam Campbell; 8 Dean Vaughan; 9 Shaun Lunt; 10 Taani Lavulavu; 11 Jamie Beaumont; 12 Jon Roper; 13 Craig Walsh. Subs (all used): 14 Steve Kirkbride; 15 Dean Burgess; 16 Darren King; 17 Steve Ormesher. **Tries:** Walsh (24, 27, 41), Dawes (33, 54), Forber (37); **Goals:** Forber 2/6. **On report:** Whitworth (70) – alleged spear tackle. **PANTHERS:** 1 Chris Brand; 2 Chris Ramsdale; 3 Chris Maye; 4 Eddie Kilgannon; 5 Mark Leigh; 6 Steven Brown; 7 Martin Gambles; 8 Lee Rowley; 9 Phil Cantillon; 10 Rob Lamb; 11 Jon Chamberlain; 12 Kris Ratcliffe; 13 Deon Duell. Subs (all used): 14 Safraz Patel; 15 Luke Murfin; 16 Gareth Jones; 17 Danny Barton. **Tries:** Maye (16), Cantillon (46, 64), Brown (76); **Goals:** Brand 2/4. **Rugby Leaguer & League Express Men of the Match:** *Town:* Craig Walsh; *Panthers:* Martin Gambles. **Penalty count:** 15-13; **Half-time:** 20-4; **Referee:** Andrew Grundy; **Attendance:** 464.

GROUP 6

CELTIC CRUSADERS 22 LEIGH CENTURIONS 14

CRUSADERS: 1 Tony Duggan; 2 Grant Epton; 3 Rob Toshack; 4 Mark Dalle Cort; 5 Richard Johnston; 6 Luke Young; 7 Jace Van Dijk; 8 Josh Cale; 9 Neil Budworth; 10 Gareth Dean; 11 Terry Martin; 12 Dean Fitzgerald; 13 Damien Quinn. Subs (all used): 14 Paul Ballard; 15 Jamie I'Anson; 16 Phil Cushion; 17 Hywel Davies. **Tries:** Dalle Cort (16), Toshack (28), Epton (58),

Ballard (68); **Goals:** Quinn 3/4.
CENTURIONS: 1 Miles Greenwood; 2 Rob Smyth; 3 Danny Speakman; 4 Adam Hughes; 5 David Alstead; 6 Martin Ainscough; 7 Aaron Heremaia; 8 Warren Stevens; 9 John Clough; 10 John Hill; 11 Tim Jonkers; 12 Tommy Grundy; 13 Anthony Stewart. Subs (all used): 14 Sam Butterworth; 15 Daryl Kay; 16 Chris Hill; 17 John Cookson.
Tries: Ainscough (16, 75), Smyth (63);
Goals: Hughes 1/3.
Rugby Leaguer & League Express Men of the Match: *Crusaders:* Mark Dalle Cort; *Centurions:* Martin Ainscough.
Penalty count: 7-4; **Half-time:** 10-6;
Referee: Craig Halloran; **Attendance:** 440.

LONDON SKOLARS 0 WIDNES VIKINGS 66

SKOLARS: 1 Pete Hodgkinson; 2 Corey Simms; 3 Joe Price; 4 Steve Green; 5 William Webster; 6 Jamie Nowland; 7 Paul Thorman; 8 Richard Louw; 9 Kurt Pittman; 10 Dave Ellison; 11 Dave Brown; 12 Lydan Maitua; 13 Jermaine Coleman. Subs (all used): 14 Frank Reid; 15 Chris Shears; 16 Dene Miller; 17 Alan Barker.
VIKINGS: 1 Scott Grix; 2 Andy Kirk; 3 Toa Kohe-Love; 4 Mick Nanyn; 5 Dean Gaskell; 6 Dennis Moran; 7 Ian Webster; 8 Jordan James; 9 Mark Smith; 10 Oliver Wilkes; 11 Lee Doran; 12 Paul Noone; 13 Bob Beswick. Subs (all used): 14 Daryl Cardiss; 15 Adam Sidlow; 16 Gavin Dodd; 17 Mike Morrison.
Tries: Wilkes (4, 11), Moran (9, 24, 80), Webster (30, 35, 39), Kohe-Love (43, 63), Nanyn (51), Kirk (73);
Goals: Nanyn 7/9, Noone 2/3.
Rugby Leaguer & League Express Men of the Match: *Skolars:* Jermaine Coleman; *Vikings:* Ian Webster.
Penalty count: 11-6; **Half-time:** 0-42;
Referee: Ashley Klein; **Attendance:** 789.

GROUP 7

BRAMLEY BUFFALOES 40 HEMEL STAGS 8

WEEK 6

Friday 23rd March 2007

GROUP 1

SHEFFIELD EAGLES 32 FEATHERSTONE ROVERS 8

EAGLES: 1 Johnny Woodcock; 2 Greg Hurst; 3 Damien Reid; 4 Richard Newlove; 5 James Ford; 6 Brendon Lindsay; 7 Dominic Brambani; 8 Jack Howieson; 9 Paul Pickering; 10 Tom Buckenham; 11 Ged Corcoran; 12 Tommy Trayler; 13 Adam Hayes. Subs (all used): 14 Gavin Brown; 15 Jon Aston; 16 Dale Holdstock; 17 Mitchell Stringer.
Tries: Newlove (10), Reid (17), Lindsay (23), Woodcock (54, 60); **Goals:** Woodcock 6/7.
ROVERS: 1 Nathan Larvin; 2 Danny Kirmond; 3 Wayne McHugh; 4 Jon Whittle; 5 Dean Colton; 6 Richard Blakeway; 7 Paul Handforth; 8 Gareth Handford; 9 Paul Hughes; 10 Stuart Dickens; 11 Jamie Field; 12 Steve Dooler; 13 Tom Haughey. Subs (all used): 14 Chris Ross; 15 Ian Tonks; 16 James Houston; 17 Dale Cardoza.
Tries: McHugh (72), Larvin (79);
Goals: Dickens 0/1, Larvin 0/1.
Sin bin: Whittle (9) – professional foul; Haughey (39) – holding down; P Hughes (50) – high tackle.
Rugby Leaguer & League Express Men of the Match: *Eagles:* Johnny Woodcock; *Rovers:* Nathan Larvin.
Penalty count: 10-14; **Half-time:** 20-0;
Referee: Jamie Leahy; **Attendance:** 1,196.

Saturday 24th March 2007

GROUP 7

WARRINGTON WIZARDS 24 BRAMLEY BUFFALOES 44

Sunday 25th March 2007

GROUP 1

CASTLEFORD TIGERS 64 DONCASTER LAKERS 8

TIGERS: 1 Tom Saxton; 2 Richard Owen; 3 Ryan Clayton; 4 Kirk Dixon; 5 Michael Wainwright; 6 Ryan McGoldrick; 7 Danny Brough; 8 Liam Higgins; 9 Andrew Henderson; 10 Craig Huby; 11 Awen Guttenbeil; 12 Dwayne Barker; 13 Peter Lupton. Subs (all used): 14 Tere Glassie; 15 Joe Westerman; 16 Michael Knowles; 17 Sean Johnson.
Tries: Saxton (10), Wainwright (18, 42), Clayton (23), Barker (32), Guttenbeil (46, 56), Lupton (48), Dixon (52), Owen (68, 77), Brough (71);
Goals: Brough 6/10, Dixon 2/2.
LAKERS: 1 Loz Wildbore; 2 Rikki Sheriffe; 3 Dean Gorton; 4 Chris Buttery; 5 Danny Mills; 6 Joe McLocklan; 7 Brett Turner; 8 Craig Lawton; 9 Peter Green; 10 Alex Benson; 11 Adam Robinson; 12 Joe Mbu; 13 Adam Scott. Subs (all used): 14 John Okul; 15 Mark Castle; 16 James Garmston; 17 James Endersby.
Try: McLocklan (38); **Goals:** Wildbore 2/2.
Sin bin: Wildbore (45) - professional foul.
Rugby Leaguer & League Express Men of the Match: *Tigers:* Danny Brough; *Lakers:* Joe McLocklan.
Penalty count: 8-8; **Half-time:** 20-8;
Referee: Robert Hicks; **Attendance:** 4,613.

GROUP 2

GATESHEAD THUNDER 26 KEIGHLEY COUGARS 30

THUNDER: 1 Neil Thorman; 2 Matt Walton; 3 Graham Stephenson; 4 Pat Williamson; 5 Danny Wilson; 6 Kevin Till; 7 Jono Rolfe; 8 Jonny Scott; 9 Tim Martin; 10 Steven Bradley; 11 Shane Wooden; 12 Nick Hyde; 13 Odell Harris. Subs (all used): 14 Ryan Clarke; 15 Damian Martinez; 16 Steve Rutherford; 17 Tony Doherty.
Tries: Williamson (4, 77), Stephenson (10), Wilson (40), Scott (65); **Goals:** Rolfe 1/2, Clarke 2/3.
Sin bin: Walton (15) - holding down.
COUGARS: 1 Matt Foster; 2 Sam Gardner; 3 Michael Hastings; 4 Mick Fogerty; 5 Alex Brown; 6 Craig Fawcett; 7 Barry Eaton; 8 Simon Bissell; 9 James Feather; 10 Tom Palmer; 11 Greg Nicholson; 12 Richard Knight; 13 Chris Redfearn. Subs (all used): 14 Gavin Duffy; 15 Wayne Sutcliffe; 16 Brendan Rawlins; 17 Luke Sutton.
Tries: Hastings (33), Bissell (43), Redfearn (60), Duffy (72), Fogerty (80); **Goals:** Eaton 5/5.
Rugby Leaguer & League Express Men of the Match: *Thunder:* Pat Williamson; *Cougars:* Barry Eaton.
Penalty count: 5-6; **Half-time:** 14-6;
Referee: James Child; **Attendance:** 389.

YORK CITY KNIGHTS 20 HALIFAX 60

CITY KNIGHTS: 1 Alex Godfrey; 2 Lee Mapals; 3 Kyle Palmer; 4 Ian Brown; 5 Lee Lingard; 6 Scott Rhodes; 7 Anthony Thackeray; 8 Toby Williams; 9 Jamaine Wray; 10 Adam Sullivan; 11 Ryan Esders; 12 Rob Spicer; 13 Stephen Grundy. Subs (all used): 14 Jon Liddell; 15 Jimmy Elston; 16 Dave Buckley; 17 Liam Watling.
Tries: Grundy (16), Lingard (55), Thackeray (65), Elston (79); **Goals:** Wray 2/3, Lingard 0/1.
HALIFAX: 1 Shad Royston; 2 Damian Gibson; 3 Mark Roberts; 4 Richard Varkulis; 5 Lee Greenwood; 6 Paul White; 7 Ian Watson; 8 Paul Southern; 9 Sean Penkywicz; 10 Aaron Trinder; 11 David Larder; 12 Damian Ball; 13 Phil Joseph. Subs (all used): 14 Tim Hartley; 15 Danny Heaton; 16 David Wrench; 17 Frank Watene.
Tries: White (3), Penkywicz (10), Royston (19, 21), Watson (30), Gibson (33), Roberts (45), Larder (62), Ball (70, 74), White (76); **Goals:** Watson 3/6, Hartley 5/5.
Rugby Leaguer & League Express Men of the Match: *City Knights:* Anthony Thackeray; *Halifax:* Sean Penkywicz.
Penalty count: 12-10; **Half-time:** 6-30;
Referee: Jamie Leahy; **Attendance:** 1,729.

GROUP 3

DEWSBURY RAMS 83 HUNSLET HAWKS 6

RAMS: 1 Ian Preece; 2 Bryn Powell; 3 Andrew Bostock; 4 Danny Maun; 5 Kane Epati; 6 Francis Maloney; 7 Dean Lawford; 8 Andy Hobson; 9 Joe Waters; 10 Dominic Maloney; 11 Kevin Crouthers; 12 Alex Bretherton; 13 Josh Weeden. Subs (all used): 14 Liam Finn; 15 Andy Spink; 16 Martin Robinson; 17 David Bates.
Tries: Bostock (9, 14), Preece (18), Crouthers (19), Epati (24), Lawford (36, 51), Robinson (38), Bates (39), Powell (46, 76), Maun (47), Weeden (58), Waters (65);
Goals: F Maloney 13/14; **Field goal:** Crouthers (78).
Sin bin: Hobson (11) - use of the elbow.
HAWKS: 1 Matt Bramald; 2 Andy Robinson; 3 Nick Walker; 4 Danny Cook; 5 Mark Cunningham; 6 Darren Robinson; 7 Mark Moxon; 8 Danny Ekis; 9 Luke Blake; 10 Danny Murgatroyd; 11 Ben Walkin; 12 Will Cartledge; 13 Gareth Greenwood. Subs (all used): 14 Aaron Dobek; 15 Matt Carbutt; 16 Karl Gunney; 17 Scott Houston.
Try: Murgatroyd (69); **Goals:** Bramald 1/1.
Rugby Leaguer & League Express Men of the Match: *Rams:* Dean Lawford; *Hawks:* Danny Ekis.
Penalty count: 9-7; **Half-time:** 46-0;
Referee: Gareth Hewer; **Attendance:** 824.

GROUP 3 v GROUP 4

BATLEY BULLDOGS 10 ROCHDALE HORNETS 13

BULLDOGS: 1 Ashley Lindsay; 2 Alex Clemie; 3 Jason Mossop; 4 Chris Langley; 5 Oliver Marns; 6 Lee Paterson; 7 Ian Gordon; 8 David Rourke; 9 Kris Lythe; 10 Jack Watson; 11 Phil Farrell; 12 Tim Spears; 13 John Gallagher. Subs (all used): 14 Luke Stenchion; 15 Anthony Murray; 16 Anthony Henderson; 17 Jon Simpson.
Tries: Langley (3), Watson (65); **Goals:** Gordon 1/2.
HORNETS: 1 Chris Giles; 2 Eric Andrews; 3 Lee Patterson; 4 Kevin King; 5 Nick Johnson; 6 Simon Svabic; 7 Phil Hasty; 8 Rob Ball; 9 Gary Hulse; 10 Ryan Benjafield; 11 Simon Baldwin; 12 Mark Blanchard; 13 Tommy Goulden. Subs (all used): 14 Wayne Corcoran; 15 Byron Smith; 16 John Gledhill; 17 Craig Robinson.
Try: Giles (15); **Goals:** King 4/5; **Field goal:** Svabic (20).
Rugby Leaguer & League Express Men of the Match: *Bulldogs:* Kris Lythe; *Hornets:* Gary Hulse.
Penalty count: 6-10; **Half-time:** 4-9;
Referee: Mike Dawber; **Attendance:** 489.

GROUP 4

SWINTON LIONS 18 OLDHAM 42

LIONS: 1 Wayne English; 2 Andy Saywell; 3 Darren Woods; 4 Mark Brocklehurst; 5 Desi Williams; 6 Martin Moana; 7 Chris Hough; 8 Gareth Hayes; 9 Liam McGovern; 10 Dave Newton; 11 Craig Farrimond; 12 Mike Smith; 13 Lee Marsh. Subs (all used): 14 Ben Williamson; 15 Craig Ashall; 16 Matt Bryers; 17 Chris Morley.
Tries: Saywell (12, 73), English (20);
Goals: McGovern 3/3.
Sin bin: Morley (54) - holding down; Moana (58) - high tackle.
OLDHAM: 1 Paul O'Connor; 2 Gareth Langley; 3 Craig Littler; 4 Drew Houston; 5 Alex Wilkinson; 6 Mark Ogden; 7 Neil Roden; 8 Jason Boults; 9 Simeon Hoyle; 10 Richard Mervill; 11 Lee Wingfield; 12 Ian Sinfield; 13 Kris Smith. Subs (all used): 14 Ian Hodson; 15 Said Tamghart; 16 Wes Rogers; 17 Lee Sanderson.
Tries: Hoyle (5), Roden (24), Sinfield (34), O'Connor (40), Smith (46), Wilkinson (60, 64); **Goals:** Ogden 7/8.
Rugby Leaguer & League Express Men of the Match: *Lions:* Andy Saywell; *Oldham:* Neil Roden.
Penalty count: 6-17; **Half-time:** 12-22;
Referee: Peter Brooke; **Attendance:** 555.

GROUP 5

BLACKPOOL PANTHERS 22 BARROW RAIDERS 78

PANTHERS: 1 Chris Brand; 2 Mark Leigh; 3 Steven Brown; 4 Eddie Kilgannon; 5 Chris Ramsdale; 6 Safraz Patel; 7 Martin Gambles; 8 Lee Rowley; 9 Phil Cantillon; 10 Rob Lamb; 11 Jon Chamberlain; 12 Kris Ratcliffe; 13 Deon Duell. Subs (all used): 14 Chris Maye; 15 Luke Murfin; 16 Gareth Jones; 17 Richard Rafferty.
Tries: Brown (15, 52), Ratcliffe (21), Maye (39);
Goals: Brand 3/4.
RAIDERS: 1 Mike Basan; 2 Nick Beach; 3 Phil Atkinson; 4 Liam Harrison; 5 James Nixon; 6 Liam Finch; 7 Darren Holt; 8 Paul Raftrey; 9 Andy Ellis; 10 Brett McDermott; 11 Martin Ostler; 12 Dave Armistead; 13 Mike Whitehead. Subs (all used): 14 Jamie Marshall; 15 Paul Wilcock; 16 Geoff Luxon; 17 Lee Dutton.
Tries: McDermott (6, 30), Ostler (8), Ellis (25), Beach (27, 55, 77), Marshall (33, 43, 48, 58), L Finch (71, 78), Raftrey (79); **Goals:** Holt 4/6, Atkinson 3/4, Beach 4/4.
Rugby Leaguer & League Express Men of the Match: *Panthers:* Steven Brown; *Raiders:* Jamie Marshall.
Penalty count: 7-9; **Half-time:** 18-32;
Referee: Paul Stockman; **Attendance:** 358.

WHITEHAVEN 58 WORKINGTON TOWN 12

WHITEHAVEN: 1 Gary Broadbent; 2 Craig Calvert; 3 Scott McAvoy; 4 Derry Eilbeck; 5 Steve Maden; 6 Carl Rudd; 7 Marc Bainbridge; 8 Marc Jackson; 9 Aaron Smith; 10 Steve Trindall; 11 Spencer Miller; 12 Richard Fletcher; 13 Aaron Lester. Subs (all used): 14 Graeme Mattinson; 15 Leroy Joe; 16 Howard Hill; 17 Scott Teare.
Tries: Broadbent (14), Rudd (20, 59), Hill (24), S McAvoy (29, 74), Fletcher (31, 36, 64), Bainbridge (70);
Goals: Rudd 9/10.
TOWN: 1 Liam Bretherton; 2 Matthew Woodcock; 3 Franco Kmet; 4 Andrew Beattie; 5 Martyn Wilson; 6 Steve Kirkbride; 7 Liam Campbell; 8 Dean Vaughan; 9 Shaun Lunt; 10 Taani Lavulavu; 11 Jamie Beaumont; 12 Steve Ormesher; 13 Craig Walsh. Subs (all used): 14 Carl Forber; 15 Allan McGuiness; 16 Jon Roper; 17 Matthew Tunstall.
Tries: Campbell (45), Wilson (55); **Goals:** Kirkbride 2/2.
Sin bin: Campbell (24) - interference.
Rugby Leaguer & League Express Men of the Match: *Whitehaven:* Richard Fletcher; *Town:* Craig Walsh.
Penalty count: 11-10; **Half-time:** 36-0;
Referee: Craig Halloran; **Attendance:** 2,636.

GROUP 6

LEIGH CENTURIONS 60 LONDON SKOLARS 22

CENTURIONS: 1 Miles Greenwood; 2 Rob Smyth; 3 David Alstead; 4 Adam Hughes; 5 Leroy Rivett; 6 Martin Ainscough; 7 Aaron Heremaia; 8 Warren Stevens; 9 John Clough; 10 Dana Wilson; 11 Chris Hill; 12 Tommy Grundy; 13 Anthony Stewart. Subs (all used): 14 Sam Butterworth; 15 Danny Speakman; 16 Tim Jonkers; 17 John Cookson.
Tries: C Hill (5), Rivett (11), Ainscough (15, 24), Greenwood (17, 48), Alstead (22, 38, 66), Grundy (42, 55); **Goals:** Hughes 8/11.
SKOLARS: 1 Ashley Tozer; 2 Corey Simms; 3 Chris Shears; 4 Steve Green; 5 Johnny Williams; 6 Jamie Nowland; 7 Paul Thorman; 8 Martyn Benson; 9 Gareth Honor; 10 Richard Louw; 11 Mike Castle; 12 Jake Kerr; 13 Lydan Maitua. Subs (all used): 14 Frank Reid; 15 Kurt Pittman; 16 Dave Brown; 17 Warren Heilig.
Tries: Thorman (34), Green (52), Brown (57), Honor (71); **Goals:** Nowland 3/4.
On report: Nowland (78) - alleged high tackle on C Hill.
Rugby Leaguer & League Express Men of the Match: *Centurions:* Aaron Heremaia; *Skolars:* Jamie Nowland.
Penalty count: 5-6; **Half-time:** 38-6;
Referee: Phil Bentham; **Attendance:** 1,277.

WIDNES VIKINGS 32 CELTIC CRUSADERS 10

VIKINGS: 1 Scott Grix; 2 Damien Blanch; 3 Daryl Cardiss; 4 Andy Kirk; 5 Gavin Dodd; 6 Andy Kain; 7 Ian Webster; 8 Jordan James; 9 Bob Beswick; 10 Oliver Wilkes; 11 Rob Draper; 12 Lee Doran; 13 Paul Noone. Subs (all used): 14 Adam Bowman; 15 Adam Sidlow; 16 Dean Gaskell; 17 Mike Morrison.
Tries: Bowman (26), Draper (38), Grix (48, 53, 78), Cardiss (58); **Goals:** Dodd 4/6.
CRUSADERS: 1 Tony Duggan; 2 Grant Epton; 3 Mark Dalle Cort; 4 Damien Quinn; 5 Richard Johnston; 6 Luke Young; 7 Jace Van Dijk; 8 Josh Cale; 9 Neil Budworth; 10 Gareth Dean; 11 Terry Martin; 12 Dean Fitzgerald; 13 Darren Mapp. Subs (all used): 14 Paul Ballard; 15 Jamie I'Anson; 16 Phil Cushion; 17 Hywel Davies.
Tries: Duggan (8, 23); **Goals:** Quinn 1/2.
Sin bin: Budworth (69) - dangerous tackle.
Rugby Leaguer & League Express Men of the Match: *Vikings:* Andy Kain; *Crusaders:* Tony Duggan.
Penalty count: 11-6; **Half-time:** 8-10;
Referee: Dave Merrick; **Attendance:** 2,540.

GROUP 7

DEWSBURY CELTIC 32 HEMEL STAGS 8

FINAL TABLES

GROUP 1

	P	W	D	L	BP	F	A	Diff	Pts
Castleford	6	6	0	0	0	246	58	188	18
Featherstone	6	2	1	3	1	130	164	-34	9
Sheffield	6	2	0	4	1	110	176	-66	7
Doncaster	6	1	1	4	2	86	174	-88	7

GROUP 2

	P	W	D	L	BP	F	A	Diff	Pts
Halifax	6	6	0	0	0	242	70	172	18
York	6	4	0	2	0	188	144	44	12
Keighley	6	2	0	4	1	136	184	-48	7
Gateshead	6	0	0	6	1	68	236	-168	1

GROUP 3

	P	W	D	L	BP	F	A	Diff	Pts
Dewsbury	6	5	0	1	1	228	64	164	16
Batley	6	2	0	4	2	100	137	-37	8
Hunslet *	6	2	1	3	0	74	187	-113	8

GROUP 4

	P	W	D	L	BP	F	A	Diff	Pts
Rochdale	6	5	0	1	1	164	78	86	16
Swinton	6	2	1	3	0	118	172	-54	8
Oldham	6	1	0	5	3	104	150	-46	6

GROUP 5

	P	W	D	L	BP	F	A	Diff	Pts
Whitehaven	6	5	1	0	0	234	76	158	17
Barrow	6	3	1	2	2	210	108	102	13
Workington *	6	3	0	3	0	136	210	-74	9
Blackpool	6	0	0	6	2	92	278	-186	2

GROUP 6

	P	W	D	L	BP	F	A	Diff	Pts
Widnes	6	5	0	1	0	256	70	186	15
Celtic Crusaders	6	4	0	2	0	136	156	-20	12
Leigh *	6	3	0	3	2	192	120	72	11
London Skolars	6	0	0	6	0	72	310	-238	0

GROUP 7

	P	W	D	L	BP	F	A	Diff	Pts
Bramley Buffaloes	6	6	0	0	0	204	94	110	18
Warrington Wizards	6	2	0	4	2	170	158	12	8
Dewsbury Celtic	6	2	0	4	1	142	180	-38	7
Hemel Stags	6	2	0	4	0	106	190	-84	6

Quarter Final Qualifying Round:
Group 1-6 winners and runners-up.
Group 7 winners.
Best three third-placed teams (*), Group 1-6.

QUARTER FINAL QUALIFYING ROUND

Saturday 21st April 2007

HUNSLET HAWKS 14 CELTIC CRUSADERS 28

HAWKS: 1 Matt Bramald; 2 Andy Robinson; 3 David Foster; 4 Eddie Mack; 5 Steve Morton; 6 Mark Moxon; 7 Matt Firth; 8 Danny Ekis; 9 Gareth Greenwood; 10 Wayne Freeman; 11 Danny Cook; 12 Will Cartledge; 13 Darren Robinson. Subs (all used): 14 David Gibbons; 15 Mark Holmes; 16 Gareth Naylor; 17 Matt Carbutt. **Tries:** Morton (2), Ekis (17), D Robinson (79); **Goals:** D Robinson 1/3.
CRUSADERS: 1 Richard Johnston; 2 Lee Williams; 3 Dean Fitzgerald; 4 Paul Ballard; 5 Owen Lewis; 6 Anthony Blackwood; 7 Tony Duggan; 8 Hywel Davies; 9 Andy Boothroyd; 10 Jamie I'Anson; 11 Geraint Davies; 12 Chris Beasley; 13 Darren Mapp. Subs (all used): 14 Tom Burnell; 15 Lee Jones; 16 Gareth Dean; 17 Chris Vitalini. **Tries:** Johnston (12), I'Anson (12), Duggan (51, 66), Blackwood (73); **Goals:** Williams 4/5.
Rugby Leaguer & League Express Men of the Match: *Hawks:* Danny Ekis; *Crusaders:* Tony Duggan.
Penalty count: 9-6; **Half-time:** 10-12;
Referee: Mike Dawber;
Attendance: 222 *(at Tetley's Stadium, Dewsbury).*

Sunday 22nd April 2007

DEWSBURY RAMS 30 LEIGH CENTURIONS 46

RAMS: 1 Ian Preece; 2 Bryn Powell; 3 Pat Walker; 4 Ryan Glynn; 5 Lee Close; 6 Josh Weeden; 7 Dean Lawford; 8 Andy Hobson; 9 Luke Haigh; 10 Dominic Maloney; 11 Kevin Crouthers; 12 Martin Robinson; 13 Liam Finn. Subs (all used): 14 John Oakes; 15 Rob Kelly; 16 Liam Crawley; 17 David Bates. **Tries:** Crouthers (11), Powell (38), Preece (54), Kelly (61), Walker (65); **Goals:** Finn 5/5.
CENTURIONS: 1 Miles Greenwood; 2 Leroy Rivett; 3 Damien Couturier; 4 Danny Halliwell; 5 David Alstead; 6 Martin Ainscough; 7 Aaron Heremaia; 8 Sean Richardson; 9 Sam Butterworth; 10 Dana Wilson; 11 Tommy Grundy; 12 Robert Roberts; 13 Anthony Stewart. Subs (all used): 14 Adam Hughes; 15 James Taylor; 16 Mailangi Styles; 17 Chris Hill. **Tries:** Greenwood (24), Heremaia (28, 77), Taylor (34), Roberts (41), Ainscough (45), Wilson (50), Couturier (77); **Goals:** Couturier 7/8.
Rugby Leaguer & League Express Men of the Match:
Rams: Bryn Powell; *Centurions:* Aaron Heremaia.
Penalty count: 8-7; **Half-time:** 12-18;
Referee: Ronnie Laughton; **Attendance:** 1,070.

HALIFAX 76 FEATHERSTONE ROVERS 16

HALIFAX: 1 Paul White; 2 Marcus George; 3 Mark Roberts; 4 Richard Varkulis; 5 Lee Greenwood; 6 Tim Hartley; 7 Ian Watson; 8 Paul Southern; 9 Sean Penkywicz; 10 Frank Watene; 11 David Larder; 12 Danny Heaton; 13 Phil Joseph. Subs (all used): 14 Danny Jones; 15 Scott Law; 16 Aaron Trinder; 17 David Wrench. **Tries:** Penkywicz (3), Joseph (11, 71), Heaton (17), Varkulis (21, 44), Hartley (37), Trinder (39), Greenwood (50, 65), Law (61), White (67), Jones (69); **Goals:** Hartley 12/13.
ROVERS: 1 Craig Bower; 2 Wayne McHugh; 3 Jon Whittle; 4 Dale Cardoza; 5 Dean Colton; 6 Richard Blakeway; 7 Chris Ross; 8 Gareth Handford; 9 Paul Hughes; 10 Stuart Dickens; 11 Steve Dooler; 12 James Houston; 13 Jamie Field. Subs (all used): 14 Gavin Swinson; 15 Ian Tonks; 16 Craig Cawthray; 17 Carl Hughes. **Tries:** Ross (26), Field (30), Colton (76); **Goals:** Dickens 2/3.
Dismissal: Handford (10) - head butt.
Rugby Leaguer & League Express Men of the Match: *Halifax:* Sean Penkywicz; *Rovers:* Chris Ross.
Penalty count: 6-7; **Half-time:** 34-12;
Referee: David Halloran; **Attendance:** 1,318.

ROCHDALE HORNETS 30 SWINTON LIONS 16

HORNETS: 1 Gary Hulse; 2 Eric Andrews; 3 Lee Patterson; 4 Kevin King; 5 Bolu Fagborun; 6 Simon Svabic; 7 Phil Hasty; 8 Simon Baldwin; 9 Dave McConnell; 10 Byron Smith; 11 Andy Gorski; 12 John Gledhill; 13 Mark Blanchard. Subs (all used): 14 Wayne Corcoran; 15 Andy Bailey; 16 Craig Robinson; 17 Paul Norman. **Tries:** Andrews (5), Hasty (18), Hulse (43), Robinson (47), Gledhill (78); **Goals:** King 5/5.
LIONS: 1 Wayne English; 2 Desi Williams; 3 Darren Woods; 4 Mark Brocklehurst; 5 Marlon Billy; 6 Mark Ogden; 7 Liam McGovern; 8 Bruce Johnson; 9 Phil Wood; 10 Rob Line; 11 Matt Bryers; 12 Mike Smith; 13 Martin Moana. Subs (all used): 14 Dave Ashton; 15 Chris Morley; 16 Dave Newton; 17 Gareth Hayes. **Tries:** Billy (22), P Wood (30), Moana (60); **Goals:** Ogden 2/3.
Rugby Leaguer & League Express Men of the Match: *Hornets:* Simon Svabic; *Lions:* Phil Wood.
Penalty count: 9-7; **Half-time:** 12-10;
Referee: Jamie Leahy; **Attendance:** 501.

WHITEHAVEN 52 BRAMLEY BUFFALOES 4

WHITEHAVEN: 1 Gary Broadbent; 2 Craig Calvert; 3 Steve Maden; 4 Derry Eilbeck; 5 Craig Benson; 6 Carl Rudd; 7 John Duffy; 8 Steve Trindall; 9 Aaron Smith; 10 Marc Jackson; 11 Spencer Miller; 12 Ricky Wright; 13 Leroy Joe. Subs (all used): 14 Daniel Smith; 15 David Ford; 16 Scott Farmer; 17 Scott Teare. **Tries:** Calvert (8, 36, 63), Eilbeck (23, 78), Duffy (27, 67), Broadbent (30), A Smith (33); **Goals:** Rudd 5/5, M Jackson 1/1, Duffy 0/1, Ford 2/2.
Dismissal: M Jackson (57) - fighting.
Sin bin: Trindall (75) - persistent offside.
BUFFALOES: 1 Shaun Flynn; 2 Nicky Fontaine; 3 Matt Mulholland; 4 Paul Coates; 5 John Richardson; 6 Brad Asquith; 7 Marc Glover; 8 Chris Gardner; 9 Kevin O'Hare; 10 Mark Butterill; 11 Graham Harrison; 12 Simon Speight; 13 Scott Pendlebury. Subs (all used): 14 Tom Webb; 15 Paul Drake; 16 Danny Mitchell; 17 Neil Hesketh. **Try:** Coates 0/1. **Goals:** Coates 0/1.
Dismissal: Flynn (67) - high tackle.
Sin bin: Butterill (54) - high tackle; Drake (57) - fighting.

Sean Penkywicz makes a break during Halifax's big win over Featherstone

Rugby Leaguer & League Express Men of the Match:
Whitehaven: David Ford; *Buffaloes:* Marc Gibson.
Penalty count: 14-9; **Half-time:** 36-4;
Referee: Dave Merrick; **Attendance:** 858.

WIDNES VIKINGS 62 BATLEY BULLDOGS 6

VIKINGS: 1 Scott Grix; 2 Dean Gaskell; 3 Toa Kohe-Love; 4 Andy Kirk; 5 Gavin Dodd; 6 Dennis Moran; 7 Andy Kain; 8 Jordan James; 9 Mark Smith; 10 Oliver Wilkes; 11 Lee Doran; 12 Paul Noone; 13 Bob Beswick. Subs (all used): 14 Aaron Summers; 15 Mick Cassidy; 16 Damien Blanch; 17 Gareth Price. **Tries:** Kain (19, 32), Cassidy (22), Gaskell (29, 56), Moran (37), Smith (44), Beswick (47), Wilkes (53), Noone (71), Kirk (75); **Goals:** Moran 5/6, Kirk 2/3.
BULLDOGS: 1 Craig Lingard; 2 Ashley Lindsay; 3 Jason Mossop; 4 Chris Langley; 5 Oliver Marns; 6 Ian Gordon; 7 Mark Barlow; 8 David Rourke; 9 Kris Lythe; 10 David Best; 11 Leigh Cooke; 12 Tim Spears; 13 Phil Farrell. Subs (all used): 14 John Rourke; 15 Luke Menzies; 16 Anthony Henderson; 17 Jon Simpson. **Try:** Lythe (65); **Goals:** Gordon 1/1.
Rugby Leaguer & League Express Men of the Match: *Vikings:* Oliver Wilkes; *Bulldogs:* Kris Lythe.
Penalty count: 10-9; **Half-time:** 28-0;
Referee: Peter Taberner; **Attendance:** 2,140.

YORK CITY KNIGHTS 16 BARROW RAIDERS 18

CITY KNIGHTS: 1 George Rayner; 2 Lee Mapals; 3 Dan Potter; 4 Chris Spurr; 5 Tom Dunmore; 6 Scott Rhodes; 7 Jimmy Elston; 8 Tabua Cakacaka; 9 Jamaine Wray; 10 Adam Sullivan; 11 Dave Buckley; 12 Ian Brown; 13 Ryan Esders. Subs (all used): 14 Jon Liddell; 15 John Smith; 16 Nathan Priestley; 17 Joe Helme. **Tries:** Rhodes (13), Brown (37), Dunmore (68); **Goals:** Wray 1/3, Dunmore 1/1.
RAIDERS: 1 Lee Norman; 2 Nick Beach; 3 Phil Atkinson; 4 Liam Harrison; 5 James Nixon; 6 Mike Basan; 7 Darren Holt; 8 Paul Rattrey; 9 Andy Ellis; 10 Jamie Butler; 11 Michael Smith; 12 Paul Wilcock; 13 Pat Weisner. Subs (all used): 14 Jamie Marshall; 15 Shane Irabor; 16 James Finch; 17 Anthony Horton. **Tries:** Holt (5), Basan (18); **Goals:** Holt 4/4; **Field goal:** Holt (41), Weisner (47).
Sin bin: Smith (67) - holding down.
Rugby Leaguer & League Express Men of the Match: *City Knights:* Scott Rhodes; *Raiders:* Darren Holt.
Penalty count: 15-13; **Half-time:** 10-16;
Referee: Robert Hicks; **Attendance:** 658.

CASTLEFORD TIGERS 50 WORKINGTON TOWN 24

TIGERS: 1 Tom Saxton; 2 Richard Owen; 3 Stuart Donlan; 4 Kirk Dixon; 5 Michael Wainwright; 6 Ryan McGoldrick; 7 Danny Brough; 8 Liam Higgins; 9 Sean Johnson; 10 Craig Huby; 11 Mark Leafa; 12 Tere Glassie; 13 Dwayne Barker. Subs (all used): 14 Joe Westerman; 15 Jason Payne; 16 Michael Knowles; 17 Ryan Boyle. **Tries:** Dixon (3), Saxton (7, 47), Barker (9), Knowles (38, 44), McGoldrick (54), Owen (60), Leafa (62); **Goals:** Brough 7/9.
TOWN: 1 Rob Lunt; 2 Matthew Woodcock; 3 Andrew Beattie; 4 Neil Frazer; 5 Stephen Dawes; 6 Carl Forber; 7 Liam Campbell; 8 Allan McGuiness; 9 Darren King; 10 Dean Burgess; 11 Steve Ormesher; 12 Dexter Miller; 13 Garry Purdham. Subs (all used): 14 David Whitworth; 15 Martyn Wilson; 16 Franco Kmet; 17 James Robinson. **Tries:** Forber (30, 33), Kmet (41), Beattie (73); **Goals:** Forber 4/4.
Rugby Leaguer & League Express Men of the Match: *Tigers:* Michael Knowles; *Town:* Liam Campbell.
Penalty count: 10-6; **Half-time:** 22-12;
Referee: Thierry Alibert; **Attendance:** 3,610.

Danny Brough upended by Mark Smith, as Oliver Wilkes moves in, during Widnes' semi-final win against Castleford

QUARTER FINALS

Saturday 26th May 2007

HALIFAX 30 CELTIC CRUSADERS 18

HALIFAX: 1 Damian Gibson; 2 Marcus George; 3 Tim Hartley; 4 Richard Varkulis; 5 Lee Greenwood; 6 Graham Holroyd; 7 Ian Watson; 8 Paul Southern; 9 Sean Penkywicz; 10 Andy Shickell; 11 Phil Joseph; 12 Paul Smith; 13 Damian Ball. Subs (all used): 14 Mark Roberts; 15 David Larder; 16 David Wrench; 17 Frank Watene.
Tries: Varkulis (11), Penkywicz (17), Greenwood (39, 75), Hartley (44), Joseph (63);
Goals: Hartley 1/4, Holroyd 2/3.
CRUSADERS: 1 Paul Ballard; 2 Grant Epton; 3 Anthony Blackwood; 4 Mark Dalle Cort; 5 Craig Richards; 6 Luke Young; 7 Damien Quinn; 8 Josh Cale; 9 Andy Boothroyd; 10 Hywel Davies; 11 Geraint Davies; 12 Chris Beasley; 13 Dean Fitzgerald. Subs (all used): 14 Neale Wyatt; 15 Jamie I'Anson; 16 Lee Jones; 17 Phil Cushion.
Tries: Boothroyd (21), Epton (27), Fitzgerald (60);
Goals: Quinn 3/4.
Sin bin: Ballard (36) - time wasting.
Rugby Leaguer & League Express Men of the Match:
Halifax: Damian Ball; *Crusaders:* Mark Dalle Cort.
Penalty count: 6-5; **Half-time:** 14-14;
Referee: Dave Merrick; **Attendance:** 1,086.

Sunday 27th May 2007

ROCHDALE HORNETS 0 WIDNES VIKINGS 24

HORNETS: 1 Gary Hulse; 2 Eric Andrews; 3 Lee Patterson; 4 Kevin King; 5 Bolu Fagborun; 6 Simon Svabic; 7 Phil Hasty; 8 Andy Bailey; 9 Dave McConnell; 10 Byron Smith; 11 Andy Gorski; 12 Simon Baldwin; 13 Tommy Goulden. Subs (all used): 14 Chris Giles; 15 Iain Marsh; 16 Wayne Corcoran; 17 Ryan Benjafield.
VIKINGS: 1 Scott Grix; 2 Damien Blanch; 3 Andy Kirk; 4 Mick Nanyn; 5 Gavin Dodd; 6 Dennis Moran; 7 Ian Webster; 8 Mick Cassidy; 9 Mark Smith; 10 Oliver Wilkes; 11 Lee Doran; 12 Paul Noone; 13 Bob Beswick. Subs (all used): 14 Aaron Summers; 15 Jordan James; 16 Dean Gaskell; 17 Danny Lima.
Tries: Blanch (17, 35), Kirk (59), Webster (67);
Goals: Nanyn 4/4.
Rugby Leaguer & League Express Men of the Match:
Hornets: Simon Svabic; *Vikings:* Dennis Moran.
Penalty count: 8-12; **Half-time:** 0-12; **Referee:** Thierry Alibert; **Attendance:** 2,362 (at Halton Stadium).

WHITEHAVEN 34 BARROW RAIDERS 14

WHITEHAVEN: 1 Gary Broadbent; 2 Craig Calvert; 3 David Seeds; 4 Derry Eilbeck; 5 Rob Jackson; 6 Carl Rudd; 7 John Duffy; 8 Steve Trindall; 9 Aaron Smith; 10 David Fatialofa; 11 Steve Bannister; 12 Richard Fletcher; 13 Aaron Smith. Subs (all used): 14 Graeme Mattinson; 15 Leroy Joe; 16 Ricky Wright; 17 Scott Teare.
Tries: Fletcher (9, 32, 38), Duffy (53, 76),

Seeds (61, 80); **Goals:** Fletcher 2/6, Rudd 1/1.
RAIDERS: 1 Mike Basan; 2 Nick Beach; 3 James Finch; 4 Liam Harrison; 5 James Nixon; 6 Liam Finch; 7 Darren Holt; 8 Paul Raftrey; 9 Andy Ellis; 10 Brett McDermott; 11 Mike Whitehead; 12 Dave Armistead; 13 Pat Weisner. Subs (all used): 14 Jamie Marshall; 15 Paul Wilcock; 16 Lee Dutton; 17 Ian Rawlinson.
Tries: Nixon (2), J Finch (39, 70);
Goals: Holt 1/3, Weisner 0/1.
Rugby Leaguer & League Express Men of the Match:
Whitehaven: Richard Fletcher; *Raiders:* Brett McDermott.
Penalty count: 4-4; **Half-time:** 14-10;
Referee: Ronnie Laughton; **Attendance:** 1,484.

CASTLEFORD TIGERS 42 LEIGH CENTURIONS 6

TIGERS: 1 Tom Saxton; 2 Stuart Donlan; 3 Michael Shenton; 4 Kirk Dixon; 5 Michael Wainwright; 6 Ryan McGoldrick; 7 Peter Lupton; 8 Ryan Boyle; 9 Andrew Henderson; 10 Mark Leafa; 11 Awen Guttenbeil; 12 Dwayne Barker; 13 Chris Charles. Subs (all used): 14 Joe Westerman; 15 Ryan Clayton; 16 Michael Knowles; 17 Richard Owen.
Tries: Wainwright (3), M Shenton (7), Barker (18, 29), Leafa (33), McGoldrick (37), Clayton (59), Donlan (61);
Goals: Dixon 5/8.
CENTURIONS: 1 Miles Greenwood; 2 Leroy Rivett; 3 Damien Couturier; 4 Danny Halliwell; 5 David Alstead; 6 Martin Ainscough; 7 Aaron Heremaia; 8 Warren Stevens; 9 Sam Butterworth; 10 Matt Astley; 11 Adam Rudd; 12 James Taylor; 13 Anthony Stewart. Subs (all used): 14 Adam Thomas; 15 Mailangi Styles; 16 John Cookson; 17 Dana Wilson.
Try: Couturier (46); **Goals:** Couturier 1/1.
Sin bin: Heremaia (5) – holding down.
Rugby Leaguer & League Express Men of the Match:
Tigers: Peter Lupton; *Centurions:* Leroy Rivett.
Penalty count: 7-6; **Half-time:** 32-0;
Referee: Mike Dawber; **Attendance:** 3,205.

SEMI-FINALS

Sunday 24th June 2007

WHITEHAVEN 34 HALIFAX 19

WHITEHAVEN: 1 Gary Broadbent; 2 Craig Calvert; 3 Rob Jackson; 4 Derry Eilbeck; 5 Steve Maden; 6 Carl Rudd; 7 John Duffy; 8 Steve Trindall; 9 Aaron Smith; 10 David Fatialofa; 11 Spencer Miller; 12 Richard Fletcher; 13 Leroy Joe. Subs (all used): 14 Carl Sice; 15 Graeme Mattinson; 16 Marc Jackson; 17 Scott Teare.
Tries: Joe (31), Sice (50), Duffy (56), Rudd (61), Eilbeck (69), A Smith (78); **Goals:** Rudd 4/5, Fletcher 1/1.
HALIFAX: 1 Shad Royston; 2 Damian Gibson; 3 Mark Roberts; 4 Richard Varkulis; 5 Lee Greenwood; 6 Graham Holroyd; 7 Ian Watson; 8 Paul Southern; 9 Sean Penkywicz; 10 Frank Watene; 11 Danny Heaton; 12 Paul Smith; 13 Phil Joseph. Subs (all used): 14 Sam Hoare; 15 Damian Ball; 16 David Larder; 17 Andy Shickell.

Tries: Varkulis (17), Greenwood (22), Smith (28);
Goals: Holroyd 3/5; **Field goal:** Watson (39).
Rugby Leaguer & League Express Men of the Match:
Whitehaven: John Duffy; *Halifax:* Richard Varkulis.
Penalty count: 8-6; **Half-time:** 6-19;
Referee: Jamie Leahy; **Attendance:** 2,246.

WIDNES VIKINGS 18 CASTLEFORD TIGERS 12

VIKINGS: 1 Scott Grix; 2 Damien Blanch; 3 Toa Kohe-Love; 4 Mick Nanyn; 5 Gavin Dodd; 6 Dennis Moran; 7 Joel Penny; 8 Mick Cassidy; 9 Mark Smith; 10 Oliver Wilkes; 11 Aaron Summers; 12 Paul Noone; 13 Bob Beswick. Subs (all used): 14 Ian Webster; 15 Lee Doran; 16 Jordan James; 17 Danny Lima.
Tries: Wilkes (9), Nanyn (19); **Goals:** Nanyn 5/5.
TIGERS: 1 Tom Saxton; 2 Stuart Donlan; 3 Michael Shenton; 4 Kirk Dixon; 5 Mike Wainwright; 6 Ryan McGoldrick; 7 Danny Brough; 8 Mark Leafa; 9 Andrew Henderson; 10 Craig Huby; 11 Awen Guttenbeil; 12 Chris Charles; 13 Ryan Clayton. Subs (all used): 14 Joe Westerman; 15 Tere Glassie; 16 Ryan Boyle; 17 Liam Higgins.
Tries: Boyle (30, 36); **Goals:** Brough 2/2.
Rugby Leaguer & League Express Men of the Match:
Vikings: Mick Nanyn; *Tigers:* Stuart Donlan.
Penalty count: 10-7; **Half-time:** 14-12;
Referee: Gareth Hewer; **Attendance:** 5,388.

FINAL

Sunday 15th July 2007

WHITEHAVEN 6 WIDNES VIKINGS 54

WHITEHAVEN: 1 Gary Broadbent; 2 Craig Calvert; 3 Derry Eilbeck; 4 Rob Jackson; 5 Steve Maden; 13 Carl Rudd; 7 John Duffy; 8 Steve Trindall; 9 Aaron Smith; 10 David Fatialofa; 11 Spencer Miller; 12 Richard Fletcher; 6 Leroy Joe. Subs (all used): 14 Carl Sice; 15 Graeme Mattinson; 16 Marc Jackson; 17 Scott Teare.
Try: Rudd (62); **Goals:** Rudd 1/1.
Sin bin: Broadbent (10) - punching.
On report: Brawl (10).
VIKINGS: 1 Scott Grix; 2 Damien Blanch; 3 Toa Kohe-Love; 4 Mick Nanyn; 5 Dean Gaskell; 6 Dennis Moran; 7 Joel Penny; 8 Mick Cassidy; 9 Mark Smith; 10 Oliver Wilkes; 11 Lee Doran; 12 Paul Noone; 13 Bob Beswick. Subs (all used): 14 Aaron Summers; 15 Jordan James; 16 Ian Webster; 17 Gareth Price.
Tries: Kohe-Love (6), Grix (14), Blanch (21, 47), Nanyn (29), Doran (33), Smith (43), Moran (71), Gaskell (76);
Goals: Nanyn 9/12.
On report: Brawl (10).
Rugby Leaguer & League Express Men of the Match:
Whitehaven: Carl Rudd; *Vikings:* Dennis Moran.
Penalty count: 3-12; **Half-time:** 0-30;
Referee: Jamie Leahy; **Attendance:** 8,236 (at Bloomfield Road, Blackpool).

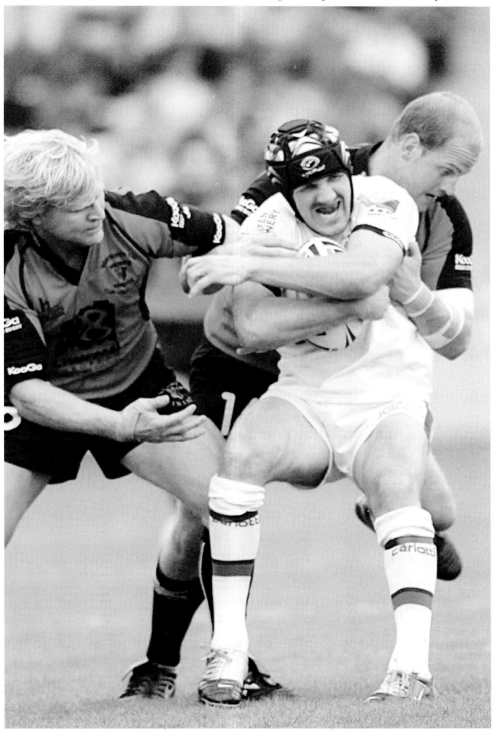

Whitehaven's Gary Broadbent wrapped up by Widnes duo Mick Cassidy and Aaron Summers during the National League Cup Final

CHALLENGE CUP 2007
Round by Round

ROUND 3

Saturday 10th March 2007

EAST HULL 10 OLDHAM 26

EAST HULL: 1 Phil Batty; 2 Jason Abdul; 3 Martin Johnson; 4 Lewis Lilley; 5 Mike McGowan; 6 Gary Blanchard; 7 Stuart Coates; 8 Lee Brown; 9 Shaun Painter; 10 Michael Docherty; 11 Ian Madley; 12 Craig Bassett; 13 Gary Noble. Subs (all used): 14 Mark Moore; 15 Liam Cunningham; 16 Mark Woodcock; 17 James Ransley.
Try: Docherty (18); **Goals:** Docherty 3/3.
OLDHAM: 1 Paul O'Connor; 2 Gareth Langley; 3 Drew Houston; 4 Said Tamghart; 5 Alex Wilkinson; 6 Mark Ogden; 7 Neil Roden; 8 Jason Boults; 9 Simeon Hoyle; 10 Wes Rogers; 11 Kris Smith; 12 Ian Sinfield; 13 Chris Baines. Subs (all used): 14 Craig Littler; 15 Andy Crabtree; 16 Mike Stout; 17 Paul Ashton.
Tries: Ogden (5), Roden (23), Stout (35), Wilkinson (72, 76); **Goals:** Ogden 3/3, Ashton 0/2.
Rugby Leaguer & League Express Men of the Match: *East Hull:* Lee Brown; *Oldham:* Neil Roden.
Penalty count: 9-10; **Half-time:** 8-18; **Referee:** Charlie Neilsen; **Attendance:** 300 *(at Hull Ionians RUFC).*

WEST BOWLING 8 LONDON SKOLARS 24

WEST BOWLING: 1 Michael Derrick; 2 Gareth Cullington; 3 Martin Tordoff; 4 Tim Sutcliffe; 5 Elliott Whitehead; 6 Peter Simpson; 7 Steve Illingworth; 8 Andrew Senior; 9 Daniel Ramsden; 10 Paul Hutchinson; 11 Nigel Halmshaw; 12 Liam Martin; 13 Ricky Helliwell. Subs (all used): 14 John Metcalfe; 15 Michael Kyte; 16 Philip Chappell; 17 Sha Basha.
Tries: Derrick (30), Cullington (67);
Goals: Illingworth 0/2.
SKOLARS: 1 Pete Hodgkinson; 2 Johnny Williams; 3 Chris Shears; 4 Ashley Tozer; 5 Austen Aggrey; 6 Kurt Pittman; 7 Paul Thorman; 8 Alan Barker; 9 Gareth Honor; 10 Martyn Benson; 11 Dave Brown; 12 Lydan Maitua; 13 Jermaine Coleman. Subs (all used): 14 Frank Reid; 15 Mike Castle; 16 Joe Price; 17 Richard Louw.
Tries: Brown (26), Tozer (45, 78), Reid (55), Aggrey (59); **Goals:** Thorman 2/4, Coleman 0/1.
Rugby Leaguer & League Express Men of the Match: *West Bowling:* Steve Illingworth; *Skolars:* Austen Aggrey.
Penalty count: 5-10; **Half-time:** 4-6; **Referee:** Andrew Grundy; **Attendance:** 230 *(at Old Brodleians RUFC).*

BLACKPOOL PANTHERS 18 PIA 42

PANTHERS: 1 Chris Brand; 2 Mark Leigh; 3 Chris Maye; 4 Chris Ramsdale; 5 Steven Brown; 6 Safraz Patel; 7 Martin Gambles; 8 Lee Rowley; 9 Phil Cantillon; 10 Daniel Palmer; 11 Eddie Kilgannon; 12 Kris Ratcliffe; 13 Deon Duell. Subs (all used): 14 Jon Chamberlain; 15 Luke Murfin; 16 Danny Barton; 17 Gareth Jones.
Tries: Leigh (12), Ramsdale (75), Cantillon (77, 78);
Goals: Brand 1/4.
Sin bin: Duell (28) - persistent offending;
Cantillon (51) - high tackle; Patel (53) - fighting.
PIA: 1 Anthony Carrere; 2 Nicolas Piquemal; 3 Josh Tatupu; 4 Florian Chaubet; 5 Nicolas Athiel; 6 Maxime Greseque; 7 Franck Traversa; 8 Dean Bosnich; 9 Mathias Garrabe; 10 Matt Kennedy; 11 Guillaume Knecht; 12 Gareth Turton; 13 Aaron Smith. Subs (all used): 14 Patrick Cala; 15 Manu Fort; 16 Sebastien Martins; 17 Maxime Pradal.
Tries: Tatupu (1, 17, 63, 66), Greseque (18), Athiel (28), Bosnich (49), Smith (70); **Goals:** Greseque 5/8.
Sin bin: Piquemal (2) - holding down; Athiel (38) - holding down; Cala (53) - fighting; Smith (74) - dissent.
Rugby Leaguer & League Express Men of the Match: *Panthers:* Phil Cantillon; *Pia:* Josh Tatupu.
Penalty count: 16-16; **Half-time:** 6-22;
Referee: Craig Halloran; **Attendance:** 327.

CELTIC CRUSADERS 50 EASTMOOR DRAGONS 10

CRUSADERS: 1 Paul Ballard; 2 Lee Williams; 3 Rob Toshack; 4 Mark Dalle Cort; 5 Craig Richards; 6 Luke Young; 7 Tony Duggan; 8 Josh Cale; 9 Andy Boothroyd; 10 Gareth Dean; 11 Terry Martin; 12 Dean Fitzgerald; 13 Jamie I'Anson. Subs (all used): 14 Tom Burnell; 15 Chris Vitalini; 16 Geraint Davies; 17 Phil Cushion.
Tries: Cale (15), Ballard (27, 75), Young (39), Dean (42), Duggan (58, 71), Richards (69, 77); **Goals:** Young 7/9.
Dismissals: G Davies (65) - fighting;
Martin (65) - fighting.
DRAGONS: 1 Jamie Barraclough; 2 Michael Jedynak; 3 Leigh Joyce; 4 Andrew Philips; 5 Michael Brown; 6 Adrian Mulcahy; 7 Kevin Brown; 8 Philip Hodgson; 9 Carl Saville; 10 Adam Endersby; 11 Andrew Fisher; 12 Gregory Fisher; 13 Richard Colley. Subs (all used): 14 Mathew Rogers; 15 Chris Hayward; 16 Robert Ramsden; 17 James Ganley.
Tries: M Brown (5, 31); **Goals:** Joyce 1/2.
Dismissal: Barraclough (65) - fighting.
Rugby Leaguer & League Express Men of the Match: *Crusaders:* Paul Ballard; *Dragons:* Michael Brown.
Penalty count: 7-6; **Half-time:** 16-10;
Referee: Peter Brooke; **Attendance:** 300.

GATESHEAD THUNDER 38 LIMOUX 22

THUNDER: 1 Neil Thorman; 2 Robin Peers; 3 Graham Stephenson; 4 Pat Williamson; 5 Danny Wilson; 6 Kevin Till; 7 Jono Rolfe; 8 Jonny Scott; 9 Tim Martin; 10 Steven Bradley; 11 Shane Wooden; 12 Nick Hyde; 13 Odell Harris. Subs (all used): 14 Ryan Clarke; 15 Steve Rutherford; 16 Matt Barron; 17 Richie Metcalfe.
Tries: Stephenson (5), Rolfe (39, 70), Williamson (43, 46), Till (64), Clarke (75); **Goals:** Rolfe 5/7.
LIMOUX: 1 Herve Marrot; 2 Mathias Pala; 3 Mathieu Mayans; 4 Harry Aonga; 5 Farid Goutta; 6 Nicolas Piccolo; 7 Sylvain Teixido; 8 Jerome Gout; 9 Brendan Solomon; 10 Taei Junior Aoese; 11 Guillaume Reffle; 12 Iosua Segi; 13 Yannick Brousse. Subs: 14 Joris Casal; 15 Mickael Simon; 16 Florent Gallo (not used); 17 Mickael Murcia.
Tries: Marrot (10), Mayans (53, 66), Goutta (80);
Goals: Mayans 3/5.
Sin bin: Solomon (72) - holding down.
Rugby Leaguer & League Express Men of the Match: *Thunder:* Neil Thorman; *Limoux:* Nicolas Piccolo.
Penalty count: 13-8; **Half-time:** 10-8;
Referee: Gareth Hewer; **Attendance:** 211.

Sunday 11th March 2007

BATLEY BULLDOGS 60 WIDNES ST MARIES 6

BULLDOGS: 1 Ashley Lindsay; 2 Alex Clemie; 3 Jason Mossop; 4 Chris Langley; 5 Oliver Marns; 6 Ian Gordon; 7 Jay Duffy; 8 David Rourke; 9 Kris Lythe; 10 Martin McLoughlin; 11 Phil Farrell; 12 Tim Spears; 13 John Gallagher. Subs (all used): 14 Anthony Murray; 15 Anthony Henderson; 16 Jack Watson; 17 Jon Simpson.
Tries: D Rourke (6), Spears (10), J Gallagher (21), Murray (29), Mossop (35, 40), Simpson (38), Lindsay (60, 67), Marns (72), Henderson (76); **Goals:** Gordon 8/11.
ST MARIES: 1 Scott Harland; 2 Darren McKinnon; 3 Kieran McDonnell; 4 David Welsh; 5 Mike Lamb; 6 Lee Birdseye; 7 Matt Viggers; 8 Andy Hibbert; 9 Anthony Hollins; 10 Graham Buck; 11 Mike Gill; 12 Peter Hyland; 13 Mark Birmingham. Subs (all used): 14 Jamie Rowlands; 15 Tevita Liku; 16 Tony Kirwan; 17 Andy Benson.
Try: Birdseye (42); **Goals:** Birdseye 1/1.
Rugby Leaguer & League Express Men of the Match: *Bulldogs:* Ashley Lindsay; *St Maries:* David Welsh.
Penalty count: 6-3; **Half-time:** 40-0;
Referee: Paul Stockman; **Attendance:** 407.

WEST HULL 18 BARROW RAIDERS 70

WEST HULL: 1 Paul Kirby; 2 Chris Lee; 3 Lee Moreton; 4 Dean Thompson; 5 Lee Craig; 6 Mark Hewitt; 7 Carl Puckering; 8 Carl Bristow; 9 Steve Stamp; 10 Casey Garrigan; 11 Brian Newby; 12 Brett Robinson; 13 Mark Cassidy. Subs (all used): 14 Dave Roberts; 15 James Wright; 16 Mike Caville; 17 Aiden Morton.
Tries: Lee (40), A Morton (49), Newby (61);
Goals: Puckering 3/3.
Sin bin: Bristow (16) - interference.
RAIDERS: 1 Khamal Ganley; 2 Nick Beach; 3 Phil Atkinson; 4 Liam Harrison; 5 James Nixon; 6 Liam Finch; 7 Darren Holt; 8 Paul Raftrey; 9 Andy Ellis; 10 Brett McDermott; 11 Martin Ostler; 12 Dave Armistead; 13 Mike Whitehead. Subs (all used): 14 Jamie Marshall; 15 James Finch; 16 Paul Wilcock; 17 Geoff Luxon.
Tries: McDermott (11), Holt (16), Ganley (18, 21, 43), Ellis (24), Atkinson (46), Nixon (53, 56), J Finch (69), Marshall (75, 77); **Goals:** Holt 11/13.
Rugby Leaguer & League Express Men of the Match: *West Hull:* Mark Hewitt; *Raiders:* Darren Holt.
Penalty count: 11-10; **Half-time:** 6-30; **Referee:** Chris Dean; **Attendance:** 450 *(at Hull Ionians RUFC).*

DEWSBURY RAMS 36 LEIGH CENTURIONS 34

RAMS: 1 Ryan Glynn; 2 Lee Close; 3 Andrew Bostock; 4 Chris Hall; 5 Danny Maun; 6 Francis Maloney; 7 Dean Lawford; 8 Andy Hobson; 9 Luke Haigh; 10 Dominic Maloney; 11 Kevin Crouthers; 12 Alex Bretherton; 13 Josh Weeden. Subs (all used): 14 Liam Finn; 15 Rob Kelly; 16 Martin Robinson; 17 David Bates.
Tries: F Maloney (8), Bretherton (15), Lawford (27), Bostock (41), Weeden (72), Crouthers (78);
Goals: F Maloney 6/7.
Sin bin: Finn (39) – persistent offside.
CENTURIONS: 1 Miles Greenwood; 2 Rob Smyth; 3 David Alstead; 4 Adam Hughes; 5 Leroy Rivett; 6 Robert Roberts; 7 Aaron Heremaia; 8 Warren Stevens; 9 Paul Rowley; 10 John Hill; 11 Mailangi Styles; 12 Tommy Grundy; 13 Tim Jonkers. Subs (all used): 14 John Clough; 15 Sam Butterworth; 16 Chris Hill; 17 John Cookson.
Tries: Grundy (11), Hughes (23), Cookson (33), Styles (44), Jonkers (65), Greenwood (67);
Goals: Heremaia 4/7, Hughes 1/2.
Rugby Leaguer & League Express Men of the Match: *Rams:* Francis Maloney; *Centurions:* Aaron Heremaia.
Penalty count: 6-10; **Half-time:** 20-18;
Referee: Robert Hicks; **Attendance:** 1,131.

FEATHERSTONE ROVERS 52 DRIGHLINGTON 10

ROVERS: 1 Nathan Larvin; 2 Danny Kirmond; 3 Wayne McHugh; 4 Dale Cardoza; 5 Craig Moss; 6 Andy Speake; 7 Paul Handforth; 8 Ian Tonks; 9 Paul Hughes; 10 Stuart Dickens; 11 Jamie Field; 12 Richard Blakeway; 13 Tom Haughey. Subs (all used): 14 Chris Ross; 15 Steve Dooler; 16 James Ward; 17 Gareth Handford.
Tries: Field (2, 15), McHugh (53, 72), Dickens (30), Dooler (35), Cardoza (38), Haughey (47), Ross (67), Handford (75); **Goals:** Dickens 5/9, Speake 1/1.
Sin bin: Speake (43) – holding down.
DRIGHLINGTON: 1 Kevin Doyle; 2 Chris Dyson; 3 Andy Jackson; 4 Dave Patterson; 5 Sean Coughlan; 6 Adam Newton; 7 Nathan Hallas; 8 Glen Pennington; 9 Sam Pickles; 10 Andy Brierley; 11 Luke Pennington; 12 Lee Mulhern; 13 Andy Kay. Subs (all used): 14 Ben Kerr; 15 Owen Buckley; 16 Paul Hustler; 17 Chris Hill.
Tries: Coughlan (5), L Pennington (18); **Goals:** Hallas 1/2.
Rugby Leaguer & League Express Men of the Match: *Rovers:* Jamie Field; *Drighlington:* Andy Kay.
Penalty count: 8-14; **Half-time:** 28-10;
Referee: Ashley Klein; **Attendance:** 1,161.

HALIFAX 86 ECCLES & SALFORD JUNIORS 12

HALIFAX: 1 Brad Attwood; 2 Marcus George; 3 Mark Roberts; 4 James Haley; 5 Lee Greenwood; 6 Danny Jones; 7 Ian Watson; 8 Andy Shickell; 9 Sam Hoare; 10 Aaron Trinder; 11 David Larder; 12 Damian Ball; 13 Phil Joseph. Subs (all used): 14 Sean Penkywicz; 15 Paul Southern; 16 Scott Law; 17 Frank Watene.
Tries: George (4, 8, 44), Greenwood (14, 18, 22, 40), Larder (30, 36, 48, 80), Attwood (38), Roberts (41, 58), Hoare (68), Haley (71); **Goals:** Haley 11/15, Jones 0/1.
ECCLES & SALFORD: 1 Paul Morgan; 2 Stuart Hudson; 3 Mike O'Boyle; 4 Andrew Muscat; 5 Dave Critchley; 6 Jake Johnstone; 7 John McAtee; 8 Glynn Watson; 9 Jason Viller; 10 Neil McPherson; 11 Jason Carter; 12 Carl Mort; 13 Marc Gilligan. Subs (all used): 14 John Basson; 15 Stafford Lloyd; 16 Adam Taher; 17 Paul Verdon.
Tries: McAtee (55), Muscat (77);
Goals: Basson 1/1, Taher 1/1.
Rugby Leaguer & League Express Men of the Match: *Halifax:* Ian Watson; *Eccles & Salford:* Glynn Watson.
Penalty count: 13-6; **Half-time:** 48-0;
Referee: Pascal Mombet; **Attendance:** 825.

KEIGHLEY COUGARS 34 THORNHILL TROJANS 6

COUGARS: 1 Gavin Duffy; 2 Sam Gardner; 3 Matt Foster; 4 Michael Hastings; 5 Ryan Smith; 6 Craig Fawcett; 7 Barry Eaton; 8 Simon Bissell; 9 James Feather; 10 Gareth English; 11 Greg Nicholson; 12 Richard Knight; 13 Chris Redfearn. Subs (all used): 14 Alex Brown; 15 Wayne Sutcliffe; 16 Tom Palmer; 17 Luke Sutton.
Tries: Knight (28), Foster (34, 45), Sutcliffe (65), Gardner (68), Hastings (70), R Smith (76);
Goals: Eaton 1/3, Knight 2/4.
On report: Brawl (57).
TROJANS: 1 Craig Holmes; 2 Robert Copley; 3 Matt Roberts; 4 George Mack; 5 Scott Redgwick; 6 Scott Dyson; 7 Liam Morley; 8 James Folan; 9 Richard Pachniuk; 10 Danny Lee; 11 Scott Woodcock; 12 Lee Schofield; 13 Anthony Broadhead. Subs (all used): 14 Daniel Annakin; 15 Vinnie Johnson; 16 Lee Smith; 17 Simon Haigh.
Try: Roberts (37); **Goals:** Holmes 1/1.
Sin bin: Holmes (57) - fighting.
On report: Brawl (57).
Rugby Leaguer & League Express Men of the Match: *Cougars:* James Feather; *Trojans:* Scott Woodcock.
Penalty count: 20-6; **Half-time:** 10-6;
Referee: Stephane Vincent; **Attendance:** 868.

LEIGH MINERS RANGERS 18 SHEFFIELD EAGLES 46

MINERS RANGERS: 1 Darren Pilkington; 2 Tom Draper; 3 Paul Wingfield; 4 John Woods; 5 Mark Jones; 6 Garry Fitzmartin; 7 Scott O'Brien; 8 Dean Balmer; 9 Aaron Gorton; 10 Danny Mole; 11 David Patterson; 12 Simon Warhurst; 13 David Radley. Subs (all used): 14 Martin Lewis; 15 Adam Higson; 16 Adam Teece; 17 Craig Wingfield.
Tries: Woods (8), Gorton (33), Pilkington (38);
Goals: Radley 3/3.
EAGLES: 1 Johnny Woodcock; 2 Greg Hurst; 3 Neil Law; 4 Richard Newlove; 5 James Ford; 6 Brendon Lindsay; 7 Gavin Brown; 8 Jack Howieson; 9 Paul Pickering; 10 Tom Buckenham; 11 Dale Holdstock; 12 Ged Corcoran; 13 Adam Hayes. Subs (all used): 14 Dominic Brambani; 15 Tommy Trayler; 16 Caldon Bravo; 17 Mitchell Stringer.
Tries: Hayes (2, 47), Law (6, 60), Woodcock (49), Bravo (67), Newlove (72), Hurst (77); **Goals:** Woodcock 7/8.
Sin bin: Lindsay (32) - holding down.
Rugby Leaguer & League Express Men of the Match: *Miners Rangers:* Simon Warhurst;
Eagles: Johnny Woodcock.
Penalty count: 7-7; **Half-time:** 18-12; **Referee:** Gareth Hewer; **Attendance:** 499 *(at Hilton Park, Leigh).*

NORMANTON KNIGHTS 10 WIDNES VIKINGS 78

KNIGHTS: 1 Michael Butterfield; 2 Kevin Bateman; 3 Joseph Hurst; 4 Chris Lewis; 5 Andrew Greaves; 6 Liam Atkinson; 7 Michael Hill; 8 Phil Newsome; 9 Chris Woolford; 10 Patrick Waterton; 11 Paul Statham; 12 Ryan Tilford; 13 Lee Aspinall. Subs (all used): 14 Richard Dobson; 15 Mark Webster; 16 James Smith; 17 Gavin Barrett.
Tries: Greaves (73), Hill (78); **Goals:** Hill 1/2.
VIKINGS: 1 Scott Grix; 2 Damien Blanch; 3 Andy Kirk; 4 Mick Nanyn; 5 Dean Gaskell; 6 Dennis Moran; 7 Ian Webster; 8 Jordan James; 9 Mark Smith; 10 Gareth Price; 11 Paul Noone; 12 Oliver Wilkes; 13 Bob Beswick. Subs (all used): 14 Daryl Cardiss; 15 Rob Draper; 16 Mick Cassidy; 17 Lee Doran.
Tries: Gaskell (1, 41), Wilkes (10), Noone (14), Webster (17, 43), Smith (26, 36), Kirk (28, 49), Moran (33, 51, 61, 71); **Goals:** Nanyn 11/14.
Rugby Leaguer & League Express Men of the Match: *Knights:* Richard Dobson; *Vikings:* Ian Webster.
Penalty count: 4-5; **Half-time:** 0-44; **Referee:** Ian Smith; **Attendance:** 1,606 *(at Halton Stadium).*

ROCHDALE HORNETS 48 SADDLEWORTH RANGERS 6

HORNETS: 1 Gary Hulse; 2 Eric Andrews; 3 Lee Patterson; 4 Kevin King; 5 Bolu Fagborun; 6 Simon Svabic; 7 Phil Hasty; 8 Rob Ball; 9 Dave McConnell; 10 Ryan Benjafield; 11 Matt Whitaker; 12 Paul Anderson; 13 Tommy Goulden. Subs (all used): 14 Wayne Corcoran; 15 Craig Robinson; 16 John Gledhill; 17 Paul Norman.
Tries: Hulse (10), Hasty (30, 73), Anderson (39), Andrews (44), King (47, 63), Corcoran (66),

Gledhill (78); **Goals:** King 6/9.
RANGERS: 1 Kevin Fitzpatrick; 2 Fraser Coley; 3 Ben Pritchard; 4 James Whalley; 5 Danny Attersall; 6 Mick Coates; 7 Chris Garforth; 8 Gary Walkden; 9 Neil Kirwan; 10 Emerson Jackman; 11 Tom Kilgannon; 12 James Rogers; 13 Philip Wood. Subs (all used): 14 Steven Jagger; 15 Simon Parrish; 16 Lars Haigh; 17 Lee Baker.
Goals: Coates 3/3.
Rugby Leaguer & League Express Men of the Match: *Hornets:* Kevin King; *Rangers:* Mick Coates.
Penalty count: 14-6; **Half-time:** 18-6;
Referee: Dave Merrick; **Attendance:** 552.

SWINTON LIONS 60 LOKOMOTIV MOSCOW 20

LIONS: 1 Wayne English; 2 Andy Saywell; 3 Darren Woods; 4 Dave Ashton; 5 Marlon Billy; 6 Liam McGovern; 7 Chris Hough; 8 Bruce Johnson; 9 Phil Wood; 10 Gareth Hayes; 11 John Walker; 12 Dave Newton; 13 Craig Ashall. Subs (all used): 14 Martin Moana; 15 Craig Farrimond; 16 Paul Alcock; 17 Chris Morley.
Tries: Saywell (2, 33, 56), Ashall (12, 62), P Wood (14), D Woods (16, 42), English (50), Johnson (60), McGovern (77); **Goals:** McGovern 8/11.
LOKOMOTIV: 1 Oleg Logunov; 2 Nikolay Zagoskin; 3 Sergey Dobrynin; 4 Andrey Zdobnikov; 5 Valentin Baskakov; 6 Viktor Nechaev; 7 Artem Grigoryan; 8 Andrey Medvedev; 9 Roman Ovchinikov; 10 Vitaly Gusev; 15 Sergey Matveev; 12 Andrey Koltykov; 13 Vladimir Odnosumov. Subs (all used): 14 Sergey Bychkov; 11 Oleg Smirnov; 16 Sergey Sidorov; 17 Denis Meshkov.
Tries: Ovchinikov (8), Zagoskin (25, 36), Dobrynin (70);
Goals: Zdobnikov 2/4.
Rugby Leaguer & League Express Men of the Match: *Lions:* Phil Wood; *Lokomotiv:* Sergey Dobrynin.
Penalty count: 3-7; **Half-time:** 28-16;
Referee: Jean-Pierre Boulagnon; **Attendance:** 331.

WHITEHAVEN 24 DONCASTER LAKERS 10

WHITEHAVEN: 1 Gary Broadbent; 2 Craig Calvert; 3 Scott McAvoy; 4 Rob Jackson; 5 Steve Maden; 6 Carl Rudd; 7 John Duffy; 8 Steve Trindall; 9 Graeme Mattinson; 10 Scott Teare; 11 Spencer Miller; 12 Richard Fletcher; 13 Aaron Smith. Subs (all used): 14 Carl Sice; 15 Leroy Joe; 16 Marc Jackson; 17 Howard Hill.
Tries: Fletcher (6, 55), Sice (24), S McAvoy (68);
Goals: Rudd 4/5.
LAKERS: 1 Loz Wildbore; 2 Rikki Sheriffe; 3 Dean Gorton; 4 Chris Buttery; 5 Danny Mills; 6 Joe McLocklan; 7 Joel Penny; 8 Craig Lawton; 9 Brett Turner; 10 Ryan Tandy; 11 Joe Mbu; 12 Neil Lowe; 13 Peter Green. Subs (all used): 14 Alex Rowe; 15 Adam Robinson; 16 Mark Castle; 17 Adam Scott.
Tries: D Mills (43), Mbu (63); **Goals:** Wildbore 1/2.
Rugby Leaguer & League Express Men of the Match: *Whitehaven:* Richard Fletcher; *Lakers:* Joe Mbu.
Penalty count: 9-6; **Half-time:** 14-0;
Referee: Mike Dawber; **Attendance:** 1,268.

WORKINGTON TOWN 18 OULTON RAIDERS 10

TOWN: 1 Liam Bretherton; 2 Stephen Dawes; 3 Andrew Beattie; 4 David Whitworth; 5 Martyn Wilson; 6 Carl Forber; 7 Liam Campbell; 8 Dean Vaughan; 9 Shaun Lunt; 10 Taani Lavulavu; 11 Jamie Beaumont; 12 Jon Roper; 13 Craig Walsh. Subs (all used): 14 Steve Kirkbride; 15 Garry Purdham; 16 Allan McGuiness; 17 Tom Armstrong.
Tries: Walsh (16), Campbell (23), Whitworth (51);
Goals: Forber 3/4.
RAIDERS: 1 Tommy Skerrett; 2 Chris Dunhill; 3 Danny Hardy; 4 Steve Jakeman; 5 Lee Hall; 6 Gavin Wood; 7 Scott Goodall; 8 Lee Williamson; 9 Aidan Bowen; 10 Carlos Sanchez; 11 Sasch Brook; 12 Billy Kershaw; 13 Andy Williamson. Subs (all used): 14 Tommy Griffiths; 15 Alan White; 16 Matt Handforth; 17 Ian Booth.
Tries: Goodall (11), White (60); **Goals:** Skerrett 1/3.
Sin bin: Brook (37) - dissent.
Rugby Leaguer & League Express Men of the Match: *Town:* Craig Walsh; *Raiders:* Scott Goodall.
Penalty count: 18-10; **Half-time:** 10-6;
Referee: Matthew Thomasson; **Attendance:** 529.

YORK CITY KNIGHTS 54 TOULOUSE 28

CITY KNIGHTS: 1 George Rayner; 2 Lee Mapals; 3 Dan Potter; 4 Chris Spurr; 5 Lee Lingard; 6 Scott Rhodes; 7 Anthony Thackeray; 8 Toby Williams; 9 Jamaine Wray; 10 Adam Sullivan; 11 Ian Brown; 12 Dave Buckley; 13 Rob Spicer. Subs (all used): 14 Jimmy Elston; 15 John Smith; 16 Ryan McDonald; 17 Nathan Priestley.
Tries: Buckley (2), Brown (9, 13, 19, 23), Mapals (26, 67), C Spurr (51, 73), Thackeray (71);
Goals: Thackeray 7/10.
Sin bin: McDonald (30) – fighting.
TOULOUSE: 1 Nicolas De Martini; 2 Cedric Olieu; 3 Sylvain Houles; 4 Sebastian Planas; 5 Fourcade Abasse; 6 Luke Branighan; 7 Constant Vilegas; 8 Jamie McDonald; 9 James Wynne; 10 Jamie Small; 11 David Delpoux; 12 Mathieu Almarcha; 13 Matthew Jobson. Subs (all used): 14 Nicolas Faure; 15 Peter Lima; 16 Cedric Prizzon; 17 Jerome Fabre.
Tries: Delpoux (4), De Martini (36, 49), Planas (59), Lima (65), Branighan (76); **Goals:** Branighan 2/6.
Sin bin: Small (30) - fighting; Jobson (30) - fighting.
Rugby Leaguer & League Express Men of the Match: *City Knights:* Lee Mapals; *Toulouse:* James Wynne.
Penalty count: 9-4; **Half-time:** 36-8;
Referee: Jamie Leahy; **Attendance:** 701.

CASTLEFORD TIGERS 88 CASTLEFORD LOCK LANE 10

TIGERS: 1 Richard Owen; 2 Alex Shenton; 3 Dwayne Barker; 4 Michael Knowles; 5 Adam Jones; 6 Ryan McGoldrick; 7 Eddie Croft; 8 Liam Higgins; 9 Sean Johnson; 10 Ryan Boyle; 11 Jason Payne; 12 Ryan Clayton; 13 Joe Westerman. Subs (all used): 14 Matthew Duckworth; 15 Nathan Massey; 16 Liam Watts; 17 Craig Potter.
Tries: A Shenton (8, 65), Westerman (13), Owen (16), Barker (24), Clayton (29), Johnson (32), Croft (42, 45), Jones (48, 80), Watts (54), Knowles (60), Duckworth (69), Boyle (72, 75);
Goals: Westerman 12/13, Owen 0/1, Knowles 0/2.
LOCK LANE: 1 Steven Bolderson; 2 John Bassinder; 3 Chris Chen; 4 Chris Stockton; 5 Craig Bettison; 6 John Astbury; 7 Robbie Mawson; 8 Wayne Hardy; 9 Joe Wilkinson; 10 Craig Jeffels; 11 Jamie Price; 12 Chris Tudor; 13 Mark Spears. Subs (all used): 14 Carl Robinson; 15 Paul Crouch; 16 James Rayner; 17 Richard Potts.
Tries: Bettison (2), Robinson (62); **Goals:** Hardy 1/2.
Sin bin: Tudor (52) – holding down.
Rugby Leaguer & League Express Men of the Match: *Tigers:* Dwayne Barker; *Lock Lane:* Mark Spears.
Penalty count: 11-4; **Half-time:** 36-4;
Referee: James Child; **Attendance:** 3,948.

HUNSLET HAWKS 40 ROCHDALE MAYFIELD 22

HAWKS: 1 Matt Bramald; 2 Andy Robinson; 3 Eddie Mack; 4 Danny Cook; 5 Steve Morton; 6 Mark Moxon; 7 Matt Firth; 8 Danny Ekis; 9 Darren Robinson; 10 Danny Murgatroyd; 11 Wayne Freeman; 12 Will Cartledge; 13 Gareth Greenwood. Subs (all used): 14 Nick Walker; 15 Karl Gunney; 16 Ben Walkin; 17 Matt Carbutt.
Tries: D Robinson (38), Freeman (40), Cook (45), A Robinson (50), Mack (64, 67), Bramald (77);
Goals: D Robinson 3/4, Bramald 3/3.
MAYFIELD: 1 Komah Naumatua; 2 Lepani Fugawai; 3 Chris Hilton; 4 Steve Wood; 5 Janan Billings; 6 Steve Gartland; 7 Pete Draper; 8 Chris Brett; 9 Neil Ramsden; 10 Tony Hilton; 11 Matt Williams; 12 Sam Wynn; 13 Matt Calland. Subs (all used): 14 Todd O'Brien; 15 Matt Gartland; 16 Terry Whaley; 17 Liam Hall.
Tries: Calland (5), Naumatua (20), S Gartland (23), Wood (72); **Goals:** S Gartland 3/3, M Gartland 0/1.
Rugby Leaguer & League Express Men of the Match: *Hawks:* Darren Robinson; *Mayfield:* Matt Calland.
Penalty count: 10-5; **Half-time:** 12-18;
Referee: Clint Sharrad; **Attendance:** 282.

ROUND 4

Friday 30th March 2007

BRADFORD BULLS 24 CASTLEFORD TIGERS 16

BULLS: 1 Marcus St Hilaire; 2 Nathan McAvoy; 3 Ben Harris; 17 James Evans; 5 Lesley Vainikolo; 6 Iestyn Harris; 7 Paul Deacon (C); 8 Joe Vagana; 9 Terry Newton; 10 Andy Lynch; 26 David Solomona; 11 Chris McKenna; 12 Glenn Morrison. Subs (all used): 14 Chris Feather; 15 Matt Cook; 16 Ian Henderson; 18 Sam Burgess.
Tries: Morrison (2), St Hilaire (19), Vainikolo (34), Solomona (66); **Goals:** Deacon 4/4.
TIGERS: 1 Tom Saxton; 2 Stuart Donlan; 3 Michael Shenton; 4 Kirk Dixon; 5 Michael Wainwright; 6 Ryan McGoldrick; 7 Danny Brough; 8 Liam Higgins; 9 Andrew Henderson; 10 Craig Huby; 11 Awen Guttenbeil; 12 Chris Charles; 13 Peter Lupton. Subs (all used): 14 Mark Leafa; 15 Tere Glassie; 16 Dwayne Barker; 17 Ryan Clayton.
Tries: Wainwright (9), M Shenton (53), Lupton (59);
Goals: Brough 2/3.
Rugby Leaguer & League Express Men of the Match: *Bulls:* David Solomona; *Tigers:* Danny Brough.
Penalty count: 13-11; **Half-time:** 18-6;
Referee: Ashley Klein; **Attendance:** 6,748.

GATESHEAD THUNDER 4 SALFORD CITY REDS 64

THUNDER: 1 Neil Thorman; 2 Matt Walton; 3 Graham Stephenson; 4 Pat Williamson; 5 Danny Wilson; 6 Tim Martin; 7 Kevin Till; 8 Jonny Scott; 9 Ryan Clarke; 10 Steven Bradley; 11 Shane Wooden; 12 Nick Hyde; 13 Odell Harris. Subs (all used): 14 Richie Metcalfe; 15 Steve Rutherford; 16 Matt Barron; 17 Tony Doherty.
Try: Clarke (60); **Goals:** Clarke 0/1.
CITY REDS: 2 David Hodgson; 15 Gray Viane (D); 22 Danny Halliwell; 23 Jordan Turner; 5 John Wilshere; 6 Luke Dorn; 7 Luke Robinson (C); 10 Michael Korkidas; 26 Stefan Ratchford (D); 14 Paul Highton; 19 Stuart Littler; 8 Andy Coley; 13 Simon Finnigan. Subs (all used): 20 David Gower; 16 Andrew Brocklehurst; 21 Stephen Nash (D); 17 Gareth Haggerty.
Tries: Coley (3), Hodgson (8, 63), Halliwell (16), Highton (21), Finnigan (25), Robinson (28, 34, 42, 50), Brocklehurst (53); **Goals:** Wilshere 10/11.
Rugby Leaguer & League Express Men of the Match: *Thunder:* Odell Harris; *City Reds:* Luke Robinson.
Penalty count: 8-6; **Half-time:** 0-40; **Referee:** Mike Dawber; **Attendance:** 1,283 *(at The Willows, Salford).*

LEEDS RHINOS 72 WORKINGTON TOWN 10

RHINOS: 23 Jordan Tansey; 2 Scott Donald; 3 Clinton Toopi; 20 Ashley Gibson; 5 Lee Smith; 6 Danny McGuire; 7 Rob Burrow; 15 Jamie Thackray; 9 Matt Diskin; 16 Ryan Bailey; 14 Ali Lauitiiti; 18 Ian Kirke; 13 Kevin Sinfield (C). Subs: 22 Carl Ablett; 8 Kylie Leuluai; 11 Jamie Jones-Buchanan; 10 Jamie Peacock (not used).
Tries: Donald (1, 15, 18, 22), Tansey (4, 29), Sinfield (35), Burrow (39, 45, 66), Lauitiiti (42), Ablett (53), Diskin (64); **Goals:** Sinfield 8/11, Burrow 2/2.
TOWN: 1 Rob Lunt; 2 Stephen Dawes; 3 Franco Kmet; 4 Andrew Beattie; 5 Martyn Wilson; 6 Carl Forber; 7 Steve Kirkbride; 8 Dean Vaughan; 9 Shaun Lunt; 10 Taani Lavulavu; 11 Darren King; 12 Jamie Beaumont; 13 Craig Walsh. Subs (all used): 14 James Robinson; 15 Allan McGuiness; 16 Garry Purdham; 17 Dean Burgess.
Tries: Dawes (71), King (75); **Goals:** Kirkbride 1/2.
Sin bin: Vaughan (63) – interference.
Rugby Leaguer & League Express Men of the Match: *Rhinos:* Rob Burrow; *Town:* Dean Burgess.
Penalty count: 14-2; **Half-time:** 42-0;
Referee: Jamie Leahy; **Attendance:** 3,576.

ST HELENS 78 BATLEY BULLDOGS 14

SAINTS: 1 Paul Wellens; 2 Ade Gardner; 3 Matt Gidley; 24 Steve Tyrer; 5 Francis Meli; 6 Leon Pryce; 7 Sean Long (C); 8 Nick Fozzard; 9 Keiron Cunningham; 18 Bryn Hargreaves; 11 Lee Gilmour; 15 Mike Bennett; 12 Jon Wilkin. Subs (all used): 17 James Graham; 20 Scott Moore; 22 Paul Clough; 23 Maurie Fa'asavalu.
Tries: Gardner (4), Wellens (6, 38), Meli (10, 69), Gilmour (13, 16), Gidley (18), Cunningham (26), Fa'asavalu (28, 31), Graham (43), Clough (45), Wilkin (51); **Goals:** Tyrer 11/14.
BULLDOGS: 1 Ashley Lindsay; 2 Alex Clemie; 3 Jason Mossop; 4 Chris Langley; 5 Oliver Marns; 6 Ian Gordon; 7 Jay Duffy; 8 David Best; 9 Kris Lythe; 10 Luke Stenchion; 11 Jack Watson; 12 Tim Spears; 13 Lee Paterson. Subs (all used): 14 Mark Barlow; 15 Jon Simpson; 16 Anthony Henderson; 17 Luke Menzies.
Tries: Spears (22), Lythe (34), Mossop (49);
Goals: Gordon 1/3.
Rugby Leaguer & League Express Men of the Match: *Saints:* Nick Fozzard; *Bulldogs:* Kris Lythe.
Penalty count: 10-4; **Half-time:** 56-10;
Referee: Robert Hicks; **Attendance:** 4,335.

Saturday 31st March 2007

WARRINGTON WOLVES 38
HULL KINGSTON ROVERS 10

WOLVES: 1 Stuart Reardon; 2 Henry Fa'afili; 3 Martin Gleeson; 5 Brent Grose; 18 Richie Barnett; 6 Chris Bridge; 9 Jon Clarke; 8 Chris Leikvoll; 14 Mark Gleeson; 16 Paul Wood; 12 Ben Westwood; 23 Mike Wainwright; 13 Vinnie Anderson. Subs (all used): 17 Michael Sullivan; 15 Rob Parker; 10 Paul Rauhihi (C); 19 Steve Pickersgill.
Tries: Grose (10, 78), Reardon (36), Anderson (49, 79), Bridge (58), Rauhihi (79); **Goals:** Bridge 5/7.
On report: Westwood (66) - alleged elbow on Gallagher.
ROVERS: 1 Ben Cockayne; 2 Jon Steel; 21 Luke Dyer; 22 Andreas Bauer; 5 Byron Ford; 6 Scott Murrell; 19 Matty Brooks; 8 Makali Aizue; 9 Ben Fisher; 15 Jim Gannon; 16 Jason Netherton; 18 Danny Ward (C); 13 Tommy Gallagher. Subs (all used): 4 Gareth Morton; 26 Dave Wilson; 27 Kirk Netherton; 10 David Tangata-Toa.
Tries: Tangata-Toa (13), K Netherton (69);
Goals: Murrell 0/1, Morton 1/1.
Rugby Leaguer & League Express Men of the Match: *Wolves:* Jon Clarke; *Rovers:* Ben Fisher.
Penalty count: 12-7; **Half-time:** 10-4;
Referee: Richard Silverwood; **Attendance:** 4,523.

PIA 8 HARLEQUINS 64

PIA: 1 Craig West; 2 Stephane Muniesa; 3 Josh Tatupu; 4 Florian Chaubet; 5 Nicolas Athiel; 6 Maxime Greseque; 7 Aaron Smith; 8 Sebastien Martins; 9 Mathias Garrabe; 10 Yannick Bois; 11 Maxime Pradal; 12 Guillaume Knecht; 13 Anthony Leger. Subs (all used): 14 Anthony Carrere; 15 Sylvain Fruteau; 16 Gregory Gimenez; 17 Nicolas Piquemal.
Tries: Carrere (61), Muniesa (66); **Goals:** Greseque 0/2.
HARLEQUINS: 16 Chris Melling; 24 Andy Smith; 3 Paul Sykes; 4 Tyrone Smith; 18 Matt Gafa; 7 Danny Orr; 1 Mark McLinden; 17 Louie McCarthy-Scarsbrook; 9 Chad Randall; 10 Daniel Heckenberg; 13 Rob Purdham (C); 12 Lee Hopkins; 6 Scott Hill. Subs (all used): 14 Julien Rinaldi; 15 David Mills; 20 Jon Grayshon; 23 Henry Paul.
Tries: Hill (9), Randall (13), Gafa (17), Sykes (27, 46), Hopkins (50), McCarthy-Scarsbrook (69, 76, 78), A Smith (72, 80); **Goals:** Purdham 3/4, Paul 7/7.
Rugby Leaguer & League Express Men of the Match: *Pia:* Maxime Greseque;
Harlequins: Louie McCarthy-Scarsbrook.
Penalty count: 6-8; **Half-time:** 0-22;
Referee: Ian Smith; **Attendance:** 300.

CATALANS DRAGONS 70 FEATHERSTONE ROVERS 12

DRAGONS: 14 Thomas Bosc; 25 Younes Khattabi; 18 Vincent Duport; 4 Adam Mogg; 5 Dimitri Pelo; 3 John Wilson; 7 Stacey Jones (C); 8 David Ferriol; 16 Lionel Teixido; 24 Remi Casty; 28 Andrew Bentley (D); 17 Cyril Gossard; 10 Jerome Guisset. Subs (all used): 20 Adel Fellous; 19 Alex Chan; 21 Julien Touxagas; 27 Kane Bentley (D).
Tries: Duport (4), A Bentley (11), Ferriol (14), Fellous (21), Khattabi (26), Chan (37), Gossard (50, 57), Bosc (62), Mogg (67, 80), Casty (77); **Goals:** Bosc 11/12.
ROVERS: 1 Nathan Larvin; 2 Danny Kirmond; 3 Jon Whittle; 4 Craig Bower; 5 Dean Colton; 6 Scott Glassell; 7 Paul Handforth; 8 James Houston; 9 Paul Hughes; 10 Stuart Dickens; 11 Jamie Field; 12 Steve Dooler; 13 Tom Haughey. Subs (all used): 14 Brian Sutton; 15 Gary Ellery; 16 Craig Cawthray; 17 James Ward.
Tries: Glassell (8), Dooler (70);
Goals: Dickens 1/1, Glassell 1/1.
Rugby Leaguer & League Express Men of the Match: *Dragons:* Stacey Jones; *Rovers:* Jamie Field.
Penalty count: 16-6; **Half-time:** 34-6;
Referee: Phil Bentham; **Attendance:** 1,545.

Sunday 1st April 2007

WIDNES VIKINGS 24 WIGAN WARRIORS 34

VIKINGS: 1 Scott Grix; 2 Damien Blanch; 3 Toa Kohe-Love; 4 Mick Nanyn; 5 Gavin Dodd; 6 Dennis Moran; 7 Andy Kain; 8 Jordan James; 9 Mark Smith; 10 Oliver Wilkes; 11 Lee Doran; 12 Paul Noone; 13 Bob Beswick. Subs (all used): 14 Aaron Summers; 15 Adam Sidlow; 16 Daryl Cardiss; 17 Mike Morrison.
Tries: Kohe-Love (8), Grix (60), James (75), Noone (79); **Goals:** Nanyn 4/6.
WARRIORS: 1 Chris Ashton; 2 Mark Calderwood; 3 Phil Bailey; 20 Darrell Goulding; 5 Pat Richards; 6 Trent Barrett; 7 Thomas Leuluai; 8 Stuart Fielden; 9 Mick Higham; 10 Iafeta Palea'aesina; 11 Gareth Hock; 12 Bryan Fletcher; 13 Sean O'Loughlin (C). Subs (all used): 16 Shane Millard; 18 Paul Prescott; 19 Harrison Hansen; 21 Danny Hill.
Tries: O'Loughlin (20), Leuluai (44), Richards (65, 72), Goulding (67), Barrett (70); **Goals:** Richards 5/6.
Rugby Leaguer & League Express Men of the Match: *Vikings:* Bob Beswick; *Warriors:* Gareth Hock.
Penalty count: 8-8; **Half-time:** 8-4;
Referee: Steve Ganson; **Attendance:** 6,006.

DEWSBURY RAMS 28 SHEFFIELD EAGLES 46

RAMS: 1 Ian Preece; 2 Bryn Powell; 3 Andrew Bostock; 4 Danny Maun; 5 Lee Close; 6 Francis Maloney; 7 Dean Lawford; 8 Andy Hobson; 9 Liam Finn; 10 Dominic Maloney; 11 Kevin Crouthers; 12 Alex Bretherton; 13 Josh Weeden. Subs (all used): 14 Luke Haigh; 15 Andy Spink; 16 Martin Robinson; 17 David Bates.
Tries: Crouthers (4), Bretherton (11), Weeden (19), Maun (25), Close (57), Preece (62);
Goals: F Maloney 2/5, Lawford 0/1.
Sin bin: F Maloney (50) – fighting.
EAGLES: 1 Johnny Woodcock; 2 Greg Hurst; 3 Damien Reid; 4 Richard Newlove; 5 James Ford; 6 Brendon Lindsay; 7 Gavin Brown; 8 Jack Howieson; 9 Paul Pickering; 10 Tom Buckenham; 11 Tommy Trayler; 12 Ged Corcoran; 13 Adam Hayes. Subs (all used): 14 Neil Law; 15 Jon Aston; 16 Dale Holdstock; 17 Mitchell Stringer.
Tries: Hurst (7, 72), Pickering (14), Holdstock (29, 76), Woodcock (47, 55); **Goals:** Woodcock 9/10.
Dismissal: Reid (25) – striking.
Sin bin: Holdstock (50) – fighting.
Rugby Leaguer & League Express Men of the Match: *Rams:* Liam Finn; *Eagles:* Johnny Woodcock.
Penalty count: 6-11; **Half-time:** 18-20;
Referee: Dave Merrick; **Attendance:** 1,038.

HUDDERSFIELD GIANTS 74 YORK CITY KNIGHTS 4

GIANTS: 7 Robbie Paul; 2 Martin Aspinwall; 5 Shane Elford; 11 Chris Nero; 1 Paul Reilly; 4 Kevin Brown; 9 Brad Drew (C); 16 Keith Mason; 19 Ryan Hudson; 10 John Skandalis; 20 Steve Snitch; 3 Jamahl Lolesi; 12 Andy Raleigh. Subs (all used): 8 Eorl Crabtree; 13 Stephen Wild; 14 Stuart Jones; 18 Darrell Griffin.
Tries: Skandalis (3), Snitch (20, 34, 62), Reilly (23, 50), Aspinwall (37), Lolesi (44), Paul (54), Hudson (57), Elford (71, 74), Nero (78); **Goals:** Drew 11/14.
CITY KNIGHTS: 1 George Rayner; 2 Lee Mapals; 3 Ryan Esders; 4 Chris Spurr; 5 Lee Lingard; 6 Scott Rhodes; 7 Andy Gargan; 8 Tabua Cakacaka; 9 Jamaine Wray; 10 Adam Sullivan; 11 Dave Buckley; 12 Nathan Priestley; 13 Jon Liddell. Subs (all used): 14 Jimmy Elston; 15 John Smith; 16 Ryan McDonald; 17 Toby Williams.
Try: C Spurr (67); **Goals:** Wray 0/1.
Rugby Leaguer & League Express Men of the Match: *Giants:* Steve Snitch; *City Knights:* Scott Rhodes.
Penalty count: 10-3; **Half-time:** 30-0;
Referee: Ben Thaler; **Attendance:** 2,137.

KEIGHLEY COUGARS 16 OLDHAM 26

COUGARS: 1 Matt Foster; 2 Sam Gardner; 3 Michael Hastings; 4 Mick Fogerty; 5 Gavin Duffy; 6 Craig Fawcett; 7 Barry Eaton; 8 Simon Bissell; 9 James Feather; 10 Tom Palmer; 11 Greg Nicholson; 12 Richard Knight; 13 Chris Redfearn. Subs (all used): 14 Andy Feather; 15 Wayne Sutcliffe; 16 Brendan Rawlins; 17 Luke Sutton.
Tries: Duffy (28), Nicholson (33), Knight (54);
Goals: Eaton 2/4.
OLDHAM: 1 Paul O'Connor; 2 Gareth Langley; 3 Craig Littler; 4 Drew Houston; 5 Alex Wilkinson; 6 Mark Ogden; 7 Neil Roden; 8 Jason Boults; 9 Simeon Hoyle; 10 Richard Mervill; 11 Ian Hodson; 12 Ian Sinfield; 13 Kris Smith. Subs (all used): 14 Wes Rogers; 15 Said Tamghart; 16 Andy Crabtree; 17 Paul Ashton.
Tries: Langley (45, 69), Ashton (49), Smith (74, 77);
Goals: Ashton 3/5.
Rugby Leaguer & League Express Men of the Match: *Cougars:* Matt Foster; *Oldham:* Ian Sinfield.
Penalty count: 8-8; **Half-time:** 8-0;
Referee: Paul Carr; **Attendance:** 1,039.

ROCHDALE HORNETS 20 CELTIC CRUSADERS 16

HORNETS: 1 Chris Giles; 2 Eric Andrews; 3 Lee Patterson; 4 Kevin King; 5 Bolu Fagborun; 6 Simon Svabic; 7 Gary Hulse; 8 Simon Baldwin; 9 Dave McConnell; 10 Byron Smith; 11 Paul Anderson; 12 Mark Blanchard; 13 Tommy Goulden. Subs (all used): 14 Phil Hasty; 15 Craig Robinson; 16 Andy Gorski; 17 Paul Norman.
Tries: Giles (19), Patterson (28), Hulse (44), Andrews (79); **Goals:** King 2/4.
CRUSADERS: 1 Damien Quinn; 2 Grant Epton; 3 Rob Toshack; 4 Mark Dalle Cort; 5 Craig Richards; 6 Luke Young; 7 Jace Van Dijk; 8 Josh Cale; 9 Neil Budworth; 10 Gareth Dean; 11 Terry Martin; 12 Dean Fitzgerald; 13 Darren Mapp. Subs (all used): 14 Richard Johnston; 15 Jamie I'Anson; 16 Phil Cushion; 17 Hywel Davies.
Tries: Richards (3), Quinn (7), Cushion (34);
Goals: Quinn 2/3.
Rugby Leaguer & League Express Men of the Match: *Hornets:* Gary Hulse; *Crusaders:* Jace Van Dijk.
Penalty count: 6-6; **Half-time:** 8-16;
Referee: Peter Taberner; **Attendance:** 482.

SWINTON LIONS 14 BARROW RAIDERS 47

LIONS: 1 Wayne English; 2 Andy Saywell; 3 Darren Woods; 4 Mark Brocklehurst; 5 Desi Williams; 6 Martin Moana; 7 Liam McGovern; 8 Bruce Johnson; 9 Phil Wood; 10 Gareth Hayes; 11 Mike Smith; 12 Chris Morley; 13 Lee Marsh. Subs (all used): 14 Craig Ashall; 15 Craig Farrimond; 16 Dave Newton; 17 Rob Line.
Tries: D Woods (28), Morley (63), Smith (72);
Goals: McGovern 1/3.
RAIDERS: 1 Khamal Ganley; 2 Nick Beach; 3 Phil Atkinson; 4 Liam Harrison; 5 James Nixon; 6 Liam Finch; 7 Darren Holt; 8 Paul Raftrey; 9 Andy Ellis; 10 Brett McDermott; 11 Martin Ostler; 12 Dave Armistead; 13 Mike Whitehead. Subs (all used): 14 Jamie Marshall; 15 Geoff Luxon; 16 Paul Wilcock; 17 Lee Dutton.
Tries: Nixon (11, 69), Wilcock (24), Atkinson (33), Holt (43), Ostler (54), Marshall (77), Ganley (80);
Goals: Holt 7/10; **Field goal:** Holt (61).
Rugby Leaguer & League Express Men of the Match: *Lions:* Lee Marsh; *Raiders:* Darren Holt.
Penalty count: 9-9; **Half-time:** 4-18;
Referee: Pascal Mombet; **Attendance:** 596.

WHITEHAVEN 36 HALIFAX 8

WHITEHAVEN: 1 Gary Broadbent; 2 Craig Calvert; 3 Scott McAvoy; 4 Derry Eilbeck; 5 Steve Maden; 6 Carl Rudd; 7 Marc Bainbridge; 8 Steve Trindall; 9 Aaron Smith; 10 Scott Teare; 11 Spencer Miller; 12 Richard Fletcher; 13 Aaron Lester. Subs (all used): 14 Carl Sice; 15 Leroy Joe; 16 Graeme Mattinson; 17 Howard Hill.
Tries: Fletcher (9, 29), Rudd (52), S McAvoy (56), Sice (74); **Goals:** Rudd 8/8.
HALIFAX: 1 Damian Gibson; 2 Damian Munro; 3 Mark Roberts; 4 Richard Varkulis; 5 Marcus George; 6 Tim Hartley; 7 Ian Watson; 8 Andy Shickell; 9 Sam Hoare; 10 Aaron Trinder; 11 David Wrench; 12 Damian Ball; 13 Phil Joseph. Subs (all used): 14 Sean Penkywicz; 15 Paul Southern; 16 Danny Heaton; 17 Frank Watene.
Try: Wrench (27); **Goals:** Hartley 2/2.
Rugby Leaguer & League Express Men of the Match: *Whitehaven:* Carl Rudd; *Halifax:* Tim Hartley.
Penalty count: 12-14; **Half-time:** 14-8;
Referee: Ronnie Laughton; **Attendance:** 2,128.

HUNSLET HAWKS 0 HULL FC 78

HAWKS: 1 Matt Bramald; 2 Andy Robinson; 3 David Foster; 4 Gareth Naylor; 5 Steve Morton; 6 Mark Moxon; 7 Matt Firth; 8 Danny Ekis; 9 Gareth Greenwood; 10 Scott Houston; 11 Wayne Freeman; 12 Will Cartledge; 13 Darren Robinson. Subs (all used): 14 Danny Cook; 15 Ben Walkin; 16 Matt Carbutt; 17 Danny Murgatroyd.
HULL: 1 Shaun Briscoe; 2 Matt Sing; 20 Richard Whiting; 3 Kirk Yeaman; 22 Craig Hall (D); 14 Motu Tony; 7 Richard Horne; 8 Ewan Dowes; 18 Wayne Godwin; 26 Scott Wheeldon; 11 Lee Radford (C); 17 Willie Manu; 12 Shayne McMenemy. Subs (all used): 13 Danny Washbrook; 25 Matty Dale; 19 Graeme Horne; 21 Hutch Maiava.
Tries: Yeaman (4, 27), McMenemy (7), Hall (13, 17, 54), R Horne (23), Wheeldon (30), Sing (34), Manu (36, 74), Dale (58), Godwin (62, 69); **Goals:** Hall 11/14.
Rugby Leaguer & League Express Men of the Match: *Hawks:* Danny Ekis; *Hull:* Craig Hall.
Penalty count: 2-8; **Half-time:** 0-52;
Referee: Craig Halloran; **Attendance:** 5,062
(at Kingston Communications Stadium, Hull).

LONDON SKOLARS 4
WAKEFIELD TRINITY WILDCATS 52

SKOLARS: 1 Pete Hodgkinson; 2 Corey Simms; 3 Chris Shears; 4 Ashley Tozer; 5 Johnny Williams; 6 James Nowland; 7 Paul Thorman; 8 Alan Barker; 9 Gareth Honor; 10 Richard Louw; 11 Kurt Pittman; 12 Lydan Maitua; 13 Jermaine Coleman. Subs (all used): 14 Frank Reid; 15 William Webster; 16 Dave Brown; 17 Warren Heilig.
Try: Shears (13); **Goals:** Nowland 0/1.
Sin bin: Thorman (28) – professional foul.
WILDCATS: 21 Matt Blaymire; 22 Peter Fox; 1 Mark Field; 4 Ryan Atkins; 2 Waine Pryce; 14 Paul March; 7 Ben Jeffries (C); 10 Danny Sculthorpe; 17 Kevin Henderson; 19 Danny Lima; 11 Ned Catic; 23 Jason Golden; 13 Brett Ferres. Subs (all used): 24 Dale Ferguson (D); 25 Richard Moore; 27 Austin Buchanan; 31 Aaron Murphy (D).
Tries: Fox (5), Pryce (22), Golden (25), P March (29), Catic (34), Ferres (46), Henderson (51, 59), Murphy (67), Jeffries (73), Buchanan (79);
Goals: P March 3/5, Ferres 1/6.
Rugby Leaguer & League Express Men of the Match: *Skolars:* Jermaine Coleman; *Wildcats:* Brett Ferres.
Penalty count: 6-6; **Half-time:** 4-22; **Referee:** Gareth Hewer; **Attendance:** 2,427 *(at Belle Vue, Wakefield).*

ROUND 5

Friday 11th May 2007

SALFORD CITY REDS 10 HUDDERSFIELD GIANTS 36

CITY REDS: 2 David Hodgson; 15 Gray Viane; 19 Stuart Littler; 3 Kevin McGuinness; 5 John Wilshere; 6 Luke Dorn; 7 Luke Robinson; 24 Lee Jewitt; 9 Malcolm Alker (C); 10 Michael Korkidas; 8 Andy Coley; 16 Andrew Brocklehurst; 13 Simon Finnigan. Subs (all used): 17 Gareth Haggerty; 20 David Gower; 26 Stefan Ratchford; 11 Mark Edmondson.
Tries: Dorn (24), Littler (63); **Goals:** Wilshere 1/2.
GIANTS: 6 Chris Thorman (C); 1 Paul Reilly; 3 Jamahl Lolesi; 11 Chris Nero; 2 Martin Aspinwall; 4 Kevin Brown; 9 Brad Drew; 16 Keith Mason; 19 Ryan Hudson; 10 John Skandalis; 20 Steve Snitch; 12 Andy Raleigh; 13 Stephen Wild. Subs (all used): 7 Robbie Paul; 8 Eorl Crabtree; 15 Paul Jackson; 18 Darrell Griffin.
Tries: Brown (28, 39), Wild (53), Paul (67), Lolesi (76), Nero (80); **Goals:** Thorman 6/7.
Rugby Leaguer & League Express Men of the Match: *City Reds:* Malcolm Alker; *Giants:* Brad Drew.
Penalty count: 1-4; **Half-time:** 6-14;
Referee: Richard Silverwood; **Attendance:** 2,694.

ST HELENS 70 ROCHDALE HORNETS 10

SAINTS: 1 Paul Wellens; 2 Ade Gardner; 3 Matt Gidley; 4 Willie Talau; 5 Francis Meli; 6 Leon Pryce; 21 Matty Smith; 17 James Graham; 14 James Roby; 10 Jason Cayless; 12 Jon Wilkin; 13 Paul Sculthorpe (C); 18 Bryn Hargreaves. Subs (all used): 8 Nick Fozzard; 9 Keiron Cunningham; 22 Paul Clough; 23 Maurie Fa'asavalu.
Tries: Meli (9, 53), Wilkin (15, 48, 79), Graham (25), Wellens (32, 36), Gardner (39, 44), Sculthorpe (60), Fa'asavalu (75); **Goals:** Sculthorpe 11/12.
HORNETS: 1 Gary Hulse; 2 Eric Andrews; 3 Lee Patterson; 4 Kevin King; 5 Bolu Fagborun; 6 Simon Svabic; 7 Phil Hasty; 8 Andy Bailey; 9 Wayne Corcoran; 10 Byron Smith; 11 Andy Gorski; 12 John Gledhill; 13 Tommy Goulden. Subs (all used): 14 Dave McConnell; 15 Iain Marsh; 16 Craig Robinson; 17 Ryan Benjafield.
Tries: Fagborun (55), Andrews (66); **Goals:** King 1/2.
Rugby Leaguer & League Express Men of the Match: *Saints:* Paul Sculthorpe; *Hornets:* Tommy Goulden.
Penalty count: 4-2; **Half-time:** 36-0;
Referee: Ronnie Laughton; **Attendance:** 3,586.

Saturday 12th May 2007

LEEDS RHINOS 18 WIGAN WARRIORS 22

RHINOS: 1 Brent Webb; 2 Scott Donald; 3 Clinton Toopi; 4 Keith Senior; 5 Lee Smith; 6 Danny McGuire; 7 Rob Burrow; 10 Jamie Peacock; 9 Matt Diskin; 8 Kylie Leuluai; 11 Jamie Jones-Buchanan; 12 Gareth Ellis; 13 Kevin Sinfield (C). Subs (all used): 15 Jamie Thackray; 16 Ryan Bailey; 14 Ali Lauitiiti; 18 Ian Kirke.
Tries: Toopi (4), Webb (30, 60); **Goals:** Sinfield 3/3.
WARRIORS: 1 Chris Ashton; 2 Mark Calderwood; 3 Phil Bailey; 14 David Vaealiki; 5 Pat Richards; 6 Trent Barrett; 7 Thomas Leuluai; 8 Stuart Fielden; 16 Shane Millard; 10 Iafeta Palea'aesina; 11 Gareth Hock; 12 Bryan Fletcher; 13 Sean O'Loughlin (C). Subs (all used): 24 Eamon O'Carroll; 9 Mick Higham; 19 Harrison Hansen; 20 Darrell Goulding.
Tries: Ashton (9), O'Loughlin (21), Calderwood (51);
Goals: Richards 5/5.
On report: Bailey (44) - alleged dangerous tackle.
Rugby Leaguer & League Express Men of the Match: *Rhinos:* Brent Webb; *Warriors:* Trent Barrett.
Penalty count: 12-5; **Half-time:** 12-12;
Referee: Phil Bentham; **Attendance:** 9,612.

Sunday 13th May 2007

OLDHAM 6 HARLEQUINS 66

OLDHAM: 1 Paul O'Connor; 2 Gareth Langley; 3 Craig Littler; 4 Drew Houston; 5 Alex Wilkinson; 6 Neil Roden; 7 Paul Ashton; 8 Jason Boults; 9 Simeon Hoyle; 10 Wes Rogers; 11 Chris Baines; 12 Geno Costin; 13 Andy Crabtree. Subs (all used): 14 John Hough; 15 Said Tamghart; 16 Richard Mervill; 17 Andy Gorey.
Try: Ashton (35); **Goals:** Ashton 1/1.
HARLEQUINS: 16 Chris Melling; 2 Jon Wells; 3 Paul Sykes; 4 Tyrone Smith; 24 Andy Smith; 7 Danny Orr; 1 Mark McLinden; 8 Karl Temata; 9 Chad Randall; 10 Daniel Heckenberg; 13 Rob Purdham (C); 12 Lee Hopkins; 6 Scott Hill. Subs (all used): 14 Julien Rinaldi; 15 David Mills; 20 Jon Grayshon; 26 Joe Walsh.
Tries: Melling (1, 55), Sykes (12, 18, 31), Temata (20, 79), McLinden (25, 67), Grayshon (46), A Smith (65, 76); **Goals:** Purdham 9/12.
Rugby Leaguer & League Express Men of the Match: *Oldham:* Geno Costin; *Harlequins:* Karl Temata.
Penalty count: 6-8; **Half-time:** 6-34; **Referee:** Craig Halloran; **Attendance:** 559 *(at Park Lane, Sedgley Park).*

WAKEFIELD TRINITY WILDCATS 4
BRADFORD BULLS 14

WILDCATS: 6 Jamie Rooney; 3 Jason Demetriou (C); 26 Luke George (D); 4 Ryan Atkins; 28 Paul White; 14 Paul March; 9 Sam Obst; 25 Richard Moore; 15 David March; 12 Duncan MacGillivray; 17 Kevin Henderson; 11 Ned Catic; 13 Brett Ferres. Subs (all used): 21 Matt Blaymire; 7 Ben Jeffries; 23 Jason Golden; 16 Ricky Bibey.
Try: White (28); **Goals:** Rooney 0/1.
BULLS: 19 Michael Platt; 2 Nathan McAvoy; 3 Ben Harris; 17 James Evans; 5 Lesley Vainikolo; 6 Iestyn Harris; 7 Paul Deacon (C); 18 Sam Burgess; 16 Ian Henderson; 10 Andy Lynch; 26 David Solomona; 12 Glenn Morrison; 13 Jamie Langley. Subs (all used): 1 Marcus St Hilaire; 14 Chris Feather; 11 Chris McKenna; 15 Matt Cook.
Tries: Vainikolo (7, 23), Cook (70); **Goals:** Deacon 1/3.
Rugby Leaguer & League Express Men of the Match: *Wildcats:* Jamie Rooney; *Bulls:* Lesley Vainikolo.
Penalty count: 4-10; **Half-time:** 4-10;
Referee: Ian Smith; **Attendance:** 3,700.

WARRINGTON WOLVES 48 BARROW RAIDERS 16

WOLVES: 1 Stuart Reardon; 2 Henry Fa'afili; 3 Martin Gleeson; 5 Brent Grose; 18 Richie Barnett; 13 Vinnie Anderson; 7 Lee Briers (C); 10 Paul Rauhihi; 9 Jon Clarke; 11 Adrian Morley; 12 Ben Westwood; 4 Paul Johnson; 23 Mike Wainwright. Subs (all used): 8 Chris Leikvoll; 14 Mark Gleeson; 15 Rob Parker; 22 Ben Harrison.
Tries: Anderson (12, 16, 45), Martin Gleeson (32, 63), Mark Gleeson (39), Grose (42), Barnett (68, 71);
Goals: Briers 6/9.
RAIDERS: 1 Khamal Ganley; 2 Nick Beach; 3 James Finch; 4 Liam Harrison; 5 James Nixon; 6 Mike Basan; 7 Liam Finch; 8 Paul Raftrey; 9 Andy Ellis; 10 Lee Dutton; 11 Paul Wilcock; 12 Dave Armistead; 13 Mike Whitehead. Subs (all used): 14 Jamie Marshall; 15 Shane Irabor; 16 Brett McDermott; 17 Ian Rawlinson.
Tries: McDermott (24), Ganley (54), Beach (78);
Goals: Beach 2/3.
Rugby Leaguer & League Express Men of the Match:
Wolves: Vinnie Anderson; *Raiders:* Liam Finch.
Penalty count: 6-3; **Half-time:** 22-6;
Referee: Thierry Alibert; **Attendance:** 4,184.

WHITEHAVEN 14 CATALANS DRAGONS 24

WHITEHAVEN: 1 Gary Broadbent; 2 Craig Calvert; 3 Derry Eilbeck; 4 Rob Jackson; 5 Steve Maden; 6 Carl Rudd; 7 John Duffy; 8 Steve Trindall; 9 Graeme Mattinson; 10 David Fatialofa; 11 Spencer Miller; 12 Richard Fletcher; 13 Aaron Smith. Subs (all used): 14 Carl Sice; 15 Leroy Joe; 16 Ricky Wright; 17 Scott Teare.
Tries: Calvert (29), R Jackson (70), Maden (79);
Goals: Rudd 1/3.
DRAGONS: 1 Clint Greenshields; 2 Justin Murphy; 3 John Wilson; 4 Adam Mogg; 18 Vincent Duport; 14 Thomas Bosc; 7 Stacey Jones (C); 10 Jerome Guisset; 27 Kane Bentley; 19 Alex Chan; 21 Julien Touxagas; 17 Cyril Gossard; 13 Gregory Mounis. Subs (all used): 8 Mathieu Griffi; 6 Casey McGuire; 16 Lionel Teixido.
Tries: Bosc (7), Duport (37), Touxagas (45), K Bentley (73); **Goals:** Bosc 4/4.
Sin bin: K Bentley (22) - interference.
Rugby Leaguer & League Express Men of the Match:
Whitehaven: John Duffy; *Dragons:* Thomas Bosc.
Penalty count: 12-9; **Half-time:** 4-12;
Referee: Ben Thaler; **Attendance:** 3,008.

HULL FC 44 SHEFFIELD EAGLES 6

HULL: 1 Shaun Briscoe; 2 Matt Sing; 22 Craig Hall; 3 Kirk Yeaman; 14 Motu Tony; 7 Richard Horne; 23 Tommy Lee; 10 Garreth Carvell; 18 Wayne Godwin; 26 Scott Wheeldon; 11 Lee Radford (C); 17 Willie Manu; 13 Danny Washbrook. Subs (all used): 25 Matty Dale; 20 Richard Whiting; 21 Hutch Maiava; 15 Paul King.
Tries: Godwin (5), Hall (21, 61, 76), R Horne (31), Briscoe (56), Yeaman (58), Maiava (79); **Goals:** Hall 6/8.
EAGLES: 1 Johnny Woodcock; 2 James Ford; 3 Damien Reid; 4 Caldon Bravo; 5 Zac Hill; 6 Brendon Lindsay; 7 Dominic Brambani; 8 Tom Buckenham; 9 Craig Cook; 10 Mitchell Stringer; 11 Tommy Trayler; 12 Ged Corcoran; 13 Adam Hayes. Subs (all used): 14 Gavin Brown; 15 Grant Edwards; 16 Paul Pickering; 17 Ryan Hepworth.
Try: Buckenham (34); **Goals:** Woodcock 1/1.
Rugby Leaguer & League Express Men of the Match:
Hull: Willie Manu; *Eagles:* Brendon Lindsay.
Penalty count: 8-3; **Half-time:** 18-6;
Referee: Gareth Hewer; **Attendance:** 4,363.

QUARTER FINALS

Friday 8th June 2007

WIGAN WARRIORS 25 HARLEQUINS 6

WARRIORS: 1 Chris Ashton; 2 Mark Calderwood; 3 Phil Bailey; 14 David Vaealiki; 5 Pat Richards; 6 Trent Barrett; 7 Thomas Leuluai; 8 Stuart Fielden; 9 Mick Higham; 10 Iafeta Palea'aesina; 11 Gareth Hock; 12 Bryan Fletcher; 13 Sean O'Loughlin (C). Subs (all used): 25 Michael McIlorum (D); 19 Harrison Hansen; 20 Darrell Goulding; 18 Paul Prescott.
Tries: Ashton (5), Calderwood (47), O'Loughlin (80); **Goals:** Richards 4/5;
Field goal: Barrett (76).
HARLEQUINS: 16 Chris Melling; 24 Andy Smith; 3 Paul Sykes; 4 Tyrone Smith; 2 Jon Wells; 7 Danny Orr; 1 Mark McLinden (C); 8 Karl Temata; 9 Chad Randall; 15 David Mills; 18 Matt Gafa; 12 Lee Hopkins; 23 Henry Paul. Subs (all used): 14 Julien Rinaldi; 17 Louie McCarthy-Scarsbrook; 22 Michael Worrincy; 30 Steve Bannister (D).
Try: Bannister (43); **Goals:** Sykes 1/1.
Dismissal: Wells (53) - use of the elbow.
Rugby Leaguer & League Express Men of the Match:
Warriors: Sean O'Loughlin; *Harlequins:* Julien Rinaldi.
Penalty count: 4-5; **Half-time:** 12-0;
Referee: Ben Thaler; **Attendance:** 10,835.

Saturday 9th June 2007

ST HELENS 25 WARRINGTON WOLVES 14

SAINTS: 1 Paul Wellens; 2 Ade Gardner; 3 Matt Gidley; 4 Willie Talau; 5 Francis Meli; 6 Leon Pryce; 7 Sean Long (C); 8 Nick Fozzard; 9 Keiron Cunningham; 10 Jason Cayless; 11 Lee Gilmour; 12 Jon Wilkin; 22 Paul Clough. Subs (all used): 14 James Roby; 17 James Graham; 23 Maurie Fa'asavalu.
Tries: Gilmour (1, 60), Talau (42), Gardner (47), Roby (75); **Goals:** Long 0/1, Wellens 2/5;

Catalans' Vincent Duport holds off Wigan's Mark Calderwood to score

Field goal: Long (72).
WOLVES: 5 Brent Grose; 26 Kevin Penny; 4 Paul Johnson; 2 Henry Fa'afili; 24 Chris Riley; 9 Jon Clarke; 7 Lee Briers (C); 16 Paul Wood; 14 Mark Gleeson; 11 Adrian Morley; 12 Ben Westwood; 15 Rob Parker; 23 Mike Wainwright. Subs (all used): 10 Paul Rauhihi; 22 Michael Sullivan; 21 Andy Bracek; 19 Steve Pickersgill.
Tries: Penny (27), Fa'afili (30); **Goals:** Briers 3/3.
Rugby Leaguer & League Express Men of the Match:
Saints: Lee Gilmour; *Wolves:* Paul Wood.
Penalty count: 8-6; **Half-time:** 4-12;
Referee: Richard Silverwood; **Attendance:** 8,503.

Sunday 10th June 2007

BRADFORD BULLS 52 HUDDERSFIELD GIANTS 20

BULLS: 19 Michael Platt; 1 Marcus St Hilaire; 2 Nathan McAvoy; 3 Ben Harris; 5 Lesley Vainikolo; 6 Iestyn Harris; 7 Paul Deacon (C); 8 Joe Vagana; 9 Terry Newton; 10 Andy Lynch; 26 David Solomona; 11 Chris McKenna; 12 Glenn Morrison. Subs (all used): 18 Sam Burgess; 13 Jamie Langley; 16 Ian Henderson; 20 Tame Tupou (D).
Tries: B Harris (5, 49), Solomona (13), Henderson (28), St Hilaire (37), Burgess (42), Tupou (60, 80), Newton (65); **Goals:** Deacon 8/10.
GIANTS: 6 Chris Thorman (C); 2 Martin Aspinwall; 11 Chris Nero; 3 Jamahl Lolesi; 1 Paul Reilly; 4 Kevin Brown; 9 Brad Drew; 16 Keith Mason; 19 Ryan Hudson; 10 John Skandalis; 20 Steve Snitch; 13 Stephen Wild; 8 Eorl Crabtree. Subs (all used): 7 Robbie Paul; 15 Paul Jackson; 24 Rod Jensen (D); 18 Darrell Griffin.
Tries: Nero (30), Lolesi (67), Paul (71), Hudson (73); **Goals:** Thorman 0/1, Drew 2/3.
Sin bin: Lolesi (13) - alleged late challenge on Deacon.
On report: Lolesi (13) - alleged late challenge on Deacon.
Rugby Leaguer & League Express Men of the Match:
Bulls: Ian Henderson; *Giants:* Brad Drew.
Penalty count: 6-6; **Half-time:** 24-4;
Referee: Phil Bentham; **Attendance:** 7,811.

HULL FC 23 CATALANS DRAGONS 26

HULL: 1 Shaun Briscoe; 2 Matt Sing; 4 Sid Domic; 3 Kirk Yeaman; 14 Motu Tony; 6 Richard Horne; 23 Tommy Lee; 8 Ewan Dowes; 18 Wayne Godwin; 10 Garreth Carvell; 11 Lee Radford (C); 17 Willie Manu; 16 Danny Tickle. Subs (all used): 14 Motu Tony; 13 Danny Washbrook; 15 Paul King; 21 Hutch Maiava.
Tries: Briscoe (34), King (50), Domic (80);
Goals: Tickle 5/5; **Field goal:** R Horne (61).
Sin bin: Godwin (69) - late challenge on Jones.
DRAGONS: 1 Clint Greenshields; 2 Justin Murphy; 3 John Wilson; 4 Adam Mogg; 25 Younes Khattabi; 14 Thomas Bosc; 7 Stacey Jones (C); 10 Jerome Guisset; 26 Luke Quigley; 15 Mathieu Griffi; 21 Julien Touxagas; 17 Cyril Gossard; 19 Alex Chan. Subs (all used): 28 Andrew Bentley; 27 Kane Bentley; 8 David Ferriol; 16 Lionel Teixido.
Tries: Mogg (5, 29), Wilson (15), Greenshields (72);
Goals: Bosc 4/5; **Field goals:** Guisset (67), Bosc (75).
Rugby Leaguer & League Express Men of the Match:
Hull: Willie Manu; *Dragons:* Clint Greenshields.
Penalty count: 5-7; **Half-time:** 8-16;
Referee: Ashley Klein; **Attendance:** 7,441.

SEMI-FINALS

Saturday 28th July 2007

BRADFORD BULLS 14 ST HELENS 35

BULLS: 19 Michael Platt; 1 Marcus St Hilaire; 3 Ben Harris; 17 James Evans; 20 Tame Tupou; 6 Iestyn Harris; 7 Paul Deacon (C); 8 Joe Vagana; 9 Terry Newton; 10 Andy Lynch; 26 David Solomona; 11 Chris McKenna; 12 Glenn Morrison. Subs (all used): 2 Nathan McAvoy; 16 Ian Henderson; 18 Sam Burgess; 23 Matt James.
Tries: Evans (16), Tupou (55), Vagana (67);
Goals: Deacon 1/3.
SAINTS: 1 Paul Wellens; 2 Ade Gardner; 3 Matt Gidley; 4 Willie Talau; 5 Francis Meli; 6 Leon Pryce; 7 Sean Long (C); 8 Nick Fozzard; 9 Keiron Cunningham; 17 James Graham; 11 Lee Gilmour; 15 Mike Bennett; 12 Jon Wilkin. Subs (all used): 14 James Roby; 18 Bryn Hargreaves; 22 Paul Clough; 23 Maurie Fa'asavalu.
Tries: Talau (3), Meli (21), Gidley (33), Clough (57), Pryce (69), Bennett (74); **Goals:** Long 4/5, Wellens 1/1;
Field goal: Long (40).
Rugby Leaguer & League Express Men of the Match:
Bulls: Ian Henderson; *Saints:* Sean Long.
Penalty count: 11-10; **Half-time:** 4-17;
Referee: Richard Silverwood; **Attendance:** 14,316
(at Galpharm Stadium, Huddersfield).

Sunday 29th July 2007

CATALANS DRAGONS 37 WIGAN WARRIORS 24

DRAGONS: 1 Clint Greenshields; 18 Vincent Duport; 3 John Wilson; 4 Adam Mogg; 25 Younes Khattabi; 6 Casey McGuire; 7 Stacey Jones (C); 19 Alex Chan; 26 Luke Quigley; 10 Jerome Guisset; 11 Sebastien Raguin; 12 Jason Croker; 13 Gregory Mounis. Subs (all used): 8 David Ferriol; 15 Mathieu Griffi; 17 Cyril Gossard; 21 Julien Touxagas.
Tries: McGuire (3), Wilson (9), Mogg (14), Duport (19, 49), Croker (72); **Goals:** Jones 6/7;
Field goal: Jones (54).
Sin bin: Jones (62) - delaying restart.
WARRIORS: 5 Pat Richards; 2 Mark Calderwood; 3 Phil Bailey; 14 David Vaealiki; 23 Liam Colbon; 6 Trent Barrett; 7 Thomas Leuluai; 8 Stuart Fielden; 9 Mick Higham; 10 Iafeta Palea'aesina; 11 Gareth Hock; 12 Bryan Fletcher; 13 Sean O'Loughlin (C). Subs (all used): 18 Paul Prescott; 19 Harrison Hansen; 20 Darrell Goulding; 25 Michael McIlorum.
Tries: Leuluai (38), Higham (56), Calderwood (64), Goulding (67); **Goals:** Richards 4/4.
Rugby Leaguer & League Express Men of the Match:
Dragons: Stacey Jones; *Warriors:* Stuart Fielden.
Penalty count: 6-8; **Half-time:** 24-6;
Referee: Steve Ganson; **Attendance:** 10,218
(at Halliwell Jones Stadium, Warrington).

FINAL

Saturday 25th August 2007

CATALANS DRAGONS 8 ST HELENS 30

DRAGONS: 1 Clint Greenshields; 2 Justin Murphy; 11 Sebastien Raguin; 3 John Wilson; 25 Younes Khattabi; 4 Adam Mogg; 7 Stacey Jones (C); 10 Jerome Guisset; 26 Luke Quigley; 19 Alex Chan; 12 Jason Croker; 17 Cyril Gossard; 13 Gregory Mounis. Subs (all used): 8 David Ferriol; 18 Vincent Duport; 24 Remi Casty; 27 Kane Bentley.
Tries: Khattabi (37), Murphy (58); **Goals:** Jones 0/2.
SAINTS: 1 Paul Wellens; 2 Ade Gardner; 3 Matt Gidley; 4 Willie Talau; 5 Francis Meli; 6 Leon Pryce; 8 Nick Fozzard; 9 Keiron Cunningham; (C); 10 Jason Cayless; 15 Mike Bennett; 12 Jon Wilkin. Subs (all used): 14 James Roby; 17 James Graham; 22 Paul Clough; 23 Maurie Fa'asavalu.
Tries: Roby (33), Gardner (40, 78), Wellens (46), Clough (51); **Goals:** Long 5/6.
Rugby Leaguer & League Express Men of the Match:
Dragons: Jason Croker; *Saints:* Paul Wellens.
Penalty count: 9-12; **Half-time:** 4-12; **Referee:** Ashley Klein; **Attendance:** 84,241 *(at Wembley Stadium).*

St Helens' Matt Gidley looks to break free against Catalans during the Challenge Cup Final

CO-OPERATIVE RLC NATIONAL

FINAL TABLE

	P	W	D	L	F	A	D	Pts
Bramley Buffaloes	16	14	0	2	714	192	522	44 (2)
Featherstone Lions	16	13	0	3	636	326	310	41 (2)
Warrington Wizards	16	12	0	4	512	327	185	38 (2)
Dewsbury Celtic	16	9	0	7	516	412	104	30 (3)
Hudds-Underbank	16	7	0	9	359	433	-74	25 (4)
Hemel Stags	16	6	0	10	431	461	-30	24 (6)
Leeds Akkies	16	4	0	12	291	556	-265	15 (3)
East Lancs Lions	16	4	0	12	338	622	-284	15 (3)
Gateshead Storm	16	3	0	13	292	760	-468	12 (3)

*Cottingham Phoenix withdrawn in June
(Bonus points in brackets)

ELIMINATION PLAY-OFFS
Saturday 15th September 2007
Warrington Wizards 52 ....Hemel Stags 22
Dewsbury Celtic 24 ....Hudds Underbank 34

QUALIFYING SEMI-FINAL
Sunday 23rd September 2007
Bramley Buffaloes 36 ....Featherstone Lions 12

ELIMINATION SEMI-FINAL
Saturday 22nd September 2007
Warrington Wizards 54 ....Hudds Underbank 14

FINAL ELIMINATOR
Saturday 29th September 2007
Featherstone Lions 40 ....Warrington Wizards 14

GRAND FINAL
Sunday 7th October 2007
Bramley Buffaloes 30 ....Featherstone Lions 42
Buffaloes: T - Fontaine 2, O'Connor, Hayes, Webb, Drake; G - Drake 3/6
Lions: T - Tepper, Pearson, Smeaton 2, Hulme 2, Froggatt; G - Pearson 7/9
Half-time: 4-30   *(at Headingley Carnegie, Leeds)*

NATIONAL CONFERENCE

PREMIER DIVISION

	P	W	D	L	F	A	D	Pts
Leigh Miners	26	19	0	7	604	417	187	38
Skirlaugh	26	16	4	6	538	306	232	36
East Hull	26	17	2	7	489	385	104	36
West Hull	26	16	2	8	624	466	158	34
Hull Dockers	26	14	1	11	563	416	147	29
Wigan St Pats	26	14	0	12	601	414	187	28
Oulton Raiders*	26	13	2	11	527	443	84	26
Thornhill Trojans**	26	14	1	11	544	513	31	25
Siddal	26	12	1	13	520	585	-65	25
Eastmoor*	26	13	1	12	446	559	-113	25
West Bowling	26	9	2	15	389	544	-155	20
Wath Brow Hornets	26	8	1	17	372	534	-162	17
Shaw Cross Sharks	26	7	1	18	331	522	-191	15
Oldham St Annes	26	1	0	25	311	755	-444	2

**4pts deducted
*2pts deducted

ELIMINATION PLAY-OFFS
Saturday 28th April 2007
West Hull 28 ....Hull Dockers 18
East Hull 24 ....Wigan St Patricks 6

QUALIFYING SEMI-FINAL
Saturday 5th May 2007
Leigh Miners Rangers 10 ....Skirlaugh 18

ELIMINATION SEMI-FINAL
Saturday 5th May 2007
East Hull 34 ....West Hull 24

FINAL ELIMINATOR
Saturday 12th May 2007
Leigh Miners Rangers 59.............................East Hull 8

GRAND FINAL
Saturday 19th May
Leigh Miners Rangers 6 ....Skirlaugh 8
Miners: T - Bradbury (55); G - Woods 1/1
Skirlaugh: T - Lewis; G - Precious 2/2
(at Spotland, Rochdale)

DIVISION ONE

	P	W	D	L	F	A	D	Pts
Rochdale Mayfield	24	20	0	4	863	419	444	40
Castleford Panthers	24	17	2	5	599	391	208	36
Leigh East	24	16	2	6	686	465	221	34
Wigan St Judes	24	14	1	9	610	442	168	29
Ince Rosebridge	24	14	1	9	526	478	48	29
Widnes St Maries *	24	13	1	10	544	477	67	25
Thatto Heath	24	9	1	14	489	547	-58	19
York Acorn	24	9	0	15	562	573	-11	18
Eccles and Salford	24	8	1	15	456	529	-73	17
East Leeds	24	8	1	15	432	672	-240	17
Ovenden	24	8	1	15	429	707	-278	17
Milford Marlins	24	7	1	16	418	619	-201	15
Lock Lane	24	6	2	16	385	680	-295	14

*2pts deducted

DIVISION TWO

	P	W	D	L	F	A	D	Pts
Waterhead	22	19	0	3	786	225	561	38
Bradford Dudley Hill	22	16	0	6	583	322	261	32
Saddleworth	22	14	0	8	613	311	302	28
Stanningley	22	14	0	8	453	277	176	28
Millom	22	12	1	9	494	346	148	25
Normanton Knights	22	12	1	9	506	443	63	25
Heworth	22	11	1	10	441	510	-69	23
Egremont Rangers	22	8	1	13	366	710	-344	17
Brighouse Rangers	22	8	0	14	388	475	-87	16
Crosfields	22	8	0	14	342	543	-201	16
Hull Isberg	22	4	0	18	346	622	-276	8
Askam	22	4	0	18	250	784	-534	8

GMB NATIONAL CUP

QUARTER FINALS
Saturday 24th March 2007
Saddleworth Rangers 32 ....Blackbrook 30
Ince Rose Bridge 18 ....Waterhead 14
Leigh Miners 12 ....Halton Simms Cross 32
West Hull 10 ....East Hull 26

SEMI-FINALS
Saturday 7th April 2007
Ince Rosebridge 10 ....East Hull 8
Saturday 14th April 2007
Halton Simms Cross 33 ....Saddleworth Rangers 18

FINAL
Saturday 26th May 2007
Ince Rosebridge 8 ....Halton Simms Cross 23
(at Woodlands, Fylde)

TOTALRL.COM CONFERENCE

SOUTHERN PREMIER

	P	W	D	L	F	A	Pts
St Albans Centurions	14	12	0	2	552	242	24
South London Storm	14	10	1	3	522	250	21
London Skolars	14	10	1	3	587	342	21
Ipswich Rhinos	14	7	1	6	429	298	15
West London Sharks	14	5	1	8	396	406	11
Kingston Warriors	14	2	0	12	322	550	4
Kent Ravens	14	1	0	13	124	846	2

MIDLANDS PREMIER

	P	W	D	L	F	A	Pts
Coventry Bears	14	14	0	0	696	167	28
Nottingham Outlaws	14	10	1	3	494	188	21
Gloucestershire W	14	8	1	5	418	298	17
Somerset Vikings	14	7	3	4	335	354	17
Derby City	14	6	1	7	381	378	13
Birmingham Bulldogs	14	5	1	8	299	349	11
Telford Raiders	14	4	1	9	302	528	9
Leicester Phoenix	14	0	0	14	95	746	0

NORTHERN PREMIER

	P	W	D	L	F	A	Pts
Carlisle Centurions	14	13	0	1	744	128	26
Billingham Lions	14	10	0	4	638	310	20
Peterlee Pumas	14	8	4	2	546	282	20
Copeland Athletic	14	8	1	5	452	429	17
Newcastle Knights	14	7	2	5	421	336	16
Sunderland Nissan	14	7	0	7	350	459	14
Jarrow Vikings	14	5	1	8	431	346	11
Durham Tigers	14	4	0	10	215	539	8
Gateshead Storm "A"	14	2	0	12	200	426	4
Whitley Bay Barbarians	14	1	0	12	128	850	2

HARRY JEPSON TROPHY - GRAND FINAL
Sunday 9th September 2007
Coventry Bears 20 ....St Albans Centurions 28
(at Broadstreet RFC, Coventry)

CONFERENCE REGIONAL LEAGUES

YORKSHIRE & LINCOLNSHIRE

	P	W	D	L	F	A	Pts
Bridlington Bulls	12	11	1	0	435	173	23
Lincoln City Knights	12	9	1	2	388	227	19
Rossington Sharks	12	9	0	3	413	194	18
Moorend Thorne M	12	6	0	6	278	266	12
South Humberside	12	5	0	7	306	414	10
Leeds Akkies	12	2	2	8	226	334	6
Scunthorpe Barbarians	12	1	3	8	318	366	5
Scarborough Pirates	12	0	1	11	126	516	1

WEST MIDLANDS

	P	W	D	L	F	A	Pts
Burntwood Bulldogs	12	10	0	2	467	232	20
Bristol Sonics	12	8	1	3	461	246	17
Coventry Bears	12	6	1	5	468	273	13
Redditch Ravens	12	5	1	6	328	484	11
Oxford Cavaliers	12	4	0	8	338	346	8
Wolverhampton W	12	1	1	10	158	629	3

CHESHIRE

	P	W	D	L	F	A	Pts
Macclesfield	12	8	1	3	350	201	17
Winnington Park	12	8	1	3	366	249	17
Runcorn Vikings	12	6	0	6	302	310	12
Crewe Wolves	12	5	0	7	166	499	10
North Wales Coasters	12	1	0	11	150	392	2

NORTH WEST

	P	W	D	L	F	A	Pts
Liverpool Buccaneers	12	11	0	1	431	188	22
Widnes Saints	12	10	0	2	560	159	20
Blackpool Sea Eagles	12	7	0	5	326	248	14
Warrington Wizards "A"	12	4	0	8	184	305	8
Ormskirk Heelers	12	0	0	12	74	354	0

SOUTH WEST

	P	W	D	L	F	A	Pts
Plymouth Titans	10	9	0	1	534	155	18
East Devon Eagles	10	6	0	4	404	240	12
Devon Sharks	10	5	2	3	322	304	12
Somerset Vikings "A"	10	2	1	7	184	376	5
Exeter Centurions	10	1	1	8	145	515	3

EAST

	P	W	D	L	F	A	Pts
Bedford Tigers	12	10	0	2	459	188	20
St Ives Roosters	12	8	0	4	400	311	16
Greenwich Admirals	12	8	0	4	402	324	16
Thetford Titans	12	5	0	7	370	332	10
Colchester Romans	12	5	0	7	346	418	10
Cambridge Eagles	12	0	0	12	150	452	0

SOUTH

	P	W	D	L	F	A	Pts
Gosport & Fareham	6	5	1	0	298	106	11
Farnborough Falcons	6	3	1	2	186	176	7
Finchley	6	2	0	4	160	212	4
London Griffins	6	1	0	5	108	262	2

WALES

	P	W	D	L	F	A	Pts
Bridgend Blue Bulls	7	6	0	1	248	137	12
Torfaen Tigers	7	5	0	2	195	209	10
Newport Titans	7	4	0	3	252	152	8
Blackwood Bulldogs	7	4	0	3	261	209	8
Valley Cougars	7	3	1	3	215	198	7
Cardiff Demons	7	2	1	4	201	191	5
Neath Port Talbot S	7	2	0	5	150	241	4
West Wales Sharks	7	1	0	6	133	316	2

SCOTLAND

	P	W	D	L	F	A	Pts
Fife Lions	8	7	0	1	418	111	14
Edinburgh Eagles	7	5	0	2	228	152	10
Paisley Hurricanes	7	3	0	4	178	261	6
Moray Eels	8	3	0	5	160	306	6
Easterhouse Panthers	8	1	0	7	150	302	2

* Glasgow withdrawn

REGIONAL LEAGUES - GRAND FINAL
Sunday 9th September 2007
Bedford Tigers 18 ....Widnes Saints 27
at Broadstreet RFC, Coventry

WELSH PREMIER DIVISION - GRAND FINAL
Saturday 4th August 2007
Bridgend Blue Bulls 24.......................Newport Titans 18

SCOTLAND - GRAND FINAL
Saturday 4th August 2007
Edinburgh Eagles 30..Fife Lions 6

SENIOR ACADEMY

SENIOR ACADEMY CHAMPIONSHIP

ELIMINATION PLAY-OFFS
Thursday 13th September 2007
Leeds Rhinos 31 ....Salford City Reds 16

Saturday 15th September 2007
Bradford Bulls 32 ....St Helens 26

QUALIFYING SEMI-FINAL
Sunday 23rd September 2007
Wigan Warriors 12 ....Hull FC 20

ELIMINATION SEMI-FINAL
Thursday 20th September 2007
Leeds Rhinos 22 ....Bradford Bulls 18

FINAL ELIMINATOR
Saturday 29th September 2007
Wigan Warriors 32 ....Leeds Rhinos 38

GRAND FINAL
Saturday 6th October 2007
Hull FC 38..Leeds Rhinos 22
(at the KC Stadium, Hull)

SENIOR ACADEMY FIRST DIVISION

ELIMINATION PLAY-OFFS
Friday 7th September 2007
Widnes Vikings 52..............................Batley Bulldogs 18

Saturday 8th September 2007
Dewsbury Rams 48 ....Whitehaven 12

QUALIFYING SEMI-FINAL
Saturday 15th September 2007
Leigh Centurions ....22 Halifax 24

ELIMINATION SEMI-FINAL
Saturday 15thSeptember 2007
Widnes Vikings 32 ....Dewsbury Rams 16

FINAL ELIMINATOR
Saturday 22nd September 2007
Leigh Centurions 16 ....Widnes Vikings 20

GRAND FINAL
Saturday 29th September 2007
Halifax 32 ....Widnes Vikings 18
(at the Shay, Halifax)

SENIOR ACADEMY UNDER 21'S CHAMPIONSHIP

	P	W	D	L	F	A	D	Pts
Wigan Warriors	20	19	0	1	724	354	370	38
Hull FC	20	15	0	5	776	437	339	30
Leeds Rhinos	20	12	0	8	742	467	275	24
Bradford Bulls	20	11	0	9	535	491	44	22
St Helens	20	9	1	10	539	512	27	19
Salford Reds	20	9	1	10	460	507	-47	19
Harlequins RL	20	9	0	11	491	550	-59	18
Wakefield T	20	8	0	12	514	506	8	16
Hull KR	20	7	0	13	433	700	-267	14
Warrington W	20	7	0	13	425	723	-298	14
Huddersfield	20	3	0	17	332	724	-392	6

SENIOR ACADEMY UNDER 21'S FIRST DIVISION

	P	W	D	L	F	A	D	Pts
Leigh Centurions	17	14	0	3	613	261	352	28
Halifax RLFC	17	13	1	3	576	216	360	27
Widnes Vikings	17	13	0	4	658	299	359	26
Dewsbury Rams	17	13	0	4	447	280	167	26
Whitehaven	17	10	0	7	514	422	92	20
Batley Bulldogs	17	10	0	7	382	339	43	20
Hunslet Hawks	17	8	0	9	341	423	-82	16
Castleford Tigers	17	8	0	9	412	507	-95	16
Sheffield Eagles	17	7	1	9	499	566	-67	15
Barrow Raiders	17	7	0	10	455	346	109	14
Rochdale Hornets	17	7	0	10	449	499	-50	14
Featherstone	17	7	0	10	376	524	-148	14
York Knights	17	6	1	10	323	525	-202	13
Workington Town	17	5	0	12	264	537	-273	10
Keighley Cougars	17	3	1	13	274	588	-314	7
Swinton Lions	17	3	0	14	349	630	-281	6

JUNIOR ACADEMY

JUNIOR ACADEMY UNDER-18 CHAMPIONSHIP

ELIMINATION PLAY-OFFS
Saturday 15th September 2007
Castleford Tigers 16 ....Widnes Vikings 36

Monday 17th September 2007
Wigan Warriors 30 ....Salford City Reds 8

QUALIFYING SEMI-FINAL
Saturday 22nd September 2007
St Helens 18 ....Leeds Rhinos 25 aet

ELIMINATION SEMI-FINAL
Saturday 22nd September 2007
Wigan Warriors 42 ....Widnes Vikings 6

FINAL ELIMINATOR
Saturday 29th September 2007
St Helens 40 ....Wigan Warriors 14

GRAND FINAL
Friday 5th October 2007
Leeds Rhinos 26.....................................St Helens 16
(at Headingley Carnegie, Leeds)

JUNIOR ACADEMY UNDER 18'S CHAMPIONSHIP

	P	W	D	L	F	A	D	Pts
St Helens	20	20	0	0	851	263	588	40
Leeds Rhinos	20	16	0	4	592	361	231	32
Wigan Warriors	20	14	1	5	676	320	356	29
Castleford Tigers	20	11	1	8	596	512	84	23
Widnes Vikings	20	11	1	8	478	489	-11	23
Salford Reds	20	10	0	10	426	512	-86	20
Hull FC	20	9	0	11	525	583	-58	18
Wakefield Trinity	20	9	0	11	438	538	-100	18
Bradford Bulls	20	7	0	13	426	496	-70	14
Huddersfield	20	5	1	14	518	683	-165	11
Warrington Wolves	20	4	0	16	447	676	-229	8
Harlequins RL	20	2	0	18	336	876	-540	4

Hull's Danny Houghton is tackled by the Leeds defence during the Senior Academy Championship Grand Final

SUPER LEAGUE 2008 FIXTURES

ROUND 4

Weekend of 1-3 February
Leeds Rhinos v Hull Kingston Rovers ..TBC

ROUND 1

Saturday 9 February
Harlequins v Wigan Warriors..............15:00
Sunday 10 February
Hull Kingston Rovers v St Helens 15:00
Warrington Wolves v Hull FC..............15:00
Huddersfield Giants v Leeds Rhinos ..15:00
Castleford Tigers v Catalans Dragons 15:30
Wakefield T Wildcats v Bradford Bulls15:30

ROUND 2

Friday 15 February
St Helens v Warrington Wolves 20:00
Wigan Warriors v Castleford Tigers 20:00
Saturday 16 February
Catalans Dragons v Hull KR................19:30
Sunday 17 February
Bradford Bulls v Huddersfield Giants..15:00
Hull FC v Harlequins 15:15
Wakefield T Wildcats v Leeds Rhinos 15:30

ROUND 3

Friday 22 February
Leeds Rhinos v Catalans Dragons 20:00
Saturday 23 February
Harlequins v Wakefield T Wildcats......15:00
Sunday 24 February
Bradford Bulls v St Helens...................15:00
Hull KR v Warrington Wolves 15:00
Huddersfield Giants v Castleford Tigers ..15:00
Hull FC v Wigan Warriors 15:15

Friday 29 February
CARNEGIE WORLD CLUB CHALLENGE

ROUND 4

Sunday 2 March
St Helens v Wakefield T Wildcats 20:00
Wigan Warriors v Bradford Bulls........20:00
Warrington Wolves v Catalans Dragons ..15:00
Huddersfield Giants v Hull FC 15:00
Castleford Tigers v Harlequins............15:30

ROUND 5

Friday 7 March
St Helens v Hull FC 20:00
Saturday 8 March
Harlequins v Huddersfield Giants 15:00
Catalans Dragons v Bradford Bulls 19:30
Sunday 9 March
Warrington Wolves v Wigan Warriors 15:00
Castleford Tigers v Leeds Rhinos 15:30
Wakefield T Wildcats v Hull KR 15:30

ROUND 6

Friday 14 March
Leeds Rhinos v Harlequins 20:00
Saturday 15 March
Catalans Dragons v St Helens 19:30
Sunday 16 March
Bradford Bulls v Warrington Wolves ..15:00
Hull KR v Castleford Tigers 15:00
Huddersfield Giants v Wigan Warriors 15:00
Hull FC v Wakefield Trinity Wildcats ..15:15

ROUND 7

Friday 21 March
Harlequins v Catalans Dragons ....TBC
Hull Kingston Rovers v Hull FC ....TBC
Leeds Rhinos v Bradford Bulls..............TBC
St Helens v Wigan Warriors ....TBC
Wakefield T Wildcats v Castleford Tigers TBC
Warrington Wolves v Huddersfield Giants..TBC

ROUND 8

Monday 24 March
Bradford Bulls v Harlequins ....TBC
Castleford Tigers v Warrington Wolves TBC
Hull FC v Leeds Rhinos ....TBC
Wigan Warriors v Hull Kingston RoversTBC
Huddersfield Giants v St Helens............TBC
Catalans Dragons v Wakefield T WildcatsTBC

ROUND 9

Friday 28 March
St Helens v Leeds Rhinos 20:00
Wigan Warriors v Wakefield T Wildcats20:00
Saturday 29 March
Catalans Dragons v Hull FC 19:30
Sunday 30 March
Bradford Bulls v Castleford Tigers 15:00
Hull KR v Huddersfield Giants 15:00
Warrington Wolves v Harlequins 15:00

ROUND 10

Friday 4 April
Leeds Rhinos v Wigan Warriors 20:00
Saturday 5 April
Harlequins v Hull Kingston Rovers 15:00
Sunday 6 April
Huddersfield Giants v Catalans Dragons 15:00
Hull FC v Bradford Bulls 15:15
Castleford Tigers v St Helens..............15:30
Wakefield T Wildcats v Warrington Wolves 15:30

ROUND 11

Friday 11 April
Leeds Rhinos v Warrington Wolves....20:00
St Helens v Harlequins 20:00
Wigan Warriors v Catalans Dragons ..20:00
Sunday 13 April
Hull Kingston Rovers v Bradford Bulls 15:00
Huddersfield Giants v Wakefield T Wildcats15:00
Castleford Tigers v Hull FC 15:30

Weekend of 20 April
CARNEGIE CHALLENGE CUP - ROUND 4

ROUND 12

Saturday 26 April
Catalans Dragons v Castleford Tigers 19:30
Sunday 27 April
Bradford Bulls v Wigan Warriors 15:00
Hull Kingston Rovers v Leeds Rhinos 15:00
Warrington Wolves v St Helens 15:00
Hull FC v Huddersfield Giants 15:15
Wakefield Trinity Wildcats v Harlequins 15:30

ROUND 13 - MILLENNIUM MAGIC

Saturday 3 May
Bradford Bulls v Leeds Rhinos..............TBC
Castleford Tigers v Wakefield T Wildcats TBC
Huddersfield Giants v Warrington Wolves..TBC
Sunday 4 May
Catalans Dragons v Harlequins ....TBC
Hull FC v Hull Kingston Rovers ....TBC
St Helens v Wigan Warriors ....TBC

Weekend of 11 May
CARNEGIE CHALLENGE CUP - ROUND 5

ROUND 14

Friday 16 May
Leeds Rhinos v Wakefield T Wildcats 20:00
St Helens v Catalans Dragons 20:00
Wigan Warriors v Warrington Wolves 20:00
Sunday 18 May
Harlequins v Hull FC 15:00
Huddersfield Giants v Hull KR 15:00
Castleford Tigers v Bradford Bulls 15:30

ROUND 15

Saturday 24 May
Catalans Dragons v Huddersfield Giants 19:30
Sunday 25 May
Bradford Bulls v Leeds Rhinos 15:00
Hull Kingston Rovers v Harlequins 15:00
Warrington Wolves v Castleford Tigers 15:00
Hull FC v St Helens 15:15
Wakefield T Wildcats v Wigan Warriors15:30

Weekend of 1 June
CARNEGIE CHALLENGE CUP
- QUARTER FINALS

ROUND 16

Friday 6 June
Leeds Rhinos v Hull FC 20:00
St Helens v Hull Kingston Rovers 20:00
Wigan Warriors v Huddersfield Giants 20:00
Sunday 8 June
Bradford Bulls v Catalans Dragons 15:00
Harlequins v Warrington Wolves 15:00
Castleford Tigers v Wakefield T Wildcats 15:30

ROUND 17

Friday 13 June
St Helens v Bradford Bulls..................20:00
Saturday 14 June
Catalans Dragons v Wigan Warriors ..20:00
Sunday 15 June
Harlequins v Leeds Rhinos 15:00
Warrington Wolves v Hull KR 15:00
Hull FC v Castleford Tigers 15:15
Wakefield T Wildcats v Huddersfield Giants 15:30

ROUND 18

Friday 20 June
Leeds Rhinos v St Helens 20:00
Saturday 21 June
Catalans Dragons v Warrington Wolves 20:00
Sunday 22 June
Bradford Bulls v Hull FC 15:00
Hull KR v Wakefield T Wildcats 15:00
Huddersfield Giants v Harlequins 15:00
Castleford Tigers v Wigan Warriors 15:30

ROUND 19

Friday 27 June
Leeds Rhinos v Castleford Tigers 20:00
St Helens v Huddersfield Giants 20:00
Wigan Warriors v Harlequins..............20:00
Sunday 29 June
Bradford Bulls v Hull Kingston Rovers 15:00
Hull FC v Warrington Wolves..............15:15
Wakefield T Wildcats v Catalans Dragons15:30

ROUND 20

Friday 4 July
Wigan Warriors v Leeds Rhinos 20:00
Sunday 6 July
Harlequins v St Helens 15:00
Warrington Wolves v Wakefield T Wildcats 15:00
Huddersfield Giants v Bradford Bulls..15:00
Hull FC v Catalans Dragons 15:15
Castleford Tigers v Hull KR 15:30

Weekend of 13 July
INTERNATIONAL WEEKEND

ROUND 21

Friday 11 July
Leeds Rhinos v Huddersfield Giants ..20:00
St Helens v Castleford Tigers.............20:00
Saturday 12 July
Catalans Dragons v Harlequins 20:00
Sunday 13 July
Hull KR v Wigan Warriors 15:00
Warrington Wolves v Bradford Bulls ..15:00
Wakefield Trinity Wildcats v Hull FC ..15:30

ROUND 22

Friday 18 July
Wigan Warriors v St Helens................20:00
Saturday 19 July
Catalans Dragons v Leeds Rhinos 20:00
Sunday 20 July
Bradford Bulls v Wakefield T Wildcats 15:00
Harlequins v Castleford Tigers............15:00
Huddersfield Giants v Warrington Wolves 15:00
Hull FC v Hull Kingston Rovers 15:15

Weekend of 27 July
CARNEGIE CHALLENGE CUP
- SEMI FINALS

ROUND 23

Friday 1 August
Wigan Warriors v Hull FC 20:00
Sunday 3 August
Harlequins v Bradford Bulls................15:00
Hull KR v Catalans Dragons...............15:00
Warrington Wolves v Leeds Rhinos....15:00
Castleford Tigers v Huddersfield Giants 15:30
Wakefield Trinity Wildcats v St Helens 15:30

ROUND 24

Friday 8 August
Leeds Rhinos v Bradford Bulls 20:00
St Helens v Warrington Wolves 20:00
Saturday 9 August
Catalans Dragons v Wigan Warriors ..20:00
Sunday 10 August
Hull Kingston Rovers v Harlequins 15:00
Hull FC v Huddersfield Giants 15:15
Wakefield T Wildcats v Castleford Tigers 15:30

ROUND 25

Friday 15 August
Leeds Rhinos v Castleford Tigers 20:00
Wigan Warriors v Wakefield T Wildcats 20:00
Sunday 17 August
Bradford Bulls v Hull FC 15:00
Harlequins v St Helens 15:00
Warrington Wolves v Hull KR 15:00
Huddersfield Giants v Catalans Dragons 15:00

ROUND 26

Friday 22 August
Wigan Warriors v Leeds Rhinos............TBC
Saturday 23 August
Catalans Dragons v Wakefield T Wildcats ..TBC
Sunday 24 August
Bradford Bulls v Hull Kingston Rovers..TBC
Huddersfield Giants v St Helens............TBC
Hull FC v Harlequins.............................TBC
Castleford Tigers v Warrington Wolves TBC

Saturday 30 August
CARNEGIE CHALLENGE CUP FINAL

ROUND 27

Friday 5 September
St Helens v Wigan Warriors................20:00
Sunday 7 September
Harlequins v Catalans Dragons 15:00
Hull Kingston Rovers v Hull FC 15:00
Warrington Wolves v Huddersfield Giants15:00
Castleford Tigers v Bradford Bulls 15:30
Wakefield T Wildcats v Leeds Rhinos 15:30

PLAY-OFFS

Weekend of Friday 12 September
ELIMINATION PLAY-OFFS

Weekend of Friday 19 September
QUALIFYING/ELIMINATION SEMI-FINALS

Weekend of Friday 26 September
FINAL ELIMINATOR

Saturday 4 October
SUPER LEAGUE XIII GRAND FINAL

GRAND FINALS
1998-2006

1998

DIVISION ONE GRAND FINAL

Saturday 26th September 1998

FEATHERSTONE ROVERS 22 WAKEFIELD TRINITY 24

ROVERS: 1 Steve Collins; 2 Carl Hall; 3 Shaun Irwin; 4 Danny Baker; 5 Karl Pratt; 6 Jamie Coventry; 7 Ty Fallins; 8 Chico Jackson; 9 Richard Chapman; 10 Stuart Dickens; 11 Gary Price; 12 Neil Lowe; 13 Richard Slater. Subs: 14 Paddy Handley for Coventry (70); 15 Asa Amone for Lowe (50); 16 Micky Clarkson for Jackson (50); 17 Steve Dooler (not used). **Tries:** Baker (15), Jackson (45), Collins (49), Hall (69); **Goals:** Chapman 3.
TRINITY: 1 Martyn Holland; 2 Josh Bostock; 3 Adam Hughes; 4 Martin Law; 5 Kevin Gray; 6 Garen Casey; 7 Roger Kenworthy; 8 Francis Stephenson; 9 Roy Southernwood; 10 Gary Lord; 11 Ian Hughes; 12 Sonny Whakarau; 13 Matt Fuller. Subs: 14 Sean Richardson for I Hughes (32); 15 Andy Fisher for Lord (26); 16 David Mycoe (not used); 17 Wayne McDonald for Whakarau (70); Lord for Stephenson (40); Stephenson for Lord (70). **Tries:** Southernwood (2), Bostock (7, 25), Casey (58), Stephenson (76); **Goals:** Casey 2.
League Express Men of the Match:
Rovers: Richard Chapman; *Trinity:* Garen Casey.
Penalty count: 8-3; **Half time:** 6-12; **Referee:** Nick Oddy (Halifax); **Attendance:** 8,224 *(at McAlpine Stadium, Huddersfield).*

SUPER LEAGUE GRAND FINAL

Saturday 24th October 1998

LEEDS RHINOS 4 WIGAN WARRIORS 10

RHINOS: 1 Iestyn Harris (C); 22 Leroy Rivett; 3 Richie Blackmore; 4 Brad Godden; 5 Francis Cummins; 13 Daryl Powell; 7 Ryan Sheridan; 8 Martin Masella; 21 Terry Newton; 25 Darren Fleary; 11 Adrian Morley; 17 Anthony Farrell; 12 Marc Glanville. Subs: 20 Jamie Mathiou for Masella (25); 24 Marcus St Hilaire for Powell (40); 14 Graham Holroyd for Newton (49); 27 Andy Hay for Fleary (54); Powell for Godden (58); Masella for Mathiou (71). **Try:** Blackmore (20).
WARRIORS: 1 Kris Radlinski; 2 Jason Robinson; 3 Danny Moore; 4 Gary Connolly; 5 Mark Bell; 6 Henry Paul; 7 Tony Smith; 16 Terry O'Connor; 9 Robbie McCormack; 10 Tony Mestrov; 20 Lee Gilmour; 17 Stephen Holgate; 13 Andy Farrell (C). Subs: 8 Neil Cowie for O'Connor (18BB, rev 48); 14 Mick Cassidy for McCormack (19BB, rev 27); 25 Paul Johnson for Moore (37); 12 Simon Haughton for Gilmour (27BB, rev 33); Haughton for Holgate (33); Cowie for Mestrov (54); Cassidy for Haughton (64); Holgate for Cowie (68); Haughton for Gilmour (71BB, rev 75); Mestrov for O'Connor (75BB). **Try:** Robinson (37); **Goals:** Farrell 3.
League Express Men of the Match:
Rhinos: Iestyn Harris; *Warriors:* Jason Robinson.
Penalty count: 7-13; **Half-time:** 4-6; **Referee:** Russell Smith (Castleford); **Attendance:** 43,553 *(at Old Trafford, Manchester).*

1999

NORTHERN FORD PREMIERSHIP GRAND FINAL

Saturday 25th September 1999

DEWSBURY RAMS 11 HUNSLET HAWKS 12

RAMS: 1 Nathan Graham; 2 Alex Godfrey; 3 Paul Evans; 4 Brendan O'Meara; 5 Adrian Flynn; 6 Richard Agar; 7 Barry Eaton; 8 Alan Boothroyd; 9 Paul Delaney; 10 Matthew Long; 11 Andy Spink; 12 Mark Haigh; 13 Damian Ball. Subs: 14 Brendan Williams for Eaton (5BB, rev 15); 15 Sean Richardson for Haigh (50); 16 Simon Hicks for Long (25); 17 Paul Medley for Spink (50); Williams for Evans (61); Long for Boothroyd (71); Spink for Long (78). **Tries:** Flynn (27), Ball (54); **Goal:** Eaton; **Field goal:** Agar.
HAWKS: 1 Abraham Fatnowna; 2 Chris Ross; 3 Shaun Irwin; 4 Paul Cook; 5 Iain Higgins; 6 Marcus Vassilakopoulos; 7 Latham Tawhai; 8 Richard Hayes; 9 Richard Pachniuk; 10 Steve Pryce; 11 Rob Wilson; 12 Jamie Leighton; 13 Lee St Hilaire. Subs: 14 Mick Coyle for Wilson (57); 15 Phil Kennedy for Pryce (35); 16 Jamie Thackray for St Hilaire (25); 17 Richard Baker for Higgins (55); Higgins for Fatnowna (62); Pryce for Kennedy (65). **Tries:** Cook (31), Higgins (46); **Goal:** Ross; **Field goals:** Tawhai, Leighton.
League Express Men of the Match:
Rams: Barry Eaton; *Hawks:* Latham Tawhai.
Penalty count: 8-5; **Half-time:** 7-7; **Referee:** Steve Ganson (St Helens); **Attendance:** 5,783 *(at Headingley Stadium, Leeds).*

SUPER LEAGUE GRAND FINAL

Saturday 9th October 1999

BRADFORD BULLS 6 ST HELENS 8

BULLS: 28 Stuart Spruce; 2 Tevita Vaikona; 20 Scott Naylor; 5 Michael Withers; 17 Leon Pryce; 6 Henry Paul; 1 Robbie Paul (C); 10 Paul Anderson; 9 James Lowes; 29 Stuart Fielden; 15 David Boyle; 23 Bernard Dwyer; 13 Steve McNamara. Subs: 14 Paul Deacon for R Paul (53); 4 Nathan McAvoy (not used); 12 Mike Forshaw for McNamara (18); 22 Brian McDermott for Anderson (18); Anderson for Fielden (61); Fielden for Dwyer (65); R Paul for Deacon (72). **Try:** H Paul (18); **Goal:** H Paul.
SAINTS: 1 Paul Atcheson; 14 Chris Smith; 3 Kevin Iro; 4 Paul Newlove; 5 Anthony Sullivan; 13 Paul Sculthorpe; 20 Tommy Martyn; 8 Apollo Perelini; 9 Keiron Cunningham; 10 Julian O'Neill; 2 Fereti Tuilagi; 21 Sonny Nickle; 11 Chris Joynt (C). Subs: 26 Paul Wellens for Martyn (52); 6 Sean Hoppe for Newlove (43); 16 Vila Matautia for O'Neill (20); 7 Sean Long for Perelini (24); Perelini for Matautia (46); O'Neill for Perelini (69). **Tries:** Iro (65); **Goals:** Long 2.
League Express Men of the Match:
Bulls: Henry Paul; *Saints:* Kevin Iro.
Penalty count: 4-7; **Half-time:** 6-2; **Referee:** Stuart Cummings (Widnes); **Attendance:** 50,717 *(at Old Trafford, Manchester).*

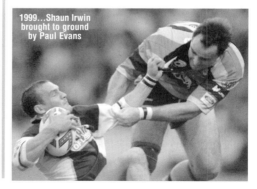

1998...Andy Farrell and coach John Monie toast Wigan's victory

1999...Shaun Irwin brought to ground by Paul Evans

2000

NORTHERN FORD PREMIERSHIP GRAND FINAL

Saturday 29th July 2000

DEWSBURY RAMS 13 LEIGH CENTURIONS 12

RAMS: 1 Nathan Graham; 2 Richard Baker; 4 Dan Potter; 3 Brendan O'Meara; 5 Adrian Flynn; 6 Richard Agar; 7 Barry Eaton; 8 Shayne Williams; 9 David Mycoe; 10 Mark Haigh; 11 Sean Richardson; 12 Daniel Frame; 13 Damian Ball. Subs: 14 Gavin Wood (not used); 15 Paul Delaney for Mycoe (53); 16 Ryan McDonald for Haigh (30); 17 Matthew Long for Williams (23); Haigh for McDonald (64).
Tries: Eaton (2), Long (23); **Goals:** Eaton 2; **Field goal:** Agar.
Sin bin: Williams (66) - use of the elbow.
On report: Richardson (20) - high tackle on Donlan.
CENTURIONS: 1 Stuart Donlan; 5 David Ingram; 3 Paul Anderson; 4 Andy Fairclough; 2 Alan Cross; 6 Liam Bretherton; 7 Kieron Purtill; 8 Tim Street; 9 Mick Higham; 10 Andy Leathem; 11 Simon Baldwin; 12 Heath Cruckshank; 13 Adam Bristow. Subs: 14 James Arkwright for Cross (68); 15 Paul Norman for Street (36); 16 Radney Bowker (not used); 17 David Whittle for Leathem (24); Street for Norman (62).
Tries: Higham (29, 69); **Goals:** Bretherton 2.
Sin bin: Whittle (66) - retaliation.
League Express Men of the Match:
Rams: Richard Agar; *Centurions:* Mick Higham.
Penalty count: 4-4; **Half-time:** 10-6; **Referee:** Robert Connolly (Wigan); **Attendance:** 8,487 *(at Gigg Lane, Bury).*

SUPER LEAGUE GRAND FINAL

Saturday 14th October 2000

ST HELENS 29 WIGAN WARRIORS 16

SAINTS: 17 Paul Wellens; 24 Steve Hall; 3 Kevin Iro; 15 Sean Hoppe; 5 Anthony Sullivan; 20 Tommy Martyn; 7 Sean Long; 8 Apollo Perelini; 9 Keiron Cunningham; 10 Julian O'Neill; 11 Chris Joynt; 22 Tim Jonkers; 13 Paul Sculthorpe. Subs: 14 Fereti Tuilagi for O'Neill (20); 12 Sonny Nickle for Perelini (28); 26 John Stankevitch for Jonkers (50); 23 Scott Barrow (not used); Perelini for Nickle (52); Jonkers for Stankevitch (66); Stankevitch for Perelini (67BB); O'Neill for Hall (74).
Tries: Hoppe (7), Joynt (28, 50), Tuilagi (69), Jonkers (80); **Goals:** Long 4; **Field goal:** Sculthorpe.
WARRIORS: 5 Jason Robinson; 2 Brett Dallas; 1 Kris Radlinski; 3 Steve Renouf; 26 David Hodgson; 6 Tony Smith; 7 Willie Peters; 8 Terry O'Connor; 9 Terry Newton; 10 Neil Cowie; 11 Mick Cassidy; 12 Denis Betts; 13 Andy Farrell (C). Subs: 23 Brady Malam for Cowie (30); 17 Tony Mestrov for O'Connor (43); 19 Chris Chester for Cassidy (47BB, rev 69); 14 Lee Gilmour for Betts (51); O'Connor for Mestrov (61); Cowie for Malam (67); Chester for Newton (75).
Tries: Farrell (13), Hodgson (58), Smith (61); **Goals:** Farrell 2.
League Express Men of the Match:
Saints: Chris Joynt; *Warriors:* Andy Farrell.
Penalty count: 10-6; **Half-time:** 11-4; **Referee:** Russell Smith (Castleford); **Attendance:** 58,132 *(at Old Trafford, Manchester).*

2001

NORTHERN FORD PREMIERSHIP GRAND FINAL

Saturday 28th July 2001

OLDHAM 14 WIDNES VIKINGS 24

OLDHAM: 1 Mark Sibson; 2 Joey Hayes; 3 Anthony Gibbons; 4 Pat Rich; 5 Joe McNicholas; 6 David Gibbons; 7 Neil Roden; 8 Leo Casey; 9 Keith Brennan; 10 Paul Norton; 11 Phil Farrell; 12 Bryan Henare; 13 Kevin Mannion. Subs: 14 Mike Ford for Mannion (27); 15 Jason Clegg for Casey (18); 16 John Hough for Brennan (44); 17 Danny Guest for Norton (40BB, rev 54); Mannion for Henare (66); Guest for Clegg (73).
Tries: Brennan (9), Ford (74), Mannion (80); **Goal:** Rich.
VIKINGS: 1 Paul Atcheson; 2 Damian Munro; 3 Craig Weston; 4 Jason Demetriou; 5 Chris Percival; 6 Richard Agar; 7 Martin Crompton; 8 Simon Knox; 9 Phil Cantillon; 10 Stephen Holgate; 11 Steve Gee; 12 Sean Richardson; 13 Tommy Hodgkinson. Subs: 14 Andy Craig for Percival (65); 15 Chris McKinney for Gee (41); 16 Joe Faimalo for Knox (32); 17 Matthew Long for Holgate (23); Knox for Long (49BB, rev 61); Holgate for Long (74).
Tries: Gee (17), Demetriou (38, 60), Cantillon (50), Munro (69); **Goals:** Weston 2.
League Express Men of the Match:
Oldham: Jason Clegg; *Vikings:* Phil Cantillon.
Penalty count: 8-5; **Half-time:** 4-10; **Referee:** Steve Ganson (St Helens); **Attendance:** 8,974 *(at Spotland, Rochdale).*

SUPER LEAGUE GRAND FINAL

Saturday 13th October 2001

BRADFORD BULLS 37 WIGAN WARRIORS 6

BULLS: 5 Michael Withers; 2 Tevita Vaikona; 20 Scott Naylor; 23 Graham Mackay; 3 Leon Pryce; 6 Henry Paul; 1 Robbie Paul (C); 8 Joe Vagana; 9 James Lowes; 22 Brian McDermott; 11 Daniel Gartner; 19 Jamie Peacock; 12 Mike Forshaw. Subs: 29 Stuart Fielden for McDermott (21BB, rev 65); 10 Paul Anderson for Vagana (22); 15 Shane Rigon for Pryce (40); 7 Paul Deacon for R Paul (69); Vagana for Anderson (53); Fielden for Gartner (72); Anderson for Vagana (74).
Tries: Lowes (9), Withers (11, 27, 31), Fielden (65), Mackay (72); **Goals:** H Paul 5, Mackay; **Field goal:** H Paul.
WARRIORS: 1 Kris Radlinski; 2 Brett Dallas; 4 Gary Connolly; 3 Steve Renouf; 5 Brian Carney; 6 Matthew Johns; 7 Adrian Lam; 8 Terry O'Connor; 9 Terry Newton; 20 Harvey Howard; 11 Mick Cassidy; 14 David Furner; 13 Andy Farrell (C). Subs: 15 Paul Johnson for Carney (12BB); 10 Neil Cowie for Howard (17); 12 Denis Betts for O'Connor (32); 19 Chris Chester for Farrell (59); O'Connor for Cowie (55); Howard for Newton (64); Cowie for Cassidy (72).
Try: Lam (63); **Goal:** Furner.
League Express Men of the Match:
Bulls: Michael Withers; *Warriors:* Adrian Lam.
Penalty count: 6-7; **Half-time:** 26-0; **Referee:** Stuart Cummings (Widnes); **Attendance:** 60,164 *(at Old Trafford, Manchester).*

2000...
Fereti Tuilagi
bursts past
Tony Smith

2001...Joe Faimalo goes past Danny Guest and Mike Ford

2002

NORTHERN FORD PREMIERSHIP GRAND FINAL

Saturday 12th October 2002

HUDDERSFIELD GIANTS 38 LEIGH CENTURIONS 16

GIANTS: 1 Ben Cooper; 2 Hefin O'Hare; 3 Eorl Crabtree; 4 Graeme Hallas; 5 Marcus St Hilaire; 6 Stanley Gene; 7 Chris Thorman; 8 Michael Slicker; 9 Paul March; 10 Jeff Wittenberg; 11 David Atkins; 12 Robert Roberts; 13 Steve McNamara. Subs: 14 Heath Cruckshank for Roberts (24BB); 15 Chris Molyneux for Slicker (53); 16 Darren Turner for March (21); 17 Andy Rice for Cruckshank (57); Roberts for Wittenberg (34); Wittenberg for Roberts (74).
Tries: O'Hare (12, 78), St Hilaire (34, 53), Thorman (46), Gene (57); **Goals:** McNamara 7.
Sin bin: Roberts (47) - fighting.
CENTURIONS: 1 Neil Turley; 2 Leon Felton; 4 Jon Roper; 3 Dale Cardoza; 5 Oliver Marns; 6 Willie Swann; 7 Bobbie Goulding; 8 Vila Matautia; 9 Paul Rowley; 10 David Bradbury; 11 Simon Baldwin; 12 Andrew Isherwood; 13 Adam Bristow. Subs: 14 Gareth Price for Bradbury, rev 35); 15 John Duffy for Swann (32); 16 John Hamilton for Bristow (46BB, rev 57); 17 David Whittle for Matautia (22); Matautia for Bradbury (53BB); Swann for Goulding (58); Hamilton for Whittle (67); Bradbury for Turley (72); Goulding for Swann (75).
Tries: Cardoza (9), Marns (18), Hamilton (70); **Goals:** Turley 2.
Sin bin: Whittle (47) - fighting; Bristow (74) - interference.
On report: Isherwood (66) - high tackle on Roberts.
Rugby Leaguer & League Express Men of the Match:
Giants: Chris Thorman; *Centurions:* Adam Bristow.
Penalty count: 11-11; **Half-time:** 14-10;
Referee: Karl Kirkpatrick (Warrington);
Attendance: 9,051 *(at Halton Stadium, Widnes).*

SUPER LEAGUE GRAND FINAL

Saturday 19th October 2002

BRADFORD BULLS 18 ST HELENS 19

BULLS: 6 Michael Withers; 2 Tevita Vaikona; 20 Scott Naylor; 15 Brandon Costin; 5 Lesley Vainikolo; 1 Robbie Paul (C); 7 Paul Deacon; 8 Joe Vagana; 9 James Lowes; 29 Stuart Fielden; 11 Daniel Gartner; 12 Jamie Peacock; 13 Mike Forshaw. Subs: 14 Lee Gilmour for Gartner (21); 10 Paul Anderson for Vagana (25); 22 Brian McDermott for Fielden (34); 3 Leon Pryce for Vainikolo (53); Fielden for Anderson (55); Vainikolo for Paul (77).
Tries: Naylor (3), Paul (44), Withers (47); **Goals:** Deacon 3.
SAINTS: 1 Paul Wellens; 5 Darren Albert; 3 Martin Gleeson; 4 Paul Newlove; 19 Anthony Stewart; 13 Paul Sculthorpe; 7 Sean Long; 8 Darren Britt; 9 Keiron Cunningham; 10 Barry Ward; 23 Mike Bennett; 15 Tim Jonkers; 11 Chris Joynt (C). Subs: 2 Sean Hoppe for Wellens (3); 12 Peter Shiels for Ward (27); 14 John Stankevitch for Britt (31BB, rev 58); 17 Mick Higham for Joynt (54); Stankevitch for Shiels (58); Joynt for Britt (75); Shiels for Jonkers (77).
Tries: Bennett (24), Long (32), Gleeson (56);
Goals: Long 3; **Field goal:** Long.
Rugby Leaguer & League Express Men of the Match:
Bulls: Paul Deacon; *Saints:* Mike Bennett.
Penalty count: 5-4; **Half-time:** 12-8; **Referee:** Russell Smith (Castleford); **Attendance:** 61,138 *(at Old Trafford, Manchester).*

2002...Martin Gleeson slides over to score as Robbie Paul looks on

2003

NATIONAL LEAGUE TWO GRAND FINAL

Sunday 5th October 2003

KEIGHLEY COUGARS 13 SHEFFIELD EAGLES 11

COUGARS: 1 Matt Foster; 2 Max Tomlinson; 3 David Foster; 4 James Rushforth; 5 Andy Robinson; 6 Paul Ashton; 7 Matt Firth; 8 Phil Stephenson; 9 Simeon Hoyle; 10 Danny Ekis; 11 Oliver Wilkes; 12 Ian Sinfield; 13 Lee Patterson. Subs (all used): 14 Chris Wainwright; 15 Richard Mervill; 16 Mick Durham; 17 Jason Ramshaw.
Tries: M Foster (7), Robinson (74); **Goals:** Ashton 2;
Field goal: Firth.
EAGLES: 1 Andy Poynter; 2 Tony Weller; 3 Richard Goddard; 4 Tom O'Reilly; 5 Greg Hurst; 6 Gavin Brown; 7 Mark Aston; 8 Jack Howieson; 9 Gareth Stanley; 10 Dale Laughton; 11 Andy Raleigh; 12 Craig Brown; 13 Wayne Flynn. Subs (all used): 14 Peter Reilly; 15 Simon Tillyer; 16 Nick Turnbull; 17 Mitchell Stringer.
Try: O'Reilly (51); **Goals:** G Brown 3; **Field goal:** Reilly.
Rugby Leaguer & League Express Men of the Match:
Cougars: Simeon Hoyle; *Eagles:* Andy Raleigh.
Penalty count: 6-8; **Half-time:** 9-4; **Referee:** Peter Taberner (Wigan). *(At Halton Stadium, Widnes).*

NATIONAL LEAGUE ONE GRAND FINAL

Sunday 5th October 2003

LEIGH CENTURIONS 14 SALFORD CITY REDS 31

CENTURIONS: 1 Neil Turley; 2 Damian Munro; 3 Alan Hadcroft; 4 Danny Halliwell; 5 Leroy Rivett; 6 John Duffy; 7 Tommy Martyn; 8 Sonny Nickle; 9 Patrick Weisner; 10 Paul Norman; 11 Sean Richardson; 12 Willie Swann; 13 Adam Bristow. Subs (all used): 14 David Bradbury; 15 Lee Sanderson; 16 Bryan Henare; 17 Ricky Bibey.
Tries: Richardson (33), Halliwell (38), Swann (65); **Goal:** Turley.
On report: Nickle (60) - late tackle on Clinch.
CITY REDS: 1 Jason Flowers; 2 Danny Arnold; 3 Stuart Littler; 4 Alan Hunte; 5 Andy Kirk; 6 Cliff Beverley; 7 Gavin Clinch; 8 Neil Baynes; 9 Malcolm Alker; 10 Andy Coley; 11 Simon Baldwin; 12 Paul Highton; 13 Chris Charles. Subs (all used): 14 Steve Blakeley; 15 David Highton; 16 Martin Moana; 17 Gareth Haggerty.
Tries: Hunte (3, 52), Beverley (23), Littler (73);
Goals: Charles 6, Blakeley; **Field goal:** Blakeley.
Rugby Leaguer & League Express Men of the Match:
Centurions: Willie Swann; *City Reds:* Gavin Clinch.
Penalty count: 10-10; **Half-time:** 10-16;
Referee: Richard Silverwood (Dewsbury);
Attendance: 9,186 *(at Halton Stadium, Widnes).*

SUPER LEAGUE GRAND FINAL

Saturday 18th October 2003

BRADFORD BULLS 25 WIGAN WARRIORS 12

BULLS: 17 Stuart Reardon; 2 Tevita Vaikona; 6 Michael Withers; 4 Shontayne Hape; 5 Lesley Vainikolo; 15 Karl Pratt; 7 Paul Deacon; 8 Joe Vagana; 9 James Lowes; 29 Stuart Fielden; 11 Daniel Gartner; 12 Jamie Peacock; 13 Mike Forshaw. Subs (all used): 10 Paul Anderson; 18 Lee Radford; 3 Leon Pryce; 1 Robbie Paul (C).
Tries: Reardon (51), Hape (59), Lowes (75);
Goals: Deacon 6/6; **Field goal:** Deacon.
WARRIORS: 1 Kris Radlinski; 5 Brian Carney; 18 Martin Aspinwall; 14 David Hodgson; 2 Brett Dallas; 15 Sean O'Loughlin; 20 Luke Robinson; 30 Quentin Pongia; 9 Terry Newton; 10 Craig Smith; 11 Mick Cassidy; 12 Danny Tickle; 13 Andy Farrell (C). Subs (all used): 4 Paul Johnson; 8 Terry O'Connor; 23 Gareth Hock; 17 Mark Smith.
Tries: Tickle (17), Radlinski (72); **Goals:** Farrell 2/3.
Rugby Leaguer & League Express Men of the Match:
Bulls: Stuart Reardon; *Warriors:* Kris Radlinski.
Penalty count: 7-6; **Half-time:** 4-6; **Referee:** Karl Kirkpatrick (Warrington); **Attendance:** 65,537 *(at Old Trafford, Manchester).*

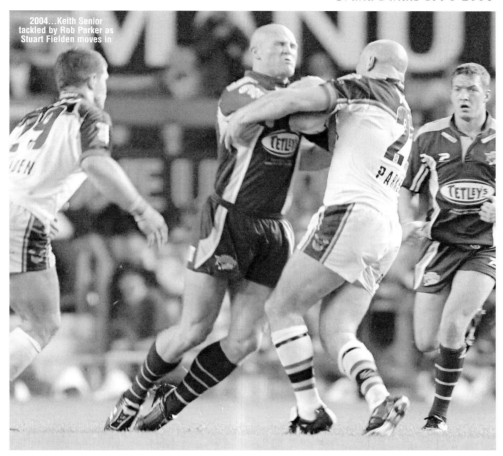

2004...Keith Senior tackled by Rob Parker as Stuart Fielden moves in

2004

NATIONAL LEAGUE ONE GRAND FINAL

Sunday 10th October 2004

LEIGH CENTURIONS 32 WHITEHAVEN 16
(After extra time)

CENTURIONS: 1 Neil Turley; 2 Rob Smyth; 3 Danny Halliwell; 4 Ben Cooper; 5 David Alstead; 6 John Duffy; 7 Tommy Martyn; 8 Simon Knox; 9 Paul Rowley; 10 Matt Sturm; 11 David Larder; 12 Oliver Wilkes; 13 Ian Knott. Subs (all used): 14 Dave McConnell; 15 Heath Cruckshank; 16 Richard Marshall; 17 Willie Swann.
Tries: Cooper (27, 83), Martyn (61), Turley (87);
Goals: Turley 6/8; **Field goals:** Turley 2, Rowley, Martyn.
WHITEHAVEN: 1 Gary Broadbent; 2 Craig Calvert; 3 David Seeds; 4 Mick Nanyn; 5 Wesley Wilson; 6 Leroy Joe; 7 Sam Obst; 8 Marc Jackson; 9 Aaron Lester; 10 David Fatialofa; 11 Paul Davidson; 12 Howard Hill; 13 Craig Walsh. Subs (all used): 14 Spencer Miller; 15 Carl Sice; 16 Chris McKinney; 17 Ryan Tandy.
Tries: Wilson (2, 71), Calvert (45); **Goals:** Nanyn 2/6.
Rugby Leaguer & League Express Men of the Match:
Centurions: Neil Turley; *Whitehaven:* Aaron Lester.
Penalty count: 5-9; **Half-time:** 7-6;
Referee: Ronnie Laughton (Barnsley).
Attendance: 11,005 *(at Halton Stadium, Widnes).*

SUPER LEAGUE GRAND FINAL

Saturday 16th October 2004

BRADFORD BULLS 8 LEEDS RHINOS 16

BULLS: 6 Michael Withers; 17 Stuart Reardon; 16 Paul Johnson; 4 Shontayne Hape; 5 Lesley Vainikolo; 18 Iestyn Harris; 7 Paul Deacon; 8 Joe Vagana; 1 Robbie Paul (C); 29 Stuart Fielden; 12 Jamie Peacock; 13 Logan Swann; 11 Lee Radford. Subs: 10 Paul Anderson for Vagana (14); 15 Karl Pratt for Paul (23); 27 Rob Parker for Anderson (24); 19 Jamie Langley for Peacock (32); Paul for Withers (ht); Peacock for Radford (48); Radford for Swann (54); Vagana for Parker (56); Parker for Fielden (63); Fielden for Vagana (67); Swann for Langley (68).
Tries: Vainikolo (7), Hape (43); **Goals:** Deacon 0/2.
RHINOS: 21 Richard Mathers; 18 Mark Calderwood; 5 Chev Walker; 4 Keith Senior; 22 Marcus Bai; 13 Kevin Sinfield (C); 6 Danny McGuire; 19 Danny Ward; 9 Matt Diskin; 8 Ryan Bailey; 3 Chris McKenna; 29 Ali Lauitiiti; 11 David Furner. Subs: 16 Willie Poching for Furner (19); 10 Barrie McDermott for Ward (22); Ward for Bailey (29); 7 Rob Burrow for Lauitiiti (30); Bailey for McDermott (41); 20 Jamie Jones-Buchanan for McKenna (48); Lauitiiti for Ward (50); Furner for Sinfield (60); McKenna for Poching (63); Sinfield for Diskin (67); Poching for McKenna (72); Ward for Bailey (73).
Tries: Diskin (15), McGuire (75); **Goals:** Sinfield 4/4.
Rugby Leaguer & League Express Men of the Match:
Bulls: Lesley Vainikolo; *Rhinos:* Richard Mathers.
Penalty count: 5-5; **Half-time:** 4-10; **Referee:** Steve Ganson (St Helens); **Attendance:** 65,547 *(at Old Trafford, Manchester).*

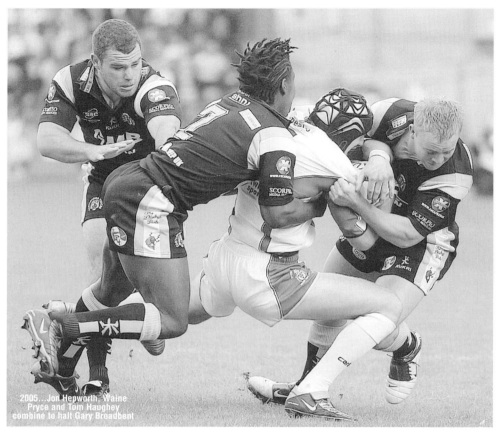

2005...Jon Hepworth, Waine Pryce and Tom Haughey combine to halt Gary Broadbent

2005

NATIONAL LEAGUE ONE GRAND FINAL

Sunday 9th October 2005

CASTLEFORD TIGERS 36 WHITEHAVEN 8

TIGERS: 1 Michael Platt; 2 Waine Pryce; 3 Michael Shenton; 4 Jon Hepworth; 5 Damien Blanch; 6 Brad Davis; 7 Andrew Henderson; 8 Adam Watene; 9 Aaron Smith; 10 Richard Fletcher; 11 Tom Haughey; 12 Steve Crouch; 13 Deon Bird. Subs (all used): 14 Paul Handforth; 15 Craig Huby; 16 Adrian Vowles; 17 Frank Watene.
Tries: Huby (22), Crouch (24), Blanch (26), Davis (33, 45), Haughey (52); **Goals:** Fletcher 2/3, Huby 3/4, Hepworth 1/1.
WHITEHAVEN: 1 Gary Broadbent; 2 Craig Calvert; 3 David Seeds; 4 Mick Nanyn; 5 Wesley Wilson; 6 Leroy Joe; 7 Joel Penny; 8 Ryan Tandy; 9 Carl Sice; 10 David Fatialofa; 11 Spencer Miller; 12 Howard Hill; 13 Aaron Lester. Subs (all used): 14 Carl Rudd; 15 Aaron Summers; 16 Craig Chambers; 17 Marc Jackson.
Tries: Seeds (56), Calvert (78); **Goals:** Nanyn 0/2.
Sin bin: Joe (16) - late tackle on Davis.
On report: Joe (16) - late tackle on Davis;
Sice (40) - alleged biting.
Rugby Leaguer & League Express Men of the Match:
Tigers: Brad Davis; *Whitehaven:* Wesley Wilson.
Penalty count: 4-9; **Half-time:** 26-0;
Referee: Steve Ganson (St Helens);
Attendance: 13,300 *(at Halton Stadium, Widnes).*

SUPER LEAGUE GRAND FINAL

Saturday 15th October 2005

BRADFORD BULLS 15 LEEDS RHINOS 6

BULLS: 6 Michael Withers; 3 Leon Pryce; 13 Ben Harris; 4 Shontayne Hape; 5 Lesley Vainikolo; 18 Iestyn Harris; 7 Paul Deacon; 12 Jamie Peacock (C); 9 Ian Henderson; 29 Stuart Fielden; 16 Paul Johnson; 10 Brad Meyers; 11 Lee Radford. Subs (all used): 24 Adrian Morley for Johnson (5); 19 Jamie Langley for Peacock (24); 8 Joe Vagana for Fielden (24); Johnson for Radford (24); 1 Robbie Paul for Henderson (31); Peacock for Vagana (45); Fielden for Morley (49); Henderson for Paul (54); Radford for Meyers (60); Morley for Peacock (62); Meyers for Langley (73); Peacock for Johnson (74).
Tries: L Pryce (29), Vainikolo (53); **Goals:** Deacon 3/5;
Field goal: I Harris.
RHINOS: 1 Richard Mathers; 2 Mark Calderwood; 3 Chev Walker; 12 Chris McKenna; 5 Marcus Bai; 6 Danny McGuire; 7 Rob Burrow; 8 Ryan Bailey; 14 Andrew Dunemann; 15 Danny Ward; 20 Gareth Ellis; 16 Willie Poching; 13 Kevin Sinfield (C). Subs (all used): 10 Barrie McDermott for Ward (17); 11 Ali Lauitiiti for Poching (21); 18 Jamie Jones-Buchanan for Bailey (31); Ward for McDermott (34); 9 Matt Diskin for Ellis (48); Poching for Lauitiiti (48); McDermott for Ward (54); Ellis for Poching (54); Lauitiiti for McDermott (61); Poching for Dunemann (65); Ward for Jones-Buchanan (68); Dunemann for Ellis (71).
Try: McGuire (22); **Goals:** Sinfield 1/2.
Rugby Leaguer & League Express Men of the Match:
Bulls: Leon Pryce; *Rhinos:* Danny McGuire.
Penalty count: 6-8; **Half-time:** 8-6; **Referee:** Ashley Klein (Keighley); **Attendance:** 65,537 *(at Old Trafford, Manchester).*

2006

NATIONAL LEAGUE TWO GRAND FINAL

Sunday 8th October 2006

SHEFFIELD EAGLES 35 SWINTON LIONS 10

EAGLES: 1 Johnny Woodcock; 5 Greg Hurst; 4 Jimmy Walker; 3 James Ford; 2 Rob Worrincy; 6 Brendon Lindsay; 7 Gavin Brown; 8 Jack Howieson; 9 Paul Pickering; 10 Mitchell Stringer; 11 Andy Hay; 12 Dale Holdstock; 13 Andy Smith. Subs (all used): 14 Craig Poucher; 15 Martin Ostler; 16 Sean Dickinson; 17 Waisale Sovatabua.
Tries: Worrincy (21, 43), Lindsay (38), Woodcock (39), Walker (51), Hay (60); **Goals:** Woodcock 5/6;
Field goal: G Brown.
LIONS: 1 Wayne English; 2 Andy Saywell; 3 Darren Woods; 4 David Alstead; 5 Marlon Billy; 6 Martin Moana; 7 Chris Hough; 8 Bruce Johnson; 9 Phil Wood; 10 Dave Newton; 11 Kris Smith; 12 Ian Sinfield; 13 Lee Marsh. Subs (all used): 14 Liam McGovern; 15 Chris Morley; 16 Danny Aboushakra; 17 Ian Parry.
Tries: Saywell (35), Alstead (74); **Goals:** McGovern 1/2.
Rugby Leaguer & League Express Men of the Match:
Eagles: Johnny Woodcock; *Lions:* Wayne English.
Penalty count: 3-4; **Half-time:** 16-4;
Referee: Peter Taberner (Wigan).
(at Halliwell Jones Stadium, Warrington).

NATIONAL LEAGUE ONE GRAND FINAL

Sunday 8th October 2006

HULL KINGSTON ROVERS 29 WIDNES VIKINGS 16

ROVERS: 1 Ben Cockayne; 2 Leroy Rivett; 3 Gareth Morton; 4 Jon Goddard; 5 Byron Ford; 6 Scott Murrell; 7 James Webster; 8 Makali Aizue; 9 Ben Fisher; 10 David Tangata-Toa; 11 Iain Morrison; 12 Michael Smith; 13 Tommy Gallagher. Subs (all used): 14 Pat Weisner; 15 Dwayne Barker; 16 Jason Netherton; 17 Dave Wilson.
Tries: Ford (6), Goddard (18, 36), Murrell (24), Weisner (43); **Goals:** Morton 4/6; **Field goal:** Murrell.
VIKINGS: 1 Gavin Dodd; 2 Damien Blanch; 3 Sean Gleeson; 4 Daryl Cardiss; 5 John Kirkpatrick; 6 Dennis Moran; 7 Ian Watson; 8 Terry O'Connor; 9 Mark Smith; 10 Barrie McDermott; 11 Mick Cassidy; 12 David Allen; 13 Bob Beswick. Subs (all used): 14 Aaron Summers; 15 Oliver Wilkes; 16 Jordan James; 17 Ryan Tandy.
Tries: Dodd (32), Tandy (57), Blanch (70); **Goals:** Dodd 2/3.
Rugby Leaguer & League Express Men of the Match:
Rovers: James Webster; *Vikings:* Mark Smith.
Penalty count: 8-5; **Half-time:** 22-4;
Referee: Phil Bentham (Warrington);
Attendance: 13,024 *(at Halliwell Jones Stadium, Warrington).*

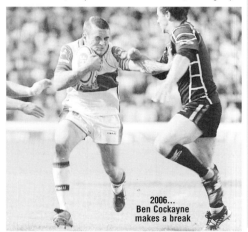

2006...
Ben Cockayne
makes a break

2006...James Roby and Ade Gardner celebrate

SUPER LEAGUE GRAND FINAL

Saturday 14th October 2006

HULL FC 4 ST HELENS 26

HULL: 1 Shaun Briscoe; 14 Motu Tony; 4 Sid Domic; 3 Kirk Yeaman; 5 Gareth Raynor; 13 Paul Cooke; 7 Richard Horne; 8 Ewan Dowes; 9 Richard Swain (C); 10 Garreth Carvell; 11 Lee Radford; 12 Shayne McMenemy; 24 Danny Washbrook. Subs: 15 Paul King for Carvell (17); 19 Graeme Horne for Radford (23); 26 Scott Wheeldon for Dowes (27); 6 Richard Whiting for McMenemy (29); Dowes for Wheeldon (49); Carvell for King (49); Radford for G Horne (51); McMenemy for Whiting (54); King for Carvell (68); Wheeldon for Dowes (73); Whiting for Tony (76); G Horne for Radford (77).
Try: Domic (24); **Goals:** Cooke 0/1.
SAINTS: 1 Paul Wellens; 2 Ade Gardner; 3 Jamie Lyon; 4 Willie Talau; 5 Francis Meli; 6 Leon Pryce; 7 Sean Long (C); 17 Paul Anderson; 9 Keiron Cunningham; 10 Jason Cayless; 11 Lee Gilmour; 12 Jon Wilkin; 16 Jason Hooper. Subs: 23 Maurie Fa'asavalu for P Anderson (12); 19 James Graham for Cayless (25); 15 Mike Bennett for Fa'asavalu (28); 14 James Roby for Cunningham (31); P Anderson for Wilkin (33); Cunningham for Gilmour (49); Cayless for P Anderson (52); Wilkin for Hooper (56); Fa'asavalu for Cayless (58); Gilmour for Graham (66); Cayless for Fa'asavalu (72); P Anderson for Wilkin (75).
Tries: Meli (17), Pryce (29), Talau (49), Gardner (52), Cunningham (62); **Goals:** Lyon 3/5.
Rugby Leaguer & League Express Men of the Match:
Hull: Shaun Briscoe; *Saints:* Paul Wellens.
Penalty count: 4-2; **Half-time:** 4-10;
Referee: Karl Kirkpatrick (Warrington);
Attendance: 72,582 *(at Old Trafford, Manchester).*

2007 SEASON
Stats round-up

SUPER LEAGUE

Paul Wellens

Kevin Sinfield

TRIES *(play-offs in brackets, included in total)*

1	Brent Webb	Leeds Rhinos	24 (3)
	Paul Wellens	St Helens	24 (0)
3	Henry Fa'afili	Warrington Wolves	22 (-)
4	Ade Gardner	St Helens	21 (0)
	Francis Meli	St Helens	21 (0)
6	Scott Donald	Leeds Rhinos	20 (1)
7	Lesley Vainikolo	Bradford Bulls	19 (0)
8	Paul Sykes	Harlequins	18 (-)
	Leon Pryce	St Helens	18 (1)
	Trent Barrett	Wigan Warriors	18 (0)

GOALS *(play-offs in brackets, included in total)*

1	Kevin Sinfield	Leeds Rhinos	128 (15)
2	Pat Richards	Wigan Warriors	112 (10)
3	Paul Deacon	Bradford Bulls	98 (0)
4	Chris Thorman	Huddersfield Giants	96 (2)
5	Danny Tickle	Hull FC	85 (6)
6	Lee Briers	Warrington Wolves	84 (-)
7	Jamie Rooney	Wakefield Trinity Wildcats	82 (-)
8	John Wilshere	Salford City Reds	61 (-)
9	Paul Cooke	Hull Kingston Rovers	51 (-)
		(includes 15 for Hull FC)	
10	Thomas Bosc	Catalans Dragons	49 (-)

GOALS PERCENTAGE *(play-offs included)*

			G	Att	%
1	Brad Drew	Huddersfield Giants	12	14	85.7
2	Stacey Jones	Catalans Dragons	22	26	84.6
3	Paul Deacon	Bradford Bulls	98	118	83.0
4	Kevin Sinfield	Leeds Rhinos	128	155	82.5
5	Pat Richards	Wigan Warriors	112	137	81.7
6	Iestyn Harris	Bradford Bulls	26	32	81.2
7	Danny Tickle	Hull FC	85	106	80.1
8	Stephen Tyrer	St Helens	36	45	80.0
9	Chris Thorman	Huddersfield Giants	96	123	78.0
10	Rob Purdham	Harlequins	14	18	77.7

(10 minimum attempts to qualify)

POINTS *(play-offs in brackets, included in total)*

			T	G	FG	Pts
1	Kevin Sinfield	Leeds Rhinos	5	128	3	279 (32)
2	Pat Richards	Wigan Warriors	13	112	2	278 (30)
3	Chris Thorman	Huddersfield Giants	11	96	2	238 (4)
4	Lee Briers	Warrington Wolves	12	84	5	221 (-)
5	Paul Deacon	Bradford Bulls	5	98	0	216 (0)
6	Jamie Rooney	Wakefield Trinity Wildcats	11	82	6	214 (-)
7	Danny Tickle	Hull FC	9	85	0	206 (12)
8	John Wilshere	Salford City Reds	12	61	0	170 (-)
9	Thomas Bosc	Catalans Dragons	11	49	0	142 (-)
10	Paul Sykes	Harlequins	13	38	1	129 (-)

CONSECUTIVE APPEARANCES
(Super League, including play-offs, and Challenge Cup)

1	Stuart Fielden	Wigan Warriors/BradfordBulls	133
2	Stuart Littler	Salford City Reds	100
3	Michael Korkidas	Salford City Reds/ Wakefield Trinity Wildcats	75
4	Mick Higham	Wigan Warriors/St Helens	69
5	Scott Donald	Leeds Rhinos	65
6	Sean O'Loughlin	Wigan Warriors	60
7	David Solomona	Bradford Bulls/ Wakefield Trinity Wildcats	53
8	Chad Randall	Harlequins	52
9	Ben Jeffries	Wakefield Trinity Wildcats	50
10	Jamie Jones-Buchanan	Leeds Rhinos	49
11	Stephen Wild	Huddersfield Giants	48
12	Chris Nero	Huddersfield Giants	47
13	Kevin Sinfield	Leeds Rhinos	41
	Keiron Cunningham	St Helens	41
15	Clinton Toopi	Leeds Rhinos	39
	John Wilshere	Salford City Reds	39
17	Luke Dorn	Salford City Reds/Harlequins	37
18	Danny McGuire	Leeds Rhinos	34
	Phil Bailey	Wigan Warriors	34
	Thomas Leuluai	Wigan Warriors	34

Brent Webb

Stuart Fielden

FINAL TABLE

	P	W	D	L	F	A	D	Pts
St Helens	27	19	0	8	783	422	361	38
Leeds Rhinos	27	18	1	8	747	487	260	37
Bradford Bulls *	27	17	1	9	778	560	218	33
Hull FC	27	14	2	11	573	553	20	30
Huddersfield Giants	27	13	1	13	638	543	95	27
Wigan Warriors **	27	15	1	11	621	527	94	27
Warrington Wolves	27	13	0	14	693	736	-43	26
Wakefield Trinity Wildcats	27	11	1	15	596	714	-118	23
Harlequins	27	10	3	14	495	636	-141	23
Catalans Dragons	27	10	1	16	570	685	-115	21
Hull Kingston Rovers	27	10	0	17	491	723	-232	20
Salford City Reds	27	6	1	20	475	874	-399	13

* 2 points deducted for 2006 salary cap breach
** 4 points deducted for 2006 salary cap breach

AVERAGE ATTENDANCES

	2007 Avg	2006 Avg	Diff
Leeds Rhinos	17,416	15,338	+2,078
Wigan Warriors	16,040	14,464	+1,576
Hull FC	14,553	11,211	+3,342
Bradford Bulls	11,873	11,287	+586
Warrington Wolves	10,510	10,406	+104
St Helens	9,813	11,022	-1,209
Catalans Dragons	8,181	6,542	+1,639
Hull Kingston Rovers	7,160	3,330	+3,830
Huddersfield Giants	7,083	5,857	+1,226
Wakefield Trinity Wildcats	6,783	5,449	+1,334
Salford City Reds	5,188	4,820	+368
Harlequins	3,395	4,917	-1,522

2007 Average	9,833
2006 Average	9,121
Difference	+712

BEST ATTENDANCES

		Round	Date
71,352	Leeds v St Helens	GF	13/10/07
	(at Old Trafford, Manchester)		
24,028	Wigan v St Helens	8	6/4/07
23,004	Hull v Hull KR	25	2/9/07
23,002	Hull v Hull KR	9	9/4/07
22,031	Wigan v St Helens	27	14/9/07
22,000	Leeds v Bradford	18	29/6/07
21,975	Leeds v St Helens	11	21/4/07
21,693	Wigan v Warrington	1	9/2/07
19,226	Leeds v Wakefield	27	14/9/07
18,659	Leeds v Hull	2	16/2/07

WORST ATTENDANCES

		Round	Date
2,346	Harlequins v Catalans	19	7/7/07
2,347	Harlequins v Salford	26	8/9/07
2,478	Harlequins v Huddersfield	21	21/7/07
2,532	Harlequins v Wakefield	10	14/4/07
3,132	Harlequins v Warrington	4	3/3/07
3,200	Harlequins v Wigan	24	18/8/07
3,278	Harlequins v Hull KR	18	30/6/07
3,379	Salford v Huddersfield	15	25/5/07
3,438	Salford v Bradford	21	21/7/07
3,515	Harlequins v Salford	2	17/2/07

CHALLENGE CUP

TRIES

1	Craig Hall	Hull FC	6
	Ade Gardner	St Helens	6
3	Khamal Ganley	Barrow Raiders	5
	Adam Mogg	Catalans Dragons	5
	Paul Sykes	Harlequins	5
	Francis Meli	St Helens	5
	Paul Wellens	St Helens	5
	Vinnie Anderson	Warrington Wolves	5

GOALS

1	Thomas Bosc	Catalans Dragons	19
2	Darren Holt	Barrow Raiders	18
	Pat Richards	Wigan Warriors	18
4	Craig Hall	Hull FC	17
	Johnny Woodcock		
		Sheffield Eagles	17

POINTS

			T	G	FG	Pts
1	Craig Hall	Hull FC	6	17	0	58
2	Pat Richards	Wigan Warriors	3	18	0	48
3	Thomas Bosc	Catalans Dragons	2	19	1	47
4	Johnny Woodcock					
		Sheffield Eagles	3	17	0	46
5	Darren Holt	Barrow Raiders	2	18	1	45

BEST ATTENDANCES

		Round	Date
84,241	Catalans v St Helens	F	25/8/07
	(at Wembley Stadium)		
14,316	Bradford v St Helens	SF	28/7/07
	(at Galpharm Stadium, Huddersfield)		
10,835	Wigan v Harlequins	QF	8/6/07
10,218	Catalans v Wigan	SF	29/7/07
	(at Halliwell Jones Stadium, Warrington)		
9,612	Leeds v Wigan	5	12/5/07

WORST ATTENDANCES

		Round	Date
211	Gateshead v Limoux	3	10/3/07
230	West Bowling v London Skolars	3	10/3/07
282	Hunslet v Rochdale Mayfield	3	11/3/07
300	Pia v Harlequins	4	31/3/07
300	Celtic Crusaders v Eastmoor	3	10/3/07
300	East Hull v Oldham	3	10/3/07

NATIONAL LEAGUE CUP

TRIES

1	Tony Duggan	Celtic Crusaders	9
	Craig Calvert	Whitehaven	9
	Scott Grix	Widnes Vikings	9
	Toa Kohe-Love	Widnes Vikings	9
5	Stuart Donlan	Castleford Tigers	8
	Shad Royston	Halifax	8
	Miles Greenwood	Leigh Centurions	8

GOALS

1	Carl Rudd	Whitehaven	44
	Mick Nanyn	Widnes Vikings	44
3	Danny Brough	Castleford Tigers	37
4	Kevin King	Rochdale Hornets	31
5	Francis Maloney	Dewsbury Rams	27

POINTS

			T	G	FG	Pts
1	Carl Rudd	Whitehaven	7	44	0	116
2	Mick Nanyn	Widnes Vikings	5	44	0	108
3	Danny Brough	Castleford Tigers	3	37	0	86
4	Kevin King	Rochdale Hornets	3	31	0	74
5	Francis Maloney	Dewsbury Rams	3	27	0	66

BEST ATTENDANCES

		Round	Date
8,236	Whitehaven v Widnes	F	15/7/07
	(at Bloomfield Road, Blackpool)		
6,871	Castleford v Featherstone	2	18/2/07
5,388	Widnes v Castleford	SF	24/6/07
5,108	Castleford v Sheffield	3	25/2/07
4,613	Castleford v Doncaster	6	25/3/07

WORST ATTENDANCES

		Round	Date
222	Hunslet v Celtic Crusaders	QFQ	21/4/07
	(at Tetley's Stadium, Dewsbury)		
289	London Skolars v Celtic Crusaders	4	4/3/07
301	Celtic Crusaders v London Skolars	2	18/2/07
335	Blackpool v Workington	3	25/2/07
358	Blackpool v Barrow	6	25/3/07

2007 Season - Stats round-up

NATIONAL LEAGUE ONE

Mick Nanyn

TRIES *(play-offs in brackets, included in total)*

1	Mick Nanyn	Widnes Vikings	23 (2)
2	Kirk Dixon	Castleford Tigers	18 (0)
	Craig Calvert	Whitehaven	18 (3)
4	James Ford	Sheffield Eagles	16 (2)
5	Michael Shenton	Castleford Tigers	15 (1)
	Gavin Dodd	Widnes Vikings	15 (0)
7	Damien Blanch	Widnes Vikings	14 (0)
	Joel Penny	Widnes Vikings	14 (0)

(includes 4 for Doncaster Lakers)

9	Stuart Donlan	Castleford Tigers	12 (0)
	Michael Wainwright	Castleford Tigers	12 (2)
	Lee Greenwood	Halifax	12 (0)
	Shad Royston	Halifax	12 (4)
	Danny Halliwell	Leigh Centurions	12 (0)
	Dennis Moran	Widnes Vikings	12 (0)

GOALS *(play-offs in brackets, included in total)*

1	Mick Nanyn	Widnes Vikings	102 (11)
2	Danny Brough	Castleford Tigers	84 (11)
3	Graham Holroyd	Halifax	80 (13)

(includes 8 for Doncaster Lakers)

4	Carl Rudd	Whitehaven	68 (5)
5	Johnny Woodcock	Sheffield Eagles	47 (3)
6	Damien Couturier	Leigh Centurions	46 (0)
7	Francis Maloney	Batley Bulldogs	38 (-)

(includes 24 for Dewsbury Rams)

8	Kirk Dixon	Castleford Tigers	32 (0)
9	Kevin King	Rochdale Hornets	26 (-)10
	Liam Finn	Dewsbury Rams	25 (-)

POINTS *(play-offs in brackets, included in total)*

			T	G	FG	Pts
1	Mick Nanyn	Widnes Vikings	23	102	0	296 (30)
2	Danny Brough	Castleford Tigers	8	84	2	202 (24)
3	Graham Holroyd	Halifax	6	80	1	185 (26)

(includes 17 (8g, 1fg) for Doncaster Lakers)

			T	G	FG	Pts
4	Carl Rudd	Whitehaven	9	68	1	173 (23)
5	Kirk Dixon	Castleford Tigers	18	32	0	136 (0)
6	Johnny Woodcock	Sheffield Eagles	7	47	0	122 (6)
7	Damien Couturier	Leigh Centurions	6	46	0	116 (0)
8	Francis Maloney	Batley Bulldogs	6	38	0	100 (-)

(includes 72 (6t, 24g) for Dewsbury Rams)

			T	G	FG	Pts
9	Gavin Dodd	Widnes Vikings	15	13	0	86 (0)
10	Kevin King	Rochdale Hornets	6	26	0	76 (-)

FINAL TABLE

	P	W	D	L	BP	F	A	D	Pts
Castleford Tigers	18	17	0	1	0	860	247	613	51
Widnes Vikings	18	16	0	2	2	740	220	520	50
Halifax	18	12	0	6	2	616	421	195	38
Whitehaven	18	11	0	7	5	474	342	132	38
Leigh Centurions	18	9	0	9	4	454	474	-20	31
Sheffield Eagles	18	6	1	11	4	414	527	-113	24
Dewsbury Rams	18	5	0	13	6	346	572	-226	21
Batley Bulldogs	18	5	1	12	2	372	645	-273	19
Rochdale Hornets	18	3	0	15	1	302	700	-398	10
Doncaster *	18	5	0	13	1	348	778	-430	10

* 6 points deducted

AVERAGE ATTENDANCES

	2007 Avg	2006 Avg	Diff
Castleford Tigers	5,037	7,096	-2,059
Widnes Vikings	3,329	3,645	-316
Doncaster	1,986	1,006	+980
Whitehaven	1,848	1,961	-113
Leigh Centurions	1,834	2,238	-404
Halifax	1,822	1,593	+229
Dewsbury Rams	1,369	878	+491
Sheffield Eagles	1,155	892	+263
Batley Bulldogs	1,023	927	+96
Rochdale Hornets	923	920	+3

2007 Average	2,033
2006 Average	1,824
Difference	+209

BEST ATTENDANCES

		Round	Date
20,814	Castleford v Widnes	GF	7/10/07

(at Headingley Carnegie, Leeds)

		Round	Date
6,528	Doncaster v Castleford	2	12/4/07
6,284	Castleford v Halifax	1	6/4/07
6,179	Castleford v Widnes	QSF	20/9/07
6,007	Castleford v Widnes	6	17/5/07
5,525	Castleford v Leigh	17	2/9/07
5,223	Castleford v Batley	3	15/4/07
4,902	Castleford v Whitehaven	10	1/7/07
4,879	Widnes v Rochdale	10	1/7/07
4,739	Castleford v Dewsbury	8	10/6/07

WORST ATTENDANCES

		Round	Date
503	Rochdale v Sheffield	15	12/8/07
532	Batley v Rochdale	17	2/9/07
555	Rochdale v Whitehaven	16	19/8/07
644	Rochdale v Batley	9	17/6/07
650	Rochdale v Leigh	13	29/7/07
667	Batley v Sheffield	2	9/4/07
682	Batley v Whitehaven	4	29/4/07
732	Batley v Doncaster	15	12/8/07
754	Dewsbury v Rochdale	5	6/5/07
820	Rochdale v Halifax	3	15/4/07

NATIONAL LEAGUE TWO

TRIES *(play-offs in brackets, included in total)*

1	Tony Duggan	Celtic Crusaders	29 (-)
2	Danny Kirmond	Featherstone Rovers	23 (2)
3	Adam Hughes	Oldham	22 (7)
4	Paul Ballard	Celtic Crusaders	21 (-)
5	Khamal Ganley	Barrow Raiders	20 (0)
6	Wayne McHugh	Featherstone Rovers	18 (3)
	Lucas Onyango	Oldham	18 (3)
8	Damien Quinn	Celtic Crusaders	17 (-)
9	Tom Haughey	Featherstone Rovers	16 (0)
10	Pete Hodgkinson	London Skolars	15 (-)
	Shaun Lunt	Workington Town	15 (0)

GOALS *(play-offs in brackets, included in total)*

1	Carl Forber	Workington Town	110 (9)
2	Darren Holt	Barrow Raiders	104 (3)
3	Stuart Dickens	Featherstone Rovers	103 (11)
4	Damien Quinn	Celtic Crusaders	65 (-)
5	Jace Van Dijk	Celtic Crusaders	62 (-)
6	Lee Marsh	Swinton Lions	61 (1)
7	Paul Thorman	London Skolars	47 (-)
8	Darren Robinson	Hunslet Hawks	43 (-)
9	Gareth Langley	Oldham	35 (8)
10	Richard Knight	Keighley Cougars	34 (-)

318

POINTS *(play-offs in brackets, included in total)*

			T	G	FG	Pts
1	Carl Forber	Workington Town	4	110	0	236 (18)
2	Stuart Dickens	Featherstone Rovers	7	103	0	234 (22)
3	Darren Holt	Barrow Raiders	3	104	1	221 (6)
4	Damien Quinn	Celtic Crusaders	17	65	0	198 (-)
5	Jace Van Dijk	Celtic Crusaders	7	62	0	152 (-)
6	Lee Marsh	Swinton Lions	7	61	0	150 (2)
7	Tony Duggan	Celtic Crusaders	29	0	0	116 (-)
8	Adam Hughes	Oldham	22	12	0	112 (34)
9	Richard Knight	Keighley Cougars	10	34	0	108 (-)
10	Gareth Langley	Oldham	9	35	0	106 (28)

FINAL TABLE

	P	W	D	L	BP	F	A	D	Pts
Celtic Crusaders	22	19	0	3	3	918	345	573	60
Featherstone Rovers	22	18	0	4	2	819	366	453	56
Barrow Raiders	22	17	0	5	4	769	387	382	55
Oldham	22	16	0	6	5	661	420	241	53
Workington Town	22	12	0	10	7	655	515	140	43
York City Knights	22	10	0	12	6	488	470	18	36
Swinton Lions *	22	11	0	11	6	605	649	-44	33
Hunslet Hawks	22	8	0	14	7	368	591	-223	31
London Skolars	22	8	1	13	4	448	610	-162	30
Keighley Cougars	22	6	1	15	4	407	692	-285	24
Gateshead Thunder	22	6	0	16	3	381	822	-441	21
Blackpool Panthers	22	0	0	22	6	332	984	-652	6

* 6 points deducted

AVERAGE ATTENDANCES

	2007 Avg	2006 Avg	Diff
Featherstone Rovers	1,504	1,069	+435
Barrow Raiders	1,431	1,042	+389
Oldham	1,179	942	+237
York City Knights	1,119	1,682	-563
Celtic Crusaders	1,070	671	+399
Workington Town	906	854	+52
Keighley Cougars	766	845	-79
Swinton Lions	493	569	-76
London Skolars	479	455	+24
Hunslet Hawks	423	426	-3
Blackpool Panthers	356	481	-125
Gateshead Thunder	349	352	-3

2007 Average	840
2006 Average	711
Difference	+129

BEST ATTENDANCES *(figure unavailable for Grand Final)*

		Round	Date
4,327	Oldham v Celtic Crusaders	21	30/8/07
3,441	Celtic Crusaders v Oldham	5	4/5/07
2,993	Featherstone v Celtic Crusaders	17	26/7/07
2,805	Celtic Crusaders v Blackpool	2	9/4/07
2,771	Barrow v Oldham	FE	30/9/07
1,924	York v Featherstone	12	24/6/07
1,901	Barrow v Featherstone	22	8/9/07
1,806	Barrow v Celtic Crusaders	18	5/8/07
1,792	Featherstone v Barrow	QSF	23/9/07
1,714	Barrow v Workington	1	6/4/07

WORST ATTENDANCES

		Round	Date
145	Gateshead v Blackpool	14	7/7/07
211	London Skolars v Celtic Crusaders	1	6/4/07
219	Gateshead v Swinton	16	21/7/07
263	Blackpool v London Skolars	20	19/8/07
273	Hunslet v London Skolars	18	5/8/07
275	Blackpool v Gateshead	9	3/6/07
275	Gateshead v Workington	17	29/7/07
276	Gateshead v Hunslet	12	23/6/07
276	Blackpool v Celtic Crusaders	16	22/7/07
277	Gateshead v Keighley	8	27/5/07

2007 TOP SCORERS - ALL COMPETITIONS

Tony Duggan

TRIES

1	Tony Duggan	Celtic Crusaders	40
2	Craig Calvert	Whitehaven	28
	Mick Nanyn	Widnes Vikings	28
4	Khamal Ganley	Barrow Raiders	27
5	Paul Ballard	Celtic Crusaders	26
6	Danny Kirmond	Featherstone Rovers	25
	Adam Hughes	Oldham	25

(includes 3 for Leigh Centurions)

8	Wayne McHugh	Featherstone Rovers	24
	Brent Webb	Leeds Rhinos	24
	Paul Wellens	St Helens	24

GOALS

1	Mick Nanyn	Widnes Vikings	161
2	Kevin Sinfield	Leeds Rhinos	139
3	Darren Holt	Barrow Raiders	138
4	Carl Forber	Workington Town	133
5	Pat Richards	Wigan Warriors	130
6	Stuart Dickens	Featherstone Rovers	128
7	Carl Rudd	Whitehaven	125
8	Danny Brough	Castleford Tigers	123
9	Paul Deacon	Bradford Bulls	112
10	Chris Thorman	Huddersfield Giants	102

POINTS

			T	G	FG	Pts
1	Mick Nanyn	Widnes Vikings	28	161	0	434
2	Pat Richards	Wigan Warriors	16	130	2	326
3	Carl Rudd	Whitehaven	17	125	1	319
4	Kevin Sinfield	Leeds Rhinos	6	139	3	305
5	Darren Holt	Barrow Raiders	6	138	3	303
6	Carl Forber	Workington Town	8	133	0	298
7	Danny Brough	Castleford Tigers	11	123	2	292
8	Stuart Dickens	Featherstone Rovers	8	128	0	288
9	Damien Quinn	Celtic Crusaders	20	86	0	252
10	Chris Thorman	Huddersfield Giants	11	102	2	250

FIELD GOALS

1	Sean Long	St Helens	6
	Jamie Rooney	Wakefield Trinity Wildcats	6
3	Lee Briers	Warrington Wolves	5
4	Stacey Jones	Catalans Dragons	4
	Simon Svabic	Rochdale Hornets	4
	Trent Barrett	Wigan Warriors	4
7	Darren Holt	Barrow Raiders	3
	Pat Weisner	Barrow Raiders	3
	Richard Horne	Hull FC	3
	Darren Robinson	Hunslet Hawks	3
	Kevin Sinfield	Leeds Rhinos	3
	Liam McGovern	Swinton Lions	3